INDIA'S
EMERGING
NUCLEAR
POSTURE

**Between Recessed Deterrent
and Ready Arsenal**

Ashley J. Tellis

D0181106

Prepared for the United States Air Force

Project AIR FORCE

RAND

The research reported here was sponsored by the United States Air Force under Contract F49642-96-C-0001. Further information may be obtained from the Strategic Planning Division, Directorate of Plans, Hq USAF.

Library of Congress Cataloging-in-Publication Data

Tellis, Ashley J.
    India's emerging nuclear posture : between recessed deterrent and ready arsenal / Ashley J. Tellis.
      p. cm.
    "MR-1127-AF."
    Includes bibliographical references and index.
    ISBN 0-8330-2774-3 (hc)—ISBN 0-8330-2781-6 (pbk)
    1. India—Military policy. 2. Nuclear weapons—India. 3. Deterrence (Strategy) I. Title.

UA840 .T45 2001
355.02'17'0954—dc21

                           00-045883

RAND is a nonprofit institution that helps improve policy and decisionmaking through research and analysis. RAND® is a registered trademark. RAND's publications do not necessarily reflect the opinions or policies of its research sponsors.

Cover design by Peter Soriano

Published 2001 by RAND
1700 Main Street, P.O. Box 2138, Santa Monica, CA 90407-2138
1200 South Hayes Street, Arlington, VA 22202-5050
201 North Craig Street, Suite 102, Pittsburgh, PA 15213
RAND URL: http://www.rand.org/
To order RAND documents or to obtain additional information, contact Distribution Services: Telephone: (310) 451-7002;
Fax: (310) 451-6915; Internet: order@rand.org

For Snuffles, Arthur, Athena, and Dhun—in partial recompense
for many lost weekends

The resumption of nuclear testing in South Asia in May 1998 came as a surprise to many in the United States. In the aftermath of these tests, India declared itself to be a "nuclear weapon state" and formally announced its intention to develop a nuclear deterrent. These events have significant implications both for regional security and for the future of the evolving international order. In particular, they require that American policymakers and defense planners understand the motivations behind India's decisions as well as the nature of Indian thinking about nuclear weaponry and the character of the evolving Indian deterrent—especially insofar as these issues affect U.S. diplomatic initiatives, nonproliferation policy, and regional strategy.

This book describes India's emerging nuclear posture in the context of a broader assessment of its strategic interests, institutional structures, and security goals. It seeks to explicate the prevailing attitudes toward nuclear weaponry among Indian security managers because such attitudes, more than anything else, will ultimately determine New Delhi's future decisions with regard to its doctrine, capabilities, and force posture. Since the principal objective of this book is to prepare U.S. policymakers in particular and the American strategic community in general for prospective developments in these three issue areas, a critical understanding, reconstruction, and synthesis of the "official mind" on key questions pertaining to nuclearization remain the most appropriate methodological device for assessing New Delhi's strategic choices.

Toward that end, the book draws deeply from the best of the vast number of Indian writings available on issues surrounding nuclear weaponry. In fact, all the data and information pertaining to the Indian nuclear program have been drawn from open sources, primarily Indian and Western newspapers, books, and journal articles. The author also benefited greatly from extensive interviews with important Indian political figures (both in the current government and in the opposition) as well as with high-ranking officials in the Prime Minister's Office, the Ministries of External Affairs and Defence (including the Defence Research and Development Organization), and senior Indian military officers, both current and retired. This exclusive reliance on open-source and interview materials implies that some factual information appearing in this book may be imperfect but does not fundamentally compromise either the principal analytical conclusions drawn or the policy implications for the United States. The writing of this book was substantially completed by October 2000.

This study is part of an ongoing analysis of emerging strategic trends in Asia and their implications for the U.S. Air Force. This research is conducted in the Strategy and Doctrine Program of Project AIR FORCE under the sponsorship of the Deputy Chief of Staff for Air and Space Operations, U.S. Air Force (AF/XO), and the Commander-in-Chief, Pacific Air Forces (PACAF/CC). This book should be of interest to the U.S. national security community, regional military and intelligence analysts, the nonproliferation establishment, and academics in general.

PROJECT AIR FORCE

Project AIR FORCE, a division of RAND, is the Air Force federally funded research and development center (FFRDC) for studies and analyses. It provides the Air Force with independent analyses of policy alternatives affecting the development, employment, combat readiness, and support of current and future aerospace forces. Research is performed in four programs: Aerospace Force Development; Manpower, Personnel, and Training; Resource Management; and Strategy and Doctrine.

CONTENTS

FIGURES

TABLES

I have incurred many debts in the writing of this book. First and foremost, I am deeply grateful to my principal sponsors in the Air Force: Both General Patrick K. Gamble, Commander-in-Chief, Pacific Air Forces, and Lieutenant General Marvin R. Esmond, Deputy Chief of Staff for Air and Space Operations, United States Air Force, were extraordinarily generous in their support of this work. They spent many hours listening to the briefings associated with this book, actively discussed the methodology of the research and its principal conclusions, and enthusiastically encouraged the dissemination of its findings throughout the intelligence and policymaking communities in the United States government.

This book also benefited greatly from the time spent and the questions posed by three other senior officers: General Michael E. Ryan, Chief of Staff, United States Air Force; General John A. Gordon, Deputy Director of Central Intelligence; and Brigadier General Timothy J. McMahon, USAF/XON, all helped greatly by prodding me to think more deeply about certain technical issues within the Indian nuclear program that have a significant bearing on both regional stability and U.S. interests.

The support offered by many individuals on the Air Force staff was also critical to the successful completion of this work. James W. Hertsch, Jr., South Asia Branch Chief, National Air Intelligence Center, began as the intelligence point of contact for this project and—despite having had to read this dense volume while it was still in manuscript form—has, much to my delight, remained a dear and steadfast friend. His thoughtful advice and gentle criticism improved this book considerably. Robert S. Boyd, Director, National Air Intelligence Center, provided several helpful criticisms as well, and Gerald J. Butkus, Major Mark Westergren, and Lieutenant Colonel James Nees, also of the National Air Intelligence Center, gave generously of their time (and patience) on several occasions. At the Headquarters, USAF/XOXX, first Lieutenant Colonel Milton Johnson and later Lieutenant Colonel Max Hannesian, Chiefs, Regional Plans and Issues, Asia-Pacific Branch, helped connect me to other individuals and resources within the Air Force family whenever that was required by the exigencies of my research. All in all, the institutional support offered by the United States Air Force to Project AIR FORCE at RAND in general and to this research effort in particular went above and beyond what one is allowed to expect of a sponsor: It made the task of writing this lengthy book much easier and even pleasurable.

A book of this kind could in principle have been written at other scholarly institutions in the United States, but there is still no better place than RAND to pursue research relating to nuclear deterrence. Despite all the changes that have taken place in global politics over the past decade, RAND remains—thanks to the diverse technical skills of its researchers, its continued emphasis on interdisciplinary research, and its institutional memory on many matters relating to Cold War nuclear deterrence—the best institution for studying the strategic postures of the emerging nuclear states. I have benefited greatly from RAND's unique resources in the writing of this book. My greatest debt here is to Zalmay M. Khalilzad, Director of the Strategy and Doctrine Program within Project AIR FORCE, who supported this research project from its inception and encouraged me—despite my many other commitments at RAND—to produce a substantial monograph that would illuminate the unique characteristics of the emerging Indian nuclear posture. In addition to providing all the bureaucratic support associated with this effort, Dr. Khalilzad brought to bear his own past work on the nuclear programs in Southern Asia and his great familiarity with the region to lend unique assistance; in numerous hours of meetings, conversation, and travel, he helped me think through many of the issues addressed in this work, and the book as a whole is all the better for it.

Several other individuals in Project AIR FORCE also deserve mention for supporting this work in other ways. C. Richard Neu read the entire manuscript critically and lightened several burdens associated with RAND's formal review process. Donald V. Palmer was helpful in more ways than can be detailed here; among other things, he arranged for my research to be widely disseminated throughout the Air Force, particularly within its nuclear community, and shepherded this volume through the security review process conducted by the Office of the Secretary of Defense prior to its publication. Natalie W. Crawford, Vice-President, Project AIR FORCE, not only has strongly supported my research interests in general but has also enthusiastically championed this book both within RAND and before several Air Force audiences. I owe Project AIR FORCE a great deal for the freedom and support it has extended me in connection with many of my endeavors at RAND, and it remains a pleasure to work in this division on several other research projects currently under way.

Working on research projects at RAND invariably means working with many other analysts, some of whom are nationally recognized experts in their fields—and thanks to their generosity, this book has profited in many ways: sometimes through formal consultations, sometimes through conversations in hallways, sometimes through critical comments on the manuscript and on briefings, and sometimes simply through the mirth and laughter found in collegiality and friendship. Among those I must particularly mention are John Baker, Anil Bamezai, Glenn Buchan, Brian Chow, Lynn Davis, Carol Fair, Andrea Gabbitas, Mark Gabriele, Jerrold Green, Jeff Hagen, Edward Harshberger, Jeff Isaacson, Stuart Johnson, David Kassing, Benjamin Lambeth, Ian Lesser, Thomas McNaugher, Charles Meade, Richard Mesic, James Mulvenon, Bruce Nardulli, Kevin O'Connell, David Orletsky, Jonathan Pollack, Kevin Pollpeter, James Quinlivan, David Shlapak, Abram Shulsky, Michael Swaine, and Alan Vick. For a book that relied so heavily on printed documents, many of which were published abroad, special thanks are owed to the librarians at RAND, who routinely produced hundreds of newspaper reports, journal articles, and government documents without which this work could not have been completed. They remain the silent heroes behind much of the best research done at RAND.

As the writing of this manuscript progressed, I enjoyed the benefit of discussing its general argument and conclusions with several individuals in the U.S. government, academia, and other think tanks both in the United States and abroad. For all the support, comments, reactions, and good advice—even when not taken—I thank Matthew Daley, Laura DeWeese, Alan Eastham, Robert Einhorn, Edward Fei, Steven Ghitelman, Rose Gottermoeller, William Hatchett, Richard Hegmann, Karl Inderfurth, Robert Levine, Douglas Makeig, Fred Miller, Randall Romo, Caroline Russell, Adam Scheinman, Waheguru P.S. Sidhu, and Douglas Wade.

Several other individuals took the time to read part or all of the manuscript, offering detailed comments and suggestions that not only saved me from much embarrassment but also improved the content considerably. Given the size of this book and the density of its analysis, such assistance went far beyond the formalities of collegiality: I am grateful to Walter Andersen, Sumit Ganguly, Lieutenant Colonel Jack Gill, Gregory Jones, Peter Lavoy, Fred Mackie, George Perkovich, Lieutenant Colonel Anne Rieman, Leo Rose, and Ambassador Frank Wisner for their critical reading of the manuscript and, more important, for their continuing friendship and support. In Stephen P. Cohen and Neil Joeck I found two thoughtful formal reviewers who not only reviewed the manuscript for RAND quickly and with their customary high standards but also continued to assist me throughout the postreview process by offering good advice on a host of matters.

Several individuals played a critical role in preparing the manuscript for publication after the review processes at RAND and at the Office of the Secretary of Defense were completed. My editor, Andrea Fellows, nimbly transformed a dense text into readable prose: Besides making numerous stylistic improvements to the manuscript, she created the bibliography, cleaned up the footnotes, and clarified scores of ambiguous locutions that surfaced in the text. Patricia Bedrosian did a yeoman's job typesetting hundreds of marked-up manuscript pages speedily and with incredible care; Bruce Cheeks transformed the graphics into printable files; Kristin Leuschner drafted the research brief that accompanies this volume; Judy Larson helped greatly in producing the briefing that summarized the arguments found in this book for several high-level audiences throughout the United States government; and Jeanne Heller, David Bolhuis, John Warren, and Jane Ryan oversaw the production and distribution of this volume with an efficiency that all RAND researchers now simply take for granted. Over the past two years, a variety of wonderful assistants at RAND—Joan Myers, Joanna

Alberdeston, Luetta Pope, Viki Halabuk, Natalie Ziegler, and especially Karen Echeverri—not only kept the flow of paper connected with this book moving efficiently but also helped me keep my sanity in the face of all the bureaucratic minutiae surrounding such a project.

A book on India's nuclear posture simply could not have been written without the support of, and access to, numerous serving and retired officials in India who gave generously of their time during my many visits to New Delhi. Their thoughts, and particularly their writings, remain the raw material from which the substance of this book has been fashioned, even though they are not responsible—obviously—for any of the interpretations I may have overlaid on their arguments or the way in which I may have used their work to derive my own conclusions. At the political level, I am deeply grateful to Jaswant Singh, the Minister of External Affairs, and to George Fernandes, the Minister of Defence, who made generous time available to meet me and explain at some length the nature of India's strategic concerns and policy preferences. K. C. Pant, the current Deputy Chairman of the Planning Commission; I. K. Gujral, the former Indian Prime Minister; and Pranab Mukherjee, a former Minister of External Affairs in a previous Congress government, were also helpful with their assessments.

Many officials in the senior bureaucracy were extraordinarily generous as well. Both the former Foreign Secretary, K. Raghunath, and the present incumbent, Lalit Mansingh, have been highly supportive of my research efforts, and both spent a great deal of time educating me about the attitudes and perceptions of India's political leadership toward nuclear deterrence. I also owe Alok Prasad, Joint Secretary (Americas), Ministry of External Affairs a great debt. During the two-odd years that it took to complete this book, he spent considerable time with me—always pleasurable, I might add—and set up numerous meetings with key individuals in the Ministries of External Affairs, Defence, and Home, as well as in the Prime Minister's Office. He remains a dear friend. I am also delighted to acknowledge the friendship, assistance, and intellectual support offered by Raminder Jassal when he was first Joint Secretary, Plans and Coordination, Ministry of Defence, and later the Principal Spokesman in the Ministry of External Affairs. Other Indian civil servants who have been helpful both professionally and personally include Satish Chandra,

Dilip Lahiri, Prabhat Shukla, Rakesh Sood, T.C.A. Rangachari, and Bambit Roy, all of whom spent several hours with me discussing the future of the emerging Indian deterrent and how this evolving capability might affect India's strategic relations with key countries and with the international community. Only space limitations prevent me from more explicitly acknowledging their generous individual contributions.

I also had the good fortune to meet and interact with five key Indian officials located at the interstices of foreign and defense policy. K. Santhanam, Chief Adviser, Technologies, at the Defence Research and Development Organization; Raja Rammana, formerly Scientific Adviser to the Defence Minister and a former Minister of State for Defence; P. K. Iyengar, formerly Chairman of India's Atomic Energy Commission; V. Arunachalam, formerly Scientific Adviser to the Defence Minister; and Arun Singh, formerly Minister of State for Defence, all spent much time and energy helping me appreciate India's unique approach to the challenges embodied by nuclear weaponry. India's nuclear capabilities today and the strategies for managing those capabilities owe a great deal to these five individuals, and it was a rewarding experience indeed to discuss the country's emerging nuclear posture with those who were, in a manner of speaking, "present at the creation."

Even though the Indian armed services have been some degrees removed from the creation of the country's nuclear capability, several military officers took the time to discuss their perceptions of the strategic challenges facing New Delhi. I place on record my gratitude to several of them for their willingness to discuss a wide range of security issues that included, but was not limited to, nuclear weaponry. Generals V. P. Malik and S. Padmanabhan, Chiefs of Army Staff; Air Chief Marshal Anil Y. Tipnis, Chief of Air Staff; Admiral Sushil Kumar, Chief of Naval Staff; Lieutenant Generals R. K. Sawhney and O. S. Lohchab, Directors General, Military Intelligence; Major General Shantanu Chaudhry, Additional Director General, Military Intelligence; Air Vice Marshal S. K. Tyagi, Assistant Chief of Air Staff (Operations); Brigadier P. K. Singh, Deputy Director General, Foreign Military Intelligence; Air Commodore R. V. Phadke; Commodore C. Uday Bhaskar; and Colonel Gurmeet Kanwal all gave graciously of their time and ideas.

This book could not have been completed without the generosity of many members of the Delhi intelligentsia. Although the pages of this text are filled with numerous citations referring to their work, many of them discussed my interest in India's nuclear capabilities and its grand strategy in much greater detail than is evident here. My deep gratitude goes first to K. Subrahmanyam, Air Commodore (retired) Jasjit Singh, M. K. Narayanan, P. R. Chari, Lieutenant General (retired) V. R. Raghavan, Brigadier (retired) Vijai Nair, C. Raja Mohan, Rear Admiral (retired) Raja Menon, Lieutenant General (retired) Satish Nambiar, and Kanti Bajpai, all of whom either met me repeatedly or hosted me in New Delhi—both professionally and socially—on several occasions. I also wish to thank G. Balachandran, Sanjaya Baru, Rahul Bedi, Raj Chengappa, Giri Deshingkar, J. N. Dixit, Sujit Dutta, Manoj Joshi, Air Vice Marshal (retired) Kapil Kak, Bharat Karnad, Bhashyam Kasturi, Amitabh Mattoo, Admiral K. K. Nayyar, Rahul Roy-Chaudhury, and Matin Zuberi for sharing ideas and information and generously indulging me even when they disagreed with my arguments.

Finally, my research in India would have been impossible without the support and hospitality offered by the U.S. Embassy in New Delhi and, in particular, the warmth and encouragement of Ambassador Richard F. Celeste and Deputy Chief of Mission Ashley Wills. The arguments elaborated in this book were, in fact, first inflicted on the embassy's country team in late 1998, and I am grateful for all the suggestions, queries, and advice (and laughter!) that emerged from that meeting. Over the years, several embassy officials, taking special interest in my work, have gone out of their way to extend me various courtesies; special thanks go to Robert Boggs, Geeta Pasi, Mary Kirby, Colonel Mark Parnell, Sheetal Patel, Major Richard White, Major Jeffery Wright, and particularly Colonel Wilhelm Merkel.

The burdens that an author faces are often best appreciated by those who live around him. My darling family—Snuffles, Arthur, Athena, and Dhun—has had to suffer my long abdication from familial duties during the last two years. And they not only put up with my restlessness, inattentiveness, and long hours of withdrawal with much more equanimity than I have a right to expect but also helped me survive the process of writing through their joyous presence even when I was little more than a distracted bore. It is to them that this book is gratefully dedicated.

ABM   Antiballistic missile

ACOAS   Assistant Chief of Air Staff

AD   Assured destruction, air defense

ADE   Aeronautics Development Establishment

ADGES   Air Defense Ground Environment System

ADRDE   Aerial Delivery Research and Development Establishment

AEC   Atomic Energy Commission

AEWC&C Airborne early-warning command and control

AOC-in-C Air Officer Commanding-in-Chief

ARDE   Armament Research and Development Establishment

ARTRAC [Indian] Army's Training Command

ASAT   Antisatellite

ASLV   Advanced Satellite Launch Vehicle

ASTE   Aircraft System and Testing Establishment

ASW   Antisubmarine warfare

ATACM   Advanced Tactical Missile

ATBM	Anti–tactical ballistic missile
ATV	Advanced Technology Vessel
AVLIS	Atomic vapor laser isotope separation
AWACS	Airborne Warning and Control System
BAI	Battlefield air interdiction
BARC	Bhabha Atomic Research Center
BDA	Battle damage assessment
BJP	Bharatiya Janata Party
C^3I	Command, control, communications, and intelligence
C^4I^2	Command, control, communications, computing, intelligence, and information
CANDU	Canada Deuterium Uranium [reactor]
CAP	Combat air patrol
CAS	Close air support
CCNS	Cabinet Committee on National Security
CDS	Chief of Defence Staff
CEP	Circular error probable
CID	Criminal Investigation Department
CIRUS	Canada-Indian Reactor–United States
CM	Cruise missile
COAS	Chief of Air Staff
CRS	Congressional Research Service
CSC	Chiefs of Staff Committee
CTBT	Comprehensive Test Ban Treaty
CWC	Chemical Weapons Convention

DAE	Department of Atomic Energy
DAMA	Demand assigned multiple access
DARIN	Display Attack and Ranging Inertial Navigation
DCNP	Defence Communication Network Project
DEFCON	Defense condition
DIT	Department of Information Technology
DM	Defence Minister
DOT	Department of Telecommunications
DRDE	Defence Research Development Establishment
DRDO	Defence Research and Development Organization
DSWA	Defense Special Weapons Agency
EAM	External Affairs Minister
ECM	Electronic countermeasure
ELINT	Electronic intelligence
EMP	Electromagnetic pulse
ENDC	Eighteen-Nation Disarmament Committee
ENDS	Enhanced nuclear detonation safety [system]
ESM	Electronic support measure
FLAG	Fiber Optical Link Around the Globe
FM	Finance Minister
FMCT	Fissile Material Cutoff Treaty
GEO	Geosynchronous [orbit]
GMPCS	Global mobile personal communications by satellite
GPS	Global Positioning System

GSLV	Geosynchronous Satellite Launch Vehicle
GSQR	General Staff Quality Requirement
HEU	Highly enriched uranium
HF	High frequency
HM	Home Minister
H-NSC	Head, National Security Council
H-NSNC	Head, National Strategic Nuclear Command
HUD	Head-up display
HUMINT	Human intelligence
IAD	Integrated air defense
IADGES	Integrated Air Defense Ground Environment System
IAEA	International Atomic Energy Agency
IB	[Central] Intelligence Bureau
ICBM	Intercontinental ballistic missile
ICF	Inertial confinement fusion
IFF	Identification friend or foe
IGMDP	Integrated Guided Missile Development Programme
INS-RLG	Ring-laser gyro-based inertial navigation system
IRBM	Intermediate-range ballistic missile
IRS	Indian Remote Sensing
ISRO	Indian Space Research Organization
IT	Information technology
JIC	Joint Intelligence Committee
KRL	Khan Research Laboratories

kt	Kiloton
LAC	Line of actual control
LANTIRN	Low-altitude navigation and targeting infrared for night
LEO	Low-earth orbit
LEU	Low enriched uranium
LF	Low frequency
MAD	Mutual assured destruction
MEECN	Minimum essential emergency communications network
MI	[Directorate of] Military Intelligence
MOD	Ministry of Defence
MOPP	Mission-oriented protective posture
MR/ASW	Maritime reconnaissance/antisubmarine warfare
MRTD	Monopolistic and Restrictive Trade Practices [Committee]
Mt	Megaton
MTE	Megaton equivalent
MUCD	Military Unit Cover Designator
NBC	Nuclear, biological, and chemical
NCA	National Command Authority
NCP	National Command Post
NDA	National Democratic Alliance
NDC	National Development Centre
NEACP	National Emergency Airborne Command Post

NFU	No first use
NMCL	National Military Command Link
NMD	National missile defense
NORAD	Northern Region Air Defense
NPT	Non-Proliferation Treaty
NSA	National Security Adviser
NSAB	National Security Advisory Board
NSC	National Security Council
NSNC	National Strategic Nuclear Command
NUTS	Nuclear use theorists
OCP	Operations command post
OMT	Other military target
PAEC	Pakistan Atomic Energy Commission
PALS	Permissive action links
PHOTINT	Photographic intelligence
PLA	People's Liberation Army
PLAAF	People's Liberation Army Air Force
PM	Prime Minister
POC	Point of contact
PPBS	Planning Program Budgeting System
PR	Photo reconnaissance
PSLV	Polar Satellite Launch Vehicle
Pu	Plutonium
PWR	Pressurized water reactor

RAW	Research and Analysis Wing
RDT&E	Research, development, test, and evaluation
RMA	Revolution in military affairs
RSTA	Reconnaissance, surveillance, and target acquisition
RV	Reentry vehicle
RWR	Radar warning receiver
SAC	Strategic Air Command
SAFF	Safing, arming, fuzing, and firing
SAM	Surface-to-air missile
SC/ST	Scheduled Caste/Scheduled Tribe
SEAD	Suppression of Enemy Air Defense
SHF	Superhigh frequency
SIGINT	Signals intelligence
SIOP	Single Integrated Operations Plan
SLBM	Sea-launched ballistic missile
SLV	Satellite Launch Vehicle
SNEP	Subterranean Nuclear Explosion Project
SNL	Strategic Nuclear Link
SPG	Strategic Policy Group
SRBM	Short-range ballistic missile
SSBN	Nuclear-propelled ballistic missile submarine
SSGN	Nuclear-propelled guided missile submarine
SSM	Surface-to-surface missile
SUPARCO	Space and Upper Atmosphere Research Organization

TACAMO   "Take Charge and Move Out"

TAR   Tibetan Autonomous Region

TEL   Transporter-erector-launcher

TES   Test Evaluation Satellite

TMD   Theater missile defense

TNW   Tactical nuclear weapon

TREE   Transient radiation effects on electronics

U   Uranium

UAV   Unmanned aerial vehicle

UF   United Front

UHF   Ultrahigh frequency

VCOAS   Vice-Chief of Air Staff

VLF   Very low frequency

VSAT   Very small aperture terminal

VSNL   Videsh Sanchar Nigam Ltd.

WLL   Wireless local loop

WWMCCS   World Wide Military Command and Control System

Chapter One

INTRODUCTION

After a hiatus of almost 24 years, India once again startled the world by resuming nuclear testing at a time when the international community had solemnly expressed a desire, through the Comprehensive Test Ban Treaty (CTBT), to refrain from the field testing of nuclear explosives.[1] On May 11, 1998, Indian Prime Minister Atal Bihari Vajpayee tersely announced that New Delhi had conducted three nuclear tests, one of which involved the detonation of a thermonuclear device. As a stunned global community struggled to respond to this development, India announced two days later that it had conducted two more detonations that purportedly "completed

---

[1]The CTBT, by calling on every signatory state not to "carry out any nuclear weapon test explosion or any other nuclear explosion," is intended to be a "zero-yield" treaty. For a variety of reasons, however, the CTBT does not define what a "nuclear weapon test explosion or any other nuclear explosion" actually is—at least for the purpose of specifying in technical terms what is prohibited by the treaty. Thus, while the CTBT clearly prohibits nuclear explosions, it does not prohibit all activities involving a release of nuclear energy, including experiments using fast-burst or pulse reactors; experiments using pulse power facilities; inertial confinement fusion (ICF) and similar experiments; the research of material properties, including high-explosive and fissile materials; and hydrodynamic experiments, including subcritical experiments involving fissile materials. Since none of these activities necessarily constitute a nuclear explosion, they are not prohibited by the CTBT. For a useful analysis of what activities are regulated by the CTBT, see the Federation of American Scientists, "Article-by-Article Analysis of the Comprehensive Nuclear Test Ban Treaty,"available at http://www.fas.org/nuke/control/ctbt/text/artbyart/art01.htm. Since the CTBT, as it currently stands, therefore allows for a variety of activities that contribute to the maintenance and possibly the development of nuclear weaponry (at least in theory), India opposed the treaty *inter alia* on the grounds that the "technologies relating to subcritical testing, advanced computer simulation using extensive data relating to previous explosive testing, and weapon-related applications of laser ignition will lead to a fourth generation of nuclear weapons, even with a ban on explosive testing." Cited in Dinshaw Mistry, *India and the Comprehensive Test Ban Treaty*, ACDIS Research Report (Urbana, IL: University of Illinois, September 1998), p. 19.

the planned series of underground tests."[2] Dismayed by these developments, the United States responded by imposing economic sanctions on India in a manner consistent with its domestic laws while simultaneously engaging in diplomatic entreaties toward Pakistan, India's archrival, in the hopes of dissuading the latter from responding with nuclear tests of its own. This feverish activity, which dominated American diplomatic efforts for the better part of three weeks, unfortunately came to naught as Pakistan, seeking to validate its nuclear weapon designs, buttress the credibility of its deterrent vis-à-vis India, and appease its restive domestic polity, responded on May 28, 1998, with an announcement that it had conducted five nuclear tests of its own.[3] This announcement was followed by claims of yet another two tests on May 30, 1998, suggesting that Pakistan's total of seven tests against India's history of six signaled Islamabad's own political confidence and perhaps even its technological superiority.[4]

Not surprisingly, the resumption of nuclear testing in India resulted in a highly charged regional atmosphere: Indian Defence Minister George Fernandes sought to elaborate on his earlier public claim that "China is potential threat No. 1";[5] Indian Home Minister L. K. Advani threatened to "deal firmly" with Pakistan if it did not roll back its proxy war in Kashmir in light of "the change in the geostrategic situation in the region";[6] and Indian Minister of State for Science and Technology Murli Manohar Joshi announced that

---

[2]"Suo Motu Statement by Prime Minister Atal Bihari Vajpayee in the Indian Parliament on May 27, 1998," *India News*, May 16–June 15, 1998, p. 1.

[3]For an assessment of the calculus behind Pakistan's decision to respond to India's nuclear tests, see Samina Ahmed, "Pakistan's Nuclear Weapons Program," *International Security*, 23:4 (Spring 1999), pp. 178–204; Neil Joeck, "Nuclear Developments in India and Pakistan," *AccessAsia Review*, 2:2 (July 1999), pp. 22–30; and Samina Yasmeen, "Pakistan's Nuclear Tests: Domestic Debate and International Determinants," *Australian Journal of International Affairs*, 53:1 (1999), pp. 43–56.

[4]The initial reports, which claimed seven tests, were later withdrawn, and the final Pakistani claim stood at six nuclear tests: five conducted on May 28, 1999, and the sixth on May 30, 1999. Assertions about the superiority of the Pakistani nuclear weapon program in general can be found in "Pakistan Used Sophisticated Technology, Says Qadeer," *Dawn*, June 1, 1998; *Pakistan: "Nuclear and Missile Superiority" over India Claimed*, FBIS-TAC-98-169, June 18, 1998; and *Pakistan: Gohar Ayub on Next India-Pakistan War*, FBIS-NES-98-228, August 16, 1998.

[5]Manoj Joshi, "George in the China Shop," *India Today International*, May 18, 1998, p. 11.

[6]Kenneth J. Cooper, "Indian Minister Warns Pakistan," *Washington Post*, May 19, 1998.

India's missiles would be armed and deployed with the country's new nuclear weapons.[7] This rhetoric was matched by that emerging from Pakistan: Former Prime Minister Benazir Bhutto fervently pleaded with the West for a preemptive military strike on India;[8] then–Prime Minister Nawaz Sharif announced in a solemn television address on the day of Islamabad's tests that "today we have made history . . . we have settled the score with India";[9] and senior Pakistani officials (including the creator of Pakistan's first uranium enrichment facility, Dr. A. Q. Khan), responding to rumors of an imminent Indian attack, claimed that Pakistan's new Ghauri intermediate-range ballistic missiles (IRBMs) would be immediately armed with nuclear warheads in the face of the manifest Indian threat.[10] Altogether, a cacophony of rhetoric and unsubstantiated claims emerged from both India and Pakistan in the month of May, leading the South Asian correspondent of the *Washington Post* to conclude laconically but accurately that "confusion dominates [the] arms race" in South Asia.[11] Amid all this excitement, however, Indian Prime Minister Vajpayee took the time to emphatically claim—in an overt challenge both to the global nonproliferation regime in general and to U.S. nonproliferation policy in particular—that "India is now a nuclear weapons state."[12] Quite predictably, this claim was matched by that of Vajpayee's Pakistani counterpart, who also asserted that his country's nuclear tests demonstrated that "we have become a nuclear power."[13]

---

[7]"India Will Cap Missiles with Nuclear Warheads: Minister," AFP Wire, May 12, 1998.

[8]Benazir Bhutto, "Perspective on South Asia—Punishment: Make It Swift, Severe," *Los Angeles Times*, May 17, 1998.

[9]John F. Burns, "Pakistan, Answering India, Carries Out Nuclear Tests," *New York Times*, May 29, 1998.

[10]Umer Farooq, "Pakistan Ready to Arm Ghauri with Warheads," *Jane's Defence Weekly*, June 3, 1998, p. 4; Faraz Hashmi, "Mass-Scale Production of Ghauri Begins," *Dawn*, June 1, 1998; and Umer Farooq, "Pakistan Warned India of 'Massive' Retaliation," *Jane's Defence Weekly*, July 15, 1998, p. 16.

[11]John Ward Anderson, "Confusion Dominates Arms Race," *Washington Post*, June 1, 1998.

[12]"Interview: Atal Bihari Vajpayee," *India Today International*, May 25, 1998, p. 29.

[13]Burns, "Pakistan, Answering India, Carries Out Nuclear Tests."

These developments, among many others, moved one of India's leading strategic commentators to reflect on the momentous events of May 1998 in the following terms:

> The world knew for quite some time that both India and Pakistan have been in possession of atomic weapons, although they were not formally recognized as nuclear weapon powers. The great powers have hoped that the anomalous nuclear standing of India and Pakistan in the international nuclear system could be fudged. They have striven hard to keep the Indian and Pakistani nuclear capabilities under wraps forever. But the hot summer of 1998 has finally vapourised [sic] the veil of nuclear ambiguity in the Indian subcontinent. As a consequence, the security situation in the subcontinent and the global nuclear order are unlikely to be the same ever again.[14]

In the same time frame, another prominent Indian analyst concluded that the triple tests at Pokhran (the field site where the Indian nuclear tests took place) had brought to an end not only "three decades of nuclear debate, self-denial, and fence-sitting" but also the perception of Indian "weakness and hypocrisy." In this analyst's view, the nuclear tests had allowed India to become "a willing and active player in the international nuclear arms control regime," but with a difference: "The difference now is that India seeks to play that game as a *nuclear weapons power*. This is the end of ambiguity—and hypocrisy" (italics added).[15]

The notion that the 1998 South Asian nuclear tests not only altered the strategic environment in the region (and, perhaps, globally) but also transformed New Delhi into a "nuclear weapons power" of some standing appears repeatedly in Indian strategic and political analyses. Yet while the former proposition is arguable, the latter may be somewhat dubious—and the truth of the matter is much more complex than most Indian analysts believe. This volume will suggest that despite having demonstrated an ability to successfully undertake nuclear explosions—including nuclear weapon test explosions—India still has some way to go before it can acquire the

---

[14]C. Raja Mohan, "Living in a Nuclear South Asia," *The Hindu*, May 28, 1998.

[15]Shekhar Gupta, "Road to Resurgence," *Indian Express*, May 12, 1998.

capabilities that would make it a significant nuclear power.[16] The analysis will further demonstrate that in many ways India remains at a crossroads with respect to its nuclear weapon program. In contrast to much of the superficial commentary that appeared in the wake of the May 1998 tests, however, it will argue that the challenges facing India are not as onerous as they are often assumed to be, although they will compel New Delhi to move—at least initially—in a direction quite different from that which most previous nuclear weapon states have taken. It will be posited that this nuclearization process will in all probability involve a large but finite number of steps that will occur covertly rather than overtly. In short, it will be argued that India's emergence as a true nuclear weapon power will more likely be a slow, gradual, and distinctive process, thanks to a number of factors—including India's traditional and highly publicized commitment to disarmament; its continuing economic and developmental constraints; its susceptibility to pressures emanating both from existing nuclear weapon states and from the global nonproliferation regime in general; its singular view of nuclear weapons as "pure deterrents" rather than as war-fighting instruments; its unique civil-military system, which has few parallels in the Third World; and, finally, the fact that its adversaries' coercive capabilities, while significant, can be countered by a minimal, albeit perhaps not a token, deterrent.

This book will assess India's emerging nuclear posture in the aftermath of the May 1998 tests. It focuses on India primarily because of its geopolitical weight and because New Delhi's choices—and others' perception of those choices—will remain among the key drivers influencing the future strategic environment in South Asia. Given this assumption, Pakistani and Chinese nuclear programs and capabilities will be addressed as well, but more with a view toward illuminating India's strategic choices and future directions than as independent objects of analysis.[17] At the same time, however, the as-

---

[16]In legal terms, India can never be a "nuclear weapon state" under the definition of that term enunciated in the Non-Proliferation Treaty (NPT). Whenever India is referred to as a nuclear weapon state in this book, however, the phrase is intended to convey not a legal status but merely a description of fact.

[17]Other RAND research has assessed China's nuclear, space, and information warfare capabilities in some detail. These findings are summarized in Zalmay M. Khalilzad, Abram N. Shulsky, Daniel Byman, Roger Cliff, David T. Orletsky, David Shlapak, and Ashley J. Tellis, *The United States and a Rising China: Strategic and*

sessment of India's future nuclear posture requires a level of detail that is often lacking in such analyses, which generally treat "going nuclear" simply as synonymous with the ability to set off nuclear explosions. As early as 1977, Lewis Dunn and William Overholt persuasively argued that proliferation research should incorporate more analytically powerful frameworks that can discriminate between "the acquisition of increasing levels of nuclear capability,"[18] such as that relating to the character of research on nuclear explosives or the procurement of specific weapon systems, or the development of command, control, and communications procedures or the enunciation of a strategic doctrine.

This book will investigate the issues outlined above by seeking a broader understanding of India's strategic interests, institutional structures, and security goals. Toward this end, it will attempt to reconstruct the logic of the choices India faces *from New Delhi's perspective* in efforts to discern which future courses of action appear most appealing to India's civilian security managers—i.e., India's elected political leadership and the senior bureaucrats who occupy critical institutions such as the Prime Minister's Office, the Cabinet Secretariat, and key ministerial departments (e.g., Finance, Defence, and Home [internal affairs]). It will then assess how such choices, if acted upon, would affect the United States and its strategic interests. This methodological decision was driven primarily by the objective of better understanding the worldview of India's security managers such that the U.S. policymaking and defense-planning communities may more effectively anticipate future developments in India's nuclear program in particular and its strategic capabilities in general.

This book is therefore divided into five chapters. Chapter Two surveys the strategic factors conditioning India's choices with respect to its future nuclear posture. Chapter Three analyzes five specific nuclear "end states" that India has debated since its independence in 1947 and that have acquired particular salience since New Delhi first demonstrated its nuclear capabilities in 1974; this analysis is in-

---

Military Implications, MR-1082-AF (Santa Monica: RAND, 1999). Both the Pakistani nuclear weapon program and the challenges of Sino-Indian-Pakistani nuclear stability are currently the focus of ongoing RAND research.

[18]Lewis A. Dunn and William H. Overholt, "The Next Phase in Nuclear Proliferation Research," in William H. Overholt (ed.), *Asia's Nuclear Future* (Boulder, CO: Westview Press, 1977), pp. 1–2.

tended to assess both the extent of the shift in India's nuclear posture after the recent tests and the implications of what the search for a "minimum credible deterrent"[19] could entail in the years to come. Chapter Four describes the nuclear posture India is likely to adopt over the next decade or two; it explicates India's evolving nuclear doctrine and describes how the force posture that is likely to be created will service this doctrine in the contexts of strategic needs that are specific to New Delhi. Chapter Five examines the operational capabilities India's desired nuclear posture will demand in light of its technical achievements and limitations and ends by assessing the adequacy of the evolving Indian deterrent in terms of the criteria offered by various nuclear deterrence theories. The conclusion, Chapter Six briefly surveys the consequences of the anticipated changes in India's nuclear posture for local security competition with Pakistan and China, the international nuclear proliferation regime, and the ongoing dialogue in U.S.-Indian relations.

---

[19]This phrase has been used repeatedly by Indian leaders to define their conception of the country's future nuclear capabilities. See, for example, Mahesh Uniyal, "No Cap on Fissile Material, Says Vajpayee," *India Abroad*, December 25, 1998.

Chapter Two

STRATEGIC FACTORS AFFECTING
INDIA'S NUCLEAR POSTURE

In assessing the variables that have influenced India's nuclear posture and the role these variables might play in shaping the country's future choices, it is useful to begin by summarizing what India's strategic posture has been for most of the postindependence period. Summarizing the complex evolution of Indian attitudes and capabilities during this time frame will necessitate the omission or oversimplification of certain historical details. This shortcoming can be tolerated, however, because the intention here is *not* to provide a comprehensive narrative describing the evolution of the Indian nuclear program given that such reconstructions are already widely available.[1] Rather, the objective is to *define a benchmark* that will al-

---

[1]Among the best sources for reconstructing the history of the Indian nuclear program are Ashok Kapur, *India's Nuclear Option* (New York: Praeger Publishers, 1976); Shyam Bhatia, *India's Nuclear Bomb* (Ghaiziabad, India: Vikas Publishing House, 1979); G. G. Mirchandani, *India's Nuclear Dilemma* (New Delhi: Popular Book Services, 1968); N. Seshagiri, *The Bomb! Fallout of India's Nuclear Explosion* (Delhi: Vikas Publishing House, 1975); Sampooran Singh, *India and the Nuclear Bomb* (New Delhi: S. Chand, 1971); J. P. Jain, *Nuclear India*, Vols. 1 and 2 (New Delhi: Radiant, 1974); and Roberta Wohlstetter, *"The Buddha Smiles": Absent-Minded Peaceful Aid and the Indian Bomb* (Los Angeles: Pan Heuristics, 1977). The best contemporary survey, which is in fact likely to become the definitive statement of the history of India's nuclear program, can be found in George Perkovich, *India's Nuclear Bomb* (Berkeley, CA: University of California Press, 1999). Itty Abraham, *The Making of the Indian Atomic Bomb: Science, Secrecy and the Post-Colonial State* (New York: Zed, 1998), represents an interesting effort to relate the nuclear program to the larger struggles with reason, modernity, and violence as embodied by the modern state. Peter R. Lavoy, *Learning to Live with the Bomb? India and Nuclear Weapons, 1947–1974*, unpublished doctoral dissertation, University of California, Berkeley, May 1997, remains a good argument about the role of personalities and the myths they created in

low analysts to judge the degree of movement that India's most recent policy shift—as exemplified by its nuclear tests and subsequent claims to nuclear status—represents when measured against the background condition of "nuclear ambiguity"[2] that ended with its resumption of nuclear testing in May 1998.

EXPLAINING THE HERITAGE OF NUCLEAR AMBIGUITY

It is important to recognize that while the history of the Indian nuclear program predates the country's independence in 1947, the strategic environment India faced for most of its independent life did not demand that any clear-cut decisions be made regarding its nuclear status. To be sure, the attitudes of India's leadership toward nuclear weaponry evolved gradually over the years. Strident opposition to nuclear weapons and all forms of competition involving nuclear weaponry was most visible during the 1950s, when India, having recently emerged from the colonial era, sought to articulate on the global stage a highly moralistic brand of politics that emphasized comprehensive economic development and, toward that goal, the harnessing of atomic energy for peaceful purposes.[3] India's approach toward nuclear power during this period was in fact Janus-faced in that its fervid enthusiasm for nuclear energy as a cost-effective solution to its vast developmental problems was matched only by its repeatedly expressed repugnance toward nuclear weaponry of all kinds. This uncompromising opposition to nuclear weapons and to nuclear weaponry per se as instruments of "high politics," subtly mutated during the 1960s when India—having become conscious both of the Chinese threat and of China's nuclear prowess following its defeat in the Sino-Indian border war of 1962—

---

the making of India's atomic bomb. Raj Chengappa, *Weapons of Peace* (New Delhi: HarperCollins Publishers, 2000), is a fascinating anecdotal history of the Indian atomic program with myriad new revelations but with much that is suspect as well.

[2]The notion of "nuclear ambiguity" refers to the condition wherein the nuclear option was "kept open but in a state of suspended animation" such that the capacity to make nuclear weapons was "neither expressed nor foreclosed." A good description of "nuclear ambiguity," from which these quotes are derived, can be found in P. R. Chari, *Indo-Pak Nuclear Standoff: The Role of the United States* (New Delhi: Manohar, 1995), p. 102ff.

[3]Sumit Ganguly, "Why India Joined the Nuclear Club," *Bulletin of the Atomic Scientists*, 39:4 (April 1983), p. 30.

began to flirt with the possibility of extending civilian nuclear technology to defense applications through its Subterranean Nuclear Explosion Project (SNEP).[4] This attempt to exploit the civilian nuclear energy and research infrastructure for strategic purposes reached its peak in 1974, when India carried out its first atomic test. In efforts to ward off Western pressures in the wake of this test, however, India affirmed its right to engage in "peaceful nuclear explosions" while simultaneously reiterating its opposition to nuclear weaponry.[5] The uncomfortable ambiguity that arose from India's demonstrated ability to make nuclear weapons, even as it persisted in its claims that it had no nuclear arsenal, continued throughout the 1980s and well into the 1990s.[6] In fact, even in the aftermath of the May 1998 nuclear tests, India's new claims to nuclear status did not elucidate whether India already possessed a ready inventory of nuclear warheads or whether it intended to create such an inventory, to be maintained and deployed at certain minimal standards of readiness.[7]

All in all, India's official attitude toward nuclear weapons evolved slowly over the years, but these shifts were insufficient to motivate the national leadership to make a deliberate decision favoring the acquisition of a nuclear arsenal or declaring India's status to be that of a nuclear weapon state. This lack of movement in the direction of overt nuclearization ultimately stemmed from the perception that

---

[4]Chari, *Indo-Pak Nuclear Standoff,* pp. 12–13.

[5]See, by way of example, Rikhi Jaipal, "The Indian Nuclear Explosion," *International Security,* 1:4 (Spring 1977), pp. 44–51.

[6]In early 1983, for example, Indira Gandhi, in an interview with the French newspaper *Le Monde,* stated during a discussion about nuclear weaponry that "we have no intention of manufacturing them. We do not manufacture them and we will not utilise them." Reproduced in Indira Gandhi, *Statements on Foreign Policy, January–April 1983* (New Delhi: Government of India, Ministry of External Affairs, 1983), p. 27. In 1985, Rajiv Gandhi indirectly reiterated this theme when he noted that U.S. unwillingness to stop the Pakistani nuclear weapon program would result in "the introduction of nuclear weapons in our area, [which] will completely change the whole region." See Maynard Parker, "Rajiv Gandhi's Bipolar World," *Newsweek,* June 3, 1985. Even as recently as 1996, then–Prime Minister I. K. Gujral, in an interview with a leading Indian newsmagazine, asserted that "at the moment, the agenda to weaponise our nuclear capability is not there." See "Interview: I. K. Gujral," *India Today International,* September 15, 1996, p. 78.

[7]Anderson, "Confusion Dominates Arms Race," and Kenneth J. Cooper, "Nuclear Dilemmas—India," *Washington Post,* May 25, 1998.

despite all the strategic challenges it faced, the security environment India had confronted for most of the postindependence period had in general been benign. The political cover provided by American strength during the early part of the Cold War and by Soviet support during the later part of that epoch further buttressed New Delhi's ambiguous attitude toward nuclear weaponry, as did India's own advantages vis-à-vis Pakistan, China's weakness as a regional adversary, and the relatively innocuous disposition of both superpowers toward India. The Nehruvian legacy of suspicion about militarized power politics and its attendant distaste of nuclear weaponry as the "currency of global power" interacted with the older Gandhian moral synthesis, which emphasized "community" over "state" and "service" over "coercion," to reinforce this ambiguous stance.[8] Finally, even when the temptation to demonstrate an overt nuclear weapon capability became more alluring than usual—e.g., from the 1970s onward—India's weakness as a center of power in international politics guaranteed that it would continue to show restraint out of fear that international pressures might impede the attainment of critical strategic objectives such as economic development.[9]

Thanks to all these factors, India's traditional nuclear posture continued to pivot simply on "keeping the option open."[10] And sustaining this posture involved, among other things, maintaining a large strategic establishment to produce fissile materials, design nuclear weaponry, and develop various delivery systems while simultaneously continuing to refrain from any public decision to create and

---

[8]B. M. Jain, *Nuclear Politics in South Asia* (New Delhi: Rawat Publications, 1994), pp. 53–77. It is important to note, however, that Nehru and perhaps even Gandhi, though not pronuclear by any means, were often ambivalent about whether nuclear weaponry would be required by Indian security interests in an anarchic international environment. A good analysis of Nehru's ambivalence can be found in Kapur, *India's Nuclear Option*, pp. 47–82, and in Perkovich, *India's Nuclear Bomb*. For an interesting albeit controversial assessment of Gandhi's attitude toward nuclear weaponry, see K. Subrahmanyam, "Hedging Against Hegemony: Gandhi's Logic in the Nuclear Age," *The Times of India*, June 16, 1998. An excellent summary that captures the complexity of Gandhi's attitude toward nonviolence can be found in V. R. Mehta, *Foundations of Indian Political Thought* (New Delhi: Manohar, 1996), pp. 217–234.

[9]The effect of foreign pressures on India's nuclear choices during the 1970s and 1980s has been analyzed in detail in Perkovich, *India's Nuclear Bomb*, pp. 190–292.

[10]See the discussion in K. Subrahmanyam, "India: Keeping the Option Open," in Robert M. Lawrence and Joel Larus (eds.), *Nuclear Proliferation: Phase II* (Wichita, KS: University Press of Kansas, 1974), pp. 112–148.

deploy a real nuclear arsenal—understood as an "organic ensemble"[11] of weaponry, delivery capabilities, supporting infrastructure, and procedural and ideational systems—that would allow a variety of deliberate and perhaps even preplanned nuclear operations to be undertaken in an emergency. This peculiar approach, which consisted of developing some components of an arsenal while desisting from creating the arsenal itself—and, indeed, publicly denying the intention to create such an arsenal—derived from India's calculated assessment that "preserving the option," in the sense understood above, would provide deterrence advantages without imposing any of the costs and risks associated with actually deploying nuclear weaponry in the context of an overt assertion of India's nuclear status. Such a posture also had the advantage of underscoring India's sovereign right to create such an arsenal at some point in the future if national security considerations so warranted, while in the interim requiring that Indian strategic policy simply preserve, both legally and technically, the capability to formally deploy nuclear weapons should that become necessary.[12]

Not surprisingly, Indian strategic policy for much of the Cold War period and thereafter focused on attaining two sets of objectives. The first set of objectives—pursued mainly at the diplomatic level—consisted of espousing the global abolition of nuclear weaponry.[13] These calls for abolition were often couched either in moralistic terms drawn from indigenous traditions or in the secular language of liberal internationalism, both of which, by imparting a strong "idealistic" flavor to Indian rhetoric, rendered such comments mis-

---

[11]Ashton B. Carter, "Introduction," in Ashton B. Carter, John D. Steinbruner, and Charles A. Zraket (eds.), *Managing Nuclear Operations* (Washington, D.C.: Brookings, 1987), p. 1.

[12]Onkar Marwah, "India's Nuclear Program: Decisions, Intent and Policy, 1950–1976," in William H. Overholt (ed.), *Asia's Nuclear Future* (Boulder, CO: Westview Press, 1977), pp. 161–196, and Raju G.C. Thomas, "India's Nuclear and Space Programs: Defense or Development?" *World Politics*, 38 (1986), pp. 315–342.

[13]A concise survey of Indian initiatives in this regard can be found in Manpreet Sethi, "The Struggle for Nuclear Disarmament," in Jasjit Singh (ed.), *Nuclear India* (New Delhi: Knowledge World, 1998), pp. 75–95, and *Disarmament: India's Initiatives* (New Delhi: Ministry of External Affairs, Government of India, 1988). The worldview that bred these initiatives can be found in *India and Disarmament: An Anthology of Selected Writings and Speeches* (New Delhi: Ministry of External Affairs, Government of India, 1988).

placed in the highly competitive arena of international politics. Yet while genuine idealism did in fact underlie India's calls for global denuclearization (especially in the early years of the Cold War), it would be a mistake to reduce India's motivations to altruistic impulses alone. In fact, these calls were equally grounded in a soberly realistic assessment of India's own condition—i.e., in the recognition that the global abolition of nuclear weaponry was essential precisely because only in a world without nuclear weapons would India be freed from the obligation to develop antidotes to possible nuclear threats at a time when it was both economically vulnerable and politically fragile. In short, New Delhi yearned to abolish the arms race because it was a race that India could not run—and did not wish to run—given its conspicuous internal weaknesses during most of the Cold War period. Because this objective could not be attained, however—thanks both to the logic of technology and to political resistance on the part of the established nuclear powers—India gradually settled for a fallback option: preventing any external political or legal restraints from encumbering its right to formally develop a nuclear arsenal when that might be required.[14]

These political goals were complemented by a second set of objectives geared toward sustaining India's capability to produce fissile materials for nuclear weapons as well as a wide range of delivery technologies that a full-fledged deterrent would require. Pursuing these objectives implied increased commitment on India's part

---

[14]The desire to maintain India's autonomy with respect to its nuclear choices existed since the beginning of its nuclear program. This desire was manifestly demonstrated first during the international discussions over the International Atomic Energy Agency (IAEA) safeguards system, where official Indian attitudes clearly reflected the "desire to avoid international safeguards against India so that [its] military option could be developed if the need arose to start a weapons program." See Kapur, *India's Nuclear Option*, p. 107. This desire to preserve national autonomy would be confirmed again during the negotiations leading up to the NPT (where India took the position that a distinction could be made between nuclear explosions for peaceful purposes and nuclear weapon tests). See the statement by Representative Azim Husain in the Eighteen-Nation Disarmament Committee (ENDC), February 27, 1968, reproduced in Jain, *Nuclear India*, Vol. 2, pp. 332–335. Most recently, the desire to preserve Indian autonomy in nuclear matters was exhibited during the CTBT negotiations, where, after much internal debate, India finally blocked the CTBT in the Conference on Disarmament. For a good statement explicating the reasoning behind this action, see Arundhati Ghose, "Negotiating the CTBT: India's Security Concerns and Nuclear Disarmament," *Journal of International Affairs*, 51:1 (Summer 1997), pp. 239–261.

to domestic research-and-development organizations both in the atomic energy arena and in the defense arena in general. The desire to possess adequate fissile materials in turn resulted in the large-scale use of foreign technologies—acquired through direct purchase, licensed reproduction, or indigenous application of information from Western sources—to produce significant quantities of weapons-usable plutonium,[15] and more recently, enriched uranium, tritium, beryllium, and other materials as well. The pursuit of adequate delivery systems resulted in a similar strategy that coupled domestic research and development with the outright purchase (sometimes involving coproduction), reverse-engineering, or modification of systems obtained from abroad—all married together through large and highly publicized domestic systems integration efforts.[16] India's defense and space research organizations have all used some variant of the above strategy, yielding several successes along with many failures that have gone unacknowledged both by Indian technologists and by their supporters in the national bureaucracy.[17] The pursuit of this strategy has in turn resulted in heightened resistance on India's part to international technology-control regimes, which are widely perceived as impediments that could prevent India from enhancing its strategic capability.

Although both objectives identified above have been actively pursued since India's independence, their success has clearly been mixed. Indian successes appear most conspicuous at the political level, where New Delhi—despite having failed to engineer any realistic international commitments to nuclear abolition—has at least succeeded in preventing external legal constraints from limiting its freedom of choice. India has not signed the Non-Proliferation Treaty (NPT)—and, despite having been one of its original votaries, has thus

---

[15]For details, see Bhatia, *India's Nuclear Bomb;* Wohlstetter, *"The Buddha Smiles": Absent-Minded Peaceful Aid and the Indian Bomb*; and David Hart, *Nuclear Power in India* (Boston: G. Allen & Unwin, 1983).

[16]For a good discussion of how these approaches were manifested in Indian missile R&D, see Timothy V. McCarthy, "India: Emerging Missile Power," in William C. Potter and Harlan W. Jencks (eds.), *The International Missile Bazaar: The New Suppliers' Network* (Boulder, CO: Westview Press, 1994), pp. 201–233.

[17]Eric Arnett, "Military Technology: The Case of India," *SIPRI Yearbook 1994* (Oxford, UK: Oxford University Press, 1994), pp. 343–365.

far refused to sign the CTBT.[18] Similarly, India remains committed in principle to supporting a Fissile Material Cutoff Treaty (FMCT), assuming that a suitable instrument can be negotiated, but is unlikely to sign any agreement that would require full transparency of past stockpiles. At a purely formal level, India's nuclear program therefore remains unconstrained by any legal obligations that would prevent it from developing a full-fledged nuclear arsenal in the future.

At a substantive level, however, such freedom of action has by no means gone unbridled. Through the indefinite extension of the NPT and the overwhelming consensus underlying the CTBT, the existing nuclear powers have substantially delegitimized the "natural right" of states to acquire any weaponry of their choice and have thus burdened holdouts like India with an inhospitable international environment within which future nuclear deployment decisions must be made. Furthermore, a variety of legislative constraints have arisen within the United States that in effect require that the U.S. government penalize—unilaterally if necessary—any state other than the Permanent Five that acquires new nuclear capabilities.[19] The sanctions imposed on India and Pakistan in the aftermath of their recent nuclear tests were in fact mandated by one or more of these legislative constraints. Since the United States will remain the only hegemonic power in the international system for at least another two decades, its ability to inhibit foreign choices with respect to nuclear

---

[18]As a result of the protracted U.S.-Indian dialogue that followed the May 1998 nuclear tests, India has agreed in principle to sign the CTBT when a national consensus in support of such an action can be achieved. In practice, however, the prospect that India will become a signatory to the treaty is contingent on the extent of support it can secure from the United States in various issue areas of importance to New Delhi. Further, senior Indian officials have explicitly stated that signing the CTBT, if and when it occurs, does not automatically imply ratification and deposit of the signed instrument—a new political strategy developed in response to the U.S. Senate's decision to eschew treaty ratification. India's becoming a signatory, therefore, is merely a preliminary step, since the obligations imposed by the treaty will not fully constrain it until the deposit of the ratified instrument is finally concluded. See "India Not to Engage in a N-Arms Race: Jaswant," *The Hindu*, November 29, 1999.

[19]These constraints are detailed in Jeanne J. Grimmett, "Nuclear Sanctions: Section 102(b) of the Arms Export Control Act and Its Application to India and Pakistan," *CRS Report for Congress* (Washington, D.C.: Library of Congress, updated October 30, 1998), and in "India-Pakistan Nuclear and Missile Proliferation: Background, Status, and Issues for U.S. Policy," *CRS Report for Congress*, Foreign Affairs and National Defense Division, Environment and Natural Resources Policy Division (Washington, D.C.: Library of Congress, December 16, 1996).

decisionmaking cannot be underestimated and must in fact be recognized as an even more significant hindrance on any freedom of
choice that India notionally enjoys. At the very least, this constraint
could materialize in the form of a continuation of the stringent U.S.
controls that currently restrict access to high technology and advanced weaponry.[20] All things considered, therefore, India has secured and maintained its formal freedom of action with respect to its
nuclear status, but such liberties are by no means untrammeled or
cost-free.

A similar assessment holds with respect to India's technological
achievements. India has certainly succeeded in maintaining the capacity to produce fissile materials—mostly weapons-usable plutonium—in the absence of external constraints. In fact, India today is
probably at the point where it faces no *technological* constraints on
its ability to produce any level of weapons-usable (including
weapons-grade) plutonium it desires for the purposes of fabricating
nuclear weaponry.[21] Indeed, the principal constraints India faces in
this context are *efficiency* constraints—and though these are by no
means notional or illusory, the implication is that India has not been
handicapped (as Pakistan traditionally was) by a lack of availability of
fissile materials. Whether India did in fact stockpile ready nuclear
weapons itself prior to May 1998 is anyone's guess. Most official U.S.
estimates suggest that India could fabricate complete weapons at
short notice, but the safety, efficiency and reliability of such weapons

---

[20]One U.S. official, Matthew P. Daley, has noted that "even if current problems
following the Indian nuclear tests are resolved, India will not get access to nuclear aid
and other high tech on the same basis as China so long as she does not sign the NPT."
See "U.S. High Tech to Remain 'Out of Bounds' for India," *Hindustan Times*, January
15, 1999. Whether this conclusion continues to hold, of course, rests largely on American choices in the years ahead—choices that will be influenced in large part by competing concerns over limiting proliferation on the one hand while preserving the future balance of power in Asia on the other. If U.S. grand strategy comes around to
viewing a strong and capable India as a necessary ingredient of a well-ordered Asian
future, U.S.-Indian cooperation in the arena of strategic technology could well begin.
Such a development would hearken back to U.S. debates in the early 1960s, when several elements of the U.S. government at least contemplated, if not argued for, supporting an Indian nuclear program in order to contain the Chinese. This chapter in the
evolution of U.S. nonproliferation policy is detailed in Perkovich, *India's Nuclear
Bomb*, pp. 86–105.

[21]Brian G. Chow, Richard H. Speier, and Gregory S. Jones, *The Proposed Fissile-
Material Production Cut-Off: Next Steps*, MR-586-OSD (Santa Monica: RAND, 1995),
pp. 43–45.

(even in the wake of the May 1998 tests) continue to be the subject of debate both within and outside India.[22]

India has also steadily developed a variety of delivery systems. Some of these capabilities, however (e.g., aircraft), may have been more presumptive than real in that they were simply conventional platforms that could be—but by some public accounts have yet to be—configured for nuclear delivery.[23] Even if some aircraft were configured for nuclear operations—as is likely the case—they would probably be effective against only one of India's two competitors: Pakistan and not China. The other Indian delivery systems are even more notional at present; India's long-range missile system, the Agni, is still in the engineering development phase, while its current shorter-range system, the Prithvi family of missiles, was originally not intended to play and will probably not have a nuclear delivery role, except perhaps in a grave emergency. Besides these inchoate capabilities at the level of weapons and delivery systems, there is no public evidence that India had developed either the supporting capabilities or the procedural and ideational frameworks that together would allow various individual components of a deterrent system to work coherently. On balance, therefore, India's capabilities prior to the May 1998 tests seem to justify the conclusion that New Delhi possessed a "nuclear option" in the form of latent and, in some areas, rudimentary capabilities but had no effective nuclear arsenal, implying that—at least by traditional Cold War standards—it had no "credible deterrent."[24]

To be sure, this conclusion does *not* imply that India possessed no retaliatory capabilities whatsoever prior to May 1998 or that these capabilities were of necessity politically and militarily ineffective vis-à-vis its principal threats, Pakistan and China. Rather, it is meant to suggest that New Delhi's latent deterrent capabilities were not—and

---

[22]Office of the Secretary of Defense, *Proliferation: Threat and Response* (Washington, D.C.: USGPO, 1996), p. 37.

[23]Dinesh Kumar, "IAF Still Lacks N-Capability," *The Times of India*, October 19, 1998.

[24]The best Indian source that affirms such a judgment is Chari, *Indo-Pak Nuclear Standoff*. The best concurring American assessment of India's (and Pakistan's) traditional nuclear posture can be found in Neil Joeck, *Maintaining Nuclear Stability in South Asia*, Adelphi Paper No. 312 (London: IISS, 1997).

perhaps are not—configured in a way that comports with the "classical" Cold War standard of what constitutes an "adequate" or a "credible" deterrent. During the Cold War, four generic criteria were advanced for deterrent adequacy and, by implication, strategic stability: the guaranteed presence of sufficient second-strike weapon reserves; a history of credible, communicated deterrent threats; the existence of survivable command, control, communications, and intelligence (C^3I) assets and supporting infrastructure; and a multitude of preplanned nuclear employment options that could be executed as part of a retaliatory strike.[25] Whether and to what extent these criteria are in fact appropriate to the South Asian region is a separate issue that will be discussed in some detail in Chapters Four and Five, but for the moment, the principal conclusion that bears restatement is that India's traditional nuclear posture, wrapped as it was in deliberate ambiguity, sought to derive deterrence benefits from the possession of latent nuclear capabilities rather than from the flaunting of ready, deployed nuclear forces.

Since maintaining the "nuclear option" and eschewing the creation of a ready arsenal have thus been the product of a deliberate political choice that remained at least formally entrenched until May 1998, it must be admitted that New Delhi's core political preferences prevailed throughout the Cold War era and beyond—at least in the main, if not in all the details. India preserved its legal freedom to develop a nuclear arsenal in the face of its failure to engineer the global abolition of nuclear weaponry, even as it concomitantly developed and maintained certain pockets of technical capability that would allow it to develop a deterrent of some kind in the future. The 1998 nuclear tests have, however, muddied this picture somewhat. Clearly, the tests themselves—assuming that they were as successful as India has claimed—have simply corroborated what most observers already believed to be true: that India was in fact capable of detonating nuclear explosives more or less successfully, as previously

---

[25]For more on the classical standards of deterrence adequacy (and the controversies that accompanied them), see, among many others, Thomas Schelling, *The Strategy of Conflict* (Cambridge, MA: Harvard University Press, 1960); Thomas Schelling, *Arms and Influence* (New Haven, CT: Yale University Press, 1966); John D. Steinbruner, "National Security and the Concept of Strategic Stability," *Journal of Conflict Resolution*, 22:3 (September 1978), pp. 411–428; and especially Charles L. Glaser, *Analyzing Strategic Nuclear Policy* (Princeton, NJ: Princeton University Press, 1990), pp. 19–60.

demonstrated in 1974. Hence, India's claim of being a nuclear weapon state may not alter any realities at the factual level but it certainly poses a political challenge for the global nonproliferation regime—for by claiming such status overtly through a series of nuclear detonations, India has in effect placed the existing nuclear weapon states on notice that their efforts to restrict the number of *acknowledged* nuclear powers to those that had "manufactured and exploded a nuclear weapon or other nuclear explosive device prior to January 1, 1967,"[26] would not be accommodated without further bargaining over India's own status in the global political order.[27] Yet while this issue represents a serious matter in its own right, it has little bearing on the central concern of this research effort—i.e., what the claim "India is now a nuclear weapons state" implies for the country's future deterrent. Before this issue is investigated in any detail, however, it is important to identify and assess those variables which are likely to have the most impact on India's future decisions about the shape and orientation of its nuclear posture.

UNDERSTANDING THE VARIABLES AFFECTING INDIA'S NUCLEAR POSTURE

In general, there are four variables that will influence the direction, extent, and patterns of change in India's nuclear posture over time: the character of the global nuclear regime; the demands imposed by regional security and, in particular, regional nuclear threats; the character of India's bilateral relations with key powers in the international system; and the opportunities offered by indigenous performance and capabilities in the context of domestic political debates about nuclearization. Each of these factors merits closer examination.

---

[26]This is the legal definition of a nuclear weapon state encoded in Article IX of the Non-Proliferation Treaty of 1967. The text of the treaty can be found in Leonard S. Spector and Mark G. McDonough (with Evan S. Medeiros), *Tracking Nuclear Proliferation* (Washington, D.C.: Carnegie Endowment for International Peace, 1995), pp. 21–24.

[27]See, for example, Muchkund Dubey, "The World Nuclear Order and India," *The Hindu*, May 27, 1998, and M. K. Narayanan, "It Takes More Than Two to Tango in Nuclear Club," *Asian Age*, May 31, 1998.

The Global Nuclear Regime

The character of the global nuclear regime is the first critical factor that will determine the direction, extent, and patterns of change in India's nuclear posture. The global regime is important in the first instance simply because of India's traditional position that the status of nuclear weaponry is a global rather than a regional problem.[28] The rhetorical dimensions of this stance are, however, less significant than its strategic consequences, which imply that critical decisions relating to further "horizontal proliferation" in South Asia—that is to say, decisions bearing on both the number and kind of strategic technologies acquired—will ultimately be linked to larger Indian perceptions about issues relating to "vertical proliferation" and, by extension, the structure of the global nuclear regime in general.[29] This in turn implies that as long as Indian decisionmakers perceive that the existing nuclear weapon states either will not or cannot move toward deeper stockpile reductions that will ultimately lead to nuclear abolition, India (and, by implication, Pakistan) will not countenance the prospect of rolling back its own nuclear programs. This obduracy is linked both to strategic concerns about perceived threats emerging from some of the nuclear weapon states—China in particular in the case of India—and to ideational fears about enshrining "discriminatory" organizational regimes such as the NPT in international politics.[30]

To be sure, the *pace* of India's (and Pakistan's) movement toward further nuclearization may be successfully moderated, assuming that a suitable combination of blandishments and penalties can be fashioned by some or all of the nuclear weapon states. However, this success will not extend to convincing either state to move in the direction of denuclearization so long as the existing international nuclear order remains structurally intact. Thanks to its size and geostrategic weight, India possesses the requisite autonomy to resist most if not

---

[28]For a recent restatement of this position, see Jaswant Singh, *What Constitutes National Security in a Changing World Order? India's Strategic Thought*, Occasional Paper No. 6 (Philadelphia: Center for the Advanced Study of India, 1998), pp. 23–26.

[29]Sandy Gordon, "Capping South Asia's Nuclear Weapons Programs: A Window of Opportunity?" *Asian Survey*, 34:7 (July 1994), pp. 662–667.

[30]Jaswant Singh, "Against Nuclear Apartheid," *Foreign Affairs*, 77:5 (September–October 1998), pp. 41–52.

all political pressures that the existing nuclear weapon states might impose on it to roll back its nuclear program. While Pakistan, for its part, may not be similarly robust, its overwhelming fear of India more than suffices to ward off the worst political pressures imaginable; Pakistan will risk internal stagnation and decay if necessary but will not exacerbate its external vulnerability by succumbing to any pressures for denuclearization as long as India, its archrival, refuses to move in a similar direction first. India, of course, will in turn refuse to contemplate any such step as long as China, its principal long-range threat, remains a significant nuclear power—and China, it may be surmised, would decline to consider denuclearization as long as Russia and the United States, its strategic rivals, refuse to consider denuclearization themselves. Thanks to this long and extended chain of consequences, no movement toward denuclearization should be expected in South Asia within the policy-relevant future.[31] This simple but consequential conclusion would not merit repetition but for the fact that in the aftermath of the May 1998 tests, there has been a renewed chorus of calls both within the United States and from abroad exhorting India and Pakistan to roll back their nuclear programs and sign the NPT as non–nuclear weapon states.[32]

The current global nuclear regime therefore influences the future direction of India's nuclear posture in at least one straightforward manner: It makes denuclearization impossible and, to the extent that it allows the existing nuclear weapon states to continually maintain and perhaps improve their arsenals even if only in qualitative terms, makes further Indian movement in the direction of nuclearization all the more likely. This assessment by no means implies that Indian

---

[31]The implication of the interaction between global politics and regional security in the context of the Indian subcontinent has been usefully explored in Gordon, "Capping South Asia's Nuclear Weapons Programs," pp. 662–673. See also Raju G.C. Thomas, "Security Relationships in Southern Asia: Difference in the Indian and American Perspectives," *Asian Survey*, 21:7 (July 1981), pp. 689–709.

[32]See, by way of example, the P-5 and G-8 statements issued in the aftermath of the May 1998 nuclear tests and, especially, *Security Council Resolution 1172 (1998) on International Peace and Security*, adopted by the U.N. Security Council at its 3890th meeting on June 6, 1998, available at http://www.un.org/Docs/scres/1998/sres1172.htm, which "urges India and Pakistan, and all other States that have not yet done so, to become Parties to the Treaty on the Non-Proliferation of Nuclear Weapons and to the Comprehensive Nuclear Test Ban Treaty without delay and without conditions."

(and Pakistani) policymakers are unaware of the changes that have occurred in the global nuclear order since 1991. They do recognize, for example, that "the nuclear arsenals of the two superpowers have shrunk several-fold"[33]—but they simply consider these changes to be insufficient, at least as far as the impact on their own strategic condition is concerned.[34]

The present global nuclear regime is in fact viewed within India as embodying a mixed blessing. Clearly, the salience of nuclear weapons as the "currency of global politics" has progressively declined over time, particularly with the passing of the Cold War. Both U.S. and Russian arsenals have, moreover, diminished considerably both in size and in terms of their strategic salience. In the United States in particular, the roles formerly allocated to nuclear weapons have in many instances been handed over to newer generations of improved conventional munitions, although the "repackaging" of some older nuclear weapons to perform those roles still lying beyond the capacity of improved conventional munitions points to the enduring importance of nuclear weaponry even in the context of the evolving "revolution in military affairs"(RMA).[35] In general, however, the significance accorded to nuclear weapons has radically diminished since the end of the Cold War, and U.S. and Russian policymakers currently appear to be contemplating even steeper reductions in their strategic nuclear capabilities—reductions that will eventually bring the size of their arsenals down to a historic low of

---

[33]Manpreet Sethi, "The Status of the Nuclear World at the Close of the Century," *Strategic Analysis*, 22:10 (January 1999), pp. 1483–1495.

[34]See Jasjit Singh, "India's Nuclear Policy: The Year After," *Strategic Analysis*, 23:4 (July 1999), pp. 509–530, for a clear statement of this theme. See also Barbara Crossette, "Why India Thinks Atomic Equation Has Changed," *New York Times*, June 15, 1998.

[35]William M. Arkin, "What's 'New?'" *Bulletin of the Atomic Scientists*, 53:6 (November–December 1997), pp. 22–27. This argument has been amplified by many Indian analysts who use it, first, as evidence of the continuing addiction to nuclear weapons on the part of the established nuclear weapon states, and second, as a justification for the distension of their own country's nuclear capabilities. See, for example, Vijai K. Nair, "Indian Nuclear Doctrine: Domestic and External Challenges," *Agni*, 4:2 (May 1999), pp. 10–28.

some 2000 warheads once the START III negotiations have success-fully concluded.[36]

Such a movement toward a "low salience nuclear environment"[37] is clearly perceived by Indian policymakers as being in their strategic interests. To the degree that superpower arms reductions help lessen nuclear competition worldwide and, in particular, decrease the in-centives for subsidiary nuclear powers like China to continually augment their nuclear capabilities, they can only serve to increase India's sense of security. For this reason, Indian strategists in general argue that the core arrangements governing U.S.-Russian arms re-duction should be progressively broadened to include the smaller nuclear powers and eventually the threshold states as well as part of a progressive drive toward global nuclear abolition. The most recent such call in fact emanated from India in the aftermath of the May 1998 nuclear tests, when the Indian government called on "all nu-clear weapons states . . . to join with it in opening early negotiations for a Nuclear Weapons Convention so that these weapons can be dealt with in a global, nondiscriminatory framework as other weapons of mass destruction have been . . . [dealt with in the past]."[38] While this invitation appears self-serving, coming as it did on the heels of the 1998 nuclear tests, it was certainly consistent with India's past proposals and represented a continuation of traditional Indian policy, which has always held out the threat of overt nucle-arization so long as the global nuclear order remained unreformed.[39]

From New Delhi's perspective, however, several critical impedi-ments have materialized in the arena of global nuclear reform—despite all the other beneficial developments that have occurred in the aftermath of the Cold War. For example, neither Russia nor the smaller nuclear powers, the United Kingdom and France, appear

---

[36]A useful survey of the prospects for, and the challenges accompanying, such re-ductions can be found in Larry D. Welch, *John J. McCloy Roundtable on the Elimina-tion of Nuclear Weapons* (New York: Council on Foreign Relations, 1998).

[37]This phrase appears in Michael MccGwire, "Is There a Future for Nuclear Weapons?" *International Affairs*, 70:2 (April 1994), pp. 211–228.

[38]John F. Burns, "India Calls for Talks on New Treaty Limiting Nuclear Arms," *New York Times*, June 1, 1998.

[39]Perkovich, *India's Nuclear Bomb*, pp. 444–468.

willing to contemplate reductions in nuclear capabilities as part of some larger process that will eventually culminate in nuclear abolition.[40] Even the United States, where the debate about nuclear abolition has perhaps reached its most sophisticated level, seems to have demurred about carrying nuclear arms reduction to its logical terminus, preferring instead to pursue a "lead and hedge" policy well into the future.[41] In every case, a number of considerations have been brought into play: Concerns about maintaining great-power status indefinitely, fear of the consequences of cheating, apprehension about prospective proliferation involving rogue states and perhaps nonstate actors, and old-fashioned considerations about security itself have combined to render comprehensive nuclear disarmament a remote and illusory goal.[42] Indeed, even moral arguments—especially those emanating from both the Christian churches and secular institutions in the United States—have failed to demonstrate that nuclear abolition is a desirable objective that should be pursued in concert with the other nuclear weapon states.[43] Taking their cue from such debates, Indian policymakers have concluded that preserving their nuclear option has become all the more necessary, since the principal condition that would enhance

---

[40]This reluctance centers on the desire to ensure permanent security in the first instance but in the final analysis is driven considerably by concerns about prestige, since given their current and projected economic standing, each of these countries would be hard-pressed to sustain its claims to great-power status in the absence of nuclear weaponry. Good discussions about how status and prestige figure in the British and French decisions to maintain a nuclear force can be found in Stuart Croft and Phil Williams, "The United Kingdom," and in Klaus Schubert, "France," in Regina Cowen Karp (ed.), *Security with Nuclear Weapons?* (Oxford, UK: Oxford University Press, 1991), pp. 145–188. In the case of Russia and China, nuclear weapons remain the principal source of security given that their conventional military capabilities are less than impressive. The increased Russian emphasis on its nuclear capabilities in the post–Cold War era is analyzed in the context of changing military doctrine in Mary C. FitzGerald, "Russia's New Military Doctrine," *Naval War College Review*, 46:2 (Spring 1993), pp. 24–44, while Chinese attitudes toward nuclear reductions are assessed in Michael D. Swaine and Alastair Iain Johnston, "China and Arms Control Institutions," in Elizabeth Economy and Michel Oksenberg (eds.), *China Joins the World* (New York: Council on Foreign Relations Press, 1999), pp. 90–135.

[41]See the analysis in Stephen A. Cambone and Patrick J. Garrity, "The Future of U.S. Nuclear Policy," *Survival*, 36:4 (Winter 1994–1995), pp. 73–95.

[42]For a good analysis of why comprehensive nuclear disarmament may be a bad thing, see Glaser, *Analyzing Strategic Nuclear Policy*, pp. 166–203.

[43]Ashley J. Tellis, "Nuclear Arms, Moral Questions, and Religious Issues," *Armed Forces & Society*, 13:4 (Summer 1987), pp. 599–622.

Indian security—global reductions leading to abolition—will probably never be fulfilled at any point in the near or distant future.

It is in this context that the long-standing U.S. effort to curtail the proliferation of nuclear weapons in South Asia is viewed uneasily in New Delhi. Clearly, even India—which often appears to be an object of American nonproliferation efforts—has a vested interest in the overall success of U.S. nonproliferation policies. Indian policymakers certainly recognize that a world of "high-entropy"[44] proliferation— i.e., a highly proliferated world with few "rules of the nuclear road"[45]—would be a dangerous one indeed as well as one in which Indian security would be reduced rather than enhanced. Consequently, there is no reason—in principle—why Indian interests and U.S. objectives with respect to proliferation should conflict. The primary reason for discord from New Delhi's perspective, however, arises not from principle but rather from practice. This is because Indian strategic managers believe that American nonproliferation policies, although laudable for all the benefits they could confer, should not apply to India because its difficult strategic environment—defined among other things by its close proximity to one nuclear weapon state and to another de facto nuclear state—as well as its general political conservatism, historic restraint with respect to the use of force, democratic character, and strategic importance to the United States (especially with respect to the issue of stability in Asia writ large), justify its treatment as the singular exception to the nonproliferation regime.[46]

The heart of New Delhi's opposition to the U.S. nonproliferation policy is therefore directed more toward that policy's application

---

[44]Roger C. Molander and Peter A. Wilson, *The Nuclear Asymptote: On Containing Nuclear Proliferation*, MR-214-CC (Santa Monica: RAND, 1993), p. xiii.

[45]Ibid.

[46]This argument was most cogently articulated by the former Indian Foreign Secretary, Maharajakrishna Rasgotra, at the RAND-RGICS Workshop on U.S.-South Asian Relations held at Jawahar Bhawan, New Delhi, February 28–29, 1996. It can also be found in Jasjit Singh, "South Asian Nuclear Scene," *The Times of India*, May 2, 1994, and in Maharajakrishna Rasgotra, "Nuclear India Must Engage the U.S.," *The Times of India*, May 29, 1998. The most authoritative affirmation of this argument can be found in "Address by Prime Minister Atal Bihari Vajpayee to the Joint Session of the United States Congress," Washington, D.C., September 14, 2000, available at http://www.meadeve.gov.in/speeches/j-session.htm.

than toward its general logic. The discomfort with its logic arises only to the degree that the policy implicitly encodes a permanent, discriminatory hierarchy in international politics. While the Nehruvian tradition in Indian policymaking might find this effect disconcerting, the more dominant realist strains today accept the reality of a two-tiered, "have/have not" system—at least as far as nuclear issues are concerned. Consequently, their principal worry centers on which side of the divide India would be locked into given its belief that nuclear weapons *do* enhance the security of some states and therefore cannot be either wished or abolished away.[47]

Since this logic cannot be applied to India without reference to Pakistan, Indian policymakers have increasingly been willing to concede that Pakistan too should be exempted from the burdens of U.S. nonproliferation efforts, albeit for different reasons. While India views Pakistan as a hostile and often irresponsible state, this volatile behavior is now acknowledged to be as much a product of Pakistan's insecurity as it is a fruit of its mendacity—although many Indians argue that mendacity will continue to dominate Islamabad's decisionmaking toward India by virtue of the peculiar internal political structures of the Pakistani state. However, to the extent that Pakistan's hostility is rooted in its perceptions of irredeemable vulnerability vis-à-vis India, the acquisition of nuclear weapons by Islamabad should serve to boost Pakistan's confidence about its security and, by implication, offer the best hope for stabilized relations with India.[48] Because attaining this goal remains fundamental to achieving peace and security in the region, most Indian policymakers today would argue that Pakistan's acquisition of nuclear weapons should also be condoned by the United States as a means of enhancing strategic stability in South Asia.

---

[47]This issue became particularly critical during the negotiations leading up to the CTBT as seen, for example, in J. N. Dixit, "The Indian Dilemma," *Indian Express*, January 9, 1996.

[48]See General K. Sundarji's views on this matter in Chidanand Rajghatta, "The Country's Foreign and Military Policies Need to Be Disciplined," *The Times of India*, January 1, 1991; K. Subrahmanyam, "Pak Nuclear Programme," *The Times of India*, February 28, 1987; and K. Subrahmanyam, "Indo-Pak Nuclear Stand-Off," *The Times of India*, May 6, 1988.

The ideal Indian rank-ordering of preferences would thus take the following form:

- The first preference would be a nuclear-capable India but not a nuclear-capable Pakistan. Under this preference, the United States would seek to prevent Pakistan from acquiring effective nuclear capabilities, thereby allowing India to provide a modicum of hegemonic stability to the subcontinent.

- The second preference would be a nuclear-capable India and a nuclear-capable Pakistan. Under this preference, the United States would ideally tolerate nuclear capabilities on both sides and perhaps even assist their management, since Indian nuclear capabilities serve to safeguard a regionally important power against both Pakistan and China while Pakistani nuclear capabilities serve to secure a weaker and more volatile state against the worst depredations that might be imagined to emerge from India. The Indian leadership certainly recognizes that one consequence of accepting Pakistan's nuclear capabilities would be an increased propensity on Islamabad's part to engage in nuclear brinkmanship through low-intensity conflicts with India. The only truly effective antidote to such Pakistani behavior—in Indian reasoning—lies in the United States' choosing to pursue some variant of the first preference. However, since Washington is unlikely to choose this alternative for both historical and political reasons, New Delhi appears resigned to the idea that its second preference—with all its disadvantages—will define the reality with which it must cope in the future. Given this fact, Indian policymakers have sought to persuade Washington that although Pakistan's nuclear capabilities ought to be tolerated as such, Islamabad's egregious political adventurism should nonetheless be sanctioned by a variety of political means.

- The third and fourth alternatives, respectively—no nuclear weapons in India and Pakistan, and no nuclear weapons in India but nuclear weapons in Pakistan—are deemed to be beyond the pale of consideration and hence are not treated seriously by Indian policymakers and analysts in general.

The bottom line, therefore, is that Indian commentators are often willing to countenance nuclear capabilities in Pakistan if such capabilities imply the removal of U.S. political pressures on India coupled with a recognition on the part of the United States that India's independent foreign policy and its emergence as a regional hegemon are ultimately beneficial to U.S. global interests. These considerations invariably underlie all New Delhi's efforts to convince Washington that a nuclearized subcontinent remains the desirable exception to its otherwise-stringent nonproliferation policy. The tensions that may arise in the process of accommodating such exceptions, especially at the level of U.S. declaratory policy, are rarely examined by Indians in any detail, leaving the impression that since nonproliferation is an American cause, managing its contradictions is best left to the Americans as well. In these circumstances, Indian security managers seek only to ensure that the global nuclear regime does not place India at a permanent disadvantage, even if they have given up all hope that it will benefit India through the outcome of complete abolition.

While the global nuclear order thus has the immediate effect of reinforcing Indian decisions against denuclearization, it affects the future Indian nuclear posture in other derivative but nonetheless important ways.

To begin with, the composition of the global order serves to define India's threat environment insofar as it provides the medium for identifying both present challenges and future threats. Mercifully, India's current readings of its nuclear threat environment, although tinged with some uncertainty when the distant future is taken into account, are relatively limited. Of the eight nuclear weapon states in the global system, four—Russia, Israel, the United Kingdom, and France—are generally regarded as posing no nuclear threat to India. Russia continues to remain an important source of military equipment, and New Delhi longs for the day when a revitalized Moscow will again be a source of political and strategic support.[49] Israel has in recent years become an increasingly important source of critical military technologies as well, and its own preoccupation with the Arab states, some of which are friendly toward Pakistan, has created a "checkerboard pattern" of strategic alignments that makes Israeli

---

[49]Anita Inder Singh, "A New Indo-Russian Connection," *International Affairs*, 71:1 (January 1995), pp. 69–81.

and Indian objectives more compatible than they are competitive.[50] Both the United Kingdom and France, despite being allies of the United States, are viewed as having a somewhat independent foreign policy where India is concerned: Both remain important sources of military equipment, with France steadily becoming more important than Great Britain, especially as a supplier of strategic technologies; each has either historical or ideological ties with India; and both have strategic concerns that, being sufficiently removed from India's, do not lock them into any directly competitive relationship with New Delhi.[51]

In stark contrast to the four states above, which do not figure into any Indian threat assessment worth naming, two other states—China and Pakistan—will continue to be regarded as straightforward nuclear threats well into the distant future. This is because both states have fought wars with India in the past; both target India with nuclear and conventional weapons; both have a variety of border disputes with New Delhi that are unlikely to be resolved soon; and each, in different ways, is likely to persist as a political rival to India as far as physical security and political eminence are concerned. This leaves the United States, the world's foremost political power, in a category by itself. Clearly, India's strategic managers—in contradistinction to some of New Delhi's vociferous elites—do not view the United States as posing a nuclear threat to India today. To be sure, U.S.-Indian relations have often been fraught with suspicion, but this discord has never reached the point at which the United States has been perceived as a real military threat—a condition that probably held even during the tempestuous days of 1971. The 1971 Indo-Pakistani war certainly represented the nadir of U.S.-Indian relations, and President Nixon's gunboat diplomacy, as exemplified by the steaming of the USS *Enterprise* into the Bay of Bengal, still ran-

---

[50]P. R. Kumaraswamy, *India and Israel: Evolving Strategic Partnership* (Ramat Gan, Israel: BESA Center for Strategic Studies, 1998).

[51]On the evolving Indian relationship with France, see Dipankar Banerjee (ed.), *Security in the New World Order* (New Delhi: Institute for Defence Studies and Analyses, 1994), and "India, France to Expand Defence Co-operation," *Jane's Defence Weekly*, January 20, 1999, p. 4.

kles many Indians.[52] Indeed, it has even been argued that this event may have had some bearing on Indira Gandhi's later decision to authorize India's first nuclear explosion,[53] and it certainly provided significant impetus for the major Indian naval modernization that began in 1978. Yet even this exercise of gunboat diplomacy was viewed by most Indian policymakers—as opposed to Indian commentators, the general public, and the Indian Navy—as more a symbolic affront than an operational challenge, albeit one that justified the creation of some strategic deterrent against the threat of extraregional intervention in the affairs of the subcontinent.[54]

In short, for much of the time since 1964, India has doubtless perceived the United States as an overbearing power—a perception influenced both by Washington's policies and by its overwhelming strength. Rarely, however, has New Delhi viewed the United States as a true *nuclear* threat. Indeed, even during the late 1970s and early 1980s, when India's concerns about the U.S. presence in the Indian Ocean reached their zenith, New Delhi's criticisms of American naval operations were driven primarily by the fear that these activities had precipitated a competitive Soviet response, thereby resulting in an unwelcome proliferation of extraregional navies close to the Indian peninsula. It is unlikely that New Delhi ever believed that U.S. naval operations either were intended to pose or actually posed a direct nuclear threat to the Indian heartland, although numerous Indian ideologues were happy to level just such charges whenever U.S.-Indian relations became problematic. It is also unlikely that India will view the United States as a nuclear opponent in the future, even though India will at some point acquire the capability to target U.S. facilities and forces at various sites along the Asian periphery. Whether India actually acts in accordance with its capabilities here

---

[52]A good narrative of this episode can be found in Barry M. Blechman and Stephen S. Kaplan (eds.), *Force Without War: U.S. Armed Forces as a Political Instrument* (Washington, D.C.: Brookings, 1978), pp. 175–221.

[53]Stephen P. Cohen, *Perception, Influence, and Weapons Proliferation in South Asia*, Report No. 1722-920184 (Washington, D.C.: Bureau of Intelligence and Research, U.S. Department of State, August 20, 1979), p. 4ff.

[54]Not surprisingly, the Indian Navy in particular perceived the political challenge of deterring such extraregional intervention in highly operational terms that are described in some detail in Ashley J. Tellis, "Securing the Barrack: The Logic, Structure and Objectives of India's Naval Expansion," Parts I and II, *Naval War College Review*, 43:3 and 43:4 (Summer and Autumn 1990), pp. 77–97 and 31–57.

will therefore be determined by New Delhi's perception of U.S. attitudes toward India and, more particularly, by its assessment of America's willingness and desire to intervene militarily in South Asian affairs to India's detriment. To the degree that India concludes that such intervention is likely or even possible over the long term, it will be given sufficient incentive to develop a range of strategic capabilities that guard against this possibility.[55] Throughout the 1980s, for example, Indian strategic literature focused on how naval instruments could be employed to "raise the cost" of potential superpower

---

[55]This issue is of critical concern to most Indian elites because the Indo-Pakistani dispute over Kashmir is often seen as providing the United States with just such an opportunity for unwelcome intervention. These fears are only exacerbated by Pakistan's persistent desire to involve Washington in resolving the Kashmir dispute. The possibility that the United States might some day choose to intervene in internal South Asian disputes conditions India's responses to all American interventionary efforts worldwide. Thus, one Indian diplomat, commenting on New Delhi's fierce criticism of the U.S.-led NATO campaign in Kosovo, noted that "the Indian reaction to Kosovo has been conditioned by its own problem of containing separatism in Kashmir. Both issues involve separatist insurgencies encouraged and supported from outside in areas where the majority of the population is Muslim." See A.N.D. Haksar, "Parallel Seen Between Kosovo Crisis and Kashmir," *India Abroad*, May 21, 1999.

While the Indian condemnation of NATO military efforts has therefore been based largely on the fear that a hegemonic United States might use the violation of human rights as a pretext for "external intervention in affairs of other countries grappling with regional disaffection," several Indian commentators have concluded that the only way to immunize India against similar American depredations in the future is to develop a "strong defence," which includes, among other things, nuclear weapons and long-range ballistic missiles. See, for example, Saumitra Mohan, "The Agni Sermon," *The Pioneer*, May 1, 1999.

Even the current Indian Chief of Air Staff, Air Chief Marshal Ashok Yashwant Tipnis—noting that "assertive diplomacy is becoming prominent and there is talk of how extraregional influences could be used here [meaning South Asia]"—has stated that "he would like the IAF to take possession of the indigenously developed Agni intermediate-range ballistic missile" in addition to the larger numbers of long-range Sukhoi-30s and Mirage-2000 multirole fighters already on order. He has further asserted that the Indian Air Force will "build up both offensive and defensive capabilities to counter 'extraregional influences,'" thus confirming the anxiety felt by Indian security managers who have attempted to defend the Pokhran tests "in the light of developments in Kosovo." See "Don't Justify Nuclear Plan, Urges China," *Hindustan Times*, May 19, 1999. Tipnis' extended statement can be found in Dinesh Kumar, "Let's Be Stronger and Smarter, Says IAF Chief," *The Times of India*, May 16, 1999.

Many of these concerns about possible U.S. intervention diminished after the 1999 Kargil crisis, when, to the surprise of many Indian policymakers and the general public, Washington publicly rejected both Pakistani rationalizations about its role in precipitating the conflict and Islamabad's invitation to intervene in order to resolve the Kashmir dispute.

intervention.[56] All things considered, there is no reason why aircraft- and missile-delivered nuclear weapons could not be envisaged for a similar role in the future, especially if the United States were perceived to be both hostile to India and unchallenged in its global hegemony. Clearly, treating the United States as a strategic threat to be countered through Indian nuclear responses is only a remote possibility at present, but because it cannot bc discounted altogether, it is in the United States' interest to condition both the political and technical choices available to India so as to prevent this from coming to pass.[57]

While the character of the global regime thus affects India's future nuclear posture in the first instance by providing opportunities for threat definition (against which evolving Indian nuclear capabilities would have to be metered), it also affects these capabilities to the extent that it produces "positive externalities" that various weaker states, including India, could exploit. The existence of such positive externalities derives from the fact that first, nuclear deterrence in many instances exhibits the characteristics of a "public good," and second, interlocking political competition in a world of nuclear multipolarity provides significant opportunities for second- and third-tier states to remain secure even if they possess less-than-adequate deterrents of the sort that would be required under conditions of pure bipolarity. These processes were in fact exploited by the British, French, and Chinese throughout the Cold War, when each of these states remained content with having minimal nuclear capabilities (despite possessing no alliance commitments, for example, in the case of China) simply because they benefited from the vast U.S. efforts at deterring the Soviet Union. Further, these states could rest

---

[56]See Tellis, "Securing the Barrack: The Logic, Structure and Objectives of India's Naval Expansion," pp. 31–57 and 77–97.

[57]Many Indian as well as U.S. commentators argue that the best solution for dealing with any misperceptions in this regard is to develop a joint U.S.-Indian understanding of the role New Delhi's nuclear weapons can play in the evolving Asian balance of power. Part of this process may include orchestrating a "grand bargain" whereby India eschews the development of certain nuclear capabilities in exchange for preferential access to American resources, technology, and political support. For different versions of this solution, see Selig S. Harrison, "Cut a Regional Deal," *Foreign Policy*, 62 (Spring 1986), pp. 126–147; Selig S. Harrison, "The United States and South Asia: Trapped by the Past?" *Current History*, 96:614 (December 1997), pp. 401–406; and C. Raja Mohan, "Nuclear Balance in Asia," *The Hindu*, June 11, 1998.

assured that their loss to the Soviets would place the United States at a severe disadvantage in the regional and global balances of power and that therefore their defense against Soviet depredations was guaranteed purely on the basis of U.S. self-interest *even if they possessed no nuclear weapons whatsoever.*[58] This phenomenon, which many theorists have concluded could lead to "free riding" by alliance partners,[59] could also be exploited by India at some point in the future, irrespective of whether India develops a close relationship with the United States.

The benefits of deterrence externalities would best obtain, however, if China were to emerge over time as a strategic rival of the United States in Asia and beyond. Should such a condition arise, U.S. efforts to deter China will inevitably provide a measure of safety to the various smaller states in Asia, including India—none of which may actually contribute to the sustenance of that larger goal. Since the United States would most likely seek to preserve the security of these states in the face of Chinese blandishments or aggression in efforts to prevent the balance of power in Asia from deteriorating to its disadvantage, it is possible that states like India would not find it necessary to develop the panoply of deterrent capabilities they might otherwise have had to cultivate. Thus, the configuration of the global nuclear order and the character of the competitive relationships between the most important states in that order will greatly influence India's future nuclear posture. To be sure, the externalities flowing from these "superpower" relationships will not result in India's outright abdication of nuclear arms because a country of India's size and geopolitical weight is seen to require some minimum deterrent to independently deter Pakistan, to ensure its own freedom of action vis-à-vis China and the United States, and to ensure the possibility of interventionary responses by other countries to possible Chinese aggression. Such factors will, however, influence India's decisions relating to the size, structure, and orientation of its nuclear arsenal.

---

[58]This calculation in fact underwrote in part the Swedish decision to give up its nuclear program. See Paul M. Cole, *Sweden Without the Bomb: The Conduct of a Nuclear-Capable Nation Without Nuclear Weapons*, MR-460 (Santa Monica: RAND, 1994).

[59]This argument was first proffered by Mancur Olsen, Jr., and Richard Zechauser, "An Economic Theory of Alliances," *Review of Economics and Statistics*, 48:3 (August 1966), pp. 266–279.

This influence will be most clearly evident (as it was in the case of China during the Cold War years) not in decisions relating to initial force architecture but rather in the subsequent choices relating to force improvement and modernization that will arise as a result of progress in its adversaries' nuclear capabilities over time. The pressure to respond nervously to every improvement in China's nuclear arsenal may simply be muted if New Delhi perceives that the commonality of interests it shares with the United States vis-à-vis China allows it to "free ride" off the counterresponses that would most probably be undertaken by the United States as the key hegemonic power in international politics.[60]

---

[60]Obviously, the types of counterresponses that the United States launches to the potential Chinese threat—if such a threat should emerge over time—would play a critical role at least with respect to the manner in which U.S. defensive efforts could influence New Delhi's future nuclear architecture and force posture. If, for example, Washington were to concentrate on developing a purely ground-based terminal defense system aimed primarily at protecting the continental United States, such a force architecture is likely to provide few positive externalities that countries such as India could exploit. The deployment of other capabilities, however—such as airborne or space-based boost-phase interceptors, airborne lasers, and sea-based theater missile defenses—could make a significant political difference to countries like India not because protection by such systems would be assured but because a potentially aggressive Chinese regime could not assume that these capabilities would not be made available to the rimland Asian powers in an emergency. Because these systems need not be either politically or physically transferred to the protectee (and may not even need to be deployed on the protectee's territory) in order for them to be effective, their deployment by the United States could allow Washington to credibly influence proliferation decisions in many countries, including some current U.S. allies, over the long term.

All such capabilities, however, bring along difficult strategic dilemmas. Besides the obvious challenges posed to the nature of the global nuclear regime as a result of such technological innovations, the potential protectees will also face painful predicaments of their own. The acquisition of strategic defenses by the United States may, for example, provide positive externalities that can be exploited by third parties, including small nuclear powers, but the latter will have to face the prospect that their own limited arsenals might become even more insignificant than would otherwise be the case—first because the major nuclear powers would be tempted to further expand their own arsenals to cope with American strategic defenses, and second because the United States itself could use its strategic defenses—in tandem with its conventional and offensive nuclear capabilities—to drastically attenuate the threat posed by many small nuclear forces around the world.

Thanks to these factors, most small nuclear powers, including India, are likely to exploit American strategic defenses, if available, to the degree they can politically while always seeking to maintain the most effective offensive nuclear force possible within their circumstances. Since India is most likely to follow this path—especially in the context of a rising, potentially aggressive China—it implies the return of one more

While the character of the global nuclear order and the relationships between the principal actors within that order thus offer opportunities for the exploitation of deterrence externalities, they also
affect India's future nuclear posture in another way: by influencing
the nature of the nuclear deterrence regime. The current nuclear
deterrence regime is an "offense-dominant" one whose stability is
ultimately grounded in the capacity of a nuclear power to readily inflict horrific damage on the population centers of an adversary.[61]
This condition, which is enshrined in the concept of "mutual assured
destruction" (MAD), holds even in the context of limited nuclear use,
since the "limited nuclear options" proposed by "nuclear use theorists" (NUTS), generally remain—after all is said and done—attempts
at strategic bargaining in order to enforce war termination on favorable terms at the earliest opportunity.[62] Indeed, nuclear weapons of
the sort currently possessed by the superpowers embody such fearsome potency that their actual use could rapidly escalate to the
large-scale employment of central strategic systems which, even if
used purely in a counterforce mode, would wreak such catastrophic
damage as to trivialize the distinction between strategic counterforce
and strategic countervalue attacks. Even nuclear-use theorists would
therefore be forced to concede that "deterrence by denial" in the
nuclear realm remains a modest innovation that is still firmly embedded in the larger reality of "deterrence by punishment."[63]

---

dilemma that Washington never satisfactorily resolved during the Cold War: whether
the United States ought to "contain" the power of its principal adversary by building
up the nuclear capabilities of the states lying on that adversary's periphery or whether
it ought to emphasize extended deterrence in order to discourage the peripheral states
from developing their own nuclear capabilities. While it is probable that many small
formal allies of the United States may be satisfied with the latter solution, larger and
more capable allies, large neutrals, and small states that may feel an acute sense of
threat are more likely to gravitate in the direction of acquiring nuclear capabilities
even as they exploit whatever forms of American protection might be available.

[61]Michael Mandelbaum, *The Nuclear Revolution* (New York: Cambridge University
Press, 1981), and Robert Jervis, *The Meaning of the Nuclear Revolution* (Ithaca, NY:
Cornell University Press, 1989).

[62]This insight was first explored systematically in Morton Kaplan, *The Strategy of
Limited Retaliation*, Policy Memorandum No. 19 (Princeton, NJ: Woodrow Wilson
School of Public and International Affairs, 1959).

[63]This claim is defended most cogently in Spurgeon M. Keeny, Jr., and Wolfgang
K.H. Panofsky, "MAD Versus NUTS: Can Doctrine or Weaponry Remedy the Mutual
Hostage Relationship of the Superpowers?" *Foreign Affairs*, 60:2 (Winter 1981–1982),
pp. 282–304.

The advantage of an offense-dominant regime is that it requires only modest nuclear arsenals for purposes of deterrence, especially on the part of emerging nuclear powers, since relatively small nuclear forces can hold at risk a large number of their adversaries' population centers.[64] So long as the delivery force is relatively survivable and the warhead yields significant enough, a horrendous amount of damage can be inflicted even with relatively modest nuclear capabilities. Small nuclear forces can therefore function as highly credible deterrents in an offense-dominant regime. As long as the present regime, which ultimately derives its efficacy from MAD, remains intact, it is therefore likely that the future Indian nuclear arsenal would remain relatively modest, at least by the standards of the Cold War—although it would stay within the same order of magnitude, at least as far as numbers go, as those of the other second-tier nuclear powers. The problem, however, is that MAD, while remaining an effective background condition, is generally a poor (and perhaps even an immoral) *strategy* in the face of deterrence breakdown. Consequently, repeated efforts have been made over the years, especially within the United States, to shift nuclear strategy in the direction of a "defense-dominant" regime in which potential nuclear aggression is contained not by the threat of assured retaliation but by assured neutralization of the adversary's nuclear attack.[65]

The instruments of such neutralization consist of various forms of strategic defense. The character and phenomenology of these systems are, however, less relevant than their consequences. A shift to a defense-dominant regime by the United States, even if undertaken

---

[64]The main reason this outcome did not obtain during the Cold War was that the United States and the Soviet Union sought to use their nuclear forces for purposes other than simply dyadic deterrence. Once nuclear weapons were seen as having utility for extended deterrence and conventionalized "denial" strategies, the resulting emphasis on nuclear war fighting ultimately led to the creation of large and diversified nuclear arsenals. Good analyses of the factors leading to this outcome can be found in William H. Kincade, "The United States: Nuclear Decision Making, 1939–89"; Robert J. Art, "The United States: Nuclear Weapons and Grand Strategy"; Allen Lynch, "The Soviet Union: Nuclear Weapons and Their Role in Security Policy"; and Sergey Koulik, "The Soviet Union: Domestic and Strategic Aspects of Nuclear Weapon Policy," in Regina Cowen Karp (ed.), *Security with Nuclear Weapons?* (Oxford, UK: Oxford University Press, 1991), pp. 21–56, 57–99, 100–123, and 124–144.

[65]For arguments in defense of such a shift on both strategic and moral grounds, see Colin Gray, "Strategic Defense, Deterrence, and the Prospects for Peace," *Ethics*, 95:3 (April 1985), pp. 659–672.

only in certain peripheral areas for purposes of safeguarding power projection forces, could lead to an expansion of the nuclear forces maintained by all other nuclear competitors. This dynamic will in turn affect the size and configuration of India's nuclear arsenal because New Delhi will be forced to respond to the expansion of those nuclear forces which, while intended mainly to enhance penetrativity in the face of an American defensive umbrella, will nonetheless result in an expanded nuclear threat leveled at the Indian heartland. While this dynamic will in all probability manifest itself only vis-à-vis China, the underlying principle will remain the same: If the global nuclear deterrence regime, led by the United States, were to shift incrementally in the direction of a defense-dominant posture, the emerging Indian nuclear arsenal would end up being much larger than most current estimates anticipate. Under such conditions, Indian policymakers would seek to increase the number, kind, and diversity of their delivery systems, boost the quantity of their fissile-material stockpile, and place increased emphasis on denial and deception operations, penetrating aids, and the like in efforts to ensure minimally effective standards of penetrativity in the face of a pure defense-dominant regime as well as a minimal force size in the face of a mixed offense-defense regime.[66]

India's security managers have already signaled their concern about these developments. In private conversations, they have revealed great interest in understanding the intent, scope, and time lines surrounding ongoing U.S. efforts to develop a thin national missile defense (NMD) system and a localized theater missile defense (TMD) system that may be deployed first in East Asia and then elsewhere. Their concern about these systems is driven not by an interest in U.S. strategic planning per se but rather by a desire to anticipate China's strategic responses to such developments. This issue is perceived to be critical because Beijing's responses to Washington's strategic defense initiatives affect India's local strategic environment and, by implication, its own future deterrence requirements

---

[66]Highlighting precisely these consequences, one prominent Indian hawk has argued, for example, that "India will have to arm its ballistic missiles with decoys and other countermeasures." Further, he notes, "The Agni-2 . . . can only be a stepping stone to other policy choices . . . how long can India do without cruise missiles that have emerged as the favoured instruments of combat and precision strike?" See Brahma Chellaney, "Playing with Fire," *Hindustan Times*, March 10, 1999.

as well. This private concern is now being articulated at a public level, albeit elliptically.[67] In contrast to the early notions expressed in the aftermath of the May 1998 tests—that the very presence of Indian nuclear weapons somehow assured successful deterrence—more recent statements suggest greater sensitivity to the challenges posed by the quality of the strategic environment. Thus, the Indian Foreign Minister noted in a recent interview that the eventual size of India's nuclear arsenal would be determined largely by the overall "strategic environment, technological imperatives, and national security needs,"[68] with the second phrase—technological imperatives—assumed to connote the critical importance placed on ensuring not only the survivability of India's nuclear assets but also the penetrativity of its strategic systems in the face of possible changes in the character of the evolving nuclear regime.

All in all, then, the global nuclear order will affect India's future nuclear posture in significant ways. It will define the potential for further nuclearization or denuclearization and, more specifically, will determine the character of the threat; may provide opportunities for exploiting deterrence externalities; and will certainly influence the extent, structure, and diversity of the future Indian arsenal.

The Regional Nuclear Threat Environment

As stated previously, Indian policymakers view the global nuclear regime as something of a mixed bag in that the benefits accruing from the progressive reduction of the most important nuclear arsenals worldwide coincide uneasily both with the de facto refusal by the Permanent Five to consider the complete abolition of nuclear weaponry and with continuing uncertainties about the identity of future nuclear threats, the prospects for exploiting deterrence externalities, and the evolving nature of the deterrence regime. In contrast, Indian policymakers view the character of the regional nuclear environment to be considerably more ominous.

Pakistan. To begin with, India's traditional challenger, Pakistan, is now clearly a nuclear weapon power. Whatever uncertainties may

---

[67]"India Asks U.S. to Give Up Missile Testing," *The Hindu*, July 4, 2000.

[68]"India Not to Engage in a N-Arms Race: Jaswant."

have existed about Islamabad's nuclear capabilities in the subcontinent and beyond were permanently laid to rest in May 1998, when Pakistan demonstrated that it possessed nuclear devices that were capable of producing militarily significant yields. In the eyes of Indian policymakers, this represented a qualitative change from the situation that existed a little over a decade ago, when Pakistan's nuclear capabilities were uncertain and its ability to mount serious threats was for all practical purposes nonexistent.

To be sure, several Indian officials—especially those associated with the civilian atomic energy establishment—argue to this day that Pakistan's nuclear capabilities remain only modest.[69] Indeed, even after Islamabad's nuclear tests on May 28, 1998, many prominent individuals associated with India's atomic program expressed doubts about Pakistan's technological prowess. Shortly after these tests were conducted, for example, P. K. Iyengar, former Chairman of India's Atomic Energy Commission (AEC), flatly declared that "Pakistan doesn't have an indigenous capability to design and fabricate nuclear weapons,"[70] while Raja Ramanna, another former Chairman of India's AEC and currently a member of the same body, asked rhetorically, "Where is the hydrogen bomb?" and concluded that "the two tests [conducted by India and Pakistan] are not comparable at all."[71] This skepticism about Pakistan's nuclear capabilities has also found voice elsewhere: One distinguished expatriate military analyst, for example, commenting on Islamabad's nuclear tests, astonishingly declared that Pakistan's "ability to explode a crude device has no military significance." This analyst went on to say, "Frankly, I did not think Pakistan could stage even one test—not because it lacked the expertise to undertake the explosions, but because of the lack of fissile material. I did not believe, and still do not, that Pakistan was able to obtain weapon-grade uranium from its Kahuta centrifuge project."[72] Other Indian commentators concurred: A major Indian

---

[69]See the discussion in W.P.S. Sidhu, "Pakistan's Bomb: A Quest for Credibility," *Jane's Intelligence Review*, 8:6 (June 1996), pp. 278–280.

[70]"Indian Scientists Throw Questions at Pakistani Experiments," *Dawn*, May 30, 1998.

[71]Ibid.

[72]Ravi Rikhye, "Pakistan N-Tests Seen as Having Little Military Value," *India Abroad*, July 24, 1998.

newspaper, in an editorial titled "Pak Pinpricks," claimed that "seismological data points to the failure of at least three of the five tests allegedly conducted on May 26 [sic],"[73] and another leading Indian analyst of nuclear weapon issues, Brigadier (retired) Vijai Nair, who earlier had done extensive work on nuclear requirements for the Indian Army, concluded that "Pakistan's failure to come forth with instant technical details of the five nuclear explosions on May 28, unlike India, have [sic] strengthened the experts' assessment that in technological terms Pakistan lags behind India, and it would need quite some time to achieve the requisite expertise for nuclear weaponization."[74] All in all, then, significant portions of the Indian strategic community—including India's nuclear scientists—have argued that Pakistan's nuclear capabilities have been exaggerated primarily to secure political advantages.

Such attitudes, however, are not shared by the Indian military. Since the early 1980s, Indian military thinkers, particularly individuals like General K. Sundarji, former Chief of Staff of the Indian Army, have focused on the challenge of prosecuting conventional operations in the context of "nuclear asymmetry"[75]—that is, a situation involving war-fighting operations between a nuclear-armed adversary and a conventionally armed force. Yet while studies of this sort continue to this day, they are restricted for the most part to the military's command schools and service headquarters. Indeed, the armed services as a combat force have *not* prepared in any significant way for war-fighting operations in a nuclear environment despite several reports to the contrary,[76] as they do not have the equipment, training, or doctrine that would allow for the conduct of military operations on a nuclear battlefield. One Indian analyst has argued, however,

---

[73]*India—Editorial: Pakistan's N-Tests "Pinpricks,"* FBIS-NES-98-152, June 1, 1998.

[74]Vijai K. Nair, "Pak Weaponization Not So: Experts Doubt Blast Potency," *Sunday Observer,* May 31–June 6, 1998.

[75]The best publicly available analysis emerging from Sundarji's early efforts remains *Effects of Nuclear Asymmetry on Conventional Deterrence,* Combat Paper No. 1 (Mhow, India: College of Combat, 1981) and *Nuclear Weapons in a Third World Context,* Combat Paper No. 2 (Mhow, India: College of Combat, 1981). Sundarji continued this analytical effort while he served as Chief of Army Staff, but the products emerging from this work are not publicly available.

[76]See, by way of example, *India: Indian Army Trains for N-Contingencies,* FBIS-TAC-98-194, July 13, 1998.

that since the early 1980s the Indian military has "indeed geared up psychologically and to some extent technically to operate in an NBC [nuclear, biological, and chemical] environment."[77] The principal evidence adduced for this claim is the fact that the Indian Army in particular focused on acquiring armored vehicles with integral NBC protection while steadily moving toward maneuver doctrines in place of the attrition-intensive strategies that dominated earlier. However, both pieces of evidence are at best ambiguous, and when scrutinized closely it is hard to sustain the claim that the Indian Army in particular and the Indian armed services in general seriously prepared themselves for operations in an NBC environment.[78] The

---

[77]W.P.S. Sidhu, *The Development of an Indian Nuclear Doctrine Since 1980,* unpublished doctoral dissertation, Emmanuel College, University of Cambridge, February 1997, p. 350. A similar though more tendentious claim can be found in Sanjay Badri-Maharaj, "The Nuclear Battlefield," *Indian Defence Review,* 14:2 (April–June 1999), pp. 75–90.

[78]The claim that the Indian Army's desire to acquire modern armored fighting vehicles with NBC protection suggests preparation for nuclear battlefield operations is simply an exaggeration. Most modern armored vehicles, both tanks and infantry/cavalry fighting vehicles, are designed with integral (passive) NBC protection (as are all modern warships). The fact that the Indian Army specified such protection as a requirement in its new mechanized acquisitions simply suggests that the service sought to acquire technologies that would enable it to remain current. In fact, the Indian Army possessed this technology before the 1980s, since its T-55 and P-76 tanks, which have been in service since the late 1960s, were already equipped with integral NBC protection; consequently, the desire to retain these capabilities in follow-on systems does not permit the inference that the Indian Army was now preparing for operations on a nuclear battlefield any more than the fact that the older T-55s came equipped with this technology justifies the inference that the Indian Army has been preparing for nuclear war-fighting operations since the late 1960s. If the Army was in fact serious about combat operations in an NBC environment, it would have acquired many other kinds of technologies that, in contrast to the views of Badri-Maharaj, it did not acquire and still does not possess in any significant quantities to this day—including mission-oriented protective posture (MOPP) gear for all troops at least in the Strike Corps; fixed decontamination equipment at the brigade level; and portable decontamination capabilities at the regimental level.

The other claim—that a shift to a maneuver doctrine suggests a desire to prepare for operations in an NBC environment—is also overstated. The Indian Army has no doubt struggled to develop and institutionalize a maneuver war-fighting doctrine since the early 1980s, but this development was driven primarily by the recognition that India may not have the luxury of overwhelming its adversaries through superior numbers or pervasively superior technology in the context of a "no-notice" short war. The shift to a maneuver doctrine was thus driven by the need to resolve critical *conventional war-fighting challenges*—brought about in part by the Indian Army's desire to extend the subcontinental battlefield to new geographic areas that were hospitable to the large-scale employment of armored forces, such as the deserts of Rajasthan and

discussion in Chapter Four will in fact demonstrate that India's civilian security managers are extremely reluctant to support any nuclear war-fighting strategies programmatically, and it is not at all clear that acquiring any operational capabilities other than the minimum required to preserve the integrity of an Indian military force in

---

Sind—rather than as a solution to addressing the challenges of a nuclear battlefield. For the genesis and logic of the shift to a maneuver doctrine, see Ashley J. Tellis, *India: Assessing Strategy and Military Capabilities in the Year 2000*, P-7978 (Santa Monica: RAND, 1996).

Clearly, the ability to successfully operate maneuver forces provides *some* benefits for nuclear war-fighting operations that no doubt place a premium on the possession of high degrees of self-protection and the ability to engage in relentless movement. Operations on a nuclear battlefield, however, require much more than the ability to engage in maneuver operations. To the contrary, they require an organizational structure differing from the current "triangular" formations employed by the Indian Army; a highly decentralized command style that is alien to current Indian Army practices; a heavy investment in real-time C^3I *within* maneuver formations, coupled with a substantial increase in the firepower of battle groups compared to what the regimental level currently possesses in the field; an entirely different logistical structure compared to that which currently services army field combat operations; and, finally, repeated exercises that focus on perfecting the "accordion" effect of cyclic dispersal and concentration, which the Indian Army has never practiced hitherto, except cosmetically as part of its routine training cycle.

Since the 1998 nuclear tests, the Indian Army has begun to pay increasing attention to the challenges of operating on a nuclear-shadowed battlefield, and it is reasonable to expect that future Army exercises will systematically incorporate new and more demanding routines designed to increase the survivability of deployed conventional forces in the face of possible nuclear attacks. Several elements of this effort are significant. First, Indian military exercises that seriously incorporate nuclear threats in order to devise new solutions for both force protection and the preservation of operational coherence in the face of adversary nuclear attacks are a new development in the Indian Army's training regimen, and these innovations are by no means either complete or institutionalized throughout the war-fighting formations of the service as a whole. Second, the emphasis—as evidenced in both Indian military exercises and the statements of senior Indian Army leaders—is primarily on force protection and the preservation of operational coherence in the face of an adversary's nuclear threat, *not* on integrating "theater" and "tactical" nuclear fire support in furtherance of either offensive or exploitative battlefield military operations. Third, a critical objective of the Army's emerging interest in the nuclear environment is to understand the research and development, acquisition, and integration requirements pertaining to the various new technologies that the service must acquire if it is to successfully preserve its conventional war-fighting capability in the face of potential nuclear use by an adversary. Pursuing such conservative objectives is a far cry from the expansive nuclear ambitions and capabilities sometimes attributed to the Indian Army as it struggles to cope with the challenges of maintaining its effectiveness in the new nuclear environment. For more on this issue, see Rahul Bedi, "Interview: Gen. Sunderajan Padmanabhan, India's Chief of Army Staff," *Jane's Defence Weekly*, January 17, 2001, and Raj Chengappa, "Pakistan Threatened India with Nuclear Attack During Kargil War: Army Chief," *The Newspaper Today*, January 12, 2001.

the face of an adversary's nuclear attack and to mount an adequate retaliatory response after absorbing such an attack is actually favored by the current senior leadership of India's armed services.[79] Indeed, if the historical record is anything to go by, the senior Indian military leadership has for the most part focused its attention on demanding that the country not employ its combat forces under conditions of strategic disadvantage.[80] As several service chiefs have publicly indicated, this has mainly involved pleading with civilian decisionmakers for the development of a national deterrent in the hope that the uniformed services may somehow be formally integrated into the country's grand strategy at the highest level. In consonance with these invocations, a recent Chief of Staff of the Indian Army, speaking in the aftermath of Pakistan's test of its new Ghauri IRBM, formally reiterated the need for "a 'strategic deterrence' capability to counter the emerging 'nuclear and missile challenges' to India's security,"[81] while the current Chief of Staff reassuringly stated that "the Army will be prepared to tackle [the] nuclear threat."[82]

---

[79]See Chengappa, "Pakistan Threatened India with Nuclear Attack During Kargil War: Army Chief."

[80]Manoj Joshi, "Deadly Option," *India Today International*, May 4, 1998, pp. 38–40.

[81]"Army Chief Calls for Steps to Counter N-Threats," *The Hindu*, April 21, 1998.

[82]"Army Will Be Prepared to Tackle Nuclear Threat," *Hindustan Times*, September 29, 2000. Specifying precisely what this entails, the current Chief of Army Staff, General S. Padmanabhan, asserted that

> I am looking at the whole range that constitutes the spectrum. You have the low-level conflict on the one end and on the other end you have the nuclear war scenario. In between this spectrum is a whole amount of strategic space. This is the space in the middle for conventional operations. As and when we come to the other end of the spectrum [i.e., the nuclear-shadowed battlefield] our tactics will change, our main systems will change. Our logistics will have to undergo a considerable change. Even your communications philosophy will have to undergo a change. There will be subtle changes as well on depth and range of our strikes. What objective we move for will change. How we maneouvre in the battlefield . . . these are things that we are looking at. *I am not for one moment suggesting that we are going to be indulging in nuclear war fighting. Nuclear war fighting is perhaps the last thing in anybody's mind. What we are looking at is to get an optimal return from conventional warfare* [italics added].

Given the many nuclear-related developments in Pakistan during the last decade, Indian policymakers have slowly come around to adopting a stance more closely allied with that of the senior leadership of its armed services. When confronted by disagreements between civilian scientists and uniformed experts about the extent of Pakistan's nuclear capabilities, for example, India's security managers have simply chosen to presume that Pakistan's nuclear capability exists at some significant level, even if many disputes have arisen about the particulars of that capability. From this presumption, they have concluded that India does in fact face a nuclear threat of some magnitude from Pakistan. This threat significantly circumscribes India's political and military freedom of action on the one hand, but it also justifies the need for continued development of India's nuclear and strategic capabilities on the other.[83] Thus, after a decade of some hesitation and ambiguity, India's civilian leadership has clearly accepted and affirmed the emergence of Pakistan's evolving nuclear capabilities even if many uncertainties remain about what that implies in terms of the balance of power vis-à-vis India.[84]

Pakistan's nuclear potential, as exemplified both by its weaponry and by the plethora of delivery systems it is developing or has already acquired, is certainly problematic in that for the first time in India's postindependence history, its immediate—and weaker—rival has acquired the ability to hold at risk significant national assets such as major population and industrial centers, critical military facilities, and strategic infrastructure assets located great distances from the frontier. This new vulnerability to standoff attack by weapons of mass destruction represents a dramatic change in the strategic balance vis-à-vis Pakistan. Whatever the minutiae relating to this balance traditionally may have been, the one single and incontrovertible manifestation of New Delhi's superiority was India's

---

See Chengappa, "Pakistan Threatened India with Nuclear Attack During Kargil War: Army Chief."

[83]An early justification of this conclusion can be found in "Pakistan Nuclear Development Leaves India No Choices," *The Times of India*, November 5, 1986.

[84]Joshi, "Deadly Option," and Patralekha Chatterjee, "Amid Blaring Headlines, India Mum on U.S. Nuclear Report," available at http://www.msnbc.com/news/418094.asp.

ability—however notional—to threaten assets throughout the depth of Pakistan's territory while remaining immune to any comparable attack directed against India. To the degree that Pakistan could mount any credible threats at all, these were restricted to challenges leveled at the frontiers, with the vast depth of India's heartland remaining a protected sanctuary lying beyond Pakistan's reach. The addition of long-range missile-delivered nuclear weapons to Pakistan's arsenal, however, has overturned this traditional Indian advantage. In the process, it has also altered the larger strategic equations in the greater South Asian region: India still cannot reach Chinese strategic targets, although it remains abundantly vulnerable to Beijing's coercive reach, while Pakistan has now extended its strategic reach to the depths of the Indian heartland, thereby forever erasing the last bastion of immunity that New Delhi once enjoyed.[85] In effect, then, Pakistan—the traditionally weaker adversary—has now neutralized India's conventional and geostrategic advantages, while India remains weaker than its other major adversary, China, by most indices of strategic capability—including geopolitical importance, economic growth, and nuclear capacity.

The Sino-Pakistani connection, which has steadily strengthened since the early 1980s, is seen in this context as placing Islamabad at an additional advantage. According to authoritative sources in the West, China has been involved in a significant degree of nuclear cooperation with Pakistan.[86] Whether Indian intelligence discerned the extent and significance of this cooperation early on is uncertain, but its task was certainly eased by the U.S. nonproliferation community's scrutiny of the Sino-Pakistani relationship. Thanks to the work of this interest group, it has been widely reported that China has provided Pakistan with specific technologies such as ring magnets, diagnostic equipment, and special furnaces; special nuclear materials such as

---

[85]This point is underscored in Brahma Chellaney, "India's Strategic Depth Lies Shattered," *The Pioneer*, April 14, 1998.

[86]The myriad details pertaining to the Sino-Pakistani nuclear relationship can be found in "China's Nuclear Exports and Assistance to Pakistan," Center for Nonproliferation Studies, Monterey, CA, available at http://cns.miis.edu/research/india/china/npakpos.htm; "China's Nuclear Exports and Assistance to Pakistan—Statements and Developments," Center for Nonproliferation Studies, Monterey, CA, available at http://cns.miis.edu/research/india/china/npakchr.htm; and "China's Nuclear Exports and Assistance to South Asia," Center for Nonproliferation Studies, Monterey, CA, available at http://cns.miis.edu/research/india/china/nsaspos.htm.

heavy water, highly enriched uranium, and tritium; integrated nuclear facilities, including the Khushab research reactor, for the production of weapons-grade plutonium; and, most problematically of all, complete nuclear weapon designs, including one design that is reported to have involved a 20- to 25-kiloton (kt) solid-core implosion device derived from China's fourth nuclear test.[87]

China has also helped Pakistan acquire reasonably efficient missile delivery systems—weapons that Islamabad had always desired because of the high degree of assured penetrativity they represented in the face of India's relatively superior air defense network.[88] Indeed, Chinese assistance is suspected even in the development of Pakistan's first indigenous missiles, the Hatf-1 and Hatf-2, both of which derived from the sounding rocket technologies imported from France by Pakistan's Space and Upper Atmosphere Research Organization (SUPARCO) in the 1960s. This assistance reached its high point in 1992 or thereabouts, when Beijing sold 34 M-11 ballistic missiles to Islamabad.[89] These missiles, which are capable of a range of 300 km while carrying an 800-kg payload (or 250 km with a 1000-kg payload), represented the first Pakistani missile system that was capable of carrying nuclear weapons. Given Islamabad's perceptions of its hostile threat environment, it is therefore not surprising that U.S. intelligence agencies reportedly concluded in 1996 that Pakistan probably "had finished developing nuclear warheads for these mis-

---

[87]Patrick E. Tyler, "China Raises Nuclear Stakes on the Subcontinent," *New York Times*, August 27, 1996.

[88]The myriad details pertaining to the Sino-Pakistani missile relationship can be found in "China's Missile Exports and Assistance to Pakistan," Center for Nonproliferation Studies, Monterey, CA, available at http://cns.miis.edu/research/india/china/mpakpos.htm; "China's Missile Exports and Assistance to Pakistan—Statements and Developments," Center for Nonproliferation Studies, Monterey, CA, available at http://cns.miis.edu/research/india/china/mpakchr.htm; and "China's Missile Exports and Assistance to South Asia," Center for Nonproliferation Studies, Monterey, CA, available at http://cns.miis.edu/research/india/china/msaspos.htm.

[89]R. Jeffrey Smith, "Report Cites China-Pakistan Missile Links," *Washington Post*, June 13, 1996, and Bill Gertz, "China Summit Missile Pact Unlikely; 'Incremental Progress' Not Ruled Out," *Washington Times*, June 21, 1998. This sale has now been offi-cially confirmed by the U.S. intelligence community. See National Intelligence Council, *Foreign Missile Developments and the Ballistic Missile Threats to the United States Through 2015*, September 1999, available at http://www.cia.gov/cia/publications/nie/nie99msl.html.

siles."[90] The delivery of the M-11s, a transaction that clearly skirted the Missile Technology Control Regime even if it did not directly violate it, was apparently followed by extensive Chinese assistance in the establishment of a missile production complex at Tarnawa outside Rawalpindi—where, through the provision of blueprints, equipment, and possibly machine tools, Pakistan would be able to domestically produce the M-11s, now designated the Hatf-3.[91] Thanks to these transactions coupled with other indigenous R&D contributions, Pakistan has managed to acquire a reliable, solid-fueled, short-range ballistic missile (SRBM) that could assuredly deliver either conventional or nuclear ordnance to any point at operational depths along the eastern frontier with India.

Yet while SRBMs like the M-11 were discussed extensively in the Indian press as a result of revelations in the United States, a more recent Pakistani acquisition—the 1500-km, liquid-fueled Ghauri IRBM—came as a complete shock to the Indian body politic. Although Pakistan had anounced the Ghauri's presence long before it was tested, Indian analysts discounted the veracity of such claims because of the assertion that it was an indigenously produced weapon.[92] One Indian analyst, for example, asserted that the Ghauri was "a long way from being in a position of undergoing test flights" and argued that Pakistan's announcement of its existence mainly represented a "psychological effort to seek . . . parity with India on the missile front."[93] When the reality that Pakistan actually pos-

---

[90]Smith, "Report Cites China-Pakistan Missile Links."

[91]Steven Erlanger, "U.S. Wary of Punishing China for Missile Help to Pakistan," *New York Times*, August 27, 1996.

[92]In fact, even after the Ghauri's test firing was displayed on national television, Indian analysts refused to believe that a live test had occurred—a judgment influenced by the fact that Indian early-warning radars apparently did not detect it. See David C. Wright, "An Analysis of the Pakistani Ghauri Missile Test of April 6, 1998," *Science and Global Security*, 7:2 (1998), pp. 227–234. In the West, too, the test firing of the Ghauri gave rise to some preposterous reporting even by otherwise-respectable sources. One report in *Jane's Missiles & Rockets*, for example, claimed that "officials in Pakistan faked pictures and the date of the Ghauri intermediate range ballistic missile launch." The date of the test was allegedly fudged "because a deal had been struck between Washington and Islamabad to delay the launch date until after the Indian elections" so as to prevent giving the Bharatiya Janata Party (BJP) "a larger mandate" than it would have received. See Paul Beaver, "Pakistan 'Faked Ghauri Missile Picture,'" *Jane's Missiles & Rockets*, 2:6 (June 1998), p. 4.

[93]Aabha Dixit, "How Real Is the Ghauri Scare?" *The Pioneer*, January 24, 1998.

sessed the Ghauri began to sink in, however, there was a hasty rush to judgment: The Indian Defence Minister, articulating a widespread belief in India, claimed that "China is the mother of this missile,"[94] and a chorus of Indian opinion makers followed suit.[95] Later Western reporting, corroborating the judgment of India's premier strategic analyst,[96] revealed conclusively that the missile was a Nodong that had been sold by the North Korean Changgwang Sinyong Corporation to Pakistan's Khan Research Laboratories (KRL) in what appeared to have been a private transaction between the two entities.[97] While the extent of Chinese involvement in this transaction is still unclear, the fact remains that the Ghauri signaled Pakistan's growing ability to strike deep at strategic levels along the Indian landmass. In the aftermath of the May 1998 tests, the head of Pakistan's Atomic Energy Commission disclosed the presence of a new 700-km solid-fueled missile, the Shaheen-1, which was supposedly "on the launch pad" awaiting a political decision before being field tested.[98] The same report also suggested that a newer, longer-range (2000-km) version of the same missile—dubbed the Shaheen-2—might be available within a year.

Between KRL and the Pakistan Atomic Energy Commission (PAEC)–SUPARCO–National Development Centre (NDC) complex, Pakistan now appears to have at least two long-range missiles, the Ghauri and the Shaheen-1, ready at hand, with many more even longer-range systems—the Ghaznavi, the Shaheen-2, and the Abid Ali—said to be in the pipeline. The Shaheen-1, which was finally tested in April 1999, is probably the same missile that one U.S. official has identified as the Tarmuk,[99] but the truth about the other

---

[94]"Fernandes Sees No Threat from Ghauri," *The Hindu*, April 10, 1998.

[95]For a good example of such claims, see Chintamani Mahapatra, "The U.S., China and the Ghauri Missile," *Strategic Analysis*, 22:3 (June 1998), pp. 363–372.

[96]K. Subrahmanyam, "Global Watch: Pakistani Missile," *Economic Times*, February 20, 1998. See also the pertinent comments in C. Raja Mohan, "Ghauri Missile: India in Denial," *The Hindu*, April 9, 1998.

[97]Paul Beaver, "Pakistan's Missile 'Was a Nodong,'" *Jane's Missiles & Rockets*, 2:5 (May 1998), pp. 1–2.

[98]John Ward Anderson, "Pakistan Claims It Has New Missile," *Washington Post*, June 2, 1998.

[99]Bill Gertz and Ernest Blazar, "Pakistan May Have Nuclear Tips for Rockets: New Test Blasts, Missile Firings Are Imminent," *Washington Times*, May 30, 1998.

missiles is difficult to discern, given both organizations' interest in competitively touting their wares. Even if some of these systems turn out to be largely fictitious, however, the fact remains that the capabilities represented by the M-11/Shaheen and the Ghauri families are already formidable enough. Pakistan has acquired the ability to reliably target most Indian fixed assets at great distances from the frontier, and this capability will only grow over the years, thereby reducing the size of the Indian sanctuary even further.[100] This growing strategic reach—coupled with the fact that a high degree of integration exists between the Pakistani armed services (the end users) and the civilian-led but military-supervised nuclear and missile establishments (the producers)—bequeaths a certain coherence to Islamabad's strategic planning that renders it significant as a nuclear adversary. Both nuclear weapons and ballistic missiles are treated seriously as military instruments of deterrence in Pakistan because Islamabad's fears about Indian intentions and its dread of the large and diversified Indian military-industrial complex are seen as leaving it no other choice but to urgently develop a range of war-fighting systems that possess both high survivability and high penetrativity vis-à-vis its principal adversary, India.

In contrast, India's traditional reliance on air-breathing systems for nuclear delivery, its robust separation between the uniformed military and the civilian nuclear establishment, its insular decision-making with respect to the nuclear program, and its lack of institutionalized mechanisms for managing nuclear strategy are viewed by many knowledgeable analysts as placing New Delhi at somewhat of a disadvantage with respect to Islamabad.[101] These problems notwithstanding, many Indian commentators still judge the emergence of Pakistan's nuclear capabilities to be a manageable problem, at least in the short run. In no small measure, this is simply a matter of pride. For many Indians, admitting that Pakistan—a weak, smaller, and defeated neighbor—might pose an irresolvable threat to Indian security is tantamount to admitting a political equivalence that could

---

[100]Aabha Dixit, "Flying Tackle: Pakistan's Missile Program Now Represents a Serious Threat to India," *The Telegraph*, September 2, 1996, and "The Missile Race," *Hindustan Times*, April 8, 1998.

[101]See the remarks in George Perkovich, "South Asia: A Bomb Is Born," *Newsweek*, January 24, 2000, p. 52.

negate all of New Delhi's claims to preeminence in the region. Not surprisingly, many Indian analysts—especially those connected with the nuclear establishment, the armed forces, and some sections of the media—simply tend to dismiss the Pakistani threat as inconsequential even while admitting many of the details that should otherwise serve to undercut that judgment.[102]

When hubris is not the issue, however, the claim regarding Pakistan's insignificance can be seen as having been asserted on other, perhaps more tenable grounds. To begin with, India is believed to possess greater nuclear weapon *potential* even if it may not be as far along as Pakistan where weaponization is concerned. This belief is grounded in the fact that India has a larger and more diversified nuclear and defense research establishment, probably possesses more sophisticated nuclear weapon designs (including, perhaps, some advanced weapon designs) and a larger stockpile of fissile materials, and could develop a greater range of indigenous delivery systems over time.[103] All these potentialities taken together would enable India, in the words of one analyst, to develop the requisite capabilities "to administer retribution of a magnitude that would demolish the national fabric of [Pakistan]."[104]

More significantly, however, claims about Pakistan's relative insignificance are often rooted in the existing asymmetry in relative vulnerability between the two states. This asymmetry effectively implies that any security competition which leads to a nuclear exchange would ultimately result in the complete destruction of Pakistan but in only limited, albeit grave, damage to India. As if confirming this judgment, one analyst has noted that the destruction of just seven dams and barrages in Pakistan even by conventional weapons would lead to "the total disruption of control over irrigation

---

[102]See, for example, Bharat Karnad, "Going Thermonuclear: Why, with What Forces, At What Cost," *Journal of the United Services Institution of India,* 127:533 (July–September 1998), pp. 310–311 and 318–320, and Vijai K. Nair, "The Structure of an Indian Nuclear Deterrent," in Amitabh Mattoo (ed.), *India's Nuclear Deterrent* (New Delhi: Har-Anand Publications, 1999), pp. 74–78.

[103]E. A. Vas, "India's Nuclear Options in the 1990s and Its Effects on India's Armed Forces," *Indian Defence Review,* 1:1 (January 1986), p. 20ff.

[104]Vijai K. Nair, *Nuclear India* (New Delhi: Lancer International, 1992), p. 137.

in the Indus Valley"[105] and, by implication, the destruction of the most important parts of the Pakistani state.

Further, the asymmetry in postconflict reconstitution capability, which favors India, is viewed as setting additional limits on Pakistan's ability to bear risks, thereby rendering Islamabad's nuclear capabilities manageable, at least in the short term. As one analyst laconically put it, "In the event of nuclear aggression, India's size and resources place it in a favourable situation in relation to its neighbours. The political leadership must realise this."[106] Such arguments in effect imply that India's greater size, resources, and level of industrialization would allow it to recover from nuclear attacks much more rapidly and coherently than could Pakistan, thus enabling it to survive the post–nuclear attack environment better than would its smaller adversary.

Finally, of course, many Indian analysts' rhetorically sanguine attitudes toward Pakistan's nuclear capabilities are rooted in an awareness that India has little reason to undertake any political-military action that would imperil Islamabad to the point at which the latter would be forced to bring its currently significant nuclear capabilities into play.[107] Since New Delhi has long held that neither subjugating nor fractionating Pakistan is in its strategic interests, Indian policymakers could claim to be reassured by the fact that nothing *they* do could lead Pakistan to nuclear use—and, as such, these policymakers might seem less than impelled to respond to Pakistan's nuclear achievements with a corresponding increase in their own nuclear readiness.[108]

---

[105]Ibid., p. 141.

[106]Satinder Singh, "Nuclear War in South Asia—The Worst Case," *Indian Defence Review*, 2:1 (January 1987), p. 74.

[107]K. Subrahmanyam, "Dealing with Pakistan," *The Times of India*, June 26, 1990. This argument may be correct as it goes, but its weakness derives from the premise that Pakistan would use nuclear weapons *only* in response to certain Indian actions and never as a result of causes such as adventurism on the part of Islamabad; pre-emptive Pakistani action precipitated by misperception or miscalculation; or a state breakdown or regime collapse in Pakistan.

[108]The growing disenchantment with Pakistan arising from its continued support for the Kashmiri insurgency has led various commentators to argue for a new Indian policy that includes cross-border operations aimed at making Pakistan "pay the price" for its misadventures. See Gurmeet Kanwal, "Pay-Back Time on the LOC," *Indian Ex-*

These four considerations are usually interpreted to mean that while Pakistan constitutes a nuclear threat to India, it is not an over-whelming one at this point. Here again, there is some truth to this judgment—but as always, the devil lurks in the details. Unfortu-nately, none of these details can be discussed here at any length. It may be noted, however, that whatever India's advantages may be in the realms of nuclear potential, postconflict reconstitution, and po-litical initiative with respect to conflict, the advantages India cur-rently enjoys in relative vulnerability over Pakistan will slowly decay over time as Islamabad develops a larger nuclear arsenal and pro-gressively longer-range delivery systems—and at some stage, there will come a point where Pakistan, despite its relative disadvantage in size, will be able to comprehensively target the Indian landmass and inflict such horrific levels of damage as to make any distinction in relative vulnerability more or less academic. For this reason, it is likely that—however dismissive Indian commentators may be today—India's security managers will treat Pakistan's nuclear capa-bilities more and more seriously over time. They will, for example, seek to avoid overt forms of political provocation; will attempt to de-velop a superior nuclear deterrent to the degree possible; will con-tinue to focus substantial resources on conventional military mod-ernization vis-à-vis Pakistan; and will pursue the acquisition of the best technical antidotes available to them in the form of anti–tactical ballistic missile (ATBM) and integrated air defense (IAD) systems. Unlike the newly enfranchised strategic community in and around New Delhi, the Indian government is responsible for the security of its citizenry, and to the degree that even modest Pakistani nuclear capabilities could place those obligations at risk, India's security managers will demonstrate more respect for those capabilities than even their rhetoric may on occasion suggest.

Given this judgment, it is clear that for at least two reasons, India will move further in the direction of nuclearization *based on the Pak-istan threat alone*. The first reason is grounded not in Pakistan's nu-clear capabilities per se but in how it is perceived to be using those capabilities with respect to India. A sturdy, nuclear-capable Pakistan

---

press, June 27, 2000, and Satish Nambiar, "Make the Army Fighting Fit, Paddy," *Hin-dustan Times*, August 20, 2000. Should such sentiments come to dominate Indian policymaking toward Pakistan, they are likely to propel greater movement in the direc-tion of nuclearization.

that focuses on economic renewal to the neglect of security competition with India represents an outcome that would cause New Delhi little grief. This may in fact be the best outcome possible, because insofar as nuclear weapons bequeath on Pakistan the security it has sought since its founding but could never be attained through external alliances, such weapons will have served the desirable purpose of reducing Pakistan's vulnerability, thus making stability in South Asia possible. If the record of the past decade is any indication, however, nuclear weapons can also have the opposite effect—that is, they could embolden Pakistan to carry on active security competition with India not through the medium of direct high-intensity conventional wars but rather through low-intensity conflicts waged by proxy that, in effect, challenge India's core objective: preserving a stable multiethnic state with claims to greatness.[109]

If Pakistan perceives its nuclear capabilities as providing, among other things, the requisite strategic cover with which to immunize it against any military counteraction in the context of some ongoing unconventional conflict with India, New Delhi will face strong pressure to shift its overall nuclear posture to cope with the challenges of nuclear coercion. This revision would not necessarily be predicated on the desire to achieve a "splendid first strike" capability, although that might suggest itself as an attractive proposition in some instances, but would likely be based instead on the need to develop an *arsenal* that is sufficiently effective to prevent strategic coercion by Islamabad, enable India to engage in "tit-for-tat" strategies of subconventional retaliation, and allow India's conventional forces the freedom of action they need to complete both counterinsurgency and, possibly, cross-border operations without fear of paralyzing counterthreats. In other words, to the degree that continued Pakistani support for Indian insurgencies results in high burdens for

---

[109]This phenomenon is well known to students of international politics since it was first identified as the "stability-instability" paradox in Glenn Snyder, "The Balance of Power and the Balance of Terror," in Paul Seabury (ed.), *The Balance of Power* (San Francisco: Chandler, 1965). For an assessment of how this paradox has materialized in South Asia with special reference to the interaction of nuclear and conventional military capabilities, see Ashley J. Tellis, *Stability in South Asia*, DB-185-A (Santa Monica: RAND, 1997). See also Sumit Ganguly, "Indo-Pakistani Nuclear Issues and the Stability/Instability Paradox," *Studies in Conflict & Terrorism*, 18:4 (1995), pp. 325–334. For an Indian perspective on this issue, see Jasjit Singh, "Pakistan's Fourth War," *Strategic Analysis*, 23:5 (August 1999), pp. 685–702.

New Delhi, there is every possibility that India's nuclear posture will shift in the direction of developing a more ambitious and complex nuclear capability. Such a reorientation—which could include having a diverse nuclear arsenal composed of different kinds of warheads, various discrete and limited-use options, and greater integration between civilian authority and military users—would be seen as progressively more necessary in the context of possible armed responses to Pakistani "needling" even if the same was otherwise unwarranted in the context of a purely nominal nuclear standoff with Islamabad. The Indian nuclear posture, even in such circumstances, would not be oriented toward nuclear war-fighting operations but would instead be aimed at developing a capability that would allow New Delhi to plan for and mount sophisticated counterthreats at varying levels of violence so as to circumvent the actual use of any nuclear weapons in favor of other kinds of subconventional or conventional military strategies.[110]

Just as Indian policymakers would be inclined to slowly transform their present strategic posture if the incidence of nuclear-shadowed proxy wars waged by Pakistan were to increase, so too are they likely to expand their nuclear capabilities if Islamabad dramatically distends its own nuclear production potential. This is the second reason India could move slowly in the direction of expanded capabilities over time. India's traditionally relaxed attitude toward Pakistan's nuclear capabilities derived in great measure from the belief that Islamabad's stockpile of fissile materials, and consequently its notional-weapon inventory, was rather small. Most public estimates assess Pakistan's inventory of fissile materials circa 1995 as being in the region of 200 kg of uranium 235.[111] Assuming that 15 kg of highly enriched uranium (HEU) are used to produce a single weapon, this inventory would suffice to produce some 13 fission bombs of a nominal 10- to 20-kt yield. India's inventory of fissile materials circa 1995, in contrast, was assessed to be roughly 450 kg of weapons-grade plu-

---

[110]For an example of strong advocacy in this direction, see M. D. Nalapat, "No More Waffling," *The Times of India*, January 18, 2000, and Nambiar, "Make the Army Fighting Fit, Paddy." See also C. Raja Mohan, "Fernandes Unveils 'Limited War' Doctrine," *The Hindu*, January 25, 2000, and "Jawing About War," *The Times of India*, January 29, 2000.

[111]All the figures in this paragraph are based on Chow et al., *The Proposed Fissile-Material Production Cut-Off*, pp. 9–15.

tonium (Pu). At a rate of 5 kg of Pu^{239} per weapon, the notional Indian stockpile would thus consist of approximately 90 fission bombs of a nominal 10- to 20-kt yield. Calculating these data for circa 1999 is more complicated, especially for Pakistan, since it is unclear whether Pakistan simply terminated enrichment at the Kahuta facility in the post-1991 period or whether it continued to produce an intermediate product consisting of medium-enriched uranium in order to substantiate its promise to the United States of not producing weapons-grade material.[112]

Since India is presumed by many of the sources cited below to produce about 30 kg of weapons-grade plutonium annually, it could have possessed an additional 120 kg of weapons-grade plutonium circa 1999 to yield a total of some 570 kg. This is sufficient to produce approximately 115 fission bombs of a nominal 10- to 20-kt yield. If Pakistan produced medium-enriched uranium during its post-1991 moratorium at Kahuta, as is likely, it could resume HEU production rapidly enough to produce an additional 175 to 200 kg of HEU in a matter of weeks. These levels would give Pakistan a notional arsenal of some 23 to 26 fission bombs of a nominal 10- to 20-kt yield, also suggesting in the process that the moratorium on HEU production that has ostensibly been in place since 1991 would have little effect on the size of Pakistan's weapons stockpile over the long term.[113] This uranium inventory will be further supplemented over time by weapons-grade plutonium produced by the new unsafeguarded re-

---

[112]By most authoritative Pakistani claims, Islamabad's fissile-material production program was never "frozen," at least in the ordinary sense of the term. See *Pakistan: Beg Says Nuclear Program "Never Frozen,"* FBIS-NES-96-165, August 22, 1996. More recent Pakistani reports clearly indicate that Islamabad continued to produce either low-enriched or medium-enriched uranium even after 1991, thus allowing it to rapidly increase the quantity of weapons-grade fissile materials in the future. See "Pakistan, India to Sign CTBT This Month," *The Muslim*, August 12, 1998. Despite some problems with the estimates therein, a good analysis of the factors involved in fissile-material production in South Asia can be found in A. H. Nayyar, A. H. Toor, and Zia Mian, "Fissile Material Production Potential in South Asia," *Science & Global Security*, 6 (1997), pp. 189–203. For Pakistan specifically, see David Albright and Kevin O'Neill, "ISIS Technical Assessment: Pakistan's Stock of Weapon-Grade Uranium," June 1, 1998, available at http://www.isis-online.org/.

[113]Nayyar et al., for example, correctly note that it would take Pakistan between five and ten weeks to produce an additional 200 kg of weapons-grade uranium if the feed material was already enriched to the 20 percent levels that are the upper limits at which the material is still classified as low enriched uranium (LEU). See Nayyar et al., "Fissile Material Production Potential in South Asia," p. 201.

actor at Khushab, which was commissioned in April 1998 and is believed to be capable of producing between 10 and 15 kg of weapons-grade plutonium, sufficient to produce two to three additional weapons per year. When the cumulative fissile-material stocks and weapon potentials of both countries are thus considered as a whole, the commonly assumed Indian lead as far as the weapon stockpile is concerned could fall off dramatically within the decade as the new Pakistani production capabilities come on line. One U.S. analyst thus concluded that "although India is estimated, as of early 1998, to possess seven times more nuclear weapons than Pakistan, . . . Pakistan could reduce that margin to a factor of less than two over the next eight years. If India wanted to maintain a significant lead over Pakistan, it would be forced to dramatically increase its fissile material production. Pakistan, however, is capable of matching such an increase."[114]

Despite this otherwise correct conclusion, it must be remembered that all the numbers relating to the size of Indian and Pakistani fissile-material inventories and nuclear weapon stockpiles are inherently speculative. After various production inefficiencies and internal program decisions are taken into account, it is likely that—at least where India is concerned—New Delhi's inventory of weapons-grade material is much smaller than the generally higher estimates circulating in the public domain.[115] Consequently, the size of the notional-weapon stockpile is probably smaller than the numbers derived from these estimates. In the case of India particularly, three different factors account for this outcome: First, the separation of weapons-grade plutonium from reactor discharges has proceeded at

---

[114]David Albright, *Fact Sheet: India and Pakistan—Current and Potential Nuclear Arsenals* (Washington, D.C.: Institute for Science and International Security, May 13, 1998), available at http://www.isis-online.org/.

[115]The most widely circulated public estimates remain Chow et al., *The Proposed Fissile-Material Cut-Off*, pp. 9–15, and David Albright, William Walker, and Frans Berkhout, *Plutonium and Highly Enriched Uranium 1996: World Inventories, Capabilities and Policies* (Oxford, UK: Oxford University Press, 1997). Authoritative Pakistani assessments of the Indian fissile stockpile tend to be even more exaggerated than the numbers produced by Western analysts; former PAEC Chairman Munir Ahmed Khan, for example, claimed that in 1990 India had 400 kg of weapons-grade plutonium—enough to make 50 to 70 nuclear bombs—and that its stockpile of plutonium the following year had reached a total of 1300 kg. See Rauf Siddiqi, "Khan Says India Has Plutonium to Make 50–70 Atom Bombs Anytime," *Nucleonics Week*, June 20, 1991, pp. 18–19.

a much slower pace than is usually assumed.[116] Second, production inefficiencies, structural bottlenecks, and other nuclear research endeavors have resulted in a smaller inventory of readily available weapons-grade materials.[117] Finally, of all the numerous plutonium-producing facilities that are up and running, only the outputs of the Canada-Indian Reactor–United States (CIRUS) and Dhruva reactors, if that, are used for the weapon program.[118] The bottom line, therefore, is that historically India has not felt compelled to rapidly accelerate the expansion of its weapons-grade plutonium inventory, first because the number of notional Pakistani weapons itself was believed to be small, and second because the ratio of existing relative capabilities implied an asymmetry that was clearly to India's advantage. As Pakistan changes this balance by expanding the size of its fissile-material inventory, either by increasing the number of centrifuges operating at Kahuta, Sihala, and Golra Sharif or by initiating the reprocessing of spent fuel from its new dedicated plutonium production reactor at Khushab,[119] the traditional Indian calculations that justified its slow pace in nuclear materials production are likely to be rendered anachronistic. In fact, as Pakistan moves toward producing the arsenal of 70-odd weapons that its strategic managers are supposed to have concluded is necessary for its national safety,[120] the Indian government is certain to shift toward more concerted efforts at bolstering both its materials inventory and its overall nuclear posture.

China. While Pakistan's exploitation of its nuclear capability and growth in the size of its arsenal would be two critical factors affecting India's traditional nuclear posture, strategic developments in China—India's larger and more significant nuclear rival—will have even more consequential effects. There is little doubt that Chinese

---

[116]Mark Hibbs, "Indian Pu Production Overstated, No Pit Production, Iyengar Says," *Nucleonics Week*, April 9, 1992, p. 6.

[117]R. R. Subramanian, "India's Nuclear Weapons Capabilities: A Technological Appraisal," in P. R. Chari, Pervaiz Iqbal Cheema, and Iftekharuzzaman (eds.), *Nuclear Non-Proliferation in India and Pakistan* (New Delhi: Manohar, 1996), pp. 21–41.

[118]Ibid.; Chari, *Indo-Pak Nuclear Standoff*, pp. 38–41.

[119]"Pakistan Starts Producing Plutonium," *The Nation*, November 17, 1998.

[120]Umer Farooq, "Pakistan Needs up to 70 Nuclear Warheads," *Jane's Defence Weekly*, June 10, 1998, p. 3.

nuclear capabilities are significant. Beijing already possesses a rudimentary strategic triad consisting of long-range bombers, one nuclear ballistic missile submarine, and several classes of nuclear-armed ballistic missiles ranging from theater to intercontinental systems.[121] The bombers and the sea-based nuclear force, however, represent capabilities that should be of minimal concern to India. The Chinese bomber fleet, consisting mostly of antiquated H-6 bombers carrying gravity weapons, will be incapable of penetrating Indian air defense systems, when alerted, along the Sino-Indian border. This force lacks the technology and training to fly nap-of-the-earth profiles, the only operating regime that would allow it to exploit the shadow zones in the Indian early-warning radar chain in order to proceed unmolested to its targets.[122] Currently, the Chinese ballistic missile submarine, too, is of suspect capability. Its principal battery, the CSS-N-3, would be unable to interdict any of the desired Indian targets from its notional patrol areas in the East China Sea, and while operating in the Indian Ocean remains a theoretical possibility, it is unlikely that China would deploy its sole subsurface strategic capability in waters with which it has little familiarity simply to interdict a target set that could be amply covered by its many land-based systems.

It is China's land-based ballistic missile force, together with the kinds of warheads this component can assuredly carry to target, that remains India's principal concern in the near term. The exact nature of this threat, however, seems to have been misconstrued by Indian policymakers and analysts who claim that it derives, among other things, from Chinese IRBMs deployed in Tibet. As early as 1988, a senior Indian military officer analyzed in some detail how the Chinese missile deployments supposedly occurring in Tibet could

---

[121]A good survey of China's present and prospective nuclear capabilities can be found in John Caldwell and Alexander T. Lennon, "China's Nuclear Modernization Program," *Strategic Review*, 23:4 (Fall 1995), pp. 27–37. A more recent assessment of China's strategic capabilities can be found in Bates Gill and James Mulvenon, "The Chinese Strategic Rocket Forces: Transition to Credible Deterrence," in *China and Weapons of Mass Destruction: Implications for the United States, Conference Report* (Washington, D.C.: National Intelligence Council, November 5, 1999), pp. 11–57.

[122]This reality will not change until China's new tactical bomber, the B-7, is fully operational sometime early in the 21st century, and it is simply unclear today whether the other tactical aircraft in the Chinese inventory—such as the Q/A-5—actually have a nuclear mission worth the name.

undercut larger Indian defense strategies in the region.[123] The following year, then–Indian Defence Minister K. C. Pant affirmed that China had in fact deployed missiles in Tibet oriented primarily against India.[124] In the week prior to the May 1998 nuclear tests, the present Indian Defence Minister reiterated the position that "China has deployed missiles with nuclear warheads in Tibet targeting India,"[125] while former Indian Foreign Secretary J. N. Dixit, writing in the same time frame, confirmed that Indian policymakers "have been generally aware of the 'tactical' missiles in Tibet."[126] One knowledgeable Indian military officer, in a piece written several years earlier that relied on the campaign literature of Western supporters of Tibet, emphatically asserted that "China has medium-range, intermediate-range, and intercontinental ballistic missiles [ICBMs] deployed on the Tibetan Plateau at Da Qaidam (37.50N, 95.18E), Xiao Qaidam (37.26N, 95.08E), and Delingha (37.6N, 97.12E), and along the Qinghai-Sichuan border."[127] This description, which apparently relies on the Indian conception of "historical" Tibet, includes both the present Tibetan autonomous region and Qinghai Province, located between Tibet and Xinjiang, to substantiate the charge that the Chinese nuclear threat to India emanates from deployments—including both missile and tactical nuclear weapons in some readings—in the Tibetan region.[128]

---

[123]Narendra Gupta, "Nuclear Missiles in Tibet," *The Times of India*, March 24, 1988.

[124]"Testing Reaction," *Far Eastern Economic Review*, June 8, 1989, p. 39.

[125]Cited in Kenneth Allen and JoEllen Gorg, "Nuclear Weapons and Sino-Indian Relations," *South Asian Policy Brief* (Washington, D.C.: Henry L. Stimson Center, June 15, 1998), available at http://www.stimson.org/cbm/sapb/brief2.htm.

[126]Ibid.

[127]Vijai K. Nair, "Nuclear Proliferation: U.S. Aims and India's Response," *Studies in Conflict and Terrorism*, 17:2 (1994), p. 169.

[128]Many Tibetan writers have also claimed the same. See Dawa Norbu, "Strategic Developments in Tibet: Implications for Its Neighbors," *Asian Survey*, 19:3 (March 1979), pp. 245–259. Reviewing some of these claims, one Indian analyst correctly noted that a great deal of confusion has arisen because of the "lack of clarity by what is meant by 'Tibet.' It has been used interchangeably both for the Tibetan Autonomous Region (TAR) and the Tibetan plateau. The Tibetan plateau is a much larger geographic area, encompassing parts of other adjoining provinces such as Qinghai, Sichuan, and Yunan. The TAR represents Inner Tibet earlier under the Dalai Lama. Lack of a clear delineation in Indian minds has often caused avoidable confusion." See Dipankar Banerjee, "The New Strategic Environment," in Amitabh

Such claims, however, have generally been greeted with skepticism in the West. One scholar, in fact, flatly asserted that "there is no Chinese nuclear threat to India, and no plan to create one."[129] This assertion, deriving from the fact that the Chinese DF-25, a 1700-km-range missile, was canceled prior to 1996, led to the following conclusion:

> The demise of the Dong Feng 25 says a lot about the state of China's strategic planning and where India figures in it. China considered developing the missile, which would have had precisely the range needed to strike key targets in India, and decided not to. The implication is that China no longer formulates strategic military plans with India in mind. . . . In abandoning the Dong Feng 25, the Chinese government has effectively reiterated that nuclear missile forces are irrelevant to Sino-Indian relations and to Chinese military planning. The 3A, the missile that the 25 would have replaced, is obsolete, and no other Chinese missiles can reach major targets in India—China's strategic missiles would overshoot them, and the M-9 and M-11 would fall short—even if they were based in Tibet, which is unlikely.[130]

This claim is problematic because it is based, among other things, on the premise that long-range ballistic missiles cannot be targeted at aim points short of their maximum range—a problem compounded by the speculation that Chinese M-9s and M-11s are in fact the relevant embodiments of threat vis-à-vis New Delhi.

Other analysts have been more measured in their conclusions. Although all agree that "there is no hard evidence that . . . China has placed IRBMs in Tibet," one thoughtful Australian analyst concluded that "China . . . can target India's heartland from existing locations near Chengdu in Sichuan, whereas India would need an ICBM capability [which it currently does not possess] to reach China's industrial heartland."[131] Two other U.S. analysts, in a fairly detailed as-

---

Mattoo (ed.), *India's Nuclear Deterrent* (New Delhi: Har-Anand Publications, 1999), p. 274.

[129]Eric Arnett, "What Threat?" *Bulletin of the Atomic Scientists*, 53:2 (March–April 1997), p. 54.

[130]Ibid., pp. 53–54.

[131]Gordon, "Capping South Asia's Nuclear Weapons Programs," p. 666.

sessment of China's strategic missile order of battle, have identified five brigades at Base 56 at Xining, Qinghai Province, and at Base 53 in Kunming, Yunnan Province, as having nuclear targeting responsibilities vis-à-vis India.[132] This assessment has been confirmed by Bates Gill and James Mulvenon in their more recent work on China's strategic forces, which concludes that the location of these bases and the types of missiles deployed therein, together with other indicators, strongly suggest that China targets India with nuclear missiles—just as it does many other potential adversaries, including nonnuclear states like Japan along its periphery and competitors beyond distant shores like the United States.[133]

Based on the detailed reconstruction of Chinese missile deployments summarized in Table 1,[134] Gill and Mulvenon conclude that

> from the locations of these bases and the ranges of their deployed missiles, several inferences can be drawn about the likely target for these missiles. The DF-3s and DF-21s of Base 80301 are likely targeted on Japan, Korea, Okinawa, or the Russian Far East. The DF-15s of Base 80302 are almost certainly aimed at Taiwan. The DF-3s and DF-21s of Base 80303 are likely targeted against countries south and southwest of China, including the Philippines, Vietnam, and India. The DF-5s of Base 80304 are the major CONUS-oriented systems, while the DF-4s of both Base 80304 and Base 80305 might be aimed at Hawaii. Finally, the DF-3s and DF-4s of Base 80306 are targeted at sites in the former Soviet Union, including Moscow, or possibly India.[135]

This conclusion has been further corroborated by news reports that, drawing on leaked American intelligence documents, have described in detail how China's missile forces are committed even

---

[132]Allen and Gorg, "Nuclear Weapons and Sino-Indian Relations."

[133]Gill and Mulvenon, "The Chinese Strategic Rocket Forces: Transition to Credible Deterrence," pp. 38–45.

[134]This table is reproduced from Gill and Mulvenon, "The Chinese Strategic Rocket Forces: Transition to Credible Deterrence," p. 39. The authors note that reports also cite the following launch sites: DF-5—Jiuquan (war reserves) and Wuzhai (war reserves).

[135]Ibid., pp. 39–40.

Table 1

Suspected Chinese Strategic Missile Bases

Base Number	Base MUCD[a]	Base and Selected Brigade Locations	Reported Missile Types
51	80301	Headquarters: Shenyang, Jilin Province Brigades: Tonghua (DF-3 and DF-21), Dengshahe (DF-3)	DF-3 (CSS-2) DF-21 (CSS-5)
52	80302	Headquarters: Huangshan (Tunxi), Anhui Province Brigades: Leping (DF-15), Lianxiwang (DF-3)	DF-15 (CSS-6) DF-3 (CSS-2)
53	80303	Headquarters: Kunming, Yunnan Province Brigades: Chuxiong (DF-21), Jianshui (DF-3)	DF-3 (CSS-2) DF-21 (CSS-5)
54	80304	Headquarters: Luoyang, Henan Province Brigades: Luoning (DF-5), Sundian (DF-4)	DF-4 (CSS-3) DF-5 (CSS-4)
55	80305	Headquarters: Huaihua, Hunan Province Brigades: Tongdao (two brigades of DF-4)	DF-4 (CSS-3)
56	80306	Headquarters: Xining, Qinghai Province Brigades: Datong (DF-3), Delingha (DF-4), Da Qaidam (DF-4), Liujihou (DF-3)[b]	DF-3 (CSS-2) DF-4 (CSS-3)
N/A	80310	Headquarters: Baoji, Shanxi Province	N/A
N/A	N/A	Headquarters: Yidu, Hubei or Shandong Province	DF-3 (CSS-2)

[a]MUCD = Military Unit Cover Designator.

[b]The Liujihou brigade was not listed with the other brigades of Base 80306, but its proximity to Qinghai suggests that it should be part of this base.

in peacetime to servicing a fairly extensive target set throughout continental and maritime Asia, Europe, and the United States[136]— commitments that render irrelevant the narrow and misleading debate about whether China actually deploys any ballistic missiles in "Tibet."

This debate is particularly meaningless from a technical point of view in light of the fact that, of the several missile systems deployed by China, the three that have been identified as systems employed

---

[136]Bill Gertz, "New Chinese Missiles Target All of East Asia," *Washington Times*, June 10, 1997, and Bill Gertz, "China Targets Nukes at U.S.," *Washington Times*, May 1, 1998. See also Caldwell and Lennon, "China's Nuclear Modernization Program," pp. 27–37.

for the nuclear targeting of India—the CSS-2, CSS-5, and CSS-3—are all sufficiently long-range to preclude their deployment from inhospitable, sparsely developed, and possibly vulnerable bases in the Tibetan autonomous region (see Maps 1a–f).[137]

China is reputed to possess 38-odd "movable" CSS-2 IRBMs, each armed with a 1- to 3-megaton (Mt) warhead and capable of interdicting targets out to a range of 2800 km. The eight-odd CSS-5 IRBMs are shorter-range weapons that are capable of interdicting targets at a range of about 1800 km, but unlike the CSS-2, they are true mobile missiles armed with a warhead of at least 200 to 300 kt and are capable of cold launch from a transporter-erector-launcher (TEL). Thanks

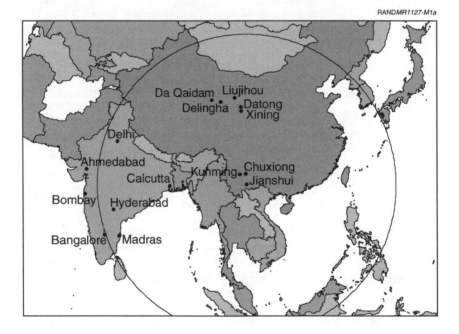

RAND*MR1127-M1a*

Map 1a—CSS-2 Coverage from Jianshui

---

[137]For a slightly different perspective on Chinese targeting, see "India–China–Pakistan Missile Ranges," in W.P.S. Sidhu, *Enhancing Indo-U.S. Strategic Cooperation*, Adelphi Paper No. 313 (Oxford, UK: Oxford University Press/IISS, 1997), p. 17.

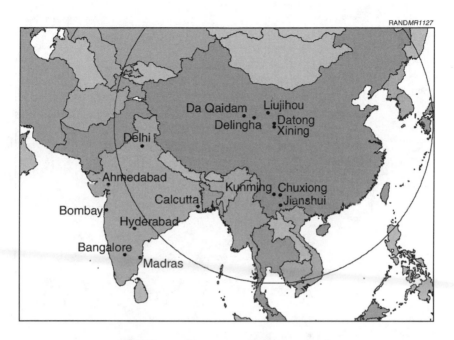

Map 1b—CSS-2 Coverage from Datong

to their deployment at the sites identified previously, both of these missile systems are capable of covering most of the principal Indian targets of interest to any Chinese planner. Even those targets which are located along the southern tip of India and which lie beyond the range of the CSS-2 and CSS-5 can be covered by the ten-plus CSS-3s known to exist in the Chinese inventory. The CSS-3, which has an enormous range of 4750 km or more and is armed with a 1- to 3-Mt warhead, in effect ensures complete targeting coverage of the Indian subcontinent.[138] One news report, based almost entirely on a leaked

---

[138]Details about the capabilities and range of the Chinese strategic weapons of relevance to South Asia have been drawn from Gertz, "New Chinese Missiles Target All of East Asia"; Gertz, "China Targets Nukes at U.S."; Allen and Gorg, "Nuclear Weapons and Sino-Indian Relations"; Caldwell and Lennon, "China's Nuclear Modernization Program"; Gill and Mulvenon, "The Chinese Strategic Rocket Forces: Transition to Credible Deterrence," pp. 38–45; and *The Military Balance, 1997–98* (Oxford, UK: Oxford University Press/IISS, 1997), p. 176.

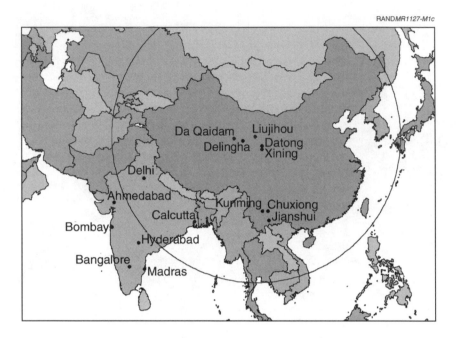

RANDMR1127-M1c

Map 1c—CSS-2 Coverage from Liujihou

American intelligence assessment of China's medium-range missile force, has described in quite astonishing detail how the CSS-2s and the CSS-5s have been deployed in targeting India. The report further reveals that, despite the fact that the CSS-2 is scheduled to be replaced by the CSS-5, small numbers of CSS-2s continue to be maintained in the interior of the country because of their range advantages vis-à-vis India. It is also asserted that these batteries are likely to remain in service until around 2002, when they will be replaced by the longer-range CSS-5 Mod 1s and Mod 2s, which would allow for the targeting of the Indian heartland despite their deployment in rearward Chinese bases.[139] The weight of the evidence thus appears to confirm the judgment offered by one Indian commentator that

---

[139]Gertz, "New Chinese Missiles Target All of East Asia."

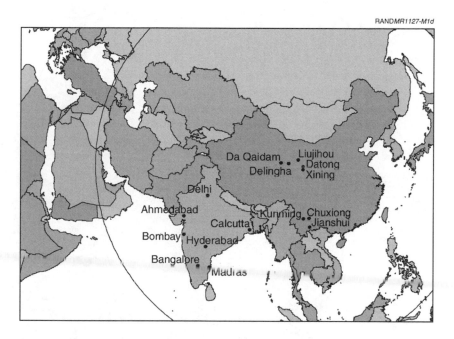

RANDMR1127-M1d

Map 1d—CSS-3 Coverage from Delingha

"China has currently a comprehensive nuclear weapon capability against India."[140]

Given the range, diversity, and lethality of these capabilities, it is not surprising to find many Indian strategic (especially military) analysts listing China as the principal security threat facing India both today and in the long term. Irrespective of whether one concurs with this judgment, the fact remains that China's current nuclear capabilities eclipse those of India. The relatively significant size of the Chinese land-based missile force is already sufficient to ensure coverage of critical Indian targets even after all the other competing target sets—relating to Russia, Japan, Taiwan, the continental United States, and American facilities in Asia—are accounted for. The diverse character of the missile force also ensures that China has an appropriate weapon for each target located within a given range

---

[140]Banerjee, "The New Strategic Environment," p. 276.

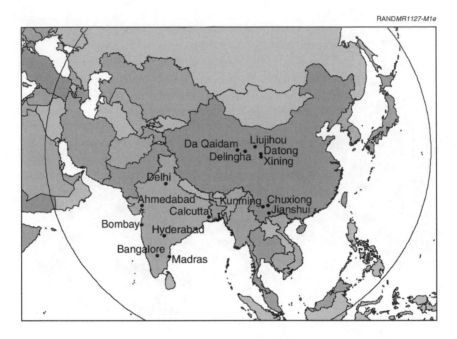

RAND*MR1127-M1e*

Map 1e—CSS-3 Coverage from Da Qaidam

circle, and the current deployment pattern of the CSS-2, -3 and -5 missiles fully ensures that the principal Indian targets can be readily interdicted if necessary. The high kiloton-to-megaton yields of the warheads deployed aboard these missiles additionally ensures that a wide range of damage requirements can readily be satisfied, and the fact that these warheads have been repeatedly tested bequeaths to them a reliability that the current Indian nuclear stockpile does not possess. At the highest end, the yields of several Chinese warheads are large enough to enable true "single bomb–single city" busting capabilities. Moreover, their carriage by tested ballistic missiles implies assured penetrativity: qualities that India's nuclear weaponry, with its relatively low-kiloton yields—which would presumably be delivered by relatively vulnerable, short-legged, air-breathing systems—simply cannot match in the near term. What rankles Indian analysts, therefore, is not the fact that a modest proportion of the

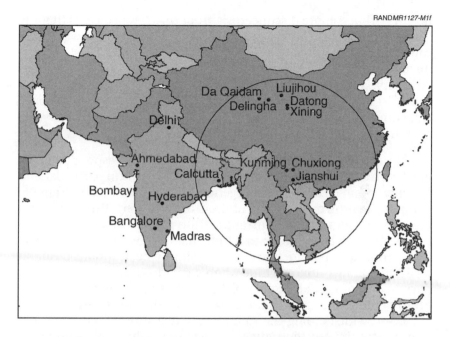

Map 1f—CSS-5 Coverage from Chuxiong

Chinese land-based missile force effectively targets India, but that New Delhi currently has no comparable deterrent whatsoever.[141]

All these realities add up in many Indian eyes to one simple conclusion: Where nuclear weapons are concerned, India is essentially defenseless, and consequently the "China threat" exists here and

_____

[141]In attempting to discredit this conclusion, Eric Arnett has argued that "India's Soviet-supplied Tupolev bombers are capable of flying anywhere in China with little fear of interception, but they are assigned instead to fly patrols over the Indian Ocean." See Arnett, "What Threat?" p. 54. This claim is misleading. The Tu-142s currently operated by India are dedicated long-range maritime reconnaissance/ antisubmarine warfare (MR/ASW) platforms that are neither designed nor optimized for attack operations deep inside enemy airspace. The avionics, sensors, and weapons carried by these aircraft are radically different from the Tu-95 strategic bomber variants currently in service with Russian strategic aviation. Given the kinds of Chinese early-warning systems and fighter aircraft that would be deployed in the western and southwestern portions of the country in an emergency involving India, it is unlikely that the Indian Tu-142s would survive for more than a few tens of minutes if they were ever employed in strategic strike missions against China.

now.[142] What is more disconcerting from this perspective is that the Chinese missile threat will only increase over time as newer, more sophisticated, land-based systems like the DF-31 and DF-41 are inducted into China's arsenal to bolster all the other connectivity, penetrativity, and survivability improvements that are already under way.[143] That these improvements are ongoing even though the principal nuclear threats to China have themselves abated in recent years gives Indian analysts some reason for pause.

Thus far, however, Indian policymakers have not responded to the ongoing modernization of Chinese nuclear systems in particular and its conventional capabilities in general by launching any dramatic countermodernization efforts of their own. In part, this is because the current Chinese modernization effort merely represents a continuation of the latent threat that India has lived with since 1964. The more important reason, however, has simply been India's desire to avoid alienating China at a time when it can do without increased security competition along its northern frontier. Indeed, the steady improvement that has characterized Sino-Indian relations since 1979—notwithstanding the momentary disruptions that occurred around the time of the Indian nuclear tests—has only reinforced New Delhi's proclivity to adopt a muted response to China's nuclear modernization. This improvement has led both sides to make deliberate efforts to avoid publicly alienating one another. For example, the resolution of local border disputes has been put off until some undefined future point, and both China and India have carefully adopted positions that limit their support for domestic challengers in each other's territory, whether in Xinjiang, Tibet, or Kashmir.[144]

Such a pattern of engagement suits both sides perfectly at this point, since each party currently seeks in its own way to create the

---

[142]See, by way of example, Ranjit Kumar, *China's Military Designs*, FBIS-NES-98-131, May 11, 1998.

[143]These upgrades are described in James Mulvenon, "Chinese Nuclear and Conventional Weapons," in Elizabeth Economy and Michel Oksenberg (eds.), *China Joins the World* (New York: Council on Foreign Relations Press, 1999), pp. 326–338, and in Gill and Mulvenon, "The Chinese Strategic Rocket Forces: Transition to Credible Deterrence," pp. 11–57.

[144]This dynamic has been well described in Surjit Mansingh, "India-China Relations in the Post–Cold War Era," *Asian Survey*, 34: 3 (March 1994), pp. 285–300.

requisite breathing room that will allow its program of national economic renewal to be brought to completion without any enervating military distractions. Both China and India stand to benefit from ensuring at least transient local tranquillity, since in doing so China has one less landward sector to worry about as it shifts its strategic focus to more pressing maritime challenges relating to Taiwan and the South China Sea, while India enjoys the liberty of actually redeploying forces from border defense operations in the northeast to counterinsurgency duties elsewhere in India, including Kashmir.[145] Consequently, India's security managers—despite their disquiet about China's growing military capabilities, Beijing's covert assistance to Pakistan, and China's increased presence along India's periphery—have continued to maintain a muted political response that, in the eyes of many local commentators, appears to border on strategic paralysis. The highly publicized statement by India's outspoken Defence Minister, George Fernandes, that "China is potential threat No. 1"[146] represents the exception to this rule—an exception not because the sentiments it expressed are uncommon among Indian political leaders but because such sentiments were articulated publicly and in such a direct fashion.

Not surprisingly, subsequent statements by the Indian leadership, including Prime Minister Vajpayee himself, appear to have shifted in tone to something approaching the previous norm: steady composure in New Delhi's public statements about China coupled with lingering suspicion of Beijing in private. This equanimity at the public level has only been reinforced as China's initial furor over India's resumption of nuclear testing has slowly died down.[147] Beijing's refusal to support Islamabad's rather blatant attempt at changing the status quo in Kargil further underscored the value of returning to the more nuanced policy India had sought to pursue vis-à-vis China since 1988. Indeed, India's subtlety toward Beijing has now reached

---

[145]As one Indian Army officer argued, "We simply cannot afford to antagonize the Chinese at this point. . . . We are fully stretched in combating insurgency in the country, and if we have to deal with renewed tension on the Line of Actual Control (LAC), the army could well break down." Quoted in Joshi, "George in the China Shop," p. 15.

[146]Joshi, "George in the China Shop," p. 12.

[147]For more on these developments, see Mark W. Frazier, "China-India Relations Since Pokhran-II: Assessing Sources of Conflict and Cooperation," *AccessAsia Review*, 3:2 (July 2000), pp. 5–35.

the point where, even with respect to nuclear weaponry, New Delhi has artfully shifted its position from that articulated during the May 1998 tests. Instead of restating the argument that India's resumption of testing was motivated by the fear of China—an argument contained in Prime Minister Vajpayee's official letter to President Clinton—the revised Indian position now rather blandly asserts that "these tests were not intended to threaten any country but to address the security concerns of the Indian people and provide them with necessary assurance."[148]

This polite attitude toward China is not unique to India. Rather, it characterizes the public diplomacy of many of China's neighbors, who generally presume that naming enemies makes enemies. In India's case, this politeness is driven particularly by the perception that for all of China's power capabilities, including those in the nuclear realm, the window of vulnerability from New Delhi's perspective is less open today than it could be tomorrow. This concern about future vulnerability derives from the recognition that with every passing day, the relative balance of power between China and India appears to change even more dramatically in favor of the former, thanks to China's high levels of sustained economic growth. This, in turn, implies that when the contested border issues—which are postponed at the moment—are eventually revisited, such visitation will take place at a time when the relative balance of power has clearly and unambiguously shifted in favor of China.[149] The general trend toward asymmetry in Sino-Indian power, which many Indian elites fear represents the face of the future, becomes all the more disturbing in light of the fact that it could extend to the one arena where India has a clear advantage today: the balance of conventional capability along the contested Sino-Indian border. For this reason, growing Chinese capabilities not simply in the nuclear realm but more significantly in the conventional arena are being watched closely in India, at times with consternation. This is because the trends suggest a variety of significant changes in combat technology,

---

[148]Singh, *What Constitutes National Security in a Changing World Order?* p. 31.

[149]C. Raja Mohan, "India, China Power Equations Changing," *The Hindu*, December 2, 1996. As one insightful Indian analysis argued, "Indian policymakers do not see China as a threat [today], but the big question is what kind of China will emerge 10 or 20 years from now and what are its implications for India." See "SAPRA Backgrounder: The China Poser," *SAPRA India Monthly Bulletin*, April–May 1996, pp. 1–6.

operational doctrine, and logistical structure that could result in increased Chinese war-fighting capabilities in the Himalayan region during the 2010-plus time frame—changes that would cause India grave concern because they would undercut its present strategy for dealing with a superior nuclear-armed power like China.[150]

India's strategy for dealing with a nuclear China today consists simply of maintaining superior conventional capabilities along the contested border. These capabilities encompass several well-equipped and highly trained mountain divisions manning a series of carefully prepared positional defenses, all backed by superior tactical airpower.[151] Indian strategists believe that a robust forward defense of this sort provides the best means of defending their territorial interests in that it can prevent China from making any significant territorial gains and, to the degree that such a defense is successful in the context of a conflict, can place the onus for initiating nuclear use—either to prevent defeat or to break up entrenched Indian defenses by other means—squarely on Chinese shoulders. Given China's present nuclear capabilities, a nuclear-use decision could involve a variety of options ranging from the discrete use of tactical nuclear weapons at the low end all the way to strategic countervalue attacks at the high end.[152] While the latter would be improbable given the stakes involved in the border dispute, Indian security planners have concluded that only a nuclear deterrent of some kind would suffice to prevent both the possibility of Chinese blackmail and actual nuclear use. This is because whatever the incentives for the other nuclear powers to checkmate any blatant Chinese effort at coercion, India simply cannot "rel[y] on the actions of other states to resolve its nuclear dilemmas"[153] in perpetuity. Accordingly, the continued success of the current *conventional deterrence* strategy requires that India acquire a range of nuclear capabilities comparable to those of

---

[150]These issues are insightfully explored in Bhashyam Kasturi, "The Looming Chinese Threat," *The Pioneer*, August 19, 1995. See also William W. Bain, "Sino-Indian Military Modernization: The Potential for Destabilization," *Asian Affairs*, 21:3 (Fall 1994), pp. 131–147.

[151]A summary description of these capabilities can be found in K. Subrahmanyam, "India's Security: The North and North-East Dimension," *Conflict Studies*, 215 (London: Centre for Security and Conflict Studies, 1988), pp. 18–22.

[152]Subrahmanyam, "India: Keeping the Option Open," pp. 117–120.

[153]Mohan, "India, China Power Equations Changing."

China or at least pursue the "ambivalent deterrence [capability that] could develop in a few years when India has missiles of 2500-km range which are under development."[154]

The more capable China envisaged in the future is seen to make a robust Indian nuclear posture even more necessary. If increased Chinese capabilities imply a vigorous modernization of China's conventional forces such that India's current advantages along the border are significantly diminished, the necessity for a ready Indian nuclear reserve might be seen as the only means by which this unfavorable battlefield situation could be redressed. Alternatively, if Chinese nuclear modernization involves the deployment of tactical weapons along the Himalayan battlefronts—implying that Chinese nuclear options in the face of a robust Indian conventional defense would not now require those incredible countervalue threats that New Delhi could either discount or use to secure external support—India would be pressed to accelerate its shifting nuclear posture into something that more clearly resembles a capacity for proportionate response. This is because Chinese tactical nuclear capabilities would allow Beijing to issue battlefield nuclear-use threats that would force India—if it lacked comparable capabilities—to submit to the threat of such nuclear use, absorb the attacks irrespective of their cost without comparable retaliation, or respond by issuing the same kinds of countervalue threats (assuming it had the delivery capabilities) that today would be deemed incredible if issued by the Chinese. None of these three outcomes would appear to be particularly attractive to New Delhi.[155]

A shift toward a more capable and transparent Indian nuclear posture could also come about simply as a result of the same contingency referred to earlier, but discounted in this analysis: a Chinese countervalue capability that is used for purposes of nuclear coercion in a manner similar to, or different from, the present Pakistani exploitation of its limited nuclear capabilities. These countervalue

---

[154]Subrahmanyam, "India's Security: The North and North-East Dimension," p. 20.

[155]See the analysis in Subrahmanyam, "India: Keeping the Option Open," pp. 117–120, and in Shankar Bhaduri, "The One and a Half Front Scenario," *SAPRA India Monthly Bulletin* (April–May 1996), pp. 14–20.

capabilities—which exist today—matter less so long as China remains politically quiescent. In such circumstances, India could steadily move toward altering its nuclear capabilities at a relatively slow pace and without much fanfare—as it seems to be doing today. Should this situation change in the future, however, either because China chooses to resurrect its support for the insurgencies in the Indian northeast[156] or because India, succumbing to the pressures of the increasingly restive community of Tibetan exiles in India, begins to support Tibetan independence,[157] the pressures on New Delhi to develop a nuclear posture that embodies flexible response capabilities would only increase.

It can therefore be concluded that the steady transformation of India's nuclear posture in the direction of continued weaponization will be driven to a significant extent by the growing perception among Indian policymakers that while Pakistan represents a "clear and present danger" to Indian security today, China could readily evolve into a similar threat over the next two decades. At the moment, the rationale for the current shift in India's strategic posture is grounded primarily in a prudential reasoning that seeks to create a deterrent aimed at insulating India against either Pakistani or Chinese nuclear coercion. However, the pressures on India to create a large and diversified deterrent may well prove overwhelming if the future behavior of both Pakistan and China is transformed in the direction of active militancy with respect to their territorial claims; if New Delhi perceives even greater Sino-Pakistani collusion than is the case at present; if Sino-U.S. relations are perceived as developing rapidly at India's expense; if Sino-Indian interests begin to manifestly clash in the Asian region at large; or if China's strategic modernization results in significant changes in the relative balance of conventional capability, the deployment of tactical nuclear weapons in the Himalayan borderlands, or the conspicuous expansion of China's present strategic nuclear capabilities.

---

[156]The history of Chinese support for Indian insurgencies is explored in Subrahmanyam, "India's Security: The North and North-East Dimension," pp. 11–18.

[157]For a good analysis of the angst experienced by Tibetan exiles in India, see Sudeep Chakravarti, "Restless Rage," *India Today International*, May 18, 1998, pp. 18–21.

Relations with Key Countries

While developments in the regional security arena relating principally to China and Pakistan would be the most important factors underlying any further alterations in India's nuclear posture, this movement would by no means depend on the local environment alone. Rather, the burdens imposed by the regional situation would be assessed in the context of a larger set of considerations, the most important being the state of India's relations with key actors in the international arena. The two critical actors here will be the United States and Russia, although other Asian centers of power, such as Japan and the various Southeast Asian states, will also factor into India's calculations. In all instances, New Delhi will accommodate the preferences of these key countries only to the degree that each is seen as being sensitive both to India's security concerns and to its desire for great-power status while also offering opportunities for a relationship based on friendship and sympathy toward Indian aims.

It is important to recognize, however, what can and cannot be expected to result from the maintenance of good relations with these countries. India's preference for a "credible minimum deterrent" of some sort is simply nonnegotiable. In fact, if India's 1998 nuclear tests reveal anything at all, it is that New Delhi did not consider the generally good relations it enjoyed with most major countries to be a good enough substitute for ensuring India's strategic autonomy. Even previous non-BJP governments in New Delhi, while avoiding testing, were adamant about retaining India's nuclear capabilities.[158] Consequently, India is unlikely to entertain any suggestions that lead to the divestiture of its nuclear weapon program, and it is also unlikely to be persuaded to permanently forgo any technical options that impinge on its ability to maintain a limited deterrent. That having been said, however, the direction India takes in pursuing weaponization, the pace at which this process is undertaken, and the kinds of force postures India develops can all be influenced by the relationships New Delhi enjoys with these key states. It is thus possible, for example, that improved relations with the United States

---

[158]This was true even of unquestionably moderate regimes like the United Front. See the remarks of the former Prime Minister, I. K. Gujral, in *India: Gujral Says Indians Cannot Give Up Nuclear Option*, FBIS-TAC-97-002, December 2, 1996.

could lead India to sign the CTBT at some point so long as conforming to this regime is not perceived as undercutting India's ability to sustain its deterrent capability. There is clearly a floor below which no policy options can be conditioned or negotiated away, and this floor is defined by whatever it takes to maintain a "minimum credible deterrent" of one sort or another. Above this floor, however, lies significant room for maneuver, and New Delhi might be willing to accommodate external preferences if such preferences are viewed as providing sufficient compensating benefits.

In many ways, developing a nuclear arsenal remains a *constrained* preference for India—which is to say that if New Delhi could avoid acquiring this capability in any maximal form, it would probably do so. In part, this is because of India's long-standing obsession with universal disarmament. Yet concerns about the requirements of a comprehensive nuclear arsenal also derive from more pressing considerations. Indian policymakers harbor no illusions about what the financial costs of such a strategic choice would be, notwithstanding the soothing estimates of numerous local nuclear weapon devotees. At a time when India is preparing to consolidate its long-awaited and much-postponed economic "takeoff," Indian security managers in general would prefer to minimize defense expenditures—including spending on a nuclear arsenal—to the maximum extent possible, since many development objectives affecting large portions of the populace have yet to be attained.[159]

At the same time, India's preference for these dual objectives— creating a minimum deterrent while minimizing defense expenditures—has been placed under increasing stress as a result of pressures emerging both from dissidents within the country (sometimes within the government itself) and from unfavorable external circumstances. The serious neglect of India's conventional forces since the early 1990s, the high levels of war wastage that resulted from the limited war with Pakistan in Kargil in 1999, and the continuing toll imposed by relentless counterinsurgency operations in various parts of the country—particularly in Kashmir—have already resulted in a sharp spike in defense expenditures in FY 2000. Whether such in-

---

[159]Singh, *What Constitutes National Security in a Changing World Order?* pp. 12– 15.

creases will be sustained in the years to come is difficult to predict, as India's traditional defense expenditure patterns are almost as cyclic as those of the United States—but Indian policymakers are acutely conscious of the financial burdens that investments in nuclear weaponry will impose on the competing obligations of conventional modernization and economic development. At a time of increasing criticism both from "hawks" outside the government and from within the government itself over poor performance in various contingencies (e.g., the intelligence failure at Kargil and the poor crisis response during the hijacking of an Indian Airlines jet at Kandhahar in December 1999), these policymakers have responded by increasing budgetary allocations on what they deem is unavoidable—maintaining superior conventional capabilities—while remaining cautious with regard to their spending on emerging strategic capabilities.[160] Critical to this strategy of minimizing resource expenditures on strategic programs until truly necessary is a pervasive ambiguity about India's nuclear development and acquisition efforts, its current and future force levels, and its organizational structures. Indian policymakers believe that the less that is said about these issues publicly, the better, as this quiescent posture allows them to maintain some semblance of moderation that may immunize them against pressures from the hawks at home while simultaneously serving to defuse external anxieties that might arise were they compelled to expand either the size or the pace of their strategic weapon programs.

Consequently, India's first preference would be to retain a minimal nuclear capability that is still ambiguous in many of its details while relying as much as it could on the possibility of "strategic coordination" with other important states—thereby avoiding those additional expenditures that it would incur if it had to develop a fully transparent and diversified nuclear arsenal that is both invulnerable

---

[160]The bulk of the sharp defense increases in the FY 2000 budget, for example, was allocated to conventional modernization, fuel, spares, and paramilitary forces rather than to strategic projects, leading one commentator to note that "limited funding for Research and Development . . . has raised eyebrows here as the Defence Research and Development Organization (DRDO) is spearheading the missile and nuclear submarine programme, the key to India's acquisition of a credible minimum nuclear deterrent." See Atul Aneja, "Army Gets Lion's Share of Funds," *The Hindu*, March 1, 2000. See also "More Allocation for Para-Military Forces," *The Hindu*, March 1, 2000.

and maintained at high levels of operational readiness. To the degree that India could secure additional margins of safety through close relations with important states in the international system—relations that would yield increased political cover, preferential access to high technology and advanced conventional weaponry, and greater recognition of its status—New Delhi might be willing to trade in its pursuit of *marginal* nuclear capabilities. Such a trade, far from being automatic, would involve extensive negotiations, but it would nonetheless be feasible provided that the right combination of blandishments and incentives could be fashioned by the major states of importance to India.[161]

Clearly, this possibility of a trade arises only because preserving the existing nuclear order is not a "zero-sum" affair when viewed in game theoretic terms.[162] Neither the existing great powers nor India (nor, for that matter, Pakistan) has an interest in any "corner solutions" that involve the complete "defeat" of the other. To the contrary, the great powers, who possess the largest stakes in preserving the existing nuclear order, simply lack the inclination (and perhaps the wherewithal) to bring India to heel by rolling back its nuclear program, especially after the events of May 1998. India, in turn, can comprehensively threaten the global nonproliferation order through its actions but lacks the incentive to do so if its own security concerns can be accommodated. These divergent but not fundamentally opposed interests create a "solution space" that could enable India to maintain a certain nuclear posture without wrecking the global nuclear regime as well as to receive various political, economic, and technological considerations from the great powers in return. This kind of solution is exactly what the present BJP-dominated National Democratic Alliance (NDA) government in New Delhi has been seeking in the aftermath of its nuclear tests. Previous Indian governments sought similar considerations as well, but being more risk-averse, they had hoped that these considerations would be forthcoming

---

[161] For an effort at conceptualizing the nature of feasible bargains, see Clifford E. Singer, Jyotika Saksena, and Milind Thakar, "Feasible Deals with India and Pakistan After the Nuclear Tests," *Asian Survey*, 38: 12 (December 1998), pp. 1161–1178.

[162] An interesting attempt at applying game theory to South Asian proliferation dilemmas can be found in Jocelyn M. Boryczka, M. K. Mohanan, and Jeffrey D. Weigand, "Cultural and Strategic Factors in South Asian Nuclear Arms Control," *Journal of Political and Military Sociology*, 25 (1997), pp. 279–303.

simply as a reward for India's traditional restraint in the realm of nuclear testing. The new NDA government, being more risk-acceptant in the face of India's perceived failure to secure these considerations, appears willing to actively bargain for them using the threat of further weaponization to achieve its larger objectives.

United States. This dynamic will be most clearly evident in India's relations with the United States because New Delhi perceives the latter as possessing most of the resources India desires, even if it is unwilling to freely part with them. "Bargaining" with the United States is therefore seen to be necessary, since "engaging" it has simply not yielded the kinds of returns that New Delhi expected early on.[163] In the waning years of the Cold War, India responded eagerly to American overtures to cement a new relationship between the two countries.[164] This enthusiasm was initially driven by India's desire to moderate its dependence on the Soviet Union but was later colored by the reality of the Soviet collapse. In any case, it was hoped that a deepening association with the United States across multiple dimensions—growing economic interaction, enhanced political understanding, increasing intelligence exchanges, and greater military-to-military ties—would provide India with a high level of strategic reassurance that would minimize the need for "go it alone" strategies, including the necessity for dramatic changes in India's nuclear posture. Clearly, if American perceptions of China as a potential threat moved in the direction of greater congruity with that of India, the need for a significant shift in Indian nuclear strategy might have become less urgent, among other things, because New Delhi could have benefited from the positive externalities generated by any efforts the United States might have made to penalize China for hostile actions—just as China benefited from U.S. containment of the Soviet Union during the Cold War.[165]

---

[163]Ramesh Thakur, "India and the United States: A Triumph of Hope over Experience?" *Asian Survey*, 36:6 (June 1996), p. 574.

[164]This interaction is summarized in Shekhar Gupta, *India Redefines Its Role*, Adelphi Paper No. 293 (London: IISS, 1995), pp. 58–60.

[165]This opportunity presented itself in concrete fashion when U.S. intelligence agencies reported China's sale of M-11s to Pakistan. By refusing to penalize China for this act in accordance with the requirements of its own law, the United States unwittingly communicated an insensitivity about Indian security concerns that contributed in part to the "go it alone" strategies represented by the nuclear tests in May 1998.

India's economic reforms, begun in 1991, were also seen to provide a significant opportunity for enhancing U.S.-Indian relations. Indian calculations, in fact, centered on this phenomenon, as it was hoped that expanded American trade and investments would amplify the U.S. stake in Indian security and stability. In this context, India's elites actually viewed increased economic intercourse as an opportunity to strike some strategic bargains: to convince the United States to relax its restrictive policies on transferring sophisticated technologies that might have civilian, dual-use, or straightforward military applications; to make the United States comfortable with the idea of assisting the Indian military in reforming its force structure and supporting capabilities as well as helping it develop proficiency in certain critical war-fighting competencies; and, finally, to persuade the United States to view a strong, capable, and independent India with an autonomous managerial role in South Asia as something that is not simply inevitable but actually desirable within the framework of American global interests.[166]

Although the U.S.-Indian relationship certainly moved in this general direction following the end of the Cold War, the pace of change was not swift enough from New Delhi's perspective. In part, this was because both India and the United States, despite engaging one another, sought to service divergent interests from inherently different levels of strength. The United States, appropriately enough, viewed its evolving relationship with India from the perspective of a global power; it sought to acquaint itself with India as a regionally influential state that might some day become more powerful and, to the degree possible, sought to incorporate India into its vision of furthering regional stability in Asia. Toward that end, it gradually distanced itself from the overly militarized relationship it had previously cultivated with Pakistan but simultaneously pressed India to adhere to the international nonproliferation regimes managed by the United States. Moreover, while on balance relations with India did improve, Washington did not feel any compulsion to accelerate this change beyond the levels that the traffic could bear, largely because India was perceived to be less important today than it could be in the

---

[166]This logic has been explored further in Ashley J. Tellis, "South Asia," in Zalmay Khalilzad (ed.), *Strategic Appraisal 1996*, MR-543-AF (Santa Monica: RAND, 1996), pp. 283–307.

future. As a consequence, the United States' efforts to improve relations with New Delhi inevitably took the form of an *evolutionary* process that was to be cemented piecemeal over an extended period of time. This incremental approach was viewed in Washington as a means of offering the United States time to gradually adjust its own policies to accommodate India's regional primacy—policies that had implications for U.S. relations with both Pakistan and China as well as for its ability to accommodate India's claims to great-power status—as well as to clarify what the overarching strategic necessity for improved U.S.-Indian relations actually was. In the meantime, modest arms sales and technology transfers, occasional military exercises, and a limited "strategic dialogue" would come to represent the official component of improved U.S.-Indian relations.

While these relations rapidly became "privatized"[167] in that growing society-to-society interactions conducted in the arenas of trade and investment gradually became the dominant component of U.S.-Indian familiarity, New Delhi was disappointed to discover that increased private economic relations with the United States did not automatically translate into political benefits in the issue areas that mattered most to India. The fact that the American state was highly autonomous in the national security arena, for example, implied that the U.S. government would not comply with New Delhi's implicit (and sometimes explicit) demands for anti-Pakistani and anti-Chinese policies merely by virtue of its growing commercial contact with India. The same held true for India's increasingly vocal demands for great-power status, especially as manifested in its desire for a permanent seat on the U.N. Security Council: All these demands could be serviced, but only if they were congruent with America's own interests over time. Since such a congruence did not exist, however, it is not surprising that on many strategic issues of importance to New Delhi—such as China's transfers of nuclear and missile technologies to Pakistan—Washington simply did not respond in the manner that India had hoped it would. In short, given the "getting to know you" premise underlying America's original overtures to India, Washington did not feel compelled to open its floodgates of high technology; recognize New Delhi's managerial status in South Asia

---

[167]This term has been used by Richard Haass and appears in Sidhu, *Enhancing Indo-U.S. Strategic Cooperation*, p. 70.

before its time; or harshly penalize India's competitors for their infractions of U.S. nonproliferation policies when imposing such penalties may not have been in Washington's larger interests. This reticence was only reinforced by what was perceived to be India's own obduracy in the nuclear and missile realms. Taken together, then, Washington's policies vis-à-vis New Delhi undercut the latter's desire to quickly acquire advanced technological and military capabilities and, far from exemplifying the rapid and revolutionary transformation in bilateral relations that India had sought as means of acquiring great-power status, yielded a cautious approach in which the United States sought to preserve good relations both with India and with its neighbors simultaneously.

Although such an approach made sense from America's point of view given that its relations with many of India's neighbors, especially China, were of greater importance than that with India, New Delhi read this policy as implying a lack of sensitivity to India's concerns.[168] In essence, Indian policymakers took it to mean that they were essentially on their own. Thus, while several Indian governments toyed with the idea of altering India's nuclear posture only to be stymied by their fear of U.S. pressure, the first risk-acceptant party to attain power in Delhi changed that posture decisively through the nuclear tests conducted in May 1998.[169] India's nuclear decisions henceforth can be moderated, at least with respect to their pace and direction, but such alterations will have to be negotiated and will involve the use of those positive incentives which the United States may have been unwilling to consider thus far. The principal instruments in the American tool kit continue to be its advanced technology and its ability to bestow political recognition in a way that yields strategic benefits. Whether the United States is willing to trade some of these assets for certain desired changes in India's future nuclear posture remains to be seen, but this is clearly one

---

[168]As noted earlier, this issue really became significant in the context of Washington's unwillingness to chastise China for transferring M-11 missiles to Pakistan. See the trenchant Indian comments on this question in K. Subrahmanyam, "Missile Proliferation: U.S. Must Heed India's Concerns," *The Times of India,* July 13, 1995, and Jasjit Singh, "Pakistan's Missiles: U.S. Turning a Nelson's Eye," *The Times of India,* July 19, 1995.

[169]The history of Indian dalliances with nuclear testing during the early to mid-1990s is detailed in Perkovich, *India's Nuclear Bomb,* pp. 318–377.

variable that will condition New Delhi's future strategic choices. To be sure, Indian elites, being aware of all these possibilities and mindful of the strategic uncertainties of the future, will continue to seek improved relations with the United States because deepened ties promise benefits whether India chooses to further develop its nuclear arsenal or not—so long as neither U.S.-Indian relations nor critical Indian strategic capabilities are sacrificed in the interim.

Russia. Maintaining a secure relationship with Russia is motivated by similar calculations. Because Russia is a pale shadow of its former incarnation, the Soviet Union, India's links with Russia do not and cannot have the same political content as its old Indo-Soviet tie.[170] Yet Indian analysts are acutely aware that for simple geopolitical reasons, "Russia, in the long run, will remain a natural strategic partner of India."[171] This judgment is driven by the perception that countries like Russia and Japan share certain common interests with India vis-à-vis China and that while both relate differently to Beijing today—Russia as a major arms supplier and Japan as a major foreign investor—neither can afford to be indifferent to the growth of Chinese power over time. For this reason, India's cultivation of close relations with both states is deemed to be critical, and the Russian connection is viewed to be particularly important even though it is acknowledged that Moscow will remain closely linked with the West and that Indo-Russian economic relations will be driven entirely by the laws and logic of the market.[172]

It is this latter reality, however, that makes Russia so interesting in the near term. For while Moscow has become increasingly sensitive to the problem of nuclear proliferation, its own precarious economic condition and its willingness to treat India as different from other proliferators (for both geopolitical and historical reasons) have given New Delhi critical opportunities to acquire Russian technology in support of its future nuclear posture. Unlike other bilateral relationships, Delhi's Russian connection can thus be seen as vital in that it

---

[170]Igor Khripunov and Anupam Srivastava, "Russian-Indian Relations: Alliance, Partnership, Or?" *Comparative Strategy*, 18:2 (April–June 1999), pp. 153–171.

[171]Brahma Chellaney, "Shoring Up Indo-Russian Ties," *The Pioneer*, July 16, 1997.

[172]Vidya Nadkarni, "India and Russia: The End of a Special Relationship?" *Naval War College Review*, 48:4 (Autumn 1995), pp. 19–33.

directly advances the development of India's strategic capabilities and, by implication, determines the kind of nuclear force architecture that India could develop over time. Russian technology here is not used in the production of nuclear weapons per se, although changes could occur in this realm as well over time. Rather, Moscow's technology is currently used largely to develop the delivery systems that could carry either conventional or nuclear payloads as the situation requires. In this context, Russian assistance has been publicly identified as supporting the development of the Indian nuclear submarine program, its indigenous sea-based cruise missile, and perhaps both its land- and sea-based ballistic missile programs.[173] In each of these programs, Russian technology transfers have not taken the form of direct sales but have instead occurred through the provision of technical assistance in support of India's own indigenous development efforts. This kind of technology transfer is more difficult to detect, since knowledge transfers conducted through personnel exchanges, linkages between specific research institutions, and mutual review and assessment of ongoing R&D work are inherently less visible than direct arms transfers but ultimately more consequential in the long run.[174]

India's relationship with Russia also allows for direct sales, but these would most likely occur in the realm of conventional weaponry, where international technology-control regimes may not apply.[175] Some of these sales, however, will directly affect India's future strategic posture, as would be the case if current discussions between New Delhi and Moscow for Russian ATBM systems like the S-300V-Antey 2500 as well as other components for developing an Indian IAD network bear fruit. A future Indian decision to purchase a long-range theater bomber like the TU-22M3 or the Su-34, which is based on the successful Su-27 design, would have a similar effect.

---

[173]Steven Lee Myers, "Russia Helping India Extend Range of Missiles, Aides Say," *New York Times*, April 27, 1998.

[174]Precisely because of this fact, the ongoing U.S.-Indian dialogue about institutionalizing a restraint regime in South Asia has included discussions about "virtual technology transfers" occurring through scientific exchanges, professional meetings, and the like.

[175]Gary K. Bertsch and Anupam Srivastava, "Weapons Proliferation and Export Controls in the Former Soviet Union: Implications for Strategic Stability in Asia," *AccessAsia Review*, 3:1 (December 1999), pp. 5–69.

Since Russia's penury coincides with its military sophistication thanks to its inheritance of the former Soviet Union's industrial base, it is likely that numerous weapon technologies will continue to be available to India, at least in the near term. In many cases in which direct sales are not at issue, these technologies will be transferred in the form of subsystems and specific assemblies, or they may take the form of knowledge transfers between private and governmental institutions in Russia and private firms or governmental research agencies in India.

In fact, some Indian analysts have berated their government for not exploiting Russia's military technology resources more systematically, noting that while "China was quick to tap the new cash-and-carry opportunities . . . India's ability to exploit the remaining though limited opportunities remains seriously constrained due to its proverbial red tape, preference for government-to-government contracts, and a defense budget with a paltry provision for capital expenditure."[176] Whatever the merits of this criticism, it is clear that India's interests will in the near term consist principally of securing continued access to Russian high-technology weaponry, which is relatively inexpensive in comparison to that of other suppliers and with which the Indian armed forces are already familiar.[177] A loss of access either for economic reasons (because the Indian economy sputters or the costs of Russian equipment simply become prohibitive) or for political reasons (Russia loses interest in supplying advanced weapons to India because of constraints imposed by potentially bigger customers such as China) would have devastating effects. It would result in the steady enervation of India's conventional military capabilities, which in turn would make the imperative

---

[176]Chellaney, "Shoring Up Indo-Russian Ties."

[177]It is worth noting that India's interest in Russian strategic technology is accompanied by a growing interest in French and Israeli technology. The parallelism in these cases is fascinating: All three states are seen as repositories of critical strategic technologies of interest to India; all three states are seen to be sufficiently independent of U.S. political pressures as far as transferring many technologies to India is concerned; and all three states are perceived to be driven more by commercial considerations than by ideological interests, and even these, to the degree that they exist, are viewed as aligned with rather than opposed to Indian perceptions. Consequently, it is not unreasonable to expect that India's strategic ties with each of these countries will grow both in connection with its strategic programs and otherwise.

of developing a larger but more transparent nuclear arsenal even more pressing.[178]

Beyond such immediate concerns, India remains reluctant to jettison the political dimensions of ties with Russia mainly for long-term security reasons. In fact, the potential rise of China itself is seen as an issue that would effectively engage Russian security interests, and to the degree that Russian nuclear capabilities vis-à-vis China remain sufficiently robust, close Indo-Russian relations are seen as having the potential to provide New Delhi with certain positive externalities that would prove most useful in restraining China from pursuing objectives that may be inimical to India. This does not imply, however, that India would seek extended deterrence guarantees either from Russia or, for that matter, from the United States. A strong and prosperous India would in all probability seek to maintain its political autonomy in much the same way that it did throughout the Cold War. The success of India's economic transformation, then, has become more crucial than ever because it will determine the degree of political autonomy that India can maintain in the face of other competing centers of power in the international system. A strong and capable India would have both a lesser need for extended nuclear guarantees from others and a diminished incentive to develop an extensive nuclear arsenal intended for war-fighting purposes as a substitute for weakened conventional forces. By contrast, an infirm India not only would have a greater need for extended security guarantees but would also experience strong pressure to develop such an arsenal in order to prevent a total loss of political autonomy in the face of growing conventional weaknesses.

Maritime Asia. It is in the context of developing comprehensive Indian strength that New Delhi's relations with the countries of mar-

---

[178]Despite all the sentiments expressed in India after the collapse of the Soviet Union, India today is no more autonomous with respect to critical high-value conventional weapon systems than it was during the Soviet era. In fact, this dependency might even increase if the ten-year defense deal concluded with Russia yields all the equipment desired by the Indian military. See Rahul Bedi, "India to Sign New 10-Year Defence Deal with Russia," *Jane's Defence Weekly*, July 1, 1998, p. 16, and Sadanand Dhume, "Arming India," *Far Eastern Economic Review*, October 12, 2000, p. 20.

itime Asia become particularly important.[179] The most significant of these countries is Japan, which is already the most important economic power in Asia and is currently India's largest aid donor. Inasmuch as Japan is viewed as having the potential to become a nuclear weapon power like India and remains China's most conspicuous regional adversary, the Indo-Japanese relationship could become a significant variable affecting India's strategic direction in the long term. For this reason, New Delhi has sought to maintain correct relations with Tokyo. Despite the latter's displeasure with India's 1998 nuclear tests, for example, New Delhi—treating this reaction, among other things, as a product of U.S. pressures—has attempted to encourage Japan to continue its private investments in India while struggling for a way to make the latent convergence of interests in the political realm more manifest in bilateral terms.[180] In the immediate future, India simply seeks more commercial interaction in order that Japanese innovation and investment may contribute to growing Indian economic prowess. Japan's willingness to steeply increase its investments in a reforming India is seen as inexorably motivating greater Indo-Japanese strategic interaction, where concerns over China's growing conventional and nuclear capabilities, the problems of freedom of navigation in the Indian Ocean, and the dependence of both countries on the Persian Gulf for energy supplies could, taken together, result in a greater appreciation of India's nuclear capabilities as serving a common interest. A similar set of considerations drives India's efforts to improve ties with other East Asian states, including Indonesia, Singapore, Malaysia, and the Philippines. Clearly, then, India's recent "look East" initiatives have both economic and political components.

Even when considered as a whole, however, it is clear that India's elites do not view their country's international relationships with key countries like the United States, Russia, and the states of maritime Asia as a *substitute* for the political autonomy that is ultimately

---

[179]V. Jayanth, "India's 'Look East' Policy," *The Hindu*, April 2, 1998. For a systematic analysis of this policy shift, see Sandy Gordon, *India's Rise to Power* (New York: St. Martin's Press, 1995), pp. 290–317.

[180]C. Raja Mohan, "Managing Indo-Japanese Nuclear Divergence," *The Hindu*, March 6, 1999.

undergirded by the possession of adequate military capabilities.[181] They readily admit, however, that a wide range of models encoding different levels of nuclear readiness are compatible with the need to maintain adequate military capabilities. The necessity for any one particular nuclear architecture will therefore be determined first by the nature of the specific threats facing the country and second by the available alternatives to that architecture. These alternatives will have to include some consideration of the relationships India enjoys with key states in the international system. These relationships will not *a priori* offer a perfect substitute for credible nuclear capabilities, but they will certainly influence the character of the capabilities required and the urgency with which these capabilities are procured. After due consideration of the costs and benefits associated with the various alternative nuclear postures, they may also determine *a posteriori* the necessity for procuring something that resembles an overt, transparent, and full-fledged nuclear arsenal.[182]

Domestic Politics and National Economic Performance

The fourth and final variable that will influence India's decision to pursue further changes in its nuclear posture centers on the pressures emanating from domestic politics in the context of the country's overall economic performance. In contrast to the other three factors examined earlier—all of which relate in some way to the international environment and as such, constitute the external drivers influencing Indian policymakers' decisions—the network of bureaucratic organizations involved in producing India's nuclear capabilities, the major political parties and key elements of the civil services, popular preferences at large, and national economic performance together constitute the internal drivers that will determine India's future nuclear posture. Each of these constituent elements merits brief examination.

Strategic Enclaves. Although India's nuclear capabilities are still primitive by the standards of the nuclear weapon states, these capabilities have been created by a fairly large and powerful bureau-

---

[181]Mohan, "Nuclear Balance in Asia."

[182]For an Indian perspective that speaks to some of these issues, see C. Raja Mohan, "India and the Nuclear Oligarchy," *The Hindu*, June 6, 1998.

cratic structure centering on three principal complexes. These complexes—the atomic energy establishment, the defense research and development organizations, and the space research program—have been termed "strategic enclaves"[183] because they focus on producing the most advanced technological devices necessary for national security in an environment that is "institutionally, spatially, and legally . . . distinct and different from the existing structure of the Indian military-security complex."[184] These enclaves are distinguished from the rest of the military-security complex by their concentration on developing "high-leverage" technological systems; their relatively flexible internal organizational structures; the high degree of cross-connectivity they enjoy across institutions; their ability to garner privileged political and budgetary support from India's state managers; and their minimal accountability to the body politic at large.[185] Since these enclaves had their origins in Jawaharlal Nehru's dream of science providing the sinews of the modern state, they have slowly come to dominate both India's attempts at economic modernization and its efforts to achieve autonomous security.[186] Thanks to the importance accorded to the latter objective, these complexes have also become important centers of power in their own right; indeed, their monopoly over technical knowledge pertaining to India's strategic capabilities, the lack of comparable expertise on the part of their civilian masters, and the extraordinarily small set of political managers tasked with regulating their activities all combine to make India's strategic enclaves a force to reckon with.[187] Not surprisingly, they have acquired interests distinct and apart from other critical institutions of state, including the armed forces—which, at least historically, have been cast in the role of hapless consumers unable to control in any significant way the development of those systems

---

[183]Itty Abraham, "India's 'Strategic Enclave': Civilian Scientists and Military Technologies," *Armed Forces & Society*, 18:2 (Winter 1992), pp. 231–252.

[184]Ibid., p. 233.

[185]Ibid.

[186]Itty Abraham, "Science and Power in the Postcolonial State," *Alternatives*, 21(1996), pp. 321–339.

[187]T. V. Satyamurthy, "India's Post-Colonial Nuclear Estate," *Radical Science*, 14 (1984), pp. 106–116.

that they will be ultimately responsible for using.[188] Any assessment of India's future nuclear posture must therefore take into account the interests and contributions of its three strategic enclaves.

Atomic Energy Establishment. The first complex—the atomic energy establishment—consists of a vast array of nuclear facilities that includes power and research reactors; uranium mining, processing, and enrichment facilities; plutonium-reprocessing plants; and heavy water production facilities.[189] While these physical capabilities bear on the ability to produce nuclear weapons, the key elements affecting India's future nuclear posture reside mainly at or around the Bhabha Atomic Research Center (BARC) in Bombay. India's nuclear design teams are reportedly located at this facility, and according to published reports, the "physics package" for the weapons used in the 1998 nuclear tests was fabricated here as well.[190] The contributions of this complex to the future Indian nuclear posture will in all probability be silent but significant. They will be silent because the process of producing weapon cores is essentially a covert endeavor, and barring any information released by India itself or acquired by others through clandestine means, the exact nature of India's nuclear devices will continue to remain free from scrutiny. These silent artifacts are nonetheless significant, however, because their type, quality, reliability, number, size, and yield ultimately form the basis of India's nuclear deterrent.

Given this fact, the nuclear weapon enclave is likely to push for three distinct policies that will have a significant impact on India's future posture. First, it will press for continued research and development on weapon designs. This effort will focus on developing a small number of distinctly different types of nuclear weapons, each of a different class of yields and capable of carriage by a variety of

---

[188]For an excellent analysis of the relations between the uniformed military and the strategic enclaves, see Arnett, "Military Technology: The Case of India," pp. 343–365. See also Eric Arnett, "And the Loser Is . . . the Indian Armed Forces," *Economic and Political Weekly*, September 5–12, 1998.

[189]A useful though jaundiced survey of India's atomic energy establishment can be found in Dhirendra Sharma, *India's Nuclear Estate* (New Delhi: Lancer's, 1983). See also Spector et al., *Tracking Nuclear Proliferation.*

[190]Raj Chengappa, "The Bomb Makers," *India Today International*, June 22, 1998, p. 31.

delivery systems. The former head of India's AEC, R. Chidambaram, has claimed that India currently possesses "three robust bomb designs"[191] that presumably remain the nucleus of its strategic deterrent. Irrespective of whether this claim is true, continued work on advanced nuclear designs—primarily boosted fission and thermonuclear weapons—will be high on the list of R&D priorities, since these devices were not tested at full yield (and perhaps were even tested unsuccessfully) during the May 1998 tests.[192]

Second, the enclave will press for a continuation of different kinds of nuclear tests. Since the "peaceful nuclear explosion" carried out in 1974, the nuclear design establishment has been at the forefront of internal debates arguing for a resumption of hot testing. While the May 1998 test series met those demands in some measure, it is unclear whether this establishment will be truly satisfied with a permanent moratorium on hot testing, particularly if India's advanced designs are actually to be certified (via a process analogous to the General Staff Quality Requirement [GSQR] currently used for conventional weapons) as fit for integration into the arsenal.[193] This problem can be mitigated to some extent if India acquires good simulation capabilities, but in the absence of full-up testing it is uncertain whether the weapon establishment could acquire full confidence in its more sophisticated designs.[194] Consequently, no matter what the inclinations of India's political leadership may be, it is likely that this community—and its supporters in the press—will

---

[191]Nirmala George, "No More N-Tests Needed: AEC," *Indian Express*, February 4, 1999.

[192]More on Indian views about desired nuclear capabilities and requirements can be found in George, "No More N-Tests Needed: AEC"; G. Balachandran, "A Consensus or a Sell-Off?" *The Hindu*, December 14, 1999; and M. R. Srinivasan, "CTBT: A Phony Consensus?" *The Hindu*, January 19, 2000.

[193]See the views of P. K. Iyengar, former Chairman of India's AEC, in Bharat Karnad, "Policy on CTBT," *Hindustan Times*, November 4, 1999; Iyengar has argued—in Karnad's words—that "because reliable performance of weapons is the key to nuclear deterrence, testing is essential for every new type or genus of weapon." See also P. K. Iyengar, "Nuclear Nuances," *The Times of India*, August 22, 2000. For the views of other Department of Atomic Energy (DAE) scientists endorsing the need for explosive tests in the future, see Srinivas Laxman, "India Should Retain Option to Carry Out More N-Tests," *The Times of India*, November 1, 2000.

[194]On this point, see Srinivasan, "CTBT: A Phony Consensus?"

advocate further hot tests of nuclear weaponry in addition to pursuing other types of subcritical and hydronuclear testing.[195]

Third, the enclave will press India to continue its refusal to comply with the U.S. request for a moratorium on the production of fissile material pending the conclusion of an FMCT.[196] Given that the

---

[195]Since late 1998, senior Indian scientists, including the Scientific Adviser to the Defence Minister, Dr. A.P.J. Kalam, have repeatedly stated that India could do without further hot tests. See "No Contradiction with Kalam's Views," *The Hindu*, September 24, 1998. Throughout 1999, the former Chairman of India's AEC, R. Chidambaram, also repeatedly affirmed that "as a result of these [May 1998] tests, we have now generated a very valuable scientific database on which we have a credible nuclear deterrent. . . . That is why we advised the Government that it could now declare a moratorium on further testing." See "Signing CTBT Will Not Weaken Country," *Indian Express*, May 10, 1999. See also Nirmala George, "India Now Within CTBT Rules: Chidambaram," *Indian Express*, April 22, 1999. Indian National Security Adviser Brajesh Mishra further claimed that India had acquired so much data as a result of its five nuclear tests in May 1998 that it actually aborted a planned sixth test, since it "did not need any more data to strengthen the nation's nuclear capability." See "India Aborted 6th N-Test: Mishra," *The Pioneer*, October 4, 1999. Irrespective of what one makes of Mishra's claim, Chidambaram's assertion is indeed interesting because the moratorium on testing announced on May 13, 1998 (the day on which India undertook its second round of tests), was offered far too quickly for India's nuclear scientists to have reached a considered determination that their tests did in fact satisfactorily bequeath the kind of "valuable scientific database" that would obviate the need for further testing. In all likelihood, therefore, the Indian nuclear research establishment would still jump at the chance to conduct further nuclear tests if it were offered that alternative, but mindful of the political pressures on the government of India from the United States and elsewhere, this establishment has perhaps found it convenient to endorse the government's desire to sign the CTBT so long as sufficient funding is made available to pursue other developmental alternatives to full-up hot testing. In the aftermath of the May 1998 tests, the budgetary allocations to the nuclear program have in fact risen considerably—perhaps in recognition of the fact that the decision to forgo further hot testing requires additional investments in theoretical research, computer simulation, cold testing, and subcritical experiments as well as a sop to the Indian nuclear establishment for its "expert" support of the government's political decision to continue with the current moratorium on hot testing.

[196]When publicly questioned about the sufficiency of India's fissile-material stockpile, the Indian atomic energy establishment has generally declined to provide any quantitative information, arguing instead that it is "a political question." See "What More Do You Want? We've Got All the Scientific Data We Needed," *Indian Express*, December 4, 1999. Separately, however, India's political leadership has intimated on several occasions that India will not enforce an immediate moratorium on the production of fissile materials "even if [the] legitimate nuclear powers and Pakistan agreed to the proposition." See "Fissile Material: India Against Moratorium Now," *The Hindu*, April 2, 1999.

extraction of weapons-grade plutonium from irradiated reactor fuel has proceeded much more slowly in India than outside observers usually recognize, the nuclear weapon enclave will argue strongly against any domestic inclination to terminate the production of fissile materials. While this stance is aimed primarily at developing the stockpile necessary to create the arsenal India may require in the future, it is also driven by the bureaucratic necessity of keeping several institutional components of the nuclear establishment in business. In any event, the enclave's strong preference for less-than-full accounting of past reprocessing and extraction efforts will remain the country's international position as the fissile-material cutoff negotiations get under way.

Defense Research and Development Organizations. The second complex, consisting of the defense research and development organizations, is in many ways similar to the nuclear enclave. Although it consists of some 50 separate defense laboratories and institutions engaged in developmental activities relating to aeronautics, electronics, weapon systems, naval technologies, engineering equipment, material sciences, life sciences, and systems analysis, training, and information, most of these institutions are oriented toward producing a wide range of conventional technologies required by India's armed forces.[197] A much smaller subset of institutions within this complex, however, is tasked with developing the specific safing, arming, fuzing, and firing (SAFF) systems necessary to make nuclear devices into usable weapons. This subset shares responsibility with the nuclear weapon enclave for ensuring that the completed warhead can adequately mate with the delivery systems ultimately chosen for serial production, while a much larger subset of the defense research and development complex will be responsible for designing and developing (and, whenever necessary, modifying) those delivery systems thought to be necessary for a future Indian arsenal. Other elements of this complex are tasked with developing the technical subsystems required for effective command and control, including

---

[197]Ron Matthews, *Defence Production in India* (New Delhi: ABC Publishing House, 1989); "Defence Research & Development Organisation," in R. K. Jasbir Singh (ed.), *Indian Defence Yearbook, 1997–98* (Dehra Dun, India: Natraj Publishers, 1997), pp. 427–494; and http://www.drdo.org.

physical safety devices, special communications links, and other associated technologies.[198]

So long as India's nuclear posture consisted of simple ambiguity, the defense research and development complex could continue its efforts at a languid pace. The decision to become a declared nuclear state, however, imposes new obligations on India, and these will be manifested in many different ways in the future. First, this complex will focus on continuing to develop a range of delivery systems that are resistant to interception. This implies a renewed effort in the area of long-range ballistic and cruise missiles aimed primarily at China but secondarily at Pakistan as well. India's achievements in these areas have thus far been modest, and consequently, the defense research complex will push for long-term development and testing of such systems if the country is to satisfy its desire for a limited nuclear deterrent of some sort in the future.[199]

Second, this complex will continue to modify India's ground attack aircraft to carry nuclear weapons if such efforts have not already been completed. This step would provide a modest deterrent capability immediately, and unless the deployment and operating procedures relating to these weapon carriers are changed, such modifications would probably go unnoticed on the outside. As newer delivery platforms are integrated into service, this complex will be tasked with modifying these new entrants as well while continuing to oversee all the other upgrades that will be necessary to ensure that India's manned strike platforms are capable of carrying out their nuclear strike mission in the face of a changing threat environment.[200]

---

[198]Some of these institutions are identified in *India: India's Nuclear Weapons Plan Examined*, FBIS-NES-98-190, July 9, 1998.

[199]This will necessarily be the case given "the consistent [historical] failure of the Indian defence research establishment to put into production any significant weapons systems that it develops." Gupta, *India Redefines Its Role*, p. 44.

[200]These activities come under the purview of the Chief Adviser (Technologies), DRDO, who oversees the Directorate of Aeronautics and its key institutions, the Aerial Delivery Research and Development Establishment (ADRDE), the Aircraft System and Testing Establishment (ASTE), and the Aeronautics Development Establishment (ADE), as well as the Special Adviser to the Chief of Air Staff, who is formally responsible for all liaison with the Indian Air Force. See http://www.drdo.org.

Third, this complex will embark on a series of development efforts associated with the construction of a nuclear arsenal. Many of these initiatives will relate to specific components such as safety systems. However, the most important activities will pertain to readying existing nuclear designs for carriage by specific delivery systems—and toward this end, the growing symbiosis between selected subsets of the defense research and the nuclear weapon communities will continue. The general changes in India's nuclear posture presaged by the 1998 tests only imply that the defense research community, which traditionally played second fiddle to the nuclear establishment, is likely to supplant the latter in importance over time. In many ways, this is because that community still has the bulk of its work cut out for it and, unlikely to complete these tasks anytime soon, will continue to garner both resources and national attention as its efforts slowly begin to bear fruit.[201]

Space Research Programs. The third complex, the space research organizations, is responsible for overseeing India's space programs, which consist of developing a variety of launch vehicles; acquiring systems engineering expertise; producing remote sensing, communications, and meteorological satellites; and maintaining the organizational and technical infrastructure for controlling its space assets.[202] For a variety of historical reasons, most associated with the emphasis placed on economic development by its founding father Vikram Sarabhai, the Indian space community has shied away from institutional participation in any of the country's military programs and to this day carefully maintains formal firewalls separating it from the strategic activities of the other two complexes. This separation, already reinforced by the normal processes of bureaucratic competi-

---

[201]There is already some evidence that the growing attention enjoyed by the defense research establishment has become an object of some concern within the atomic research complex. See Pallava Bagla, "Pokharan: DRDO Limelight Hurt DAE," *Indian Express*, December 10, 1998.

[202]Useful surveys of India's space capabilities can be found in Anita Bhatia, "India's Space Program," *Asian Survey*, 25:10 (October 1985), pp. 1013–1030; Dinshaw Mistry, "India's Emerging Space Program," *Pacific Affairs*, 71:2 (Summer 1998), pp. 151–174; *India, Its Space Program, and Opportunities for Collaboration with NASA* (Arlington, VA: ANSER, 1999); and Deborah J. Foster, "The Indian Space Program," in John C. Baker, Kevin M. O'Connell, and Ray A. Williamson (eds.), *Commercial Observation Satellites: At the Leading Edge of Global Transparency*, MR-1229 (Santa Monica: RAND/ASPRS, 2001), pp. 247–262.

tion, takes on more urgency because the increasing international collaboration pursued by the space research complex would be imperiled if its relationship with India's nuclear and defense research establishments were perceived to be too close.[203] In any event, the space research program—through a combination of foreign technology injections and indigenous efforts—has developed an "end-to-end space capacity"[204] that has resulted in the ability to build a variety of space launch vehicles and communications, meteorological, and earth observation satellites. As part of this process, the space research program has also developed excellent test and launch facilities close to the equator, thereby creating a boon for space systems intended for geosynchronous orbit.[205] India's achievements in the space arena have become significant enough to make the country a serious candidate in the commercial satellite launch market, and its investments in the realm of space-based remote sensing have made it a potential resource for many U.S. and European customers.

With these impressive achievements, the space research program—despite its early institutional intentions—will wind up actively supporting the Indian nuclear posture, even if only indirectly. To begin with, several of the specific technologies required to develop a credible deterrent are space-related, and it will not be surprising to find India's atomic and defense research complexes leaning on its space research organizations for solid fuel rocketry, satellite-based reconnaissance, communications, and meteorology packages, and ground-based surveillance, control, and telemetry systems. The space complex's achievements in solid-fuel rocketry, for instance, are of critical interest to organizations that have been tasked with developing long-range ballistic missiles. As an example, the Polar Satellite Launch Vehicle (PSLV), a booster with a 20-meter-long and 2.8-meter-wide five-segment solid-rocket motor in its first stage, is in the same payload-carrying class as the U.S. Atlas E launch

---

[203]This dynamic is well understood as described in "Indian Space Program," U.S. Embassy Political Section, Cable to U.S. Department of Defense No. 30510, New Delhi, January 6, 1988, paragraph 62, cited in McCarthy, "India: Emerging Missile Power," p. 205.

[204]Jon Fairall, "India's Global Aims," *Space*, January 1, 1995, p. 17.

[205]Michael Mecham, "India Builds a 'Crown Jewel,'" *Aviation Week & Space Technology*, August 12, 1996, pp. 56–57.

vehicle and, if developed into a ballistic missile, could easily carry a 1-ton military payload out to intercontinental ranges.[206] Such capabilities would be of great interest to defense technologists attempting to improve on the new all-solid-fueled Agni IRBM currently being tested by India. Beyond solid-fuel rocketry, the space complex's ever-improving earth observation satellites would also be attractive technologies for absorption—particularly as the IRS-P6, with its 2.5-meter-resolution panchromatic imaging capability, and the Cartosat-2, with its 1-meter-resolution capability, become operational in the next few years.[207]

Given the past record, however, it is unlikely that any of these technologies will be transferred directly to the military sector. Rather, new patterns relating to internal technology diffusion are likely to become evident. The most obvious and already established conduit centers on the transfer of personnel with specific skills to the other complexes as the need for their services arises. A.P.J. Kalam, previously the highly visible manager of the Indian Integrated Guided Missile Program, for example, was a space engineer who transferred to the Defence Research and Development Organization (DRDO) in order to head the new missile R&D effort. Less obvious but equally critical exchanges will take place in the form of knowledge transfers carried out through collaborative work at the interindividual or intergroup level across various complexes.[208] If these forms of collaboration turn out to be insufficient, new institutional arrangements enabling joint access to space-related technologies are likely to emerge. This is most probable where access to satellite systems is concerned; since satellites are high-value

---

[206]The Geosynchronous Satellite Launch Vehicle (GSLV), which is slated for launch in 2001, will have an even bigger solid-fuel first stage consisting of the PSLV's first-stage motor and a 275,000-lb, 9.2-foot-diameter booster that produces one million pounds of thrust, clustered by six PSLV strap-on motors, making it capable of carrying 5500-lb payloads to intercontinental ranges.

[207]"Growing Pains," *Aviation Week & Space Technology*, October 13, 1997, p. 17, and Mistry, "India's Emerging Space Program," p. 161.

[208]As one U.S. analyst noted, "Although the [Indian defense research and space] organizations are competitive, it is most natural for scientists and engineers working on similar problems (particularly if working for the same employer of last resort) to discuss problems and success, sharing information about their projects." Telegram No. 31294, paragraph 96, U.S. Embassy, New Delhi, telegram to the U.S. State Department, in National Security Archives, Washington, D.C.

systems that exist in small numbers and remain under the control of the Indian Space Research Organization (ISRO) for both technical and operational reasons, new institutional arrangements allowing the atomic energy and defense research establishments (and even the armed forces) to access their data streams are likely to be developed. This will allow the satellite itself to remain under the control of a civilian research organization while its onboard capabilities (and data outputs) can be shared with a variety of strategic users, sometimes through straightforward commercial arrangements.

The bottom line, therefore, is that the space research complex, which has benefited over the years from the investments in high technology associated with India's strategic enclaves, will soon be confronted with an opportunity to contribute substantially to the work that will be carried out by these enclaves. Even though it will still be inclined both by institutional temperament and by necessity to stay as far away from military-strategic endeavors as possible, that complex is likely to become more and more involved in the same. In fact, it is doubtful that India will be able to develop an effective nuclear posture without meaningful contributions from its space research complex: As one of India's leading newsmagazines noted, "A separate component to the space programme is overdue. In fact, so is a new space policy."[209]

Implications for India's Nuclear Posture. The importance of the country's three strategic complexes is thus likely to increase over time, with significant implications for India's nuclear posture. Despite the fact that the track record of these complexes has been less than stellar in several issue areas, each of these complexes is widely viewed within the country (and increasingly outside) as being on the leading edge of Indian technology. That alone gives them great bureaucratic weight where influencing political decisions is concerned. Further, most Indians appear to be noticeably proud of the enclaves' achievements, viewing the capabilities these organizations nurture as safeguarding both national security and political autonomy in an international environment that is often perceived as hostile to the

---

[209] "India's Pies in the Sky," *India Today International*, October 20, 1997, p. 5.

ascendance of Indian power.[210] The utterances of India's top scientists and technologists are therefore treated with considerable public respect. Since these individuals are all civilians, their statements—even on matters at the interstices of science, defense, and national policy—fall within the realm of permissible discourse in the Indian context and can therefore influence public expectations with respect to national policy, even if they do not determine those policies independently.[211]

It is clear that at least two of the three strategic enclaves have already successfully altered Indian national policy. The atomic energy establishment, which had long argued publicly for renewed nuclear testing, certainly felt vindicated by the consultative processes that led up to the 1998 Indian decision to test its nuclear weapons.[212] The defense research establishment, in turn, having succeeded in developing an SRBM in the face of complete disinterest on the part of the Indian armed forces, is now focusing on developing more capable, longer-range ballistic and cruise missiles that will almost certainly become the mainstay of an Indian nuclear deterrent when such a deterrent is completed.[213] The success of these two enclaves thus augurs well for their continued influence, but the limits of such influence must be recognized as well. Thus far, for example, India's political leaders have succeeded in preventing technological determinism from running amok by carefully directing the pace of research and development through stringent control of funding and by basing all testing and deployment decisions on political necessity

---

[210]See the comments in R. Chidambaram and V. Ashok, "Embargo Regimes and Impact," in Deepa Ollapally and S. Rajagopal (eds.), *Nuclear Cooperation: Challenges and Prospects* (Bangalore, India: National Institute of Advanced Studies, 1997), and in A.P.J. Abdul Kalam (with Y. S. Rajan), *India 2020* (New Delhi: Viking, 1998), pp. 187–216.

[211]For a trenchant commentary on the pernicious consequences of this process, see "Democracy of Science," *The Times of India*, January 7, 2000.

[212]On the processes of consultation leading up to the May 1998 tests, see Manoj Joshi, "Nuclear Shock Waves," *India Today International*, May 25, 1998, pp. 12–20.

[213]The strategic and bureaucratic logic beneath the development of the Integrated Guided Missile Development Programme (IGMDP)—note the lack of a General Staff Requirement for any of the surface-to-surface missiles developed under the program—has been explicated in Sidhu, *The Development of an Indian Nuclear Doctrine Since 1980*, pp. 248–274, and in Sidhu, *Enhancing Indo-U.S. Strategic Cooperation*, pp. 21–27.

rather than merely on technical capability—and this dynamic is unlikely to change in the future. However, to the extent that India's indigenous achievements occur in the context of a deteriorating regional environment and the rise of a global regime marked by ever more restrictive technology flows, the definition of political necessity itself will expand to accommodate the views of India's strategic enclaves even more systematically. In a world where India increasingly sees autarkic solutions as the only way to preserve its security and autonomy, considerations about the morale of its enclaves will interact with the intuition that these organizations represent the best route to great-power capabilities, thereby making India's strategic enclaves even more signficant players than before.[214]

Political Parties. As the enclaves press to advance India's nuclear capabilities further over time, the breakwaters that previously served to resist such pressures at the political level will continue to fissure. So long as the Congress Party was assured control of the national polity, its traditional preference for nuclear ambiguity automatically became India's national policy as well. It must be remembered, however, that even the Congress government came close to changing that posture several times after 1992, at least as far as testing was concerned; the national test site at Pokhran was continually prepared, and on the two occasions when India seemed ready to test, only strong U.S. political pressures succeeded in averting that outcome.[215] The subsequent United Front (UF) regimes in New Delhi also appear to have toyed with the idea of testing but ultimately demurred; as former Indian Prime Minister I. K. Gujral later acknowledged, these "no-test" decisions were reached under pressure even though it was "conceded that . . . [testing] . . . had to be done at sometime or the other."[216] The evidence thus suggests that even the Congress and UF governments—regimes that were unquestionably moderate in their political inclinations—had contemplated the idea of altering India's nuclear posture and would probably have done so in the absence of pressures emanating from the United States. In any

---

[214]See the interesting, albeit somewhat self-serving, arguments in Brahma Chellaney, "An Indian Critique of U.S. Export Controls," *Orbis*, 38 (1994), pp. 439–456.

[215]Joshi, "Nuclear Shock Waves," p. 18.

[216]*India: Indian Nuclear Tests Planned Since 1995*, FBIS-NES-98-138, May 18, 1998.

event, the Congress Party's traditional lock on power has all but evaporated, and the UF has been similarly marginalized in Indian politics. Moreover, the rise of new national parties such as the BJP, which have already declared India to be a nuclear weapon state, implies that future debates about the country's nuclear posture will probably pivot on what kind of deterrent should be created, what forms that deterrent capability should take, and over what time frames these capabilities should materialize.

The actions of the BJP-dominated NDA government have thus forced the center of the Indian nuclear debate substantially to the right, leaving all the other political parties struggling to respond to the new strategic realities.[217] Both the major opposition groupings, the Congress Party and the UF, felt uneasy about supporting the BJP-dominated government's surprise decisions to resume testing and to declare India as a nuclear weapon state. This unease, however, derived not so much from a judgment that such actions ran counter to the national interests as from a recognition that these decisions, being immensely popular in domestic political terms, would serve only to remind voters that the opposition parties lacked the courage to take on the established nonproliferation order and do what most Indian elites believed was necessary for the country's safety when they were in power.[218] A different and more subtle private criticism offered by some opposition leaders who had served in high government positions centered on the claim that the Vajpayee government's decision to test only compromised what the country had been secretly doing all along and, by opening the door to renewed external pressures, actually compromised India's ability to continue the covert development of its nuclear weaponry.[219]

Whatever the merits of such concerns, the decision to test rattled all the opposition parties, who scrambled to position themselves

---

[217]John F. Burns, "Nuclear Blasts Put India's Opposition Parties in a Bind," *New York Times*, May 14, 1998. See also C. Raja Mohan, "Nuclear Politics—I: Playing Football with Nuclear Weapons," *The Hindu*, May 25, 1998.

[218]As one Indian commentator noted, "For forty years, no political party had the guts to take the nuclear process to its logical conclusion." T.V.R. Shenoy, "Why the Buddha Smiled," *Indian Express*, May 20, 1998.

[219]Private conversations with the author, January 1999. See also Mani Shankar Aiyar, "A Bang or a Whimper?" *India Today*, June 1, 1998, p. 20.

so that they could bask in the glow of the country's achievements even as they sought to avoid endorsing the decisions of the BJP-dominated government in power. Not surprisingly, the Congress Party initially responded to the tests by claiming that they were simply the culmination of a long-standing policy initiated by previous Congress governments. This position was later refined to hold that the tests represented a national achievement and, as such, could not be treated as a trophy to be claimed by any single political party. The UF similarly chimed in by congratulating the country's scientists and technologists, and while its most visible member, I. K. Gujral, initially insinuated that India's tests were motivated by domestic politics, he too subsequently sought—at least in public forums—to justify them as having been made necessary by changes in India's strategic environment. Most opposition parties would thus have endorsed the sentiments expressed by one Indian observer who, seeking to deflate the BJP-dominated government's claims of political courage, argued succinctly that "the bomb . . . has many fathers. The Congress conceived it. The UF nurtured it. The BJP delivered it. Let us not give the obstetrician any more credit than is due."[220]

Whether the twin decisions to resume testing and to declare India a nuclear weapon state were substantially motivated by domestic political considerations, as many commentators both in India and abroad have alleged, remains yet another issue that will be debated for years to come and may never be conclusively resolved.[221] Irre-

---

[220]A. Surya Prakash, "All Were Party to the Nuclear Gatecrash," *The Pioneer*, May 25, 1998.

[221]A short summary of the positions taken by the principal Indian opposition parties to the test can be found in Joshi, "Nuclear Shock Waves," p. 20. The claim that the May 1998 tests were motivated simply by domestic politics in different ways is assessed and—correctly—dismissed in Sumit Ganguly, "India's Pathway to Pokhran II: The Prospects and Sources of New Delhi's Nuclear Weapons Program," *International Security*, 23:4 (Spring 1999), pp. 171–175. The conclusion offered and defended later in this monograph is that the May 1998 tests provided some domestic political benefits to the BJP-dominated government, but that these benefits were welcome by-products of a decision made primarily on grounds of national security. The validity of these grounds may be contested, but the fact that they did motivate India's national leadership seems compelling given the changing character of the country's security debate since 1995 and the BJP's distinctive vision of Indian security needs. For more on the latter, see Jaswant Singh, *Defending India* (Chennai, India: Macmillan, 1999), pp. 1–60 and 306–338. For other views on the role of domestic politics, see Hilary Synnott, *The Causes and Consequences of South Asia's Nuclear Tests*, Adelphi Paper No. 332 (London: IISS, 1999).

spective of the position one takes on this question, the fact remains that the BJP-dominated government has bequeathed to India a strategic situation differing significantly from that which existed prior to its entry into office. It is, moreover, unlikely that any future government, irrespective of how it is constituted within the political spectrum, will roll back the clock and return India to the condition that obtained prior to May 1998—assuming that is at all possible. As one Indian commentator noted, "No government in India will go against the consensus in favour of creation of an adequate nuclear deterrent."[222] In fact, as the analysis in Chapter Five will demonstrate, the alterations that are likely to occur in India's nuclear posture will be either covert changes or mutations that can be readily disguised under the rubric of conventional force modernization. Thanks to this fact, future Indian governments, whether they are formed by the Congress Party, by the UF, or by any of the regional parties now proliferating around the country, *can derive all the international benefits that come from the appearance of "moderation" while still pursuing the development of exactly the same kind of deterrent that a BJP-dominated government would probably pursue if it were assured many years in power*. The implications of this judgment should be sobering for all who have set their hearts on ridding South Asia of its nuclear weaponry and, at the very least, should caution those who believe that the present regime's departure will inevitably usher in a new era of nuclear equipoise in the subcontinent.

Popular Preferences. While all the major political parties likely to form a government in the future would thus carry the country's strategic posture further toward a nuclear arsenal, albeit covertly and with much ambiguity, the final ratification of this direction will of course come from India's body politic itself—both its elites and its increasingly sophisticated mass of ordinary voters. The best studies of Indian public opinion on the nuclear question indicate that the elite population believes that the country's weapon option should not be divested.[223] Given the progressive changes in Pakistan's and China's nuclear posture, a smaller but still substantial proportion of

---

[222]M. D. Nalapat, "Eagle's Eye View: Isolating India to Help China," *The Times of India,* June 25, 1998.

[223]David Cortright and Amitabh Mattoo, "Elite Public Opinion and Nuclear Weapons Policy in India," *Asian Survey,* 36:6 (June 1996), pp. 545–560.

those polled argued that India should develop a nuclear arsenal immediately. In fact, in the aftermath of the nuclear tests, most reports suggested that Indian elites were ready to endorse development of a ready nuclear arsenal right away. This position, driven by post-test euphoria, was also influenced by concerns about national self-respect and the desire to prove—first and foremost to themselves—that India is autonomous, can stand up to the great powers, and is worthy of being treated as a regional hegemon.[224]

This enthusiasm for nuclear weapons by Indian elites is, however, somewhat misleading. To begin with, it may simply be a transient phenomenon precipitated by the events of May 1998. Further, the elite population itself consists of at least two broad groups: those involved in economic affairs and those connected to the political and strategic establishments. The former subset is unlikely to support nuclear weaponization if it undercuts the prospects for growth and investment;[225] in contrast, some of the latter would most likely argue that India's size and capabilities allow it to pursue further nuclearization with minimal damage to the prospects for continued growth.[226] Finally, it is unclear whether the vast majority of the voting masses share the Indian elites' enthusiasm for nuclear status and, in particular, for a large and ready arsenal. While most Indians traditionally have endorsed the idea of maintaining the nuclear option as a hedge against an uncertain future, few have actually been enamored of more complex nuclearization when the costs of the weapon program become apparent to them. Popular opinion and, for that matter, most elite opinion as well thus support maintaining a national nuclear capability but seek to preserve this "on the cheap"— and certainly not at the expense of economic development and technological modernization.[227] Only a small subset of the security elite has argued for complete nuclearization no matter what the cost, and even here, this support is often rationalized by the claim that an ar-

---

[224]"Thrilled Experts Say Nation Has Strength to Take On World," *Economic Times*, May 12, 1998, and Chandan Mitra, "Explosion of Self-Esteem," *The Pioneer*, May 12, 1998.

[225]Jayati Ghosh, "The Bomb and the Economy," *Frontline*, May 8–21, 1999.

[226]Karnad, "Going Thermonuclear: Why, with What Forces, at What Cost," pp. 327–330.

[227]Perkovich, *India's Nuclear Bomb*, pp. 451–452.

senal in the Indian context would be relatively inexpensive to create and maintain in comparison with the West.[228]

Where the influence of elite and mass opinion on nuclear weapon choices is concerned, perhaps the most critical fact, then, is that the former group (in its security-related incarnation) dominates the political debate and defines the range of preferred choices but has remarkably little power to force policymakers to act in support of those preferences. The actual policy choices are determined by the autonomous interests of the Prime Ministers in office, who, while taking into account the preferences of the strategic enclaves, the political elites, and various political parties, have generally been acutely sensitive to the impact of the nuclear issue on economic development and foreign relations precisely because these variables most affect the living conditions of the large voting populace and, by implication, the political survival of the politician. Given that there has never been a clamor for a nuclear arsenal at the popular level, thanks both to a lack of popular interest in these issues and to the costs involved, India's security managers are unlikely to feel compelled to accelerate nuclearization because of any public pressure. All decisions here will be essentially private ones that can be made without fear of any adverse popular opinion so long as they do not involve a surrender of India's nuclear options. This gives Indian decisionmakers great latitude—because no matter whether their choices are excoriated or lauded by the elites, the latter are essentially incapable of forcing the pace of weaponization in any practical terms, and the large voting masses continue to be relatively uninterested in all security-related issues. All this implies that popular opinion will not drive future Indian choices about the shape and pace of nuclearization. To the contrary, so long as Indian capabilities are not perceived to be surrendered, such opinion is likely to remain neutral and may function as a modest brake on weaponization if the cost of creating a nuclear arsenal threatens to exacerbate economic difficulties.[229]

---

[228]See the claims adduced in Manoj Joshi, "Marginal Costing," *India Today*, June 1, 1998, pp. 22–23.

[229]The relationship between economic pressures, public opinion, and Indian decisionmaking with respect to India's nuclear capabilities was manifested most acutely during the 1964 debates, which are examined insightfully in Perkovich, *India's Nuclear Bomb*, p. 74ff.

Economic Performance. India's economic performance may well have a significant effect on India's future strategic direction. On a fundamental level, this would seem to pertain primarily to how much a nuclear arsenal costs in both absolute and relative terms. Unfortunately, however, no authoritative estimates of the costs of an effective nuclear force are available, in part because the secrecy enveloping India's strategic enclaves makes it difficult to compute the true burdens of many of their programs. Although the Indian government's official defense, atomic energy, and space budgets are publicly disseminated, these are usually of little help because the relevant grant requests invariably identify only gross amounts associated with various heads of expenditure rather than the specific amounts allocated for individual projects or systems. This paucity of authoritative information has resulted in a variety of private estimates about the costs of a nuclear arsenal, most of which represent either Western estimates (sometimes modified) or simply back-of-the-envelope calculations provided by military officers or budget analysts.[230]

These figures, at any rate, embody enormous variation. As early as 1966, Major-General Som Dutt, in an analysis based on Western writings of the time, suggested that "even a modest retaliatory force with a sophisticated delivery system"[231] would cost India between $230 and $300 million annually for at least a decade. Even these figures, he admitted, were probably underestimated, since France and Britain were reported to have spent between $300 and $340 million on their nuclear arsenals for well over two decades. In 1968, the doyen of India's strategic analysts, K. Subrahmanyam, estimated more realistically that an Indian nuclear deterrent could cost $1.5 billion annually (presumably in 1968 dollars) over a ten-year period, while Vice-Admiral K. K. Nayyar, who participated in a secret internal study of this issue in the mid-1980s, claimed more recently that a limited nuclear arsenal would cost approximately $1 billion (Rs. 4000

---

[230]For some Western figures and comments on this issue, see Paul Mann, "Subcontinent Poised for Nuke Deployment," *Aviation Week & Space Technology*, August 3, 1998, pp. 24–26.

[231]D. Som Dutt, *India and the Bomb*, Adelphi Paper No. 30 (London: IISS, 1966), p. 7.

crore) annually for a decade.[232] In his published recollections of India's nuclear policy, Subrahmanyam asserted that the internal study referred to by Admiral Nayyar concluded that "India could have a balanced deterrent programme within ten years at a cost of Rs. 7000 crore"[233] ($1.6 billion). It is unclear whether this figure represents total costs or simply annual costs spread out over a period of ten years. If it is the latter, the total cost of the arsenal at $16.3 billion (Rs. 70,000 crore) would constitute the high—but probably more honest—end of the estimates currently populating Indian discussions;[234] if it is the former, it would be in line with other more optimistic assessments claiming that a modest arsenal could be constructed "within five years" and "would not exceed Rs. 5000 crore"[235] ($1.2 billion) in aggregate costs. Cost figures of the sort offered by Admiral Nayyar, which represent roughly 10 percent of the 1998–1999 Indian defense budget (which itself constitutes less than 3 percent of the country's GNP), have thus led many Indian commentators to argue that the expenses of full nuclearization remain well within India's economic capacity.

A cursory examination of the Indian defense budget initially appears to justify such optimism. The Indian defense budget in 1998–1999 was approximately $9.5 billion[236]—which, for the sake of discussion, was probably about 3 percent of the country's GNP during that year. If it is assumed that this GNP will grow at about 5.5 percent for another decade—with defense expenditures held constant as a percentage of GNP—the Indian defense budget will be a little over $16 billion by 2008–2009. If such growth and expenditure levels actually obtain, the *cumulative marginal increase* in Indian defense resources will be approximately $34 billion a decade or so from now. If it is further assumed that all marginal increases in defense expendi-

---

[232]Joshi, "Marginal Costing," pp. 22–23.

[233]K. Subrahmanyam, "Indian Nuclear Policy—1964–98,"in Jasjit Singh (ed.), *Nuclear India* (New Delhi: Knowledge World, 1998), p. 41.

[234]A similar accounting has also been offered by C. Rammanohar Reddy, "The Wages of Armageddon—I–III," *The Hindu*, August 31–September 2, 1998. The author also offers an excellent survey of other Indian estimates together with a critique of these judgments.

[235]Joshi, "Marginal Costing," p. 22.

[236]Calculated at an exchange rate of roughly $1 = Rs. 40.

tures are set aside only for the nuclear arsenal, then it is possible—based on the cost estimates one relies on—to argue that the arsenal can be financed solely out of the marginal increases in defense expenditures that will accrue as a result of normal economic growth alone. Of course, this claim assumes that India will grow constantly at a rate of at least 5.5 percent annually; that defense expenditures as a percentage of GNP will remain constant over time; and that no dramatic changes will occur in the rates of exchange relative to internal prices during this period. All these are no doubt significant assumptions, but if they are presumed to hold for the sake of argument, then it is possible to assert that at least Admiral Nayyar's arsenal, coming in at $10 billion, and one of Subrahmanyam's estimates of Nayyar's arsenal, coming in at $16.3 billion, could be financed by the marginal increase in defense expenditures alone over the next decade.

There are many reasons, however, to be skeptical of such a conclusion.

First, a great deal of uncertainty exists about the accuracy of all the cost estimates proffered above, in part because they are often advanced by individuals who have publicly advocated the acquisition of a full-fledged nuclear arsenal. The temptation to understate costs for the purpose of enticing the Indian government to embark on certain courses of action thus cannot be underestimated, especially because it is recognized that the decision to create an arsenal would be irreversible once it is embarked on, despite whatever its true costs eventually turned out to be.[237]

Second, the absence of true cost information relating to the component parts from which any aggregate numbers are derived is as serious a problem as lack of scrutiny on the part of budget analysts outside the government. In effect, this problem boils down to the fact that real information about program costs is unavailable to non-

---

[237]See the apt comments of Peter Lavoy in this regard, cited in Mann, "Subcontinent Poised for Nuke Deployment." One recent news report, for example, has indicated that India has drafted a $3.75 billion nuclear C^3I plan to be completed over the next five years ("India Drafts New N-Command, Control System," *Hindustan Times*, January 12, 2000). If true, this represents a substantial increase over the $112 million (or thereabouts) that previous Indian estimates of the sort found in Joshi, "Marginal Costing," p. 23, had asserted would be required by a nuclear C^3I system.

governmental entities and, because of genuine methodological difficulties, may even be unavailable to the Indian government itself. This peculiar problem is caused largely by the fact that the Indian defense budgeting process did not adopt the Planning Program Budgeting System (PPBS), which would have allowed security managers to assess the true costs of any given system in its entirety as well as its cost-effectiveness in relation to some alternatives.[238]

Third, if the history of India's military R&D programs is any indication, no major development effort has been successfully completed on schedule and in line with expenditure forecasts.[239] This implies that even if the estimates currently offered represent honest appraisals, the sorry record of simpler projects undertaken in the past should give decisionmakers reason for pause, since the currently advertised costs of the arsenal will in all probability turn out to be gross underestimates as development efforts take longer than expected and as national macroeconomic conditions change over the ten-year time frame incorporated in these calculations. It is worth remembering that developing a nuclear arsenal—even one that comports with India's minimal needs—would involve not only producing dozens of individual systems but also integrating such systems into an organic structure that renders all previous military development projects and their associated cost overruns trifling by comparison.[240]

---

[238]Consequently, Indian security managers can discern total program costs *post factum* better than they can assess individual and comparative project costs in real time because the detailed breakdown of costs in terms of capital outlays and labor distinguished by skill levels is rarely available for all defense programs across the board. Consequently, it is impossible to apply the standard cost-benefit analysis techniques detailed in I.M.D. Little and J. A. Mirrlees, *Project Appraisal and Planning for Developing Countries* (London: Heinemann, 1974), to compute the real costs of the development and deployment of India's desired nuclear posture. This difficulty, as well as the consequences thereof, is assessed in detail in Amiya Kumar Ghosh, *India's Defence Budget and Expenditure Management in a Wider Context* (New Delhi: Lancer Publishers, 1996).

[239]Arnett, "Military Technology: The Case of India," pp. 343–365. See also Chris Smith, *India's Ad Hoc Arsenal* (Oxford, UK: Oxford University Press, 1994), pp. 144–178.

[240]This reality is already becoming apparent if recent news reports are to be believed. For example, the Su-30 MKI aircraft, which many Indian analysts claim will become the air-breathing component of their future triad, is already facing difficulties, as its surface attack capabilities are apparently not as effective as expected. With production difficulties afflicting the Sukhoi plants in Russia, it is not clear whether the

Fourth, even if some of the more modest cost estimates relating to the arsenal turn out to be correct, it must be recognized that the costs associated with funding a nuclear arsenal cannot supplant those associated with personnel expenditures, conventional modernization, ongoing military operations, and routine cyclical training. All four of these heads of account have suffered greatly during the last decade, and if the Indian armed services are to maintain their operational proficiency in the obligations they are currently servicing, the anticipated marginal increases in military expenditure arising from normal economic growth will have to be allocated in growing proportion to the conventional elements of the existing military force rather than to any new nuclear-related systems. In fact, one Indian analysis has suggested that conventional modernization alone would require $16.8 to $35 billion (Rs. 72,200–1,51,700 crores) over the next five years[241]—clearly a figure that would substantially erode (if not wipe out entirely) the $34 billion notionally available for a nuclear arsenal over the next decade.

The immensity of India's conventional defense needs cannot be underestimated, and if the Indian military is to be modernized sufficiently to exploit the evolving RMA even as New Delhi proceeds to develop a robust nuclear arsenal simultaneously (especially in the form of the triad urged by most Indian security elites), it would require increases in defense expenditures over and above those enlargements which accrue simply as a result of a growing GNP.[242] It is unclear at this point whether such increases could be undertaken

---

Indian Air Force will be able to acquire the contingent it needs on time with the spares, avionics, and weapon package it has contracted for. See Suman Bhattacharyya, "Time to Crash Land," *Outlook*, March 13, 2000.

[241] Bharat Karnad, "Cost-Effective Budgeting: Getting the Priorities Right," *Indian Defence Review*, 13:1 (January–March 1998), pp. 8–23.

[242] See the analysis in Jasjit Singh, "Budgeting for Security Needs," *Frontline*, July 18–31, 1998. It must be remembered that India already lacks many of the advanced technological capabilities necessary for effective counterinsurgency operations—already the biggest consumer of India's large military manpower pool and its most demanding security challenge on an ongoing basis—and that New Delhi will soon have to reinvest in modernizing India's northern defenses if it is to maintain its current margin of conventional superiority vis-à-vis China. Meeting both of these challenges will only burden the Indian exchequer further as it attempts to satisfy other demands relating to the need for a large quantum of conventional stores, the investment choices imposed by the emerging RMA, and the burdens exacted by the desire for a nuclear deterrent.

without having a deleterious effect on the larger processes of economic growth itself. The challenge of sustaining rising levels of economic growth in fact remains the principal problem facing New Delhi, and it is by no means obvious that India has yet surmounted the impediments to generating high, self-sustaining growth. As an editorial in a major Indian newspaper put it in the aftermath of the government of India's record 2000–2001 defense budget,

> The unprecedented increase in the defence budget is worrisome because it goes against a long trend of declining or standstill defence expenditure. It has been a deliberate matter of policy to try and contain defence expenditure in order to leave more resources for social sectors such as education and health. If anything has changed in the non-defence sectors in the last decade of structural adjustments and economic reform, it is the squeeze on resources for social sectors and the sharp decline in capital formation. . . . Runaway defence expenditures are not what this country needs.[243]

While most economists believe that India would have to grow at a pace of at least 7 percent per annum if it is to simultaneously beat absolute poverty and develop great-power capabilities by the year 2015, these growth rates simply cannot be sustained if India is forced to increase nondevelopmental expenditures at a time when it seems unable to enforce further structural changes in its economic institutions for political reasons.[244] Further, the achievement of these growth rates is clearly contingent on expanding the economy's connectivity with the global system. Yet this connectivity, which is required to underwrite the vast investments necessary in infrastructure, power, agriculture, and human development, cannot be achieved in the face of continued Western opposition to Indian nuclearization, especially when coupled with domestic decisionmaking failures relating to further economic liberalization. Given these facts, the costs of developing a nuclear arsenal are likely to be much greater when the opportunity costs of nuclearization are factored in, and to the degree that they contribute to depressing India's economic performance, they will have had a more lasting effect on

---

[243]"Sinha's Defence," *Indian Express,* March 2, 2000.

[244]On India's failures in this regard, see "A Decade of Economic Reforms: Political Discord and the Second Stage," *Doing Business in India,* 2:1 and 2:2 (Fall 1999), pp. 1–42.

India's security than the mere presence or absence of the arsenal itself.[245]

None of this is meant to suggest that India will simply be unable to afford a nuclear arsenal. It is meant to suggest, however, that an arsenal could be much more expensive than is currently imagined in that it would require greater defense burdens than the country has borne over the past decade; could cut into critical expenditures on conventional forces; and, finally, would retard India's capacity to grow rapidly if it cements Western reluctance to support the country's economic modernization in the face of continued domestic failure to pursue the economic reforms necessary for sustained future growth. It is the twin components of this last variable that will have a substantial effect on the course India pursues with respect to nuclearization. If its arteriosclerotic domestic economic policies can be reformed successfully, New Delhi might be able to ward off the most painful consequences of Western governmental pressure that have materialized in the aftermath of the 1998 nuclear tests.[246] Continued economic reform would allow private interests abroad to dominate the opposition of their governments and enable India to sustain the economic performance that would be necessary to generate larger defense budgets, including those additional expenditures required for a nuclear arsenal. Failure to sustain high growth rates, however—whether rooted in domestic malaise or in indifferent foreign participation—will have exactly the opposite effect: It would result in an inability to develop a deterrent of the kind India's security elites

---

[245]Not surprisingly, a leading Indian newsmagazine argued that the NDA government should have used the 1998 nuclear tests "to push ahead with [the] tough economic measures" that were necessary to ensure increases in the country's "true strength." See "Nuclear Afterglow," *India Today International*, May 25, 1998, p. 7. The NDA regime's failure to accelerate the program of structural reforms pertaining to the economy—as evidenced by its three lackluster national budgets in 1998, 1999, and 2000—will have more serious consequences for India's claims to great-power capabilities than will its refusal to develop a ready arsenal of the sort demanded by one Indian hawk. See Brahma Chellaney, "For India, the Big Nuclear Breakthrough Has Fizzled," *International Herald Tribune*, May 13, 1999.

[246]A good assessment of the impact of U.S. sanctions against India can be found in R. Ramachandran, "Sanctions: The Bark and the Bite," *Frontline*, May 8–21, 1999, and Daniel Morrow and Michael Carriere, "The Economic Impacts of the 1998 Sanctions on India and Pakistan," *Nonproliferation Review*, 6:4 (Fall 1999), pp. 1–16. See also G. Balachandran, "India's Nuclear Option: Economic Implications," *Strategic Analysis*, 19:2 (May 1996), pp. 143–156.

believe is necessary. Even worse, such failure might result either in the creation of a ragged nuclear capability or in a gradual political retrenchment at a time when New Delhi's adversaries, having anticipated a distension in India's nuclear arsenal, appear well along the road to developing even more significant capabilities of their own. India's economic performance, and the perceptions of that performance by the country's voting masses, will thus condition the pattern of nuclearization that New Delhi could pursue in the future.

On balance, then, how do these four structural factors affect India's future nuclear direction? Although this question cannot be answered with certainty, the most reasonable conclusion at this point is that these factors will interact, as Indian Defence Minister George Fernandes put it, to make "nuclear weaponization . . . necessary and, in the ultimate analysis, inevitable."[247] To be sure, the forms, pace, and manifestations of weaponization are still not fully settled, but this certainly seems to be the *direction* in which New Delhi is headed—as opposed to the reverse course, which involves denuclearization and India's possible accession to the NPT as a non-nuclear weapon state. This should not be surprising given the character of the four issues analyzed above. Despite recognizing the significant improvement in the global nuclear regime, Indian elites view the reluctance to carry the process forward toward complete abolition as implying that international politics has not been transformed in any fundamental way, or at least not in any way that requires India to contemplate moving further away from the acquisition of nuclear weaponry. The steady increases in Pakistan's nuclear capability, coupled with the extant Chinese nuclear threat, are seen to demand changes in India's traditional policy of merely "keeping the option open" to the neglect of other alternatives that may include developing a full-fledged arsenal. India's relations with key states in Asia and beyond are viewed as either good or steadily improving, but no single dyadic relationship, including that with the United States, is seen at this point as providing the strategic resources—political, economic, or technological—that make a change in India's traditional nuclear posture unnecessary. Finally, pressures from the scientific establishment and national elites

---

[247] "Moratorium Will Not Affect N-Weaponisation: Fernandes," *The Times of India*, May 27, 1998.

compete with the many views of India's political parties and their mass following—and while the resulting vectors do not inevitably translate into the demand for a ready arsenal, the fact remains that if national economic performance allows it, India would move in such a direction rather than away from it. All things considered, therefore, a shift toward further nuclearization seems inescapable, although the exact predicates of that dynamic remain to be discerned.

Chapter Three

ASSESSING ALTERNATIVE INDIAN NUCLEAR POSTURES

This analysis has thus far suggested that a variety of external and internal pressures will force a shift in India's nuclear posture in the years ahead. The May 1998 tests, in fact, represented merely the beginnings of change, and the culmination of this sequence is not yet clear despite the many rhetorical flourishes that have issued from New Delhi. At the same time, even if India were to move further in the direction of weaponization, as the last chapter suggested will be the case, it is worth remembering that weaponization represents not a step but a process. This process embodies many constituent moves, some of which may be unobservable to casual viewers both in India and abroad and many of which will actually be disguised even as they occur. The very prospect of such movement, however, has energized the United States; operating on the assumption that weaponization in any form is deleterious to South Asia's stability, U.S. diplomats and policymakers have begun earnest discussions with their Indian and Pakistani counterparts in the hope first that weaponization itself may be eschewed and ultimately that the nuclear programs themselves will be terminated in both countries.[1]

---

[1]This intention has been expressed most clearly in John Holum's speech to the Defense Special Weapons Agency (DSWA) International Conference on Controlling Arms, Philadelphia, Pennsylvania, June 10, 1998, available at http://www.acda.gov/speeches/holum/dswahol.htm. For a later statement, see Ramesh Chandran, "U.S. Has Not Accepted India's Need for Nuclear Deterrent: Holum," *The Times of India*, December 11, 1999, which quotes Holum as stating that "the U.S. has not accepted the idea that India needs to have a credible minimum nuclear deterrent in its arsenal. . . . A core point of our dialogue with India has been our belief that every country determines its own security requirements. But we think that from our perspective,

These objectives, consistent as they are with the larger U.S. interest in nonproliferation, once again raise the question of the choices facing New Delhi (and, for that matter, Islamabad). This chapter seeks to identify and assess the various strategic nuclear options facing New Delhi, some of which entail weaponization and some of which do not. The purpose of this exercise is primarily heuristic but nonetheless has important policy-related implications. By analyzing the full range of alternatives facing India, it seeks to understand which choices remain fundamentally unacceptable to New Delhi and why, and which options will be pursued in the future and how. Therefore, scrutiny of even those alternatives already rejected by South Block is necessary because it sheds light on how India will orient its preferred choices to service those problems which made the discarded alternatives unacceptable to begin with. Only then will it be possible in any analytical sense to identify what the operational predicates of India's preferred future posture will be.

In consonance with this logic, this chapter identifies five distinct nuclear postures from amid a continuum of possibilities, each with varying degrees of acceptability to India (see Figure 1). These postures, referring to critical equilibrium points along that continuum, are conceived primarily as Weberian "ideal types." An ideal type, in Weber's sociology, is an artificially created mental construct that attempts to order diffuse and complex phenomena *by isolating and accentuating certain key characteristics into a distinct but internally consistent conceptual representation*. Each of the alternatives described below therefore focuses on making explicit the "unique particularity" inherent in a given nuclear posture and, as such, remains an "exaggerating abstraction" created by systematically isolating one unique facet of that posture and carrying it to its logical

---

India's security requirements are . . . best served without a nuclear capability. . . . [Consequently, the United States does not] acquiesce in or accept [India's emerging nuclear] capability." It is still not clear whether remarks such as these are meant to communicate the "true" and perhaps hidden contours of U.S. policy toward India (and Pakistan, for that matter) or whether they are intended mainly to signal to the international community that, whatever accommodation Washington may reach with India and Pakistan, the United States remains committed to upholding the architecture of the global nonproliferation regime. At the very least, they signal that the Clinton administration had not conclusively resolved the internal debates between the nonproliferation and regional bureaucracies with respect to American strategies for dealing with India's nuclear weapon program.

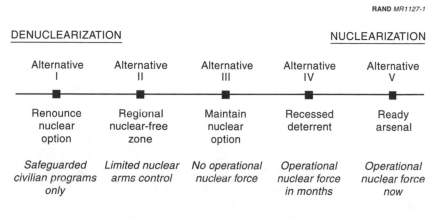

Figure 1—Alternative Indian Nuclear Postures

extreme.[2] Consequently, the five alternatives—when treated separately—are heuristic fictions but are nonetheless necessary fictions insofar as they provide a means of identifying the range of choices open to India, analyzing the extent of change likely in India's future posture, and explicating the content through which such change might be manifested.

Alternative I: Unilaterally renounce the nuclear option after obtaining positive and negative security guarantees. This alternative implies that India would formally "give up" its sovereign right to develop a nuclear arsenal after (1) obtaining from each declared nuclear power negative security guarantees—i.e., that nuclear weapons would never be used against India; and (2) obtaining from at least some of the existing nuclear weapon states positive security guarantees—i.e., that a nuclear umbrella would protect India in the event of a nuclear threat. India's formal renunciation of the option to create a nuclear arsenal would not necessarily entail actually signing the NPT, even though in principle that remains Washington's long-term goal. Indeed, India could decline to become an NPT signatory, thereby

---

[2]This logic of the "ideal type" is explicated in Max Weber, *The Methodology of the Social Sciences*, translated and edited by Edward A. Shils and Henry A. Finch (New York: The Free Press, 1949), pp. 50–112, and the quotations in this sentence are drawn from Weber's description in the pages cited.

symbolically affirming its traditional concerns about legitimizing nuclear inequality. This alternative would, however, require that India place all of its nuclear facilities under safeguards and subject its entire fissile-material inventory to strict accounting.[3] Alternative I would therefore appear to make India a de facto signatory to the NPT even if it chose to formally remain outside what it considers to be a discriminatory regime. In a strict sense, however, this alternative does not actually do so because the renunciation it demands does not involve any *legal* commitments to the international community to eschew the production of nuclear weapons; it simply involves a *national* decision to renounce the development of nuclear arms, with the accession to international safeguards being primarily a guarantee of good faith on New Delhi's part. Alternatively, India could simply choose to sign the NPT as a non–nuclear weapon state, but because this would imply a symbolic acquiescence to an "unequal" global regime, the weaker of the two variants is selected for consideration here.

Alternative II: Orchestrate a regional nuclear control regime that obviates the need for developing a nuclear arsenal. This alternative would also require that India renounce its right to develop operational nuclear capabilities, but such a renunciation would not be unilateral. Instead, it would be part of a regional nuclear management regime that would aim to reduce the threat each of the participating countries—India, Pakistan, and China—posed to each other and, to the degree possible, reduce the costs of a potentially open-ended arms race, especially between India and Pakistan. This alternative, which has been conceptualized as viable "in conjunction with some definite moves on the global scale toward substantial nuclear arms reduction and disarmament,"[4] would require negotiated and verifiable agreements that committed both India and Pakistan to eschewing the development of nuclear weaponry while simultaneously constricting both the pattern and type of Chinese nuclear deployments in proximity to the subcontinent. Such a limited nuclear arms

---

[3]This and other variants of nuclear foreclosure are discussed in P. R. Chari, "India's Nuclear Option: Future Directions," in P. R. Chari, Pervaiz Iqbal Cheema, and Iftekharuzzaman (eds.), *Nuclear Non-Proliferation in India and Pakistan* (New Delhi: Manohar, 1996), pp. 60–86.

[4]Praful Bidwai, "Nuclear Policy in a Mess," *The Times of India*, November 27, 1991.

control regime could consist of either multiple bilateral arrangements or a single trilateral agreement that in effect binds all three states to the maintenance of a South Asian nuclear-free zone supported, if necessary, by security guarantees and/or other political commitments from the other nuclear powers.[5] Strictly speaking, this nuclear-free zone would result only in India's and Pakistan's eschewing the production and deployment of nuclear weaponry; China would remain a nuclear weapon state but would undertake binding obligations that would diminish the nuclear threat it posed to India in the context of an overall resolution of the current Sino-Indian territorial dispute. China's residual nuclear capabilities would then by implication be reserved only for contingencies involving the United States and Russia and their treaty-bound allies in Asia. While a nuclear-free zone of this sort has never been formally tabled for discussion at the diplomatic level, the idea that this alternative embodies has been advocated by some Indian analysts who oppose nuclearization.[6] It also underlies the occasional calls that have emerged for a "five-party or multilateral conference"[7] on nuclear issues in South Asia, and it therefore merits consideration as a nonunilateral option to Alternative I.

Alternative III: Maintain the nuclear option *qua* option indefinitely. This alternative simply requires that India maintain the status quo as it existed prior to May 11, 1998, without any revision. Under this alternative, India would neither exercise its option to create a nuclear arsenal nor renounce its sovereign right to develop such an arsenal in circumstances of grave national danger. Maintaining the nuclear option implies that India would continue to produce weapons-grade plutonium at the relatively low rates it has in the past; engage in theoretical work relating to nuclear weapon design and perhaps continue to develop or even produce the nonnuclear SAFF mechanisms required by a nuclear weapon; and research and develop various delivery systems as technology demonstrators. This

---

[5]The logic of nuclear-free zones in general is discussed in O. Sukovic, "The Concept of Nuclear Free Zones," in D. Carlton and C. Schaerf (eds.), *Perspectives on the Arms Race* (London: Macmillan, 1989), pp. 267–285.

[6]Bidwai, "Nuclear Policy in a Mess." See also Praful Bidwai, "India and NPT Review: Grasping the Disarmament Nettle," *The Times of India*, September 22, 1994.

[7]The logic and limitations of these calls have been discussed in Chari, *Indo-Pak Nuclear Standoff*, p. 82ff.

alternative also implies, however, that India would *not* create an arsenal of standardized, completed nuclear weapons; deploy dedicated nuclear delivery systems; configure dual-use systems for nuclear delivery; or develop the supporting infrastructure necessary for pre-planned nuclear operations. Such an approach would no doubt result in the creation of certain latent capabilities but, from the perspective of nuclear operations, would embody the *potential* for a nuclear arsenal rather than a ready capacity for discrete nuclear use or sustained nuclear war fighting.

By constituting the entry point to that part of the decision spectrum pertaining to nuclearization, Alternative III can be seen to possess a certain fuzzy and uncertain quality. This is because "maintaining the option"—understood as "continuing the . . . nuclear ambiguity despite its unsatisfactory aspects"[8]—essentially involves a posture that cannot be independently verified save for its more obvious elements, such as producing and deploying dedicated nuclear delivery systems. Nonetheless, this alternative may be summarized as denoting a posture best described by the phrase "no operational nuclear force." As such, it constitutes an equilibrium point worthy of examination because it can resolve some kinds of strategic problems facing India and because it appears to have been a relatively stable political preference for most of the post-1974 period.

Alternative IV: Develop a "recessed deterrent" as part of maintaining a credible option to create a full-fledged nuclear arsenal if required.   This alternative requires that India move beyond simply maintaining a set of latent, and in some areas embryonic, nuclear capabilities. Instead, it would place India on a path leading to the development of a nuclear arsenal *without* actually arriving at that goal. This alternative presumes that effective nuclear capabilities derive not merely from the possession of a small number of nuclear weapons but rather from an integrated capability that includes actual nuclear weapons and their delivery systems as well as supporting technologies such as a C^{3}I apparatus, procedural systems that regulate the custody and release of nuclear weapons, and ideational systems that define the doctrines governing both the acquisition and

---

[8]Ibid., p. 82.

use of nuclear weapons as well as strategies for war termination.[9] As such, Alternative IV would require that India put in place the plans, procedures, and organizations that are necessary for effective nuclear operations in an emergency; for example, it would permit the continued design and cold testing of nuclear weapons and their components under laboratory conditions and would allow for the continued design and testing of various delivery vehicles. At the same time, however, it would prohibit the fabrication of completed nuclear weapons, the production and/or deployment of dedicated or dual-capable nuclear delivery systems, and the mating of weapons with delivery systems that are then maintained even at low levels of readiness. In effect, Alternative IV would bequeath on India an incipient nuclear capability that would derive from its having developed the various parts necessary for an effective deterrent, but it would not produce a standing force capable of carrying out nuclear operations *immediately*. This alternative may thus be summarized as denoting a posture best described by the phrase "operational nuclear force available in months" in that its effectiveness derives from the fact that it could be constituted into a viable nuclear arsenal under deteriorating political circumstances—and because this capability is recognized as such, it can serve to deny even stronger adversaries the freedom to use their strength exploitatively.[10]

Alternative V: Initiate development of a robust and ready nuclear arsenal immediately. This alternative would carry the strategy of maintaining recessed nuclear capabilities to its maximal conclusion. Under this posture, India would in effect work toward acquiring the kinds of nuclear capabilities the declared nuclear powers possess

---

[9]As early as 1957, Henry Kissinger noted in his seminal work *Nuclear Weapons and Foreign Policy* (New York: Harper & Brothers, 1957), p. 197, that "it is important to distinguish . . . between the possession of nuclear weapons and their strategic effectiveness. By themselves, nuclear weapons have a considerable nuisance value. But, unless they are coupled with sophisticated delivery means, highly complex communications systems and appropriate tactics, it will be difficult to utilize them effectively. Unless the whole military establishment is geared to nuclear tactics, nuclear war becomes a highly dangerous adventure."

[10]One variant of this alternative has been advocated most persuasively by one of India's most respected strategic commentators, Jasjit Singh, in his essay "A Nuclear Strategy for India," in Jasjit Singh (ed.), *Nuclear India* (New Delhi: Knowledge World, 1998), pp. 306–324.

and would create a sizable inventory of nuclear weapons with vary-ing yields *ready for immediate use* when sanctioned by the national command authority. This alternative may in fact be summarized by the phrase "ready and operational nuclear force available now." Having such capabilities implies that the relevant delivery systems, be they aircraft or missile, would be acquired as well and that such systems would be readily available for any combat missions together with all the diverse enabling capabilities that are necessary to trans-form a nuclear weapon stockpile into a credible nuclear arsenal. By further implication, this alternative would require that India's nu-clear deterrent be "militarily serviceable"[11] and thus within the im-mediate reach of the armed services, who would maintain it at the high levels of readiness demanded of any technology intended for the conduct of prompt operations. Possessing such a robust set of capabilities, however, does not necessarily imply that the arsenal would be visible and transparent. To the contrary, these capabilities, even when acquired, could well be hidden under a veil of opacity. Consequently, it is important to distinguish between the fact of an arsenal's existence and its disposition; while the creation of an arse-nal in the systemic sense understood above would present several telltale signs that disclosed its existence, it could still remain highly enigmatic with respect to its force architecture, doctrinal underpin-nings, and command-and-control arrangements—especially in their details. Therefore, the creation of the full-fledged, fully deployed nu-clear arsenal that this alternative entails does not require that India reveal its force structure and deterrence doctrine (although neither of these alternatives is precluded) even if it has already proclaimed itself to be a "nuclear weapon state."

Assessing India's future direction on the basis of the alternatives presented above requires an analysis of how New Delhi would view each option in the context of three specific criteria, First, does the specified alternative increase India's security? Security in this context would imply enhancing India's physical safety and decisional auton-omy, which in turn speaks to the question of managing current as well as future threats that may result from the selection of a given alternative. Second, does the specified alternative bequeath strategic

---

[11]Bharat Karnad, "A Thermonuclear Deterrent," in Amitabh Mattoo (ed.), *India's Nuclear Deterrent* (New Delhi: Har-Anand Publications, 1999), p. 111.

flexibility to India's security managers? Strategic flexibility in this context implies the ability to change or even reverse course at a relatively low cost should the exigencies of international politics so demand. Third, does the specified alternative promise to improve India's status? Status in this context implies at least preserving, if not bettering, the country's relative standing in international politics.

ALTERNATIVES INVOLVING DENUCLEARIZATION

Viewed in the context of the three questions posed above, Alternatives I and II are greeted with skepticism in New Delhi today. By contrast, the United States—driven by a desire to buttress the global nonproliferation order—still espouses a policy that is at least formally anchored in encouraging India and Pakistan to adopt one or the other of these alternatives. And while the intensity of this pressure has varied as a function of the personalities on both sides, the political atmosphere in South Asia, the competing demands on Washington's time and attention, and the overall status of U.S.-Indian (and U.S.-Pakistani) relations, the United States remains committed, at least in principle, to shepherding both India and Pakistan into joining the NPT regime as non–nuclear weapon states. To be sure, there have been many changes with respect to how this goal has been pursued over the past decade, but America's general commitment to it is a logical by-product of its desire to preserve a robust global nonproliferation order—a desire that is reinforced by the belief that nuclear weapons do little to resolve and much to exacerbate the security challenges facing India (and, for that matter, Pakistan).[12] New Delhi, as might be expected, disagrees vehemently with this judgment, but most Indian analysts have failed to systematically assess precisely how nuclear capabilities can enhance (or subvert) the three objectives—security, flexibility, and status—identified earlier. To the contrary, most local analysts have simply been content to assert the benefits of nuclear weaponry without in any way attempting to determine whether these benefits are uniform or, given India's grand strategic objectives, are worth the trade-offs

---

[12]Strobe Talbott, "Dealing with the Bomb in South Asia," *Foreign Affairs*, 78:2 (March–April 1999), pp. 110–122.

they demand.[13] When a systematic analysis of the kind conducted below is completed, however, it becomes evident that *New Delhi may have good reasons to reject denuclearization, although these reasons are much narrower than commonly supposed and are in fact somewhat ambiguous on the margins.*

Alternative I: Renounce the Nuclear Option

To begin with, Alternative I—although generally mocked within India as an idealistic Gandhianism that has no place in modern international politics—does not subvert the three criteria identified above as readily as is often imagined. This is particularly true if this alternative, once adopted, is accompanied by the striking of certain strategic bargains with existing nuclear powers such as the United States and Russia, which have a substantial stake in maintaining a stable global nonproliferation regime. Before Alternative I is even contemplated, however, New Delhi must assume a number of characteristics of the international system to be increasingly valid. First, New Delhi must assume that nuclear weapons are of decreasing value in the international arena and that all actions furthering this trend—including its own—are by definition in its national interests. This perception would enable New Delhi to realistically expect Pakistan to renounce its nuclear option in tandem with India, thereby diminishing the range of threats India faced even if not quite eliminating them. Second, New Delhi must assume that nuclear weapons have real utility only in situations where the homeland of a state is threatened, and not as instruments for the extraction of political concessions. This expectation would allow India to see nuclear weapons in the hands of its potential adversaries as being less useful than is often feared, thereby permitting New Delhi to proceed with

---

[13]Oddly, serious analyses of this kind today have been undertaken mostly by Indian "doves" who invariably conclude that India's security, far from being enhanced, is only compromised by its acquisition of nuclear weapons. For good examples of such work, see Kanti Bajpai, "Secure Without the Bomb," *Seminar*, 444 (August 1996), pp. 57–60, and Kanti Bajpai, "The Fallacy of an Indian Deterrent," in Amitabh Mattoo (ed.), *India's Nuclear Deterrent* (New Delhi: Har-Anand Publications, 1999), pp. 150–188. The few exceptions at the other end of the Indian political spectrum are Nair, *Nuclear India*, and Karnad, "A Thermonuclear Deterrent," pp. 108–149, where the differences in premises and logic vis-à-vis the arguments of the Indian doves are clearly evident.

its act of renunciation with far less "fear and trembling" than might otherwise be the case.

At present, however, many influential Indian strategic analysts are not convinced that either of these conditions applies. On the first issue, for example, K. Subrahmanyam has emphatically argued that nuclear weapons continue to be the "currency of global power"— and that although these weapons "are not military weapons" in the conventional sense, their value derives precisely from the fact that they are instruments of high politics and are therefore the means by which power and prestige are allocated in the global order. Consequently, Subrahmanyam notes, India has no choice but to acquire these weapons to the extent that it "wants to be a player and not an object of this global nuclear order."[14] On the second issue, another prominent Indian analyst, Bharat Karnad, has argued that irrespective of whether nuclear weapons have operational utility for war fighting, they are eminently useful for what Carl von Clausewitz once called "such warfare as consists in a mere threatening of the enemy and in negotiating."[15] So long as nuclear weapons are seen to retain their utility for such forms of strategic coercion—an issue that greatly exercises Indian analysts of all political stripes—the likelihood that the country will endorse denuclearization, either unilaterally or regionally, becomes highly remote.

In any event, and irrespective of whether these two expectations obtain among policymakers in New Delhi, a potential decision on India's part to renounce its nuclear capabilities would be plausible only if it were accompanied by several strategic, albeit perhaps tacit, agreements with important actors like the United States and Russia to the effect that New Delhi would be given preferential access to political and financial resources as well as to a range of advanced civilian, dual-use, and military technologies. To be effective, these technologies should not only allow India to adequately defend its national interests in the absence of nuclear weapons but also enable it to improve its relative power position in the international arena. At

---

[14]See Amitav Ghosh, "A Reporter at Large: Countdown," *The New Yorker,* October 26–November 2, 1998, p. 189.

[15]Cited in Bharat Karnad, "Politics of 'Militarised' States," *Hindustan Times,* January 22, 1983. This article also has an extensive discussion on the utility of nuclear weapons for strategic coercion.

the very least, then, access to such resources and technologies must enable India to advance its developmental goals more efficiently than before. Moreover, if such an outcome is to be consummated, it must be reinforced by India's accretion of increased status in international politics and by greater accommodation of its preferences in those great-power activities which affect New Delhi's interests and sensitivities. Indeed, only a "grand bargain" of this sort—i.e., one that trades India's renunciation of nuclear weapons for both positive and negative security guarantees as well as enhanced access to great-power resources in the form of either a seat on the U.N. Security Council or preferential access to high technology—would stand some chance of securing India's consideration.[16] Whether New Delhi would ultimately find such a bargain acceptable, however, is unclear. Thus, it is worth exploring whether a unilateral renunciation of nuclear weapons—in the form described earlier and accompanied by just such bargains—would be deleterious to India's security, its desire for strategic flexibility, and ultimately its status.

Security Considerations. It is clear that both now and in the foreseeable future, India will face only two major strategic threats: a nuclear-armed Pakistan and a nuclear-armed China. To be sure, some Indian strategists have argued that nuclear developments in more remote areas like the Middle East and Northeast Asia—as well as those of the established nuclear weapon powers, especially the United States—may affect Indian security as well.[17] However, these claims are generally somewhat tenuous, based as they are on the theoretically plausible but practically inconsequential proposition that "anarchy is seamless." In fact, the best theoretical work that has addressed this issue has concluded that "security complexes" defined by regional amity-enmity considerations will continue to be the principal drivers of threat planning—and that although more

---

[16]Such a deal has, in fact, been proposed by two American scholars. See Harrison, "Cut a Regional Deal"; Harrison, "The United States and South Asia: Trapped by the Past?"; and Stephen P. Cohen, "A Way Out of the South Asia Arms Race, "*Washington Post*, September 28, 1992. Another American scholar argued that the opportunities offered by formally accepting denuclearization for the attainment of (nonnuclear) great-power capabilities remain precisely the reasons why India ought to have signed the NPT. See Raju G.C. Thomas, "Should India Sign the NPT/CTBT?" in Raju G.C. Thomas (ed.), *The Nuclear Non-Proliferation Regime* (New York: St. Martin's Press, 1998).

[17]See, for example, Karnad, "Going Thermonuclear: Why, with What Forces, at What Cost," pp. 313–314, and Karnad, "A Thermonuclear Deterrent," p. 128ff.

generalized security challenges might well arise, such challenges will rarely if ever be salient enough to warrant serious programmatic responses by countries other than the great powers.[18] In India's case, this implies that the nuclear capabilities now becoming evident in the Levant and Northeast Asia as well as those in Europe and the Americas are less relevant for assessing how nuclear weapons might resolve New Delhi's security dilemmas and, as such, can be disregarded for now. One Indian analyst, Vijai Nair, summed up this more restricted criterion of adequacy succinctly when he noted that while

> the U.S. deterrent philosophy is complex and directed to achieve a large number of variable objectives . . . this philosophy is not applicable to the Indian nuclear deterrent, which is required purely as a defensive instrument to ensure that no outside power is tempted to coerce the country or initiate a nuclear strike in a conflict situation. Therefore, the size (numbers) and capability (range) of [India's] strategic forces need to be limited to deterring *regional nuclear powers* by holding hostage to nuclear retaliation, major assets in those states [italics added].[19]

The threats emanating from regional nuclear powers like Pakistan and China must therefore be accorded the most serious consideration, especially given the rivalries that exist between each of these two states and India.[20] These threats could be manifested in three ways. First, both states could threaten to use nuclear weapons either to avert battlefield defeat or to accelerate battlefield victory in the context of a local conventional war. Second, they could engage in blatant nuclear blackmail in the context of some crisis (or even outside a crisis) in efforts to force India to make political concessions. Third, they could exploit the perceived immunity conferred by their nuclear arsenals to engage in low-intensity conflicts with India, secure in the knowledge that New Delhi could not threaten nuclear or perhaps even conventional retaliation.[21]

---

[18]Barry Buzan, *People, States and Fear,* 2nd ed. (Boulder, CO: Lynne Rienner Publishers, 1991), pp. 186–229.

[19]Nair, "The Structure of an Indian Nuclear Deterrent," p. 83.

[20]This premise forms the explicit basis of Vijai Nair's interesting book on Indian nuclear strategy. See Nair, *Nuclear India,* pp. 7–77.

[21]These three categories of nuclear threats essentially span the spectrum that defines the utility of these weapons. The first contingency incorporates the notion of nu-

1. Averting defeat or accelerating victory in a conventional war. The effects of each of these contingencies would be different in the case of Pakistan and China thanks to differences in their relative capabilities vis-à-vis India, and hence they must be considered separately in the context of how they could threaten the denuclearized India that would be assumed to exist under Alternative I. As far as Pakistan is concerned, it is unlikely that the first form of threat—the use of nuclear weapons to either avert defeat or accelerate victory in the context of a conventional war of unlimited aims—would acquire any real significance because of the generally low probability that such premeditated conflicts will arise in South Asia today. Indeed, since 1971 the declining utility of unlimited-aims war in the region has slowly become a strategic fact of life that has been widely acknowledged both by the U.S. government and by the strategic elites in South Asia, if not by some Western commentators. The logic underlying this phenomenon has already been articulated elsewhere[22] and hence will not be repeated here except for two summary statements bearing on this issue: First, rapidly diminishing political incentives in both India and Pakistan interact with conditions of high defense dominance on both sides to make premeditated wars of unlimited aims only a remote possibility. Second, fears about operational ineffectiveness on both sides coupled with concerns about the inability to enforce war termination at the desired moment interact to minimize

---

clear weapons as effective war-fighting instruments; the second contingency involves the idea of nuclear weapons as tools of coercion; and the third contingency refers to nuclear weapons as umbrellas that could engender instability at lower levels of conflict. The fourth contingency would refer to nuclear weapons as pure deterrents against attack. This contingency is not addressed here because nuclear weapons in the hands of Pakistan and China would be oriented toward deterring *Indian* threats, and as such this category is more relevant when analyzing Islamabad's and Beijing's decisions to maintain an arsenal rather than New Delhi's. To the degree that this issue is relevant to New Delhi's decision to denuclearize, its relevance is grounded mainly in the benefits that Indian nuclear weapons would have in deterring those Pakistani and Chinese nuclear attacks aimed at decisively eliminating India as a competitor. To the degree that such attacks are aimed at securing certain specific political goals short of outright elimination, they are analyzed under the rubric of the three contingencies noted above. Other kinds of hypothetical attacks, including those intended to definitively obliterate India's existence as a politico-physical entity, are so beyond the pale of possibility as to merit no systematic consideration whatsoever.

[22]Tellis, *Stability in South Asia,* pp. 2–33 and 55–62.

the probability of most though not all premeditated conflicts of limited aims.[23]

The localized conflict at Kargil in 1999 remains an apt example of the kind of limited-aims war that could still occur under conditions of "ugly stability"[24] in South Asia. Unlike most limited-aims wars, which are aimed at securing finite portions of intrinsically valuable territory, Pakistan's military operations at Kargil may well have focused at least as much on precipitating international intervention in support of its claims over Kashmir as they did on securing marginal pieces of Indian territory. If this was in fact the case, the Kargil crisis could well be viewed as a good example of nuclear-shadowed brinkmanship aimed at securing foreign intervention in an ongoing dispute rather than a purely limited-aims war as it is traditionally understood in the literature.[25] This peculiar kind of conflict, which might be termed "catalytic war" in that it is deliberately initiated with the intent of inveigling third parties to enter the fray in order to force the resolution of an ongoing political dispute, could recur in the future if the power transitions currently under way within the Indian subcontinent continue to gather force. Under such conditions, Pakistani desperation coupled with factors such as decreasing state capacity, the rise of a risk-acceptant national leadership, and the prospect of serious international attention could combine to create conditions in which premeditated catalytic conflicts might actually become an attractive option.[26]

The opportunities for such types of limited war, however, would constantly fluctuate, since the background conditions required to spark such conflicts are likely to remain persistently in flux. As a result, the "ugly stability" that normally defines strategic interactions in the Indian subcontinent could be interrupted by intense and episodic "crisis slides" that—if all went well—would gradually abate, returning both competitors to their preexisting pattern of "ugly

---

[23]Ibid.

[24]Ibid., pp. 30–33.

[25]John Mearsheimer, *Conventional Deterrence* (Ithaca, NY: Cornell University Press, 1983), pp. 53–56.

[26]For more on these possibilities, see Tellis, *Stability in South Asia*, pp. 56–59.

stability" (which may subsist, however, at higher and higher plateaus of relative violence in the aftermath of each successive crisis). Yet while all these crises will certainly have tense and unsettling moments, perhaps including limited conventional military operations of some intensity, they are unlikely to precipitate the actual use of nuclear weapons—as opposed to nuclear signaling or nuclear brandishment—mainly because the likely initiator of these crises, Pakistan, recognizes that none of its desired political goals is worth a nuclear war.[27] Clearly, Islamabad's (and, for that matter, New Delhi's) ability to prevent such a war from resulting from inadvertence, miscalculation, misperception, or accident in the midst of a crisis may be suspect, but it is reasonable to conclude—*at least at the level of intentionality*—that neither Pakistan nor India would stand to gain much if the crisis they precipitated for whatever reason degenerated into an all-out war involving the actual use of nuclear weaponry. Since this recognition is likely to inhibit both sides' risk-taking propensities, the possibility of escalation to actual nuclear use is likely to be minimal even though the prospect for acute political crises and some limited conventional military operations may well increase in the future. This reality, in turn, immediately reduces the opportunities for Pakistan to engage in any nuclear use vis-à-vis India, either to avert battlefield defeat or to accelerate battlefield victory in the context of a local conventional war.

Even if this conclusion is held in abeyance, however, it is clear that Pakistan's incentives to actually *use* nuclear weapons have always been somewhat constrained. Indeed, the use of nuclear weapons to accelerate the prospects of a battlefield victory in an otherwise conventional war is all but impossible for Pakistan given the relative balance of power in South Asia; Islamabad is simply too weak to reach out for victory in a war of unlimited aims, and while it could attain early if transient success in some kinds of limited-aims conflicts (e.g., the operations at Kargil), it is unclear how nuclear weapons as warfighting instruments would contribute to such success in these contingencies.[28] Even in the few instances where Pakistan's use of

---

[27]A. R. Siddiqi, "Balancing the Nuclear Debate," *Defence Journal*, 19:11–12 (1994), pp. 3–11, and Afzal Mahmood, "What Nuclear Sanity Demands," *Dawn*, May 31, 1999.

[28]Badri-Maharaj, "The Nuclear Battlefield," pp. 86–87.

nuclear weapons would actually bequeath it some clear operational advantages—as, for example, in interdicting the Banihal tunnel to prevent Indian reinforcements from reaching northern and western Kashmir during a surprise attack—India would have at its disposal a variety of conventional solutions that could prevent Islamabad from exploiting the fruits of such discrete operational use. At the very least, India could simply prolong the war, mobilize to amass the requisite force superiority over time, and destroy the flower of Pakistan's military capabilities, perhaps irrevocably.

To prevent just such an outcome, any Pakistani effort to harness nuclear weaponry for purposes of ensuring a conventional victory on the battlefield would have to be comprehensive, involving the widespread use of such weapons on several strategic and multiple battlefield targets. At the very least, it would require a readiness to employ nuclear weapons extensively in order to produce militarily significant operational effects. If, for example, Pakistan sought to destroy even a single Indian armored division advancing along a frontage of 15 km with its constituent elements spread out to a depth of 25 km—that is, to destroy at least 50 percent of the 500-odd armored vehicles within the formation—it would need to employ between 436 and 257 nuclear weapons of 15-kt yield, depending on the hardness estimates selected for armored vehicles. Even if Pakistan settled for killing merely 50 percent of the division's personnel in their vehicles as opposed to destroying the vehicles themselves in order to secure a "mission kill" rather than a "hard kill," it would require about 37 nuclear weapons of 15-kt yield just to operationally disable a single Indian armored division. This calculation of weapon expenditures is in fact conservative because it is predicated on the assumption of perfect circular-error-probable (CEP), zero weapon failure rates and on relatively modest frontages derived from the historical example of the First Indian Armored Division's advance in the Shakargarh sector during the 1965 war. If any of these assumptions are altered in the direction of greater realism, the number of Pakistani nuclear weapons required to either destroy or disable even a single Indian armored formation would be even greater.[29]

---

[29]If, for example, it is assumed that Pakistan possesses only 8-kt weapons as opposed to the 15-kt devices used in the calculation above, the number of weapons required to destroy an armored division increases considerably—all other assumptions

It must be noted, however, that Pakistan today simply does not possess a nuclear arsenal of the size that would make these employment options possible, and it is unlikely to acquire the capabilities that would enable it to do so at any point in the future. Further, it seems doubtful that Pakistan has any political interests in South Asia—including those linked to recovering disputed territories such as Kashmir—that would warrant either the comprehensive use of nuclear weapons or the readiness to escalate such use in the face of initially discrete nuclear applications. This is especially relevant in situations where even a nonnuclear India could respond by altering its war aims, invoking external security guarantees, or simply fabricating nuclear weapons in an emergency and using them to destroy Pakistan despite having absorbed what may be its consequential first strike(s). This hypothetical conclusion assumes, of course, that Pakistan's nuclear arsenal would remain a small one given the presumption of a unilaterally denuclearized India of the sort called for by Alternative I. The presumption of a small Pakistani nuclear arsenal here is justified simply by the expectation that Islamabad would have no incentive to produce anything more than a token nuclear force—primarily for political reassurance—if India did in fact divest itself of its nuclear weaponry through the adoption of comprehensive safeguards over its nuclear facilities and a full accounting of its past fissile-material and weapon inventory.

The contingency of Pakistan using nuclear weapons as warfighting instruments to prevent a battlefield defeat is somewhat more plausible, but there are no political reasons today—and few that can be envisaged for the future—why New Delhi would want to place Islamabad in a position where, fearing for its very survival, it must use nuclear weapons to prevent strategic defeat. Indeed, the evolution of such a contingency presupposes great rapacity on New Delhi's part, and while India could conceivably become more bellicose in the future, it is difficult to imagine such bellicosity taking the form of a war

---

held constant. With 8-kt devices in its inventory, Pakistan would need to expend between 663 and 391 weapons in order to destroy 50 percent of the armored vehicles and some 57 weapons in order to kill 50 percent of the personnel in their vehicles. The bottom line therefore remains the same: If nuclear weapons are to be employed in war fighting for purposes of achieving specific operational-tactical ends, a large number of weapons is necessary. The calculations here were performed using psi requirements for damage; if vulnerability numbers are used instead, the number of nuclear weapons varies somewhat but the general conclusions remain unchanged.

initiated by New Delhi to threaten the survival of the Pakistani state.[30] This would be all the more true if Pakistan was known to have nuclear capabilities, implying that the very factors that could force the use of such capabilities would not be presented by India. This, at any rate, appears to be the assumption underlying the current Indian discussion about the possibility of waging a limited war in South Asia.[31] Precisely because they recognize that nuclear weapons in South Asia deter all-out war, Indian security managers are struggling to escape from the straitjacket of self-deterrence, since it is widely believed that Pakistan's possession of nuclear weaponry has in fact provided Islamabad with the license to needle New Delhi without fear of Indian military counterresponses.[32] The underlying premises of this new debate in India clearly suggest that avoiding most if not all of the contingencies that would precipitate Pakistan's defensive use of nuclear weapons is well within New Delhi's control,[33] at least in theory. Hence it is not unreasonable to presume that if an India possessing nuclear capabilities has been so careful to prevent nuclear deterrence breakdown from coming to pass, an India that unilaterally renounced its nuclear option would become more careless and thereby precipitate the same undesirable outcome it has avoided thus far.[34]

---

[30]Tellis, *Stability in South Asia*, pp. 30–31.

[31]Mohan, "Fernandes Unveils 'Limited War' Doctrine."

[32]Ibid.

[33]See the thoughtful arguments in V. R. Raghavan, "Limited War and Strategic Liability," *The Hindu*, February 2, 2000.

[34]It should be noted, however, that this discussion about Indian control over the possibilities of Pakistani nuclear use is predicated on the standard assumptions of rational deterrence theory and focuses only on the *purposeful* use of nuclear weapons in the context of deliberate wars that can be imagined in the region. It is not intended to suggest that a denuclearized India would be immune to *every* Pakistani nuclear-use contingency imaginable. Thus, for example, a collapsing Pakistan may still choose to use nuclear weapons as part of a vengeful attack on India even if New Delhi had little or no role in the failure of the Pakistani state. Alternatively, Pakistan could use nuclear weapons on India because its strategy of nuclear brinkmanship—the attempt to invoke international intervention by deliberately precipitating conventional or subconventional military crises with India—results in a substantial Indian military riposte that Islamabad then mistakes for an unlimited-aims war justifying recourse to its strategic reserves. Contingencies of this type obviously cannot be neutralized by an India that adopts Alternative I as its preferred strategy, and as a later discussion in this section will establish, it remains an important reason New Delhi cannot comply with the international desire for denuclearization in the form represented by this

A similar set of considerations applies to contingencies involving China. There is little doubt that many Indian policymakers fear China's intentions over the long term, and the prospect of a powerful China "returning" to complete its "national reunification" agenda with respect to its territorial disputes with India remains disconcerting to New Delhi.[35] Indeed, it is in this context that China's possible use of nuclear weapons in South Asia becomes relevant. A closer examination of this issue, however, reveals that there are in fact few circumstances under which China's use of nuclear weapons as warfighting instruments would be either plausible or advantageous to it in the context of a conventional conflict with India. This judgment essentially hinges on an assessment of the Sino-Indian military balance that exists along the Himalayan border separating India from China. This military balance cannot be discussed in detail here, but its general condition can be summarized in the following terms. Unlike 1962, when the Indian Army was completely outclassed by the Chinese People's Liberation Army (PLA) with regard to both equipment and performance, the situation today has shifted substantially in India's favor. It is in fact possible to assert that India now enjoys relative superiority to China—not necessarily in numbers because that is affected by both sides' ability to bring in reinforcements from outside the theater, but clearly as far as the quality of its personnel, training, infrastructure, and logistics is concerned.[36] More important, India possesses unqualified superiority in tactical airpower, and it is likely that at least for the next decade, the Indian Air Force will be able to secure complete air supremacy along the Himalayan frontier within a few days of the outbreak of conflict.[37]

---

alternative. I am grateful to Stephen P. Cohen for drawing these contingencies to my attention.

[35]Subrahmanyam, "India: Keeping the Option Open," p. 118; "SAPRA Backgrounder: The China Poser," pp. 2–6; Jasjit Singh, "Why Nuclear Weapons?" in Jasjit Singh (ed.), *Nuclear India* (New Delhi: Knowledge World, 1998), pp. 14–20; and Mohan, "India, China Power Equations Changing."

[36]Jasjit Singh, "Nuclear Diplomacy," in Jasjit Singh (ed.), *Nuclear India* (New Delhi: Knowledge World, 1998), p. 290.

[37]"Defending India's Frontiers," *Air International*, 33:6 (December 1987), pp. 267–296. The only circumstance under which this conclusion would be weakened is in the case of a simultaneous high-intensity, two-front war vis-à-vis China and Pakistan. India would require about two weeks to establish air superiority against Pakistan alone, and this timetable would certainly be disrupted if key strike assets must be simultaneously allocated to the Himalayan theater. While such contingencies are al-

The nature of India's general military superiority must, however, be qualified with reference to the objectives New Delhi seeks to attain—for while India's combat forces in the theater, both land and air, are superior to their Chinese counterparts where *defending* territorial interests is concerned, such forces are for all practical purposes incapable of conducting any sustained offensives aimed at capturing new territories at significant distances from the forward edge of the current frontier. At the same time, this limitation holds equally for Chinese forces already deployed or intended for deployment along the border. Thanks to the terrain, weather, and general levels of military preparedness on both sides, the net result of this symmetry is that an extremely robust condition of defense dominance prevails along the Sino-Indian border. The nature of this defense dominance is in fact even sturdier than that along the Indo-Pakistani frontier because unlike the latter case, where New Delhi would gradually acquire an offensive edge in the event of a lengthy conflict,[38] no comparable transmutation is likely to occur even in an extended Sino-Indian border war for a variety of operational and technical reasons. This implies that both India and China have highly durable defensive capabilities that are unlikely to erode at any time soon. Indeed, even when China's war-fighting capabilities improve several decades from now as a result of its current military modernization, this condition of defense dominance is unlikely to change, as the Himalayan frontier will remain as foreboding as ever. Moreover, even if New Delhi fails to secure all the military technologies it desires from the United States and Russia—its presumptive conditions for nuclear renunciation—the Indian military will certainly not stand still as the PLA improves its capacity to prosecute limited high-technology wars. In fact, the weather, the terrain, and the advantages accruing to the defense will all interact to ensure that *even with incremental improvements in force capability*, the Indian Army and Air Force will be more than capable of offsetting any advanced technological capabilities

---

ways possible, the Indian Air Force has never seriously planned a full-blown offensive counterair campaign against both China and Pakistan simultaneously because it has judged—correctly—that such a collusive attack is highly improbable in the post-1971 environment.

[38]See Tellis, *Stability in South Asia*, pp. 19–22.

that the PLA might acquire as a result of China's growing economic prowess.[39]

Taken together, all these judgments imply that although a Chinese invasion might result in a battlefield defeat for the PLA, the latter would be deprived of the value of any battlefield nuclear use so long as the Indian Army did not attempt to exploit its successful forward defense through pursuit at the operational level deep behind China's front lines. Since India does not possess and lacks the political interests to develop the logistical capacity for such actions—assuming that they can in fact be executed in the terrain concerned—the situational necessity for Chinese nuclear use even in the context of a battlefield defeat is unlikely to materialize. Hence, given the exceedingly conservative operational goals that characterize India's forward defense strategy in the Himalayan theater, the fears some Indian military officers have expressed that "China may use TNWs [tactical nuclear weapons] in the defensive mode to neutralise China's own lifelines such as the Aksai Chin highway or the arterial roads supplying Tibet"[40] would appear to be overstated.

China's use of nuclear weapons to advance the prospects of a battlefield victory is just as unlikely. The Himalayan battlefield is often said to lend itself to effective discrete nuclear use in that its numerous valleys and watersheds form enclosed spaces that could maximize the operational effects of nuclear weapons while simultaneously containing radioactive fallout. At the same time, however, the employment of nuclear weapons to destroy entrenched Indian formations[41] presumes that the PLA's war-fighting objectives in some future conflict are not restricted to making marginal gains along the existing frontiers but are aimed instead at invading and occupying all of the disputed territories—including, for example, the entire state of Arunachal Pradesh in the Indian northeast.

---

[39]Singh, "Nuclear Diplomacy," pp. 289–291. This issue also remains the subject of current research at RAND.

[40]Arun Sahgal and Tejinder Singh, "Nuclear Threat from China: An Appraisal," *Trishul*, 6:2 (1993), p. 32.

[41]Nuclear weapon effects on a mountain battlefield are illustrated in Sundarji, *Effects of Nuclear Asymmetry on Conventional Deterrence*, pp. 12–13.

Assuming this to be the case for the moment, the use of Chinese tactical nuclear weapons in this context would most likely take place during breakthrough battles in the high mountain passes[42]—but even in this situation the advantages of nuclear use, although theoretically attractive, are less than clear. This is because the problem of transiting through heavily contaminated chokepoints is compounded by the fact that the features of this complex terrain may shield large groups of defenders from weapon effects in relatively close proximity to ground zero. Such defenders could thus offer effective resistance despite the previous use of nuclear weapons by their adversary, with the result that actual nuclear employment might have to be much more extensive than initially intended so as to suppress resistance both quickly and irrevocably.[43] It is unclear whether the PLA is capable of conducting such offensive combat operations on a nuclear battlefield. Moreover, even if one assumes that China's nuclear capabilities— especially tactical—would indeed suffice to neutralize the heaviest concentrations of Indian defenders en route to the plains, they would still be unequal to the principal operational challenge the PLA would face after its initial success: effectively sustaining both a war-fighting force and an occupation regime in the conquered territories situated far from their bases of support at a time when Indian special forces and regular small-unit detachments could exploit their knowledge of the terrain to unleash a reign of terror on their Chinese adversaries. In such circumstances, the Indian Air Force, operating from secure bases in both the lower northeast and the Gangetic plains, would only add to the PLA's difficulties in sustainment and control.

If all of these threats are to be neutralized, Chinese nuclear weapons—as in the Pakistani contingency considered above—would have to be employed not merely on battlefield targets but on strate-

---

[42]One Indian military analysis has claimed that "as per unconfirmed information, 203-mm guns with 5-kt warheads are distributed in 90 artillery battalions. The PLA also has S-23 Soviet-type 180-mm artillery and T-5 short-range ballistic missiles . . . 10-kt bombs are [also] carried by A-5 fighter bombers and M-series missiles (M-9, M-11) carry tactical nuclear warheads," all of which presumably could be used for securing tactical gains on the Himalayan battlefields. See Sahgal and Singh, "Nuclear Threat from China: An Appraisal," p. 31.

[43]D. Som Dutt, *The Defense of India's Northern Borders*, Adelphi Paper No. 25 (London: IISS, 1966), pp. 8–9.

gic ones as well. As one Indian military analysis argued, these weapons "could be used to facilitate offensive designs [and to] neutralise enemy threat[s] and target communication centers"[44]—which, in the context of a ground offensive against India, would entail a large number of Chinese strikes in the Sikkim, Arunachal Pradesh, and Ladakh sectors as follows:

> **Sikkim Sector.** The strategic aim would be to slice the northeast from the rest of India by linking up with Bangladesh through the strategic Chumbi Valley. Bagdogra airfield could be a quasi-strategic target. Tactical nuclear strikes could be launched on important localities.
>
> **Arunachal Pradesh.** The strategic aim could be to block the Siliguri Corridor by a nuclear strike on a suitable road-rail bottleneck. The rest of the tactical scenario could be the same as for the Sikkim sector.
>
> **Ladakh Sector.** Routes into Ladakh could be blocked by suitable low-yield TNWs, thus severely restricting the Indian Army's ability to reinforce forward localities. A Sino-Pak collusion in this sector cannot be ruled out.[45]

While such contingencies are certainly within the realm of possibility when viewed at an abstract level, they do invoke the question previously raised about proportionality: Which of China's political interests in South Asia demand the use of strategic nuclear weaponry and toward what end? Even assuming that the existing nuclear powers do not intervene in such a context—thereby going against both their own self-interest and the negative and positive security guarantees accorded to India as part of its decision to renounce nuclear acquisition—China's actual use of nuclear force in either a battlefield or a strategic context for the purpose of increasing the prospects of conventional victory borders on the incredible given its marginal territorial interests in South Asia. It is therefore the character of these interests more than any other that serves to nullify Indian claims

---

[44]Sahgal and Singh, "Nuclear Threat from China: An Appraisal," p. 32.

[45]Ibid.

asserting that the "Chinese threat of low-yield nuclear weapons usage on the Himalayan battlefield is real."[46]

It should also be noted that in all contingencies relating to Pakistani or Chinese nuclear use or to the threats thereof, the international community—especially the other established nuclear powers—would have compelling reasons to intervene on behalf of a nonnuclear India in the event of a conflict. This is not because the latter would simply invoke its security guarantees—as is loosely presumed by Alternative I—but more significantly because it is in the great powers' interests to prevent nuclear coercion so as to ensure the viability of the global nonproliferation regime. Any nuclear use or threats thereof would imperil the existing nonproliferation order, and any successful use or threats thereof would imperil it even more. Consequently, the great powers would have substantial cause to intervene on behalf of a nonnuclear state threatened by another not merely out of political or legal obligation but also out of fundamental self-interest.[47] An India that renounced its nuclear option—as would be required by Alternative I—would therefore preserve its security first by maintaining robust conventional capabilities but second by exploiting the great powers' interest in preserving an international order in which nuclear weapons have diminished significance.

This conclusion is vulnerable, of course, to two kinds of criticisms: first, that a nonnuclear India would be placed at a disadvantage simply because no matter how substantial the interests of the great powers might be, New Delhi could never be certain that they would intervene—and that in effect would restrict India's security choices. Second, even if India could obtain ironclad guarantees of intervention (assuming that all the reliability issues connected with such

---

[46]Pravin Sawhney, "Himalayan Conflict Forges Artillery Doctrine," *Jane's International Defence Review*, 32:3 (1999), p. 56. Not surprisingly, India's premier strategic commentator, K. Subrahmanyam, acknowledged, "It is not a question of Chinese aggression or military threat" but rather the Indian desire for a "balancing arrangement vis-à-vis [growing] Chinese power and influence" that really drives the demand for an Indian nuclear deterrent. See K. Subrahmanyam, "Nuclear India in Global Politics," *World Affairs*, 2:3 (July–September 1998), p. 22.

[47]See the pertinent comments in Fred Charles Iklé, "The Second Coming of the Nuclear Age," *Foreign Affairs*, 75:1 (January–February 1996), pp. 119–128.

guarantees are resolved *ex hypothesi)*, the character and extent of this intervention would become clear only as a crisis evolved. The uncertainties associated with this process, especially if India is not an active part of some alliance, would be disconcerting to New Delhi and would thus make nuclear renunciation less attractive than it first appeared even in the presence of security guarantees. Both of these difficulties, it must be recognized, are essentially grounded in the *levels of risk* India appears willing to bear. This issue will be discussed again later, but the important point is that New Delhi would not be unambiguously vulnerable to nuclear weapons as war-fighting instruments even if it renounced the right to develop such weapons in the face of comparable capabilities possessed by its adversaries.

2. Engaging in blackmail for political concessions. If the first kind of threat to security—the use of nuclear weapons in the context of war—is seen on balance to be less serious than is sometimes imagined, the second kind of threat is more problematic, for it is indeed possible, at least theoretically, that either Pakistan or China could engage in certain blatant forms of nuclear brandishing for purposes of blackmail in the context of a political crisis with India. In the most extreme version of this scenario, a risk-acceptant Pakistani or Chinese decisionmaker might demand that India settle some outstanding political dispute such as Kashmir or the status of the McMahon line on terms issued by the former—or else risk the loss of some major Indian city. Even lesser threats could possibly prove unnerving, as Major General Som Dutt, in one of the earliest and most prescient Indian discussions about the utility of nuclear weapons in the context of a Chinese threat, noted:

> Admittedly, it would hardly be necessary for China actually to use nuclear weapons to achieve such limited aims; but both China and India value a position of influence in Asia, and a process of competition could ensue in which the border states might be a focal point. Thus if China has strategic options which India does not have—or denies herself—then not only is China likely to win the psycho-political game, but she could precipitate a crisis over the border states or elsewhere in which India could be blackmailed into paralysis.[48]

---

[48]Dutt, *India and the Bomb*, p. 1.

Given that Pakistan could easily be substituted for China throughout this passage with no harm to the author's intent, it is obvious that as early as the 1960s several thoughtful analysts were already concerned about the threat of blackmail emanating "from two directions"—challenges that "might develop separately or could combine in a single dangerous threat, in which case India would find herself in an extremely difficult position."[49]

While the problem of nuclear blackmail is indeed serious, the difficulties it would pose should not be overstated, especially in the context of "compellance" strategies geared toward the pursuit of limited aims. In fact, an India that renounced nuclear weapons under the terms of Alternative I could respond to even the most extreme intimidation in one or more ways. To begin with, it could simply disregard such blackmail and challenge its assailants to make good on their threats.[50] Alternatively, it could respond by declaring that any use of nuclear force by either state would be dealt with "appropriately"—which, in the case of Pakistan, could involve a conventional response that would end only with the permanent subjugation and occupation of Pakistan itself. A Pakistani decisionmaker who proceeded to act on his threat in the face of such a counterthreat may not be deterred by an Indian nuclear arsenal either, and hence deterrence breakdown in this instance may not be a product of New Delhi's renunciation of its nuclear option. Whether Pakistan's efforts at compellance are deterred in this instance would admittedly be a function of the size and character of Islamabad's nuclear arsenal in relation to India's conventional capabilities, India's nuclear defense preparedness, and, finally, the balance of resolve present on both sides.

A Chinese nuclear threat, however, could not be dealt with in a similar manner because an Indian counterthreat that proposed conventional retaliation in response to Beijing's nuclear brandishing would simply be meaningless. In this instance, India would therefore need to invoke the positive security assurances derived from the

---

[49]Ibid. For more on this issue, see also Sisir Gupta, "The Indian Dilemma," in Alastair Buchan (ed.), *A World of Nuclear Powers?* (Englewood Cliffs, NJ: Prentice-Hall, 1966), pp. 55–67.

[50]Major General S. N. Antia, in Sundarji, *Effects of Nuclear Asymmetry on Conventional Deterrence*, pp. 21–22.

nuclear-armed great powers—the condition that made its nuclear renunciation operative in the first place—to checkmate China's efforts at blackmail. Such an option would of course be available even in a contingency involving Pakistan, but the need to invoke such protection would be less pressing in the case of Pakistan than for China. Here again, a prudent Indian security manager who might otherwise justifiably doubt the credibility of such guarantees would have less cause to do so for two reasons.

First, it should be obvious that since the success of nuclear blackmail would seriously undermine the stability of the global nonproliferation regime, this is one instance in which the established nuclear powers—especially the United States—would have a vested interest in intervening on India's behalf. Indeed, successful Chinese or Pakistani blackmail would simply provide an object lesson to other states, *including those already within the existing nonproliferation regime*, that acquiring nuclear weapons pays off—i.e., that such weapons do in fact allow certain desired political objectives to be attained, and that any renunciation of these weapons must therefore be reconsidered in light of the potential benefits that can be derived from their acquisition.

Second, so long as positive security guarantees are secured from states more powerful and capable than either China or Pakistan, there should be every reason for India to expect such guarantees to be credible. Indeed, the problem with extended deterrence in general lies not in the extension of nuclear guarantees per se but rather in whom those guarantees are directed against. U.S. nuclear guarantees to Europe during the Cold War, for example, became less and less credible over time because the assailant the United States sought to contain gradually grew more and more powerful, finally reaching parity with the United States at least as far as its nuclear capabilities were concerned.[51] By contrast, neither China nor Pakistan is likely to reach parity with the United States or, for that matter, with Russia in the foreseeable future, assuming that one or both of these states would in fact serve as guarantors of India's security if the latter decided to renounce its nuclear weapon option under Alternative I.

---

[51]The challenges the United States faced as parity unfolded are explored in Anthony H. Cordesman, *Deterrence in the 1980s: Part I, American Strategic Forces and Extended Deterrence*, Adelphi Paper No. 175 (London: IISS, 1982).

In these circumstances, extended deterrence would not be im-plausible, but the assumption would be that both the United States and Russia would continually preserve their existing nuclear superi-ority vis-à-vis a rising China. This could prove more problematic than it appears, however, because it could require that both great powers violate one of the assumptions inherent in India's choice of Alternative I—i.e., that both the United States and Russia accelerate the pace of reductions in their nuclear arsenals.[52] Choosing Alterna-tive I thus requires that India accept the fact that decreasing the size and capabilities inherent in some nuclear stockpiles may not be so desirable after all—which of course suggests in turn that there is at least one less reason for New Delhi to choose Alternative I to begin with.

In any event, this analysis suggests that coping with nuclear blackmail in the absence of one's own nuclear capabilities remains a thorny problem for India. To be sure, the most extreme forms of nu-clear brandishing by China or Pakistan could be dealt with, but only if India's leadership remained sufficiently risk-acceptant to challenge either assailant to make good on their threats. If China in particular were to carry through with these threats, however, India would sim-ply lose, since it would possess no conventional or nonconventional countervailing capability to punish China in return—at least imme-diately. Because India possesses significant conventional punish-ment capabilities vis-à-vis Pakistan, coping with the maximal threats that could emerge from Islamabad could be a lesser problem for New Delhi so long as Pakistan's nuclear arsenal remained minuscule. This would not be the case, however, if Pakistan's nuclear capabilities were to increase over time or if India's leadership turned out to be susceptible to paralysis in the event of a crisis. A steely resolve and strong conventional forces would thus be essential for coping with blatant coercion on the part of either China or Pakistan, but in both cases India would remain relatively vulnerable if it lacked nuclear weaponry of its own. India could even win some "games of chicken" in these circumstances, but it is unlikely that its leadership would be

---

[52]This is in fact one of the principal arguments advanced in the United States against nuclear abolition. See, for example, Kathleen C. Bailey, "Proliferation: Impli-cations for U.S. Deterrence," in Kathleen C. Bailey (ed.), *Weapons of Mass Destruction: Costs Versus Benefits* (New Delhi: Manohar, 1994), pp. 133–143.

content with the kind of security that would derive primarily from self-restraint exercised by its adversaries.[53]

Where less-than-maximal threats are concerned, the issue of New Delhi's immunity to coercion is equally problematic. To be sure, India does possess the requisite conventional capabilities that would deny either of its adversaries the gains it might seek on the battlefield, but the effectiveness of this force in the presence of even modest nuclear threats is limited.[54] India's current land and air forces do not possess the intelligence, mobility, protection, and reconstitution capabilities at the operational level that would allow them to maintain high levels of war-fighting effectiveness even in the face of limited nuclear threats. Therefore, neutralizing such threats would again require that India gamble on its advantages (if any) in the balance of resolve or, more significantly, rely on external guarantees to ensure its safety. Only durable external support could decisively resolve the problem of blackmail in such circumstances—but as Indian policymakers are acutely aware, relying on such assistance brings with it a new set of uncertainties while also implying the loss of political autonomy—a prospect that is not at all attractive to India, given its considerable size and past experience of colonialism.[55]

3. Low-intensity conflicts. The third form of manifested threat—subtle nuclear coercion through low-intensity conflict, waged with the expectation that New Delhi could not threaten nuclear or possibly even conventional retaliation—further illustrates the tensions inherent in relying on extended deterrence. Nuclear-shadowed low-intensity conflicts represent a highly subtle form of strategic coercion in that they do not exemplify manifest nuclear threats; rather, they involve the support of domestic dissidence in the targeted country, with the assailant's nuclear capabilities serving primarily as the strategic cover preventing the targeted state from directly retaliating

---

[53]On the logic of such games, see Schelling, *Arms and Influence*, pp. 116–120.

[54]This, at any rate, appears to be the dominant view in the Indian military, as expressed through the arguments found in Sundarji, *Effects of Nuclear Asymmetry on Conventional Deterrence*.

[55]The critical importance of both these variables insofar as they influence the desire for autonomy in Indian grand strategy is explored in detail in Kanti Bajpai, "India: Modified Structuralism," in Muthiah Alagappa (ed.), *Asian Security Practice* (Stanford, CA: Stanford University Press, 1998), pp. 157–197.

through conventional or nuclear means because of the unacceptable costs that such retaliation would presumably entail. Both China and Pakistan have engaged in such unconventional conflicts with India in the past: China supported various insurgency groups in the Indian northeast until about the 1980s, and Pakistan supported the Sikh insurgency in the Punjab during the mid- to late 1980s, subsequently shifting its support to the Kashmiri insurgency that continues to the present day.[56]

India's traditional response to such unconventional challenges has consisted primarily of a reactive strategy. This strategy, which has included a combination of co-optation and coercion, is distinctive because all the violence the latter element entails has been directed exclusively toward the insurgents and not toward their foreign supporters. Therefore, India's reactive strategy has always involved a conscious effort to maintain peace at the interstate level, even as frenetic military operations are conducted domestically.[57] This activity, which has consisted mainly of small-unit operations within Indian territory alone, deliberately precludes cross-border operations of any kind. To be sure, these operations have often been accompanied by cross-border exchanges of fire, especially in the context of insurgencies receiving support from Pakistan—but such exchanges have been primarily a function of larger Indo-Pakistani disputes and not simply a tactical consequence of the counterinsurgency operations themselves. An India that chose to renounce its nuclear capabilities as required by Alternative I would not find itself handicapped with respect to the pursuit of a reactive strategy in the context of any future

---

[56]India too engaged in low-intensity conflicts (though not nuclear-shadowed low-intensity conflicts) vis-à-vis China and Pakistan in the past. The most prominent example of such activity versus China remains the Indian support (with the collaboration of the CIA) of the Khampa rebellion in the late 1950s and early 1960s in Tibet, and the best example of such activity versus Pakistan remains the assistance offered to the Mukti Bahini in the months leading up to the 1971 war. Since then, however, Indian activities vis-à-vis these two countries appear to have been more restrained; although it is often alleged, especially in Pakistan, that India has supported dissidence both in the Sind and in Karachi, no clear-cut evidence of these activities has publicly surfaced thus far.

[57]An analysis of the larger strategy, including the co-optational political efforts mandated by it, can be found in Gupta, *India Redefines Its Role*, pp. 23–33. The military dimensions of the strategy are well described in Rajesh Rajagopalan, "'Restoring Normalcy': The Evolution of the Indian Army's Counterinsurgency Doctrine," *Small Wars and Insurgencies*, 11:1 (Spring 2000), pp. 44–68.

unconventional challenges. This is because India's possession of nuclear weapons would play little role in such a strategy, which hitherto has been dictated primarily by political factors.[58] In fact, to the extent that India's renunciation of nuclear weapons results in increased economic and conventional military capabilities—flowing from increased cooperation with friendly great powers—New Delhi's ability to execute such a reactive strategy might actually be enhanced.

Against this beneficial effect of renunciation, however, arise two possibly deleterious consequences that must also be considered. First, India's renunciation of its nuclear option may lead its adversaries to increase the pace or level of their support to dissidents within India. This course of action may in fact become attractive if the ongoing security competition in South Asia leads India's adversaries to conclude that increased unconventional challenges can now be pursued without any fear of nuclear retaliation and—to the degree that the absence of Indian nuclear capabilities would strip New Delhi of its strategic cover against an adversary's nuclear threats—with less fear of conventional retaliation as well. To be sure, no adversary is likely to increase its unconventional challenges merely because India has renounced its nuclear option. However, India must reckon with the possibility that its adversaries would now possess more opportunities to engage in unconventional conflicts without fear of retaliation than might have been the case had it continued to nurture some kinds of nuclear capabilities. Second, India's renunciation of the nuclear option implies that New Delhi could never shift away from its reactive counterinsurgency strategy in the direction of a more proactive one even if required to do so *in extremis*. Besides merely increasing the intensity of violence directed against the insurgents domestically, a proactive strategy could include cross-border operations such as "hot pursuit" as well as punitive retaliation or shallow joint and combined-arms penetrations into enemy territory. Lacking the requisite nuclear cover, India would be unlikely to contemplate such operations against either a nuclear Pakistan or China without assuming a relatively high degree of risk because it would now be placed in the position of deliberately

---

[58]The reasons beneath the Indian preference for a reactive as opposed to a proactive strategy are explored in Tellis, *Stability in South Asia*, pp. 47–50.

escalating a conflict even if strategic necessity so dictated. It is uncertain whether the positive security guarantees offered by friendly great powers, which are assumed to exist under Alternative I, would be considered operative in the face of such a contingency or even if the negative security assurances previously offered by potential adversaries such as China would be deemed to hold in the context of some hypothetical Indian conventional counterinsurgency operations on Chinese territory.[59]

When the security dimensions of a possible nuclear renunciation by India are therefore taken into account, an apparently paradoxical outcome obtains. Specifically, India appears to be more safe at the high-intensity end of the conflict spectrum than at the low-intensity end: It is safest when an adversary might be tempted to use nuclear weapons as war-fighting instruments in the context of conventional military operations against India; it is less safe when nuclear threats are used as instruments of blackmail; and it is least safe when nuclear weapons become subtle tools of coercion by abetting unconventional conflicts. Renouncing nuclear weapons thus places India at a lesser disadvantage where pure conventional conflicts are concerned and at a greater disadvantage at the level of political crises and unconventional, low-intensity conflicts. On reflection, however, this should not be surprising in that the evolution in political attitudes toward nuclear weapons since the end of World War II has resulted in the diminishing credibility of nuclear use for any contingencies other than stark homeland defense.[60] Since India is unlikely to be confronted by such a contingency, the utility of a nuclear capability is thus lowest in this regard. No evolution in political attitudes, however, can reduce the value of nuclear weapons as more or less subtle instruments of coercion in the context of both unconventional conflicts and political interactions between states. As Paul Bracken noted, "More than anything else, weapons of mass destruction use intimidation and threat for their effect. As in the first nuclear age, brandishing them for political uses is their most potent effect. It

---

[59]For other arguments relating to this issue, see Subrahmanyam, "India: Keeping the Option Open," pp. 133–134.

[60]T. V. Paul, "The Paradox of Power: Nuclear Weapons in a Changed World," *Alternatives*, 20:4 (October–December 1995), pp. 479–500.

is this political effect that is so troubling."[61] What may be more problematic, however, is that nuclear weapons may not even have to be formally brandished in order to secure certain desired political effects; in many instances, their mere presence may suffice to express threats, convey signals, enlarge freedom of action, and bestow psychological advantages on their possessors. As Bracken has correctly argued,

> The Asian states have learned from the West. They have learned how to use nuclear weapons without actually detonating them in an attack, for political maneuvers, implicit threats, deterrence, signaling, drawing lines in the sand, and other forms of psychological advantage. The United States now forgets how it "used" nuclear weapons for forty years to reshape international politics to its advantage—when it deterred Soviet conventional attack on Europe, for instance, or when it went on high alert during the Cuban Missile Crisis and the 1973 Middle East War. The same pattern is appearing in Asia. North Korea uses its (implied) nuclear weapons to thwart outside pressure for reform and to extort free food and oil from the West. India uses nuclear weapons to send a wake-up signal to the United States about its relationship with China, its refusal to accept second-class status among the world's powers. Israel uses nuclear weapons to intimidate the Arabs and to play on their subconscious sense of inferiority. Whether these uses are successful or prudent is beside the point.[62]

What is very much to the point, however, is that the capacity for using nuclear weapons in these subtle but politically effective ways derives from the "residual" potentialities inherent in the possession of nuclear weapons—and consequently it is not surprising that the coercive advantages accruing merely from the ownership of such instruments are manifested more conspicuously when the level of actual violence is itself otherwise restricted.

Concerns about physical safety—half of the security problem—are exacerbated by difficulties with respect to political autonomy, the other dimension of security for all states in the international system. Clearly, nuclear abdication, as defined under the terms of Alternative

---

[61] Paul Bracken, *Fire in the East* (New York: HarperCollins Publishers, 1999), p. xv.
[62] Ibid., p. 97.

I, reduces India's autonomy in a number of ways: It makes New Delhi dependent on the choices, actions, and policies of others, however well intentioned they may be, for its safety; it limits India's own freedom to pursue policies that it may want to undertake for various reasons; and it may even limit India's choice of allies, since not many states are both willing and able to provide the kinds of guarantees that would be necessary to make nuclear abdication a worthwhile option for India. This last consideration is not a trivial one because even the United States—the country most capable of providing nuclear guarantees to India—has historically declined to do so for New Delhi even when the latter was eager to explore this alternative in lieu of developing its own nuclear deterrent (e.g., during the 1960s).[63] Indeed, the preoccupation with autonomy continues to dominate policymaking in New Delhi with respect to nuclear issues. In part, this is because of the country's legacy of colonialism, which reinforces India's determination never to become subject again to the control of outsiders—but it is also a function of New Delhi's perceptions of India's size and potential power, which, taken together, reinforce its basic beliefs about the country's greatness and claims to recognition. Together, these factors combine to make a return to dependence on others distasteful—and hence any alternative that entails a loss of autonomy, in addition to the foregoing concerns about safety, is unlikely to dominate the decision space with respect to future nuclear capabilities in India. India's Foreign Minister, Jaswant Singh, reaffirmed this conclusion in the following words:

> We cannot have a situation in which some countries say, "We have a permanent right to these symbols of deterrence and of power; all of the rest of you . . . do not have that right. We will decide what your security is and how you are to deal with that security." A country the size of India—not simply a sixth of the human race, but also an ancient civilization—cannot in this fashion abdicate its responsibility.[64]

---

[63]For an assessment of past Indian efforts to obtain security guarantees, see A. G. Noorani, "India's Quest for a Nuclear Guarantee," *Asian Survey*, 7:7 (July 1967), pp. 490–502.

[64]Mike Shuster, interview with Jaswant Singh, *All Things Considered,* National Public Radio, June 11, 1998. Not surprisingly, similar sentiments are held by other nuclear powers who have perceived their nuclear weaponry as providing, besides strategic deterrence and political prestige, the ultimate guarantee of political independence

Recognizing these myriad considerations with respect to physical safety and political autonomy is finally important for one additional reason that is of particular significance to this book: that India's perceptions of its vulnerabilities will define the kinds of nuclear capabilities New Delhi will seek to develop, and perhaps make manifest, in the future. In that sense, understanding the nature of the multiple challenges India faces with respect to nuclear abdication provides a good indication of the ends to which its future nuclear efforts are likely to be directed, especially if the second alternative involving denuclearization—a regional nuclear weapon–free zone (to be discussed below)—is also perceived to be untenable.

Flexibility. If the security implications of nuclear renunciation embodied in Alternative I are thus seen to be something of a mixed bag, how does this alternative hold up when measured against the criterion of strategic flexibility? Here the answer is as unambiguous as it should be reassuring to New Delhi: India's strategic flexibility is abundantly preserved under Alternative I. Under this alternative, India can continue to produce plutonium for its fissile-material stockpile; can continue to develop various delivery systems and even deploy some of them, if necessary, with advanced conventional warheads; and can continue to think about and debate the conditions that may require a reversal of its nuclear policy, even as it could begin to develop the enabling systems that would increase its nuclear effectiveness if such a breakout becomes necessary. Thus, India's renouncement of the nuclear option under the terms of Alternative I does not in any sense strip it of its nuclear capabilities permanently. In fact, choosing this alternative may not materially alter very much in comparison to India's condition of being a de facto nuclear state, at least as that was expressed between 1974 and 1992. India will retain physical possession of its nuclear materials, its research establishment, and its development complexes. It will simply subsist as a "virtual nuclear power" like Japan or Germany today—i.e., as a state that has the ability to rapidly develop a nuclear arsenal but that chooses not to do so for political reasons.[65] If strategic necessities

---

and decisional autonomy. See Ian Smart, "The Great Engine: The Rise and Decline of a Nuclear Age," *International Affairs*, 51 (October 1975), pp. 544–553.

[65]These states were in fact presumed to be prime examples of "latent proliferation" in the 1970s, and concerns about their "latent arsenals" occasionally surface to this day. See Ted Greenwood, Harold A. Feiveson, and Theodore B. Taylor, *Nuclear*

demand it, this posture can always be reversed. While a decision to that effect should not and certainly would not be made lightly, it would not violate any international agreements; it would merely entail a reversal of national policy. And while such a reversal may not be cost-free, depending on the circumstances under which it is made, it nonetheless does not involve any permanent constraints on India's freedom of action with respect to nuclear choices—something New Delhi is always suspicious about—except those it voluntarily accedes to and that in the larger framework of international politics cannot be truly permanent anyway.

Status. Although Alternative I does not constrain India's strategic flexibility, it would not necessarily result in a clear improvement of India's status in the international system. The claim that this proposition embodies should not be misunderstood. An India that renounces nuclear weapons—as is sought, for example, by the traditional U.S. policy toward South Asia—can improve its status in international politics, but a great deal depends both on whether the existing great powers are capable of supporting a redefinition of global preeminence and on India's own domestic achievements in the interim. Since the beginning of modernity, great-power status in the international system has been defined primarily by a state's possession of comprehensive military capabilities, which today include, among other things, the possession of nuclear weapons. These capabilities bequeath to great powers a qualitatively different kind of autonomy from that which other states enjoy, and these differential levels of autonomy are institutionally recognized through the veto system in the U.N. Security Council.[66]

To be sure, it is possible that the great powers today could move in the direction of changing the prevailing force-centered concept of power in international politics. They could, for example, institution-

---

Proliferation: Motivations, Capabilities, Strategies for Control (New York: McGraw-Hill, 1977); Harold Feiveson, "Proliferation Resistant Nuclear Fuel Cycle," *Annual Review of Energy*, 3 (1978), pp. 357–394; and Motoya Kitamura, "Japan's Plutonium Program: A Proliferation Threat?" *Nonproliferation Review*, 3:2 (Winter 1996), pp. 1–16.

[66]John Lewis Gaddis has in fact argued that nuclear weaponry embodied a power gradient that helped distinguish the superpowers from the rest of the global system. See John Lewis Gaddis, "Nuclear Weapons, the End of the Cold War, and the Future of the International System," in Patrick Garrity and Steven A. Maaranen (eds.), *Nuclear Weapons in a Changing World* (New York: Plenum Press, 1992), p. 24.

ally include states that have demonstrated great economic achievements, such as Japan and Germany, or states that possess great potential capabilities—such as Brazil, India, and Indonesia—into the *sanctum sanctorum* of international governance, giving such entities the full veto powers enjoyed by the existing nuclear weapon states. Such a movement would clearly indicate that the great powers are prepared to concede that a broader view of global status can reap benefits for international politics, including the preservation of a structurally unequal but desirable nuclear regime. Whether such a restructuring is appropriate all told is a separate issue, but the fact remains that if carried out, it would constitute a radical reform of the global hierarchy of prestige and, as such, could result in India's renouncement of its nuclear option in the manner envisaged in Alternative I in exchange for the attainment of great-power status.

It is highly unlikely, however, that such a restructuring of the international order could in fact be carried out—for even if the United States, in a moment of optimism, were to successfully complete some of the many plans now being contemplated for the expansion of the U.N. Security Council, it is likely that the resulting reorganization will become increasingly incongruous over time. This incongruity will result from the fact that because international politics has not been radically transformed with respect to its "deep structure"[67]—meaning that self-regarding states and their relative distribution of capabilities will remain central to the ordering of international affairs—any expansion of the "superstructure" of international governance to include countries that do not possess comprehensive military power will be condemned to failure or eventual irrelevance.[68] This disjuncture will be less problematic as long as the new entrants' interests coincide with those of the United States, but should such interests diverge over time, these entrants will be forced to acquire new military capabilities of the sort they had previously eschewed in order to maintain their security, status, and autonomy independent of U.S. support. Over the long run, therefore, the true

---

[67]For more on this notion, see John Gerard Ruggie, "Continuity and Transformation in the World Polity: Toward a Neorealist Synthesis," in Robert O. Keohane (ed.), *Neorealism and its Critics* (New York: Columbia University Press, 1986), pp. 131–157.

[68]For an excellent discussion of how power and prestige are related in international politics, see Robert Gilpin, *War and Change in International Politics* (Cambridge, UK: Cambridge University Press, 1981).

great powers in international politics will continue to be those that possess an abundance of military capabilities, and any interim efforts to abridge this fundamental reality are likely to enjoy only transient success.

Where India is concerned, this simply means that New Delhi will be reluctant to trade its military power—including its nuclear capabilities—for a great-power status that is artificially constructed as a result of prevailing U.S. strategic imperatives. This kind of status, which would ultimately be viewed as impermanent, would only strengthen New Delhi's resolve to develop those capabilities which would assure "true" great-power status over time and would thus render New Delhi likely to further pursue rather than abdicate the acquisition of comprehensive national power. Because acquiring these capabilities is fundamentally linked to how successfully India can complete its own internal economic transformation, it is likely that New Delhi, despite both the domestic obstacles to reform and the multiple trade-offs it confronts between acquiring military power and economic strength, will ploddingly pursue the former while attempting as best it can to minimize the difficulties caused by the latter. The benefits of choosing Alternative I will thus continue to be uncertain as far as India's desire to enhance its status is concerned, because the fundamental transformation of international politics is still improbable. Consequently, India is unlikely to divest itself of its nuclear capabilities even if that might allow for more rapid economic growth in the short run.[69]

Alternative II: A Regional "Nuclear-Free Zone"

In contrast, Alternative II—developing regional arrangements to enforce denuclearization—could in principle provide a better solution to India's strategic quandaries, but it too is unlikely to come to fruition for reasons that have as much to do with Indian preferences and those of its partners as with the structural contradictions inherent in the idea itself. In effect, Alternative II requires that India eschew its nuclear weapon program in the context of developing a regional nuclear control regime that binds Pakistan, its near-term

---

[69]For a succinct report of Indian perceptions on this issue, see Crossette, "Why India Thinks Atomic Equation Has Changed."

competitor, to an identical obligation while merely restraining China, its long-term competitor, from mounting nuclear threats through constraints on the deployment of its weaponry. Many variants of this idea have been discussed within the nonproliferation community as well as by various official U.S. spokesmen over the years. Indeed, these ideas were fairly common throughout the 1970s and early 1980s, when the U.S. government began to invest considerable energy in attempting to roll back the growing momentum toward South Asian nuclearization. Interestingly, the earliest demands for a South Asian nuclear-free zone emanated from some of the regional states themselves; Zulfikar Ali Bhutto in particular— despite having initiated Pakistan's own nuclear weapon development program in January 1972 (immediately after its defeat in the 1971 war)—is credited with "work[ing] very hard for the establishment of a nuclear-free zone in the area."[70]

Pakistan's calls for regional denuclearization—which grew in intensity throughout the 1970s, especially after India's first nuclear test in 1974—were enthusiastically supported by China, in part because these early formulations explicitly excluded Beijing from the obligations they imposed and, as such, did not burden China with any requirement to modify its own nuclear posture vis-à-vis India.[71] China's support was also influenced by the existing antagonisms of the time, as an early Chinese commentary made amply evident:

> We hold the Pakistan proposal for the establishment of a nuclear-free zone in South Asia is just and reasonable. . . . The South Asian subcontinent has seen the intensifying contention between the two superpowers, one of which has supported the expansionist policies of a certain country in the region . . . if the desire for the establishment of a nuclear-free zone in South Asia is to be realized, it is imperative to guard against and oppose the superpower intervention and the expansionist acts of any country.[72]

---

[70]Pervaiz Iqbal Cheema, "Pakistan's Quest for Nuclear Technology," *Australian Outlook*, 34:2 (1980), p. 194.

[71]J. Mohan Malik, "China and South Asian Nuclear-Free Zone," *China Report*, 25:2 (1989), pp. 113–119.

[72]"Proposals for Establishing Nuclear-Free Zones," *Peking Review*, 50 (December 13, 1974), pp. 15–16.

Predictably, all such proposals were immediately rejected by India, which viewed Beijing's support for these initiatives as being opportunistic.[73] As K. Subrahmanyam argued,

> [Chinese] nuclear missiles on the Tibetan plateau are sitting ducks vis-à-vis the USSR but terrifying instruments of intimidation in respect of India. Half of China lies south of Kashmir and geographically China is part of South Asia. Pakistanis always insist that China is a South Asian country with legitimate interests in the area. Therefore leaving China out of a regional nuclear security arrangement can only be intended to disarm India vis-à-vis China and subject it to the latter's domination.[74]

The complications caused by China's presence as a nuclear weapon state abutting the South Asian landmass gradually began to be appreciated in Pakistan as well, and subsequent formulations of Pakistan's nuclear-free zone proposal thus incorporated additional safeguards that were intended to make the idea palatable to India, at least at a rhetorical level. General Zia-ul-Haq's version of the concept, for example—first advanced in 1979—required that "the Indian Ocean, the entire region, be declared a denuclearized zone, and . . . that the have-not . . . be granted guarantees by the countries having such weapons."[75] Pakistani Foreign Minister Shahabzada Yakub Khan further developed this idea when he proposed in 1987 not only that the established regional nuclear weapon states—meaning China—provide legally binding assurances never to use or threaten to use nuclear weapons against the South Asian countries but also that "they . . . be asked not to deploy nuclear weapons adjacent to the region or to remove them where such deployments already exist."[76]

This latest version of Pakistan's proposal, which exemplifies the idea of limited regional nuclear arms control, is attractive for purposes of discussing the prospect that India might adopt some variant

---

[73]P. S. Jayaramu, "Nuclear Weapons–Free Zone, Non-Proliferation Treaty and South Asia," *IDSA Journal*, 13:1 (July–September 1980), pp. 133–147.

[74]K. Subrahmanyam, "Countering Zia's Proposals," *The Times of India*, July 4, 1987.

[75]Joint Publications Research Service, *Worldwide Report: Nuclear Development and Proliferation*, 36 (March 28, 1980), pp. 34–35.

[76]Cited in Malik, "China and South Asian Nuclear-Free Zone," p. 117.

of Alternative II, since it attempts to address the most pressing concerns that New Delhi has articulated almost continuously since 1964. Not surprisingly, some version of this idea arises every now and then, often in association with the occasional calls for a dialogue between China, India, and Pakistan on nuclear and other strategic issues.[77] Most of these proposals require that China's nuclear capabilities be constrained simply because they cannot be eliminated in that China, by an accident of history, became a full-fledged nuclear power before India did. Restricting but not eliminating China's nuclear weapon program is also implicitly justified by the common strategic belief that the Indian subcontinent represents a security complex in which the principal amity-enmity relationship is defined by India and Pakistan, with China simply abutting the subcontinent rather than being a direct participant within it. Since China's own strategic focus appears to be directed more toward East Asia than to its southwest, the rationale for such a belief would appear to be reinforced. As noted earlier, one analyst has in fact argued that Beijing's cancellation of the DF-25 missile implies that China no longer poses a nuclear and missile threat to the subcontinent and thus should not serve as an excuse for India to continue its own nuclear weapon programs.[78] Such assessments, some Indian analysts have argued, require that New Delhi seriously consider the opportunity offered by a regional nuclear control regime of the kind embodied in Alternative II.[79]

It is indeed certain that India's security would be enhanced by institutionalizing robust regional nuclear constraints that would free India from becoming a target of its competitors' nuclear weapons. The only problem with such a solution, however—at least in the first instance—resides in the preferences of those competitors. It is unlikely, for example, that Pakistan—which has traditionally claimed that it would be willing to give up its nuclear option "one minute" after India does so—would actually accede to any proposals for regional denuclearization even if India were suddenly to accept such

---

[77]See, for example, Kathleen Bailey and Satoshi Morimoto, "A Proposal for a South Asian Intermediate Nuclear Forces Treaty," *Comparative Strategy*, 17:2 (1998), pp. 185–195.

[78]Arnett, "What Threat?"

[79]Bidwai, "Nuclear Policy in a Mess," and Achin Vanaik, "Since the Pokhran Tests," *Seminar*, 485 (January 2000), pp. 51–56.

arrangements for its own reasons. This reluctance on Islamabad's part is rooted not in mendacity but rather in old, self-interested reasons of survival. Given Pakistan's strategic circumstances, it should not be surprising to find that almost all Pakistanis believe—using the words of Zafar Iqbal Cheema—that

> only Pakistan's ability to build . . . a [nuclear] deterrent can neutralize India's broad regional dominance. In their calculations, the acquisition of a nuclear weapons capability can deter India's conventional military threat by raising the cost of conflict to unacceptably high levels. The historical record of Pakistan's alliances with the U.S. and the West, where the big powers have not shown any willingness to become embroiled militarily in the Indo-Pakistani conventional wars, also confirms the belief . . . that no state will safeguard Pakistan's security in a confrontation with India. Nuclear proponents in Pakistan believe that nuclear weapons provide the ultimate guarantee of regional security. The recent Sino-Indian rapprochement also makes Pakistanis feel increasingly insecure. If realized, the stipulated Sino-Indian accords could chip away Pakistan's margin of diplomatic maneuvering. *Envisioning this, Pakistanis are unlikely to show great willingness to abandon the nuclear option* [italics added].[80]

To be sure, most Pakistani elites understand that a subcontinent freed of nuclear weapons would certainly spare their state the horror of absorbing nuclear attacks in the context of an all-out war with India. Yet while the threat of such attacks is indeed disconcerting, Pakistan's special vulnerabilities—flowing from its smaller size, the heavy concentration of its population and industrial assets within a very small target set, and its extreme vulnerability to destruction caused by the interdiction of a few critical nodes relating to irrigation, communications, and power generation—make its security managers especially sensitive to the consequences of strategic inter-

---

[80]Zafar Iqbal Cheema, "Pakistan's Nuclear Policies: Attitudes and Posture," in P. R. Chari, Pervaiz Iqbal Cheema, and Iftekharuzzaman (eds.), *Nuclear Non-Proliferation in India and Pakistan* (New Delhi: Manohar, 1996), p. 120. It should be noted that although Cheema's conclusion, save for the last sentence in the quotation, originally described the position of the "pro-bomb" lobby in Pakistan, this conclusion could be safely deemed to describe the attitude of the vast majority of Pakistani citizens today. See Zafar Iqbal Cheema, "Pakistan's Nuclear Use Doctrine and Command and Control," in Peter R. Lavoy, Scott D. Sagan, and James J. Wirtz (eds.), *Planning the Unthinkable* (Ithaca, NY: Cornell University Press, 2000), pp. 158–181.

diction.[81] Not surprisingly, then, Pakistani policymakers have traditionally sought to cope with this problem by developing a modest nuclear deterrent of their own even as they have simultaneously put forth an array of nuclear arms control proposals designed to limit the size and shape of India's nuclear capabilities. This response in fact led one prominent U.S. analyst to argue that Islamabad's efforts to "advance the prospects of mutual nuclear restraint" in South Asia have been so numerous as to constitute the "second track of its nuclear policy for more than a decade."[82] This effort was obviously seen as being "aimed at placing limits on India's nuclear potential, even as Pakistan sought to achieve a nuclear weapons capability of its own."[83]

While a nuclear-free South Asia would certainly relieve Islamabad of many of the unnerving burdens arising from its possession of nuclear weaponry—i.e., high costs, enhanced vulnerability, and deepening immizerization—it is unclear in the final analysis whether such a scenario would improve Pakistan's security across the board. This is because a nuclear-free Pakistan would still have to contend with the specter of India's conventional superiority, which has only been further enhanced—especially in the realms of air and naval power—since the Pressler Amendment's restrictions became operative in 1990. Islamabad is thus confronted by a difficult conundrum in the context of a possible war with India: In effect, nuclear weapons in South Asia increase the risks that could lead to Pakistan's utter and irrevocable demise, but the absence of such weapons also increases the risk of its loss of autonomy and perhaps even physical security. Given this dilemma, it is unlikely that Pakistan has any serious incentive to make good on the many nuclear arms control proposals it has put forth in the past, even if such proposals were somehow to be accepted by India[84]—as such an outcome would only institutionalize

---

[81]See, for example, Kamal Matinuddin, "The Missile Threat," *The News*, March 2, 1997, and Ayaz Ahmed Khan, "Countering the Prithvi Threat," *The Nation*, June 30, 1997.

[82]Leonard S. Spector, *The Undeclared Bomb* (Cambridge, MA: Ballinger Publishing Company, 1988), p. 130.

[83]Leonard S. Spector (with Jacqueline R. Smith), *Nuclear Ambitions* (Boulder, CO: Westview Press, 1990), p. 98.

[84]A useful survey of Pakistan's arms control proposals can be found in Niaz A. Naik, "Towards a Nuclear-Safe South Asia: A Pakistani Perspective," in David O. Smith

India's threatening military superiority. Consequently, Islamabad's arms control proposals have probably been more of a diplomatic exercise than an agenda designed to increase its security. So long as Islamabad was certain that India would reject such proposals, thanks to its own concerns about China and its obsession with redressing global inequality, there was every reason to offer numerous nuclear arms control measures with alacrity, since Pakistan could be fully confident that it would never have to make good on any of its proposed commitments. This strategy, in effect, suggests that Dr. A. Q. Khan's celebrated claim that "Pakistan's future policy is to remain closely tied to Indian actions"[85] was true but held in only one direction: further nuclearization and not the other way around.

This judgment is corroborated by crucial Pakistani decisions reached after Pakistan's own May 1998 tests at Chagai: Faced with the prospect that New Delhi might sign the CTBT in the aftermath of its second test series, Islamabad for the first time formally unlinked its own position on the treaty from that of India.[86] This in effect implies that even if India were to accede to the CTBT for its own reasons, there would be no such automatic accession on the part of Pakistan, since the effects of a permanent moratorium on nuclear testing are perceived to be sufficiently deleterious to warrant forgoing even those benefits that may accrue from marching in lockstep with New Delhi on this issue. On balance, these considerations imply that nuclear weapon capabilities will continue to exist in South Asia—an outcome that is certainly not cost-free for Pakistan but is still better than most other conceivable alternatives (especially when viewed over the long term) as nuclear weapons simply provide the best means of preserving Pakistan's security without compromising its autonomy. Indeed, this is an outcome that Pakistan has always

---

(ed.), *From Containment to Stability: Pakistan–United States Relations in the Post–Cold War Era* (Washington, D.C.: National Defense University, 1993), pp. 41–50.

[85]A. Q. Khan, "The Spread of Nuclear Weapons Among Nations: Militarization or Development," in Sadruddin Agha Khan (ed.), *Nuclear War, Nuclear Proliferation and Their Consequences* (Oxford, UK: Clarendon Press, 1986), p. 423.

[86]Shaheen Sehbai, "Pakistan Reassessing Position on CTBT," *Dawn*, July 1, 1998. The implications of this event are analyzed in Agha Shahi, "Talbott's Visit: Would Delinking Pakistan's Signing of CTBT with India's Signing Serve the National Interest?" *Pakistan Link*, July 24, 1998.

longed for, especially since it has learned that even its previous sacrifice of autonomy, undertaken in the days of its dependence on foreign allies, was ultimately insufficient to the task of preserving its security. Thus, so long as the actual *use* of nuclear weapons can be avoided, these devices will continue to provide Pakistan with a degree of reassurance that it would not be willing to sacrifice through any regional—or even global—agreements pertaining to nuclear disarmament.[87]

While Pakistan's reasons for rejecting a regional nuclear arms control regime—including those that Pakistan itself may have proposed—ultimately hinge on perceptions of its strategic weakness, China's reasons for rejecting such an arrangement would probably be rooted in its strength. Indeed, a regional nuclear regime that placed restraints on Chinese nuclear deployments—for example, on the Tibetan plateau or elsewhere—would be uninteresting to Beijing simply because it would entail giving up actual capabilities merely to avoid a notional counterthreat from India.[88] Complicating matters further, no deployment restrictions whatsoever would eliminate the Chinese nuclear threat, since Beijing already possesses delivery systems of sufficiently long range to make all geographic restrictions on deployment utterly meaningless.[89] Moreover, many Chinese nuclear delivery systems are mobile, meaning that deployment constraints could be rapidly circumvented in a crisis. All future modernization of China's land-based strategic forces will, in fact, center on the deployment of true road-mobile, solid-fueled missile systems like the DF-31 and DF-41, both of which would be

---

[87]See the comments in Neil Joeck, "Nuclear Proliferation and Nuclear Reversal in South Asia," *Comparative Strategy*, 16 (1997), pp. 263–273.

[88]This proposition, of course, has never been seriously tested because China has never treated India as a nuclear state even in the context of its ongoing bilateral dialogue with New Delhi. Despite the fact that this dialogue continued for at least a decade, it is interesting to note that nuclear issues were raised by the Indian delegation publicly—though not really discussed by both sides—for the first time in March 2000. The Chinese response to this issue was simply dismissive of Indian concerns. See "India Rejects China's Call for Rollback," *Hindustan Times*, March 9, 2000.

[89]As one Chinese analyst noted, "China never deployed nuclear weapons in Tibet because of . . . the geographical difficulties of doing so. Nor does China need to do so, since its long-range missiles can reach India from far outside Tibet." Ming Zhang (ed.), *China's Changing Nuclear Posture* (Washington, D.C.: Carnegie Endowment for International Peace, 1999), p. 45.

able to target the entire Asia-Pacific region from any point on the Chinese landmass. The possibility that preagreed deployment constraints could be rapidly circumvented in a crisis either does not apply to sea-based nuclear forces or applies *a fortiori* to air-breathing nuclear carriers. Either way, the problem of regulating Chinese nuclear deployments through spatial restrictions thus invites no easy or useful solutions that might interest India—rendering the notion of a South Asian nuclear-free zone a victim of irresolvable structural contradictions.[90]

Even if some deployment constraints could be negotiated between New Delhi and Beijing despite these problems, the difficulties of verifying Chinese compliance with such agreements would not disappear. India currently has no operational capabilities that could attest to Beijing's adherence to any restricted deployment regime except those involving systematic intrusions into Chinese airspace. While the Mig-25RB aircraft, India's dedicated strategic reconnaissance platform, has optical systems of relatively high (< 1 meter) resolution that are capable of detecting and generally identifying missile TELs, in the absence of cuing by other intelligence sources these aircraft would require repeated surveillance flights over large areas of southwestern and southeastern China if Beijing's missile deployment patterns were to be verified with reasonable confidence.[91] To the extent that the principal Chinese missile systems targeted at India consist of either fixed weapons or merely "movable" systems, verifying their presence at the usual locations would not be unduly difficult—so long as it is presumed, at least for the sake of argument, that the Chinese would tolerate Indian intrusions on their airspace in order to verify compliance with a regional nuclear arms control regime of the sort envisaged by Alternative II. Once China replaces its current weapons with the true road-mobile missile systems envisaged in the

---

[90]For a discussion of these and other structural contradictions in a larger context, see C. Raja Mohan, "Nuclear Free Zones: Illusion and Reality," in K. Subrahmanyam (ed.), *India and the Nuclear Challenge* (New Delhi: Lancer International, 1986), pp. 143–167.

[91]The Indian Mig-25RB's photo-reconnaissance suites are described in Jon Lake, "Mikoyan Mig-25 'Foxbat' and Mig-31 'Foxhound' Variants," *World Air Power Journal*, 34 (Autumn–Fall 1998), p. 115. See also Peter Steinemann, "IAF Recce Intrusion," *Air Power International*, 2:3 (1998), pp. 46–47, for another useful description of Indian Air Force reconnaissance capabilities.

future, however, India's air-breathing reconnaissance systems could well become less effective because in the absence of external cuing, they might not be able to localize these mobile systems independently.[92]

Because India's satellite systems currently cannot provide any effective cuing either, a regional regime of the sort envisaged by Alternative II would require by definition external guarantors who would monitor compliance on a regular basis and provide all parties with impartial evidence about possible ambiguities and violations. Yet it is unlikely that such guarantors could be found, at least at present, because concerns about revealing the quality of one's own surveillance capabilities would prevent even technically proficient states from providing the kind of information that would be necessary to make such a regional arms control agreement hold. As commercial satellite imagery of sufficient resolution—such as that available from the IKONOS system—becomes readily available and as the resolution of India's own remote-sensing systems improves over time, this problem could become less significant—but both of these emerging solutions may still be limited by the challenges of cost, coverage, timeliness, and reliability, not to mention the myriad problems associated with interpreting, analyzing, and integrating the received data at the user end.[93] The issue of whether India can be confident about verification, preferably by its own national technical means,

---

[92]If it is assumed that the 300-mm oblique cameras in the Mig-25RB allow the aircraft to cover a ground swath equal to five times the aircraft's operating altitude of, say, 21,000 meters, the aircraft would be able to cover roughly 200,000 km^2 on a single mission, assuming that the aircraft flies a straight-line 1000-km subsonic patrol over Chinese territory. No mission in practice would follow such a flight profile, and consequently actual coverage would be considerably less than these figures suggest. In any event, even with such coverage India's Mig-25RBs would probably be unable to independently verify the location of all China's mobile missiles in the future—the probability of detection here being greatly influenced by the spatial distribution of these missiles, the extent and quality of their ground mobility, their operational posture in peacetime and during a crisis, the deception and denial practices operationalized by the Second Artillery Corps, and India's ability to sustain unhindered, repetitive reconnaissance missions over large portions of Chinese territory.

[93]See *From Surprise to Reckoning: The Kargil Review Committee Report* (New Delhi: Sage Publications, 2000), pp. 95–136, for a survey of both the technical limitations of India's current reconnaissance systems and the numerous problems India has had in managing intelligence data thus far.

thus remains a significant impediment to the successful conclusion of any agreement of the sort envisaged by Alternative II.

Even if these verification issues can be resolved satisfactorily, however, it is likely that Alternative II, in whatever variant imaginable, will ultimately be doomed in practice because of China's consistent refusal to accept that its strategic capabilities have any bearing on the nuclear programs in South Asia.[94] Indeed, at a diplomatic level China has never considered India to be a nuclear weapon state even though it apparently treats India as a nuclear adversary in the context of its own strategic deterrence posture. This schizoid attitude has led Beijing to consistently attribute India's drive for nuclear capabilities to New Delhi's competition with Islamabad and to its quest for global recognition, neither of which is presumed to have any relationship whatsoever to China, its regional behavior, or its strategic nuclear capabilities. China's dismissive attitude toward India did not change even in the aftermath of the May 1998 tests, but it has been supplemented by a determination to avoid formally granting New Delhi anything that even remotely resembles recognition as a de facto nuclear state.[95] Despite the gradual stabilization of Sino-Indian diplomatic relations, the background condition of mutual suspicion thus remains intact. As one perceptive analyst concluded almost a decade ago,

> the Sino-Indian relationship is . . . an uneasy one. India still regards nuclear China as a major threat to its security. It sees China's South Asian policies as anti-Indian, divisive, opportunistic, and interfering. China for its part perceives India to be an ambitious, overconfident, yet militarily powerful neighbor with whom it may eventually have to have a day of reckoning.[96]

---

[94]The peculiar relationship of China to the Indian subcontinent, especially in nuclear matters, is cogently explored in Jonathan Pollack, "China and Asia's Nuclear Future," in Francine Frankel (ed.), *Bridging the Nonproliferation Divide* (Lanham, MD: University Press of America, 1995), pp. 97–118.

[95]"Give Up N-Programme, China Tells India," *The Hindu*, March 8, 2000.

[96]Gary Klintworth, "Chinese Perspectives on India as a Great Power," in Ross Babbage and Sandy Gordon (eds.), *India's Strategic Future* (New York: St. Martin's Press, 1992), p. 96.

With attitudes such as these continuing to define the tenor of Sino-Indian relations, it is not surprising that China would have little interest in supporting a South Asian nuclear-free zone that involves a cooperative redeployment of its nuclear capabilities, just as it is equally certain that India would reject any solution that relied entirely on the presumption of Chinese strategic restraint for its security.

The most attractive element of Alternative II—its potential acceptability to India—thus stands nullified, at least in the first instance, because New Delhi would be unable to find strategic partners with which to consummate such a deal. Pakistan would simply be unable to live with unfettered Indian conventional superiority in perpetuity, while a reliable deployment restriction regime would be unacceptable to Beijing because China considers itself to be irrelevant to nuclear politics in South Asia. Furthermore, such a deployment regime would turn out to be unacceptable to India as well because the range advantages of some present and most future Chinese land-based nuclear systems would make spatial deployment restrictions irrelevant even if the verification challenges associated with such a regime were surmounted.

In the final analysis, however, even if all these problems were somehow to disappear, India's old obsession with countering global "nuclear apartheid" would ultimately put to rest any solution based on a variant of Alternative II. This judgment is corroborated by India's negotiating record in the years leading up to the conclusion of the NPT in 1967, when Indian security managers—faced with the challenge of seeking a creative solution to the emerging nuclear threat embodied by China's embryonic nuclear arsenal—focused not on regional responses of the sort exemplified by a "nuclear weapon–free zone" but rather on global antidotes requiring that "the nuclear threat itself be addressed and eliminated."[97] In this solution, India's traditional opposition to a world characterized by "a nuclear weapon apartheid,"[98] was bolstered by its past failure to secure effective nuclear guarantees from the superpowers, its frustration at being un-

---

[97]Perkovich, *India's Nuclear Bomb*, p. 115.

[98]This phrase was first used by India's representative to the ENDC, V. C. Trivedi, on May 23, 1967, and is cited in Perkovich, *India's Nuclear Bomb*, p. 138.

able to secure an effective global commitment to comprehensive nuclear disarmament, and its growing concern about the nuclear threat emanating from its northern neighbor. As a result, New Delhi was forced to adopt a nuclear posture that effectively provided it with all the moral and political justification it needed to avoid entering into any "discriminatory" agreements that might suggest acquiescing to the permanent possession of nuclear weapons by some while accepting their indefinite abdication by others.

To be sure, it is sometimes suggested that New Delhi might in fact be willing to mute its opposition even to discriminatory arrangements of the sort encoded in a South Asian nuclear-free zone if such arrangements were actually capable of providing India with durable security. However, this proposition has never been formally tested and in fact may even be impossible to test because India's demand for security has at least since 1964 been inextricably linked to the larger problem of affirming its claims to status in the context of a search for global equity.[99] Not surprisingly, then, Alternative II has traditionally been rejected by Indian security managers, at least rhetorically, on the grounds of security alone, even though this opposition actually masks a complex, many-sided calculus that incorporates numerous elements relating to India's postcolonial identity, the burdens of its colonial past, its yearning for a new normatively driven international political order, and more unexceptional concerns about political and strategic safety. This fact notwithstanding, it must be recognized that despite its lack of utility with respect to satisfying India's concerns about security, Alternative II in its best variants would preserve India's strategic flexibility, since it does not require that New Delhi give up its nuclear potential permanently. This potential could always be maintained in some latent form and transformed into nuclear weaponry if circumstances so demanded, albeit at some cost in the context of the prevailing nonproliferation order. These costs, however, would probably be no greater and no less than they are today, so the choice of Alternative II per se cannot be said to significantly impede India's flexibility. Its effects on India's desire to maintain and improve its status, however, are uncertain, as these would depend on the twin considerations identified earlier: the

---

[99]See the arguments in Gordon, "Capping South Asia's Nuclear Weapons Programs," pp. 664–667, and in Perkovich, *India's Nuclear Bomb*, pp. 444–468.

nature of the future international system and India's own political-economic performance. In the final analysis, however, these considerations are less relevant given that the high price of this alternative for both India and its partners would ultimately make it unacceptable as a serious policy alternative for either.

Evaluating Denuclearization

All things considered, therefore, there would seem to be understandable reasons New Delhi has not moved in the direction of denuclearization. This policy shift should not, however, obscure an important insight that emerges from the analysis of the challenges posed by denuclearization: that when all is said and done, nuclear weapons provide India with only ambiguous benefits, not clear and uncontestable advantages. Moreover, such weapons have the least comparative advantage as deterrents to actual nuclear violence by India's adversaries, because so long as New Delhi maintains its traditional policy of military restraint vis-à-vis China and Pakistan, neither of these competitors is well served even by the token use of nuclear weaponry in the face of India's conventional force superiority and in light of the political goals that each has traditionally sought to attain within the subcontinent. Nuclear weapons in the hands of New Delhi have a somewhat greater comparative advantage at deterring any nuclear blackmail that may be mounted by China and Pakistan; however, the more blatant the blackmail, the more incredible the threat, and hence, by implication, the less pressing the need for Indian nuclear weapons. In contrast, the more subtle the blackmail, the more valuable Indian nuclear weapons turn out to be. Even here, however, the primary utility of such weapons derives more from their "psycho-political" value—that is, their potential ability to strengthen the resolve of Indian policymakers in standing up to the sources of blackmail—than from their operational value as instruments of conflict. India's success in vacating such threats will in most instances derive from the effectiveness of its other assets, such as the quality of its diplomacy, the effectiveness of its conventional forces, the robustness of its national cohesion, the adroitness of its elected leadership, and the extent of support it garners from its international allies. Finally, Indian nuclear weapons have the greatest comparative advantage where denying India's adversaries the freedom to wage low-intensity war against India is concerned. Yet even this advantage constitutes a sharp double-edged sword in that New Delhi's nuclear weapons cannot eliminate the freedom enjoyed by India's adversaries to wage subconventional wars against India; they can only eliminate the immunity India's adversaries may believe they enjoy as a result of their asymmetric possession of nuclear weaponry. To the degree that India's nuclear weapons allow New Delhi to compete with its adversaries in like or greater-than-comparable measure—that is, either through the support of subconventional conflicts in their territory or through the prosecution of punitive conventional military operations—New Delhi's nuclear assets could also function as the means by which Indian security sharply deteriorates. This would be particularly true if India's nuclearization engenders strategic responses whose action sequences lead to the actual use of nuclear weapons on one or both sides. In such circumstances, it matters little if the nuclear use arose from rational reasons or as an unfortunate consequence of misperception, miscalculation, or accident, since the net result would in both cases be an unspeakable diminution in India's safety and well-being.

Therefore, even when India's possession of nuclear weapons may have some utility, such weapons appear to bring with them multiple burdens that immediately devalue their attractiveness. When other consequences—such as the high financial burdens of sustaining effective nuclear capabilities, the corrosive effects of those weapons on India's conventional military standing, and the damage wrought by the possession of those weapons to India's claims to exceptionalism in international politics—are factored into the evaluation, the attractiveness of nuclear weapons for India's security, standing, and freedom of action turn out to be narrow indeed.[100] Clearly, where ensuring security is concerned, Alternative I could leave New Delhi more secure than Indian elites generally suggest would be the case, although it would perhaps leave India less secure than the American nonproliferation community is wont to believe. Nonetheless, it would preserve India's strategic flexibility even as its effects on India's future status remain somewhat ambiguous. On balance,

---

[100]As one of India's best younger strategic analysts, C. Raja Mohan, echoing this judgment, pointed out, "It is necessary for India to understand at once the limited role of nuclear weapons in the country's grand strategy and the severe limitations they impose on its immediate security policy." See C. Raja Mohan, "Grand Strategy: Back to Basics," *The Hindu*, January 20, 2000.

therefore—and barring any dramatic changes in the global nuclear environment—India would continue to reject this alternative as a viable end state despite any American entreaties that may be issued in this regard from time to time. Alternative II, for its part, would probably be pursued in principle if it could be translated into a viable solution that adequately addressed both security and equity. Its viability in this regard, however, is precisely the issue—and consequently New Delhi is unlikely to expend much political and diplomatic energy in pursuing it.

Several observers, especially in the United States, have argued that New Delhi's reluctance to pursue denuclearization through either Alternative I or any variant of Alternative II is ultimately linked to India's overweening desire for status, which India sees inextricably linked to the possession of nuclear weapons.[101] While consideration of status will certainly play a role in any decision to eschew Alternative I in the future, what is more likely to be a determining factor is not status or even the pressures of domestic politics, as still others have argued,[102] but rather India's familiar and habitual risk aversion. Given that India is a relatively young and weak state, the country's security managers have generally exhibited a highly conservative approach toward international politics. This trait has usually manifested itself in the form of sluggardly decisionmaking, a general reluctance to use force, and an emphasis on conciliation.[103] In the arena of nuclear politics, high risk aversion, more than any other variable, not only explains why India did not persist with its nuclear testing program after the first detonation in 1974 but also explains why India went to great lengths to depict that test as a "peaceful nuclear explosion" and why, despite many obvious indications to the contrary, India declined until recently to claim that it was a "nuclear weapon state."

---

[101]See, for example, Fareed Zakaria, "Becoming a Great Power, Cheap," *Newsweek*, May 25, 1998, p. 34.

[102]Atul Kohli, "Know India; Don't Overreact," *Christian Science Monitor*, May 18, 1998, and Andrew Mack, "What India Did Was Right for Indians," *Asian Age*, May 21, 1998.

[103]These traits are discussed at some length in Gordon, *India's Rise to Power*, pp. 3–5.

The lack of confidence that India often displays in international politics has led many of its own elites to describe it as a "soft state."[104] While this trait has had many beneficial effects and, indeed, has often been responsible for the perception of India as a moderate entity in world politics, it now turns out to be the very characteristic that prevents New Delhi from taking the bold leap called for by those alternatives involving denuclearization—even if it were possible to convince Indian policymakers that the deleterious effects of their decisions would be marginal compared to their benefits. Being highly risk-averse at least collectively, they are unable to shake off the discomfort that accompanies any surrender of the proverbial "bird in hand" for even greater benefits still out "in the bush." It is here that the sheer uncertainties of an age in transformation weigh most heavily on Indian minds. For while Indian security managers recognize that preserving their nuclear capabilities has cost them much thus far and could cost them even more in the future, they still see these capabilities as worth holding onto because no matter how inadequately they perform the role, nuclear weapons remain the best hedge against such an apprehension as arises from the uncertainties concerning the capabilities and intentions of both adversaries and allies.

While a more risk-acceptant group of security managers might have opted for some forms of denuclearization, there is no arguing the fact that accepting any such alternative implies that India would forgo another of its cherished values: its desire for autonomy. Even Alternative II implies some diminution in autonomy to the extent that India would have to rely on the capabilities of others to both guarantee and verify an agreement that affects its security. Such a sacrifice, however, might well be accepted in light of the great benefits this alternative offers were it to be made available without sacrificing other values relating to global equality. The sacrifice of autonomy entailed in Alternative I, however, is an entirely different matter, as it clearly seeks to preserve security and status by depending largely on the actions of others—which, even if these are only security guarantees that may never be actualized, still appear in New Delhi's eyes to be a radical diminution of its self-worth. It is here that

---

[104]Brahma Chellaney, "India's Nuclear Planning, Force Structure, Doctrine and Arms-Control Posture," *Australian Journal of International Affairs*, 53:1 (1999), p. 57.

the heritage of several centuries of subordination interact with the constant recognition of India's size, history, and "call to greatness" to produce an instinctive refusal on India's part to agree to any policies that entail a return to systematic dependence on another state, be it for security, prosperity, or any other reason. India's desire to sustain its political autonomy—which implies the freedom to choose friends, strategic policies, and its way of doing things without restraint by another—thus remains a goal that is almost conjoint with preserving physical security.[105] Clearly Alternative I does not allow such autonomy because it makes India either dependent on the resources of others for its freedom or beholden to others for actions that would in the end preserve its safety. Therefore, for a combination of reasons that are rooted first in risk aversion and ultimately in a desire to preserve strategic autonomy, India has not embarked and will not embark on any alternatives that resemble denuclearization—irrespective of the pressures from the United States and elsewhere that may be brought to bear on it—even if the net benefit from nuclearization is, in the final analysis, smaller than usually believed.

ALTERNATIVES INVOLVING NUCLEARIZATION

If India's movement toward denuclearization is all but impossible in the foreseeable future, assessing future directions from among the alternatives involving nuclearization becomes all the more relevant. The alternatives discussed here represent relatively fine distinctions in nuclear posture from the standpoint of policy, but it is critical that these differences be explored if policymakers both in the United States and in India are to avoid locking themselves into simplistic dichotomies involving "nuclear" versus "nonnuclear" states of being. Although this analysis has thus far identified reasons India is unlikely to pursue various nonnuclear alternatives (some of which may in fact be preferred by the United States), it has not yet assessed which nuclear postures are desirable from New Delhi's perspective and which are likely to be settled for given the various constraints India confronts with respect to strategic issues. The analysis has, however, identified the ends to which India's nuclear capabilities would be

---

[105]The best analysis of the sources, manifestations, and consequences of this position remains Bajpai, "India: Modified Structuralism," pp. 157–197.

directed based on an assessment of its structure of vulnerability. Specifically, it has established that India does not require nuclear weapons for war-fighting purposes because it is neither inferior, in conventional military terms, to its principal adversaries nor faced with any threats emanating from the prospect of effective battlefield nuclear use by its competitors. India may, however, require some strategic reserves that serve to immunize it against the possibility of blatant blackmail and subtle coercion (carried out either through conventional diplomatic instruments or through the mechanism of subconventional conflicts)—and the kind of nuclear posture that New Delhi eventually settles for will thus be one that preserves its security, flexibility, and status in the face of precisely such threats. The obvious point of departure, then, consists of examining the nature of India's traditional posture—Alternative III, defined as maintaining the nuclear option *qua* option—and assessing why it did not hold indefinitely as many observers both in India and the United States hoped it would.[106]

Alternative III: Maintaining the Nuclear Option

As defined earlier, "maintaining the nuclear option" essentially entailed producing the fissile materials required for nuclear weaponry and continuing to design nuclear weapons and develop various delivery systems, but refraining from creating or deploying a ready arsenal in the form of completed nuclear weapons that, taken together with their supporting infrastructure and procedural and ideational systems, would enable India's national leadership to undertake prompt nuclear operations in the event of an emergency. This definition of the option implied that even if India had some nuclear weapons—understood as either fully assembled weapons or merely components of such weapons—it would still not be deemed to possess operational nuclear capabilities as long as "the physical network . . . [and] . . . the plans, procedures, organizations, and

---

[106]A good survey of American and Indian desires and expectations with respect to India's future nuclear posture on the eve of the May 1998 tests can be found in "The Future of Nuclear Weapons: A U.S.-India Dialogue," in *Proceedings of the Center for the Advanced Study of India, University of Pennsylvania*, held at the Wharton Sinkler Conference Center, May 5–8, 1997, available at http://www.sas.upenn.edu/casi/nuclear97.html.

widely shared assumptions that allow the parts to work together coherently"[107] did not exist or were not developed in advance. The absence of these supporting elements (and perhaps the weapons themselves) meant that the country's nuclear potential was not "weaponized"—and while this appeared to be a source of great consternation to many Indian commentators, this unusual form of "nonweaponized deterrence"[108] was widely held to describe how India's nuclear option stood incarnated since its initial test in 1974.[109] Thus, in response to an interviewer's question about why India did not change its nuclear posture, former Indian Prime Minister I. K. Gujral cogently responded as late as 1996 that "at the moment the agenda to weaponise our nuclear capability is not there. Whether there will be such an agenda depends on the security threats we face. What we have done is retained the nuclear option. In that sense, we have opted for a status quo approach."[110]

These remarks on Gujral's part could have implied any of the following propositions, among many others:

1. India had the requisite capability to develop nuclear weapons, but it did not possess any weapons at the time (= no weaponry whatsoever).

2. India had the requisite capability to develop nuclear weapons and probably possessed some weapons in unassembled form (= suspicion about weaponry).

3. India had the requisite capability to develop nuclear weapons and probably possessed some weapons in unassembled form, but it probably did not possess the supporting infrastructure normally required for the conduct of nuclear operations (= suspicion about weaponry and uncertainty about the existence of other auxiliary capabilities).

---

[107]Carter, "Introduction," p. 1.

[108]George Perkovich, "A Nuclear Third Way in South Asia," *Foreign Policy*, 91 (Summer 1993), p. 86.

[109]See the discussion in Chari, *Indo-Pak Nuclear Standoff*, pp. 53–80.

[110]"Interview: I. K. Gujral," p. 78.

4. India had the requisite capability to develop nuclear weapons and possessed several weapons, but it did not possess the supporting infrastructure normally required for the conduct of nuclear operations (= absolute certainty about weaponry coupled with certainty about the lack of other auxiliary capabilities).

Which of these propositions applied to India's nuclear capabilities is difficult to say, since the issue relates in part to the meaning of the term *weaponization*. This term—coined by Sandia National Laboratories in the United States—was originally intended to describe the process of developing, testing, and integrating nuclear payloads with the delivery vehicles intended to carry such payloads to their targets in the event of war. The notion of weaponization, in its strict, narrow sense, would therefore refer to all the myriad details relating to the transformation of some specific nuclear device into a usable weapon system that would then be available for the prosecution of nuclear operations. However, the term *weaponization* can also be used in a broader sense in which it would simply refer to the development of the technologies, plans, procedures, and organizations necessary for effective nuclear operations in the event of conflict—a usage that derives from the idea that nuclear capabilities become consequential only through the existence of a complex, integrated deterrent system rather than merely as a result of the isolated presence of some discrete technologies. Recognizing the distinction between the narrow and broad sense of the term *weaponization*, illustrated in Figure 2, is important when one is assessing both the past and the future of India's nuclear weapon program.

Clearly, Gujral's simple statement—like similar statements by other Indian Prime Ministers in the past—is difficult to interpret because it is not clear which concept of weaponization is implied. Many Indian policymakers, especially its politicians, would argue that "maintaining the option" entailed proposition one and no other. Thus, for example, a long line of Indian Prime Ministers—including Indira Gandhi, Rajiv Gandhi, and finally I. K. Gujral—repeatedly affirmed that while India certainly possessed the capabilities to develop

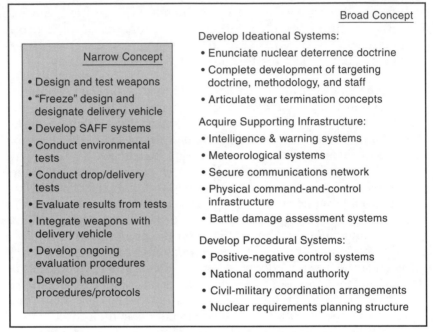

Figure 2—Two Concepts of Weaponization

nuclear weaponry, it did not possess any nuclear weaponry whatsoever.[111]

By contrast, many Indian and foreign academics, following the judgments advanced by observers inside the U.S. government, would associate "maintaining the option" with some variant of proposition two: They would affirm India's ability to produce nuclear weaponry and suggest that the country even possessed such weapons but would assert that these weapons probably existed in unassembled form. The uncertainty about India's nuclear capabilities here derived in large measure from the semantic problem of whether unassembled weapons could be said to constitute real nu-

---

[111] See, for example, Gandhi, *Statements on Foreign Policy, January–April 1983*, p. 27; Parker, "Rajiv Gandhi's Bipolar World"; and "Interview: I. K. Gujral," p. 78. See also Perkovich, "A Nuclear Third Way in South Asia," pp. 85–104.

clear capability—a question answered in the affirmative by the Director of the Central Intelligence Agency, R. James Woolsey, when he argued that "the distinction between whether or not these weapons are, in fact, assembled or only able to be assembled within a few days is a very small distinction. But the key point is that it's our view that they can be assembled, the few that each could put together, quite quickly."[112]

Other foreign analysts, including those associated with the U.S. government, as well as some Indian analysts—especially those with close connections to the uniformed military or the defense research establishment—would expand the thesis summarized in proposition two to include an assessment of India's supporting capabilities. These analysts would assert that proposition three in fact provided a more accurate depiction of what maintaining the option really entailed: It accepted the notion that India possessed nuclear weapons and perhaps maintained these weapons in disassembled form but highlighted the fact that New Delhi had not yet developed all the technologies, plans, procedures, and organizations that would be necessary for the effective conduct of nuclear operations in the event of a conflict.[113] Accepting proposition three would therefore imply that India could still—somewhat truthfully—claim to be maintaining its option even if it possessed nuclear weapons in complete or disassembled form so long as it remained relatively unprepared for the wide variety of nuclear operations that it might have to undertake in a crisis.

It is generally difficult to identify individuals or agencies who would argue in favor of proposition four as it is described above. In most cases, this is because information about the status of India's nuclear weapon stockpile is closely safeguarded. Indeed, while many sources have speculated about the size and quality of India's arsenal, no public sources have authoritatively described either the disposition of that arsenal or the extent of India's nuclear

---

[112]See, for example, testimony of R. James Woolsey, Director, Central Intelligence Agency, U.S. Congress, Hearings of the Senate Governmental Affairs Committee on Nuclear Proliferation, 103rd Congress, 1st Session, February 24, 1993, p. 16.

[113]See, for example, Joeck, *Maintaining Nuclear Stability in South Asia*, and Manoj Joshi, "In the Shadow of Fear," *India Today International*, July 21, 1997, pp. 50–53.

operations architecture. The U.S. government, for example, described India's posture as being one in which nuclear weapons could be readily fabricated at short notice but remained silent about the extent of auxiliary capabilities that India had in place for the conduct of nuclear operations.[114] K. Subrahmanyam corroborated this view by concluding that "successive [Indian] Prime Ministers were technically truthful when they asserted that India did not have a nuclear weapon because the nuclear core and the rest of the weapon assembly were kept separate and, therefore, no weapon existed."[115] Subrahmanyam does not, however, describe whether any auxiliary capabilities were developed, asserting only that "since India was committed to no-first-use, the [need for] retaliation was not time critical."[116] This laconic remark presumably implies that the ancillary capabilities India required for nuclear operations either were not developed or existed only in embryonic form because the irrelevance of prompt retaliation allowed such capabilities to be either improvised or formalized whenever necessary.

Irrespective of what India's nuclear posture precisely was for most of the post-1974 period, the consensus among observers—at least within the United States—was that India did in fact possess nuclear capabilities in some form. The consensus further held that these capabilities included, at least after 1990, the possession of unassembled nuclear weapons that were not deployed with their eventual end users—the armed services—and that were maintained without a large and complex set of ancillary capabilities dedicated to the conduct of nuclear operations.[117] If this judgment is true, it would imply that—at least in terms of the definitions offered previously—India had weaponized its nuclear capabilities prior to May 1998, even if only in the narrow sense of the term.[118] This conclusion seems to be

---

[114]Office of the Secretary of Defense, *Proliferation: Threat and Response*, pp. 35–41.

[115]Subrahmanyam, "Indian Nuclear Policy—1964–98," pp. 49–50.

[116]Ibid.

[117]Perkovich, "A Nuclear Third Way in South Asia," pp. 85–104.

[118]Despite his earlier (1996) remarks, I. K. Gujral himself seemed to confirm this judgment when, in an interview granted after the May 1998 tests, he commented, "We were moving in this direction. If you look at the entire history of acquisition of this deterrence—the minimum necessary deterrent—it was a response to a situation . . . that was building around us from the eighties onward. I would say, to the credit of my

confirmed by the Kargil Review Committee Report, which notes that the "Indian nuclear programme was weapon-oriented at least since 1983"[119] and, further, that weaponization itself, at least in the narrow sense, "took place between 1992 and 1994."[120] The disadvantages of this equilibrium—covertly developing the weapons themselves without comparable attention to both developing the formal structures associated with their management and publicly announcing the existence of these capabilities—have been described *ad nauseam* by many Indian commentators, especially those who have sought to move the country's national posture beyond maintaining the option to some other, more assertive form of nuclearization. The important point, however, is that most Indian analysts (and some even in the United States) agreed that this was in fact where the Indian nuclear program stood prior to the events of May 1998, although there were disagreements about the details pertaining to the country's precise nuclear status.[121] George Perkovich summed up this consensus accurately when he concluded in 1993 that "despite all their expense and effort . . . India and Pakistan have *not* yet deployed nuclear arsenals or even declared themselves to be nuclear weapon states."[122]

The critical question therefore consists of explaining why maintaining the option did not constitute a stable equilibrium—that is, an end state that attracted neither exogenous nor endogenous pressures for change. Several scholars, both Indian and American, argued quite cogently that maintaining the option *could* constitute an equilibrium position if India was not pressured by the international community, since absent such pressures this alternative—Alternative III—did not unduly prejudice Indian security, flexibility, or status and conse-

---

predecessors in office, that each one of us sustained that practice—from Rajiv Gandhi down. And no Prime Minister, after demitting office, let the country down by revealing what he should not. That is a great compliment to the Indian system in which I take great pride." See "Interview of the Week: Inder Kumar Gujral," *Sunday Observer*, September 20–26, 1998.

[119] *From Surprise to Reckoning: The Kargil Review Committee Report*, p. 206.

[120] Ibid., p. 205.

[121] Joshi, "In the Shadow of Fear," pp. 50–53.

[122] Perkovich, "A Nuclear Third Way in South Asia," p. 87.

quently engendered few reasons for moving away from the status quo that emerged in the post-1974 period.[123]

The claim that Indian security stood unimpaired as a result of simply maintaining the nuclear option derives from two arguments, both of which must be held conjointly if the claim is to remain effective. The first such argument is that *all* nuclear weapons—irrespective of their size, type, or quality—embody such fearsome destructive power that their only rational purpose can be to avert war. As K. Subrahmanyam put it, "The power to impose intolerable pain or unacceptable destruction irrespective of the outcome of conventional military operations, and the certainty of destruction"[124] are what make nuclear weapons in general and nuclear deterrence in particular unique. Consequently, as the former Chief of Staff of the Pakistan Army, General Mirza Aslam Beg, opined, "It is not their numbers that matter, but [merely] the destruction that can be caused by even a few [such devices]"[125] that gives nuclear weapons their unique effectiveness. These beliefs, in turn, lead inexorably to the substantive claim that "a small number of such weapons are sufficient for mutual annihilation of countries, and this itself [provides] sufficient deterrence to cast doubts on the outcome of a nuclear military adventure."[126] The presumption that makes this claim tenable, of course, is that the nuclear weapons a state possesses actually work—that is, that they are capable of being successfully detonated under operational conditions and would produce the requisite yields sought by their designers. Only if this presumption held could the possessor be confident—irrespective of what others believed—that its nuclear holdings per se would ensure its national safety.

The second argument, which undergirds the logic of "maintaining the option" as a means of effectively preserving security, is that the destructiveness of nuclear weapons is so absolute that *all* the re-

---

[123]See, among other discussions, the pertinent remarks of V. Arunachalam, K. Santhanam, and P. K. Iyengar in "The Future of Nuclear Weapons: A U.S.-India Dialogue," available at http://www.sas.upenn.edu/casi/nuclear97.html.

[124]K. Subrahmanyam, "Nuclear Force Design and Minimum Deterrence Strategy for India," in Bharat Karnad (ed.), *Future Imperilled* (New Delhi: Viking, 1994), p. 178.

[125]Cited in Perkovich, "A Nuclear Third Way in South Asia," p. 89.

[126]Raja Ramanna, "Security, Deterrence, and the Future," *Journal of the United Services Institution of India*, 122:509 (July–September 1992), pp. 282–292.

quirements otherwise considered to be necessary for stable deterrence—enunciated doctrine, robust command and control, suitable targeting, and adequate crisis management and war termination planning—are rendered infructuous because the fearsome power inherent in these devices produces a deterrent effect that cannot be supplemented or undermined by any other institutional or ideational artifacts pertaining to their use. As Marc Trachtenberg articulated this claim, "The mere existence of nuclear forces means that, whatever we say or do, there is a certain irreducible risk that an armed conflict might escalate into a nuclear war."[127] Thus, the presence of nuclear weapons per se is seen to produce, as McGeorge Bundy phrased it, a kind of "existential deterrence"[128] that suffices in itself to discourage any adversary from challenging the values held by their possessors even if the latter do not have "adequate" doctrines of deterrence or possess all the physical and institutional instruments that may be promulgated by some theory as necessary for effective retaliation.[129]

If this logic is carried one step further in the South Asian context, it becomes obvious that "existential deterrence" may not require "effective" weapons either—that is, weapons that will always successfully detonate on command with certain assured yields, or even weapons that physically exist. For if deterrence derives simply "from a fear of escalation [that is inexorably] factored into [the] political calculations"[130] of all states faced with a potential nuclear adversary, even the mere suspicion that nuclear weapons might exist in the latter's armory should suffice to make all assailants "more cautious and

---

[127]Marc Trachtenberg, "The Influence of Nuclear Weapons in the Cuban Missile Crisis," *International Security*, 10:1 (Summer 1985), p. 139.

[128]McGeorge Bundy, "Existential Deterrence and Its Consequences," in Douglas MacLean (ed.), *The Security Gamble: Deterrence Dilemmas in the Nuclear Age* (Totowa, NJ: Rowman & Allanheld, 1984), pp. 3–13.

[129]It should be noted, however, that Bundy's concept of existential deterrence, developed as it was in the context of the U.S.-Soviet confrontation, was predicated on the presence of truly large arsenals that were substantially survivable and built around the enormously destructive power of thermonuclear weaponry. See Bundy, "Existential Deterrence and Its Consequences," pp. 8–9.

[130]Trachtenberg, "The Influence of Nuclear Weapons in the Cuban Missile Crisis," p. 139.

more prudent than they otherwise would be."[131] This prudence would be inevitable given the high costs of miscalculation that obtain in the nuclear realm, and by implication national security could be adequately preserved even when no nuclear weapons actually exist except in the psychological realms of suspicion and uncertainty. Satisfactory deterrence, in this reading, could thus be generated even by pure bluff or, as one analyst insightfully phrased it, through "the power of suggestion"[132]—because any potential assailant confronted with even the possibility of unacceptable destruction would have few incentives to pursue a revisionist strategy that resulted in its own (or in mutual) destruction.

The implicit marriage of these two claims—the destructiveness of all nuclear weapons and the effectiveness of existential deterrence—gave rise to the expectation that India could maintain its nuclear option indefinitely while still adequately preserving its security. The simple suspicion that India might have nuclear weaponry in some form was seen as sufficient to prevent its competitors from mounting any critical challenges to its core interests.

Maintaining the option, by this logic, not only preserved India's security but had the added advantage of preserving its flexibility as well, as it did not in any way abridge India's right to change course at some point down the line. It could not, for example, restrict India's abilities to pursue more assertive forms of nuclearization if the regional environment called for such measures, and it allowed equally for the possibility that India could give up its nuclear program entirely—without having to bear the costs involved in developing an arsenal in the interim—if it was reasonably satisfied that global trends toward nuclear disarmament were evolving at a reasonable pace. In fact, if married "to the moral, as distinct from [the] militarist, route to credibility and high global stature,"[133] this alternative could, according to some Indian analysts, allow India to pursue its agenda with respect to global disarmament in an even more authentic and

---

[131]Ibid.

[132]Devin T. Hagerty, "The Power of Suggestion: Opaque Proliferation, Existential Deterrence, and the South Asian Nuclear Arms Competition," *Security Studies*, 2:3/4 (Spring–Summer 1993), pp. 256–283.

[133]Bidwai, "India and NPT Review: Grasping the Disarmament Nettle."

purposeful way. Further, India's desire for status was also arguably not compromised by maintaining the option—for to the degree that the distribution of prestige in the international arena is determined by the possession of nuclear weaponry, the presumption of possession arising from maintaining the option allowed India to reap some of the benefits of being cast as a nuclear power. Moreover, to the degree that the distribution of prestige is determined by achievements other than nuclear capability, India's claims to prestige were in no way diminished by continuing to maintain the option, at least so long as this course of action did not compromise the country's ability to achieve those other goals which also regulate the international distribution of status.[134]

There is little doubt that maintaining the option, thus, had minimal effect on India's flexibility and perhaps only ambiguous effects on its status. The ambiguity here derived mainly from the fact that the presumption of possessing nuclear weapons—a transparent consequence of maintaining the option—resulted in India's subjection to the restrictions of several international technology-control regimes. To the extent that such restrictions prevented the country from being able to increase its economic and technological capabilities, maintaining the option contributed to decreasing India's international status *if this status was based on criteria other than the possession of nuclear weaponry*. If the opposite was true, however, India's desire for status remained more or less unhampered as a result of keeping the option open.[135] The real difficulty with

---

[134]Many Indians, however, have doubted whether this is in fact the case. As Partha Ghosh put it, "Nuclear parity is the easiest thing to achieve; the difficult task is to match the adversaries in economic development." See Partha S. Ghosh, "Bomb, Science and the State," *The Hindu*, June 9, 1998.

[135]In effect, the traditional strategy of maintaining the option allowed India to split the difference between these two competing bases of status in international politics, since it was never quite clear to New Delhi whether India's status inconsistency could best be resolved by either purely economic or purely strategic means. In a U.S.-Indian symposium in 1997, Kirit Parekh, one of India's best development economists, framed this issue in the following way:

I've been hearing various kinds of strategy arguments . . . but I just heard some economic arguments and I thought maybe I should join that. One argument was that maybe India should really develop, or at least sell, its option. I think one should also look in terms of what it is that India would gain if India were to go nuclear, which is being supported in various stages. One should factor in a few things: what are the gains and what are the costs in doing that? On the cost

sustaining Alternative III as a stable equilibrium therefore stemmed primarily from what was perceived to be its corrosive effects on the nation's security. This perception—which had steadily gained currency among Indian elites, the higher leadership of the armed forces, and sections of the leading political parties, including the Congress Party—derived from the limitations inherent in the notion of existential deterrence as well as from specific features of India's evolving strategic environment.

To begin with, the expectation that maintaining the option *qua* option could subsist as an equilibrium end state presupposes that the thesis "nuclear weapons have an unacceptably destructive power uniformly," holds true. This thesis in fact made sense during the Cold War, when the superpowers' arsenals were heavily populated with extremely high-yield weapons, any one of which could have caused "unacceptable" damage if used against a strategic target.[136] The superpowers, however, also possessed large numbers of smaller nu-

---

side, of course, there's obviously the cost of development of the hardware but also the cost of manpower. What is important is that some of the brightest and the best men go into this, and the opportunity cost of using them somewhere else should be properly reckoned in. Other costs would be that if you go publicly and overtly nuclear, there might be retaliation costs of various kinds. There may be trade sanctions, there may be technology embargoes. There may be reduction of inflows of aid, of foreign institutional investment, as well as of various kinds of capital flows, including foreign investment. One might be able to make some estimates of this.

On the other hand, there may be some gains, which also one should think about. Obviously, the most important would be the psychological satisfaction the Indian elites would get, that they've been able to thumb their nose at those bullying Americans. Then there will be technological fallout and spin-offs, which can be very sizable and substantial, I grant that. And the third would be security gains. From what I am hearing, security gains seem to be somewhat of a question mark; one is not clear what the security gains are. Maybe there are some, maybe there aren't any, and there is a lot of discussion of it. I'm willing to believe that yes, there are some security gains by having a nuclear option. *It seems to me that one can also have these technological spin-offs by doing all the research and all the work that it requires without going really fully nuclear. So I would think that the option in which you do all the development but not the last few steps of putting the system together seems to me to be, at least from an economist's perspective, a better option* [italics added].

See "The Future of Nuclear Weapons: A U.S.-India Dialogue," available at http://www.sas.upenn.edu/casi/reports/nuclear/panel4.html.

[136]For a succinct survey of the kinds of nuclear capabilities possessed by the United States and the Soviet Union during the height of the Cold War, see John M. Collins, *Imbalance of Power* (San Rafael, CA: Presidio Press, 1978).

clear weapons, none of which could cause "unacceptable" damage but all of which ultimately relied for their effectiveness on the potential for escalation to truly horrific levels of violence. In such circumstances—when the arsenals consisted of tens of thousands of nuclear weapons, many thousands of which were high-yield devices—the notion of existential deterrence held a certain logic. After all, the damage that could be wrought by the discrete use of some of these weapons as well as the escalatory consequences of using many smaller weapons either simultaneously or in sequence created "existential" deterrence effects that transcended both the use doctrines and the organizational arrangements put in place by their possessors.[137]

A similar situation, however, did not obtain in South Asia. Nuclear weapons here do not exist in large numbers and, by the most reliable estimates, consist of a few tens in number, and none is believed to be of very high destructive capability. In fact, it is not at all clear even from the tests conducted in May 1998 whether Indian nuclear designs (or Pakistani designs, for that matter) have the destructive power to yield the "one target–one bomb" capability that most people, harking back to Hiroshima and Nagasaki, have come to associate with nuclear use (a misleading piece of imagery to begin with given the relatively small size of the Japanese targets in comparison with the cities of South Asia).[138] All this implies that if Indian nuclear weapons have less-than-fearsome capabilities, and if these capabilities have existed in only limited numbers since 1974, the overwhelming destructiveness of nuclear weapons that undergirds the classic conception of existential deterrence may not have applied to South Asia. As General A. M. Vohra, arguing precisely this point, noted, "In a situation of low-level nuclear symmetry, the danger of a nuclear holocaust does not exist"[139]—and to that degree the presumed existence of nuclear weapons per se could not have provided the stability that the devotees of existential deterrence claim automatically exists

---

[137]Bundy, "Existential Deterrence and Its Consequences," pp. 8–9; Keeny, Jr., and Panofsky, "MAD Versus NUTS," pp. 282–304.

[138]Gregory S. Jones, *From Testing to Deploying Nuclear Forces: The Hard Choices Facing India and Pakistan*, IP-192 (Santa Monica: RAND, 2000), p. 7.

[139]A. M. Vohra, chapter in K. Sundarji (ed.), *Nuclear Weapons in a Third World Context*, Combat Paper No. 2 (Mhow, India: College of Combat, 1981), p. 39.

in the Indian subcontinent.[140] This was particularly true because, as subsequent discussions will indicate, the effectiveness of India's nuclear devices—especially that tested in 1974—was suspect to begin with and consequently could not have given New Delhi the assurance it needed to make existential deterrence a viable national security strategy.

Further, nuclear weapons, however powerful they may be, have political uses that go beyond simply deterring aggression.[141] If this were the only goal sought to be serviced by nuclear weaponry, existential deterrence might suffice. But nuclear weaponry has other effects, among the more corrosive of which is the so-called stability-instability paradox.[142] This paradox describes a condition whereby nuclear weapons prevent nuclear war, but only at the cost of opening the door to other conventional or subconventional conflicts. Because conventional conflict is perhaps both cost- and mission-ineffective in South Asia today, it has been replaced for the most part by unconventional wars taking the form of externally supported domestic challenges to state authority.[143] Nuclear weapons in this context become subtle instruments of coercion, as they enable their possessors to support various dissatisfied groups involved in internal conflicts abroad with the expectation of relative immunity to retaliation. Deterrence breakdown in such situations may not occur primarily because of the premeditated choices of state rivals but rather because nonstate actors "capable of pressuring both India and Pakistan [and] unaffected by their nuclear capabilities"[144] achieve success that they might not otherwise have enjoyed in the absence of foreign support. The unintended success of domestic dissidence could thus precipitate interstate conflicts even between nuclear-capable rivals because the state threatened with unacceptable political losses might feel

---

[140]In fact, Vohra goes on to claim that "prima facie nuclear weapons of low yield may be used particularly if their use is restricted to tactical targets. Militarily the employment of such nuclear weapons would be very effective against say a bridgehead and there need be no collateral damage."

[141]Subrahmanyam, "Nuclear Force Design and Minimum Deterrence Strategy for India," pp. 185–188.

[142]Snyder, "The Balance of Power and the Balance of Terror."

[143]Tellis, Stability in South Asia, pp. 2–33.

[144]Joeck, Maintaining Nuclear Stability in South Asia, p. 27.

compelled to use all the means at its disposal, including nuclear weapons, to stave off impending defeat.[145]

Deterring nuclear coercion of this sort, especially when carried out by either more risk-acceptant or more powerful adversaries, requires more than latent nuclear capabilities or even assembled weapons; to the contrary, it may require an explicit strategy that involves mounting credible threats. Mounting credible threats in turn requires more than completed nuclear weapons *simpliciter;* it requires additional physical accoutrements, command systems, and decision rules that can tailor those threats to the challenges expected, the ability to assess and choose between multiple alternatives, and the development of strategies and institutions for crisis management and conflict termination. In other words, responding to nuclear coercion may require capabilities that move beyond simply maintaining a nuclear option.[146] This issue becomes particularly relevant because existential deterrence, if it works at all in the presence of modest nuclear capabilities, provides adequate deterrence only so long as deterrence does not break down. This may sound tautological, but it is not. So long as the competing political wills in any relationship are not actively engaged in violence—which may occur through deliberate choice, accident, irrationality, or miscalculation—or, when engaged in violence, do not face the prospects of unacceptable losses, existential deterrence may suffice to preserve security. Under all other conditions, the limitations of existential deterrence will be seen in stark relief, as even nuclear-capable states will have to do something "more" than simply rely on the psychological benefits of presumed nuclear possession when faced with either the possibility of a serious nuclear crisis or the prospect of a serious political loss.[147] The reliability of existential deterrence as an effective long-term equilibrium thus becomes suspect especially in a region where the prospects of

---

[145]For an argument as to why states threatened with loss are more likely to embark on extreme responses—including, for example, the use of nuclear weapons—see the discussion in Kenneth Watman, Dean Wilkening, John Arquilla, and Brian Nichiporuk, *U.S. Regional Deterrence Strategies*, MR-490-A/AF (Santa Monica: RAND, 1995), pp. 13–26, and Dean Wilkening and Kenneth Watman, *Nuclear Deterrence in a Regional Context*, MR-500-A/AF (Santa Monica: RAND, 1994), pp. 1–30.

[146]Joeck, *Maintaining Nuclear Stability in South Asia*, pp. 35–64.

[147]See the apt discussion in Dinshaw Mistry, "What If Deterrence Fails?" available at http://www.ipcs.org/issues/articles/132-ndi-dinshaw.html.

interstate crises are ever-present thanks to the active and ongoing security competition between India and Pakistan and the latent suspicions between India and China.

Given the modest nuclear capabilities residing in South Asia and the limitations of existential deterrence as a security strategy, Alternative III—continuing to maintain the nuclear option *qua* option—could have remained a stable equilibrium only so long as the following conditions were obtained:

1. There were no attempts at nuclear coercion through unconventional forms of violence;

2. There were no crises that could make demands beyond the ability of India's traditional nuclear posture;

3. The nuclear programs of India's principal competitors, Pakistan and China, were relatively stable and not increasing either in size or in effectiveness;

4. Indian security managers remained confident about the operational effectiveness of their latent nuclear capabilities over time;

5. The global nuclear regime remained relatively tolerant of India's continued maintenance of its nuclear option; and

6. Indian decisionmakers remained generally sanguine about both the intensity of the security threats facing the country and their ability to contain these threats by means other than nuclear weapons.

From India's point of view, however, all these conditions steadily eroded in varying degrees during the last decade—and consequently it turned out to be only a matter of time before New Delhi embarked on a course of action that would move it beyond the traditional posture of keeping the option open. Each of these issues will be discussed briefly below.

To be sure, India has thus far not faced the contingency of successful nuclear coercion carried out through unconventional forms of violence, but this is not to say that it has not been tried. In fact, the support Pakistan extended to the Sikh insurgency during the latter half of the 1980s and to the Kashmiri insurgency since the early

1990s remain good examples of attempted nuclear coercion.[148] None of these contingencies, however, was threatening enough to require that India change its nuclear posture or mount credible counterthreats necessitating the brandishing of its nuclear weaponry. In large part, this is because India's large size and signifi cant reserve of domestic resources allowed it to absorb the costs of Pakistan's needling without recourse to more provocative alternatives.[149] At the same time, Pakistan's own relatively risk-averse behavior also helped preempt the need for any change in India's nuclear posture. There is no guarantee, however, that future domestic challenges to the Indian state will echo those of the past or that India will be able to undercut future attempts at nuclear coercion simply by exploiting its relatively large size, its significant economic and conventional military capabilities, and its great political endurance. Another significant uprising in Kashmir or elsewhere—especially one abetted by a more risk-acceptant Pakistani leadership that "persuade[s] itself that India has been battling cross-border terrorism without exercising the right of hot pursuit, as any other country would have, because of its fear of the Pakistani bomb"[150]—could thus result in a situation where New Delhi would need an extensive menu of responses, including the ability to issue credible nuclear threats. And while it is unlikely that Pakistan would renew its support for domestic Indian dissidence in such a way as to provoke these threats, such a resumption of support cannot be ruled out by Indian elites over the long term, especially if a potentially successful Indian achievement of hegemony provokes Pakistan to undertake some dramatic but risky attempts at counteraction.[151]

Even more significant than Pakistan's choices, however, would be China's future decisions with respect to nuclear coercion—for if

---

[148]A useful survey—from an Indian perspective—of past attempts at Pakistani coercion through unconventional means can be found in Vijay Karan, *War by Stealth* (New Delhi: Viking, 1997). For a good survey on how Pakistani nuclear coercion fits into Pakistan's larger grand strategy, see Eric Arnett, "The Future Strategic Balance in South Asia," in Herro Mustafa (ed.), *The Balance of Power in South Asia* (Abu Dhabi, UAE: Emirates Center for Strategic Studies and Research, 2000), pp. 95–108.

[149]Tellis, *Stability in South Asia*, pp. 47–50.

[150]R. D. Kwatra, "From Deterrence to Blackmail: Pakistan's Nuclear Agenda," *Indian Express*, January 20, 1996.

[151]Subrahmanyam, "Indian Nuclear Policy—1964–98," pp. 48–49.

China, having successfully completed its economic renewal, chose to pursue its desire for "national reunification" by supporting domestic insurgencies in India (as was the case throughout the 1960s and 1970s in the Indian northeast), it is uncertain whether New Delhi would believe that simply maintaining the nuclear option could provide it with sufficient cover to ward off Chinese aggression. To be sure, such aggression is by no means inevitable and depends largely on the quality of Sino-Indian relations over time, the character of internal Chinese politics, and the larger patterns of security competition in Asia. It does, however, remain one possible outcome, especially if a belligerent Chinese leadership calculates that its greater economic and military (including nuclear) capability provides it with substantial political leverage vis-à-vis India and leaves New Delhi with few of the advantages the latter enjoys in similar circumstances vis-à-vis Pakistan.[152] Indeed, the prospect of such an eventuality does concern New Delhi, and although most Indian policymakers are currently circumspect about the Chinese threat—George Fernandes' exceptional remarks in May 1998 notwithstanding—the future of the Chinese challenge 20-odd years out appears more disconcerting. In large measure, this is because many Indians perceive that China's incentives to maintain its reticence with respect to the disputed border will lessen once it has successfully concluded its economic reform program and become a true superpower.[153] Even more perniciously, the very anticipation of such future discord—assuming that China's economic ascendancy and military growth continue on a more or less even keel—has become a powerful motivating force that argues for a shift in India's nuclear posture purely as a prudential measure long before any significant Chinese challenge to New Delhi becomes palpable.[154]

A similar set of considerations relates to the occurrence of nuclear-shadowed crises. Thus far, India has not had to confront any significant nuclear crisis. Indeed, the country's worst defeat in war occurred in 1962, well before it possessed any significant nuclear

---

[152]Indian concerns here are usefully summarized in Subrahmanyam, "India's Security: The North and North-East Dimension," pp. 8–22.

[153]Amitabh Mattoo, "Chinese Takeaway," *The Telegraph*, August 8, 1997.

[154]Mohan, "India, China Power Equations Changing."

capability (and also before it faced any nuclear threats). Similarly, the two political crises that took place during the nuclear era in South Asia made few demands on India's nuclear capabilities; the 1987 Brasstacks crisis, for example, involved no nuclear threats, and even the veiled warnings allegedly communicated by A. Q. Khan in his celebrated interview of January 28, 1987, were not made public until well after the crisis had abated. Even if Khan's threats had been privately communicated to New Delhi before the crisis ended, however, India would have been unlikely to have taken them seriously because almost all senior Indian nuclear scientists at that point believed that Pakistan had no nuclear capabilities worth the name. Thus, irrespective of what Pakistani capabilities actually were, they were not seen (or at least were unlikely to have been seen) as relevant to India's immediate strategic choices.[155]

A different kind of problem materialized during the 1990 crisis. Although precise details about these events are classified, several public reports suggest that Pakistani nuclear activities were detected during this crisis.[156] And while it is unclear whether India perceived those developments or whether it was even intended to be made aware of them, suffice it to say that the United States reacted and intervened diplomatically to defuse the situation. India for its part appeared to be unconcerned about Pakistan's actions, since as one authoritative source described, "there was a top secret analysis in India on the probability of the Pakistani nuclear threat and it was concluded that it was not very significant."[157] Whatever else New Delhi may have learned from that crisis, its *public* appearances at the time suggested that it did not perceive the need for any rapid revision of its traditional posture toward nuclear weaponry. There is now good evidence, however, that key thresholds relating to weaponization were in fact crossed sometime in the aftermath of the 1990 crisis, when India's strategic enclaves formally completed the process of

---

[155]A good assessment that affirms the irrelevance of nuclear weaponry during the 1987 crisis can be found in Devin T. Hagerty, *The Consequences of Nuclear Proliferation: Lessons from South Asia* (Cambridge, MA: MIT Press, 1998), pp. 91–116.

[156]The most widely publicized, albeit inaccurate, report about these events remains Seymour M. Hersh, "On the Nuclear Edge," *The New Yorker*, March 29, 1993.

[157]Subrahmanyam, "Indian Nuclear Policy—1964–98," p. 45.

fabricating nuclear weapons as a prudential response to future nuclear threats that might be levied against India.[158]

The anticipation of future crises seems to have further reinforced India's commitment to acquire more manifest forms of nuclear capability. In part, this is because the technologies of warfare in the subcontinent have progressively changed from air-breathing platforms to ballistic missiles that place a high premium on rapid responsiveness and preplanned operations.[159] Even more significant, however, is the fact that future nuclear crises involving Sino-Indian relations—irrespective of the technologies involved—would be entirely different from those that have occurred in the context of Indo-Pakistani encounters. Specifically, a crisis here would involve a declared nuclear power with capabilities several orders of magnitude greater than those of India. Consequently, any confrontation between Beijing and New Delhi would be seen as inevitably redounding to the disadvantage of the latter were India to persist with its strategy of simply maintaining the option, at least in the sense understood prior to the events of 1990. As former Chief of Army Staff General K. Sundarji argued:

> The argument that China has not employed nuclear blackmail against us from 1964 to date and therefore is unlikely to do so in the future is questionable. During this period, China was a fledgling nuclear weapon power with missiles deployed in soft ground launchers, which were totally vulnerable to Soviet nuclear attacks. . . . Today, she has nuclear-powered submarines capable of carrying nuclear ballistic missiles. . . . With the passage of time this capability will continue to grow, and with the acquisition of a minimum deter-

---

[158]In his revealing essay, "Indian Nuclear Policy—1964–98," K. Subrahmanyam states that Rajiv Gandhi issued the orders to weaponize India's nuclear capability in the aftermath of the Third U.N. Special Session on Disarmament in 1988, but that "in the period 1987–90, India [remained] totally vulnerable to the Pakistani nuclear threat." When India formally completed the process of fabricating its weaponry is not clear from this published account, but it leaves no doubt that at least by 1991, the process of weaponization, understood in the narrow sense again, was well under way. See Subrahmanyam, "Indian Nuclear Policy—1964–98," pp. 43–50. In *From Surprise to Reckoning: The Kargil Review Committee Report,* a document substantially authored by K. Subrahmanyam, it is revealed officially for the first time that India did in fact weaponize its nuclear capabilities sometime between 1992 and 1994. See *From Surprise to Reckoning: The Kargil Review Committee Report,* p. 205.

[159]Joeck, *Maintaining Nuclear Stability in South Asia,* pp. 47–48.

rent in the second strike mode against the USSR and the USA, it is probable that China might indulge in nuclear blackmail when dealing with nonnuclear countries.[160]

The implications of this argument, among many others, for Sundarji and others like him is that India ought to change its traditional nuclear posture of simply maintaining the option—and in a hurry.[161]

While concerns about nuclear coercion and nuclear-shadowed crises were critical enough to precipitate silent changes in India's nuclear posture at least since the early 1990s, what became increasingly obvious beginning in the mid-1990s was that the challenges imposed by conditions three to six, taken together, would lead these changes to become the focus of intense public scrutiny.

India's perception of Pakistan's and China's growing strategic capabilities was already sketched out in the previous chapter. Throughout the 1990s, however, Indian policymakers were steadily barraged by news reports, drawn from leaked American intelligence documents, vividly describing the growing nuclearization taking place around the country's periphery. Where Pakistan was concerned, for example, Indian security elites—feeding on a steady diet of stories appearing in the American press—constantly sought to remind their government about the new improvements in Islamabad's enrichment capabilities flowing from China's sale of the more sophisticated samarium-cobalt ring magnets to Pakistan; the development of a new uranium enrichment facility at Golra Sharif with Chinese assistance; and Islamabad's most recent efforts at simultaneously pursuing the "plutonium route" in order, as one Western analyst phrased it, "to develop nuclear weapons that are lighter and easier to miniaturize than ones based on HEU."[162] The steady improvement in delivery capabilities from aircraft to missiles like the M-11, the Ghauri, and the Shaheen, all of which could in principle

---

[160]Cited in Gregory F. Giles and James E. Doyle, "Indian and Pakistani Views on Nuclear Deterrence," *Comparative Strategy*, 15:2 (1996), p. 137.

[161]K. Sundarji, "Declare Nuclear Status," *India Today*, December 31, 1990, p. 73, and K. Sundarji, *Blind Men of Hindoostan* (New Delhi: UBS Publishers, 1995).

[162]Andrew Koch, "Pakistan Persists with Nuclear Procurement," *Jane's Intelligence Review*, 9:3 (March 1977), p. 132.

carry Pakistan's basic nuclear designs, also raised concern, since they allowed for the assured interdiction of most high-value targets deep within the Indian heartland while simultaneously signaling that New Delhi "not only ha[d] frittered away its twenty-year lead over Pakistan, but ha[d] fallen substantially behind it."[163]

Yet even these spectacular increases in prowess paled in comparison to those Indian commentators perceived China as having made during the same period. These included improvements in nuclear modernization resulting from a series of low-yield nuclear tests concluded just prior to the CTBT; the significant infrastructure modernization undertaken throughout the Chinese mainland, particularly along the Himalayan border; the dramatic upgrades in command-and-control systems regulating both nuclear and conventional forces; and, finally, doctrinal modifications that, following Western analyses, were seen as heralding a transition to a "limited" deterrence strategy that would diminish the incredibility of those strategic threats on which weaker competitors like India had long relied for their own safety. These developments were summed up by one Indian military analyst who declared that "the PLA as constituted today is a palpable first-order strategic threat [to India] now and not in the future."[164]

Although India's politicians probably did not understand the significance of many of these technical details, the same could not be said of the higher bureaucracy in New Delhi. Civilian bureaucrats in the Ministry of Defence, the DRDO, and the office of the Scientific Adviser to the Defence Minister clearly grasped the implications of the nuclear modernization under way in both Pakistan and China. Since these details were probably transmitted to the Cabinet through various option papers prepared by the relevant ministries, the dominant impression India's political masters came away with was that of growing Pakistani and Chinese nuclear capabilities as well as increasing collusion between Pakistan and China in support of a

---

[163] Prem Shankar Jha, "Nuclear Blackmail," *Hindustan Times*, April 17, 1998.

[164] Bhaduri, "The One and a Half Front Scenario," p. 20. See also Sahgal and Singh, "Nuclear Threat from China: An Appraisal," pp. 27–38.

subtle encirclement strategy masterminded by Beijing.[165] This encirclement—executed through the creation of a nuclear-armed rival within South Asia, a refusal to resolve outstanding territorial disputes with New Delhi, and the gradual penetration of Myanmar—was perceived as being intended to lock India into the confines of the subcontinent by generating security challenges that served to distract New Delhi when it could otherwise be preparing to play a larger role in Asia and beyond.[166] Irrespective of the veracity of these perceptions, the net result was that many Indian policymakers began to perceive malign intentions on the part of China—a problem that only became more disconcerting when it was recognized that the United States would play no helpful role either by thwarting the growing Sino-Pakistani collusion on the nuclear issue or by offering increased reassurance to New Delhi in the form of expanded political, technological, or strategic ties.[167] Faced with such a "deteriorating" regional environment—especially one in which India's decisionmakers became increasingly conscious of the country's new vulnerability to standoff attack from Pakistan—New Delhi's traditional nuclear posture became a candidate ripe for public change.

This prospect of change was only magnified by an unnerving scientific reality that several Indian policymakers were aware of but could never bring themselves to publicly admit: that India's 1974 test was a preliminary but less-than-successful experiment that accordingly called into question the very basis for believing that the alternative of "keeping the option open" could remain a viable form of existential deterrence in perpetuity. In point of fact, the first Indian test in 1974 was a "nuclear explosion" but was emphatically not a

---

[165]The most sophisticated treatment of the "encirclement" thesis can be found in Yaccov Vertzberger, *China's Southwestern Strategy: Encirclement and Counterencirclement* (New York: Praeger, 1985). This theme would be reiterated by Indian policymakers in formal statements released during the May 1998 nuclear tests.

[166]Good examples of the arguments underlying such perceptions can be found in Bidanda M. Chengappa, "Playing Chinese Checkers," *Indian Express*, May 5, 1998, and *India: Indian Article Views Chinese Threat*, FBIS-NES-98-131, May 10, 1998.

[167]K. Subrahmanyam, "History Repeats Itself," *Economic Times*, July 27, 1998; J. N. Dixit, "China-U.S. Equations," *The Hindu*, July 10, 1998; and Anand K. Sahay, "Emerging Power Equations," *The Pioneer*, July 8, 1998.

"nuclear weapon test explosion."[168] To the contrary, it essentially represented the culmination of an experimental effort—dubbed the Subterranean Nuclear Explosion Project and sanctioned by Indian Prime Minister Lal Bahadur Shastri in 1964 after the first Chinese nuclear test—whose objective was to demonstrate that Indian nuclear science had reached the point where it could exploit the processes of nuclear fission to initiate the explosive release of energy. In effect, this test was aimed at establishing a proof of principle and, despite its larger political implications, primarily represented an attempt by the atomic energy establishment to validate the maturity and sophistication of its scientific skills before the Indian political leadership and the country at large.[169] Consequently, as W.P.S. Sidhu accurately noted, "Indian scientists have always referred to the plutonium-implosion package that was detonated in 1974 as a 'device'"[170] because it was neither intended to be nor had it reached "the status of an operational weapon"[171] at the time.

Dr. Raja Rammana, the chief scientist under whose direction the test occurred, subsequently claimed that the 1974 explosion did involve an actual nuclear weapon. This claim was repudiated, however, by Dr. Homi Sethna, the former Chairman of India's AEC under whose aegis the entire Indian nuclear program operates—who succinctly and accurately asserted that the device tested in 1974 had neither the shape nor the portability required for use as a weapon of war.[172] Indeed, Rammana's claim—which was obviously motivated by a desire to influence political debates within the country—hinges on the notion that the 1974 device confirmed the theoretical and physical characteristics required for a successful nuclear detonation and hence ought to be considered a usable "bomb." Yet the fact remains that this design was of greater interest to physicists than to

---

[168]This distinction is appropriately emphasized in Donald R. Westervelt, "The Role of Laboratory Tests," in Jozef Goldblat and David Cox (eds.), *Nuclear Weapons Tests: Prohibition or Limitation?* (Oxford, UK: Oxford University Press, 1998), p. 47.

[169]For an excellent survey of the events leading up to and surrounding this event, see Perkovich, *India's Nuclear Bomb*, pp. 60–189.

[170]W.P.S. Sidhu, "India's Nuclear Tests: Technical and Military Imperatives," *Jane's Intelligence Review*, 8:4 (April 1996), p. 170.

[171]Ibid.

[172]Mini Pant Zachariah, "Indian Scientist Says Ramanna Wrong About 1974 'Bomb,'" *Asian Age*, October 12, 1997.

weaponeers in that the former could declare any device that successfully generated fission energy through a controlled detonation to be an effective "nuclear bomb," whereas the latter would reserve such an appellation only for a device that conformed to certain shape, weight, and stability parameters and that would detonate successfully on command in the face of all the stresses associated with the operation of its carrier system.[173]

In point of fact, India certainly did not possess a nuclear bomb of this sort in 1974, and the test conducted that year was not designed to validate any dedicated weapon design. Consequently, Pokhran I remained a "nuclear explosion" but was not a "nuclear weapon test explosion" of the kind that would have generated confidence in the claim that India possessed a usable nuclear weapon requiring no further testing for its deterrent efficacy. Even more problematically, however, the 1974 test, while validating the design of the implosion system in principle, failed to produce the kinds of yields that its designers had intended or that the popular literature has attributed to it. This fact has never been publicized by Indian policymakers for obvious reasons—it would require that they engage in further nuclear testing despite the great political costs the country incurred in the aftermath of its first test—but news of the less-than-desirable yields generated by the 1974 explosion nonetheless circulated *sotto voce* in the Indian strategic community for more than two decades. One Indian commentator, in fact, baldly asserted that

> The test in Pokharan in 1974 was basically a "dud." Other than exploding, it failed on almost all other scientific counts and, most important, it yielded very little data. It would have been very difficult to serialize production of nuclear weapons on the basis of the 1974 test, and—in any case—the reliability of those weapons would have been in question.[174]

---

[173]In the United States, these variables are termed "military characteristics" and are prepared by the Department of Defense for each nuclear warhead taking into account its intended delivery system. For a good account of how nuclear testing fits into this process, see P. S. Brown, "Nuclear Weapons R&D and the Role of Nuclear Testing," *Energy and Technology Review*, UCRL-52000-86-9 (September 1986), pp. 6–18.

[174]Amitabh Mattoo, "Enough Scientific Reasons Seen for Conducting Tests," *India Abroad*, May 15, 1996.

While the claim that India's 1974 test was a "dud" is clearly hyper-bole—the test did, after all, meet Mark's criterion for a successful nuclear explosion, defined as producing "at least three orders of magnitude more energy per pound than would be available from high explosives"[175]—the fact remains that it provided a much smaller yield than the 10–15 kt commonly reported by most public sources. How much smaller has never been authoritatively stated, al-though one 1981 Indian news report claimed that "some sources at the BARC maintain that independent measurements by some scien-tists put the yield at Pokhran to be as low as 2000 tons of TNT."[176] As recently as 1998, this conclusion was corroborated by one of India's leading journalists, who noted that "there has been no explanation of the low-yield, nor refutation of the story—long known in some circles—that Pokharan-I's yield was not 10–20 kt as claimed but 2–4 kt."[177] This failure to secure the desired yield through a single test explosion should not be surprising, however, since as one authority on nuclear weapon design noted, "the principal uncertainty to be addressed by a weapon test explosion . . . [is] . . . that of yield (or of performance in a complete delivery system)."[178] Developing a nu-clear weapon that consistently provides assured yields usually re-quires many hot tests or, at the very least, numerous heavily instru-mented high-explosive and/or hydrodynamic experiments—and even these may be insufficient to resolve the problems associated with the timing of initiation, which often accounts for the less-than-desired yields in a nuclear explosion. Not surprisingly, the United States alone—by official count—conducted 1054 low- or full-yield hot tests simply to certify fewer than 100 nuclear designs as reliable enough for stockpiling in its arsenal during the Cold War.[179] Cer-

---

[175]J. Carson Mark, "Nuclear Weapons Technology," in B. T. Feld, T. Greenwood, G. W. Rathjens, and S. Weinberg (eds.), *Impact of New Technologies on the Arms Race* (Cambridge, MA: MIT Press, 1971), p. 137.

[176]Cited in Perkovich, *India's Nuclear Bomb*, p. 182, with a detailed discussion of this question on pp. 181–183.

[177]Praful Bidwai, "Regaining Nuclear Sanity," *The Times of India*, June 6, 1998.

[178]Westervelt, "The Role of Laboratory Tests," p. 51.

[179]See "Gallery of U.S. Nuclear Tests" for a survey of all American nuclear tests conducted since 1945: http://www.fas.org/nuke/hew/Usa/Tests/index.html. The en-tire inventory of U.S. nuclear weapon designs is surveyed at http://www.fas.org/nuke/hew/Usa/Weapons/Allbombs.html. Today, the United States has roughly ten major types of nuclear weapons in its enduring stockpile.

tainly India could not be expected to better this record with a single nuclear experiment.

It is not remarkable, therefore, that the 1974 explosion, which confirmed that India's device had in fact gone supercritical and had by implication produced a nuclear explosion, also confirmed that the design of the implosion system was not as good as it might have been. Consequently, what began as an experiment turned out to be a proof test that forced India's nuclear design establishment to work further on improving the yield while reducing the weight and size of the overall device.[180] These developments, however, created new structural uncertainties in that Indian security managers could never be confident that their principal nuclear weapon design would be reliable—i.e., that it would assuredly generate the yields its creators sought or that the design improvements undertaken after 1974 would actually produce the intended corrective effects.[181] This concern about the efficiency of India's weapons haunted the country's political and scientific leadership, or at least those who cared, for the better part of the post-1974 period—and while periodically there were strong political reasons for resuming nuclear testing, it is important to remember that the 1974 experiment also generated considerable technical uncertainties that had to be resolved if India was to possess an effective nuclear arsenal, be it real or virtual, at some point in the future. Not surprisingly, one of India's premier nuclear scientists has thus gone on record as asserting that, irrespective of the political imperatives involved, the nuclear tests conducted in May 1998 "were [an] absolute technical necessity."[182] At the same time, Indian Foreign Minister Jaswant Singh—alluding to precisely the political consequences of the technical uncertainty arising from the 1974 test—asserted that "the restraint exercised for twenty-four years, after having demonstrated our capability in 1974,

---

[180]Chengappa, "The Bomb Makers," pp. 29–31.

[181]In fact, if the corrective measures focused primarily on improving the timing of initiation, the effectiveness of these measures could be conclusively validated *only* by hot testing in that both hydrodynamics and neutronics could be assessed by laboratory experiments, but ensuring appropriate timing of initiation and guaranteed device yields usually require hot testing of one sort or another. See Westervelt, "The Role of Laboratory Tests," pp. 47–58.

[182]Girish Kumar, "Pokhran-II Is a Turning Point in Raising National Morale" (interview with Anil Kakodkar), *The Times of India*, July 30, 1998.

is in itself a unique example. Restraint, however, has to arise from strength. It cannot be based upon indecision or doubt. The series of tests recently undertaken by India [in 1998] has led to the removal of doubts. The action involved was balanced, in that it was the minimum necessary to maintain what is an irreducible component of our national security calculus."[183]

The uncertainties about the efficiency of India's principal device design, primarily with respect to assured yield, would probably have been accommodated by India's policymakers had they been convinced that the global nuclear regime would not unduly penalize New Delhi for retaining its ambiguous status indefinitely. Consequently, successive Indian Prime Ministers toyed with the idea of resuming nuclear testing beginning in 1982–1983 but did not actually do so, motivated as they were primarily by a desire to secure domestic political gains. In 1995, however, a series of changes in the global nuclear regime marked the beginning of the end of India's nuclear ambiguity on purely strategic grounds. The indefinite extension of the NPT in 1995 in fact turned out to be the first step in what India perceived to be a growing constriction of its ability to maintain its nuclear option.[184] New Delhi resisted the indefinite extension of the NPT on the grounds that such an outcome would allow the existing nuclear weapon states to disregard their treaty obligations to work toward universal disarmament without incurring serious penalties. In effect, the NPT's indefinite extension implied that the world would be permanently divided into nuclear "haves" and "have-nots"—and whatever New Delhi's discomfort with global discrimination may previously have been, Indian security managers saw the permanent ratification of this divide as a strategic threat insofar as it provided neither benefits nor legitimacy for countries that chose to maintain an ambiguous nuclear status indefinitely.[185] Moreover, since only three countries were affected by these developments—Israel, India, and Pakistan—and since Israel was presumed to be for all practical purposes a de facto American ally, Indian policymakers read U.S. ef-

---

[183]Singh, *What Constitutes National Security in a Changing World Order?* pp. 31–32.

[184]Jasjit Singh, "India, Europe and Non-Proliferation: Pokhran II and After," *Strategic Analysis*, 22:8 (November 1998), pp. 1111–1122.

[185]Ibid., pp. 1114–1116.

forts with respect to the NPT extension as part of a larger nonproliferation initiative directed primarily at India and Pakistan. What
made the effort to secure such an extension all the more unsettling
from New Delhi's standpoint, however, was the persistent undercur-
rent of international reporting suggesting that even as the legitimate
nuclear powers sought to provide the nonnuclear powers political
assurances against nuclear use (as a quid pro quo for support of the
permanent extension of the NPT), they not only continued to develop new nuclear weapon technologies but also attempted to devise
more flexible and effective ways of using those technologies to
counter a new range of "regional nonproliferation threats."[186] One
Indian commentator, reiterating the dominant view among Indian
policymakers at the time, thus concluded that "given their plans for
new warheads and weapon-testing facilities, the call by the nuclear
haves for an unconditional extension of the NPT appears hypocritical
at best and sinister at worst. Their 'security assurances' are pitifully
inadequate."[187]

This perception was even more strongly reinforced by U.S. efforts
to conclude the CTBT in the aftermath of the indefinite extension of
the NPT. One prominent Indian analyst assessed these efforts in the
following terms: "The United States has been moving decisively to
impose qualitative and quantitative limits on India's nuclear capabilities. After failing to constrain India's nuclear programme through
a regional nonproliferation framework, the Clinton Administration
has decided to use the global route to cap India's nuclear programme."[188] By this analyst's reading, the CTBT posed an even
greater threat to the viability of the Indian nuclear option than the
NPT because the former treaty, by forbidding further nuclear testing,
would prevent New Delhi from ever being able to achieve confidence
in the technical effectiveness of its nuclear weaponry—an issue of
some concern given both the problematic legacy of the 1974 test and
the significant improvements in weapon technology that India would

---

[186]V. Siddharth, "NPT Extension: Safer World Only for U.S.," *Indian Express*, May
4, 1995.

[187]Ibid.

[188]C. Raja Mohan, "India's Nuclear Options," *The Hindu*, December 20, 1995.

potentially require vis-à-vis China in the future.[189] The inability to test its improved devices at some future point could render the Indian nuclear deterrent inutile, at least as far as the confidence of the national leadership in its nuclear capabilities was concerned. This constraint became even more worrisome, India's premier strategic commentator argued, because the treaty's effect of capping India's nuclear weapon capability would not extend symmetrically to Pakistan "because Chin[ese]-Pakistan[i] transactions could include complete [nuclear] weapons [transfers], since there is no verification system to monitor that such transactions do not take place"[190] among signatories to the treaty.

Consequently, it was not surprising that in the negotiations leading up to the treaty in Geneva in 1996, "India for the first time stated that the nuclear issue is a national security concern . . . and advanced that as one reason why [it] was unable to accede to the CTBT."[191] In any event, India would probably have been content to quietly sit out the CTBT with no subsequent changes in its nuclear posture (just as it had done earlier with the NPT) had Article XIV's "entry into force" clause—introduced at Russian, British, and Chinese insistence—not surfaced at the last minute in the draft text.[192] In essence, this clause made the treaty's effectiveness contingent on the accession of 44 states—including India—that were specially named in Annex 2 of the document, providing for a review conference in 1999 if the treaty had not entered into force three years after the date of the anniversary of its opening for signature. The purpose of this review conference was to enable "the States that have already deposited their instruments of ratification" to examine the extent to which the basic objectives of the treaty had been met and to "consider and decide by consensus what measures consistent with international law may be undertaken to accelerate the ratification process in order to facilitate the early entry into force of this Treaty." The prospect of such a review

---

[189]Raj Chengappa, "Playing the Spoiler," *India Today*, September 15, 1996, pp. 76–78.

[190]K. Subrahmanyam, "India and CTBT," *The Times of India*, February 21, 1996.

[191]Singh, "Against Nuclear Apartheid," p. 46.

[192]Official Indian perceptions of the CTBT and the effects of the "entry into force" clause have been detailed in Ghose, "Negotiating the CTBT: India's Security Concerns and Nuclear Disarmament," pp. 239–261.

conference, which under the terms of the treaty could be repeatedly convened "at subsequent anniversaries of the opening for signature of this Treaty, until its entry into force,"[193] greatly agitated most Indian strategic elites, who feared that this mechanism was little more than a back door to enforce the treaty by a majority vote if accession to the document by some of the 44 states specified in Annex 2 was not forthcoming in the interim. Indeed, one former Indian Foreign Secretary—echoing the sentiments of many Indian policymakers—publicly asserted that the "one feature of the CTBT which is different from the NPT is that once the CTBT as proposed by the United States is adopted, even countries not adhering to the treaty will be subject to sanctions [under Article XIV]."[194] To be sure, the United States attempted to assure India, through a series of diplomatic notes, that coercive sanctions were emphatically not the purpose of the review conferences, but such assurances failed to allay Indian suspicions—and many Indian policymakers thus began to view the interval between the CTBT's conclusion and the convening of the first review conference as the closing window of opportunity within which India would have to change its traditional nuclear posture.[195] Brajesh Mishra, for example—then a member of the BJP's cell on foreign affairs and currently Principal Secretary to Indian Prime Minister Atal Bihari Vajpayee—argued prophetically, while commenting on the Congress government's stand on the CTBT, that India should "'immediately' go ahead with 'one or two nuclear tests' to help develop 'nuclear warheads for our missiles' . . . [since] the longer we wait, the more dangerous will it be for us, and the longer we delay (carrying out the tests), the more pressure will be brought on us."[196] Other Indian analysts argued for less dramatic but equally significant responses, enjoining New Delhi "to declare that India is a

---

[193] The relevant text of the treaty from which these quotations are drawn is available at http://www.fas.org/nuke/control/ctbt/text/ctbt1.htm.

[194] J. N. Dixit, "Stand Up or Put Up," *Indian Express*, April 16, 1996.

[195] The most apt characterization of Indian fears about the "entry into force" clause can be found in Mohammed Ayoob, "Nuclear India and Indian-American Relations," *Orbis*, 43:1 (Winter 1999), p. 66.

[196] *India: BJP Demands "Two Nuclear Tests" to Develop Warheads,* FBIS-NES-96-155, August 9, 1996.

nuclear weapons state and that it reserves the right to acquire, improve and augment nuclear weapons."[197]

As it turned out, the BJP government accepted both suggestions on May 11, 1998. But with sentiments such as these dominating India's political discourse—sentiments that grew out of a fear that India's ability to maintain its option indefinitely was steadily eroding even as grave uncertainties persisted with respect to the technical efficacy of its weaponry—it was only a matter of time before India shifted from its traditional posture of maintaining the option. When these sentiments were combined with other variables—such as concerns about the growing nuclear and missile programs in Pakistan and China, the perceptions of increased Sino-Pakistani technological collusion, the United States' apparent apathy with respect to enforcing its own nonproliferation laws vis-à-vis Beijing, and other, more nebulous fears about future nuclear coercion and nuclear crises involving China and Pakistan—it became increasingly obvious that the old posture of maintaining the option was poised for change. When this change would occur and what form it would take could not yet be discerned, but in retrospect it appears evident that at least the timing of change would be determined simply by an alteration in the last condition identified earlier: the ascendancy to power of the BJP, a more risk-acceptant party that simply did not believe either that the security threats facing the country had dissipated or that India possessed the ability to defuse those threats by any means other than nuclear weapons.[198]

At the time of the BJP's accession to power, the policy consequences of these beliefs were neither obvious nor self-evident, even to Indians. In the aftermath of India's nuclear tests, many American commentators, including elected officials, heaped scorn on the U.S. intelligence community for failing to see the obvious: that the BJP-led coalition's own National Agenda for Governance promised to "exercise the option to induct nuclear weapons." Yet however clear these promises seem in retrospect, they were certainly not unmistakable at the time they were first issued. *India Today*, for example— widely regarded as one of the country's most respected news-

---

[197]Rakshat Puri, "Another Approach to CTBT," *Hindustan Times*, August 14, 1996.

[198]Singh, *Defending India*, pp. 290–291 and 306–338.

magazines—summarized the National Agenda with the headline "Words, Words, Words: The BJP-Led Alliance's National Agenda for Governance Confuses Rather Than Clarifies."[199] Commenting on what it termed "the [BJP's] breathtaking promise to 're-evaluate the nuclear policy and exercise the option to induct nuclear weapons,'" the magazine wryly asserted that "the second clause only makes the first one entirely redundant." Indeed, even the doyen of India's strategic commentators, K. Subrahmanyam, was not impressed; writing soon after the NDA government's ascension to office, he concluded after extensive analysis of the nuclear posture that "there may not be a radical change in policy between the policy of the earlier governments and the National Agenda."[200] Other Indian analysts offered similar judgments. P. R. Chari, for example, noted that "the BJP's nuclear agenda has not attracted much attention"[201] and offered three plausible reasons why this was in fact the case:

> First, nobody takes election manifestos seriously in India. Experience informs that these declarations of intent are designed to garner votes. Politicians in power have more important things to do than pursue election promises. Second, BJP leaders have reiterated their nuclear intentions for years. This pursues the line defined by its earlier avatar [incarnation]—the Jan Sangh—that had also advocated its favouring India's nuclear weaponization. Third, the BJP in power has acted very differently from their rhetoric when out of power. Apropos, the BJP and the Jan Sangh were in power in earlier coalition governments. Why did they not press for India weaponizing its nuclear programme?[202]

Reasoning from this rather sensible premise, Chari concluded that "the BJP may not change India's nuclear policy," in part because "opinion is sharply divided among the experts whether more nuclear tests are necessary . . . for India to weaponize its 'open' nuclear op-

---

[199]"Words, Words, Words," *India Today*, March 30, 1998, p. 5.

[200]K. Subrahmanyam, "Nuclear Option and Agenda," *Economic Times*, March 20, 1998.

[201]P. R. Chari, "BJP's Nuclear Agenda," February 20, 1998, available at http://www.ipcs.org/issues/articles/060-ndi-chari.html.

[202]Ibid.

tion."[203] If these assessments are anything to go by, the BJP's decision to resume nuclear testing came as a surprise even to many Indians—who, with the exception of some commentators on the Left, would doubtless have agreed with one analyst who exclaimed, "The unthinkable has happened. India's decision to conduct three tests, including one thermonuclear test, has surprised most and shocked at least a few."[204]

That these decisions occurred at the time they did, however, can be explained mainly by the risk-accepting propensities of the BJP in contrast to India's other political parties. To be sure, the various factors analyzed earlier all contributed to the perception that India's external security environment had evolved in an unfavorable direction. This pernicious evolution was assisted in part by some of India's own strategic choices—the effect of the 1974 nuclear test and the Integrated Guided Missile Program on Pakistan's own nuclear and missile acquisition decisions being just two examples—but since their long-range consequences were either overlooked or accepted to begin with,[205] it is not surprising that the BJP found itself in power at a time when pressure to change the country's traditional nuclear posture was steadily mounting. What had prevented these changes from coming about even more hastily than they did was simply differences in risk tolerance among the various political parties,

---

[203]Ibid.

[204]Mattoo, "Enough Scientific Reasons Seen for Conducting Tests."

[205]India often contributes to its own misfortunes because of its strategic solipsism. Many Indian technical initiatives, such as the 1974 nuclear test, the missile development program, and the pursuit of advanced nuclear weaponry, were initiated primarily as "technology demonstrators" intended to showcase the quality of India's scientific prowess. Despite the fact that many of these initiatives were actually less successful than advertised, their effect on Pakistan has often been more arresting than intended; in many cases, they have unnerved Islamabad sufficiently to cause it to initiate major counterresponses that have had the end result of actually overtaking India in several issue areas where New Delhi originally possessed both the lead and the initiative. When faced with subsequent evidence of Pakistan's unbelievable progress, Indian decisionmakers often fail to recognize the deleterious consequences of their own actions: Their "technology demonstrators" invariably alarm Islamabad sufficiently into mounting formidable counterresponses even as their own passionate belief in the success of these demonstrations lulls them into a complacency that prevents them from bringing these experimental initiatives to an effective and successful conclusion in the field.

especially as far as individual leaders were concerned.[206] Yet at the same time, the pressure for change had already begun to dominate the domestic debate about security policy. Indeed, this changing national mood was captured succinctly by a report jointly issued in 1995 by two of India's most prestigious think tanks, the Institute for Defence Studies and Analyses and the Centre for Policy Research, which—after considering many of the alterations occurring in the six conditions identified above—argued that ". . . in this changed situation, the present position of keeping the nuclear option open has become meaningless. There is need now to examine how best to translate this into effective deterrence and to safeguard our vital interests, in political and military terms."[207]

When combined with other endogenous factors—such as continuing pressure from the Indian scientific establishment and the uniformed military's new but fervent urging for greater clarity in the country's nuclear capability and deterrence doctrines—such judgments ensured that Alternative III would subsist only as an unstable equilibrium that was fated to collapse when the preferences of key decisionmakers happened to align with some external events signaling a further deterioration in the country's security environment. And indeed, Pakistan's decision to test the Ghauri IRBM, the rash and provocative rhetoric emerging from Islamabad in the aftermath of that test, and the muted U.S. response to this new distension in Pakistani capabilities turned out in retrospect to be just such events. As one Indian news report summarized it, "Vajpayee walked into South Block on March 19 with his mind fully made up. But events did shape the timing: Operation Shakti was authorised two days after the

---

[206]As I. K. Gujral would remark in an interview after the nuclear tests, "The option of testing a nuclear device has been before every Prime Minister since the time of Rajiv Gandhi but they chose not to exercise it. It is up to the judgment of the Prime Minister to work out the concerned mathematics as far as the cost-benefit ratio is concerned and arrive at his own conclusions. . . . For me economic and social development was of vital importance. Each one of us has our own value sheet of cost-benefit valuation in terms of economic development." See "We Have It, They Have It, That's All," *The Times of India*, May 16, 1998.

[207]"Summary of Recommendations," presented at the Institute for Defence Studies and Analyses—Centre for Policy Research Joint Seminar, India International Centre, New Delhi, September 24, 1995.

Ghauri test-firing in Pakistan."[208] Thus, while the cluster of events relating to the Ghauri demonstration certainly did not *cause* the Indian nuclear test, they undoubtedly *occasioned* it, and the BJP government's strong determination ensured that when faced with a choice of possibilities—including a comparable resumption of Indian missile tests, a formal declaration of India's nuclear status, a covert development of a full-fledged arsenal, and a resumption of overt nuclear testing—India would in fact "go for broke" in efforts to simultaneously validate the technical quality of its own nuclear arsenal, reassure its own populace, and communicate to Pakistan, China, and the United States that India would take care of its own interests no matter what the costs might be to each of these states.[209]

The events that occurred in May 1998 lent substance to this decision, and the analytical issue at this juncture therefore lies in understanding India's future choices now that the "veritable middle

---

[208]Joshi, "Nuclear Shock Waves," p. 14. Even as moderate a commentator as Prem Shankar Jha argued that "India's response to the launching of the Ghauri should . . . be unequivocal. Instead of pretending that nothing much has happened, or worse, that the Pakistanis may be lying . . . [India] should shed its indecision and do whatever is needed to restore credibility to its nuclear deterrence capability. This requires . . . when it becomes absolutely necessary, the resumption of nuclear testing." See Prem Shankar Jha, "India Must Resume N-Tests," *Hindustan Times*, April 18, 1998.

[209]In hindsight, this BJP decision seems obvious in part because it was revealed in the aftermath of the May 1998 tests that the BJP government had in fact authorized a resumption of nuclear testing during the 12 days that it was in office during May 1996. For details about this extraordinary episode, which the United States government did not then know, see Perkovich, *India's Nuclear Bomb*, pp. 371–377. This episode has now been used by several analysts (see, for example, Joeck, "Nuclear Developments in India and Pakistan," pp. 6–14) to argue the point that the BJP-dominated government's decision to renew nuclear testing in 1998 had less to do with India's security concerns and more to do with the BJP's long-standing conviction that India needed nuclear weapons in order to overcome its strategic immobility and to underwrite its claims to greatness. This conclusion is not entirely obvious, however, since it fails to explain why the BJP in its earlier incarnation—the Jan Sangh—did not even argue for a resumption of nuclear testing when it was an equally, if not more, important part of a previous coalition government in 1977. The only explanation satisfying these facts is therefore that, whatever the BJP's traditional preferences about nuclearization might have been, India's strategic environment in 1998 presented certain incentives which enabled the BJP to act on its long-standing beliefs without giving the appearance of pursuing a fundamentally irrational course of action. To that degree, the "deterioration" in India's strategic environment—which could certainly not be asserted in 1977 in the manner in which it could be argued in the post-1995 period—played a critical *permissive* role in enabling the BJP to act on what may have been its political prejudices but could nonetheless be defended as a justifiable policy made necessary by India's national interest.

path,"[210] Alternative III, has finally collapsed. To be sure, some Indian commentators still hope that a new version of Alternative III might be resuscitated.[211] Praful Bidwai, for example, has argued emphatically that despite the events of May 1998, "there must be no weaponisation and no [more] tests."[212] Tracing the burdens both to India's traditional commitment to a nuclear weapon–free world and to its security, Bidwai has consistently maintained that India "must never test again nor make weapons that are . . . [both] . . . illegal and strategically irrational."[213] Elaborating on this theme, Bidwai's colleague Achin Vanaik has defended the thesis that "nuclear deterrence is a deeply immoral doctrine," further asserting that New Delhi's readiness to countenance new patterns of nuclearization would result only in a "persistent involvement in this discourse [that] debases a nation."[214] Consequently, Vanaik argues, any solution to India's strategic conundrum that produces further nuclearization would have the effect of ensuring that "India has now become part of the problem of global nuclear disarmament and not part of the solution."[215]

Some Indian analysts have therefore argued against moving away from Alternative III on the grounds that such actions would undermine the eventual possibility of global nuclear disarmament. At the same time, still others have chosen to defend this conclusion primarily on the basis of India's own strategic interests. The latter arguments, which are driven largely by a sobering view of what nuclearization would entail for India's broader political objectives, have been articulated by a former Director General of Military Operations, Lieutenant General V. R. Raghavan, and by a former Chief of Naval Staff, Admiral L. Ramdas.

Raghavan, for example—arguing against the larger tide—has asserted that the optimal direction for India at present is not "to stay

---

[210]Singh, "Why Nuclear Weapons?" p. 20.

[211]Kamal Mitra Chenoy, "India Should Beat the Nuclear Club, Not Join It," *Asian Age*, July 23, 1998.

[212]Praful Bidwai, "Sign the Test Ban Treaty," *The Times of India*, July 14, 1998.

[213]Bidwai, "Regaining Nuclear Sanity."

[214]Achin Vanaik, "Hotter Than a Thousand Suns," *The Telegraph*, May 26, 1998.

[215]Achin Vanaik, "Drawing New Lines," *The Hindu*, May 23, 1998.

the nuclear weapons course, bear the costs and create the credible deterrence necessary to engage in a dialogue of equals . . . [but rather] . . . to use the nuclear tests as a loud and clear message from India for ending nuclear double-talk and obfuscation and securing India's security."[216] Recognizing that the May 1998 nuclear tests cannot be undone in either a physical or a political sense, Raghavan noted that "the way to avoid the dilemmas . . . [imposed by unfavorable] . . . nuclear choices lies in taking the focus back to economic growth and political stability."[217] Since "India's national interests would be best safeguarded by demonstrating nuclear weapons readiness without be[coming] a nuclear threat,"[218] the most sensible solution at this juncture, according to Raghavan, would consist of reviving Alternative III, but in a new guise that would entail "converting the moratorium on tests announced by the Prime Minister into binding agreements, stopping the process of tests from going into a weapons production cycle, and . . . restoring relations with other countries which have been allowed to get tangled by the [May 1998] tests."[219] This course of action was obviously justified on the premise that Indian security and status "essentially depends on regional stability and economic growth" and that tightly "integrating India globally in economic and technological terms" rather than "getting isolated" from the international system consequently remained India's most important immediate strategic objective. Given this understanding, Raghavan maintained that the nuclear tests ought to be used as diplomatic instruments to force "the nuclear five to find ways of accommodating Indian interests [by] using the negotiating value of nuclear weapons instead of their deterrent value,"[220] since "an undue weightage to the arguments [about] deterrence and force structures w[ould] leave [Indian] leaders vulnerable to overplaying the nuclear gambit."[221]

---

[216]V. R. Raghavan, "The Indian Nuclear Gambit," *The Hindu*, August 5, 1998.

[217]V. R. Raghavan, "India's Nuclear Dilemma," *The Hindu*, August 6, 1998.

[218]V. R. Raghavan, "Nuclear Insecurity," *Hindustan Times*, June 11, 1998.

[219]Ibid.

[220]Ibid.

[221]Raghavan, "The Indian Nuclear Gambit."

Admiral Ramdas has similarly argued that because "neither India nor Pakistan has, or can afford, what real nuclear weaponization takes, . . . the need of the hour is to restructure the national agenda to meet th[e] new challenge" of producing "real power and strength [that] will come only when we can give all our people their basic needs like food, drinking water, health, education, clothing and housing."[222] Along with some others, both analysts have in effect argued for turning the clock back to the maximum extent possible. They urge the Indian government to use its nuclear tests as a bargaining chip to accelerate the processes of global nuclear disarmament, ensure that India's security and status concerns are taken seriously, and solidify the country's integration into the global economy in order to further its developmental goals rather than simply treating the events of May 1998 as a stepping stone along the path toward further nuclearization.[223]

Alternative IV: A Recessed Deterrent

These views, however—no matter how cogent they may be—represent a distinct minority in India today, and given the predilections of both the present Indian government and the higher bureaucracy, it is most likely that all future choices will run even further in the direction of nuclearization rather than away from it. Indeed, of the two broad termini imaginable, the more minimalist choice embodied by Alternative IV has already found surprising support—at least in the main, if not in all the details—from one of India's best-known strategic commentators, Jasjit Singh, who has argued that India's "interim needs . . . could be met by a doctrine and strategy of 'recessed deterrence.'"[224] This position has also been defended by a few other Indian commentators, who have similarly argued, albeit less clearly,

---

[222]L. Ramdas, "Pokhran-II and Its Fallout," *Frontline*, July 7–17, 1998.

[223]For other views affirming this position, see "In Arms Way," *The Telegraph*, May 28, 1998; Ramachandra Guha, "And Now, the Test of Sanity," *The Telegraph*, June 8, 1998; and Arjun Makhijani, "A Disarming Offer No One Can Refuse," *The Times of India*, September 3, 1998.

[224]Singh, "A Nuclear Strategy for India" p. 318.

that striving for robust nuclear deterrence could at this stage turn India into little more than a nation of "beggars with the bomb."[225]

All such views—which, it must be noted, are not popular among Indian security elites (who believe that the May 1998 nuclear tests have provided the country with the best opportunity to strike out as a full-fledged nuclear weapon state)—are grounded in three important assumptions. The first of these assumptions, while conceding that nuclear capabilities of some sort are essential for Indian security, holds that the notion of security itself ought to be framed in inclusionary terms centering on a concept that goes "back to economic growth and political stability."[226] The implication of this vision is that India's nuclear capabilities, while made necessary by its uncertain strategic environment, still cannot function as the "be-all and end-all" of its strategic preparedness. Hence, to the degree that robust nuclearization actually undercuts the objective of securing a "comprehensive, durable and integrated peace . . . [which ensures the] . . . socio-economic growth and development of India,"[227] this assumption argues that the burdens imposed by such nuclearization simply ought to be minimized. The second assumption holds that the extant global nuclear order is heading inexorably toward a "decaying of deterrence"[228] in that the use of nuclear weapons and the issuance of nuclear threats have become less and less credible for a variety of reasons, ranging from growing distaste for all things nuclear to the decreasing utility of war as a method for resolving disputes to the high costs of using nuclear weaponry as instruments of war fighting and coercion. Because nuclear weapons in such circumstances have "utility more in terms of political deterrence rather than . . . military deterrence,"[229] the net implication of this insight is that India's immediate strategic objective should consist of developing a recessed capability that could "represent an end-state

---

[225]This phrase is borrowed from Bhaskar Dutta, "Beggars with the Bomb," *The Telegraph*, May 26, 1998. For a critique of even minimal weaponization, see also Praful Bidwai, "Beggared by the Bomb: Dangerous Shift in Nuclear Doctrine," *The Times of India*, April 21, 1998.

[226]Raghavan, "India's Nuclear Dilemma."

[227]Singh, "A Nuclear Strategy for India," p. 313.

[228]Ibid., p. 308.

[229]Ibid., p. 309.

itself before India starts to reverse its own capability in proportion to the process of abolition by other weapon states."[230] Finally, the third assumption is that at least in the foreseeable future, India is not likely to face any strategic challenges that will require it to possess a large, ready arsenal capable of promptly executing nuclear operations in the context of a crisis. This assumption concedes that such threats could materialize over time, but because they are "unlikely to arise very rapidly"[231] and because "significant early warning will be available"[232] when they do, there is no compelling need for India to lock itself into an interim nuclear posture that is costly, demanding, and escalatory. Given these assumptions, Indian strategists who argue for postures resembling Alternative IV treat nuclear capabilities essentially as a hedge against strategic uncertainty: They seek to preserve Indian security at the lowest possible cost, but because they also value the benefits of a denuclearizing international order, they reason that a recessed deterrent represents the best choice for New Delhi even in the aftermath of the recent nuclear tests in South Asia.[233]

Thanks to such concerns, Alternative IV fits the bill admirably. This alternative centers on making Indian deterrence capabilities more *credible* not by pursuing more overt and provocative components such as further nuclear testing, the assembly-line production of nuclear weapons, or the deployment of nuclear-armed delivery systems, but rather by developing the crucial albeit hidden and oft-forgotten command-and-control structures as well as the organizational and ideational elements relating to sufficiency requirements, use doctrine, targeting options, and conflict termination. Since effective deterrence derives in the final analysis not simply from the possession of some completed nuclear weapons and dedicated delivery systems but also from an integrated capability

---

[230]Ibid., p. 318.

[231]Ibid.

[232]Ibid.

[233]This position has been affirmed most clearly, and at some political cost, only by Jasjit Singh. But echoes of this position can also be found in the writings of other Indian commentators. These are explored in the context of the wider Indian debate on nuclear weapons in Kanti Bajpai, "India's Nuclear Posture After Pokhran II," *International Studies*, 37:4 (October–December 2000), pp. 267–301.

that includes both effective C^{3}I and adequate planning mechanisms, the recessed deterrent Alternative IV prescribes requires that India develop these latter dimensions of national capability *while still refraining from the serial production of new nuclear weapons and the deployment of dedicated nuclear delivery systems.*

On the premise that a nuclear arsenal is ultimately a systemic artifact as opposed to a disparate collection of discrete components, Alternative IV would obligate India to initiate the development of those ancillary elements which make a nuclear arsenal *possible*—should that be required at some point in the future—but without producing such an arsenal immediately. Thus, as far as fissile-material production is concerned, the recessed deterrent would not only allow for the continuation of spent-fuel reprocessing, as is currently occurring in the facilities at Trombay, Tarapur, and Kalpakkam,[234] but would also permit the continued enrichment of uranium, assuming that such is already occurring on a pilot scale in facilities at Trombay and Rattehali. This uranium enrichment appears to be intended primarily for fueling India's future nuclear submarines—a capability that would prove useful both for conventional warfare and for a future deterrent if required.[235] In point of fact, both the production of plutonium and the enrichment of uranium continued even when India's nuclear posture consisted simply of maintaining the option, and the recessed deterrent does not entail any departure from this practice, although it would prefer that no changes be made in the *pace* at which these materials are accumulated. This variable, however, is beyond the control of any outside entity, and many sources have suggested that India already has a sufficient inventory of fissile materials to service its future deterrence needs.[236] This view also seems to have informed New Delhi's decision to allow the discussions on the FMCT to begin in Geneva.

Where nuclear weapons themselves are concerned, the recessed deterrent would also allow BARC and other centers to continue both

---

[234]Manoj Joshi, "India's Nuclear Estate," *India Today International*, May 4, 1998, p. 40.

[235]T.S. Gopi Rethinaraj, "ATV: All at Sea Before It Hits the Water," *Jane's Intelligence Review*, 10:6 (June 1998), pp. 31–35.

[236]Jones, *From Testing to Deploying Nuclear Forces*, p. 8.

theoretical and laboratory experimentation relating to nuclear weapon design.[237] This work—which India has now acknowledged includes research relating to the development of boosted fission and fusion weapons in addition to pure fission devices—would proceed as usual except for the fact that no hot testing of these devices would be permitted. The May 1998 tests obviously violated this stipulation, so acceding to Alternative IV today would require no *further* testing of any nuclear devices. As Jasjit Singh, accepting such a constraint as integral to his version of the recessed deterrent, noted:

> There is no doubt that we have the wherewithal to make plutonium-based 15–30 kiloton yield nuclear warheads. A thermonuclear bomb would be desirable but will require testing. We have the sovereign right to test, but the costs of likely international response outweigh the benefits, at least at this stage. The 1974 peaceful explosion provided us with enough basis for a credible capability. It also needs to be remembered that the Hiroshima bomb was not tested but it was not any less effective because of that. A nuclear test, therefore, remains a desirable measure but not a necessity. A test will define the quality of the deterrent but not the credibility of [that] deterrent.[238]

It can thus be seen that the stipulation of "no further tests" essentially formalizes India's voluntary moratorium on future nuclear testing. In the aftermath of the May 1998 tests, India indicated that laboratory tests of the nonnuclear components of its nuclear devices (primarily SAFF components), subcritical nuclear tests, and computer-aided simulations would continue.[239] Presuming that these are already occurring, the recessed deterrent Alternative IV envisages would allow them to continue first because they may not be detected by external entities and second because they do not embody a manifest challenge to the international nonproliferation order (since, among other things, the existing nuclear weapon states also perform such tests on a regular basis). Alternative IV would therefore permit India to maintain its existing—small—stockpile of nuclear weapons

---

[237] See *India: India's Nuclear Weapons Plan Examined.*

[238] Jasjit Singh, "The Nuclear Option," *Hindustan Times,* March 21, 1998.

[239] "Planned Series of Nuclear Tests Completed," *India News,* May 16–June 15, 1998, p. 8.

but would forbid the production of new weapons (either individually or through assembly-line methods) and the explosive testing of both current and improved nuclear weapon designs.

The recessed deterrent would also leave inviolate the country's traditional efforts to develop its nuclear delivery systems. It would, for example, permit the DRDO to continue its development of potential delivery systems such as the Agni, Sagarika, and follow-on Prithvi missiles. At the same time, however, it would require that India abjure the production and deployment of all nuclear systems, be they dedicated vehicles like the Agni or Agni follow-on missile or dual-capable systems like the Prithvi (SS-150/250/350), Jaguar, Mirage 2000, and Su-30, which are capable of carrying nuclear weapons. Since the latter are already present in the inventory and operational, having been acquired for a conventional war-fighting role, Alternative IV would also require that India eschew any modifications that would render some or all of these platforms true nuclear delivery systems. This would include abstaining from both hardware and software modifications as well as from command changes that would reconstitute these platforms into new organizational structures relevant to nuclear operations. In this issue area as well, the demands of a recessed deterrent *may* represent little more than a variation of the posture associated with maintaining the option, but it is worth noting that such requirements do run counter to both U.S. and Indian preferences expressed in the aftermath of the May 1998 tests.

To be sure, the United States would prefer to see all Indian ballistic missile research, development, test, and evaluation (RDT&E) programs either terminated outright or at least frozen until a clear and present danger appears to confront New Delhi.[240] Such a preference could, however, strip India of its ability to operationalize a deterrent *in extremis,* since developing effective missile delivery vehicles is essentially a time-consuming process with a maturation period that runs into years if not decades. Because this outcome would be inconsistent with developing a recessed deterrent, Alternative IV would allow continued RDT&E activities relating to all India's missile pro-

---

[240]"Remarks to Stimson Center," Secretary of State Madeleine K. Albright, Washington, D.C., June 10, 1998, available at http://secretary.state.gov/www/statements/1998/980610.html.

grams but would prohibit both the production of such missiles, either individually or serially, and their deployment as nuclear vehicles ready for war. Jasjit Singh, too, has emphasized that his version of a recessed deterrent requires a vigorous missile RDT&E program, although he hedges on the question of missile production; while he seems to endorse such production on the grounds that "the advantage of investment in . . . missiles is that they can always be used with conventional warheads also," he simultaneously asserts that India "should be willing to forgo ballistic missiles if all countries are willing to abolish them."[241] Alternative IV, as described here, would permit a variety of Indian missile RDT&E activities and the acquisition of long-lead items required to produce these missiles when necessary, but it would proscribe the production of any missiles that were meant to serve primarily as nuclear delivery vehicles. Since India has already produced some missile systems that are notionally capable of delivering nuclear ordnance—principally the Prithvi SSM (SS-150)—Alternative IV would require that these vehicles be maintained purely as conventional systems, in line with what appear to be India's original intentions.[242] Consistent with this interest, Alternative IV would, however, reject India's preference for modifying some of its dual-capable systems for nuclear delivery missions. Since the objective of a recessed deterrent is to enable India to prepare itself for the burdens of security management in the nuclear age without actually creating an arsenal before it is truly necessary, Alternative IV would also reject any proposals to configure for nuclear delivery missions either some of its conventionally armed ballistic missiles, such as the Prithvi, or its attack aircraft, because this would run counter to the objective just enunciated. To be sure, detecting such modifications may be difficult if not impossible, but the intent of maintaining a potential as opposed to an actual arsenal requires the rejection of all proposals leading to the creation of a relatively ready strike force. Moreover, unlike the long lead times necessary for developing a missile capability, the modification of

---

[241] Singh, "The Nuclear Option."

[242] The issue of the Prithvi as a nuclear system will be further discussed in Chapter Five, but the initial Indian intention in developing this system revolved primarily around utilization for conventional war-fighting purposes. See Indranil Banerjie, "The Integrated Guided Missile Development Programme," *Indian Defence Review*, 5:2 (July 1990), pp. 103–105.

strike aircraft for nuclear missions can be undertaken more or less quickly in an emergency; consequently, it makes sense to forbid such activities even though it simultaneously permits RDT&E efforts and long-lead acquisition activities in the missile realm.

Alternative IV as described above may thus embody few changes from the traditional posture as far as the production of fissile materials, the development and production of nuclear weapons, and the acquisition of delivery systems are concerned. At the same time, however, it does entail new and potentially far-reaching changes with respect to the development of both the supporting infrastructure and the procedural and ideational systems associated with a nuclear deterrent—changes that are deemed to be vital because, as Neil Joeck succinctly phrased it, they "enhance stability in a crisis and improve the ability to avoid nuclear use in the event of war."[243] Several Indian analysts have argued for these changes—some well before the May 1998 nuclear tests occurred—on the grounds that "Indian defence [has heretofore subsisted] in an unreal world not prepared for the threat of nuclear weapons and missiles" and, as such, required a reorientation that would help "assure India's security in the nuclear *kaliyug.*"[244] Still other analysts have pleaded for these changes in the hope that they would lead to an overhaul of the entire defense decisionmaking system—an overhaul that, while intended to immunize India against the worst effects of existing nuclear threats in the first instance, would ultimately lead to a greater appreciation of military power where enhancing the country's desire for safety, power, and prestige is concerned.[245] Irrespective of the motivations underlying these arguments, most Indian security managers would agree with Joeck's assessment that the most compelling reason for adopting a posture closer to what is called a recessed deterrent (as opposed to merely maintaining the option) is "to reduce nuclear risks"—i.e., to "help . . . reinforce deterrence at ground level

---

[243]Joeck, *Maintaining Nuclear Stability in South Asia,* p. 13.

[244]Joshi, "In the Shadow of Fear," pp. 50 and 53. The term *kaliyug* refers, in Hinduism, to the last of the four ages—*yugas*—that make up one cycle of creation. The Kali-Yuga, which Hinduism believes refers to the present age, is characterized by wickedness and disaster that lead to the destruction of the world in preparation for a new cycle of creation and with it a new cycle of yugas.

[245]Vijay Kiran, "Strategic Failure," *Hindustan Times,* July 25, 1998.

and ensure that both sides are not left with a choice between suicide and surrender."[246]

Alternative IV therefore requires specific changes in India's nuclear posture, all of which lie outside the obvious realms of weapon capabilities and delivery systems. The first such cluster of changes—material improvements—are connected to the development of an adequate *supporting infrastructure* that would help decisionmakers assess an adversary's capabilities and intentions as well as execute any proportionate responses that may be appropriate if deterrence fails. Among other things, this would require that India reconfigure its intelligence and warning systems—understood here mainly in terms of technical equipment—so that it could effectively monitor and assess the range of threats facing the country on a day-to-day basis in peacetime as well as provide careful evaluations of possible breaking events during a crisis.[247] Other associated requirements would include modernizing India's communications network, investing in a survivable chain of command centers, and reconfiguring the meteorological and space systems to provide timely support both to political decisionmakers and to civilian and military personnel tasked with carrying out nuclear operations.[248]

Since such capabilities already exist, however—if only in rudimentary form and driven primarily by the demands of conventional warfighting operations—the changes this alternative would require at the level of infrastructure may be less important than those demanded by the second cluster, which is associated with the development of *procedural systems*. Procedural systems here refer specifically to schemes that govern the management and use of the country's nuclear capabilities, among the most critical of which are those aimed at ensuring adequate positive and negative control over the nuclear inventory. Positive control in this context implies that weapons must be readily available when required by the legitimate authority, while negative control implies that weapons must be us-

---

[246]Joeck, *Maintaining Nuclear Stability in South Asia*, p. 13.

[247]Singh, *Defending India*, pp. 287–289.

[248]See the discussion in Kapil Kak, "Command and Control of Small Nuclear Arsenals," in Jasjit Singh (ed.), *Nuclear India* (New Delhi: Knowledge World, 1998), pp. 266–285.

able only by those specifically authorized to do so.[249] At a purely technical level, both forms of control are not as difficult to achieve in India as is sometimes imagined in the West, but whether the *legitimacy* of the prevailing arrangements can be sustained in the context of strategic decapitation—especially in a democratic country like India, where such issues have thus far not become the staple of the nuclear debate—remains an open question. Other procedural matters that must be resolved include the structure of the nation's national command authority; the chain of command, control, and custody in the event of strategic decapitation; the structural arrangements for civil-military coordination relating to nuclear use, including the vexing issue of predelegation; and the creation of a formal nuclear requirement-planning structure that includes both civilian scientists and military planners.[250]

Associated with procedural systems but quite distinct from them lies a third cluster of changes predicated by Alternative IV that, because they remain entirely in the realm of concepts, might be referred to as the *ideational system*. The ideational system in the context of nuclear deterrence is fundamentally concerned with defining the political utility of nuclear weapons for a particular country and, thereafter, with translating that definition into a deterrence doctrine that governs nuclear acquisitions and force-structure planning, the choice of targets and targeting strategies, and, finally, issues of war termination and postconflict recovery. The ideational system is in this context intimately connected with the procedural system described earlier in that the concepts governing the effective acquisition and employment of nuclear force can be derived only through an established institutional system that is capable of acquiring information, assessing choices in the wake of bureaucratic and public debate, and promulgating decisions that are recognized as legitimate and authoritative by all the subordinate echelons in the establishment.[251] In a more fundamental sense, however, the ideational system remains the bedrock on which all other dimensions of the nu-

---

[249]Peter D. Feaver, *Guarding the Guardians* (Ithaca, NY: Cornell University Press, 1992), pp. 12–13.

[250]Kak, "Command and Control of Small Nuclear Arsenals," pp. 266–285.

[251]K. Subrahmanyam, "Nuclear Policy and Political Culture," *Economic Times*, August 20, 1998.

clear posture will be built. This is because the country's perception of nuclear weapons and their utility will remain the foundation on which all the procedural and infrastructural capabilities necessary to transform the nuclear potential into an effective deterrent will be constructed.[252]

By requiring that India pay more attention to the supporting infrastructure necessary to deal with the technological problems of the nuclear age—as well as by mandating that India pay heed to procedural and ideational systems that serve to transform brute weapons into effective deterrents—the proponents of Alternative IV appear to be seeking a way to enhance Indian security by developing its latent capabilities without simultaneously contributing to a subversion of the international disarmament process, which in fact serves Indian interests. This by necessity requires a two-track strategy—one that demands on the one hand that India "get all the elements of potential nuclear capability in place at an early date" but on the other hand that India eschew "overt weaponization" so long as "drastic reduction and elimination of nuclear weapons, along with . . . chang[es in] the attitudes and belief systems that justify the utility and usability of nuclear weapons,"[253] remain possible. By advocating simply a recessed deterrent at this stage, analysts like Jasjit Singh essentially argue that a "nonweaponized" posture, in which the "option to weaponise [understood in the strict, narrow sense] is kept open and

---

[252]While the procedural systems in India historically have been both informal and idiosyncratic, varying from regime to regime (with the only exception being the constancy of final control in the person of the Prime Minister), the Indian government traditionally did not articulate any authoritative ideational framework in any detail. This has changed slowly in the aftermath of the May 1998 tests, and the details are discussed at great length in the next chapter. Even before these pronouncements were available, however, the utility of nuclear weapons and the derivative questions of doctrine and employment were discussed mainly by think tanks, retired and serving military officers, and journalists, not by knowledgeable officials associated with the civilian DAE (which operates the nuclear weapon program) or by political functionaries such as serving Cabinet Ministers, senior bureaucrats, or technologists conversant with the extent of India's nuclear capabilities. This led to recurrent American calls for better clarification of India's strategic intentions, and even India's most respected strategic analyst, K. Subrahmanyam, concluded before the 1998 tests that whatever India's nuclear policy and its requirements may be, "it cannot be kept in sealed covers" (see Joshi, "In the Shadow of Fear," p. 53) if it is to effectively cope with the terrible dilemmas that any democratic polity faces in the nuclear age.

[253]Singh, "A Nuclear Strategy for India," p. 303.

[is] linked to [a] rise in [the] threat levels [facing the country],"[254] best serves India's interests at this time.

If the processes of global denuclearization gather steam as this recessed deterrent is being developed, India could simply "reverse the nuclearisation at its early stages, or [even] forgo it in the interest of greater security, which is not built on generating insecurity of the most acute kind."[255] If, however, global disarmament efforts were unfortunately to fail, Indian security would still not be unduly imperiled, since "there [would] be time enough and [the] basic capability [in place] to transform [the] recessed deterrence into a full-fledged minimum deterrence."[256] Thanks to this vision of strategic hedging, Alternative IV is seen as providing a means by which the collateral requirements associated with possessing a credible nuclear capability can be steadily acquired—to the advantage of Indian defense preparedness in general and its deterrent capabilities in particular—even as the country begins to "focus [its] energies and expertise [on] the central goal of global abolition of nuclear weapons."[257] This posture is viewed by many "owls" in the Indian strategic debate as optimal because it improves the country's security without in any way undermining its desire for both flexibility and status.

The claim that Alternative IV improves Indian security is predicated on the belief that approaching nuclear deterrence in a systematic way—including understanding and coherently responding to its multifaceted demands—actually contributes to its success. By implication, this alternative therefore presumes that existential deterrence is itself a myth—i.e., that nuclear weapons *simpliciter*, at least of the kind and numbers subsisting in South Asia, do not deter, and consequently that acquiring an adequate deterrent requires attention to those complementary variables that render such weapons politically useful. It is further argued that these complementary variables can in fact spell the difference between the success or failure of deterrence. At a perceptual level, for example, they serve to enhance the value of

---

[254]Ibid., p. 310.
[255]Ibid., p. 304.
[256]Ibid.
[257]Ibid.

the hidden capabilities insofar as they help to communicate the extent of Indian resolve and the degree to which its leaders take their stewardship seriously.[258] At an operational level, they similarly enhance the value of the hidden inventory by ensuring that the capabilities in place are adequate to the political tasks concerned and are safe and secure both in peacetime and during a crisis. This view of the benefits of Alternative IV has considerable merit, making it difficult to conclude that the ideational, institutional, and perhaps even physical improvements that would result from choosing this option would be deleterious either to Indian security or to South Asian stability in general. So long as the crucial caveat associated with Alternative IV is respected—that no significant changes be made in India's traditional posture with respect to both the fabrication of additional nuclear weapons and the production, modification, and deployment of delivery systems—it is therefore likely that a recessed deterrent would in fact enhance rather than detract from Indian security.

This conclusion is further reinforced by the fact that none of the improvements this alternative entails—with the exception of continued missile testing—would run afoul of the global nonproliferation efforts mounted by the United States. Indeed, undertaking these improvements would certainly indicate that India takes the problems of nuclear deterrence seriously. To the extent that such preparations might be perceived as moving the subcontinent further down the nuclear road of no return, they might increase the misgivings of U.S. constituencies concerned about nonproliferation. But since nuclear reversal is all but impossible at this stage of the game in both India and Pakistan, any responsible improvement in decisionmaking structures and crisis management capability in one or both states—if accompanied by restraint in the production and deployment of nuclear weapons and their associated delivery systems—would probably be viewed by most U.S. security managers as the "second best" outcome.[259] This applies even to the problem of missile testing:

---

[258]Raj Chengappa, "Worrying over Broken Arrows," *India Today International*, July 13, 1998, p. 30.

[259]Secretary of State Madeleine Albright summarized this position when she stated that "we really have three goals for Geneva, and that is to make sure that this does not escalate, which really means that there should be no further testing of any kind; that there not be any capability of deployment in any way; and no mating of the

While most U.S. policymakers would prefer that India (and Pakistan, for that matter) cease all missile testing permanently, they would find ways to live with this problem if India could provide an authoritative, binding commitment that it would not pursue the development of intercontinental-range ballistic missiles as well as other ballistic and cruise missiles beyond those already in the pipeline, and that the ballistic missiles currently in engineering development would be neither produced nor deployed for now. Any commitments that go beyond these limits would be impossible to obtain from India and, even if they were obtained, could not be expected to hold unaltered into the distant future. Even with these commitments, however, it is clear that Alternative IV promises great benefits for Indian security in that it would minimize the extent of international (including U.S.) discomfort with its strategic programs while allowing India to steadily develop the ancillary capabilities that would make its deterrent viable if required in a crisis, even as it pursues the objective of global disarmament that may ultimately make that deterrent unnecessary.

It is obvious that India's flexibility will also remain uncompromised by a recessed deterrent. Since all the changes this alternative entails are either procedural or ideational, with the material innovations consisting solely of upgrades in supporting infrastructure rather than increases in raw deliverable capability, the country's flexibility—understood here as its ability to change course down the line—should generally be unaffected. It can be argued, of course, that a state which makes all the investments called for by a recessed deterrent would be loath to denuclearize at some future point because, among other things, it will have invested too much by then

---

missiles with nuclear capability. *So basically, we are somewhere now between having a capability and deployment. We don't want this to move any further.* We also want to make sure, as a part of that first point, that there is no arms race in the region. We also are going to talk about trying to turn around some of the points of the underlying conflict between the two, which obviously does mean talking about Kashmir; and then doing what we can to shore up, reaffirm the international non-proliferation system." See "Press Remarks on India and Pakistan," Secretary of State Madeleine K. Albright, Washington, D.C., June 3, 1998, available at http://secretary.state.gov/www/statements/1998/980603.html. See also Strobe Talbott, "Address at Conference on Diplomacy and Preventive Defense," cosponsored by the Carnegie Commission on Preventing Deadly Conflict and the Stanford-Harvard Preventive Defense Project, Stanford University, Palo Alto, CA, January 16, 1999, available at http://www.state.gov/www/policy_remarks/1999/990116_talbott_sa.html.

simply to turn around and quit. Yet while such an argument appears to have some merit, it is both false empirically and superficial at a practical level. Indeed, the historical record suggests that states which have concluded that they were better served by denuclearization have not hesitated to abandon their nuclear programs, irrespective of how much they had previously invested in them.[260] India's own record in the realm of chemical weaponry is also relevant here: Despite having invested significant resources in covertly developing a stockpile of chemical weapons, India committed itself to the divestiture of these capabilities when ratification of the Chemical Weapons Convention (CWC), a nondiscriminatory international accord, was perceived as being in its national interests.[261] At a practical level, too, the investments Alternative IV entails have multiple uses beyond nuclear deterrence, so their costs are unlikely to become the principal stumbling block to any future decision to denuclearize—so long as the latter is seen to be in India's larger interests when viewed on its own terms. On balance, therefore, India's desire for flexibility would probably remain untrammeled.[262]

Finally, the development of a recessed deterrent is unlikely to have any significant impact on India's status. Since it does not increase the size or quality of India's nuclear stockpile in any manner different from what might have occurred under the choice of maintaining the option, all the benefits and costs associated with the traditional posture of nuclear ambiguity remain unchanged.

Alternative V: Developing a Ready Nuclear Arsenal

Since Alternative IV generally increases the credibility of India's nuclear option but does not produce a ready arsenal, a large and vocal subset of the country's security elites has argued for a shift to Al-

---

[260]See Joeck, "Nuclear Proliferation and Nuclear Reversal in South Asia," pp. 263–273. See also Mitchell Reiss, *Bridled Ambition: Why Countries Constrain Their Nuclear Capabilities* (Washington, D.C.: Woodrow Wilson Center Press, 1995).

[261]Manoj Joshi, "Chemical Weapons Convention: Under Scrutiny," *India Today*, May 31, 1997, pp. 58–60.

[262]If flexibility is understood in a different sense, however—i.e., as the ability to conduct controlled nuclear operations rather than simply execute some kind of "Samson option"—the capabilities acquired as a result of Alternative IV would actually increase Indian flexibility.

ternative V, which calls for the development of a relatively small but nonetheless robust nuclear arsenal immediately.[263] Advocates of this alternative essentially believe that all the innovations a recessed deterrent entails are necessary but insufficient so long as India's fissile-material production base, weapon stockpile, and associated delivery systems are not improved commensurately. Proponents of this alternative recognize that all such improvements will require many years, if not decades, to come to fruition. Nonetheless, they believe that these improvements should be accelerated with a view toward deploying not merely a recessed deterrent but a ready nuclear arsenal at the earliest possible opportunity. Bharat Karnad, arguing for the latter, compared the two choices by asserting that merely developing the capacity to produce, "depending on which Western source one wants to give credence to, 60 to 120 nuclear warheads . . . is not so much a recessed or opaque deterrent as a phantom deterrent good enough to spin theories with but damned thin pretence to base the country's ultimate defense on."[264] This view holds, in other words, that India's security requirements demand not simply the presence of potential nuclear capabilities but rather manifestly deployed arsenals that, even if relatively small, are substantial enough to neutralize the worst intentions that India's largest adversary may harbor. Brahma Chellaney further emphasized the need for just such a capability when, commenting on a parliamentary discussion about India's emerging nuclear posture, he declared that "the nation now knows that its minimum deterrent, based on modest capabilities, will perforce involve deployment of nuclear weapons. This would greatly disappoint those who have been [advocating] Made-in-USA concepts fashioned exclusively for the Indian sub-continent, such as "recessed deterrence."[265] And

---

[263]See, for example, N. C. Menon, "Subtleties of Sagarika," *Hindustan Times*, May 11, 1998; S. Chandrashekar, "In Defense of Nukes," *Economic Times*, May 17, 1998; M. D. Nalapat, "India Needs to Expand Scope of Nuclear Diplomacy," *The Times of India*, December 18, 1998; Karnad, "A Thermonuclear Deterrent," pp. 108–149; Nair, *Nuclear India*, pp. 152–172; Brahma Chellaney, "Nuclear-Deterrent Posture," in Brahma Chellaney (ed.), *Securing India's Future in the New Millennium* (New Delhi: Orient Longman, 1999), pp. 141–222; and, Raja Menon, *A Nuclear Strategy for India* (New Delhi: Sage Publications, 2000), pp. 177–234.

[264]Bharat Karnad, "Contenting Scenarios," *Hindustan Times*, January 7, 1997.

[265]Brahma Chellaney, "Expert Comment: New Nuclear Clarity with Old Waffle," *Hindustan Times*, January 3, 1999.

while sentiments such as these—which favor a ready arsenal as opposed to some alternative demonstration of nuclear capabilities— have had a place in the Indian nuclear debate at least since 1964, they have grown far more prominent since the nuclear tests of May 1998. Indeed, these tests and India's subsequent declaration of its nuclear status have been widely viewed as the last hurdles India has faced en route to full nuclearization—and accordingly, advocates of this posture believe that New Delhi, having crossed the Rubicon, should now proceed inexorably toward developing and deploying a full-fledged arsenal of the kind (if not the numbers) maintained by other nuclear weapon states.[266]

At one level, this view represents merely an "evolutionary" expectation, as advocates for Alternative V argue that the opprobrium India incurred for having resumed its nuclear testing in May 1998 would not be worth the trouble if the process of nuclearization were suddenly to be short-circuited and transmuted into a new kind of ambiguity that lasts for another 25-odd years. The middling posture advocated by protagonists of Alternative IV is seen in this context as confining New Delhi to a "nuclear limbo" of sorts[267] that will improve neither its security nor its standing in the global order but will only reinforce the view that India is a "soft state" unable to make the hard decisions its own self-interest mandates. Precisely because such images would be deleterious to Indian security writ large, advocates of full nuclearization argue that New Delhi, having finally bitten the bullet, should now proceed to develop a robust and ready arsenal even in the face of strong foreign pressure to the contrary.[268] As a former Indian Foreign Secretary argued,

What was the point of Pokhran II, of unveiling our nuclear muscle, if we are now to submit to the indignity of reversion, for purposes of the CTBT and the NPT, to a non-nuclear weapon state status? Doing so will bring our entire nuclear establishment under international safeguards and lay our country open to intrusive monitoring and inspections by, or at the behest of, the five acknowledged nuclear

---

[266]Bharat Karnad, "Fuelling Strategic Fatalism," *Hindustan Times*, May 7, 1999.

[267]The phrase, though not the argument, is borrowed from C. Raja Mohan, "India in a Nuclear Limbo," *The Hindu*, August 21, 1997.

[268]Brahma Chellaney, "The Real Battle Has Just Begun," *The Pioneer*, May 13, 1998.

weapons powers. There are bound to follow even stronger pressures
on us to sign the NPT and to desist from testing, developing, and
deploying missiles, without which there can be no credible nuclear
deterrent. Surely, all this is a recipe for making India a nuclear eunuch.[269]

Obviously, such arguments mask a deep albeit often unstated fear
that the 1998 nuclear tests—dubbed "Pokhran-II"—may turn out to
resemble the first nuclear test, "Pokhran-I," in more ways than is currently recognized: as a gigantic tempest that, while followed by
decades of indecision, nonetheless rattles India's adversaries sufficiently to precipitate feverish counterresponses that only leave New
Delhi worse off than before. In their zeal to avert such problems
down the line, a significant segment of India's security elites today
thus argue not only for the development of the ancillary capabilities
mandated by Alternative IV but also for an expansion of the country's
weapon stockpile and the accelerated development and production
of new delivery systems—changes that would carry the process of
nuclearization to its conclusion and presumably bequeath to New
Delhi the kinds of deterrent capabilities, if not the numbers, that the
declared nuclear powers possess.[270]

Fissile-Material Production and Composition. The first set of
changes Alternative V entails pertains to the rate at which India
produces fissile materials as well as the composition of the materials
themselves. Although most observers believe that India has a large
fissile-material production complex that can in theory produce
substantial stocks of weapons-grade plutonium, the actual size of
this inventory has traditionally been much smaller than is usually
suspected. R. R. Subramanian, for example—one of the country's
leading nuclear experts—has pointed out that India has thus far used
only its CIRUS (40-MW) and Dhruva (100-MW) reactors for
producing weapon-related plutonium despite the fact that it could in
theory use all its other unsafeguarded power reactors as well should

---

[269]Maharajakrishna Rasgotra, "Making India a Nuclear Eunuch," *The Pioneer*,
April 1, 1999.

[270]See, for example, Karnad, "Going Thermonuclear: Why, with What Forces, at
What Cost?" pp. 310–337, and Brahma Chellaney, "India's Trial by Atom," *Hindustan
Times*, November 4, 1998.

this prove necessary.[271] This restricted use has been attributed to India's taking its bearings from nuclear developments in Pakistan rather than China. The end result of this effort has in any case been a smaller stock of weapons-grade plutonium than would technically be feasible for India to produce. Indeed, when the materials diverted for neutron flux studies, the fast-breeder program, and medical and industrial uses are taken into account in conjunction with the losses incurred during separation and reprocessing, Subramanian concludes that India's 1991 stockpile probably did not exceed 200-odd kilograms—a figure that is much smaller than the estimates of organizations like the Carnegie Endowment for International Peace.[272] A careful examination of the efficiency factors governing the operation of India's two weapon reactors suggests that Subramanian's estimates may be closest to the truth, but this in turn implies that the notional Indian stockpile—estimated in 1991 to consist of some 20 weapons of approximately 15–20 kt—is also much smaller than is usually imagined. Irrespective of what New Delhi's fissile-material inventory is today (an issue discussed in greater detail in Chapter Five), the reports appearing in the Western press crediting India with an inventory that could yield more than 300 nuclear weapons—comparable to the present nuclear stockpiles of Great Britain and France—can thus be seen to border on fantasy.[273]

Recognizing that India's fissile-material inventory is much smaller than it could be, a more robust version of Alternative V would call for the quantity of weapons-grade materials to be increased considerably so as to allow India to service deterrence requirements relating to both Pakistan and China. This would in turn require improving the efficiency of India's two weapon reactors and perhaps even increasing the number of reactors dedicated to producing weapons-grade plutonium—if the country is to avoid the economic burden of

---

[271]Subramanian, "India's Nuclear Weapons Capabilities: A Technological Appraisal," p. 23.

[272]Ibid., pp. 24–25; "Report of the Carnegie Task Force on Non-Proliferation and South Asian Security," in *Nuclear Weapons and South Asian Security* (Washington, D.C.: Carnegie Endowment for International Peace, 1988), p. 11.

[273]See the data referred to in W.P.S. Sidhu, "India Sees Safety in Nuclear Triad and Second Strike Potential," *Jane's Intelligence Review*, 10:7 (July 1998), p. 23. See also Ian Steer, "Asia's Rival Reactors a Cause for Concern," *Jane's Intelligence Review*, 10:10 (October 1998), pp. 26–29.

operating its power reactors in a "low-burnup" mode or the technical disadvantages of using reactor-grade plutonium produced by its nuclear power plants. Alternatively, India could simply decline to sign the FMCT now being discussed in Geneva until such time as it produces fissile materials in the quantity it believes to be adequate for its deterrent. For a brief period during the Gujral regime, India contemplated just such a course of action,[274] but its recent decision consenting to the initiation of the FMCT discussions suggests either that New Delhi is confident that its limited inventory suffices for the deterrence of both adversaries or, more likely, that the FMCT is sufficiently far from completion to allow India to produce an inventory of the size it desires. In any event, concerns about the size of the country's fissile-material inventory have already resulted in calls from some of the country's leading commentators for a careful review of whether India has sufficient nuclear materials at hand to constitute a credible deterrent.[275] On occasion, such concerns have also provoked criticism of the Indian government for having allowed the FMCT discussions to proceed without first having secured compensating benefits for such a concession.[276]

Other observers have suggested different ways around the problem of limited fissile materials. The former head of Pakistan's Atomic Energy Commission, Munir Ahmed Khan, for example, has argued that India has developed its enrichment capabilities precisely in order to produce highly enriched uranium for weapon purposes.[277] The belief that India's enrichment facilities are intended to provide the HEU necessary to make composite plutonium-uranium weapons is especially popular in Pakistan, but adding enriched uranium to a basic fission design intended to incorporate weapons-grade plutonium in its core is unlikely to bestow any advantage on India (although it would allow for some increase in the total numbers of weapons produced, depending on the relative inventories or pro-

---

[274]Brahma Chellaney, "A New Nuclear Dividing Line," *The Pioneer*, June 4, 1997.

[275]C. Raja Mohan, "Rethinking CTBT and FMCT," *The Hindu*, June 16, 1998, and Chellaney, "India's Trial by Atom."

[276]Brahma Chellaney, "How Pokhran II Has Bombed," *Asian Age*, May 25, 1999.

[277]Munir Ahmed Khan, "Future of Indian and Pakistani Nuclear/WMD Programmes," unpublished background paper prepared for the RAND-IRS Colloquium, February 25–26, 1996, Islamabad, Pakistan, pp. 2–3.

duction rates of the two materials, if India were to use HEU to produce a new class of basic, uranium-based fission weapons). To be
sure, the possession of HEU would certainly assist India in the production of advanced nuclear weapons in that it could be used as a
"spark plug" to help ignite the lithium deuteride "fuel" in the
secondary stage of a thermonuclear device. Even this application,
however, is not strictly necessary, since modest quantities of
weapons-grade plutonium can be readily substituted for HEU without diminishing the effectiveness of the spark plug and, by implication, without reducing the prospect of achieving a successful fusion
reaction.[278] Indeed, even other advanced designs, such as boosted
fission weaponry, can be built around plutonium cores exclusively.
Using deuterium-tritium in gaseous or other forms in order to inject
fusion neutrons into the core, these designs may incorporate natural
uranium tampers, but they do not require enriched uranium either
for their effectiveness or for their efficiency.[279] As noted earlier,
highly (or medium) enriched uranium is relevant for fueling nuclear
submarines, a platform India has sought to develop since the late
1980s—and if India's enrichment capabilities are enlarged for this
purpose, they would contribute more to developing a potential delivery system than to enlarging the weapon inventory itself. Thus,
if increasing the inventory of fissile materials is India's objective,
this objective will for all practical purposes have to be pursued
through the plutonium economy alone—and this will require in turn
additional plutonium production reactors as well as increased efficiency throughout the production cycle if a dramatically larger
fissile-material inventory is to be acquired in a hurry.[280]

---

[278]A good description of the "spark plug" and the role it plays in the overall design
of a thermonuclear weapon can be found in Carey Sublette, *Nuclear Weapons Frequently Asked Questions*, "Section 4:4: Elements of Thermonuclear Weapons Design,"
available at http://www.fas.org/nuke/hew/Nwfaq/Nfaq4-4.html#Nfaq4.4.

[279]Carey Sublette, *Nuclear Weapons Frequently Asked Questions*, "Section 4.0:
"Engineering and Design of Nuclear Weapons, Section 4.3.1—Fusion Boosted Fission
Weapons," available at http://www.fas.org/nuke/hew/Nwfaq/Nfaq4-3.html#
Nfaq4.3.1.

[280]If India continues to produce HEU, however, and thereby manages to create a
large inventory of HEU over and above that required for fueling submarine reactors
(which might require only medium enriched uranium depending on the reactor design chosen for the vessel), it could choose to utilize all its "excess" HEU to create an
entirely new class of pure HEU-based fission weapons conforming to the "gun-barrel"
design demonstrated in the nuclear weapon used at Hiroshima. As noted above, this

Increasing Nuclear Weapon Types. A more significant alteration in India's national posture may be mandated by the second set of changes Alternative V implicitly entails—namely, increasing the types of nuclear weapons India possesses to match the capabilities of its larger competitor, China. The character and effectiveness of India's current nuclear designs will be analyzed in Chapter Five, but for now it should be noted that if India sought to match Chinese nuclear designs, New Delhi would be required to end its self-imposed moratorium and conduct additional nuclear tests[281]—a proposal already advocated by the National Executive of the BJP[282]—since it is unlikely that laboratory simulations of true multistage weapons would provide sufficient confidence about their effectiveness in practice.[283] Irrespective of whom these capabilities are actually designed against, however, India's boosted fission and thermonuclear weapon designs would invariably require hot testing if the national command authority is to be assured that its nuclear inventory actually works. This holds true irrespective of how these weapons are to be delivered because the extreme pressures and temperature changes associated with missile launch acceleration, payload reentry, and aircraft jinking in flight all make heavy physical demands on the integrity of the warhead. Although many of the warhead components can be thoroughly validated without explosive testing, and although most of these components may not even be part of what are otherwise fully instrumented underground tests, the implosion systems in India's aircraft- and missile-delivered boosted fission and thermonuclear weapons *will* have to be explosively tested until its

---

would allow it to increase the total numbers of weapons in its arsenal, and such weapons are unlikely to require hot testing for their validation. It is improbable that India would choose to go this route in the near future, however, although it cannot be ruled out as a long-term possibility if New Delhi succeeds in producing large quantities of HEU in the face of what continues to be a relatively small inventory of weapons-grade plutonium. In an effort to correct this last problem, India has announced the construction of a new unsafeguarded reactor, thereby suggesting that plutonium continues to be the material of choice for its weapon program.

[281]P. R. Chari, "Misgivings on CTBT," *Hindustan Times*, January 4, 2000.

[282]Angana Parekh, "BJP Asks Centre to Review Move on CTBT, Moratorium," *Indian Express*, August 23, 1998.

[283]Richard L. Garwin, "Maintaining Nuclear Weapons Safe and Reliable Under a CTBT: What Types of Weapons Can Be Developed Without Nuclear Explosions?" available at http://www.fas.org/rlg/000531-ctbt.htm.

developers are satisfied that such weapons can perform adequately in the face of hostile environmental conditions.

As a complement to increasing India's fissile-material production capability and continuing with its nuclear tests, Alternative V would also require the development and production of relevant delivery systems, both aircraft and missile. As far as the former are concerned, India's needs vis-à-vis Pakistan can be fulfilled simply through the use of equipment currently in its conventional inventory. These aircraft—mainly the Jaguar, the Mirage 2000, and eventually the Su-30—can be employed in surface strike operations. If committed to a nuclear delivery role, however, such aircraft would have to be configured specifically for that purpose, and this would require hardware modifications that relate both to navigation equipment and to the carriage of weaponry as well as software modifications that allow for the safing, arming, and fuzing of the weapon just prior to release. Even more significantly, however, these modified aircraft and their crews would have to be specially secured, withheld from conventional operations, and possibly based at airfields located in close proximity both to the weapon assembly areas and to their intended targets.

It should also be noted that while India already has the latent capability to deliver nuclear weapons against Pakistan through air-breathing platforms, it currently lacks a comparable capability vis-à-vis China. Indeed, all Indian strike aircraft are relatively short-legged in comparison to the vast depth of the Chinese heartland, and therefore, there appear to be few alternatives available to India other than to acquire long-range theater bombers or switch entirely to missiles where nuclear operations against its northern neighbor are concerned. Because the former systems are too expensive and the latter capabilities are currently nonexistent, however, it is not surprising that Indian defense analysts have unequivocally argued that the focus of India's future weaponization efforts "must shift to [the] Agni."[284]

The Agni missile, currently India's principal IRBM system, was initially intended to serve mainly as a test bed for validating certain

---

[284]Pravin Sawhney, "India's Missile Policy: Focus Must Shift to Agni," *The Times of India*, March 4, 1997.

key technologies relating to missile guidance and reentry. In its original form, the missile was simply a technological monstrosity: It was a hybrid vehicle based on the marriage of a solid-fueled first stage (derived from the civilian Satellite Launch Vehicle [SLV]) with a liquid-fueled second stage (derived from the Prithvi missile) and, as such, suffered from all the readiness and safety limitations that still affect the Prithvi SRBM. Further, the range capabilities demonstrated by the Agni-I test bed, some 1000 km, effectively precluded the weapon's use to interdict the most important Chinese targets of interest to any Indian force planner—presumably the chief reason IRBMs were developed in the first place. Consequently, several Indian analysts argued long before the May 1998 nuclear tests that the original test bed should become a precursor for a new missile, Agni-II, to be "powered by newer and better solid propellants and having a longer range."[285] This new missile, argued Lieutenant General J.F.R. Jacob, the distinguished architect of India's 1971 victory in the east, should possess an operational range of at least 5000 km and be a "rugged system capable of quick firing from silos, truck chassis or railway carriages."[286] The Agni-II was finally tested in April 1999 and, while still not meeting all criteria laid out by Jacob and others, has nonetheless demonstrated several advances that augur well for India's desire to create a land-based missile force: The new variant is entirely solid-fueled; is designed as a rail-mobile system; has demonstrated a 2000-km range; is equipped with a maneuvering reentry vehicle; and has been "designed to carry a nuclear warhead if required,"[287] with the warhead itself having been tested as part of the May 1998 series.

It is therefore evident that operational missiles such as the Agni-II and its follow-on versions, whether based in hardened silos or deployed in road- or rail-mobile modes, would represent an enormous leap in India's nuclear capability. At the same time, however, some analysts have called on India—even more ambitiously—to move away from land-based systems altogether. In an effort to reduce the possibility of splendid counterforce strikes as well as to minimize the

---

[285]Manoj Joshi, "Operation Defreeze," *India Today*, August 11, 1997, p. 68.

[286]Ibid.

[287]Raj Chengappa, "Boom for Boom," *India Today International*, April 26, 1999, pp. 28–31.

threat facing the Indian heartland more generally, these analysts have argued that "deterrence must shift underwater."[288] The cultivation of such capabilities would, however, require an acceleration of the country's nuclear submarine program, the development of a new ballistic and/or cruise missile capable of submerged launch, and the design of a new class of compact but relatively high-yield warheads in addition to all the associated command-and-control systems and positive and negative controls associated with sea-based weapons.[289] And while such capabilities are clearly several decades away, they do demonstrate that developing a robust nuclear arsenal as called for by Alternative V will demand a substantial increase in the effort India devotes to its nuclear estate, especially when viewed against its past record.

Even as these technologies are steadily acquired, however—assuming that India does in fact opt for Alternative V—literally thousands of other decisions and investments must be made in the arena of systems integration if the resulting arsenal is to be maintained at reasonable levels of responsiveness. Clearly, for example, it is not sufficient for India to have nuclear systems that embody high penetrativity if such systems are vulnerable to accidents at home or to unauthorized or mistaken use, as any of these outcomes could have catastrophic effects that would affect the nation's ability and willingness to maintain such expensive deterrents over the long term. This immunity to accidents and to unauthorized or mistaken use must also coexist with a high level of prelaunch survivability, which implies in turn that the deterrents must be safe against *any* actions that may be undertaken by an adversary. The deterrent must also possess sufficient connectivity with its command authorities at all times so that it can operate as intended even amid the chaos of warfare and destruction. Safety, survivability, connectivity, and penetrativity thus remain the quadrangle of effective deterrence, and to the degree that the force is expected to remain highly responsive

---

[288]Raja Menon, "Deterrence Must Shift Underwater," *The Times of India*, March 23, 1995.

[289]"N-Submarine Best Bet Against Nuclear Attack, Says Navy," *Indian Express*, December 12, 1999.

and ready for the conduct of nuclear operations, the tensions inherent in these four variables will only become more manifest.[290]

To be sure, these tensions can be resolved, but not cheaply. In fact, it has been demonstrated that during the Cold War the bulk of nuclear-related expenditures incurred by both sides arose not from specific weapon systems as such but from the complex supporting and procedural systems that were designed to resolve some of the tensions among these four variables.[291] Even if the arsenal India eventually develops is not maintained at levels of readiness approaching that of the U.S. or Soviet arsenals, the trade-offs imposed by these variables will still need to be resolved, and while their solutions may prove less costly than in the U.S.-Soviet case, such solutions will nonetheless require significant resources of the kind not applied before. In any event, developing a robust and reasonably ready arsenal of the sort Alternative V embodies will also involve a number of additional steps that must be completed before India can produce a credible deterrent that is visible to adversaries and bystanders alike.[292]

First and foremost, this process would involve choosing an appropriate deterrence doctrine that would in turn drive considerations such as the choice of weapon design, force architecture, and command-and-control systems. Even if these efforts are for the most part surreptitious, the range of activities required to make Alternative V viable implies that India's actions and intentions could not remain entirely ambiguous. While an increase in fissile-material production, for example, could be disguised somewhat, it is still likely to be noticed, especially if India were to exploit its power reactors to produce the increased levels of plutonium desired. In any event, increasing the production of fissile materials is the easiest element to disguise. By contrast, a new generation of nuclear weapon designs, especially those involving complex multistage configurations, would have to be serially hot tested if the high levels of confidence associated with a

---

[290]Some of these tensions are explored in John D. Steinbruner, "Choices and Trade-offs," in Ashton B. Carter, John D. Steinbruner, and Charles A. Zraket (eds.), *Managing Nuclear Operations* (Washington, D.C.: Brookings, 1989), pp. 535–554.

[291]See the discussion in Stephen I. Schwartz (ed.), *Atomic Audit* (Washington, D.C.: Brookings, 1998), pp. 1–31.

[292]Chellaney, "India's Trial by Atom."

robust nuclear arsenal are to be attained by India's security managers—and going to the trouble of developing such capabilities would in fact be inexplicable were they not to be confirmed through full-up testing and communicated to potential adversaries as part of the logic of deterrence. Finally, developing the kinds of long-range delivery systems exemplified by both ballistic and cruise missiles would inescapably involve a range of observable activities relating to their testing, production, and eventual deployment. Consequently, if India opts for Alternative V in the manner described earlier, the enigmatic dimensions of its previous nuclear capability—i.e., those relating to employment doctrine, command and control, and perhaps even some elements of force structure—could not be entirely sustained in its new strategic posture. The selection of Alternative V would therefore represent a considered, conspicuous, and deliberate alteration in national strategy—and would be interpreted as such by friends, neutrals, and adversaries alike.

While Alternative V would clearly make India a traditional nuclear power over time, the question of how this alternative would affect its security, flexibility, and status today remains open. Advocates of Alternative V, of course, believe that the country's security environment has deteriorated so significantly that developing a full-blown nuclear arsenal would represent little more than a long-overdue increase in national security. Such an argument holds true, however, only if security is defined as the possession of clear and robust immunity to nuclear attack or coercion by other states. If this narrow definition of security is sustained, India's safety will probably be enhanced by the possession of a full-fledged nuclear arsenal—but by the same token it may be undermined if a broader notion of security is admitted for consideration. If security is held to consist of preserving national integrity against *all* threats, both foreign and domestic, and is seen as deriving from the possession of comprehensive capabilities that include economic development, technological strength, and political coherence, then the selection of Alternative V—especially in the form of a full-fledged "triad" developed immediately—may in fact contribute to the diminution of India's security at this time.[293]

---

[293]Lieutenant General V. R. Raghavan summarized this argument when he argued that "the challenge [facing India] lies in getting out of the nuclear maze the

Several analysts sensitive to this concern point out that a reduction in security would occur because Alternative V would precipitate the countervailing targeting of India by the declared nuclear powers, especially China.[294] As such, these analysts maintain, India would be no better off than before and might in fact be worse off as a result of possessing a nuclear deterrent. This argument is less attractive than it first appears and consequently is unlikely to commend itself to Indian strategic planners, who would argue that the country is already targeted by its presumed adversaries, China and Pakistan, for strategic reasons and is unlikely to be targeted by the other nuclear powers—the United States, Russia, Great Britain, and France—simply because the power-political interests of these countries do not collide in any meaningful way with India's strategic concerns.[295] While there is probably considerable truth to this rejoinder, the fact remains that developing a robust and ready nuclear arsenal today could still undermine Indian security, broadly understood, for reasons that have little to do with being a strategic target of the nuclear operations conducted by other states. Rather, the burdens of Alternative V are a function of four different but related concerns that strike closer to home.

First, opting for Alternative V will impose both high direct costs and high opportunity costs, neither of which India can afford to incur at the present time. Depending on the deterrence posture to be serviced, the direct costs of a robust Indian arsenal could be considerable.[296] Most Indian analysts dispute this claim on the grounds that several of the expenses associated with a nuclear arsenal could be treated as sunk costs that have already been borne as part of

---

Government has built around itself [after the May 1998 tests]. This has happened because of nuclear weapons having been granted an unwarranted centrality in India's security discourse. The way out lies in placing a new perspective on nuclear weapons. *There is more to national security than nuclear weapons alone. The Government needs to decide not so much the extent as the limits of India's nuclear deterrent.* The problem is less with nuclear weapons and more of a lack of conceptual clarity. In the interim, the dangerous uncertainty is not going to diminish" (italics added). See V. R. Raghavan, "Dangerous Nuclear Uncertainties," *The Hindu*, March 13, 2000.

[294]Zia Mian and A. H. Nayyar, "A Time of Testing?" *Bulletin of Atomic Scientists*, 52:4 (July–August 1996), pp. 35–40.

[295]See the remarks in K. Sundarji, "Indian Nuclear Doctrine—I: Notions of Deterrence," *Indian Express*, November 25, 1994.

[296]Reddy, "The Wages of Armageddon."

India's preparations for conventional warfare.[297] Consequently, the additional expenditures required are seen to consist simply of the cost of a few dozen or so missiles—if the most modest example proffered of an Indian nuclear arsenal is taken as the benchmark. Unfortunately, even in this case the low direct costs advertised are deceptive because the final costs of any arsenal would include not only the cost of preparing the warheads and delivery systems (which might be written off as partially sunk) but also expenditures associated with the deployment regime, with safety, security, and training procedures, and with command, control, and communications arrangements. These requirements are immense where a full-fledged arsenal is concerned and are not comparable to the relative modest arrangements associated with the traditional posture of maintaining the option. Moreover, none of these supporting investments has thus far been made, and hence they would constitute entirely new expenditures that cannot be lightly dismissed as sustainable under the rubric of sunk costs.[298] The experience of other nuclear powers in fact suggests that the most expensive component of a nuclear program is not the "business end" of the arsenal per se but rather the acquisition and maintenance of the supporting infrastructural and procedural systems that make the business end effective.[299] These costs have never been systematically analyzed in the Indian context, however, and therefore all claims relating to the allegedly modest costs of a nuclear arsenal must be taken with a large grain of salt—especially because those estimates that do break down the costs of the arsenal suggest, for example, that command-and-control capabilities could be purchased for less than 15 percent of the total costs.[300]

The opportunity costs of a nuclear arsenal must also be considered in this context. This concern is particularly critical today, a time when India, seeking to undo the stagnation of the past several decades, has deliberately chosen to deemphasize accelerated military spending in favor of comprehensive economic restructuring. It is

---

[297]Joshi, "Marginal Costing."

[298]"India Eyes $3.75 Billion Nuclear Command Plan," *Defense News*, January 17, 2000, p. 2.

[299]Schwartz (ed.), *Atomic Audit*, pp. 1–31.

[300]See the breakdown in Joshi, "Marginal Costing," p. 23.

unclear whether increasing nuclear-related expenditures at a time when this process has just begun to bear fruit is either appropriate or rational given that India already faces competing and perhaps more pressing demands for public investment in infrastructural capacity, power generation, human capital, and agriculture. Moreover, India's most pressing security problems currently center on combating domestic insurgencies and maintaining internal order, both of which place heavy demands on its conventional forces—and to the degree that the latter capability is degraded thanks to investments in an expanded nuclear force structure, India may well end up exposing its security to greater risks than might otherwise have been necessary.[301] The opportunity costs of a robust nuclear arsenal may therefore turn out to be too high and much more subversive of Indian security when added to the already-steep direct costs of weaponization.

Second, India's shift to a full-fledged arsenal would clearly imply that it has decided to forgo one of the two objectives sought by the strategy of maintaining the option—namely, supporting a relatively stable global nonproliferation order that provides significant benefits for Indian security. Opting for an arsenal today could contribute to the progressive and possibly irreparable weakening of this order, thus forcing the existing nuclear powers—especially the United States—to subject India to even more stringent constraints than those that currently apply. Such constraints would further impede India's access to economic resources, technological expertise, and political support from abroad and would undercut the vital connectivity India needs to make its new strategy of participating in the global economy successful.[302] A forced return to autarky at a time when globalization holds promise of helping India emerge from poverty and underdevelopment not only would be tragic from the perspective of economic modernization but would also be highly significant when viewed from the standpoint of India's future capacity to compete with China and other countries in the arena of power politics.

---

[301] M. L. Thapan, "Nuclear Games," *The Statesman*, September 29, 1999.

[302] P. R. Chari, "What Is the Future of Nuclear India?" *The Times of India*, May 17, 1998.

Third, the decision to develop a robust nuclear arsenal immediately could well contribute to a deterioration in India's immediate regional security environment. At the very least, it would provoke a charged Pakistani response and quite possibly open the door to an undesirable arms race. This is of import because any arms race within the subcontinent would have both conventional and nuclear dimensions—and although India would probably "win" such a race eventually given its larger resource base, the critical question is whether this is a race that India should even contemplate.[303] The concern here cannot simply be Indocentric, as any arms race that involves asymmetric overexertion by Pakistan cannot be in New Delhi's interests if the end result is increased insecurity and heightened risk taking on Islamabad's part. A nuclear competition between India and Pakistan would also prejudice the possibility of reconciliation with respect to outstanding political disputes; would retard the latter's progressive if reluctant acceptance of its inferior bargaining position; and would distort the overall priority relating to development throughout the South Asian region. It could also have corrosive effects beyond South Asia proper in that a sudden rush to develop a nuclear arsenal would reinforce similar efforts already under way in Iran and Iraq. These programs, which the United States is currently attempting to terminate, could exacerbate security dilemmas in the Persian Gulf and throughout the Middle East and possibly create unforeseeable complications with regard to energy access that may ultimately come to haunt the South Asian states themselves.[304]

Fourth and finally, India's decision to develop a nuclear arsenal would impede its efforts to develop a sturdier political relationship with the United States. U.S.-Indian relations, which often seem crisis-prone even in the best of times, were on the verge of reaching a profitable equilibrium prior to India's 1998 nuclear tests. After much soul searching, the United States had for all practical purposes abandoned its earlier efforts at rolling back the nuclear programs in South Asia. In part, this was because the United States had acquired a better appreciation of the strategic compulsions that motivated both India and Pakistan to begin their programs in the first place. This gradual acceptance has been held at risk by the 1998 nuclear tests

---

[303]Achin Vanaik, "Danger of an Arms Race," *Hindustan Times*, May 14, 1998.

[304]Ed Blanche, "Nuclear Reactions," *Jane's Defence Weekly*, June 17, 1998, p. 22.

and has given rise to new U.S. efforts to restrain the nuclear programs in the subcontinent. And while the United States is still struggling—in concert with both India and Pakistan—to develop a new equipoise with respect to nuclearization in South Asia, it is important to recognize that Washington is unlikely to take kindly to a runaway expansion of India's (or, for that matter, Pakistan's) strategic programs, especially if this expansion threatens larger nonproliferation interests that go well beyond the Indian subcontinent.[305] Even apart from the issue of proliferation, however, India seeks U.S. support in a variety of endeavors ranging from securing a permanent seat on the U.N. Security Council to greater strategic understanding to expanded economic intercourse. All these efforts would be held at risk—to New Delhi's great disadvantage—if India were to press ahead in developing a robust and ready arsenal at a time when the threats justifying such a posture are not obvious to all either within or outside India.[306]

When these four counts are carefully assessed, it is hard to justify the claim that a robust nuclear arsenal, if developed today, would enhance India's security. In a similar manner, such an arsenal is unlikely to increase India's flexibility. Acquiring an arsenal of the kind described earlier would in fact imply that India has embarked on the road of no return. Once instituted in full-fledged form, this arsenal would be difficult and costly to draw down, and such a drawdown

---

[305]Secretary Albright enunciated this concern clearly when she noted that

The fundamental goal of President Clinton's visit to India was to set our course for a qualitatively different and better relationship with India, not a simple return to the status quo before its nuclear tests. The limits on our ability to cooperate with India, and Pakistan, are a matter of U.S. law, as well as our international obligations. Achieving the level of cooperation with India that we both desire will depend on progress made toward nonproliferation.

The United States' approach to nonproliferation is global. We cannot abandon it simply because we desire an improved relationship. Any other stance would break faith with all the nations—from South Africa to South America to the former Soviet Republics—who have made difficult decisions to strengthen their own security and the cause of nonproliferation by joining the NPT.

See Secretary of State Madeleine K. Albright, "Op-Ed on the President's Trip to South Asia," printed in *Diario las Americas*, April 2, 2000, available at http://secretary.state.gov/www/statements/2000/000402.html.

[306]"Early Solution to Nuclear Issues Will Help: Talbott," *The Hindu*, January 14, 2000.

would probably never occur except as part of a global agreement on denuclearization—an outcome that, even if possible, is many decades away. Any hope that it could be used in the interim to extract concessions from the declared nuclear states (with respect to global denuclearization or otherwise) would be illusory as well, since few tangible inducements could be offered in exchange for an Indian promise to forgo its nuclear weaponry. All that might be possible are simply bilateral nuclear arms control agreements with Pakistan—but surely if this were the goal, it could be achieved without having to traverse the circuitous route of developing a full-fledged arsenal. India's quest for status may remain similarly unfulfilled despite its choice of a nuclear arsenal. The latter will bequeath to it the distinction of being both a de facto nuclear state and a militarily significant entity (a status it already enjoys), but if such recognition were to come at the cost of economic weakness and technological hurdles, it would be but an empty accomplishment. As one of India's best-known advocates of a ready arsenal concluded,

> [The] glaring mismatch India has to tackle is between its economic capacity and security needs. Without economic power, India can have no security, even with nuclear weapons. The way Pakistan has sunk economically since conducting its tests should serve as a lesson to India to accord the highest priority to putting its economic house in order. India should also be cognizant of the danger that nuclear weapons in the hands of a soft state can invite greater insecurity.[307]

Precisely because this very outcome could result from the pursuit of Alternative V today, it seems reasonable to conclude that a ready arsenal would appear to promise only pernicious consequences for security and, at best, ambiguous benefits where India's flexibility and status are concerned.

WHAT WILL INDIA CHOOSE?

Given this range of alternatives, what will India choose? Clearly, there appear to be three distinct though closely related options available to it, each with a differing set of predicates (see Table 2).

---

[307] Chellaney, "India's Trial by Atom."

Table 2
Synoptic Comparison of the Three Possible Nuclear Postures

	Alternative III: Continue to Maintain Nuclear Option	Alternative IV: Initiate Development of "Recessed Deterrent"	Alternative V: Acquire Robust and Ready Nuclear Arsenal
Fissile-material production base	Produce and separate weapons-grade plutonium at low rates; continue production of enriched uranium at low rates.	Produce and separate weapons-grade plutonium at low rates; continue production of enriched uranium at low rates.	Accelerate production and separation of weapons-grade plutonium; accelerate production of enriched uranium.
Nuclear weapons	Design work; theoretical research; no hot testing; fabricated components but no completely assembled weapons?	Design work; theoretical research; no hot testing; maintain existing stockpile of unassembled weapons but no "serial production" of new devices.	Hot testing of current and advanced nuclear designs; "serial production" of completely assembled weapons.
Delivery capabilities	RDT&E only; no production and deployment of dedicated nuclear delivery systems; no modification of dual-use systems.	RDT&E primarily; acquisition of long-lead items but no production and deployment of dedicated nuclear delivery systems; no modification of dual-use systems.	RDT&E, "serial production," and deployment of dedicated nuclear delivery systems; modification of dual-use systems with new deployment arrangements.
Supporting infrastructure	No action	Initiate development of intelligence and warning systems, meteorological systems, secure communications network, physical command-and-control infrastructure, BDA systems.	Comprehensive acquisition of intelligence and warning systems, meteorological systems, secure communications network, physical command-and-control infrastructure, BDA systems.

Table 2 (continued)

	Alternative III: Continue to Maintain Nuclear Option	Alternative IV: Initiate Development of "Recessed Deterrent"	Alternative V: Acquire Robust and Ready Nuclear Arsenal
Procedural systems	No action	Initiate development of positive-negative control systems, national command authority, civil-military coordination arrangements, nuclear requirements planning structure.	Complete development of positive-negative control systems, national command authority, civil-military coordination arrangements, nuclear requirements planning structure.
Ideational systems	No action	Initiate development of nuclear deterrence doctrine; targeting doctrine, methodology, and staff; war termination concepts.	Enunciate nuclear deterrence doctrine; complete development of targeting doctrine, methodology, and staff; articulate war termination concepts.
Strategic defense	No action	Initiate development of civil defense procedures; modernize IADGES; acquire ATBMs; reorganize disaster management organizations.	Systematic acquisition of ATBMs and comprehensive modernization of the IADGES; refine civil defense procedures and reorganize disaster management organizations.

These positions are sometimes so similar that a casual observer might be tempted to dismiss their differences altogether. This attitude is understandable given the inherent complexity of the larger process of nuclearization. Yet these options must be understood for what they are: "ideal types" that attempt to give policymakers on both sides room to maneuver while simultaneously providing analysts with the kinds of fine-grained distinctions that, as Dunn and Overholt lamented more than two decades ago, can seldom be found in proliferation studies.[308] In any event, these options are best viewed as a heuristic device for framing future Indian choices—and taken as such, the analysis above suggests that despite the 1998 nuclear tests, New Delhi remains at a crucial crossroads with respect to its nuclear posture. India has tested weapons and has declared itself to be a nuclear weapon state. This declaration suggests that New Delhi will continue to develop and maintain a stockpile of assembled nuclear weapons, but even this outcome does not automatically follow from the declaration of nuclear status.[309]

When the three nuclear postures outlined in Table 2 are closely examined, it becomes obvious that India's present posture locates the country slightly to the right of Alternative III. India possesses nuclear weapons, even if only in disassembled form, but it still does not possess the panoply of delivery capabilities it desires or the supporting infrastructure and procedural and ideational systems necessary for the effective conduct of a wide range of nuclear operations. This implies in turn that India's claim to have become a significant nuclear power as a result of its tests is at best premature and at worst preposterous.[310] Indeed, it is not even clear whether these tests changed anything as far as India's raw strategic capabilities are concerned, since the development of both nuclear weapons and assorted delivery systems, together with their potentially slow production, would have continued even if the 1998 nuclear tests had not taken place. And while these tests will no doubt enhance both India's and Pakistan's ability to pursue some of these objectives, it is too

---

[308]Dunn and Overholt, "The Next Phase in Nuclear Proliferation Research."

[309]For a good discussion about the uncertainties associated with the declaration of nuclear status, see John F. Burns, "In Nuclear India, Small Stash Does Not an Arsenal Make," *New York Times*, July 26, 1998.

[310]Chellaney, "How Pokhran II Has Bombed."

early to argue that they have engendered a qualitative change in the regional environment at least as far as both states' technical proficiency is concerned; if anything, they have merely confirmed capabilities that most observers had long suspected existed in the region. By contrast, the 1998 tests do affect U.S. nonproliferation policy, which had sought to maintain India and Pakistan in an ambiguous status so as to sustain the façade of a global nuclear order consisting of only five legitimate nuclear weapon states. Secondarily, they affect the global nuclear regime insofar as they could create demonstration effects that lead other states to pursue their nuclear weapon programs more vigorously. At the same time, they have not altered, as many Indian analysts have claimed, either the global balance of power or the evolving regional power-political order in South Asia.

All of this implies that India still confronts a set of choices similar to those it faced prior to the tests: It could return to a new version of simply maintaining the option; it could switch to a recessed deterrent that involves no serial production or new deployment of nuclear devices and delivery systems but requires improvements in ideational resources, organizational capacity, and supporting infrastructure; or it could move toward a robust arsenal that calls for the development of all the war-fighting capabilities necessary for the prompt conduct of a wide variety of nuclear operations. Although the first alternative has more proponents than the second in the domestic arena, most Indian security elites seem wedded to some version of the third. The government of India itself has not formally announced its own preferences in any detail except to suggest that India will create a "minimum, but credible, nuclear deterrent"[311] at some point in the future. It is clear, however, that whatever the exact predicates of this deterrent may eventually be, India's emerging nuclear posture will be determined by three issues.

The first issue centers on India's intuitions about what really deters. This is an issue with which both the United States and the Soviet Union struggled throughout the Cold War, and while all the major theories of deterrence—that nuclear weapons per se deter, that assured punishment deters, and that assured denial deters—had their

---

[311]Tarun Basu, "Nuclear Doctrine Emerges, but Tension Mounts on Border," *India Abroad*, August 14, 1998.

protagonists, only the third school finally won out, at great cost to both sides. *All* Indian elites seem determined to avoid traversing this historical route and while the first two schools are well represented among India's security elites—with the former favoring a return to maintaining the option and the latter arguing for some manifest deterrent force—it is most likely that some solution offered by the latter will finally prevail.

The second issue relates to India's assessment of the direct and opportunity costs of creating a deterrent. The first of these issues is easier to assess than the second, but only slightly. What seems clear, however, is that given India's developmental imperatives, its national leadership will seek to purchase deterrence at minimal cost. This gives rise to legitimate fears about an unstable deterrent, or at least a deterrent that serves more as an invitation to attack than as an antidote to it. Since most of the standard solutions to this problem are both capital-intensive and costly, it is likely that India will develop a nontraditional deployment and operational posture that attempts to obviate the problems of instability while still acquiring some sort of a deterrent at low cost.

The third issue pivots on India's willingness to accept risks that will define the form and readiness levels of the deterrent it seeks to create. In this context, the more risk-averse the leadership is about positive control over its nuclear arsenal—i.e., about ensuring reliable launch on command—the more likely it will be to move in the direction of developing a large and complex deterrent force consisting of a significant number of nuclear weapons and delivery systems coupled with an elaborate command-and-control structure. Because this posture is expensive and goes against the grain of traditional civil-military relations in India, however, a future Indian deterrent will likely seek to maximize simplicity while aiming for a level of readiness that ensures better negative control—i.e., preventing unwanted launch of nuclear weaponry—rather than positive control in the sense defined above.

Each of these three variables obviously embodies a wide spectrum of options, and unfortunately there are no "correct" answers to any of the difficult issues they pose. More significantly, even those answers proffered today may not hold as new governments take the helm in New Delhi tomorrow. The desire for a minimum deterrent, however, suggests at least this much: that the present government believes that actual nuclear weapons, not simply existential nuclear capabilities, are critical for deterrence but that the costs of a deterrent are significant enough to prevent it from being conceived as an open-ended force that must be maintained both at high absolute levels and at high relative levels in comparison to the capabilities of India's adversaries. On this question at least, it appears that both the present government and the principal opposition party, the Congress, are agreed.[312]

This implies that Alternative III is no longer viable, at least for now. India will not return to maintaining the option, whatever its merits may be, and, if anything, the present regime is likely to initiate activities that will make it difficult (and perhaps even unnecessary) for its successors to retreat from its chosen course. The pace of movement may be altered and the degree of visibility accorded to certain actions may be muted by subsequent governments, but the general direction will probably not be altered radically, since retrenchment is costly in both international and domestic terms. The desire for a minimum deterrent also suggests that New Delhi is not satisfied by the alternative of a recessed deterrent *as an end state*. However, given the critical issues of cost and risk tolerance, it is not clear that a minimum deterrent will eventuate in Alternative V—a robust and ready arsenal—either. In fact, it is most likely that New Delhi, following its ingrained habit of seeking the "veritable middle path," will over the next several years split the difference further and adopt a nuclear posture that begins with creeping weaponization— now understood in the broad sense—but ultimately ends somewhere between Alternatives IV and V. This peculiar Indian equilibrium, illustrated in Figure 3 and dubbed a "force-in-being," will be examined in some detail in the next chapter in the context of a larger discussion about Indian attitudes toward nuclear deterrence.

---

[312] "Cong Parroting BJP on Minimum Nuclear Deterrent," *The Pioneer*, March 23, 2000.

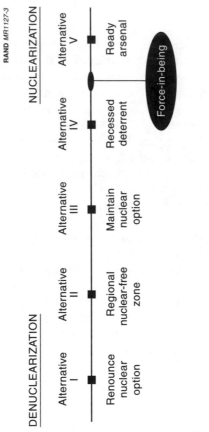

RAND *MR1127-3*

Figure 3—India's Emerging Nuclear Posture

TOWARD A FORCE-IN-BEING (I): UNDERSTANDING INDIA'S NUCLEAR DOCTRINE AND FUTURE FORCE POSTURE

Any discussion of India's nuclear doctrine and future force posture is by definition fraught with uncertainty. This uncertainty arises first because India is still at the initial stages of developing a nuclear deterrent. Since this will be a long and drawn-out process that will probably require decades to complete, a multitude of factors could intervene to either modify the doctrine or change the pace and direction of India's nuclear posture in the future. The experience of previous nuclear powers has further demonstrated that doctrinal innovations usually occur in the aftermath of technological breakthroughs that, by their very nature, are often unanticipated.[1] A "late nuclearizer" like India, however, is unlikely to reap the benefits of a similar "product cycle" because current international pressures against nuclearization have already compelled it to engage the question of appropriate doctrine well before all the technological prerequisites necessary to service such a doctrine are at hand. Consequently, future technological surprises or failures—as they occur—could result in significant modifications of any doctrine that

---

[1]As one scholar phrased it, at least in the United States, "a new weapon starts with a technological idea rather than as a response to a specific threat or as a means to fulfill a long-standing mission." And while in the erstwhile Soviet Union "external factors play[ed] an early role in stimulating weapons innovation and internal forces act[ed] later to influence the way a directive to implement a certain innovation [was] carried out," doctrinal systems in both cases appeared to succeed technological innovation, not the other way around. See Matthew Evangelista, *Innovation and the Arms Race* (Ithaca, NY: Cornell University Press, 1988), p. x.

may currently be contemplated or advanced by elites and security managers in New Delhi.

It also remains uncertain whether the objectives India seeks to pursue with respect to nuclearization today represent an ironclad national consensus that will survive immutably over time. At the moment, there is good reason to believe that the desire for a minimum deterrent—one that takes the form of creeping weaponization in its initial stages but ends up as a force-in-being sometime over the next several years—represents a doctrinal vision that is shared by most key security managers in the present government as well as by influential decisionmakers within the main opposition parties outside of the extreme Left.[2] This could change, however, depending on the vicissitudes of domestic politics, the performance of the Indian economy, and the international security environment.

Finally, India's nuclear doctrine and its desired force posture have never been spelled out in any significant detail by New Delhi. Although a variety of official statements relating to these issues have appeared, such statements are by no means complete and do not address those details that are of most interest to analysts of nuclear deterrence.[3] This in itself should not be surprising, since most policymakers outside the United States usually describe the contours of their nuclear doctrine and force posture in only broad terms. However, this tendency toward generality is even more pronounced in India, where it represents a conscious and deliberate effort on the part of India's security managers—thus making it all the more difficult to describe the nation's nuclear worldview in any comprehensive way.

This judgment applies even to that now well-publicized document, the "Draft Report of [the] National Security Advisory Board on Indian Nuclear Doctrine," which was officially released on August 17,

---

[2]C. Raja Mohan, "Vajpayee's Nuclear Legacy," *The Hindu*, April 21, 1999.

[3]See, for example, "Suo Motu Statement by Prime Minister Atal Bihari Vajpayee in the Indian Parliament on May 27, 1998," pp. 1–2; "Paper Laid on the Table of the House on Evolution of India's Nuclear Policy," *India News*, May 16–June 15, 1998, pp. 3–6; "Press Statements on India's Nuclear Tests Issued on May 11 and 13, 1998," *India News*, May 16–June 15, 1998, p. 8; "Prime Minister's Reply to the Discussion in Lok Sabha on Nuclear Tests on May 29, 1998," *India News*, May 16–June 15, 1998, pp. 9–10; and "India Not to Engage in a N-Arms Race: Jaswant."

1999.[4] This report, which is perhaps the single most coherent statement on nuclear doctrine ever to have been produced in India, still suffers from some internal tensions and, more important, from continuing ambiguity with respect to its status as a policy document. The report was issued by the National Security Advisory Board, formally an official body that is part of the country's newly established National Security Council.[5] This board, however, is located along the outer tier of a complex hierarchical political structure and is intended to be a vehicle through which senior government decision-makers can draw on the advice, judgment, and counsel of the nation's more prominent academics, retired civil servants, retired diplomats, and retired military officers. The documents issued by the board therefore do not constitute settled policy as such but strictly represent recommendations formulated for the consideration of the "principals" who constitute the core of the National Security Council itself. Consequently, the Advisory Board's report on nuclear doctrine should not be treated as representing India's nuclear doctrine per se but should be viewed as a reasoned judgment offered by some of the nation's leading experts about what that doctrine ought to be.

Regardless of its status, however, the Advisory Board's report turned out to be highly controversial at the time of its initial release. Besides causing panic in Pakistan[6] and exacerbating prevailing suspicions in China,[7] it riled many Indian security specialists and commentators, who lambasted it for a variety of reasons ranging from poor grammar and syntax to internal inconsistency to unrealistic albeit ambitious posturing.[8] The principal opposition party,

---

[4]For the text of this document, see "Draft Report of [the] National Security Advisory Board on Indian Nuclear Doctrine," *India News*, October 1, 1999, pp. 2–3.

[5]The structure and functions of this council are discussed further in Chapter Five.

[6]For a good example of Islamabad's reaction, see "Pakistan Reacts Strongly to India's Assertion," *The Times of India*, August 19, 1999, and "Pak to Raise Nuclear Doctrine Issue at UN," *Asian Age*, August 28, 1999.

[7]Chen Yali, "Nuclear Arms Race Looms," *China Daily*, August 24, 1999, and "India's Proposed Nuclear Doctrine Likely to Figure in Sino-Russian Talks," *Hindustan Times*, August 25, 1999.

[8]Examples of such critiques can be found in P. R. Chari, "The Nuclear Doctrine," August 24, 1999, available at http://www.ipcs.org/issues/articles/252-ndi-chari.htm; Kuldip Nayar, "Between Welfare and Weapons," *Indian Express*, August 31, 1999; Savita Pande, "It's a Bit of a Hogwash, This Doctrine," *Indian Express*, August 30, 1999; Raja Menon, "The Nuclear Doctrine," *The Times of India*, August 26, 1999; Manoj

the Congress, was also incensed by its circulation; seeing the document as merely an electoral ploy to garner public attention and possibly votes in the upcoming national election, a senior Congress leader and former Indian Foreign Minister, Pranab Mukerjee, indignantly remarked that "the caretaker government has no business, politically [or] morally, to bring out [a] document of this nature, which will affect the life of the entire subcontinent. The basic question is how can a government which has lost its mandate bring out such a document. . . . They are not running a college union, but a federal government."[9]

More to the point, however, the Indian government itself, somewhat taken aback in the face of both domestic and international criticism, moved deftly to distance itself from the report. Thus, what had originally been intended—at least in the minds of its creators—to be a definitive statement about India's prospective nuclear posture was now redefined by the government of India as merely a "draft."[10] Not content with this relabeling, however, Indian Prime Minister Atal Bihari Vajpayee further devalued the report by arguing that "there is nothing new in the policy announced by us. . . . We have talked about command and control in the new policy, but it is a draft policy which can be changed."[11] Indian Foreign Minister Jaswant Singh quickly followed suit, announcing that he had "no inhibitions in discussing all [the report's] aspects" with his American interlocutors, "as the document is meant for public discussion."[12] Finally, in an elaborate but obviously planted interview a few months later, Singh further attempted to "dispel the widespread misconcep-

---

Joshi, "The ABC and Whys of India's N-Doctrine," *The Times of India*, August 22, 1999; K. K. Katyal, "A Motivated Exercise?" *The Hindu*, August 23, 1999; W.P.S. Sidhu, "This Doctrine Is Full of Holes," *Indian Express*, September 8, 1999; Sat Pal Sharma, "A Faulty Doctrine," *The Pioneer*, September 16, 1999; G. Balachandran, "What Is the Relevance of a Triad?" *The Hindu*, September 10, 1999; M. V. Ramana, "A Recipe for Disaster," *The Hindu*, September 9, 1999; Kanti Bajpai, "A Flawed Doctrine," *The Times of India*, September 7, 1999; and Bharat Wariavwalla, "Are They Really MAD?" *Indian Express*, September 7, 1999.

[9]"Congress Flays Nuclear Doctrine," *Asian Age*, August 19, 1999.

[10]Mallika Joseph, "India's Draft Nuclear Doctrine," report of the IPCS seminar held on August 27, 1999, available at http://www.ipcs.org/issues/articles/255-ndi-mallika.htm.

[11]"N-Doctrine Adheres to Old Policy: Atal," *The Pioneer*, August 21, 1999.

[12]"Jaswant Rejects U.S. Concern," *The Hindu*, August 20, 1999.

tions on Indian nuclear doctrine"[13] by providing a critical restatement that appeared to diverge significantly from the contents of the Draft Report. This interview sought to soften the impact of many of the report's original recommendations and even offered a new gloss on some of its linguistic formulations, but a careful reading of this redaction suggests that despite the government's attempts to publicly distance itself from the document, there remained at least some points of convergence that must be engaged by any analysis of India's nuclear doctrine and emerging force posture.

At one level, this evidence of convergence is not surprising in that the Draft Report had an inexorable internal logic that, although unpalatable to many both in India and in the United States (including the U.S. government, which has been justifiably critical of the document on many counts), appealed to many decisionmakers in critical loci of power—including the Prime Minister's Office and the Ministries of External Affairs and Defence. This partial convergence of ideas, however, makes the task of analysis all the more difficult, because while the openly available Draft Report has not been formally endorsed by any Indian policymakers—except perhaps by National Security Adviser Brajesh Mishra, and here, too, only by implication[14]—various public and private comments on the part of such policymakers do suggest an acceptance of at least some of its key tenets. Yet this acceptance has not yet translated—and may never translate—into a willingness to enunciate India's *real* nuclear doctrine in any clear, comprehensive, and publicly accessible way, despite the fact that a general set of principles and perhaps even a doc-

---

[13]"India Not to Engage in a N-Arms Race: Jaswant."

[14]See "Opening Remarks by National Security Adviser Mr. Brajesh Mishra at the Release of Draft Indian Nuclear Doctrine," available at http://www.meadev.gov.in/govt/opstm-indnucld.htm. One of India's leading journalists, Kuldip Nayar, for example, responding to Mishra's actions and remarks, stated that "I would not have bothered a bit about the draft 'Nuclear Doctrine' if it had not been released by the Prime Minister's secretary, Brajesh Mishra. The National Security Advisory Board had issued it for 'debate and discussion' [Nayar errs on this point: The board prepared the report as a mandated, confidential recommendation to the government] and it should have been treated that way. But Mishra made it official. What it means is that the government had decided to weaponise its nuclear capability without even building a consensus on the important issue. . . . The government has used the board only as a cover. It could easily do so because it appointed on the board such members as were on the same level of hawkishness as the BJP men." See Nayar, "Between Welfare and Weapons."

ument reflecting those principles have been formally developed by India's senior security managers.

It thus becomes evident that the details which would make India's nuclear doctrine and emerging force posture coherent have not been furnished by any official statements and have been made available only to a limited extent by nominally official but unauthoritative documents like the Draft Report (whose internal coherence at least validates its probative value even if it does not offer conclusive proof). Consequently, such details must instead be supplied by analysts who are tasked with interpreting the few authentic declarations available in the context of a larger understanding of Indian attitudes toward nuclear deterrence, the country's existing military and technical capability, and the challenges facing its desired force posture over time. This chapter is intended to provide just such an understanding, with the caveat that it represents an early view of India's evolving preferences—which, because of the various intervening circumstances cited earlier, could eventually be incarnated in somewhat different form. Despite such cautionary notes, this chapter will describe India's evolving nuclear doctrine, and the nuclear force posture predicated by that doctrine, in a much more systematic way than its security managers and strategic commentators have ever articulated. In fact, most of the analysis that follows will be characterized by a much greater order and coherence than can actually be found in reality.

The conclusions this research effort offers are also much more conditional than the declarative tone in which they are expressed might suggest. This is because the official Indian view on many of the details subsumed by the phrase "nuclear doctrine and force posture" is simply not available and, in some instances, has not even been formulated, since decisionmakers in New Delhi are just beginning to appreciate some of the more remote implications—be they political, technical, or operational—of their preferences. Despite these problems, the analytical coherence and declamatory style this chapter adopts, though artificial and perhaps premature, is nonetheless desirable insofar as it allows India's future nuclear posture and the logic underlying its creation, maintenance, and utility to be presented in as lucid a manner as possible. This clarity of expression, which is designed to avoid equivocation, caveats, and ambiguity as much as possible even though they may be justified, is aimed at providing a better assessment of India's evolving deterrent than is currently available while simultaneously generating a better appreciation of the consequences of that deterrent for U.S. interests both in the region and around the globe.

Three other methodological issues are also worthy of recognition in this context, the first of which pertains to the level of analytical detail that is pursued. The discussion throughout this chapter will for the most part remain abstract because the nature of the subject at hand seldom permits unclassified analysis at a level that would meet the standards of operations research.[15] Even if issues of classification did not intrude, it is simply too early to analyze India's nuclear posture at the level of operations analysis because many of India's weapon and delivery systems, training and deployment postures, and general operational routines have not yet been developed and institutionalized. Consequently, even when it touches on military-technical issues, this discussion will focus on uncovering problems relating to successful deterrence rather than on operational minutiae that either have been classified by the government of India or, more often than not, have simply not been developed.

The second issue pertains to the method of analysis. The discussion on India's nuclear doctrine and force posture is derived primarily from *static* analysis. That is, its attempts to explicate New Delhi's requirements are based on an understanding of factors that are critical to India but do not integrate the capabilities, doctrines, and force postures of India's competitors, China and Pakistan. This is because integrating the latter variables would require a level of dynamic analysis—especially if a net assessment of deterrence stability is required—that lies beyond the scope of this work.[16] The issue of Chi-

---

[15]A good discussion of the type of information required to support operations research and the limitations of such research can be found in E. S. Quade and W. I. Boucher (eds.), *Systems Analysis and Policy: Planning Applications in Defense* (New York: Elsevier, 1968).

[16]Strategic nuclear net assessment was obviously a staple of Cold War analysis and was possible, among other things, because both sides had nuclear arsenals with well-understood physical and organizational characteristics. For a useful survey of such work together with an example of a software program that allows nonspecialists to dynamically model a simple nuclear exchange scenario in the U.S.-Soviet context, see Lynn Eden and Steven E. Miller (eds.), *Nuclear Arguments* (Ithaca, NY: Cornell University Press, 1989).

nese and Pakistani nuclear capabilities is therefore discussed only when it is necessary either to illustrate points of comparison or to ascertain whether such capabilities impinge on the adequacy of the Indian deterrent *in principle*.

The third issue pertains to the subject of standards. Whenever discussions about nuclear deterrence involving technologies, operations, or doctrine are conducted, the U.S.-Soviet experience throughout the Cold War looms large in the consciousness of most Western analysts. This is understandable not only because that experience once served as a yardstick for evaluating the adequacy, effectiveness, and stability of various deterrent architectures but also—and perhaps more perniciously—because it has survived as the dominant framework for thinking about nuclear deterrence in general.[17] The temptation to view nuclear deterrence in South Asia through the lens of U.S.-Soviet competition should be resisted, however, because the objectives both India and Pakistan have sought to attain through nuclear capabilities are very different from those historically pursued by the United States and the former Soviet Union. If the Indian deterrent is assessed in relation to the nuclear architectures epitomized by U.S.-Soviet competition, it will therefore be found wanting—but this is the wrong test of its adequacy, effectiveness, or stability. The appropriate measure in this instance is not whether India's deterrent is good by the standards of the Cold War but rather whether it is *appropriate and good enough for New Delhi* given the latter's objectives, resources, traditions, and constraints—all these understood, of course, in the context of those "eternal" verities about nuclear weapons so clearly illuminated as a result of superpower competition in the postwar period.[18] Since this criterion is

---

[17]For more on this issue, see the remarks of Regina Cowen Karp in Serge Sur (ed.), *Nuclear Deterrence: Problems and Perspectives in the 1990s* (New York: UNIDIR, 1993), pp. 122–124.

[18]There is obviously great debate about what the verities distilled from the experience of the "first nuclear age" actually are. For two good studies that revisit this issue from the perspective of principle and practice, respectively, see Robert Jervis, "Strategic Theory: What's New and What's True," *Journal of Strategic Studies*, 9:4 (December 1986), pp. 135–162, and David A. Shlapak and David E. Thaler, *Back to First Principles: U.S. Strategic Forces in the Emerging Environment*, R-4260-AF (Santa Monica: RAND, 1993).

fundamental to any worthwhile analysis of nuclear deterrence in South Asia, it will suffuse all subsequent discussions about India's future nuclear doctrine and force posture.

INDIA'S NUCLEAR DOCTRINE: CONCERNS, CONTEXTS, AND CONSTRAINTS

There is no accepted definition of "doctrine" in modern strategic thought. In the West, the concept usually refers to those "fundamental principles by which military forces or elements thereof guide their actions in support of national objectives."[19] This definition implies that doctrine pertains first and foremost to the conduct of military forces in the field and, as such, functions as a unifying agent that regulates all the collective actions oriented toward securing specific operational objectives within a given battle space. Wayne Hughes succinctly summarized this notion when he concluded that "doctrine is the glue of tactics,"[20] but this conception, being limited to the operational and tactical levels of war, turns out to be unduly restrictive for purposes of this analysis. The old Soviet definition may in fact be more appropriate here, since the concept of doctrine was understood expansively as a hierarchic structure of principles anchored fundamentally in the grand strategic objectives and material capabilities of the state. Beginning at the national level, the authoritative *Dictionary of Basic Military Terms* thus defined doctrine as

> A nation's officially accepted . . . views on the nature of modern wars and the use of the armed forces in them, and also on the requirements arising from these views regarding the country and its armed forces being made ready for war. . . . Military doctrine has two aspects, political and military-technical. The basic tenets of a military doctrine are determined by a nation's political and military leadership according to the sociopolitical order, the country's level of economic, scientific, and technological development, and the

---

[19]Department of Defense, *Dictionary of Military and Associated Terms* (Washington, D.C.: USGPO, 1984), p. 113.

[20]Wayne P. Hughes, Jr., *Fleet Tactics: Theory and Practice* (Annapolis, MD: U.S. Naval Institute Press, 1986), p. 28.

armed forces' combat material, and with due regard to the conclusions of military science and the views of the probable enemy.[21]

This conception of doctrine is attractive because it reaches to the level of grand strategy, thereby providing an opportunity to depict India's own evolving nuclear doctrine as the supreme national view of its nuclear capabilities—a view that, despite having been articulated in only piecemeal fashion by its many security managers, is deeply rooted in its understanding of the nature and limits of nuclear war as an instrument of policy, the role of its own military forces in the political life of the state, the country's current and future levels of economic and technological modernization, and the demands imposed both by military science insofar as it pertains to nuclear weapons and by the attitudes and capabilities of its principal adversaries, China and Pakistan. Despite the lack of a formal creed that speaks to these issues comprehensively, a doctrine that is grounded in precisely these considerations can be identified from several official pronouncements, understood in the context of the larger strategic debates taking place among the "rejectionists," "pragmatists," and "maximalists" within the country.[22]

Explicating the doctrine in these terms allows it to be seen not as a narrow set of tactical rules governing nuclear operations in practice—as would be the case if Western notions of doctrine were adopted in this analysis—but rather as a worldview that first defines the core question of what purposes are served by the acquisition of nuclear weapons and then addresses all the important subsidiary issues pertaining to force posture, concepts of operations, and weapon employment. In so doing, India's nuclear doctrine can be seen as a system of beliefs that both describes the utility of nuclear weapons to the state and identifies the manner in which these weapons will be deployed and used consistent with the purpose for which they have been acquired.

---

[21]Soviet Faculty of the General Staff Academy, *Dictionary of Basic Military Terms: A Soviet View* (Washington, D.C.: USGPO, 1976), p. 37.

[22]These labels have been used by one Indian scholar to describe the character of the Indian strategic debate insofar as it pertains to nuclear weapons. This debate has been summarized in Kanti Bajpai, "The Great Indian Nuclear Debate," *The Hindu*, November 12, 1999. See also Bajpai, "India's Nuclear Posture After Pokhran II," pp. 267-301.

The Declaratory Level of Policy

The most significant and distinguishing facet of India's nuclear doctrine is its consistent claim that nuclear weapons are above all else political instruments rather than military tools. At first sight, this claim might not appear to be either interesting or of consequence, since all weapons are ultimately political to the extent that they exist to serve the interests of the state. The Indian conception of the utility of nuclear weapons, however, has a more specific and substantive meaning: Nuclear weapons are understood to be properly political instruments because they are emphatically not *usable* weapons in any military sense. Indian Prime Minister Atal Bihari Vajpayee attempted to capture this understanding when he stated that "nuclear weapons are weapons of mass destruction,"[23] implying thereby that they cannot be used, must not be used, and will never be used as instruments of war fighting by New Delhi. Indian President K. R. Narayanan, addressing the nation on the occasion of the golden jubilee of India's independence, reiterated this view when he solemnly stated that "nuclear weapons are useful only when they are not used. They can only be a deterrent in the hands of a nation."[24] A prominent Indian analyst, Jasjit Singh, amplified this argument when he asserted that despite the existence of many superpower doctrines projecting "a military role for nuclear weapons," it has become obvious over time that "[a] nuclear war cannot be won, and therefore must never be fought."[25] Carrying this thesis to its logical end, Singh concludes that "nuclear weapons [are] more an instrument of politics . . . than a military instrument of war fighting."[26] Affirming this conclusion in the context of a comparison with the doctrines of other nuclear powers, K. Subrahmanyam asserted simply that "India does not subscribe to the outmoded war-fighting doctrine [followed by the United States and the U.S.S.R.], and [in contrast to the doctrines

---

[23]"Prime Minister's Reply to the Discussion in Lok Sabha on Nuclear Tests on May 29, 1998," p. 9.

[24]"Address to the Nation by Shri K.R. Narayanan, President of India, on the Occasion of the Closing Function of the Golden Jubilee of India's Independence, Central Hall of Parliament, New Delhi—August 15, 1998," *India News*, July 16–August 15, 1998, p. 3.

[25]Singh, "Why Nuclear Weapons?" p. 11.

[26]Ibid.

upheld by these states] the Indian nuclear weapons are meant solely for deterrence."[27]

Nuclear weapons, in Indian readings, are thus seen as having functional utility *more as pure deterrents than as implements of war.* Because these weapons embody enormous destructive capability—a capability often greater than that required by most rational political ends—they are perceived as having relatively low utility in situations where all the antagonists possess similar technologies. In such situations, any use or attempted use of nuclear weapons by one state against another would be countermanded by the symmetrical use, or threatened use, of these weapons by their competitors. The net result—either a devastating war arising from actual use or a political standoff arising from prevented use—implies that the efficacy of nuclear weapons per se is least when all other states have comparable capabilities. Under situations of asymmetry, however, nuclear weapons could have remarkable efficacy as instruments of coercion because nonnuclear states would be highly vulnerable to threats that might be issued by their nuclear-armed adversaries—or so it is argued. Most Indian analysts appear to be greatly exercised by this class of contingencies, and it is therefore not surprising that Jasjit Singh, surveying 47 incidents involving the threat of nuclear weapons since 1946, concluded that "nuclear weapons played an important political role rather than a military one"[28]—a role in which "the threatened party could ignore the threat only at its peril."[29] Drawing similar conclusions, K. Subrahmanyam asserted that "the main purpose of a third world arsenal is deterrence against blackmail,"[30] since this presumably constitutes the principal problem affecting nonnuclear powers in situations of nuclear asymmetry.

Irrespective of whether the historical analysis underlying these conclusions is accurate, the belief that nuclear weapons are most

---

[27]K. Subrahmanyam, "Talbott Is Stuck in Pre-'85 Nuclear Groove," *The Times of India*, November 17, 1998.

[28]Singh, "Why Nuclear Weapons?" p. 13.

[29]Ibid.

[30]K. Subrahmanyam, "Nuclear Policy, Arms Control and Military Cooperation," paper presented at the Carnegie Endowment for International Peace–India International Centre conference on India and the United States after the Cold War, New Delhi, March 7–9, 1993, p. 7.

useful as antidotes to blackmail is deeply embedded in the Indian psyche. This obsession with neutralizing blackmail, threats, and compellance is ultimately rooted in India's long historical memory of constant invasion and repeated subjugation by foreign powers, and New Delhi's strategic weakness for most of its independent life has only reinforced it. And while both the specific sources of threat and the level of concern about threats have varied considerably over time, the general preoccupation with negating coercion and black-mail has remained more or less constant in India's strategic policy, deriving sustenance today from the potential for misuse arising from the nuclear capabilities India's principal adversaries, Pakistan and China, now possess. Most security managers in New Delhi would in fact argue that their decision to acquire nuclear weaponry—that is, to move beyond simply maintaining the nuclear option—is itself a constrained choice in that they would prefer not to have any nuclear weapons to begin with if the global environment and their regional situation so permitted.[31] At the same time, however, the absence of this alternative and the consequent decision to pursue nucleariza-tion do not imply, as Subrahmanyam put it, that India ought to mimic "the U.S. nuclear strategic theology, [even though it has thus far] dominated all thinking in matters nuclear."[32] Elaborating on this notion, Subrahmanyam asserted that "India has the benefit of the

---

[31]This argument, in fact, forms the preamble to the "Draft Report of [the] National Security Advisory Board on Indian Nuclear Doctrine," which asserts that "the use of nuclear weapons in particular as well as other weapons of mass destruction constitutes the gravest threat to humanity and to peace and stability in the inter-national system. Unlike the other two categories of weapons of mass destruction, biological and chemical weapons, which have been outlawed by international treaties, nuclear weapons remain instruments for national and collective security, the possession of which on a selective basis has been sought to be legitimised through permanent extension of the NPT in May 1995. Nuclear weapon states have asserted that they will continue to rely on nuclear weapons with some of them adopting policies to use them even in a nonnuclear context. These developments amount to virtual abandonment of nuclear disarmament. This is a serious setback to the struggle of the international community to abolish weapons of mass destruction. . . . Autonomy of decision making in the developmental process and in strategic matters is an inalienable democratic right of the Indian people. India will strenuously guard this right in a world where nuclear weapons for a select few are sought to be legitimised for an indefinite future, and where there is growing complexity and frequency in the use of force for political purposes." See "Draft Report of [the] National Security Advisory Board on Indian Nuclear Doctrine," p. 2.

[32]K. Subrahmanyam, "Educate India in Nuclear Strategy," *The Times of India*, May 22, 1998.

wisdom drawn from the highly risky and totally non-viable policies of nuclear deployment followed by the United States and the USSR. It has, therefore, no intention of repeating those blunders."[33]

Most Indian elites would assert that New Delhi can afford to deviate from the received wisdom pertaining to the management of nuclear weaponry—even as it acquires a nuclear arsenal—because the Indian strategic problematic is unique in many ways, at least in relation to the United States vis-à-vis the Soviet Union during the Cold War. Unlike the United States, for example—which developed its nuclear arsenal during a period of intense superpower competition and amid clear and present danger to its security—India has set out to develop a nuclear capability at a time when the global strategic environment is much less intense and when there is a clearer recognition that any nuclear use would be highly escalatory and therefore "should not be initiated."[34]

Further, unlike the United States during the Cold War, India does not suffer any conventional inferiority vis-à-vis either Pakistan or China. Since it is therefore unlikely to be at the receiving end in a conventional conflict with either of these two states, it is spared the imperative of thinking about nuclear weapons as usable instruments of war fighting that may have to be harnessed *in extremis* to stave off potential defeat on the battlefield.[35] This by no means eliminates the problem of responding to the first use of nuclear weapons by India's adversaries, but at least this obstacle represents a different class of challenges than that arising from the need to use one's own nuclear weapons first because of serious conventional weaknesses in the face of a highly revisionist threat.

Finally, unlike the United States during the Cold War, India does not have to service any obligations relating to the extended deterrence of allies located far from its own territories, and it does not face a formidable military machine against which it has poor or, at worst, no conventional antidotes. The only object of concern here is India's own security, and given its at least nominal conventional military

---

[33]Subrahmanyam, "Talbott Is Stuck in Pre-'85 Nuclear Groove."

[34]Subrahmanyam, "Educate India in Nuclear Strategy."

[35]Singh, "Nuclear Diplomacy," pp. 289–291.

superiority vis-à-vis both Pakistan and China (in the theater), the only contingency left for nuclear weapons to service is that of immunization to blackmail arising from either its adversaries' threat of nuclear use or the political exploitation of their own nuclear assets in some abnormal political circumstances.[36]

India's simple—and perhaps even simplistic—conception of the value of nuclear weapons thus derives fundamentally from the fact that the country does not face any onerous security challenges that would demand a more expansive view of the utility of nuclear weaponry. One of India's leading strategic commentators, C. Raja Mohan, explicated this judgment clearly when, in the context of the ongoing Indian debate about the nature and utility of nuclear weaponry, he noted that

> India has taken too long to come to terms with the nuclear revolution and its impact on world military affairs. But the technology underlying the atomic revolution is 50 years old, and a continuing obsession with it will prevent India from making crucial investments and policy decisions on the new revolution in military affairs. The dramatic advances in information and communication technologies and their application to warfare will increasingly determine the locus of military power in the coming century. Worship of the old nuclear gods and the reluctance to pay attention to the impact of [information technology] on the conduct of future wars will put India back in the position of global irrelevance with or without nuclear weapons. . . . Nuclear weapons are certainly important. And India's decision to acquire them was long overdue. But in the flush of becoming an atomic power, India could easily overstate the significance of nuclear weapons. They can only serve a limited purpose for India—of preventing the use or threat of use of nuclear weapons by its adversaries against it. There is little else that nuclear weapons can do. . . . Even the most sophisticated and expansive nuclear arsenal will not propel India into the ranks of great powers. Mindless obsession with nuclear weapons will instead push India down the ruinous path that the Soviet Union went. Having acquired

---

[36]Jasjit Singh, for example, has argued that the only reason India needs nuclear weapons "is to provide insurance against nuclear threat ('blackmail' or hegemony, as the Chinese describe it) and possible use. We do not need them for power or prestige. India's status in the final analysis will be governed by how successfully we solve our problems." See Jasjit Singh, "Nukes Have No Prestige Value," *Indian Express*, June 4, 1998.

an insurance policy through nuclear weapons, India must now pursue the arduous domestic agenda of economic modernisation, political reform, and social advancement. . . . The productive economic and political engagement of the world must remain the bedrock of nuclear India's diplomacy. A paranoid reading of external threats to security and an overdetermination of the role of nuclear weapons in national strategy will drive India into a needless confrontation with most nations and undermine New Delhi's efforts to expand its regional influence and global standing.[37]

Confirming such sentiments about the limited utility of nuclear weapons to India, Prime Minister Vajpayee too summarily concluded that New Delhi "do[es] not intend to use these weapons for aggression or for mounting threats against any country; these are weapons of self-defense, to ensure that India is not subjected to nuclear threats or coercion."[38]

The view that nuclear weapons are exclusively political instruments whose efficacy derives from their possession but not their use (as opposed to military tools, whose efficacy derives primarily from how they might potentially be used in operational terms) places Indian nuclear doctrine squarely at the deterrence end of the "deterrence-defense continuum" that Glenn Snyder so clearly described 40 years ago.[39] Being located at this end implies that nuclear weapons are treated, in Bernard Brodie's words, as "absolute"[40] weapons that can inflict excruciating and perhaps even fatal pain on all antagonists irrespective of their relative national strength. Such weapons are also viewed as impossible to defend against in any meaningful way and consequently their presence is perceived as radically transforming the traditional ends to which force may be applied. As Brodie put it, "Thus far, the chief purpose of a military

---

[37] C. Raja Mohan, "Beyond the Nuclear Obsession," *The Hindu*, November 25, 1999.

[38] "Suo Motu Statement by Prime Minister Atal Bihari Vajpayee in the Indian Parliament on May 27, 1998," p. 2.

[39] See Glenn H. Snyder, *Deterrence and Defense* (Princeton, NJ: Princeton University Press, 1961), pp. 3–51. A more systematic and elaborate version of this continuum has been elaborated by William R. van Cleave, "The Nuclear Weapons Debate," *U.S. Naval Institute Proceedings*, 92:5 (May 1966), pp. 26–38.

[40] Bernard Brodie (ed.), *The Absolute Weapon: Atomic Power and World Order* (New York: Harcourt, Brace, 1946).

establishment has been to win wars. From now on its chief purpose must be to avert them. It can have no other useful purpose."[41] This claim about the absolute character of nuclear weaponry, which makes only deterrence and not defense viable, has been contested from the very beginning of the nuclear age[42]—and these debates obviously have implications, some of which will be explored later, even in the Indian context today. For the moment, however, suffice it to say that Indian security managers appear to have rejected the U.S. solution that finally prevailed during the Cold War: By refusing to treat deterrence as an outcome that is best assured by developing various strategies of defense, such as preemptive attacks, limited nuclear options, or robust strategic defenses, New Delhi has adhered to the traditional opposition that theorists like Snyder have postulated to exist between deterrence and defense, coming down strongly in favor of the former and rejecting the latter, at least at the level of declaratory policy.[43]

Dr. Raja Ramanna, one of India's foremost nuclear weapon scientists and a former Minister of State for Defence, reaffirmed Brodie's original insight about the absolute character of nuclear weaponry and conveyed Indian views about the illogic of transforming the challenge of deterrence into problems of defense in a speech delivered as early as 1992:

> Since the end of the Second World War, the problem of security has become aggravated because of two reasons: military power has become synonymous with technological and industrial power, and new developments in technology have brought the situation to a state where weapons of destruction have not merely been improving in potency in some linear manner, but a fundamental change in overall capability has taken place. Besides being assisted by automation, never dreamt of before, some of them have reached the status of what is known as "ultimate" weapons, i.e., their individual destructive power is more than what the world can bear. The "ultimate" weapon has the power of destroying vast areas of the earth and making them uninhabitable in a matter of a few seconds.

---

[41]Ibid.

[42]See the discussion about William Liscum Borden and his arguments in particular in Jervis, "Strategic Theory: What's New and What's True," pp. 135–137.

[43]"India Not to Engage in a N-Arms Race: Jaswant."

In spite of this, the "ultimate" nature of modern weapons does not by itself seem sufficient for countries to give up further development of more efficient weapons. Greater effort is being put on defense research and the testing of weapons continues as before. In some countries the burden of deterrence has messed up not only their entire economic structure, but even their very integrity as nations.[44]

Even India's hawks are usually agreed on this issue: that nuclear deterrence ought not to be treated as a problem that lends itself to solutions based on defense, as the United States held during the Cold War. Indeed, such individuals might passionately argue for a larger nuclear weapon stockpile and a technically more diverse set of weapon types than even their country's security managers consider necessary, but these capabilities are justified mainly on the grounds of enhancing the credibility of deterrence rather than in support of any sustained nuclear war-fighting strategy. Thus, for example, even Bharat Karnad, who argues for a diverse nuclear arsenal consisting of atomic demolition munitions at one end all the way to high-yield thermonuclear weapons at the other, ultimately comes down on the side of a nuclear doctrine centering on *deterrence by punishment,* which requires, in his view, a stockpile of some 330 nuclear weapons by the year 2030—clearly a minuscule force if the requirements of nuclear war fighting as understood during the Cold War are anything to go by.[45] In any event, Karnad remains more or less the exception among Indian elites: Most Indians are content to eschew any nuclear weaponry that might even hint of a willingness to contemplate a war-fighting posture, and this sentiment is shared both by critical decisionmakers within the Indian government and by the top brass of the Indian armed forces today. Consequently, while all the hawks invariably assert that India needs readily available nuclear weapons for its security, almost all of them—if Karnad is treated as the exception—also believe that these capabilities ought to be subordinated, as one of the more prominent hawks phrased it, to "a doctrine that eschews both a war-fighting approach and the . . . recessed

---

[44]Ramanna, "Security, Deterrence, and the Future," p. 283.

[45]Karnad, "A Thermonuclear Deterrent," pp. 140–149.

or non-deployed deterrence advocated by the United States and its friends."[46]

Since India's preferred outcome is thus defined solely in terms of deterrence (understood as a rejection of defense in the context of the deterrence-defense continuum), the possession of even a few survivable nuclear weapons capable of being delivered on target, together with an adequate command system, is seen as sufficient to preserve the country's security. Preserving safety in the face of blackmail and coercion does not, however, require any additional *pronouncements* about the size of the nuclear stockpile, theories of deterrence, use doctrines, targeting philosophy, or operational posture. As one highly placed manager associated with India's nuclear program pointed out, "We don't fall into the standard pattern of declared doctrines, specific weapons, delivery capabilities or force postures," since the very recognition that India possesses nuclear weapons suffices to ensure that all "aggressive acts" would be adequately deterred even without the promulgation of any particular doctrine of deterrence.[47]

When viewed against this background, the ideas articulated in the "Draft Report of [the] National Security Advisory Board" no doubt constitute a genuine exception to the official Indian preference for silence on all details relating to its nuclear strategy. Even the volubility of the Advisory Board in this instance, however, can be attributed to a concatenation of three distinct factors: first, the understandable but misguided pressure emanating from Washington for an Indian "nuclear doctrine" in the aftermath of the tests of May 1998; second, the absence of any individuals on the Advisory Board charged with actually carrying out the recommended doctrine outlined in the Draft Report; and third (and perhaps most important), the Advisory Board's expectation that the report would remain a confidential recommendation to the government of India rather than a draft paper released for public debate. Absent these three conditions, it is unlikely that any detailed public articulation of India's nuclear doctrine

---

[46]Chellaney, "India's Trial by Atom."

[47]See the remarks of S. Rajagopal cited in Deepa M. Ollapally, "India's Strategic Doctrine and Practice: The Impact of Nuclear Testing," in Raju G.C. Thomas and Amit Gupta (eds.), *India's Nuclear Security* (Boulder, CO: Lynne Rienner Publishers, 2000), p. 79.

would have been offered by the Indian government, since the latter, by all evidence thus far, appears to believe that a global recognition of the country's nuclear capabilities suffices for effective deterrence. Defence Minister George Fernandes affirmed this judgment when he noted that "being a nuclear weapon state was a [sufficient] deterrent for [India's] enemies, and that was the entire aim of [India] declaring itself [to be] one."[48]

This conservative view of sufficiency requirements, at least at the level of declaratory policy, is strongly influenced by the belief that, as Thomas Schelling once put it, "what makes atomic weapons different is a powerful tradition that they *are* different."[49] This claim, which all Indian security managers would readily understand, accept, and make their own, is perceived as reinforcing the extant *tradition of nonuse of nuclear weaponry*—a tradition that centers on the "jointly recognized expectation that [these weapons] may not be used in spite of declarations of readiness to use them, even in spite of tactical advantages in their use."[50] Anticipating that this tradition will continue to hold robustly as a background condition even amid the unsettled political conditions in the subcontinent and its environs, Indian policymakers believe that extended discussions about India's nuclear capabilities, doctrine, and force posture are both unnecessary and counterproductive—unnecessary because India would rarely find itself in a position where it would have to actively exploit its nuclear reserves for defensive purposes, and counterproductive because articulating the character of India's nuclear capabilities, doctrine, and posture in any detail could precipitate probing tests on the part of its adversaries, who may seek to discern both its limits and its vulnerabilities. Indian Defence Minister George Fernandes provided an inkling of these sentiments when he argued that "when people keep commenting that the nation is divided on the nuclear tests and that it has become a contentious issue, then we are only providing our opponents an assurance that they don't have much to

---

[48]"Kargil Shouldn't Bias Western View of India's N-Policy: George," *The Times of India*, July 21, 1999. Indian Prime Minister Vajpayee echoed these sentiments when he too declared in Parliament that the "fact that we've become a nuclear weapons state should be a deterrent itself." See "PM Declares No-First Strike," *Indian Express*, August 5, 1998.

[49]Schelling, *The Strategy of Conflict*, p. 260.

[50]Ibid.

worry [about]; that we are not even united on our own survival. . . . A nation can be at war on issues like what should be our priorities, on issues relating to social justice, etc. But on our very survival, never."[51]

Official exhortations to silence such as those expressed by Fernandes have been criticized by India's free and often feisty media[52]—and once even by the Parliamentary Standing Committee on Defence, which urged the government "to move away from [the] conservative concept of keeping everything behind the veil of secrecy," since India's adversaries could contemplate mounting nuclear attacks only if they "underestimated the robustness of our preparedness."[53] The fact remains, however, that senior Indian security managers have continued to maintain a deliberate silence about all the *details* relating to these issues, preferring instead to leave most analysis to the imagination in efforts to exploit whatever deterrence benefits can be derived from uncertainty, opacity, and ambiguity. Indeed, even when they have spoken about nuclear matters, such individuals have sought to describe not what India might do in the event of a deterrence breakdown but rather what needs to be done to prevent such a breakdown from occurring. And even these declamations—offered in sparse and general terms—usually turn out to be little more than either repeated justifications of why India needs a minimum but credible nuclear deterrent or pleas to the international

---

[51]Dinesh Kumar, "National Debate on N-Tests Hurts Security Concerns: Fernandes," *The Times of India*, October 12, 1998.

[52]A leading national daily, *The Times of India*, for example, in a pointed editorial aimed at Fernandes' remarks, noted that while Fernandes "may have reasons for taking such a position . . . given the demands and sensitivities of the portfolio that [he] is handling, . . . the position taken by Mr. Fernandes is itself highly debatable. . . . While opinion is divided on the May 1998 nuclear tests and their diplomatic and economic fallout, there has been a heartening unanimity on the view that the issue should be discussed. In fact, this continuing debate is a matter of singular pride for India. . . . In this regard, India has distinguished itself from most other nuclear powers whose deterrence needs and capabilities have seldom, if ever, been publicly discussed with such passionate and informed zeal." See "Silent Thunder," *The Times of India*, October 13, 1998.

[53]"Declare Our Nuclear Capability to Deter Strike," *Asian Age*, December 26, 1998. For other exhortations in a similar vein, see also Ashok K. Mehta, "Preparing for a Nuclear Future," *Hindustan Times*, June 19, 1998, and Ranjit B. Rai, "Nuclear Strategy," *The Pioneer*, September 7, 1998.

community to restrain India's adversaries, particularly Pakistan.[54] Even the Draft Report, in the section titled "Objectives," does not add much more to that which might already be presumed about Indian thinking on this question: After affirming that "India's peacetime posture aims at convincing any potential aggressor that . . . any threat of use of nuclear weapons against India shall invoke measures to counter the threat," it simply declares that "any nuclear attack on India and its forces shall result in punitive retaliation with nuclear weapons to inflict damage unacceptable to the aggressor."[55]

This laconic attitude, which essentially repeats what most Indians already presume to be the essential characteristics of nuclear weaponry anyway—the ability to inflict unacceptable damage even in the context of the most limited use—stands in sharp contrast to the loquacity about nuclear doctrine and force posture that characterized the United States during the Cold War. These attitudinal differences are in turn rooted in diametrically opposed intuitions about the question "What deters?" During the Cold War, the United States—operating on the intuition that achieving successful nuclear deterrence was a difficult task requiring both extensive capabilities and credible threats—created a sizable and redundant nuclear arsenal coupled with relatively transparent nuclear-use doctrines, all designed to communicate the character of its nuclear capabilities and to ensure that its otherwise-incredible strategic threats would actually be carried out in response to any attack.[56] India, in contrast—operating on the intuition that achieving successful

---

[54]See, for example, the tenor of the remarks offered by both Jaswant Singh and George Fernandes in their interviews with Tim Sebastian of the BBC as reported in Surya Prakash, "We Sleep Well Mr. Sebastian, Thank You," *The Pioneer*, July 28, 1999.

[55]"Draft Report of [the] National Security Advisory Board on Indian Nuclear Doctrine," p. 2. The expanded discussion of various dimensions of retaliation in the Draft Report occur only in the sections on India's desired force structure, and they cannot be treated by any means as an exhaustive statement of how India might respond in the context of a nuclear attack. These issues will be discussed in more detail in the subsequent section of this chapter, which focuses on the operational level of policy.

[56]In his classic work *The Strategy of Conflict*, for example, Thomas Schelling assessed at some length many of the techniques that a deterrer could use to communicate its commitment to carrying out what might otherwise be dismissed as incredible threats because of their inherent painfulness. See Schelling, *The Strategy of Conflict*, pp. 119–161. See also Schelling, *Arms and Influence*, pp. 1–125.

nuclear deterrence is a relatively easier matter, thanks both to the absolute character of nuclear weaponry and the relatively robust tradition of nonuse already in place—appears content to settle for a simpler set of nuclear capabilities while remaining silent with respect to many of the details pertaining to its ability to retaliate. This response is quite logical, since India seems to be satisfied by the belief that even a ragged nuclear response would suffice to deter its adversaries given that this response would inflict more damage than *any of the political objectives sought by its competitors* is worth.[57]

Understanding this criterion is critical to comprehending India's evolving nuclear doctrine and force posture because it suggests that no matter how serious the increase in Pakistani and Chinese nuclear capabilities may be, New Delhi believes that it faces a reasonably permissive geopolitical environment—at least insofar as this environment influences *the prospects for nuclear use by India's adversaries*.[58] This judgment is not unreasonable given the fact that the most likely use of nuclear weapons against India would emanate from Pakistan, not China. The Indo-Pakistani rivalry involves dynamic security competition: It entails a high degree of routine violence; is manifested through active struggle over a disputed territory; and involves in Pakistan a weak state that is highly sensitive to Indian threats to its security. Given these considerations, any conflict between India and Pakistan—even one stemming from miscalcula-

---

[57]K. Subrahmanyam formulated this criterion succinctly when he noted that war, including nuclear war, "does not make sense as an instrument of policy, if there is no worthwhile gain or if the costs of it will not be commensurate to the results expected or achieved." See K. Subrahmanyam, "In Dubious Battle: How War Became Obsolete," *The Times of India*, May 9, 1995. Since even limited nuclear—countervalue—attacks can be extraordinarily costly *in terms of the casualties suffered by the victim*, the possibility of even a ragged nuclear response ought to suffice to make the achievement of stable deterrence a relatively simple task. See K. Subrahmanyam, "Nuclear Defence Philosophy: Not a Numbers Game Anymore," *The Times of India*, November 8, 1996. This understanding has also been explicated in some detail in K. Sundarji, "Changing Military Equations in Asia: The Role of Nuclear Weapons," in Francine Frankel (ed.), *Bridging the Nonproliferation Divide* (Lanham, MD: University Press of America, 1995), pp. 119–149.

[58]For a good discussion of the rationale underlying this judgment, see Singh, "A Nuclear Strategy for India," pp. 306–324. See also Subrahmanyam, "Nuclear Force Design and Minimum Deterrence Strategy for India," pp. 177–189.

tion—is likely to produce nuclear brandishing by Islamabad and, in the limiting case, even some kinds of nuclear use.[59]

Despite the challenges such a contingency poses, however, New Delhi appears to be sanguine about the problem of Pakistani nuclear use for three reasons. First, India is unlikely to ever pursue any course of action that would place Pakistan in a situation where the latter felt it had no alternative but to use its nuclear weapons in anger.[60] Second, even if Pakistan were to use its nuclear weapons extensively against India, the stark geographic vulnerabilities of the former imply that even a relatively small Indian residual reserve would more than suffice to destroy Pakistan as a functioning state. As one Indian analyst phrased this judgment, "The logic of Pakistan's nuclear [posture] rests in the assumption that the only way to counter India's size and might rests in acquiring a first-strike nuclear capability, forgetting that Pakistan cannot survive even the second strike option that the Indian nuclear doctrine has reserved for itself."[61] Third, it is increasingly believed that even in the context of a limited conventional war with Islamabad, a nuclear-armed Pakistan would not be able to use its nuclear weapons with impunity against India. While these capabilities might be brandished and their political effects exploited for purposes of signaling, many Indian analysts argue that Pakistan would be unlikely to conclude such stratagems by actually using its nuclear weaponry either because the costs of doing so would far exceed its benefits in the context of a limited confrontation[62] or because the superpowers—especially the United

---

[59]For a discussion of such contingencies, see Tellis, *Stability in South Asia*, pp. 55–62. This conclusion is decisively rejected by some Indian hawks like Karnad, who, thanks both to an ignorance about Pakistan's true nuclear capabilities vis-à-vis India and to a somewhat patronizing belief that Islamabad's "nuclear forces may even be complementary should the unitary strategic space of the subcontinent ever be reclaimed with the seeding of an *entente cordiale*," conclude simply that "Pakistan is not too weighty a nuclear threat" to India. See Karnad, "A Thermonuclear Deterrent," pp. 135–136.

[60]See Sundarji, "Changing Military Equations in Asia: The Role of Nuclear Weapons," pp. 125–128.

[61]D. N. Moorthy, "Ambiguity Is India's New Nuclear Agenda," *Jane's Intelligence Review*, 11:11 (November 1999), p. 49.

[62]V. K. Grover, "Nuclear Bluff," *The Pioneer*, February 12, 2000.

States—would be unlikely, out of pure self-interest, "to permit Pakistan to get away with [such] a nuclear strike."[63]

Irrespective of the veracity of each of these three claims, the bottom line is that New Delhi refuses to be unsettled even by the more likely contingency pertaining to nuclear use in Southern Asia: threats emanating from Pakistan. In large part, this is because all three considerations interact to produce an expectation that whatever Islamabad may say, it will not actually make good on any of its threats to use nuclear weapons—above all, because any nuclear exchange, while certainly painful for India, could quite simply obliterate Pakistan. Consequently, the prospect of just such an outcome should suffice to prevent Islamabad from initiating any nuclear use to begin with—or so many Indian analysts are wont to argue.[64]

This calculus does not carry over to China in an identical way, but even here New Delhi can afford to be reasonably sanguine as far as the fear of nuclear first use against India is concerned. To begin with, Sino-Indian competition, despite all its ebbs and flows over the past five decades, has never involved the routinely high levels of violence that obtain in the case of India and Pakistan. China does lay claim to some 90,000 km^2 of Indian territory in the eastern sector and occupies parts of the Aksai Chin that lie within the northern Indian state of Jammu and Kashmir. For all practical purposes, however, New Delhi is reconciled to this occupation, since the more valuable real estate claimed by China—in the eastern Indian state of Arunachal Pradesh—is already under effective Indian control.[65] By contrast, the dispute over Aksai Chin, where China controls a modest portion of territory claimed by India, represents an area of greater value to Beijing because the critical land line of communication between Xinjiang and Tibet happens to run through this region. The character of the respective Chinese and Indian occupations therefore produces a certain equilibrium from the perspective of stability: China has defined Aksai Chin in the western sector—which it already occupies—

---

[63]"Nuclear Follies," *The Times of India*, July 2, 1999.

[64]"Stale Tale," *The Times of India*, June 30, 1996, and Nair, *Nuclear India*, pp. 137–142.

[65]For a useful overview of these issues, see Sumit Ganguly, "The Sino-Indian Border Talks, 1981–1989: A View from New Delhi," *Asian Survey*, 29:12 (December 1989), pp. 1123–1135.

as strategically vital to its security interests, although it claims that the eastern sector is crucial to the solution of the border issue, while India has defined the eastern sector—which it already occupies—as strategically vital to its security interests, although it claims that Aksai Chin is crucial to the solution of the border issue.[66] As a result, neither state has any real incentive either to give up the areas each currently occupies or to usurp control over the areas currently held by the other.

Consequently, although Beijing's refusal to abdicate its claims over the eastern sector often rankles New Delhi, it is clear that these holdings are simply not considered to be *intrinsically valuable*, at least in the way that they are to India. In China's eyes, these territories do not represent the political equivalent of Taiwan or Hong Kong, and therefore Beijing has not considered it worth their reintegration through either the threat or the use of force. Thus, what is intrinsically valuable for India is simply marginal for China, and given these contrasting valuations, it is not surprising to find that India has developed a robust conventional military capability designed explicitly to frustrate any Chinese attempts at altering the status quo in the Indian northeast through forcible means. To be sure, China could use its superior nuclear capabilities—ranging from tactical nuclear weapons all the way to its strategic systems—to neutralize Indian conventional defenses in an effort to wrest control of these territories, as some Indian observers often fear.[67] The critical question, however, remains why. These disputed territories are so marginal to Beijing's strategic calculations that it is not likely to fight a conventional war, let alone risk nuclear use and subsequent nuclear retaliation by New Delhi, in efforts to change the existing equities in the area.[68]

---

[66]This parallelism is borrowed from Xuecheng Liu, *The Sino-Indian Border Dispute and Sino-Indian Relations* (Lanham, MD: University Press of America, 1994), p. 178.

[67]See, for example, Sahgal and Singh, "Nuclear Threat from China: An Appraisal," pp. 27–38.

[68]The late General K. Sundarji affirmed this judgment by quoting Kenneth Waltz approvingly when he asked, "What issue between the latter [referring to India and China] could justify Chinese leadership in risking a city or two?" See Sundarji, "Changing Military Equations in Asia: The Role of Nuclear Weapons," p. 138.

China's refusal to formally retract its claims over this territory does serve the purpose of needling India and, more justifiably, functions as a bargaining chip useful to secure New Delhi's consent to Beijing's claims over Aksai Chin. At the same time, however, there is clearly a difference between asserting territorial claims for psychopolitical advantage and threatening an armed conflict involving nuclear use for the purpose of recovering what are otherwise simply marginal territories. Not surprisingly, then, Beijing appears content to pursue the former course of action, and New Delhi has in turn judged correctly that the prospects of Chinese nuclear first use in support of a conventional offensive designed to recover these territories are minimal—despite Beijing's overall nuclear superiority and the otherwise ongoing Sino-Indian strategic competition—since the value of the disputed territories for China in no way warrants issuing nuclear threats, let alone using nuclear weapons first, against India. As K. Subrahmanyam concluded as early as 1970, "Even the most ardent advocate of an Indian [nuclear] weapon programme does not visualise . . . the Chinese threat in terms of China using ballistic missiles to destroy Indian cities."[69] More recently, Subrahmanyam excluded even other subsidiary kinds of potential Chinese nuclear use when he argued that "it is not a question of Chinese aggression or threat" that warrants the creation of an Indian nuclear force, but rather "the need for a stable, Asian balance of power."[70] Other Indian observers, including Jasjit Singh, have further refined this rationale by noting that the presence of Indian nuclear weapons vis-à-vis China should be viewed primarily as a hedge against the "strategic uncertainties"[71] in Beijing's future political direction. Consequently, these weapons exist principally to provide political "insurance"[72] because in their absence the "continuing asymmetry in nuclear weapons capability [between India and China] would make [the hope for] equal security [merely] a mirage."[73] Another Indian scholar reiterated this argument in similar terms: "There is one major strategic rationale for the

---

[69]K. Subrahmanyam, "Options for India," *Institute for Defence Studies and Analyses Journal*, 3 (1970), p. 102.

[70]Subrahmanyam, "Nuclear India in Global Politics," pp. 22–23.

[71]Singh, "Why Nuclear Weapons?" *Nuclear India*, p. 16.

[72]Ibid, p. 19.

[73]Ibid, p. 20.

construction of a credible and effective Indian nuclear weapon posture: to provide a hedge—an insurance policy—against the possibility of a belligerent China in an uncertain anarchic world."[74]

Both the Pakistani and the Chinese challenges have thus been viewed as posing only modest strategic problems for New Delhi, at least as far as the use of nuclear weapons against India is concerned. Both states certainly have nuclear weapons and thus place India in a situation where it is required to have comparable capabilities for purposes of deterrence and self-assurance. The low likelihood that either adversary will use its weapons in anger against India, however, implies that New Delhi need not rely heavily on its nuclear assets. In the case of Pakistan, Islamabad's structural weakness makes all but the most token Pakistani nuclear use highly improbable as a matter of national policy. In the case of China, the problem of proportionality between means and ends in territorial disputes between China and India produces exactly the same outcome despite Beijing's otherwise overwhelming nuclear superiority. It is therefore possible to argue, simply in terms of these readings, that nuclear weapons are in fact unnecessary for India,[75] but the validity of such a conclusion ultimately hinges on the risk tolerance of security managers in New Delhi. Being risk averse, Indian policymakers have by now made it abundantly clear that they would prefer to acquire nuclear weapons for purposes of both deterrence and self-assurance because, as Subrahmanyam framed their reasoning, "while [nuclear] deterrence may be fragile, [the] absence of [nuclear] deterrence will make the situation even more fragile."[76] These policymakers are not convinced, however, given the relatively low prospects for nuclear use by an adversary, that India requires much more than the possession of a modest but secure deterrent to ensure its national safety.

Given this minimalist notion about what it takes to deter successfully, it is obvious that India will continue to distinguish itself from

---

[74]Amitabh Mattoo, "India's Nuclear Policy in an Anarchic World," in Amitabh Mattoo (ed.), *India's Nuclear Deterrent* (New Delhi: Har-Anand Publications, 1999), pp. 18–19.

[75]Such an argument has in fact been advanced most cogently in Bajpai, "The Fallacy of an Indian Deterrent," pp. 150–188.

[76]K. Subrahmanyam, "The Nuclear Bomb: Myths and Reality," *Economic Times*, June 22, 1998.

both Pakistan and China by retaining a highly distinctive view about nuclear weaponry. If the term *nuclear weaponry* is treated as the framework of analysis, New Delhi is likely to place its greatest emphasis on the adjective *nuclear,* as in "*nuclear* weaponry," thereby using this term to connote national political assets that insure against strategic blackmail and potential nuclear use. This emphasis stems directly from the belief that the absolute rather than relative performance of these weapons, coupled with the horrendous consequences of even limited use, more than suffices to make them potent deterrents against any of India's competitors—deterrents that do not even require explicit threats of use to guarantee their political efficacy given the highly remote circumstances under which they might become relevant.[77] Islamabad, in contrast, is more likely to place greater emphasis on the noun *weaponry,* as in "nuclear *weaponry,*" thus using this term to refer to military instruments that might have to be employed *in extremis* for purposes of ensuring national safety. This emphasis stems in turn from Pakistan's strategic inferiority vis-à-vis India and from its ever-present fear of being overwhelmed by Indian military action—factors that, taken together, create greater incentives for systematically integrating nuclear weapons *qua* weapons into its operational military planning.[78] In contrast to both India and Pakistan, Beijing is likely to emphasize both adjective and noun uniformly, meaning that it will interpret the term *nuclear weaponry* to refer both to national assets constituting insurance against strategic blackmail *and* to military instruments that might have to be employed operationally *in extremis* against more capable powers. This emphasis on both the political-psychological and the military-operational predicates of nuclear weaponry grows directly out of China's status as a legitimate nuclear weapon state and as an acknowledged albeit relatively weak great power—factors that interact to bequeath to China a politically useful nuclear weapon status even as they compel it to consider the potential usability of these instruments against other, more capable great powers in the international system.[79]

---

[77]See the discussion in Singh, "Why Nuclear Weapons?" pp. 9–25.

[78]See the discussion in Agha Shahi, Zulfiqar Ali Khan, and Abdul Sattar, "Securing Nuclear Peace," *The News International,* October 5, 1999.

[79]See Michael D. Swaine and Ashley J. Tellis, *Interpreting China's Grand Strategy,* MR-1121-AF (Santa Monica: RAND, 2000), pp. 121–123.

The emphasis on *nuclear* weaponry as political instruments and pure deterrents in India, in sharp contrast to the differing emphases placed by its competitors, is obviously grounded first and foremost in structural constraints—that is, in the specific objectives these weapons are called on to service in the context of India's grand strategic needs. This factor represents only part of the story, however, as India's inordinate emphasis on the political as opposed to the military character of nuclear weapons also stems from three distinct but separate strands of political thought that are uniquely rooted in India's strategic traditions and domestic circumstances.

The first reason for India's refusal to treat nuclear weapons as military tools is rooted in the tightly interwoven strands of idealist and liberal thought that defined the country's political culture in its formative years. Despite the many changes in New Delhi's nuclear policy since 1947, the one underlying element of continuity in India's strategic attitudes lies in its consistent refusal to invest nuclear weapons with any axiological legitimacy. Holding that such weapons are "morally, legally and politically indefensible,"[80] India led the charge for "universal and non-discriminatory disarmament" in all international forums since the beginning of the nuclear age. Indeed, even when India opposed disarmament treaties like the NPT and the CTBT, it did so on the grounds that these solutions created more problems than they remedied; in India's view, the former legitimized the entitative status of nuclear weaponry as acceptable instruments of international competition even as it enshrined a permanently discriminatory international regime, while the latter did not go far enough in the direction of disarmament even as it created new opportunities for the nuclear weapon states to maintain and improve their existing arsenals. Consistent with this belief, India argued before the International Court of Justice that "any use of nuclear weapons . . . to promote national policy objectives would be unlawful"[81] and that therefore the use or threat of use of nuclear weapons should be declared illegal under international law. Hence, India's

---

[80]Praful Bidwai, "BJP's Nuclear Stance Seen as Undermining Security," *India Abroad*, April 10, 1998.

[81]"Annexure II, Indian Memorial Submitted to the International Court of Justice, Status of Nuclear Weapons in International Law: Request for Advisory Opinion of the International Court of Justice," *Indian Journal of International Law*, 37:2 (April–June 1997), p. 244.

general attitude toward nuclear deterrence as a system of regulating interstate behavior has always been antagonistic. Indeed, even as late as the discussions leading up to the CTBT, India held that nuclear weapons were "not essential to the security of any nation" and that the threat of inflicting mass destruction to control state behavior was invariably an "abhorrent" doctrine.[82]

Given this tradition, India's decision to finally acquire nuclear weapons created considerable dilemmas for New Delhi, leading numerous Indian commentators and strategic analysts to struggle with the challenge of reconciling this decision with India's long-standing commitment to disarmament. At the level of doctrine, however, policymakers see only one defensible way out of this predicament: to treat the acquisition of nuclear weapons as a *maximin* strategy—that is, as the "best of the worst" choices facing India—while simultaneously refusing to define the value of these instruments in militarily translatable terms. Indeed, only a worldview that treats nuclear weapons as political devices as opposed to military tools can emphasize the radical inutility of such weapons and thereby salvage something resembling fidelity to the country's larger commitment to nonviolence as an ordering principle of political life. Nonetheless, the difficulty of reconciling the demands of technology in general with the ideals of political morality has continued to pose a challenge to India since its independence[83]— and nuclear weapons, as the acme of technology, have only heightened this challenge. Indian security managers today believe that the solution to this conundrum cannot consist of rejecting the technology itself, since ideals, however attractive, cannot survive without power. Power without ideals, on the other hand, is draconian and dangerous, and to the degree that nuclear weapons must be possessed, their power can be tamed only by ideationally denaturing them in a way that is consistent with India's larger moral principles. India's exaggerated emphasis on nuclear weapons as political rather than military instruments must therefore be seen as a solution that derives from more than just a specific strategic

---

[82]Bidwai, "BJP's Nuclear Stance Seen as Undermining Security."

[83]This theme has been addressed at some length and with great sophistication in Ashis Nandy (ed.), *Science, Hegemony and Violence: A Requiem for Modernity* (Delhi: Oxford University Press, 1988).

problem. Its viability is ultimately ensured by the fact that it tolerates the possession of such weapons only so long as possession itself is grounded in the rationale that nuclear weapons cannot be treated as weapons per se and used as such.[84] It comes as little surprise, then, that even the Draft Report on Indian Nuclear Doctrine—perhaps uniquely among all such documents in the world—begins with a lengthy preamble that sings the praises of universal nuclear disarmament and, even as it defines the structure of what could become a significant Indian nuclear force, ends by admonishing the country's security managers "to continue [their] efforts to achieve the goal of a nuclear weapon-free world at an early date" while working to secure, in the interim, both "an international treaty banning [the] first use [of nuclear weaponry]" and "internationally binding unconditional negative security assurances by nuclear weapon states to non-nuclear weapon states."[85]

While the demands emanating from India's larger philosophic and political traditions function as the first reason for treating nuclear weapons as something other than operationally usable military implements, the second reason is rooted in the more prosaic institutions of domestic politics, especially India's peculiar organization of civil-military relations. It is often insufficiently recognized that India

---

[84]This position riles some Indian hawks like Bharat Karnad, who would prefer that India jettison its heritage of commitment to nonviolence and simply acquire nuclear weapons in order to enhance its security and buttress its claims to great-power status. As he phrased his larger critique, "This will require the will to power which the politically correct, if impractical, ideology of world peace through disarmament married to an inert, self-deluding, national security policy has so far made impossible." See Bharat Karnad, "India's Weak Geopolitics and What to Do About It," in Bharat Karnad (ed.), *Future Imperilled* (Delhi: Viking, 1994), pp. 66–67. In another place, Karnad reaffirms this position even more emphatically: "[India] relies on deterrence and seeks to obtain disarmament, when these two are, in realistic military terms, at the two ends of the pole. . . . For a self-proclaimed 'Nuclear Weapons State,' disarmament is a manifestly counterproductive policy thrust. . . . Alas, Delhi hangs on to the vestiges of the past by conjoining its imperative to weaponise with the sentimental craving to advance disarmament. This is a somewhat quixotic and contrarian effort, especially in a milieu where military power is the fulcrum of international diplomacy." See Karnad, "A Thermonuclear Deterrent," p. 114.

[85]"Draft Report of [the] National Security Advisory Board on Indian Nuclear Doctrine," pp. 2–3. As one Indian commentator caustically observed, "Nuclear doctrines normally deal with the deployment of nuclear arsenals. They never advocate abolition. The draft Indian nuclear doctrine [manages to] deal with not only complete nuclear disarmament but also nuclear warfighting [simultaneously]." See Sidhu, "This Doctrine Is Full of Holes."

has one of the most rigid and ironclad systems in the world for ensuring *absolute* civilian control over the military. This institutional structure was developed early in the postindependence period, when the country's founding fathers—fearful of the threat posed by the "man on horseback"—created a bureaucratic framework, first through the Constitution and later through a series of administrative orders, that completely subordinated the uniformed services to a variety of civilian political and bureaucratic masters.[86] The Constitution of India vests control of the Indian military with the President, who exercises that control through the Prime Minister and the Cabinet. Within the Cabinet itself, a subcommittee called the Cabinet Committee on Political Affairs (now renamed the Cabinet Committee on National Security [CCNS]), which consists of the Prime Minister, the Home (Interior), Finance, External Affairs (Foreign), and Defence Ministers, serves as the principal decisionmaking body on all matters of national security. The deliberations of the CCNS are assisted in practice by the two most important civil servants in the government: the Principal Secretary to the Prime Minister (who currently holds the position of National Security Adviser as well) and the Cabinet Secretary, both of whom are supported by the Strategic Policy Group (which consists of the Cabinet Secretariat by another name, the three service chiefs, the heads of the Department of Atomic Energy [DAE], the DRDO, and the intelligence services, and the Governor, Reserve Bank of India) and the Joint Intelligence Committee (which has now been reincarnated as the National Security Council Secretariat).

The decisions of the CCNS, insofar as they involve the armed forces, are transmitted through the Ministry of Defence, which is headed by civilian politicians at the apex. These politicians—the Defence Minister and the Minister of State for Defence—are assisted in turn by four key civilian bureaucrats: the Defence Secretary; the Secretary, Defence Production; the Defence Finance Adviser (a Secretary-level office); and the Scientific Adviser to the Defence Minister (who is also simultaneously the Secretary, Defence Research and Development). Under these principal secretaries are several

---

[86]The seminal work on the unique character of Indian civil-military relations remains Stephen P. Cohen, *The Indian Army: Its Contribution to the Development of a Nation* (Berkeley, CA: University of California Press, 1971). See also Veena Kukreja, *Civil-Military Relations in South Asia* (New Delhi: Sage Publications, 1991).

additional and joint secretaries, each in charge of special functional portfolios (see Figure 4).

The most interesting element of this organizational structure is that the three Indian armed forces, each with separate service headquarters, are *not* part of the Ministry of Defence. They ultimately report to the Defence Minister only through a Chiefs of Staff Committee, which in practice reports immediately to the Defence Secretary. Thus, although the three service chiefs in principle have policymaking access both to the Prime Minister (through their representation on the Strategic Policy Group) and to the Defence Minister (through their representation on the Defence Minister's Committee), their access is in practice severely constrained by mores and institutional traditions that are not revealed on any organizational chart. What complicates matters further is that both bodies wherein the service

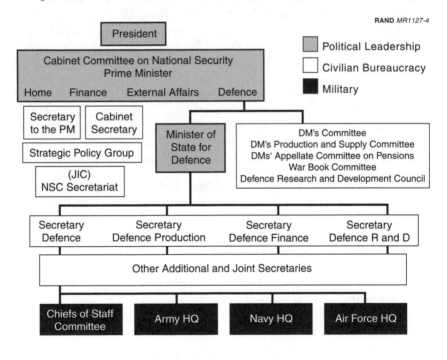

Figure 4—India's Higher Defense Organization

chiefs are represented have problematic histories: The Strategic Policy Group is a fairly new institution, and to the degree that it is dominated by the Cabinet Secretariat, it is almost certain to cement the
marginalization of India's senior most military leadership; whereas
the Defence Minister's Committee is an old institution but is for all
practical purposes a moribund one that, despite the present Defence
Minister's attempts to resuscitate it, continues to be less than fully
effective because of the great dependence of the elected politician
who holds the post of Defence Minister on the civilian bureaucrats
who staff the Defence Ministry. Consequently, despite the nominal
representation of India's senior military leaders in such august bodies, the thorough subordination of the military to the civil is ultimately ensured by the fact that *all* strategic, budgetary, acquisition,
and personnel decisions are controlled by the Indian Administrative
Service, the civilian bureaucracy that consists of the principal, additional, and joint secretaries, who "play a dominant middle role and
insulate professional men in uniform from [the] political leadership."[87] The opinions, requests, and recommendations of the
service chiefs are thus vetted by civil servants, who, thanks to their
ability to control the flow of paperwork, formulate budgets, and
influence senior service promotion decisions, remain ultimately
responsible for the military posture of the Indian state despite the
fact that they may "have neither the knowledge nor the perspective
to assume such responsibility."[88] To be sure, the weaknesses of this
control system are widely recognized in India, but being content with
the protection afforded by the country's great size and inherent
strength relative to its adversaries, Indian security managers—
historically—have consciously refrained from altering the structure
of strict civilian control no matter what benefits in increased military
efficiency might accrue as a result. The experience of Pakistan, where
the armed forces have routinely captured the management of state,
has only strengthened their resolve to maintain this ironclad
supremacy, and it has in fact consolidated the "fairly effective
alliance between the civil service and politicians, an alliance created

---

[87]Kotera Bhimayya, "Nuclear Deterrence in South Asia," *Asian Survey*, 34:7 (July
1994), p. 649.

[88]Ibid.

for the purpose of reducing the role of the military in the decision-making process."[89]

While the armed forces are thus separated from the locus of national security decisionmaking, they are even further removed from the nuclear weapon program. In fact, even the civilian-controlled Ministry of Defence—as a corporate entity—has never been traditionally connected to the weapon program as such; instead, all decisions pertaining to this program have been made solely—and often orally—by India's Prime Ministers, relying on the advice of a few close advisers who can seldom be identified by their position on an organizational chart alone.[90] The Prime Ministers, using their Secretariat as a functional clearinghouse, have in turn controlled the nuclear weapon program through the DAE, which functions as the bureaucratic parent of the AEC. The AEC, which is responsible for overseeing the country's vast nuclear estate, including institutions like BARC in Bombay (where India's nuclear weapons have traditionally been designed), is composed entirely of civilian scientists and managers who constitute the highest scientific-regulatory body in the nuclear realm. As such, the AEC also functions as the "brain trust" on which successive Indian Prime Ministers have relied for advice in connection with decisions pertaining to nuclear issues. To the degree that the Ministry of Defence is involved corporately in the weapon program, it has been involved mainly through the DRDO, which is headed by the Scientific Adviser to the Defence Minister, also a civilian. Between the DAE, which ultimately produces the nuclear components, and the DRDO, which is responsible for both producing the nonnuclear components of the country's nuclear devices and transforming these devices into usable weapons, the entire Indian nuclear weapon program can thus be seen to be controlled, manned, and operated by civilians.[91]

---

[89]Cohen, *The Indian Army*, p. 171.

[90]See the most revealing description of this pattern in Subrahmanyam, "Indian Nuclear Policy—1964–98," pp. 26–53, and episodically throughout Perkovich, *India's Nuclear Bomb*.

[91]The history of this development and the gradual integration of the DRDO into what was originally only a DAE-managed program is well described in Perkovich, *India's Nuclear Bomb*, pp. 261–317.

India's recent decision to formally acquire nuclear weapons is in no way intended to disturb the fundamental structure of civil-military relations, at least to the degree that such is possible. If anything, acquiring nuclear weapons has made India's leadership even more sensitive to the need for maintaining strict civilian control over its armed forces. The experience of Pakistan once again looms large in Indian consciousness, since it is remembered that Zulfikar Ali Bhutto's nuclear weapon program, although originally intended to serve as a civilian counterweight to the Pakistani military, was ultimately hijacked by the latter and transformed into a trump card that was used against both its civilian masters and, ultimately, India.[92] Acutely conscious of this political history, Indian security managers appear determined to regulate the role of the military in nuclear matters to the maximum extent possible. This determination has only been fortified by the public ruminations of several retired service officers who see in India's decision to declare its nuclear status a new opportunity for the military to actively participate in the country's national security decisionmaking. Indian policymakers, at least thus far, appear to hold exactly the opposite view: They seem ready to sacrifice the increases in operational coherence and efficiency that might stem from unobstructed military involvement in nuclear command, control, and operations for the safety that comes with restricted military participation occurring primarily under conditions of extreme emergency.[93]

---

[92]Ibid., pp. 204–205.

[93]Not recognizing that this is in fact a conscious decision on the part of India's civilian security managers, at least one Indian hawk, Brahma Chellaney, has concluded that the country's "minimum deterrent" has more bark than bite, as "the military continues to be shut out from nuclear-deterrent planning and operations." Continuing, Chellaney argues, "There [is] no explanation as to what could be the security benefits of weapons the military d[oes] not know about and ha[s] not trained to use. . . . The Vajpayee government, without giving the military any role in nuclear deterrence, claims India can deter any threat. Will civilians by themselves prepare targeting strategies for war scenarios or do what the Prime Minister has identified as an essential minimum-deterrence requirement—maintain deployed nuclear weapons? Will the DRDO, which has devised a nuclear doctrine and command-and-control system, fire nuclear weapons when India suffers a first strike? The paradox of a country proclaiming a nuclear deterrent without the necessary military underpinnings can only make it more vulnerable in a regional situation where it confronts a well-armed, ambitious nuclear power and a state whose nuclear-weapons programme has always been run by the military." See Brahma Chellaney, "Woolly Diplomacy," *Hindustan Times*, May 5, 1999.

How this division of labor might be operationalized will be discussed later, but it suffices for now to conclude that precisely because maintaining strict civilian control over the military is a continuing national security requirement in India, the incentive to treat nuclear weapons as anything other than political instruments for pure deterrence is nonexistent. If it were imagined, even for a moment, that these weapons could have operational military use, the need to integrate the uniformed services as full partners into the national nuclear command-and-control apparatus would become obligatory. Such integration, however, would inevitably destroy the traditional framework of civil-military relations that India's security managers have worked so hard to entrench over the last 50 years, as it would distend the military's dominion over highly powerful weapons that affect the nation's survival in ways that conventional military capabilities never could. Not surprisingly, then, one of the BJP's most prominent national security specialists, Mohan Guruswamy, concluded simply that "these are not weapons to be issued to the existing armed services."[94] Given that New Delhi never risked integrated military participation in national security decisionmaking even when all India had were conventional weapons, it is therefore unlikely, despite the imperatives of the nuclear age, that India will enthusiastically enhance the role of the military in this sphere—*at least until it has tried and run out of all other feasible alternatives.*

If recent reports are to be believed, the new recommendations made by the Group of Ministers with respect to reforming India's higher defense organization continue to reflect the ambivalence of Indian security managers about enlarging the role of the armed forces in the management of India's national security affairs, including those aspects related to the control of its nuclear weapons. On the face of it, these recommendations appear to be, as one Indian commentator put it, "sweeping" in nature, suggesting "an altogether new architecture for managing national security."[95] This conclusion is derived from the fact that the Group of Ministers has apparently recommended, among other things, the appointment of a Chief of

---

[94]Cooper, "Nuclear Dilemmas—India," May 25, 1998.

[95]Atul Aneja, "Towards a New Security Architecture," *The Hindu,* February 28, 2001.

Defence Staff (CDS) who "will serve as the 'single point' military adviser"[96] to the government of India; the creation of a new unified command that, headed by the new CDS, will oversee the country's "nuclear forces, which [will] include delivery systems based on land, air and the sea"[97]; the creation of a new triservice Defence Intelligence Agency that will report to a new National Intelligence Board to be headed by the National Security Adviser; and the formalization of a new joint command in the far eastern theater headquartered in the Andaman Islands.[98]

The implications of these recommendations for change in India's higher military decisionmaking cannot be analyzed here in detail but the innovations noted above may not be as dramatic as they first appear—at least as far as the command, control, and custody of India's nuclear assets are concerned.

First, the new CDS, although intended to be the single-point adviser to the government of India on all matters pertaining to defense, replaces, for all practical purposes, the current Chairman of the Chiefs of Staff Committee. To be sure, the new CDS will possess augmented powers relative to the erstwhile chairman, among other things because he will "report directly to the Defence Minister"[99] and will have the power to adjudicate many kinds of interservice disputes. This power, however, may not be as decisive as it appears, because each of the three service chiefs, even under the new arrangements, will have independent access to India's highest civilian authorities and can convey their claims, judgments, and opinions— including dissenting opinions—autonomously to these authorities.

Second, the new CDS will have *no* operational control over any conventional military forces whatsoever. The operational command over all of India's conventional forces will continue to reside in the three service chiefs, who will control the employment of these components in all war-fighting operations. The primary role of the new

---

[96]Aneja, "GoM for Revamp of Defence Management," *The Hindu*, February 27, 2001.

[97]Ibid.

[98]Ibid.

[99]"Service Chiefs to Plan on Control of N-Forces," *The Times of India*, March 5, 2001.

CDS will therefore be restricted principally to overseeing the planning, organization, training, and equipage of these forces (in coordination with the three service chiefs) while assuming additional responsibility for the overall direction, coordination, and approval—not execution—of the joint war-fighting plans that must be developed if the Indian military is to respond coherently in the face of the new challenges specific to the nuclear age. Over a period of time—perhaps after the first five-year review—the CDS *could* acquire some forms of operational control over India's conventional forces at the expense of the existing service chiefs, but this development is expressly not mandated in the current slate of recommendations.

Third, the only operational role that the new CDS is supposed to acquire is supervision of India's nuclear capabilities, and this function is likely to be expressed through the mechanism of a new unified (actually triservice) command that could be created for this purpose. This is certainly an important innovation, but its significance ought not to be exaggerated. For starters, it is unclear, as yet, whether the Prime Minister will finally accept this recommendation. Further, the creation of a new unified command overseeing India's nuclear assets does *not* imply that the country's civilian authorities will actually transfer completed nuclear weapons into the custody of this body during peacetime. Rather, the new command will oversee only the delivery systems currently maintained by the various war-fighting arms, and even its ability to discharge this function adequately is still unclear. This is because the CDS, lacking any operational authority over India's conventional forces, will nonetheless be required to plan, procure, and operate many kinds of military assets that have both conventional and nuclear uses: With the exception of those missile systems dedicated solely to the nuclear role (and which will be available only many years from now), various other war-fighting systems, such as combat and transport aircraft, communications equipment, surveillance and battle damage assessment (BDA) assets, and automated mission-planning tools, are all dual-capable in nature. How the CDS, who has no operational control over these assets insofar as they are earmarked for conventional operations, will acquire jurisdiction over them in connection with nuclear missions remains a knotty organizational problem that will have to be ironed out.

Fourth and finally, the relationship between the CDS (in both his advisory and his operational roles) and the country's national command authority, which hitherto has been constituted exclusively by civilians, remains an issue that is not yet authoritatively clarified. If the historical record is anything to go by, however, this relationship will be reaffirmed in favor of enduring civilian supremacy, with the CDS continuing to remain responsible to the Prime Minister and to the Cabinet.[100]

Even if all these bureaucratic challenges are satisfactorily resolved, the creation of a new unified command headed by the CDS and tasked with overseeing India's nuclear assets will not be as dramatic an innovation as it first appears: It will result primarily in centralized planning for nuclear operations and could over time pave the way for centralized procurement, maintenance, and deployment of the delivery vehicles that are currently operated separately by the three Indian armed services. To be sure, both the centralized planning for nuclear operations and the systematic allocation of strategic assets for nuclear missions through the mechanism of a unified command would represent a significant improvement in India's capacity for effective retaliatory response. As subsequent discussions will reveal, however, this innovation only standardizes what has already been occurring secretly within India at different levels and in different ways. Consequently, so long as these developments do not extend to the military bureaucracies dominating nuclear decisionmaking institutions in India, the military acquiring peacetime custody over completed Indian nuclear weapons, and the armed services obtaining autonomous authority over nuclear-use decisions both in peacetime and in a crisis, the baseline conclusion explicated and defended earlier—that India's nuclear weapons are primarily national political assets intended to perform as instruments of deterrence rather than war fighting—remains entirely intact. In this context, even the most relevant new innovations—the unified command headed by the CDS and tasked with overseeing India's strategic assets, joint planning, and nuclear operations—can be appreciated as a skillful political

---

[100]When commenting on the recommendation of the Group of Ministers, Indian Defence Minister George Fernandes noted that the Prime Minister will continue to be the final authority on all matters referred to in their report, including the issue of whether the recommendations themselves ought to be accepted. See "PM Will Decide on GoM Report: Fernandes," *The Hindu*, February 28, 2001.

strategy for eliminating all the potential interservice rivalries that are likely to emerge over India's developing nuclear capability. Simultaneously, they represent the minimally necessary adjustments India must make in addressing the exigencies of the nuclear age—but precisely because they have materialized in such a hesitant, incremental, and evolutionary form, they effectively serve to attenuate any stronger military claims over the possession, control, oversight, and employment of India's nuclear reserves as a whole.[101]

The third reason India has treated nuclear weapons as political instruments focused solely on deterrence as opposed to defense pertains to cost issues that are linked in turn to some dimensions of civil-military relations. It should be noted that the issue of cost here does not refer to the price tag of the nuclear deterrent writ large, as this cost, whatever it may be, will be borne by India given its determination to acquire a nuclear arsenal of some sort in the future.[102] India recognizes, however, that the ultimate price tag for its deterrent will be determined to a significant extent by the specific kind of force architecture that it creates. And it is in this context that the distinctive conception of nuclear weapons India has adopted becomes critical, because insofar as nuclear weapons are treated as having utility as implements of war, India will have no choice but to address the many complications that arise when such weapons are viewed as "just another ingredient" in the strategic balance of power.[103] In-

---

[101]It should be noted that the "Draft Report of [the] National Security Advisory Board on Indian Nuclear Doctrine," for all its loquacity on other issues, is conspicuously silent on the question of how India's military services ought to be integrated into the preparations for nuclear operations. While it clearly states that "nuclear weapons shall be tightly controlled and released for use at the highest political level" and that "the authority to release nuclear weapons for use resides in the person of the Prime Minister of India, or the designated successor(s)," it does not speak to the questions of how the custody and release of India's nuclear weapons are to be managed at an institutional level. See "Draft Report of [the] National Security Advisory Board on Indian Nuclear Doctrine," pp. 2–3.

[102]The Finance Minister, Yashwant Sinha, affirmed this judgment in a 1999 briefing, noting that the nuclear weapon program "had been going on for long and had been built into the regular budget." Further, he noted that although this would be a costly endeavor, these costs would be accepted because the long time frames governing such outlays and India's high growth rates would interact to make these expenditures bearable. See Sridhar Krishnaswami, "N-Programme Not a Burden, Says Sinha," *The Hindu*, October 1, 1999.

[103]In their classic 1971 work, Enthoven and Smith lamented the use of "comparison games" that "are virtually meaningless" but nonetheless served to drive

deed, the resolution of this problem in the United States not only led to the creation of a large and costly nuclear force posture but also diluted the strict civilian control the United States initially maintained over its nuclear assets.[104] Indian security managers would prefer to avoid being trapped by either of these possibilities, so to the degree that treating nuclear weapons as political instruments enables them to avoid the development of a nuclear inventory of the sort demanded by highly competitive balance-of-power models of international politics, New Delhi will continue to emphasize the political rather than the military character of its nuclear assets. As Jaswant Singh phrased it,

> the Indian thinking is different principally because we have discarded the Cold War reference frame of nuclear war fighting. In our view, the principal role of nuclear weapons is to deter their use by an adversary. For this, India needs only that strategic minimum which is credible. . . . Therefore, the question of an arsenal larger than that of country X or Y becomes a nonquestion. For India, the question is only one of adequacy that is credible and thus defines our "minimum."[105]

This disinclination to treat nuclear weapons as anything other than political instruments frees India from continually having to contemplate the relative balance of nuclear capabilities existing around its periphery or to prepare *ex ante* for the kinds of nuclear war-fighting operations that would burden it with developing an extremely sophisticated nuclear deterrent, cultivating the requisite managerial competencies to direct such a complex force, and contemplating the prospect of intense military involvement in the day-to-day management of its national deterrent.

India's reluctance to view nuclear weapons as usable military instruments also stems from other cost concerns. Specifically, if New Delhi's nuclear weapons—or those of its adversaries, for that matter—were treated as offensive war-fighting implements, India's

---

the U.S.-Soviet nuclear arms race by their obsessive focus on comparative "bean counts." See Alain Enthoven and K. Wayne Smith, *How Much Is Enough? Shaping the Defense Program, 1961–69* (New York: Harper & Row, 1971), p. 179.

[104]How this process evolved is described in Feaver, *Guarding the Guardians*.

[105]"India Not to Engage in a N-Arms Race: Jaswant."

conventional military forces would have to be radically redesigned and reequipped for the conduct of military operations on a nuclear battlefield. This task would in turn require not only new organizational structures and tactical doctrines but also enormous financial investment in new technologies in order to enhance the mobility, protection, and firepower of India's maneuver formations.[106] Some Indian military analysts, succumbing to wild flights of fancy, have already begun arguing the need for modifying the country's conventional force posture to accommodate the prospect of nuclear warfighting operations in all three combat media (land, sea, and air[107]), and elements of the three Indian armed services have already begun privately arguing the case—with the help of various allies within the Indian nuclear and defense research establishments—for a variety of nuclear weapons, some of which may be appropriate only for specific war-fighting missions.[108] Such recommendations, however—which inevitably arise from the perception of nuclear weapons as war-fighting instruments—would saddle the Indian exchequer with even greater burdens than those associated with the development of a pure deterrent. Recognizing the implications for both India's fiscal health and its national security, New Delhi has refused to endorse such ideas, in part because it seeks to avoid making the kinds of investments that, by allowing India's military forces to integrate offensive nuclear and conventional capabilities, actually increase the prospect that nuclear weapons will be used in a subcontinental

---

[106]As described earlier, one scholar, W.P.S. Sidhu, has argued that India's land force modernization, which began in the mid- to late 1980s, was designed to prepare the Indian Army for military operations on the nuclear battlefield. Irrespective of the veracity of this claim, such nuclear-related modernization has still not materialized in any meaningful sense at the empirical level, and to the degree that it is being pursued, the focus today appears to be mainly on defensive NBC operations.

[107]See, for example, J. K. Dutt, "The Army in the Nuclear Age," *The Statesman*, August 10, 1998; Sat Pal, "Nuclear Onus on Navy," *The Pioneer*, October 11, 1999; and Sharad Dixit, "IAF, the Pivot of Nuclear Power," *The Pioneer*, October 25, 1999.

[108]Rare public evidence of such exhortations was provided by one of India's most well-known nuclear scientists, P. K. Iyengar, who argued that India ought to develop and test a neutron bomb before formally acceding to any obligations under the CTBT. See "India Must Test N-Bomb Before Signing CTBT," *The Hindu*, May 2, 2000. In a similar vein, individual components within the Indian Army, Navy, and Air Force have each begun making private representations to the government of India for their preferred kinds of nuclear weapons on the assumption that such devices ought to be produced to meet various operational needs specific to each service.

war. This desire to avoid the "conventionalization"[109] of nuclear weaponry—as well as to avoid the considerable costs associated with developing a force posture capable of conducting tactical nuclear operations on a subcontinental battlefield—thus constitutes the final reason India has insisted that nuclear weapons remain nothing more than political instruments of statecraft.

India's effort to depict nuclear weapons as purely political instruments is thus rooted in the multiple objectives and constraints relating to its national security policy. New Delhi's reluctance—and perhaps inability—to pursue a conventional war that threatens either Pakistani or Chinese national survival is seen to result in its being spared the prospect that either of its adversaries will actually use nuclear weapons in anger against India. Nor do India's own relatively benign political objectives require it to contemplate using nuclear weapons against its adversaries. The principal utility of an Indian nuclear arsenal, then, consists of providing New Delhi with the self-assurance that flows from the possession of such "absolute" or "ultimate" weapons—a self-assurance that would enable Indian decisionmakers both to stand up to attempted nuclear coercion by Pakistan and China and to deter possible nuclear use by either antagonist within the context of some escalating "crisis slides"[110] that might occur within the Southern Asian region (as opposed to being available for exploitative purposes in support of some premeditated, predatory wars of unlimited or limited aims). Given the narrow benefits sought from the possession of nuclear weaponry, Indian security managers, at least at the declaratory level, can afford to treat their nuclear reserves as political instruments whose utility derives solely from nonuse rather than as military tools that acquire utility only in the context of operational employment on the battlefield.

This predilection is only reinforced by the fact that while India seeks to preserve its immunity to blackmail and destruction, it also endeavors to secure other objectives of national policy simultaneously. To the extent it can do so, for example, India still hopes to

---

[109]Hans Morgenthau, "The Fallacy of Thinking Conventionally About Nuclear Weapons," in David Carlton and Carlo Schaerf (eds.), *Arms Control and Technological Innovation* (New York: Wiley, 1976), pp. 256–264.

[110]C. Bell, *The Conventions of Crisis: A Study in Diplomatic Management* (Oxford, UK: Oxford University Press, 1971), p. 17.

goad the international order into progressively eliminating all nuclear weaponry; still desires to maintain the stigma attached to nuclear weapons as implements of war; still seeks to preserve the existing standards of civilian supremacy over the military, which, among other things, requires minimizing the role of the latter with respect to the management of nuclear weaponry; and still yearns to minimize the costs associated with a nuclear deterrent by avoiding doctrines that require large and redundant nuclear capabilities as well as extensive modernization of its conventional military assets for purposes of integrating battlefield nuclear capabilities into its maneuver formations.

Since none of these multiple objectives can be secured by treating nuclear weapons as military instruments, the strategic necessity of treating these devices as political instruments alone—intended for and useful only as instruments of deterrence—is reinforced even further at the level of declaratory policy. And while this policy can change over time, such an alteration is unlikely to occur so long as the three domestic constraints examined above do not disappear, and so long as the present offense-dominant global nuclear regime remains more or less intact.

The Operational Level of Policy

While the analysis above suggests that there are good reasons for treating nuclear weapons solely as political instruments at the level of declaratory policy, it is obvious to many Indian security managers—particularly those in the higher bureaucracy—that such a posture may not be sustainable at the level of operational policy. The first reason for this disjuncture derives simply from the fact that India subsists in a regional environment populated by other nuclear states, some of which may possess different notions about the utility of nuclear weapons. It is likely that Pakistan, for example, and possibly China as well, would treat its nuclear weapons as war-fighting instruments to be actively integrated into its defensive preparations vis-à-vis India. While still oriented toward deterring war in general, such a posture would locate Islamabad (and possibly Beijing) at the defense end of the deterrence-defense continuum described by Snyder.[111] The fact that at least one of India's adversaries treats its nuclear assets in a somewhat different way thus resurrects the old question of whether the existence of opposing doctrinal traditions actually undermines stability between two similarly armed adversaries, forcing even the side that prefers not to think of nuclear weapons *qua* weapons to take operations planning and weapon employment more seriously than would otherwise be the case. As Colin Gray framed this issue in the U.S.-Soviet context, "If one side to the competition pursues the assured destruction path, how great a risk is it taking should the other side, for whatever blend of reasons, choose differently?"[112]

This question was in fact debated at great length throughout the Cold War, when a second generation of theorists in the United States, including Richard Pipes, attacked the existing U.S. declaratory policy as being obsessed with conflict avoidance when Soviet military theory was in contrast designed "to fight and win a nuclear war."[113] The arguments of critics like Richard Pipes, Paul Nitze, Colin Gray, and others essentially boiled down to the belief that the willingness of one side to countenance the conventionalization of nuclear strategy resulted not only in the destruction of strategic stability but also in the loss of political competition, since the state that planned for the

---

[111]A brief survey of Pakistani writings on nuclear strategy and its relationship with conventional war fighting can be found in "Epilogue to the 1998 Edition" in Stephen P. Cohen, *The Pakistan Army, 1998 Edition* (Karachi, Pakistan: Oxford University Press, 1998), pp. 177–179. At least one scholar has argued that Beijing too may be moving in the direction of integrating nuclear weapons into conventional war-fighting strategies. See Alastair Iain Johnston, "China's New 'Old Thinking': The Concept of Limited Deterrence," *International Security*, 20:3 (Winter 1995–1996), pp. 5–42. The empirical evidence that China is moving in such a direction, however, is currently quite ambiguous, and it is not at all clear that the current focus of Chinese nuclear modernization, centered as it is on improving the reliability, survivability, and responsiveness of its strategic nuclear assets, will ultimately translate into a shift from "minimum deterrence" into some other strategies of deterrence by denial involving the integrated use of nuclear weapons for war-fighting purposes. See Swaine and Tellis, *Interpreting China's Grand Strategy*, pp. 121–123 and 165.

[112]Colin Gray, "Nuclear Strategy: The Case for a Theory of Victory," *International Security*, 4:1 (Summer 1979), p. 59.

[113]This phrase is taken from the title of Richard Pipes' celebrated essay, "Why the Soviet Union Thinks It Could Fight and Win a Nuclear War," *Commentary*, 64:1 (July 1977), pp. 21–34.

possibility of nuclear weapon use would seek and find extraordinary ways to employ those instruments so as to confront its opponents with little more than a choice between surrender and suicide in the event of a crisis.[114] Yet while efforts at averting this outcome preoccupied the United States throughout the latter half of the Cold War, it is still not clear whether the Soviets' attempt at conventionalizing nuclear strategy could ever have succeeded: Although there is substantial evidence that the Soviet leadership planned to fight nuclear wars in order to win,[115] the existence of large, diversified, and complex nuclear arsenals on both sides also effectively guaranteed that any deliberate nuclear use in a major war, especially on the scale contemplated by the Soviet Union, would eventually degenerate into a mutually assured genocide that could not serve any useful policy ends.[116] This insight, however, has unsettling implications for South Asia, because even if the presence of asymmetric doctrines does not subvert deterrence—an issue that is by no means settled[117]—the Indian subcontinent certainly lacks the large, diversified, and redundant nuclear killing capabilities that ultimately guaranteed stability in the U.S.-Soviet context. India's desire to treat nuclear weapons as political instruments oriented purely toward deterrence might therefore prove insufficient if it is not accompanied by large numbers

---

[114]This notion underlay Paul Nitze's famous article, "Deterring Our Deterrent," *Foreign Policy*, 25 (Winter 1976–1977), pp. 195–210.

[115]See, for example, Beatrice Heuser, "Warsaw Pact Military Doctrines in the 1970's and 1980's: Findings in the East German Archives," *Comparative Strategy*, 12:4 (1993), pp. 437–457.

[116]See Robert Jervis, "Why Nuclear Superiority Doesn't Matter," *Political Science Quarterly*, 94 (Winter 1979–1980), pp. 617–633.

[117]The critical issue in the South Asian context is whether nuclear deterrence in the subcontinent can be stable if India holds onto a doctrine that nuclear weapons are solely political instruments useful only for deterrence but not defense while Pakistan, in contrast, adheres to a doctrine that views nuclear weapons as militarily useful with great utility for defense. This asymmetry in doctrinal beliefs, mirroring a similar debate in the U.S.-Soviet context during the Cold War, cannot be resolved without reference to the political objectives and military strategies pursued by both India and Pakistan. When these are analyzed in some detail—unfortunately a task that cannot be undertaken here—it is *possible* that the problem of doctrinal asymmetry in South Asia would lose some of its edge and that its greatest potential for destabilization might be minimized *if both sides were to adopt nonprovocative military strategies even as they continue to disagree about the territorial status quo*. An extended demonstration of this conclusion requires a dynamic analysis of the conventional and nuclear balances as well as the extant military strategies in the subcontinent.

of nuclear weapons, assuredly survivable delivery systems, and extremely high-yield warheads that together create presumably self-equilibrating forms of "true" existential deterrence.[118]

The second reason devising an operational policy is necessary derives from the fact that despite the good intentions of India and its adversaries, deterrence *can* break down, and consequently the relationship between deterrence breakdown and potential nuclear use merits serious consideration. To be sure, it is unlikely that a deterrence breakdown will occur in South Asia because of any premeditated decision to launch unlimited-aims wars. Indeed, other RAND research has demonstrated that neither India nor Pakistan currently has the political incentive or the military capabilities to pursue many of the revisionist strategic goals that are often attributed to them.[119] In general, this also holds true in the Sino-Indian case, at least in the near term.[120] A deterrence breakdown is therefore less likely to occur as a result of premeditated choice than through miscalculation, desperation, or catalytic causes, with the last precipitant probably appearing in the form of unexpected success enjoyed by domestic dissidents who receive foreign support.[121] If a deterrence breakdown does occur as a result of such causes, however, the conventional forces of any two sides (or even all three, in some implausible scenarios) could in fact find themselves engaged in an armed conflict. Depending on the political exigencies of the moment, these forces may be tasked to attain specific operational objectives, many of which may be in support of some larger damage-limiting strategies. Irrespective of what the actual aims of such force employment might be, however, they could conceivably be perceived as threatening the viability of the defenders' state writ large if conventional op-

---

[118]These characteristics are clearly inherent in McGeorge Bundy's conception of existential deterrence. See Bundy, "Existential Deterrence and Its Consequences," pp. 3–13.

[119]Tellis, *Stability in South Asia*, pp. 13–33.

[120]Ashley J. Tellis, Chung Min Lee, James Mulvenon, Courtney Purrington, and Michael D. Swaine, "Sources of Conflict in Asia," in Zalmay Khalilzad and Ian O. Lesser (eds.), *Sources of Conflict in the 21st Century*, MR-897-AF (Santa Monica, RAND, 1998), pp. 148–164.

[121]Tellis, *Stability in South Asia*, pp. 55–62, and Joeck, *Maintaining Nuclear Stability in South Asia*, pp. 16–34.

erations were to deliberately or inadvertently dent the nuclear reserves deployed in the region.[122]

It is in such circumstances that recourse to nuclear weapons, either for purposes of brandishing or for actual use, would become most relevant in South Asia. Coping with such a contingency would require an operational policy that explicitly addressed the question of nuclear use, since a declaratory posture pivoting on the utility of nuclear weapons as political instruments would become infructuous with the actual outbreak of conflict. This issue was widely addressed during the Cold War, especially by theorists such as Colin Gray, who argued that the disproportionate attention "directed towards the effecting of pre-war deterrence at the cost of the neglect of operational strategy" had had "extremely deleterious effects upon the quality of Western strategic thinking and hence upon Western security."[123] Gray, in fact, explicitly asserted that doctrines of the sort advanced by Bernard Brodie, which stressed the "utility in nonuse of nuclear weaponry,"[124] were *astrategic* because they failed to address the question of what constituted an optimal response if deterrence broke down despite the best intentions of all the antagonists involved. The challenge of devising a rational military response in the face of deterrence breakdown involving the possible use of nuclear weapons is therefore one that India cannot avoid either through rhetoric or through repeated assertions of its declaratory posture.[125] Indeed, this is one of those conundrums that inevitably comes in the wake of possessing nuclear weapons, and the obligation to address all the

---

[122]The prospect of such eventualities has already become a source of concern to Pakistani strategists, who view their country's conventional weaknesses as increasing the vulnerability of their nuclear assets to Indian attempts at conventional counterforce. See, for example, Talat Masood, "Evolving a Correct Nuclear Posture," *Dawn*, August 21, 1998. This issue also became a subject of some concern during the later years of the Cold War. See Barry R. Posen, *Inadvertent Escalation* (Ithaca, NY: Cornell University Press, 1991).

[123]Gray, "Nuclear Strategy: The Case for a Theory of Victory," p. 62.

[124]This phrase is in fact the title of Chapter 9 in Bernard Brodie, *War and Politics* (New York: Macmillan, 1973).

[125]On precisely this score, one Indian analyst correctly criticized the "Draft Report of [the] National Security Advisory Board on Indian Nuclear Doctrine" as being "a totally harmless document that is of little or no use to anyone involved in translating a doctrine into a workable operational plan." See G. Balachandran, "India's Nuclear Doctrine," available at http://www.ipcs.org/issues/articles/254-ndi-bala.htm.

dilemmas it entails cannot be escaped so long as there is even a minuscule prospect that nuclear weapons might actually be employed in anger. Moreover, these dilemmas must be confronted expressly at the level of operational policy—although this policy will in India's case be grounded more or less consistently in the assumptions of its declaratory policy: that nuclear weapon use cannot be contemplated for rational political ends and, by implication, that there can never be an appropriate operational posture and employment doctrine designed to support the intelligent conduct of a nuclear war.[126]

Given this overarching belief—a view also held, incidentally, by most U.S. devotees of mutual assured destruction during the Cold War—India has approached the issue of operational policy reluctantly, almost as a concession to the ruthless imperatives accompanying the possession of nuclear weaponry. This operational policy—which, it may be argued, consists of four distinct components—has not yet been articulated in its entirety by any official spokesmen. What follows, therefore, is a reconstruction based on some authoritative Indian declarations combined with insights gleaned from other nonofficial Indian commentary and several private conversations with high-level Indian politicians, bureaucrats, and military officers.

The premise underlying India's operational policy, grounded as it is in the country's declaratory posture, is that the presence of nuclear weapons heralds the end of strategy as it is traditionally understood. All Indian security managers would thus heartily endorse Leon Sigal's claim that "the sheer destructiveness of nuclear war has [not only] invalidated any distinction between winning and losing . . . [but] . . . it has [also] rendered meaningless the very idea of military strategy as the efficient employment of force to achieve a state's objectives."[127] Confirming just such sentiments, G. Balachandran, a well-known Indian operations research analyst, prefaced his own

---

[126]The Indian case thus differs from that of the United States with respect to the relationship between declaratory and operational policy. For a good analysis of why and how declaratory and operational policies diverged in the case of the United States, see Desmond Ball, "U.S. Strategic Forces: How Would They Be Used?" *International Security*, 7:3 (Winter 1982–1983), pp. 31–60.

[127]Leon V. Sigal, "Rethinking the Unthinkable," *Foreign Policy*, 34 (Spring 1979), p. 39.

analysis of India's nuclear requirements with the admonition that a nuclear weapon "is truly a weapon of mass destruction . . . whose use can only be a measure of last resort."[128] This judgment, which corroborates the public statements of many Indian policymakers, implies that because nuclear weapons cannot be used in pursuit of any *offensive* ends through war and because nuclear war itself cannot be prosecuted for any rational political objectives, the use of nuclear weapons *in extremis* can have only *retributive* utility. This suggests that the sole circumstances justifying the threat of use of nuclear weapons would be to prevent an adversary from pursuing a course of action that, if completed, would radically abridge India's physical security and decisional autonomy.

No First Use. Under the aegis of this fundamentally defensive outlook, *the first component of India's nuclear doctrine at the level of operational policy is its insistence on the no first use of nuclear weaponry.* This emphasis on no first use is remarkably pervasive in Indian strategic thought. It was officially proposed to Pakistan first in 1994 as a formal arms control measure and has been affirmed on several occasions since that time by leading Indian political leaders in Parliament. The official paper on the "evolution of India's nuclear policy," for example—issued in the aftermath of the country's nuclear tests—once again repeated the Indian government's "readiness to discuss a 'no-first-use' agreement with . . . [Pakistan], as also with other countries bilaterally, or in a collective forum."[129] This commitment was reiterated in Parliament by Indian Prime Minister Vajpayee, who spelled out its two components—the no first use of nuclear weapons against nuclear states coupled with the nonuse of nuclear weapons against nonnuclear states—by avowing that India "will not be the first to use nuclear weapons. Having stated that, there remains no basis for their use against countries which do not have nuclear weapons."[130] This willingness to formally adhere to a

---

[128]G. Balachandran, "Nuclear Weaponization in India," *Agni*, 5:1 (January–April 2000), p. 37.

[129]"Paper Laid on the Table of the House on Evolution of India's Nuclear Policy, May 27, 1998," pp. 4–5.

[130]"India Evolves Nuclear Doctrine," *The Times of India*, August 5, 1998, and "PM Declares No-First Strike." Vajpayee's statement, and Indian policy in general on this issue, therefore directly contradict the conclusion drawn by one analyst, who argued that "if the [Indian] 'no first use' offer is not taken up and no agreement is reached,

policy of not using nuclear weapons first under any circumstances (and not using them at all where nonnuclear powers are concerned) has also been endorsed by many Indian strategic analysts, including K. Subrahmanyam, who has argued that India ought to have "a totally uncaveated policy, with no reservation whatsoever on no first use."[131] Asserting that "India should not be the first to use nuclear weapons under any circumstances," Subrahmanyam has gone to great lengths to remind both domestic and foreign audiences that "the nuclear weapons of India are meant for a punishing retaliation only if India is hit [first by a nuclear attack]."[132] These sentiments, which are fairly widespread in India and shared by most of the country's senior security managers, have not, however, prevented some Indian analysts—including Subrahmanyam himself—from succumbing on occasion to the temptation to trumpet these claims more vociferously than usual in order to embarrass Pakistan, which has thus far refused to countenance a similar policy thanks to its fears of India's conventional superiority.[133]

In any event, the biggest challenge to the strict no-first-use policy articulated by senior Indian security managers, including the Prime Minister, ironically emerged from the National Security Advisory Board, headed by Subrahmanyam himself. In language that was as revealing of the political rifts within the board as it was of the animus harbored toward this component of India's operational policy by a small group of "maximalists" within the strategic community, the "Draft Report of [the] National Security Advisory Board on Indian Nuclear Doctrine" subtly altered New Delhi's traditional position on this subject by asserting that "India will not resort to the use or threat of use of nuclear weapons against States which do not possess nu-

---

then clearly India reserves the right of nuclear first use, particularly against those countries that have not even entered into discussion on the subject." See Sidhu, "India Sees Safety in Nuclear Triad and Second Strike Potential," p. 25.

[131] K. Subrahmanyam, "Nuclear Tests: What Next?" *IIC Quarterly*, Summer/ Monsoon 1998, p. 57.

[132] Ibid.

[133] See K. Subrahmanyam, "Building Trust on the Bomb," *The Times of India*, July 7, 1985; K. Subrahmanyam, "Kashmir 1948–1998," *The Times of India*, June 26, 1998; and Subash Kapila, "India and Pakistan Nuclear Doctrine: A Comparative Analysis," available at http://www.ipcs.org/issues/articles/260-ndi-kapila.html. For a Pakistani view, see Ejaz Haider, "No-First-Use vs. No-War-Pact, or Both?" *Friday Times*, October 20–26, 2000.

clear weapons, *or are not aligned with nuclear weapon powers"* (italics added).[134] With the addition of this qualifying clause, the Draft Report radically expanded in one fell swoop the number of countries that would potentially be threatened by India's emerging nuclear arsenal. Under the strict no-first-use assurances provided by India's Prime Minister in Parliament, only the eight nuclear powers—the United States, Russia, China, the United Kingdom, France, China, Pakistan, and North Korea—could in principle find themselves subjected to Indian nuclear threats, and that too, only if they were to attack India first. Under the board's new formulation, however, even allies of these powers that did not possess nuclear weapons—for example, the thirteen nonnuclear allies of the United States in NATO, the two nonnuclear allies of the United States in the ANZUS treaty, and the three nonnuclear allies of the United States in the Five Power Defense Agreement, the six or more nonnuclear allies and partners of the United States in East Asia, and the eleven nonnuclear partners of Russia in the CIS—could now be subjected to Indian nuclear threats in some extreme circumstances.

This dramatic enlargement of India's pool of potential adversaries was privately justified on two grounds, one formal and one substantive. The formal argument centered on the claim that the recommended nuclear doctrine was intended to be a permanent document that would provide policy guidance for the widest variety of contingencies imaginable. Although it was not expected that any of these additional states would ever fall victim to an Indian nuclear threat, the board reasoned that a strategic guidance of the sort represented by the Draft Report ought to cover even remote contingencies should those materialize at some distant point. The substantive argument, which was more unsettling, centered on the belief that if a major nuclear power were ever to threaten India's security and autonomy, its nonnuclear allies should be prevented from concluding that they could support such coercive actions with impunity under the assumption that their own nonnuclear status would effectively bestow on them an immunity to any nuclear threats India might levy in its

---

[134]"Draft Report of [the] National Security Advisory Board on Indian Nuclear Doctrine," p. 2.

own defense. Such reasoning, whether formal or substantive, served only to demonstrate how insensitive the Draft Report was both to the domestic political context and to the international political constraints facing Indian decisionmaking in the realm of nuclear policy.[135] Even worse, it opened the door to expanding India's targeting requirements—if only at a conceptual level—at the same time some of the country's best analysts were conclusively demonstrating that New Delhi's current and prospective nuclear stockpile might be unable to service even some variants of the minimal targeting requirements deemed necessary to deter India's immediate adversaries, China and Pakistan.[136]

Not surprisingly then, this Draft Report recommendation engendered great controversy both within India, where many viewed it as needlessly pompous and overly provocative, and abroad, where it was viewed in many Western capitals as well as in Islamabad and Beijing as evidence of a reckless commitment to the kind of irresponsible nuclearization that was both unwarranted and destabilizing in the strategic environment of Southern Asia. Recognizing these criticisms, the government of India, in the person of Minister for External Affairs Jaswant Singh, moved quickly to stem the erosion of India's traditional position on this question by declaring simply and unambiguously—in the redaction later published in *The Hindu*—that "India has declared a no first use doctrine. This has implicit in it the principle that India shall not use nuclear weapons against non-nuclear weapon states."[137] This reaffirmation, which confirmed the strict no-first-use assurance that Prime Minister Atal Bihari Vajpayee had formally presented in Parliament after the nuclear tests in August 1998, continues to be attacked episodically by Indian hawks like Bharat Karnad, who stated quite baldly that the Indian "no first use

---

[135]On the question of context and constraints, see the remarks of Frank Wisner, "India's Nuclear Posture: Taking a Fresh Look," remarks delivered at the CII Round Table on Indo-U.S. Relations: Challenges and Opportunities, New Delhi, October 20, 1999.

[136]On this issue, see Balachandran, "Nuclear Weaponization in India," pp. 37–50, and Gurmeet Kanwal, "India's Nuclear Force Structure," *Strategic Analysis*, 24:6 (September 2000), pp. 1039–1075.

[137]"India Not to Engage in a N-Arms Race: Jaswant."

doctrine . . . is something of a hoax. It is one of those restrictions which countries are willing to abide by except in war!"[138]

There is little doubt that the no-first-use pledge remains an unverifiable tenet of New Delhi's operational policy. But this promise, contrary to the opinions of Karnad and others, is likely to prove valid in India's case for several reasons. First, it is consistent with India's nuclear doctrine at the declaratory level as well as its traditional attitudes toward nuclear disarmament and its established refusal to legitimize nuclear weapons as ordinary instruments of war (all these three components, in turn, being sensible precisely because they accord with India's core security interests). Second, it allows New Delhi to underscore its pacific intentions vis-à-vis Pakistan and China and thereby reap all the political benefits that accrue from being perceived as a moderate, responsible, and peace-loving state in the international system. Third, it is consistent with the emerging Indian nuclear posture, which, taking the form of a force-in-being, provides at least some assurance (though not conclusive proof) that India is not committed to the rapid—including first—use of nuclear weapons in the event of a deterrence breakdown. Fourth and most important, it is unlikely to be violated because India's strategic circumstances are favorable enough to prevent New Delhi from ever having to use nuclear weapons *first* against any of its adversaries. This issue requires further elaboration because it goes to the heart of why India can make good on its no-first-use promise while simultaneously revealing the circumstances under which New Delhi would in fact resort to the actual employment of nuclear weapons in anger.

As earlier discussions indicated, there are only two broad contingencies that could activate New Delhi's reliance on its nuclear weaponry: nuclear coercion and nuclear use by its adversaries. The first contingency relates to nuclear coercion carried out either through the support of domestic dissidence in India on the expectation that India cannot retaliate militarily or through direct—be it manifest or subtle—nuclear brandishing intended to force New Delhi into making some sort of political concessions. The first category of coercion simply requires that India be able to cope with its

---

[138]Karnad, "A Thermonuclear Deterrent," p. 120. The challenges imposed by the no-first-use policy for India are usefully explored in Gurmeet Kanwal, "'No First Use' Doctrine: India's Strategic Dilemma," *The Tribune*, July 15, 2000.

domestic dissidence through a combination of political and economic co-optation and military repression, as it has traditionally done.[139] This "reactive" solution allows New Delhi to ignore the nuclear capabilities of its foreign adversaries altogether. Even if a "proactive" solution consisting of shallow cross-border operations is required, India's nominal military superiority over Pakistan and local military superiority over China allow such operations to be conducted by conventional means alone.[140] To be sure, any moves of this sort might require that India rely on its nuclear assets, if only to prevent Pakistan and China from employing their nuclear capabilities in response to India's conventional actions, and this in turn might require that India signal its willingness to pursue strategies of "escalation dominance"—but it would not require that New Delhi contemplate any first *use* of its own nuclear weaponry. It could be argued, of course, that the prospect of Indian first use clearly becomes plausible in this context because successful preemptive strikes might turn out to be the only means by which New Delhi could secure the escalation dominance necessary to resolve the issue on its own terms. While this argument is plausible in theory, however, it is unlikely to hold in practice, because it is inconceivable that India will ever engage in *any* proactive solutions to domestic insurgencies that require accompanying nuclear first use to begin with. Even if it were to contemplate such strategies, it currently lacks (and will continue to lack well into the future) the kind of nuclear weaponry that would allow it to execute the effective damage-limiting preemptive strikes that are necessary for successful escalation dominance.[141] The net result, therefore, is that no feasible contingency exists that would require India to engage in nuclear first use where combating nuclear

---

[139]Gupta, *India Redefines Its Role*, pp. 23–33.

[140]The character and difference between "reactive" and "proactive" strategies in the Indo-Pakistani context are discussed in Tellis, *Stability in South Asia*, pp. 47–54.

[141]This will certainly continue to be the case where nuclear operations against an alerted adversary are concerned. The only forms of Indian nuclear preemption that stand some chance of operational success from a damage-limiting perspective are those undertaken as pure "bolts out of the blue," and even here, success is anything but assured given the pervasive opacity that envelops both the Pakistani and the Chinese nuclear arsenals. In all other circumstances—including crisis situations wherein proactive operations might be conducted—opacity, deception, and mobility all combine to make most Pakistani and Chinese nuclear systems relatively immune to Indian attempts at damage-limiting preemption—and for this reason among many others, such strategies are unlikely to be pursued by New Delhi in the first place.

coercion, carried out through the abetting of domestic dissidence, is concerned.

This conclusion, it must be admitted, would be severely tested if India were faced with the prospect of imminent state breakdown resulting from domestic dissidence supported by foreign powers. If India were to face a situation similar to that which Pakistan confronted in 1971, where a constituent state of the union was on the verge of successfully seceding, the question of whether a possible Indian proactive solution to this contingency would require the first use of its nuclear weaponry purely for damage-limiting purposes would certainly become relevant. The few Indian theorists who have thought about this problem, such as General K. Sundarji, have essentially dismissed it by arguing that the presence of nuclear weapons essentially ensures that no foreign power would support a domestic secessionist movement to the point of success precisely because the shadow of possible nuclear weapon use would curb all such adventurism to begin with.[142] Unfortunately, the historical record in South Asia offers little support for such optimism. Pakistan, for example, has not only continued to support various secessionist movements within India even as the presence of nuclear weapons was abundantly obvious to both sides but also, more flagrantly, actually initiated a limited-aims war at Kargil in May 1999, at least partly because it was convinced that nuclear weapons would immunize it against the worst imaginable forms of Indian retaliation.[143] Despite this fact, it is possible to suggest that the prospect of India facing a situation similar to that which Pakistan confronted in 1971 is highly unlikely because India's large size, significant economic and military capabilities, democratic political order, numerous mediating institutions, vibrant civil society, and great institutional endurance all combine to prevent the "million mutinies"[144] that always appear to be breaking out from ever reaching the point at which state break-

---

[142]Sundarji, "Changing Military Equations in Asia: The Role of Nuclear Weapons," p. 127ff.

[143]Afzal Mahmood, "From the Pakistani Press: The Nuclear Option," *The Times of India*, July 18, 1999.

[144]This phrase is borrowed from V. S. Naipaul, *India: A Million Mutinies Now* (London: Heinemann, 1990).

down becomes a realistic possibility.[145] Consequently, it is unlikely that India will face a situation analogous to the 1971 crisis faced by Pakistan in the future—and by implication, India is also unlikely to be tested by the challenge of averting nuclear use as part of a comprehensive proactive response aimed at remedying the threat of imminent national disintegration.

The second category of nuclear coercion refers to either manifest or subtle nuclear brandishing that may be carried out by India's adversaries in efforts to intimidate New Delhi. Should such eventualities arise, India is likely to rely heavily on its nuclear assets for strategic reassurance. This comfort will, however, derive simply from the fact that India already possesses nuclear weaponry, and possession of these devices more than any manipulation of them should suffice to bolster Indian resolve given the kinds of issues that remain unsettled between Islamabad and Beijing on the one hand and New Delhi on the other.[146] Indeed, even in the worst circumstances imaginable, nuclear brandishing by Pakistan and China would provoke counterbrandishing by India—and while such a situation is likely to have both tense and unsettling moments, involving as it does an elaborate *pas de deux* aimed at manipulating threats and risks, it is unlikely to require any Indian first use of its nuclear weapons. This conclusion is reinforced by the fact that all the imaginable incentives for nuclear first use in this context—the temptation to unleash damage-limiting preemptive strikes or the pressures building up to a "use or lose" employment decision—simply would not obtain in the Indian case for a variety of technical and operational reasons. These include the fact that no Southern Asian state currently appears to possess nuclear weaponry capable of counterforce attacks; to be capable of satisfactorily piercing the veil of opacity maintained over the nuclear capabilities of its competitors; to be interested in operationalizing a deployment posture that exacerbates

---

[145]For a good analysis that speaks to this issue, see James Manor, "'Ethnicity' and Politics in India," *International Affairs*, 72:3 (1996), pp. 459–475, and James Manor, *Collective Conflict in India*, *Conflict Studies*, 212 (London: Centre for Security and Conflict Studies, 1988).

[146]This point is made so emphatically by one Indian scholar, Kanti Bajpai, that he in fact concludes that India may not need a nuclear deterrent altogether. See Bajpai, "The Fallacy of an Indian Deterrent," pp. 150–188.

"use or lose" conundrums; or to be willing to accept the kinds of uncertainties and losses that would arise even from modest nuclear use given the nature of political competition within the region.[147]

If both manifestations of nuclear coercion therefore do not require India to respond with first use of its nuclear weaponry, it becomes obvious that New Delhi can provide credible assurances of no first use—and can in fact make it part of its operational policy—because no other contingencies exist that would require it to violate this policy. This judgment holds even when the second contingency—which requires that New Delhi rely on its nuclear reserves in the face of potential nuclear use by its adversaries—is investigated. The discussion in Chapter Three and elsewhere established that India possesses an effective superiority over both Pakistan and China where defense of its territories is concerned. India does not, however, possess a similar superiority in the offense, meaning that it would be likely to fail if it sought to acquire significant chunks of Pakistani and Chinese territory and hold onto them by force. Recognizing this operational fact in the context of larger political considerations, New Delhi has long eschewed the pursuit of policies designed to secure additional territory.[148] To the degree that it seeks local hegemony in South Asia, it has emphasized its geopolitical weight and its symbols of power but has by and large refrained from enforcing its writ through the constant use of force. This implies that India is unlikely to apply its military power—including its nuclear weapons—either to enlarge its territorial holdings or to cement its hierarchic status, although it would certainly prefer to secure the latter simply by dint of its recognized size, inherent potentialities, and past achievements. Even if India were to violate this expectation in the future, it would most likely be confronted by its adversaries, particularly Pakistan, using *their* nuclear weapons first rather than by any contingency that compelled it to resort to the initial employment of nuclear weaponry. This judgment, once again, is grounded in the realization that New Delhi does not possess nuclear weapons, delivery vehicles, or a command sys-

---

[147]For a discussion that speaks to some of these issues, see the treatment in Hagerty, *The Consequences of Nuclear Proliferation: Lessons from South Asia*, pp. 56–59.

[148]Tellis, *Stability in South Asia*, pp. 30–33.

tem capable of conducting "splendid"[149] first strikes—the only condition under which a first use of nuclear weapons might be attractive to India.

It is in this context that some observers fear that even if India cannot execute "splendid" first strikes satisfactorily, it may still be compelled in some circumstances to use its nuclear weapons first if, for example, it were to be confronted by reasonable evidence that its adversaries were readying themselves for a prospective nuclear attack on India. These arguments, derived straightforwardly from the classical problem of the "reciprocal fear of surprise attack,"[150] usually presume that New Delhi may be forced to violate its otherwise well-intentioned no-first-use pledge in some exceptional scenarios if initiating preemptive, not preventive, nuclear attacks appears better than absorbing imminent first strikes. These contingencies have received serious attention in New Delhi, and Indian strategic planners have responded in three ways.[151] First, they argue that any information about imminent nuclear attack, if such is available at all, is likely to be more ambiguous and incomplete than transparent and conclusive given the nature of the strategic capabilities, force architectures, and deployment postures maintained on all sides. Thanks to this fact, incomplete information ought to warrant reticent responses rather than hasty overreaction, especially given the high costs of mistaken action in the nuclear realm. Second, they note that even if credible information about an imminent attack is available, it is still prudent for India *not* to respond preemptively because preemption would only ensure that an attack, which was only probable up to that point, actually became inescapable. Because the difference between probable and inescapable attack embodies enormous consequences for both Indian and regional security, policymakers in New Delhi argue that prudence and moral sensibility would demand responses that decelerate the pace of escalation, not speed it up—as preparations for preemptive responses ineluctably do. Third and fi-

---

[149]This term, popularized by Herman Kahn, refers to a situation in which one side can dramatically reduce damage to itself if and only if it strikes first. See Shlapak and Thaler, *Back to First Principles*, p. 30.

[150]Schelling, *The Strategy of Conflict*, pp. 207–229.

[151]I am deeply grateful to K. Subrahmanyam for discussing this issue with me in some detail. See also Manoj Joshi, "India Must Have Survivable N-Arsenal," *The Times of India*, April 30, 2000.

nally, they assert that the very challenge that such contingencies pose places special obligations on India and its no-first-use pledge: It requires New Delhi to ensure that its strategic assets are survivable enough that even if its adversaries are tempted to unleash first strikes, *India* will never feel compelled to use its nuclear weapons first merely because the vulnerability of its strategic reserves produces enormous differences between the expected costs of striking first and those of striking last.[152] Indian policymakers thus appear to be cognizant of the challenges associated with the temptations of preemption, but they remain convinced—correctly—that so long as their own nuclear assets are properly safeguarded through a combination of concealment, deception, and mobility, they could escape the burdens of acting precipitously even though the temptations themselves are unlikely to disappear so long as nuclear weapons exist in Southern Asia.

Use as Instruments of Punishment. The above analysis therefore suggests that since India's nuclear weapons cannot be used to resolve the problem of nuclear coercion and will not be used to underwrite either territorial or political expansionism, they can serve only as antidotes to the threats of use by its adversaries or as punishments if these weapons are in fact employed against India. Under the aegis of this essentially retributive concept—which is designed primarily to prevent deterrence breakdown from occurring but, failing that, to prevent the country from becoming a helpless victim to nuclear attack by others—*the second component of India's nuclear doctrine at the level of operational policy is its insistence that nuclear weapons, when used, will be oriented to punishment alone.* This conception of nuclear weapons as instruments of punishment was advanced by the adherents of the assured-destruction school during the Cold War because they believed that the horrendous character of nuclear

---

[152]For more on this issue, see Glenn A. Kent and David E. Thaler, *First-Strike Stability: A Methodology for Evaluating Strategic Forces*, R-3765-AF (Santa Monica: RAND, 1989). The "Draft Report of [the] National Security Advisory Board on Indian Nuclear Doctrine" explicitly reflects this concern when it notes that "India shall pursue a doctrine of credible minimum nuclear deterrence. In this policy of 'retaliation only,' the survivability of our arsenal is critical. This is a dynamic concept related to the strategic environment, technological imperatives and the needs of national security. The actual size components, deployment and employment of nuclear forces will be decided in the light of these factors." See "Draft Report of [the] National Security Advisory Board on Indian Nuclear Doctrine," p. 2.

weapons allowed them to be used only for purposes of deterring conflict through the threat of inflicting catastrophic damage should deterrence fail. In the event of deterrence failure, a genocidal level of damage might be inflicted by each antagonist on the other, but it was precisely this fear of annihilation that was expected to shore up the structure of deterrent threats and prevent the outbreak of hostilities.[153] It was recognized, of course, that the act of retaliation in the face of a prior nuclear attack might be absurd, irrational, and possibly even immoral, since the retaliatory response could neither undo the catastrophic damage the defendant had already suffered nor procure any positive gains of its own. All retaliation could do was intensify the catastrophe through an act of vengeance, pure and simple. While an attacker could hope that the defendant, seeing the sheer irrationality of striking back, would refrain from responding in kind, he could not *count* on the defendant being restrained by any concerns about rationality—and fears of compounding the catastrophe that would be unleashed by such retaliation were supposed to prevent the initial shot from being discharged in the first place.[154]

This logic has been adopted by India in its entirety at the operational level of policy. As a doctrine, it has a distinguished pedigree, and the spectrum illustrated in Figure 5 indicates that it is but one of three different orientations that India could have adopted with respect to the *telos* of its nuclear use.[155] At one end, nuclear weapons can be used in an offensive mode in which the principal intention consists of disarming the adversary. Nuclear-use strategies predicated on this orientation treat nuclear weapons as war-fighting

---

[153]The most articulate expositions of this view in the U.S.-Soviet context can be found in, among many other writings, Brodie, *The Absolute Weapon: Atomic Power and World Order*; Bernard Brodie, "The Development of Nuclear Strategy," *International Security*, 2:4 (Spring 1978); Bernard Brodie, *Escalation and the Nuclear Option* (Princeton, NJ: Princeton University Press, 1966); Robert Jervis, *The Illogic of American Nuclear Strategy* (Ithaca, NY: Cornell University Press, 1984); Jervis, *The Meaning of the Nuclear Revolution*; and McGeorge Bundy, *Danger and Survival: Choices About the Bomb in the First Fifty Years* (New York: Random House, 1988).

[154]Snyder, *Deterrence and Defense*, p. 6.

[155]For a somewhat different characterization of these schools with further elaboration, see Charles L. Glaser, "Disputes over the U.S. Military Requirements of Nuclear Deterrence," in Charles L. Glaser (ed.), *Analyzing Strategic Nuclear Policy* (Princeton, NJ: Princeton University Press, 1990), pp. 19–60.

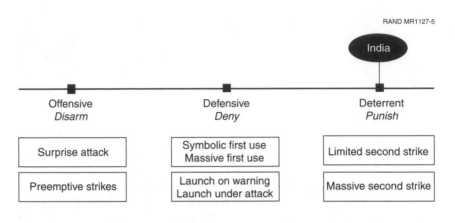

Figure 5—Indian Choices Amid the Spectrum of Nuclear Strategies

instruments par excellence and include surprise attacks in which "bolt-out-of-the-blue" strikes (or BOOB attacks, as they are known in the trade) are used to interdict an adversary's nuclear forces and C³I systems with the intent of eliminating his ability to retaliate effectively. These attacks could occur without any strategic warning or without a formal declaration of war. Preemptive strikes also constitute an example of offensive use, except that in this case the first use of nuclear weapons, although aimed at the same set of targets as in a surprise attack, would occur under conditions of tactical warning and perhaps even after the conventional forces of both antagonists are already engaged on the battlefield. Irrespective of how nuclear weapons are employed in such instances, the offensive use of nuclear weapons is predicated on the belief that these devices are the most effective instruments of war-fighting imaginable and, as such, can be used to "paralyze and intimidate any resistance"[156] through the preplanned, purposeful, and comprehensive use of such weapons in war.[157]

---

[156]This phrase is borrowed from Rostow's description of Soviet strategic objectives, appearing in Eugene V. Rostow, "Of Summitry and Grand Strategy," *Strategic Review*, 14 (Fall 1986), p. 14.

[157]The best examples of such a conception of the utility of nuclear weapons can be found in Soviet military writings during the Cold War: A. A. Sidorenko, *The Offensive: A Soviet View* (Washington, D.C.: USGPO, 1973); *Marxism-Leninism on War and Army: A Soviet View* (Washington, D.C.: USGPO, 1974); A. S. Milovidov (ed.), *The Philosophical*

In contrast to such expansive applications of force, nuclear weapons can also be used in a defensive mode—a category located in the middle of the spectrum—in which the principal intention consists of denying the assailant either his operational objectives on the battlefield or his strategic interests in seeing the defendant's nuclear reserves effectively eliminated. Nuclear weapons in this conception are treated as war-fighting instruments as well but are intended less for exploitation and more to reinforce deterrence and/or to avert military defeat, with all the disastrous political consequences that flow from the last outcome. Many nuclear-use strategies are predicated on this posture, including (1) symbolic first use, designed mainly to warn the assailant to terminate his aggressive actions while signaling the defendant's resolve to escalate to higher levels of violence if aggression is not vacated; (2) limited or massive first use, designed either to stop an operational offensive in the absence of a robust conventional defense or to communicate, through selective theater or strategic counterforce attacks, a willingness to ratchet up the level of resistance in order to credibly force war termination short of all-out genocide or political defeat; and (3) launch-on-warning or launch-under-attack, where the defendant releases his nuclear weapons in the face of attacks that are either imminent or under way.[158]

Even more strongly in contrast to these middling uses, nuclear weapons can finally be used in a deterrent mode, where the principal intention consists simply of punishing the assailant if deterrence failure results in any nuclear attack on the defendant. Nuclear weapons in this context are treated not as war-fighting instruments intended to either disarm the adversary or deny him his political or

---

Heritage of V. I. Lenin and Problems of Contemporary War: A Soviet View (Washington, D.C.: USGPO, 1974); V. E. Savkin, *The Basic Principles of Operational Art and Tactics: A Soviet View* (Washington, D.C.: USGPO, 1974); and S. P. Ivanov, *The Initial Period of War: A Soviet View* (Washington, D.C.: USGPO, 1986).

[158]During the Cold War, this approach toward strategy was most closely reflected in official U.S. nuclear doctrine since the early 1970s, and it received its most systematic justification in policy statements of Secretary of Defense Harold Brown in the various annual reports of the Department of Defense issued during Brown's years in office. See also United States Congress, Senate Committee on Foreign Relations, *Nuclear War Strategy*, Hearing before the Committee on Foreign Relations, 96th Congress, Second Session, on Presidential Directive 59, September 16, 1980 (Washington, D.C.: USGPO, 1981).

military objectives but merely as punitive instruments to be applied in retaliation for his first use of nuclear weapons. Nuclear use strategies based on this posture include all manner of pure second-strike doctrines where the emphasis on retaliating after the defendant absorbs a first strike is modulated primarily by the extent and density of the attack. The degree of retaliation chosen, be it symbolic or massive, would thus be determined by the extent of damage suffered by the defendant in tandem with other considerations, such as the pressures for war termination, the size and composition of the surviving fraction of the retaliatory force, and the extent of assistance and/or assurance that may be available from other nuclear powers.[159]

From amid the three choices offered by this spectrum, India appears to have chosen the third alternative, with its nuclear use oriented solely toward punishing an adversary who employs his nuclear weapons to attack India. As the "Draft Report of [the] National Security Advisory Board on Indian Nuclear Doctrine" phrased it, "Any nuclear attack on India and its forces shall result in punitive retaliation with nuclear weapons to inflict damage unacceptable to the aggressor."[160] This implies that Indian retaliation would occur only *after* the country has absorbed—suffered—a nuclear first strike at the hands of its adversaries. Indian policymakers recognize, however, that the language of "first and second strikes" has a certain antiseptic quality that obscures the vast amounts of damage all antagonists would suffer in the course of such operations, and they have thus deliberately shied away from such language even in private conversations, believing it to be tainted by the offensive and defensive conceptions of nuclear use inherited from the Cold War. Being conscious of the fact that they are trying to steer a new course with respect to nuclear doctrine, given India's unique strategic needs and its limited resources, Indian strategic managers consistently emphasize that the

---

[159]The clearest example of such a strategy historically has been that followed by China. See, among others, Harry Gelber, *Nuclear Weapons and Chinese Policy*, Adelphi Paper No. 99 (London: IISS, 1973); Banning N. Garrett and Bonnie S. Glaser, *War and Peace: The Views from Moscow and Beijing*, Policy Paper in International Affairs No. 20 (Berkeley, CA: Institute of International Studies, University of California, 1984); and John C. Hopkins and Weixing Hu (eds.), *Strategic Views from the Second Tier: The Nuclear Weapons Policies of France, Britain, and China* (New Brunswick, NJ: Transaction Publishers, 1995).

[160]"Draft Report of [the] National Security Advisory Board on Indian Nuclear Doctrine," p. 2.

concept of "retaliation only"[161]—understood as punishment for a nuclear attack—suffices to describe the ultimate objective of India's nuclear use even though it is well understood that such a policy in effect refers to a second-strike posture of one sort or another.

There is little reason to disbelieve Indian officials when they argue that the most suitable nuclear-use policy for New Delhi is one that treats nuclear weapons as deterrents suitable only for punishment. This is because India does not possess the capabilities to use its nuclear weapons in either an offensive or a defensive mode except in the most trivial operational sense. An offensive use of nuclear weapons would require a large nuclear arsenal and incredibly accurate delivery systems maintained at high levels of readiness, a real-time intelligence-gathering capability, a highly automated mission-planning system, and robust strategic defenses capable of coping with the ragged retaliation that would inevitably occur in the aftermath of any disarming attack. It would also require great proficiency in planning complex offensive military operations. Developing such a strategic infrastructure would be extraordinarily costly and would involve high levels of military participation in both national security planning and day-to-day control over the nuclear arsenal.[162] These are exactly the outcomes Indian policymakers seem intent on

---

[161]Both the "Draft Report of [the] National Security Advisory Board on Indian Nuclear Doctrine," p. 2, and Singh's interview in *The Hindu*, "India Not to Engage in a N-Arms Race: Jaswant," repeat this expression.

[162]It has sometimes been asserted that this is in fact the strategy the United States intended to follow in the event of nuclear war. Irrespective of the veracity of this claim, there is little doubt that the United States did develop an enormous variety of nuclear capabilities that made such a strategic alternative an option for policy. These details are described in Robert C. Aldridge, *First Strike!: The Pentagon's Strategy for Nuclear War* (Boston: South End Press, 1983). On a more scholarly note, these capabilities are also described in great detail in Bruce G. Blair, *Strategic Command and Control: Redefining the Nuclear Threat* (Washington, D.C.: Brookings, 1985), and in Bruce G. Blair, *The Logic of Accidental Nuclear War* (Washington, D.C.: Brookings, 1993). The sheer scale and complexity of these capabilities, however, ought to suggest that even though the "Draft Report of [the] National Security Advisory Board on Indian Nuclear Doctrine," pp. 2–3, somewhat grandiosely argues for "effective command, control, communications, computing, intelligence and information (C^4I^2) systems" as well as "space-based and other assets . . . [for] . . . early warning, communications, [and] damage/detonation assessment," it does not argue similarly for any counterforce weaponry, thus leading ineluctably to the conclusion that even the supporting capabilities deemed to be necessary by the Draft Report are not intended to support any offensive nuclear strategies by India. This issue is discussed further in Chapter Five.

avoiding, and consequently they will neither encourage the military to walk down this path nor provide it with the resources that would enable it to do so.

A defensive use of nuclear weapons aimed at denying the adversary his objectives is only mildly less demanding. Denial operations at the tactical or operational level require large numbers of variable-yield weapons, permanent military custody of the devices, a real-time surveillance system, predelegated authority for the use of nuclear weapons to field commanders, and an operational infrastructure designed for effective command and control over a nuclear battlefield.[163] Denial operations at the strategic level require robust early-warning and attack characterization systems, nuclear forces maintained at hair-trigger levels of alert, a complex set of standard operating procedures, and complete civil-military integration at the levels of command, custody and execution.[164] Again, these are capabilities that India currently lacks, and many will deliberately not be acquired because they run counter to the financial and domestic-political imperatives of the Indian state.

Nuclear weapons acquired solely as a deterrent for purposes of punishment embody much less onerous demands. To be sure, the burdens associated with this posture are no doubt substantial, but they are less so than those associated with the offensive and defensive uses of nuclear weapons. A nuclear-use posture that focuses on punishment can make do with small numbers and primitive types of nuclear weapons, simpler standard operating procedures, relatively

---

[163]For a useful survey that speaks to some of these issues in the U.S. context, see *Challenges for U.S. National Security: Nuclear Strategy Issues of the 1980s: Strategic Vulnerabilities, Command, Control, Communications, and Intelligence, Theater Nuclear Forces: A Third Report*, prepared by the staff of the Carnegie Panel on U.S. Security and the Future of Arms Control (Washington, D.C.: Carnegie Endowment for International Peace, 1982); William R. van Cleave and S. T. Cohen, *Tactical Nuclear Weapons: An Examination of the Issues* (New York: Crane, Russak, 1978); and Stephen D. Biddle and Peter D. Feaver (eds.), *Battlefield Nuclear Weapons: Issues and Options*, CSIA Occasional Paper No. 5 (Boston: Center for Science and International Affairs, Harvard University, 1989).

[164]These dimensions are detailed in Blair, *Strategic Command and Control.*

higher levels of civilian custody and control, and fewer financial resources allocated to strategic deterrence.[165]

The emphasis on punitive retaliation as the focus of India's operational policy appears reasonable when it is understood that India's leadership seeks to develop a modest nuclear deterrent that suffices to protect the country against relatively remote threats without bankrupting the exchequer or radically transforming the Indian domestic structures of governance in the process. Consequently, it is obvious that Indian strategic planning focuses fundamentally on shaping its nuclear threats to deter *any* nuclear use by its adversaries; this objective retains priority because averting nuclear use remains the most advantageous outcome for India given that its relative military superiority and its restrained political goals vis-à-vis both China (in the theater) and Pakistan do not require it to contemplate initiating either exploitative or defensive operations with nuclear weaponry. If this objective cannot be attained, the employment of nuclear weapons for punishment remains the *only* alternative available to a state that seeks both to eschew nuclear war fighting and to avoid offering its adversaries the hope that they could pursue their strategic goals by means of some limited forms of nuclear use.

Given the challenges associated with these two objectives, Indian strategic thinking has deliberately refused to specify publicly and in advance what the dimensions of its punitive retaliation would be in the event of a nuclear attack. Thus, it has not addressed any questions pertaining to the character, extent, or weight of Indian retaliatory action if an adversary's nuclear use were, for example, to be restricted to the detonation of nuclear weapons on its own territory, either as part of a symbolic demonstration or in order to secure specific operational objectives; if the "use" of nuclear weapons arose as a result of an accidental detonation involving its adversaries' nuclear forces in the course of an ongoing conventional war; if the detonation of nuclear weapons resulted from the actions of foreign terrorists or nonstate actors; or if the employment of nuclear weapons

---

[165]The clearest exposition of this argument in the Indian context can be found in Sundarji, "Changing Military Equations in Asia: The Role of Nuclear Weapons," pp. 119–149, and in Nair, *Nuclear India*, pp. 78–193.

arose as a result of the dissolutive processes of state failure or institutional collapse in either Pakistan or China. Referring to such lacunae in the context of a critique of Indian pronouncements on this subject, especially the Draft Report, one Indian analyst asked rhetorically, "How will India respond to a nuclear attack by a non-state entity? Where will India's retaliatory strike be targeted? What happens if a rogue entity is spread over a number of states?"[166]

Clearly, the answers to all these questions are not publicly available today. In part, this is because India's operational policy has not yet been fully developed, at least with respect to those problems Indian policymakers currently deem excessively abstract, more or less remote, or simply implausible. On other, more pressing contingencies, however, they *have* developed embryonic solutions, but whether these plans will hold amid the actual pressures of conflict is anyone's guess. These plans, however, are unlikely to be openly articulated, mainly because India's security managers do not want to provide any opportunities for other states to test India's resolve to use its nuclear weapons in the case of strategic attack. Hence, on the rare occasions policymakers do choose to amplify their thinking, they are likely to simply reiterate in one form or another the bland formulation that "India can and will retaliate with sufficient nuclear weapons to inflict destruction and punishment that the aggressor will find unacceptable if nuclear weapons are used against India and its forces"[167] without attempting to further specify the extent, mode, and limits of any Indian attempts at punishment. On this issue, India's approach to the problem of punitive retaliation mirrors that of France during the Cold War, when Raymond Barre, for example, argued that "it is not possible nor desirable" to define punitive retaliation exhaustively, since "employment policy is not fixed and remains sufficiently supple to respond in a rational fashion to all requirements of our security and to the diversity of marginal situations"[168]—or when Valéry Giscard d'Estaing decried the exhortations

---

[166]Balachandran, "India's Nuclear Doctrine."

[167]"Draft Report of [the] National Security Advisory Board on Indian Nuclear Doctrine," p. 3.

[168]Cited in David S. Yost, "French Nuclear Targeting," in Desmond Ball and Jeffrey Richelson (eds.), *Strategic Nuclear Targeting* (Ithaca, NY: Cornell University Press, 1986), p. 148.

to specify the nature and magnitude of punishment in advance on the grounds that an adversary "must not be able to calculate what would be the reaction to this or that initiative that he might take."[169] Since these sentiments are shared by Indian security managers, all of New Delhi's pronouncements about its operational policy of "retaliation only" will continue to be deliberately ambiguous, but the principal Indian objective of shoring up deterrence without endorsing nuclear war fighting in any form implies that its strategic orientation will remain focused—for good reason—solely on nuclear strategies that emphasize punishment.[170]

Delayed but Assured Retaliation. Since Indian nuclear use will remain directed to punitive operations for all the reasons outlined above, *the third component of India's nuclear doctrine at the level of operational policy is its belief that "delayed—but assured—retaliation" suffices as a response to the question of when punishment ought to be meted out.* This notion of delayed but assured retaliation suggests that Indian security managers believe that the ability to retaliate is more important for purposes of deterrence than when the retaliation actually occurs.[171] The extent of the permissible delay in carrying out the retaliatory response has not yet been specified, in part because Indian policymakers probably do not know the answer themselves. This issue is conditioned first by several technical realities relating to the state of India's future nuclear deterrent. These include the number of weapon and delivery systems of which the deterrent force will eventually be composed; the differences in the types of delivery systems and the time to full readiness associated with each type of system; the precise command, control, and custody arrangements that will be institutionalized over time; and the kind of peacetime posture that Indian policymakers will define for each specific component of the deterrent force. Since this deterrent writ large is still in the process of being developed and its final disposition is as yet unclear, it should not be surprising if Indian security man-

---

[169]Ibid.

[170]For more on this issue, see Gurmeet Kanwal, "Nuclear Targeting Philosophy for India," *Strategic Analysis*, 24:3 (June 2000), pp. 459–473, and Kanwal, "India's Nuclear Force Structure," pp. 1039–1075.

[171]"India Not to Engage in a N-Arms Race: Jaswant."

agers cannot assess *a priori* how long it would take to mount a credible retaliatory response.[172]

The second point that bears on this issue is the extent of damage that India will suffer when absorbing an adversary's first strike. Depending on the adversary's goals in a war, its attacks could affect India's nuclear production facilities, known or suspected weapon storage sites, military facilities and bases, key nodes in the command-and-control network, and major transportation links, all of which would affect not only India's ability to retaliate but also the time frame within which any retaliation could be unleashed. The less effective or more limited the first strike, the greater the country's reconstitution capability and, by implication, the shorter the time frame for executing the retaliatory response. Variables such as these, however, can be predicted only imperfectly, and while the planning cells both in various service headquarters and in the Indian Ministry of Defence will no doubt identify various time lines—depending on the state of the strategic infrastructure that survives the initial attack—the "real" answer to the question of how quickly India could retaliate will become available only amid the carnage of war. There may, in fact, be many real answers, depending on the kind of nuclear weapon use employed by the adversary. Discrete, symbolic use, for example, could allow for relatively quick, "tit-for-tat" responses, since India's strategic capabilities would survive more or less intact. By contrast, more substantial first strikes could result in greater delays, as the country would need additional time to reconstitute its surviving capabilities before it could unleash its weapons of vengeance.

The third factor bearing on the question of when India might retaliate is simply political. The character of the circumstances surrounding the conflict and the initial use of nuclear weapons, the perceived war aims of the adversary and India's own strategic

---

[172]This issue is related substantially to the problem of readiness, which varies both with the technological peculiarity of different types of weapon systems and with the organizational structure of the deterrent as a whole. For a good description of how the readiness of various U.S. strategic forces was expected to change in response to the five-tier defense condition (DEFCON) alerting system developed during the Cold War, see Bruce G. Blair, "Alerting in Crisis and Conventional War," in Ashton B. Carter, John D. Steinbruner, and Charles A. Zraket (eds.), *Managing Nuclear Operations* (Washington, D.C.: Brookings, 1987), pp. 75–120.

intentions, and the quality of support available from important states in the international system would all affect the urgency with which New Delhi felt compelled to issue its retaliatory response. This is another variable, however, that is impossible to estimate in advance. Consequently, even if Indian decisionmakers had perfect, real-time information about the state of their arsenal and could model their postattack strategic capabilities accurately, the uncertainty that *always* attends political events would prevent them from being able to provide any unique answers to the question of how quickly a retaliatory response could be mounted in the aftermath of a nuclear first strike.

Even if this answer were known to New Delhi, however, it is unlikely that Indian policymakers would choose to reveal it publicly. Again, this is because they would not want to provide their adversaries with any information that would enable the latter to minimize the retributive consequences of an Indian counterattack; all they would wish to convey is that retaliation is certain and that it would be devastating irrespective of when and how it was actually inflicted. As one Indian analyst phrased this requirement, the "intent for immediate and instantaneous reaction must be replaced by a mechanism which automatically becomes operative in response to a nuclear attack against the state. [India's eventual nuclear] doctrine should guarantee that such a rejoinder cannot be repealed."[173] In other words, it is more important for India to develop a response system that guarantees successful retaliation once nuclear attacks have occurred than to focus on developing the capability for meting out "immediate and instantaneous" reprisals. It is ironic that this facet of Indian operational doctrine is in fact similar to Chinese nuclear doctrine, which also stresses the certitude rather than the alacrity of retaliation. In words that could have been uttered by many Indian security managers dealing with this question, one Chinese strategist, describing Beijing's nuclear-use doctrine in the context of the Soviet Union, was reported by two Western analysts to have declared that

> Chinese deterrent strategy is based on "launch at any uncertain time." He noted that the Soviets—who cannot preempt all of

---

[173]Nair, *Nuclear India,* p. 104.

China's nuclear missiles, which are carefully stored in caves or otherwise protected and camouflaged—would have to continue to worry about Chinese retaliation "perhaps hours, days, weeks, months or even years later." Even if China's leadership is destroyed in a decapitating nuclear attack, "the Chinese people would not lose confidence. They will be able to wait even three months or more until a new leadership is formed. In the United States, if the government did not retaliate in 24 hours, the people would panic. But the Chinese people can wait until a new leadership is capable of ordering retaliation. Orders could even be sent by foot. The Soviet Union cannot help but be uncertain. Therefore," he concluded, "China does not need an invulnerable C^3 system" to ensure the viability of its nuclear deterrent.[174]

While these sentiments may not hold up under the radioactive debris of a nuclear attack, they are certainly shared, even if unknowingly, by many Indian security managers and strategic elites. The idea that India ought not to develop a nuclear posture that is oriented toward the goal of prompt retaliation—understood in the Western sense as the necessity for retaliating with nuclear weapons within an hour or so of suffering an attack—has remained a key item of agreement between Indian and American diplomats in the ongoing discussions about institutionalizing a restraint regime in South Asia.[175] Indian policymakers, in particular, understand especially well that because their public commitment to a no-first-use policy cannot be objectively verified by any of the conventional instruments of arms control, the character of their nuclear weapon deployment posture is a critical indicator of how genuine their commitment to such a policy actually is. Given this consideration among many others, they have gone out of their way to emphasize that any posture which intimates a capability to engage in prompt retaliation—be it launch on warning, launch under attack, or simply instantaneous reprisal—is unlikely to find favor in New Delhi.[176] Based on the belief that eschewing prompt retaliation not only is in India's interests but actually constitutes a desirable objective for the entire international

---

[174]Garrett and Glaser, *War and Peace: The Views from Moscow and Beijing*, p. 129.

[175]For a good Indian view of its government's position on this issue, see Dilip Lahiri, "Formalizing Restraint: The Case of South Asia," *Strategic Analysis*, 23:4 (July 1999), pp. 563–574.

[176]Ibid.

nuclear order, New Delhi has in fact taken the lead in calling for a "global de-alerting, de-targeting and de-activating"[177] of all nuclear weapons as a confidence-building measure to help reduce the salience of nuclear weaponry in world politics.

These efforts, which are viewed in New Delhi as contributing to the progressive delegitimization of nuclear weapons as a necessary precondition for their eventual elimination,[178] suffered a setback when the "Draft Report of [the] National Security Advisory Board on Indian Nuclear Doctrine" publicly repudiated the official preference for "delayed—but assured—retaliation." Arguing that India's future nuclear posture ought to be centered on the "capability to shift from peacetime deployment to fully employable forces in the shortest possible time,"[179] the Draft Report urged that "India's nuclear forces and their command and control . . . be organized for very high survivability against surprise attacks and *for rapid punitive response*" (italics added).[180] This recommendation, which certainly runs counter to other evidence about official Indian preferences on this issue, has been privately defended by many members of the Advisory Board on three grounds. First, it is held that a rapid convertibility from the de-alerted and possibly demated peacetime nuclear posture to full wartime readiness is essential to preserve the credibility of India's retaliatory capabilities; the ability to prepare for speedy nuclear retaliation, according to this line of argument, could turn out to be critical in retarding any emerging preferences on the part of the adversary for mounting first strikes against the backdrop of possible conventional deterrence breakdown. Second, it is maintained that the rapid convertibility to a wartime posture alone holds promise of denying the adversary any hope that it could count on the international community to restrain India's retaliatory strike on the grounds that such action would serve no positive purpose and would only compound the tragedy engendered by the initial attack. This consideration is seen to be particularly significant vis-à-vis Pakistan, which

---

[177]For a discussion of this proposal, see P. R. Chari, "India's Global Nuclear Initiative," available at http://www.ipcs.org/issues/articles/157-ndi-chari.htm.

[178]"Disarming Argument," *The Times of India*, May 11, 2000.

[179]"Draft Report of [the] National Security Advisory Board on Indian Nuclear Doctrine," p. 3.

[180]Ibid.

is often viewed as being reckless enough to consider unleashing a first strike were it to be entranced by the possibility that strong international pressures could restrain India from unsheathing its otherwise-slow nuclear sword. Third, swift convertibility to a wartime posture along with readiness to unleash a rapid punitive response is seen as possibly the only alternative available to India in situations where the preferences of the international community and New Delhi happen to diverge on the question of what constitutes the most appropriate response to an attack on India. Because the international community may be more concerned about minimizing the damage to the taboo against nuclear use or because it judges that an Indian nuclear counterresponse would undercut any prospects of restoring regional order at a time when all New Delhi cares about is vengeance for having suffered a nuclear attack, many Indian elites believe that preserving the country's freedom of action requires it to possess the capability for rapid retaliation so that New Delhi may enjoy the option of inflicting reprisals—if it so chooses—well before its hand is possibly stayed by superior coercive pressures building up from the outside.

Irrespective of how these rationales are evaluated, the fact remains that these concerns reflect both a profound lack of confidence in India's ability to make the hard decisions required during a nuclear crisis and an unsettling fear that the international community may seek to press its own interests even when India has suffered the trauma of nuclear attack. Not surprisingly, then, many of the Advisory Board's recommendations veer in the direction of ensuring an automatic retributive response because of what appears to be an unstated fear that, absent some kind of a "doomsday machine" which takes either mechanical or organizational form, India may be sufficiently paralyzed in the event of a nuclear attack that it might actually contemplate abdicating its option to retaliate *in extremis*. Since this fear resonates deeply with the widespread suspicion among local elites that India is on balance a "soft state," the Draft Report emphasizes that in addition to all other material accoutrements, successful deterrence finally requires "the will to employ nuclear forces and weapons."[181]

---

[181]"Draft Report of [the] National Security Advisory Board on Indian Nuclear Doctrine," p. 3.

At a more analytical level, however, the Draft Report's recommendations about the need to shift speedily from peacetime deployment to wartime employability in support of rapid punitive responses must be viewed as an effort to address two separate but related operational questions. The first of these pertains simply to the pace at which India's nuclear force-in-being adjusts from its low-readiness posture in peacetime to meeting the exigencies of war, whereas the second pertains directly to the issue of how rapidly India ought to retaliate, irrespective of how fast or how slow the process of increasing force readiness actually turns out to be. Although the answer to the second question may in many instances turn out to be dependent on the first, there is no reason—at least in principle—why this should invariably be so. This is because it is possible to imagine a situation where a fully ready and alerted Indian nuclear force is *not* committed to rapid reprisals even in the aftermath of absorbing a nuclear attack either because New Delhi cannot execute significant retaliation with the forces it has left or because it seeks to orchestrate some other kind of international political response that would be even more damaging to its assailant's interests than that produced by Indian nuclear retribution. Although what these responses might be cannot be speculated on beforehand, it is worth emphasizing that the failure to reiterate the distinction between the issues of rapid convertibility from one readiness state to another and the relative speed of retaliation can leave the question of how delayed Indian retaliation would be in actuality somewhat ambiguous.

Indian Foreign Minister Jaswant Singh attempted to clarify this issue by restating what was previously described as the general preference of Indian security managers. While discussing the relationship between survivability and the speed of retaliation, he repudiated the Advisory Board's recommendation that India plan for a "rapid punitive response," noting that "retaliation does not have to be instantaneous, [but] it has to be effective and assured."[182] Amplifying this theme, Singh asserted that neither the effectiveness nor the credibility of a retaliatory response need be contingent on the speed with which the readiness levels of a force are altered; since "mobility and dispersal [by themselves] improve survivability,"[183] he argued that

---

[182] "India Not to Engage in a N-Arms Race: Jaswant."
[183] Ibid.

focusing on force protection was sufficient to enhance credibility because a retaliatory capability that remained inviolate was more useful for purposes of deterrence than an obsession with rapidly raising readiness or mounting quick punitive responses. Both of these solutions could turn out to be subversive of crisis stability and, even worse, might serve to precipitate the very first strikes that the Advisory Board's recommendations sought to deter. Thus, Singh noted that while the requisite operating procedures would be put in place to "ensure the transition from peacetime deployment modes to a higher state of readiness when required," these procedures would be designed to ensure that they "do not tempt an adversary to preemption but strengthen deterrence by underlying the political resolve for effective retaliation."[184] The sum and substance of Singh's clarifications therefore suggest that India's operational policy does not emphasize prompt retaliation—understood as launch on warning, launch under attack, or any other kind of speedy reprisals[185]—but still leaves unclear what the pace of change in readiness levels would be and, more important, what the relationship between changes in readiness levels and the various thresholds characterizing the process of deterrence breakdown might be in practice.[186]

While Jaswant Singh thus affirms "delayed—but assured—retaliation" to be a key tenet of India's operational policy—in effect echoing the views of the moderates among Indian strategic elites[187]—the question of how much delay ought to be tolerated in the retaliatory response remains unanswered. To be sure, many Indian security

---

[184]Ibid.

[185]It is interesting to note that similar postures have increasingly become a subject of discussion in the United States. Two U.S. Navy analysts, for example, have argued that U.S. strategic deterrence in the post–Cold War era should also emphasize certitude rather than urgency of retaliation. See T. R. Bendel and W. S. Murray, "Response Is Assured," *U.S. Naval Institute Proceedings*, 125:6 (June 1999), pp. 34–37.

[186]This critical issue is discussed in further detail later in this chapter.

[187]The moderates who have addressed this issue in some detail include K. Sundarji, "Imperatives of Indian Minimum Nuclear Deterrence," *Agni*, 2:1 (May 1996), pp. 17–22; "India and the Nuclear Question: An Interview with General K. Sundarji, PVSM (Retd)," *Trishul*, 7:2 (1994), pp. 45–56; Sundarji, "Changing Military Equations in Asia: The Role of Nuclear Weapons," pp. 119–149; Subrahmanyam, "Nuclear Force Design and Minimum Deterrence Strategy for India," pp. 177–195; Nair, *Nuclear India*, pp. 78–194; and, by implication, Singh, "A Nuclear Strategy for India," pp. 306–324.

managers have clear preferences, and some have argued privately that India should aim to be able to execute its retaliatory response "within hours" of suffering a nuclear attack. This time line must, however, be understood—at least at present—as an aspiration rather than a reality because many of the desired delivery systems do not yet exist, the myriad organizational and procedural details relating to force employment have not yet been completely worked out (at least as far as future weapon systems are concerned), and India's capacity to execute retaliation within some specified time frame will be fundamentally conditioned by the extent and weight of the first strike unleashed by its adversaries.[188] This yardstick—the ability to retaliate "within hours"—is intended, however, to suggest that ideally India would aim to develop a deterrent posture that would allow it to respond as rapidly as its command authority deems fit. The capacity for instantaneous retaliation is obviously not favored—as Jaswant Singh has made clear—but an organized structure allowing for quick retaliation measured in at most a few days, if not several hours, is deemed to be most appropriate because such levels of responsiveness are seen as essential to insulating the national command authority from any foreign political pressures to eschew retaliation in the aftermath of a nuclear attack on India. Whether such pressures actually arise will obviously be determined by the density of the attack itself, but Indian security managers—always sensitive to the desire to maintain their freedom of action—would prefer to configure a nuclear posture that allows for a relatively quick response even if they choose not to exercise it, so long as this posture does not fundamentally subvert their larger preferences for lower system costs, enduring civilian control over critical components of their nuclear reserves, and high degrees of crisis stability. In practical terms, therefore, the outer boundaries with respect to the permissible delay in executing retaliation would probably be defined by hours to days rather than by weeks to months, as the Chinese strategist quoted earlier argued would suffice in the case of Beijing. The late General Sundarji captured this sentiment when he concluded that India's

---

[188]This does not imply, however, that India cannot retaliate with its nuclear weapons today. It must be noted emphatically that India currently possesses both the plans and the ability to retaliate with its air-breathing systems, and it is likely to have possessed such capabilities at least since the early 1990s. How these systems will be used in the event of deterrence breakdown has been the object of much internal discussion within the DRDO and the senior leadership of the Indian Air Force.

retaliatory response "can be a good few hours or even perhaps a day after the receipt of the first strike."[189]

The ability to execute expeditious retaliation of this sort, it must be understood, is a desire that falls under the category of "nice to have" but is emphatically not a demand that will be institutionalized in terms of either force structure or operational procedures *if it undercuts the larger objectives of the Indian state*. Indian security managers are well aware of all the burdens inherent in the desire for relatively rapid retaliatory capabilities. The intention to construct a nuclear-use strategy built around the notion of "delayed—but assured—retaliation" in fact constitutes an explicit effort to avoid just such burdens. Maintaining forces on ready alert and perhaps even on hair-trigger readiness, developing complex C^3I systems, acquiring sophisticated negative control technologies, building an elaborate physical command infrastructure, *and* distributing completely assembled nuclear weapons to the armed services—who then acquire both custody and practical control over the entire deterrent system—are just some of the practical consequences that follow from the desire for a force structure designed for overly rapid retaliation. However, since these ingredients are costly, are subversive of India's traditional arrangements for political control, and violate its fundamental intuitions about the utility of nuclear weaponry, New Delhi will err in the direction of tolerating delays in executing its retaliatory responses so long as it can preserve the capacity to retaliate in ways that do not either bankrupt the country or undermine its traditional desire for strict civilian control over all the strategic instruments the state possesses.[190]

Tolerating such delays—and, in fact, planning for them—actually makes sound strategic sense in that it allows New Delhi to operationalize solutions that would enhance the survivability of what would ultimately be its relatively small nuclear force. There is, on balance, no good reason India should seek to develop even a force posture that would allow it "to move from concealed, separate, stor-

---

[189]"India and the Nuclear Question: An Interview with General K. Sundarji, PVSM (Retd)," p. 51.

[190]See the remarks in "India Not to Engage in a N-Arms Race: Jaswant."

age of nuclear components to a fielded force within 24 hours."[191] Meeting the demands imposed by even such a more relaxed time frame would, however, require greater centralization of India's nuclear assets, thus increasing their vulnerability to interdiction by an adversary. Even if the components constituting these assets are dispersed, the constraints imposed by a 24-hour retaliatory window implies that they cannot be dispersed very far and, in many instances, may simply be distributed in different locales close to a small number of relatively salient and obvious nodes. Such localized distribution, while probably effective against Pakistan, could be ineffective against China, as the large damage radii obtaining from Beijing's high-yield weapons could easily negate all the benefits that might otherwise accrue to such compact patterns of dispersal.

Where the length of the retaliatory window is concerned, Indian policymakers are confronted with a set of trade-offs. A shorter retaliatory window may insulate them against pressures from the international community, but it could result in a force posture that is relatively more vulnerable to interdiction. This conclusion, of course, would not hold if the nuclear attacks on India were merely token attacks or if they were, at best, relatively small in number; if India's concealment, deception, and denial practices were robust enough to offset any attempts made by an adversary to strip its nuclear reserves of their protective opacity; or if the kinds of nuclear weapons used to attack Indian targets were relatively small in yield and thus incapable of interdicting multiple targets through the destructive effects of a detonation occurring at any single given aim point. Precisely because New Delhi can never be certain that these assumptions will hold vigorously over time, it makes most sense for India to plan on a deployment posture that, despite extending the length of time required to retaliate, actually serves to decrease an adversary's incentives to attack. In many instances, these incentives can be decreased most easily by adopting a deployment posture that forces the adversary to increase the number of nuclear weapons it must lay down in order to minimize the pain that would accompany any expected Indian retaliatory action. Pursuing this objective may, however, require that India emphasize a greater dispersal of components, higher levels of mobility, and more stringent forms of opacity, camouflage, decep-

---

[191]Giles and Doyle, "Indian and Pakistani Views on Nuclear Deterrence," p. 143.

tion, and denial, all of which may in turn increase the length of the retaliatory window required to mount a successful punitive counter-response. And while this lengthier retaliatory window may give the international community more time to influence India in directions that it may prefer not to go *a priori*, it nonetheless allows New Delhi to put in place a distributed deployment posture that may actually increase the survivability of its retaliatory assets, especially against formidable nuclear adversaries like China.[192]

Given the costs and benefits of these two alternatives, it is obvious that coping with international pressures is a risk that India should be willing to take, especially if it increases the survivability of its relatively small nuclear forces. Having survivable forces is necessary to prevent attacks on India to begin with, but if such attacks—especially extensive strikes—occur nonetheless, the most pressing strategic problem facing New Delhi will be whether it has the requisite residual capability to retaliate, not the extent of international pressure that may be brought to bear on it or the length of time within which retaliation ought to take place. When the survivability of the force is at a premium—as all Indian security managers acknowledge today[193]—trading away the capacity for expeditious retaliation, as represented by the criterion of a 24-hour window, is a small price to pay, especially since New Delhi resolutely seeks to avoid all high-cost antidotes to the problems of survivability, pervasive military control over its national deterrent, and any technical solutions that are likely to exacerbate the problem of crisis stability. Indian policymakers recognize this already, and while they are content to entertain arguments in support of rapid retaliation emanating, for example, from sections of the uniformed military and the National Security Advisory

---

[192]Whether this conclusion holds in practice and to what degree will have to be verified by applying various techniques of operations research. All that can be said in the abstract is that applying the logic of a "shell game" increases the coordination costs of mounting a retaliatory response and, by implication, expands the time interval required to mount such a strike, but this solution could contribute to increasing the survivability of the retaliatory force as a whole. In other words, if there is a trade-off between relatively rapid retaliation—understood here as occurring within 24 hours—and enhanced survivability, India ought to settle for the latter in order to enhance both its own safety *and* regional stability as a whole.

[193]"India Not to Engage in a N-Arms Race: Jaswant"; Lahiri, "Formalizing Restraint: The Case of South Asia," pp. 563–574; and Joshi, "India Must Have Survivable N-Arsenal."

Board, it is unlikely that they will be swayed because the costs and risks such preferences embody clearly overwhelm their presumed benefits.

This willingness to stand up to the assorted pressures for rapid retaliation may not, however, withstand the test of time. While India's emerging nuclear forces are still embryonic in form and there is no pressing predatory threat on the horizon, the Indian government can continue to enjoy the manifold benefits of settling for a relatively relaxed nuclear response posture. But as Indian nuclear capabilities gradually distend, its investments in C^3I slowly mature, and the patterns of civil-military coordination required to execute retaliatory acts progressively stabilize, it is increasingly likely that New Delhi will steadily move toward creating a readiness posture that enables it to unleash full-scale retaliation within 24 hours or so of suffering a nuclear attack even though it will continue to be reticent about publicly disclosing this or any other preferred time frame despite the calls for such disclosure that have already emerged in the Indian strategic debate.[194] More important, India will continue to be even more tight-lipped about any details pertaining to the nature of its retaliatory response. Clearly, the principal question here consists of whether India would—within the limits of its doctrine of "delayed—but assured—retaliation"—choose to respond in a graduated fashion, where the punishment meted out was intended to be proportionate to the attack suffered, or whether it would react with a single spasm of nuclear violence designed to exact ultimate retribution once and for all. On this question more than any other, Indian security managers are likely to be even more taciturn than usual because their desire to maximize deterrence effectiveness translates into a refusal to assist any adversary's calculations with respect to possible Indian reactions to a contemplated attack. Thus, even if it were possible to communicate what the pattern of retaliation might be in advance, New Delhi would consider such communication to be highly undesirable insofar as it might enable Pakistan or China to plan a series of

---

[194]Manoj Joshi, "From Technology Demonstration to Assured Retaliation: The Making of an Indian Nuclear Doctrine," *Strategic Analysis*, 22:10 (January 1999), pp. 1467–1482.

counterresponses which, even if eventually unsuccessful, might contribute to a costly deterrence breakdown in the interim.[195]

Although the reasons for India's official silence are thus understandable, it is possible to speculate about what the structure of New Delhi's retaliatory response might be simply by understanding India's strategic objectives and the relative balance of capabilities in Southern Asia. Put simply, the principal Indian strategic objective in the context of all matters nuclear consists of avoiding nuclear attack (or nuclear coercion) at all costs (since the threat of conventional attack has essentially been defanged as a result of New Delhi's local military superiority). Since effective offensive and defensive nuclear strategies essentially do not exist as far as India is concerned, stable deterrence requires it to possess the ability and willingness to inflict horrific pain on any adversary who dares to cross the nuclear-use threshold. Despite the current belief on the part of many experts that Pakistan possesses some sort of lead vis-à-vis India as far as strategic capabilities go,[196] Pakistan's geographic vulnerability coupled with India's greater nuclear potential implies that New Delhi could eventually acquire the kind of nuclear superiority that is consistent with its greater resources and relative strength. In contrast to China, however, India will always remain the weaker nuclear power; not only will Beijing possess a larger nuclear inventory and more powerful nuclear weapons, but it will also maintain a more diversified set of delivery capabilities vis-à-vis New Delhi indefinitely. India's operational challenge therefore lies in devising a retaliatory response that suffices to penalize two different kinds of adversaries—one possibly weak and the other certainly strong—in a wide range of circumstances. This implies that even as it seeks to avoid suffering nuclear

---

[195]This reticence should not be surprising given that Indian Defence Minister George Fernandes, when asked in Parliament about whether nuclear weapons would be inducted into the armed forces, declared that it was "not wise" to make any statement in this regard. See "Govt. Will Not Bow to Pressure on N-Arms," *The Hindu*, July 24, 1998. For a critique of this policy emphasizing uncertainty, see Joshi, "From Technology Demonstration to Assured Retaliation: The Making of an Indian Nuclear Doctrine," pp. 1476–1479.

[196]See, for example, Perkovich, "South Asia: A Bomb Is Born," p. 52; John Donnelly, "Official: Pakistan's Nuclear Warheads Outpace India's," *Defense Week*, July 27, 1998; Joshi, "Deadly Option," p. 39; and Robert Windrem and Tammy Kupperman, "Pakistan Nukes Outstrip India's, Officials Say," *MSNBC International News*, June 6, 2000, available at http://www.msnbc.com/news/417106.asp.

attack, India must be capable of inflicting the requisite punishment should deterrence fail while still working toward attaining effective intrawar deterrence and speedy conflict termination.

Given these constraints, it is possible to suggest—at least as a first cut—that India, while developing retaliatory capabilities that allow it to execute both "massive" retaliation and "graduated" nuclear responses (these terms understood, of course, in the suitably denatured forms appropriate to the South Asian context), could end up in practice carrying out proportionate retaliation if deterrence failed. New Delhi can afford to consciously pursue a range of options involving graduated responses vis-à-vis Islamabad *if* it eventually acquires a larger and more capable nuclear arsenal that provides it with opportunities for escalation dominance over Pakistan. Obviously, the possibility of this outcome obtaining hinges on the following conditions:

1. That New Delhi acquires sufficient nuclear superiority over Pakistan, understood in terms of both the number and yield of the weapons present in its stockpile;

2. That both New Delhi and Islamabad recognize India's relative superiority as far as the nuclear balance is concerned; and

3. That the Pakistani first strike which precipitates Indian retaliation is essentially a symbolic or limited attack that is viewed as such both in New Delhi and in Islamabad.

Under such circumstances, India could choose to respond only in proportion to the Pakistani attack, using its superior nuclear reserves to enforce intrawar deterrence and speedy conflict termination on its own terms.

There are, in fact, sound practical reasons why massive retaliation vis-à-vis Islamabad may be unnecessary if the above conditions hold, most deriving from Pakistan's relative strategic vulnerabilities. These vulnerabilities—manifested by Pakistan's narrow geographic depth, the high concentration of its national assets along a very small target array, and the significant threat posed to the Punjabi heartland by even localized infrastructure attacks—imply that even relatively modest levels of Indian nuclear retaliation could result in catastrophic damage that could push Pakistan well beyond the pale of speedy recovery. Thanks to these structural weaknesses, even low levels of Indian retaliation would suffice to inflict relatively high levels of punishment on Islamabad especially where population losses and critical assets destroyed are concerned, thus making massive retaliation unnecessary and possibly counterproductive.[197] On balance, however, it is not at all clear that the three conditions identified as necessary for the outcome of limited or proportionate Indian retaliation actually obtain in South Asia today, and consequently the prospect of a massive nuclear counterresponse by New Delhi vis-à-vis Islamabad deserves at least passing attention.

The temptation for India to respond to a Pakistani nuclear attack with massive retaliation would arise under one or more of the following conditions:

1. The Pakistani first strike turns out to be large in scope and weight, suggesting either an attempt at damage limitation pursued through widespread counterforce attacks or the execution of a "Samson option"[198] involving widespread countervalue or countermilitary attacks as a last roll of the dice. Under such circumstances, India's nuclear response is likely to consist of large-scale retaliation with everything deployed in New Delhi's arsenal and then some.

2. The Pakistani first strike turns out to be relatively limited but occurs in the context of a general misperception in New Delhi about Pakistan's strategic intentions relating to the conflict. If New Delhi perceives any Pakistani first use as merely the opening salvo in what could turn out to be a series of sequential attacks, Indian policymakers are likely to respond with a "massive" use of their own reserves the first time around so as to eliminate the threat of expected future attacks while they can.

3. The Pakistani first strike turns out to be relatively limited but occurs in the context of a pervasive misperception in New Delhi

---

[197]The logic of limited retaliation vis-à-vis Pakistan is discussed in H. K. Srivastava, "Nuclear India: Problems and Praxises," *Combat Journal*, April 1987, pp. 30–40.

[198]This phrase is borrowed from Seymour M. Hersh, *The Samson Option: Israel's Nuclear Arsenal and American Foreign Policy* (New York: Random House, 1991), which describes Israeli nuclear strategy as essentially a Wagnerian *Götterdämmerung* executed *in extremis*.

about its own relative capabilities vis-à-vis Islamabad. If Indian policymakers believe that the nuclear balance in South Asia favors them asymmetrically over Pakistan—despite uncertainty elsewhere about this issue—they could be tempted to respond even to modest Pakistani nuclear use with substantial counter-responses of their own, intending these counterresponses to severely punish Islamabad for its breach of the nuclear-use taboo and executing them on the solipsistic assumption that New Delhi possesses the strategic wherewithal to ratchet the levels of punishment even higher if Islamabad should choose to mount further nuclear attacks.

All in all, it is reasonable to conclude that both proportionate and massive Indian retaliation are equally possible in the context of a subcontinental nuclear war, with the probability of one occurring over the other being determined principally by the validity of the three pairs of boundary conditions delineated above.[199]

A different logic—as well as a different conclusion altogether—dominates the calculus vis-à-vis China but produces in the process a more assured outcome. India is clearly the weaker state in the Sino-Indian dyad and may eventually turn out to be just as insubstantial vis-à-vis China as many Indian hawks believe Pakistan would be against India in matters of nuclear capability. In the context of a Chinese nuclear attack (assuming, of course, that this was something less than all-out nuclear use), an Indian attempt at executing massive retaliation would be futile because the disparity in Sino-Indian nuclear capabilities could result in an overwhelming Chinese rejoinder that destroys Indian society in exchange for at best only catastrophic damage to the Chinese polity.[200] Accepting such an exchange ratio would be illogical even by an otherwise reasonable theory of punishment. The differential in the relative ability to punish is in fact so great in the Sino-Indian case that when retaliation must actually be executed—as opposed to merely being threatened—India either would be self-deterred or would engage only in proportionate pun-

---

[199]On this issue, see also Kanwal, "Nuclear Targeting Philosophy for India," pp. 459–473.

[200]For a good discussion about the weight of possible Chinese nuclear attacks on India, see Jones, *From Testing to Deploying Nuclear Forces*, p. 4.

ishment designed to satisfy the demand for retribution as a prelude to speedy war termination. The strategic objective of preserving Indian safety against nuclear attack in the face of the country's own relative weakness vis-à-vis China almost guarantees that if the fateful demand for nuclear retaliation were to confront Indian decision-makers, they would settle for limited, proportionate, or graduated rather than massive retaliation precisely because it was the prudent thing to do: It would satisfy the need for punishment without in any way precluding the possibility of an even greater catastrophe for both sides should a speedy termination of conflict elude the antagonists.[201]

The actual Indian retaliatory response vis-à-vis both Pakistan and China could therefore be similar in some instances and radically different in others, though—as the analysis indicates above—for different reasons in each case. In any event, prewar Indian declaratory policy will certainly continue to insinuate the prospect of sure "massive" retaliation because security managers in New Delhi would seek to deny both Islamabad and Beijing the hope that they could pursue nuclear aggression while accommodating some low and manageable levels of Indian retribution. Thus, for example, during the Kargil crisis with Pakistan in May and June of 1999, Brajesh Mishra, the Indian National Security Adviser, asserted, "Let me make one thing absolutely clear. We have a policy of no first use. . . . But if any attempt is made against us, God forbid, we will go all out."[202] Indian policymakers are also likely to devalue the significance of an adversary's nuclear threats whenever possible in order to underscore their own composed posture and to minimize the prospects of self-deterrence in a crisis. Thus, for example, Brajesh Mishra decried Pakistan's nuclear threats on several occasions during the Kargil crisis as "border[ing] on lunacy,"[203] while Prime Minister Vajpayee,

[201]Except for K. Subrahmanyam, Bharat Karnad, Vijai Nair, and Gurmeet Kanwal, Indian analysts have not discussed targeting challenges vis-à-vis China in any detail, thereby suggesting either that China is not an imminent nuclear threat or that there is not much India can do about China, at least in the near term, except to deploy the best deterrent it possibly can in the hope of immunizing itself against potential Chinese threats.

[202]Praful Bidwai, "Nuclear Weapons Seen as Having Enhanced Insecurity," *India Abroad,* July 16, 1999.

[203]"Pak N-Threat Borders on Lunacy: Brajesh," *Hindustan Times,* July 5, 1999.

when asked about Pakistan's reported nuclear threats, serenely replied that "we are prepared for all eventualities."[204]

Such prewar declaratory postures, however, are not the same as wartime operational policies, and while Indian decisionmakers may certainly execute massive retaliation—especially if they either absorbed an immense first strike that left them with little other choice or sought to punish a weaker state like Pakistan on the presumption that they possessed the capability for escalation dominance—it is possible that in many other circumstances India would settle for a limited or proportionate retaliation that, while embodying retribution and perhaps signaling its inherent capabilities, threatens to escalate to even higher levels of violence in the hope of enforcing a speedy termination of conflict.[205] Of course, since an adversary cannot be confident that India would respond in this measured fashion and no other, the emphasis on deterrence by punishment is likely to suffice as an effective antidote to adventurism. Indian

---

[204] "India Not Daunted by Pak Nuke Threat: PM," *The Times of India*, July 1, 1999.

[205] This formulation, of course, raises another interesting possibility: Could India avoid nuclear retaliation altogether even if it has suffered a modest nuclear attack by an adversary? This possibility has been raised by both Indian and American scholars— see Srivastava, "Nuclear India: Problems and Praxises," p. 36; Sharad Dixit, "A Nuclear Strategy for India," *The Pioneer*, September 3, 1998; and Joeck, *Maintaining Nuclear Stability in South Asia*, p. 57—and represents an intriguing though in the final analysis somewhat unlikely possibility. One reason for this judgment is that no Indian government is likely to survive politically if it fails to respond to a nuclear attack by mounting at least token retaliation. More significantly, however, the alternative of avoiding a nuclear response would become plausible if India could retaliate by alternative means such as altering its war aims vis-à-vis the immediate adversary. During the Gulf War, such an alternative was bruited by the U.S. leadership in the event Saddam Hussein used weapons of mass destruction on Coalition forces. In the South Asian case, however, few possibilities of this sort present themselves. For example, India could not respond to limited nuclear attacks by threatening to occupy Pakistan or China physically, since it not only lacks the conventional resources to do so but would actually precipitate further nuclear attacks if it ever attempted such solutions. In theory, it could also attempt to retaliate by supporting secessionist movements in both countries after the cessation of hostilities, but such solutions too are slow, may not succeed, and, even if successful, may only provoke a resumption of nuclear attacks on India. Thus, except for the plausible but unlikely solution that posits the international community banding together to inflict political and military reprisals on the attackers coupled with a large-scale reassurance effort aimed at preventing New Delhi from seeking individual retribution, it is difficult to imagine any kind of satisfaction that could be dangled before India to induce it to accept a policy of nonretaliation in the event of suffering a nuclear attack. For more on this issue, see Dixit, "A Nuclear Strategy for India."

policymakers, in turn, will only seek to reinforce the robustness of this strategy by refusing to clearly specify their nuclear employment policy *a priori* in any detail and, if they do, will tend to emphasize its overwhelmingly painful consequences, even if at the moment of truth they find it counterproductive to carry out their own prewar ultimatums.[206]

---

[206]The resemblance of this strategy to that pursued by both the British and the French "independent deterrents" during the Cold War is more than just coincidental, having all arisen from similar strategic circumstances. Both British and French efforts in this regard are reviewed in Lawrence Freedman, "British Nuclear Targeting," and Yost, "French Nuclear Targeting," both appearing in Desmond Ball and Jeffrey Richelson (eds.), *Strategic Nuclear Targeting* (Ithaca, NY: Cornell University Press, 1986), pp. 109–126 and 127–156.

It is important to recognize, however, that India's prewar emphasis on "massive" punishment for any infraction of the no-nuclear-use rule could in some situations precipitate the very outcome India sought to avoid—namely, massive employment of nuclear weapons by India's adversaries in the event of a deterrence breakdown. This unintended outcome could occur if Pakistan, for example, were to reason that because even the most token nuclear use in the context of a conventional war would precipitate a massive Indian nuclear counterresponse anyway, it might as well go first with an overwhelming nuclear attack of its own—when its nuclear weapons reserves are still secure and its C^3I systems are operationally coherent in a way that they would not be in the aftermath of the large expected Indian riposte. This incentive to unleash a massive nuclear attack—when only token nuclear employment might otherwise have sufficed—would not exist if Pakistan were to be convinced about the survivability of its nuclear reserves in the face of even a potentially massive Indian response. In such circumstances, Islamabad could use its nuclear weapons in the modest fashion appropriate to its strategic situation while waiting to see whether New Delhi would in fact make good on its threat to unleash massive nuclear punishment. Since Pakistan's nuclear capabilities would by definition be secure in these circumstances, it could afford to ride out Indian retaliation and then proceed to escalate in an appropriate fashion depending on what India's retaliatory response actually was—as opposed to unleashing a massive nuclear strike to begin with simply for the prudential reason of limiting the damage that would be caused by the anticipated Indian reaction. This logic, then, serves to highlight three important issues: First, India's insistent prewar emphasis on massive retaliation, although understandable as a strategy for shoring up deterrence, could precipitate the very phenomenon it seeks to avoid: a nuclear attack on India that takes on even greater proportions than might otherwise have been the case. Second, the survivability of Pakistan's nuclear assets (and Islamabad's confidence about that survivability) makes a critical difference to whether Pakistan executes limited or massive nuclear first-use strategies. Parenthetically, it also suggests that—for purely self-interested reasons—Islamabad would be better off investing in enhancing the survivability of its nuclear reserves rather than pursuing nuclear strategies aimed at eroding India's capability to retaliate if it is to avoid being put in a situation where it has to choose committing suicide simply for fear of death. Third, the paradoxes of rationality that cause perverse outcomes in the Indo-Pakistani case do not obtain in the Sino-Indian dyad because Beijing's existing nuclear superiority and the high survivability of its strategic assets vis-à-vis New Delhi's make

Strategic Nuclear Targeting. The logic of "delayed—but as-sured—retaliation" satisfactorily addresses the question of when punishment might be executed if deterrence breakdown were to result in nuclear weapon use by an adversary against India. It does not specify, however, what the targets of such retaliation might be, and consequently *the fourth component of India's nuclear doctrine at the level of operational policy relates to the "countervalue plus" targeting strategy that New Delhi is likely to pursue in support of a posture of mutual assured vulnerability that simultaneously embodies some targeting flexibility.* This dimension of operational policy—the intended target set that is the object of any retaliatory action—has not been discussed publicly by any Indian security managers and probably never will be for the reasons alluded to earlier. New Delhi's discomfort with nuclear weapons reinforces its inclination to brush all the unsavory dimensions of nuclear strategy under the table. And while Indian security managers recognize that strategic targeting has to be carried out precisely because it remains the price of effective deterrence, they will be satisfied by modest efforts carried out in complete secrecy. In fact, these activities are already under way: Various planning cells in the Indian Ministry of Defence, particularly the DRDO, and in the service headquarters have begun to examine targeting requirements in some detail, although the scale of effort, the extent of direction from the civilian leadership, and the degree of coordination between the civilian nuclear weapon designers and civilian and uniformed operational planners are not known.[207] In any event, the secrecy that accompanies this effort is driven first and foremost by the political imperative of not giving needless offense to any adversaries while simultaneously seeking to minimize the concerns of the Indian public about their own relative vulnerability—concerns that would arise if any discussions about nuclear targeting were to be carried out publicly. Indian policymakers have, in fact, consciously sought to avoid replicating the provocative rhetoric that emerged from Pakistan in the aftermath of its Ghauri missile test, when a number of Pakistani politicians took the stage in order to gloat about their new offensive reach—some even publicly identify-

---

any Indian threats of massive retaliation incredible—irrespective of the kinds of Chinese nuclear-use strategies that are at issue.

[207]The author is deeply grateful to an Indian scholar who has requested anonymity for sharing his understanding of these efforts.

ing a host of cities in India that would supposedly be targeted by Islamabad's new strategic systems.[208]

While the desire to avoid agitating public sentiment in the region at large represents the political reason for refusing to discuss India's targeting policy publicly, there is also a sound strategic reason for New Delhi's continued silence on this issue. Because Indian strategic managers have consistently held that their nuclear deterrent is oriented fundamentally toward the political management of crises rather than toward the achievement of some military objectives on the battlefield, they have consciously sought to avert all attention from the operational issues surrounding nuclear weapon employment, such as targeting requirements, damage expectancy calculations, and the criteria for assured destruction. In fact, this aversion to operational issues is best illustrated by the fact that India's Foreign Minister, Jaswant Singh, is reported to have "decried"—on the record—"[even] the use of the word 'arsenal,' terming it as 'a throwback to the years of the Cold War.'"[209] This conscious disregard of operational issues *in public discussion* is grounded on the premise that these problems represent narrow and secondary concerns that cannot be allowed to dominate the central strategic problem facing India: legitimizing the need for a modest but capable nuclear force to guarantee India's strategic independence in the face of any nuclear threats, blackmail, and coercion that may be mounted by its adversaries. Since defending this objective against both domestic skeptics and a hostile international community remains a challenging endeavor in its own right,[210] Indian policymakers have sought to avoid any discussions that would feed public controversy and debate about the country's evolving nuclear posture. The only external discussions of such matters have been conducted off the record by some Indian think tanks and by a few defense analysts writing for national newspapers and magazines. Among the more significant of these must be counted General K. Sundarji, the late Chief of Staff of the Indian

---

[208] *Pakistan: Nuclear Scientist: Pakistan Can Hit Many Indian Cities,* FBIS-NES-98-217, August 5, 1998, and *Pakistan: Gohar Ayub on Next India-Pakistan War.*

[209] Joshi, "From Technology Demonstration to Assured Retaliation: The Making of an Indian Nuclear Doctrine," p. 1471.

[210] See the remarks of Prime Minister Vajpayee in "N-Deterrence a Must: PM," *The Pioneer,* May 13, 2000.

Army, and Brigadier Vijai Nair, whose work on India's nuclear policy, despite being incomplete in some areas, represents the best early discussion of the country's nuclear requirements and strategy.[211] A more recent contribution that is both sophisticated and interesting (but that is clearly embedded in the classical approach to nuclear deterrence familiar in the West and hence is unlikely to command the allegiance of Indian policymakers in all its details) is Admiral Raja Menon's *A Nuclear Strategy for India*.[212]

Since this last dimension of operational policy—targeting doctrine—is not publicly discussed by Indian policymakers, all the assertions that follow are proffered purely on the basis of logical deduction supplemented by insights gained from conversations with Indian security managers and elites. In this instance, though, deductive claims are generally adequate because targeting policies are invariably a complex function of a country's grand strategy and overarching nuclear doctrine, the size of its arsenal, the quality of its nuclear weapons and delivery systems, and the number, hardness, relative concentration, and intrinsic mobility of the potential targets to be interdicted. A good deal of general information about most of these variables in Southern Asia is publicly available, and while these data may not suffice to forecast any *actual* targeting plans, they are more than sufficient to describe the broad orientation of Indian targeting that is likely to obtain both in the near term and over time.[213]

Figure 6 identifies a range of targeting options subsumed by a variety of nuclear strategies. While these options are identified as distinctly as possible for purposes of analysis, it is likely that most war plans would in practice cover a mix of target sets, with each plan probably dominated by an emphasis on one particular targeting orientation to the relative neglect of others. This emphasis is usually

---

[211]Sundarji, "Changing Military Equations in Asia: The Role of Nuclear Weapons," pp. 119–149, and Nair, *Nuclear India*, pp. 133–151. See also Kanwal, "Nuclear Targeting Philosophy for India," pp. 459–473.

[212]Menon, *A Nuclear Strategy for India*.

[213]Much of this information is usefully collected in S. Rashid Naim, "Aadhi Raat Ke Baad ('After Midnight')," in Stephen P. Cohen (ed.), *Nuclear Proliferation in South Asia* (Boulder, CO: Westview Press, 1991), pp. 23–61; Nair, *Nuclear India*, pp. 133–151; and http://www.fas.org/nuke/guide/china/index.html, http://www.fas.org/nuke/guide/india/index.html, and http://www.fas.org/nuke/guide/pakistan/index.html.

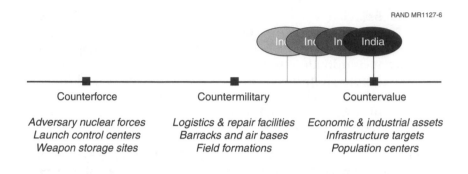

Figure 6—India's Likely Targeting Strategies

conditioned by both the grand strategy of the state concerned and the size and quality of its nuclear arsenal—a fact that allows its targeting policy to be described in terms of some specific orientation despite all the complexities that may otherwise characterize its war plans.[214]

At one extreme, strategic nuclear targeting could be oriented toward interdicting "counterforce" targets.[215] This target set usually consists of the adversary's nuclear weapons themselves, the storage sites at which the weapons are located, the delivery systems slated to carry the weapons (if these are not already mated to the warheads), the bases that host the delivery systems, and the command-and-control architecture that directs the operations of the entire force. Counterforce targets thus consist of both hard and soft systems that may in turn be either fixed or mobile. ICBMs deployed in fixed, fully hardened silos and strategic submarine bases represent examples of hard fixed targets; manned bombers and submarines at sea, in contrast, are example of soft targets that are also mobile; and missile

---

[214]This argument is borne out in the survey of targeting polices followed by the great powers during the Cold War, which, with the conspicuous exception of China, are described in Desmond Ball and Jeffrey Richelson (eds.), *Strategic Nuclear Targeting* (Ithaca, NY: Cornell University Press, 1986), pp. 35–156.

[215]The nature of these targets and their relevance, for example, in the U.S.-Soviet context are well described in Desmond Ball, *Targeting for Strategic Deterrence*, Adelphi Paper No. 185 (London: IISS, 1983).

storage facilities, above-ground C^3I sites, and strategic surface-to-air missile (SAM) installations remain good examples of soft fixed targets. Irrespective of the specific attributes of a given system, counterforce targets as a whole share certain characteristics: They exist in relatively significant number; they are relatively small in size; and they enjoy a relatively high degree of protection against nuclear effects either because they are hardened by design or because their inherent mobility allows them to escape beyond the lethal radii of an attacking weapon. Both offensive and defensive nuclear strategies can emphasize counterforce targeting because they seek to disarm the adversary of his coercive capabilities either to secure counterforce-countercontrol preeminence or to limit the extent of damage that may be inflicted as a result of an assailant's first strike.[216]

In the middle of the spectrum lies a vast range of assorted "countermilitary" targets that consist for the most part of the myriad instruments required for the successful prosecution of high-intensity combat.[217] These targets include all the conventional military forces of the adversary, especially high-value resources such as armored and mechanized divisions, capital ships and submarines, and strategic air capabilities in the form of both combat aircraft and support platforms. Countermilitary targets also include the strategic infrastructure required to enable these high-value resources to operate effectively. Some of the principal kinds of countermilitary targets include barracks, supply depots, and marshaling yards; tank, vehicle, and ammunition storage facilities; transportation assets and military communications facilities; naval bases and shipbuilding and repair yards; and conventional air bases, command posts, and early warning and air defense facilities. These targets obviously embody disparate characteristics—some are hard, some are soft, some are fixed, and some are mobile—but the most distinguishing feature of the set as a whole is the vast number of its constituent parts, each of which

---

[216]A good general discussion of this issue with an assessment of its benefits, challenges, and limitations for strategic stability can be found in Albert Legault and George Lindsey, *The Dynamics of the Nuclear Balance* (Ithaca, NY: Cornell University Press, 1976).

[217]On the characteristics of these targets, which used to be generically described as "other military targets" (OMT), and the challenges of interdicting them in the U.S.-Soviet context, see Jeffrey Richelson, "The Dilemmas of Counterpower Targeting," *Comparative Strategy*, 2:3 (1980), pp. 223–237.

is defined by its relatively small size. Both offensive and defensive nuclear strategies incorporate significant countermilitary targeting, although the latter are more likely to stress such targets, especially at the operational level, given their emphasis on denying the adversary his war aims on the battlefield.[218]

At the other end of the spectrum, strategic nuclear targeting could focus mainly on "countervalue" targets, which, broadly defined, are targets that host most of the resources necessary for the sustenance of a modern society.[219] The most conspicuous countervalue targets are population centers such as cities, which contain significant portions of the workforce in an industrialized economy as well as most of the critical economic and industrial capabilities that constitute either the war-supporting capability of a country or the resources bearing on its ability to recover in the aftermath of a nuclear attack. The former category would include, for example, petroleum refineries, industrial plants, and arms and munitions production facilities, while the latter category would include all facilities pertaining to the production of coal, steel, aluminum, cement, and electric power. Countervalue targets may also encompass specific national infrastructure assets such as the communications system, the transportation network, and the power grid, including switching stations, space control facilities, dams, rail junctions and switching yards, bridges and tunnels, and generating stations and nuclear power plants, all of which help maintain the connectivity modern societies require for their survival and functioning.[220]

---

[218]During the Cold War, the need to interdict these kinds of targets gave rise to an entire class of specialized "theater" and "tactical" nuclear weapons. The multifaceted rationale for these systems is explored in Ashley J. Tellis, "NATO and Theater Nuclear Force Modernization: Looking Backward, Looking Forward," *Journal of East and West Studies*, 15:2 (Fall–Winter 1986), pp. 101–126.

[219]On the characteristics of "countervalue" targets and attacks involving such targets, see Office of Technology Assessment, *The Effects of Nuclear War* (Montclair, NJ: Allanheld, Osmun, 1980). Studies that assessed attacks on such targets in the U.S.-Soviet context are usefully reviewed and summarized in Michael Salman, Kevin J. Sullivan, and Stephen van Evera, "Analysis or Propaganda? Measuring American Strategic Nuclear Capability, 1969–88," in Lynn Eden and Steven E. Miller (eds.), *Nuclear Arguments* (Ithaca, NY: Cornell University Press, 1989), pp. 172–245.

[220]The author is deeply grateful to David Shlapak for sharing his unpublished RAND work on effective air campaigns, which examines attacks on this class of targets in detail.

The organization of modern societies often results in the concentration of many countervalue targets in a few geographic locations with large populations, and consequently even a strategy that seeks to avoid population targeting per se could generate enormous fatalities simply by virtue of the collocation of critical economic and industrial targets with dense pockets of habitation.[221] Such fatalities are often the result of peculiar interactions ensuing from the complex physical effects of a nuclear explosion. The human body, for example, can withstand simple overpressures of 30 psi, but winds associated with as little as 2–3 psi could blow people out of buildings, causing instant death. Consequently, many nuclear damage calculation models simply assume that minimum overpressures of 5 psi would suffice to kill at least half the population located within the 5-psi ring of a nuclear detonation.[222] Since high population fatalities would inevitably accompany any nuclear strategy oriented toward countervalue targeting—even if populations per se are not targeted—this kind of targeting doctrine best supports a deterrent strategy aimed mainly at punishment. In fact, observers such as Bernard Brodie have argued that so long as an adversary's cities are targeted by a retaliatory strategy, the distinction between counterforce, countermilitary, and countervalue targeting could simply break down because if these targets are collocated, "it can hardly mean much to the population involved whether the destruction of cities is a by-product of, [for example], the destruction of airfields or vice versa."[223]

Confronted with a choice of these three options, India is almost certain to settle for countervalue targeting and, by implication, seek to service a nuclear strategy centered on some kind of mutual assured vulnerability.[224] While such a targeting posture follows directly from India's operational policy, which focuses on deterrence

[221]Jeffrey Richelson, "Population Targeting and U.S. Strategic Doctrine," in Desmond Ball and Jeffrey Richelson (eds.), *Strategic Nuclear Targeting* (Ithaca, NY: Cornell University Press, 1986), p. 248.

[222]Office of Technology Assessment, *The Effects of Nuclear War*, pp. 15–26.

[223]Bernard Brodie, *Strategy in the Missile Age* (Princeton, NJ: Princeton University Press, 1959), p. 156.

[224]The most systematic Indian justification for this targeting strategy can be found in Nair, *Nuclear India*, pp. 133–151; Sundarji, "Changing Military Equations in Asia: The Role of Nuclear Weapons," pp. 119–149; and K. Sundarji, "Nuclear Deterrence: Doctrine for India—Part 2," *Trishul*, 6:1 (1993), pp. 67–86.

based on threats of punishment, it is more fundamentally grounded in the character of the country's nuclear capabilities—or lack thereof. These capabilities will be discussed in some detail in the next chapter, but a summary description at this point should suffice to clarify why countervalue targeting is most logical for India vis-à-vis both China and Pakistan, though New Delhi would certainly possess greater targeting flexibility in the case of the latter. India's nuclear capabilities essentially reside in a small inventory of relatively low-yield nuclear weapons that will be delivered, at least in the foreseeable future, primarily by tactical strike aircraft. This inventory will likely not exceed 150 to 175 weapons by the year 2010, with the most reliable designs today producing yields in the 10- to 20-kt range.[225] Although Indian scientists have claimed that they can produce boosted fission weapons with yields of some 200 kt[226] and even thermonuclear weapons with megaton-sized yields, these capabilities have not yet been demonstrated to the universal satisfaction of others, especially India's adversaries. Consequently, it is reasonable—at least for heuristic purposes—to base the analysis on nuclear capabilities that have been unambiguously demonstrated thus far while simply alluding to the likely consequences if these capabilities were to change in the future. These demonstrated capabilities, which consist of levitated versions of the basic fission design tested in 1974 and are capable of producing yields in the range of 20 kt *at best*, essentially imply that both significant counterforce and countermilitary targeting are ruled out for all practical purposes—especially in the case of nuclear operations against China—because of the limited yields and relatively small number of nuclear weapons that India will eventually acquire.[227]

To begin with, most of the primary Chinese counterforce targets, consisting of nuclear-tipped ballistic missiles, are either mobile or

---

[225]The primary Indian fission design, the levitated "flying plate" version of the device tested in 1974, is credited with being capable of producing yields in the 10- to 20-kt class and is believed to have produced most of the recorded yield during the 1998 test series. This design and its expected yield are described in Raj Chengappa, "Is India's H-Bomb a Dud?" *India Today International*, October 12, 1998, pp. 22–28.

[226]"India Can Produce N-bomb of 220 Kiloton: Chidambaram," *The Times of India*, May 23, 1998, cited in Karnad, "A Thermonuclear Deterrent," p. 117, and "India Can Make 200 Kilotons of Nuke Weapons," *Hindustan Times*, October 31, 2000.

[227]This issue is discussed in greater detail in Chapter Five.

deployed in hardened silos and caves. While some missiles are maintained in soft garrisons, these systems would disperse in periods of crisis or on receipt of strategic warning.[228] Since Indian nuclear use will only be retaliatory, meaning that it would occur after China used nuclear weapons first, it is reasonable to presume that all of Beijing's mobile missiles (primarily CSS-5s) will be flushed from their peacetime locations and dispersed to their wartime hides as part of normal preparation for nuclear combat. India's military forces lack, both currently and prospectively, the ability to detect, track, and target any of these mobile missiles, while those weapons maintained in fixed hardened silos (some CSS-3s) or stored in caves or tunnels (primarily CSS-2s and some CSS-3s) would be invulnerable even to direct nuclear attack because the small yields of India's weapons would simply be unable to generate the overpressures necessary to neutralize these protected assets.[229] Thus, even if India could somehow reach the missile deployment sites, launch control centers, or weapon storage facilities either by aircraft or by ballistic missile, it would most likely be unable to eliminate China's strategic nuclear reserves even with the standard two-on-one attacks that were commonly assumed during the Cold War. This is because aircraft delivery bequeaths greater accuracy, but penetrativity is uncertain, and the

---

[228]Details about the CSS-2s, -3s, and -5s most relevant to India are discussed in Gill and Mulvenon, "The Chinese Strategic Rocket Forces: Transition to Credible Deterrence," pp. 27–45, with additional information about both the missiles and their basing postures available in Robert S. Norris, Andrew S. Burrows, and Richard W. Fieldhouse, *British, French, and Chinese Nuclear Weapons, Nuclear Weapons Databook*, Vol. 5 (Boulder, CO: Westview Press, 1994), pp. 338–341 and 358–397, and at http://www.fas.org/nuke/guide/china/facility/missile.htm.

[229]By way of comparison, during the high tide of the Cold War, both the United States and the Soviet Union assigned weapon systems with relatively high yields and accuracies to the hard-target counterforce role. The principal U.S. missile systems allocated for this mission were equipped with warheads that had yields in the hundreds of kilotons and were capable of accuracies down to a few hundred feet. Soviet missiles too had more or less comparable accuracies and were equipped with warheads that often had yields going up to several megatons. In contrast, a 3500-km Indian Agni armed with New Delhi's primary fission design would be able to muster yields roughly similar to that of a Nagasaki-class nuclear weapon (~20 kt) with an accuracy that would probably run close to many hundreds of feet—if the accuracy of the missile was presumed to be simply 0.1 percent of its range. Details about U.S. and Soviet nuclear weapons and missiles can be found in Thomas B. Cochran, William M. Arkin, and Milton M. Hoenig, *U.S. Nuclear Forces and Capabilities, Nuclear Weapons Databook*, Volume 1 (Cambridge: Ballinger Publishing Company, 1984), and Thomas B. Cochran, William M. Arkin, and Milton M. Hoenig, *Soviet Nuclear Weapons, Nuclear Weapons Databook*, Vol. 4 (Cambridge, MA: Ballinger Publishing Company, 1989).

yields of India's air-dropped weapons would at any rate be rather small, whereas missile delivery solves the penetrativity problem but would be additionally limited by the relatively poor accuracy of the system. What complicates matters finally is the small current and projected size of the Indian nuclear stockpile relative to the number of Chinese counterforce targets.

Where counterforce attacks are concerned, the effectiveness against hard targets appears to be more sensitive to accuracy than to yield by a ratio of approximately 5:1.[230] This implies that India's intermediate-range missile force, if and when deployed, would have to be extraordinarily accurate even at relatively long distances, and attaining such accuracies would not only require Global Positioning System (GPS)-aided inertial guidance systems—which India will probably obtain—but also advanced (not strapdown) inertial guidance capabilities, which are likely to lie beyond India's reach for some time to come.[231] In any event, if missiles or advanced strike aircraft are intended to be the systems of choice for counterforce targeting, all successful attacks would likely require much larger weapon yields than those assumed above and possibly earth-penetrating warheads as well in order to exploit the superior coupling effects offered by the latter to achieve at least "mission kills" that neutralize Chinese missile silos and storage caves, weapon storage bunkers, and launch control centers. Since India has all but eschewed further nuclear testing, however, it is unlikely that such capabilities can be developed, and thus, by implication, significant hard-target counterforce kill capability will remain beyond New Delhi's reach.[232]

---

[230]See the discussion in William T. Lee, "Soviet Nuclear Targeting Strategy," in Desmond Ball and Jeffrey Richelson (eds.), *Strategic Nuclear Targeting* (Ithaca, NY: Cornell University Press, 1986), p. 104ff.

[231]The quality of guidance systems in Indian missiles is discussed in Janne E. Nolan, *Trappings of Power: Ballistic Missiles in the Third World* (Washington, D.C.: Brookings, 1991); Aaron Karp, *Ballistic Missile Proliferation: The Politics and Technics* (Oxford, UK: Oxford University Press, 1996); and Eric Arnett, "Military Research and Development in Southern Asia: Limited Capabilities Despite Impressive Resources," in Eric Arnett (ed.), *Military Capacity and the Risk of War* (Oxford, UK: Oxford University Press, 1997), pp. 243–276.

[232]If India resumes nuclear testing, however, and such testing results in the successful validation of its advanced nuclear designs—boosted fission or thermonuclear weapons—New Delhi could move somewhat in the direction of acquiring

This conclusion holds equally if India attempted to attack other fixed targets, such as submarine bases or airfields: Neither kind of target would suffer significant damage even if India's small nuclear weapons were accurately delivered by aircraft, for example, unless it was presumed that New Delhi would be willing to expend nontrivial numbers of multiple weapons per target. The large number of potential targets in this set, however, implies that the total number of weapons India would have to allocate to prosecuting such missions could easily exceed the size of its entire nuclear stockpile—and consequently the strategic wisdom of planning such attacks *for purposes of retaliation* remains an open question. In any case, there is no guarantee that China's nuclear submarines and nuclear-capable aircraft would actually be destroyed by such attacks, since these platforms could be rapidly relocated during a crisis; and even if some of these capabilities were destroyed, the small size of the Indian nuclear inventory makes such attacks a relatively wasteful proposition since they would not result in great and unacceptable damage to the Chinese state. Interdicting Chinese counterforce targets is therefore a losing proposition because there are probably more such targets than there will be Indian nuclear weapons; because China's relatively hardened systems could survive an Indian counterforce strike, while its softer mobile systems would simply be beyond the reach of Indian targeting capabilities; and, finally, because modest counterforce attacks would be strategically irrelevant either for true damage limitation or for effective retribution. The same judgment holds to an even greater extent where countermilitary targeting is concerned because the target set here consists of literally thousands of aim points that are clearly orders of magnitude larger than Indian nuclear capabilities would ever be. Even if many of these systems could be successfully destroyed, it is not clear whether their destruction would constitute adequate punishment for China's prior use of nuclear weapons against India.

---

modest counterforce capabilities. In the final analysis, however, success here would be contingent on India's ability to improve the accuracies of its missiles through the incorporation of advanced guidance systems and vastly increasing the number of nuclear weapons deployed in its stockpile. Because the former is likely to be easier than the latter, it is possible that significant counterforce capabilities, at least vis-à-vis China, will continue to elude New Delhi. Because of India's larger nuclear doctrine and the other components of its operational policy, this lack of counterforce capabilities is unlikely to become very troublesome to New Delhi.

Given these considerations, countervalue targeting alone holds promise of inflicting "destruction and punishment that the adversary will find unacceptable"[233] for any nuclear transgressions committed against India—at least in the context of an all-out war.[234] If China's vital centers—understood primarily as the cities that host significant fractions of its population, industry, and economic life—are treated as the principal foci of this countervalue targeting doctrine, it is easy to see why India's nuclear capabilities stand some chance of being both useful and effective instruments of punitive retaliation. To begin with, urban centers are generally soft targets that can be readily pulverized by overpressures as low as 5 psi. These levels of overpressure will kill large numbers of people while also contributing to additional casualties caused by the synergistic effects of blast, thermal radiation, nuclear fallout, and electromagnetic pulsation. Cities are also large targets, which makes them less sensitive to the accuracy constraints of India's present and future delivery systems. This implies that they can be held at risk even by relatively small and inaccurate weapons so long as these are employed in multiple numbers with the designated ground zeros adequately spaced in relation to the target perimeter—and even multiple weapon allocations may be unnecessary if the primary objective is simply to inflict significant numbers of casualties rather than attempting to destroy the city itself. Further, urban centers are fixed targets: They are easy to find using primitive methods of navigation and thus lend themselves to attack by a variety of delivery systems, including unconventional technologies in an emergency. Finally, and perhaps most important, urban centers offer maximum "bang for the buck" in that they represent concentrated targets hosting large fractions of several kinds of national resources, all located within a relatively compressed geographic locale. Even a cursory glance, for example, at China's five most heavily populated metropolitan complexes—Beijing, Shanghai, Hong Kong, Tianjin, and Shenyang—suggests that these cities represent principal concentrations of China's industrial capabilities, con-

---

[233]"Draft Report of [the] National Security Advisory Board on Indian Nuclear Doctrine," p. 3.

[234]Nair, *Nuclear India*, pp. 142–143, and Kanwal, "Nuclear Targeting Philosophy for India," pp. 459–473.

tribute disproportionately to its national income, and remain dense hubs for transport and communications.[235]

Successful nuclear attacks on such centers, therefore, would certainly constitute significant punishment in terms of the casualties suffered, and even the ensuing damage, though likely modest, would probably be far greater than the value of the objectives China presumably sought to obtain through its nuclear first use against India. This, at any rate, remains the judgment of some of India's most respected strategic thinkers, including K. Subrahmanyam and the late General Sundarji,[236] and it is therefore reasonable to suppose that India's targeting strategy vis-à-vis China would consist primarily of countervalue attacks aimed heavily at its vital centers in order to inflict massive casualties with the smallest possible expenditure of nuclear fires in case of any all-out war. While such punishment would certainly not destroy the Chinese polity—given the relative balance of power in the Sino-Indian case, no punishment that India could apply ever would—the strategic objective of such all-out attacks would nonetheless be to inflict such penalties as would threaten "to generate dangerous imbalances between that country and her primary adversaries [like the United States and Russia] and to seriously retard her economic growth to further aggravate [the postwar] global imbalances"[237] of power in the international system. This logic is highly reminiscent of British and French targeting doctrine vis-à-vis the Soviet Union during the Cold War, as defense planners in London and Paris would insistently suggest that the postwar "world geopolitical context"[238] always remained relevant to their nuclear strategy because "the adversary [would have to] consider the situation in which he would find himself after having suffered the destruction of a non-negligible part of his cities, of his industrial and administrative means, and of his communications, when the other great

---

[235]For details, see *The National Economic Atlas of China* (New York: Oxford University Press, 1994).

[236]Subrahmanyam, "Nuclear Defence Philosophy: Not a Numbers Game Anymore," and "India and the Nuclear Question: An Interview with General K. Sundarji, PVSM (Retd)," pp. 45–56.

[237]Nair, *Nuclear India*, p. 145.

[238]Yost, "French Nuclear Targeting," p. 134.

nuclear powers would retain the economic and military potential intact."[239]

Indian strategists who reiterate such arguments certainly exaggerate the geopolitical effects that New Delhi's relatively small nuclear strikes would have on China, but their understanding of why countervalue targeting is sensible for countries with small nuclear arsenals is reasonable. As early as 1947, when nuclear weapons were still limited in number and small in effect, U.S. strategists recognized that countervalue targeting would have significant deterrent effects because even small devices of the sort used on Hiroshima and Nagasaki could inflict significant casualties in highly compressed time frames and, as a result,

> would create a condition of chaos and extreme confusion. Not least of this would be an increased element of hopelessness and shock resulting from the magnitude of destruction; the fear of the unknown; the actual lingering physical after effect of atomic explosions; the psychological effect arising from the necessity to evacuate large densely populated areas; and the attendant psychological state which these factors create.[240]

A deeper appreciation of these consequences have subsequently led all the smaller nuclear powers to emphasize targeting cities per se as part of their ultimate punishment strategies because, as one French spokesman noted at the height of the Cold War,

> these targets are easy to reach, without great accuracy in the missiles required, and especially because one can thus cause important damage with a limited number of weapons. . . . It is only in the framework of an anticities strategy that the desirable level of damage can be guaranteed with the means that remain in proportion to the scientific, industrial, and economic possibilities of France. Any other strategy would necessitate much more important

---

[239]Ibid.

[240]"Strategic Implications of the Atomic Bomb, August 29, 1947, United States Joint Chiefs of Staff Modern Military Section," in Gregg Herken, *The Winning Weapon: The Atomic Bomb in the Cold War, 1945–1950* (New York: Vintage Books, 1981), p. 271.

means, without doubt beyond our reach, and could not but weaken deterrence.[241]

Because the smaller nuclear powers like France, the United Kingdom, and China possessed both a larger number of nuclear weapons and weapons that produced much higher yields in comparison to India's current and prospective strategic holdings, they could pursue true countervalue targeting strategies that focused on physically obliterating an adversary's principal conurbations. India's modest nuclear capabilities cannot be directed toward achieving identical effects, however, and to that degree the analogy with French nuclear doctrine vis-à-vis the Soviet Union breaks down because Paris, for all its weaknesses, had many more high-yield nuclear weapons than India would probably possess eventually. These capabilities made the French threats of inflicting real countervalue punishment much more credible against the Soviet Union than India's threats would be against China. Even in the French case, however, the analytical consensus was that Paris' deterrent threats were in practice quite incredible, and they obtained whatever efficacy they did, in the final analysis, only because of the positive externalities arising from the massive American deterrence of the Soviet Union.[242] Positive externalities of this sort may not be available in the Sino-Indian case, as Beijing could prosecute a war limited to India alone without involving any other potential nuclear adversaries—and consequently New Delhi, so long as it pursues an independent foreign policy, may not be able to always "free ride" under the deterrence umbrellas that may otherwise exist between the United States or Russia and China.

Recognizing all these facts, strategic thinkers like Subrahmanyam and Sundarji—reflecting the judgments of India's strategic managers on this issue—have argued not for an anticities strategy in the strict sense of the term but rather for an *antipopulation strategy* focusing on inflicting a high level of demographic damage relative to their estimation of the benefits an adversary could gain by nuclear use against India. Consequently, both Subrahmanyam and Sundarji con-

---

[241]Guy Lewin, "La dissuasion française et la stratégie anti-cités," *Défense Nationale*, January 1980, pp. 24 and 31, cited in Yost, "French Nuclear Targeting," p. 143.

[242]Yost, "French Nuclear Targeting," pp. 154–156.

stantly refer to the high costs of Hiroshima and Nagasaki in their writings, noting that "we know the results"[243] of even such limited nuclear use. This conclusion appears reasonable, however, only because it is explicitly based on the presumption that there are few benefits any adversary could gain through the use of nuclear weapons against India to begin with and, consequently, that even the high casualties caused by small nuclear attacks on civilian centers—at least relative to the historical norm in South Asia—would more than suffice to achieve effective deterrence. Other Indian analysts, however—not convinced either by this logic or by the deterrence value of such a targeting strategy—argue for true anticity capabilities instead and, accordingly, urge their government to induct high-yield nuclear weapons into the country's evolving stockpile.[244] One analyst summarized these demands succinctly by arguing that "the first requirement . . . for an effective and credible nuclear deterrent is the need for the Indian nuclear arsenal to be based on high yield thermonuclear weapons. . . . The second requirement, for an effective Indian nuclear deterrent force . . . is to accelerate the missile development programme, especially the development of ICBMs."[245] Demands such as these, however, are so fundamentally at odds with India's currently demonstrated capabilities that they are likely to remain simply exhortations emanating from yet another interest group in New Delhi, since India's security managers thus far appear to be satisfied that an antidemographic strategy—with the high costs it would impose on India's adversaries relative to the goals they might seek in their struggles with New Delhi—suffices to procure the kind of deterrence that would safeguard India's vital interests in all the feasible "unlimited" conflicts that can be imagined with Beijing and Islamabad.

The technical reasons India would continue to pursue a countervalue strategy *of this sort* vis-à-vis China also apply in the case of Pakistan, which has even fewer vital centers. The most populous

---

[243]"India and the Nuclear Question: An Interview with General K. Sundarji, PVSM (Retd)," p. 51, and Subrahmanyam, "Nuclear Defence Philosophy: Not a Numbers Game Anymore."

[244]See, by way of example, Nair, *Nuclear India*, p. 181; Karnad, "A Thermonuclear Deterrent," pp. 128–149; and Balachandran, "Nuclear Weaponization in India," pp. 47–48.

[245]Balachandran, "Nuclear Weaponization in India," pp. 47–48.

urban concentrations, such as Karachi, Lahore, Faisalabad, Rawalpindi, and Hyderabad, are also critical centers for heavy and light industry and for the processing of agricultural goods.[246] Any attacks on these cities would thus devastate both the economic fabric and the ideational embodiment of Pakistan. While it is logical, therefore, for India to systematically target these vital centers, the potentially larger size of New Delhi's nuclear inventory vis-à-vis Islamabad—at least eventually—and Pakistan's narrow geographic depth and high strategic vulnerabilities all interact to allow India to prosecute a wider range of countervalue options besides simply anticity targeting. This, at any rate, seems to be the judgment of Indian analysts like Nair and perhaps Karnad as well.[247] Pakistan's irrigation and water control systems in the Punjab and its main rail hubs in the central and southern portion of the country at Bahawalpur, Dera Ghazi Khan, and Hyderabad stand out as tempting targets in that attacks on the former would result in substantial damage to the heartland of the Pakistan state, whereas attacks on the latter would destroy the connectivity between the northern and southern portions of the country.[248] Many of these targets, however, are extraordinarily hard and, often requiring more than one weapon per aim point, become attractive magnets for interdiction if and only if India builds up a large enough arsenal that enables coverage of even marginal targets once its primary antidemographic orientation is satisfied.[249] If an inventory of such size is created, it is possible for New Delhi to consider even some countermilitary targeting vis-à-vis Islamabad. This requirement, however, is unlikely to acquire any priority—except in the case of a limited war—because countermilitary targeting can quickly degenerate into a bottomless sink in which a disproportionately large number of nuclear weapons must be expended in exchange for potentially meager operational results.[250]

---

[246]Surveyor General of Pakistan, *Atlas of Pakistan* (Rawalpindi, Pakistan: Survey of Pakistan, 1990), pp. 60–64 and 67–90.

[247]This issue is explored in some detail in Nair, *Nuclear India*, pp. 137–142, and elliptically in Karnad, "A Thermonuclear Deterrent," pp. 135–143.

[248]Nair, *Nuclear India*, pp. 137–142.

[249]See the discussion in Balachandran, "Nuclear Weaponization in India," pp. 42–47.

[250]For a brief description of the number of U.S. and Soviet weapons assigned to this role during the Cold War, see Salman et al., "Analysis or Propaganda? Measuring

Counterforce targeting is likely to receive even less attention from India simply because Pakistan's nuclear forces, which are steadily migrating to mobile ballistic missiles, will be largely undetectable in a conflict. India may slowly acquire the ability to detect and identify Pakistan's fixed nuclear storage sites over time, but attacking such sites—or the airfields thought to host nuclear-capable aircraft, for that matter—would be irrelevant in the context of a retaliatory response. If India were to use its nuclear weapons first and in a pre-emptive strike mode, counterforce attacks—assuming these could be executed flawlessly—might make some sense, but even these would require many more nuclear weapons than India might eventually possess, particularly if it seeks to comprehensively interdict the entire range of suspected targets with the intent of achieving damage limitation.[251] The Indian commitment to delayed retaliation, however, implies that attacking these facilities in the aftermath of absorbing a first strike is tantamount to closing the barn well after the horse has escaped. A doctrine of delayed retaliation effectively makes counterforce strikes anachronistic, and as long as Pakistan has minimal strategic warning, it is likely to rapidly disperse its nuclear forces to their wartime hides so as to frustrate any Indian temptation at launching a counterforce attack.[252] It is important to recognize that India currently has no capabilities whatsoever to detect critical mobile targets and it is unlikely to acquire such detection capabilities for many decades to come—and it will take just as long, if not longer, for India to develop the force architecture that enables it to success-

---

American Strategic Nuclear Capability, 1969–88," pp. 260–261. Even this description does not capture the 7000-odd theater and tactical nuclear warheads that NATO had judged to be essential for successfully interdicting Soviet theater nuclear forces and other military targets.

[251]Thus, for example, Indian analysts themselves note that attacking a single Pakistani air base with 20-kt weapons, assuming relatively small circular error probables (CEPs) of about 200 meters, would require the use of approximately four nuclear weapons in order to be assured a damage expectancy of 90 percent. See Balachandran, "Nuclear Weaponization in India," p. 44. Based on this calculation, attacks on the 26 Pakistani facilities supposedly capable of handling jet aircraft in 1988—see Eric Arnett, "Conventional Arms Transfers and Nuclear Stability in South Asia," in Eric Arnett (ed.), *Nuclear Weapons and Arms Control in South Asia After the Test Ban* (Oxford, UK: Oxford University Press, 1998), p. 81—would alone require at least 104 weapons or, equivalently, more than what is believed to be the entire Indian nuclear stockpile today.

[252]Arnett, "Conventional Arms Transfers and Nuclear Stability in South Asia," p. 84.

fully interdict such targets. Even when it does acquire such capabilities, these will be *relatively* more useful for attrition in the context of a protracted war than for executing damage-limiting strategies or increasing the effectiveness of Indian retaliation. This latter objective can be fulfilled productively only by countervalue targeting (which does not require a sophisticated C^3I system to begin with), and given India's overriding objective of avoiding nuclear attack, its targeting strategy will focus predominantly on inflicting punishment through strikes on Islamabad's vital centers even though it will have other marginal options vis-à-vis Pakistan. The strategic objective of any all-out Indian retribution in the case of Pakistan, however—unlike China—would be to simply destroy the state of Pakistan once and for all or, as Vijay Nair put it more delicately, "to inflict damage to the extent of degrading that country's capability of continuing as a socioeconomic entity."[253]

Since Indian targeting of Pakistan and China, and Pakistani and Chinese targeting of India in return, all ultimately rely on the ability to punish an assailant by holding at risk his most precious and vulnerable societal assets—populations residing in cities—the dominant nuclear strategy in South Asia is likely to remain one of mutual assured vulnerability. This is emphatically true in the case of India, which, by both design and circumstances, is wedded to a strategy of "delayed—but assured—retaliation" emphasizing varying levels of punishment. Whether this punishment is applied proportionately or massively, in graduated form or in a single spasm, will be determined only by the actual circumstances of conflict, even though India's prewar doctrine is likely to allude to the prospect of massive punishment executed "in one fell swoop telescoping mass and time."[254] To be sure, the Indian arsenal is not and never will be large enough to inflict comprehensive societal destruction on China, although it may be able to attain some analog of this outcome against Pakistan. Pakistan, in contrast, may not be able to inflict comprehensive societal destruction on India, although China would certainly be able to

---

[253]Nair, *Nuclear India*, p. 144. See also S. Gupta and W.P.S. Sidhu, "The End Game Option," *India Today*, April 30, 1993.

[254]The phrase is Curtis LeMay's and appears in David Alan Rosenberg, "The Origins of Overkill," in Steven E. Miller (ed.), *Strategy and Nuclear Deterrence* (Princeton, NJ: Princeton University Press, 1984), p. 39.

administer some facsimile of such punishment on India were it to allocate vastly larger numbers of its nuclear assets for this purpose than it presumably does today. The net result is that some version of mutual assured vulnerability, perhaps best described as "MAD Lite," will eventually obtain in the greater South Asian region even if it is not exactly defined in such terms either by India or by its other competitors.

This slow and gradual emergence of pervasive mutual vulnerability—a condition engendered as much by Indian operational policies as by those of its adversaries—not only represents a new strategic situation in Southern Asia but also heralds a transformation in India's own traditional attitude toward the morality of conflict. As many Indians are proudly wont to point out, "The region has [had] a record of responsibly conducted wars,"[255] since during all previous conflicts in Southern Asia, New Delhi, Islamabad, and Beijing "have displayed enormous restraint in willfully targeting civilians, industry or economic infrastructure, which is more than many in the West have done."[256] Such claims often overlook the fact that, historically, none of these three contestants ever possessed the technical wherewithal to prosecute such attacks—even on a smaller scale in comparison to, say, the Allied air campaigns over Germany and Japan during the Second World War—in the face of the competing demands made by other war-fighting missions. Nor were these adversaries ever locked into any "absolute" conflicts that required them to pursue war aims involving the kind of destruction that was inflicted, for example, during the Iraqi occupation of Kuwait, the Coalition's air offensive over Iraq, or the Allied bombing of Serbia over Kosovo. The presence of nuclear weapons in Southern Asia nonetheless promises to alter the traditional restraints with respect to all the *jus in bello* conditions elaborated by just-war theory insofar as New Delhi's operational strategy (and presumably those of its antagonists) would deliberately kill individuals instead of merely restraining them; attack noncombatants as a direct object of state policy; inflict wanton destruction and great suffering indiscriminately;

---

[255]Brahma Chellaney, "South Asia's Passage to Nuclear Power," *International Security*, 16:1 (Summer 1991), p. 68.

[256]Sundarji, "Changing Military Equations in Asia: The Role of Nuclear Weapons," p. 135.

and perhaps violate the principles of proportionality depending on the kinds of strategic responses unleashed in the face of an adversary's attack.[257]

Thoughtful Indians who have confronted this issue have attempted to defang the moral implications inherent in any countervalue targeting strategy by suggesting that India will seek ways to circumvent population attacks and may actually be compelled to do so because of peculiar problems associated with geographical proximity, uncertain meteorological factors, and cross-national kinship ties in the subcontinent.[258] However valid these arguments may be in the Indo-Pakistani context, they certainly do not carry over to a Sino-Indian conflict. Even so, they are not particularly persuasive because the technical quality and numerical limitations that define India's emerging nuclear capabilities (and Pakistan's, for that matter) leave New Delhi no alternative—for all the reasons described earlier—but to focus resolutely on population targeting as the ultimate guarantee of regional deterrence stability. To be sure, all political entities in Southern Asia could focus on using their nuclear weapons solely for countermilitary targeting in an effort to avoid the many moral conundrums arising from anticity or antipopulation targeting strategies. In India's case, however, such a solution is unlikely to be viewed as particularly efficacious either for bolstering deterrence or for inflicting retribution, and consequently New Delhi will most likely be compelled to emphasize countervalue targeting strategies as part of its retaliatory response in the context of an all-out subcontinental war. Thanks to the presence of nuclear weapons, India will consequently be faced—for the first time—with the burden of planning a military strategy that runs counter probably to its own instincts and certainly to its own history. Not surprisingly, then, a military officer like Sundarji, when addressing the question of the morality of Indian nuclear strategy, could do little more than rationalize its benefits by arguing that "however morally repugnant it might be, there is no choice but to target cities in the hope that these plans would never

---

[257]For more on these conditions see James F. Childress, "Just-War Criteria," in Thomas A. Shannon, *War or Peace? The Search for New Answers* (New York: Orbis Books, 1980), pp. 40–58.

[258]Chellaney, "South Asia's Passage to Nuclear Power," pp. 68–69.

need to be executed."[259] In reiterating this argument, he and other Indian security managers, who would argue similarly, clearly indicate that nuclear weapons *will* cause New Delhi to move away from its own traditional moral preferences and closer to the Western justification, which affirms the permissibility of nuclear threats directed at civilians by arguing, in the words of Michael Novak, that "those who intend to prevent the use of nuclear weapons by maintaining a system of deterrence in readiness for use do *intend* to use such weapons, but only in order not to use them, and do threaten to use them, but only in order to *deter* their use."[260]

When all is said and done, however, it is important to recognize that the countervalue targeting doctrine described above refers only to the *peacetime* preferences of policymakers in New Delhi. What exactly may occur under conditions of deterrence breakdown is anyone's guess. As James Schlesinger once noted, "Doctrines control the minds of men only in periods of non-emergency. They do not necessarily control the minds of men during periods of emergency. In the moment of truth, when the possibility of major devastation occurs, one is likely to discover sudden changes in doctrine."[261] It should not be surprising, therefore, to find that under conditions of actual war, Indian policymakers may behave quite differently than their prewar doctrines suggest. In all likelihood, though, such deviation would occur in the direction of reducing the quantum of punishment applied initially, not increasing it—particularly if New Delhi were to suffer a less-than-all-out attack at the hands of a superior power. Even if discrete attacks were to be undertaken by a weaker power like Pakistan, it is not at all clear whether India would in fact respond

---

[259]Sundarji, "Changing Military Equations in Asia: The Role of Nuclear Weapons," p. 136.

[260]Michael Novak, *Moral Clarity in the Nuclear Age* (Nashville: Thomas Nelson, 1983), p. 59. For an extended analysis of this issue, see Tellis, "Nuclear Arms, Moral Questions, and Religious Issues," pp. 599–622.

[261]United States Congress, Senate Committee on Foreign Relations, Subcommittee on United States Security Agreements and Commitments Abroad, *Nuclear Weapons and Foreign Policy*, hearings before the Subcommittee on U.S. Security Agreements and Commitments Abroad and the Subcommittee on Arms Control, International Law and Organization of the Committee on Foreign Relations, United States Senate, 93rd Congress, Second Session, on U.S. Nuclear Weapons in Europe and U.S.-U.S.S.R. Strategic Doctrines and Policies, March 7, 14, and April 4, 1974 (Washington, D.C.: USGPO, 1974) p. 160.

"massively" so long as the constraining conditions described earlier continue to hold. On those rare occasions where they might actually choose to address such matters, however, Indian policymakers will most likely continue to harp on the prospect of massive punishment whenever delivered. This declamatory position is logical given India's strong desire to prevent any breach of the existing breakwaters that restrain nuclear weapon use.[262]

As their nuclear arsenal matures over time, however, Indian policymakers—like their U.S. counterparts during the Cold War—will most likely formally develop some modest options that seek to preserve targeting flexibility. These options will not take the same form as they did in the case of the United States, where enormous resources were poured into developing varied Selective, Limited, and Regional Nuclear Options, together with gigantic investments in strategic connectivity, designed for the conduct of a protracted nuclear war.[263] Targeting flexibility in India's case will most likely involve the ability to execute discrete, possibly graduated responses that allow for something other than immediate anticity targeting so that Indian security managers will have options that enable them to equalize damage if need be while simultaneously signaling their resolve to escalate to even higher levels of violence in order to bring about a rapid termination of conflict.[264]

This does not imply the need for any specialized tactical weapons, however, and Jaswant Singh in particular has explicitly ruled out the acquisition of all such devices by asserting, "Regarding tactical nuclear weapons, let me remind you that we do not see nuclear

---

[262]For a good survey of Indian views on this issue, see Kanwal, "Nuclear Targeting Philosophy for India," pp. 459–473.

[263]Desmond Ball, "The Development of the SIOP, 1960–1983," in Desmond Ball and Jeffrey Richelson (eds.), *Strategic Nuclear Targeting* (Ithaca, NY: Cornell University Press, 1986), p. 81ff.

[264]For a good discussion about the dynamics of terminating nuclear conflicts, albeit in the U.S.-Soviet context, see Stephen J. Cimbala and Sidney R. Waldman (eds.), *Controlling and Ending Conflict* (New York: Greenwood Press, 1992).

weapons as weapons of warfighting."[265] Therefore, if India finally ends up possessing some "tactical" weapons, they will be owed more to the emerging pressures of bureaucratic politics and to the determination of India's "strategic enclaves" to prove their worth than to any coherent national strategy demanding such devices as necessary to sustain a strategy of proportionate retaliation. What is in fact more likely is that if India sought to respond to a limited attack proportionately, it would seek to use its existing fission weapons in controlled but operationally creative ways with the intention of forcing speedy war termination. Jasjit Singh corroborated this when he argued that specialized tactical weapons are unnecessary for India because "in reality, it is the effect of the use of [nuclear] weapons that must determine the definition of whether they are tactical or strategic."[266] Sundarji addressed this problem as well by noting that even if a limited nuclear attack does occur at a tactical level, India's standard fission devices of 10- to 20-kt yield would suffice for a limited counterresponse: As he framed the issue, if deterrence fails because an adversary has used its weapons in a limited way to secure either some symbolic or battlefield advantages, "the second strike [may] not be on tactical point targets but on tactical area targets that abound in the combat zone. Most of these are optimally attacked by weapons of yields of 10–20 kt fired as low air bursts (producing hardly any fallout). Hence, there is no need to produce unique tactical nuclear weapons."[267] What is most significant about Singh's and Sundarji's position, in the final analysis, is that even at the tactical level the philosophy is not nuclear war fighting in the event of nuclear deterrence breakdown but rather the application of that minimal level of force—using only the standard weapons already possessed by New Delhi—to permit a restoration of the prior condition of nuclear deterrence leading up to conflict termination. As Sundarji phrased it simply, "at the tactical level also, the philosophy is nuclear deterrence."[268]

---

[265]"India Not to Engage in a N-Arms Race: Jaswant."

[266]Singh, "A Nuclear Strategy for India," p. 317.

[267]Sundarji, "Changing Military Equations in Asia: The Role of Nuclear Weapons," p. 135.

[268]Ibid. See also Singh, "A Nuclear Strategy for India," p. 317.

On balance, therefore, these arguments suggest that if restricted Indian retaliatory responses are required in the face of limited attacks for purposes of enforcing intrawar deterrence, Indian policymakers could find appropriate solutions within the constraints of their existing nuclear inventory. And since the possibility of limited attacks on India cannot be ruled out—these kinds of attacks being, in fact, the most probable, according to Indian readings of the threat[269]—it is likely that New Delhi will formalize a variety of strategic plans over time that enable it to respond *proportionately* both to maintain the credibility of its retaliatory threats—"the power to hurt [which] is most successful when held in reserve"[270]—and to minimize the extent of damage India could suffer in the event that deterrence breaks down. Even as they develop such solutions in private, however, Indian policymakers will strive to avoid conveying any impression that they are contemplating nuclear war-fighting strategies involving the discrete use of their strategic weaponry. Thus, the mental images underlying all their public discussions will continue to insinuate that *any* nuclear use against India would invoke massive and catastrophic counterattacks, irrespective of when they were delivered. This emphasis on large-scale retaliation in the face of any nuclear attack, reminiscent of French nuclear doctrine during the Cold War, is obviously designed primarily to shore up deterrence and avert the prospect that India will fall victim to any kind of nuclear threat. While such an emphasis is understandable, it is unlikely to be useful in the context of deterrence breakdown that results in any actual nuclear use—especially low levels of use—by a superior or an equal adversary.[271]

In such circumstances, New Delhi's primary objective may consist of inflicting retribution, but this objective will have to be balanced against what it takes to achieve speedy war termination at minimal cost to India. This issue will certainly remain most relevant vis-à-vis

---

[269]K. Subrahmanyam, "A Credible Deterrent: Logic of the Nuclear Doctrine," *The Times of India*, October 4, 1999.

[270]Schelling, *Arms and Influence*, p. 3.

[271]K. Subrahmanyam, in fact, argues that limited attacks alone remain the only serious possibilities that India ought to plan for and contend against. See Subrahmanyam, "A Credible Deterrent." See also Singh, "Why Nuclear Weapons?" and Singh, "A Nuclear Strategy for India," pp. 9–25 and 306–324.

China but will rapidly become relevant vis-à-vis Pakistan as well, as Islamabad continues to accumulate the nuclear weapons required to comprehensively target more and more Indian urban centers deep within the subcontinental landmass. In such circumstances, responding to limited nuclear attacks with "massive retaliation" will only precipitate strategically meaningless forms of mutual devastation. Given these considerations, it is reasonable to expect that India's nuclear doctrine will eventually incorporate something akin to a "countervalue plus" targeting orientation that still presupposes mutual assured vulnerability at bottom but integrates the capacity for more flexible responses in order to ensure that punishment, whenever inflicted, can be proportionate and lead eventually to speedy conflict termination at the most minimal cost to India. This capability obviously inheres in India's nuclear reserves even today, but it will only become more salient in the country's strategic planning as India's nuclear doctrine and force structure mature over time.

FASHIONING A DETERRENT: THE LOGIC AND STRUCTURE OF THE EVOLVING FORCE-IN-BEING

The character of India's nuclear doctrine, explored in the last section, clearly suggests why the traditional alternative of "maintaining the option"—Alternative III described in Chapter Three—cannot be a destination to which New Delhi will return in the aftermath of its May 1998 tests. This alternative, by eschewing the development of an arsenal of *any* sort, simply renders the doctrine elaborated above irrelevant and consequently will not be pursued, since New Delhi has already determined that a real nuclear capability is essential for its security. Alternative IV—the "recessed deterrent"—will be rejected as well, since its emphasis on supporting capabilities to the exclusion of producing nuclear weapons and delivery systems prevents the development of those critical components that India's larger doctrine requires. In contrast, Alternative V—a "robust and ready arsenal"—clearly enables New Delhi to pursue the strategy encoded by its nuclear doctrine but, by being too expensive, violating its desire for strict civilian control, and possibly being subversive of crisis stability, represents a posture that is much too extravagant to suit India's deterrence needs.

The idea of a nuclear "force-in-being"[272] as a middling option between Alternatives IV and V—illustrated in Figure 3—is therefore particularly attractive to New Delhi because it bequeaths to India a deterrent capability against strategic coercion and blackmail without all the attendant problems of exorbitant cost and diluted civilian control. These advantages accrue directly from the character of a nuclear arsenal maintained as a force-in-being: The weapons and delivery systems *are* developed and produced, with key subcomponents maintained under civilian custody, but these assets as a whole are *not* deployed in any way that enables the prompt conduct of nuclear operations. Such assets are, in fact, sequestered and covertly maintained in distributed form, with different custodians exercising strict stewardship over the components entrusted to them for safekeeping.

This distributed posture can be maintained indefinitely, with the various parts never reconstituted to form a true war-fighting force except in the aftermath of a nuclear attack against India. This specific posture, exemplifying the "base case" that defines the routine disposition of India's nuclear assets, allows for several variations that will be discussed in greater detail later. But the key idea encompassed by the notion of a force-in-being is that the entire "arsenal," understood as the sum of its component parts, functions as a *strategic reserve* that is neither fully visible nor operationally ready habitually yet is nonetheless present and available for employment—after some preparation—when strategic necessity so dictates. Such a force, by definition, will not be maintained regularly on high levels of alert. Indeed, it may hardly ever be reconstituted in peacetime in its entirety except for purposes of an exercise, and when such activity occurs, it would in all probability take place without any notice or fanfare un-

---

[272]The phrase "force-in-being" occurs in passing and only once in Nair, *Nuclear India*, p. 96, but the concept is not developed and has no analytical significance in his work. The concept of the force-in-being elaborated here, however, is compatible with many of Nair's ideas and comports broadly with the notions of deterrence sufficiency held by most of the "pragmatists" in the Indian strategic debate, whence it has migrated into the official depiction of India's nuclear posture as elaborated both in public statements and in high-level talks carried out with the United States.

less it is consciously intended to be an effort at "deliberate capability revelation."[273]

Its key distinguishing characteristic, therefore, is quiescence at the operational level—which does not, however, translate into inactivity at the strategic level of politics. A force-in-being is indeed highly active at the grand strategic levels of diplomacy and political choice, but this activity is manifested not so much by its tempo as by its effects. Its very existence as a potentially complete—but dormant—capability serves as a deterrent to possible adventurism by an adversary: It constantly hovers in an adversary's consciousness, commands its attention, keeps it at bay, and prevents it from attempting anything that would result in risk and hazard to itself while constantly obliging it to think of nothing but being on guard against the terrible attack that would follow in retaliation against any of its provocations.[274]

The nuclear force-in-being is therefore a deterrent whose effectiveness derives from its ability to be constituted into a viable retaliatory instrument under conditions of supreme emergency—usually, but not invariably, understood to mean after a nuclear attack on India has occurred. And because it is recognized that such reconstitution could occur in hours to days rather than in months to years—and would embody fairly unacceptable levels of destruction relative to the political goals sought to be secured by force—it can serve to deny even stronger or more ready adversaries the freedom to exploit the fruits of their nuclear threats or use. A robust and ready arsenal would obviously achieve these goals just as effectively as a force-in-being, but it would do so at a much higher cost to India. A recessed deterrent, in contrast, would be highly inadequate because the time required to generate the retaliatory response could take months or perhaps even years and, as such, would allow a potential adversary to discount the penalties of long-postponed retaliation and embark on a course of action that promised to yield relatively painless rewards in the near term. A nuclear force-in-being strikes a convenient mid-

---

[273]For more on this, see Kevin N. Lewis, *Getting More Deterrence Out of Deliberate Capability Revelation*, N-2873-AF (Santa Monica: RAND, 1989).

[274]This sentence is based on Captain Richard Kempenfelt's famous description of a fleet-in-being, cited in Geoffrey Till, *Maritime Strategy and the Nuclear Age*, 2nd ed. (New York: St. Martin's Press, 1984), p. 114.

dle ground: It avoids interminable delays in retribution, thus solving the "discounting problem"[275] associated with a recessed deterrent, while escaping all the financial costs and political burdens that arise from the demand for prompt punishment, which necessarily requires a robust and ready arsenal.

Not surprisingly, a deterrence posture modeled on the notion of a force-in-being also seems to function as the template governing the disposition of other Indian strategic assets. Two examples are particularly relevant here for the light they shed on the problem of how India's nuclear forces are deployed today and how they would be deployed in the future. The first example pertains to the manner in which New Delhi acquired and deployed its chemical weaponry. India covertly pursued a large chemical weapon research, development, and production program for almost two decades prior to the conclusion of the CWC, which banned all such weapons universally. Although this effort was tracked by the American intelligence community[276] and was even identified by knowledgeable public sources in the United States,[277] the Indian government consistently denied the existence of a chemical weapon program in the early years of the negotiations leading up to the CWC.[278] The research, development,

---

[275]The discounting problem arises as a result of the belief that because rational actors prefer benefits in the present rather than in the future, they are more likely to choose courses of action that generate benefits "today" if the costs of such actions can be deferred until "tomorrow." This process of "discounting" future costs or penalties often lies at the root of many pathologies of rationality, and any good deterrence strategy has to find ways of minimizing these discounted future costs if it is to be effective in the present. For more on the discounting problem at a theoretical level, see Robert Sugden and Alan Williams, *The Principles of Practical Cost-Benefit Analysis* (Oxford, UK: Oxford University Press, 1978).

[276]See the discussion in E. J. Hogendoorn, "A Chemical Weapons Atlas," *Bulletin of the Atomic Scientists*, 53:5 (September 1997), p. 38.

[277]Office of Technology Assessment, *Proliferation of Weapons of Mass Destruction: Assessing the Risks*, OTA-ISC-559 (Washington, D.C.: USGPO, 1993).

[278]The Federation of American Scientists notes that "when the Third UN Disarmament Conference, held in 1988, decided that the next logical step in the disarmament process would be measures to halt production of chemical weapons, Indian diplomats responded by claiming that India had no chemical weapons. Foreign Minister K. Natwar Singh repeated this claim in 1989 in the Paris Conference of the State Parties to the Geneva Protocol of 1925, as did Minister of State Eduardo Faleiro . . . at the January 1993 Paris Conference CWC signing ceremony." See "India: Chemical Weapons," available at http://www.fas.org/nuke/guide/india/cw/, which remains the best summary description of India's chemical weapon program.

and production activities associated with this effort were conducted exclusively at civilian facilities owned and operated by the DRDO, and one Indian source has identified the Defence Research Development Establishment (DRDE) in Gwalior as the principal center for "research on physical and medical protection against chemical weapons."[279] The Indian military, which presumably would have been the end user of these weapons in an emergency, was largely in the dark about the character and the extent of these capabilities and was never tasked with the obligation of integrating these weapons into existing contingency plans. This led one serving officer to erroneously conclude in 1989 that "India has very patently no chemical warfare capability and no design whatsoever to acquire such weapons."[280] In any event, instead of being distributed to the end users in peacetime, India's chemical weapons—which included artillery shells—were treated as *strategic national assets*, maintained completely under the control of the civilian Ministry of Defence and intended for transfer to the uniformed military only when its security managers in New Delhi determined that these weapons were to be used as part of a retaliatory response in the aftermath of a chemical attack on India.[281]

Since the defense services had neither the information nor the control or custody of these weapons, they could not be used in the conduct of routine military operations. Their use was reserved instead for retaliatory purposes only, and the necessity and circumstances of such use were to be determined solely by India's civilian security managers at the highest reaches of the government. It is most likely that New Delhi's chemical weapon program would never have become public knowledge had it not been for India's accession to the CWC. As part of the ratification process institutionalized by this convention, India was required to identify its chemical weapon production facilities and storage sites, and only when it did so did information about New Delhi's chemical capabilities become news

---

[279]Joshi, "Chemical Weapons Convention: Under Scrutiny," p. 60.

[280]D. Banerjee, "The Future of Chemical Warfare and India," *Combat Journal*, August 1989, p. 84.

[281]See *India: Report Views Country's Stockpile of Chemical Weapons*, FBIS-TAC-97-182, July 1, 1997; *India: Article Views Posture on CWC, Real Case*, FBIS-TAC-97-189, July 8, 1997; and Manoj Joshi, "Chemical Confessions," *India Today*, July 7, 1997, p. 76.

both to the rank and file of India's military and to the country at large.[282]

The Indian government's handling of its chemical weaponry illustrates the kind of response that is likely to mark its handling of the nuclear arsenal as well. Obviously, there are important differences with respect to the latter: Here, the quest for a deterrent of some sort and the fact that India is already known to possess nuclear weapons in some form are extremely relevant. In contrast, India's desire for and ownership of chemical weapons was a state secret unknown to all but a few in India and in the United States. Consequently, India's chemical weaponry could not serve as a force-in-being in the same way that its nuclear weapons actually will in the future. This critical difference, however, should not be allowed to obscure the important similarities that the two cases share, especially with respect to New Delhi's continuing determination to provide minimal information about its capabilities while exercising maximal control over its weaponry. The example of India's chemical weapon program in fact remains a good baseline for describing India's future approach to and control over its nuclear force-in-being, for as one Indian commentator noted, it makes "the telling point that notwithstanding the deception, which was in any case in the national interest, the declared possession of chemical weapons will be a deterrent to those who think India's posture on such issues is all a bluff. No one, least of all the prime minister, wants to talk about nuclear weapons. But the implications are obvious."[283]

Another example that is relevant to understanding how India's nuclear force-in-being may eventually be configured derives from its handling of its SRBMs, notably the land-based versions of the Prithvi. The Prithvi SRBM is intended to be a conventional deep attack system that will eventually be available in three different range variants with five alternative types of conventional warheads.[284] Although these systems were originally envisaged to be mere corps-level assets

---

[282]See Joshi, "Chemical Weapons Convention: Under Scrutiny," and Joshi, "Chemical Confessions."

[283]Ibid.

[284]The history of the Prithvi program is recounted in Sidhu, *The Development of an Indian Nuclear Doctrine Since 1980*, pp. 246–268.

similar to the Advanced Tactical Missile (ATACM) system deployed by the U.S. Army, fears about the Prithvi's nuclear potential, raised by both Pakistan and the United States, led India to treat its Prithvi force as if it were a strategic asset held in inert reserve. The Indian Army's missile inventory, for example, is not deployed in the accepted sense of the term—that is, maintained by its controlling units in their designated area of operation. The unit slated to operate the missiles, the 333rd Missile Group, is in fact based in Secunderabad in South India, far from its wartime operating location, while the missiles themselves are secured in storage bunkers—unfueled—close to the Indo-Pakistani border.[285] This separation of the operating units from their weaponry—and the storage of the weapons themselves in dormant status—creates together a force-in-being. This missile force is certainly not ready for prompt operations: The operating unit would require a few days to arrive at the front line from its peacetime locations in southern India, and many hours would then be needed to recover the weapons from storage, mate them with the launch equipment, test the reconstituted systems, and disperse to various presurveyed firing locations, followed by a few more hours to fuel the missiles and actually launch them.[286] The Prithvi force therefore remains a good example of a weapon system held in operational reserve. Even as it exists in a dormant state, however, the missiles are *strategically* active in that they serve as visible, recognized reminders of India's capability to inflict punishment and, to that degree, presumably contribute to maintaining stable deterrence in South Asia.[287]

Both the chemical weapon program and the Prithvi SRBM force highlight two separate but related characteristics of the future Indian nuclear force-in-being. The former example suggests that the nuclear arsenal will be highly opaque, with great deception, denial, conceal-

---

[285]Greg J. Gerardi, "India's 333rd Prithvi Missile Group," *Jane's Intelligence Review*, 7:8 (August 1995), pp. 361–364; R. Jeffrey Smith, "India Moves Missiles Near Pakistani Border," *Washington Post*, June 3, 1997; and "India's Missile Move," *Washington Post*, June 9, 1997.

[286]For details, see Pravin Sawhney, "How Inevitable Is an Asian Missile Race?" *Jane's Intelligence Review*, 12:1 (January 2000), p. 31.

[287]For a good argument on how nondeployment could contribute to stability, see Gaurav Kampani, "Prithvi: The Case for 'No-First-Deployment,'" *Rediff on the Net*, available at http://www.rediff.com/news/jul/10kamp.htm.

ment, and mobility used to hide the location of critical assets like weapons, delivery systems, assembly sites, and wartime command posts. Information about all the details pertaining to these assets will be hidden from most, including the rank and file of the Indian military, whose senior officers will be told primarily what they need to know in order to develop contingency plans relating to retaliation in the aftermath of a nuclear attack. In this context, the leadership and the senior staff of the new unified command—which may be created to oversee the delivery systems earmarked for nuclear missions—and the senior leadership of the three Indian armed services (together with their staffs) would be the most likely agents entrusted with the information necessary to plan the conduct of nuclear operations. The latter example suggests that the nuclear arsenal will be distributed with weapons, and possibly even parts of weapons, kept separate both from one another and from the delivery systems. While the delivery vehicles will remain in military custody because they are war-fighting instruments per se, their final organizational disposition is as yet unclear: The delivery vehicles may be routinely maintained by their parent services and earmarked for reallocation to the prospective unified command in the event of deterrence breakdown, or, albeit less probably, they may be sequestered, maintained, and deployed routinely by the new command that may be created to oversee India's strategic assets. The resolution of this issue will no doubt be conditioned substantially by the kinds of delivery systems in question: Dual-capable aircraft of the sort currently in the Indian inventory will likely be retained by the Indian Air Force both in peacetime and in war, with some units earmarked for allocation to the unified command in the event that nuclear operations become necessary. In contrast, the dedicated nuclear missile systems of the sort not yet present in the Indian inventory are likely to be procured and routinely maintained by the new unified command for use in the event of a nuclear deterrence breakdown. Irrespective of which organizational model is followed in the details, India's dedicated nuclear delivery systems are in general likely to be deployed primarily in standby condition (except for combat aircraft, which, almost by definition, are dual-capable systems) at locations that will be neither openly acknowledged nor perhaps close to the borders with Pakistan and China. Only when these systems are required in moments of supreme emergency would the various component parts of the deterrent writ large be brought together, integrated, and formally released to the end user—the uniformed military—with the objective of executing the acts of vengeance demanded by India's retaliatory response.[288]

Both of these examples therefore serve to limn the future shape of India's nuclear deterrent, which may be summarily described as *a force-in-being that will be limited in size, separated in disposition, and centralized in control.* Each of these variables will be analyzed further in some detail. Before that investigation is undertaken, however, one important inference ought to be underscored. The Indian decision to develop a force-in-being implies that New Delhi's post-1998 nuclear posture—despite all the contrary rhetoric and expectations aired in New Delhi, Islamabad, and elsewhere in the world—will not be *radically* different from that which has been in place since 1992–1994. The biggest difference, of course, is that India today is a declared nuclear weapon power, and as such its national leadership can openly discuss its nuclear capabilities both in Parliament and with external interlocutors if they so choose. The myriad research-and-development efforts pertaining to India's emerging nuclear capabilities can also be carried out without the pervasive subterfuge of the past, and planning for strategic nuclear operations (including completing the organizational changes mandated by these efforts) can similarly be pursued far more systematically and without hesitation, embarrassment, or dissembling. Although these differences are not trivial, they will for all practical purposes define the outer limits of change that are likely to become manifest with India's new declaration of nuclear status. On all other matters, however, the continuities between India's post-1992–1994 variant of "maintaining the option" and its post-1998 posture of developing a force-in-being will be far greater and much more significant than most public commentators in India, Pakistan, and the United States often seem to recognize.

Limited in Size

All Indian discussions about their future force posture uniformly emphasize one element: that the desired nuclear deterrent will be

---

[288]For an excellent summary of this particular posture, see K. Sundarji, "Prithvi in the Haystack," *India Today International*, June 30, 1997, p. 49.

limited in size. Prime Minister Atal Bihari Vajpayee, using language that is by now fairly common among the country's strategic community, authoritatively staked out this position in Parliament when he asserted that India would not seek more than a "minimum, but credible, nuclear deterrent."[289] A senior government official, believed to be National Security Adviser Brajesh Mishra, elaborated on this locution by observing that a minimum deterrent implied "a defensive orientation for India's nuclear forces and a commitment to avoid a nuclear arms race."[290] Leading strategic analysts have amplified this leitmotif, with K. Subrahmanyam, for example, arguing that India is now "in a position to avoid all the disastrous mistakes of the nuclear theologians and to think through [its] own strategy in the light of recent nuclear strategic wisdom."[291] This strategy, he avers, is centered "on minimum deterrence combined with no-first use."[292] Jasjit Singh, corroborating this argument, has asserted that "even in the worst case scenario, the maximum capability that India would ever need is that of minimum deterrence. There is, thus, virtually no risk of an open-ended arms race in the subcontinent."[293]

Very rarely, some commentators have given vent to dissenting views on this question. Brigadier V. P. Naib, for example, asserted that

> Security depends upon assuming the worst possible case and developing the ability to cope with it. We must be able to absorb the total weight of a nuclear attack on our nuclear stockpiles and installations, on our air ground and naval capacity to make war, our vital industrial complexes, oil installations, on our cities and on our people. We can only do this by having in readiness a reliable ability to inflict unacceptable damage at any time during the strategic exchange, or as Mr. McNamara termed it, "an assured destruction capability." This is the true meaning of deterrence, and *it cannot be achieved by the so-called minimum deterrence nor by the govern-*

---

[289]Basu, "Nuclear Doctrine Emerges, but Tension Mounts on Border," p. 26.

[290]C. Raja Mohan, "India Committed to Minimum N-Deterrence," *The Hindu*, December 7, 1998.

[291]Subrahmanyam, "Educate India in Nuclear Strategy."

[292]Ibid.

[293]Singh, "South Asian Nuclear Scene."

*ment's bland assurances that "it will be able to retaliate at short no-
tice, when the need arises"* [italics added].[294]

In a similar vein, one of India's most prominent civilian hawks,
Bharat Karnad, chastised the Indian government for pursuing "policy
constructs found in the 'lamplight' of 'minimum deterrence' [when]
other, more effective, solutions lie shimmering in the broad 'daylight'
of deterrence history."[295] These more effective solutions are personified by what Karnad calls a "maximally strategic"[296] deterrence
posture built around multiple kinds of high-yield nuclear weapons
and numerous diverse delivery systems that, taken together, would
create the "full and robust deterrent"[297] deemed essential for the
success of India's national purpose.

Such arguments, however, constitute the outer limits of the Indian
strategic debate and do not appear to command a strong following
among the civilian leadership at the political and the bureaucratic
levels, the higher leadership of the armed services, or the more numerous retired service officers who have written on this subject.
Among this last group, a more typical example is represented by
Major General (retired) Ashok Mehta, who noted that "minimum deterrence and an NFU [no-first-use] policy allow for the maintenance
of a limited nuclear arsenal—warheads and delivery systems—and a
small, not-too-elaborate command and control structure. This
makes the strategic deterrent affordable and prevents a nuclear arms
race."[298] In a similar but even more relaxed vein, former Indian Chief
of Army Staff General V. P. Malik seemed to suggest that India's May
1998 nuclear tests themselves functioned as some sort of limited
deterrent, since they demonstrated the country's nuclear weapon
capability and in so doing "had fulfilled a long-standing demand of
the armed forces."[299]

---

[294]V. P. Naib, "The Nuclear Threat," *Indian Defence Review*, 8:1 (January 1993),
pp. 61–62.

[295]Karnad, "A Thermonuclear Deterrent," p. 108.

[296]Ibid., p. 135.

[297]Ibid., p. 133.

[298]Ashok K. Mehta, "Case for a Nuclear Doctrine with Minimum Deterrence,"
India Abroad, August 28, 1998.

[299]*India's Malik Satisfied with N-Weaponry*, FBIS-NES-98-149, May 29, 1998.

While the general consensus in India, both among civilian commentators and within the armed services, thus seems to converge on the desirability of a "minimum deterrent," it is not surprising to find that Indian "defence experts . . . seem to be divided over . . . what constitutes a minimum deterrent."[300] This should not be startling because the concept of minimum deterrence—having been borrowed from Western debates on the subject—has been controversial from the very beginning of its history. The simplest conceptions of minimum deterrence have defined it as a "nuclear strategy in which a nation (or nations) maintains the minimum number of nuclear weapons necessary to inflict unacceptable damage on its adversary even after it has suffered a nuclear attack."[301] Intuitively, this definition suggests that such a nuclear force would be oriented toward countervalue targeting, since the small number of weapons presumably implied by the qualifier "minimum" ultimately requires "city-busting" strategies if the necessity for "unacceptable damage" is to be adequately satisfied. This predicate of minimum deterrence, however, left many theorists dissatisfied on both moral and prudential grounds, and consequently a number of alternatives ranging from "finite counterforce" to "limited nuclear options" were advanced to allow for the possibility of limiting damage and controlling escalation if deterrence were ever to fail.[302] Each of these alternatives, however, brought new problems in their wake, none of which was satisfactorily resolved during the Cold War. Not surprisingly, then, the notion of "minimum deterrence," defined as "a secure second-strike force of sufficient size to make threats of AD [assured destruction] credible,"[303] came to be seen more as an ideal type that was valuable because it provided an eidetic image that contrasted strongly with its polar opposite, "maximum deterrence," which, defined as a posture

---

[300] *India: Defense Experts Differ on Nuclear Deterrence,* FBIS-NES-98-167, June 16, 1998.

[301] H. B. Hollins, Averill L. Powers, and Mark Sommer, *The Conquest of War: Alternative Strategies for Global Security* (Boulder, CO: Westview Press, 1989), pp. 54–55.

[302] See, for example, David Lewis, "Finite Counterforce," in H. Shue (ed.), *Nuclear Deterrence and Moral Restraint* (Cambridge, UK: Cambridge University Press, 1989), pp. 51–115, and Lawrence Martin, *Minimum Deterrence,* Faraday Discussion Paper No. 8 (London: Council for Arms Control, 1987).

[303] Barry Buzan, *Strategic Studies: Military Technology and International Relations* (London: Macmillan, 1987), p. 193.

"capable of fighting, and in some sense winning, nuclear wars across a spectrum of contingencies,"[304] was thought to better define the orientation of both U.S. and Soviet nuclear forces during the high point of superpower competition.

Since the notion of minimum deterrence did not (and could not) define any unique force size or structure, it was compatible with numerous nuclear architectures ranging from a few dozen warheads through a few hundred to perhaps even a few thousand weapons, all depending on the strength, resilience, and risk-taking propensities of the adversary. Irrespective of the number of weapons deemed to be dictated by this conception, however, what was most conspicuous about Western views on minimum deterrence was the unifying belief that "the main challenge [was how] to achieve [stability] at lower nuclear force levels,"[305] since managing the system of nuclear deterrence remained the key concern of high politics, particularly among the great powers. The specific problem, then, consisted of appreciating the limits of "successive build-down"[306]—in other words, the floor beyond which progressively deeper cuts in the number of nuclear weapons could not be safely undertaken because there was an "expectation of a critical threshold below which strategic stability would be uncertain."[307] In contrast to such Western concerns, the Indian approach toward minimum deterrence involves the opposite problem. Although most Indian strategists would readily admit, in the words of Uday Bhaskar, that minimum deterrence is a "relative term" and that "every country has to have its own minimum deterrent based on an empirical analysis of [the] regional strategic scenario and the enemy's potential,"[308] the specific challenge facing New Delhi today is that of a *buildup*—not a drawdown—of its nuclear forces, given that its strategic deterrent hitherto has been largely latent, symbolic, and nominal. This challenge of finding an appropriate ceiling to bound India's nuclear capabilities, however, generates a question similar to that engendered by the Western de-

---

[304]Ibid., p. 194.

[305]Karp, in Sur (ed.), *Nuclear Deterrence: Problems and Perspectives in the 1990s*, p. 122.

[306]Ibid., p. 123.

[307]Ibid.

[308]*India: Defense Experts Differ on Nuclear Deterrence.*

bate—namely, how much is enough for purposes of both deterrence and stability.

This question exercised Western strategists greatly during the Cold War, and a variety of sophisticated analytical techniques were developed in efforts to satisfactorily address it.[309] And while a consensus solution proved elusive despite these labors, at least the framework governing the solution became clear: The number of nuclear weapons deemed to be sufficient was seen to be a complex function of the type, yield, and reliability of the weapons themselves and the number of targets needed to be held at risk, with this last variable being affected in turn by the number, types, and reliability of the weapons the adversary possessed and the nuclear strategy it was expected to pursue. Because U.S. and Soviet nuclear strategy quickly took a turn in the direction of war fighting, the requirements of sufficiency came to be steadily defined by the challenges of counterforce and countermilitary targeting, and the various debates that followed about the "bomber gap," the "missile gap," and "ICBM vulnerability" have now become part of Cold War lore.[310] Although Indian nuclear strategy will not be similarly saddled by the need to accommodate constantly changing counterforce and countermilitary requirements, it will still have to address the central problem pertaining to the relationship between the number of weapons possessed or sought to be procured by India and the number of adversary targets these weapons are expected to interdict. This relationship will in turn be critically influenced by the yields of India's nuclear weapon designs, the expected reliability and survivability of the deterrent force as a whole, and the damage criteria sought to be satisfied with respect to the designated target

---

[309]The history of this search to define nuclear sufficiency, together with a review of all the intellectual innovations it produced, is reviewed in Fred Kaplan, *The Wizards of Armageddon* (New York: Simon and Schuster, 1983).

[310]A good analysis of how sufficiency came to be characterized in the United States until the 1970s can be found in Jerome H. Kahan, *Security in the Nuclear Age* (Washington, D.C.: Brookings, 1975); from the 1970s until the end of the Cold War, see John M. Collins, *U.S./Soviet Military Balance Statistical Trends, 1970–1981* (Washington, D.C.: Congressional Research Service, Library of Congress, 1982), and John M. Collins, *U.S./Soviet Military Balance Statistical Trends, 1980–1989* (Washington, D.C.: Congressional Research Service, Library of Congress, 1990). See also John M. Collins, *U.S.-Soviet Military Balance: Concepts and Capabilities, 1960–1980* (New York: Aviation Week, 1980).

set. This last variable, by itself, can dramatically alter the terms of "minimum deterrence" because for any given reliability and yield combination—particularly at the lower end—the number of nuclear weapons required, for example, to physically obliterate a city could be very different from, say, attempting to destroy that city as a functioning entity or, to take the simplest objective, simply seeking to kill large numbers of people in the shortest possible time frame. The requirements of sufficiency, even as far as relatively simple nuclear strategies centered on countervalue targeting are concerned, thus turn out to be inordinately contingent not only on the technical characteristics of one's own nuclear forces and those of the adversary but also on the precise operational objectives these forces are expected to service in the event of deterrence breakdown.[311]

Indian security managers thus far have not publicly defined their requirements with respect to any of these issues and will probably never do so openly in the future. The overt definition of such requirements would yield important clues about where India stood in relation to its adversaries in capability and could thus open the door to public pressure to maintain an effective "strategic balance" of some sort, thereby leading to possible arms racing. It would also generate further controversies about the appropriateness of India's nuclear strategies and its desired force levels—and such controversies would invariably engage both India's adversaries and external interlocutors like the United States in a discussion that would disturb the "atmospherics" in Southern Asia, ultimately subverting New Delhi's interest in maximizing, not minimizing, the uncertainties its adversaries face in the nuclear realm. Finally, these pressures, taken together, could decrease the pervasive opacity and systemic doubt

---

[311]The failure to accommodate the distinctions relating to operational objectives often results in analysts reaching opposite conclusions. Thus, for example, Jordan Seng argues that minor nuclear powers will invariably be satisfied with modest nuclear arsenals—less than 100 20-kt-type weapons—because it is assumed that maximizing population casualties will suffice as the goal of any countervalue targeting strategy. G. Balachandran, in contrast, concludes that India, for example, would require more than 800 20-kt-type weapons to interdict a small set of some 24 assorted targets because it is presumed, *inter alia*, that stable deterrence in this instance requires the physical obliteration of each of these targets. See Jordan Seng, *Strategy for Pandora's Children: Stable Nuclear Proliferation Among Minor States*, unpublished doctoral dissertation, University of Chicago, 1998, pp. 1–104, and Balachandran, "Nuclear Weaponization in India," pp. 42–47.

that Indian policymakers believe is important for successful deterrence among weaker powers—and consequently they have shied away from providing any authoritative indication about the numbers and types of weapons predicated by their vision of "minimum, but credible, deterrence." Thus, while the upper and lower bounds of India's strategic requirements are unknown, what is clear is that New Delhi believes that successful deterrence "is not dependent on matching weapon to weapon, but [rather hinges] on the ability to retaliate with a residual capability."[312] Indian Prime Minister Vajpayee, when faced with insistent U.S. demands that India quantify its minimum deterrent, in fact carried this otherwise sensible notion to an extreme by stating in Parliament that minimum deterrence "is not a question of numbers"[313] but represents instead a force posture that "implies [the] deployment of [nuclear] assets in a manner that ensures survivability and [the] capacity [for] an adequate response."[314]

This position is obviously borrowed from the writings of K. Subrahmanyam, who had earlier argued, also in response to U.S. demands for a quantification of India's deterrent, that both

> those against India being a nuclear weapon state and those conditioned by U.S. nuclear strategic theology . . . raise the question of what minimum nuclear deterrent the Indian Government has adopted as its declaratory policy. [This] is an arcane question and cannot be answered in precise numerical terms like 30, 300, 3,000 or 30,000. The very idea that there must be a precise numerical value to the deterrent arsenal is part of the sedulously fostered nuclear theology of former U.S. defence secretary Robert McNamara, who has now abjured it. However, his legacy lives on. . . . *Minimum deterrence is not a numerical definition but a strategic approach. If a country is in a position to have a survivable arsenal, which is seen as capable of exacting an unacceptable penalty in retaliation, it has a minimum deterrence [as] opposed to an open-ended one aimed at*

---

[312]Singh, "Nukes Have No Prestige Value."

[313]Cited in Kapil Sibal, "Toy Gun Security: Flaws in India's Nuclear Deterrence," *The Times of India*, January 13, 1999.

[314]"Deterrence to Be Evaluated Time to Time: Govt," *Economic Times*, December 17, 1998.

matching the adversary's arsenals in numerical terms [italics added].[315]

This notion that minimum deterrence is a strategic approach and hence beyond quantification has been criticized vehemently by other Indian analysts, who note that "for deterrence to be credible, it has, ultimately to be based on numbers."[316] Any other conception is "even worse than it looks. This is not deterrence, but a joke."[317]

Such criticisms overlook the subtlety of the official Indian position, which is based on Subrahmanyam's writings. Clearly, both Subrahmanyam and India's security managers amply recognize that deterrence, in the final analysis, *is* about numbers: the number of weapons that India possesses, the number of weapons that can survive a first strike, the numbers of weapons that could be successfully carried to and detonated on target, and the number of weapons required to wreak unacceptable damage on an adversary who threatens Indian security. All these facts are readily understood by policymakers in New Delhi. Therefore, what the policymakers are attempting to suggest through their claims that deterrence is not about numbers is merely that the number of nuclear weapons judged to be essential to Indian security is not something they are willing to disclose to their own body politic, to their adversaries, or to any other interested interlocutors, including the United States. In part, this response is influenced by the fact that Indian policymakers cannot be certain today what their eventual stockpile of fissile materials and the quality of their future nuclear weapon designs—the two crucial variables that will determine the size of the Indian deterrent—will be. The accumulation of fissile materials could, for example, be constrained by technical failures or by continued inefficiency within the Indian nuclear estate as well as by changes in the international nuclear regime—primarily those relating to the obligations that may be imposed on India by the successful conclusion of an FMCT in the fu-

---

[315]K. Subrahmanyam, "Not a Numbers Game: Minimum Cost of N-Deterrence," *The Times of India*, December 7, 1998.

[316]Sibal, "Toy Gun Security: Flaws in India's Nuclear Deterrence."

[317]Ibid.

ture.[318] The quality of India's future nuclear weapon designs and the amount of fissile materials these designs require may also change dramatically if India were to resume nuclear testing at some point or, more remotely, if its weapon designers were to make the risky switch from their basic fission design to some other kind of device without benefit of further hot testing.[319] All these contingencies imply that India's security managers today simply cannot be confident about what their nuclear weapon inventory will look like a decade or so from now, and even though they probably have a good idea where they would prefer to end up, they are unlikely to reveal this information—for reasons relating both to the exigencies of public diplomacy and to the requirements of deterrence stability—to anyone who might have the temerity to ask.

Indeed, even when sorely pressed on this question, Indian policymakers have traditionally responded in a very bland and uninformative fashion, stressing that their "approach is not expansive or aggressive" and that it would be limited to acquiring "the means to deter present and future threats."[320] In their public statements, they have continued to emphasize that the relative number of nuclear weapons India possesses vis-à-vis its adversaries is less important than the fact that even a few surviving weapons would cause more pain than any of the objectives sought by the latter is worth. In some instances, going even further, they have explicitly affirmed that India is in fact content to accept nuclear inferiority vis-à-vis China, in terms of both numbers and qualitative capability because such inferiority in no way prejudices their ability to preserve India's security and autonomy.[321] Whether a similar position would be maintained vis-à-vis Pakistan is unclear despite Jaswant Singh's insistence that "the question of an arsenal larger than that of country X or Y [is] a

---

[318]For a general survey of what the FMCT obligations might entail, see Frank N. von Hippel, "The FMCT and Cuts in Fissile Material Stockpiles," *Disarmament Forum*, 2 (1999), pp. 35–44.

[319]The relationship between weapon designs and fissile-material stockpiles is examined in Balachandran, "Nuclear Weaponization in India," pp. 42–47.

[320]"Deterrence to Be Evaluated Time to Time: Govt."

[321]Joshi, "India Must Have Survivable N-Arsenal."

non-question."[322] This issue does not seem to have received much attention in New Delhi because it is presumed that India already possesses nuclear superiority over Pakistan in both number and qualitative capability—and even if this is untrue by some criteria today, it remains almost an article of faith among Indian policymakers that India will enjoy such superiority over Pakistan eventually.

Whether New Delhi's position on the irrelevance of nuclear superiority would change if Pakistan gained nuclear superiority in the future is therefore an interesting question, but one that cannot be answered with any certainty today. The only thing worth stating on this matter is that Indian security managers have always believed that New Delhi's strategic preeminence vis-à-vis Islamabad was not simply a fact of life but an operating condition that had to be assiduously maintained because of their view of Pakistan as a risk-acceptant, if not an irresponsible, state. This view was most clearly articulated by Indian Defence Minister George Fernandes when he argued that "Pakistan is an irresponsible country . . . [that] has lost . . . three conflicts with India, and in case of a fourth conflict, [it] could be tempted to push the nuclear button."[323] Given such views, India's security managers have gone to great lengths—especially in their discussions with the United States—to implicitly justify their supposed nuclear superiority over Pakistan by asserting that a view of these capabilities which pushed them "below [their] security requirements and limit[ed] them to a purely Indo-Pak context is unacceptable."[324]

On the assumption that India continues to enjoy nuclear superiority over Pakistan even as it remains inferior to China by many comparable measures, New Delhi has therefore repeatedly affirmed that the very notions of superiority and inferiority are politically irrelevant so long as the residual capability to devastate a certain fraction of the adversary's assets always remains inviolate even amid the carnage of

---

[322]"India Not to Engage in a N-Arms Race: Jaswant."

[323]"Pakistan May Use N-Weapons, Fears Fernandes," *Hindustan Times*, June 30, 1999.

[324]Mohan, "India Committed to Minimum N-Deterrence."

war.[325] Although influenced in part by the confidence that they already possess nuclear superiority over Pakistan, this affirmation also draws sustenance from a variety of larger beliefs held in India about the gradual decay in the efficacy of nuclear threats since the beginning of the nuclear era; the strong presumption already held against any nuclear use; and the progressively declining thresholds that define unacceptable damage as societies continue to modernize economically. All these perspectives combine to suggest that New Delhi would finally settle for a relatively small nuclear force that, even if numerically and qualitatively inferior to those of an adversary like China, remains sufficient to insure India against blackmail, coercion, and the threat of exploitative use emerging from both Beijing and Islamabad. Even a modest number of nuclear weapons is deemed to be adequate for this purpose because no disputes requiring the extensive use of Chinese nuclear weapons against India are seen to exist, while India's strategic inferiority vis-à-vis China is believed to remain sufficient in itself for strategic superiority over Pakistan.

Irrespective of whether this expectation turns out to be correct, however, it must still be translated into a weapon inventory that is consistent with the overarching concept of minimum deterrence, and Vijai Nair, one of India's most widely read commentators on nuclear matters, has attempted to provide just such a numerical estimate of how the country's evolving deterrent ought to be sized. Nair estimates that with regard to Pakistan, a nominally weaker nuclear adversary, India should acquire the ability to target

> six metropolitan centers including port facilities; one corps-sized offensive formation in its concentration area; three sets of bottlenecks in the strategic communications network; five nuclear-capable military airfields; two hydroelectric water storage dams. A total of 17 nuclear engagements.[326]

With regard to China, a superior nuclear adversary, Nair argues that India ought to focus not on discrete attacks but on large punishing strikes that would retard postwar Chinese capabilities relative to its other adversaries. This implies that

---

[325]"India Not to Engage in a N-Arms Race: Jaswant."

[326]Nair, *Nuclear India*, p. 170.

> Initially, India needs to create a weapons capability to pull out five to six major industrial centers plus two ports to service China's SSBN [nuclear-propelled ballistic missile submarine] fleet. This makes a total of eight nuclear strikes.[327]

Against such a target array, Nair argues that

> the ideal configuration of warhead numbers and yield would be: two strikes of one megaton each for metropolitan centres and port facilities; two strikes of 15 kt each for battlefield targets; one strike with a yield of between 200 and 500 kt each for dams; one strike of 20 to 50 kt each for military airfields; and one strike each of 15 kt for strategic communication centres.[328]

After reliability parameters are factored in at the rate of two weapons for each autonomous strike, with 20 percent of the entire force structure maintained as a postwar reserve, the 25 designated targets in China and Pakistan are calculated as requiring an overall Indian arsenal of 132 weapons of varying size and yield.[329] Nair's accounting, summarized above, represents the most detailed example of an Indian effort to justify a nuclear force structure on the basis of some idealized sufficiency requirements.

Other commentators have offered similar albeit sometimes less detailed assessments. General K. Sundarji, for example, concluded that against a small country like Pakistan "up to 1 MTE [megaton equivalent] (say, 50 × 20 kt weapons) might do. Even for deterring a large country, one is most unlikely to require more than 4 MTE."[330]

---

[327]Ibid.

[328]Ibid., pp. 170–171.

[329]Ibid., p. 181. As Balachandran's analysis points out, however, these small inventory sizes are crucially dependent on India's possession of the high-yield weapons called for in Nair's calculations. Absent such weapons, the number of nuclear weapons required to obliterate these targets immediately goes up from the few tens in Nair's analysis to many hundreds—or, more precisely, from 132 weapons of varying yields to upwards of 800 20-kt-size weapons. See Balachandran, "Nuclear Weaponization in India," pp. 42–47.

[330]K. Sundarji, "Nuclear Deterrence: Doctrine for India—Part 1," *Trishul*, 5:2 (December 1992), p. 48. In later writings, Sundarji reduced these requirements even further, arguing that "all that is needed to deter a small to medium-sized country would be about 20 weapons of about 20 kiloton yield each [0.4 MTE], and about 50

These totals are difficult to translate into specific numbers of weapons because the design yields of India's nuclear weaponry are not publicly known. Sundarji suggests, however, that targeting 15 conurbations in both Pakistan (5) and China (10) should suffice for minimum deterrence: Each of these targets could be attacked with "three fission warheads of 20 kt each, detonated as low airbursts,"[331] and from this requirement he deduces that India "would need 45 warheads (and their delivery means) to survive an adversary first strike"[332]—numbers that are explicitly based on weapon designs producing nominal yields in the 20-kt range. After factoring in reliability parameters and possible losses to an adversary's first strike, Sundarji concludes that "a low estimate of 90 weapons and an upper estimate of 135 weapons would be reasonable" because, given basing modes that exploit opacity and mobility, "adequate numbers [of weapons] would survive"[333] any of the expected attacks emanating from either China or Pakistan. K. Subrahmanyam, too, argues for a comparable class of numbers: In 1994 he declared that India needed only "sixty deliverable warheads"[334]—which in practice probably meant some larger number if the reliability quotient and the possible attrition of these assets are taken into account. These weapons were presumably still 20-kt-class fission weapons, since Subrahmanyam not only rejected the need for both megaton-range thermonuclear weapons and neutron bombs but also argued that India's standard design, which was tested in 1974, did not need any further tests and could, if needed, "be boosted with some addition of thermonuclear materials."[335] Other observers have expressed different yet comparable views about Indian requirements. General V. N. Sharma, a former Indian Army Chief of Staff, for example, asserted that "around 50 bombs should do" but called for "going the whole hog" in delivery

---

such weapons [1 MTE] for even a large country." See K. Sundarji, "The CTBT Debate: Choice Before India," *Indian Express*, December 4, 1995.

[331]K. Sundarji, "CTBT and National Security: Options for India," *Indian Express*, April 6, 1996.

[332]Sundarji, "Imperatives of Indian Minimum Nuclear Deterrence," p. 18.

[333]Ibid.

[334]Subrahmanyam, "Nuclear Force Design and Minimum Deterrence Strategy for India," p. 189.

[335]Ibid., p. 190.

systems.[336] In sharp contrast to these more moderate estimates, Bharat Karnad has argued that strategic sufficiency for India cannot consist of anything less than the ability to interdict some 60 primary and secondary targets in China and Pakistan, thereby necessitating a nuclear force of well over 300 weapons by the year 2030—most of which must be high-yield thermonuclear devices.[337]

Although the size of India's weapon inventory has thus received considerable attention, the number of desired delivery systems has not yet been specified in comparable detail. In part, this is because deducing the minimal number of delivery vehicles necessary requires complex operations research and analysis as well as prior knowledge of several parametric variables, including basing modes, relative hardness and mobility, and estimates of success accruing to deception and denial. The kind of delivery system chosen also affects the final force size: While ballistic and cruise missiles, which are single-use vehicles, would correlate with their nuclear payloads in a one-to-one relationship, strike aircraft, being reusable, do not lend themselves to such a simple force-sizing metric. The lower penetrativity of aircraft, on the other hand, can increase the gross numbers required, and complex planning tools are therefore necessary if good estimates of operational requirements are to be derived—even if issues like procurement and operational and life-cycle costs are not treated as constraints *a priori*. Given the lack of access to such planning tools and the information required to use them effectively, however, it is not surprising that various Indian commentators have advanced different estimates of the delivery systems required to carry their preferred inventory. In 1994, for example, K. Subrahmanyam argued that his force of about 60 nuclear weapons be carried on 20 Prithvi SRBMs and 20 Agni IRBMs and the rest on strike aircraft.[338] Two years later, Sundarji, in contrast, argued for a force of some 150 warheads carried on 45 Prithvi SRBMs and 90 Agni IRBMs, with the balance carried by aircraft.[339] Vijai Nair has argued for at

---

[336]Raj Chengappa and Manoj Joshi, "Future Fire," *India Today*, May 25, 1998, p. 23.

[337]Karnad, "A Thermonuclear Deterrent," p. 143.

[338]Subrahmanyam, "Nuclear Force Design and Minimum Deterrence Strategy for India," p. 193.

[339]Joshi, "Marginal Costing," pp. 22–23.

least five SSBNs in order to maintain 48 sea-launched ballistic missiles (SLBMs) ready at all times for use against China and Pakistan, in addition to 36 SRBMs and IRBMs and various other unspecified numbers of manned aircraft.[340] And in the most expansive version of all, Bharat Karnad has argued for a force of four SSBNs contributing a total of 48 SLBMs, 25 ICBMs, 40 IRBMs, and 70 manned aircraft, all to be complemented by another 70 air-to-surface missiles and 25 atomic demolition munitions.[341] The exact nature of the calculations leading up to these force architectures is not known and in all probability represent either "back-of-the-envelope" computations or simply wild to educated guesses about what seems to be strategically desirable and politically feasible in the Indian milieu.[342]

To be sure, differences also exist among all the conceptions of sufficiency proffered in Indian discussions. Some, for example, require thermonuclear weapons while others do not presume their availability; some emphasize a larger numbers of weapons while others stress a smaller inventory; and some emphasize the need for more long-range missiles while others maintain that fewer will suffice. What is more interesting, however, are the similarities of these conceptions. All, for example, posit essentially finite arsenals—that is, weapon inventories and delivery systems that do not inexorably grow in size once the ability to service certain destruction requirements is assured, this finitude obviously being conditioned by the requirements of both ensuring survivability in the face of adversaries' force levels and guaranteeing penetrativity in the face of technological change. Further, the level of destruction thought to be sufficient for successful deterrence is relatively small, generally centering on the ability to destroy 8 to 15 target complexes in China and Pakistan. What is regarded as constituting destruction, however, may vary from analyst to analyst. Many accept a certain redundancy in capabilities to allow for reliability constraints, attrition as a result of first strikes, and delivery failures, yet none argues for a force posture that is in any way automatically or consistently keyed to the size and character of the

---

[340]Nair, *Nuclear India*, pp. 171–172.

[341]Karnad, "A Thermonuclear Deterrent," p. 146.

[342]For still another set of desired numbers pertaining to delivery systems, see Kanwal, "India's Nuclear Force Structure," pp. 1039–1075.

adversaries' nuclear capabilities. A few even undertake some sort of systematic analysis to justify the desired stockpile and delivery systems based on their estimate of what it takes to inflict "unacceptable damage" as understood within the geopolitical context of Southern Asia, with some analysts emphasizing the need for thermonuclear weapons if they believe these requirements to be high and others appearing content with small fission devices if they believe that population targeting suffices for the same purpose. These analyses, mostly carried out by retired service officers like Nair, Sundarji, and Menon, reflect the Weberian legal-rational orientation that characterizes the uniformed military's approach to operational planning, and it is not surprising that most Indian commentators who have seen active service tend to analyze nuclear requirements in the same way they would approach conventional military operations.

The exceptions to this rule remain Bharat Karnad and G. Balachandran. Although both are civilians, Karnad's accounting of India's nuclear requirements is driven as much by his understanding of what it takes to effectively deter in the Southern Asian context as it is conditioned by a political desire to promote India's strategic independence and its standing as a great power.[343] Karnad's accounting of India's nuclear requirements, however (and, to some extent, Nair's and Menon's as well), remains at substantial variance with the country's currently demonstrated technical capacity, the history of its resource allocations to defense, the size of its resource base relative to other competing social claims, and its doctrine regarding the utility of nuclear weapons. Of all the Indian analysts who have articulated specific conceptions of what minimum deterrence entails in numerical form, only Subrahmanyam and Sundarji have proffered an accounting of nuclear requirements that comports perfectly with India's currently demonstrated technical capacity and its larger doctrine about the value of nuclear weaponry.[344]

---

[343]Karnad in fact explicitly admits this objective up front, and his discussion leaves the reader with no doubt that sufficiency for him means deterring not just China and Pakistan but also the great powers. See Bharat Karnad, "Needed: An 'India First' Nuclear Policy," *The Pioneer*, July 27, 2000, and Bharat Karnad, "Next, a Series of Thermonuclear Tests," *The Pioneer*, July 28, 2000.

[344]The character of India's demonstrated technical capabilities will be discussed at greater length in the next chapter.

Several commentators, especially those with military backgrounds, have thus focused on explicating India's nuclear requirements through use of simple quantitative analysis. It is not clear, however, whether a similar approach has been taken by the atomic energy establishment, the civilian bureaucracy that ultimately manages India's nuclear weapon program. What is most likely, at least in the near term, is that legal-rational analytical approaches relating to the issue of sufficiency will be pursued independently either by individual analysts in their private capacity outside the government or by small planning cells in the DRDO and in the three service headquarters. Their findings will then be disseminated through both formal and informal means to Indian decisionmakers, including senior political figures and key bureaucrats. These individuals may use such findings for their own ends—to assess funding requirements; to influence the thinking of weapon designers at BARC and within the DRDO; or to define India's negotiating postures in bilateral discussions with the United States and in various international forums.

Such analytic efforts—whether undertaken by private individuals or by government employees—will therefore play a role in India's nuclear requirements planning process in the immediate future. In all probability, however, most decisions about the size of India's nuclear arsenal will ultimately pivot on considerations *other than merely operational requirements.* It is, in fact, possible that the size of the nuclear weapon stockpile will eventually be defined mainly by the quantum of fissile materials available to India—and not necessarily by the size of the target set defined by India's numerous security commentators. Similarly, the yield of the nuclear weapons themselves will be determined fundamentally by the designs that Indian scientists have thus far been able to validate or appear to have the greatest preference for—and not necessarily by the demands imposed by the technical characteristics of the target array. On all these matters, India's nuclear estate traditionally has been highly solipsistic, pursuing its research, development, and production activities mainly in light of the technical and bureaucratic challenges confronting Indian nuclear science rather than by the operational imperatives deriving from the nation's nuclear strategy.[345]

---

[345] On this issue, the classic work remains Perkovich, *India's Nuclear Bomb*, pp. 444–468. There is also little evidence that suggests things have changed radically since

This implies that the chief constraint on developing an arsenal of the size, shape, and form preferred by analysts like Karnad and Nair may be India's smaller-than-usually-estimated fissile-material inventory and its poorly validated nuclear weapon design base. If India agrees to a cutoff in the production of fissile materials after a successful conclusion of the FMCT in Geneva, continues with its self-imposed moratorium on nuclear testing indefinitely, and signs and ratifies the CTBT at some point in the future, these policy choices—more than any operational requirements—will define the kind of nuclear arsenal that India would eventually possess.[346]

India's delivery systems may not be similarly constrained, but the strategic consequences of this freedom are ambiguous. There is no reason, for example, why India cannot in time develop and produce a class of reasonably effective SRBMs and IRBMs; continue to purchase the best advanced combat aircraft available on the international market; and eventually even acquire a nuclear-powered missile submarine. All these vehicles may even be procured in significant numbers, since there are only economic but effectively no physical constraints on their acquisition in the long run. These systems will, however, be limited in potency, since they will carry only a small number of possibly low-yield nuclear weapons. This is because the number of weapons will be constrained by the fact that at some point in the foreseeable future India might have to terminate the production of fissile materials (or at least account for future production, de-

---

India's May 1998 nuclear tests; see "Pakistan, India 'Have Not Moved Very Far' to Field Nukes: Cohen," *The News International*, May 13, 2000, and P. R. Chari, "India's Slow-Motion Nuclear Deployment," *Carnegie Endowment for International Peace Proliferation Brief*, 3:26 (September 7, 2000). It should be recognized, however, that the judgments of the uniformed military, as expressed both privately and through interfacing mechanisms like the DRDO, have steadily grown in relevance as far as designing the structure and quality of India's prospective nuclear arsenal and its managerial institutions are concerned. As is usually the case, however, the uniformed military's contributions on this subject are absorbed mainly through informal channels in great secrecy, involving a minuscule number of individuals.

[346]This is well recognized by many Indian analysts, who have therefore argued that the Indian government ought not to sign the CTBT even as they berate it for enabling the FMCT negotiations to begin in the Conference on Disarmament. See Brahma Chellaney, "Caution on CTBT," *Hindustan Times*, November 3, 1999; Karnad, "Policy on CTBT"; Balachandran, "A Consensus or a Sell-Off?"; Rajesh Rajagopalan, "The Question of More Tests," *The Hindu*, December 17, 1999; Bharat Karnad, "A Sucker's Payoff," *Seminar*, 485 (January 2000), pp. 45–50; Chellaney, "How Pokhran II Has Bombed"; and Chellaney, "India's Trial by Atom."

pending on what a final negotiated text of the FMCT requires),[347] while the yield of the weapons will be constrained by the fact that India's prospective decision to formalize its moratorium on nuclear testing would leave it with high confidence mainly in a set of simple fission designs.[348] Thus, even if India mounts higher-yield (or more sophisticated) weapons on these delivery vehicles over time, the quality of these weapons will not have been fully validated, since they will not have been hot tested as such. Consequently, the deterrent effects that flow from the acknowledged possession of such weapons will not accrue to India, since it will not be clear to India's adversaries that New Delhi in fact possesses sophisticated nuclear weapons that would inflict catastrophic and possibly fatal damage in the event of war. On balance, then, India will possess a nuclear deterrent, but this deterrent—at least as far as outsiders are concerned—will consist mainly of small numbers of relatively simple nuclear weapons.

This conclusion, however, should not be misconstrued. India's political leadership is *not* seeking to create a large and complex nuclear arsenal, even if its scientific community seeks to push the envelope with respect to increasingly sophisticated weapon designs. Even when India ceases to produce fissile materials and "freezes" its existing weapon designs, policymakers in New Delhi believe that India will still have sufficient nuclear capabilities to immunize it against the threats of blackmail and potential use emanating from China and Pakistan. This is because the principal criterion for strategic adequacy in India's eyes is not that the damage inflicted by its weapons be greater than that which can be inflicted by an adversary but only that the costs resulting from Indian retaliation be greater than any political benefits accruing to the adversary as a result of its nuclear threats or first use. The requirements for effective deterrence in the Indian context are thus truly low because state managers in New Delhi have already concluded that few political benefits could be secured by any adversary through aggression—with or without nuclear

---

[347]On the debate about what the FMCT should regulate and how, see Tariq Rauf, "Fissile Material Treaty: Negotiating Approaches," *Disarmament Forum*, 2 (1999), pp. 17–28, and Victor Bragin and John Carlson, "Some Significant Divisions in the Scope Debate," *Disarmament Forum*, 2 (1999), pp. 29–34.

[348]Rajagopalan, "The Question of More Tests"; Iyengar, "Nuclear Nuances"; and Karnad, "Needed: An 'India First' Nuclear Policy."

weapons—against India. Those that could be secured subsist entirely in the psychic realms of coercion and blackmail, but the acknowledged possession of nuclear weapons by India—irrespective of their numbers or quality—should more than suffice to neuter such threats.[349] Outside of these psycho-political contingencies, no real and lasting benefits are perceived to accrue from any active aggression against India. Strategists in New Delhi would thus assert that even the loss of a single Chinese or Pakistani city like Chengdu or Lahore would not be worth the benefits of war, since in every conceivable scenario the predicted benefits are invariably less than the price that might have to be paid if the offensive involves a first use of nuclear weapons against India.[350]

Given this generally modest criterion of strategic adequacy, even small numbers of relatively low-yield fission bombs could suffice to provide India with the deterrence it desires—or so Indian policymakers argue *sotto voce*. In fact, Karnad's estimate of requirements, centering on a few hundred thermonuclear weapons, actually constitutes the *maximal* variant of sufficiency yet advanced in the Indian debate, and it is entirely plausible that New Delhi would be satisfied with a much lower number of nuclear weapons, most of which may have yields that barely rise above the smallest devices that analysts like Karnad (or Nair, Balachandran, and Menon, for that matter) consider to be absolutely necessary. As Jasjit Singh phrased this expectation, "It is difficult to visualise an arsenal with anything more than a double-digit quantum of warheads" over the next few years, and "it may [actually] be prudent to even plan on the basis of a lower end figure of say 2–3 dozen nuclear warheads by the end of 10–15 years . . . [since] with the passage of time, deterrence decay factors will lead to the requirements of a smaller arsenal rather than a larger one."[351] Where types of weapons are concerned, Sundarji, for ex-

---

[349]K. Subrahmanyam, "Arms Race Myth: Fallout of Overactive Minds," *The Times of India*, May 30, 1998.

[350]Subrahmanyam, "Nuclear Defence Philosophy: Not a Numbers Game Anymore."

[351]Singh, "A Nuclear Strategy for India," p. 315. Such beliefs also suggest how closely Indian requirements mirror, however imperfectly, the expectations of other smaller nuclear powers during the Cold War. Referring to British nuclear requirements, for example, Colonel Jonathan Alford argued that "there was no real need . . . to increase the capability, as defined in terms of the number of targets in the Soviet

ample (and Subrahmanyam as well), has consistently argued that "there is no need for fusion (hydrogen bomb) or enhanced-yield fission (tritium) warheads,"[352] since even allocating three simple fission warheads of 20 kt each per city has been deemed to be adequate for purposes of deterrence. India already possesses this class of capabilities, however, and consequently Indian policymakers will seek as best they can to avoid succumbing to various domestic pressures to enhance their strategic capabilities through what would be seen abroad as provocative political acts like resuming nuclear testing, accelerating the missile development program, and overtly inducting nuclear weapons alongside its conventional defense capabilities.

Therefore, although India's nuclear force may eventually be defined more by technical limitations and political constraints than by strict operational requirements of the sort articulated by Karnad, Nair, Balachandran, and Menon, Indian policymakers today believe that prudence requires that they keep all their options open even if their modest capabilities are currently judged to be sufficient for effective deterrence and even if they now feel less than compelled to pursue the kinds of technologies favored by the most zealous domestic advocates of advanced nuclear weaponry.[353] On this issue, both the Indian government and security elites within the country at large appear to be of one mind. Both groups are agreed that India's strategic policies with respect to matters affecting the size and quality of its future deterrent ought to have three components.

- *First, don't foreclose any possibilities unless the payoffs from foreclosure incontrovertibly exceed the costs.* In practical terms, this implies that India will be loath to make good on its commitment to quickly sign and ratify the CTBT and assist the FMCT negotia-

---

Union, that the United Kingdom should hold at risk—and we felt that the requirement to hold some 12 major Soviet conurbations hostage to the British nuclear forces would remain adequate." See "Alford Testimony in the House of Commons, Fourth Report from the Defence Committee, Session 1980–81," *Strategic Nuclear Weapons Policy* (London: HMSO, 1981), p. 26. The French similarly believed that as few as 12 anticity strikes would suffice to deter the Soviet Union from unacceptable behavior. See Yost, "French Nuclear Targeting," p. 140.

[352]Sundarji, "Imperatives of Indian Minimum Nuclear Deterrence," p. 18.

[353]The real problem here, of course, may be India's scientists, who in their zeal for the fanciest devices imaginable may fail to produce even simple devices that are reliable, consistent in quality and yield, and operationally adequate.

tions to a speedy and successful conclusion because surrendering the benefits embodied by such actions would occur only if there were some prospect of securing suitable political blandishments that would compensate for whatever technical weaknesses may ail the emerging Indian nuclear deterrent.

- *Second, don't make any formal commitments to limit the upper bounds of strategic capability.* In practical terms, this implies that Indian security managers will not provide any binding assurances either to the United States or to the international community that their desired force-in-being will not exceed certain quantitative or qualitative thresholds even if in practice they do convey some such understandings tacitly and informally.

- *Third, don't restrain domestic research, development, and production activities relating to nuclear weapons, fissile materials, and delivery systems.* In practical terms, this implies that India will press ahead with its existing efforts in all three arenas. And while these efforts may be accelerated in some areas (e.g., the production of fissile materials) while remaining more or less constant in others (e.g., the development of delivery systems), this will not extend to reducing the quantum of effort applied overall no matter what pressures may emerge from the international community.

This threefold strategy is clearly intended on the one hand to minimize the extent of the formal obligations restraining India's emerging strategic capabilities while on the other hand to produce the largest and most effective deterrent force possible within the limits of India's current capabilities.[354] The objective of producing the largest and most effective deterrent force, in turn, is not simply to expand the size of the nuclear weapon inventory for its own sake but rather to increase the extent of the residual fraction that would survive a nuclear strike that might be mounted by its adversaries. The "Draft Report of [the] National Security Advisory Board on Indian Nuclear Doctrine" captured this requirement succinctly when it noted that India's operational policy of "retaliation only" makes "the

---

[354]The entire nuclear infrastructure is detailed in Perkovich, *India's Nuclear Bomb*, pp. 469–472, and the portions relevant to the nuclear weapon production program are briefly described in Joshi, "India's Nuclear Estate."

survivability of our arsenal . . . critical."[355] Further, it stated that survivability—and, by implication, the size of the arsenal—constituted a "dynamic concept related to the strategic environment, technological imperatives, and the needs of national security."[356] The report consequently concluded that "the actual size, components, deployment and employment of nuclear forces [ought to] be decided in the light of these factors."[357] In point of fact, the Advisory Board may well have exaggerated how much flexibility India possesses with respect to increasing the survivability of its nuclear forces—at least insofar as this survivability can be manipulated through increases in the number of nuclear weapons given both the technical status of the country's nuclear production infrastructure and its commitment to adhering to a fissile-material cutoff if such a treaty is successfully concluded in the future. It did point out quite accurately, however, that the size of India's nuclear force would eventually be influenced by many variables, including the capability and disposition of the nuclear forces maintained by India's adversaries (the "strategic environment"); the demands levied on penetrativity in the face of incipient transformations in the present offense-dominant global nuclear regime ("technological imperatives"); and the state of political relations between India and its immediate adversaries, among those adversaries themselves, and between India and other key powers in the global system (the "needs of national security").

A recognition of these factors led the Advisory Board to insinuate that the size of India's emerging nuclear force could not be fixed *a priori* but would have to be sufficiently variable to ensure survivability in light of the changes that could occur in the issue areas noted above.[358] The prospect of such variability, however, cannot imply that the size of India's nuclear force would by definition be open-ended. Even though some of the Advisory Board's original members

---

[355]"Draft Report of [the] National Security Advisory Board on Indian Nuclear Doctrine," p. 2.

[356]Ibid.

[357]Ibid.

[358]This has also been affirmed by Indian security managers like Jaswant Singh, who noted that "this 'minimum' . . . cannot be a fixed physical quantification." See "India Not to Engage in a N-Arms Race: Jaswant." See also Prime Minister Vajpayee's statement in "Deterrence to Be Evaluated Time to Time: Govt."

would in fact prefer just such an interpretation and would consequently argue that India ought not to participate in the FMCT negotiations currently occurring in Geneva,[359] most Indian security managers recognize that at some point in the future an FMCT, if successfully concluded, would compel them to either terminate the production of weapon-usable materials or at least transparently account for all their future inventories.[360] This fact, coupled with the constraints imposed by the parlous state of India's nuclear infrastructure, sets a ceiling on the size of India's future nuclear arsenal that cannot be negotiated away unless the country is willing to make a massive investment in new nuclear production facilities right away in the hope that it can dramatically distend its potential arsenal before the decade is out (i.e., when the constraints emerging from an FMCT could conceivably kick in).[361] There is no empirical evidence thus far that India is willing to make such investments, although it is reasonable to assume that it would bend over backwards to increase the efficiency of its fissile-material production cycle, supplemented by increased reliance on its civilian nuclear power infrastructure to support its weapon needs and perhaps complemented by a few discrete investments in new plants and equipment at critical points in the weapon production process—all in order to build up its strategic

---

[359]See, for example, the position affirmed early on in Brahma Chellaney, "India's Crucial Role," *Indian Express,* April 21, 1995, and Brahma Chellaney, "India's Wrong Signal on Fissile Cut-Off," *Indian Express,* April 22, 1995.

[360]As Jaswant Singh phrased it, "We have, after the tests last year, announced our readiness to engage in multilateral negotiations in the Conference on Disarmament in Geneva for a nondiscriminatory and verifiable treaty to ban future production of fissile materials for nuclear weapon purposes. *This decision was taken after due consideration, which included an assessment of time frames for negotiations and entry into force of an FMCT.* At this stage, India cannot accept a voluntary moratorium on production of fissile materials. Let me add that FMCT negotiations are a complex exercise. It will be important, therefore, as we go along to constantly monitor the pace, direction and content of these negotiations" (italics added). See "India Not to Engage in a N-Arms Race: Jaswant."

[361]For more on the state of India's nuclear infrastructure, see Nayan Chanda, "The Perils of Power," *Far Eastern Economic Review,* February 4, 1999, pp. 10–17. The disrepair of both civilian and weapon programs has been further described in T.S. Gopi Rethinaraj, "In the Comfort of Secrecy," *Bulletin of the Atomic Scientists,* 55:6 (November 1999), pp. 52–57.

material inventory to the desired size before it is constrained by emerging changes in the global nuclear regime.[362]

It is interesting to note that Foreign Minister Jaswant Singh reiterated the Advisory Board's published position on the variables defining the size of the Indian arsenal virtually word for word in his own redaction of the Draft Report.[363] Most knowledgeable strategic commentators, however—including K. Subrahmanyam—recognize that for all the homage paid to the principle that "the minimum deterrent cannot be a fixed physical quantification," there is in fact some sort of outer bound that defines the size of India's minimum deterrent, at least over the next decade. This judgment has been confirmed by Singh himself, who declared that "[India] shall not . . . pursue an open-ended programme."[364] K. Subrahmanyam sought to clarify in concrete terms what the outer limits of the Indian minimum deterrent might be by affirming that the country's emerging arsenal will probably be pegged at approximately 150 nuclear weapons[365]—a judgment obviously based on the premise that no FMCT restrictions will be operational for at least another decade *and* that India can increase its plutonium production for weapon purposes in the interim. If both assumptions fail to hold, however, India's nuclear inventory could grow larger—or perhaps remain smaller—than the 150 weapons currently forecast, with the odds being that it would stay smaller rather than larger if India's past

---

[362]This appears to be corroborated by the recent decision to remove BARC from the purview of the Atomic Energy Regulatory Board in order to provide the former "a free hand in going ahead with its programme of developing nuclear weapons." See "Atomic Energy Watchdog Won't Bark at BARC," *Indian Express*, June 1, 2000.

[363]The relevant portion of Singh's statement read: "India needs only that strategic minimum which is credible. With the policy of 'retaliation only,' survivability becomes critical to ensure credibility. This 'minimum,' however, cannot be a fixed physical quantification; it is a dynamic concept but firmly rooted in the strategic environment, technological imperatives, and national security needs, and the actual size, components, deployment and employment of nuclear forces will be decided taking into account all these factors." See "India Not to Engage in a N-Arms Race: Jaswant."

[364]"India Not to Engage in a N-Arms Race: Jaswant."

[365]Subrahmanyam, "A Credible Deterrent."

efforts at accumulating weapons-grade plutonium are any indication.[366] Recognizing this, Subrahmanyam caustically concluded that "today for many Americans who pride themselves in leading their country towards disarmament and who have a lot of admirers among the anti-nuclear lobbyists in India, reducing their stockpile to zero means bringing it down to 200 warheads. On the basis of this standard, perhaps the Indian nuclear deterrent will be less than zero."[367]

All this implies that the emerging Indian nuclear deterrent will by the year 2010 be a relatively small force consisting of 150-odd weapons (and possibly even less), most of which will likely be capable of producing comparatively small yields of some 20 kt (if New Delhi persists with its current moratorium on nuclear testing). India will continue to pursue a variety of delivery systems, especially ballistic and cruise missiles, and will acquire as many of these systems as necessary to deliver its nuclear weapons under a wide variety of operational contingencies. Because none of its current missiles is an ideal vehicle for nuclear payloads, however, India will likely continue to develop these systems to reach ranges that will probably not exceed 3500 km, even as it persists in experimenting with a variety of unorthodox basing modes, in efforts to gradually migrate from its current reliance on air-breathing vehicles (which will nonetheless remain the primary carriers of India's nuclear weaponry for some years to come). In any event, the size and configuration of the Indian arsenal writ large and the character of the nuclear weaponry deployed within it will be defined less by operational requirements of the sort adduced by military analysts than by internal and external technical and political constraints—but this fact should not hamper New Delhi's efforts to produce the minimum deterrent that it believes is sufficient for its specific needs. Even though such a force structure—based mainly on a modest number of small nuclear weapons together with their associated delivery systems—will in all probability satisfy Indian security managers, they will resolutely refuse to provide any formal assurances in a bilateral context to the

---

[366]For more on this issue, see R. Ramachandran, "Pokhran II: The Scientific Dimensions," in Amitabh Mattoo (ed.), *India's Nuclear Deterrent* (New Delhi: Har-Anand Publications, 1999), pp. 34–38. This question is also discussed in much greater detail in Chapter Five.

[367]Subrahmanyam, "A Credible Deterrent."

United States (or anyone else, for that matter) that have the effect of limiting their options in the face of future uncertainties.

Separated in Disposition

The fact that India will probably settle for a relatively small nuclear arsenal consisting of 150-odd weapons, together with a number of delivery vehicles to carry such an inventory to target—all oriented toward holding between 8 and 15 target sets in China and Pakistan at risk—provides a more concrete image of the Indian version of minimum deterrence. To be sure, such a force does not yet exist and probably will not exist in full form for at least another decade or two. In the interim, there is little evidence that New Delhi is pursuing these capabilities at an accelerated pace across the board, because India believes, despite occasional claims to the contrary,[368] that it is already ahead of Pakistan where nuclear weapons are concerned and does not expect serious strategic competition with China for another 15 to 20 years.[369] At that point China, having completed its economic reform program, may be comfortably ensconced along the path of self-sustained growth and might have completed its logistical and infrastructure modernization in Tibet. These two developments taken together would allow it—at least theoretically—to mount some kinds of no-notice challenges to India along the disputed border and to that degree could make India's reliance on its nuclear capabilities for reassurance more necessary. None of these contingencies, however, is likely to materialize before the next two decades—and until then, China's nuclear arsenal will continue to pose more of a latent than a manifest threat.[370] The slowly developing Indian nuclear capabilities are thus designed, as far as Beijing is concerned, to neutralize any Chinese challenges that may arise over the long term, under-

---

[368] Perkovich, "South Asia: A Bomb Is Born"; Donnelly, "Official: Pakistan's Nuclear Warheads Outpace India's"; and Windrem and Kupperman, "Pakistan Nukes Outstrip India's, Officials Say."

[369] For more on this issue, see Singh, "Why Nuclear Weapons?" and Singh, "A Nuclear Strategy for India," pp. 9–25 and 306–324.

[370] On the evolution of Chinese military capabilities and the relevant time lines for the development of various military capabilities, see Swaine and Tellis, *Interpreting China's Grand Strategy*, pp. 159–169, and Khalilzad et al., *The United States and a Rising China*, pp. 37–62.

stood as 20 to 30 years out, since the nuclear threat from Pakistan is deemed to be manageable thanks to the nuclear capabilities India already possesses.[371]

Even when the Indian arsenal matures over the next decade, it will, for all the reasons explicated earlier, remain a relatively small force consisting of some seven-score weapons together with their associated delivery systems. By the very fact of its existence, however, it will become a source of threat to both China and Pakistan, which in the event of deterrence breakdown may be forced to contemplate a variety of preemptive damage-limiting strategies purely for defensive reasons.[372] A nuclear force of any sort inevitably becomes a magnet for such strategies because of the cataclysmic power it represents. A *small* nuclear force of the kind that would be developed by India (and by Pakistan, for that matter) exemplifies an even greater enticement, however, because it serves to make "splendid first strikes" feasible at least in principle.[373] An important challenge facing India's evolving arsenal therefore consists of ensuring its survivability against any first-strike temptations on the part of an adversary, and neutralizing such temptations successfully represents the first key to successful deterrence. This challenge boils down to the question of how a small nuclear force may be preserved inviolate such that a substantial portion of its nuclear assets will survive, ready to be reconstituted for the devastating retribution to follow, even if first strikes are unleashed *in extremis.*

In general, states that already possess nuclear arsenals have adopted a combination of solutions to ensure survivability. Each of these solutions—"physical hardening, geographic dispersion, mobility, redundancy, secrecy, and the active interdiction of attacking weapons"[374]—embodies different benefits and costs, and their selection must ultimately be based on the value placed on the purposes

---

[371]"India on U.S. Report," *The Statesman*, June 9, 2000; and Patralekha Chatterjee, "Amid Blaring Headlines, India Mum on U.S. Nuclear Report."

[372]Jones, *From Testing to Deploying Nuclear Forces*, pp. 3–4.

[373]Lewis A. Dunn, *Controlling the Bomb: Nuclear Proliferation in the 1980s* (New Haven, CT: Yale University Press, 1982), pp. 69–94, and Scott D. Sagan and Kenneth N. Waltz, *The Spread of Nuclear Weapons: A Debate* (New York: W. W. Norton, 1995), pp. 55–57.

[374]Steinbruner, "Choices and Trade-offs," p. 546.

they are meant to serve as well as on their overall effect on the nuclear posture. Since India has eschewed the development of a robust and ready arsenal (Alternative V in the previous chapter) in favor of a force-in-being (a middling choice between Alternatives IV and V), it is unlikely to pursue either physical hardening or active interdiction of attacking weapons as its *primary* means of ensuring survivability.

Physical hardening of India's nuclear assets, a solution most relevant to the land-based air and missile force and to the physical C^3 infrastructure, is an extraordinarily expensive and complex endeavor.[375] The complexity of this effort essentially derives from the fact that successful hardening requires that *every* critical component of a given system be made immune to the damage mechanisms associated with a nuclear detonation: air blast, ground shock, electromagnetic pulse (EMP), radiation, and thermal effects. Coping with each of these mechanisms requires different, specially designed solutions for every kind of component that might be at risk. As far as missile systems go, for example, a missile might have to be physically encased in a special silo that is deliberately hardened to high levels of overpressures through use of advanced materials technology, and within the silo itself the missile, perched in a "rattle space," will have to be braced by special suspension devices that absorb the violent ground motion accompanying a surface detonation. Sealing to high tolerances would also be required to protect the missile and its integral launch and operational support equipment against thermal effects, while the power supplies, communications, environmental and launch control hardware, and crew and maintenance support equipment would have to be hardened in still others ways against EMP and radiation effects.[376] If a mobile missile system is to be made survivable in the event that continuous dispersal or dispersal-on-warning cannot be assured, then the entire missile and its erector-launcher

---

[375]Kanti Bajpai, "India's Diplomacy and Defence After Pokhran II," in *Post Pokhran II: The National Way Ahead* (New Delhi: India Habitat Centre, 1999), p. 41.

[376]The multifaceted challenges associated with system hardening in the face of nuclear attack are detailed in United States Air Force, *Systems Applications of Nuclear Technology: Effects of Airblast, Cratering, Ground Shock and Radiation on Hardened Structures*, AFSCM-500-8 (Washington, D.C.: Headquarters, Department of the Air Force, 1976). See also S. Schuster (ed.), *The Air Force Manual for Design and Analysis of Hardened Structures*, Vols. I and II (Chatsworth, CA: California Research & Technology, Inc., 1987).

may have to be buried in some sort of trench system with requirements similar to those noted above.[377] Aircraft, too, may require similarly recessed or semirecessed shelters, while protecting the C^3I infrastructure necessitates a different set of hardening techniques in the face of the threats posed by physical destruction, EMP and TREE effects (transient radiation effects on electronics), ionospheric disruption, and jamming. The latter may also require redundancy in the form of multiple links, subject to different failure modes, and the capacity of reconstitution if it is to be effective in the face of a nuclear attack. [378]

Investing in capabilities of this sort not only may lie beyond New Delhi's technical and fiscal capacity but also could be insufficient in the face of the nuclear threats India confronts. Both the kinds of warheads deployed aboard the Chinese missile force and the accuracies that can be attained by Chinese missiles through the use of GPS and differential GPS supplements ensure that Beijing's hard-target interdiction capabilities—which already benefit from high-yield warheads—will improve faster than any Indian advances in hardening technology.[379] The evidence collected by Mark Stokes and others already suggests that China has embarked on a significant missile modernization program that is focused, among other things, on increasing missile accuracy through the exploitation of new onboard and external navigational systems.[380] And while these

---

[377]Such a system was in fact considered by the United States as a possible basing mode for its MX missile during the 1980s. See, Office of Technology Assessment, *MX Missile Basing* (Washington, D.C.: USGPO, 1981), pp. 97–101.

[378]These issues are discussed in J. G Hammer, C. A. Sandoval, and A. Laupa, *Installation Hardening Concepts for Manned Bomber Systems*, RM-3239-PR (Santa Monica: RAND, 1962); Francis R. Eldridge, *Protection of Communications and Electronic Systems*, P-1657 (Santa Monica: RAND, 1959); and J. Bower and P. A. Goldberg, *British Directions in Hardening Missile Bases Against Electromagnetic Effects from Nuclear Explosions*, D-7226 (Santa Monica: RAND, 1960).

[379]China's nuclear interdiction capabilities vis-à-vis certain classes of hard targets such as airfields is usefully assessed in Bruce Bennett, "The Emerging Ballistic Missile Threat: Global and Regional Implications," in Natalie W. Crawford and Chung-In Moon (eds.), *Emerging Threats, Force Structures, and the Role of Air Power in Korea*, CF-152-AF (Santa Monica: RAND, 2000), pp. 181–217.

[380]Mark Stokes, *China's Military Modernization: Implications for the United States* (Carlisle Barracks, PA: Strategic Studies Institute, 1999), pp. 79–108, and Bernard D. Cole and Paul H.B. Godwin, "Advanced Military Technology and the PLA: Priorities and Capabilities for the 21st Century," in Larry M. Wortzel (ed.), *The Chinese Armed*

initiatives do not by any means portend a shift in the direction of nuclear war fighting on the part of Beijing, they do suggest that China could gradually acquire the capability for at least some limited kinds of nuclear counterforce attacks against weaker competitors like India.[381]

In this context, it is also not clear whether the interdiction of attacking weapons through active defenses in the form of both long- and short-range terminal intercept systems would be the best mechanisms for ensuring the survivability of New Delhi's emerging nuclear deterrent, as has been suggested by some Indian analysts.[382] During the Cold War, a variety of high- and low-altitude ballistic missile defense systems were investigated—and, in some instances, even deployed—as a means of enhancing the survivability of land-based nuclear assets. These systems were attractive in many situations where the assets to be defended were either small, hard, and fixed or mobile only over certain narrow and predefined swaths of territory. When the targets had such characteristics—the former, for example, describing the Minuteman missile bases at Grand Forks, North Dakota, and the latter describing the multiple protective shelters concept suggested for the Peacekeeper missile—both the Safeguard and the Low Altitude Defense Systems had some utility.[383]

It is not clear, however, whether active defense systems of these kinds would offer similar benefits in the case of India. To be sure, there are some kinds of assets—such as nuclear production facilities, command bunkers, airfields for nuclear-capable aircraft, and peace-

---

Forces in the 21st Century (Carlisle Barracks, PA: Strategic Studies Institute, 1999), pp. 159–215.

[381] Bennett demonstrates this clearly in the context of air base attacks, for example, in Bennett, "The Emerging Ballistic Missile Threat: Global and Regional Implications," pp. 181–217.

[382] Bajpai, "India's Diplomacy and Defence After Pokhran II," pp. 42–43, and Praful Bakshi, "Nuclear Euphoria and Harsh Realities," *Hindustan Times*, July 14, 1998. See also "India to Design ABM on U.S. Lines: Kalam," *The Times of India*, January 5, 2000.

[383] For more on this issue, see Ashton B. Carter, "BMD Applications: Performance and Limitations," and David N. Schwarz, "Past and Present: The Historical Legacy," in Ashton B. Carter and David N. Schwarz (eds.), *Ballistic Missile Defense* (Washington, D.C.: Brookings, 1984), pp. 98–181 and 330–349. See also Raymond E. Starsman, *Ballistic Missile Defense and Deceptive Basing: A New Calculus for the Defense of ICBMs* (Washington, D.C.: National Defense University Press, 1981).

time missile garrisons—that would benefit from effective missile defenses *if such were to be available.* Their availability, however, is precisely what is at issue, because although New Delhi—seeking to indigenize an advanced IAD network to provide secondary protection against tactical ballistic missiles[384]—has attempted to procure the Russian S-300 system, it is unclear whether these systems will be acquired with the most sophisticated detection and tracking radars available for reasons of both high cost and constrained access. It is also unclear whether such systems—even if acquired in their best available variant—would suffice to protect Indian assets against the high reentry speeds of many Chinese ballistic missiles (and possibly some future Pakistani systems as well).[385] The acquisition of active defenses designed specifically to cope with *strategic* ballistic missiles has not received much attention in India primarily because of concerns about cost, availability, and technical value—even the best Russian technologies here, such as the ABM-3 system incorporating the SH-04 and -08 missiles, are now several decades old—and their effectiveness, at any rate, is suspect if the acquisition of such systems is not predicated on the creation of a larger "overlay" defense architecture integrating different kinds of exoatmospheric sensors and components.[386] What complicates matters further is that even *good* terminal missile defenses, however effective they may be against substrategic ballistic missiles, could actually subvert the goal of protecting some kinds of Indian nuclear assets, such as command facilities that might rely primarily on concealment and deception for their survivability—and they could simultaneously remain ineffective in protecting the large dispersal areas in which India's rail- and road-mobile missile systems would necessarily operate once they were flushed from their peacetime garrisons upon receipt of strategic warning. Active defenses, in any event, are extraordinarily expensive,

---

[384]N. K. Pant, "Ruling over the Skies," *The Pioneer*, February 8, 1997.

[385]On Indian claims in this regard, see *India: "Major" Indo-Russia Defense Pact Reported*, FBIS-NES-98-174, June 23, 1998. For more on this issue, see Gregory Koblentz, "Theater Missile Defense and South Asia: A Volatile Mix," *Nonproliferation Review*, 4:3 (Spring–Summer 1997), pp. 54–62.

[386]Victor Smirnov, "Space Missile Defense Forces: Yesterday, Today, Tomorrow," *Military Parade*, 16 (July–August 1996), available at http://www.milparade.com/1996/16/72-73.htm. See Stephen Weiner, "Systems and Technology," in Ashton B. Carter and David N. Schwarz (eds.), *Ballistic Missile Defense* (Washington, D.C.: Brookings, 1984), pp. 49–97.

could be defeated by relatively simple countermeasures, and would function more as symbols of reassurance in the context of domestic politics than as effective operational antidotes to the kinds of weapons that China possesses today and that Pakistan may possess tomorrow.[387]

Not surprisingly, then, Indian security managers will likely avoid most of the onerous hardening and active defense solutions that some security analysts in New Delhi have proposed. Their preferred solution, heavily emphasizing concealment, deception, and mobility, will focus instead on configuring the force-in-being in such a way as to feature *pervasively distributed capabilities in order that no completed strategic systems actually exist routinely as transparent targets for potential interdiction.* This does not imply, of course, that hardening and active defenses will have no place whatsoever in India's evolving nuclear architecture. Various components of that architecture—C^3I networks and storage facilities, for example—will be progressively hardened as required, and some kinds of active defenses will also be incorporated whenever appropriate. Neither of these two solutions, however, will define the structuring orientation of the deterrent as a whole. Instead, this orientation will be defined primarily by the emphasis on distributed capabilities—and it is this feature that not only makes the Indian deterrent a force-in-being as opposed to, say, a robust and ready arsenal but also broadly contributes to resolving its problems of survivability, at least in principle.[388] Both the National Security Advisory Board and India's security managers have implicitly affirmed that distributed capabilities of one sort or another will characterize the emerging Indian force-in-being. The draft doctrine released by the Board obliquely referred to this idea when it drew a distinction between normal "peacetime deployment" and "fully employable forces" that would be required in times of either crisis or war.[389] Jaswant Singh

---

[387]On the limitations of active (terminal) defenses against missile attack, see Richard L. Garwin, "Technical Aspects of Ballistic Missile Defense," *APS Forum on Physics and Society*, 28:3 (July 1999). For more on this issue, see also Richard L. Garwin, "Effectiveness of Proposed National Missile Defense Against ICBMs from North Korea," March 17, 1999, available at http://www.fas.org/rlg/990317-nmd.htm.

[388]Bajpai, "India's Diplomacy and Defence After Pokhran II," pp. 39–45.

[389]"Draft Report of [the] National Security Advisory Board on Indian Nuclear Doctrine," p. 3.

also affirmed this distinction more directly when, in response to a question about whether it "would . . . be correct to deduce that India will follow different peacetime and wartime deployment/postures," he answered in the affirmative, emphasizing that different "operating procedures will ensure the transition from peacetime deployment modes to a higher state of readiness when required."[390]

The concept of distributed capabilities, which lies at the heart of the idea of a force-in-being, implies that the normal peacetime posture of India's nuclear deterrent will consist of deliberately separated components maintained under conditions of great secrecy. For purposes of analysis, these components may be treated as encompassing the weapon's core, which consists of some kind of fissile material and is usually referred to as the "pit"; the weapon assembly, which consists of all the other nonnuclear elements of the device, including the SAFF subsystems; and the delivery platform, be it aircraft or missile. If the delivery platform is a missile, there are, strictly speaking, two components—the missile itself and the launch system—and the technical characteristics of the latter will vary depending on whether the missile is designed for road or rail mobility or if it is intended for basing on a surface or a subsurface platform. Irrespective of the precise basing mode, however, the distinction between the missile and the launch system—which is analogous to the gravity bomb-strike aircraft combination—is relevant for purposes of understanding the concept of distributed capabilities as the central organizing principle underlying India's current and prospective peacetime nuclear posture.

In a conceptual sense, the notion of distributed capabilities implies that all the distinct and separate components identified above will be stored independently and with the highest level of secrecy consistent with the character of each.[391] The exact extent of separation that will be operationalized in practice, however, is unknown

---

[390]"India Not to Engage in a N-Arms Race: Jaswant."

[391]For a good description that provides a flavor of how this system has been operationalized in the past, see Chengappa, *Weapons of Peace*. The logic of such a system for purposes of deterrence received its fullest articulation first in the writings of Sundarji; for a good summation, see Sundarji, "Indian Nuclear Doctrine—I: Notions of Deterrence," and K. Sundarji, "Indian Nuclear Doctrine—II: Sino-Indo-Pak Triangle," *Indian Express*, November 26, 1994.

and will never be revealed by India's security managers. Yet it is possible to abstractly identify at least six distinct degrees of separation that could define the routine configuration of India's nuclear deterrent on the assumption that this force will eventually include only gravity bombs and warheads to be carried either by land-based aircraft or by land- and sea-based ballistic missiles. If the inventory were to include cruise missiles of different sorts and various kinds of tactical nuclear weapons, the postures described below would have to be further modified, but since it is likely that India's nuclear systems will in the foreseeable future consist mainly of land- and sea-based ballistic missiles—the Agni and possibly the Prithvi in several variants—along with land-based aircraft of different kinds, the postures described below should suffice for purposes of analysis (see Figure 7).

Posture I involves a systematic separation of the pit from the weapon assembly, both of which, in turn, are stored away from their aircraft delivery system. Posture II also involves a systematic separation of the pit from the weapon assembly, both of which are stored away from the delivery system. Since the delivery system in this case is a missile, however, Posture II describes a condition where the missile and its launch system are stored separately as well. This configuration obviously applies only to the land-based component of the deterrent force, since a sea-based deterrent, whether centered on surface ships or on submarines, either does not permit such a degree of separation or permits it only under outlandish technical and operational assumptions so as to render it infeasible.

In contrast to Postures I and II, which describe extremely high degrees of separation among components and entail significant organizational and procedural complexity as far as the management and reconstitution of such a force are concerned, the other postures describe various modes of deployment involving smaller degrees of separation. Posture III involves separating the pit from the weapon assembly and storing these separately from the missile delivery systems—which are maintained, however, in integrated form, with both missiles and launchers mated routinely. Posture IV involves a further diminution in the degree of separation, with the missile, its launcher, and the weapon assembly routinely maintained in integrated form

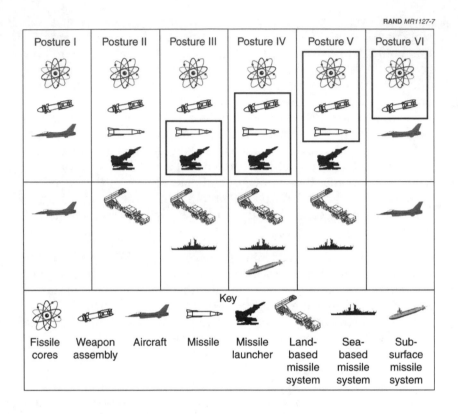

Figure 7—Alternative Postures Defining the Concept of Distributed
Capability

minus only the nuclear pit, which is stored separately and away from
the rest of the integrated system. Although this mode of separation
can be used with respect to both land- and sea-based systems, it is
likely that in the case of the latter both the pits and the missile together with its launch equipment would be aboard the same vessel—
in contrast to a land-based system, where these components could
be stored at some distance from one another. Posture V represents
an alternative form of separation that is broadly comparable to Posture IV in that it would involve the complete mating of the nuclear
pit, the weapon assembly, and the missile itself, but with these completed units stored separately and away from their associated launch
system. This mode of separation is most feasible where land-based

missiles are concerned; is less so in the case of surface ship-based systems; and is practically impossible in the case of submarines, since the loading equipment required to make such a deployment mode viable would be unavailable on subsurface platforms. Posture VI represents a version of separation analogous to Posture V but applies to aircraft; in this deployment mode, the pit and the weapon assembly are fully integrated to form complete and ready gravity bombs, but these units are stored separately from their delivery aircraft, which, being dual-use platforms, are maintained at relatively high levels of readiness.

Several Indian analysts have discussed the notion of distributed capabilities when they have argued either for or against the idea of a "demated" nuclear force.[392] This idea, which in the Indian context derives largely from the intellectual contributions of General Sundarji,[393] K. Subrahmanyam,[394] and Jasjit Singh,[395] has not, however, been discussed in the extensive form elucidated above, and consequently it is difficult to assess which model of distributed capability Indian analysts would either approve or disapprove when they argue about the desirable character of their evolving force posture. In any event, Indian security managers appear to believe that their strategic interests would be best served by some kind of opaque distributed posture that helps preserve the inviolability of their modest nuclear capabilities while simultaneously enhancing crisis stability and reducing the risks associated with the threats of accidental detonation, unauthorized use, mistaken authorized use, and terrorist seizure.[396] The choice of any particular mode of separation, however, depends to a large extent on which of the above objectives is to be

---

[392]W.P.S. Sidhu, "A Virtual De-alert in South Asia," *UNIDIR-Newsletter*, 38 (1998), pp. 27–31; R. Rajaraman, "Delay Deployment: Towards Nuclear Risk Reduction," *The Times of India*, October 1, 1999; Bajpai, "India's Diplomacy and Defence After Pokhran II," pp. 32–45; and Menon, *A Nuclear Strategy for India*, pp. 171–173.

[393]Sundarji, "Indian Nuclear Doctrine—I: Notions of Deterrence," and "Indian Nuclear Doctrine—II: Sino-Indo-Pak Triangle"; Sundarji, "Prithvi in the Haystack"; and Sundarji, "Changing Military Equations in Asia: The Role of Nuclear Weapons," pp. 119–149.

[394]Subrahmanyam, "Nuclear Force Design and Minimum Deterrence Strategy for India," pp. 176–195.

[395]Singh, "A Nuclear Strategy for India" pp. 306–324.

[396]"India Not to Engage in a N-Arms Race: Jaswant."

maximized relative to all others, since there exist intricate trade-offs between survivability, operational flexibility, and risk avoidance in the context of all the threats identified above.

Indian policymakers thus far have not provided any public indication about which objective they would seek to maximize. Nonetheless, their statements suggest an inordinate albeit justifiable concern about the survivability of their nuclear assets.[397] Such remarks, however, should be treated as indicating their recognition of the more obvious problems rather than as considered judgments about how the resolution of such problems will be reconciled with the demands emerging from other less obvious but equally exigent challenges. If their concerns about the priority of ensuring the survivability of the force above all else are taken at face value, then it is likely that they will settle for a deployment posture that incorporates higher degrees of separation. In this context, it is important to recognize that the fact or extent of distribution per se does *not* enhance survivability: Survivability is best ensured by lack of transparency about the location of the nuclear assets. If these assets cannot be located by an adversary because of successful deception, camouflage, or mobility, their survivability is assured irrespective of whether they are deployed in distributed or integrated form. However, because not all the components of a nuclear force can be obscured with equal efficiency—nuclear weapons and their constituent parts, for example, can be hidden far more effectively than delivery systems or the parts thereof—this focus on preserving opacity must be supplemented by a dispersal of components in order to ensure that an adversary's success in locating some elements will not result in a potential loss of the more valuable assets, the nuclear weapons themselves (as would be the case if the relatively more detectable delivery systems were constantly mated with their nuclear payloads).[398]

---

[397] See "Draft Report of [the] National Security Advisory Board on Indian Nuclear Doctrine," pp. 2–3; "India Not to Engage in a N-Arms Race: Jaswant."

[398] This difference in valuation arises because it is presumed that at some point in the future a variety of constraints arising from the CTBT and FMCT regimes will interact to restrict the qualitative and quantitative characteristics of India's nuclear weapon stockpile, thus making the weapons per se far more valuable than the delivery systems, which could be improved in quality or expanded in number without being afflicted by any comparable restrictions.

In order to maximize the success of preserving opacity while simultaneously effecting the distribution of components, force planners would need to acquire a far larger number of potentially more detectable delivery systems than the size of their nuclear weapon stockpile would actually necessitate. Recognizing this fact, the "Draft Report of [the] National Security Advisory Board" argues that in addition to "mobility, dispersion and deception," the "survivability of [India's nuclear] forces will [have to] be enhanced by . . . [the presence of] . . . multiple redundant systems."[399]

While this argument is certainly correct, the key analytical problem identified earlier remains unresolved. If the only objective is to maximize survivability, it is logical for India to focus on acquiring a larger number of delivery systems than is strictly justified by the size of its weapon stockpile coupled with a force posture that emphasizes higher degrees of separation among components—as is exemplified, for instance, by Postures I and II. However, if the objective of maximizing survivability is to be pursued in tandem with some other objective—for example, the ability to shift quickly from peacetime deployment to wartime readiness, as is recommended by the draft doctrine issued by the National Security Advisory Board[400]—then it would be logical for India to consider alternative postures such as Postures V and VI, which incorporate lower degrees of separation. In the end, it would require sophisticated operations research to discern the optimal choices among these various alternatives, and the answers would be greatly conditioned by, among other things, the designs of India's nuclear weapons, the number of India's deterrent assets, the extent of attack envisaged or the extent of attack against which the deterrent is sought to be immunized, and the desired time lines for retaliation.

A complete solution to the problem of assessing the appropriate degree of distribution, however, will require not only an analysis of the trade-offs between the survivability–rapid retaliation dilemma but also an analysis of how any solution adopted to deal with this issue affects India's ability to cope with other challenges, such as the

---

[399]"Draft Report of [the] National Security Advisory Board on Indian Nuclear Doctrine," p. 3.

[400]Ibid.

threats posed by accidental detonation, unauthorized use, mistaken authorized use, and terrorist seizure. When these challenges are incorporated into the analysis, it becomes obvious that Postures V and VI may quickly subvert stability insofar as they require nuclear devices to routinely subsist in completed form. The threats emerging from such a posture can be mitigated considerably if the nuclear weapon designs incorporate some sort of enhanced nuclear detonation safety system (ENDS) and various kinds of permissive action links (PALs)[401]—but if such technologies are not available (or are available in only primitive form), other alternatives will have to be relied on. An alternative that resolves the survivability–rapid retaliation dilemma together with the other challenges of nuclear possession, then, can be found only among Postures I, III and IV, with Posture I being optimal for the air-breathing arm and Posture IV being optimal for the land- and sea-based missile arms of the force. Both of these postures would require nuclear weapons based on "insertable pit"[402] designs—hardly the acme of safety technology today—but if India possesses such devices or can create them, its force-in-being could routinely enjoy the benefits of increased survivability, the ability to generate rapid increases in readiness when required, and great immunity to all the assorted challenges accompanying the possession of nuclear weapons simultaneously.

Irrespective of which of the above postures Indian security managers prefer for their force-in-being, it is obvious that these will be operationalized in dynamic rather than static form: that is, the many components of the deterrent force which are stored separately may be covertly moved from location to location periodically. Moreover, the relatively small size of many of the components, coupled with the fact that a ready physical infrastructure already exists for storing, maintaining, and readying these elements, makes a distributed solu-

---

[401]For more on these technologies, see United States Congress, House Committee on Armed Services, Panel on Nuclear Weapons Safety, *Nuclear Weapons Safety: Report of the Panel on Nuclear Weapons Safety of the Committee on Armed Services*, House of Representatives, 101st Congress, Second Session (Washington, D.C: USGPO, 1990), and Donald Cotter, "Peacetime Operations: Safety and Security," in Ashton B. Carter, John D. Steinbruner, and Charles A. Zraket (eds.), *Managing Nuclear Operations* (Washington, D.C.: Brookings, 1987), pp. 17–74.

[402]For more on such designs, see Chuck Hansen (ed.), *The Swords of Armageddon*, Vol. 8 (Sunnyvale, CA: Chukelea Publications, 1995), pp. 11–36.

tion to India's strategic problem eminently feasible. In this context, there are three general conditions that are necessary for the success of such an arrangement: First, there must be a large number of storage sites under the effective control of the state; second, the number of individuals with information about the physical location of the actual holdings must be small; and third, there must be an organizational system capable of handling both the storage and the episodic but covert movements of various components.

All three conditions obtain abundantly in the case of India. To begin with, the DAE and the DRDO, which will presumably retain physical control of the nuclear pits and weapon assemblies for at least some time to come, control more than 100 major complexes between them, many of which have multiple physical structures where various kinds or combinations of critical components could be stored in complete secrecy.[403] Of course, there is nothing that prevents either of these two organizations from requisitioning other government facilities for purposes of covert storage, but even if DAE and DRDO facilities alone are considered, the candidate storage sites could easily run into well over a few hundred specific hides if not more.[404] It is very difficult even for a superpower like the United States—let alone China and Pakistan—to continuously monitor and identify the status of India's nuclear components if they are stored in some separated form in different locations, many of which may not even be identified. Obviously, the effectiveness of this solution does not accrue from the "atomic" distribution of components per se; these components may in fact be physically concentrated at fewer

---

[403]The DAE, for example, oversees more than 60 major complexes in India; see O. P. Sabherwal, "India's Nuclear Strategy: Peaceful and Weapon Capability," *World Focus*, 21:4 (April 2000), p. 22. The DRDO similarly oversees approximately 50 major complexes; see R.K. Jasbir Singh (ed.), *Indian Defence Yearbook, 1997–98* (Dehra Dhun, India: Natraj Publishers, 1997), pp. 438–442. There are still many other complexes controlled by various defense production and supply entities that do not come under the administrative control of either the DAE or the DRDO but are nonetheless fully under the control of the government of India.

[404]The overhead imagery of some Indian research and development facilities published by the Federation of American Scientists amply demonstrates that even singular complexes relating to the nuclear weapon program contain numerous individual, dispersed facilities that can be used as potential hides. See Federation of American Scientists, "A View of Non-NPT Nuclear States from Space: Nuclear and Missile Facility Satellite Images and Their Implications for the NPT," available at http://www.fas.org/eye/3nws.htm.

than a dozen or so facilities. But because there are so many potential hides to begin with and because the dispersal of components is operationalized in utmost secrecy, the disadvantages otherwise accruing to even such a "molecular" dispersal of assets are minimized.[405]

The same logic applies to the delivery systems, but the issues here are more complex. Since the delivery platform is actually an aircraft or a missile, it will be maintained by the military itself in operating, standby, or inert status. Neither aircraft nor missiles need be routinely maintained in operating condition, and if minimizing costs is a critical objective, the prepared delivery systems can be maintained either in a standby or in an inert mode. Missiles, once produced, can be maintained together or apart from their launcher-transporters in inert status for fairly long periods of time so long as diagnostic checks of both components and the overall system are regularly carried out.[406] Aircraft, in contrast, require regular start-ups, routine proving flights, and constant maintenance if they are to be made available for normal combat operations at relatively short notice. Indian decisionmakers, of course, may not require even such minimal levels of availability and may rest content with maintaining their nuclear strike aircraft in "cocooned" conditions, depending on the desired time frame for conducting retaliatory strikes. Such a deployment mode, however, is highly unlikely, because the Indian combat aircraft slated for the nuclear mission are essentially dual-capable platforms that have primary obligations relating to conventional war fighting in the event of deterrence breakdown. Consequently, they will be maintained in normal operating conditions and at relatively high levels of readiness most of the time. Therefore, unlike the land-based missile arm, which can be maintained at various degrees of dormancy in peacetime, India's air-breathing systems will be routinely maintained in operating condition to the benefit of their sec-

---

[405]Indian efforts to disguise their weapon-related storage, test, and operational activities are described intermittently throughout Chengappa, *Weapons of Peace.*

[406]In the aftermath of the Cold War, France considered maintaining its Hades SRBMs in such a condition and was prepared, until procurement of this system was canceled, to sustain such a posture indefinitely. See Yves Boyer, "Questioning Minimum Deterrence," in Serge Sur (ed.), *Nuclear Deterrence: Problems and Perspectives in the 1990s* (New York: UNIDIR, 1993), pp. 101–104.

ondary nuclear role.[407] For technical reasons associated in part with the demands of sea keeping, India's sea-based missile arm—if and when such is operational—will also be maintained at a high level of readiness, at least when the vessels hosting such systems are under way on patrol.

In any event—and irrespective of the readiness status of these platforms—there are more than 50 major Indian Air Force bases and forward support facilities where nuclear-capable aircraft and land-based missiles can be bivouacked in peacetime.[408] The aircraft themselves will be constantly rotated between facilities and may even be "randomly" shifted in formations of varying size between different air bases in an emergency. So long as some air bases (and the aircraft on them) survive an attack, the latter will be available for mounting retaliatory strikes using, if necessary, other civilian airfields and facilities to marry up with their weapons prior to executing the retaliatory strike.[409] Since land-based missile systems, in contrast, do not require special operating facilities such as runways and control towers, they could be stored covertly at many more locations, including the hundreds of cantonments, bases, and facilities operated by all three Indian armed services. So long as their wartime operating sites are presurveyed and the launch coordinates known ahead of time, the land-based missiles and their TELs can be stored anywhere, although they might require various kinds of intratheater airlift to carry them to their launch points when the decision is made to unleash the punitive response. Rail-mobile systems may be able to avoid such demands altogether if the extra, separately stored missiles, pits, warheads, and other components can be brought to the reconstitution point by rail itself. A similar judgment applies to road-

---

[407]This is certainly the case today, as was demonstrated during the Kargil crisis, when India apparently readied at least some Mirage aircraft for possible nuclear missions against Pakistan. See Chengappa, *Weapons of Peace*, p. 437.

[408]For more details, see Jon Lake, "Indian Air Power," *World Air Power Journal*, 12 (Spring 1993), pp. 138–157.

[409]There are 449 airports/airstrips in India. These include five international airports, 87 domestic airports, and 28 civil enclaves at military airfields in addition to India's other dedicated military air bases. More than 67 of these civilian facilities are equipped with a variety of navigational aids and radars, as are all India's dedicated military air bases. For details, see "Indian Airports," available at http://civilaviation.nic.in/aai/airport.htm.

mobile missiles, but since these conclusions hinge heavily on the extent of the nuclear attack on India and, by implication, on both the quality of the surviving infrastructure and the size and composition of the residual fraction of the force, Indian force planners would most likely arrange for the availability of intratheater airlift or some other forms of surface transportation in support of their retaliatory operations.[410]

Ironically, the sea-based component of the Indian deterrent—both surface ships and submarines—may be the most handicapped *from the perspective of covert basing.* The number of ports in India where nuclear assets might be housed are relatively few. There are, for example, some 14 major and 29 minor ports, and many of the latter have neither the size nor the draft to berth any major surface combatants, let alone submersible platforms, although some could support offshore berthing in an emergency.[411] In any event, both surface ships and submarines are difficult to disguise while berthed, and unlike aircraft or land-based missiles, which can be quickly redeployed or flushed out from their hides in an emergency, ships and submarines require significant preparation time prior to egress from their home ports. Both ships and submarines are also relatively slow and can be trailed, and ships are particularly vulnerable to wide-area search and track operations. These disadvantages can be compensated for by clever operational practices, including continuous cyclic deployments, but even these techniques do little to alter the fact that ships and submarines have to preserve survivability by means other than covert basing and, unlike aircraft and land-based missiles, may actually be somewhat more vulnerable in peacetime because their presence at a few clearly identified and specialized facilities is difficult to obscure.[412]

---

[410]This, at any rate, was explicitly envisaged in Sundarji's conception of how a force-in-being would operate (see Sundarji, "Indian Nuclear Doctrine—I: Notions of Deterrence"), and the various passages in Chengappa, *Weapons of Peace*, that describe the conduct of India's nuclear activities amply corroborates this expectation.

[411]Details about Indian ports, together with details about berthing facilities, can be found at http://www.indiaport.com. See also Satkartar Batra, *The Ports of India*, 3rd ed. (Kandla, India: Kandla Commercial Publications, 1982).

[412]A good survey of how the United States responded to the threats facing its sea-based strategic forces can be found in T. A. Heppenheimer, *Anti-Submarine Warfare: The Threat, the Strategy, the Solution* (Arlington, VA: Pasha Publications, 1989). See also Donald C. Daniel, *Anti-Submarine Warfare and Superpower Strategic Stability*

Despite this challenge, which may or may not be oppressive depending on the circumstances, the fact remains that all prewar storage facilities in India—both civilian installations overseen by the DAE and the DRDO and military facilities—are relatively secure, since all enjoy high levels of physical protection against penetration and unauthorized access.[413] Moreover, the sheer size, number, and location of these facilities render them ideal sanctuaries for all kinds of critical strategic components. Given the operating practices in both the atomic energy establishment and the military at large, clandestine storage—with minimal revelation of all the related physical, operational, and inferential signatures—can thus be successfully effected outside the prying eyes of observers both within and beyond these installations. This fact makes the objective of preserving location uncertainty eminently feasible, which in turn increases the survivability of the deterrent as a whole. At a conceptual level, this strategy of storing a relatively small set of components or entire systems in a potentially large set of protecting hides forces an attacker to target all or most of these facilities if it is not known *a priori* which of them contain what components and in what number. By immersing critical elements of the force—in peacetime and, perhaps, even during a crisis—in a sea of hides, the logic of distributed capabilities then forces an attacker to expend a larger quantum of assets than it otherwise would to ensure the high levels of attrition that are obviously necessary to make any first strike worthwhile.[414]

While the number of facilities at which India's strategic assets could be distributed is therefore potentially large, the number of individuals with information about the location and status of these

---

(Urbana, IL: University of Illinois Press, 1986) and Tom Stefanick, *Strategic Antisubmarine Warfare and Naval Strategy* (Lexington, KY: Lexington Books, 1987).

[413]Peter R. Lavoy, "Civil-Military Relations, Strategic Conduct, and the Stability of Nuclear Deterrence in South Asia," in Scott Sagan (ed.), *Civil-Military Relations and Nuclear Weapons* (Stanford, CA: Center for International Security and Arms Control, Stanford University, 1994), p. 84, and P. R. Chari, *Protection of Fissile Materials: The Indian Experience*, ACDIS Occasional Paper (Urbana, IL: University of Illinois, September 1998).

[414]This was precisely the logic that underlay the initial U.S. interest in mobile basing of its ICBMs. See Office of Technology Assessment, *MX Missile Basing*, pp. 34–45.

component parts is, by contrast, small.[415] Unlike U.S. nuclear weapon programs, for example, which are organized as gigantic bureaucracies oriented toward achieving order and efficiency, the Indian program involves a relatively small number of people and is oriented toward the strict maintenance of secrecy. It has been estimated, for example, that the Indian nuclear tests in May 1974 did not involve more than 75 scientists and engineers[416] and that the May 1998 tests probably involved fewer than 250 people at various levels.[417] Those who possess a "God's eye view" of the entire weapon program are probably fewer than two dozen in number, although perhaps many more may be aware of bits and pieces of information pertaining to the general effort.[418] Moreover, it is almost impossible for outsiders to determine who has full knowledge of the program, since no organizational chart of India's "nuclear weapon program" actually exists, and even if it did, such a chart would obscure almost as much as it revealed.[419] This is because administrative structures in India—especially those relating to the nuclear weapon effort—cut across organizational realms, and operational directives are invariably communicated informally without any written record whatsoever.[420] These arrangements work only because the Indian administrative structure spawns effective but shadowy core *networks* that are superimposed on the existing *institutions*. In such circumstances, strategic decisionmaking is transacted within the small network,

---

[415]See the discussion at various points in Chengappa, *Weapons of Peace*, and Perkovich, *India's Nuclear Bomb*.

[416]Perkovich, *India's Nuclear Bomb*, p. 172.

[417]Rahul Bedi, "As Nuclear Test Preparations Avoid Detection," *Jane's Defence Weekly*, May 20, 1998, p. 5.

[418]Chengappa, *Weapons of Peace*, pp. xv–xvi.

[419]Chengappa's narrative, in his *Weapons of Peace*, notes at various points that even those individuals who one might assume would know about India's nuclear weapon program—at least when judged from the outside—often did not know any details or even basic facts about some of the key decisions made by India's Prime Ministers and their often idiosyncratically selected band of close advisers. According to Chengappa, these individuals included at various times the Cabinet Secretary, the Defence Minister, and the Chiefs of Staff.

[420]See Subrahmanyam, "Indian Nuclear Policy—1964–98," pp. 26–53, and episodically throughout Perkovich, *India's Nuclear Bomb*, and Chengappa, *Weapons of Peace*.

while the larger institutional apparatus is simply relegated to the business of routine management.[421]

The overall bureaucratic structure, however, serves the critical purpose of weeding out individuals who fail to appreciate the "rules of the game," thereby contributing to the success of the core network insofar as it serves to bring together a small group of individuals at the very top who trust one another, share a common conception of the national interest, and can execute complex decisions secretly and in a way that does not necessarily involve the rest of the organizational apparatus. To be sure, this modus operandi certainly does not preclude the development of more formal and institutionalized procedures for managing the Indian nuclear deterrent over time—and the prospective creation of a new unified command headed by the CDS and tasked with overseeing India's strategic assets could provide Indian state managers with just the institutionalized structures necessary to plan, procure, organize, and train the various components of the evolving deterrent force.

In the interim, however, it does suggest that the security of the control and oversight arrangements will be difficult to compromise because low-level actors will *not* possess sufficient information about the status and disposition of *all* the constituent parts of the deterrent, while the high-level actors will be difficult to identify exhaustively and, even if identified, will not reveal anything more than they choose to about India's nuclear posture writ large.[422]

---

[421]The failure to distinguish between informal networks and formal institutions as far as decisionmaking with respect to the Indian nuclear weapon program is concerned often leaves many Western and even Indian analysts puzzled and confused. See, for example, Jonathan Karp, "India Faces Task of Creating Nuclear-Weapons Doctrine," *Wall Street Journal*, May 27, 1998. By looking hard for formal institutions and not finding them, such analysts are often led to the erroneous conclusion that an effective Indian nuclear command system does not currently exist. This conclusion holds only if it is believed that formal institutions are essential for the success of all kinds of decisionmaking. If networks suffice, however, at least in some issue areas, it is possible that India could have an effective command system without all the accoutrements otherwise associated with formal institutional arrangements. For good theoretical work that highlights the distinction between institutions and networks, see Manuel Castells, *The Informational City: Information Technology, Economic Restructuring, and the Urban-Regional Process* (Cambridge, UK: Blackwell, 1989).

[422]Chengappa, for example, points out how even India's Defence Ministers, service chiefs, and important senior bureaucrats often knew what they did about India's nuclear weapon program and activities only because they were specifically told

This simple fact makes any countercontrol targeting strategy difficult if not impossible to execute even by an advanced nuclear power, because even the destruction of every identifiable technical node within the command system may not suffice to prevent control from being reestablished by more primitive means and through the coordinated actions of a relatively small number of individuals who know each other intimately. Since the entire organizational structure places a premium on extreme secrecy, extensive countercontrol targeting may also not suffice for perfect damage limitation, since any potential adversary has to reckon with the prospect that there could always be some further strategic capabilities or technical resources held in reserve—capabilities that are unknown even to those few individuals otherwise thought to possess "perfect" knowledge about the status and disposition of India's distributed strategic assets. It is this uncertainty which ultimately neutralizes the challenges posed by any potential compromise from within, not to mention the fact that an adversary who receives such information will still have to grapple with the uncertainties associated with the reliability of covert information, since the costs of mistaken action could be high.[423]

---

what they needed to know in the context of some incipient nodal event and not because they were entitled to know merely because of the position they held within the Indian state. Thus, he describes one instance when in the context of preparation for India's nuclear tests the Chief of Army Staff did not know about the impending tests (except whatever he may have picked up informally because his regiment was tasked with preparing the test shafts), while his subordinate, the Director General, Military Operations, was provided with the minimal information necessary so that the requisite tasking could be issued to the engineer regiments at Pokhran ordering them to prepare the shafts in anticipation for the forthcoming tests. Whether these details are apocryphal is less relevant than the fact that "need to know" rather than seniority often determined the fact and extent of knowledge about the Indian nuclear weapon program even among the most senior functionaries of the Indian state. See Chengappa, *Weapons of Peace*, pp. 1–14.

[423]This difficulty, in effect, helps resolve what was called the "clever briefer" problem during the Cold War. This problem refers to a hypothetical contingency in which a "clever" military briefer could accost the national command authority with the claim that a prompt preemptive damage-limiting attack on the adversary ought to be considered because a sudden intelligence windfall resulted in complete information about the size, disposition, and readiness of the adversary's nuclear forces. This information would be complemented by the presentation of a clever operational plan that arguably would achieve complete success only if the attack was launched "immediately," since the information that guaranteed success would become obsolete if it were not acted upon within the narrow (present) window of opportunity.

Finally, what makes the distributed posture potentially effective from the standpoint of survivability is the fact that routine standard operating procedures already exist in both the civilian and military realms. The Indian nuclear program, for example, already has a working set of institutional procedures that regulate the transfer of critical nuclear materials between various facilities and sites as well as a physical infrastructure that allows for the appropriate handling of all such materials.[424] A similar set of procedures and infrastructure exists in the DRDO. Since these communities have primary responsibility for the custody, storage, and handling of both nuclear pits and weapon assemblies in peacetime, it is not unreasonable to believe that these components would be secured (or moved, as the case may be) without any security lapses or compromise. As the components themselves are relatively small and can be moved by ordinary forms of transportation, the likelihood that a potential adversary would be able to locate all or many of the storage sites associated with the concealment of these components is extremely remote. If anything is detected at all, it is likely to be the delivery systems rather than the fissile cores and weapon assemblies, but detecting such components is unlikely to be of great consolation to potential adversaries such as China and Pakistan because it is possible that all they would gain for the trouble of attempting a first strike against such a target set is delayed retaliation coupled with a sure and certain war with India.[425]

As if to inure against this possibility, the Indian military, too, has a comparable set of procedures and infrastructure governing the storage and movement of critical war materials.[426] If anything, these organizational capabilities are even better developed because the peacetime dispersal of India's military capabilities across vast distances of the hinterland has required that its armed services develop

---

[424]Chari, *Protection of Fissile Materials: The Indian Experience*, pp. 5–7.

[425]Whether delayed retaliation is at all possible, of course, obviously hinges on whether an adversary can destroy all or most of the Indian delivery systems involved. This contingency is implausible as far as Pakistan is concerned and even in the case of China would demand a large weapon allocation that raises all manner of questions about the strategic utility of such actions. For one Indian assessment of this exchange calculus, see Menon, *A Nuclear Strategy for India*, pp. 177–234.

[426]Ibid., pp. 235–261.

both the physical infrastructure and the organizational routines that pertain to the rapid movement of military equipment in an emergency. Thus, for example, combat aircraft routinely stage out to forward operating facilities for exercises; major land formations rotate episodically to training locations at the frontier; and the forward defenses in remote border areas are kept supplied by complex support services that move large amounts of stores, supplies, and equipment. Therefore, organizing the storage and episodic movement of nuclear-capable aircraft and ballistic missiles will not be an insurmountable problem for the Indian military. To be sure, such activities can be detected because military movements often release characteristic physical, technical, and inferential signatures. Such detection, however, may not occur in real time and, in fact, may not occur at all, as the Indian military's proficiency at camouflage, deception, and denial has vastly improved in recent years. And while it is possible that many activities pertaining to the covert storage and movement of nuclear-capable platforms might be detected by advanced powers such as the United States, the same does not hold true for India's principal adversaries, China and Pakistan.[427]

It should also be noted that even if India's regional adversaries detected these platforms, they would be confronted with the same uncertainties noted earlier in the context of detecting distributed nuclear weapons: They could never be sure that they had identified all of India's nuclear strike assets, and even if they did, the separation of weapons from weapon carriers implies that retaliation could be fur-

---

[427]The critical detection systems necessary for such purposes are imagery, electronic, and signal intelligence systems. Because both ground- and air-based systems have significant operational limitations, space-based systems become particularly critical. Pakistani capabilities in these areas are not worth mention. While Chinese capabilities are certainly superior in all three collection media, they are significantly handicapped as far as real-time collection, assessment, and dissemination of data are concerned. While these capabilities will certainly improve over the next decade, it is still unclear whether such improvements will actually allow for an effective counterforce war-fighting strategy. For more on Pakistani and Chinese capabilities in this regard, see Desmond Ball, *Signals Intelligence in the Post–Cold War Era: Developments in the Asia-Pacific Region* (Singapore: Institute of Southeast Asian Studies, 1993); Desmond Ball, *Signals Intelligence (SIGINT) in South Asia: India, Pakistan, Sri Lanka (Ceylon)* (Canberra: Strategic and Defence Studies Centre, Australian National University, 1996); Khalilzad et al., *The United States and a Rising China*, pp. 57–59; and the FAS websites on Pakistan and China at http://www.fas.org/spp/guide/pakistan/index.html and http://www.fas.org/spp/guide/china/index.html, respectively.

ther delayed but not avoided. If India adopted patterns of distribution of the kind represented by Postures I, II, III, and VI, the fissile cores and weapon assemblies would still exist inviolate even if the more translucent delivery systems were detected, identified, and successfully attacked. If, however, the weapon assemblies minus the cores were mated to the delivery systems in advance—as would be the case if Postures IV and possibly V were adopted—this advantage would be lost, which is one more reason India ought to consider distributing and maintaining both the fissile core and the weapon assembly separately from the delivery vehicle and/or launch equipment. Since the last two components are more likely to be detected than the first two, it does not make sense to imperil these secure elements by prematurely mating them to a potentially more vulnerable system. This posture would no doubt delay any retaliatory response, but depending on the size, extent, and density of the anticipated threat, New Delhi might find it worthwhile to emphasize a strategic disposition that increases survivability rather than alacrity of response within the overall framework of a force-in-being. Thus, even if the delivery vehicles were to be destroyed, the surviving pits and weapon assemblies would allow India to consider the possibility of unconventional means of delivery and would not prevent New Delhi from hastily reconfiguring additional delivery vehicles, especially aircraft, for purposes of retaliation if *all* its primary designated carriers were destroyed—against all odds—in a first strike.

The virtue of the distributed force-in-being that is likely to be operationalized by India is that it resolves the vexing problem of survivability at low cost, since many of the other solutions, such as hardening and active defenses, are beyond New Delhi's financial and technical reach. Further, it allows India to exploit all the comparative advantages that accrue to both its size and its patterns of organization: The large number of potential sanctuaries coupled with the extreme secrecy surrounding nuclear decisionmaking and operations will allow Indian security managers to develop an effective solution that preserves the survivability of its nuclear assets by refusing, in effect, to present any worthwhile targets. In a strict sense, the distributed solution represents a shell game in that there *are* plenty of potential targets—in fact, far more than there are deliverable nuclear weapons in Pakistan and possibly in China as well. Even if many of these suspected sanctuaries could be successfully attacked, the adversary could not be sure that these strikes would de-nature the Indian nuclear force and thereby prevent the costly retaliation that would result from such attacks. Indeed, the dis-tributed solution makes it difficult even for advanced nuclear powers to effectively target such architectures, since with it there is pervasive uncertainty about both the organizational arrangements relating to command and control and the locations of the numerous separated components that, when reconstituted, would make up a viable retal-iatory force. As Sundarji put it, "It is not just a question of [finding] 'needles in haystacks,' but parts of many needles in many haystacks which might be brought together when required within hours to days, to form full needles in yet many more different haystacks."[428] The targeting challenges facing adversaries like China and Pakistan would be even greater than those facing an advanced nuclear power, and consequently it is not unreasonable to expect that these adver-saries would be deterred from attempting damage-limiting strikes in the first place.

All strategic solutions to the problem of survivability involve trade-offs, and the Indian concept of a distributed force-in-being is no ex-ception. The critical weakness of this posture is not its susceptibility to accidents—since completed nuclear weapons probably would not exist as such in peacetime—but rather its potential inability to effec-tively reconstitute in the aftermath of a nuclear attack in order to carry out the retaliation ordered by the national command authority. While it is difficult to imagine any successful damage-limiting strikes conducted by either China or Pakistan simply because of the ratio of potential targets to weapons involved, not to mention the intelli-gence requirements needed to support such strikes, it should be rec-ognized that such eventualities are possible at least theoretically and could impose great burdens on India's capacity to retaliate. Although Indian nuclear assets may not be entirely obliterated by such strikes, the resulting damage could cause ample dislocation in the coordi-nating mechanisms, thereby either delaying retaliation interminably or reducing its effectiveness considerably.

Should this outcome obtain, it would be obvious that India's ef-forts at ensuring the survivability of its nuclear capabilities were less

---

[428]Sundarji, "Indian Nuclear Doctrine—I: Notions of Deterrence."

than effective to begin with. This is, however, a risk that Indian decisionmakers seem willing to take for three reasons: first, because the requirements for successful disarming strikes are deemed to be so large as to render them beyond the pale of possibility in the real world, especially in the context of India's competition with China and Pakistan;[429] second, because neither Pakistan nor China has demonstrated either the technical capabilities or the doctrinal interest in executing damage-limiting first strikes as a matter of operational policy;[430] and third, because the circumstances under which Indian nuclear weapon use becomes realistic are so remote that the risk of being unable to reconstitute effectively becomes a secondary problem, given New Delhi's more pressing interest in ensuring the safety of its weaponry, minimizing the costs of the arsenal, and maintaining continual civilian control over its strategic assets.[431]

What makes a difference in the end is that India does *not* seek to deter formidable nuclear powers like the United States and Russia, but merely lesser adversaries like China and Pakistan. Even in these instances, nuclear weapons do not represent New Delhi's first line of defense but remain merely *political instruments of deterrence and reassurance* that acquire effectiveness because the devastation that even one of India's modest weapons could cause would be far greater than any of the benefits its adversaries sought through war. Given these realities, the risk of being unable to reconstitute an overwhelming retaliatory response because of an excessively distributed force-in-being is something that New Delhi can live with. The Indian state will in fact attempt to mitigate this problem by *not* distributing excessively but simply by exploiting the *possibilities* of extensive distribution through the use of secrecy, deception, and mobility to mask the few locations where its strategic reserves are actually hidden. Sundarji confirmed India's calculations in this regard when he noted that "with any such deployment, an Indian planner may not have the degree of assurance that he would like about the survival of the In-

---

[429]Ibid.

[430]Subrahmanyam, "Nuclear Force Design and Minimum Deterrence Strategy for India," pp. 186–191. On this issue, see also Shahi, Khan, and Sattar, "Securing Nuclear Peace," and Robert A. Manning, Ronald Montaperto, and Brad Roberts, *China, Nuclear Weapons, and Arms Control* (New York: Council on Foreign Relations, 2000).

[431]Subrahmanyam, "Nuclear Force Design and Minimum Deterrence Strategy for India," pp. 176–195.

dian second strike. However, with such a deployment no Chinese planner can be certain that no Indian second strike will survive that could devastate a few major Chinese cities. [Consequently] there will be enormous reluctance to go in for such a Chinese first strike. This is what deterrence is all about."[432]

Centralized in Control

While maintaining opacity, supplemented if necessary by the separation of components, constitutes the first level of protection against interdiction by an adversary, the discussion above indicates that the issue of survivability constitutes only one of the many challenges an emerging nuclear power faces. Among other critical issues is the security of the nuclear force—that is, its resistance to efforts by unauthorized individuals to acquire custody of the weaponry and discharge them without legitimate sanction. Dealing with this problem remains the province of the control system, which regulates both the patterns of custody surrounding nuclear weapons and the extent of autonomy these custodians enjoy with respect to the issue of legitimate use. The challenges arising from these issues have traditionally been termed the dilemma of "positive" and "negative" control. As Peter Feaver summarized it, positive control refers to the fact that "leaders want a high assurance that the weapons will always work when directed,"[433] while negative control refers to the equally high degree of reassurance sought by the national leadership that "the weapons will never be used in the absence of authorized direction."[434] Since positive and negative control must be accomplished simultaneously, there has always been a certain degree of tension between these two demands, as the requirements of safety could undercut the requirements of survivability and vice versa. Thus, for example, concentrating all nuclear weapons in a single location would enhance safety considerably insofar as these weapons could be better guarded against threats of theft, loss, and unauthorized use, but their very concentration would increase their susceptibility to inter-

---

[432]Sundarji, "Indian Nuclear Doctrine—I: Notions of Deterrence."

[433]Peter D. Feaver, "Command and Control in Emerging Nuclear Nations," *International Security*, 17:3 (Winter 1992–1993), p. 163.

[434]Ibid.

diction in a first strike. The dispersal of nuclear weapons, in contrast, could immunize them against the threat of easy interdiction insofar as dispersal dramatically increases the level of resources required for a splendid first strike but could increase the risks of "nuclear inadvertence, that is, the risk that nuclear weapons may be used by accident; by third parties, such as terrorists; or without authorization."[435] These safety-survivability trade-offs traditionally resulted in the development of various innovations intended to safeguard nuclear weapons while preserving their effectiveness—and although different nuclear powers adopted alternative solutions depending on the political and operational goals they wished to pursue, all control systems eventually came to display a certain bias that was "reflected in the[ir] relative emphasis on either positive or negative control."[436]

The United States, for example—operating on the premise that achieving successful nuclear deterrence against a revisionist power like the Soviet Union was a difficult and demanding task—attempted to resolve this dilemma by a combination of technical and organizational solutions which always sought to ensure that a sufficient number of nuclear weapons would remain constantly available and ready for instant use even after absorbing a Soviet first strike. To ensure ready availability—or in other words, continuing positive control—the United States developed an elaborately dispersed force in which ready nuclear weapons were deployed on board a multiplicity of platforms such as land-based missiles, submarines, and bombers just to ensure that sufficient nuclear warheads survived any attempted Soviet attack. Because this solution centering on dispersal essentially implied that the uniformed services had *completed nuclear weapons* (at varying levels of readiness) in their possession at all times, the problem of negative control—that is, the prevention of mistaken or unauthorized use—became a critical issue. The United States addressed this challenge through a combination of technical responses—e.g., designing its nuclear weapons to incorporate ENDS systems supplemented by PALs, permissive enable systems, and elaborate physical launch and firing sequences—that were designed

---

[435]Bradley A. Thayer, "The Risk of Nuclear Inadvertence: A Review Essay," *Security Studies*, 3:3 (Spring 1994), p. 429.

[436]Feaver, "Command and Control in Emerging Nuclear Nations," p. 168.

to disable either the weapon or its launch system in the event of unauthorized or improper attempts at use.[437]

These technical solutions, which were often highly sophisticated and costly, were complemented by organizational innovations, such as the personnel reliability program and the "two-man rule," which were designed to prevent unreliable individuals from gaining access to the weaponry while simultaneously prohibiting even otherwise trustworthy custodians from executing unauthorized launches.[438] Since the fear of a successful Soviet preemptive (or decapitating) strike was always present in the consciousness of American planners, the overall command system was biased in the direction of positive control, and this tendency was reflected most conspicuously in the highly "delegative"[439] patterns of authority that were institutionalized throughout the system. This meant not only that the custodians of the weaponry—the uniformed military—enjoyed a high degree of autonomy with respect to the use of nuclear weapons in their possession but also, as one authority put it, that the "decentralization [which] ha[d] been literally wired into the strategic communications network [actually left] national officials without the physical means they would need to bring strategic operations under firm control."[440] Since delegative control implied that there were few *physical* constraints on the release of these weapons, several military operators—especially those in the air defense and ballistic missile submarine community—could independently launch their weaponry if they were confronted by special circumstances such as a surprise attack or if they had good reason to believe that a prior Soviet strike had decapitated the national civilian leadership.[441]

In the case of India, the control system would be biased in exactly the opposite direction because New Delhi's strategic requirements

---

[437]The best description of these efforts remains Feaver, *Guarding the Guardians*.

[438]For more of these innovations and their limitations, see Scott D. Sagan, *The Limits of Safety: Organizations, Accidents, and Nuclear Weapons* (Princeton, NJ: Princeton University Press, 1993). See also William A. Hodgson, "Nuclear Weapons Personnel Reliability Program," *Combat Edge*, 4:1 (June 1995), pp. 22–23.

[439]The term comes from Feaver, "Command and Control in Emerging Nuclear Nations," p. 170.

[440]Blair, *Strategic Command and Control*, p. 51.

[441]Feaver, "Command and Control in Emerging Nuclear Nations," p. 169.

differ from those the United States faced during the Cold War.[442] To be sure, there are some superficial similarities between the two—India will probably also pursue some kind of distributed solution to the problem of survivability—but the nature of the assets distributed and the pattern of control exercised over these assets will be radically different. The United States distributed *complete* nuclear weapons across diversified delivery systems possessed, maintained, and manned by a variety of end users in the uniformed military. India is likely to distribute only discrete components of its nuclear "arsenal" across different locations, with the uniformed military—either through the prospective new unified command or through the existing armed services—tasked principally with storing, maintaining, and manning the delivery systems. These stored delivery systems may not be mated with any weapon assemblies, and the fissile cores necessary to transform these assemblies into completed nuclear weapons are likely to be stowed covertly in still other locations separate from the delivery system and probably from the nonnuclear weapon assembly as well. The exact degree of separation, of course, will depend on which of the six models of distributed capability the Indian state finally chooses, but completed nuclear weapons are in any case unlikely to be distributed to any of the uniformed end users for custodial purposes in peacetime.

This separation by components—which lies at the heart of the Indian version of the distributed solution—will probably be further complemented by a partitioning by organization: The DAE and the DRDO, both civilian agencies, are likely to retain custody of the fissile core and the weapon assembly (either jointly or separately), while the nuclear-capable delivery system, be it aircraft or missile, will remain in the custody of the uniformed military, since there is in effect no viable alternative arrangement as far as the dual-capable delivery systems are concerned. Thus, neither the DAE nor the DRDO

---

[442]In fact, it is likely that, after accounting for all their relevant differences, the Indian command system will more closely resemble the Soviet command system during the Cold War than the American system at least to the extent that the latter's obsession with system survivability and adequacy of target coverage will be replaced, as in the Soviet model, by equal if not greater emphasis on "geopolitical considerations, self-preservation, and negative control as [on] damage expectancy." Blair, *The Logic of Accidental Nuclear War*, p. 59. The Soviet command system and its contrasting biases are reviewed in some detail on pages 59–167 of this work.

nor the uniformed military would be able to launch a nuclear weapon independently, since none of these organizations—acting autonomously—would have all the necessary components to assemble a completed weapon and deliver it to target without explicit authorization from the national leadership.

Without such authorization, it would in fact be impossible for the various custodial teams to even assemble together, since there is a high degree of organizational separation between the civilian nuclear scientists, the civilian defense technologists, and the uniformed military. Even if the two former groups—exploiting their common civilian status—could somehow get together and fabricate a nuclear device clandestinely, they would at worst end up with a nuclear weapon that could not be delivered. If, on the other hand, the latter two groups—exploiting their common involvement in matters relating to the military—could somehow get together and mate their respective assets, they would at worst end up with a weapon assembly on a delivery system but not a nuclear weapon, since the final product would continue to lack a fissile core. Unauthorized assembly of nuclear weapons would therefore require all three groups to collude effectively if deployment postures involving a high degree of separation among components are chosen by the national leadership. This is almost impossible in India's case, however, because the custodians of these components, being few in number and knowing each other intimately, share an extraordinarily high commitment to the Indian state and, as such, would be unlikely to undertake any course of action that would imperil the national interest. Only fairly senior governmental employees with long and distinguished records of service would have the knowledge or the physical access relating to India's nuclear components.[443] And while collusion leading to unauthorized use is theoretically possible in such a system, it is highly unlikely, since such individuals would have no reason to pursue a course of action that leads to the destruction of the state that they have long served and that, by giving them positions of authority, has also served them well in return. The lengthy process of socialization that occurs in the civilian bureaucracies, the nuclear weapon re-

---

[443]See the descriptions at various points in Chengappa, *Weapons of Peace*, for more on this issue. See also Chari, *Protection of Fissile Materials: The Indian Experience*, pp. 5–6.

search program, the defense scientific establishment, and the uniformed services thus serves in effect as a de facto personnel reliability program, since only those individuals who survive the extended novitiate successfully on their way to the top would be entrusted with either decisionmaking responsibilities or organizational custody of the various components that make up India's strategic capabilities.[444]

The multiple levels of distribution—first by component and then by organization—that will most likely be institutionalized by the Indian system of managing its nuclear assets (even in the context of the new unified command that might be set up to oversee and coordinate nuclear operations) thus effectively serve as a "super PAL"[445]—an elaborate set of physical and organizational constraints on the unauthorized creation of a nuclear weapon when such is not required by the demands of national policy. It is possible that in addition to such constraints, stemming from the disassembled stocking of key components, each individual nuclear weapon might also have some kinds of PALs. The joint statement issued by the DAE and the DRDO in the aftermath of the Indian tests referred to "safety interlocks"[446] and other security devices. These could be constraining locks built into the design of the weapon itself, similar to the Category A and B PALs that were designed for U.S. nuclear weapons in

---

[444]Some Indian scholars have argued for a formalization of this process through the institutionalization of something akin to a two-man rule (see *India: Study Recommends Two-Person Rule for Using Nuclear Arms*, FBIS-TAC-98-261, September 18, 1998). Indian policymakers, however, while not ruling out such solutions eventually, emphasize in private that their current arrangements in fact afford far greater protection than would be offered by a two-man rule, since the necessity for collaboration between at least two organizations to ready India's nuclear weapons itself ensures that more than two individuals would be required to prepare these weapons for delivery. The description at various points in Chengappa, *Weapons of Peace*, clearly corroborates this claim. If the new unified command charged with overseeing India's nuclear delivery systems actually materializes and the Indian state chooses a model of distributed capability that minimizes separation between components, new technical and organizational safeguards will have to be developed in order to preserve the safeguards that India's nuclear capabilities traditionally enjoyed.

[445]This concept, although not this term, is discussed at length in Scott Sagan, "The Origins of Military Doctrine and Command and Control Systems," in Peter R. Lavoy, Scott D. Sagan, and James J. Wirtz (eds.), *Planning the Unthinkable* (Ithaca, NY: Cornell University Press, 2000), pp. 16–46.

[446]"Joint Statement by the Department of Atomic Energy and Defence Research and Development Organization," *India News*, May 16–June 15, 1998, p. 12.

the early 1970s.[447] In any event, it is most likely that India would seek to physically safeguard its arsenal against unauthorized use, at least in the near term, through organizational solutions that reinforce separation rather than through technological solutions alone, which in their most sophisticated form may be both costly and beyond reach. Whatever the technologies incorporated in terms of control features, however, it is reasonable to expect that New Delhi will place greater faith in the integrity of its custodians, both civilian and military—given the small, secretive nature of the program—for purposes of ensuring safety against unauthorized use. This assurance is further reinforced by the fact that any attempt to fabricate a weapon from disassembled components would require a larger number of individuals to collude than are needed simply for assuring safe custody of the parts, implying that in turn whistle-blowers could emerge as an additional check if a small cabal of traitorous individuals attempted to assemble completed nuclear weapons without specific authorization. Since this problem is not very serious to begin with, the Indian preference for organizational solutions to the problems of unauthorized use will likely prevail because it also comports with the need to minimize costs and maintain continuing civilian control.

While the character of distribution—both by component and by organization—will remain a key difference between the U.S. and Indian solutions to the problems of survivability and unauthorized use, the pattern of ultimate control with respect to the question of who can legitimately order nuclear use will also be divergent. Unlike the United States, the Indian system of control will be highly "assertive,"[448] meaning that the civilian leadership at the very top, in the person of the Prime Minister and his Cabinet, will continue to exercise strict and pervasive control over the structure of nuclear asset distribution, the authorization pertaining to the marriage of various strategic components in an emergency, and the decision to actually use nuclear weapons as part of a retaliatory response. Even the Draft Report issued by the National Security Advisory Board, for all of its

---

[447]For more on this subject, see Robert S. Norris, "U.S. Nuclear Weapons Safety and Control Features," *Bulletin of the Atomic Scientists*, 47:8 (October 1991), pp. 48–49, and Feaver, *Guarding the Guardians*, p. 212.

[448]The term comes from Feaver, "Command and Control in Emerging Nuclear Nations," p. 170.

concerns about the survivability of India's nuclear assets, did not argue for a "delegative" control system, asserting instead that "nuclear weapons shall be tightly controlled and released for use at the highest political level. The authority to release nuclear weapons for use resides in the person of the Prime Minister of India, or the designated successor(s)."[449] The key to such ironclad control, both in peacetime and in wartime, lies in the power that India's Prime Ministers have traditionally exercised over both the nuclear program and the military. By being able to directly oversee the affairs of the DAE while controlling both the DRDO and the armed services through the civilian Ministry of Defence, India's Prime Ministers have always been able—whenever they so chose—to exercise close and continuing authority over any developments occurring in these organizations.[450] The acquisition of nuclear weaponry is likely to make this traditionally tight control even tighter, first because nuclear weapons embody special risks and second because, unlike the United States, the strategic circumstances India faces do not require it to develop a delegative command system in which the custodians of various strategic components would be empowered to employ these capabilities at their own discretion.

As an earlier discussion elaborated, India is conventionally strong enough that it is unlikely to contemplate any first use of nuclear weaponry against either Pakistan or China. The strategic contests between India on the one hand and China and Pakistan on the other also do not require the latter to use nuclear weapons in anger against New Delhi—so long as the latter hews to its traditional policy of strategic restraint. Since India's nuclear weapons are intended primarily as political instruments of deterrence and reassurance in the face of possible threats and secondarily as instruments of retribution in the event of actual use, policymakers in New Delhi believe that

---

[449]"Draft Report of [the] National Security Advisory Board on Indian Nuclear Doctrine," p. 3. This affirmation clearly repudiates the ill-justified claims made by some Western observers that India is likely to settle for a "delegative" system of control. See Thomas Withington, "Nuclear Dilemmas Seize Asia," *Jane's Intelligence Review—Pointer*, December 1998, pp. 13–14.

[450]This fact is corroborated at various points in Perkovich, *India's Nuclear Bomb*, and in Chengappa, *Weapons of Peace*. The capability of the Prime Minister to control the entire defense establishment, both institutionally and operationally, is emphasized in Kukreja, *Civil-Military Relations in South Asia*, pp. 185–228.

their interests are not at all well served by opting for a completely "delegative" command system where a significant number of completed nuclear weapons are distributed to the uniformed military for routine custody and safekeeping, with this end user being granted the "predelegated"[451] authority for the use of such weapons in an emergency.[452] There is good reason to believe that such judgments are in fact justified, since India's declaratory doctrine of "delayed—but assured—retaliation" can be preeminently satisfied by more or less strong forms of "assertive" control, where both the peacetime custody of weapons (or their component parts) and the routine authority over nuclear-use decisions are retained by civilian institutions, with the devolutionary rather than predelegated transfer of resources and authority taking place only under conditions of supreme emergency. Such a command arrangement could be satisfactory so long as an adequately distributed nuclear posture, which can assure the survivability of a significant fraction of India's nuclear assets, exists in some form and is complemented by effective procedures for postattack reconstitution. If these conditions obtain, the weak time urgency of retaliation should provide the Indian state with the margins of safety it needs to effectively generate its punitive capabilities prior to executing its retaliatory attack.[453]

Any assertive command system of the sort associated with centralized control obviously suffers from one specific weakness: its vulner-

---

[451]On the logic and practice of "predelegation" during the Cold War, see Feaver, *Guarding the Guardians*, pp. 44–54. It is important to recognize the distinction between "devolution" and "predelegation" of command authority: The former refers to the "orderly transfer of the entire command function, along with a preset chain of command, when the superior in the hierarchy is incapacitated," while the latter refers to the "a priori delimitation of circumstances under which subordinates in the chain of command can assume that the authorization to use nuclear weapons has been given to them." Feaver, *Guarding the Guardians*, p. 44.

[452]At least one serious Indian analyst has made a systematic argument for what appears to be a partially delegative command system in which the uniformed services possess custody of completed nuclear weapons in peacetime. Whether such a demand for custody is complemented by a demand for predelegated use authority is less clear, but it may be implied by the requirement for a launch-on-warning capability discussed in Menon, *A Nuclear Strategy for India*, pp. 177–282.

[453]"India and the Nuclear Question: An Interview with General K. Sundarji, PVSM (Retd)," pp. 45–56.

ability to "strategic decapitation."[454] Strategic decapitation refers to the destruction of the national command authority as a result of enemy action that is intended to paralyze a state's ability to respond rapidly and coherently. The sudden destruction of the leadership can result in the defendant's loss of ability to react in an organized fashion, particularly when time is at a premium, because of the specific operational characteristics of the nuclear forces facing off on both sides. This was a critical concern during the Cold War given the nature of both U.S. and Soviet war-fighting strategies, but in this instance as in many others there was no consensus on whether successful decapitation—understood as the ability to effectively blunt retaliation through countercontrol attacks—was feasible in practice or even appropriate as a deliberate strategy.[455] Preparing for this contingency certainly concentrates the minds of many Indians; the "Draft Report of [the] National Security Advisory Board on Indian Nuclear Doctrine," for example, affirmed that the requisite "procedures for the continuity of nuclear command and control" ought to be created in order to "ensure a continuing capability to effectively employ nuclear weapons" even in the face of "surprise attacks" and "repetitive attrition attempts" by an adversary.[456]

While such directives are appropriate, there is good reason to believe that the threat of strategic decapitation may not be as overpowering as is sometimes imagined, at least in the case of conflict scenarios in Southern Asia. To begin with, there is no reason Pakistan or China should pursue strategies of nuclear decapitation even if they are able to do so. If they were ever in a situation where their nuclear weapons actually had to be used, both states would most likely employ their weapons for purposes of strategic signaling rather than in pursuit of countercontrol objectives. The intent of such use would be to communicate resolve and threaten escalation to even higher

---

[454]This concept is systematically discussed in John D. Steinbruner, "Nuclear Decapitation," *Foreign Policy*, 45 (Winter 1981–1982), pp. 16–28.

[455]For opposing opinions on this matter, see Ashton B. Carter, "Assessing Command System Vulnerability," in Ashton B. Carter, John D. Steinbruner, and Charles A. Zraket (eds.), *Managing Nuclear Operations* (Washington, D.C.: Brookings, 1987), pp. 555–610; Blair, *Strategic Command and Control*, pp. 208 and 282–283; and Shlapak and Thaler, *Back to First Principles*, pp. 25–31 and 73–83.

[456]"Draft Report of [the] National Security Advisory Board on Indian Nuclear Doctrine," p. 3.

levels of violence if the Indian state did not back down from the course of action that led either Pakistan or China to use its nuclear weapons in the first place. Such employment requires that the attacker deliberately eschew decapitating strikes because the national leadership of the adversary must remain intact if a tacitly or explicitly negotiated termination of conflict is to occur. The only time decapitating strikes make sense is when the assailant—determined to "go for broke"—visualizes its nuclear use to be part of an all-out disarming attack intended to destroy the adversary once and for all. This logic, however, may not be particularly compelling in any circumstances short of all-out nuclear war, since as Shlapak and Thaler argue, "eliminating the very people with whom war termination might be arranged in a probably futile attempt to prevent a devastating . . . counterblow would be a very poor gamble"[457] indeed.

The circumstances and war aims that would justify such kinds of nuclear first use on the part of either Pakistan or China are hard to imagine in the South Asian context. Any Pakistani nuclear first use would almost by definition be a constrained action designed to limit predatory Indian behavior and, as such, would be intended "to signal as much as to punish, to bargain as much as [to] batter."[458] Not only are decapitation strategies counterproductive in such circumstances, but the character of Pakistan's emerging nuclear capabilities, at least over the next decade, also provides no assurance that such strategies could even be successfully executed. The quality of Chinese capabil-

---

[457] Shlapak and Thaler, *Back to First Principles*, p. 80.

[458] Ibid., p. 25. The only exception to this rule consists of those situations where Islamabad, believing that India would retaliate massively irrespective of how Pakistan's nuclear first use unfolded, would be tempted to consider decapitating attacks as part of its initial nuclear employment merely to minimize the damage that would be inflicted by the anticipated Indian counterattack. The temptation to unleash decapitating attacks in such circumstances would be rational and would obviously be precipitated by Pakistan's taking Indian threats of "massive" punishment at face value. Even in such situations, however, Pakistan may still not need to execute decapitating strikes if its nuclear reserves are survivable enough and can ride out the expected Indian counterattack; if it lacks the resources and the intelligence required to successfully execute such attacks with a high degree of confidence; and if there is a nontrivial probability that India may in fact not make good on its prewar threats of "massive" punishment in the event of limited Pakistani nuclear first use. When all these factors are taken into account, there is good reason to believe that the incentives for Pakistan to unleash decapitating strikes are actually less significant in practice than they might sometimes appear in theory.

ities, on the other hand, leaves no doubt that decapitation attacks on India could be mounted quite successfully *in extremis*, but the wisdom of pursuing such a course of action—except in retaliation for a comparable attempt on India's part—remains to be demonstrated. While it is therefore possible to conjure up a variety of scenarios involving attempted decapitation attacks that might be mounted by both Islamabad and Beijing, it is extremely hard to explain convincingly whether and why such outcomes would obtain in practice. Not surprisingly, then, Giles and Doyle, in their extensive survey of Pakistani writings on nuclear strategy, note that "there appears to be little interest among Pakistani analysts in a decapitation strategy"[459]— and even those scholars who argue that Chinese nuclear doctrine is on the cusp of significant change do not marshal any evidence suggesting that Beijing appears to be contemplating decapitation strategies of the kind that were greatly feared during the Cold War.[460]

This does not imply that India should not treat the possibility of decapitation seriously. It should, and if Indian discussions are any indication, it probably will.[461] The solution to potential decapitation, however, does not lie in having a delegative command system, where completed nuclear weapons are distributed to the uniformed services *a priori* and the individual custodians are authorized to employ these weapons on their own initiative in the absence of positive directives from the national command authority in the aftermath of a nuclear attack. Rather, the solution lies in developing a proper system for devolving authority and transferring strategic assets in an emergency. The former would regulate how the legitimate power to authorize the employment of nuclear weapons passes seamlessly from the prewar leadership to various survivors in accordance with some preestablished and publicly recognized procedures, while the latter would regulate the myriad procedures defining how nuclear weapons (or the components thereof) would be transferred from their peacetime custodians, assembled for possible use, and finally reassigned to their wartime users for final delivery to target when ordered to do so by the national leadership. This is precisely the solu-

---

[459] Giles and Doyle, "Indian and Pakistani Views on Nuclear Deterrence," p. 154.

[460] See Johnston, "China's New 'Old Thinking': The Concept of Limited Deterrence," pp. 5–42.

[461] Giles and Doyle, "Indian and Pakistani Views on Nuclear Deterrence," p. 154.

tion that New Delhi is likely to refine over the next decade, and some elements of this system have been advocated by leading Indian thinkers such as K. Subrahmanyam and Jasjit Singh.[462] Other commentators, such as Raj Chengappa, have claimed—with some plausibility—that India has had just such a command system, albeit secretly and perhaps only informally developed, since at least 1989.[463] Whether this has been the case is difficult to verify, but other scholars have also referred to the existence of some kind of devolutionary system that would allow for the use of nuclear weapons in the event of an attack on the leadership in New Delhi.[464]

When faced with the set of choices illustrated in Figure 8, India will therefore institutionalize—if it has not done so already—a highly assertive system that involves strict centralized control over both the distributed arsenal and nuclear-use decisions in peacetime, with authority and resources steadily devolving to various legitimate successors and operational users, respectively, in the event of strategic decapitation. Operationalizing this preference, of course, has numerous practical implications (some of which will be discussed in

RAND MR1127-8

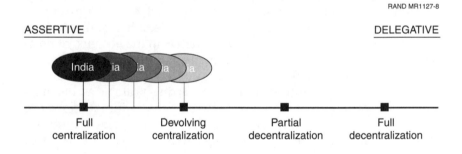

Figure 8—India's Likely Command Arrangements

---

[462]K. Subrahmanyam, "After Pokhran-II," *Economic Times*, May 14, 1998, and Singh, "A Nuclear Strategy for India," pp. 306–324.

[463]Chengappa, *Weapons of Peace*, pp. 335–336.

[464]This is described in almost hyperbolic form by Stephen Peter Rosen, *Societies and Military Power* (Ithaca, NY: Cornell University Press, 1996), pp. 251–252.

the next chapter), but it subsists as an effective solution that allows India to maintain its cherished tradition of civilian control over strategic capabilities without any of the risks that accompany a delegative system. This is particularly true because a delegative system is currently unnecessary given the nature of both the capabilities of India's adversaries and the likeliest circumstances under which these capabilities might be used. Further, a delegative system might actually be dangerous if India does not possess all the safety and control capabilities that permit completed nuclear weapons to be routinely maintained in such form. In practice, the lack of safety technologies is likely to be more problematic than the possible absence of control capabilities, since the threat of unauthorized access is for the most part less significant in the case of India. Safety issues, however, are an entirely different matter, as there is no evidence that India's nuclear weapon designs incorporate advanced safety features like strong-weak links, insensitive high explosives, and fire-resistant pits.[465] Moreover, the only narrative that engages such issues—Chengappa's *Weapons of Peace*—actually provides a somewhat pessimistic picture when it describes how India's nuclear scientists, during their preparations for the May 1998 tests, were inordinately concerned about electrical mishaps that "could mess up the[ir] [assembled] device[s] or even in an extreme case detonate one of them."[466] If India's nuclear weapons are not designed to achieve "one-point safety,"[467] maintaining them routinely in completed form—either clandestinely or in elaborate storage igloos—does not appear to be an attractive proposition even if all the targeting vulnerabilities associated with the latter kind of storage are not taken into account.[468]

When all these factors are taken into account, it seems most likely that India will settle—and with good reason—for an assertive com-

---

[465]These technologies are detailed in Cotter, "Peacetime Operations: Safety and Security," pp. 17–74.

[466]Chengappa, *Weapons of Peace*, p. 423.

[467]For a description of this concept, see Cotter, "Peacetime Operations: Safety and Security," p. 43.

[468]Storage igloos may compromise survivability in the Indian case because their distinctive physical characteristics and associated C^3 equipment would actually reduce the location uncertainty critical to the viability of India's hidden nuclear assets.

mand system in peacetime with fully centralized control over both custodial arrangements and use decisions. This centralization would shift, however, toward more devolutionary alternatives with respect to decisionmaking in the event of decapitation, just as the custodial arrangement would also mutate as a crisis evolves to the point at which India might choose to ready its nuclear weapons for possible use. Figures 9 to 13 attempt to describe in iterations of increasing complexity how the assertive Indian command system might operate in a variety of strategic circumstances. They also include a brief assessment of some of the key alternatives proposed to the current and prospective arrangements that appear to dominate the thinking of decisionmakers in New Delhi.

The model of assertive control illustrated in Figure 9 suggests how India might maintain its distributed deterrent both in peace and in war, at least at a macro level—that is, without reference to the exact degree of microseparation that will be maintained with regard to the weapon components (described previously in terms of the six postures illustrated in Figure 7). This figure attempts to identify the broad pattern of responsibilities both within the civilian and across the civil-military realms in efforts to further clarify the logic of the

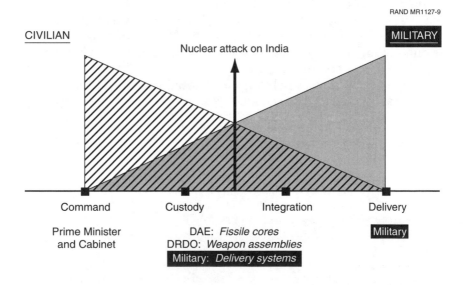

Figure 9—India's Assertive Command System—The "Baseline" Model

evolving force-in-being and to evaluate its prospects for success as a safe and effective deterrent. Since the emerging Indian nuclear force will not be configured as a ready arsenal primed for the prompt conduct of nuclear operations, the command system must oversee four specific operational tasks: the command of the force, which pertains to all decisions relating to the development, acquisition, deployment, and use of nuclear weapons; the custody of the distributed components, consisting of the fissile core, the weapon assembly, and the delivery systems, each of which may be maintained separately in various combinations by different custodians; the integration of the arsenal, which consists of the marriage between these variously distributed components when the decision to retaliate is arrived at in the aftermath of a nuclear attack on India; and finally the delivery of the weapons, which refers to the safe and effective detonation of the completed nuclear weapon on its intended target.

Figure 9 illustrates the "baseline" model of assertive control, based on the early work of General K. Sundarji, which knowledgeable Indian civilian strategists note has served as the generic blueprint for India's nuclear command-and-control system.[469] It also represents the received wisdom that is prevalent in the atomic energy establishment, in the higher bureaucracy, and among senior politicians in the most important political parties. Consequently, it remains the yardstick against which all future developments in India's command system can be judged. As the figure suggests, the command of India's nuclear capabilities will remain an exclusively civilian responsibility that resides primarily with the Prime Minister and the Cabinet, although it will be exercised in the name of the President of the Republic of India. Although this responsibility may devolve to other individuals in the event of strategic decapitation, the principle of civilian control will remain effective because the legal provisions that allow for such devolution will have to be ratified by civilian authori-

---

[469]The elements of this framework can be found in the many writings of K. Sundarji cited throughout this book, with quick summaries available in "India and the Nuclear Question: An Interview with General K. Sundarji, PVSM (Retd)," pp. 45–56; Sundarji, "Prithvi in the Haystack"; and Sundarji, "Nuclear Deterrence: Doctrine for India—Parts I and II." On Sundarji's contributions as constituting the baseline for India's command system and deterrence doctrines, see C. Raja Mohan, "Sundarji's Nuclear Doctrine," *The Hindu*, February 11, 1999, and Subrahmanyam, "Indian Nuclear Policy—1964–98," pp. 38–50.

ties either through a formal constitutional process or through the dissemination of formal administrative orders.[470] In peacetime, however, this command authority will remain with India's elected civilian leaders, who will be responsible for all the development, acquisition, deployment, and use decisions pertaining to nuclear weaponry. The uniformed military will probably have no *formal* role whatsoever at the level of command even though it may be consulted whenever necessary by the civilian leadership and will contribute to national decisionmaking by means of its expertise, which is available to its civilian superiors through both formal and informal channels—including the new institution of the CDS that is likely to be created in the future.[471]

The custody of the strategic components would be shared by both civilian and military organizations—perhaps under the aegis of a new unified command that may be created for this purpose—in accordance with one or more of the six distributed postures described in Figure 7. In the simplest conception imaginable, the civilians, in the form of the DAE and the DRDO, would retain control, either jointly or separately, over the fissile core and the nonnuclear weapon assembly, while the uniformed military, either through means of the new unified command or through the existing armed services, would be responsible for maintaining and stowing the delivery vehicle itself. (The military's custodial and oversight responsibilities may extend to maintaining some nonnuclear weapon components along with the delivery system, depending on which of the six microdistribution postures described in Figure 7 the Indian state eventually selects. These variations in custodial responsibilities, however, do not undercut the broad division of responsibilities outlined in this baseline model of India's command system.) All of these activities can be carried out in peacetime by each custodial agency more or less independently. The uniformed military does not need to be more than minimally involved in the day-to-day management and control of the deterrent writ large except at the level of coordination and planning. Even here, however, its involvement—in the most minimal

---

[470]This is alluded to in "India Not to Engage in a N-Arms Race: Jaswant."

[471]Empirical examples of how this process has been institutionalized historically can be found in various passages throughout Perkovich, *India's Nuclear Bomb,* and in Chengappa, *Weapons of Peace.*

versions imaginable—could consist mainly of collaborating with its civilian counterparts in defining strategic requirements, developing targeting plans, and finalizing contingency arrangements pertaining to the task of integration, which regulates the organized movement of civilian-controlled components to the assembly sites where the dispersed components—cores, weapon assemblies, and perhaps delivery vehicles—would be mated prior to weapon launch and delivery itself. In order to undertake these responsibilities satisfactorily, the military, the DAE, and the DRDO will have to collaborate in a variety of planning exercises designed to develop the appropriate contingency plans, and as far as integration is concerned they will have to jointly agree on certain emergency coordination procedures that define how various custodians would congregate at the assembly sites. This joint planning can be done formally or informally, but the critical point is that the uniformed military does not need to know exactly where the weapons and/or components are stored in peacetime but merely that the fissile cores and weapon assemblies would be available and produced by their custodians at certain predesignated points prior to integration. To the degree that these activities require the assistance of the uniformed military, greater or lesser degrees of additional information will have to be preshared with military planners—even if only informally—*a priori*. If the plans currently mooted for the creation of a new unified command, headed by the CDS and tasked with overseeing India's strategic assets, are actually implemented successfully, this organization will likely become the nodal institution where all plans and coordination pertaining to nuclear operations would be hammered out.

In this baseline model of assertive control, the integration and delivery of New Delhi's nuclear weapons do not occur *except after India has suffered a nuclear attack*. This implies that even if conventional deterrence breakdown has already occurred—as might be the case in some conflict scenarios—the baseline model advocated by Sundarji would not mandate physically preparing and integrating India's nuclear assets for possible retaliatory use.[472] Sundarji sensibly justified this restraint on the grounds of enhancing crisis stability, since the refusal to rush into integration activities in the midst of a conflict

---

[472]Sundarji, "Prithvi in the Haystack," and Sundarji, "Changing Military Equations in Asia: The Role of Nuclear Weapons," pp. 119–149.

held the best promise of dampening a potentially dangerous crisis slide that could otherwise provoke destabilizing competitive actions aimed at increasing nuclear readiness in an environment characterized by great uncertainty and tension. Consequently, the task of integration in this framework presents itself only when the decision to use nuclear weapons has been made by India's civilian leadership, and this decision is precipitated not simply by possible conventional deterrence breakdown but only by the fact of an actual nuclear attack on India. This step specifically involves physically reconstituting the nuclear deterrent and requires that all the component parts maintained by various custodial organizations be brought together in a synergistic fashion in order to prepare the nuclear arsenal for the impending retaliatory strike. Integration, which in this context refers to the many steps involved in mating the fissile core with the weapon assembly and the delivery vehicle, may involve all the custodial groups directly converging at the assembly sites (if each agency is independently responsible for assuring its own transportation) or, more likely, would require that such groups meet at some intermediate locations (where the various custodians and their components would be transported by military assets, either air or surface, to designated assembly areas likely to be located in close proximity to the launch sites). In either case, the role of the military increases disproportionately at this juncture, since orchestrating the transportation of the various strategic components, together with their custodians, at certain assured levels of security will be a demanding task matched only by the military's own exigent obligation to prepare the delivery systems in their custody for prospective nuclear operations—all amid the carnage of prior nuclear attacks and, possibly, an ongoing conventional war.[473]

When all the custodial groups have gathered together at the assembly areas and the various components have been married together to form completed nuclear weapons that are then attached to their designated delivery vehicles, the force-in-being is finally transformed into a ready nuclear arsenal. The last task in the sequence now consists of delivering the completed nuclear weapons to their targets. This stage marks the point at which civilian contributions es-

---

[473]For a brief and perhaps all too impressionistic description of how this was attempted during the Kargil crisis, see Chengappa, *Weapons of Peace*, pp. 437–438.

sentially come to an end, as military operators alone are competent to execute the mission of physically carrying out the retaliatory strikes. While these missions would obviously be carried out only in wartime (and after nuclear attacks on India have already occurred), wide-ranging peacetime preparations will be necessary for the success of such an operation. Extensive preplanning will be required to ensure that the delivery vehicles, which are either dispersed or "cocooned" in standby status, can be moved to bases near the designated assembly areas; under the baseline model, such activities can be initiated even before actual deterrence breakdown occurs so long as this preparatory dispersal does not entail any actual integration of deliverable nuclear weapons. Missile launch sites in particular will need to be presurveyed, and aircraft strike operations will require prior route planning as well as preplanned allocations of supporting systems such as escorts, tankers, jammers, and airborne early-warning command and control (AEWC&C) platforms to ensure successful ingress, attack, and egress. These are all essentially military tasks, and much of the planning, training, and organizational arrangements necessary for their success can be completed in peacetime. From the perspective of understanding the baseline model of the assertive Indian control system, however, the important point is that whether the nuclear strikes are conducted by aircraft or delivered by missile, civilian control over the nuclear payload ends only when the fabricated weapon is transferred to the uniformed operators just before final delivery.

This baseline model suggests that civilian dominance of the command system, which is maximal in peacetime, diminishes only as one moves toward the point of weapon delivery, and that up to the moment of integration—the stage where the fissile core is mated to the weapon assembly and the delivery vehicle—the civilian custodians of India's strategic components remain fully in charge of the country's nuclear reserves. Figure 10 illustrates how such a system could be—and perhaps historically has been—operationalized in practice. This illustration is based on the impressionistic descriptions found throughout Perkovich's *India's Nuclear Bomb* and Chengappa's *Weapons of Peace*, supplemented by several off-the-record conversations with civilian decisionmakers and senior military officers in New Delhi. It is also premised on the fact that India's nuclear capabilities traditionally consisted solely of air-delivered

RAND MR1127-10

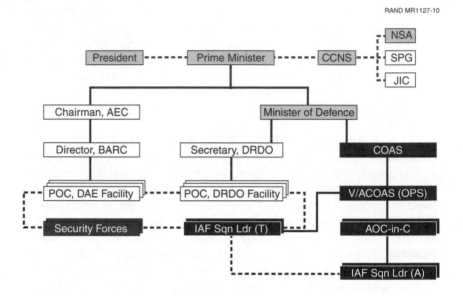

Figure 10—India's Assertive Command System—A Closer Look

weapons, and to that degree the chains of command, control, custody, and operations illustrated here will change considerably as new organizational innovations, such as the creation of a unified command possibly headed by the CDS, are institutionalized in the future and as newer strategic capabilities—such as land- and sea-based ballistic and cruise missiles—are integrated into the national deterrent force.

As Figure 10 illustrates, the orders to integrate India's nuclear assets in preparation for a retaliatory response can be issued only by the Prime Minister—the head of the government in India—who may choose to consult the President of the Republic of India and the CCNS as necessary. This decisionmaking process could be supported by advice from the National Security Adviser, the Strategic Policy Group, and the Joint Intelligence Committee (which is functionally the Secretariat for the National Security Council) if such advice is so-licited. In any event, once the decision to prepare India's nuclear weapons for retaliation is reached, the Prime Minister, by his direct authority over the DAE, can order the Chairman of India's AEC, the Director of BARC, and, through them, the various points of contact at other DAE facilities where nuclear components may be stored to prepare their distributed assets for integration. Through the civilian Minister of Defence and possibly even directly, a parallel set of orders can be issued, first to the Secretary, DRDO, and second to the Chief of Air Staff, to support—via prearranged procedures—the fabrication of India's distributed components into complete and usable weapon systems.[474] In any event, the Secretary, DRDO, would in turn charge the points of contact at the various DRDO facilities tasked with supporting the weapon program to provide all the necessary expertise, equipment, and resources relevant to completing the process of integration. The role of the Air Chief now becomes pivotal because his service would be obligated to provide all the major transportation assets necessary to completing the processes of integration as well as to generate the alerts required to prepare the designated attack (and supporting) units for the nuclear delivery mission. This tasking would probably be routed through either the Vice-Chief of Air Staff or the Assistant Chief of Air Staff (Operations) and may also include the Air Officer Commanding-in-Chief (AOC-in-C) of the relevant geographic commands, although the Indian Air Force command system is flexible enough that even the AOC-in-C can simply be bypassed by the Chief of Air Staff or his principal deputies if they desire to transmit any orders directly to the leaders of the relevant transport, attack and supporting units. The last individual relevant to completing this process—whose current role is relatively residual—is the Chief of Army Staff or the Director-General, Military Operations, who is likely to be responsible for allocating the small security details necessary to escort the various custodians en route to the assembly areas.

While these organizational arrangements exploit what are clearly formal command relationships within the Indian state, the operational dimensions of integrating India's nuclear weapons and preparing them for delivery rely greatly on *informal* albeit well-

---

[474]Since India's traditional delivery systems were exclusively aircraft, the Chief of Air Staff remained the only service chief with responsibilities to the nuclear command system. As India's delivery systems grow in diversity to include Army and possibly Navy assets, it is likely that the Chiefs of Army and Navy Staffs and, more important, the new Chief of Defence Staff, will also be included in parallel arrangements if the baseline model of assertive command survives more or less unaltered over time.

understood "standard operating procedures"[475] that regulate the actions of the various custodians and their supporting cast: the key points of contact within the DAE and DRDO communities, the Air Force transport and attack squadrons, and the Army units committed to the security detail. It is within this cycle of agents and activities that all the practical actions necessary to bring the Indian nuclear deterrent to full war-fighting readiness will be consummated. The procedures that regulate such actions have historically been quite informal, sometimes idiosyncratic, and often improvised because India's nuclear capabilities have not been either large or diverse. Moreover, they have not been oriented toward securing any demanding operational goals in the face of highly capable adversaries. Finally, they have sufficed in the past because the close-knit character of the Indian nuclear decisionmaking system has allowed their relatively simple strategies of retaliation to be carried out through even loose command arrangements of the kind illustrated in Figure 10.

What is remarkable about this system in general is how informality, unwritten rules, and "workarounds" have been used to construct a relatively flexible command system that serves the operational needs of the national leadership even as it preserves the preexisting structural balances within the Indian state.[476] Failure to appreciate the utility of such arrangements within the Indian context often leads to criticisms, both within India and abroad, of the quality of the country's command and control. These criticisms surface in different forms: Those who are obsessed with formal arrangements and organizational charts, for example—overlooking the fact that structured informality may be just as effective, even if less transparent, for purposes of command—usually insinuate that India has no effective nuclear command-and-control system whatsoever.[477] Others assert that structured informality can never be a good enough substitute for

---

[475]This term is obviously used in a very different sense from that appearing in Paul Bracken, *The Command and Control of Nuclear Forces* (New Haven, CT: Yale University Press, 1983).

[476]A good analysis of how intelligent, informal, and nonplanned interventions play a critical role in ensuring the effectiveness of even large, formal military decision systems can be found in N. F. Kristy, *Man in a Large Information Processing System— His Changing Role in SAGE*, RM-3206-PR (Santa Monica: RAND, 1963).

[477]Clayton P. Bowen and Daniel Wolven, "Command and Control Challenges in South Asia," *Nonproliferation Review*, 6:3 (Spring–Summer 1999), p. 25.

formal organization, thus concluding that so long as the Indian command system lacks the formality visible in other nuclear states, its effectiveness will be suspect and open to question.[478] Even some senior retired Indian military officers have privately raised similar charges, but their calculations often have less to do with their judgments about the effectiveness of the present arrangements than with their desire to publicly formalize the status of the uniformed services as critical and respectable arms of the Indian state.[479]

Irrespective of how such criticisms are finally evaluated, any analysis of the Indian nuclear command system must recognize several important realities: India *does* possess an excellent, entirely formal national command system. This command system regulates all the activities of the uniformed military across research, procurement, training, deployment, and operations. A different but parallel system exists—formally—where controls over the atomic energy establishment are concerned. What the country may currently lack is a formal nuclear command system—that is, an isomorphically structured system that regulates research, procurement, training, deployment, and operations in the nuclear realm through a detailed specification of functional and administrative tasks allowing routinization of performance to be pushed as far as possible under prevailing conditions.[480] Yet precisely because India does possess a formal national command system that regulates both the military and the atomic energy domains, it is possible for its elected leadership to graft informal or perhaps even secretly formal arrangements pertaining to nuclear operations onto what are otherwise two distinct but orderly organizational structures. Therefore, the extant Indian nuclear command system is emphatically not an ungrounded web of ad hoc provisions but instead remains a good example of how nested "organic" arrangements can always be embedded within, and derive their viability from, otherwise large and complex formal organizations—

---

[478]Ashok K. Mehta, "Need to Involve Services in Decision-Making Stressed," *India Abroad*, March 12, 1999.

[479]The other reasons for such charges have to do with the distinct differences in civil-military attitudes to the "always-never" dilemma, which are usefully summarized in Feaver, *Guarding the Guardians*, pp. 26–28.

[480]The distinctiveness of formal organizations, in contrast to the alternatives, is explored in some detail in Michael I. Reed, *The Sociology of Organizations: Themes, Perspectives, and Prospects* (New York: Harvester Wheatsheaf, 1992).

arrangements that, in the final analysis, can be effective only because they presuppose the prior existence of some formally constituted hosts whose resources can be drawn on for purposes of fulfilling their intended goals.[481]

Since this command system is viewed as having served India well since at least 1989—and since it offers the further advantage of preserving the autonomy of the civilian guardians of the nuclear weapon program while simultaneously minimizing the *formal* involvement of the uniformed military until late in the weapon employment cycle—India's senior security managers are attracted to the idea of institutionalizing a more sophisticated version of the framework illustrated in Figures 9 and 10 as the template for the command and control of future Indian nuclear operations. A.P.J. Abdul Kalam provided an early inkling of this position when he noted that "we have a command-and-control system in a different form . . . now we have to consolidate and establish it."[482] This template, of course, would be modified to accommodate the new delivery systems and the larger number of nuclear weapons that India will acquire over time. It would also incorporate more structured opportunities for the military's participation in affairs relating to the overall deterrent, especially with respect to refining nuclear requirements, conducting targeting analysis, completing contingency plans, and integrating the services' infrastructure, ancillary technologies, and other assorted conventional capabilities in support of nuclear operations. These changes are presaged in the recent recommendations made by the Group of Ministers with respect to restructuring India's higher defense decisionmaking organizations. And while they are significant in the context of past practices, they would still not alter the three fundamental characteristics that are central to India's emerging force-in-being: the exclusive control maintained by the nation's civilian leadership, both elected and bureaucratic, over the command function; the relative dormancy of the nuclear reserves at the operational level, assured both by the maintenance of a distributed

---

[481] The nature of "organic" arrangements, which emphasize flexibility and adaptability against a backdrop of formal bureaucratic organizations, is examined at length in Tom Burns and G. M. Stalker, *The Management of Innovation* (Oxford, UK: Oxford University Press, 1994).

[482] Karp, "India Faces Task of Creating Nuclear-Weapons Doctrine."

deployment posture in peacetime and by the continuing civilian custody of critical nuclear components in all circumstances short of a supreme emergency; and the crucial but still relatively limited role of the armed services as far as the autonomous use of India's strategic assets are concerned.[483]

The prospect of such an organizational design forming the basis of India's future command system has not been greeted favorably by many observers, who, if the reported words of India's Air Chief Marshall (retired) S. K. Mehra are any indication, appear to be concerned that despite the Prime Minister's repeated declaration that "adequate C^3I arrangements were in place, . . . the Services seemed out of the decision-making loop."[484] This theme appears to have figured prominently in an early discussion on Indian nuclear command and control held at one of New Delhi's think tanks, the Institute for Peace and Conflict Studies, where numerous military officers vociferously argued for "the need for a CDS and integration of Service HQs [headquarters] with MOD [Ministry of Defence] to evolve a single point decision-making centre"; more intimate relations between the "political executive and the military . . . to ensure quick decision making"; "proper IFF [identification friend or foe] arrangements . . . , especially to distinguish between conventional and nuclear platforms/weapons"; secure "communications . . . to ensure that unintended launches did not occur"; and preplanned "arrangements . . . either for the recall or [for the] self-destruct of platforms after their launch."[485]

While each of these suggestions is unexceptional when considered individually—and many of them are in fact reflected in the reported recommendations of the Group of Ministers—what is fascinating about the requirements *taken together* is that they presume New Delhi seeks to deploy a robust and ready arsenal, intended for the conduct of prompt operations rather than a force-in-being that, while oriented primarily toward ensuring deterrence, also remains

---

[483]"Unanswered Questions," *Financial Times*, October 26, 1998.

[484]P. R. Chari, "Command and Control Arrangements," in *Report of the Sixth IPCS Seminar on the Implications of Nuclear Testing in South Asia*, available at http://www.ipcs.org/issues/articles/135-ndi-chari.html.

[485]Ibid.

capable of executing retaliatory strikes *in extremis*. Only under such a presumption does the cumulative demand for rapid decisionmaking, recall and self-destruct technologies, IFF systems capable of distinguishing between conventional and nuclear platforms, and communications security to prevent unintended launches make any sense. To the degree that these requirements reflect official service preferences—which they may not—they serve only to suggest how poorly the Indian military at large understands both the strategic intentions of its own leadership and how the latter's desire for a force-in-being is explicitly predicated, among other things, on keeping the *routine* involvement of the uniformed services in the country's strategic programs to a minimum. It is, in fact, ironic that the Indian military—having traditionally resisted arguments in support of nuclear weaponry because of the pernicious effect of such weaponry on conventional modernization—has now spawned small constituencies both within the three services and in the community of retired military officers who have jumped into the breach with often grandiose plans that in contradistinction to the visions of civilian policymakers, treat nuclear weapons explicitly as military rather than political instruments and, accordingly, call for a set of acquisition, deployment, and operating regimes that are more consistent with this view rather than any other.[486]

A secret policy paper, *Options for India—Formation of a Strategic Nuclear Command*, reportedly prepared by the Planning Directorate of the Indian military and approved by the three service chiefs, only corroborates this conclusion (see Figure 11).[487] If the reporting about this paper is accurate, the higher leadership of the uniformed military has called for the creation of a new multiservice body, the National Strategic Nuclear Command (NSNC), which would not only control the entire gamut of nuclear operations in peace and in war

---

[486]The best example of an argument that treats nuclear weapons as military instruments—because they bring in their trail an inexorable logic that cannot be avoided—remains Menon, *A Nuclear Strategy for India*, which, viewing nuclear weapons *qua* weapons, assesses their management with the same care and sophistication found in Western discussions of nuclear deterrence during the Cold War.

[487]Manvendra Singh, "Who Should Control Nuclear Button? Armed Forces Have a Proposal," *Indian Express*, September 1, 1998, and Rahul Bedi, "India Assesses Options on Future Nuclear Control," *Jane's Defence Weekly*, September 16, 1998, p. 16.

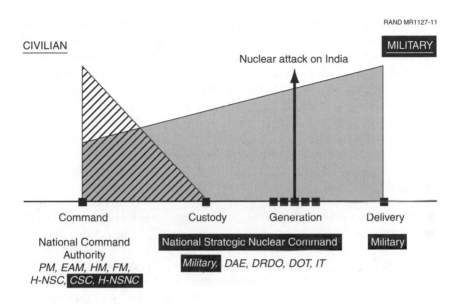

RAND MR1127-11

Figure 11—Indian Military's Suggested Command System

but, more interestingly, provide an institutional opportunity for the military's claim to representation at the highest levels of *command* itself. This level, which in the baseline model described earlier in Figure 9 was manned exclusively by civilian leaders in the person of the Prime Minister and the Cabinet, is now sought to be expanded, with the service chiefs recommending that the National Command Authority include the "head of the proposed National Security Council (NSC), the chiefs of staffs committee, and the NSNC commander"[488] in addition. Such a claim is unprecedented given the traditional pattern of civil-military relations in India and the fact that the service chiefs currently lack any national command responsibilities. What it does suggest, however, is that the Indian military is seeking to expand the sphere of its authority on the ground that nuclear weapons are different and, as such, require a "symbiosis between the political leadership and those directly involved with military operations."[489]

---

[488]Bedi, "India Assesses Options on Future Nuclear Control."
[489]Ibid.

The sketchy reporting about this policy paper further suggests that the reorganization proposed by the military would allow the armed services to acquire physical *custody* of India's nuclear weapons as well, albeit through the creation of an NSNC that would be manned by military officers in addition to other experts seconded from the DAE, the DRDO, and the Departments of Telecommunications and Information Technology. The creation of such a dedicated organization, intended to centralize all custodial, maintenance, and training responsibilities with respect to nuclear weaponry, is obviously patterned on the examples of the Strategic Air Command in the United States and the Strategic Rocket Forces in the Soviet Union (at least in their early incarnations) and possibly the Second Artillery Corps in China today.[490] The acquisition of custodial responsibilities, manifested through the creation of a new, dedicated organization like the NSNC, would obviously minimize the importance that integration enjoyed in the baseline model of control, since ready and completed (or almost completed) nuclear weapons would now be in the possession of the Indian military. Inasmuch as the responsibility for nuclear delivery operations remains unchanged in both frameworks, the new model of command recommended by the Indian military (illustrated in Figure 11) would actually result in a substantial transformation of the traditional Indian approach to nuclear weaponry, which emphasized the acknowledged possession of nuclear weapons as more important for successful deterrence than any operational plans oriented toward rapid response, prompt operations, and nuclear war fighting. As if to underscore this contrast, the military's policy paper reportedly argues that "tactical nuclear weapons [should] be released by the [National Command Authority] through the NSNC to the operational centres of the three service headquarters, *[but that] their usage . . . will be decided by the operational commands and the NSNC"* (italics added).[491] Under the new framework, the power of the uniformed military would therefore expand dramatically to include participation in both command and custodial functions while retaining all the older responsibilities (and perhaps ac-

---

[490] For a good analysis that attempts to draw lessons from the experience of these organizations, see Gurmeet Kanwal, "Command and Control of Nuclear Weapons in India," *Strategic Analysis*, 23:10 (January 2000), pp. 1707–1732.

[491] Bedi, "India Assesses Options on Future Nuclear Control."

quiring some new ones) with respect to systems integration and nuclear delivery.

This restructuring of the national nuclear command system, advocated by the uniformed military through official representations, has been echoed in other public statements authored by a variety of serving and retired military officers in India. Of the numerous writings that have surfaced on this subject since the 1998 tests, the work of three military officers—the Indian Army's Colonel Gurmeet Kanwal, the Indian Navy's Rear Admiral (retired) Raja Menon, and the Indian Air Force's Air Vice Marshal (retired) Kapil Kak—merit special mention not only because their writing reflects the distinctive views of their parent services but also because their substantive arguments embody a degree of sophistication, thoughtfulness, and *gravitas* that is rare in the context of the Indian nuclear debate.[492] There are clearly some variations in each of their proposals; Kanwal, for example, recommends the creation of a Chief of Defence Staff to oversee a triservice Strategic Force Command whose combat units would be controlled by the individual services. Menon, in contrast, recommends that the Chiefs of Staff Committee, bearing overall responsibility for defining nuclear requirements and targeting lists, should be designated the nodal organization for transmitting nuclear release orders to all combat units, which would be controlled by specifically created, integrated theater commands. Finally, Kak simply recommends that the Chairman, Chiefs of Staff Committee and the Chief of Air Staff jointly control a specially created Strategic Command that would have both possession of and authority over all of India's emerging nuclear forces. Such differences in viewpoint aside, what is remarkable are the similarities that underlie all of these proposals— similarities that ultimately lead them to advocate a command system that is radically removed from the present system, which has existed in some form or another since the early 1990s. In a significant echo of the suggestions made by the leadership of the uniformed military in their paper on *Options for India: Formation of a Strategic Nuclear Command*, all three analysts are ultimately united by the belief that:

---

[492] Kanwal, "Command and Control of Nuclear Weapons in India," pp. 1707–1732; Menon, *A Nuclear Strategy for India*, pp. 177–283; and Kak, "Command and Control of Small Nuclear Arsenals," pp. 266–285.

- Completed nuclear weapons ought to be maintained and deployed routinely as a ready deterrent to potential adversary actions;

- The armed forces ought to be seamlessly integrated into the institutions of national decisionmaking all the way from command to delivery; and

- Each of the military services, either individually or through new joint institutions, should possess custody of the relevant nuclear weapon systems even in peacetime.

While these ideas are certainly not controversial in the established nuclear states, institutionalizing such innovations would certainly run counter to the core logic embodied by the force-in-being and would also result in a remarkable enlargement of the power of the Indian military, at least when viewed in historical terms. Precisely because such a distension of military power runs counter to the established traditions of the Indian state, it is unlikely to be endorsed by India's political leadership, particularly the civilian bureaucracy. Irrespective of what the final outcome may be, the alternative model of control recommended by the senior leadership of the Indian military and their votaries in the community of retired military officers indicates that the armed services treat nuclear weapons seriously as potential instruments of war and seek to be fully involved in all decisions relating to the acquisition, deployment, operation, and use of such weaponry. It is not surprising, therefore, to find many Indian military officers expressing the expectation that although "the current command and control arrangements seemed to be that the AEC scientists/engineers had control over the nuclear devices, . . . the Services would have their command, but eventually."[493]

This expectation may, in fact, come to pass over time, and the recent recommendations of the Group of Ministers with respect to restructuring higher defense decisionmaking *could* represent the first tentative steps in that direction. In great measure, future changes in the patterns of control will depend first on what Pakistan and China do in the interim, since the nuclear force structures, technologies, and doctrines gradually becoming visible in these countries may

---

[493]Chari, "Command and Control Arrangements."

force India to modify its preferred approaches to the management of nuclear weaponry;[494] and second on the kinds of delivery systems India itself acquires over time, since the shift toward a sea-based deterrent will of necessity transform the force-in-being into something resembling a ready arsenal and, accordingly, will require new methods of management that are closer to the military's preferences than those encoded in the baseline model described earlier. This second development is critical in that irrespective of what Pakistan and China do, India is not *physically* constrained to change the methods of managing its nuclear inventory. The development of a sea-based deterrent, however, imposes unavoidable technological imperatives for change: While land-based nuclear capabilities can be maintained in distributed form, a surface ship or submarine-based deterrent presupposes complete or at least relatively high degrees of integration of the nuclear system at all times. To be sure, it can still be maintained—even if not in distributed form—as something resembling a force-in-being, but engineering such a posture would require India to develop either a complex operational system that includes both technologies and organizational arrangements allowing for the emergency integration of physically separated components while under way or sophisticated PALs that prevent the vessel's commander from being able to activate his weapons if he does not receive specific enabling codes from the national command authority. Such technologies, currently utilized by the United States to control its SSBN fleet,[495] are sophisticated and costly—but thankfully these challenges will not present themselves in the Indian context in any full-fledged form for at least another decade if not two, since an Indian SSBN capability is currently nowhere on the horizon.[496] India is likely to emplace ballistic missiles on surface ships within the next decade, but it is unlikely that these missiles will actually be armed

---

[494]In 2000 Pakistan announced the creation of its own National Command Authority, an impressive organizational structure that vests control of the country's nuclear weapons in a variety of bodies manned jointly by civilian leaders and the uniformed military. See "National Command Authority Formed," *Dawn*, February 6, 2000.

[495]See Sagan, *The Limits of Safety: Organizations, Accidents, and Nuclear Weapons*, p. 277, for a discussion of how the U.S. Navy resisted the integration of PALs on its SSBN fleet throughout the Cold War.

[496]See the remarks of C. Raja Mohan in *Post Pokhran II: The National Way Ahead*, pp. 78–79.

with nuclear warheads before a formal decision is made to transition from the current posture of a force-in-being into some alternative type of ready nuclear force.[497]

The preferences of the Indian military may therefore come to pass over the long term, but their desire to participate in the command function is far removed from the thinking about nuclear doctrine and command-and-control arrangements that currently obtains among India's civilian leaders both in the political arena and in the higher bureaucracy. In these circles, the view that India's nuclear weapons are first and foremost political instruments of deterrence seems to provide adequate justification for creating an operationally quiescent force-in-being—with all the characteristics described earlier—rather than a robust and ready arsenal designed for the prompt conduct of protracted nuclear operations. The concerns expressed by military officers about survivability, readiness, and the need to prepare seriously for nuclear operations *in extremis*, however, are not lost on India's senior security managers, and consequently it is likely that the baseline command system illustrated in Figure 9 will actually mutate considerably to accommodate different strategic circumstances even as it creates new opportunities for active military participation—although always under uncompromising civilian direction and control—in the management of the evolving Indian deterrent.

Figure 12 illustrates one possible metamorphosis from the baseline model and suggests how the Indian command system is likely to respond—within the parameters of the basic framework pertaining to the force-in-being—to contingencies that arise within a low-threat scenario.

The first modification that is likely to be institutionalized relative to the baseline model illustrated in Figure 9 is the development of institutions such as the National Security Council Secretariat and the National Intelligence Board that are charged with generating a "strategic alert,"[498] warning security managers about the possibility

---

[497] For details about this somewhat peculiar effort at basing tactical, liquid-fueled SRBMs like the Dhanush on the Indian Navy's Sukanya class offshore patrol vessels, see the description available at http://www.bharat-rakshak.com/NAVY/Sukanya.html.

[498] For more on this phenomenon in the Cold War context, see Scott Sagan, "Nuclear Alerts and Crisis Management," *International Security*, 9:4 (Spring 1985), pp.

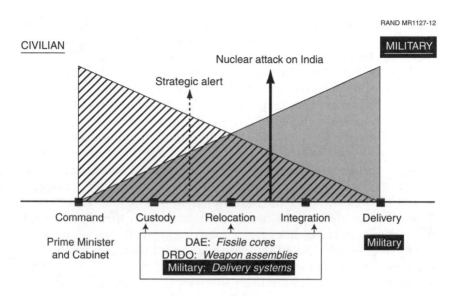

Figure 12—India's Likely Command System in a Low-Threat Scenario

of an impending crisis. Strategic alerts are different from tactical alerts in that the former signal the possibility of war, whereas the latter signal the imminence of actual military attack. Since the Indian nuclear force will be routinely maintained as a force-in-being, the possibility of strategic warning becomes critical not so much to its survival—because presumably opacity, mobility, deception, and denial in peacetime ought to suffice as far as ensuring survivability is concerned—as to the ability of the Indian leadership to deter threats through possible signaling if required and, more important, to organize for retaliatory actions should those become necessary. Given that the historical record throughout the 20th century suggests that political crises have always preceded the outbreak of war,[499] it is reasonable for Indian security managers to seek some level of warning so that they can do whatever is necessary to reinforce deterrence.

99–139; Joseph I. Kruzel, "Military Alerts and Diplomatic Signals," in Ellen P. Stern (ed.), *The Limits of Military Intervention* (Thousand Oaks, CA: Sage Publications, 1977), pp. 83–99; and Kurt Gottfried and Bruce Blair (eds.), *Crisis Stability and Nuclear War* (Oxford, UK: Oxford University Press, 1988), pp. 234–243.

[499]Richard K. Betts, *Surprise Attack: Lessons for Defense Planning* (Washington, D.C.: Brookings, 1982), pp. 4–5.

In truly low-threat scenarios, the baseline model of command is therefore likely to be modified by the search for strategic warning, which is then used to organize the relocation of India's dispersed strategic assets. This relocation could be carried out under the aegis of the new unified command headed by the CDS (if these institutions are in fact created eventually), or it could be carried out entirely under the auspices of the command-and-control system currently in place. In either case, the purpose of relocating these strategic assets would be to increase their survivability, signal the readiness to respond, or prepare for more effective retaliation. Irrespective of the intentions underlying such relocation, Indian security managers would not require the integration of their nuclear devices even if conventional deterrence breakdown occurred after the receipt of strategic warning because a low-threat scenario—almost by definition—would leave them confident that they could integrate their weapons without hindrance after riding out a first strike. This command sequence is most likely to materialize in practice if the political crisis in question appeared to be relatively insignificant and without any nuclear-shadowed dimensions; if New Delhi feared that the detectable integration of its nuclear capabilities might actually precipitate a nuclear attack that might otherwise have been avoided; or if relocating the nuclear assets was all that was required by the demands of strategic prudence in some more or less abnormal political circumstances. Should one or more of these conditions obtain, the baseline model of command could be modified in the manner suggested by Figure 12 with relatively low risk.

In a high-threat scenario, however, when none of the three moderating conditions obtain, it is likely that the baseline command system would be modified in the one consequential way illustrated in Figure 13: India's nuclear weapons would if necessary be relocated on receipt of strategic warning—again under the aegis of the new unified command (if established) or at the direction of the existing command system—but would be integrated, ready, and waiting even before nuclear attacks on India occurred—and irrespective of whether conventional deterrence broke down in the interim. As the nuclear capabilities of India's primary competitors grow in numbers, diversity, and yield, and if New Delhi were to be confronted by crises that were tinged heavily with nuclear shadows, it is most likely that the Indian command system would operate in consonance with the

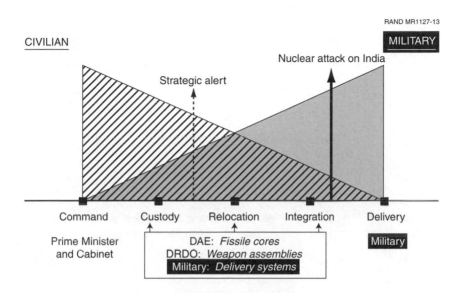

Figure 13—India's Likely Command System in a High-Threat Scenario

posture illustrated in Figure 13 as its new baseline model for situations of supreme emergency. If Chengappa's description in *Weapons of Peace* is accurate, the Indian command system did in fact operate in just this fashion during the Kargil crisis in 1998.[500] Even if these events did not occur as described, however, there is every reason to believe that some variation of the command sequence depicted in Figure 13 will turn out to be the response framework of choice during a major crisis in the future.

As time goes by, however, and as India's own nuclear capabilities mature in different dimensions, it is likely that even the prospectively new baseline illustrated in Figure 13 will give way to the more complex and sophisticated command system depicted in Figure 14. Under this model—India's most likely eventual command system—New Delhi will still maintain a force-in-being as its standard operating posture in peacetime. A formally constituted National Command Authority that is constructed principally around the Prime Minister, the Cabinet, and other civilian successors but that may include senior

---

[500]Chengappa, *Weapons of Peace*, p. 437.

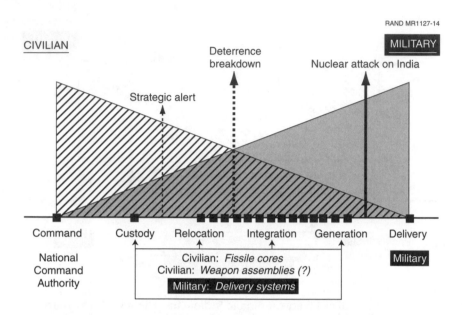

RAND MR1127-14

Figure 14—India's Likely Eventual Command System

military officers in an advisory capacity will discharge the command function. The material components of the nuclear arsenal will continue to be distributed across a variety of custodial agencies, both civilian and military, all of which are likely to be coordinated under the aegis of the new unified command headed by the CDS. On the receipt of strategic alert, however, India's National Command Authority will direct the relocation of its strategic assets if required by the specific circumstances facing the force at that point. More important, however, New Delhi will focus on developing the technical capabilities, human competency, infrastructural support, and organizational arrangements that will enable it to integrate its weapon systems and generate the requisite increases in readiness before, during, or after conventional deterrence breakdown with the intent of possessing more or less ready nuclear forces even before it absorbs what may be the first of many sequential nuclear attacks on India. Clearly, Indian security managers can use such a command model even today, but success in this regard would owe mainly to the fact that their current nuclear capabilities are relatively small and unidimensional. What they are likely to pursue, therefore, is the option of employing such a command system even when their nuclear capabilities increase in terms of the number of warheads possessed, the diversity of delivery systems employed, and the extent of distribution governing the dispersal of weapon systems and/or their components. The ability to rapidly alert, relocate, integrate, and ready a larger and more diverse nuclear force even before absorbing a first strike is a capability that Indian security managers will eventually strive for mostly for prudential reasons deriving from the belief that possessing the option for rapid response is, other things being equal, better both for the deterrence of adversaries and for the reassurance of the national leadership. This is in fact the logic that drove the National Security Advisory Board to recommend that India's future nuclear posture focus on developing the "assured capability to shift from peacetime deployment to fully employable forces in the shortest possible time."[501] In this final model of command following from the posture of a force-in-being, the actual Indian retaliation after suffering a nuclear attack may still *not* be instantaneous, since the retaliatory response time will be determined in large part by the extent of damage suffered as result of the adversary's attack. Yet this command model, more than any of the variants illustrated previously, holds the best promise of allowing Indian security managers to unleash their retaliatory response within a few hours of suffering an attack—the time frame that many Indian strategic planners consider to be most desirable in the political context of conflicts in Southern Asia—as opposed to the many-hours-to-a-few-days delay that is inherent in the initial baseline model illustrated in Figure 9.

The command system illustrated in Figure 14 thus remains the model to which the Indian nuclear deterrent will eventually conform, although policymakers in New Delhi will not publicly articulate this conception today. Even if they do not aspire to institutionalize this model at present, they are nevertheless likely to do so once their present development, acquisition, and reorganization plans in the nuclear realm come to fruition. Although this will take a decade (if not more) to be fully realized, the capabilities that they will have acquired by then will simply allow for the institutionalization of such a command system. It is also not unreasonable to believe that by this

---

[501]"Draft Report of [the] National Security Advisory Board on Indian Nuclear Doctrine," p. 3.

point the current international pressures that make for restraint will have abated somewhat or will at least have diminished in intensity as the world grows progressively used to the idea that nuclear weapons in the Indian subcontinent are here to stay. Under such circumstances, the willingness of India's security managers to countenance increasing the rate at which their force-in-being can be reconstituted in the face of imminent threats will also intensify. Even at this point, however, it is important to remember that India's nuclear deterrent—assuming that no untoward perturbations occur in the interim—will remain a force-in-being rather than a ready arsenal in that it will still have distributed components in peacetime maintained by various combinations of civilian and military organizations. These capabilities will still have to be materially integrated on the explicit directive of the National Command Authority, and this will occur only when strategic warning dictates that India's deterrent capabilities be reconstituted as a matter of political prudence. What will change as a result of the many iterations in the baseline command model, however, are the organizational patterns regulating the custody of the many force components; the sequencing of the integration process relative to the event of deterrence breakdown; the readiness of the deterrent force before nuclear attacks on India occur; and the time frame within which retaliatory actions can actually be unleashed *after the absorption of nuclear strikes on India.*

It is obvious that as India moves toward the institutionalization of such a command posture over time even while remaining grounded within the framework of a force-in-being, it *could* gradually acquire the capability for first strikes in a crisis—something that was *irrevocably* ruled out so long as the baseline command model illustrated in Figure 9 remained operational. This development could become a source of concern to India's adversaries and, if not managed appropriately, could even become subversive of crisis stability. The saving grace, however, is that even when India acquires the technical, human, infrastructural, and organizational competence to ready its forces rapidly in anticipation of an adversary's first strike, it will still lack the political incentives to initiate nuclear first use for all the reasons explored earlier in this book. More important, so long as its nuclear weaponry is more effective for countervalue rather than counterforce missions, it will continue to lack the technical incentives to engage even in preemptive strikes, despite the possible background condition of conventional deterrence breakdown.

Consequently, it is reasonable to conclude that as long as India does not possess a true sea-based nuclear deterrent, its currently desired strategic posture—a force-in-being—can endure despite the many variations in reconstitution and readiness time lines that are likely to become visible in the years ahead. The potential changes in reconstitution and readiness rates, however, do raise an interesting question about the long-term viability of the force-in-being as an equilibrium solution to India's strategic needs—a question whose answer must be deferred until the next chapter. In the interim, it may simply be noted that India's strategic development, acquisition, and deployment plans are still in their formative phase, and accordingly it will be many years before even the force-in-being—let alone some successor regime that is at present only an evanescent glimmer on a distant horizon—is complete.

TAKING STOCK

The prospective Indian nuclear deterrent, configured as a force-in-being of the kind described in this chapter, represents a unique solution to a unique set of requirements. Because New Delhi is not conventionally weaker than its principal adversaries, it does not require nuclear weaponry primarily as military instruments of defense. What it requires are political tools that immunize it against possible nuclear threats that may be mounted by its adversaries. This reassurance of immunity is sought first and foremost in the realm of psychology insofar as Indian decisionmakers seek capabilities that would enable them to face up to any potential Chinese or Pakistani challenges without fear of being utterly defenseless. Given the centrality of this "psycho-political" concern, it is not surprising that Indian policymakers view their acknowledged possession of nuclear weapons as being the single most important ingredient contributing to successful deterrence and reassurance. To be sure, they recognize that the mere possession of nuclear capabilities is inadequate for successful deterrence and reassurance over the long haul; because nuclear capabilities in the hands of one state invariably become a magnet that compels counteraction on the part of its adversaries, it is understood that India will need to develop a range of ancillary instruments that will allow its emerging arsenal to remain both lethal and reliable amid many—though not all—of the strategic circumstances that may materialize in the future.

The necessity of possessing nuclear reserves that could function as an effective deterrent not simply in the realm of psychology but also in the effective domain of operations will in fact force Indian decisionmakers to concentrate on investing resources in assuring the requisite survivability, connectivity, and penetrativity of their nuclear assets. In this context, they appreciate that numerous additional accoutrements—such as more advanced delivery vehicles, refurbished command-and-control arrangements, and additional safety protocols—are essential if their arsenal is to serve as a source of credible deterrence and reassurance over time, and these capabilities will almost certainly be developed over this decade and beyond. They do not, however, feel pressured to develop many of these ingredients urgently because the instruments India currently possesses—fission weapons and strike aircraft—are seen as sufficient to deter Pakistan. And while the ideal deterrent necessary to constrain China—high-yield weapons atop IRBMs—is certainly a long while away, Indian policymakers believe that they have at least another decade and probably two before the political need for such systems becomes truly pressing. In the interim, even modest capabilities, built around aircraft and IRBMs armed with simple fission warheads, are deemed to suffice against both adversaries irrespective of the latter's capabilities because, given New Delhi's targeting strategies, Indian policymakers are likely to ask, echoing Kenneth Waltz, "Why compare weapons with weapons when they are to be used not against each other but against cities that cannot counter them?"[502]

Even when India acquires new and more formidable nuclear assets, however, its policymakers recognize that the "order of precedence" and the "balance of power" in regional politics will not have changed considerably. India will still remain stronger than Pakistan but weaker than China. For the most part, this weakness will not derive from poor technical accomplishments per se but rather from a

---

[502]Kenneth N. Waltz, "What Will the Spread of Nuclear Weapons Do to the World?" in John K. King (ed.), *International Political Effects of the Spread of Nuclear Weapons* (Washington, D.C.: USGPO, 1979), p. 188.

lack of time and opportunity to pursue further technological advancements legitimately given the gradually tightening international nonproliferation order. If the constraints of time and circumstance did not present themselves, India could continue to produce unaccountable weapons-usable fissile materials indefinitely; could continue to develop and hot test thermonuclear as well as other types of nuclear weapons until these capabilities were fully validated in the eyes of its adversaries; and could continue to design, test, and produce a wide variety of delivery systems without fear of constraints imposed by major extraregional powers such as the United States. For good or bad, however, India does not enjoy such liberties today, and New Delhi recognizes that as it begins to fulfill the commitments it has made in principle with respect to the international nuclear control regime (and to the United States, acting as the chief steward of that regime), its ability to develop a nuclear arsenal of the sort the existing great powers possess will diminish even further.

Yet none of this unnerves New Delhi greatly because Indian policymakers are convinced that nuclear weapons—whatever their quality—represent such potent *political* tools that no matter how minuscule their operational effects may be, the very prospect of even the smallest device going off in anger should more than suffice to safeguard their interests in a crisis. This kind of confidence is not exuded by any other nuclear weapon power (save perhaps China if its traditional nuclear force posture and its putative views about nuclear weaponry are any indication), but Indian security managers appear to base their sometimes-unnerving sanguineness on two simple convictions: one, that nuclear weapons have decreasing relevance as *usable* instruments of high politics; and two, that there are simply no disputes between India and its adversaries which are worth resolving through the use of nuclear weaponry. Even where serious disputes exist, New Delhi has determined that India is so well off conventionally (and will continue to remain so with modest increments of effort) that it would never have to rely on its nuclear reserves for purposes of defense. In fact, so long as India does not use its conventional advantages in an *exploitative* mode, it would continue to enjoy the best of both worlds: It could use its defensive capabilities to preclude a reliance on nuclear weapons for purposes of survival while giving its adversaries no excuse to resort to nuclear use in support of their own defense. The other residual needs requiring nuclear weapons can be satisfied by the relatively simple fission devices India is already known to possess—and at any rate, India's adversaries have to reckon with the possibility that New Delhi may have still more lethal nuclear capabilities even if these have not been unambiguously demonstrated thus far. The only eventuality that such a modest capability cannot neutralize is when a manifestly greater power like China deliberately exploits its nuclear superiority—accepting the costs of Indian nuclear retaliation, however ragged, in the process—to engage in an unlimited-aims war against India. Since New Delhi has ruled out such a contingency as unrealistic almost by definition, however, it is believed that India does not have to develop nuclear capabilities designed to counter such a possibility.

All told, then, India's modest nuclear capabilities appear to satisfy New Delhi—even though they will be further improved along the margins as time goes by—because they are *not* intended to service any "*tous azimuts*" (all-encompassing) requirements, an adequacy criterion that is sometimes argued for by Indian hawks like Karnad, who assert that "India will . . . have to contend with [a] range of weapons from the extremely advanced held by the U.S. to the relatively effective in the Chinese inventory."[503] They are also not intended to provide deterrence benefits under *all* strategic circumstances imaginable over an indefinite period of time. Indian strategic planners in the Ministries of Defence and External Affairs strenuously insist that their nuclear resources are not designed to contend with the strategic capabilities of the United States, Russia, Britain, France, and Israel, as they have neither the financial or technical resources nor the political need to counter the nuclear capabilities of any of these states. They are also insistent that India's nuclear capabilities are not designed to deal with every strategic environment and political contingency imaginable but only against certain kinds of threats that may be mounted by two specific adversaries—China and Pakistan—within the parameters of a largely offense-dominant global nuclear regime. These threats are deemed to be manageable precisely because both adversaries are perceived to possess relatively small arsenals; be constrained by relatively strong pressures against easy recourse to nuclear use; and remain engulfed by disputes with India that do not objectively warrant any use of their own nuclear

---

[503]Karnad, "Going Thermonuclear: Why, with What Forces, at What Cost," p. 317.

weaponry. Based on this assessment, Indian security managers believe that the country is unlikely to face political situations where nuclear weapons are *actually* used against it. Even if such use were to occur in some remote circumstances, they believe that the extent of use is likely to be relatively small and limited. Further, these contingencies—being unlikely to materialize in the form of "bolt-out-of-the-blue" attacks—would occur, Indian policymakers believe, mainly in the context of a graduated process of deterrence breakdown, which is likely to be preceded by some kind of political crisis that allows for specific forms of strategic warning.

Thanks to these judgments, India's limited nuclear capabilities—so long as they meet certain minimal standards of lethality, survivability, connectivity, and penetrativity—are seen to be sufficient both to assure the country's strategic safety as well as to bequeath to it the status required to underwrite New Delhi's demands for greater recognition on the global stage. Since limited capabilities are deemed to suffice for both security and status, it is not surprising to find that New Delhi has evolved a command system premised on the belief that assured retaliation is far more important than speedy retaliation for deterrence success. Most of the established nuclear powers refrained from creating a similar and comparably structured command system because, although it was recognized that nuclear war was invariably a "low-probability/high-cost" event, they took their bearings from their fears of the high costs of unpreparedness and consequently invested heavily in complex, redundant, and expensive command systems that were oriented primarily toward maximizing the levels of damage expectancy in case of a nuclear war. India has configured, and is in the process of refining, its command system based on exactly the opposite calculus. Believing that nuclear war is not an acceptable form of political competition in the specific circumstances facing the Southern Asian region in the "second nuclear age," New Delhi has taken its bearings from the low-probability dimension of the nuclear war contingency and, accordingly, has sought to develop only such a minimally adequate command system as would give its adversaries reason to fear that even the most ragged Indian retaliation they might have to suffer would not be worth the benefits of having launched any first strike to begin with. India's civilian-dominated command system, however informal it may be in practice, is seen as sufficient to enforce such a strategic pause on the part of its adversaries, and consequently New Delhi has sought nothing more—but also nothing less—from its indigenous nuclear command system, which has no parallels anywhere else in the world.

The uniqueness of the Indian command arrangements, its deterrence posture writ large, and its attitudes toward the status and management of nuclear weaponry do, however, raise a larger and more significant theoretical question: Is the system of nuclear deterrence subject to some universal laws that, transcending space and time, demand a certain isomorphism in all deterrent architectures, postures, and strategies irrespective of where they might materialize in practice? Or is the system of nuclear deterrence a political phenomenon that is regulated by the specific character of the strategic competition in a given situation, such that a variety of deterrent architectures, postures, and strategies could in fact materialize across time and space so long as all these variables otherwise comport with some abstract, minimal standards of deterrence adequacy? Depending on how these questions are answered, the evolving Indian nuclear deterrent may be found more or less wanting. Those theorists, both Western and Indian, who believe that nuclear deterrence is a sociophysical phenomenon that is regulated by some immutable laws governing its creation and maintenance would be gravely suspicious about the adequacy of the Indian force-in-being, since this force architecture is unlikely to meet the standards embodied by the ideal-typical deterrent forces appearing on both sides of the Cold War divide during the heyday of superpower competition. Indian policymakers and their followers among the security elites would argue, on the other hand, that although all nuclear deterrents must meet certain minimal standards of adequacy, the specific forms, postures, and command arrangements governing these artifacts can vary from country to country and, even in the case of the super powers, from epoch to epoch precisely because nuclear deterrence is not an absolute sociophysical phenomenon but a contingent one that is invariably shaped by the exigencies of political competition at a given point in time and space. Accordingly, they would defend their own evolving deterrent as being perfectly suited to the specific strategic circumstances confronting *their* country and, as such, would assert that it remains the best solution for them no matter how different or peculiar it might appear in comparison to other deterrents maintained elsewhere in the world. On this question more than any other, India's security managers might turn out to be more correct than their critics, since there is an increasing recognition even in the West today that the "classical" models of nuclear deterrence may have been an aberration brought about solely by the intensity of Cold War competition and that different political circumstances in the future may in fact spawn different kinds of nuclear deterrents—deterrents that vary in size, posture, and architecture based not only on the character of political competition occurring within a given "security complex"[504] but also on the technologies, institutions, and ideas that gain dominance in a particular age.[505]

India's possession of a unique and relatively limited, even if gradually improving, deterrent is thus anchored in specific beliefs about the international environment and the demands imposed by that environment on New Delhi. These external considerations are complemented by other concerns, among the most important of which is the challenge of developing a force posture that does not subvert the traditional Indian preference for minimal military control over its strategic assets. This reticence at involving the military extensively in matters nuclear is linked to concerns about maintaining certain preferred patterns of civilian dominance while simultaneously underscoring the country's larger claim that nuclear weapons remain undesirable instruments of international politics. Only a nuclear arsenal configured as a force-in-being stands some chance of satisfying both of these constraints concurrently while also meeting the other operational demands of survivability, safety, and lethality. It also holds the additional advantage of minimizing the costs incurred in the creation of a deterrent, especially given the strong competing demands on defense resources at a time when India has still not escaped the trap of underdevelopment. The configuration of the force-in-being described in this chapter allows India to affirm that its nuclear capabilities represent political rather than military instruments in the first instance while at the same time remaining tools that can

---

[504]For the logic of this concept, see Buzan, *People, States and Fear*, pp. 186–229.

[505]The best exploration of this argument can be found in John Baylis and Robert O'Neill (eds.), *Alternative Nuclear Futures: The Role of Nuclear Weapons in the Post–Cold War World* (Oxford, UK: Oxford University Press, 2000), and in Avery Goldstein, *Deterrence and Security in the 21st Century* (Stanford, CA: Stanford University Press, 2000).

be mutated into weapons of mass destruction if the strategic circumstances so warrant. The force-in-being also lends itself to being *transformed* into a more robust and formidable posture, like a ready arsenal, if India's strategic environment demands such a response over time.

Achieving this end state, however, does not appear to be the objective right now—despite the pressures emanating from India's hawks, both civilian and military—and New Delhi will continue to resist all domestic pressures that argue for moving toward such a goal right away. While this is true even of the BJP government currently in office, it will become only more so if a Congress government or a left-of-center coalition were to return to power in the future. Indian policymakers of all stripes appear to be convinced that only benefits accrue from moving slowly and with due deliberation: A slow evolution in the country's nuclear capabilities serves as an effective learning process for both state managers and the armed services while simultaneously allowing other national entities the time they need to adjust to the new realities embodied by a nuclear India. Moving cautiously also gives Indian policymakers a much better feel for the true costs involved in creating a deterrent, especially in comparison to the absurdly low figures currently offered by devotees of nuclearization in New Delhi. For all of these reasons, the Indian nuclear posture in the years ahead is best described as a *creeping weaponization* that will eventually materialize into a force-in-being. This, rather than a ready arsenal, will remain the outcome as India continues to put the pieces together over this decade and beyond.

As this process unfolds, however, the force-in-being will continue to face the challenge of servicing two opposing orientations simultaneously: as political symbols and as weapons of retribution. Only time will tell whether the Indian deterrent will be successful in meeting these antinomous demands, for success here will depend less on the persuasiveness of the overarching concept of the force-in-being and more on how effectively this notion is translated into the many thousands of details relating to the safety, survivability, connectivity, and penetrativity of the potential force. The adequacy of this translation cannot be investigated right now because India is still a great distance away from the point where its nuclear capabilities would be fully manifested as a force-in-being. But it is not too early to identify—at least in broad generic terms—the kinds of components New Delhi would seek to develop as it proceeds to structure its future deterrent in a way that comports with some facsimile of the force-in-being described in this chapter.

Chapter Five

TOWARD A FORCE-IN-BEING (II): ASSESSING THE REQUIREMENTS AND ADEQUACY OF THE EVOLVING DETERRENT

It has long been a staple of strategic wisdom that all nuclear arsenals embody one solution or another to the competing trade-offs facing their possessors. The shapes of emerging nuclear arsenals in particular are held to be especially sensitive to the character of civil-military relations and to the time urgency of retaliation.[1] In India's case, these considerations—if present trends offer any indication—will most likely result in a nuclear posture that, taking the form of a force-in-being, will emphasize opaque and granularly distributed ingredients, assertive command structures, and more or less delayed retaliation. Such a posture could in principle satisfy India's national security requirements, but having a splendid conceptual solution does not an effective deterrent make. An effective deterrent ultimately requires appropriate material capabilities of various sorts, all organized coherently in terms of specific procedural frameworks and organizational structures. This chapter seeks to assess in preliminary fashion whether India possesses the ingredients the force-in-being concept necessitates, and it then attempts to identify what capabilities the country is likely to develop in the future if this evolving concept is to be successfully incarnated as a viable system of deterrence. This analysis therefore serves to identify the areas of activity in which India's strategic managers will probably engage over the next two decades—areas that the United States would do well to monitor. It

---

[1]Feaver, "Command and Control in Emerging Nuclear Nations," pp. 160–187.

concludes by examining whether the force-in-being, once complete, will satisfy certain critical demands that any system of nuclear deterrence would generate.

PUTTING THE PIECES TOGETHER: WHAT INDIA HAS, WHAT INDIA HASN'T

Fissile Materials

Among the first requirements for the creation of a nuclear capability, in whatever form it takes, is the availability of fissile materials. From its inception, the Indian nuclear program focused on the creation of a plutonium economy in order to sustain a three-stage production cycle aimed at exploiting mixed oxide fuels and, eventually, fast breeder reactors to create full self-sufficiency in the generation of low-cost nuclear power.[2] In consonance with this goal, India harnessed the natural uranium–fueled, heavy-water-moderated research and power reactors used in the first phase of the cycle to create a significant stock of the by-product plutonium. This plutonium was to be mixed with thorium—a resource India possesses in abundance—to fuel a series of second-stage reactors intended to produce uranium 233 (U^{233}) as a further by-product. In the third stage, fast breeder reactors using combined U^{233}-thorium fuels were to be constructed with the intention of "breeding" more U^{233} than would be consumed in the operation of such reactors. This three-stage cycle—derived from the grandiose vision of Homi Bhabha[3]—was intended to make India self-sufficient, since the country's abundant thorium reserves, when complemented by the continuous breeding of U^{233}, essentially promised an unlimited supply of nuclear fuel for the cheap generation of electricity. The centrality of plutonium in such an energy cycle, however, also implied that no matter how it was eventually used for the production of U^{233}, plutonium would always be available in the interim for the creation of nuclear weapons were

---

[2]The three-stage plan is briefly described and assessed in G. S. Bhargava, "Nuclear Power in India," *Energy Policy*, 20:8 (August 1992), pp. 735–743. See also Perkovich, *India's Nuclear Bomb*, pp. 26–34.

[3]See Ganesan Venkataraman, *Bhabha and His Magnificent Obsessions* (Hyderabad, India: Universities Press, 1994) for further details about Bhabha's plans.

India to embark on such a course of action.[4] Weapons-grade pluto-nium—Pu[239]—thus came to constitute the principal fissile material for New Delhi's nuclear weaponry, even though India would develop two experimental, pilot-stage ultracentrifuge plants for the produc-tion of highly enriched uranium along the way.[5]

Any attempt to understand the shape and structure of the future Indian deterrent raises three critical issues relating to fissile materi-als: First, what kinds of fissile materials does India possess, and what is it likely to seek? Second, what is the size of its fissile-material in-ventory? And third, what is the relationship between the size of its fissile-material inventory and its weapon stockpile?

What kinds of fissile materials does India possess, and what is it likely to seek? It is now widely known that India possesses a signifi-cant inventory of weapons-grade plutonium. Also understood is the fact that India has attempted to produce highly enriched uranium in the form of U[235] through the centrifuge process, although the extent to which this has been accomplished remains unclear, as does the size of this inventory. One RAND analysis suggests that, at most, In-dia "could currently produce only 10 kg of HEU per year."[6] India is also believed to have produced "kilogram quantities of U-233 by ir-radiating thorium in its power reactors."[7] The desire for small quantities of HEU—that is, uranium containing more than 20 per-cent U[235]—traditionally arose from the need for a fuel source for the nuclear reactors being developed to power India's future nuclear submarines. This need by itself is certain to propel India's desire for more HEU, although its claim to have tested a thermonuclear device in May 1998 could justify further acquisition of this material. Many advanced weapon designs use some combination of thermonuclear fuel and HEU in order to, as one analyst put it, "provide an extra

---

[4]The centrality of plutonium in India's early nuclear power and weapon plans has been examined in great detail in Perkovich, *India's Nuclear Bomb*, pp. 13–59.

[5]Spector et al., *Tracking Nuclear Proliferation*, pp. 89–95.

[6]Jones, *From Testing to Deploying Nuclear Forces*, p. 8.

[7]Ibid.

'kick' to get the fusion reaction going."[8] If the thermonuclear device tested in May 1998 was of such a design and if New Delhi seeks to "serial produce" this design for its inventory, India will have to greatly expand its capability to produce either U^{233} or U^{235}, since its present annual production capacity of these materials has been judged to be "significantly less than the amount needed for nuclear weapons."[9]

To be sure, there are obviously thermonuclear weapon designs that use only weapons-grade plutonium in combination with materials such as lithium deuteride.[10] There are also boosted fission designs (which reportedly served as the "primary" in India's May 1998 thermonuclear test)[11] that use weapons-grade plutonium and deuterium-tritium, usually in gaseous form.[12] If India's weapon designs are of this sort, New Delhi will likely concentrate largely on producing weapons-grade plutonium—as it has traditionally done—as well as lithium deuteride and deuterium-tritium, leaving its experimental centrifuge facilities to produce whatever HEU they can for the submarine program or other research purposes. In fact, at least one report has suggested that India has begun stockpiling highly concentrated tritium extracted from the heavy-water moderator in India's power reactors for weapon applications[13] in addition to the tritium it otherwise produces by irradiating lithium in its research reactors.[14] When combined with other information about India's continuing lithium 6 purification and production program,[15] these re-

---

[8]David Albright, "India and Pakistan's Nuclear Arms Race: Out of the Closet but Not in the Street," *Arms Control Today*, 23:5 (June 1993), p. 13.

[9]Ibid.

[10]See Sublette, *Nuclear Weapons Frequently Asked Questions*, "Section 4.4: Elements of Thermonuclear Weapons Design."

[11]Chengappa, "Is India's H-Bomb a Dud?" p. 28.

[12]See Carey Sublette, *Nuclear Weapons Frequently Asked Questions*, "Section 4.3: Fission-Fusion Hybrid Weapons," available at http://www.fas.org/nuke/hew/Nwfaq/Nfaq4-3.html#Nfaq4.3.1.

[13]T. S. Gopi Rethinaraj, "Tritium Breakthrough Brings India Closer to an H-Bomb Arsenal," *Jane's Intelligence Review*, 10:1 (January 1998), pp. 29–31.

[14]David Albright and Tom Zamora, "India, Pakistan's Nuclear Weapons: All the Pieces in Place," *Bulletin of the Atomic Scientists*, 45:5 (June 1989), p. 25.

[15]Albright, "India and Pakistan's Nuclear Arms Race: Out of the Closet but Not in the Street," p. 14.

ports suggest that India will persist with its plutonium-based designs even in its advanced weapon program to the further neglect of HEU—an inference supported by India's reported disinclination to begin serial production of ultracentrifuges for large-scale uranium enrichment.[16] On balance, then, it would appear that India will continue to emphasize weapons-grade plutonium as the principal nuclear material for its fission designs and will supplement it with deuterium, tritium, and lithium deuteride whenever its boosted fission and thermonuclear requirements so warrant while continuing to produce other special materials, such as beryllium and polonium, for the tampers and/or initiators its weaponry requires.[17]

What is the size of the fissile-material inventory? The size of India's fissile-material inventory is of more than academic interest because of its general relationship to the size of India's present and prospective stockpile of nuclear weaponry. Unfortunately, however, accurate information about this inventory is hard to come by. Indeed, the open literature provides a bewildering array of values that makes reliable conclusions difficult to reach. In addition, the literature often fails to distinguish weapons-grade plutonium that is immediately separated from that which is produced through irradiation but is not separated either because of capacity constraints in the reprocessing facilities or because of bottlenecks at other points in the fuel cycle. By assuming that all of India's weapons-grade plutonium is immediately separated, most analyses thus fail to distinguish between fissile-material production capacity in general and the actual quantities of fissile materials that are immediately available for the fabrication of nuclear weaponry.[18] This difficulty is exacerbated by the fact that even serious scholars rarely examine India's capacity to produce the other special materials necessary to manufacture nuclear weapons. As a result, the size of India's presumed weapon stockpile is often straightforwardly derived from the quantity of fissile materials alone without any thought given to the other con-

---

[16]Ibid., 13.

[17]The special materials produced in India for its nuclear weapon program are discussed in Albright and Zamora, "India, Pakistan's Nuclear Weapons: All the Pieces in Place," and Albright, "India and Pakistan's Nuclear Arms Race: Out of the Closet but Not in the Street."

[18]The only work that has recognized the sensitivity of this question is Albright, *Fact Sheet: India and Pakistan—Current and Potential Nuclear Arsenals.*

straints that might limit the size of this stockpile. None of these difficulties can be resolved here, however, and consequently this analysis
will simply identify some of the most prominent assessments available about India's fissile-material inventory with the intent of suggesting the future courses of action New Delhi might pursue as far as
the production of fissile materials—primarily weapons-grade plutonium—is concerned.

The earliest estimates appearing in the West provided an unreal-
istically high assessment of India's fissile-material production capability. Assuming that significant portions of the Indian nuclear
complex (including many power reactors) would be dedicated to
producing weapons-grade plutonium, Arnold Kramish forecast in
1984 that by the year 2000 India would possess the equivalent of 1100
critical masses (or some 8800 kg of Pu^{239} at the rate of 1 critical mass
= 8 kg Pu^{239}), since it was believed to be capable of producing up to
100 critical masses annually.[19] In the early 1980s, the Congressional
Research Service (CRS), among others, similarly calculated that India
would be able to sustain an annual production rate of some 127 kg of
Pu^{239} to yield an inventory of approximately 1600 kg by the year
2000—a figure that would suffice to create some 400 simple fission
weapons (at the rate of 1 critical mass = 4 kg Pu^{239}).[20] This figure or
some variant thereof is still favored by some media reports and has
become the fulcrum on which Indian hawks have occasionally
placed their demand for a large nuclear arsenal.

Estimates such as these, however, have been sharply reduced in
recent years. On the basis of one of the most detailed unclassified
analyses of fissile-material holdings available, for example, David Albright estimated in 1998 that

> India has about 370 kilograms of weapon-grade plutonium, or the
> equivalent of about 74 nuclear weapons. India relies principally on
> the Dhruva reactor for weapon-grade plutonium, and can increase
> its stock of weapon-grade plutonium at a rate of about 20 kilograms

---

[19]Arnold Kramish, "The Bombs of Balnibarbi," in Rodney W. Jones (ed.), *Small
Nuclear Forces and U.S. Security Policy* (Lexington, KY: Lexington Books, 1984), pp. 26–
30.

[20]Rodney W. Jones, *Small Nuclear Forces*, Washington Paper No. 103 (New York:
Praeger, 1984), p. 17, cited in Karnad, "A Thermonuclear Deterrent," p. 129.

per year. This amount corresponds to roughly four nuclear weapons per year. At this rate, in 2005 India is estimated to have enough weapon-grade plutonium for over 100 nuclear weapons. India could produce significantly more weapon-grade plutonium by using its CANDU [Canada Deuterium Uranium] power reactors, although it may not have sufficient facilities to separate significant quantities of plutonium from the irradiated CANDU fuel.[21]

In a similar vein, Gregory Jones at RAND updated earlier calculations to conclude that India possesses

about 450 kg of separated weapons-grade plutonium, which would allow the manufacture of about 90 simple fission weapons. India is currently producing about 25 kg of weapons-grade plutonium per year, which could be increased to about 100 kg per year if India felt it to be necessary. This stockpile of plutonium and its current production rate are probably enough to supply India with an adequate supply of fission weapons.[22]

While both of these midrange estimates represent a vast improvement over earlier ones, many authoritative Indian sources suggest that they still overestimate the size of India's actual inventory (even if the issues of production versus separation and availability of other special materials are left aside). This overestimation generally results from optimistic assumptions about efficiency factors and capacity constraints pertaining to various phases of the Indian fissile-material production cycle.

Correcting for these factors, some well-placed Indian analysts have offered even smaller estimates of their country's fissile-material stockpile. Savita Pandey at the Institute for Defence Studies and Analyses in New Delhi—a think tank funded by the Indian Ministries of Defence and External Affairs—concluded that after all other activities requiring fissile materials are taken into account, the inventory available for the production of nuclear weapons in 1995 stood at some 170 kg of Pu^{239}—and from this figure she inferred that India would have "enough weapons grade plutonium by the turn of the

---

[21]Albright, *Fact Sheet: India and Pakistan—Current and Potential Nuclear Arsenals.*

[22]Jones, *From Testing to Deploying Nuclear Forces*, pp. 14–15.

century to produce [just] about 50 nuclear weapons."[23] In an article reportedly written after the author was given access to various government briefings, R. Ramachandran similarly argued that the fissile-material inventory available for weapon production from India's two research reactors, CANDU (operational since 1960) and Dhruva (operational since 1985), could not exceed 280 kg of Pu^{239} in 1998—which, on his assumption that 8 kg are required per critical mass, turns out to be sufficient for a maximum of 35 nuclear weapons.[24] David Albright's more recent reassessment of India's nuclear stockpile comes much closer to these more conservative estimates. Using a sophisticated Monte Carlo approach, Albright's assessment focuses on providing a range of possibilities that allow for "central" or "best" estimates of India's fissile-material stockpile to be derived. Through use of such a methodology, the Indian inventory of weapons-grade plutonium—derived by estimating total production in its reactors minus drawdowns from nuclear testing, processing losses, and civil uses of weapons-grade plutonium—was estimated to stand at some 290 kg at the end of 1998. This inventory size represents the median value of a range of estimates, and if each of India's fission weapons is assumed to incorporate a critical mass consisting of somewhat less than 5 kg of Pu^{239}, the total Indian weapon stockpile would consist of approximately 60 nuclear weapons at the end of 1998.[25]

On balance, therefore, the most reliable estimates of India's fissile-material stockpile today seem to cluster around the smallest numbers that have been articulated over the years. Unfortunately, however, many of these estimates are not directly comparable owing to differing assumptions about the capacity and efficiency of the reactors and reprocessing facilities, the extent of consumption attributable to other nuclear endeavors, and the varying figures used to define the plutonium requirements per critical mass. These methodological complications notwithstanding, the fact remains that an increasing number of Western and Indian commentators

---

[23]"India Will Have Plutonium for 50 N-Weapons by 2000 AD," *Hindustan Times,* October 27, 1997.

[24]Ramachandran, "Pokhran II: The Scientific Dimensions," pp. 35–36.

[25]David Albright, *India and Pakistan's Fissile Material and Nuclear Weapons Inventory, End of 1998* (Washington, D.C.: Institute for Science and International Security, October 27, 1999), available at http://www.isis-online.org/publications/southasia/stocks1099.html.

have begun to conclude that the country's fissile-material inventory is much smaller than was previously assumed—a conclusion that has occasionally been confirmed by senior officials of India's DAE.[26] As such, it is often argued that the country's readiness to engage in negotiations leading up to the FMCT should be reviewed, and Ramachandran in particular has even asserted that "there is need for at least one more Dhruva-like dedicated reactor if a weaponization programme with the minimum deterrence strategy is envisaged."[27] This conclusion, it should be remembered, is based on the assumption that India would need only 60 nuclear weapons for its minimum deterrent—an argument advanced by K. Subrahmanyam in his writings on this subject in 1994.[28] If, by contrast, it is assumed that the Indian deterrent would require closer to the 150-odd warheads that Subrahmanyam has now concluded are necessary,[29] then the need for continued or perhaps accelerated production of fissile materials prior to any accession to the FMCT would become all the more pressing.

What is the relationship between the size of the fissile-material inventory and the weapon stockpile? This issue is also of critical importance because it speaks to the size of India's potential arsenal and, by implication, to the adequacy of that arsenal vis-à-vis the capabilities of its competitors. Unfortunately, however, this issue too is difficult to resolve because even if the exact size of India's fissile-material inventory were known, the quality of its weapon designs and the types of weapons it intends to produce would affect the final solution. Since information about these variables is hard to come by, informed guesses based on the fissile-material requirements associated with some abstract weapon design will have to suffice. Even these informed guesses, however, will probably prove inadequate, because India's nuclear weapon designs could change over time. A given quantity of fissile materials could therefore be used to create many more (or fewer) nuclear weapons than the requirements asso-

---

[26]Hibbs, "Indian Pu Production Overstated, No Pit Production, Iyengar Says," p. 6.

[27]Ramachandran, "Pokhran II: The Scientific Dimensions," p 36.

[28]See Subrahmanyam, "Nuclear Force Design and Minimum Deterrence Strategy for India," pp. 176–195.

[29]Subrahmanyam, "A Credible Deterrent."

ciated with some abstract weapon design would suggest. And since improvements in weapon design through laboratory experiments, a return to hot testing, or new access to foreign assistance cannot be ruled out, the actual number of nuclear weapons that could eventually be fabricated from a given stockpile of weapons-grade plutonium would vary considerably, as illustrated in Table 3.

Also at issue is the precise amount of plutonium that is needed to produce a device with a given yield. Although International Atomic Energy Agency (IAEA) regulations assume that 8 kg of plutonium are required to produce a simple fission design with approximately 20 kt of yield, it is likely that these requirements are overstated, since, among other things, weapons-grade plutonium in such quantities is likely to be subject to severe criticality problems if kept together routinely.[30] Other analysts have estimated, however, that countries possessing "low" technical capability could build 20-kt devices with only 6 kg of weapons-grade plutonium; that countries possessing "medium" technical capability could build such devices with approximately 3.5 kg; and that countries possessing "high" technical capability could build these devices with as little as 3 kg.[31] Part of the problem with calculating India's weapon stockpile therefore arises simply from not knowing at which end of the spectrum its nuclear designs are situated. The best available evidence from Indian sources indicates that the pits used in the nuclear devices tested in May 1998 "each weighed between five to ten kilograms."[32] If this information is correct, India would have to be classified as a country with low technical capability, at least as far as the sophistication of its nuclear weapon designs is concerned. Arbitrarily translating this judgment into an assumption that its designs use some 6 kg of plutonium per weapon suggests that India's fissile-material inventory would in 1998

---

[30]It should be noted, however, that the IAEA's definition of "threshold amounts," which identifies the "approximate quantity of special fissionable material required for a single nuclear device," is intended to cover processing losses incurred during the manufacture of a fissile core and as such does not represent simply the minimum critical mass needed for an explosive chain reaction. Despite this fact, the quantity of fissile material identified by the concept of "threshold amounts" may still be far too high—a position argued cogently in Thomas B. Cochran and Christopher E. Paine, *The Amount of Plutonium and Highly Enriched Uranium Needed for Pure Fission Nuclear Weapons* (Washington, D.C.: Natural Resources Defense Council, 1995), pp. 1–5.

[31]Ibid., pp. 9–12.

[32]Chengappa, "The Bomb Makers," p. 31.

Table 3

Relating the Fissile-Material Stockpile to Varying Plutonium Masses per Weapon

Size of Weapons-Grade Pu Stockpile (kg)	Pu Mass per Weapon (kg)					
	3	4	5	6	7	8
200	66.67	50.00	40.00	33.33	28.57	25.00
210	70.00	52.50	42.00	35.00	30.00	26.25
220	73.33	55.00	44.00	36.67	31.43	27.50
230	76.67	57.50	46.00	38.33	32.86	28.75
240	80.00	60.00	48.00	40.00	34.29	30.00
250	83.33	62.50	50.00	41.67	35.71	31.25
260	86.67	65.00	52.00	43.33	37.14	32.50
270	90.00	67.50	54.00	45.00	38.57	33.75
280	93.33	70.00	56.00	46.67	40.00	35.00
290	96.67	72.50	58.00	48.33	41.43	36.25
300	100.00	75.00	60.00	50.00	42.86	37.50
310	103.33	77.50	62.00	51.67	44.29	38.75
320	106.67	80.00	64.00	53.33	45.71	40.00
330	110.00	82.50	66.00	55.00	47.14	41.25
340	113.33	85.00	68.00	56.67	48.57	42.50
350	116.67	07.50	70.00	58.33	50.00	43.75
360	120.00	90.00	72.00	60.00	51.43	45.00
370	123.33	92.50	74.00	61.67	52.86	46.25
380	126.67	95.00	76.00	63.33	54.29	47.50
390	130.00	97.50	78.00	65.00	55.71	48.75
400	133.33	100.00	80.00	66.67	57.14	50.00

have yielded approximately 266 weapons (by the old CRS estimates), some 61/75 weapons (by the 1998 Albright/Jones estimate), or some 47/48 weapons (by the Ramachandran/1999 Albright estimate)—all of these figures obviously increasing progressively if its designs used less than 6 kg of fissile material in the core (see Table 3).

If, for the sake of discussion, all of India's weapons are assumed to be entirely thermonuclear, calculation becomes even more problematic, since the precise amount of weapons-grade plutonium necessary to construct such devices is classified.[33] What complicates the calculation here is that specific information is required about the amount of plutonium necessary for both the "primary" and the "spark plug," assuming that the latter in fact incorporates weapons-

---

[33]Jones, *From Testing to Deploying Nuclear Forces*, p. 8.

grade plutonium rather than HEU.[34] Depending on the kinds of thermonuclear weapon designs at issue, such calculations can become extremely complex by virtue of the multiplicity of special nuclear materials that may be used in a given device. In India's case, however, this problem may be more tractable because the most reliable reports emerging from the May 1998 tests have suggested that its thermonuclear device is based on a version of the relatively simple Teller-Ulam staged radiation design, which uses India's preexisting simple fission (or a modified boosted fission) device as the primary.[35] This implies that the arbitrary assumption made earlier about the quantity of fissile material required by the standard Indian fission weapon may be treated as identical to the requirements of the primary and, further, that the crude information available in the literature about the quantity of fissile material required by the spark plug[36] should provide some indication of the size of India's potential thermonuclear inventory, since it is assumed that all the other special materials—such as beryllium, polonium, lithium deuteride, deuterium, and tritium—are available in the necessary quantities.[37]

Kosta Tsipis has provided some general information about the quantity of fissile materials required to construct a thermonuclear device when he noted that a 1-Mt thermonuclear weapon "contains a few kilograms of lithium deuteride and tritium, some kilograms of plutonium, and about 100 kilograms of uranium 238."[38] Discussing the same issue in the context of India's advanced designs, R. Ramachandran remarked that "even a thermonuclear weapon would

---

[34]See the discussion in Sublette, *Nuclear Weapons Frequently Asked Questions*, "Section 4.4: Elements of Thermonuclear Weapons Design," for a good survey of the kinds of materials involved in the fabrication of a thermonuclear weapon built according to the Teller-Ulam design.

[35]Ramachandran, "Pokhran II: The Scientific Dimensions," pp. 22–28.

[36]Good sources of information about the spark plug are Hansen (ed.), *The Swords of Armageddon*, Vols. 1–8, and Sublette, *Nuclear Weapons Frequently Asked Questions*, "Section 4.4: Elements of Thermonuclear Weapons Design." The spark plug used in Indian nuclear devices is discussed in passing in Iyengar, "Nuclear Nuances."

[37]If boosted fission rather than simple fission devices constitute the primary in India's thermonuclear weapons, the relationship between fissile material and the size of the weapon stockpile has to be appropriately modified, since boosted fission devices can be constructed with somewhat smaller amounts of fissile material than that used in simple fission weapons.

[38]Kosta Tsipis, *Arsenal* (New York: Simon & Schuster, 1983), p. 38.

use a trigger with [a] similar amount of Pu"[39] compared to that used by a simple fission design (~6 kg of Pu[239] by an arbitrary assumption based on the Indian reporting cited earlier). And Gregory Jones concluded more accurately that when the requirement of the primary and the spark plug are taken into account, "plutonium-only thermonuclear weapons . . . might well use more plutonium than a standard fission weapon."[40] Since it is unlikely that the spark plug in any Indian thermonuclear weapon would use as much fissile material as that residing in its primary, however, it is reasonable to conclude that the size of the hypothetical Indian thermonuclear stockpile would be more than half its inventory of pure fission weapons—although how much more than half is difficult to discern in the absence of precise information about the amount of fissile materials the spark plug actually requires.[41] This rough estimate of the hypothetical Indian thermonuclear stockpile obviously assumes that India can produce the quantities of lithium deuteride it needs to fuel the secondary stage of each of its weapons as well as all the other special materials that may be required to produce the initiators, tampers, and lenses associated with such devices. A different conclusion holds as far as a hypothetical Indian boosted fission stockpile is concerned: In this instance, the number of weapons ought to be somewhat greater than that held in an inventory of simple fission devices, since the kilogram quantities of plutonium required for the pits in such weapons would undergo marginal reductions when supplemented by the gram-quantity additions of deuterium-tritium. The potential size of India's thermonuclear and boosted fission stockpile relative to its potential stockpile of simple fission weapons can therefore be crudely characterized in the following way: For any potential stockpile of simple fission devices, x, the potential thermonuclear stockpile would be some number greater than $1/2\ x$, while the potential boosted fission stockpile would be some number greater than x—assuming that all

---

[39]Ramachandran, "Pokhran II: The Scientific Dimensions," p. 38.

[40]Jones, *From Testing to Deploying Nuclear Forces*, p. 8.

[41]This result is further affected by the uncertainty about whether India's thermonuclear weapons will incorporate simple fission or boosted fission devices as their primary, since the quantity of weapons-grade plutonium required to construct these devices is different in each case.

these advanced designs are based *entirely* on some modification of the basic fission design described in open sources.[42]

All these details reinforce the conclusion reiterated earlier: that the number of weapons in the Indian inventory is a function of their specific designs, the efficiency of those designs, and the existing inventory of fissile materials. Since no precise information about these variables is available, however, the size of the presumed inventory can be expressed only as a range of values. If the old U.N.-CRS data are disregarded as being overly optimistic, the only choices thus remain the 1998 Albright/Jones estimate of roughly 61 to 75 simple fission weapons and the Ramachandran/1999 Albright estimate of 47 to 48 simple fission weapons (all calculated for 1998 totals at 6 kg per critical mass). Since the desired Indian weapon stockpile has been defined by several knowledgeable Indian officials in private conversations with the author as "less than one half the known inventory of India's largest competitor"—referring to the Chinese nuclear arsenal, which is reputed to consist of 350-odd warheads today[43]—the eventual size of the preferred Indian arsenal must consist of fewer than 175 weapons. This figure comports with Subrahmanyam's claim that internal studies commissioned by the Indian military in the 1980s suggested "an appropriate number of warheads in low three digit figures."[44] Several Indians have in private conversation insinuated that this figure could be closer to 100 than to 175 weapons, although reaching for force totals somewhere in the region of the latter or even beyond has not been ruled out depending on how the capabilities of India's adversaries and the character of the global nuclear regime change over time. Given the evolving nuclear doctrine described in the previous chapter, however, there is no reason New Delhi should not be satisfied, at least in its present circumstances, with an arsenal

---

[42]Chengappa, "Is India's H-Bomb a Dud?" and Chengappa, *Weapons of Peace*, p. 207.

[43]This estimate of the Chinese inventory was provided by Jaswant Singh, India's Foreign Minister, in a meeting with a RAND research team in New Delhi on January 18, 1999. This figure is also held by many Indian strategic analysts who follow China. To the degree that it is contested, the disputes arise mainly on prudential grounds, as some analysts argue that the structural uncertainties about the Chinese nuclear weapon inventory should prevent India from pegging its own sufficiency criteria to any *conservative* estimates of Beijing's capabilities.

[44]Subrahmanyam, "Indian Nuclear Policy—1964–98," p. 41.

consisting of even fewer than 100 warheads, although it is practical to expect—simply for purposes of ensuring deterrence stability—that no public declaration to that effect would ever be articulated. More important, it is unlikely that New Delhi would unilaterally terminate the production of fissile materials in the interim because the demands of prudence are seen as requiring a large enough stockpile of such materials even if these are not immediately transmuted into an inventory of ready and available weapons.[45] In all probability, therefore, India will attempt to produce the largest inventory of fissile materials it possibly can prior to the conclusion of an FMCT—an inventory that could enable it to produce even more than the 100-odd weapons the pragmatists in New Delhi believe is sufficient for deterrence—in part as insurance against the possibility that its adversaries may have a larger arsenal than they are currently thought to possess.

In any event, if an arsenal of around 150 weapons is treated as desirable from New Delhi's point of view, then irrespective of which estimate of India's fissile-material inventory one accepts, India still has some way to go before it can be satisfied that its fissile-material stockpile is sufficient for its future deterrent. If the 1998 Albright/ Jones estimate is more accurate, the gap India has to close may not be as great as analysts like Ramachandran believe. If, on the other hand, the Ramachandran/1999 Albright estimate holds, then India will need to accelerate the production of fissile materials before any constraints imposed by a future FMCT become legally binding—or risk being forever condemned to a strategy of subterfuge grounded in an exaggeration of its weapons-grade material inventory. This circle, of course, can be squared simply by reducing the sufficiency requirements for deterrence, and many Indian analysts, including Jasjit Singh, have in fact argued that India's deterrence needs—which could be amply met by some "double digit quantum of warheads"— may require that New Delhi "even plan on the basis of a lower end figure of say 2–3 dozen nuclear warheads by the end of 10–15 years."[46]

If this suggestion does not find favor with India's security managers, however—as is likely—then the data in Table 4 suggest that

---

[45]"Fissile Material: India Against Moratorium Now."

[46]Singh, "A Nuclear Strategy for India," p. 315.

Table 4

Increases in Efficiency Required to Produce Various Desired Indian Nuclear Weapon Stockpiles by 2010

Desired Number of Nuclear Weapons	Number of Weapons Above Present Inventory (50 weapons in 2000)	Total Additional Fissile Material Required to Produce Number of Nuclear Weapons Above Present Inventory @ 6 kg Pu239 per Weapon (kg)	Average Annual Production Rate of Fissile Materials Required to Produce Number of Nuclear Weapons Above Present Inventory over 10 Years (kg)	Change in Efficiency Required Relative to the Traditional Annual Rate of Fissile-Material Production: 12–16 kg Pu239
~60 Subrahmanyam, 1994	10	60	6	0.5–0.3
~70–76 Traditional efficiency	20–26	120–160	12–16	1
~150 Subrahmanyam, 2000	100	600	60	5–3.7
~100–150 Improved efficiency	50–100	300–600	30–60	2.5/1.8–5/3.7
~125–200 Expanded capability	75–150	450–900	45–90	3.7/2.8–7.5/5.6
~300–330 Karnad, 1999	250–280	1500–1680	150–168	12.5/9.3–14/10.5

India's nuclear estate would indeed require dramatic changes in performance to reach the weapon inventory targets various Indian analysts have set. The baseline for the calculations codified in Table 4 is drawn from R. Ramachandran's analysis of India's fissile-material stockpile, which he argued consisted of some 280 kg of weapons-available Pu^{239} in 1998 that has been growing at the traditional rate of approximately 12–16 kg annually.[47] If these figures are extrapolated to the year 2000, India's stockpile of fissile materials would have consisted of a maximum of 304–312 kg, which for the sake of simplicity may be rounded off to 300 kg of Pu^{239}. This year 2000 total in turn yields 50-odd weapons, assuming that each device uses approximately 6 kg of plutonium in its core.

If the traditional rate of accumulation (12–16 kg annually) remains unchanged over the next decade, Table 4 suggests that India could accumulate an additional 120–160 kg of Pu^{239} by 2010—sufficient to raise its nominal weapon stockpile to a total of 70 to 76 standard fission weapons. At such rates of accumulation, India would be able to meet the 1994 Subrahmanyam target of 60 weapons over the next decade without any changes in its traditional rate of accumulation. If it is to meet Subrahmanyam's 2000 target of approximately 150 weapons, however, it would need to accumulate some 600 kg of Pu^{239} over and above its current inventory, or 60 kg annually—and generating such increases would require that India improve its accumulative efficiency by three and one-half to five times its traditional level. Yet attaining such efficiency increases through better maintenance and more effective organizational routines alone is likely to tax the Indian nuclear estate, since the prevailing infrastructure in different portions of New Delhi's fissile-material production complex is somewhat dilapidated.[48] If its newer facilities, such as the large-scale reprocessing plant at Kalpakkam, work as efficiently as desired, India could conceivably meet the efficiency increases demanded in Subrahmanyam 2000 by the year 2010. What is more likely, however, is that it will meet less ambitious requirements—say, for nuclear stockpiles ranging from 100 to 150 weapons by the year 2010—since the kinds of efficiency improvements such smaller force sizes demand, at least toward the lower end, hover around twice (or

---

[47]Ramachandran, "Pokhran II: The Scientific Dimensions," pp. 34–61.

[48]Rethinaraj, "In the Comfort of Secrecy," pp. 52–57.

slightly more than twice) the current levels of accumulative performance. In any case, the calculations in Table 4 clearly show that the arsenal sizes demanded by analysts like Bharat Karnad, which run into requirements for 300 to 330 nuclear weapons, simply cannot be attained by the year 2010, since they would require that the Indian nuclear estate produce between 9 and 14 times its current annual output of weapons-grade fissile materials.[49] Even if India were to settle for a more modest arsenal that was nonetheless larger than the one suggested in Subrahmanyam 2000—say, an arsenal consisting of 125 to 200 weapons by 2010—it would still require immense improvements in performance ranging from more than twice to almost eight times the current annual rate of accumulation of fissile materials. Such levels of performance, at least at the higher end, cannot be attained through efficiency increases alone but would instead require a progressive expansion of present capabilities in the form of new dedicated weapon reactors, further upgrades in infrastructure, an expansion of the ultracentrifuge cascades dedicated to producing HEU, and perhaps even a new reliance on India's civilian nuclear power plants for producing the quantity of fissile material such an ambitious program would require.

When the requirements identified in Table 4 are properly appreciated, it becomes obvious that India's behavior with respect to fissile-material production *would* offer evidence not only about which estimates of its fissile-material holdings are correct but also about which weapon inventory size it seeks to attain.[50] For all it is worth, India has formally declined to comply with the U.S. request for an

---

[49]It must be noted, however, that Karnad's requirement for 300-plus nuclear weapons is premised on their availability by the year 2030. Accordingly, the analysis in this paragraph should not be construed as a criticism of Karnad's requirements but merely as an indicator of the immensity of the task India would face were it to pursue a weapon stockpile of the sort Karnad recommends within the next decade. If Karnad's 30-year time frame was indeed accepted, India would need to produce between 50 and 56 kg of Pu^{239} annually for the next 30 years. This, in turn, would require an accumulative efficiency comparable to that associated with meeting the demands articulated in Subrahmanyam 2000—which, while possible, must still be counted as rather demanding, at least in relation to the historical record.

[50]This argument is premised, of course, on the assumption that India will simply settle for basic fission weapons as the mainstay of its future arsenal. Should this assumption be altered, however, it would be more difficult to assess what kind of arsenal size India would be satisfied with simply from scrutinizing its rate of accumulation of fissile materials.

immediate cessation of fissile-material production pending the conclusion of the FMCT. This could suggest a desire on India's part to continue producing fissile materials in order to meet its unfulfilled stockpile requirements, or it could represent merely a diplomatic refusal to comply with unilateral demands in the absence of a binding multilateral treaty. While there are certainly benefits to the latter posture, it is worth remembering that the real payoffs are garnered in the former issue area: India's fissile-material inventory grows progressively, if only slowly, irrespective of *why* New Delhi refrains from ceasing production. Not surprisingly, then, it is most likely that in the years ahead India will in fact participate in discussions leading to an FMCT while refusing to adhere to any interim moratorium on the production of fissile materials prior to the conclusion of such an agreement. Operating on the expectation that the negotiations leading up to the FMCT will be neither rapid nor easy, India could use the breathing space that the diplomatic process affords to steadily expand its stock of fissile materials while ultimately relying on the continued opacity of its past inventory to insinuate that it has more than ample fissile-material holdings whether or not that is actually the case.

There is already growing evidence that India has begun to focus on increasing its available stockpile of weapons-grade materials. BARC, for example, has been removed from the supervisory purview of the Atomic Energy Regulatory Board, suggesting that a wide variety of weapons-related activities will no longer be constrained by the "regulatory and safety functions . . . hitherto exercised by the Atomic Energy Regulatory Board."[51] After years of hesitation, it has also been announced that the DAE will build "one more research reactor in Trombay . . . to increase India's production capacity of unsafeguarded plutonium."[52] This new reactor, which will be similar to the 100-megawatt Dhruva that has been operating at BARC since 1985, is expected to become operational by 2010, implying that at the very least India's security managers expect to be producing weapons-grade plutonium for its arsenal even after that date. Further, the reports that emerged after May 1998 that one of the five Indian nuclear

---

[51]Ramola Talwar Badam, "BARC Now Freed of Regulatory Control," *Asian Age*, May 31, 2000.

[52]"New Reactor Being Planned in Trombay," *The Hindu*, April 28, 1999.

tests involved reactor-grade plutonium not only indirectly confirms the veracity of the smaller estimates of India's fissile-material holdings but also raises the question of whether India would actively seek to use its civilian plutonium inventory to augment its otherwise small stockpile of weapons-grade material.[53] Finally, the question of whether India would use at least some of its civilian nuclear power reactors in a "low-burnup" regime to produce additional quantities of weapons-grade plutonium for military needs remains widely discussed but not yet publicly resolved.[54] In any event, India's future actions in each of these issue areas will provide important clues to its judgment about the adequacy of its fissile-material holdings as well as about the arsenal size it deems to be appropriate for its needs.

None of these actions, however, is likely to occur transparently, and consequently India's continued concealment of its existing inventory of weapons-grade materials, its relatively opaque fissile-material accumulation activities, and its strong determination not to spell out the specific contours of its minimum deterrent will allow India to reap all the deterrence benefits that derive from its adversaries' inability to accurately estimate the true size of its relatively small nuclear stockpile. Since India's overarching strategic doctrine treats nuclear weaponry as being more efficacious as political instruments than as military tools, it would not be surprising if New Delhi were to be satisfied with even a smaller nuclear arsenal than many of its elites publicly advocate. This arsenal could consist of fewer than 100 weapons, as analysts like Jasjit Singh advocate, or could hover around 150 weapons, as recommended by K. Subrahmanyam. Whatever stockpile size finally materializes, however, it may in no way imply an endorsement of the force-sizing metric advocated by various security elites in New Delhi. Rather, it would be more likely to represent an acceptance of certain cold technical and political realities that are grounded both in the infirmities that afflict India's fissile-material production infrastructure and in external influences such as U.S. political pressure and the constraints that a successful FMCT may impose. So long as the residual fraction that

---

[53]Chengappa, "Is India's H-Bomb a Dud?" pp. 27–28, and Albright, *India and Pakistan's Fissile Material and Nuclear Weapons Inventory, End of 1998.*

[54] Albright, *India and Pakistan's Fissile Material and Nuclear Weapons Inventory, End of 1998.*

can survive a nuclear attack is believed to be high—thanks to the pervasive secrecy surrounding the entire Indian nuclear weapon apparatus—Indian policymakers would probably be content with a relatively small nuclear weapon inventory, especially if the opacity of past stockpiles allows them to garner significant deterrence benefits from the widespread public belief that the country's civilian nuclear complex "provide[s] enormous potential for the production of much larger than expected amounts of weapons-grade fissile materials."[55]

The size of India's reactor-grade plutonium inventory is the last issue of some consequence from the perspective of arsenal size, but it is one that is clouded by a great deal of uncertainty. David Albright, for one, has estimated that in 1998 India's civil plutonium inventory consisted of some 7500 kg. This figure includes the 3825 kg safeguarded by the IAEA (of which 25 kg are separated) as well as some 3700 kg of unsafeguarded plutonium (of which 700 kg are ostensibly separated).[56] If other public reports of India's fissile-material stockpile serve as any indication, however, these data too probably overstate the amount of separated, unsafeguarded, reactor-grade plutonium India possesses. In any event, reactor-grade plutonium cannot be used to make reliable, high-yield fission weapons if this material is used in place of weapons-grade plutonium within India's basic fission design. Reactor-grade plutonium *can* be used to produce reliable, high-yield fission weapons, but these would require either fast-assembling implosion systems or fusion boosting, both of which would almost certainly have to be validated through further explosive testing.[57] There is also no way for India to strip out the undesirable Pu^{240} isotopes from its stockpile of reactor-grade plutonium, since the technology best suited for this purpose—atomic vapor laser

---

[55]Nayyar et al., "Fissile Material Production Potential in South Asia," p. 202.

[56]Albright, *India and Pakistan's Fissile Material and Nuclear Weapons Inventory, End of 1998.*

[57]For more on this issue, see Carey Sublette, *Nuclear Weapons Frequently Asked Questions*, "Section 6.0: Nuclear Materials," available at http://www.fas.org/nuke/hew/Nwfaq/Nfaq6.html; Amory B. Lovins, "Nuclear Weapons and Power-Reactor Plutonium," *Nature*, 283 (February 1980), pp. 817–823; J. Carson Mark, "Explosive Properties of Reactor-Grade Plutonium," *Science and Global Security*, 4 (1993), pp. 111–128; and Richard L. Garwin, "Reactor-Grade Plutonium Can Be Used to Make Powerful and Reliable Nuclear Weapons: Separated Plutonium in the Fuel Cycle Must Be Protected as If It Were Nuclear Weapons," available at http://www.fas.org/rlg/980826-pu.htm.

isotope separation (AVLIS)—is not available to India. What this implies, therefore, is that absent fast-assembling weapon designs, fusion boosting, and AVLIS technology, reactor-grade plutonium could be used in India's standard fission weapon only if New Delhi were satisfied by the fizzle yields that would result. If this is in fact the case, the 700 kg of separated, unsafeguarded, reactor-grade plutonium India is supposed to possess would translate into some 116 small-yield nuclear weapons at a rate of 6 kg of reactor-grade material per device. The remaining 3000-odd kg of unseparated, unsafeguarded, reactor-grade plutonium translates at the same rate into another 500 devices, but this calculation makes sense only if it is presumed that India will in fact separate plutonium from the spent fuel rods before its separation plants are possibly shut down under the terms of a future FMCT. Thus far, India has shown little inclination to expand its stockpile of separated reactor-grade plutonium, and for sound strategic reasons: Given the limitations of its nuclear material production infrastructure, New Delhi is better off focusing its energies on the production and separation of weapons-grade plutonium rather than squandering its limited plant capacity on separating reactor-grade plutonium at a time when it has demonstrated neither a mastery of fusion boosting nor the ability to design fast-assembling implosion systems. To be sure, this fact has not prevented some analysts from emphasizing the significance of India's reactor-grade plutonium stockpile in their assessments of India's potential nuclear arsenal.[58] There is no conclusive evidence, however, that either the government of India or its DAE scientists adhere to a similar calculus when they evaluate the size of their desired nuclear arsenal.

Nuclear Weapons

From the perspective of ensuring adequate deterrence, the discussion about fissile-material inventories helps mainly to establish the size of the potential arsenal. The types of weapons that constitute this arsenal are only partly illuminated by such a discussion and hence merit separate treatment. The need for such treatment is based in turn on the admittedly debatable premise that the quality of

---

[58]Sidhu, "India Sees Safety in Nuclear Triad and Second Strike Potential," p. 23, and Steer, "Asia's Rival Reactors a Cause for Concern," pp. 26–29.

a state's nuclear weapons has a bearing on the durability of the deterrence it can obtain.[59] Since this premise was believed to hold true during the Cold War, both the United States and the Soviet Union developed a wide variety of sophisticated nuclear weapons ranging from multimegaton city busters at one end all the way down to sub-kiloton tactical nuclear weapons at the other. Accepting the logic that underlay these achievements, many Indian analysts have maintained that New Delhi should induct a wide variety of nuclear devices into its arsenal, among the most important of which are thermonuclear weapons.[60] These weapons find particular favor with Indian hawks such as Karnad because it is argued that, all other things being equal, thermonuclear weapons make particularly effective deterrents: Their immense destructive power makes true city-busting capabilities possible with a single bomb and, as such, would provide India with robust deterrence given the unacceptable destruction that can be inflicted even by a small residual fraction of weapons surviving an adversary's attack.[61] While they do not contest the destructive efficacy of thermonuclear weapons, Indian owls would by contrast dispute the claim that such immense destructive power is required to produce deterrence stability *in the specific circumstances facing the Indian state.*[62] While this debate ultimately relates to competing intuitions about "what deters"—an issue that will be addressed more directly later in this chapter—the discussion here focuses simply on understanding what is known and what can be inferred about the technical quality of India's nuclear weaponry.

Ordinarily, this topic would escape all public discussion, but the nuclear tests of May 1998 generated a good deal of information about India's nuclear weapon designs, much of it released by New Delhi itself in response to the controversy that surrounded Indian claims

---

[59] For a useful review of this issue in the South Asian context, see Hagerty, *The Consequences of Nuclear Proliferation: Lessons from South Asia*, pp. 39–62.

[60] P. R. Chari, "Weaponisation and the CTBT," *The Hindu*, July 5, 2000.

[61] Karnad, "Next, A Series of Thermonuclear Tests," and Pravin Sawhney, "To Test or Not to Test: The Challenge for India's Nuclear Credibility," *RUSI Journal*, 141:3 (June 1996), p. 31.

[62] See, for example, Sundarji, "Changing Military Equations in Asia: The Role of Nuclear Weapons," pp. 119–149.

about their technical achievements.[63] This discussion is not intended to resolve the controversy about the nuclear tests per se but only to clarify what the debate reveals about India's nuclear weaponry, primarily from the standpoint of assuring successful deterrence.

On May 11, 1998, India announced that it had tested three nuclear devices: a fission device with a yield of about 12 kt; a thermonuclear device with a yield of approximately 43 kt; and a subkiloton device of unspecified yield. On May 13, India announced that it had tested two more subkiloton devices with yields of 0.2 and 0.6 kt, respectively.[64] "By these tests," Dr. P. K. Iyengar, former Chairman of India's AEC, exclaimed, "we have demonstrated in an unambiguous fashion that we can make any kind of nuclear weapon."[65] Based on these remarks and others, two of India's most well-known defense reporters concluded that "Pokhran 1998 was different not just for the number of explosions but also [for] the range of weapons systems it helped to test: bombs with enormous yields of energy caused by advanced thermonuclear reactions, weapon-compatible, medium-impact bombs and, if needed, tactical ones too."[66] In effect, the earliest reports appearing after the 1998 test series concluded that India possessed at least three different kinds of nuclear weapons: first, a simple fission design, dubbed Pokhran Mark II, that was described as a "less-weight-but-more-bang version of the 1974 Pokhran bomb";[67] second, a thermonuclear bomb that Indian scientists insisted was a

---

[63]See, for example, S. K. Sikka and Anil Kakodkar, "Some Preliminary Results of May 11–13, 1998, Nuclear Detonations at Pokhran," *BARC Newsletter*, 172 (May 1998), pp. 1–4; S. K. Sikka, Falguni Roy, G. J. Nair, V. G. Kolvankar, and Anil Kakodkar, "Update on the Yield of May 11–13, 1998, Nuclear Detonations at Pokhran," *BARC Newsletter*, 178 (November 1998), pp. 1–5; S. K. Sikka, F. Roy, and G. J. Nair, "Comment on the Paper 'Monitoring Nuclear Tests' by Barker et al.—Science 25 September 1998," unpublished manuscript; and Eliot Marshall, "Did Test Ban Watchdog Fail to Bark?" *Science*, 280 (June 26, 1998), pp. 2038–2040.

[64]"Joint Statement by the Department of Atomic Energy and Defence Research and Development Organization," p. 12.

[65]Quoted in Chengappa and Joshi, "Future Fire," p. 22.

[66]Ibid., p. 24.

[67]Ibid.

true "two-stage device"[68] possessing "a fission trigger and a secondary stage"[69] and, as such, represented the acme of the country's weapon design prowess; and third, a tactical nuclear weapon that was described in press reports as a "low-yield bomb . . . meant for smaller explosions required to pulverize [a] hostile army on the battlefield."[70] In addition to the specific weapons that were tested on May 11, the low-yield detonations that occurred on May 13 were intended to support future subcritical tests that, as one report noted, would be "needed by India in case it joins [the] CTBT and has to stop [further] big bangs [in the future]."[71]

This account of India's claimed achievements has been mired in controversy for three reasons. First, the seismological signatures released by the three test series on May 11 suggested only a single detonation rather than multiple detonations.[72] Second, the body-wave magnitude resulting from this test series registered only 5.1 on the Richter scale at the Incorporated Research Institutions for Seismology's nearest monitoring station at Nilore, Pakistan, suggesting a total yield closer to 20 kt rather than the 55+ kt India originally claimed.[73] Third, the May 13 test series could not be verified through seismic data even though the combined yield of 800 tons should by rights have been, as one Los Alamos geophysicist hyperbolically put it, "visible all over the world."[74] Before this controversy is examined for the clues it might offer to India's nuclear capabilities, it is important

---

[68]Transcript of the press conference hosted by Dr. R. Chidambaram, Chairman, AEC, and Secretary, DAE; Dr A.P.J. Kalam, Scientific Adviser to the Defence Minister and Secretary, Department of Defence Research and Development; Dr. Anil Kakodkar, Director, BARC; and Dr. K. Santhanam, Chief Adviser (Technologies), DRDO, May 17, 1998.

[69]Ibid.

[70] Chengappa and Joshi, "Future Fire," p. 24.

[71]Ibid.

[72]William J. Broad, "Monitors Picked Up Only 1 of 5 India Blasts," *New York Times*, May 15, 1998.

[73]Marshall, "Did Test Ban Watchdog Fail to Bark?" pp. 2038–2040. The U.S. Geological Survey reported a final corrected m_b = 5.2 for the May 11 explosions, much smaller that the m_b = 5.76 that would be expected if the yields were in fact ~55 kt as claimed by India.

[74]Ibid., p. 2038.

to eliminate some fundamental inaccuracies that have arisen as a result of uninformed reporting.

The first such controversy centers on the claim proffered by many Indian analysts—as the defense correspondent of one major Indian newspaper phrased it—that India's testing of subkiloton nuclear devices "marks a significant technological leap, as it now provides the armed forces with the choice of having a wide array of lethal tactical nuclear weapons."[75] The fact remains that India did not test *any* such weapons during its two rounds of tests in May 1998. This conclusion, which can be inferred from the country's nuclear doctrine, was corroborated by several Indian officials (including some who were involved in the nuclear tests) in a series of conversations with the author in August 1998. India's nuclear arsenal currently has no place for tactical nuclear weapons given that the country does not require any instruments of battlefield use for purposes of ensuring its security.[76] This has been affirmed both by India's Defence Minister, George Fernandes, who has noted unequivocally that "Indian nuclear weapons are for strategic deterrence, not for tactical use,"[77] and by its Foreign Minister, Jaswant Singh, who has with equal clarity stated, "Regarding tactical nuclear weapons, let me remind you that we do not see nuclear weapons as weapons of war fighting. In fact, India sees them only as strategic weapons, whose role is to deter their use by an adversary."[78] These affirmations notwithstanding, many Indian analysts continue to believe that their country tested tactical nuclear weapons in May 1998 and consequently argue that the Indian armed forces must prepare themselves to deploy these devices effectively. One analyst affiliated with the semiofficial Institute for Defence Studies and Analyses in Delhi exemplified this point of view when he wrote:

---

[75]Dinesh Kumar, "Sub-Kiloton Devices a Technological Leap," *The Times of India*, May 14, 1998.

[76] For a systematic defense of this conclusion, see Gurmeet Kanwal, "Does India Need Tactical Nuclear Weapons?" *Strategic Analysis*, 24:2 (May 2000), pp. 221–246.

[77]Rahul Bedi, "Interview with George Fernandes," *Jane's Defence Weekly*, July 1, 1998.

[78]"India Not to Engage in a N-Arms Race: Jaswant."

With its serial nuclear tests [in May 1998], India demonstrated the ability to produce sophisticated nuclear warheads. Now the task for the country is to provide suitable carriers to these warheads to attain a credible nuclear deterrence. . . . All the nuclear warheads of . . . [the May 1998 test] . . . series can be carried by Indian Air Force aircraft, which can deliver them with some changes in configuration. Low-yield devices, such as the 0.2 kiloton [device] tested [on] May 11 and the 0.5 and 0.3 [kt devices tested on] May 13, can be mounted on any ballistic missile, but to use a ballistic missile for that purpose would be a waste. The reason is clear: A low impact would be attained at a huge cost. The best carrier for low-yield or sub-kiloton devices is artillery.[79]

All such analyses explicitly or implicitly presume that the low-yield tests conducted in May 1998 were intended to validate different designs useful for fabricating tactical nuclear weapons. One of the most knowledgeable Indian analysts who has written about this issue, however, has pointed out that "the design of these 'sub-kt' tests . . . [does] not seem to suggest that weaponization in this range of yields—artillery, tactical or field—is currently on the agenda."[80] This fact notwithstanding, several commentators, including members of the Indian armed services, regularly presume in their public writings that India possesses dedicated tactical nuclear weapons, has tested them, and is likely to integrate them into its deterrent posture.[81] Again, nothing could be further from the truth. India *may* have carried out a low-yield detonation as part of its May 11 test series. However, such a test, if it did occur, could have been undertaken for numerous reasons other than the need for tactical weapons—e.g., as part of weapon development experiments, tests of specific components or materials, or tests for system safety. In fact, the "Joint Statement by the Department of Atomic Energy and Defence

---

[79]Rajiv Nayan, "Delivery Systems Seen as Aiding Nuclear Deterrence," *India Abroad*, June 26, 1998.

[80]Ramachandran, "Pokhran II: The Scientific Dimensions," p. 50.

[81]This presumption is in fact made manifest in the military's proposal for a new command system declaring that "tactical nuclear weapons [ought to] be released by the NCA through the NSNC to the operational centers of the three service headquarters. Their usage, however, will be decided by the operational commands and the NSNC." Bedi, "India Assesses Options on Future Nuclear Control."

Research and Development Organization," issued after the test series, specifically refers to tests that "have significantly enhanced our capability in computer simulation of new designs and taken us to the stage of sub-critical experiments in the future, if considered necessary."[82] R. Ramachandran similarly points out that India's subkiloton tests could well have been used to create a database for future subcritical experiments, although he is doubtful that such a small test series would be adequate for future weapon development in lieu of further hot testing and in the absence of a large prior archive of weapon test data. In any event, he notes that India's low-yield detonations, which were intended to provide data on neutron multiplication behavior in systems that are just above criticality, could not simultaneously be used for designing nuclear weapons because the principal phenomenon of interest in the latter case is neutron multiplication in systems approaching supercritical states. From this argument, Ramachandran draws the conclusion that India's low-yield nuclear tests—whatever their purposes may have been—could not have been intended for the development of tactical nuclear weapons.[83]

In private conversations, Indian officials have referred to these low-yield tests as having contributed to validating new nuclear materials and, perhaps, corroborating various hypotheses about their equations of state. Several press reports since the May 1998 tests have described how one of India's low-yield tests involved an experiment with "dirty plutonium"—reactor-grade plutonium—as a fissile material for possible weapon applications.[84] If this is the case, it could constitute an example of what might be meant by the term "new nuclear materials" while also suggesting, incidentally, that India's stock of weapons-grade plutonium, being smaller than what is usually imagined, would warrant the investigation of such alternative materials for use in an extreme emergency.[85] In any event, the experiments involving "dirty plutonium" could have some bearing—even if unintended—on the issue of tactical nuclear weapons, as was al-

---

[82]"Joint Statement by the Department of Atomic Energy and Defence Research and Development Organization," p. 12.

[83]Ramachandran, "Pokhran II: The Scientific Dimensions," pp. 50 and 53–54.

[84]Chengappa, "Is India's H-Bomb a Dud?" p. 28.

[85]See the discussion in Perkovich, *India's Nuclear Bomb*, pp. 428–431.

luded to in the last section. As is well known, all kinds of plutonium other than weapons-grade plutonium have traditionally been shunned by weapon designers because they contain more than 7 percent of the undesirable isotope Pu^{240}.[86] Since fuel- and reactor-grade plutonium, for example, contains 7–18 percent and more than 18 percent Pu^{240}, respectively, they are particularly susceptible to the problems of preinitiation—the premature initiation of a chain reaction caused by the presence of high-neutron background materials before the desired degree of supercriticality can be achieved in the nuclear device—and, as such, have never been the materials of choice in circumstances where weapons-grade plutonium is freely available.[87] Preinitiation usually results in a sharp lowering of yields, and consequently any nuclear weapon that intends to use high-neutron background materials in its core while still seeking to reliably generate great yields must compensate for preinitiation either through sophisticated design techniques, which ensure fast assembly of the fissile materials,[88] or through boosting, which injects a stream of additional neutrons just before the moment of maximum supercriticality "so that the bomb's tendency to fly apart is partly countered by the continuing forces of convergent assembly"[89] to produce the otherwise unattainable desired yield.[90]

Even if India cannot readily exploit such solutions, it could still use "dirty plutonium" in the core of its standard fission weapons were it willing to accept relatively degraded yields as a consequence. Most authorities knowledgeable about this issue affirm that even standard fission devices that would otherwise produce 10–20 kt if constructed

---

[86]The standard sources that examine the issue of reactor-grade plutonium for nuclear weapons are Lovins, "Nuclear Weapons and Power-Reactor plutonium," pp. 817–823; Mark, "Explosive Properties of Reactor-Grade Plutonium," pp. 111–128; and Richard L. Garwin, "Reactor-Grade Plutonium Can Be Used to Make Powerful and Reliable Nuclear Weapons: Separated Plutonium in the Fuel Cycle Must Be Protected as If It Were Nuclear Weapons."

[87]The United States, for example, did develop and test a nuclear weapon made out of reactor-grade plutonium in 1962, but such devices were never certified for operational use because of the plentiful availability of weapons-grade plutonium during the Cold War.

[88]Lovins, "Nuclear Weapons and Power-Reactor Plutonium,"pp. 819–821.

[89]Ibid., p. 820.

[90]Perkovich, *India's Nuclear Bomb*, pp. 428–430.

with weapons-grade plutonium will produce "yields 3–10 times lower that those mentioned above (depending on the design), [and that] yields in the kiloton range could be accomplished."[91] One analyst, reviewing these assessments in some detail, concluded simply that "preinitiation [even] at the least favorable moment in a Trinity-type bomb would still produce reliable kiloton yields: the worst-case, minimum, 'fizzle' yield is still a 'militarily useful' ~1 kton."[92] If India's standard fission weapon using reactor-grade plutonium in its core could produce a ~1-kt yield routinely—which is "a very significant yield from a military point of view"[93]—then it is possible that even within the limits of its current technology New Delhi could produce pseudo-tactical weapons with yields that are operationally comparable to those produced by dedicated U.S. and Soviet nuclear artillery shells during the Cold War.

All this goes to reaffirm the conclusion reached in the last chapter: that India need not possess "dedicated" tactical nuclear weapons in order to employ its nuclear assets in a tactically significant way. Instead, it could achieve the capacity for "calibrated deterrence"[94] advocated by many of its security analysts, who seek to avoid "uncontrollabl[e] . . . counter-city attacks wreaking limitless destruction"[95] in the event of deterrence breakdown, either by manipulating the operational variables involved in delivering its standard fission weapons or by simply substituting reactor-grade plutonium in its existing fission devices to produce fizzle yields that nonetheless have militarily significant effects. One of the key inferences that can be drawn from the May 1998 test series, therefore, is that although India surely did not test any dedicated tactical nuclear weapons whatsoever, it could still produce tactically useful low-yield weapons if one of its subkiloton tests successfully provided the information its sci-

---

[91]Office of Technology Assessment, *Nuclear Proliferation and Safeguards* (New York: Praeger, 1977), p. 142.

[92]Lovins, "Nuclear Weapons and Power-Reactor Plutonium," p. 821.

[93]Statement of Dr. John S. Foster, Director, Defense Research and Engineering, Department of Defense, before the Subcommittee on Arms Control, Senate Foreign Relations Committee, May 1, 1973, cited in Ray E. Kidder, "Militarily Significant Nuclear Explosive Yields," *FAS Public Interest Report*, 38:7 (September 1985), p. 2.

[94]Chellaney, "Nuclear-Deterrent Posture," p. 213.

[95]Ibid.

entists sought about "dirty plutonium" as a potential nuclear weapon material. If India were to successfully design nuclear weapons capable of rapid assembly or were to master the techniques of fusion boosting over time, its "dirty plutonium" could conceivably be used even to produce reliable, high-yield nuclear weapons. Proving such innovations conclusively would almost certainly require a return to hot testing, but the May 1998 tests do not provide any incontrovertible evidence thus far that India has perfected either of these two kinds of technologies.[96]

If it is therefore concluded that the subkiloton tests of May 11 and 13 could contribute to the creation of some militarily significant low-yield devices even if they were not intended for the design of dedicated tactical nuclear weapons, then the Indian arsenal—based on what India claimed to have tested in 1998—is left with two other potentially higher-yield weapons: the simple fission design, which is generally acknowledged to be a weaponized version of the device tested in 1974, and the new thermonuclear design, which ostensibly produced a yield of some 42 kt. And it is this latter device that has been the source of even greater controversy, since its announced yield was much smaller than what most thermonuclear weapons are popularly believed to produce. As one Indian nuclear scientist is quoted as remarking, "One doesn't think of thermonuclear weapons in kilotons; it's usually done in the megaton range or multiples of megatons."[97] Yet while this is certainly the common view about thermonuclear yields (a view that appears to resonate with Pakistani scientists[98]), it is important to recognize that there is no technical reason it should be so—for it is, in fact, possible to produce thermonuclear devices that generate very low yields, and in the case of the United States at least such devices were actually certified as operational weapons by virtue of their special ability to meet the exacting safety criteria specified for nuclear weapons routinely deployed under difficult circumstances in the field.

---

[96]For a good summary of Western assessment of India's May 1998 test series, see Peter D. Zimmerman, "India's Testing: Something Doesn't Fit," *Los Angeles Times*, May 22, 1998.

[97]T.S. Gopi Rethinaraj, "Indian Blasts Surprise the World, but Leave Fresh Doubts," *Jane's Intelligence Review*, 10:7 (July 1998), p. 20.

[98]Muhammed Najeeb, "Indian H-Bomb Test a Failure, Say Pakistan Scientists," *India Abroad*, June 19, 1998.

In any event, in August 1998 Indian officials suggested in private conversations with the author that the thermonuclear device tested in May of that year was not an operational weapon—as the fission device obviously was—but rather an experiment intended primarily to establish that the designated primary would actually burn the relatively small quantities of thermonuclear fuel present in the secondary stage. R. Chidambaram, formerly Chairman of India's AEC, now appears to have confirmed this notion publicly by stating that of the five nuclear devices exploded in Pokhran in 1998, "the 15-kiloton [fission] device was a weapon [that] had been in the stockpile for several years. Others were [merely] weaponisable configurations."[99] The fact that the thermonuclear test was only an experiment and not the validation of an operational weapon, Indian officials argued in August 1998, ought to have explained the deliberately low yields that were realized in May of that year. Two other factors that are more readily appreciated also contributed to this outcome: first, the desire to minimize damage to the inhabited areas located fairly close to the test range; and second, the desire to prevent any venting of radioactive debris because of the shallow depth of burial of the test devices themselves. The constraints imposed by the shallow depth of burial in particular were driven by the decision to use the old, shallower test shafts that had been dug in the early 1980s for purposes of testing India's fission devices rather than to begin digging some new, deeper shafts, which Indian scientists feared would inevitably have signaled a possible resumption of testing and the consequent imposition of new international political pressures.[100] These facts notwithstanding, the critical question from the viewpoint of assessing India's nuclear weaponry is not whether the intended yields from the tests were kept deliberately low for what are otherwise legitimate reasons but whether the May 1998 yields announced by the Indian nuclear estate in fact comport with the various data about these events available to the international community.

On this score, there is near-unanimity within the U.S. governmental and academic communities that a substantial divergence exists

---

[99]"'Only One Device at Pokhran-II Was a Weapon,'" *The Hindu*, June 22, 2000.

[100]Many of these reasons are detailed in Chellaney, "Nuclear-Deterrent Posture," pp. 202–209.

between India's announced yield and the inferred seismic yield.[101] Indeed, the gradual changes in India's claims about what was tested, the benchmarks against which its yields were measured, and the very fact that its initial claims were advanced long before these declarations could be systematically corroborated make many of India's official assertions about its achievements suspect—a conclusion increasingly affirmed even within India today.[102] In any event, on the crucial matter of the kinds of devices actually tested in May 1998—the issue of analytical concern at the moment—India's initial claims that it had tested a thermonuclear weapon consisting of "a fission trigger and a secondary stage"[103] have now given way to the assertion that the primary stage of this device actually involved a boosted fission trigger with a yield of 12 kt[104] and not a simple 15-kt fission device, as the director of BARC's solid state and spectroscopy group,

---

[101]The best academic analyses of this discrepancy in the United States can be found in Terry Wallace, "The May 1998 India and Pakistan Nuclear Tests," *Seismological Research Letters*, 69:5 (September–October 1998), pp. 386–393; J. R. Murphy, "Seismic Yield Estimation for the Indian and Pakistani Nuclear Tests of May, 1998," paper presented at the 20th Annual Seismic Research Symposium on Monitoring a CTBT, Santa Fe, NM, September 23, 1998; Brian Barker et al., "Monitoring Nuclear Tests," *Science*, 282 (September 25, 1998), pp. 1967–1968; William R. Walter, Arthur J. Rodgers, Kevin Mayeda, Stephen C. Myers, Michael Pasyanos, and Marvin Denny, *Preliminary Regional Seismic Analysis of Nuclear Explosions and Earthquakes in Southwest Asia*, UCRL-JC-130745 (Geophysics and Global Security Division, Lawrence Livermore National Laboratory, July 1998); J. Schweitzer, F. Ringdal, and J. Fyen, "The Indian Nuclear Explosions of 11 and 13 May 1998," *NORSAR Semiannual Technical Summary*, NORSAR Scientific Report No. 2-97/98, pp. 121–130; and Marshall, "Did Test Ban Watchdog Fail to Bark?" pp. 2038–2040. U.S. governmental judgments of the tests are summarized in Perkovich, *India's Nuclear Bomb*, pp. 424–433, and in Mark Hibbs, "India May Test Again Because H-Bomb Failed, U.S. Believes," *Nucleonics Week*, November 26, 1998. The two international observers who argued in favor of India's announced yields are Jack F. Evernden, "Estimation of Yields of Underground Explosion with Emphasis on Recent Indian and Pakistani Explosions," *Physics and Society*, 27:4 (October 1998), pp. 10–11, and Roger Clark, whose views are summarized in Debora MacKenzie, "Making Waves," *New Scientist*, June 13, 1998, pp. 18–19. Evernden's estimates were apparently biased by a small northern European earthquake that occurred after the Indian tests. See Charles Meade, "Surface Wave Magnitudes and Yield Estimates for the May 11, 1998 Indian Nuclear Test," unpublished memo.

[102]For some good reporting on this issue, see D. N. Moorthy, "AEC Chief Defends Pokharan Yields," *Indian Express*, November 30, 1999.

[103]Transcript of the press conference hosted by Dr. R. Chidambaram, Chairman, AEC, and Secretary, DAE.

[104]Chengappa, "Is India's H-Bomb a Dud?" pp. 22–28; Ramachandran, "Pokhran II: The Scientific Dimensions," p. 50.

S. K. Sikka, had earlier informed the journal *Science* in a written communication.[105]

While this steadily mutating story does little to enhance the credibility of India's claims, it does suggest that any analysis of the kinds of nuclear weapons India may be presumed to possess must reckon with the prospect of not two but actually three separate designs: a fission weapon with the initially claimed yield of some 12 kt; a boosted fission weapon with a claimed yield of approximately 12 kt; and a thermonuclear device with a claimed yield of 31–36 kt, depending on whether the total yield of all devices tested on May 11 was finally either ~55 or ~60 kt. Indian officials have claimed both totals at different times and have varied the internal breakdown of these figures as well: In the final version of their claims, the simple fission device is supposed to have yielded 15 kt; the thermonuclear device 45 kt, divided between a 12-kt boosted fission trigger and a 33-kt fusion yield; and the assorted subkiloton tests 0.2 kt, 0.3 kt, and 0.5 kt, respectively, with the last two tests alleged to have been conducted on May 13, 1998.[106]

The fact that these figures suggest three nuclear designs and not two as per the earlier Indian claims has been explicitly confirmed by R. Chidambaram, who asserted that his team of scientists "obtained three robust bomb designs"[107] as a result of their May 1998 tests. Directly addressing the issue of the combined boosted-fission/thermonuclear test, Chidambaram asserted that this event was deliberately intended to "kill two birds with one stone"—i.e., to validate a boosted fission design (which in principle can provide more than a fourfold increase in yield over a simple fission bomb) while simultaneously using the energy generated from such a primary to burn the lithium deuteride that presumably constituted the ther-

---

[105]Marshall, "Did Test Ban Watchdog Fail to Bark?" p. 2039.

[106]The earlier Indian claims are recorded in John F. Burns, "Indian Scientists Confirm They Detonated a Hydrogen Bomb," *New York Times*, May 18, 1998, while the revised claims can be found in Marshall, "Did Test Ban Watchdog Fail to Bark?" pp. 2038–2040. In a later, more inexplicable accounting, Indian scientists are also supposed to have "put the yield from the fission bomb at 20 kt and the hydrogen bomb at 25 kt." Chengappa, "Is India's H-Bomb a Dud?" p. 26. These varying figures obviously cannot be reconciled and only underscore the spurious and utterly unreliable character of the official scientific claims accompanying the May 1998 tests.

[107]George, "No More N-Tests Needed: AEC."

monuclear fuel in the secondary. Admitting that "most nuclear weapon powers had gone through the traditional path of separately testing a boosted fission device,"[108] Chidambaram justified his team's approach to this issue by referring to the state-of-the-art capabilities India possessed in these areas and, accordingly, argued that "each of our tests should be considered equivalent to several carried out by other nuclear weapon states."[109] This effort at validating multiple effects through a minimum number of tests is consistent with the public claims made by other senior Indian scientists, some of whom are even reported to have suggested that "the five tests [carried out in May 1998] were equivalent in value to about 50 [tests]"[110] in terms of the experience gained.

Although these arguments advanced about the sufficiency of India's minimal number of nuclear tests are quite fraudulent, the other justifications for why Indian scientists deliberately restricted the yield of their thermonuclear weapons to relatively low levels are more plausible. It is certainly difficult to believe that Indian scientists have mastered the art of terminating the fusion burn precisely in order to obtain reliably low yields—without *any* prior hot testing of advanced weapon designs—but at least their intention to keep the overall yields low are understandable. The need to limit damage to the villages near the test site; the need to avoid venting given the relatively shallow depths of burial of the devices necessitated by the use of old shafts; and the need to limit the maximum yield given the number of multiple devices that had to be tested simultaneously from relatively closely spaced shafts for reasons of cost, political considerations, and deception and denial all converge toward a reasoned justification for lower rather than higher yields.[111] But what

---

[108]"No Compromises on N-Power: AEC Chief," *Indian Express*, February 4, 1999.

[109]Ibid.

[110]Chengappa, "Is India's H-Bomb a Dud?" p. 28. Obviously whether such a dual experiment actually took place cannot be verified through seismological means alone. In any event, whether the primary involved a boosted fission trigger or not, the entire experiment more likely than not was intended to establish a proof of principle rather than to validate a final weapon design, at least as far as the thermonuclear weapon per se was concerned.

[111]For many of these reasons, see "Weaponization Now Complete, Say Scientists," *The Hindu*, May 18, 1998; Chengappa, "The Bomb Makers," pp. 26–32; and throughout Chengappa, *Weapons of Peace*.

makes the Indian claims of unvarnished success difficult for most international observers to swallow ultimately derives from three factors: the relatively low body-wave magnitudes registered by the May 11 tests;[112] the character of the crater morphology resulting from each of the tests given the geology of the area and the relative depths of burial of the devices tested;[113] and the complete absence of seismic information pertaining to the May 13 tests.[114]

Although the May 11 tests should have registered an average body-wave magnitude of 5.76 if all the detonations produced a total yield of even ~55 kt, the actual average magnitude finally reported by the U.S. Geological Service of mb = 5.2 suggests that the total yield of all three devices could not have exceeded 9–16 kt, with the best mean estimate for the yield based on seismic sources set at around 12 kt.[115] If the total uncertainty surrounding the mean estimates is taken to be 50 percent, because of uncertainties relating to the geologic conditions of the test site, emplacement geometry, degree of coupling, and the like, the estimated yield of the May 11 tests would not exceed 24 kt, with most Western analysts holding to the claim that, as Terry Wallace put it, "you're going to be pushing 20 kilotons at most for the 11 May test."[116]

---

[112]Wallace, "The May 1998 India and Pakistan Nuclear Tests," pp. 386–393; Murphy, "Seismic Yield Estimation for the Indian and Pakistani Nuclear Tests of May, 1998"; Barker et al., "Monitoring Nuclear Tests," pp. 1967–1968; Walter et al., *Preliminary Regional Seismic Analysis of Nuclear Explosions and Earthquakes in Southwest Asia*; and Marshall, "Did Test Ban Watchdog Fail to Bark?" pp. 2038–2040.

[113]Wallace, "The May 1998 India and Pakistan Nuclear Tests," p. 389. Brief descriptions of the local geology and the effect of geology on crater formation can be found in S. K. Bhushan, "Geology Around Pokhran Nuclear Sites," *Journal of the Geological Society of India*, 52:1 (July 1998), p. 118, and A. C. McEwan, "Environmental Effects of Underground Nuclear Explosions," in Jozef Goldblat and David Cox (eds.), *Nuclear Weapons Tests: Prohibition or Limitation?* (Oxford, UK: Oxford University Press, 1998), pp. 75–91.

[114]Wallace, "The May 1998 India and Pakistan Nuclear Tests," pp. 389–390; Walter et al., *Preliminary Regional Seismic Analysis of Nuclear Explosions and Earthquakes in Southwest Asia*, p. 6. There is still no corroborating evidence for the May 13, 1998, tests; in all probability, these tests *did* take place but with much smaller yields than those suggested by India. In any case, the photographs of this event—published in Chengappa, "Is India's H-Bomb a Dud?" p. 25—are suspicious, as are many other photographs relating to the May 1998 tests found in Chengappa, "The Bomb Makers," pp. 26–27.

[115]Barker et al., "Monitoring Nuclear Tests," p. 1968.

[116]Marshall, "Did Test Ban Watchdog Fail to Bark?" p. 2039.

Indian scientists have attempted to explain this critical discrepancy by arguing that the location of many seismometers along an east-west axis biased the seismic reading, as "mb values are in general smaller at the azimuths away from the north direction."[117] After correcting for distortions introduced by azimuth, BARC scientists have argued that "a value of mb = 5.39 was obtained as the global average"—which in turn translates into "an average combined yield of 58 ± 5 kt after taking into account the geology of Pokhran test site as calibrated by our POK1 explosion."[118] Even if the significance of east-west measuring bias is disregarded,[119] this translation of magnitude-to-yield values appears to be heavily dependent on a smaller set of values attributed to the constants a and b in the magnitude-yield formula $mb = a + b \log Y$—values that are more appropriate for tectonically active regions than for the stable Indian test sites and that consequently are not used by any other observers outside India.[120] It is not clear whether manipulating the value of the constants alone always produces the kinds of yields desired by India because a quick recalculation—using one set of constants (a = 3.8, b = 0.9) attributed to BARC's experts by one knowledgeable Indian scientific commentator who has attempted to defend India's claim of success in its thermonuclear test[121]—seems to suggest that the total yield of the May 11 tests could not have exceeded 36 kt.

---

[117]Sikka et al., "Update on the Yield of the May 11–13, 1998, Nuclear Detonations at Pokhran," p. 1.

[118]Ibid., pp. 1–2.

[119]The Indian argument that mb values were generally smaller when measured by seismometers emplaced along the east-west axis is true but is fundamentally misleading. Because mb values are distorted by a variety of factors, including sensor locations and geological variations, the appropriate methodology for calculating such values consists of averaging the readings obtained by *all* reporting stations in a given seismographic network. The Indian strategy of selecting only those readings obtained from sensors located primarily away from an east-west axis amounts to little more than "cherry picking" the data in order to derive those desired mb values which translate into the higher yields that Indian scientists sought to justify in the first place.

[120]The best analysis of this issue can be found in Wallace, "The May 1998 India and Pakistan Nuclear Tests," pp. 386–393, and in Gregory van der Vink, Jeffrey Park, Richard Allen, Terry Wallace, and Christel Hennet, "False Accusations, Undetected Test and Implications for the CTB Treaty," *Arms Control Today*, 28:4 (May 1998), pp. 7–13.

[121]See the values used in R. Ramachandran, "Understanding Pokhran II & III: A Technical Appraisal," *Agni*, 3:3 (January–May 1998), pp. 12–25.

This class of yields sharply constrains the kind of weaponry India may be said to possess. If the May 11 tests are interpreted as producing a yield between 9 and 16 kt (with the best mean estimate set at approximately 12 kt with an upper bound of ~24 kt after allowance for evaluative uncertainties), either (a) the fission device detonated successfully (if it is assumed to be either 12 kt or 15 kt in yield) but both the boosted fission primary and the thermonuclear secondary failed; or (b) the fission device and the boosted fission trigger detonated more or less successfully (if both are assumed to have yielded 12 kt each, but not if the former was in fact supposed to have produced a larger yield, as the revised Indian claim suggests) while the thermonuclear secondary failed. What simply seems improbable is (c): that both the fission weapon and the thermonuclear device in its entirety detonated successfully, as the combined yields do not *unambiguously* corroborate India's claims of success even after due allowance is made for evaluative uncertainty. Even the assumption embodied in (b), that both the fission weapon and the boosted fission trigger produced their full yield as planned, is highly suspect because it presumes that the May 11 test series produced between 24 and 27 kt of yield—a conclusion that can be sustained only if one settles for the highest and most favorable estimate of yield derived from the body-wave magnitude associated with that event. Such a conclusion, besides being a suspicious deduction, is certainly not corroborated by the crater characteristics of the two test sites.[122]

Consequently, what is most likely to have occurred—when the seismic data, the crater morphology associated with each test site, knowledge about the local geology of the test range, and information about the depth of burial, including that gained from mensuration of the evacuated debris from the test shafts, are all integrated—is that the fission weapon detonated successfully (although its actual final yield is uncertain) while the boosted fission trigger almost certainly failed to boost successfully and consequently could not produce the temperatures required to ignite the thermonuclear fuel present in the secondary.[123] Clearly, the Indian photographs released of the test

---

[122]Wallace, "The May 1998 India and Pakistan Nuclear Tests," p. 389.

[123]Rethinaraj, "Indian Blasts Surprise the World, but Leave Fresh Doubts," pp. 20–21. One technical study of the value of nuclear testing for the United States concluded that a full-yield explosion of the primary, which would be necessary to successfully

sites suggest that some sort of detonation did take place in the shaft where the thermonuclear device was located, but the physical evidence suggests that the fission components of the trigger produced most of the fizzle yield, with failure to boost accounting for the inability to secure the fusion yield that Indian scientists claimed they obtained from this test.[124]

This conclusion must be carefully understood: Irrespective of what claims Indian scientists may make about the success of their thermonuclear test, the controversy surrounding this issue ought to suggest, at the very least, that India has not demonstrated *beyond a shadow of a doubt* that it has mastered the ability to produce advanced nuclear weapons even if it is presumed—against the weight of all available evidence—to actually possess such a capability. The nuclear tests conducted in May 1998 were supposed to have two specific objectives: to enhance the country's own confidence in its existing weapon designs and to communicate to its adversaries the extent of its technological prowess for purposes of ensuring deterrence stability.[125] Yet even if the first objective has been satisfactorily attained, however solipsistically—that is, because the Indian nuclear estate believes in the success of its test regime, because post-test analysis provided the data necessary to remedy the flaws discovered during explosive testing, or because India's nuclear scientists have

---

validate the "ignition of the secondary," would "generate nuclear yields in excess of approximately 10 kt." See Sidney Drell et al., "Nuclear Testing: Summary and Conclusions," *JASON Nuclear Testing Study*, JSR-95-320, August 3, 1995, available at http://www.fas.org/rlg/jsr-95-320.htm. By this conclusion, India's thermonuclear test ought to have produced a yield in excess of approximately 10 kt if its claim that the thermonuclear fuel in the secondary successfully ignited is to be believed. However, the characteristics of the crater at the thermonuclear test site, when coupled with the seismic data for *all* tests occurring on May 11, 1998, do not unambiguously corroborate India's claim.

[124]Indian nuclear scientists have published results from their radiochemical measurements, which they claim prove that the yield of the thermonuclear device tested in May 1998 was 50 ± 10 kt. See S. B. Manohar, B. S. Tomar, S. S. Rattan, V. K. Shukla, V. V. Kulkarni, and Anil Kakodkar, "Post Shot Radioactivity Measurements on Samples Extracted from Thermonuclear Test Site," *BARC Newsletter*, 186 (July 1999), pp. 1–5. Unfortunately, this paper does not reproduce the raw data gathered from the samples subjected to radiochemical testing and as a result it is difficult to conclude that the results claimed cohere with the data actually recovered from the radiochemical tests.

[125]Singh, *What Constitutes National Security in a Changing World Order?* pp. 31–32.

shifted to more conservative weapon designs to increase the probability of successful detonations in the future—the second objective has hardly been secured, since significant portions of the international community are not yet convinced about the validity of India's technical claims. It may be argued quite cogently that what observers in the United States and more generally the West may believe is irrelevant, since India's nuclear capabilities are not designed to deter those countries. By this very token, however, what the Pakistanis and the Chinese believe about India's nuclear prowess could be highly relevant, and it is here that India's ambiguous achievements would matter more than elsewhere. The Pakistani scientific community, however, has already publicly expressed its disbelief about the success of India's thermonuclear experiment,[126] and while the Chinese strategic community has made no comparable public response, there is good reason to believe that its private estimates of New Delhi's achievements do not deviate substantially from the opinions expressed in Islamabad.[127]

All these exhibitions of disbelief might have been written off within India as yet another example of foreign condescension were it not for the fact that in February 2000, P. K. Iyengar, a former Chairman of the Indian AEC and one of the key individuals associated with the 1974 test, went public—thanks to a private, ongoing rivalry with R. Chidambaram—with his claim that the Indian thermonuclear test was not as successful as had previously been affirmed. This assertion, echoing the astute assessment of Bharat Karnad in an earlier article,[128] was proffered in the context of the Indian debate about sign-

---

[126]Najeeb, "Indian H-Bomb Test a Failure, Say Pakistan Scientists."

[127]Zhang, *China's Changing Nuclear Posture*, pp. 33–34. The Indian scientific community, exasperated by the pervasive skepticism emanating from the West and often contemptuous of Pakistan's own modest achievements in the field of nuclear weaponry, has charged the West with deliberately spreading "misinformation" about India's technical achievements for political reasons (see Satyen Mohapatra, "Low Yield Reports Misleading: AEC Chief," *Hindustan Times*, January 5, 1999). Other Indian analysts have argued that while some doubt is to be expected given that "India has shown a remarkable level of capability," most Western skepticism "is politically motivated and aimed at undermining India's deterrent posture" (see Brahma Chellaney, "India's Hydrogen Bomb," *Hindustan Times*, January 13, 1999). For more along these lines, see Chellaney, "Nuclear-Deterrent Posture," pp. 141–222.

[128]See Karnad, "A Sucker's Payoff," pp. 45–50, for a good reading of what was and was not achieved by the May 1998 tests.

ing the CTBT. In urging his government not to sign the treaty, Iyengar noted that the thermonuclear design tested in May 1998 was primarily a proof of principle rather than a weaponized design; had failed to achieve a complete fusion burn that would have marked it as a viable design; had an unknown yield by virtue of having been tested simultaneously with at least another fission weapon; and, finally, was simply insufficient as a data point on which to benchmark future computer simulations of such devices.[129] Despite this critique, Iyengar sought to reconcile his claims with the DAE's announced May 1998 yields and, as a consequence, was forced to speculatively revise the breakdown of total yields in still another way: Accepting that the fission device yielded 15 kt, Iyengar concluded that the boosted fission trigger produced 20 kt and the thermonuclear fuel produced another 20 kt to reach a total of 55 kt from all tests combined.[130] This redaction obviously does not square with the evidence accepted internationally and, at any rate, appears to have left many serious Indian analysts justifiably suspicious about their country's capability to produce the kinds of advanced nuclear weapons believed to be necessary without further testing—weapons that the Indian nuclear estate repeatedly affirms it could manufacture without any difficulty whatsoever.[131]

This debate about New Delhi's technical achievements only confirms the suspicion harbored by many observers of the Indian nuclear weapon program: that India's nuclear scientists, like many weapon designers elsewhere in the world, are so fascinated by the sophistication of their conceptual designs that they often tend to overlook the more simple, pedestrian attributes invariably demanded by all end users—repeatedly tested, mechanically reliable weapons that will produce a specified yield whenever they are required to do so under any operational circumstances. Instead of focusing their energies and resources on producing these kinds of nu-

---

[129]"Indian Scientist Opposes Signing of CTBT," *Deccan Herald*, February 19, 2000.

[130]Mark Hibbs, "Because H-Bomb Fuel Didn't Burn, Iyengar Pleads for Second Test," *Nucleonics Week*, June 1, 2000.

[131]See, for example, Chari, "Weaponisation and the CTBT"; Karnad, "A Sucker's Payoff"; Rajagopalan, "The Question of More Tests"; Balachandran, "A Consensus or a Sell-Off?"; V. R. Raghavan, "Whither Nuclear Policy," *The Hindu*, July 1, 2000; and especially A. Gopalakrishnan, "How Credible Is Our Deterrence?" *The Hindu*, November 18, 1998.

clear weapons, India's nuclear scientists appear to be more seduced by the challenges of reaching out for the farthest limits of the possible rather than contenting themselves with demonstrating an incontrovertible mastery over merely the efficacious: Their quest for the best, in effect, has become the resolute enemy of the good enough.[132] Karnad in particular has noted how India's nuclear scientists have privately claimed that "the country has a dozen proven weapons configurations to choose from in structuring a nuclear deterrent."[133] While there is little reason to doubt that India does in fact possess many nuclear designs, the claim that these designs are "proven" in the sense of being capable of satisfying the end user is sheer fantasy given that, as Karnad put it, "the most decisive potential weapon, namely the thermonuclear or fusion device, may have failed in the one-off test"[134] conducted in May 1998.

The character of the comments uttered by India's nuclear scientists since these tests also suggests a disturbing sleight of hand: Weapon designs, weaponizable designs, and operational weapons all appear to be treated interchangeably in Indian rhetoric, with the result that designs that may exist merely on paper, that may have been confirmed as plausible through some theoretical calculations or computer simulations, or whose components may have been tested but only in a piecemeal fashion, are all expansively defined as "available weapons," leading one respected Indian observer to complain that the carefully worded phraseology used by Indian scientists often fails to "clarify whether more field tests would be required to fashion the devices . . . with reasonable confidence into deliverable nuclear weapons."[135] This somewhat blasé and overconfident attitude exhibited by India's nuclear scientists about their weapon technology capabilities is ultimately grounded in the sociology of India's civil-military divide: Since the responsibility for designing, developing, and maintaining India's nuclear weaponry is vested entirely in civilian authorities with little or no military collaboration, it is not surprising that design and reliability issues that should by rights be

---

[132]See the apt remarks in Manoj Joshi, "The Nuclear Maharaja Has No Clothes," *The Times of India,* June 9, 2000.

[133]Karnad, "A Sucker's Payoff," p. 47.

[134]Ibid.

[135]Chari, "Weaponisation and the CTBT."

heavily influenced by the contingencies of deterrence breakdown and actual nuclear use merit less attention as far as the Indian nuclear estate is concerned. In fact, these problems may be dismissed altogether on the grounds that nuclear weapons, being merely political instruments and not usable military tools, will never be put to the test of war anyway and hence do not warrant the time, energy, and resources that it would take to assure operational and yield reliability if such weapons were to be used *in extremis*. R. Chidambaram may have unwittingly betrayed this attitude when he argued that "in [the] two decades (after Hiroshima) nobody had to use nuclear weapons, and it is very clear in my mind that nobody is going to use them in the future too. For me knowing our history and the fact that in a thousand years we have never coveted anyone else's territory, such weapons are only a deterrent. Being such a big country, India had also to be a strong one."[136]

In any event, the debate about India's nuclear tests brings to the fore two specific sets of issues: First, what kinds of weapons can India finally be presumed to have? And second, what is India likely to do in the future?

What kinds of weapons can India finally be presumed to have? It is reasonable to presume that if only one device was successfully tested in May 1998, that device was India's fission weapon. The basic design of this weapon, presumably with a simple solid-core implosion system, was tested in 1974. The improved version, tested in 1998, was based on a levitated flying-plate design,[137] and the relative success of this test, based on both the seismic data and the test site imagery released by New Delhi, implies that India must be credited with the capability to produce at least simple fission weapons with an effective yield of some 12–15 kt. One Indian analyst has noted that militarily usable fission designs could produce a maximum yield of ~50 kt,[138] but it is unlikely that even India's 1998 flying-plate design could simply be scaled up to produce the kinds of yields—"20 to 50

---

[136]Cited in Chengappa, *Weapons of Peace*, p. 120.

[137]Ibid., pp. 207–208.

[138]Sawhney, "To Test or Not to Test: The Challenge for India's Nuclear Credibility," p. 31.

kt"[139]—that commentators often believe are possible even in the absence of boosting. India's fission weapons could certainly be engineered to produce a yield closer to (and perhaps even beyond) the high end of this spectrum, but a comprehensive redesign of the implosion system and not merely a manipulation of the existing configuration would be required if such yields were desired.[140] Such a redesign would certainly require a return to hot testing, since "increasing uncertainty would be associated with more advanced implosion systems that use less fissile material than [any] original solid-sphere design."[141] But since India has presumably eschewed this option in light of its current commitments to the United States, it is reasonable to conclude that the Indian nuclear estate can primarily produce simple fission weapons capable of yields not much beyond 15 kt.

If India's boosted fission trigger had detonated successfully in May 1998—even if the secondary failed during the thermonuclear test—this device would have offered New Delhi significant strategic advantages. For starters, it would have enabled India to dramatically increase the effective size of its weapon-usable fissile-material stockpile, since an effective boosted fission design would allow it to use even its reactor-grade plutonium to produce high-yield nuclear weapons. It would also have enabled India to increase the yields otherwise produced by its fission weaponry while simultaneously reducing their weight. Thanks to boosting, India could thus have developed a larger and a more destructive arsenal simultaneously. This fact has important strategic consequences that ought not to be overlooked in the controversy over India's thermonuclear claims.[142]

---

[139]Ibid., p. 33.

[140]If pure fission weapons yielding much greater than 70 kt have to be produced, the historical record suggests that such devices would be "very expensive due to the large amounts of Pu-239 required" and would incur severe weight penalties. The French AN 22 and MR 31 weapons, which had yields of 60–70 kt and 120 kt, respectively, are good examples of large, pure fission weapons. For details, see Norris et al., *British, French, and Chinese Nuclear Weapons, Nuclear Weapons Databook*, Vol. V, p. 185.

[141]Richard L. Garwin, "The Future of Nuclear Weapons Without Nuclear Testing," *Arms Control Today*, 27:8 (November–December 1997), pp. 3–11.

[142]See the remarks by Ray Kidder in Chengappa, "Is India's H-Bomb a Dud?" p. 28.

In part, this is because successfully boosting fission weapons is a challenging technical exercise in its own right, and although not popularly appreciated, it is no less—and in some ways may even be more—demanding than the design and construction of true two-stage thermonuclear weaponry. Not surprisingly, several Indian analysts have rushed in to claim that even if the test of the full thermonuclear device was unsuccessful, the boosted fission component certainly produced the intended yields.[143] This capacity has presumably granted India "access to weapons that have yields in excess of 150 kilotons—possibly more."[144] It has been asserted that such capabilities have enabled India to actually develop a 200-kt boosted fission warhead for the Agni,[145] and one analyst has even claimed that the country "retain[s] a capability to exercise a variety of options varying from 20 kt to 500 kt yields."[146] Such judgments find resonance among the more optimistic of India's strategic elites—and, not surprisingly, given the overconfidence of India's nuclear estate, even the architect of the May 1998 test series, R. Chidambaram, has claimed that the thermonuclear experiment has allowed India to develop weapons with yields of about 200 kt.[147] This conclusion is of interest because it does not assert that India can develop thermonuclear weapons in the megaton range without additional hot tests but merely that the ostensibly successful thermonuclear experiment has allowed for the creation of devices with yields that are popularly associated with boosted fission weaponry.[148]

---

[143] Sanjay Badri-Maharaj, "Nuclear India's Status," *Indian Defence Review*, 15:2 (April–June 2000), p. 128.

[144] Badri-Maharaj, "The Nuclear Battlefield," p. 90.

[145] Ibid., p. 126. See also Sanjay Badri-Maharaj, *The Armageddon Factor* (New Delhi: Lancer Publishers, 2000), pp. 47–97, for a collection of unsubstantiated claims about Indian nuclear prowess coupled with a pervasive underestimation of Pakistani nuclear capabilities.

[146] Sawhney, "To Test or Not to Test: The Challenge for India's Nuclear Credibility," p. 31.

[147] "India Can Produce N-Bomb of 200 Kiloton," cited in Karnad, "A Thermonuclear Deterrent," p. 117, and "India Can Make 200 Kilotons of Nuke Weapons."

[148] Sawhney, for example, notes that "militarily usable boosted weapons have explosive powers of up to about 500 kt. The yields of the most powerful boosted weapons are equal to those of low-yield thermonuclear weapons." See Sawhney, "To Test or Not to Test: The Challenge for India's Nuclear Credibility," p. 31.

There is no publicly available evidence, however, suggesting that any of these claims are true. Nor can these assertions be corroborated even inferentially from what is known from the May 1998 tests. As a result, these classes of yields must be treated as simply one of the many theoretical possibilities that may be inherent in some of India's current nuclear designs. By the standards of deductive reasoning or available evidence, however, they cannot be considered empirical capabilities that India is universally acknowledged to possess at least as far as its standing nuclear inventory is concerned. The same conclusion applies *a fortiori* with respect to India's thermonuclear weapons: The general failure of the thermonuclear test forces the conclusion that India cannot be said to possess effective thermonuclear weaponry at present, and as Indian officials pointed out first to the author in August 1998 and later publicly, the requirement for thermonuclear weapons has never been defined as a formal deterrence requirement by India's political leadership.[149] The thermonuclear test is therefore owed more to the zeal of the Indian nuclear estate and to the pressures of technological determinism within the weapon program than to a calculated assessment on the part of the national leadership about the need for such capabilities.

When all is said and done, therefore, the May 1998 tests do not validate P. K. Iyengar's early claim that Indian scientists "have demonstrated in an unambiguous fashion that we can make any kind of nuclear weapon."[150] It does, however, open the door to crediting India with possibly two kinds of nuclear weaponry: a new, arguable capability to produce pseudo-tactical nuclear weapons through the incorporation of "dirty plutonium" in the core of its standard fission design, in addition to its previously demonstrated competence to produce relatively low-yield fission weaponry. India certainly possesses additional designs for both boosted fission and thermonuclear weapons, but it cannot be credited with unambiguously demonstrating its capacity to produce such weapons through the data available to the international community as a result of the May 1998 tests. It will also be difficult to credit India with the ability to produce such advanced weapon designs in the absence of a return to field testing.

---

[149] See the discussion in Perkovich, *India's Nuclear Bomb*, p. 431.

[150] Quoted in Chengappa and Joshi, "Future Fire," p. 22.

What is India likely to do in the future? Clearly, the validation of one, and possibly the opportunity to produce another, type of nuclear weapon is only the beginning of a long process given India's decision to develop a nuclear deterrent of some sort in the future. This implies that the principal task India faces where nuclear weapons are concerned consists of completing the process of weaponization understood in the strict sense of the term. In the aftermath of the May 1998 tests, prominent Indian technologists such as A.P.J. Kalam hurriedly claimed that "our weaponization is complete."[151] Such claims, however, must be treated either as hyperbole or at best as partial truths. Weaponization in the strict sense refers to the "developing, testing, and integrating [of] warhead components into a militarily usable weapon system"[152] and, as such, is a long and drawn-out process that cannot be fully completed before the delivery systems ready to carry such payloads are at hand. But since the full range of India's delivery systems are not yet complete (as the subsequent discussion will demonstrate), it must be concluded that the process of weaponization in India has only just begun. Depending on the types of delivery systems sought over time, each carrier will inevitably impose new kinds of physical demands on the nuclear payload: Aircraft impose burdens different from those of ballistic and cruise missiles, with the basing modes associated with these systems further complicating the physical and operational demands made on the payloads. Until the entire panoply of delivery systems is therefore developed, it would at the very least be premature to conclude that Indian weaponization is in fact complete.[153]

Even before weaponization in any extended sense occurs, however, Indian scientists will most likely focus on refining their standard fission design as a result of the data gathered from the May 1998 tests. If international political constraints did not exist, these refined designs would be repeatedly hot tested until their creators were completely satisfied that the devices would work as intended with different kinds of delivery systems while still producing the desired

---

[151]*Indian Nuclear Tests Included Hydrogen Bomb,* FBIS-NES-98-138, May 18, 1998.

[152]Neil Joeck, *Nuclear Relations in South Asia,* UCRL-JC-132729, December 1998, p. 10.

[153]Raja Menon, "Not in National Interest, "*Hindustan Times,* January 5, 2000.

yields. This would be particularly true as far as the boosted fission and thermonuclear weapon designs are concerned. Since India has currently ruled out further hot testing for political reasons, however, most of these refinements will have to be carried out through laboratory experiments, computer simulations, and fully instrumented dummy tests.[154] These experiments will of necessity focus on confirming that the subsystems will work as intended in the hope that the entire system will enjoy the same reliability, when fully integrated, as each of the subsystems presumably demonstrated when they were assessed under test conditions.[155]

Even as this process is completed, however, India's designers will want to make certain that the modifications introduced into their weaponry will not compromise the ability of the existing weapon carriers—primarily aircraft—to successfully deliver these payloads. Kalam, for example, has indicated that Indian weapon designers have already been testing the "size, weight, performance and vibrations" of their devices "for quite some time."[156] This testing will obviously continue if the designs are further modified as a result of the data gleaned from both the recent nuclear tests and other continuing experiments. The larger challenge, however, will consist of readying what will by then be relatively stable fission designs for a new class of

---

[154] For a discussion of these issues together with examples of some such activities undertaken in the past, see Sawhney, "To Test or Not to Test: The Challenge for India's Nuclear Credibility," pp. 30–35; Pravin Sawhney, "Standing Alone," *Jane's International Defence Review*, 29:11 (November 1996), pp. 25–28; and Chengappa, *Weapons of Peace*, p. 418.

[155] This is an issue that speaks among other things to the reliability of the weapons and, by extension, to the level of confidence that the owners of these weapons desire from their strategic reserves. Because dilemmas of confidence lay at the heart of the U.S. deterrent, which was focused on ensuring reliable positive control, Washington pursued a large and sophisticated weapon test program that aimed at maximizing device reliability, safety, and efficiency simultaneously. See Donald R. Westervelt, "Can Cold Logic Replace Cold Feet?" *Bulletin of the Atomic Scientists*, 35:2 (February 1979), pp. 60–62, and Brown, "Nuclear Weapons R&D and the Role of Nuclear Testing," pp. 6–18. To the degree that India can live with greater uncertainty in each of these areas, its need for a return to hot testing its fission weaponry may be reduced *pari passu*. This conclusion obviously does not apply as far as boosted fission and thermonuclear devices are concerned: Neither dummy tests nor tests of subsystems would suffice to ensure the viability, let alone the reliability, of such devices. Advanced nuclear designs *have* to be repeatedly field tested, though not necessarily at full yield, if they are to be validated as worthy of induction into an operational inventory.

[156] *Indian Nuclear Tests Included Hydrogen Bomb.*

delivery systems that either are just coming on line or will be available only many years into the future. Mating these existing designs to a new set of delivery vehicles, primarily missiles—many of which do not yet exist in their final form—will thus be the principal preoccupation of Indian weapon designers over the long term.

All of this presupposes, however, that India can live quite contentedly without any advanced nuclear weapons in its inventory. Indian policymakers currently believe this to be the case, since the present and expected range of threats could be adequately deterred by New Delhi's simple fission weapons. So long as this judgment holds, India's nuclear estate will be restricted to improving its current advanced designs—to the degree that it can—by means of simulations and laboratory tests alone while constantly preparing for the possibility of renewed field testing in the event that India's political leadership should change its mind and authorize the formal development and induction of advanced weapons into the country's nuclear inventory.

None of these activities, in any event, is likely to be carried out at an accelerated pace, since many of the delivery systems that will form the mainstay of the mature Indian nuclear arsenal are probably several years away from their initial field-operational capability. Nor is India likely to build its entire stockpile of nuclear weaponry right now—even if it had the requisite inventory of fissile material—because it makes more sense to hold out on completing this process in order to garner all the benefits that may be made available from further laboratory tests, other simulations, and possibly even access to external assistance in the future. The promise of marginal improvements in India's fission weapon design base; the continued efforts at further developing advanced designs, even if only through computer simulation and laboratory experiments; and the need to more clearly define the operational, safety, and design parameters of its future delivery vehicles, together with the patterns of deployment and the reconstitution procedures for contingency operations, will all combine to compel India to engage in little more than creeping weaponization for most of the coming decade. Figure 15 reproduces

RAND MR1127-15

```
                    Technical Work in Weaponisation

    a)    Reduction in size and weight  of 1974 design

    b)    Dev of reliable detonators

    c)    Dev & clearance of
          -    new Implosion Assembly
          -    new Trigger Unit
          -    new mech & el fuzes
          -    airframe;

    d)    System Integration;   System Qualification

    e)    Platform safeties; platform mods

    e)    Design validation through  flight trials

    g)    Store Qualification with Platforms

    h)    Store Clearance and Acceptance




    drdo/shakti-98
```

Figure 15—Creeping Weaponization: A DRDO View

the DRDO vision of what weaponization entails and, to that degree, suggests what is likely to occur in the years to come.[157]

During this time, Indian weapon designers are likely to concentrate on four specific tasks: (1) to further refine their existing fission designs based on the lessons learned from the May 1998 nuclear detonations and other subcritical tests and computer simulations that

---

[157]This document comes through the courtesy of K. Santhanam, Chief Adviser (Technology), DRDO.

may be carried out in the future; (2) to establish that the delivery systems currently in India's possession and identified for the nuclear weapon delivery role can carry these refined designs without compromising safety or effectiveness; (3) to ensure that those nuclear designs selected to serve as the mainstay of India's arsenal in the near term are fully compatible with both the aircraft and the land- and sea-based missile delivery systems that will be acquired for nuclear operations over the next two decades; and (4) to pursue the development of advanced weapon designs, primarily boosted fission and thermonuclear capabilities, in the hope of reaping whatever benefits may be afforded by theoretical studies, laboratory experiments, and external assistance in the interim while waiting for the opportunity to return to renewed hot testing to conclusively validate these capabilities when the national leadership so demands. Until that point is reached, however, these four tasks will have to be performed in an environment that does not allow for any full-up tests of a complete, integrated nuclear weapon system.

Delivery Systems

Possessing the requisite inventory of fissile materials and even a stockpile of nuclear weapons is insufficient for purposes of deterrence in the absence of adequate delivery systems that can carry these weapons to target. Although it is widely believed that a "classic nuclear triad force—with distinct land, sea and air components—will eventually be created" as part of India's efforts to further its "second strike potential,"[158] the fact remains that New Delhi is many years if not decades away from acquiring such a capability in full-fledged form. This fact notwithstanding, many Indian thinkers have argued that a strategic triad is indispensable because the country's reactive-use doctrine, combined with its relatively small nuclear weapon inventory, requires that it diversify its strategic assets in such a way as to maximize its survivability.[159] Not surprisingly, the "Draft Report of [the] National Security Advisory Board on Indian Nuclear Doctrine" affirmed that India's nuclear forces "will be based on a triad of aircraft, mobile land-based missiles and sea-based assets" in order

---

[158]Sidhu, "India Sees Safety in Nuclear Triad and Second Strike Potential," p. 23.

[159]See, for example, Subrahmanyam, "A Credible Deterrent."

that they may be "effective, enduring, diverse, flexible, and responsive to the requirements . . . of credible minimum deterrence."[160] The Indian Army's Training Command (ARTRAC) is believed to have issued a similar recommendation even before the Advisory Board released its Draft Report; arguing that the Indian deterrent ought to consist at least initially of "two legs of the triad, comprising warplanes capable of carrying nuclear weapons like the Sukhoi-30, the Mirage 2000 and land-based nuclear-tipped missiles,"[161] the ARTRAC report concluded that submarine-based systems should eventually be integrated into the deterrent force because of their high survivability in the face of even dense nuclear attacks that may be mounted by an adversary.

Despite the controversy that these recommendations have provoked in the West, the Indian government appears to have accepted the overall logic they embody—at least in principle. Foreign Minister Jaswant Singh for example—attempting to strike a balance between the technical demands associated with system survivability and the diplomatic imperatives of calming the political atmospherics—did not conclusively reject the notion of a strategic triad but merely hinted at its prematurity. Addressing this issue directly, he noted that

> It is a known fact that today India has nuclear-capable aircraft and mobile land-based nuclear-capable missiles. We have an R&D programme for a naval version of Prithvi that has been a part of the IGMDP [Integrated Guided Missile Development Program] launched in 1983. It is also a fact that many analysts, particularly in Western countries, consider nuclear missiles on submarines to be the most survivable nuclear asset in the scenarios that they have thought of—first strike, second strike, war and so on. Our approach is different. It is, therefore, premature to talk of an Indian "triad." R&D programmes will certainly continue, aimed at enhancing survivability and thus, credibility, but decisions on production, deployment, and employment will be taken on the basis of factors that I have outlined earlier. In short, just as parity is not essential for deterrence, neither is a triad a prerequisite for credibility. Let me

---

[160]"Draft Report of [the] National Security Advisory Board on Indian Nuclear Doctrine," p. 3.

[161]Srinjoy Chowdhury, "Army Moots Nuclear Triad," *The Statesman*, April 6, 1999.

suggest that you look at the Indian nuclear deterrent as a "triad" based on a different set of three dimensions—a deterrent that is minimum but credible because it is survivable and backed by effective civilian command and control to ensure retaliation.[162]

Irrespective of how the last sentence in this statement is evaluated, Singh's other conclusions with respect to the triad appear fairly straightforward. The government of India already possesses various land-based deterrent systems, however incipient they may be, and will pursue a sea-based deterrence option as part of its ongoing R&D efforts simply as a hedge against strategic uncertainty. The decision to *actually* deploy nuclear weapons at sea, however, will not be made before the associated basing technologies are judged to be mature, and even then only if the threat environment India faces is seen to impose burdens of the sort that cannot be neutralized through land-based solutions alone. Indian security managers clearly recognize that sea-based nuclear capabilities hold the potential to radically transform the nature of their desired force-in-being, and while they hope to defer institutionalizing such solutions until it becomes truly necessary to do so, they also recognize that prudence requires them to investigate all such possibilities in the event that the strategic environment deteriorates to the point where they are left with no other satisfactory alternative. The current R&D efforts connected with the sea-based arm thus remain another example of how the Indian state is attempting to hedge its bets—but because of the powerful technologies involved, these efforts have given rise to the widespread yet mistaken belief that an Indian nuclear "triad" is all but imminent.[163]

A closer look at India's capabilities, however, suggests that at the moment New Delhi possesses at best a monadic delivery force consisting of relatively short-range tactical strike aircraft like the Jaguar, Mirage 2000, Mig-27, and Su-30MK. None of these platforms has been designed for the conduct of all-weather strike operations, and consequently attack missions carried out in other than daylight conditions would require high pilot skill, ingenious mission planning, and favorable environmental factors for their success. More-

---

[162]"India Not to Engage in a N-Arms Race: Jaswant."

[163]For a good example of such claims, see Badri-Maharaj, "Nuclear India's Status," pp. 124–128, and Chengappa, *Weapons of Peace*, pp. 425–438.

over, if Indian press reports are to be believed, these delivery systems are still more notional than real: These platforms were originally acquired for conventional strike operations, and although they could by that very fact be reconfigured to carry nuclear weapons, several Indian press reports have claimed that no evidence exists that any airframes have yet been modified for the conduct of nuclear operations. This situation caused one Indian analyst to lament that

> five months after India exploded five nuclear devices in May 1998, the Indian Air Force is nowhere near becoming nuclear capable. None of the IAF's approximately 17 strike squadrons have been earmarked for carrying out a nuclear strike. Nor has a training doctrine been formulated, or any of the aircraft been 'hardwired' for delivering nuclear bombs. . . . [164]

While India's tactical strike aircraft no doubt possess the potential to serve as nuclear delivery vehicles, this potential—which is inherent in almost all modern attack aircraft—must not be confused with the existence of a true delivery system. As one Indian source correctly noted, "In theory, we can carry a free fall nuclear bomb. But we have yet to earmark a squadron, an aircraft, or formulate a training doctrine for our pilots."[165]

By itself, this lack of public preparation should not be surprising in that New Delhi does not believe that transparent evidence of ready delivery capabilities is necessary for Indian security at present. This lack of transparency often leads many analysts to presume that no Indian nuclear delivery capabilities currently exist because it is usually—and incorrectly—assumed that India's claims to nuclear status must imply that the country is inexorably headed toward the development of a ready arsenal rather than simply a force-in-being.[166] Because the latter objective represents the real terminus of Indian policy at least in the policy-relevant future, it is almost certain that New Delhi has already configured a small contingent of nuclear-capable strike aircraft that, being dual-capable platforms, are de-

---

[164]Kumar, "IAF Still Lacks N-Capability."

[165]Ibid.

[166]Rahul Bedi, "India's Nuclear Prowess Remains on Paper, Official Rhetoric," *Asian Age*, November 8, 2000.

ployed without any fanfare and in exactly the same fashion as all the other conventional strike aircraft in the Air Force's inventory.[167] Several Indian reports have in fact described how their Air Force began practicing nuclear toss-bombing techniques as early as 1988,[168] and hence it is not unreasonable to presume that India had at this point equipped a small contingent of conventional strike platforms for nuclear missions—especially after the 1990 crisis, when the government of India had to face up to Pakistan's transformation into a true nuclear power.[169] The formal claims to nuclear status advanced after the May 1998 tests imply that the process of further modifying air-breathing platforms for nuclear operations will only continue— but like everything else associated with the evolving deterrent, these developments will transpire secretly and at a much slower pace than unofficial Indian commentators would desire.

This fact—which is based on the accurate official judgment that India is unlikely to require a hyper-ready nuclear force in the near future—should give reason for pause when Indian claims about being a powerful nuclear weapon state are aired too carelessly. The desire to become a more capable nuclear weapon state in the future, however, will force New Delhi in the direction of developing a variety of delivery systems, although it is likely that for at least several more years (and perhaps a decade) India's strike capabilities will continue to reside primarily in its short-legged air-breathing platforms. This near-term focus on air-delivered weaponry stems directly from the fact that India's nuclear weapons today are most easily configured as gravity bombs to be carried by the various aircraft already in its possession (though these obviously would need specific modifications if they are to deliver nuclear weapons effectively). The kinds of aircraft chosen for this mission and the strengths and weaknesses of these platforms thus assume particular importance from the perspective of ensuring adequate deterrence.

While many aircraft in the Indian inventory could in theory be configured to carry a nuclear bomb, the platforms that become most

---

[167] See the discussion in Perkovich, *India's Nuclear Bomb*, p. 295.

[168] Sawhney, "To Test or Not to Test: The Challenge for India's Nuclear Credibility," p. 32.

[169] See the discussion in Chengappa, *Weapons of Peace*, pp. 382–384.

relevant to the nuclear delivery mission are those possessing at least the following attributes: (1) they have adequate navigation capabilities and avionics that allow them both to reach their intended targets in a variety of weather conditions and to deliver their air-to-surface ordnance relatively accurately; (2) they have at least one ordnance station stressed to carry loads in excess of 1000 kg while also possessing sufficient ground clearances to allow for safe carriage of the weapon itself; (3) they are equipped with two engines, if for no other reason than to enhance survivability in combat; (4) they are capable of carrying both defensive weaponry and electronic countermeasures (ECM) equipment (in addition to their nuclear payloads) in order to ensure relatively safe transit to their payload release points; and (5) they possess the requisite operating range to bring them within reach of those targets designated by the national command authority.[170] When measured by such criteria, no aircraft currently in the Indian Air Force inventory is ideally suited to the nuclear delivery role, since the service never acquired a true theater bomber that possessed long range; was capable of carrying heavy payloads; was equipped with advanced navigation and avionics systems that allowed for all-weather operations, especially at low altitudes, without compromising aircraft safety, positional accuracy, and effective weapon delivery; and hosted sophisticated electronic penetration aids to increase platform survivability during both transit and attack. To be sure, many aircraft possessing all these attributes—for example, the Su-24 Fencer—existed in the Soviet arsenal, but the Indian Air Force, for a variety of political, financial, and doctrinal reasons, remained unequipped with any long-range strike platforms. As one respected commentator noted, "It is surprising that the [Su-24 Fencer] aircraft was never acquired by the Indian air force in the late 1980s. The aircraft could have easily struck targets throughout Pakistan and into invasion routes in Tibet and southern China, but the air force continued to soldier on with its remaining Canberras for this mission."[171] The decision not to acquire a modern theater bomber

---

[170]For a good analysis of the desirable characteristics of nuclear-capable strategic aircraft during the Cold War—in contrast to these characteristics in the South Asian context—see Alton H. Quanbeck and Archie L. Wood, *Modernizing the Strategic Bomber Force: Why and How* (Washington, D.C.: Brookings, 1976).

[171]Keith Jacobs, "Heavy Attack Aircraft," *Indian Defence Review*, 13:1 (January–March 1998), p. 75.

like the Soviet Su-24 or the Western Tornado has therefore left India with only four tactical platforms that are relevant to the nuclear delivery mission: the Jaguar, the Mirage 2000, the Mig-27, and the Su-30MK. Yet none of these aircraft is ideal for the role, and of the quartet, perhaps only two—the Jaguar and the Mirage 2000—are currently capable of performing the nuclear strike mission with a reasonable chance of success.[172]

All four platforms must nonetheless be considered candidates for the nuclear strike mission simply because, at least in the first instance, each of them possesses at least one weapon station that is stressed to carry loads of 1000 kg or greater. If it is assumed that India's nuclear weapons weigh in at some 1000 kg (a not-unreasonable assumption for first-generation devices), it becomes obvious that the Mig-27 is the least capable platform in this regard, since it has only one centerline station (which also doubles as a wet station) capable of accommodating 1000-kg loads. The Su-30MK, in contrast, has at least two pylons capable of carrying 1000-kg-class loads, while the Jaguar and the Mirage 2000 each have two pylons capable of carrying 1134- and 1800-kg loads, respectively. On the basis of load-carrying capabilities alone, therefore, the Su-30MK, the Jaguar, and the Mirage 2000 turn out to be superior to the Mig-27. This superiority is further enhanced when the combat radius of each of these aircraft is considered. Calculating the combat radius of any aircraft is a challenging exercise because the problem admits to no unique solution.[173] The attainable combat radius on any mission depends on the aircraft's fuel capacity, the efficiency of its engine, the takeoff weight (including the weight and even the aerodynamic shape of its payload), the flight profile, atmospheric conditions such as air pressure, wind speed, and temperature, the expected amount of combat time, and the level of fuel reserves desired upon recovery. Attempting to

---

[172]All data on aircraft in this section, except when specifically referenced, are derived from Paul Jackson (ed.), *Jane's All the World's Aircraft, 1998–99* (Coulsdon, UK: Jane's Information Group Ltd., 1998); Bill Gunston and Mike Spick, *Modern Air Combat* (New York: Crescent Books, 1983); and David Donald and Jon Lake (eds.), *Encyclopedia of World Military Aircraft*, Vols. I and II (Westport, CT: AIRtime Publishers, 1994).

[173]See the discussion in R. D. Shaver, *Range Enhancement Equations for Various Refueling Options*, N-1872-AF (Santa Monica: RAND, 1982), and in William Stanley and Gary Liberson, *Measuring Effects of Payload and Range Differences of Fighter Aircraft*, DB-102-AF (Santa Monica: RAND, 1993).

calculate the "true" combat radius of any aircraft can thus be seen to be a frustrating activity—and therefore the following analysis, which reproduces certain published data in order to support a rough comparison among the various aircraft identified above, must be treated as indicative rather than determinative of the mission radii that may actually be obtained in combat.

All comparisons of combat radii must also be sensitive to operational context. Since New Delhi is likely to authorize nuclear retaliatory missions only after absorbing an adversary's first strike—a response consistent with the Indian doctrine of no first use—the Indian Air Force will have to execute its reprisal operations in the face of fully alerted air defense systems maintained by the adversary. If nuclear use against Pakistan occurs at the later stages of a conventional conflict, it is likely that the Pakistani air defense net will be all but decimated by that point. Consequently, the Indian Air Force will enjoy full operational freedom of action where its nuclear missions are concerned.[174] The same conditions, however, are unlikely to obtain vis-à-vis China because irrespective of the scope or length of a conventional Sino-Indian conflict, Chinese air defense systems are likely to remain relatively unimpaired, especially along the approaches to key high-value targets. These targets, being far from the Himalayan border, will probably remain immune to any Suppression of Enemy Air Defense (SEAD) operations that may be conducted by the Indian Air Force. Consequently, nuclear operations against China will have to be conducted in the face of relatively coherent and responsive air defenses—in contrast to operations against Pakistan, which may take place in a more favorable combat environment.[175]

---

[174]For a good discussion on Pakistan's air defense capabilities and the character of the Indian air threat, see Pushpindar Singh, Ravi Rikhye, and Peter Steinemann, *Fiza'ya* (New Delhi: Society for Aerospace Studies, 1991), pp. 95–112 and 152–186, and Ashley J. Tellis, "Hawkeyes for Pakistan: Rationale and Logic of the E-2C Request," *Journal of South Asian and Middle Eastern Studies*, 10:1 (Fall 1986), pp. 36–66.

[175]The key variable that determines the ease with which Indian nuclear missions may be undertaken vis-à-vis Pakistan is the length and intensity of a conventional war prior to the point of nuclear use. A long and intense war would ensure that Pakistani air defenses are sufficiently attrited that even weak Indian penetrations would effectively go unhindered. In contrast, a short war—or even a conflict that resulted in early nuclear use—would impose great burdens on the Indian Air Force's ability to penetrate Pakistani airspace; although this objective could no doubt be achieved, the costs and complexity of assuring such penetration would increase greatly. This has less to do with the thinness of Islamabad's surface-to-air defenses than it does with Pak-

Since penetrating such alerted and perhaps unimpaired air defense systems is best done—all other things being equal—by flying lo-lo-lo profiles in order to exploit the limitations of terrestrial radars, the comparisons adduced below emphasize only this kind of flight regime—although whenever data are available, the aircraft in question are presumed to carry external fuel in addition to their nuclear, defensive weaponry, and ECM payloads. Assessing the capabilities of Indian aircraft in this flight regime alone is particularly appropriate because it allows for an assessment of aircraft quality in the most demanding nuclear operations imaginable—vis-à-vis China—without prejudicing their effectiveness against smaller and weaker adversaries such as Pakistan.[176]

When the operational radius of India's tactical aircraft is considered in the context of the lo-lo-lo flight regime, the superiority of the Mirage 2000 and the Jaguar over both the Mig-27 and the Su-30MK becomes amply evident. The Mig-27, which is a single-engine aircraft, is estimated to possess a combat radius of some 225 km, with 7 percent of its fuel held in reserve. If this radius is reduced by 20 percent to allow for the "dog legs" associated with operational routing, the radius of the Mig-27 drops to about 180 km. With external fuel, this figure could rise to as much as 430 km, but this configuration usually does not allow the aircraft to carry any external penetration aids or defensive weaponry. In effect, the aircraft thus would be "naked" except for its nuclear payload if such levels of operational reach were sought. The generally small operational radius of the Mig-27, usually classified as being in the basic 200- to 250-km class, is understandable, given that the aircraft was primarily designed as a simple platform for close air support/battlefield air interdiction

---

istan's geophysical compactness, the readiness levels and relative quality of its air force, and the effectiveness of its Air Defense Command. Given these facts, it is not at all clear, for example, whether the Indian nuclear strike package that was assembled during the Kargil crisis—described in Chengappa, *Weapons of Peace*, p. 437ff—could actually have penetrated Pakistani airspace to successfully deliver its nuclear weapons if it had to prosecute such a singular mission in the absence of a generalized, high-intensity conventional air war.

[176]For more on this flight regime and on the challenges of penetration in general, see J. R. Walker, *Air-to-Ground Operations* (London: Brassey's, 1987), pp. 35–65.

(CAS/BAI) operations rather than as a sophisticated weapon carrier for deep penetration missions at the theater level.[177]

The Su-30MK, recently acquired by India, exhibits a larger operational radius than the Mig-27.[178] Although no detailed performance figures have been released for this model, the MK version is for all practical purposes an Su-27PU (which in turn was converted from an Su-27UB) at least as far as its fuel system is concerned. If the low-altitude radius of action of the Su-27 "Flanker B" is any indication, the Su-30MK may be presumed to have an operational radius not much greater than the 420 km attributed to the "Flanker B."[179] One Indian analyst has claimed that "the Su-30 has a strike range of 5000 km with in-flight refueling,"[180] while another more credible source has described it as possessing a low-altitude range of 1390 km—implying thereby that its mission radius would be almost 700 km.[181] Unfortunately, this estimate, which was presumably supplied by the Sukhoi Design Bureau, does not describe the flight profile used to generate these figures—and thus, as one respected aviation analyst cautioned, "all of the specifications . . . [relating to the Su-27] . . . should be treated with some caution [because] Sukhoi has released widely differing performance figures on different occasions (and even releases different dimensions for the same aircraft), while rarely specifying the loads carried for particular range or performance figures."[182] From all that is known in the West about this aircraft, such figures

---

[177]Donald and Lake (eds.), *Encyclopedia of World Military Aircraft*, Vol. II, pp. 304–305.

[178]The Su-30MKs the Indian Air Force currently possesses will eventually be replaced by the Su-30MKI, which is expected to feature different design characteristics, advanced avionics, and possibly greater endurance. Since the Su-30MKI does not currently exist in its final configuration, the discussion here refers primarily to the Su-30MK model unless specified otherwise. Despite extravagant claims made by both Russia and India, the eventual specifications of the Su-30MKI remain uncertain, as do the timetables for delivery. See Fred Weir, "Can Russia Deliver on Arms Sales?" *Christian Science Monitor*, November 29, 2000.

[179]Jon Lake, "Sukhoi Su-27 Variant Briefing, Part 1," *World Air Power Journal*, 28 (Spring 1997), pp. 117–119.

[180]Rahul Bedi, "Tests Give Impetus to Agni Missile," *Jane's Defence Weekly*, May 20, 1998.

[181]"From Su-27 to Su-37: The Plane with Many Masks," *Vayu 2000 Aerospace Review*, III/1997, pp. 43–45.

[182]Lake, "Sukhoi Su-27 Variant Briefing, Part 1," p. 119.

appear to represent the high end of the aircraft's performance capabilities in the low-altitude regime. The operational radius of the MK in a consistently lo-lo-lo flight regime is likely to be closer to 500 than to 700 km, but even if both figures are accepted as a range for purposes of analysis, the effective radius drops down to roughly 400–560 km when the 20 percent margin for dog legs is factored into the calculation.[183]

This relatively low figure for the twin-engine Su-30MK in the lo-lo-lo profile might appear surprising at first sight given the aircraft's general reputation for endurance and for its ability to operate at extended distances. The Su-30MK does in fact possess all these attributes—but mainly when operating at medium to high altitudes and when employed in air superiority as opposed to surface strike missions. Overlooking this fact, some Indian analysts have mistakenly presumed that this aircraft embodies truly deep-penetration capabilities of the sort that bequeath to it "the range to cover most of China" and "deliver a nuclear payload deep into Chin[ese territory]."[184] Such conclusions appear to be justified on the presumption that the Su-30MK is in fact capable of attaining operational radii exceeding 1250–1500 km in the context of antisurface missions,[185] but these performance figures are simply illusory if a lo-lo-lo flight profile is desired. This is because the twin engines of the Su-30 rapidly lose efficiency when the aircraft operates at low altitudes, and while the avionics of the MK version have been modified for the air-to-surface role (while still retaining their original proficiency in the air-to-air mission), its airframe and engines are simply not optimized for long range while employed in the nap-of-the-earth flight regime.[186]

---

[183] Ibid. Lake notes that the Su-27 is capable of a 420-km low-altitude radius of action rising to 1090 km at high altitude.

[184] Sidhu, "India Sees Safety in Nuclear Triad and Second Strike Potential," p. 24.

[185] Bajpai, "The Fallacy of an Indian Deterrent," p. 164.

[186] As Jon Lake notes, in designing the Su-27 aircraft, "Sukhoi worked towards meeting a low-level radius of action requirement of 500 km (310 miles) (inferring a low-level range of at least 1200–1400 km/745–870 miles) and a high-level radius of 1700 km (1050 miles) (with a range of 4000 km/2485 miles)." Lake, "Sukhoi Su-27 Variant Briefing, Part 1," p. 103.

To be sure, the range limitations of the Su-30MK can be circumvented by air-to-air refueling, but because such operations cannot be carried out over enemy territory, air refueling can only marginally increase the aircraft's operational radius in the lo-lo-lo strike mission. In the specific operational circumstances India faces—where the aircraft's launch bases are generally close to the international border—the ability to carry additional fuel in external tanks would have been far more useful for purposes of extending the Su-30MK's operating radius. The original Soviet design, however, settled for air-to-air refueling rather than external fuel tanks as a means of extending its range and endurance. This solution made perfect sense in the context of Soviet needs, which centered primarily on sustaining extended air patrols over its vast remote borders. In such operations, air-to-air refueling conducted in domestic airspace provided an apt means of increasing mission radius and loiter time.[187] Since deep penetration into hostile territory was not at issue—as would be the case if New Delhi employed its Su-30MKs for nuclear strikes—the solution embodied by air-to-air refueling is less than perfect where India's operational needs are concerned. When India acquires dedicated airborne tankers (as it will over the next decade), the ability to refuel its Su-30MKs will certainly bring many advantages, but these will be realized mostly in terms of increased flexibility rather than in terms of increased range. The ability to engage in air-to-air refueling will allow India's Su-30s to be based deep in the rear, where they are likely to be less vulnerable to attacks, especially those mounted by Pakistan. From such rearward bases, the Su-30s can stage out to forward locations as required or even embark on some kinds of attack operations, refueling en route in Indian airspace whenever necessary. This solution, however, provides only minimal advantages vis-à-vis China, because the distances from the Indian border to the most attractive Chinese targets are so vast that even multiple air-to-air refuelings over Indian airspace would add little to the Su-30's operational radius when employed in a lo-lo-lo attack regime.[188]

---

[187]"Sukhoi Su-27," in Paul Jackson (ed.), *Jane's All the World's Aircraft, 1998–99* (Coulsdon, UK: Jane's Information Group Ltd., 1998), pp. 422–425.

[188]The ability to refuel the Su-30MKs would be most valuable, however, in defensive counterair operations along the border or where long-endurance combat air patrol (CAP) is required. Where nuclear strike missions vis-à-vis China are concerned, however, the operational radius of the aircraft can obviously be extended by altering its flight profile—for example, by undertaking some legs of the mission at high altitude

On balance, then, neither the Mig-27 nor the Su-30 is likely to be chosen as India's primary nuclear delivery platform. While both aircraft have pylons capable of carrying stores of some 1000 kg, the platforms themselves are unfortunately too limited in range to be able to carry such payloads to the desired distances. This is certainly true where Indian nuclear operations against China are concerned, but it may also be true against Pakistan in some exceptional circumstances. The Mig-27 in this context also has the additional disadvantage of being payload limited and, unlike the Su-30, carries little defensive armament and relatively poor penetration aids. The advantages of the Su-30 are clearest here: Being a more modern airplane, it is equipped with newer avionics (including many French and Israeli subsystems in the MKI). These include a new Russian multimode radar, guidance systems for TV-command weapons, anti-radiation missiles, assorted air-to-surface weaponry, and independent laser designation capabilities in addition to electronic support measure (ESM) systems and various types of within-visual-range and beyond-visual-range air-to-air missilery. Yet, as impressive as these capabilities may be, they are nonetheless most useful for short-range conventional strikes rather than for long-range nuclear delivery missions.[189]

Among the systems most valuable for the latter task would be a terrain-following radar that allows the aircraft to fly true nap-of-the-earth flight profiles, especially during ingress; an integrated forward-looking infrared capability; active ECM pods; and, of course, the ability to accept external fuel tanks of various sizes. The Russians have developed two Su-27 variants—the Su-34 and the Su-35[190]—with just such attributes, but the MKs currently being inducted into the Indian Air Force are not equipped with these or any of the other capabilities integral to the newest generation of Russian deep penetrators. Only

---

either en route to the target or during the return home. The ability to sustain such profiles, however, would be determined by the character of the air defense systems in the Chinese southwest during a conflict. In general, planning for such profiles could levy increased risk to the aircraft, and given the vast size of the Chinese landmass, they may not provide substantially increased reach with respect to the critical targets presumably of interest to India.

[189]For details, see "Sukhoi Su-30M," in Paul Jackson (ed.), *Jane's All the World's Aircraft, 1998–99* (Coulsdon, UK: Jane's Information Group Ltd., 1998), p. 428.

[190]See Lake, "Sukhoi Su-27 Variant Briefing, Part 1," pp. 129–135.

time will tell whether the late-series MKI airframes will be equipped with some of these new capabilities, but at the moment all the evidence suggests that despite its acquisition of some new types of Russian air-to-surface weapons, India intends to use its early Su-30MKs primarily for air superiority rather than for deep penetration missions.[191] The aircraft's secondary air-to-surface attack capabilities will no doubt contribute to making the MK a useful conventional attack platform, particularly in support of the offensive counterair doctrine the Indian Air Force plans to employ against Pakistan[192]—and by virtue of that fact, India is likely to treat the aircraft as a candidate system that can be configured for nuclear delivery *in extremis.* But for all its virtues and despite some Indian claims to the contrary,[193] the Su-30MKI is unlikely to become the primary nuclear delivery vehicle of the Indian Air Force in the near future.

In contrast to the Russian airplanes, the Mirage 2000 and the Jaguar seem better suited to the nuclear delivery role. Both aircraft have operational radii of more than 900 km in the lo-lo-lo strike regime when equipped with external tanks. Allowing for dog legs, this figure drops to some 740 km, although the actual combat radius will of course vary depending on the flight profiles flown and the combination of fuel tanks and nuclear ordnance carried by any given airplane. The Mirage 2000 in particular would benefit where both range and mission flexibility are concerned because of its ability to engage in air-to-air refueling. Both aircraft have at least three hard points capable of carrying loads in excess of 1000 kg, and both have the requisite ground clearances to carry nuclear weapons of the sort India is thought to possess. The Jaguar, some Indian assertions notwithstanding, is in fact particularly well suited as far as ground

---

[191]This judgment is based on the air defense livery of the new aircraft; the fact that the squadron (Squadron Number 24) reequipping with the Su-30s earlier flew the Mig-21 *bis* in the air defense role; and the fact that the training regime at least of the early Su-30s already in Indian Air Force employ has emphasized air defense operations rather than long-range ground attack.

[192]For details about the Indian Air Force's evolving offensive counterair doctrine vis-à-vis Pakistan, see Ashley J. Tellis, "The Air Balance in the Indian Subcontinent: Trends, Constants, Contexts," *Defense Analysis*, 2:4 (Winter 1986), pp. 263–289, and Pravin Sawhney, "India's First Airpower Doctrine Takes Shape: An Aging Air Force Looks to the Future," *Jane's International Defence Review*, 30:6 (1997), pp. 33–38.

[193]See N. K. Pant, "SU-30s: Strategic Take-off into Next Century," available at http://www.ipcs.org/issues/articles/286-mi-pant.html.

clearances are concerned, and one analysis has noted how the undercarriage legs "sit the aircraft very much higher on the ground than one expects of aircraft of this size."[194] Both aircraft clearly are excellent platforms for the surface attack mission as well. The Jaguar was designed from the ground up as a dedicated tactical strike aircraft, and its airframe, engines, and flight controls were optimized for high performance at low altitudes. The Mirage 2000, in contrast, is a true multirole fighter that, although initially designed for proficiency in the air combat mission, can effectively prosecute the surface attack mission because its fly-by-wire controls and small canard-type foreplanes on the air intake trunks allow it to secure all the advantages of a delta planform—high fuel storage, low drag, increased maneuverability, fewer control surfaces, and decreased radar detectability—while minimizing most of the instabilities that arise when the aircraft carries a large quantity of external stores during low-altitude missions.[195]

While both the Jaguar and the Mirage 2000 thus share one characteristic—their ability to carry out effective low-level attacks with relatively heavy payloads—the two airplanes differ in many other respects. The Jaguar, for example, is an older platform, but with two engines it is rugged and has an operational reliability that makes it particularly useful for high-value missions like nuclear delivery. Unfortunately, it has only modest defensive weaponry, and although it possesses both active and passive ECM suites, these capabilities are of uncertain quality. Its most critical weakness, however, lies in both the lack of a terrain-following radar, which limits its ability to fly true ground-hugging profiles, and the lack of integrated night and adverse-weather capabilities. If the aircraft does reach its target unmolested and the environmental circumstances permit adequate target sighting, the Display Attack and Ranging Inertial Navigation (DARIN) nav-attack system provides excellent weapon release solutions for accurate delivery. However, its lack of a terrain-following radar, night and adverse-weather capabilities, adequate defensive weaponry, and sophisticated ECM capabilities implies that any nuclear delivery mission the Jaguar undertakes would require a signifi-

---

[194]Arthur Reed, *Sepecat Jaguar* (London: Ian Allan, 1982), p. 101.

[195]For details, see Paul A. Jackson, *Mirage* (Shepperton, UK: Ian Allan, 1985), pp. 99–115.

cant strike package with several other aircraft flying escort and sweep missions to allow the nuclear platform unimpeded ingress and safe delivery of its ordnance.[196]

Despite its limitation of being a single-engine aircraft, the Mirage 2000 has several advantages here. It has a formidable suite of defensive weaponry, excellent ESM/ECM systems, and a superior multimode radar that provides high performance in both air-to-air and air-to-surface regimes simultaneously. If equipped with the Litening II pod, the aircraft would also acquire a formidable night and adverse-weather deep penetration capability that promises to be far more effective than the Litening laser designation pods currently in service with the Indian Air Force.[197] Although early aircraft acquired by New Delhi were usually seen in the livery associated with air-to-air combat, India has begun to experiment with Mirage 2000s in the surface attack role. It has been reported, for example, that some platforms have been equipped with the French Antilope 5 terrain-following radar, twin inertial navigation systems, and reinforced radomes, thus optimizing them for accurate nap-of-the-earth penetration and attack.[198] If so equipped, the Mirage 2000 would be an excellent platform for nuclear delivery missions carried out independently or with very small strike packages. So long as the con-

---

[196]India's newest Jaguars are expected to be retrofitted with an El-Op head-up display (HUD) with an up-front camera, a Sextant MFD 66 active-matrix moving-map liquid crystal display, digital terrain-map generator, a multichannel digital video color recorder, a ring-laser gyro-based inertial navigation system (INS-RLG) with GPS, a multimode mission computer, an ELTA-built airborne self-protection jammer, an indigenous radar warning receiver (RWR), and wiring for carrying the Litening laser designation pod. The Sextant is also expected to upgrade the autopilot system. See "SPECAT/HAL Jaguar," available at http://www.bharat-rakshak.com/IAF/Info/Specs-Combat.html#SEPECAT%20Jaguar. If these modifications are in fact incorporated, many of the aircraft's current limitations will disappear and the Jaguar could become a critical component of India's nuclear delivery force. Raj Chengappa claims, however, that the Indian Air Force examined and ultimately rejected the Jaguar as India's principal delivery platform, allegedly because the aircraft lacked the clearance to carry the country's gravity bombs. See Chengappa, *Weapons of Peace*, p. 327ff. If this information is accurate, then at least the aeroshell of India's fission weapon may have to be redesigned if the new capabilities of the aircraft are to be exploited.

[197]The superiority of the Litening II over both the Litening I and other systems like LANTIRN is described in William B. Scott, "New Targeting Pods Deliver 'Litening Strikes,'" *Aviation Week & Space Technology*, August 21, 2000, pp. 56–60.

[198]"Dassault Mirage 2000," in Paul Jackson (ed.), *Jane's All the World's Aircraft, 1998–99* (Coulsdon, UK: Jane's Information Group Ltd., 1998), p. 104.

straints imposed by a single engine are accepted—presumably because of the high quality of the M53-P2 engine—the aircraft's superior mission radius, avionics, defensive weaponry, and countermeasure systems, would make it the best platform India currently has (and it has most likely already modified) for the nuclear mission.[199]

This conclusion does not in any way undercut the broader judgment that India's current delivery vehicles, which consist principally of tactical strike aircraft, are still compromised, since these vehicles were neither designed nor acquired principally for delivering nuclear weapons at long ranges from their home bases. Even the Mirage 2000, which is the most sophisticated of the two platforms capable of decent mission radii in the lo-lo-lo strike regime, has only a single engine and may not possess the integrated terrain-following and night-vision systems that could become essential for safe penetration and effective egress. Obviously, such capabilities may or may not be relevant depending on the operational and physical environments surrounding India's decision to use its nuclear weapons, but they do imply that each of India's candidate platforms has some handicap that would prevent it from functioning effectively as a nuclear delivery system under the widest possible range of operating conditions. As the analysis above suggests, there is at present no single aircraft that offers all the following attributes: twin engines; integrated terrain-following radars and/or infrared navigation and targeting systems allowing for "blind" night and all-weather attack operations; single-point load-carrying capabilities in excess of 1000 kg with sufficient ground clearance; adequate defensive weaponry and sophisticated ECM equipment; and long mission radii that allow for deep theater reach. Because of this, India will be forced to make do with the aircraft inventory it possesses, at least in the near term, if it is serious about developing its nuclear deterrent even as a force-in-being.

What Will India Do? Over the next few years, India will most likely continue to do what it has probably done since the late 1980s to early 1990s: incrementally improve one or two of the four candidate systems examined above—probably the Mirage 2000 (with the Jaguar as backup)—in order to prepare a small number of aircraft for the nu-

---

[199]Chengappa, *Weapons of Peace*, pp. 382–384.

clear delivery mission while continuing to marginally expand the size of its inventory to maintain the minimum force size necessary in the face of peacetime attrition. At the very least, this continuing process of preparation will include modifying one or more stressed hard points on the fuselage to secure the nuclear weapon physically; adapting the cockpit controls to allow for remote arming of the weapon by the pilot at some point en route to the target; modifying the software controlling the ranging and weapons-aiming computers to enable the safe and effective release of a nuclear weapon of specified weight and yield; and integrating better navigation, targeting, ECM systems, and air defense weapons to increase the platform's survivability and penetrativity. The process of selecting a given aircraft and modifying the umbilicals and interfaces appropriately for the nuclear mission has traditionally been a DRDO task that has been and will continue to be undertaken in cooperation with the DAE and a small number of individuals associated with the Air Force.[200] This cooperative endeavor will continue covertly and without fanfare so long as the relevant nuclear-capable airframes remain in active service; there is some likelihood that India's nuclear weapons will change in physical configuration; and both the DRDO and the DAE continue to share custodial responsibilities over the nuclear warheads themselves. This ongoing effort at configuring and maintaining India's tactical strike aircraft for nuclear missions, like all the other activities connected with India's nuclear weapon program, will thus remain both low-key and highly secretive. Even the *institutional* participation of the Air Force in this endeavor has thus far been and will continue to be kept to a minimum: A few senior Air Force commanders, including the Chief of Air Staff, the Deputy/Assistant Chief of Staff (Operations), and possibly one or more AOCs-in-C with small groups of selected staff will continue their task of selecting certain aircraft, squadrons, pilots, and maintenance crews for "conversion," training, and operations in the nuclear role, with the rest of the force

---

[200]For details on how this process was carried out historically, and especially the crucial roles of the Aircraft System and Testing Establishment (ASTE) and the Armament Research and Development Establishment (ARDE), see Chengappa, *Weapons of Peace*, pp. 326ff, 359ff, and 382ff.

deliberately excluded from information about, and participation in, this effort.[201]

Irrespective of how this process unfolds, it is unlikely that India will announce any details pertaining to these activities; nor is it likely to identify the type of aircraft or the units selected for this mission. The relatively small size of the Indian deterrent—even when the force-in-being is finally completed—will make Indian policymakers acutely sensitive to the need for complete opacity, since the survival of their modest air-breathing capabilities hinges on the degree to which India's adversaries remain uncertain about the types and numbers of aircraft constituting its nuclear-capable force; the exact location of their deployment in real time; and the possibility that additional airframes might be held in reserve and perhaps distributed in or periodically rotated to locations other than their normal bases. The uncertainty arising from this basic lack of information will only be supplemented by deliberate efforts at deception and denial, since New Delhi's primary objective in every instance will be to deny its potential adversaries—Pakistan and China—any information that might fuel their temptation to unleash a nuclear attack aimed at disarming India, especially in the context of a crisis.[202]

While India is thus likely to continue to maintain an air-breathing delivery force under conditions of great secrecy, it will probably undertake several initiatives over the next decade in order to sustain the ability of its aircraft to service the nuclear mission. First, India is

---

[201]The degree of compartmentation within a given military service in India is exemplary and can be explained not so much by the hierarchic structures command but rather by the patterns of institutional culture that obtain within the Indian military. The preparations for the Indian nuclear tests in May 1998 are a good example of how such compartmentation has worked in practice: The Army's engineer units, for example, which helped prepare the Pokhran test sites for the detonations, received their orders and completed their tasks unbeknownst to both other formations and all but a narrow and short chain of command. This compartmentation is unlikely to change even if the new unified command charged with overseeing India's strategic assets finally materializes.

[202]The "Draft Report of [the] National Security Advisory Board on Indian Nuclear Doctrine" affirms that "survivability of the forces will be enhanced by a combination of multiple redundant systems, mobility, dispersion and deception." See "Draft Report of [the] National Security Advisory Board on Indian Nuclear Doctrine," p. 3.

likely to contemplate selective upgrades to the aircraft it chooses for the nuclear delivery role. The Jaguar, the Mirage 2000, and the Su-30MK, for example, would profit immensely from the integration into their existing avionics systems of terrain-following radar, GPS navigation and night-vision flight and targeting equipment, and integrated countermeasure capabilities (including active jamming), and the Su-30MK would further benefit from being plumbed for the carriage of external fuel tanks of various sizes. These technologies, taken together, would improve both penetrativity and range—the principal challenges facing any aircraft delivery system—and consequently are likely to be acquired in the years ahead.[203] Associated with this effort although distinct from it would be the acquisition of a small number of specialized supporting aircraft. The Indian Air Force has already established a requirement for six to eight tanker aircraft that will probably be configured around the IL-76 airframe.[204] The service has also invested heavily in electronic warfare programs in recent years, and it is possible that a few older long-range aircraft such as the venerable Canberra might be converted to serve as specialized jamming platforms.[205] These platforms are likely to be complemented by the creation of some kind of SEAD capability, but whether this will consist of dedicated aircraft for the mission or simply the equipping of some modified attack aircraft with antiradiation missiles is still unclear.[206] These capabilities, acquired piecemeal from France, Russia, and Israel, are likely to surface publicly sometime over the next decade but may appear sooner if the air defense systems maintained by India's principal adversaries are seen as undergoing dramatic qualitative changes in the interim.

Second, India faces critical decisions with regard to the number of aircraft it seeks to modify for the nuclear delivery role. There are essentially two paradigms here, and depending on which is chosen, the

---

[203]See, for example, "IAF Jaguars to Get New Mission Computers," *Defence Systems Daily*, August 2, 2000.

[204]"Govt. to Purchase Tanker Planes," *The Hindu*, April 26, 2000.

[205]Rupak Chattopadhyay, "The Indian Air Force: Flying into the 21st Century," *Bharat Rakshak Monitor*, 3:1 (July–August 2000), available at http://www.bharat-rakshak.com/MONITOR/ISSUE3-1/rupak.html.

[206]See ibid. and Sanjay Badri-Maharaj, "World's Fourth Largest Air Force," *Indian Defence Review*, 14:4 (October–December 1999), pp. 113–123, for more details about these programs.

deployment and operating regimen of the entire nuclear-capable force would be modified. The first paradigm consists of configuring only a few aircraft from a given class for the nuclear mission and, in effect, treating these aircraft as "precious" strategic assets—thereby withholding them from conventional operations, isolating them from the rest of the force, and securing them in special sanctuaries. Alternatively, these specially configured aircraft, however few in number, could be commingled with conventional airframes and treated as just another strike platform for purposes of disguising their true identity. Opting for such a paradigm—which essentially represents the continuation of India's present posture—would be relatively inexpensive, since only a few aircraft would be reconfigured in this way. The loss of any such modified airframe however, even as a product of normal attrition, would result in a significant diminution of strike capability.

The second paradigm consequently takes exactly the opposite tack by requiring that an entire class of aircraft selected for the nuclear role be configured to carry both conventional and nuclear ordnance interchangeably. These aircraft would then be treated like any conventional instrument of combat. They would certainly be secured, as are all lethal military assets, but the loss of a few platforms either in training or through routine attrition would in no way diminish the retaliatory capability of the deterrent, because the wasted airframes could be readily replaced by any other aircraft of the class, all of which would be equally capable of executing the nuclear mission. While this paradigm allows for tremendous operational flexibility given that no special demands would be made on the movement or the deployment of a few critical airframes, it also entails relatively high costs because it would require that all aircraft of a particular type be modified for what is ordinarily a low-probability mission.

There are, of course, many variants on each of these two models, but depending on how close each variant is to one of the two polar cases described above, each involves different costs and provides different benefits. It is unclear at this point which paradigm India will opt for over the long term, but in the near future New Delhi will most likely continue with some variant of the first model—a paradigm that should satisfy India so long as Pakistan remains its most pressing nuclear threat. As the Indian nuclear deterrent distends over time to meet various contingencies involving China, however, some variant of the second paradigm might be operationalized, particularly if Beijing becomes an active and more powerful adversary than is currently the case and if the Indian defense budget increases substantially in real terms during this and the next decade. In the meantime, India will concentrate simply on maintaining the requisite number of nuclear delivery systems. It is therefore not surprising to find that New Delhi has focused considerable attention on procuring both new two-seat Jaguars[207] and additional Mirage 2000s, the latter clearly intended to augment its stable of specialized nuclear delivery platforms.[208]

Third, India is likely to slowly increase its investments in infrastructure to support the retaliatory capabilities its air-breathing systems embody. Since the Indian nuclear deterrent will be a rather small force even when it is finally mature, and because this force is doctrinally intended to service a retaliatory role alone, New Delhi will likely pay great heed to its combat aviation infrastructure in order to ensure the survivability of its nuclear aircraft and their ability to retaliate even after absorbing a nuclear attack. Simple antidotes like securing aircraft in hardened bunkers—a regimen already followed—could be supplemented by increasingly complex organizational solutions as the number of nuclear weapons, the number and accuracy of the delivery systems, and the yield of the weapons that can be carried to Indian targets increase over time. Since the peacetime locations of all Indian air bases are well known, as are the identities of the aircraft and squadrons deployed at these bases, future organizational remedies to the twin problems of increasing survivability and ensuring adequate retaliatory capacity could consist of developing more dispersal airfields; operationalizing idiosyncratic aircraft dispersal rou-

---

[207]Hirak Choudhuri, "Nuclear-Equipped Jaguars for IAF?" *The Statesman*, February 19, 1999.

[208]Rahul Bedi, "India Seeks Mirage 2000 Nuclear Squadron," *Asian Age*, August 29, 1999. India has also announced that it will acquire four Tupolev-22M3 "Backfire" long-range bombers on lease from Russia. If and when acquired, these aircraft will constitute the first dedicated theater bombers in Indian military service. The range and sophistication of these aircraft would allow for complete coverage of both Pakistani and Chinese targets, but if Indian plans are to be believed, these aircraft are intended primarily for maritime interdiction and naval strike warfare rather than for the transcontinental nuclear attack mission. Whether India will maintain these aircraft as emergency operations–capable nuclear platforms remains to be seen. See Rezaul H. Laskar, "Navy to Get 4 Nuclear-Capable Bombers," *Asian Age*, February 14, 2000.

tines, particularly in a crisis; and preparing civilian and ancillary airfields with upgraded infrastructure, navigational equipment, and critical storage facilities to support dispersal, staging, or strike operations in an emergency.[209] The objective of all these solutions would be to complicate the nuclear targeting strategy that an adversary may develop over time while simultaneously attempting to ensure that certain critical facilities—i.e., those capable of supporting retaliatory strikes and lying within range of India's preferred targets—would survive any initial nuclear blows that might be mounted against New Delhi's force-in-being. Obviously, the need for such complex solutions is minimal today given Pakistan's relatively small nuclear arsenal and China's attention on areas other than its southwestern frontier. Should either of these two factors change significantly, however—as well they might over the next decade and beyond—the necessity for investing in more complex solutions to the problems of survivability would become readily apparent.[210]

Fourth and finally, India will continue to develop a range of delivery tactics that will be slowly codified, practiced, and disseminated throughout the nuclear-capable squadrons of the Indian Air Force. The need to systematize preparations for nuclear delivery missions simply did not exist so long as India's nuclear posture consisted of "keeping the option open." However, India's newfound desire to lay claim to being a nuclear weapon power has provided a structural opportunity for small planning arms deep inside Indian Air Force headquarters to contemplate a doctrine—in the strict Western sense of the term—relating to the conduct of nuclear missions.[211] Yet this

---

[209]If Chengappa is correct, these efforts have been under way since the early 1990s. See Chengappa, *Weapons of Peace*, pp. 355ff and 391ff.

[210]For an Indian Air Force viewpoint on this question, see B. D. Jayal, "India 2020: A Perspective on Air Power," *Indian Defence Review*, 13:4 (October–December 1998), pp. 19–25.

[211]In 1997, the Indian Air Force promulgated its first airpower doctrine that, because of its timing, focused entirely on conventional air operations. For details, see Sawhney, "India's First Airpower Doctrine Takes Shape: An Aging Air Force Looks to the Future." This effort has now extended to include planning for nuclear operations, but it is safe to say that, unlike the case of conventional planning, no document on this subject is likely to be released by the Indian Air Force any time soon. There have already been reports, however, that the Indian Air Force has finalized a nuclear doctrine in support of the country's larger deterrence strategy. One source has quoted the Indian Chief of Air Staff, Air Chief Marshal A. Y. Tipnis, as stating that "India is committed to a no-first-use policy for nuclear weapons. The only option then is to develop

doctrine is likely to evolve in a uniquely Indian fashion. Inasmuch as New Delhi's nuclear weapons are primarily political tools, for example, and as such are intended primarily to reassure the national leadership and deter their use by an adversary in a crisis, it is quite possible that the Indian Air Force planners and pilots tasked with developing such a doctrine may never be handed a real, complete Indian nuclear weapon! In any case, it is certainly unlikely that these "operators" would know much about the size, disposition, or locations of the nuclear stockpile writ large; instead, they are most likely to be either given dummy weapons or informed mainly about those critical weapon parameters that are necessary for the development of a viable doctrine, such as the shape, weight, and yield of the weapons and the general set of targets against which they are to be used.[212] Armed with this information and probably with a mockup of the weapon to validate aerodynamic effects, the Indian Air Force will be tasked with developing a nuclear delivery doctrine that, quite logically, is likely to be based on the offensive counterair doctrines already developed in the context of conventional warfare. Obviously, the precise maneuvering profiles of a nuclear delivery platform will vary greatly from those used in the discharge of conventional ordnance, but most other variables—such as the desired size and composition of the strike package, the route-planning factors, and the allocation of nontactical assets required for the success of the mission—would roughly approximate those already planned for India's conventional operations. Developing a doctrine for the delivery of nuclear weapons would be critical to the success of India's desired minimum deterrent, and hence it should not be surprising to find small groups of service planners tasked with developing, refining, and codifying this doctrine in preparation for what may ultimately be unit- and formation-size combat practice in the years ahead.[213]

---

a second strike capability. . . . How we will react, how we will operate (in the face of a nuclear threat or attack), that has been decided." See "IAF Draws Up Nuclear Strategy," *The Times of India*, October 8, 2000.

[212]For the historical record on this issue, the best source remains the descriptions at various points in Chengappa, *Weapons of Peace.*

[213]The Air Force traditionally sought full access and integration with the country's nuclear R&D efforts but according to the best histories of the Indian nuclear program was not granted such access. See Perkovich, *India's Nuclear Bomb*, pp. 296–297, and Chengappa, *Weapons of Peace*, p. 327. The current Air Force position on this issue is

Even when these initiatives are completed over the next decade, however, India's nuclear capabilities are likely to remain relatively limited as far as their strategic reach is concerned. As Maps 2–4 indicate, the air-breathing arm of the Indian nuclear force-in-being provides sufficient coverage against Pakistani targets but would be utterly incapable against China. Each of the maps provides a true measure of distance from the three representative air bases on which the equidistant azimuthal projections are centered: Ambala and Jodhpur in the west and Tezpur in the east. The range circles,

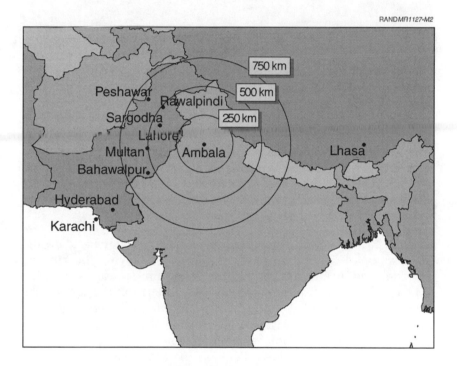

RAND*MR*1127-M2

Map 2—India's Strategic Reach from Ambala

---

described in Jayal, "India 2020: A Perspective on Air Power," pp. 19–25, and in Kak, "Command and Control of Small Nuclear Arsenals," pp. 266–285. Greater Air Force integration with future Indian nuclear R&D efforts, and with national strategic planning, is likely to occur, however, if the new unified command headed by a CDS finally materializes.

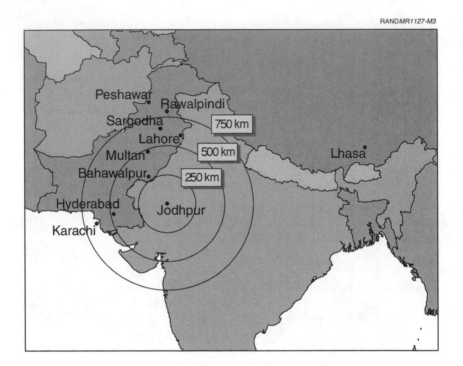

Map 3—India's Strategic Reach from Jodhpur

although based on the lo-lo-lo mission radii of the four candidate air-craft examined earlier, can also be read as displaying the kind of reach enjoyed by any aircraft capable of attaining these radii under combat conditions. Examined synoptically, the graphics suggest that any aircraft capable of a 750-km mission radius suffices to target every relevant section of Pakistan that would be of interest to an Indian force planner. These graphics may in fact *understate* the operational reach of the Indian Air Force because the relatively poor state of Pakistan's air defenses and the high attrition they may be expected to sustain within two weeks of conventional combat suggest that Indian attack squadrons, operating out of forward bases like Jodhpur and flying the hi-hi-lo profiles possible in a permissive air defense environment, would be able to range much farther afield and even strike targets deep into Baluchistan if necessary. In contrast, even lo-lo-lo profiles flown out of air bases like Ambala bring all of the critical

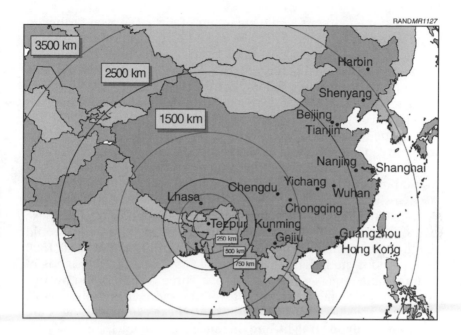

Map 4—India's Strategic Reach from Tezpur

targets in northern Pakistan within easy reach of India's air-breathing deterrent.[214]

The critical limitation, where the air-breathing force is concerned, is therefore not Pakistan but China. Map 4, with its equidistant azimuthal projection centered on Tezpur, clearly indicates that even the best Indian aircraft are probably ineffectual in this context, since the most lucrative Chinese targets lie much farther to the north and east of India's forward bases. This graphic may in fact *overstate* the reach of India's air-breathing deterrent, for even if it is assumed that

---

[214]This implies that even if Pakistan's air defense net is not sufficiently degraded, India's strike aircraft can reach every significant Pakistani target even when operating solely in lo-lo-lo flight profiles. Because such aircraft would probably be detected by the terminal radars at the end of their transit phase, they will probably require accompanying escort and electronic warfare packages to ensure unmolested delivery of their weapons, but at least the weapon carriers themselves will not be constrained by range limitations as they would be in the case of China.

nuclear-armed aircraft would stage out of air bases even farther to the northeast of Tezpur, like Chabua and Jorhat—clearly an impossibility if these airfields have been destroyed by prior Chinese attacks—the operational radius of India's air-breathing platforms does not improve appreciably so long as they are committed to a lo-lo-lo flight regime. Since it must be assumed that under conditions of conflict the Chinese Air Force would be fully alerted and would relocate many additional fighter squadrons, sensors, and air defene weaponry to the numerous reserve air bases in the Chengdu and the Lanzhou Military Regions,[215] the Indian Air Force's nuclear aircraft would probably have no choice but to fly lo-lo-lo profiles in order to survive their transit en route to Chinese targets. Map 4 clearly demonstrates that even the least attractive though nearest Chinese targets, such as Kunming, Chengdu, Chongqing, and Gejiu, would require aircraft that were capable of mission radii of at least 1500 km.[216] And if the Indian Air Force seeks to interdict other kinds of countervalue targets—like the massive Three Gorges Dam now under construction near Yichang—it would require an aircraft capable of at least a 2000-km mission radius. All these extended ranges are computed only in straight-line distances, not dog legs, and consequently the minimal effective operating radii necessary to interdict these targets would be even higher under combat conditions.

---

[215]Details about the Chinese Air Force and its peacetime basing patterns may be found in *International Air Forces and Military Aircraft Directory, 1991* (Essex, UK: Aviation Advisory Services, 1991). For Chinese airpower capabilities in general, see also John Wilson Lewis, "China's Search for a Modern Air Force," *International Security*, 24:1 (Summer 1999), pp. 64–94; Ken Gause, "PLAAF (People's Liberation Army Air Force) Continues to Modernise at a Slow yet Steady Pace," *Jane's Intelligence Review*, 10:6 (June 1998), pp. 38–43; and, Nick Cook, "Re-arming the Dragon: The New People's Liberation Army Air Force," *Interavia*, 51:604 (November 1996), pp. 31–32.

[216]The Su-30MK can attain such radii of action only if it is committed to a hi-hi-hi flight profile, clearly a risky operational regime if China deploys its Su-27/30 interceptors to the Chengdu and Lanzhou Military Regions in times of crisis. These aircraft are not currently based in either of these two military regions, but should China perceive the development of an aircraft-based nuclear threat from India over time, Beijing is likely to prepare for such deployments during an emergency. China already has standing plans that enable it to swing air defense forces from other military regions into southwestern China during any emergency. For a good description of how such a swing strategy was implemented in 1987, see Craig Covault, "Tibetan Air Operations—Part 1," *Aviation Week & Space Technology*, October 12, 1987, pp. 54–60, and Craig Covault, "Tibetan Air Operations—Part 2, *Aviation Week & Space Technology*, October 19, 1987, pp. 103–106.

Even if suitably modified, none of the strike aircraft examined above—the Jaguar, the Mirage 2000, and the Su-30MK—would be capable of such operational radii in the lo-lo-lo flight regime. The bottom line, therefore, is that India's nuclear deterrent, which in the near future will be centered exclusively on air-breathing platforms, will be utterly ineffectual against China, the country Indian strategic planners usually identify as New Delhi's most significant potential adversary. As one Indian reporter readily admitted, "The IAF possesses no aircraft that can strike at even a medium-sized Chinese city outside Lhasa,"[217] and striking Lhasa—a major Tibetan city with a very small percentage of Han Chinese—may not in any case be the best retaliatory strategy to deter Beijing. Indian policymakers no doubt recognize the limitations of these existing capabilities but do not appear to be distraught, since they seem to be operating on the assumption that an active Chinese threat will not materialize for at least another two decades. If something should go wrong during this period, India would have no choice but to use its existing aircraft as best it could, possibly even attempting one-way missions in an effort to hit any significant Chinese targets that may lie within the ferry range of its strike platforms. Because it is acknowledged that planning for one-way missions is not a desirable solution to the problem of limited reach, however,[218] it is obvious that India will concentrate on developing alternative kinds of delivery vehicles—primarily ballistic missiles—so that its nuclear weapons can be effectively targeted at the strategic assets of most value to China.

Several such missile R&D programs are already under way in India.[219] The most mature program, however, is that which is focused on the development of the Prithvi SRBM. The Prithvi SRBM is slated to appear in three variants: The 150-km version, capable of carrying a 1000-kg payload, has already been inducted into the Army inventory; the 250-km version, currently under development and slated to enter the Air Force inventory, is capable of carrying a ~500-

---

[217]Manoj Joshi, "Missile Program on Hold," *Asia-Pacific Defense Reporter*, April–May 1994, p. 20.

[218]See the perceptive comments in Bajpai, "The Fallacy of an Indian Deterrent," p. 165.

[219]Anupam Srivastava, "India's Growing Missile Ambitions: Assessing the Technical and Strategic Dimensions," *Asian Survey*, 40:2 (2000), pp. 311–341.

kg payload; and the 350-km version, currently being developed for deployment aboard some of the Indian Navy's surface combatants, will also be able to carry payloads in the ~500-kg class.[220] All three versions, the last two code-named "Dhanush," are supposedly capable of being armed with five kinds of conventional payloads: unitary high-explosive, incendiary, fuel-air explosive, cluster bomblets, and submunitions. Nonetheless, Indian plans suggest that they will be acquired in relatively small numbers: The Army is expected to purchase some 100 missiles, the Air Force approximately 25, and the Navy an unannounced but presumably comparable number,[221] although reports have speculated that a total of 300 missiles may in fact be ordered.[222] This decision to acquire such modest quantities of what are generally considered to be relatively inaccurate weapons has been a source of great bewilderment: One analysis has demonstrated that the number of conventionally armed missiles required for some of the missions contemplated for the Prithvi, such as airfield denial, is so large that the inventory currently being acquired by the Indian armed services would be woefully inadequate by any measure.[223] The implication often drawn from this conclusion is either that the development of the Prithvi in all of its variants is a bureaucratic blunder that has been pursued mostly for reasons of prestige rather than out of true operational need, or that its claimed conventional payloads are merely a subterfuge intended to obscure its true character as a nuclear delivery system. Only the latter mission, it is argued, makes the pattern of current Indian acquisitions sensible, since even small numbers of a relatively inaccurate missile would suffice if they were intended for the delivery of nuclear rather than conventional warheads.[224] This judgment derives further credibility

---

[220]"Chronology of Indian Missile Development," Center for Nonproliferation Studies, Monterey, CA, at http://cns.miis.edu/india/indiachron2.html, and Mohammed Ahmedullah, "Prithvi and Beyond—India's Ballistic Missile Programmes," *Military Technology*, 23:4 (1999), pp. 76–78.

[221]J. P. Joshi, "Employment of Prithvi Missiles," *Journal of the USI of India*, 126: 526 (October–December 1996), pp. 462–465.

[222]Vivek Raghuvanshi, "India Moves Prithvi Missile Toward Serial Production," *Defense News*, September 11, 2000, p. 11.

[223]Z. Mian, A. H. Nayyar, and M. V. Ramana, "Bring Prithvi Down to Earth: The Capabilities and Potential Effectiveness of India's Prithvi Missile," *Science & Global Security*, 7 (1998), pp. 333–360.

[224]Harwant Singh, "Only a N-Warhead!" *Vayu Aerospace Review*, IV/1994, p. 30.

from the fact that the diameter of the Prithvi's missile bus is large enough to accommodate even a relatively primitive nuclear weapon, and its throw weight, especially in the Army version, would easily allow for the carriage of a notional 1000-kg warhead. Not surprisingly, many respected Indian analysts have defined nuclear-armed versions of the Prithvi as a desirable component of their country's arsenal.[225]

Whether the Prithvi system is in fact adequate for the various conventional missions usually attributed to it is an interesting question but one that cannot be addressed here. That the Prithvi is structurally capable of carrying a nuclear warhead is also indisputable; the only issue is whether it is likely to be employed for such missions and what the consequences of its use might be for purposes of deterrence. There are two important reasons the Prithvi is undesirable as a nuclear delivery system, the first of which derives simply from India's desired nuclear posture and its existing pattern of civil-military relations. India's desire for a force-in-being rather than a ready nuclear arsenal suggests that the Prithvi SRBM would be a less-than-optimal delivery platform because the need, after absorbing a first strike, to mate nuclear warheads with many dispersed missile platforms in close proximity to the front would be extraordinarily cumbersome from an operational standpoint. Even though Indian planners appear willing to accept great inconveniences in order to maintain highly distributed nuclear capabilities, the challenge of integrating completed nuclear weapons with strike aircraft (or missiles located at existing air bases) is relatively small compared to the challenges of integrating these weapons with missile platforms that have complex prelaunch fueling sequences and are dispersed in some remote field locations but that nonetheless remain well within range of possible enemy air interdiction.[226]

Because postattack reconstitution under these conditions would be extremely difficult, New Delhi may have to contemplate arming its SRBMs with nuclear weapons even prior to absorbing an adver-

---

[225]See, for example, Subrahmanyam, "Nuclear Force Design and Minimum Deterrence Strategy for India," pp. 176–195.

[226]For more on this issue, see Harbir K. Mannshaiya, "India's Prithvi," *International Defense Review*, 28:8 (August 1995), pp. 23–25.

sary's first strike. Such a posture, however, automatically implies that the Indian armed services would have complete and ready nuclear weapons in their custody either in peacetime or during a crisis. This would certainly be true if the sea-based variants of the Prithvi were to be armed with nuclear warheads (and similar issues would become relevant to the Air Force version as well under some circumstances). While India's nuclear weapons may be equipped with some kinds of primitive PALs, New Delhi's current insistence on maintaining strict civilian custody of its nuclear inventory—until it voluntarily divests that custody prior to the actual employment of these weapons— suggests that it would rather not use any delivery systems that could compromise its preferred method of control. While the Navy version of the Prithvi would certainly subvert this preference and is therefore unlikely to be configured as a dedicated nuclear delivery platform today, the Army and Air Force versions may also embody similar problems.[227] Even if they do not, however, they certainly run up against the second reason a nuclear-armed SRBM cannot be a desirable Indian nuclear platform.

The Prithvi SRBM, in all three versions, suffers from one fundamental weakness: its extremely short range. Even the longest-range version contemplated—the Navy's Dhanush, which is supposedly capable of a 350-km range—adds nothing to India's already impressive short-range strike capabilities. Even at maximum range, the Prithvi family of missiles therefore suffices only to target Pakistan— which is already well within Indian Air Force strike coverage—but does nothing to improve India's glaring weaknesses where target coverage vis-à-vis China is concerned. To be sure, one could argue that a nuclear-armed Prithvi would assure penetrativity in a way that no nuclear-armed aircraft could emulate. This is certainly true, but uncertain penetrativity is not likely to be much of an issue vis-à-vis Pakistan under most imaginable circumstances, and while it may be a challenge vis-à-vis China, it is almost certain to be eclipsed by the problem of severely limited reach even before any other subsets of

---

[227]It is important to recognize that when the initial Indian decision to produce the Prithvi was made, the missile was not conceived of as a nuclear weapon carrier. For more on the genesis of this system and why it was not envisaged as a nuclear delivery vehicle, see Perkovich, *India's Nuclear Bomb*, pp. 244–249.

operational difficulties are admitted for analysis.[228] This basic fact all but guarantees that the Prithvi class will be an unlikely candidate for a nuclear delivery vehicle: It merely duplicates the capabilities New Delhi already has vis-à-vis Pakistan, potentially subverting its preferred command system in the process, while providing no new capabilities vis-à-vis China even though it would compromise India's command system were it to be employed along the Himalayan border.[229]

All this having been said, however, India's civilian nuclear weapon designers are still likely to develop a nuclear warhead for the Prithvi even if there is no real operational need for such a device. The divide between the DAE—which produces India's nuclear warheads—and the uniformed services that must ultimately execute military operations makes it likely that the former will attempt to develop a relatively lightweight nuclear weapon capable of being deployed aboard India's SRBMs simply to push the envelope with respect to yet another form of high technology.[230] A more charitable hypothesis might explain this development as possibly one more attempt at hedging against uncertainty. In any event, such a development now seems increasingly likely—indeed, one observer has claimed that it has already occurred[231]—and if it does come about thanks to the imperatives of technological determinism, it would not only replicate the genesis of the Prithvi missile program itself but also bequeath to India a lighter fission warhead for its SRBMs even though these ve-

---

[228]For more on this issue, see C. V. Gole, "The Prithvi—Facts and Fancies," *Vayu Aerospace Review*, IV/1994, pp. 23–30.

[229]Appreciating these considerations, Bharat Karnad has correctly argued that "not nuclearizing the short-range SSM Prithvi and, in fact, withdrawing it from [the] present near-border deployment [areas] should constitute the core concept" beneath India's strategic planning. He further argues that "a non-nuclear Prithvi makes ample military sense as well. It widens the 'firebreak' between conventional and nuclear weapons and . . . remove[s] the prospect of the unrecallable short-range ballistic missile, accidentally or inadvertently, starting a nuclear conflagration." See Karnad, "A Thermonuclear Deterrent," pp. 136–137.

[230]As of February 2000, one prominent analyst, confirming that India did not possess a lightweight nuclear warhead capable of being deployed on the Prithvi, noted that "we could, possibly, miniaturize the weapon to fit into the operationalised Prithvi missile, but that system is also restricted in range." See Premvir Das, "A Simple Solution to CTBT Problem," *The Pioneer*, February 12, 2000.

[231]Chengappa, *Weapons of Peace*, p. 418.

hicles may be both marginal and redundant to the nuclear mission from a strictly operational point of view.

The severe range limitations of the Prithvi SRBM imply that even nuclear-armed versions of the missile would not provide New Delhi with a delivery system capable of targeting important civilian and military assets within China. Recognizing these limitations, New Delhi in 1983 initiated the development of an intermediate-range missile system, the Agni—which from its inception was intended to carry a 1000-kg-class payload to ranges in excess of 1500 km.[232] The ability to deliver such a payload to these distances obviously implied the intention to prepare for the possibility of nuclear missions, and the early tests of the Agni thus appeared to focus more on perfecting separation technologies, the closed-loop guidance system, and the reentry vehicle, including a maneuverable warhead, than on improving the maximum range of the missile per se.[233] Consequently, the versions tested up to the early 1990s employed a peculiar hybrid configuration consisting of a solid-fueled booster from the Indian SLV-3 for the first stage combined with the liquid-fueled Prithvi for the second stage. Although this "technology demonstrator" was said to be capable of a range of some 2500 km, the actual performance demonstrated in flight tests was much lower; as one Indian reporter noted, "The first test of the Agni was to a range of 750 kms and the [last] one to just about 1000 kms."[234]

The Agni test program was frozen under U.S. pressure until 1995. After the May 1998 nuclear tests, however, New Delhi resurrected the program with the intent of developing a rail-mobile IRBM capable of carrying a nuclear payload to "ranges varying from 1,500 km to 2,500 km and even beyond."[235] India is seeking to attain these improved

---

[232]Amit Gupta, "Fire in the Sky: The Indian Missile Program," *Defense and Diplomacy*, 8:10 (October 1990), pp. 44–47.

[233]Government of India, *The Missile Development Programme, Backgrounder* (New Delhi: Public Information Bureau [Defence Wing]), June 25, 1992, p. 2, and Pierre Langereux (with Vivek Raghuvanshi), "Surprise: L'Inde teste sur 1200 km un nouveau missile strategique," *Air & Cosmos/Aviation International*, 1463 (March 14–20, 1994), pp. 40–41.

[234]Joshi, "Missile Program on Hold," p. 20.

[235]Dinesh Kumar, "Nuclearization Calls for Strategic Command," *The Times of India*, May 16, 1998.

ranges through the development of a two-stage, solid-fueled missile in which the liquid-fueled second stage used in the test bed is replaced with a new solid-fueled stage. This variant—which will eventually be equipped with a maneuvering reentry warhead—is currently under engineering and manufacturing development, and its first test was successfully conducted in April 1999.[236] The development program associated with this new all-solid-fueled, rail-mobile missile is likely to be approximately five years in duration, given that DRDO spokesmen have argued that the agency would "need to conduct between six to eight tests of the Agni missile system before its accuracy can be perfected."[237] Since India is not likely to conduct more than two to three missile tests in any given year, however, the development and testing process will probably take at least half a decade (if not more) once the delays associated with such programs in India are taken into account. Assuming low-rate production starts immediately—which is unlikely—it will thus be at least a decade before a complete IRBM force capable of reaching out to ~2500 km ranges becomes operational.[238]

Even when such a force is completed, however, Map 4 suggests that a ~2500-km missile will provide India with reasonable though not complete coverage of Chinese targets *if and only if* New Delhi is willing to deploy these missiles at air bases like Tezpur in the extreme northeastern portions of the country. Moreover, even if these missiles were based at such forward locations, important Chinese countervalue targets like Beijing, Tianjin, Nanjing, and Shanghai would continue to remain out of range. Interdicting such targets would require an even longer-range missile, perhaps one capable of ~3500-km range, that would also have to be based in a relatively forward location like Tezpur. While such a basing posture can no doubt be implemented, it would require much greater sensitivity to strate-

---

[236]For details, see "Agni-II Joins Nation's Missile Showcase," *Hindustan Times*, April 12, 1999.

[237]*India: DRDO Says 6–8 Tests Needed to Perfect Agni Missile*, FBIS-NES-96-156, August 12, 1996.

[238]The current Agni-II variant, however, has a range of roughly 2000 km, or at least has been tested only up to that range. It is unclear whether the missile in its present configuration could attain a range far greater than 2000 km without extensive redesign. For details on the technical characteristics of the new missile and its rail launcher, see Chengappa, "Boom for Boom," pp. 28–31.

gic warning because there are fewer bases in the northeast that can host India's IRBMs than in the rest of northern India.[239] The pressures to rapidly flush the dormant IRBMs—even if maintained routinely without complete nuclear warheads—from their peacetime locations to designated wartime hides would thus become greater if the survivability of these retaliatory systems is to be enhanced against a Chinese barrage attack.

If a ~2500-km-range Agni is based in northern or central India, the targeting coverage vis-à-vis China diminishes radically. Map 5 suggests that a 2500-km missile based in Jhansi, for example, would barely be able to target Kunming and Gejiu, although if it were based farther to the north and east of Jhansi at bases like Gorakhpur, Allahabad, and Kalaikunda, targets like Chengdu and Chongqing would

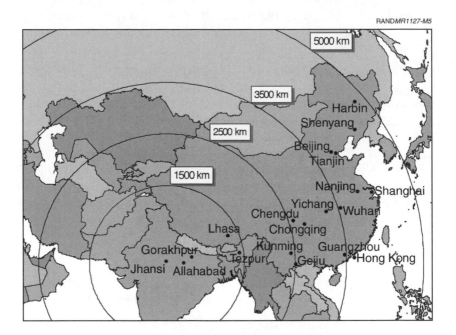

Map 5—India's Strategic Reach from Jhansi

[239]For more on this issue, see Amitabh Mattoo, "Strategic Significance of the Agni-II Test Is Stressed," *India Abroad*, April 23, 1999.

be certain to fall within range. The principal disadvantage of a ~2500-km missile, however, is that it would have to be located in a small northeastern quadrant of the Indian mainland (roughly between 25 and 28 N and between 78 and 88 E) if targets in southeastern China are to be adequately covered. Obviously, this does not imply that the missiles have to be permanently deployed here but only that they will have to reach this general area at the time of launch if the desired Chinese targets in the Sichuan, Yunnan, and Guizhou provinces (and their environs) are to be effectively attacked. If India's ballistic missiles must be be moved from outside this quadrant to predesignated launch sites within it, the burdens associated with ensuring the safe and secure transit of both missiles and launch platforms to the firing sites—as well as the challenges of safeguarding key infrastructure assets like bridges, switching stations, and rail lines along the transit corridors—increase greatly. Consequently, it is desirable that mobile missiles be located as close to their firing points as possible, but this in turn implies that the shorter the missile's range, the smaller the deployment quadrant will be (and the greater the susceptibility of the missiles to destruction by barrage attacks) if the missile systems are to remain within reach of their targets at all times.

Because shorter ranges in general tend to increase the vulnerability of a mobile missile system while decreasing its operational flexibility, New Delhi will likely continue to develop newer variants of the Agni missile that extend beyond ~2500 km in range. If the range of these follow-on variants is increased to, say, 3500 km—the maximum range that Indian planners seem to be currently contemplating[240]— the targeting coverage amply extends to aim points like Chengdu, Chonqing, and Yichang but still leaves other important targets like

---

[240]It is believed that Indian strategic planners currently have settled for an Agni variant of 3000-km range, which will be armed with maneuvering and perhaps multiple warheads, as their principal IRBM system during the next decade. See Rahul Bedi, "India Confirms Plans for Improved Agni and Naval Cruise Missile," *Jane's Missiles & Rockets*, 2:10 (October 1999), p. 6. It is important to recognize, however, that irrespective of what kind of targeting a ≤3000-km-range Agni allows vis-à-vis China, it dramatically increases the flexibility of Indian strategic planners as far as targeting Pakistan is concerned. Such a missile could target Pakistan from any point on the Indian landmass and, being rail-mobile, would be substantially immune to most conceivable forms of Pakistani interdiction. The relevance of a ≤3000-km Agni vis-à-vis Pakistan cannot, therefore, be underestimated under some scenarios, even though most public discussions about the Agni in India focus almost entirely on China.

Hong Kong, Guangzhou, Shanghai, and Beijing immune to Indian retaliation so long as these weapons are deployed in or around the military bases at Jhansi. It is here that China's large size, specific location, and superior nuclear inventory in relation to India combine to impose—at least in principle—potentially painful trade-offs on the Indian deterrent: Missile deployments along the north Indian plains and the central Indian ranges help enhance the survivability of the Indian IRBM force (essentially by increasing the area of locational uncertainty) but would severely reduce their targeting coverage. Conversely, deployments—or firing points—at northeastern locations like Tezpur improve target coverage dramatically but *may* do so only at the expense of increased inflexibility or vulnerability.[241]

This conclusion, it must be admitted, is based principally on a crude generalization. Sophisticated operations analysis would be required to assess whether actual deployments or transits to firing points closer to the Indian northeast would in fact be as problematic as the prima facie evidence suggests. This would necessitate estimating the number and yields of Chinese nuclear weapons that can be allocated to servicing Indian targets; the kinds of Chinese reconnaissance, surveillance, and target acquisition (RSTA) assets that might be available for interdicting mobile platforms in the future; the number of Indian missiles and launch platforms available; the speeds at which these platforms can be flushed from their peacetime garrisons on receipt of strategic and tactical warning; the transportation bottlenecks existing along the transit routes; and the extent of strategic and tactical warning that might be available to India. Moreover, a comprehensive analysis would have to assess the effect of these variables on potential deployments not only at sites such as Tezpur and Jhansi but also at various intermediate points between these two polar locations in order to determine how the demands of range can best be serviced with minimal constraints on survivability. Since this analysis cannot be conducted at such an early stage in the development of the Indian deterrent, however, the conclusions affirmed in the previous paragraph must be treated as preliminary rather than conclusive.

---

[241] For good Indian arguments on this issue, see Brahma Chellaney, "India's Trial by Fire," *Hindustan Times*, October 21, 1998.

In any event, concerns about the potential adequacy of targeting coverage are already being voiced in India. One Indian commentator, for example, has argued that "considering that India is still under trial by Agni (fire)," Indian Foreign Minister Jaswant Singh "ought to explain why the Indian negotiators have allowed the U.S. side in the ongoing [U.S.-Indian] talks to open a discussion on capping Agni development at 2,500 to 3,000 kilometer range."[242] This commentator further asserted that if the country is "to build an effective and flexible missile-deterrent force, India needs IRBMs with ranges in the middle to upper sections of their 1,000 to 5,000 kilometer class [if it is] to strike key Chinese strategic targets."[243] This demand for a 5000-km-class missile is echoed in several other Indian commentaries, and although some analysts, such as Lieutenant General J.F.R. Jacob, argue for such capability on the grounds that it will enhance India's strategic reach,[244] the real benefits of such a missile—if and when it becomes available—will lie not so much in its operational reach as in its operational flexibility. If Maps 4 and 6 are viewed synoptically, it is amply evident that a 5000-km Indian missile provides target coverage similar to that of a 3500-km system—at least as far as major Chinese cities are concerned—but the former weapon can be based as far south as Secunderabad, whereas the latter must be based at a northeastern site such as Tezpur in order to secure comparable coverage. This implies that a 5000-km missile can be based far deeper within India; can be moved greater distances to preserve locational uncertainty; and can be deployed in the most politically stable parts of the country without compromising in its ability to hold critical Chinese targets at risk.[245]

The key problem, however, may pivot on developing such a missile. Indian strategic planners currently appear to be content with a ballistic missile capable of reaching out to a maximum range of roughly 3500 km (and perhaps even 3000 km if published reports are

---

[242]Chellaney, "India's Trial by Fire."

[243]Ibid.

[244]See Jacob's remarks in Joshi, "Operation Defreeze," p. 68.

[245]Jones, *From Testing to Deploying Nuclear Forces*, p. 4.

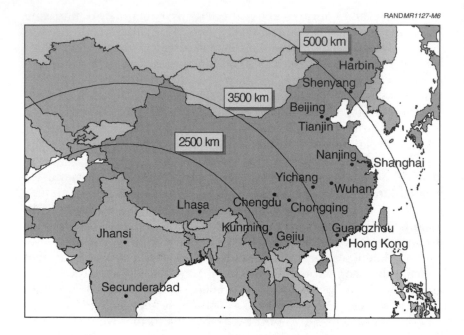

Map 6—India's Strategic Reach from Secunderabad

any indication).[246] At one level, this suggests that they are confident that such missiles, despite being based (or having their firing points located) somewhere between Jhansi and Tezpur, would still provide effective target coverage at minimal risk to their safety and survivability. This confidence is not necessarily misplaced *if*—as Indian security managers believe—the number of Chinese weapons that can be allocated to interdict Indian targets is relatively small and New Delhi's ability to assuredly target even a few large Chinese cities, such as Chengdu, Kunming, and Chongqing, suffices for effective deterrence in South Asia. Since the number of potential sanctuaries and launch points between Jhansi and Tezpur is not inconsiderable, however, Indian security managers could conclude that the targeting

---

[246]"Agni 2 Test Soon?" *Hindustan Times*, March 4, 1999, and Purnima S. Tripathi, "Agni III to Be Test Fired Soon, says Fernandes," *Asian Age*, September 23, 2000.

solutions required for a splendid first strike by China are well beyond the strategic resources Beijing is likely to possess or commit vis-à-vis India in the foreseeable future. If all these calculations are correct, it is not unreasonable for New Delhi to elect not to develop the even longer-range ballistic missiles that many Indian analysts currently appear to advocate. There is, however, another technical reason a missile with a maximum range in excess of 3500 km may not yet hold New Delhi's interest: The planform of the current Agni design has already reached the limits of its success, and even substituting new solid-fueled stages—as has already been planned—is unlikely to extend the missile's range much beyond the 3000- to 3500-km maximum currently contemplated in South Block. As Gregory Jones put it succinctly, "No upgrade of [the] Agni is likely to be able to produce a missile with a 3,500–5,000 km range. Thus, India would have to produce a whole new missile."[247]

Producing an entirely new missile is not likely to evince great enthusiasm in New Delhi today—for while the prospect of yet another R&D program may be welcomed by DRDO technologists in South Block, it is likely to provoke only consternation within the Finance Ministry in North Block. The country as a whole today is also unlikely to support the cost of developing yet another missile design from scratch, and it is therefore not surprising that analysts such as Bharat Karnad have argued that India, "as a top priority, [ought] to at least partially militarize the Indian Space Research Organization's proven space launch capabilities."[248] Karnad believes that India's "ICBM technology is, in effect, already operational" and that "all that is required is for the [standard] satellite payload to be replaced with a megaton thermonuclear warhead atop the ISRO rockets, and a redoubtable Indian ICBM force is ready."[249] Such a capability, he argues, would not only offer range and accuracy advantages over missiles like the Prithvi and Agni but also provide India with political clout and power. As another Indian commentator put it, "The development of intercontinental ballistic missiles . . . is the only way to

---

[247]Jones, *From Testing to Deploying Nuclear Forces*, p. 8.

[248]Karnad, "A Thermonuclear Deterrent," p. 139.

[249]Ibid.

command respect from the U.S. and neighbors like China and Pakistan."[250]

Despite the ISRO's otherwise-impressive capabilities, however, India's SLVs are not ICBMs in disguise, and they certainly cannot be transformed into ballistic missiles on a whim. This is because they are simply not rugged enough for military operations; cannot be rapidly transported either by road or by rail; and are too big to be carried by any of the TELs currently in Indian service or on the drawing board. Moreover, if India's SLVs, especially the Geosynchronous Satellite Launch Vehicle (GSLV) and the PSLV favored by analysts such as Karnad, were to be mated with nuclear payloads, the resulting missiles would be so large that there would be no alternative but to maintain them perpetually on launch pads, since India would probably not be able to build the huge hardened silos that would be necessary to protect them in the event of an adversary's attack. A few representative numbers help establish why the idea of transforming India's existing SLVs into ballistic missiles is so chimerical. The best road-mobile ICBM in the current Russian inventory, the SS-27, has a launch weight of some 47,000 kg. In contrast, the best rail-mobile ICBM in the same inventory, the SS-24, weighs in at about 104,000 kg—more than twice the weight of the SS-27.[251] These two systems provide some indication of the gross weights that can be transported by the best road and rail launchers available.

The ISRO's GSLV and PSLV, however, are in an entirely different league. The GSLV, which is a mixed solid- and liquid-fueled system, weighs in excess of 365,000 kg, while the PSLV, which is also a mixed solid- and liquid-fueled system, weighs approximately 283,000 kg at launch.[252] This implies that the GSLV is in effect almost eight times heavier than the SS-27 and almost three and one-half times heavier than the SS-24, while the PSLV, although lighter than its larger stablemate, is still more than six times heavier than the SS-27 and almost three times heavier than the SS-24. Only the ISRO's Advanced

---

[250]Menon, "Subtleties of Sagarika."

[251]"SS-24 'Scalpel' (RS-22/RT-23U)" and "SS-27 (Topol-M, RS-12M1/-12M2)," in Duncan Lennox (ed.), *Jane's Strategic Weapons Systems* (Coulsdon, UK: Jane's Information Group Ltd., 1999), Issue 29, January 1999.

[252]"India," in David Baker (ed.), *Jane's Space Directory, 1999–2000* (Coulsdon, UK: Jane's Information Group Ltd., 1999), pp. 185–189.

Satellite Launch Vehicle (ASLV) comes in at a more reasonable launch weight of about 41,000 kg, but this vehicle, being equipped with two solid-fuel strap-on motors, has an unwieldy planform for a mobile ballistic missile. If the two strap-on motors are removed, the ASLV's weight is reduced by almost 19,000 kg, leaving the all-solid core with a launch weight of roughly 22,000 kg[253]—a value that is closer to the desirable weight for a road-mobile ballistic missile. However, an ASLV modified in this way would simply be unable to lift a 1000-kg payload to the ranges necessary to interdict critical countervalue targets in China or beyond. All Indian SLVs are thus handicapped by their enormous weight, excessive diameter (often on account of their strap-on boosters), and extremely high weight-to-payload ratios. This last trait does not impose any penalties in the context of space launch capabilities, but it does make every one of these systems inadequate when used as a ballistic missile, especially if mobility of any sort is desired. Not surprisingly, one Indian scholar correctly concluded that, contrary to the views of Karnad, "India's subsequent space launch vehicles, the ASLV and the PSLV, despite being more powerful than the SLV-3, are unlikely to find applications as ballistic missiles."[254]

All this implies that a decade or so from now India will possess at best only a ~3000 to 3500-km Agni variant in operational service. Recent Indian analysis has further suggested that the production of this variant, dubbed the Agni III, and its induction into operational service will not commence before the missile has been fully tested and proven.[255] A missile capable of ranges between 3500 and 5000 km or beyond will, moreover, have to be designed from scratch, and although the development of such a missile lies well within India's capabilities (based simply on the proficiencies it has demonstrated in its Agni and space programs),[256] New Delhi is unlikely to embark on such an effort immediately. In principle, India already possesses the capability to develop a true ICBM, but it has few political incentives to do so given that its most important adversaries can be adequately

---

[253]Ibid.

[254]Mistry, "India's Emerging Space Program," p. 163.

[255]Sawhney, "How Inevitable Is an Asian Missile Race?" p. 32.

[256]"ICBMs Any Day, Says Kalam," *Hindustan Times*, September 18, 2000.

targeted with systems of lesser range.[257] Over the next decade, India is thus likely to focus on producing a ~3000- to 3500-km-range missile—and when such a design is finally accepted for production, it will most likely be configured for deployment in a rail-mobile mode, although a road-mobile variant could be created as well.[258] India does possess a large, fairly well-run civilian rail network, and it would therefore be possible to devise a deployment system that would allow rail-mobile missiles and launchers to use this network to create great locational uncertainty.[259] However, the costs of developing such a deployment system—which would require that special trains be *continuously* dispersed and operate alongside civilian traffic even in peacetime without compromising either the safety or the security of the launcher and the missile—would be inordinately high. Indian security managers are thus unlikely to risk such an operating regime, despite the fact that these delivery systems may *not* be routinely armed with their nuclear payloads.[260]

The rail-mobile deployment system traditionally found its greatest advocate in the late General Sundarji, who argued that India's existing investments in rail communications—and its 60,000 km of route length—offer ample opportunities for rail-mobile basing of India's strategic ballistic missiles.[261] The special trains carrying such missiles would be based in secure garrisons in peacetime and flushed into the wider rail network only on receipt of strategic warning. Such a "disperse-on-warning" deployment regime would enable the force to reap all the benefits of security in peacetime while exploiting all the advantages of locational uncertainty in times of crisis. Operationalizing this solution would require developing special, secure sidings that could host the rail-mobile platforms in peacetime while

---

[257]See the remarks of Dr. A.P.J. Kalam in "Need for ICBM Questioned," *The Times of India*, January 10, 1990.

[258]Chengappa, "Boom for Boom," and Brahma Chellaney, "India Demonstrates Its Missile Prowess," *Hindustan Times*, April 12, 1999.

[259]A good overview of the Indian railway system can be found in M. A. Rao, *Indian Railways* (New Delhi: National Book Trust, 1975), and in Rajendra Narain Saxena, *Four Decades of Indian Railways, 1950–1990* (Delhi: Academic Foundation, 1991).

[260]Amit Gupta, "South Asian Nuclear Choices," *Armed Forces Journal International*, 136:2 (September 1998), pp. 24–30.

[261]Sundarji, "Changing Military Equations in Asia: The Role of Nuclear Weapons," p. 137ff.

instituting a management system to regulate their dispersal in times of crisis. Almost all major Indian army bases are already well connected to the existing rail network, and so long as Indian security managers are satisfied with assigning oversight responsibilities to the Indian Army (as opposed to an alternate service like the Indian Air Force) either independently or under the aegis of a new unified command, there should be little difficulty with basing these systems at locations close to or within existing army garrisons.[262] Air Force custody and operation of these systems—again independently or under a unified command—may be more troublesome in comparison, because it would require that many of the generally remote airfields at which the missile systems might be based be physically connected to the existing Indian rail network.[263] Operating mobile missiles under the aegis of the Indian Air Force is thus more practical if road-mobile variants of Indian IRBMs are developed at some later date. Road-mobile systems imply that India's missile launchers would be deployed on specially designed TELs but do not imply that such TELs and their associated train—carrying reloads, meteorological and signal equipment, and command facilities—would be constantly mobile. Instead, these systems, like their rail-mobile counterparts, would be stored at several protected air (and army) bases and would be flushed from their peacetime garrisons either randomly or on receipt of strategic warning.

Irrespective of the specific form of mobility they employ, the operating patterns of these systems would be similar. When flushed from their garrisons, all dispersed road-mobile missiles and launchers would either proceed to their wartime hides or remain constantly mobile within certain designated quadrants until the emergency was lifted. Rail-mobile systems would constantly shuttle along certain predetermined routes that were previously prepared for this purpose. The missiles carried by either mobility system would be armed with their nuclear payloads just prior to launch, and on traditional Indian thinking such mating would not occur until after the country

---

[262]Pushpindar Singh, "The Indian Army Today: Colour and Firepower," *Asian Defence Journal*, April 1987, pp. 5–27, read in tandem with Survey of India, *Railway Map of India*, 14th ed. (New Delhi: Survey of India, 1989).

[263]See Lake, "Indian Air Power," pp. 138–157, in tandem with Survey of India, *Railway Map of India*.

has absorbed the adversary's first strike.[264] Only those launchers-missiles that survived the first strike would be armed with warheads (or warhead components, most likely the "pits") that were available after such an attack. The latter might, however, have to be transported from a different location before the process of mating and testing could proceed, and therefore hours if not days might elapse before any retaliatory responses could be mounted. Although the myriad details that make such an operational regime feasible have yet to be worked out in their entirety—especially insofar as such a regime would apply to the entire future Indian nuclear force in the face of different levels of threats—its general logic appeals to Indian policymakers because they believe that widespread dispersal of their rail-mobile missilery (and road-mobile platforms, if such are developed over time) should suffice to protect at least a few systems that would finally be armed with nuclear warheads (if these are not already armed prior to nuclear deterrence breakdown) and ordered to carry their payloads of retribution to target.[265]

Such a deployment regime inevitably implies that India is likely to produce many more launchers than are strictly required for purposes of interdicting a given target array—and even more missiles than there are likely to be either launchers or nuclear warheads. Producing more than the militarily required number of launchers and missiles not only addresses the derivative demands imposed by continual testing, attrition, and maintenance but also advances the strategic objective of enhancing uncertainty: It promotes the illusion that there might be more nuclear warheads than actually exist and allows for more widespread dispersal of what are ordinarily inert systems that could become lethal if suitably armed. Moreover, to the degree that such dispersal, coupled with some local mobility, increases the number of systems that survive any attempted first strike, it also contributes to deterrence stability insofar as the residual inventory suffices to interdict a significant number of enemy targets. Since New Delhi has more army and air force facilities in the relevant

---

[264]This represents the "baseline" model of control discussed in the previous chapter and exemplifies the nuclear C^2 model advocated by General Sundarji. Obviously, depending on whether the "baseline" model or its alternatives are selected in the future, the sequences described in this paragraph would vary accordingly.

[265]Gupta, "South Asian Nuclear Choices," pp. 24–30.

quadrants of the country than there are probably Chinese or Pakistani nuclear weapons available for use against India, it is likely to conclude that a static deployment of its rail-mobile missiles in protected garrisons in peacetime should suffice to ensure survivability so long as these inert delivery systems can be either readily flushed to some alternate wartime hides or committed to some predetermined mobile routines on receipt of strategic warning.[266]

Since the logic of rail (and road) mobility implies a survivable deterrent so long as the potential aim points outnumber the quantity of weapons that can be allocated by an adversary, India is unlikely to pursue any outlandish or complicated basing modes such as those that were discussed in connection with the U.S. MX missile program.[267] This may change over the very long term, but from all indications available, New Delhi appears to be attempting to cope with contingencies beyond the next 20 years by investing in the development of a sea-based capability rather than by exploring more esoteric forms of land basing. This sea-based effort includes examining options for basing ballistic missiles on board surface vessels, as exemplified by the current experiments with the liquid-fueled Dhanush missile aboard the Navy's Sukanya-class offshore patrol craft, and, more significantly, the development—now under way for almost 25 years—of a nuclear-powered submarine dubbed the Advanced Technology Vessel (ATV).[268] The Dhanush program is unlikely to result in a sea-based nuclear deterrent—at least on present plans—since it is driven primarily by the Indian Navy's interest in acquiring a land-attack capability vis-à-vis Pakistan in order to assert its own strategic relevance to the larger war-fighting outcomes within the Indian subcontinent.[269] This requirement has forced the Navy to seek a variety of standoff attack capabilities that hold promise of allowing it to replicate its 1971 achievements at Karachi, and toward

---

[266]Ibid.

[267]For details about these alternatives, see Office of Technology Assessment, *MX Missile Basing*, pp. 3–29.

[268]Rahul Bedi, "India Presses Ahead with SSN to Boost Navy's Nuclear Profile," *Jane's Defence Weekly*, July 22, 1998, p. 26.

[269]For more on this calculation, see Ninad D. Sheth, "Interview: The Depth of the Indian Navy," *India Today* Web Exclusive, available at http://www.india-today.com/webexclusive/interviews/20000520sushil.html.

that end it has begun to induct various long-range anti–surface cruise missiles on board its air, surface, and subsurface platforms as well as to deploy SRBMs aboard some of its patrol vessels in order to threaten critical Pakistani sea- and shore-based assets in times of conflict. The fact that Islamabad can never be *certain* as to whether these standoff capabilities—especially the surface ship-based ballistic missile systems—are purely conventional or nuclear-armed is seen to make such unorthodox deployment postures particularly attractive from a strategic point of view: These sea-based systems serve to levy a potential nuclear threat on Pakistan from what is otherwise a nontraditional axis and, by that very fact, compel Islamabad to allocate military resources to sanitize them even though the strike systems in question may finally turn out to be no more than conventionally armed vehicles of little strategic significance. To the degree that the Dhanush system provokes such a Pakistani response, it will have served its purpose in Indian naval calculations while simultaneously laying the groundwork for the deployment of new solid-fueled, nuclear-tipped variants in the future—that is, if Indian policymakers choose to move beyond their currently preferred model of a force-in-being to institutionalize an alternative deterrent posture at some later point.

While the Dhanush project thus seeks to exploit the ambiguity of the missile's payload to secure strategic benefits, the ATV is intended to create a nuclear-propelled submarine that can carry SLBMs of the kind associated with a true sea-based deterrent.[270] This project has reportedly gone through three major generations of design work, all of which have focused on developing a 600-ton reactor capable of being fitted within the space constraints of a relatively small submarine hull. This effort had to begin from scratch, since India had no experience whatsoever in designing maritime nuclear reactors, not to mention a nuclear submarine. Over the last two decades the project was also the subject of internecine bureaucratic wrangling between the Indian Navy (the eventual end user) and BARC, which was tasked with developing the nuclear reactor. These disputes have apparently been worked out, however, and it has now been reported that "BARC scientists, after years of struggle, have finally developed a land-based prototype of the submarine's propulsion plant, a 90-MW pressurized

---

[270]"N-Sub Project on Course: Navy," *The Times of India*, July 27, 1999.

water reactor (PWR) with turbines and propellers, and are testing it at a secret location in southern India."[271] Over the years, the objective of developing a nuclear submarine appears to have changed as well. Although originally intended as an attack boat capable of stalking superpower fleets operating in the Indian Ocean, the vessel now appears more likely to serve as a cruise or ballistic missile carrier that could one day be armed with small nuclear payloads.[272]

Since the lease of the Russian Charlie-class nuclear-propelled guided missile submarine (SSGN) was terminated in 1991, several Russian design bureaus have actively assisted the ATV program "in non-nuclear areas such as hull design and underwater navigation."[273] Even more interestingly, it would appear that Russia has been helping India develop a short-range SLBM dubbed Sagarika.[274] This missile, which one analyst notes "is universally described as having a maximum range of 300 km,"[275] reportedly relies on Russian technology "to allow the missile to be launched from underwater."[276] Beyond that, details pertaining to this weapon are scarce, and there is actually an ongoing debate about its relationship to another sea-launched cruise missile that India is ostensibly developing.[277] Irrespective of what the facts about this issue might be, the evidence suggests that India remains committed to developing both a nuclear submarine and the strategic weaponry that goes with it. The latter program is certainly immature right now, but if India is able to master the basic technologies required to successfully launch an SRBM with Russian assistance, there is no reason in principle why the range and throw weight of such a weapon cannot be increased—with much less (and possibly greater indigenous) effort—over time.

---

[271] Rethinaraj, "ATV: All at Sea Before It Hits the Water," p. 32.

[272] "N-Submarine Best Bet Against Nuclear Attack, Says Navy."

[273] Andrew R. Koch, "Nuclear-Powered Submarines: India's Strategic Trump Card," *Jane's Intelligence Review*, 10:6 (June 1998), p. 29.

[274] Myers, "Russia Helping India Extend Range of Missiles, Aides Say."

[275] Andrew R. Koch, "In Search of the Real Sagarika," *Jane's Intelligence Review*, 10:7 (July 1998), p. 24.

[276] Koch, "Nuclear-Powered Submarines: India's Strategic Trump Card," p. 30.

[277] Koch, "In Search of the Real Sagarika," p. 24.

A successful short-range SLBM could thus pave the way for other longer-range sea-based missiles in the future—a capability that will be limited only by the preferences of Indian security planners with respect to range and by the weight and volume limitations of the host submarine's hull and propulsion systems. Even if the range of these sea-based missiles is not dramatically increased, they would still have great utility because, as one Indian naval officer notes, the general invulnerability of a nuclear submarine would allow submersible platforms to operate relatively close to the coastlines of their intended targets without creating all the diplomatic problems that arise when "drawing arcs from a country's [land-based] missile sites . . . results in far too many wrong deductions"[278] about their intended targets. Since many key Pakistani and Chinese targets lie relatively close to their coastlines, even an SRBM aboard a nuclear submarine should therefore suffice for purposes of delayed retaliatory strikes in the event of deterrence breakdown.

Not surprisingly, then, New Delhi has continued to pursue its nuclear submarine project with some intensity. As one Indian reporter noted, "Although many defence projects . . . have been shelved for the time being due to funding shortages, the ATV is one project that has been receiving unflagging monetary support from the government."[279] It has further been reported that

> Plans are also under way to lay down a 2500-ton boat with the technical assistance of Russian scientists and engineers by the end of this year [1998]. With the Russians agreeing to hawk their nuclear expertise in designing and fabricating a hull, along with its subsequent integration with the propulsion plant, the long-awaited ATV project looks certain to be completed by about 2004.[280]

While these completion dates are clearly optimistic (other sources have suggested a "launch around 2006/7 and commissioning a year later"[281]), the fact remains that the ability to build a nuclear submarine more or less indigenously will open new strategic doors to India

---

[278]Menon, *A Nuclear Strategy for India*, p. 227.

[279]Rethinaraj, "ATV: All at Sea Before It Hits the Water," p. 35.

[280]Ibid., p. 32.

[281]Bedi, "India Presses Ahead with SSN to Boost Navy's Nuclear Profile," p. 26.

while also presenting new strategic conundrums. A nuclear-armed ballistic and cruise missile battery aboard a nuclear submarine would, for example, eliminate many of the vulnerability problems that could otherwise bedevil New Delhi's land-based missile force[282] *if* a truly quiet nuclear submarine—which represents a significant engineering challenge in its own right—could in fact be constructed in India. The record of past Indian performance in submarine construction does not inspire great confidence, however, and the ATV program in particular has been universally acknowledged to be "one of the most ill-managed projects of independent India."[283] Moreover, the U.S. experience has shown that the task of constructing quiet nuclear submarines is extraordinarily challenging and costly and, even if achievable, certainly does not represent an area in which India may be presumed to enjoy a comparative advantage in the face of adversaries that are likely to possess advanced diesel-electric submarines equipped with air-independent propulsion, decent sensors and fire-control systems, and adequate long-range weaponry. Even apart from these issues, however, the strategic necessity for a submarine-based deterrent arm has not yet been adequately demonstrated in the Indian context.

Most Indian observers—including the National Security Advisory Board—assert that "deterrence requires that India maintain . . . sufficient, survivable and operationally prepared nuclear forces"[284]— and from this quite reasonable requirement they quickly conclude that a "submarine based [nuclear] capability is critical" since, as the Indian Navy's Chief of Staff put it, "for one it is most capable and for another it is easier to conceal. It is a real deterrent. A submarine-based deterrent has credibility."[285] Such conclusions, which are based largely on the rationales for a sea-based deterrent proffered by the established nuclear powers, have not yet been scrutinized by In-

---

[282]Menon, *A Nuclear Strategy for India*, pp. 227–231.

[283]Pal, "Nuclear Onus on Navy."

[284]"Draft Report of [the] National Security Advisory Board on Indian Nuclear Doctrine," p. 2.

[285]Sheth, "Interview: The Depth of the Indian Navy."

dian analysts and consequently raise three important questions that remain unresolved.[286]

First, is the vulnerability of the evolving land-based Indian deterrent serious enough to warrant recourse to a sea-based option? Answering this question requires that operations analysis be conducted to gauge whether Pakistan and China do in fact possess the requisite numbers of nuclear weapons and delivery systems to successfully interdict what will eventually be an Indian force of several-score mobile ballistic missiles and probably equal numbers of advanced combat aircraft. This issue is of particular importance because senior Indian security managers and many respected strategic analysts readily admit that "no one envisages in these days [any] high density attacks with hundreds and thousands of warheads."[287] If this is the case, the evolving Indian mobile land-based deterrent is freed from the largest threat to its survival that can be envisaged and, by implication, may be far safer than proponents of a sea-based deterrent are willing to admit—especially given the fact that successfully interdicting mobile missiles is an enormously difficult technical enterprise that will remain beyond the reach of India's principal adversaries well into the foreseeable future.

Second, are the survivability and mission effectiveness of a submarine-based deterrent better than those of a mobile land-based missile? Ballistic missile submarines, which many Indian sources argue ought to be equipped with 12 to 16 missiles per boat, represent a concentrated cluster of strategic capabilities. Thus, the detection and sinking of only one such vehicle represents the loss of a significant fraction of a country's strategic reserves. In contrast, a single mobile land-based missile—when dispersed like a submarine—represents a much smaller fraction of a state's strategic capability and consequently does not embody a significant diminution of retaliatory capability even if lost to enemy attack. The established nuclear powers traditionally made up for this potentially unhealthy concentration of capabilities by incorporating highly sophisticated quieting tech-

---

[286]The exception remains Balachandran, "What Is the Relevance of a Triad?"—which contains some of the most penetrating criticisms of the justifications for a sea-based deterrent advanced in the Indian context. For a diametrically opposed viewpoint, see Menon, *A Nuclear Strategy for India*, pp. 177–283.

[287]Subrahmanyam, "A Credible Deterrent."

niques into their ballistic missile submarines and by deploying them in patrol areas relatively far from their adversaries' homelands in efforts to enhance platform survivability.[288] Even then, however, the challenges of communication with submerged submarines made these systems most effective as "barrage" firing weapons rather than as platforms optimized for flexible nuclear operations.[289] Given the current and projected levels of technology available to India, it is reasonable to assume that New Delhi will be better equipped to build and deploy an effective land-based mobile ballistic missile force than to construct and operate a quiet ballistic missile submarine armed with long-range subsurface-launched ballistic missiles. Since even the best submersible systems built in India will have some nontrivial probability of detection—especially if these systems are armed with short-range missiles that require them to operate in relatively close proximity to an adversary's coastline—it is reasonable to suggest that a comparable force of mobile land-based missiles could yield a much higher residual fraction of strategic assets when compared to a submarine that is detected and sunk in a given attack scenario. To that degree, the attractiveness of ballistic missile submarines for purposes of enhancing the survivability of India's strategic reserves remains open to debate.[290]

Third and finally, is a submarine-based deterrent more cost-effective than a mobile land-based missile? At least one Indian analyst's answer to this query, which hinges in part on the answer to the second question, has been negative. G. Balachandran, addressing this issue, notes that "in all available estimates of the cost of a nuclear weaponization programme for India, . . . the bulk of the cost, nearly two-thirds of the total cost, goes towards the provision of a

---

[288]Even these attributes, however, were insufficient to preserve the inviolability of the Soviet SSBN force against U.S. antisubmarine warfare (ASW) operations in the event of war—a clear reminder of the prospect facing countries that possess an inferior submarine fleet in an environment where even minute differences in relative technological capability can spell the difference between survival and disaster for the submarine arm. For details pertaining to this question, see Stefanick, *Strategic Antisubmarine Warfare and Naval Strategy*, and Daniel, *Anti-Submarine Warfare and Superpower Strategic Stability*.

[289]Lynn Etheridge Davis, *Limited Nuclear Options*, Adelphi Paper No. 121 (London: IISS, 1975–1976), pp. 19–20.

[290]For a brief quantitative assessment of this issue, see Balachandran, "What Is the Relevance of a Triad?"

viable and safe nuclear submarine force."[291] When these costs are assessed against the size of the residual fraction of a land- and sea-based force expected to survive an adversary attack, Balachandran demonstrates that "the cost of 20 additional [land-based] missiles will be far less than that of a nuclear ballistic missile submarine"[292] armed with 16 to 20 comparable weapons. After factoring qualitative differences in capability between the two kinds of deterrence arms, the unit costs of each missile in their alternative basing modes, and the command-and-control costs of a dyad versus a triad, Balachandran concludes that "all indications are that a nuclear ballistic missile submarine force will not confer any advantage commensurate with the [marginal] expenses involved."[293]

It is possible that this conclusion would change if India developed a different structure of comparative advantage with respect to the construction of submersible vessels in the years ahead.[294] Until that time, however, it is important to recognize that although many Indian analysts have asserted that a submarine-based deterrent is necessary for the viability of their country's evolving nuclear posture over the long term, no analysis justifying this argument has yet been adduced. If Balachandran's assessment is in fact taken seriously, the idea of a sea-based deterrent is not at all as advantageous as it is sometimes portrayed in the Indian debate. Consequently, India's strategic managers—although willing to fund this research and development program as part of their contingency planning—will likely demand further analyses before converting this endeavor into a pro-

---

[291]Ibid.

[292]Ibid.

[293]Ibid.

[294]The historical record, however, confirms that India experienced enormous technical difficulties in constructing even diesel-electric submarines, and the various convulsions affecting the ATV project do not inspire confidence that New Delhi possesses the technical and organizational capabilities required to construct quiet, safe, and effective nuclear submersibles that could hold their own in a variety of operational environments. The Indian record with respect to submarine construction is usefully summarized in Mark Gorwitz, "The Indian Strategic Nuclear Submarine Project: An Open Literature Analysis," December 1996, available at http://www.fas.org/nuke/guide/india/sub/ssn/index.html. The Indian Navy reorganized its management of the ATV project in 2000 in the hope of producing an effective nuclear platform sometime before the end of this decade. See "Nuclear Submarine Project Gets a New Head," *The Times of India*, September 30, 2000.

curement initiative that dramatically changes India's prospective nuclear architecture. Recognizing just this fact, even the most zealous advocates of a submarine-based deterrent within the Indian Navy are always careful to point out that although the ATV "will have the ability to carry nuclear weapons,"[295] the government "will [have to] decide whether these nuclear-propelled submarines, capable of carrying nuclear weapons, would actually do so."[296] This caveat is invariably emphasized in all internal service discussions about the triad precisely because it is recognized that the decision to procure a sea-based deterrent would radically alter the character of India's desired strategic posture. Specifically, it is understood that a nuclear-armed ballistic missile submarine (like a nuclear-armed ballistic missile–equipped surface combatant) could not exemplify the force-in-being that New Delhi seeks to develop today but would instead personify some kind of a robust and ready arsenal—one in which at least the custody of completed nuclear weapons and launch vehicles would reside entirely with India's uniformed services in peacetime. Although India's civilian leadership would certainly limit the decisional autonomy of these naval custodians by installing various kinds of PALs on board its sea-based weaponry, such a nuclear posture would no doubt be radically different from the operational configuration security managers in New Delhi currently seem to be contemplating.

The acquisition of a sea-based nuclear deterrent—in either surface or submersible form—will therefore come to personify India's moment of truth: While air-breathing systems and even land-based missiles do allow for the maintenance of those demated and dealerted nuclear postures which exemplify a force-in-being, a major surface combatant or ballistic missile submarine armed with nuclear weapons would only incarnate some kind of a ready arsenal, with the speed of its retaliatory response being limited primarily by the time it takes to issue the nuclear release orders, the time it takes to receive and authenticate the same aboard the vessel, and the time it takes to complete the battery firing procedures. If 10 or 20 years hence India still seeks to preserve its currently preferred posture of a force-in-being (as opposed to some version of a robust and ready arsenal), it

---

[295] "N-Sub Project on Course: Navy."

[296] "India to Produce Indigenous N-Submarine," *Hindustan Times*, July 27, 1999.

would therefore have no choice but to seek alternative, non-naval solutions to the as-yet-unanalyzed problems of force vulnerability. This might include exploring other basing modes such as continuous rail mobility or deep underground basing rather than developing a sea-based deterrent. If New Delhi does pursue such alternatives when needed in the distant future, its nuclear submarine platforms could be restricted to tactical roles only, as was intended by the Navy's expansion plans during the 1980s.[297] Whether India will eschew the acquisition of a sea-based deterrent when that option becomes available for reasons of both nuclear strategy and civil-military relations cannot yet be determined, but if New Delhi were to pursue such a solution, it would be obvious that the currently desired force-in-being would subsist only as an interim posture en route to the development of a full-fledged robust and ready arsenal.

While such an arsenal may even represent the ultimate future of the Indian deterrent, its imminence should not by any means be exaggerated. The discussion in this section clearly indicates that for all India's claims to being a nuclear weapon state, New Delhi's deterrent posture will center for a long time on a limited, monadic delivery system: short-range strike aircraft. At least another decade will elapse before a dyadic posture involving aircraft and land-based ballistic missiles becomes fully ready and operational, and it is unlikely that India will have a credible triad of any size, effectiveness, or flexibility for at least another decade and possibly two.

Supporting Infrastructure

The availability of fissile materials, nuclear weapons, and delivery systems by themselves does not suffice to produce an adequate deterrent even if such a deterrent is configured simply as a force-in-being. To the contrary, an effective deterrent requires a minimum level of supporting infrastructure in order to physically "net" the

---

[297] For more on how the Indian Navy envisaged the use of nuclear submarines during the 1980s, see Tellis, "Securing the Barrack: The Logic, Structure and Objectives of India's Naval Expansion," Parts I and II, pp. 31–57 and 77–97.

weapons and delivery systems in a coherent way.[298] This infrastructure enables the national leadership to monitor the character of the country's threat environment and the status of its own retaliatory forces while simultaneously allowing for the dissemination of appropriate operational directives if retaliatory strikes are to be conducted in the context of a deterrence breakdown. Since supporting infrastructure is therefore a key component of deterrence capability, it is not surprising that several Indian analysts have set forth fairly ambitious requirements pertaining to their country's nuclear posture[299]—requirements ranging from dedicated command centers and multiple and redundant communications systems, to complex intelligence collection and assessment technologies that include early-warning platforms, to integrated strategic defenses and large-scale civil defense measures. Many of these elements have been borrowed from existing literature on Western C3I systems, and almost all appear to be based on the premise that India's claim to becoming a nuclear weapon state requires that New Delhi create separate, *dedicated* technical capabilities to oversee the control and operation of its nuclear forces.[300]

Whatever the virtues of having such capabilities may be, this premise is highly suspect. For while Indian security managers no doubt intend to develop a "minimum, but credible, deterrent" over time, their intentions today appear focused primarily on developing a force-in-being rather than a ready arsenal. This implies in turn that India's nuclear posture will consist primarily of weapon and delivery systems that are maintained separately and in an operationally

---

[298]Indian leadership views on this issue are described in Kumar, "Nuclearization Calls for Strategic Command," and Dinesh Kumar, "No Move Yet to Set up Nuclear Command," *The Times of India*, July 2, 1998.

[299]The best analyses of Indian requirements with respect to supporting infrastructure can be found in Nair, *Nuclear India*, pp. 183–194; Bajpai, "The Fallacy of an Indian Deterrent," pp. 150–188; Narendra Gupta, "Detonations Don't Make Deterrence," *Indian Express*, May 22, 1998; Amar Zutshi, "For a Strategic Defence," *The Pioneer*, May 1, 1998; Bakshi, "Nuclear Euphoria and Harsh Realities"; Kanwal, "Command and Control of Nuclear Weapons in India," pp. 1707–1732; Menon, *A Nuclear Strategy for India*, pp. 235–283; and Kak, "Command and Control of Small Nuclear Arsenals," pp. 266–285.

[300]This premise is most clearly articulated in Nair, *Nuclear India*, pp. 183–194, and in Menon, *A Nuclear Strategy for India*, pp. 235–283.

inactive condition, at least as far as their routine disposition is concerned.[301] Since this posture explicitly rejects the maintenance of a completed and ready arsenal—i.e., one in which all components are deployed in a highly integrated state *a priori* and sustained at relatively high levels of readiness—it is unlikely that New Delhi will set out to create a separate set of technical systems dedicated solely to the control of its emerging nuclear capabilities. If in fact India seeks to maintain only a mobilizable nuclear reserve oriented toward prosecuting simple retaliatory actions involving a relatively small number of nuclear weapons—as opposed to a ready war-fighting force that will be called upon to execute complex, frequently changing plans involving a large and diversified nuclear arsenal— such dedicated capabilities would be costly and might even prove unnecessary. Consequently, while New Delhi will incrementally develop the specific organizational arrangements necessary to control its budding strategic capabilities—such as the new unified command, which will be responsible for overseeing India's strategic assets and planning for nuclear operations—it will most likely graft these new elements onto its existing command system, which regulates the disposition and movement of all Indian conventional forces, rather than develop an entirely new and specialized structure parallel to its existing system of higher defense management.[302] As Prime Minister Vajpayee put it, "India does not intend to build a large arsenal or create an elaborate command and control system like other nuclear weapon powers."[303]

This in turn implies that while India will no doubt develop some kind of supporting infrastructure over the long haul, this infrastructure is likely to be far less ambitious than that deemed essential by many unofficial Indian sources today. There is little doubt that the requirements associated with developing this infrastructure have only begun to receive attention in New Delhi, and the process of analyzing, establishing, and investing in these requirements is by no

---

[301] For more on this issue, see Kumar, "No Move Yet to Set Up Nuclear Command."

[302] Indian Defence Minister George Fernandes alludes to this prospect in the comments cited in Kumar, "No Move Yet to Set Up Nuclear Command." See also "Interview of the Week: Inder Kumar Gujral" for more on this issue.

[303] Chengappa, "Worrying over Broken Arrows," p. 30.

means complete. In part, this is because India has simply not completed the process of weaponization, and consequently the complex demands pertaining to supporting infrastructure are not yet fully understood because it remains unclear what kinds of nuclear weapons and delivery systems India will finally possess and in what numbers. Obviously, the development of a supporting infrastructure cannot be put off until after this process is complete, but by the same token it cannot be developed *ab initio* on the basis of some abstract template. Rather, the development process is likely to unfold in an evolutionary way and in a manner commensurate with the gradual acquisition of the weapon and delivery systems themselves. Not surprisingly, published reports suggest that India has already produced a $3.75 billion plan focused on the acquisition of key components related to its nuclear C^3I infrastructure over a five-year period.[304] Whether this plan has been formally approved or executed by the national leadership is not clear, but three preliminary conclusions with respect to India's supporting infrastructure can nonetheless be drawn.

First, efforts will be made to keep the costs associated with the development of such capabilities to a minimum. New Delhi is likely to spend whatever is necessary to control its nuclear forces, but necessity in this context will be defined by what satisfies decisionmakers in the world of international politics rather than by the abstract standards laid down by Indian theorists and commentators.

Second, efforts will be made to keep the configuration of the supporting infrastructure simple. This criterion of simplicity again implies that India will focus only on developing an infrastructure that is necessary to support nuclear operations relevant to the subcontinent—not one that is designed to address all nuclear operations imaginable or, for that matter, nuclear operations involving countries other than China and Pakistan. The nuclear operations for which New Delhi will prepare consist principally of *small, preplanned retaliatory attacks*. This implies that the supporting infrastructure must at a minimum be able to provide sufficient sanctuary for the national command authority; allow for incoming damage reports and roll calls of surviving forces; allow for deliberation, re-

---

[304] "India Eyes $3.75 Billion Nuclear Command Plan."

view, and selection of specific retaliatory options; and, finally, permit effective dissemination of the nuclear release order with confirming report-back from the various custodians of India's strategic reserves. The infrastructure developed for these purposes must also be able to survive relatively small nuclear attacks emanating from either China or Pakistan, which may or may not incorporate even smaller counter-C3I components. It will *not*, however, be required to support flexible or ad hoc retaliation, reoptimization of attack plans in real time, prompt counterattacks in a preemptive launch-on-warning or launch-under-attack mode, interdiction of critical mobile targets, or protracted nuclear operations—all of which represent contingencies for which the United States prepared its supporting infrastructure (with varying degrees of success) during the Cold War.[305]

Third, efforts will be made to use bits and pieces of India's existing infrastructure to the maximum extent possible. This implies that India will not develop new and dedicated capabilities if preexisting assets can be modified or used as is. Given the premium on economy, the supporting infrastructure already in place for the conduct of conventional operations will most likely be used for nuclear operations as well, although perhaps by different operators, organizations, and entities.[306]

These three considerations ought to be borne in mind when future Indian initiatives with respect to nuclear supporting infrastructure are anticipated or assessed. Since the number of technologies that fall under this rubric are numerous, however, the following analysis will focus only on four broad categories: command centers, communications systems, warning and assessment capabilities, and strategic defenses.

Command Centers. Many Indian analysts have argued that at a minimum India will require a set of dedicated command centers

---

[305]Matin Zuberi, "The Proposed Nuclear Doctrine," *World Focus*, 21:4 (April 2000), pp. 3–5.

[306]See the comments of K. Santhanam and V. Arunachalam in "Panel Four: Nuclear Weapons and the Balance of Power," in *Proceedings of the Center for the Advanced Study of India, University of Pennsylvania*, held at the Wharton Sinkler Conference Center, May 5–8, 1997, available at http://www.sas.upenn.edu/casi/reports/nuclear/panel4.html, for more on this issue.

from which the National Command Authority (NCA)—meaning the Prime Minister or his designated successors—could control the retaliatory strikes that would be mounted in the event of a deterrence breakdown. Indeed, even the earliest studies about a potential Indian deterrent, commissioned by General K. Sundarji during the early 1980s, concluded that some kind of National Command Post (NCP) would be necessary in this context, and the policy paper on nuclear command arrangements reportedly approved by India's service chiefs similarly argues that a "robust communications centre with the ability to receive information and intelligence and disseminate orders and instructions"[307] should be established. Yet another Indian analyst has actually argued for two command posts built to certain specific configurations, asserting that "in a crisis situation, the proposed NCA should be expected to operate from an underground, hardened and electro-magnetic pulse protected National Command Post. An alternative NCP located some distance away from the capital assumes equal salience."[308] Other analysts, such as Vijai Nair, have argued that such dual command posts "must have identical communication facilities" and that there should be "outstations on the National Military Command Link (NMCL) emanating from the NCA and . . . the controlling headquarters on the Strategic Nuclear Link (SNL) that would service the military requirements of the nuclear strategy."[309]

It is obvious that although these suggestions presuppose the existence of a separate, dedicated set of nuclear command links that may not be developed in the near future, a small set of underground leadership command posts is likely to be constructed—two national command posts, one outside of Delhi and one somewhere in the vicinity of the Prime Minister's Office in the heart of New Delhi, have reportedly been built already[310]—simply to minimize the worst ravages of a nuclear attack that might be mounted by Pakistan. The logic of having such dedicated command posts is not difficult to discern:

---

[307] Bedi, "India Assesses Options on Future Nuclear Control," p. 16.

[308] Kapil Kak, "Strategic Template for Nuclear India," *The Times of India*, August 11, 1998.

[309] Nair, "The Structure of an Indian Nuclear Deterrent," p. 95.

[310] Chengappa, "Worrying over Broken Arrows," p. 31, and Bedi, "India's Nuclear Prowess Remains on Paper, Official Rhetoric."

Since they would presumably be equipped with the personnel, facilities, and information systems that would allow a decisionmaker to appreciate the threat environment and respond to it appropriately, secure command posts would become critical organizational nodes for the effective execution of any military operation. In point of fact, India already possesses many such facilities; the operations centers at the three service headquarters in New Delhi, the operations center of the Director-General, Military Operations, in South Block, and the operations rooms at each headquarters associated with the services' combat commands already serve as the sinews of the national military command system, where all orders originating from the Prime Minister and the Cabinet are transmitted via the Ministry of Defence to the individual service chiefs and then to their subordinate commanders. The chief weakness of this infrastructure, however, lies in the fact that none of these key facilities is hardened and designed to operate in a nuclear environment.[311] Thus, while they do afford considerable protection against conventional threats, such facilities are unlikely to survive any nuclear attacks that might be directed at them—a vulnerability that has obviously driven analysts' repeated calls for a new set of dedicated underground command posts capable of directing nuclear operations in a protracted war. Unfortunately, however, command posts such as these would be costly to develop if they were in fact intended to be truly "capable of withstanding up to a 20 kt blast from a ground burst or from a deep penetration nuclear weapon like the U.S. B61-11 earth penetrating nuclear warhead."[312]

The United States, for example, developed a complex set of command centers during the Cold War.[313] These fixed centers were appropriate mainly for peacetime operations, since even the most hardened of them, like the Northern Region Air Defense's (NORAD's) command facility at Cheyenne Mountain and the Alternate National Military Command Center in Maryland, could not have survived the

---

[311]For details, see Gurmeet Kanwal, "Command and Control of India's Nuclear Weapons," *World Focus*, 21:4 (April 2000), pp. 9–13.

[312]Ibid., p. 12.

[313]These are described at some length in Albert E. Babbitt, "Command Centers," in Ashton B. Carter, John D. Steinbruner, and Charles A. Zraket (eds.), *Managing Nuclear Operations* (Washington, D.C.: Brookings, 1987), pp. 322–351.

kinds of nuclear attacks that the Soviets might have mounted against them. To compensate for these vulnerabilities, the United States invested in a variety of mobile centers, of which airborne command posts like the National Emergency Airborne Command Post (NEACP), the Strategic Air Command's (SAC's) "Looking Glass," and the Navy's "Take Charge and Move Out" (TACAMO) are perhaps best known. The United States also flirted with both afloat and land-based mobile command centers, but even after all these investments were made, it is not clear how robust the American command system actually was.[314] To be sure, the U.S. example may not be entirely relevant to India, since the former had to face the demanding challenge of ensuring effective control of its nuclear forces in the context of a possibly protracted war, a complex Single Integrated Operations Plan (SIOP), and many thousands of nuclear weapons that might have been exchanged between the United States and the Soviet Union. Yet the vulnerability of fixed command posts and the virtues of mobile alternatives remain a lesson that is pertinent to India even if all other aspects of the American control system are less germane.

The experience of smaller nuclear powers like France, which developed austere versions of the U.S. command system, is also instructive. Paris constructed a command post for its strategic nuclear forces at Taverny, burying it under concrete more than 60 meters below the surface. It also constructed an alternate command center at Lyon-Mont-Verdun, but after both of these major investments had been made, the transmitters necessary to send the launch codes to its SSBN fleet remained overland and, by implication, were highly vulnerable to interdiction.[315] This vulnerability led one analyst to conclude that "destroying, or simply degrading, such key C^3 centers could be functionally equivalent to destroying the nuclear weapons themselves since no French nuclear weapon could be used without redundant confirmation of launch authority from the chief of state."[316]

---

[314]The best analysis of this issue is found in Blair, *Strategic Command and Control*.

[315]Yost, "French Nuclear Targeting," pp. 136–137.

[316]Ibid.

The moral of the story is clear: Any Indian command post that is designed to function effectively in the face of even a few Pakistani or Chinese nuclear missiles, especially those that will be available 20 years hence, cannot simply be located "underground"—i.e., in the basement of a military headquarters—but will instead have to be hardened and deeply buried if it is to survive any attacks aimed at paralyzing New Delhi's C^{3}I network.[317] Yet it is unclear whether India has the technology to build such hardened and deeply buried structures, and even if this were the case, it remains unclear whether India would be able to construct an information network whose *every* node—from its point of origin at the NCA down to the multiple operators at the AEC, DRDO, military headquarters, and field units—is also buried deep enough to prevent the proverbial weak link from subverting the entire chain.[318] The challenges here are, moreover, as much technical as they are operational and financial—for the location of any fixed command post, no matter how deeply buried it may be, will sooner or later be discovered by India's adversaries, and the accuracy of at least China's nuclear missiles over the next two decades is likely to improve to a sufficient extent that accurate countercontrol attacks will be theoretically feasible. If China in fact develops deep-earth penetrating warheads, such attacks could actually be highly effective even if only a relatively small number of warheads were allocated to such missions.[319]

It can thus be seen that India will be faced with a host of unpalatable choices: For while deeply buried command centers are indeed New Delhi's best option should it settle for fixed installations, such centers are extraordinarily difficult and expensive to build, and the technical and financial burdens of deeply burying the entire information distribution network over great distances along the Indian

---

[317]This is in effect a variant of the Soviet solution followed during the Cold War. For details, see Blair, *The Logic of Accidental Nuclear War*, pp. 120–145.

[318]For an analysis of this issue in the U.S. context, see Albert J. Wohlstetter and Henry Rowen, *Objectives of the United States Military Posture*, RM-2373-PR (Santa Monica: RAND, 1959), p. 31ff.

[319]For a good example of how even highly accurate but low-yield deep penetrating warheads could destroy underground facilities, see Albert Wohlstetter and Richard Brody, "Continuing Control as a Requirement for Deterring," in Ashton B. Carter, John D. Steinbruner, and Charles A. Zraket (eds.), *Managing Nuclear Operations* (Washington, D.C.: Brookings, 1987), pp. 162–163.

landmass—so as to render it immune to deep-earth penetrating attacks—are considerable. Moreover, even if these constraints could
somehow be overcome, the presence of specialized equipment to
construct such a network would itself signal the location of various
nodes in the chain—and if these locations were eventually compromised, their survivability would always be uncertain either because
of ongoing improvements in the accuracy and lethality of Chinese
(and possibly Pakistani) ballistic missiles or because of the possibility
of deep-earth penetrating attacks. Given these considerations, New
Delhi is unlikely to embark on such ambitious projects in haste, especially when there are other solutions that would in principle offer
the prospect of mitigating command vulnerability at lower costs.

In fact, there are three solutions that can be operationalized fairly
readily and are likely to prove more attractive to New Delhi, at least
in the near term. The first and most burdensome solution consists of
configuring some kind of airborne or afloat command post. Over the
next two decades, India is likely to acquire some kind of airborne
warning and control system, probably developed with Russian and
Israeli assistance.[320] Many of the technologies that will be installed
on such an aircraft can be adapted for the command-and-control
mission, either on the Airborne Warning and Control System
(AWACS) platform itself or preferably on some other airframes dedicated to this task. These aircraft, operating in tandem with some of
the airborne tankers that India will also acquire, can be specially
dedicated to the command mission. These platforms need not be
numerous and need not be maintained on constant airborne alert;
rather, they can be deployed routinely at one or more Indian air
bases and would be required to sortie only on receipt of strategic
warning to some other facilities either to increase locational uncertainty or to pick up members of India's national command authority
in anticipation of a nuclear attack.[321] Similar technologies can be
installed on board India's larger surface ships, although for technical
and operational reasons an airborne platform might be more appropriate so long as India's retaliatory capabilities are primarily land-
based.

---

[320]Chattopadhyay, "The Indian Air Force: Flying into the 21st Century."

[321]Details on how the United States used such a system during the Cold War can
be found in Blair, *Strategic Command and Control*, pp. 127–181.

The second option, which is both more attractive and immediately available, is simply to upgrade all the communications suites, resident databases, and mission-planning equipment in existing Indian operations rooms to serve as nuclear command posts in an emergency. While these centers are no doubt soft targets that can readily be interdicted, upgrading all of them would diminish the problem of command vulnerability simply by increasing redundancy. Such a solution would effectively increase the number of nuclear munitions that an adversary must expend if it is to maximize the probability of success accruing to a counter-C3I attack aimed at paralyzing the Indian state. Moreover, this alternative does not preclude the development of several other nontraditional sites as backup command centers to be activated *only* in the aftermath of a nuclear attack. In effect, this solution would covertly create several reserve command sites that, although soft, could not be identified as such in peacetime. The success of such an effort, however, will depend on the degree to which India is able to exercise strict operational security vis-à-vis Pakistan and China during the construction, configuration, start-up, and test phases: After these processes are complete, they can be maintained indefinitely in a dormant state in the absence of conflict. Since the number of covert facilities that can potentially be developed on DAE, DRDO, and military installations alone is extremely large, the targeting requirements necessary to enforce C3I denial become so demanding as to be rendered impractical in the specific war-fighting environment in Southern Asia.

The third and possibly the most intriguing solution, especially in the intermediate term, is to develop some variety of mobile land-based command centers.[322] These centers could be deployed aboard specially constructed vehicles (or trains) that are maintained in a garrisoned posture during peacetime but are flushed to wartime hides (or dispersed amid the civilian rail net) on receipt of strategic warning. Obviously, exercising such an option would require the development of special vehicles that have sufficient reserves of power to run the complex data and communications systems on board,

---

[322]For a description and assessment of such centers, see Babbitt, "Command Centers," pp. 336–344; C. C. Mow and J. W. Workman, *Feasibility of Transportable Armored Command Posts*, RM-4422-ISA (Santa Monica: RAND, 1965); and Alan J. Vick, "Post-Attack Strategic Command and Control Survival: Options for the United States," *Orbis*, 29:1 (Spring 1985), pp. 95–117.

sufficient fuel (or access to fuel) to enable reasonably distant dispersal away from their peacetime garrisons, and sufficient habitability to allow a small cadre of staff and decisionmakers to transmit the nuclear release orders in the aftermath of a nuclear attack. The virtue of such a solution is that mobile command centers could be made reasonably small and could be equipped with all manner of long-distance, beyond-line-of-sight wireless communications equipment on board. In addition, their movements would be relatively difficult to track in real time, and they could be built relatively cheaply and in sufficient number to allow for redundancy should some of the original complement fail to survive the initial attacks.

Obviously, operations involving all these systems would require a great deal of preplanning, including but not restricted to plans relating to the relocation of the national leadership on receipt of strategic warning. The degree of preplanning here, however, is not likely to exceed the levels of forethought otherwise required to make other elements of the force-in-being operationally effective. Each of the three alternatives described above nonetheless represents a cheaper, more survivable, and more readily attainable capability than those involving the construction of deep-underground facilities dedicated to the task of managing nuclear operations. It must be remembered that the demands imposed on command facilities in the Indian case are much less than those that affected similar facilities in the United States and the Soviet Union during the Cold War.[323] Command centers in the latter cases were intended to enable command authorities to ride out nuclear attacks safely and to execute complex war-fighting strategies over an extended period of time—with as much improvisation as necessary—in the face of horrendous damage inflicted by hundreds if not thousands of nuclear weapons detonating all around them.

Nuclear attacks aimed at India would by contrast be much smaller and would not exceed a few score weapons at most. New Delhi's retaliatory responses, too—at their most demanding—would be fairly simple and would not require the kind of complex planning that characterized the primarily counterforce operations both the United

---

[323]This point is emphasized most trenchantly by Santhanam in "Panel Four: Nuclear Weapons and the Balance of Power."

States and the Soviet Union planned for at the height of their rivalry. Indian nuclear retaliatory missions, perforce, will be preplanned operations, and it is therefore unlikely, given the modesty of Indian nuclear reserves and its operational infrastructure, that its command centers will be intended to support highly improvised mission planning. Instead, the main purpose of such centers will be to provide a sanctuary where the national leadership can survive the relatively small nuclear attacks that are likely to be unleashed; can receive and assess attack and damage reports; can contemplate various preplanned courses of action; and can order fairly simple retaliatory actions that will in all likelihood take the form of a riposte more or less in slow motion.[324] Hence, command centers in India need not be as sophisticated, complex, or numerous as American and Russian facilities were during the Cold War.

Given these considerations, New Delhi is likely to pursue the second, third, and first alternatives—in that order—before it embarks on any costly schemes to build hardened and deeply buried underground command posts of the sort that were constructed by the Soviet Union during the Cold War.[325] To be sure, some facilities resembling the latter will almost certainly be constructed if they have not been completed already, but these facilities are more likely to be shallow underground structures equipped with blast doors, baffles, and labyrinth entrances intended to provide some degree of blast attenuation—and designed to provide a quick, near-term alternative to the soft above-ground facilities already existing—rather than deeply buried structures that, being impervious to indirect air-induced weapon effects and relatively resistant to direct induced violent ground motions, could actually survive a direct hit.[326] Although India's shallow underground command posts ought to suffice so long as its adversaries are armed with either relatively inaccurate or low-

---

[324] For one thoughtful view of the demands associated with this process, see Menon, *A Nuclear Strategy for India*, pp. 242–283.

[325] For an excellent description of these facilities, see the analysis in Department of Defense, *Soviet Military Power: An Assessment of the Threat, 1988*, 7th ed. (Washington, D.C.: USGPO, 1988), pp. 44–67.

[326] The differences between shallow underground and deeply buried structures are discussed in *Heating, Ventilation, and Air Conditioning of Hardened Installations, Technical Manual*, TM 5-855-4 (Washington, D.C.: Department of the Army, November 1986), pp. 1–4.

yield weapons, New Delhi will have no alternative but to consider constructing deeply buried facilities embedded in hard rock if it seeks to inure its command system against the threat of attack by megaton-class nuclear weapons *through the use of fixed, land-based alternatives*.[327] Thus far, however, Indian strategic managers have not shown any inclination to pursue solutions centered on a deep underground command system despite the fact that they are favored by many of India's strategic elites.

Communications Systems. Irrespective of what kind of protected command facility or network is ultimately developed, India will need a variety of communications systems in order to connect its command authorities with the custodians of the various components of its distributed arsenal. Ideally, these communications links should be reliable, redundant, and secure. Since no single communications system possesses all these properties simultaneously, however, most command structures settle for a multiplicity of systems, with their specific technical qualities determining whether they function as the primary, secondary, or tertiary links for a given task. Consistent with this fact, Vijai Nair has argued that India should develop and deploy "communication satellites providing real time voice and audio-visual data links based on ultrahigh and very high frequency bands; extremely low frequency communications facilities to direct subsurface forces; airborne relay stations to meet range limitations of equipment; [and] alternate ground based radio and radio relay networks."[328] Similarly, Raja Menon has asserted the need for a wide variety of communications systems, each of which would become relevant either at different stages of the alerting process or because of the differences between the various Indian deterrent arms. These systems include the civilian voice telephone net, data and image transfer components operating over a fiber-optic backbone, and radio and satellite communications, all netted together with the early-warning, attack assessment, and launch control systems that would be required, in the author's estimation, for the robust control of India's emerging deterrent.[329]

---

[327]For more on this question, see Philip M. Dadant, *Why Go Deep Underground?* P-1675 (Santa Monica: RAND, 1959).

[328]Nair, "The Structure of an Indian Nuclear Deterrent," p. 98.

[329]Menon, *A Nuclear Strategy for India*, pp. 272–283.

Clearly, the United States procured each and every one of these technologies during the Cold War. In fact, one of the greatest concerns of U.S. military planners throughout this period was ensuring stable connectivity before, during, and after a nuclear attack. In support of this objective, the World Wide Military Command and Control System (WWMCCS)—the communications system carrying peacetime and crisis traffic—slowly incorporated over time a specially segregated component called the "minimum essential emergency communications network" (MEECN), which was dedicated to transmitting nuclear launch orders through different media to the strategic force components surviving the initial Soviet attacks.[330] The challenge of connectivity facing the United States was particularly burdensome because it was assumed that a Soviet first strike would involve a relatively large number of nuclear weapons, many of which could destroy sensors, command nodes, and platforms as well as some operational military bases before the national command authorities could generate decisions based on tactical warning and initial attack assessments.[331] Furthermore, American retaliatory action, which could have been initiated simply on warning or while under attack, was oriented toward executing extraordinarily complex mission plans that required different and widely separated arms of the triad to launch their weapons rapidly but in a precisely orchestrated sequence at a highly specific set of targets. By contrast, it is unlikely that the Indian nuclear force will either have to operate in similarly demanding circumstances or be tasked to execute a similarly complex retaliatory plan. Consequently, India's needs pertaining to connectivity are much simpler, although for reasons of physics a certain degree of redundancy will of necessity be incorporated into its strategic communications network.[332]

The term "strategic communications network" itself must be recognized for what it is, however, which is to say that it should not be understood as a dedicated communications system acquired, deployed, and maintained apart from the civil networks already present within the country. Rather, it refers simply to that subset of the na-

---

[330]Vick, "Post-Attack Strategic Command and Control Survival: Options for the United States," pp. 95–117.

[331]Blair, *Strategic Command and Control*, p. 257.

[332]Zuberi, "The Proposed Nuclear Doctrine," pp. 3–5.

tional communications system which India's strategic enclaves and its uniformed military already use. To be sure, there are certainly a few dedicated links that are restricted to these end users alone, but such dedicated links are not unique to India's strategic enclaves, as many national organizations have separated communications systems. The Indian Railways, for example, have a dedicated telephone network separated by many degrees from the rest of the civilian system. In the final analysis, then, India's future investments in strategic communications, like the rest of its supporting infrastructure, will profit greatly from the modernization of its existing civilian systems. Indeed, successive Indian governments since 1991 have committed themselves to modernizing the entire national communications infrastructure over the next two decades[333]—and while this effort is intended primarily to promote economic growth and national development, the objectives of enabling remote-area access, primarily through wireless systems combining telephony, television, and computers, are an integral part of this planning. The implications of such a network, especially if it does succeed in using relatively cost-effective and innovative solutions (e.g., wireless local loop [WLL] systems and very small aperture terminals [VSATs]), for defense purposes should be obvious.

If the plans published by the government of India offer any indication,[334] India's future national communications infrastructure is likely to consist of a multilayered system.[335] At its base would be the

---

[333]The contours of the overall telecommunications modernization program are described in Stephen D. McDowell, *Globalization, Liberalization and Policy Change: A Political Economy of India's Communications Sector* (New York: St. Martin's Press, 1997). See also Peter Evans, "Indian Informatics in the 1980s: The Changing Character of State Involvement," *World Development*, 20:1 (1992), pp. 1–18, and Government of India, *Indian Telecommunications*, Report by the Telecom Commission (New Delhi: Ministry of Commerce, 1994).

[334]Ministry of Communications, *VIII Five Year Plan (1992–1997): Industrial Development for Telecom Sector* (New Delhi: Government of India, 1991); "Information Technology Action Plan," *India News*, June 16–July 15, 1998, pp. 1–3.

[335]Good surveys of the structure of the Indian telecommunications system can be found in "India: The Commercial and Regulatory Environment," *Asia Pacific Telecommunications*, March 1, 1997; Ashok Jhunjhunwala, Bhaskar Ramamurthi, and Timothy A. Gonsalves, "The Role of Technology in Telecom Expansion in India," *IEEE Communications*, November 1998, pp. 88–94; Mark Rockwell, "Telecom in India: Bring Order from Chaos," *Telephony*, 218 (June 1990), pp. 26–30; and N. Ravi, "Telecommunications in India," *IEEE Communications*, March 1992, pp. 24–29.

traditional copper landlines, albeit with increasing numbers of fiber-optic segments, that currently dominate the communications system. In 1998, India is believed to have had more than 267,000 route kilometers of coaxial cable, with 72,000-odd kilometers linked by microwave systems and another 57,000-odd kilometers linked by various ultrahigh-frequency (UHF) systems. The fiber-optic segment consisted of more than 76,000 route kilometers in 1998, and this was expected to increase to in excess of 203,000 route kilometers by 2002.[336] This system obviously represents a complex amalgam of underground and overhead lines connected to local exchanges that are in turn connected to numerous regional switching facilities through either other landlines or microwave relays.[337] Altogether, India possessed more than 23,000 exchanges in 1998 together with a switching capacity capable of managing in excess of 21.2 million lines that year. Despite its large absolute size, however, this network is generally old, prone to defects, and unreliable, with low call-completion rates—in large part because of the numerous nonelectronic exchanges embedded in the switching network. For this reason, India is gradually replacing its traditional Strowger and crossbar exchanges with digital switching, and its Eighth Five-Year Development Plan had in fact mandated that 93 percent of the network be digital by the end of 1997.[338] The reliability of this system will thus progressively improve as the local and long-distance switching systems become entirely digital. However, this architecture will nonetheless remain vulnerable to strategic attack because the most important multipurpose switching stations are relatively few and constitute soft targets that invariably exist above ground.[339]

Since the basic trunk-line system does not cover many parts of the country, especially remote areas, the Indian government has also been attempting to incorporate an intermediate technology layer

---

[336]*India—Telecommunications Market and Regulatory Overview* (Bucketty, Australia: Paul Budde Communication, 2000), p. 2.

[337]A useful map of the overall transmission network can be found in Ravi, "Telecommunications in India," p. 28.

[338]"India: The Commercial and Regulatory Environment."

[339]For details, see Ravi, "Telecommunications in India," pp. 24–29. See also *India—Telecommunications Market and Regulatory Overview*, pp. 1–8.

centered on fixed-wireless networks providing local-loop services.[340] This technology, envisaged as complementing the multichannel radio systems that traditionally served low-density areas and connected rural centers to the national trunk network, is seen as offering critical opportunities for reliable communications when "nonpremium" services like cellular and paging are at issue.[341] Increasingly, however, the government has begun to view mobile cellular systems as the wireless architecture of choice intended initially to serve the demand for rapid communications in urban areas but eventually extending to rural areas as well.[342] A new telecommunications policy implemented in April 1999 has in fact resulted in the rationalization of service, revenue, and regulatory structures and in the division of the entire country into four main cellular markets: the major metropolitan areas of Bombay, Delhi, Calcutta, and Madras; a Category A circle consisting of prosperous regional states like Maharashtra and Gujarat; a Category B circle consisting of next-tier states like Punjab, Rajasthan, and Madhya Pradesh; and a Category C circle consisting of the geographic periphery, including Jammu and Kashmir, Assam, and the Andaman and Nicobar islands.[343] This scheme is expected to intensify the demand for different kinds of wireless services—which, in the case of India, turn out to be particularly attractive because they help overcome existing infrastructure bottlenecks, preclude the need for new, expensive, and cumbersome investments in laying landlines, and allow for the rapid implementation of new connectivity technologies that bypass or replace obsolescent communications systems.[344]

Finally, the apex layer consists of dedicated satellite telephony intended to support high-speed broadband voice, data, and other

---

[340]Abhinav Taneja, "A Phone in Every Village: Taking Telecom to Rural India," *New Telecom Quarterly*, October 11, 1997, p. 9ff.

[341]"India: Fixed Wireless Communications," *Tradeport*, available at http://www.tradeport.org/ts/countries/india/isa/isar0037.html.

[342]Thomas C. Hunter, Jr., "India: Set for Wireless," *Cellular and Mobile International*, January 1, 1997.

[343]*India—Wireless and Satellite Communications* (Bucketty, Australia: Paul Budde Communication, 2000), pp. 3–5.

[344]For details on the variety of wireless systems already operational or sought in India, see "India: Wireless Communications," *Tradeport*, available at http://www.tradeport.org/ts/countries/india/isa/isar0041.html.

kinds of commercial and strategic transmissions both within the country and internationally.[345] At the commercial level, the national telecommunications provider Videsh Sanchar Nigam Ltd. (VSNL) signed important agreements early on with ICO Global Communications to establish a satellite access mode in India for global mobile personal communications, and other providers, including Iridium, Globalstar, and Constellation, also began operating (or intend to operate) services in India. Although the future of some of these programs is uncertain by virtue of Iridium's failure as a commercial project, the threatened bankruptcy of ICO, and continued fears about Globalstar's viability, general trends in the global mobile personal communications by satellite (GMPCS) regime suggest that, whatever the economic challenges facing the first generation of operators, GMPCS represents a new wave in communications that promises greater connectivity through mobile facsimile, messaging, data, two-way voice, and broadband multimedia via small, handheld phone sets, computer-mounted terminals, and laptops. These capabilities will exploit the growing availability of new satellite systems—whether geostationary or nongeostationary, fixed or mobile, broadband or narrowband, global or regional—that are capable of providing telecommunications services directly to end users from a constellation of satellites. Such systems are likely to coalesce over time into three specific categories: little low-earth-orbit satellites (little LEOs), big low-earth-orbit satellites (big LEOs), and broadband, low-earth-orbit satellites (broadband LEOs).[346] Not surprisingly, then, the first generation of GMPCS operators will soon be joined—and could probably be replaced—by regional operators such as Agrani, Thuraya, ACeS, Reliance, and Orbcomm, all of which plan to offer voice, data, and messaging communications services in various parts of India within the next few years.[347] VSNL—which will remain a monopoly only until around 2004—is also expected to in-

---

[345]*India—Wireless and Satellite Communications*, pp. 1–10, and David Benton, "MSS Systems Advance Telecommunications in India," *Satellite Communications*, November 1994, p. 18.

[346]Details on the promise of GMPCS for global communications are available in "Space Communications and Applications," in *Third United Nations Conference on the Exploration and Peaceful Uses of Outer Space*, Background Paper No. 5, A/CONF.184/BP/5, May 27, 1998, pp. 13–18.

[347]*India—Wireless and Satellite Communications*, pp. 7–8.

vest in other satellite access technologies, such as the INMARSAT Mini M connection to access the Fiber Optical Link Around the Globe (FLAG) system, as well as to continue to provide key inter-country satellite connections through INTELSAT, access to subma-rine cable systems and the international maritime network through INMARSAT, and satellite-based paging services.[348] These channels will supplement the domestic satellite communications services al-ready provided by the INSAT system to commercial, military, and national leadership users.

Most important from the perspective of defense and strategic communications, however, is India's new and growing interest in VSAT communications systems.[349] The terminals associated with these systems are relatively small in size, are vehicle portable, and, unlike fiber-optic and cable technologies, operate independently of distance; thus, they can serve as ready-made infrastructure in places where trunk lines of different sorts prove too costly or impractical. Since relatively secure satellites in geosynchronous (GEO) orbits serve as the backbone for VSAT networks, VSAT terminals can call on any available GEO satellite, passing signals when necessary in a bent-pipe configuration from one earth station to another and sometimes from satellite to satellite to establish a secure, reliable link with an-other VSAT terminal.[350] Given the advantages of this system, India has begun to invest heavily in VSAT networks for both commercial and strategic uses, opening the Ku band in addition to the C band previously available for VSAT users. In fact, it is likely that all of India's strategic institutions, including the nuclear and defense re-search and development establishments as well as the uniformed military, will settle—as more and more satellite transponder space becomes available—on VSAT technologies for their long-distance, beyond-line-of-sight communication requirements, especially when reliability, portable equipment, jam resistance, and security are nec-essary for their success.[351]

---

[348]For details, see "India: The Commercial and Regulatory Environment."

[349]See *India—VSAT Overview and Major Players* (Bucketty, Australia: Paul Budde Communication, 2000), pp. 1–6.

[350]Amy C. Cosper, "VSATs Find Their Voice," *Global Telephony*, 5:5 (September 1997).

[351]"New Satellite Communication System for Army," *The Hindu*, April 20, 2000.

When these multiple layers of infrastructure modernization are completed, the civilian communications network will give Indian decisionmakers a host of technologies with which to access their strategic enclaves and nuclear delivery assets in an emergency. The advantage New Delhi enjoys here is that its nuclear doctrine does not require rapid retaliation, and India can thus afford to delay its response in the face of significant damage to its communications systems. Therefore it is unlikely to be handicapped by waiting for the reconstitution of its transmission links, however partial, before it unleashes retribution.

There are at least four different types of communications systems available to New Delhi for this purpose. At the first level, connectivity can be established simply through landlines. While these are no doubt vulnerable because many critical components of the circuit-switched network are above ground, and because it will be some time before India develops a completely packet-switched voice and data network, neither Beijing nor Islamabad can be certain that New Delhi will be unable to use this system without expending an even larger number of weapons than they might otherwise allocate to the counter-C^3I mission.[352] Since the number of weapons that either state can allocate to such a mission is small to begin with, it is possible that at least some landline connections that survive the initial attack will enable Indian decisionmakers to establish contact with their strategic components for purposes of ordering retaliation. Neither Pakistan nor China is known to emphasize the counter-C^3I mission in their strategic targeting—and even if this changes with respect to China over time, it is unlikely that Beijing would be willing to expend a large number of warheads for such a mission given the competing demands that its relatively small strategic forces already face vis-à-vis other adversaries.[353] In any event, if India develops a completely packet-switched system over time, the damage that can

---

[352]The difference between standard circuit switching and packet switching was first described by Paul Baran at RAND in 1961, and his work is usefully summarized in Wohlstetter and Brody, "Continuing Control as a Requirement for Deterring," pp. 169–178. India's packet-switched capabilities are described in "India: The Commercial and Regulatory Environment" and in *India—Fixed Network: Voice and Data Services* (Bucketty, Australia: Paul Budde Communication, 2000), pp. 1–7.

[353]These demands are discussed in some detail in Gill and Mulvenon, "The Chinese Strategic Rocket Forces: Transition to Credible Deterrence," pp. 11–57.

be caused even by larger hypothesized Chinese attacks to its landline network would be circumvented, at least as far as issuing launch orders and receiving confirmation of receipt are concerned.[354]

In any event, there is a second communications system already in place. Should all landlines be rendered inoperable—a remote prospect to begin with—Indian decisionmakers could use other kinds of wireless transmissions, such as high-frequency (HF) broadcasting systems, to issue their launch orders. HF broadcasts, especially in the sky-wave propagation mode, can be received by receivers beyond the horizon up to many thousands of kilometers away and, as one analysis has pointed out, "have overcome [many of their] reliability problems in recent years."[355] The advantage of HF transmitters is that they are relatively small, can be made mobile, and suffice even at low power. The disadvantage of HF communications is that they can be interrupted or degraded by weather conditions, nuclear weapon effects, and jamming by hostile adversaries. Such degradation, however, is usually transient and, as such, would not eliminate the connectivity between the leadership and its strategic elements either if multiple transmitters exist or if the national command authority, being committed to a strategy of delayed retaliation, is willing to wait out the effects of degradation before issuing its retaliatory orders.[356] In general, HF communications systems thus represent a relatively flexible and easy way of contacting distant components of a dispersed force-in-being. Even more to the point, however, these systems already exist in India and are used by each of the armed services, civil aviation, the broadcasting system, and other

---

[354]Even if the increases currently hypothesized in Chinese nuclear force capabilities actually occur as a result of U.S. NMD/TMD initiatives, it is not clear whether China will be able to mount comprehensive counter-C^3I attacks against India so long as its targeting allocations vis-à-vis the latter remain more or less constant in absolute terms. Nothing in China's current or projected strategic nuclear doctrine suggests an interest in nuclear war fighting, and planning to interdict its adversaries' C^3I capabilities would in any event require far more warheads that those currently projected for China. For assessments of changes in Chinese force size as a result of U.S. NMD/TMD developments, see Steven Lee Myers, "Study Said to Find U.S. Missile Shield Might Incite China," *New York Times*, August 10, 2000.

[355]Glenn W. Goodman, Jr., "Long-Distance Communications," *Armed Forces Journal International*, 137:8 (March 2000), p. 20.

[356]For more on HF systems, see Ashton B. Carter, "Communications Technologies," in Ashton B. Carter, John D. Steinbruner, and Charles A. Zraket (eds.), *Managing Nuclear Operations* (Washington, D.C.: Brookings, 1987), pp. 240–242.

national agencies. Obviously, these technologies are not ideal for improvising complex war plans involving widely separated elements of a force, but they are sufficient for issuing brief encrypted launch orders and for confirming the receipt of the same *so long as specific retaliatory options, authenticating procedures, and coordination plans have been developed prior to a conflict.* If dissemination of the launch order and confirmation of receipt are all that India's nuclear doctrine requires for effective connectivity and assured retaliation, New Delhi need not invest in more exotic low-frequency (LF) communications technologies—as did the United States—in order to benefit from the better immunity to nuclear effects these systems offer in their ground-wave propagation mode.[357]

The third capability that New Delhi already has, and that will be made available in even better form in the future, is satellite-based communications provided either through its own dedicated space systems or through access to international satellite networks that can be readily accessed by mobile devices within India. Satellite-based communications systems, which usually operate in the superhigh-frequency (SHF) and UHF bands, are purely line-of-sight systems.[358] Ordinarily, such systems would require several relays to effectively transmit information over long distances. Since most communications satellites are placed in GEO orbit, however, they automatically acquire line-of-sight contact with more than 80 percent of the hemisphere beneath them and consequently become perfect instruments for wide-bandwidth, high-data-rate communications. Wide bandwidths and high data rates not only allow for reliable voice communications between multiple users but also allow for the transmittal of data, images, and sensor information concurrently. More important, they allow multiple users to interact simultaneously in different media, even as they exchange large quantities of data electronically—and this flexibility enables satellite communications systems to support the kind of audio- and video-conferencing capabilities that are necessary if nuclear operations are to be improvised or conducted on an ad hoc basis prior to execution. The VSAT sys-

---

[357]For details, see Jonathan B. Tucker, "Strategic Command and Control Vulnerabilities: Dangers and Remedies, *Orbis*, 27:4 (Winter 1993), pp. 941–963.

[358]Satellite-based communications systems are described at some length in Carter, "Communications Technologies," pp. 242–250.

tems in which India is increasingly investing would thus provide both clear and encrypted voice, data, fax, and video transmissions and would permit demand assigned multiple access (DAMA) capability, which allows hundreds of users to share a single satellite communication channel based on need or demand.[359]

At the present time, India does not have any dedicated military communications satellites, but it does have six multipurpose spacecraft that are currently operational. These six "birds," consisting mainly of satellites from the INSAT-2C/D/E series, provide some 80 transponders in the C, S, and Ku bands that are used for telecommunications, TV relay, data collection, search-and-rescue operations, and meteorology.[360] These capabilities will further increase with the launch of the INSAT-3 series, as it is expected that the eight or nine spacecraft in this series will provide India with some 130 transponders for ready use by the year 2002 and approximately 150 transponders through the first decade of this century. Although these INSAT spacecraft can and do support Indian military operations, they are still not dedicated military communications satellites. One authoritative Indian source has noted that the ISRO has already conducted numerous studies to define a satellite communications system appropriate for the armed services. Because such a dedicated system would need to be accessible by an extremely large number of users from a wide variety of fixed and mobile terminals, these studies have concluded that "[a] minimum [of] two full satellites at any time will be required to be produced in future."[361] It is further believed that usage requirements alone would mandate replenishment launches "every three years or so, . . . [in order] . . . to [continually] maintain the system."[362] Clearly, producing a dedicated military communications satellite is well within India's technical competency. Moreover, the advent of the GSLV will in fact enable India to launch 2.5-ton-class satellites into GEO transfer orbit, and by all in-

---

[359]"VSATs Are Very Competitive," *Indian Express*, February 4, 2000, and Dhiraj Ahuja, "The Extra Terrestrial Connection," *Dataquest India*, November 15, 1996.

[360]Mecham, "India Builds a 'Crown Jewel,'" pp. 56–57, and Raj Chengappa, "Moon Mission," *India Today International*, July 3, 2000.

[361]Pramod Kale, "Future Space Communications System for India," *IETE Technical Review*, 8:5 (September 1991), p. 273.

[362]Ibid.

dications some kind of augmented—if not dedicated—military space communications platform will certainly be deployed by New Delhi within this decade.[363]

For all their advantages, however, satellite communications systems do have vulnerabilities. For example, the uplinks and downlinks to the system can be jammed; the ground infrastructure necessary to control the satellites' operation can be interdicted by nuclear or conventional means; and the space platforms themselves can be attacked by antisatellite (ASAT) weapons. Although the last contingency could become relevant over the next two decades because of China's emerging ASAT capability, this threat would likely be least effective against communications satellites parked in GEO orbits.[364] In any event, New Delhi has already secured gateways to international satellite communications systems that can be readily accessed even by personal handsets from anywhere within India. With systems like Motorola's Iridium and Globalstar (and their commercial successors, such as Agrani, Thuraya, ACeS, Reliance, Constellation, and Orbcomm), Indian security managers will acquire fairly simple but operationally significant means of disseminating launch orders in an emergency through, if nothing else, global mobile personal communications systems. A system configured like Iridium may not require any ground stations within India for managing communications traffic and would remain immune to military attacks even in the context of a bitter Sino-Indian (or Indo-Pakistani) war simply because it represents a third-party asset that is always available for use by any subscriber.

The expected proliferation of such systems, when combined with India's growing access to other foreign commercial satellite com-

---

[363] *India: Indian Air Chief: War Success to Depend on Satellites,* FBIS-NES-98-281, October 8, 1998. Details about India's new space-based satellite communications system can be found in Vivek Raghuvanshi, "India Starts Research on Satellite Project," *Defense News,* May 29–June 4, 1995, p. 34. For more on India's military space plans, see V. Siddhartha, "Military Dimensions in the Future of the Indian Presence in Space," *Journal of the United Services Institution of India,* 130:540 (April–June 2000), pp. 243–258.

[364] Chinese interests and emerging capabilities in this area are described in Stokes, *China's Military Modernization: Implications for the United States,* pp. 117–123.

munications systems,[365] implies that New Delhi will possess additional levels of communications redundancy: So long as all the relevant custodians of New Delhi's force-in-being are equipped with portable handsets capable of accessing GMPCS satellites, the dissemination of launch orders, report-back, and even teleconferencing can be conducted prior to executing retaliation. Obviously, the presence of such capabilities in no way obviates the need for preplanned operations, but since such preplanning will presumably take place as a matter of course, India's ready access to international satellite communications systems will only enhance its capacity for nuclear retaliation despite the damage that its command system may otherwise suffer. As Jasjit Singh concluded, hyperbolically but accurately, "In today's world, a motorized cell phone connected to a satellite will do the job"[366] as far as ensuring strategic connectivity is concerned.

Finally, and in addition to the three capabilities described above, India already possesses a fourth communications system that is actually somewhat premature from the perspective of nuclear operations. As part of the ambitious naval modernization conducted during the mid-1980s, the Indian Navy constructed a very low frequency (VLF) broadcasting station at Vijayanarayanam in the southern Indian state of Tamil Nadu.[367] This VLF facility, which is currently operational, is used primarily by the Navy to communicate with its conventional attack submarines. If and when India acquires a ballistic missile submarine, this facility would become crucial because it would permit the national command authority to issue launch orders to submerged boats operating at depths of a few meters. VLF waves propagate over long distances—almost a quarter of the globe away— and are generally immune to the atmospheric disturbances caused by nuclear explosions. Their small bandwidth, however, limits the rate at which data can be transmitted, usually allowing only for the

---

[365]For an excellent examination of the utility of such systems for defense communications in the context of the United States (but with clear applications to India), see Tim Bonds, Michael G. Mattock, Thomas Hamilton, Carl Rhodes, Michael Scheiern, Philip M. Feldman, David R. Frelinger, and Robert Uy, *Employing Commercial Satellite Communications*, MR-1192-AF (Santa Monica: RAND, 2000).

[366]Cooper, "Nuclear Dilemmas—India."

[367]Tellis, "Securing the Barrack: The Logic, Structure and Objectives of India's Naval Expansion," Part II, pp. 31–57.

operation of slow teletype.[368] If India's preplanned nuclear options are appropriated coded, VLF broadcasts would allow for the dissemination of such codes slowly but fairly reliably. Thus, they could be used to transmit nuclear release orders both to submerged vessels and to land units if the latter are suitably equipped with receiver terminals capable of picking up VLF signals. This medium of transmission, however, would truly be a system of last resort because the alternative technologies available to New Delhi—landlines, HF radio, and satellite communications in the form of both global mobile systems and VSATs—are far more flexible and rapid than VLF. Because submerged vessels cannot access landlines and HF communications, however, VLF will continue to remain the transmission method of choice for naval purposes.[369] Yet when India deploys a true ballistic missile submarine it could acquire an airborne VLF transmitter similar to the U.S. Navy's TACAMO if it desires to minimize the vulnerability of the large terrestrial VLF installation currently in place at Vijayanarayanam.

In all probability, though, India is likely to forgo the acquisition of such exotic systems because, as the analysis suggests, New Delhi already enjoys several advantages with respect to strategic connectivity. First, the number of Chinese and Pakistani warheads that would be allocated to Indian targets in general and to counter-C^3I mission in particular is relatively small, implying that many of India's command assets would survive even if the face of what would otherwise be unprecedented damage in the event of a nuclear attack. Second, New Delhi already possesses several of the communications systems Indian analysts desire—and though these systems were acquired primarily for conventional military or other civil operations, they could readily be used for strategic C^3 if New Delhi made the investments required to increase their number, hardness, mobility, and distribution either in connection with nuclear mission planning or as part of ongoing improvements in India's communications infrastructure. Third, India's operational requirements with respect to ensuring connectivity are generally simple: The system must primarily be able to disseminate launch orders and receive confirmation of message receipt rather than enabling full report-back, as is required by

---

[368]Carter, "Communications Technologies," pp. 235–239.

[369]Menon, *A Nuclear Strategy for India*, pp. 279–281.

strategies emphasizing flexible or ad hoc retargeting. Fourth and finally, New Delhi benefits from its doctrine of delayed retaliation in that the advantages of not being committed to a strategy of prompt response free India from the burden of investing in complex and overly redundant communications systems, since it can take as long as it needs to reconstitute its C^3I network before it exacts nuclear retribution.

All things considered, therefore, New Delhi appears to be much better placed to execute its retaliatory strategy than many analysts give it credit for. Moreover, it often goes unrecognized that since the 1980s, all three Indian armed services have undertaken a comprehensive modernization of their C^3 systems in order to enhance their bandwith, reliability, diversity, and security. To be sure, Indian security managers will obviously undertake a thorough systems analysis of the communications vulnerabilities existing along the entire length of their command chain—especially as this might be stressed under different scenarios of nuclear conflict—but such an analysis is likely to suggest that so long as New Delhi seeks to deploy some kind of a force-in-being rather than a ready arsenal, what it probably needs are many small and focused supplementary investments as opposed to large new programs aimed at replicating some facsimile of the communications infrastructure maintained by the U.S. and the Soviet Union during the Cold War.[370]

Warning and Assessment Capabilities. A similar judgment applies to the necessity for warning and assessment capabilities. Here too, many Indian analysts have levied extensive demands on New Delhi. One senior retired military officer, for example, has argued the need for "full and continuous intelligence on the location, movement and . . . installation of the [adversaries' nuclear] SSMs [surface-to-

---

[370]This conclusion is corroborated by New Delhi's initiation of a small (Rs. 600 crore) Defence Communication Network Project (DCNP) to integrate all the existing communications systems possessed by the three armed forces, the Ministries of Defence, Home, and External Affairs, and the paramilitary forces. The DCNP is expected to focus mainly on netting together the different existing terrestrial networks and satellite overlays in order to create "synergy" between the different users and to maintain robust links between the command headquarters and their subordinate echelons through multiple open and secure voice and data links. See Srinjoy Chowdhury, "Communication Network to Link Armed Forces with Ministries," *The Statesman*, August 11, 2000.

surface missiles] along with their command and control links and or-ganization [as well as] the[ir] nuclear weapon aircraft." What is most important, he concludes, "is that there should be real time intelligence with Air HQ in peacetime and with the OCP [the nuclear operations command post] whenever it is activated."[371] Arguing this point further, Nair notes that "while satellites would be a part of the system to provide these inputs, the country needs to maintain a viable air element for both ELINT [electronic intelligence] and photo reconnaissance [PR]. The existing infrastructure with the Indian Air Force would have to be upgraded technologically to meet these demands, and suitable communications links integrated into the strategic communication network."[372] The National Security Advisory Board, in its Draft Report, also argued laconically that "deterrence requires that India maintain . . . effective intelligence and early warning capabilities."[373]

In a less ambitious vein, another scholar—reiterating some of what has been written in India on this subject—has noted that "the demands of early warning are technical in part and human in part. Early warning satellites, airborne reconnaissance and over-the-horizon radar are vital [but] human systems of a high order are a necessary supplement."[374] This judgment coheres well with the assessments of U.S. analysts like Neil Joeck, who concluded that "strategic and tactical warning must be improved"[375] if nuclear stability is to be enhanced in South Asia. Other Western commentators, however, have gone beyond Joeck's carefully limited inference to assert that "India and Pakistan have taken up nuclear positions rife with the potential for military and political miscalculation," among other things "because neither country has [a] state-of-the-art early warning and intelligence-gathering capability."[376] Such views, which are common in popular Western commentary, appear to be

---

[371]Gupta, "Detonations Don't Make Deterrence."

[372]Nair, *Nuclear India*, p. 192.

[373]"Draft Report of [the] National Security Advisory Board on Indian Nuclear Doctrine," p. 2.

[374]Bajpai, "The Fallacy of an Indian Deterrent," p. 163.

[375]Joeck, *Maintaining Nuclear Stability in South Asia*, p. 59.

[376]See the opinions recorded in Paul Mann, "Subcontinent's Nuclear Duel Raises Miscalculation Risk," *Aviation Week & Space Technology*, June 8, 1998, p. 58.

based on the somewhat dubious premise that the absence of technologies for *tactical* warning not only results in an inadequate deterrent but inevitably creates deterrence instability as well.[377]

The range of technologies, systems, and organizational issues that bear on the question of how to provide adequate warning and assessment are large and complex, and consequently it is useful to assess this problem by relating the need for such capabilities to India's specific operational requirements.

The purpose of any warning and assessment system in the nuclear realm is to enhance the survivability of a country's strategic reserves in order to preserve its capacity for inflicting unacceptable damage on an adversary so as to deter attack in the first place.[378] During the Cold War, the United States relied heavily on multiple systems to provide the tactical notice necessary to flush manned bombers from their vulnerable land bases, bring SSBNs and land-based ICBMs to ready status, and prepare the command system to execute intricate launch-on-warning or launch-under-attack retaliatory strikes if necessary. This warning and assessment complex consisted of a variety of sophisticated technologies that, taken together, were designed to provide early and reliable information about the extent, dimensions, and targets of any unfolding attack directed against the United States. Space-based satellite early-warning systems provided the first signal of ICBM and SLBM attacks because their infrared sensors could detect the intense plumes generated during the boost phase of a missile launch. From that point on, various land-based and, supplementarily, airborne radars located either along the coast or scattered throughout Alaska, Canada, Greenland, and England took over the task of detecting, tracking, and characterizing the nature of the attack mounted by various kinds of missiles and bombers, or missiles

---

[377]These arguments are misleading because they do not factor in the size and quality of the opposing nuclear arsenals in Southern Asia, the nuclear doctrines of the three contestants, and their capacity to process attack information even if tactical warning was available.

[378]See the discussion in Bruce G. Blair and John D. Steinbruner, *The Effects of Warning on Strategic Stability* (Washington, D.C.: Brookings, 1991), for a sophisticated treatment of how the presence of warning systems can affect deterrence, sometimes in dangerous ways—a point that is usually overlooked by well-meaning but often ill-informed Western observers who constantly bemoan the lack of tactical warning systems in South Asia.

alone. The data required to arrive at this determination was fused and processed at NORAD headquarters in Colorado and then rapidly disseminated to SAC headquarters at Omaha, the national command authorities, and the various unified and specified commands throughout the United States, who would then initiate diverse pre-planned responses designed to increase the survivability of the force components assigned to them—if these were not immediately committed to executing a rapid retaliatory response. Finally, as the incoming attack was consummated, various space-based multispectral sensors would identify the number, location, and yield of the nuclear detonations taking place over U.S. territory, thus completing the assessment required to enable command authorities to determine the nature and extent of their retributive response.[379]

The objective of investing in such an expensive integrated warning and assessment capability was to increase the fraction of nuclear assets that would survive a deliberate Soviet attack. Ensuring the success of this objective became particularly important because as Soviet nuclear capabilities grew in number, diversity, and accuracy, the vulnerability of U.S. strategic assets also grew proportionately, and significant portions of the triad—the manned bombers, for example—turned out to be highly dependent on reliable early warning for their survival. In any event, the desire to maximize the largest possible fraction of the force surviving a nuclear attack was fundamentally rooted in the demands of American strategy: The simple strategy of "assured destruction" could have been successfully executed even in the complete absence of strategic and tactical warning because the war loads carried by all surviving American SSBNs were more than sufficient to destroy every Soviet city of any consequence. U.S. nuclear strategy, however, was never oriented toward deterrence by punishment—that is, simply achieving "assured destruction"—as is often erroneously assumed. Rather, it focused singlemindedly on deterrence by denial, which was intended to prevent the Soviet Union from securing victory by eliminating U.S. counterforce assets, thereby compelling Washington to choose between "surrender" or

---

[379]This nuclear warning and assessment system is described in some detail in Blair, *Strategic Command and Control*, and in John C. Toomay, "Warning and Assessment Sensors," in Ashton B. Carter, John D. Steinbruner, and Charles A. Zraket (eds.), *Managing Nuclear Operations* (Washington, D.C.: Brookings, 1987), pp. 282–321.

"countervalue" attacks that would further result in the complete destruction of all American cities.[380]

Because frustrating this logic of victory was deemed to be essential for strategic stability, the United States had to preserve the largest possible fraction of its *counterforce* capabilities even in the face of a massive Soviet first strike. One way to preserve these capabilities was simply to initiate preventive or preemptive attacks designed to interdict Soviet counterforce assets before they could actually be employed. Thanks to all the political, technological, and moral burdens associated with such a course of action, American decisionmakers settled for the second, more expensive alternative: to build a massive warning and assessment capability that would provide reliable notice of an incipient Soviet strike, thereby allowing U.S. forces to disperse in order to increase survivability or be launched prior to absorbing the vast incoming attack. If such an attack was only of limited dimension, then the warning and assessment system became essential simply to ensure a proportionate retaliatory response. In all instances, however, adequate tactical warning and assessment became critical for the success of America's nuclear strategy.[381]

The demands imposed on India's strategic capabilities are dramatically different. To begin with, New Delhi does not propose to acquire an arsenal anywhere near the size or complexity of the U.S. nuclear force. Further, it does not intend to create a ready arsenal in the first instance but only a force-in-being composed of latent capabilities that could be fused together to produce a deterrent when required *in extremis*. Moreover, India also does not face any adversaries today—and will probably not face any adversaries for at least another two decades—that resemble the Soviet Union in terms of the size, quality, and depth of their nuclear capabilities. Despite these differences in circumstance, however, there is no doubt that stable deterrence in South Asia also requires that India maintain relatively survivable nuclear assets, even if only as a dispersed force-in-being. Ensuring this survivability in fact remains the *sine qua non* for India's continued safety in the nuclear age, but the challenge facing New

---

[380]Ball, "U.S. Strategic Forces: How Would They Be Used?" pp. 31–60.

[381]See the comments in Harold Brown, *Thinking About National Security: Defense and Foreign Policy in a Dangerous World* (Boulder, CO: Westview Press, 1983), p. 78ff.

Delhi is not simply that of assuring the survivability of its strategic resources but rather assuring their survivability without having to reproduce the gigantic, costly, and operationally demanding warning and assessment capabilities that the United States maintained in order to generate reliable tactical warning.[382] The logic of India's no-first-use doctrine also eliminates the prospect of ensuring survivability through preventive war or preemptive strikes. Consequently, New Delhi must resolve the challenges of survivability in a different way—and the solution represented by its force-in-being suggests that survivability will be maintained primarily through "a combination of multiple redundant systems, mobility, dispersion and deception."[383]

This insistence on thorough opacity with respect to the number, location, and disposition of various elements of its retaliatory force implies that India will seek to ensure survivability primarily by denying its adversaries the information they need to perfect the targeting strategies essential to the successful execution of a "splendid first strike." Since the survival of these elements is fundamentally dependent on uncertainty about their location either in peacetime or during a crisis, the survivability of the Indian force-in-being also turns out to be *substantially independent of warning—or, at least, tactical warning.* If so, New Delhi is freed from the burden of maintaining both the warning and assessment systems and the operational readiness postures that the United States had to sustain during the Cold War. Obviously, all other things being equal, having tactical warning about an incipient attack is better than not having such warning—but other things usually are not equal, and the huge costs associated with producing tactical warning systems would simply be wasted if the operationally dormant (i.e., the standard) disposition of the force-in-being does not allow the survivability of these reserves to be enhanced as a result of such received warning. Vijai Nair corroborated this judgment perfectly when he noted that "the time of flight of missiles from Pakistan and Tibet to targets in India is so lim-

---

[382]Chengappa, "Worrying over Broken Arrows," pp. 30–31.

[383]"Draft Report of [the] National Security Advisory Board on Indian Nuclear Doctrine," p. 3.

ited, that even if a launch is detected, not much can be done to neutralise it."[384]

In such circumstances, it is probable that New Delhi will invest the
resources it might otherwise have frittered away on extensive tactical
warning and assessment systems to further increase the locational
uncertainty surrounding its strategic reserves. To be sure, some fixed
targets by their very nature cannot be hidden from view, and this implies that large aim points like cities, air bases, and cantonments as
well as other permanent military facilities like logistics centers and
storage depots will always be vulnerable to a surprise attack. However, if India adequately disperses, conceals, and camouflages its
strategic components while maintaining strict secrecy about their
number, location, and disposition, no adversary can be certain, even
in a crisis, that the damage-limiting strikes it may contemplate
against fixed targets would in fact immunize it from the painful consequences of future Indian retaliation. Thus, even if many civilian
and military installations remained vulnerable to attack, the uncertainty with respect to whether such attacks would *eliminate* India's
nuclear reserves would contribute more to their survivability than
any acquisition of tactical warning and assessment systems.[385] Despite what some Indian military officers may say, New Delhi does *not*
require any technologies that provide "full and continuous intelligence on the location, movement and the installation" of its adversaries' nuclear capabilities to ensure the success of its force-in-being.

---

[384]Nair, *Nuclear India,* p. 192.

[385]This conclusion seems to be conceded even by Raja Menon, who, while acknowledging that "there would probably not be many in India who would positively
opt for an early warning system," nonetheless defends the acquisition of such capabilities on the grounds that the "320 seconds" of warning provided by such a system
may be worth it "if this is the only time available to sound air raid sirens, get people
into shelters and warn the target areas" of the imminent attack. See Menon, *A Nuclear
Strategy for India,* pp. 261–264. While this reasoning is sound in principle, Indian
security managers appear to have concluded today that the costs associated with truly
benefiting from the availability of tactical warning—that is, both the costs of the
tactical warning systems themselves and the enormous expenses associated with the
construction of nationwide civil defenses—are better allocated to the retaliatory
components of the nuclear deterrent itself and to other investments that better
contribute to preventing deterrence breakdown rather than to coping with the
consequences of deterrence failure. This logic of this posture, which is fully consistent
with an acceptance of mutual assured vulnerability, underlies the remarks made by
Santhanam, Iyengar, and Arunachalam in "Panel Four: Nuclear Weapons and the
Balance of Power."

Consequently, Indian security managers are unlikely to emphasize the acquisition of such capabilities over the next two decades.

So long as India's nuclear reserves are opaque and are maintained in the operationally dormant condition associated with a force-in-being, the acquisition of tactical warning and assessment systems will not enhance their survivability at all; all that such systems may do is enable Indian decisionmakers to calculate what the size of their residual force is likely to be if all the attacking weapons launched by the adversary detonate successfully on their intended targets. Having such information prior to the conclusion of an attack would be useful if India had a strategy of prompt response. With a doctrine of delayed retaliation, however, the utility of possessing such information immediately is more ambiguous. The only advantage that could be unambiguously attributed to the possession of tactical warning systems is that New Delhi would be able to conclusively determine *who* was launching a nuclear attack directed against India. And while this capability again represents an advantage of some sort, it presumes an operational environment that bears little resemblance to that perceived by New Delhi. In a practical sense, the only countries likely to launch nuclear attacks on India are China or Pakistan. Neither is believed likely to launch such attacks out of the blue, and such attacks are not expected to occur outside of an evolving political crisis or preparation for a conventional war. Consequently, determining the identity of the state launching a nuclear attack is unlikely to be a particularly difficult matter in practice and certainly does not appear to embody the kind of difficulty that should compel New Delhi to acquire the complex tactical warning systems built around distant early-warning and over-the-horizon radars, satellite-based infrared detection platforms, and other terrestrial systems that are described as being relevant for this purpose.[386]

The bottom line, therefore, is that India does *not* need tactical warning capabilities for the success of its force-in-being. Such capabilities made sense primarily in the context of the strategic

---

[386]These technologies are discussed at length in the South Asian context in Vipin Gupta, "Sensing the Threat—Remote Monitoring Technologies," in Stephen P. Cohen (ed.), *Nuclear Proliferation in South Asia* (Boulder, CO: Westview Press, 1991), pp. 225–264; in Menon, *A Nuclear Strategy for India*, pp. 235–283; and in Nair, *Nuclear India*, pp. 183–194.

predicament the United States and the Soviet Union faced and in the context of the operational postures maintained by these two states. Countries that escaped these problems did not invest in comparable kinds of warning and assessment systems. China remains a classic example here: It did not acquire such capabilities throughout the Cold War and still does not possess them.[387] This may not even change over time, but if it does, it will be because Beijing moves more closely toward a nuclear war-fighting doctrine that emphasizes limited nuclear use or damage limitation, in contrast to its traditional posture of simple countervalue retaliation executed in the context of a delayed second strike. This conclusion, however, is not intended to suggest that India needs no warning and assessment systems whatsoever; instead, it is meant to affirm that New Delhi does not need the kinds of tactical warning systems that many Indian analysts, borrowing uncritically from the American experience of the Cold War, claim it ought to acquire.

The capabilities that India needs—and that New Delhi will in fact acquire over the next few decades—are those that enable *strategic*, not tactical, warning and assessment. To reiterate a well-known distinction, strategic warning and assessment systems foretell the possibility of impending war, while tactical warning and assessment systems signal either imminent attacks or attacks already under way.[388] Most Indian analysts who argue for the latter kinds of capabilities, which allow for real-time or near-real-time updates about an adversary's military operations, presume that New Delhi will engage in preemptive strikes or even initiate nuclear wars. Referring to the first kind of response, for example, a former Indian Air Vice Marshal advocated "offensive action" claiming that "it would be logical . . . that right at the commencement of hostilities, or in pre-emptive action, the [Pakistani] Ghauri and the [Chinese] SSMs in Tibet, their installations and infrastructure, be destroyed or damaged to make them unusable."[389] Referring to the second kind of response, one Indian

---

[387] Stokes, *China's Military Modernization: Implications for the United States,* pp. 109–134, and Johnston, "China's New 'Old Thinking'": The Concept of Limited Deterrence," p. 33.

[388] Ashton B. Carter, "The Command and Control of Nuclear War," *Scientific American*, 252 (January 1985), p. 33.

[389] Gupta, "Detonations Don't Make Deterrence."

civilian analyst noted that "we may find that Pakistan poses its choices to us in a less than clear-cut manner while compelling us to react in an all-out manner, resulting in our initiation of nuclear war or [responding by] surrender."[390] While these arguments represent conundrums made familiar by the Cold War, India's nuclear doctrine and force posture are designed to avoid both alternatives to the maximum extent possible.

In fact, Indian policymakers, being overwhelmed by the political significance attributed to the possession of nuclear weapons, often tend to err in exactly the opposite direction: refusing to think seriously about the contingencies involving nuclear use rather than jumping at the prospect of designing clever nuclear-use strategies. In any event, it is important to recognize that New Delhi simply does not and will not possess the resources to engage in satisfactory damage limitation vis-à-vis China (and Pakistan, for that matter) through either preemptive action or premeditated first strikes, although some marginal attrition strategies pursued through conventional means are possible if the nuclear-use contingency is preceded by a lengthy conventional war. Beijing's nuclear superiority over New Delhi and the geographic location of China's nuclear assets vis-à-vis India's force-structure weaknesses prevent damage limitation stratagems from even being contemplated in the Sino-Indian case, while Pakistan's emphasis on producing a wide variety of mobile delivery systems in significant numbers—all tightly integrated into its strategic planning and conventional war-fighting capabilities and ready for rapid, efficient, and covert dispersal—actually ensures that even if Indian damage-limiting strikes are contemplated, successful interdiction of these reserves is unlikely unless it is presumed that New Delhi would actually unleash a bolt-out-of-the-blue attack without any provocation. While such an action is of course possible in theory, it strains credulity to think that India would ever behave this way in practice. Neil Joeck reaffirmed this conclusion in the Indo-Pakistani context by succinctly asserting that "India and Pakistan's invulnerable nuclear capabilities make it unlikely that either would plan a preemptive attack."[391]

---

[390]Joshi, "From Technology Demonstration to Assured Retaliation: The Making of an Indian Nuclear Doctrine," p. 1478.

[391]Joeck, *Maintaining Nuclear Stability in South Asia*, p. 56.

This judgment leaves India with the need mainly for strategic warning and assessment capabilities. Yet the technical components contributing to such capabilities are often difficult to describe because, as one authority put it, they "read like a Baedeker of applied science."[392] Moreover, strategic warning in itself represents a much more complicated endeavor than the technologies that support it, in part because "the signs of imminent attack are [invariably] much more varied and ambiguous than the physical signatures of missiles or aircraft in flight."[393] Strategic warning no doubt requires technology, but it is simply not as technology-dependent as tactical warning usually is; it may even use many of the same technical systems employed by the latter, but these instruments are generally organized, directed, and used in different ways. Unlike tactical warning, which concentrates on the narrow challenge of detecting specific physical signatures of weapons in operation, strategic warning addresses the wider domain of intelligence gathering and politico-military assessment and as such, requires not so much specialized gadgetry as an integrated intelligence collection and analysis capability that allows the national leadership to make informed judgments about an evolving political situation. This in turn requires, among other things, "an efficient intelligence service and research staff, dedicated to strategic and nuclear issues"[394] and an organizational structure capable of evaluating important indicators in order to "render proper advice and formulate appropriate options."[395]

The technical capabilities required to support many of these activities already exist in India in embryonic form. Although India does not possess dedicated surveillance satellites, for example, it has an impressive space-based remote sensing program. The Indian Remote Sensing (IRS) series currently in orbit have, among other things, panchromatic cameras with a resolution of 5.8 meters.[396] The

---

[392]Toomay, "Warning and Assessment Sensors," p. 283.

[393]Ibid.

[394]Bajpai, "The Fallacy of an Indian Deterrent" p. 163.

[395]Nair, *Nuclear India*, p. 117.

[396]Michael Mecham, "Cost-Conscious Indians Find Profits in Imaging Satellites," *Aviation Week & Space Technology*, August 12, 1996, pp. 59–60. This level of resolution does not imply that the satellites are unable to see objects smaller than 5.8 meters but merely signifies that they cannot distinguish between two objects that are closer than

resolutions generally necessary for any surveillance system are in principle a function of the size of the object and the level of precision required for the specific intelligence task; airfield facilities, for example, require resolutions of 6 meters for detection, 3 meters for precise identification, and 0.15 meter for technical analysis; aircraft require resolutions of 4.5 meters for detection, 1 meter for precise identification, and 0.045 m for technical analysis; missile sites require resolutions of 3 meters for detection, 0.6 meter for precise identification, and 0.045 meter for technical analysis; and nuclear weapon components require resolutions of 2.5 meters for detection, 0.3 meter for precise identification, and 0.015 meter for technical analysis.[397] While Indian satellites are certainly not capable of such performance, they will at least be able to locate many important objects of interest when their 2.5-meter-resolution panchromatic cameras are deployed aboard the IRS-P6 satellites early in this century.[398]

These improvements notwithstanding, India's current spacecraft are not ideal as military reconnaissance systems in part because their cameras operate only in the visible and near-infrared portions of the spectrum and because their revisit times are generally poor. These limitations will be redressed somewhat by the new generation of satellites likely to become available within a few years, which will carry a mix of electro-optical cameras, thermal infrared sensors, and synthetic aperture radars.[399] At the same time, however, it is believed that even if the currently operational satellites were to reach their optimal orbits, "it w[ould] cut revisit times for imaging any locale from five days to three."[400] All in all, then, India already has some modest space capabilities that can contribute to strategic warning,

---

that interval. Depending on the objects imaged, their relationship with other entities in the viewing field, and the environmental conditions prevailing at the time of scrutiny, it is quite possible that the IRS can detect even very small objects despite its less-than-optimal resolution for intelligence purposes.

[397] Senate Committee on Commerce, Science and Transportation, *NASA Authorization for Fiscal Year 1978*, pp. 1642–1643, and *Reconnaissance Handbook* (McDonnell-Douglas Corporation, 1982), p. 125.

[398] "Growing Pains," p. 17.

[399] Mecham, "Cost-Conscious Indians Find Profits in Imaging Satellites, pp. 59–60, and Bill Gertz, "Crowding In on the High Ground," *Air Force Magazine*, April 1997.

[400] "Growing Pains," p. 17.

and within the next two decades it is likely to develop a new generation of dedicated, low-earth-orbit military reconnaissance satellites that are capable of providing visual, infrared, and radar imagery. The Indian Air Force has already argued that "success in future wars will depend on the ability to deploy space-based resources for surveillance, battlefield management and communications,"[401] and it is believed that the government of India will support the acquisition of a small number of satellites dedicated to the communications and military reconnaissance mission in the near term.[402]

After the Kargil crisis of May 1999, the government of India, sensitized to the need for new surveillance and warning systems, authorized a new cluster of technology initiatives focused on rapidly increasing India's imaging capabilities through the acquisition of both high-endurance unmanned aerial vehicles (UAVs) and new space-based systems together with their associated ground-based control centers and image-processing facilities.[403] In the latter area, the most significant initiative has reportedly been the rapid reorientation of the existing IRS program to produce a new Test Evaluation Satellite (TES) capable of 1-m resolution. This imaging satellite, which is expected to be launched on India's PSLV sometime early in this decade, will apparently be based on the design of the 2.5-meter-resolution IRS-P5 Cartosat but will be deployed in a lower orbit of approximately 500 km (compared to the 800-km-odd orbit of the IRS-1C and the 700-km-odd orbit of the IRS-1D) in order to secure a 1-meter-equivalent resolution.[404] Over the longer term, Indian strategic planners have concluded that the country would require a constellation of approximately six dedicated surveillance satellites if New Delhi seeks to observe the status of critical facilities and formations in China and Pakistan twice or thrice daily.[405] Whether the new TES satellite is envisaged as being a precursor to such a surveillance

---

[401] *India: Indian Air Chief: War Success to Depend on Satellites.*

[402] Raghuvanshi, "India Starts Research on Satellite Project," p. 34, and "New Delhi Plans Missile-Monitoring Satellite for '99," *Jane's Defence Weekly*, April 29, 1998.

[403] "Israeli UAVs: Forces of the Future," *Vayu Aerospace Review*, IV/2000, pp. 50–52, and "Imaging Capability," *Aviation Week & Space Technology*, November 22, 1999, p. 17.

[404] "'Spy Satellite' Launch by Year-End," *The Hindu*, July 2, 2000.

[405] Ibid.

system is unknown, but the tenor of discussions among Indian technologists suggests that New Delhi will exploit its already-impressive remote sensing program to increasingly support its space reconnaissance activities in the future.

Even though these reconnaissance platforms will continue to lack the state-of-the-art payloads familiar in the West, they will nonetheless suffice to provide Indian decisionmakers with good information about the general status of its adversaries' military capabilities in the preattack phase, perhaps one of the most important components contributing to adequate strategic warning. It ought to be remembered, in this connection, that India already has real-time or near-real-time access to a wide variety of foreign imagery (including radar imagery) from satellites such as LANDSAT, SPOT, and ERS-1,[406] and this access will only grow in the future as the ISRO's international activities increase in both sophistication and depth. Of increasing relevance, too, is the fact that New Delhi will have ready access to a new generation of high-resolution commercial earth observation satellites like Space Imaging's 1-meter-resolution Ikonos, which will be joined by EarthWatch's QuickBird and OrbImage's OrbView-3 in the years ahead.[407] Access to the information provided by these platforms—which offer high resolution, a broad range of spectral capabilities, greater timeliness, a growing number of platforms in orbit, and worldwide accessibility—promises to revolutionize the global transparency regime and will endow countries like India, which possess the requisite ground infrastructure to receive the data, the technical expertise to process and analyze the imagery, and the resources required to purchase information about the relatively small swaths of territory of interest to their militaries, with advantages they did not possess before.[408]

---

[406]K. Kasturirangan, "Evolution of Space Based Remote Sensing in India," *IETE Technical Review*, 9:5 (1992), p. 379.

[407]The implications of new commercial observation satellites for security are examined in some detail in John C. Baker, Kevin M. O'Connell, and Ray A. Williamson (eds.), *Commercial Observation Satellites: At the Leading Edge of Global Transparency*, MR-1229 (Santa Monica: RAND/ASPRS, 2001).

[408]This issue is further explored in John C. Baker and Dana Johnson, "Security Implications," in John C. Baker et al. (eds.), *Commercial Observation Satellites: At the Leading Edge of Global Transparency*, MR-1229 (Santa Monica: RAND/ASPRS, 2001).

Data from such systems will further supplement the information already procured from India's manned airborne reconnaissance platforms, from its land- and maritime-based surveillance systems, and from its human assets in the military and civilian intelligence services—and all these resources will then collectively constitute a significant reservoir of capabilities for strategic warning. India's technical assets, including its own and foreign commercial space-based systems, will also suffice for purposes of damage assessment in the event that India does suffer a nuclear attack. So long as India's space assets and its associated infrastructure survive an adversary's first strike—an outcome that Indian policymakers would presumably wish to ensure through future efforts at building redundancy, reconstitutability, and reconfigurability in their space assets and control systems—New Delhi's IRS system should provide useful preattack information for strategic warning as well as relevant postattack imagery of the damage India sustains as a result of enemy action.[409]

India also has—or will soon acquire—several other supplementary capabilities. It already possesses space-based meteorological, environmental monitoring, and communications platforms, for example, and these too will grow in both number and quality over time.[410] These capabilities are useful for monitoring weather effects on military operations and for supporting adaptive route planning, assessing the effects of damage either suffered or inflicted, and maintaining connectivity between widely spread-out strategic forces. India also enjoys access to many foreign navigation and positioning spacecraft, including the ubiquitous GPS, which allow it to receive accurate location information as well as to deliver many kinds of ordnance, including strategic weapons, with higher degrees of accuracy. In addition, New Delhi has a wide range of terrestrial capabilities, including various kinds of ground- and air-based photographic intelligence

---

[409]India has already demonstrated this capability. In December 1998, for example, "India's reconnaissance satellite flew over Baghdad in the aftermath of Operation Desert Fox, taking pictures of Iraq's badly damaged military intelligence headquarters." Although the "images were not nearly as detailed as those released by the Pentagon," one report concluded that "the existence of Indian imagery of Baghdad shows how competition is mounting in space." Vernon Loeb, "Hobbyists Track Down Spies in Sky," *Washington Post*, February 20, 1999.

[410]These capabilities are detailed in *India, its Space Program, and Opportunities for Collaboration with NASA*, pp. 28–42.

(PHOTINT) and signals intelligence (SIGINT) systems in addition to its more traditional human intelligence (HUMINT) assets.[411] While India thus requires—and will probably develop—certain technical capabilities to support its strategic warning needs, such as high-bandwidth communications transponders and dedicated surveillance systems in low-earth orbit, the real challenges in this area will lie in the realm of reorganizing its intelligence institutions to collect and evaluate information more effectively.[412]

Strategic warning remains an arena where information fusion, evaluation, and considered judgment matter much more than simply technical data, and while remedying weaknesses in the latter realm is easier to accomplish, it will not suffice if the organizations, procedural routines, and competence required to systematically assess an adversary's capabilities and intentions remain underdeveloped. One of India's leading strategic commentators, Jasjit Singh, made this point effectively when he asked rhetorically, "How many specialists on Pakistan does the country [really] have?"[413] Even if this question could be answered in reassuring ways—which it currently cannot—the Kargil crisis amply demonstrated that the principal weaknesses in India's intelligence system, at least as far as strategic warning goes, lie in fragmentation within its intelligence collection mechanisms; a lack of institutional structures for coordinating collection requirements, collating reporting, and generating unified assessments; and finally an inability to effectively integrate intelligence judgments with decisionmaking at the highest levels of policy.[414]

The ministerial task forces set up in the aftermath of the Kargil crisis have recently made several recommendations to the Prime Minister aimed at remedying India's traditional weaknesses in the

---

[411]For a survey of these capabilities, see Ball, *Signals Intelligence in the Post–Cold War Era: Developments in the Asia-Pacific Region*, pp. 73–96, and Manoj Joshi, "Signal Wars: Indian Capability in Perspective," *Frontline*, September 10, 1993.

[412]See *From Surprise to Reckoning: The Kargil Review Committee Report*, pp. 109–117 and 233–238, for an excellent description of the current Indian intelligence-gathering, evaluation, and analysis system. See also Bruce Vaughn, "The Use and Abuse of Intelligence Services in India," *Intelligence and National Security*, 8:1 (January 1993), pp. 1–22.

[413]Manoj Joshi, "Old Body, New Name," *India Today*, December 7, 1998.

[414]*From Surprise to Reckoning: The Kargil Review Committee Report*, pp. 253–256.

area of strategic warning. Among other things, they have urged the creation of a new Defence Intelligence Agency headed by a three-star officer who would control all the technical intelligence collection efforts currently undertaken by the three armed services and the Cabinet Secretariat; the creation of a new National Intelligence Board that, composed of high-level representatives from all of India's external and internal intelligence collection agencies, would be responsible for intelligence fusion, evaluation, and dissemination at the highest levels of policy; and maintaining the office of National Security Adviser as a permanent position within the government, tasked with, among other responsibilities, heading the National Intelligence Board for purposes of delivering strategic warning to the national command authority.[415] It is currently unclear whether these recommendations will be accepted by the Prime Minister as is—odds are they will be—but the scope of the suggestions leave no doubt that the Indian state is well aware of the importance of strategic warning and will likely work hard to develop the capacity for acquiring such warning in the future.

It is important to note that even if the absence of strategic warning does not make a life-or-death difference to New Delhi's ability to execute relatively simple forms of retaliation over some extended period of time, the availability of effective strategic warning will certainly enhance its capacity for a coherent response. So long as India maintains a force-in-being, its ability to retaliate will remain a function of the level of uncertainty surrounding the true location of its strategic assets. Because some assets (e.g., nuclear pits and weapon assemblies) are easier to conceal than others (e.g., delivery systems), however, it is obvious that having some strategic warning is preferable to having no strategic warning at all. And while it is possible that even in the absence of strategic warning some elements of India's retaliatory capability would survive, it is more likely that the size of its residual force and its capacity for efficient, expedited response would greatly increase were strategic warning to be available. Thus, even if India seeks to constitute its deterrent only after it rides out an adversary's first strike, the breathing space provided by an effective anticipation of attack would enable it to increase its capability to organize

---

[415]Aneja, "Towards a New Security Architecture"; Aneja, "GoM for Revamp of Defence Management"; and "Service Chiefs to Plan on Control of N-Forces."

these residual elements. This warning time could be used, for example, to disperse strike aircraft from their traditional bases, flush rail- and road-mobile missiles from their peacetime garrisons, alert the multiple custodians of India's strategic assets to prepare for possible contingency operations, and sequester the national command authority in safe locations from which they can direct India's retaliatory actions if deterrence does in fact break down.

Generating effective strategic warning thus requires New Delhi to be sensitive both to the disposition of military capabilities and to the larger political intentions of its competitors. As part of developing this understanding, India's national leadership must be able to acquire and fuse information arriving from multiple sources—diplomatic, military, intelligence, and international—in order to generate a good assessment of an adversary's preferences and goals. One analyst has noted that this may involve, among other things, "acquir[ing] intelligence on [the] alert status of hostile nuclear forces," monitoring potential adversary "launch sites and nuclear capable airfields," and "monitoring inimical communications that may provide an indication of . . . imminent attack."[416] The object of all these endeavors, obviously, is to prepare for crisis alerting in order to enhance one's own readiness for war while simultaneously engaging in strategic signaling vis-à-vis the opponent. Strategic signaling, however, often raises concern for analysts, many of whom argue that increasing the alert status of one's own forces might appear to be escalatory insofar as it signifies a preparation for combat.[417] Yet however true this may be in principle, the best crisis management studies during the Cold War suggest that while "any decision to place nuclear forces on alert . . . [is] an extremely dangerous step, . . . it is by no means clear that the inherent risks involved with an alert will always be greater than the dangers produced by refraining from alerting forces."[418]

Alerting measures are no doubt unsettling, but if they are restrained and "controlled with the utmost prudence and disci-

---

[416]Nair, *Nuclear India,* p. 192.

[417]Jones, *From Testing to Deploying Nuclear Forces,* pp. 5–6.

[418]Sagan, "Nuclear Alerts and Crisis Management," pp. 130–131.

pline,"[419] they may in fact yield many of the benefits of crisis diplomacy with few of its disadvantages. Indeed, the most dangerous thing may not even be the decision to alert per se but rather what is done as a consequence of such an action. The ideal situation is one where nuclear alerts increase the survivability of one's own forces by mandating "reactive" behaviors like dispersal and concealment—essentially limiting the effectiveness of potential attack by an adversary—rather than propelling "proactive" responses aimed at rapidly eliminating the most exposed and vulnerable capabilities of the opponent.[420] Accordingly, the alerted posture dictated by the availability of strategic warning in India's case is almost certain to take the form of enhanced dispersal and concealment rather than accelerated efforts at preemption—and if past crisis behavior at least in Pakistan is any indication, Islamabad too is likely to disperse its forces for prudential reasons rather than contemplate any hurried preemptive attacks.[421] So long as Islamabad possesses a nontrivial number of mobile delivery systems and New Delhi continues to lack the ability to interdict critical mobile targets—both of which are likely to obtain over the next two decades—there is no need whatsoever for either Pakistan or India to contemplate any proactive responses that emphasize preemption. Even if such responses are contemplated, there is simply no way either state will be able to execute such strategies successfully, at least as far as interdicting counterforce targets is concerned.

---

[419] Ibid.

[420] The ideal system, obviously, as Gottfried and Blair phrased it, is one where "both the capability and the endurance of the command system can be significantly enhanced in a manner that does not project threat, at least at first blush." See Gottfried and Blair (eds.), *Crisis Stability and Nuclear War*, pp. 237–238.

[421] This fact is often overlooked by numerous Western commentators who, while trumpeting the supposed hair-trigger responses that would be mounted, especially by Pakistan, forget that Islamabad's past behaviors where nuclear operations are concerned have in fact been highly conservative. In the hours leading up to the Pakistani nuclear tests in May 1998, for example, Islamabad, fearing an incipient Indo-Israeli attack on its nuclear installations, generated a strategic alert. While this alert was obviously a product of bad intelligence on both Indian capabilities and intentions, it is important to note that the actions undertaken by Islamabad were reactive and not proactive in the sense described above. See Bill Gertz, "Scare Preceded Pakistan Nuke Test: Expected Strike by India, Israel," *Washington Times*, June 1, 1998, for an account of Pakistani actions.

China, too, is likely to conform to just such a behavioral pattern, even though the empirical evidence to support such a claim does not now exist.[422] This fact notwithstanding, China's general nuclear superiority over India and India's continuing inability to engage in counterforce attacks aimed at interdicting critical mobile targets even at short range, let alone targets located at vast distances inside the Chinese heartland, imply that neither side has any incentive to pursue proactive responses that would lead to preemption. Moreover, at least one side, India, and possibly both sides, India and China, will continue to lack the technical capabilities that make such alternatives feasible over the next two decades, implying thereby that neither side ought to feel compelled to strike first *simply in order to increase survivability* even if both sides were to generate strategic alerts in the context of a crisis.

The upshot of this discussion is that New Delhi's interest in supporting infrastructure will be oriented more toward providing strategic warning and less toward the tactical warning capabilities some Indian analysts advocate—and investing in such resources promises to yield significant payoffs that will enhance India's nuclear posture. Realizing these benefits, however, will require the nurturing of specialized bureaucratic competencies, focused organizational restructuring, and new policymaking structures that allow for rapid information flows, systematic scrutiny of available options, and greater decisional agility even more than large technical investments.[423]

Strategic Defense. Finally, the last ingredient of supporting infrastructure that is often advocated by some Indian analysts is strategic defense. One commentator summarized these arguments by reminding his readers that "having stepped into the nuclear arena, India has to prepare itself against a nuclear attack." This aspect, he adds, has two facets: the first consisting of "proper active AD [air defense] system[s]" capable of intercepting enemy aircraft and missiles, and the second consisting of a "suitable passive air defense system"

---

[422]Little is known about Chinese nuclear behavior in the context of a crisis, but the best analyses seem to suggest that China's nuclear posture, at least in the foreseeable future, will continue to emphasize relatively small forces capable of executing delayed second strikes. See Manning et al., *China, Nuclear Weapons, and Arms Control*, pp. 18–19 and 54–58.

[423]Vijay Karan, "Institutionalise Strategic Thinking," *Indian Express*, July 7, 1998.

capable of protecting "people in special underground shelters and bunkers."[424] Other commentators have also endorsed the need for such investments. One former Air Vice Marshal, for example, has argued that although India currently has "no antiballistic weapon system to counter . . . missiles in [their] terminal phase, . . . one can be sure that, if tasked, Abdul Kalam and his team would be able to design and produce our own indigenous and effective ABM [antiballistic missile]."[425] Another retired officer, echoing such views, asserts that "a fine tuned Indian surface-to-air missile [like] Akash . . . could prove a good match to [the capabilities of foreign systems like the] Patriot"[426] and hence should be acquired urgently. The father of the Indian missile program, Abdul P.J. Kalam, also endorsed such views by publicly claiming that India could in fact design a state-of-the-art, space-based strategic defense system that mimicked the capabilities sought by the "Star Wars" program in the United States.[427] To be sure, passive defense systems have their advocates as well. One civilian analyst, for example, citing the example of Russian and Chinese civil defense preparations, has noted that since passive protection would become viable only "if the existing civil defense plans are made nuclear-oriented . . . it is desirable that India should also build its civil defense against [the] growing menace"[428] of nuclear attack. Other, more thoughtful analysts of nuclear issues, such as Nair and Sundarji, are less convinced of the need for strategic defenses. Nair, for example, while not emphatically opposed to such defenses, is more impressed with the ability of even primitive ballistic missiles to nullify sophisticated countermeasures and therefore argues for maintaining deterrence stability primarily by offense-dominant means rather than through defense-dominant approaches centered on substantial missile and civil defenses.[429] Raja Menon, in contrast, seems more supportive of civil defenses, although he does not assess

---

[424]Bakshi, "Nuclear Euphoria and Harsh Realities."

[425]Gupta, "Detonations Don't Make Deterrence."

[426]Zutshi, "For a Strategic Defence."

[427]"India to Design ABM on U.S. Lines: Kalam."

[428]Rakesh Dutta, "Civil Defence Against Nuclear Attack," *Indian Defence Review*, 13:4 (October–December 1998), p. 90.

[429]Nair, *Nuclear India*, p. 158ff.

either the overall structure or the direct and opportunity costs of such efforts.[430]

Given the diversity of views on this question, it is unlikely that Indian decisionmakers will ally themselves publicly with any one school, although that does not appear to have stopped the local city government in New Delhi from drawing up an extravagant plan—still unfounded—to construct numerous underground bunkers within the heart of the city.[431] Although Indian policymakers are probably most sympathetic to the Nair-Sundarji view of the relative inefficacy of strategic defenses—among other reasons because of their cost implications—they are still likely to acquire some modest active defenses as part of their overall modernization of the Air Defense Ground Environment System (ADGES), an air defense net that has been in place since 1974 and that has slowly been upgraded to cope primarily with regional airborne threats.[432] The ADGES consists primarily of a chain of early-warning radars located around the Indian periphery. These radars, generally optimized for detecting high- and medium-altitude targets, feed information into various air defense control centers that control India's manned interceptors and strategic SAM batteries (primarily SA-3s) and cue the numerous Army-manned mobile SAM systems and anti-aircraft artillery deployed around many urban concentrations and military facilities. The detected intruders are then engaged by some combination of manned interceptors, SAM batteries, and anti-aircraft artillery en route to their targets. Although the Indian ADGES is fairly coherent, it is by no means a true IAD system where threat data are collected, fused, interpreted, and disseminated electronically to various components of the defensive network.[433] In addition, the detection process itself can be spotty depending on the terrain and on environmental conditions. Although the Indian Air Force has attempted to minimize these weaknesses through use of mobile observation posts

---

[430]Menon, *A Nuclear Strategy for India*, p. 264.

[431]Kota Neelima, "Either You Will Be Dead or Crammed in a Bunker with 10,000 People," *Indian Express,* July 25, 1999.

[432]The ADGES is described at some length in George Tanham and Marcy Agmon, *The Indian Air Force*, MR-424-AF (Santa Monica: RAND, 1995), pp. 47–49.

[433]Bernard Blake, "Long-Range Air-Defense Systems: A Global Survey," *International Defense Review*, 27: 5 (May 1994), p. 41.

and new, indigenously produced gap-filler radars, the ADGES is not yet a robust network capable of coping with a high-threat environment. This may not have been a problem vis-à-vis Pakistan when the latter possessed only manned aircraft, since the existing radars and the large number of manned interceptors in service with the Indian Air Force more than sufficed to bring the air-breathing threat down to manageable proportions. The system is also capable of dealing more or less effectively with intruding Chinese aircraft, although the mountainous terrain along the northern borders greatly diminishes its detection effectiveness. These limitations, however, are less consequential because the People's Liberation Army Air Force (PLAAF) presence close to the Sino-Indian border has traditionally been minimal and the platforms available for operations have for the most part been obsolete.[434]

The advent of missile threats to India, however, has changed this picture considerably. As the events surrounding the Pakistani Ghauri test demonstrated, for example, India's current early-warning radars could not detect high-speed objects with small radar cross-sections.[435] This implies that both Pakistani and to an even greater extent Chinese missile flights are currently impervious to detection. If China increases its air presence and bases more advanced aircraft near the Sino-Indian border over time, the northern early-warning net may not be able to detect all such intruders if they attempt to exploit the radar's shadow zones for purposes of ingress. Not surprisingly, then, the Indian Air Force is committed to modernizing its ADGES to cope with more complex threats.[436] This modernization has been justified primarily in terms of improving Indian conventional air warfare capabilities, although it has obvious spillover benefits in the realm of strategic defense. At the present time, the modernization effort appears to focus on three areas: improving physical infrastructure, including "establishing a number of addi-

---

[434]Not surprisingly, then, the Indian Air Force's Eastern Air Command is, as one observer put it, "more concerned with anti-insurgency operations than with anything else." Lake, "Indian Air Power," p. 148. Consistent with this threat perception, the Eastern Air Command primarily has second-line air defense aircraft like Mig-21s in its inventory.

[435]"Indians Disparage Pakistan Missile Claim," *Washington Times*, April 11, 1998.

[436]Rahul Bedi, "India Targets $1B Russian Air Defence Capability," *Jane's Defence Weekly*, April 2, 1997, p. 2.

tional airfields in order to plug gaps in the network of existing forward airfields";[437] acquiring improved equipment, which in addition to the space-based platforms referred to earlier will include new airborne early-warning systems, "powerful, long-range coastal radars," and additional radar coverage "to certain areas of north-east India";[438] and purchasing additional weaponry, the most significant of which are the six S-300 PMU-1 anti-air and ATBM systems India desires.[439] The S-300 systems are intended to be integrated into the existing ADGES, and if India purchases the best radars known to be associated with this weapon, the S-300 batteries would offer greatly enhanced capabilities against all kinds of air-breathing threats while simultaneously posing some kind of challenge to the penetrativity of Pakistan's ballistic missiles, if not China's. If India also acquires the lethal Russian SA-10/SA-15 combination for other generic air defense tasks, its ability to defend its airspace would improve even further.[440]

All these systems, however, are extremely expensive. Moreover, even if they are acquired—which at any rate will not occur imminently—they will not be inducted in more than small numbers and may enter Indian service without the best detection and fire control radars available, thanks to the extraordinarily high costs of the components involved.[441] This implies that these systems, however effective they may be against aircraft, would be less effective against missiles and, as such, would serve to provide more psychological comfort than complete defense. Even if India acquires the most

---

[437] Sawhney, "India's First Airpower Doctrine Takes Shape: An Aging Air Force Looks to the Future," p. 34.

[438] Ibid.

[439] Bedi, "India to Sign New 10-Year Defence Deal with Russia," p. 16.

[440] For details, see Christopher F. Foss, "'Grumble' on Land—SA-10," *Jane's Intelligence Review*, 3:5 (May 1991), pp. 203–206; Christopher F. Foss, "Update on SA-10b 'Grumble' Surface-to-Air Missile," *Jane's Intelligence Review*, 3:12 (December 1991), pp. 562–565; and Steven J. Zaloga, "SA-15 'Gauntlet' Air Defence Missile System," *Jane's Intelligence Review*, 5:12 (December 1993), pp. 534–538.

[441] Details about the S-300 system and its various radar and fire control systems can be found in Steven J. Zaloga, "Russian Tactical Ballistic Missile Defence: The Antey S-300V," *Jane's Intelligence Review*, 5:2 (February 1993), pp. 52–58; Steven J. Zaloga, "'Grumble': Guardian of the Skies, Pt. 1," *Jane's Intelligence Review*, 9:3 (March 1997), pp. 113–118; and Steven J. Zaloga, "'Grumble': Guardian of the Skies, Pt. 2," *Jane's Intelligence Review*, 9:4 (April 1997), pp. 153–156.

potent versions of these systems, their small numbers would suffice mainly to diminish—not eliminate—attacks that might be mounted on centers of great political and strategic importance to India, since as one analyst put it, there is no "silver bullet in missile defense."[442] In all probability, New Delhi is unlikely to acquire anything other than a thin ATBM defense capability over the next decade. Rather, it will continue to rely primarily on the logic of punishment—meaning the threat of "delayed—but assured—retaliation"—to prevent nuclear threats to the homeland, with its few defensive systems serving only to minimize attacks on critical targets and provide some forms of psychological assurance.

Since these systems essentially represent token defenses, they will almost certainly be ineffective against all Chinese strategic missiles and may be ineffective against many Pakistani ballistic missiles as well. This difference in outcome hinges in the first instance on the fact that the reentry velocity of many Pakistani systems is substantially lower than that of their Chinese counterparts. While the former threats generally fall within the target velocity intercept parameters of ATBM systems like the S-300 PMU-1, the latter clearly do not.[443] The lower reentry velocity of most Pakistani missiles does not imply, however, that such missiles can *invariably* be intercepted by India's ATBM defenses if and when these are deployed; to the contrary, the capability to successfully intercept here will be substantially diminished by India's lack of space-based missile warning systems, the technical inadequacies of its long-range early-warning radars, and the still-limited automatic data transfer capability within the ADGES, all of which would combine to deny the terminal intercept systems the cuing information they would need to maximize their effectiveness. Further, even if such information were available, otherwise effective missile defenses could also be frustrated by the presence of penetration aids and by the possibility of saturation—challenges that could become increasingly relevant in the case of both Pakistan and

---

[442]L. P. James III, "No Silver Bullet in Missile Defense," *U.S. Naval Institute Proceedings*, 125:12 (December 1999), pp. 39–43.

[443]See Koblentz, "Theater Missile Defense and South Asia: A Volatile Mix," pp. 54–62, for useful data on the reentry velocities of different Pakistani and Chinese missiles.

China a decade or so from now.[444] Consequently, all Chinese strategic missiles—and increasingly even its semistrategic missiles—are likely to remain immune to India's ATBM defenses. And while many Pakistani missiles today would in principle be comparably susceptible to interception, whether a satisfactory defense can be achieved in practice remains dependent on issues that are currently unresolved: the number and quality of the Indian ATBM systems deployed, the effectiveness of future upgrades undertaken within the ADGES, and the availability of some kinds of long-range detection capabilities for early warning and cuing.

Given the costs associated with pursuing these investments in any robust way, it is not at all clear that New Delhi will be any more enamored of thick active defense solutions tomorrow than it is today. Its continued reliance on offensive threats for deterrence stability implies that it is equally unlikely to pursue any large-scale passive defense measures either. Such efforts are, in addition, extraordinarily costly to pursue and organizationally demanding to sustain. In a situation where India relies primarily on strategic rather than tactical warning, meaningful civil defense measures involving evacuation to shelters and the like would also be chaotic and burdensome. The origins of civil defense in India go back to the air raid management efforts launched by the British government during the Second World War[445]—and while these efforts continued with some earnestness until 1971, they were for the most part superfluous during the three conventional Indo-Pakistani wars, since the Pakistan Air Force's efforts to locate targets in major urban areas were frustrated more by a lack of strategic offensive capabilities than by the valiant though usually successful efforts of local wardens to supervise neighborhood "blackouts." In the nuclear era into which the subcontinent has steadily slipped since 1974, these measures have become even more

---

[444]China is likely to respond to U.S. NMD/TMD initiatives both with a buildup of the size of its missile inventory and with increased deployment of penetration aids aboard its missile. Once Pakistan's missile production plant at Tarnawa comes on line, Islamabad will possess the capacity to produce large numbers of missiles, some of which may not even be armed with nuclear warheads but are nonetheless useful for barrage fires—and if Chinese assistance to Pakistan continues well into the indefinite future, it would not be surprising to find Islamabad capable of integrating penetration aids into its strategic payloads before long.

[445]For details, see Seth Drucquer, *Civil Defence in India* (Bombay: Oxford University Press, 1942).

superfluous to the point of being all but obsolete, and the government of India is thus unlikely to embark on any but the most token efforts to revitalize civil defense preparedness when the viability of such an investment in enhancing urban protection has yet to be demonstrated.[446] The desire for passive defenses will consequently remain the hobbyhorse of a few zealous advocates but is unlikely to become a strategic priority for the Indian state.

This discussion about supporting infrastructure suggests, on balance, that despite possessing many of its constituent components, India still stands some distance away from being a fully effective nuclear weapon state. Even though many of the technologies already exist in an embryonic condition, and despite the fact that sizable new programs may not be necessary to sustain a force-in-being, several specific initiatives are no doubt necessary for the success of this posture. These include some kinds of command facilities; different kinds of focused investments in integrating strategic communications and increasing redundancy; more mature, integrated warning and assessment systems and organizational structures; and perhaps even some modest improvements in air defense and ATBM systems. These investments will no doubt materialize in the future, but the process of accretion will be slow, relatively costly, and hesitant, because the full implications of what is actually necessary will not become apparent through a single epiphany but rather as part of a gradual process of discovery over time.

Procedural Systems

Since India has now formally claimed the status of a nuclear weapon state, little doubt remains that New Delhi will gradually acquire many of the components its force-in-being requires over the next two decades. The process of developing, producing, acquiring, and integrating these components will be measured and often difficult, but the general trend suggests a steady accumulation of strategic capabilities over time. The most conspicuous evidence of this accretion in the near term will lie in the testing of various kinds of de-

---

[446] A useful survey of the current state of India's civil defense preparedness can be found in Rajendra Prasad, *India's Civil Defence in the Nuclear Age* (Bareilly, India: Prakash Book Depot, 1988).

livery systems. As described earlier, several Indian commentators have already called for the accelerated procurement of different kinds of hardware, all of which are deemed to be necessary for the success of their country's deterrent. K. Subrahmanyam argued, for example, that the solid-fueled Agni-II IRBM represents "the crucial factor to reinforce the credibility of our credible minimum deterrent. Without Agni, India will have no credible deterrent."[447] Such an emphasis on the material accoutrements of deterrence should not be surprising given the critical lacunae in current Indian capabilities. At the same time, however, the stress that analysts have placed on material implements—i.e., weapons, delivery systems, sensors, and physical infrastructure—also derives from the fact that these components are highly visible and, as such, tend to attract more attention than other dimensions of the force. In this sense, Indian commentary about the country's strategic requirements often mirrors that of American discussions during the Cold War.[448] Indeed, such discussions once led three analysts to comment that "an imbalance exists in the study of security in the nuclear age. The process of managing the arsenals is less discussed and less familiar than either the weapons themselves or the doctrinal logic used to define their purposes."[449]

In any event, since the material accoutrements of deterrence tend to galvanize the political imagination in a way that "managerial practices for peacetime and plans for wartime"[450] often do not, it is reasonable to assume that India will in fact produce many of the technical implements required for deterrence over time—and it is likely to do so successfully because the R&D efforts related to the creation of these capabilities enjoy widespread public support as well as the support of important bureaucracies within the Indian state. In any case, the relative effectiveness of systems development

---

[447]K. Subrahmanyam, "The Smouldering Agni," *Economic Times*, March 18, 1999.

[448]A handful of Indian analysts, including K. Subrahmanyam, Jasjit Singh, C. Raja Mohan, Vijay Nair, Raja Menon, P. R. Chari, and V. R. Raghavan, remain the exception to this rule, but the vast majority of Indian strategic commentators—like their American counterparts during the Cold War—remain enthralled by the physical accoutrements of deterrence.

[449]Carter, "Introduction," p. 1.

[450]Ibid.

efforts will be easy to measure because defining success is often simply a matter of gauging whether an individual weapon system works as intended. For these reasons among others, the development of the material components of India's nuclear arsenal is likely to proceed unimpeded.

Even when this process is concluded, however, India will still not possess a complete nuclear deterrent—even if that deterrent is configured only as a force-in-being—if it has not yet developed the procedural systems necessary to direct and control the myriad material and ideational elements that, taken together, are usually viewed as embodying an effective strategic capability.[451] Procedural systems in this context refer simply to the organizational arrangements controlling the design, production, management, and use of all the material and ideational artifacts associated with a nuclear deterrent, however they may be configured.[452] The procedural system is therefore a true "system of systems" insofar as it embodies all the "plans, procedures, organizations, and widely shared assumptions that allow the parts to work together coherently."[453] Unlike the material and ideational components of the arsenal—which encompass, for example, the weapon systems and the principles of strategy and doctrine, respectively—the procedural system often remains the silent component of any command architecture. This silence is deceptive, however, because "though technology and [doctrinal] logic are important elements [for successful deterrence], security is [finally produced] by human organizations, and the results achieved [ultimately] depend on their performance."[454] For these reasons, an effective nuclear deterrent requires not only a systemically embedded set of interlocking, complex physical-technical components oriented toward servicing a particular ideational conception of deterrence but also an or-

---

[451]See the apt remarks in K. Subrahmanyam, "Challenges to Indian Security," Field Marshal K. C. Cariappa Memorial Lecture, New Delhi, October 28, 2000, unpublished manuscript, and "N-Arms Alone Not Enough: Subrahmanyam Panel," *The Hindu*, October 29, 2000.

[452]This definition of a procedural system is based on the description offered by N. Bruce Hannay and Robert E. McGinn, "The Anatomy of Modern Technology: Prolegomenon to an Improved Public Policy for the Social Management of Technology," *Daedalus*, 109:1 (Winter 1980), p. 26ff.

[453]Carter, "Introduction,"p. 1.

[454]Ibid.

ganizational and regulatory framework that controls the entire system throughout its life cycle; beginning with design, continuing through creation, production, deployment, and management, and finally ending, if necessary, in possible employment. The procedural system can thus be seen to serve as the glue that holds all the elements of the deterrence system together insofar as it binds the technology and doctrine into a coherent whole that justifies the creation, structure, management, and use of the nuclear deterrent writ large.[455]

Since all technical arrangements inevitably embody specific "forms of order,"[456] the nuclear deterrent—like any other complex technology—also requires organizational and regulatory mechanisms to lend it the coherence, pattern, and *telos* it needs if it is to be transformed into a usable instrument of national power. As the deterrent system becomes larger and more complex, these organizational and regulatory mechanisms become more numerous and more demanding. Unfortunately, for all their importance, the procedural systems India's emerging force-in-being requires cannot be definitively described here simply because the size, configuration, and deployment pattern of India's evolving arsenal have not yet been defined in detail.[457] As these variables are slowly fleshed out over time, the organizational and regulatory structures necessary to manage the various components will evolve as well and may in some cases be designed anew. The important point, however, is that configuring appropriate procedural systems is an evolutionary process that, at least in the case of the great powers, proceeded at an equal pace with the development and maturation of the nuclear arsenal itself. For this reason, many Western analyses that bemoan India's lack of "sophisticated procedures to control its fledgling nuclear arsenal"[458] are usually specious, since they fail to recognize first that

---

[455]See the discussion in Robert E. Osgood, *Nuclear Control in NATO* (Washington, D.C.: Washington Center for Foreign Policy Research, 1962), p. 21ff.

[456]Langdon Winner, "Do Artifacts Have Politics?" *Daedalus*, 109:1 (Winter 1980), p. 123.

[457]One well-thought-out example of what the Indian procedural system ought to be with respect to nuclear warhead development, production, and allocation can be found in Menon, *A Nuclear Strategy for India*, pp. 235–252.

[458]Dexter Filkins, "India Missile Test Raises Nuclear Bar for Rival," *Los Angeles Times*, April 12, 1999.

New Delhi is no worse off than most of the great powers were at a comparable point in their own history, and second that India's emphasis on producing a force-in-being rather than a ready arsenal requires organizational controls—many of which are already in place—that differ from those associated with the delegative nuclear posture maintained by the United States during the Cold War.

While it is therefore difficult to describe *every* procedural system India needs before its force-in-being fully matures, it is possible to identify three critical kinds of organizational and regulatory components that New Delhi is likely to develop or further refine in the near term: a national command authority, a national security council, and better civil-military coordination.

A National Command Authority. The first critical component necessary for the success of the Indian force-in-being is the formal constitution of something resembling a national command authority. This issue is already being discussed widely among Indian elites and the uniformed military, and the consensus throughout the country is that "the Prime Minister will exercise final control over [nuclear] weapons."[459] The National Security Advisory Board affirmed this judgment explicitly when it asserted in its Draft Report that "nuclear weapons shall be tightly controlled and released for use at the highest political level. The authority to release nuclear weapons for use resides in the person of the Prime Minister of India, or the designated successor(s)."[460] While this recommendation is consistent with the existing structure of strategic decisionmaking in India, the notion of prime ministerial control in the institutional form of a national command authority will require further systematization. This is the case because bureaucratic supervision of the "nuclear estate" in peacetime is different from preparing to develop, procure, and manage a nuclear force that may one day be committed to undertaking retaliatory operations in the event that a deterrence breakdown results in nuclear attacks on India. Transforming the existing patterns of prime ministerial control into an effective national

---

[459]Kumar, "Nuclearization Calls for Strategic Command."

[460]"Draft Report of [the] National Security Advisory Board on Indian Nuclear Doctrine," p. 3.

command authority in turn entails at least four distinct changes in institutional arrangements currently obtaining within the polity.

To begin with, the relationship of prime ministerial authority to presidential power will have to be formally clarified insofar as it pertains to activities and operations in the nuclear realm, even if this means simply explicating what already obtains as a result of tradition, established practice, and previous legislation. Under the Atomic Energy Act, the Prime Minister has formal control over all matters relating to the nuclear realm, and this implies that developing, producing, deploying, and maintaining nuclear warheads are activities overseen by the AEC under the direction of the Prime Minister.[461] This structure of control is eminently suited to the force-in-being India currently envisages in that it results in the treatment of nuclear weapons as national assets controlled by civilian security managers rather than as war-fighting instruments routinely controlled by, and under the custody of, the uniformed military. Since the purpose of acquiring nuclear weapons, however, is to maintain them in constant readiness for possible use no matter how unlikely this contingency may be, minimal but nonetheless formal coordination between prime ministerial authority and presidential power will be necessary first because only the uniformed military can actually deliver these weapons when required and second because the President of India remains the constitutionally recognized commander-in-chief of all India's armed services.[462]

In practice, this coordination is rarely a problem because by both tradition and law the President usually assents to all legitimate Cabinet directives pertaining to the use of military power. But because it is possible—though not probable—that nuclear attacks on India may occur in a highly compressed time frame or via a surprise attack, it is desirable that the nature of Prime Ministerial–Presidential consultations with respect to the question of nuclear response be thought through *a priori*. Important questions that need to be considered in

---

[461] The genesis and logic underlying this arrangement are described in Perkovich, *India's Nuclear Bomb*, pp. 17–21 and 38ff.

[462] The formal relationship between the President and the rest of the Indian executive branch on questions of war and peace is described in P. R. Chari, "India: The Policy Process," in James M. Roherty (ed.), *Defense Policy Formation* (Durham, NC: Carolina Academic Press, 1980), pp. 127–151.

this context include the legality of military responses in situations where the President or his constitutional successors are unavailable, incapacitated, or temporarily incommunicado.[463] Even aside from such contingencies, planning for consultations with the President in the event of nuclear attacks remains a sensible course of action, and these consultations would in any case help the Prime Minister and the Cabinet choose between alternative courses of action that by their very nature embody grave consequences for national security. Even if these practical benefits are overlooked, however, a minimal recourse to Presidential authority is unavoidable if war is to be declared or if India's military forces are to be committed to nuclear missions as part of its retaliatory response. Public evidence of coordination with the President in authorizing such retaliation has many benefits—especially in assuring the *legitimacy* of the selected response—but the requirement for public recognition is not strictly necessary. What is important is that all the relevant entities involved in the activities leading up to an act of retaliation harbor no doubt that the chosen course of action represents a national decision—symbolized by consultation with the President—rather than simply a partisan act ordered by an incumbent who happens to hold office.[464] This concern would not be critical if India were to become a victim of

---

[463]This problem is emblematic of a set of contingencies that India never had to face prior to its entry into the nuclear age and hence is conspicuous by its absence in all traditional discussions about higher defense organization in India. For a good survey of the traditional issues, see P. R. Chari, "Civil-Military Relations in India," *Armed Forces & Society*, 4:1 (November 1977), pp. 3–28. Unfortunately, it also seems to be missed in what are otherwise good studies of Indian higher defense organization in the nuclear age—like Kapil Kak, "Management of India's Security and Higher Defence—I," *Strategic Analysis*, 22:3 (June 1998), pp. 327–337, and Kapil Kak, "Direction of Higher Defence—II," *Strategic Analysis*, 22:4 (July 1998), pp. 501–514—suggesting thereby that the role of the President, even in its formal relationship to issues of nuclear war, has not yet received much attention in India.

[464]While there are few grounds for concern that the President might in fact oppose national security decisions made by the Prime Minister, the historical record in India suggests that presidential power has sometimes been exercised more autonomously than usual when less-than-stable governments have been in power. Given the expectation that coalition governments will continue to dominate Indian politics well into the foreseeable future, consultation with the President about potential nuclear retaliatory responses may be desirable if controversies about the wisdom of some of these actions are to be avoided under conditions of supreme emergency. For a useful survey of the exercise of exceptional presidential power in India, see Paul R. Brass, *The Politics of India Since Independence*, 2nd ed. (Cambridge, UK: Cambridge University Press, 1994), pp. 45–47.

extensive nuclear attacks. If, however, its retaliatory response was in any way disproportionate to the harm it suffered, the legitimacy of the chosen courses of action would have to be underscored by a variety of symbolic and substantive means.

While the consultations between President and Prime Minister are thus important for both legal and symbolic reasons in a democracy like India—especially where momentous decisions involving the kind of nuclear retaliation are concerned—several other issues are even more critical if the national command authority is to function effectively. The second issue in this context thus pertains to developing an appropriate division of labor within the Cabinet with respect to nuclear matters. As earlier discussions indicated, the Indian Prime Minister remains the ultimate decisionmaker with respect to all questions involving the development and acquisition of nuclear weaponry. Managing a deterrent, however, requires expertise, oversight, and judgment over many more issues than simply nuclear weapons as narrowly understood. Insofar as these questions relate to technical, ideational, and procedural systems, however, they cannot remain the responsibility of the Prime Minister alone, since this office holder is often overburdened by other political and administrative responsibilities. In theory, the corporate responsibility for such matters is ultimately held by the Cabinet Committee on Political Affairs (or the Cabinet Committee on National Security, as it has been renamed), which is composed of the Prime Minister in concert with the Ministers of Home, Finance, Defence, and External Affairs. Unfortunately, many of these office holders, being generalists, are ill equipped to understand the complex problems of nuclear technology, doctrine, or organizational structure. Indeed, the Cabinet Secretary—the principal civil servant tasked with coordinating draft documents from various ministries and submitting the same for Cabinet consideration and approval—is also a generalist who has neither the expertise to assess the challenges relating to managing a nuclear deterrent nor perhaps even the time to develop such a competency if so required.[465] These difficulties are exacerbated by the excessive secrecy and compartmentation that often plague Cabinet activities, which frequently leave nominally important ministers oblivious to

---

[465] Kak, "Management of India's Security and Higher Defence—I," pp. 333–334.

the details of key programs managed by the country's strategic enclaves.[466]

What complicates the problems engendered by secrecy is oftentimes studied ignorance and lack of interest in the larger issues of nuclear strategy.[467] Obviously, professional politicians are not expected to become experts in the minutiae of nuclear operations—yet it is not unreasonable to expect that the Indian state would always have some knowledgeable individuals at the highest reaches of government who can understand, query, and critique the positions the country's civil servants, nuclear and defense scientists, uniformed services, and strategic elites hold on nuclear issues. Unfortunately, however, this is still not the case.[468] Maintaining effective command over the evolving force-in-being would therefore require a new division of labor within the Cabinet, and this might in turn involve either the formation of new institutional structures (such as a new subcommittee) or the reordering of existing arrangements to ensure that at least a small subset of Cabinet ministers are administratively if not legally tasked with developing the expertise required to contribute to the management of India's emerging nuclear assets.[469] Many Indian analysts have argued—correctly—that acquiring such expertise does not entail tampering with any of the existing structures of authority: The prime minister would remain the sole arbiter of all matters relating to atomic energy, and the CCNS would still function as the corpo-

---

[466]Thus it is not clear, for example, whether the entire Cabinet or even key ministers were informed of the Prime Minister's decision to resume nuclear testing in May 1998 prior to the tests. Chengappa, *Weapons of Peace*, p. 6, lists only four individuals as having been consulted by the Prime Minister prior to the tests, but this account is disputed by others. The descriptions at various points in Perkovich, *India's Nuclear Bomb*, clearly corroborate the fact that throughout India's postindependence history, key decisions relating to the nuclear program were made by India's Prime Ministers often with little formal consultation and invariably in complete secrecy.

[467]Subrahmanyam, "Nuclear Policy and Political Culture."

[468]It is still not clear, for example, whether India's elected leadership appreciates the implications of the international critiques leveled at the DAE's claims with regard to the results of the May 1998 nuclear tests. It has been reported that DAE scientists briefed the national leadership in the aftermath of the tests, but there are no institutional structures that allow for any peer review of the DAE's conclusions, and the Indian Cabinet has no access to alternate sources of expertise to evaluate the claims made by the official nuclear scientific community.

[469]For some suggestions on this issue, see Kak, "Management of India's Security and Higher Defence—I," pp. 334–337.

rate guardian of India's national security.[470] Within these institutions or around them, however, could be a few individuals who would serve as the repository of expertise on nuclear issues—the National Security Adviser being a good candidate—advising the Prime Minister (if he himself is not one of these experts) on critical decisions relating to "what amount, range and variety of [nuclear] capability would be desirable, along with a doctrine which clearly spells out the why, when and how [relating to nuclear] use."[471]

If such expertise is not developed within the Cabinet or immediately around it, critical problems relating to the thrust of strategic research and development, the size of the nuclear inventory, the shape and disposition of the nuclear arsenal, the operational doctrine governing the maintenance and use of nuclear assets, and the procedural systems necessary to control India's emerging strategic capabilities would likely owe their resolution to technological momentum, fiscal constraints, bureaucratic rivalry, or mere political expediency than to careful, considered, and deliberate strategy. And should these idiosyncratic variables come to determine India's nuclear posture, the country's national command authority would slowly be reduced to the status of a nominal as opposed to a real authority; obviously it would continue to retain control over the metaphorical "button"— i.e., the decision to release nuclear weapons in anger—but it would slowly lose control over the size, structure, and disposition of the forces regulated by that button to elements lying well beyond its command.[472] And such diminishing authority would inevitably result in the replacement of effective control with the mere illusion of control—an outcome whose implications for national security, regional stability, and interstate relations warrant careful consideration in New Delhi.

---

[470]Raja Menon, "Strategic Decisionmaking," *Hindustan Times*, July 30, 1996.

[471]Kumar, "Nuclearization Calls for Strategic Command."

[472]As P. R. Chari, corroborating this argument, once noted, "Policy and strategy become the handmaid of military technology. Advances therein are then accommodated in the defence policy. Regrettably, this is precisely what is . . . occurring in India due to the absence of sufficient thought being given to expressing its defence policy with some degree of precision and comprehensiveness. This is apparent from the lack of any mention of its nuclear and missile deployment policy" in the nation's overall national security strategy. See P. R. Chari, "Defence Policy Formulation: The Indian Experience," *Indian Defence Review*, 11:1 (January–March 1996), p. 32.

If these disadvantages are to be avoided in the long term, there is simply no alternative but to ensure that most senior security managers educate themselves about the dynamics of nuclear strategy. The leadership in every existing nuclear weapon state has had to acquire such competence as part of the burden of ensuring stability in the nuclear age, and India's civilian politicians cannot remain the exception to this rule. The nurturing of such expertise at the Cabinet level or in small pockets within the Cabinet system also has other advantages; for example, it allows for seamless transitions in an emergency such as that which would occur if the Prime Minister were suddenly incapacitated. Ultimately, achieving effective command performance at the highest levels of authority in India will require a return to the collegial spirit of the cabinet system, wherein critical information necessary to make good decisions is shared freely and important choices with respect to the size, structure, and disposition of India's strategic capabilities are discussed candidly and without restraint.[473] This pattern of decisionmaking, however, went out of style with the late Prime Minister Indira Gandhi—to the lasting detriment of collective policymaking—and it simply remains unclear, given the era of coalition politics that looms over New Delhi in the foreseeable future, whether the heritage of cabinet responsibility can be recovered sufficiently to enable India to put in place an effective national command authority that can respond to evolving security challenges in a rational, disciplined, and effective manner.[474]

The third issue pertaining to the development of an effective national command authority pivots on formalizing custodial responsibilities over various nuclear assets in India. The present structure of custodial responsibilities is an inchoate product of tradition and administrative regulation. While the uniformed services are clearly charged with maintaining the delivery systems together with their associated infrastructure and supporting capabilities, the responsibility for nuclear weapons per se is shared by two civilian agencies,

---

[473]For more on this problem, see V.A. Pai Panandiker and Ajay K. Mehra, *The Indian Cabinet* (New Delhi: Konark Publishers, 1996).

[474]On this issue, see James Manor (ed.), *Nehru to the Nineties: The Changing Office of Prime Minister in India* (Vancouver, Canada: UBC Press, 1994).

the DAE and the DRDO.[475] Yet the exact division of responsibilities between these two agencies has remained a closely guarded secret, although the extent and limits of their obligations are certain to be revised as Indian capabilities mature. The character of these mutual obligations, however, will probably become more explicit over time and will in all probability become increasingly bureaucratic, running the gamut from pure research and laboratory experiments to coordinated and joint testing to prototype fabrication prior to serial production. This increasingly detailed division of responsibilities will also affect budgetary allocations as well as the commitment of specialized personnel to the various working groups that are usually set up within India's strategic enclaves.[476]

Such an increasingly bureaucratized division of responsibilities is likely to culminate in an operational plan (or a series of operational plans) specifying the patterns of command, custody, and transfer of various nuclear assets to the end operators—the military—in an emergency. This is critical to the viability of a force-in-being which is structurally centered on a system of "divided control."[477] Indeed, the Draft Report released by the National Security Advisory Board predictably endorsed this expectation, albeit in somewhat florid language, when it affirmed that "an integrated operational plan, or a series of sequential plans, predicated on strategic objectives and a targetting [sic] policy shall form part of the system."[478] Such plans probably exist today, if only in embryonic form, and most of them probably rely on the familiarity of the principal custodians with each other and their acknowledged loyalty to the Indian state to ensure the legitimate transfer of nuclear assets from one point to another within the operational structure.[479] As India's nuclear capabilities

---

[475]Chengappa, *Weapons of Peace*, p. 391, in fact asserts that the Indian custodial system required "at least three agencies . . . to combine their effort if the bomb had to be readied for a launch," but it is not clear from his description whether the armed services represent the third body insofar as they would ordinarily have control over the delivery systems.

[476]The only example of serious analysis of these issues available in the Indian public debate remains Menon, *A Nuclear Strategy for India*, pp. 235–283.

[477]Chengappa, "Worrying over Broken Arrows," p. 31.

[478]"Draft Report of [the] National Security Advisory Board on Indian Nuclear Doctrine," p. 3.

[479]See the discussion at various points in Chengappa, *Weapons of Peace*.

increase in both size and diversity, however, the personalized procedural systems currently in place will quickly reach the limits of their utility—and at that point a more bureaucratized system that relies on prespecified "standard operating procedures"[480] will be required so that the seamless transfer of custody of various nuclear components can take place during an emergency even in situations where the custodians do not personally know one another.

The creation of the new unified command tasked with overseeing India's nuclear delivery systems could provide Indian strategic managers with the institutional capabilities necessary to plan, organize, and train for this task.

Developing an effective national command authority would therefore require, as one of its most important components, a clearly specified system of command dissemination, custody controls, and preapproved procedures for the transfer of nuclear assets so that the political leadership can count on its ability to retaliate even if some of the peacetime custodians fail to survive the initial attacks. Equally important, the presence of such a system would ensure that even widely dispersed military operators could execute authentic retaliatory orders despite their lack of personal familiarity with any of the custodians who may be charged with transferring nuclear weapons or their components to these end users in the context of an emergency.[481] The new unified command headed by the CDS, if established according to expectations, will play a critical role here: It would become the main institution tasked first with overseeing the preparation of all the delivery systems and physical infrastructure that are currently procured, manned, and operated by different armed services; and second with developing all the plans—both current and prospective—pertaining both to conventional joint

---

[480]For more on the utility and the dangers of standard operating procedures (SOPs), see Bracken, *The Command and Control of Nuclear Forces*. It should be recognized, however, that the dangers of SOPs to which Bracken refers do not derive from the existence of SOPs per se—which are necessary in all complex organizations—but rather from SOPs that promoted a risk of nuclear inadvertence in the presence of two tightly coupled, opposing nuclear forces. For more on this issue, see Thayer, "The Risk of Nuclear Inadvertence: A Review Essay,"pp. 472–479.

[481]It is in such an environment that technical innovations relating to nuclear safety, such as PALs, secure container systems, and permissive enable systems, would become most relevant.

operations and to the coordination of changing control and custody procedures over nuclear weapon components in an emergency.

Finally, the last and oft-discussed component of an effective national command authority lies in the promulgation of procedures for orderly succession and for the delegation of nuclear release powers in the event of decapitation.[482] As prior analysis has argued, a critical component of India's force-in-being is its assertive command system. This implies that the authority to unleash nuclear weapons will remain tightly held by the Indian Prime Minister and will not be predelegated to any other officials—either civil or military—prior to the outbreak of conflict. Such a system of tight centralization obviously carries with it the risk of strategic decapitation—that is, the possibility that retaliation could be frustrated simply as a result of the early and sudden destruction of legitimate authority.[483] Yet this contingency, however fearsome it may be in theory, is less relevant in India's case simply because most kinds of nuclear attacks imaginable in this context—whether emanating from China or from Pakistan—would take the form of either strategic signaling or discrete tactical use.[484] Indeed, there are very few contingencies, almost all of them highly improbable, that would require either of Delhi's adversaries to unleash a surprise "last roll of the dice" nuclear attack on India—clearly the only strategy under which strategic decapitation would appear to be rational.[485] These facts notwithstanding, many Indian commentators have argued that New Delhi should nonetheless prepare for the possibility of strategic decapitation in order to guard against operational surprise.[486]

Such advice, although offered in a cautionary way, is sensible and will probably be accepted by New Delhi as part of its contingency preparations given its claims to nuclear status. Precisely how such

---

[482] See, for example, *Study Recommends Two-Person Rule for Using Nuclear Arms*, FBIS-TAC-98-261, September 18, 1998.

[483] Steinbruner, "Nuclear Decapitation," pp. 16–28.

[484] For a somewhat different view, albeit one grounded entirely in capabilities rather than in strategic judgments, see Menon, *A Nuclear Strategy for India*, pp. 254–256.

[485] Shlapak and Thaler, *Back to First Principles*, pp. 80–81.

[486] Kak, "Command and Control of Small Nuclear Arsenals," pp. 266–285, and Subrahmanyam, "After Pokhran—II."

advice is implemented, however, is an entirely different matter. While it is clear that preparing for orderly succession could be exemplified by an act of Parliament transparently specifying in advance the legitimate path for the devolution of nuclear release authority, there is no reason why this procedure should be the only option available to India. To be sure, specifying details about succession through an act of Parliament carries with it an imprimatur that no other mechanism in India's democratic polity can match. An act of Parliament also imparts the message that New Delhi is cognizant of its obligations as a nuclear weapon state and seeks to discharge those obligations fully and seriously. Full transparency about the chain of succession clearly resolves all the problems of legitimacy that may arise with respect to the question of whether certain political agents are authorized to execute those painful acts which embody grave political and moral repercussions for India. But full transparency in these matters may also be perceived as subversive of security insofar as they might reveal more about India's nuclear posture and the identity of key decisionmakers than its security managers feel comfortable disclosing.[487]

It is therefore possible that New Delhi will consider one of two other alternatives: (1) to resolve the problem of orderly succession entirely through internal administrative arrangements without any public discussion and with minimal notice, or (2) to employ a mixed solution that involves securing legal authority from Parliament to develop procedures for transferring authority while keeping most of the details relating to that process—and to the offices involved—a state secret. The first alternative obviously does not resolve the problems of legitimacy in any substantive way, although it could satisfy security concerns while ensuring an effective transfer of release authority during a national emergency. The second alternative, in contrast, strikes a better balance inasmuch as it secures many of the benefits pertaining to legitimacy while preserving the security of the succession chain and any other details that Indian policymakers may want to keep under wraps, all without prejudicing the effective devolution of release authority during a crisis.

---

[487]Kanwal, "Command and Control of Nuclear Weapons in India," pp. 1727–1728.

Irrespective of how this issue is finally resolved, the creation of a succession system itself should not be difficult in a democratic polity like India. As Figure 16 illustrates, India has traditionally had an elaborate "warrant of precedence," and thus developing a suitable system for the devolution of power among a greater or lesser number

RAND MR1127-16

1. President	16. Envoys Extraordinary accredited to India
2. Vice-President	17. Chair/Speakers of State Legislatures (w/s)
3. Prime Minister	18. State Cabinet Ministers (w/s)
4. State Governors	Chief Ministers, Union Territories
5. Former Presidents	Union Deputy Ministers
6. Deputy Prime Minister	19. Officiating Chiefs of Staff (Lieutenant General)
7. Chief Justice	20. Chair, Central Administrative Tribunal
Speaker (Lok Sabha)	Chair, Minorities Commission
8. Union Cabinet Ministers	Chair, SC/ST Commission
State Chief Ministers (w/s)	Chair, Union Public Service Commission
Deputy Chair, Planning Commission	Chief Justices, High Court (o/j)
Former Prime Ministers	Puisne Judges, High Court (w/j)
Opposition Leaders in Parliament	21. State Cabinet Ministers (o/s)
9. Bharat Ratna recipients	Chair and Speakers, State Legislatures (o/s)
10. Ambassadors, Extraordinary and	Chair, MRTP Commission
Plenipotentiary	Deputy Chair and Deputy Speakers, State
High Commissioners accredited to India	Legislatures (o/s)
11. Supreme Court Judges	State Ministers of State (w/s)
12. Chief Election Commissioner	Ministers, Union Territories
Comptroller and Auditor General	Speakers, Legislative Assemblies, Union
13. Deputy Chair, Rajya Sabha	Territories (w/t)
State Deputy Chief Ministers	22. Chief Commissioner, Union Territories (w/t)
Deputy Speaker, Lok Sabha	State Deputy Ministers (w/s)
Members, Planning Commission	Deputy Speakers, Legislative Assemblies,
Union Ministers of State	Union Territories (w/t)
14. Attorney General	23. Deputy Chair and Deputy Speakers, State
Cabinet Secretary	Legislatures (o/s)
Lieutenant Governors (w/t)	State Ministers of State (o/s)
15. Military Chiefs of Staff (General)	Puisne Judges of High Courts (o/j)
	24. Members of Parliament
	25. State Deputy Ministers (o/s)

NOTE: w/s = within their states; w/t = within their territories; o/s = outside their states; w/j = within their jurisdictions; o/j = outside their jurisdictions

Figure 16—India's Warrant of Precedence

of successors should not be inordinately difficult.[488] Some suggestions as to who should be on this list have already been proffered, mostly by military officers,[489] but given the pattern of civil-military relations in India, it is most likely that the final succession chain would be biased in favor of civilian rather than military leaders, as appears to be reflected in the warrant of precedence illustrated in this figure. In the United States at least, the succession chain in the event of nuclear attack is composed *entirely* of civilian leaders even though it is recognized that some individuals might be poorly prepared to exercise such leadership and could be either belatedly or badly connected to the military system in an emergency. Even though "delegation down the military chain of command may [thus] be more effective than the presidential succession proper," the integration of military leaders into the U.S. succession chain never occurred because "it was widely regarded as highly undesirable, even improper, for political and constitutional reasons and because of the danger of usurpation of the delegated power."[490] Given the significance of such concerns in India, it is possible and even likely that New Delhi would simply emulate the American example when devising its own system of devolving command authority for nuclear operations.

A National Security Council. Although the development of a national command authority involves the evolution of procedural systems at the highest levels of state, this development cannot be successful unless it extends to the intermediate echelons of the political structure as well, for it is here that most of the staff work relating to the analysis of policy options is concluded—options that are then transmitted with recommendations to the highest political authorities for final deliberation and sanction. Many of the most important

---

[488] This figure is drawn from "Table of Precedence: Who, Exactly, Is What," available at http://www.indiavotes.com/reference/who.shtml. Other variations on this table can be found at "Our India: Table of Precedence," available at http://www.ourindia.com/oi2.htm.

[489] See, for example, Kanwal, "Command and Control of Nuclear Weapons in India," p. 1727.

[490] Walter Slocombe, "Preplanned Operations," in Ashton B. Carter, John D. Steinbruner, and Charles A. Zraket (eds.), *Managing Nuclear Operations* (Washington, D.C.: Brookings, 1987), p. 133.

details relating to the size, structure, and disposition of India's nuclear deterrent are collected, analyzed, and collated into alternative policy choices at this level, and consequently the quality of the institutional framework at the intermediate levels of governance has an enormous bearing on the kinds of decisions ratified at the political level.[491] In general, the quality of personnel manning these levels of decisionmaking in India has been high, in large measure because of the extraordinary talent residing in its administrative and foreign services.[492] Despite this fact, however, national policies have often suffered from considerable incoherence for several reasons: The best and most competent Indian civil servants are still generalists rather than specialists in many issue areas; the organizational structure of their employment binds them to advance the specific interests of their ministries rather than those of the country as a whole; and finally, the coordinating institutions that are supposed to provide an integrated view of various options—based on the expert judgments issuing from different ministries—have never developed into robust centers of competence thanks to budgetary constraints, the constant rotation of personnel, and, on many occasions, confusion between political responsibility and administrative obligations.[493]

Many distinguished political commentators in India have therefore argued that at least where nuclear issues are concerned, potential lapses in higher decisionmaking can be averted only through the formation of a National Security Council that possesses a permanent secretariat tasked with collecting, analyzing, and disseminating relevant information pertaining to critical national choices.[494] The development of such an institution along the lines of that in the United States would improve Indian decisionmaking considerably, especially in matters relating to strategic and nuclear issues. Past efforts to create a National Security Council, however, have proved to be ar-

---

[491]Kak, "Management of India's Security and Higher Defence—I," pp. 334–337.

[492]Lloyd I. Rudolph and Susanne Hoeber Rudolph, *In Pursuit of Lakshmi* (Chicago: University of Chicago Press, 1987), pp. 2, 75–77, and 80–83; Jeffrey Benner, *The Indian Foreign Policy Bureaucracy* (Boulder, CO: Westview Press, 1985), pp. 9–61.

[493]Ibid., pp. 74–83, and Chari, "India: The Policy Process," pp. 133–144.

[494]See, for example, the remarks by J. N. Dixit in *India: Indian National Security Council Discussed*, FBIS-NES-98-147, May 27, 1998, and D. C. Pathak, "Security Concept," *The Pioneer*, December 11, 1998.

duous exercises. The first attempts at instituting such a council, for example, foundered in 1990 on the shoals of bureaucratic opposition and political indifference. Several other proposals were then intermittently aired between 1990 and 1998, but none survived to see the light of day.[495] In the aftermath of India's May 1998 nuclear tests, the BJP government set up a task force to recommend a structure for such a council, and although most of the task force's recommendations were reportedly rejected, a new National Security Council was instituted in late 1998.[496]

The institution of this new body has, however, been greeted with mixed reviews, with many Indian analyses arguing that its key weaknesses are a product of its organizational structure and of uncertain political commitments to using it effectively.[497] As constituted by the Vajpayee government, the National Security Council is essentially a three-tiered organization (see Figure 17). At its core lie the "principals"—namely, the Prime Minister, who chairs a council consisting of the Home, Defence, Finance, and External Affairs Ministers. The Principal Secretary to the Prime Minister—a position usually held by a senior bureaucrat—currently serves as the National Security Adviser, but there is no legal reason a single individual should hold both positions simultaneously in the future. Beneath this committee of principals lies a Secretariat that consists of the chiefs of the independent intelligence services and the heads of the intelligence components of various ministries, the police, paramilitary forces, and various military intelligence directorates. Arrayed on either side of this secretariat in the third tier are two other bodies: (1) the Strategic Policy Group (SPG), which is chaired by the Cabinet Secretary and incorporates the existing "committee of secretaries" composed of senior civil servants overseeing important ministries, with the addition of the heads of the armed services, the DAE and the DRDO, and the Governor of the Reserve Bank of India; and (2) the National Security Advisory Board (NSAB), which is chaired by a Convenor appointed by the government and consists of

---

[495]For a quick review of Indian efforts in this regard, see Amitabh Mattoo, "Counsel for the Defence," *The Telegraph*, November 27, 1998.

[496]Joshi, "Old Body, New Name."

[497]Mahesh Uniyal, "Mixed Reviews Greet National Security Council," *India Abroad*, November 27, 1998.

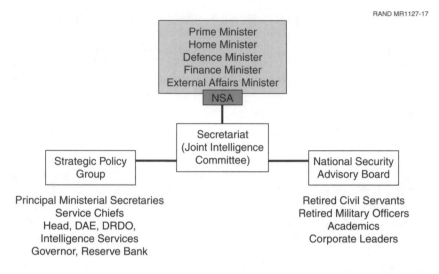

RAND MR1127-17

Figure 17—India's National Security Council

nongovernmental experts, academics, journalists, retired civil servants, and retired military officers.[498]

Each of these two bodies, the SPG and the NSAB, would convene independently to discuss various issues of national importance—often on directive from above—with the aim of channeling advice and recommendations to the National Security Adviser either autonomously or through his Secretariat. These alternatives, after due vetting, would then be passed on to the principals of the National Security Council itself for deliberation and decision. Even if they are not, the products generated by these bodies could still influence policy because their analyses and recommendations would filter to other bureaucratic arms like the Prime Minister's Office, the secretariats of the various ministries, and the working-level organs of the intelligence and military communities, where they are likely to be used in internal deliberations or absorbed into the policy-option papers prepared by these bodies for the consideration of their superiors. While such an organizational structure thus sounds eminently

---

[498]Joshi, "Old Body, New Name."

sensible in principle, it is not clear whether the new National Security Council in its totality will be effective for the dual purposes for which it is really needed: first, long-range strategic planning, and second, close day-to-day monitoring of the geopolitical and threat environments for purposes of issuing effective strategic warning.

The problems here are legion.[499] To begin with, the three most important bodies that make up the new National Security Council are simply incarnations of existing governmental institutions: The principals of the National Security Council are for all intents and purposes the Cabinet Committee on Political Affairs (now renamed the Cabinet Committee on National Security), except that the former is supposed to exercise deliberative functions in contrast to the latter's decisional responsibilities, and the SPG is with some modifications primarily the traditional "committee of secretaries" presided over by the cabinet secretary; and the new National Security Council Secretariat is simply the old Joint Intelligence Committee, which now serves as the principal staff of the National Security Adviser.[500] Clearly, all these bodies—being completely immersed in normal administrative chores—are already fully extended by the day-to-day burdens of governance and are therefore unlikely to find the time and energy to engage either in long-range planning or in any lateral, "out-of-the-box" thinking. Recognizing this fact, former Indian Foreign Secretary J. N. Dixit argued that "the council and its secretariat should be mechanisms independent of government departments dealing with day to day security functions and operations. Designating the joint intelligence committee or the defence planning staff as the secretariat for this council will not do. They [already] have their own responsibilities."[501] Since all the individuals associated with the main governmental constituents of the National Security Council—the principals, the Secretariat, and the SPG—have good access to the internal resources of the state but are overwhelmed by routine political or administrative responsibilities, it is obvious that long-range strategic planning is likely to get short shrift—as has traditionally

---

[499]For two excellent surveys of the problems associated with the National Security Council, see V. R. Raghavan, "Where the NSC Has Failed," *The Telegraph*, December 11, 2000, and J. N. Dixit, "Security Alert," *Hindustan Times*, December 7, 2000.

[500]Joshi, "Old Body, New Name."

[501]Dixit, *India: Indian National Security Council Discussed.*

been the case—simply because the key officials capable of undertaking this task lack the time to focus on long-range issues that often are not tractable, lack clear policy solutions, and demand costly initiatives that will seldom bear fruit during their term in office. Not surprisingly, then, when such problems arise, "ad hocist [sic] decision making [becomes] a heady brew and [remains] addictive."[502]

The one body that could engage in such activities is the NSAB, since it is composed primarily of individuals who do not have day-to-day responsibilities either in politics or in administration. Since the members of this body either were formerly connected with government (e.g., retired civil servants and retired military officers) or remain involved with the government but are some degrees removed owing to their current occupations (e.g., academics and corporate leaders), the NSAB could in principle undertake long-range strategic planning because it comports, at least in the first instance, with the key functional requirement of having members who are not burdened with onerous political or administrative responsibilities. It is unclear, however, whether the NSAB as it is currently constituted is the best vehicle for this task. This is because its members are *not* full-time analysts whose services are paid for and secured exclusively by the government but are instead private citizens who have been tasked with pro bono advisory responsibilities in addition to all their many other personal interests and commitments. Unlike the policy-planning staffs in the U.S. Departments of State and Defense—whose members are full-time government employees tasked with doing primarily long-term strategic planning—the NSAB does not consist of a permanent staff of full-time employees dedicated solely to the task of understanding macrostrategic trends and assessing alternative policy options relevant over the longer term. Moreover, many of the members selected during the last two iterations of the board's existence are not specialists in the truest sense of the term but merely diverse opinion makers of different stripes in national politics.[503]

---

[502]K. Subrahmanyam, "Reform Decision-Making Process," *Economic Times*, April 16, 1998.

[503]The membership of the board is identified in *India: Delhi: NSC Sets Up Missions for Strategic Defence Review*, FBIS-TAC-99-020, January 20, 1999.

It is also unclear, based on past performance, whether this body has had the requisite access to state resources—time, money, and particularly privileged information—that would enable it to support national policymaking in a useful and sustained way. Of the various bodies constituting the present National Security Council, only the principals, the Joint Intelligence Committee that functions as the Secretariat, and members of the SPG have access to classified information that affects policy choices, and it appears that the NSAB *corporately* has not been given access to this information in connection with its work on nuclear doctrine, the strategic defense review, and defense budgeting. As things currently stand, the requirement for effective long-term strategic assessments thus remains unfulfilled in India, because even the National Security Council body best suited for this purpose continues to be handicapped by various structural limitations. So long as the NSAB essentially consists of part-time outsiders, their analyses will have value primarily as a "sanity check" for India's policymakers and as an additional source of ideas emanating from societal as opposed to state institutions. This contribution is no doubt important, but it still does not represent serious long-term strategic planning of the kind New Delhi needs if it is to avoid—as Sundarji put it—the traditional "lotus-eating approach" that "gave Indian leaders a nice warm glow of righteousness and the country a bogus feeling of importance not based on reality."[504]

Success in this endeavor is therefore likely to require a full-time National Security Adviser who possesses an integrated staff consisting of civilians and military officers, both generalists and specialists, all of whom are full-time employees of the government, or civilian specialists seconded to the government on dedicated long-term contracts. This staff must, in addition, have access to multiple— including privileged—sources of information, as their principal purpose must not lie in the production of new and original research but rather in the reorganization of existing information in ways that support the creation of better policy choices over the medium to long term. The "option papers" created through this process would then be cycled both formally and informally through the existing bureaucracy and to political decisionmakers, and these products would il-

---

[504]K. Sundarji, "National Policy and Security Strategy," *The Hindu*, December 13, 1996.

luminate the long-run consequences of day-to-day decisions while simultaneously shaping the character of current decisions by reference to some desired end state obtaining over the longer term.[505]

Many Indian analysts have argued for precisely such a structure,[506] but the present National Security Council is structured in a way that does not make long-term strategic planning possible. This is because the present organization represents a failure of structure in that it commits people to do the work they are already doing while the work yet to be done remains undone. The connectivity of elements like the NSAB, which focus on issues of long-term import, with existing bureaucracies like the Cabinet and Prime Minister's Secretariat, the Defense Planning Staff, and the perspective planning cells in the various military headquarters, is also low to nonexistent, and the quality of its members is, from the perspective of technical expertise, a mixed bag. On balance, therefore, the NSAB appears to be utterly dependent on the use to which it is put by the National Security Adviser, and by implication its effectiveness is simply hostage to the political weight of the National Security Adviser (and his relationship to the Prime Minister) in national politics. In addition, the National Security Council *may* embody a failure of commitment to the extent that its legal and constitutional status remains unclear. And since the utility of the National Security Council as a whole continues to depend on the vicissitudes of "process" rather than on the strengths of "structure"—as represented by legislation and previously established practice—even the longevity of the existing structure writ large is an open question.[507] The nature of its relationship with the new bodies currently contemplated in India, such as the National Intelligence Board, the Defence Intelligence Agency, and the unified command to be headed by the CDS, is also still unclear. Such a situation cannot augur well for the development of an effective national command authority, broadly understood.

---

[505] Pramit Pal Chaudhuri, "A Question of Strategy," *Hindustan Times*, November 6, 2000.

[506] The best analysis in this regard remains Dixit, *India: Indian National Security Council Discussed*, and K. Subrahmanyam, "Planning for Security: Blueprint for an Apex Body," *The Times of India*, December 20, 1989.

[507] Thoughtful comments on how some of these challenges may be overcome can be found in K. Subrahmanyam, "National Security Council," *Economic Times*, April 2, 1998.

If the institutions for long-range strategic planning thus remain deficient, the capabilities for day-to-day monitoring of the geopolitical and threat environments for purposes of generating effective strategic warning are not particularly effective either. The task of collating all the relevant information necessary for strategic warning ultimately remains the responsibility of the Joint Intelligence Committee (JIC), which is "the highest evaluation agency in India relating to defense and security issues."[508] The reconstitution of this body into the Secretariat of the new National Security Council should therefore augur well, at least in theory, for the prospect of effective strategic warning. As it is currently constituted, however, this agency is less than adequate to the task. The principal weaknesses of the national security intelligence and warning system in India is not a lack of relevant information at the ministerial, departmental, or agency level but rather the absence of an institution that can harmonize multiple sources of information and conflicting bureaucratic interests to provide an objective assessment of the threat environment at a given point in time.

There are numerous intelligence agencies in India, but three organizations in particular share responsibility for providing information that bears on the country's ability to generate effective strategic warning: the Research and Analysis Wing (RAW), which is the main collector of external intelligence and remains the primary clandestine operations arm of the state; the Directorate of Military Intelligence (MI), which is the primary collector of tactical and, to a lesser degree, field SIGINT principally for military consumers; and the Central Intelligence Bureau (IB), which is the principal agency overseeing internal security and counterintelligence operations within India.[509] The JIC/National Security Council Secretariat is responsible for obtaining and fusing diverse information from these various sources, analyzing this information and generating assessments, and finally collating its analysis and recommendations into specific policy choices for the consideration of the National Security Adviser, the principals on the National Security Council, or the Cabinet as a whole. As the Kargil crisis amply demonstrated, however, this intelli-

---

[508]Chari, "India: The Policy Process," p. 143.

[509]Bhashyam Kasturi, *Intelligence Services: Analysis, Organization and Functions* (New Delhi: Lancer Publishers, 1995), pp. 56–78.

gence and warning system failed completely both strategically and tactically by virtue of the rivalries between the various intelligence organizations, the lack of intelligence sharing both between the various collectors and between the collectors and the JIC/ National Security Council Secretariat, the technical inadequacies of the Indian intelligence-collection apparatus, the stunning lack of redundancy in the collection efforts, and the lack of coordination between the various collectors at levels below the JIC. Such a failure would certainly be disastrous in a nuclear environment, since India's emerging deterrent relies on the expectation of strategic warning for an efficient response even if not entirely for its survivability.[510]

In the aftermath of the Kargil crisis, various proposals have been advanced for improving the collection, coordination, and analysis system with a view toward avoiding a repetition of the numerous intelligence failures that bedeviled India in the past.[511] Yet while many of the technical and some of the organizational solutions presented are likely to be incorporated into the system—if the recent recommendations of the Group of Ministers is any indication—a number of underlying problems relating to the production of effective warning remain. These involve, among other things, the challenges of improving the quality of the personnel involved in the fusion and analysis functions; improving coordination between the Ministries of External Affairs, Home, Defence, and the intelligence services; and developing mechanisms for setting requirements and mandating regular report-back and briefings both to the highest levels of the bureaucracy and to the political leadership.[512]

As more bureaucratic institutions are created to advance national security decisionmaking, however, the task of coordinating these institutions will only grow more complicated. There are already numerous bodies, such as the Cabinet Secretariat, the National Security

---

[510]*From Surprise to Reckoning: The Kargil Review Committee Report*, pp. 233–238.

[511]See, for example, Gurmeet Kanwal, "Defence Intelligence," *The Statesman*, November 20, 2000; "Defence Intelligence Agency on the Anvil," *The Hindu*, October 19, 2000; Shishir Gupta, "National Intelligence Board Mooted," *Hindustan Times*, October 1, 2000; and Shishir Gupta, "Plan to Upgrade IAF, Navy, Intelligence Chiefs' Posts," *Hindustan Times*, October 19, 2000.

[512]*From Surprise to Reckoning: The Kargil Review Committee Report*, pp. 233–238, and Chari, "India: The Policy Process," pp. 142–145.

Council Secretariat, and the Strategic Policy Group—not to mention the relevant ministries—that contribute in some way to the production of strategic warning. These institutions will probably be augmented in the future by additional organizations such as the National Intelligence Board and the Defence Intelligence Agency. Coordinating the activities of all these bodies within the framework of the existing cabinet system is likely to become a demanding task. The Cabinet Secretariat traditionally performed all the myriad tasks connected with coordinating the intelligence and warning process. In addition to all the other routine chores of maintaining records, minutes of meetings, and the like, it also performed the function of clarifying the import of national security decisions made by the Cabinet and translating the same into actionable tasks for all the relevant governmental agencies. Yet while these routine functions have remained unchanged, the critical role the Secretariat historically played—that of reconciling ministerial recommendations, flagging key issues for adjudication and decision by the political leadership, and presenting evaluated intelligence information for strategic decisions—has slowly been usurped by the Prime Minister's Office as part of the steady transfer of power from the Cabinet to the Prime Minister. While such a migration might have been quite tolerable in other circumstances, there is no evidence that the growing concentration of power in the Prime Minister's Office has resulted in the capacity for more effective intelligence and warning in the national security arena. On the contrary, it appears to have generated a widespread perception that decisionmaking in this area and elsewhere has been overly "politicized" because the Prime Minister's Office has in fact become "a parallel center of power at the cost of the institution of the Cabinet."[513] Complicating matters further is the fact that the burdens of managing a complex polity like India have led the bulk of the Prime Minister's Office time, resources, and assets to be consumed by the demands of domestic politics rather than by matters of national security. The Indian state thus appears to have garnered the worst of both worlds: The institution most capable of managing its intelligence and warning process—the Cabinet Secretariat—has experienced a steady diminution in power, effectiveness, and prestige, while the most powerful bureaucratic institution

---

[513]Cited in Panandiker and Mehra, *The Indian Cabinet*, p. 229.

within the government today—the Prime Minister's Office—finds itself overextended and incapable of controlling the intelligence and warning process with the diligence required in a nuclear weapon state. Only time will tell whether the several new bodies now being set up to assist in the production of better strategic warning will be successful in correcting this problem,.

In any event, if these problems are not rectified, India is likely to find itself in the distinctly unwelcome position of having less-than-effective policymaking institutions where both long-range and near-term strategic challenges are concerned.

Better Civil-Military Coordination. While the National Command Authority and National Security Council represent critical procedural systems at the highest and intermediate levels of state, respectively, the sound management of India's evolving nuclear capabilities also requires good procedural systems at the lower levels of its regulatory structure—and among the most important innovations needed here lies in the improvement of civil-military coordination, which in turn involves several interrelated issues. Clearly there is a need for better overall civil-military coordination within the Indian state. The world was once again reminded of the parlous condition of this relationship when in 1999 India's top political leadership summarily dismissed Chief of Naval Staff Admiral Vishnu Bhagwat for a variety of reasons, including the "defiance of civilian authority."[514] In the aftermath of this incident, the Indian Defence Minister initiated a review of possible reforms in the higher defense decisionmaking apparatus, and numerous Indian commentators—as well as the three uniformed services—proffered various suggestions in this connection.[515]

Most of the discussions prompted by this debate have focused on creating a new Chief of Defence Staff to be held in rotation by the three services; the integration of the service headquarters with the

---

[514]The details of this extraordinary episode can be found in Prabhu Chawla and Manoj Joshi, "Sunk!" *India Today*, January 11, 1999.

[515]Bedi, "Indian Forces to Be Restructured," *Jane's Defence Weekly*, October 21, 1998, p. 20. One of the most thoughtful analyses of reform in higher defense decisionmaking can be found in P. R. Chari, "Needed Radical Restructuring of the Defense Apparatus," *The Hindu*, February 16, 1999, and in K. Subrahmanyam, "Restructuring Ministry of Defence," *Economic Times*, February 8, 1999.

Ministry of Defence; the creation of a new "Procurement Executive" to oversee weapon selection and purchase negotiations; the development of a new Defence Management Service; better integration between the Ministries of Defence and Finance; increased autonomy for the service chiefs in matters of lower-level promotions; the resuscitation of the Defence Minister's Committee; and the creation of new integrated theater commands.[516] All these recommendations represent sensible, and perhaps long-overdue, innovations that are no doubt necessary for better defense management, and, not surprisingly, the Group of Ministers has already accepted many of these ideas. Yet at the same time, it is unlikely that they will by themselves lead to more effective control of India's evolving nuclear capability. This is because the relationship between competent higher defense institutions and coherence in nuclear planning, management, and operations has traditionally been indirect in India's case, because New Delhi's nuclear capabilities have historically been developed and nurtured outside the bureaucratic control of the uniformed military. Therefore, any effort to improve the management of nuclear forces cannot rely on the indirect benefits accruing from defense institutional reform but must instead focus on the specific civil-military issues that directly affect the deterrent.

It is likely that these improvements will manifest themselves in three distinct ways over time. The first and most significant manifestation of improved civil-military coordination will center on involving one or more of the relevant service chiefs and their staffs in formal planning pertaining to India's nuclear capabilities.[517] As Major General D. K. Palit noted, the "Chiefs of Staff—however relegated to the wings they might have been in the past in matters of national security formulation—will now have to be drawn into the deliberations of policy-making bodies in order to make their due contributions to

---

[516]These proposals have been summarized from Suba Chandran, "Integration of Defence Apparatus," report of an IPCS seminar held on January 22, 1999, available at http://www.ipcs.org/issues/articles/T/1-mdi-Suba.htm; Chari, "Needed Radical Restructuring of the Defense Apparatus"; Subrahmanyam, "Restructuring Ministry of Defence"; P. K. Vasudeva, "The Army Will Not Take Over," *The Hindu*, February 16, 1999; and Mehta, "Need to Involve Services in Decision-Making Stressed."

[517]See Joeck, *Maintaining Nuclear Stability in South Asia*, pp. 52–54.

nuclear war planning."[518] If past practices are any guide, this involvement could remain secret, although it is likely that such consultations will become routine, systematic, and wide-ranging over time: India's Chief of Air Staff is already believed to be part of the informal nuclear policy planning group within the government,[519] and that role will likely be extended to the other service chiefs in time. Integrated planning and consultation with the leadership of the armed services do not, however, translate into military command, control, or custody of India's nuclear assets. India's civilian security managers are anxious to safeguard their jurisdiction in all three issue areas, in part to drive home the point—both within the country and abroad—that India's nuclear weapons are not instruments usable for war fighting but merely national assets against political blackmail. Consistent with this view, even the prospective unified command that could be headed by the CDS will not acquire any command, control, or custody over nuclear weapon components in peacetime. This means that civilian custodians will maintain the fissile cores and possibly the weapon assemblies routinely. These new organizational structures would, however, provide a formal mechanism through which the higher military leadership could contribute to the management of India's nuclear deterrent in three ways: first, by providing military advice with respect to strategic requirements in order to guide the research, development, and acquisition of nuclear weapons, delivery systems, and supporting infrastructure assets; second, by overseeing the development of nuclear targeting and weapon employment plans under civilian guidance; and third, by developing and systematizing all the plans and procedures required to effectively integrate India's distributed strategic capabilities under different threat conditions. Obviously, these activities have been under way for a while, but thus far they were carried out primarily through informal means. By contrast, the new institutional arrangements—if they come to fruition in the best imaginable forms—would allow both the CDS and the three service chiefs more direct access to the highest political authorities as part of the reorganization of the

---

[518]D. K. Palit, "War in the Deterrent Age," *United Services Institution of India Journal*, 124:535 (January–March 1999), p. 21.

[519]Sawhney, "To Test or Not to Test: The Challenge for India's Nuclear Credibility," p. 32.

Ministry of Defence.[520] From a strictly operational point of view, the formal integration of India's military headquarters with its Ministry of Defence may therefore be unnecessary—at least as far as effective nuclear operations are concerned. This integration may be desirable on other grounds, but so long as India's civilian leaders create *structured opportunities* for the service chiefs to express their recommendations about the design, organization, and requirements of the country's nuclear forces (while simultaneously requiring them to plan all the details connected with the integration and employment of these forces in an emergency), they can continue to derive all the benefits of professional military advice without risking any of the liabilities they fear might arise if the uniformed military were to be formally integrated into the functions of nuclear command.[521]

For this system to work, however, there must be systematic opportunities for consultation about nuclear issues. The CDS must secure ready access to the national leadership in order to receive authoritative guidance and political endorsement of his plans, and he should be able to levy demands on the other service chiefs, since the latter are expected to remain the operational commanders possessing day-to-day control over all conventional military forces for at least the next five years. Negotiating this division of authority and finalizing the plans that regulate the detachment of various assets to the new CDS and to the new unified command that might be created will require much work and goodwill. These challenges will not be trivial because the operational command over India's nuclear delivery systems—which might be ceded to the CDS as per the recent recommendations of the Group of Ministers—could collide with the operational responsibilities of the existing service chiefs because many of India's delivery systems and almost all of its supporting infrastructure will remain, at least in the near term, essentially dual-capable assets that are already committed to conventional operations. The

---

[520]Dinesh Kumar, "Government Set to Empower Armed Forces with Policy Ammunition," *The Times of India*, November 7, 2000.

[521]For more on this, see Bhimayya, "Nuclear Deterrence in South Asia," p. 649ff. As D. K. Palit also acknowledges, India's national leadership would prefer to keep its nuclear weaponry outside of the custody and control of the uniformed military but, this fact notwithstanding, correctly argues that New Delhi would still have to adapt existing strategic institutions to ensure properly coordinated responses in the event of conflict. See Palit, "War in the Deterrent Age," p. 22ff.

CDS will also require substantial access to information about New Delhi's nuclear capabilities. India's nuclear scientists and defense technologists traditionally held this information closely, but it will now have to be more widely shared if the new unified command is to prepare a variety of "rolling" plans for nuclear operations—plans that either augment or replace those already believed to have been drawn up by the Indian Air Force.[522] Amid all these discussions about reorganization, however, it is important to remember that the instructions to specific commanders to prepare certain units for nuclear operations are almost certain to have been transmitted by now, if only informally, through the Chief of Air Staff. The need for specific equipment, resources, training, and support to carry out these missions is also likely to have been informally communicated to the relevant civilian authorities: What remains to be done is mainly to systematize existing plans and prepare for the induction of other, more capable technologies that will be available in larger numbers and that may require different readiness levels, basing modes, custodial arrangements, and organizational controls in the future. There already exists an established procedure centered on the creation of GSQRs for this purpose, and it is likely that some variant of this process will be progressively applied to nuclear-related requirements over time.[523] This cyclic process will require steady consultations between the relevant military institutions and their civilian masters even if the former are asked to independently prepare for such operations with their own resources and without any fanfare. In any event, high-level coordination between the uniformed military—personified by the CDS, the service chiefs, and their selected staffs—and the civilian authorities, both in the leadership and in the nuclear and defense research-and-development communities, will grow as the force-in-being is operationalized over time.[524]

The second significant manifestation of improved civil-military coordination will be improved coordination between the DAE, the DRDO, and uniformed services at the working level. As the previous discussion indicated, the responsibility for creating a nuclear deter-

---

[522] See "IAF Draws Up Nuclear Strategy."

[523] See, for example, Menon, *A Nuclear Strategy For India*, pp. 241–260.

[524] For Indian complaints that this is still not occurring as rapidly as it should, see "Is India a N-Weapon State?" *The Hindu*, October 1, 2000.

rent historically was borne primarily by civilian institutions, with formal military involvement occurring mainly at the tail end of the process. This unique division of labor is now likely to be tweaked in ways that allow for enhanced military participation in what were previously nontraditional areas of presence.[525] Such participation, again, may not be organized in the near term through specialized bureaucratic devices such as offices, titles, and budgets, but it *will* occur under the aegis of the CDS in at least four issue areas of importance to the future force-in-being: assessing force-structure requirements; analysis in support of R&D efforts and acquisitions; operations research in support of deployment postures; and testing and integration of systems. In each of these issue areas, the potential contributions of the military will spell the difference between symbolic and effective nuclear capabilities.

Under the aegis of the CDS in particular, it is likely that these four issue areas will receive increased attention. The analysis in support of this work may initially be conducted through informal networks, but it should not be surprising to find officers such as the Vice-Chief of Defense Staff and his deputies increasingly directing, if not entirely absorbing, the efforts already made in this regard by small existing "shops" within the Ministry of Defence (particularly the DRDO) and at the service headquarters.[526] This involvement will mainly regulate the activities of staff officers and technical specialists who perform the bulk of the analysis. The results of such analysis, in turn, will inform the conclusions of senior officers and officials from different agencies—conclusions that will then lead to the drafting of internal papers and, thereafter, to specific decisions following approval by the country's political leadership.

While this is likely to be the modus operandi on all matters requiring analysis prior to the generation of specific development or ac-

---

[525]The uniqueness of India's traditional arrangements when viewed from a comparative perspective is reviewed in Perkovich, *India's Nuclear Bomb*, pp. 444–464.

[526]At a more supervisory level, it is almost certain that officials from the Prime Minister's Office and the Ministry of External Affairs will also play a critical role in this process as will a small host of other individuals who, despite not holding any identifiable offices, will nonetheless contribute ideas, suggestions, and judgments through their close connections with key individuals in power. A Joint Secretary from the Ministry of External Affairs, for example, will be assigned to the office of the CDS.

quisition decisions, only a slightly modified procedure would obtain in the case of executing decisions already made; the testing and integration of specific weapon systems, for example, would be completed through the interaction of a small number of individuals—civilian and military—with minimal bureaucratic procedures. The objective in all instances would be to complete the task at hand with minimal visibility, minimal employment of resources, and minimal alteration of preexisting patterns of activity. Obviously, it is possible that shifting to some alternative procedures that are more visible would make for a better deterrent. Whether or not this is true, however, New Delhi's desire to possess a minimum deterrent, but not one at any price, is likely to ensure that it will focus on developing such a capability with minimal disruption of the existing patterns of civil-military relations, and there is no reason in principle why it cannot succeed in this endeavor. So long as civil-military coordination under the aegis of the CDS is ongoing, systematic, and productive, New Delhi will be able to enjoy the best of both worlds: to develop a force-in-being that comports with some desirable standards of operational utility even if it restricts the military's role in the *control* of those activities leading up to the creation of such a capability.[527]

The third and final manifestation of improved civil-military coordination will be the development of standard operating procedures relating to the management of nuclear missions in an emergency.[528] As the command system described in the previous chapter suggested, the baseline model of command envisages significant military contributions in an operational sense primarily in the aftermath of a deterrence breakdown. Prior to a deterrence breakdown, the primary operational role of the Indian military consists of maintain-

---

[527] It is important to recognize that this conclusion implies that the Indian military is already—even before the creation of the CDS—*involved* in various matters pertaining to the operation of the country's nuclear deterrent even if these forms of involvement may not comport with the traditional patterns witnessed in the history of previous nuclear powers. Further, the creation of the CDS only suggests that as India's nuclear capabilities increase in size, diversity, and complexity, the currently informal networks responsible for planning and coordination in the nuclear operations realm will slowly mutate into more institutionalized structures that are dedicated to these tasks, even if their more remote offices or agencies are not overtly identifiable.

[528] See Joeck, *Maintaining Nuclear Stability in South Asia*, pp. 61–63, and K. Sundarji, "Meeting Nuclear Threat: A Plan for India," *Indian Express*, March 11, 1996.

ing delivery systems in custody either at various levels of alert or in inactive status; practicing for nuclear missions, perhaps without actual weapons themselves; and systematically preparing for nuclear operations. After a deterrence breakdown has occurred and the decision to retaliate has been made by civilian authorities, the operational contributions of the uniformed military rise steeply as they begin to assist in the integration of relatively dispersed strategic components prior to the actual delivery of nuclear weapons against an adversary's targets. In order to make the response system associated with both this baseline and other alternative models of command viable, a significant amount of civil-military coordination in peacetime is necessary—and again, while this coordination does not have to be visible in the first instance, it does have to be systematic, preplanned, and coherent. In fact, it is all but inevitable that those procedures developed for this purpose in the past will be increasingly systematized in the form of standard operating procedures that may or may not take the form of doctrinal manuals but will in any case be comprehensive enough to allow all the relevant custodians of India's emerging nuclear assets to undertake the preplanned primary and alternate procedures for pre- or postattack reconstitution and response.[529]

Systematizing the plans required to support such a response system as India's nuclear assets grow in numbers, diversity, and complexity represents the essence of nuclear operations, and because the Indian force-in-being will be characterized by both a distributed deployment posture and an assertive command system in peacetime, the demands on civil-military coordination in preparing viable plans will be significant. To be sure, some issues—such as personnel reliability programs, ensuring physical security of components, and procedures for crisis relocation—can be independently managed by the various custodial agencies. Numerous other challenges, however—such as planning for effective targeting, developing appropriate authentication procedures, disseminating fallback plans in an emergency, and devising easily understood procedures for pre- or postattack coordination, assembly, and reconstitution of forces—will require extensive peacetime coordination between civilian and mili-

---

[529]"IAF Draws Up Nuclear Strategy" and "IAF Suggests Nuclear Air Command," *Hindustan Times*, November 28, 2000.

tary planning staffs. To the degree that such activities—which have already begun in India—are completed successfully as the country's nuclear capabilities grow in size and diversity, New Delhi will have a minimal set of procedural systems that will allow it to control its nuclear arsenal effectively in the event of a deterrence breakdown. The prospective appointment of the CDS and the likely creation of a unified command in the future are in fact designed to bequeath to India just this capability.

The discussion of procedural systems conducted here suggests that managing a nuclear force is a complex activity that spans many dimensions ranging from the design of that force to its production and deployment to its possible use. Each of these stages requires various organizational and regulatory mechanisms throughout the political system: At the highest levels, an effective National Command Authority plays a critical role in defining both the country's grand strategy and the purpose of nuclear capabilities in servicing that strategy while serving as the only agency that can legitimately authorize the use of nuclear weapons when such is required. At the intermediate level, an institution like the National Security Council (among others) could prove useful in fusing information, analyzing issues, and preparing alternatives for the consideration of senior policymakers with respect to nuclear capabilities, among other strategic issues, and in generating strategic warning. Finally, at more lower levels, the coordination of civil-military expertise would play a vital role in ensuring that specific policy choices are translated into the minutiae critical for orderly operations both in peacetime and during an emergency. Obviously, this list of desirable procedural systems does not in any way exhaust the list of organizational desiderata necessary for a safe and effective nuclear deterrent. Many of these micromechanisms will be identified only as the Indian force-in-being develops over time. All that can be done here is to focus on certain critical macrovariables that affect the prospect that these micromechanisms will be developed as time passes. When the record pertaining to the development of these procedural systems is reviewed, the evidence suggests that although India has made a start in developing some capabilities, it still has a long way to go before the organizational mechanisms that regulate its nuclear deterrent are judged to be comprehensive, effective, and complete, especially when the potential growth in the size, diversity, and complexity of India's evolving arsenal is taken into account.

MEETING THE DEMANDS OF SUCCESSFUL DETERRENCE

The analysis of capabilities undertaken in this chapter clearly demonstrates that India's claims to being a nuclear weapon state are somewhat overstated, since India continues to lack many of the components associated with a nuclear deterrent irrespective of how that deterrent is configured. At this point in time, New Delhi appears to have a small quantity of fissile materials, primarily weapons-grade plutonium, that continues to be accumulated at a relatively slow but increasing pace; a small number of nuclear weapons, which by most accounts are maintained in unassembled form; a small number of delivery systems consisting primarily of short-range tactical strike aircraft, some of which have been modified for the nuclear strike mission; an embryonic supporting infrastructure that includes many elements originally intended for the sustenance of conventional military operations, but with some other components either absent or available only in notional form; and modest procedural systems that are still more consistent with India's previous posture of "maintaining the option" than with its new desire for a "force-in-being." Given these generally limited capabilities, the assertion that India is now a nuclear weapon state[530] must be interpreted more as a symbolic challenge to the existing global nuclear regime than as an accurate descriptor of the country's present strategic capabilities.

Many of these weakness will no doubt be remedied over time. If India's security managers continue to develop its nuclear capabilities with the same resolve the BJP government demonstrated in 1998, the country could well have—as Table 5 indicates—all the essential elements its force-in-being requires over the next two decades.

Even when this process is completed, however, India will possess—at least according to its current plans—a fairly modest nuclear arsenal that will serve mainly to allow for simple forms of retaliation while minimizing the peacetime risks associated with the possession of such weaponry. In fact, maintaining a deterrent in the form of a

---

[530]Prabhu Chawla, "Interview: Atal Bihari Vajpayee," *India Today*, May 25, 1998.

Table 5

Time Frame Governing Development of India's Force-in-Being

Component	Near Term (~5 Years)	Medium Term (~5–10 Years)	Long Term (~10–20 Years)
Nuclear weapons			
Produce fissile materials	√	√	?
Improve nuclear weapon designs	√	√	√
Delivery systems			
Modify strike aircraft	√	√	√
Procure nuclear SRBMs	?	√	
Procure nuclear IRBMs		√	√
Procure nuclear ICBMs			?
Procure surface combatants with N-SLBMs/CMs[a]		?	√
Procure SSBNs with N-SLBMs/CMs			√
Upgrade physical infrastructure	√	√	√
Supporting infrastructure			
Develop command posts	√	√	√
Improve communications systems	√	√	√
Develop warning and assessment sensors	√	√	√
Incorporate thin strategic defenses	√	√	√
Procedural systems			
Institutionalize National Command Authority	√	√	
Consolidate National Security Council	√	√	
Improve joint civil-military coordination	√	√	√

[a]N = nuclear; CM = cruise missile.

force-in-being trades wartime effectiveness for enhanced peacetime safety and security, and Indian policymakers appear quite comfortable with such a compromise because they view their nuclear weapons primarily as political instruments intended to promote caution in the minds of their adversaries—while bolstering their own self-confidence—rather than as true weapons of war that are likely to see extensive use in the Indian subcontinent.[531] Since New Delhi is optimistic about the low prospects of nuclear use, it is not surprising to find—as Figure 18 depicts—that its force-in-being is almost by its very nature biased in the direction of negative as opposed to positive control.[532] In fact, the analysis that follows suggests that the force-in-being may be able to meet many of the criteria for a good deterrent precisely because it is configured along conservative lines that emphasize safety even as it seeks to fulfill the strategic purposes for which it is being acquired.

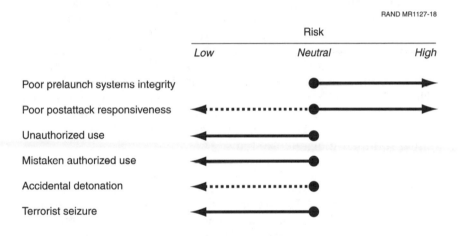

Figure 18—The Relative Vulnerability of India's Nuclear Arsenal

Prelaunch Systems Integrity. Any complicated system like a nuclear deterrent consists of a number of complex parts, all of which must function flawlessly if the deterrent is to perform as required.[533] A

---

[531]Pratap B. Mehta, "India: The Nuclear Politics of Self-Esteem," *Current History*, 97:623 (December 1998), pp. 403–406.

[532]On optimism about nuclear-use issues, see Jaswant Singh's comments in Suman Guha Mozumber, "Nation Not to Abandon Its Missile Program," *India Abroad*, June 19, 1998.

[533]Many of the relevant issues here are identified in Christopher Chant and Ian Hogg, *The Nuclear War File* (London: Ebury Press, 1983), p. 28ff.

ready arsenal, for example, benefits greatly from the fact that all of its component systems are deployed and maintained in the same physical and operational environments that surround them during actual use: Weapons are mated to launchers; launchers are integrated to physical controls and diagnostic systems; and the entire apparatus is tested and deployed in a context as close to operational conditions as possible. The Indian force-in-being, in contrast, may not enjoy many of the benefits that accrue from advance physical integration and maintenance at high levels of readiness: Components of warheads may be separated from one another; weapons are likely to be separated from delivery platforms and launchers; and missiles may be further separated from their TELs and diagnostic equipment. Many of these limitations can be overcome through repeated testing of components in different environments and through the constant maintenance of such components at high standards.[534] However, because intricate technologies often interact in unanticipated ways, there is always some likelihood that a dispersed system— when brought together—may experience a higher failure rate than other routinely integrated systems.[535]

Indian weapon technologists are well aware of this problem, as are their civilian masters; indeed, the former often distinguish between having "confidence" in the performance of a system and providing full "assurance" that the system will always work as intended.[536] While rigorous testing at the component and subcomponent level is seen as providing confidence that India's deterrent will work when required, Indian technologists recognize that they cannot offer policymakers any unconditional assurance about their products' performance because political constraints and operational practices often conspire to prevent them from conducting the kinds of tests that would allow them to do so. These concerns are often voiced with regard to nuclear weapons themselves, given New Delhi's self-

---

[534]See the examples offered in Sawhney, "To Test or Not to Test: The Challenge for India's Nuclear Credibility," pp. 30–35, and Sawhney, "Standing Alone," pp. 25–28.

[535]For a good statement about Indian concerns relating to this issue, see Karnad, "A Sucker's Payoff," pp. 46–47.

[536]I am grateful to K. Santhanam, Chief Adviser (Technologies), DRDO, for discussing the implications of this distinction with me from an operational perspective. See also Sundarji, "Indian Nuclear Doctrine—II: Sino-Indo-Pak Triangle," for additional remarks on this issue.

imposed moratorium on further testing. Indian policymakers counter, however, that while further full-up tests may in fact contribute to the quality of their deterrent, such tests may not be necessary for *deterrence stability*, since India's adversaries cannot count on the technical imperfections of its force-in-being to provide them with the immunity they need to prosecute successful acts of aggression against India given the horrendous consequences they would face if those expectations turned out to be false in a crisis situation.[537] Put another way, Indian policymakers today appear to recognize that their force-in-being as a whole may exhibit poorer systems integrity than some other conceivable variant, such as a ready arsenal, but they nonetheless believe that securing other important political objectives makes the possession of such a deterrent well worth the risk.

Postattack Responsiveness. While the conclusion that the Indian force-in-being is likely to display a bias toward poorer rather than greater systems integrity is easy to draw simply on the basis of its inherent characteristics, the quality of its retaliatory effectiveness in the postattack stage is more difficult to assess because this variable is critically influenced by the size and efficiency of an adversary's attack. A large attack conducted with scores of high-yield warheads could incapacitate India in ways lying beyond the scope of the imagination; even if these attacks did not succeed in interdicting the critical components of the deterrent per se, they could destroy the national infrastructure and the organizational structure of the Indian state to a sufficient extent to preclude any effective retaliation.[538] If, on the other hand, the attacks on India were either symbolic or modest, the Indian force-in-being should be able to reconstitute and respond effectively. The depiction of bias in Figure 18 is therefore appropriately ambivalent, since both the degree and the coherence of the force-in-being's postattack responsiveness depend in large measure on what India's adversaries do to it in the context of conflict. Despite this ambivalent characterization, Indian policymakers—as noted before—are not unduly troubled by the prospect of poor

---

[537]The clearest statement of this position can be found in Sundarji, "Changing Military Equations in Asia: The Role of Nuclear Weapons," pp. 134–135.

[538]For a pessimistic view of this problem, see Jones, *From Testing to Deploying Nuclear Forces*, p. 6.

postattack responsiveness because they believe that nuclear weapons per se have sufficient dissuasive power to prevent any adversary from testing fate in the face of their awesome capabilities.[539]

This sanguine attitude notwithstanding, it is important to recognize that the issue of postattack responsiveness is critically influenced by the degree of opacity surrounding the Indian deterrent. The success with which New Delhi is able to mask the size, location, and disposition of its nuclear assets in peacetime and the rapidity with which it can disperse these assets in a crisis will be *the* most critical variables determining whether an adversary's attack is easy or difficult, small or large. If India's competitors are able to render the country's nuclear posture transparent by some means of intelligence, they could at least in theory disarm India by mounting focused attacks in the context of a crisis. The decision to launch such focused attacks could be rationalized as a form of preemptive defense were an adversary to reason that initiating nuclear war left it better off than taking its chances with an unsteady peace. Successful opacity maintained under all circumstances, on the other hand, would undermine this calculus by forcing an adversary to confront the prospect of an unsuccessful attack and compelling it to launch a much larger strike than would otherwise be necessary, in the process raising two critical issues that could make the difference to India's safety: First, does the adversary possess the number and kinds of weapons capable of interdicting the huge target set that must necessarily be destroyed if it is to minimize the prospect of a successful Indian counteraction? And second, given the competing interests that any adversary tasked with making this decision would face, are the political goals in dispute worth the expenditure of such massive—as opposed to limited—levels of force? Successful opacity in effect holds the key to Indian security—for insofar as it requires India's adversaries to mount much larger nuclear attacks than would otherwise be the case, these attacks become increasingly disproportionate to the political issues in dispute and, as a result, become less probable as well. This beneficial outcome, then, only redounds to India's advantage where postattack responsiveness is concerned.

---

[539]The clearest statement of this position again remains Sundarji, "Changing Military Equations in Asia: The Role of Nuclear Weapons," pp. 136–138, and Sundarji, "Indian Nuclear Doctrine—I: Notions of Deterrence."

Unauthorized Use. Among the major concerns historically associated with the presence of nuclear weapons has been the fear that their enormous power might be unleashed by agents not authorized by the state; it is hypothesized that such misuse might result either because the custodians who physically possess these weapons chose (or threatened) to use them in the absence of an explicit command from state managers or because the physical control of the devices might be usurped by entities that are not organizationally part of the state.[540] The desire to avert such problems during the Cold War led to the development of both technological solutions such as PALs and organizational solutions such as the two-man rule—measures that may eventually be incorporated in some form into the Indian nuclear arsenal as well. At the same time, however, the currently anticipated configuration of India's force-in-being makes it highly resistant to unauthorized use, in large part because it ensures that no completed nuclear weapons will exist in peacetime or at least prior to any official directive to integrate separated components into completed weaponry.[541] Since India's nuclear reserves in their "normal" status would thus take the form of separated components, the problem of unauthorized use would be minimized because illegitimate entities would face the onerous task of locating, identifying, recovering, and reconstituting the separate, secretly stowed components into completed devices. Orchestrating this process would therefore require assistance from individuals associated with the weapon program and might in fact require many custodians—possibly from several different organizations who may not know one another personally—to conspire to fabricate such a device. Alternatively, it would require that a device somehow fall into the wrong hands after it had been legitimately reconstituted on receipt of a proper directive from the national command authority.

It is extremely unlikely that either of these contingencies could occur given the organizational structure of India's strategic enclaves. Covertly reconstituting completed nuclear weapons, for example,

---

[540] For a good review of the numerous issues related to this problem, see Paul Leventhal and Yonah Alexander (eds.), *Preventing Nuclear Terrorism* (Lexington, KY: Lexington Books, 1987).

[541] This statement obviously does not apply to devices reconstituted for experimental or testing purposes.

would be extremely difficult by virtue of the relatively large number of individuals required for such an operation. Moreover, if such devices were to be used (as opposed to being merely reconstituted) in any politically significant way, the burden of carrying out this operation would be further magnified, since it would require the acquiescence if not the cooperation of a wide variety of individuals ranging from scientists and technologists to armed guards and truck drivers. Because the organizational demands associated with hatching such a conspiracy and carrying it to a successful conclusion are so great, it is highly improbable that the Indian force-in-being would be subjected to the threat of unauthorized reconstitution of its weaponry leading to some form of use—unless it is assumed that a significant portion of India's strategic enclaves would for some reason elect to rebel against the state. While such an outcome is possible in theory, there is no reason to believe that it is likely.

Nor is the second contingency—properly reconstituted weapons falling into the wrong hands—a plausible outcome. If the country's evolving doctrine serves as any indication, India's nuclear weapons would be reconstituted primarily in the aftermath of a nuclear attack—and in such circumstances reconstitution, being merely a prelude to retaliation, would present minimal opportunity for any loss of such devices, since the time that would elapse between reconstitution and use would be quite short. It is also likely that the assembly areas where final integration of weapon components takes place would be in close proximity to the location where delivery operations are initiated. Even if Indian nuclear weapons are reconstituted on strategic warning as a prudential measure—prior to any attack on India—these weapons may not be delivered to their final operators—the uniformed military—except prior to authorized use. Moreover, even if they were delivered prior to authorized use, the risk involved would be minimal because the Indian military's past record of loyalty to the state is exemplary despite its modest status in the national hierarchies of prestige and power. Shekhar Gupta captured both of these dimensions succinctly when he noted that "in no other major democracy are the armed services given so insignificant a role in policymaking as in India. [Yet] in no other country do they accept it with the docility they do in India."[542] Consequently, even if

---

[542]Cited in Kak, "Direction of Higher Defence—II," p. 504.

completed nuclear weapons are transferred to the uniformed military in the context of a crisis, the ingrained loyalty of the armed services, combined with specific organizational safeguards designed for just such an eventuality, ought to suffice to prevent unauthorized use.[543] Therefore, irrespective of the specific sequences followed in connection with the processes of reconstitution, it is almost certain that India will use a combination of secrecy, enhanced security arrangements, and physical safety devices to prevent any entities—including the uniformed military—from acquiring material custody of completed weapons ahead of the time deemed appropriate by civilian authorities. The same safeguards should also suffice to prevent unauthorized entities from securing access to any completed nuclear weapons.

None of these intrinsic safeguards prevents Indian security managers from developing additional solutions to the already-manageable challenge of unauthorized use. While most solutions suggested in the Western literature gravitate toward the development of advanced mechanical safeguards such as PALs, numerous additional measures could be instituted at relatively low cost. Given the structure of the force-in-being, the most effective measure in all such instances would lie in further strengthening the strong sense of identification with national purpose that already prevails within India's strategic enclaves. This solution, which the Indian state has in fact adopted since its independence,[544] in itself minimizes the possibility of unauthorized use, since it further diminishes the already-minuscule incentive for organized revolt. Beyond reliance on loyalty, however, the Indian state has many other bureaucratic tools at its disposal to increase safety. The local Criminal Investigation Department (CID) and the Intelligence Bureau, for example, already perform background checks of all personnel assigned to security duties in sensitive locations.[545] And while there is little that would prevent these ac-

---

[543]Chengappa, *Weapons of Peace*, pp. 437–438, suggests that during the Kargil crisis, for example, DRDO custodians, maintaining physical custody of the warheads at all times, in fact "headed to where the Prithvi missiles were deployed," as four of these systems were allegedly being "readied for a possible nuclear strike."

[544]See Abraham, *The Making of the Indian Atomic Bomb: Science, Secrecy and the Post-Colonial State*, for an excellent discussion of how this solution was operationalized in India.

[545]Kasturi, *Intelligence Services: Analysis, Organization and Functions*, p. 64.

tivities from being extended to many more individuals associated with the force-in-being, these efforts may actually prove unnecessary, since both the DAE/DRDO and the uniformed military already have their own versions of a "personnel reliability program" that, by incorporating both informal and formal reviews, have thus far been remarkably effective. There is no reason, however, why the internal surveillance responsibilities borne by these institutions, together with others like the Intelligence Bureau and the Central Bureau of Investigation, cannot be expanded so that any individuals confronted by suspicious or unexplained occurrences within their programs have access to institutionalized means of reporting potential challenges to state authorities.

Mistaken Authorized Use. While the Indian force-in-being is thus highly resistant to unauthorized use in both structure and practice, it is even more strongly biased against the possibility of mistaken authorized use. To be sure, the potential for mistaken authorized use generally inheres in a nuclear posture designed for the conduct of prompt operations. Specifically, when nuclear weapons are already in the custody of the end user, when predelegated authority to use such weapons is disseminated to lower echelons of the command chain, and when nuclear operations are designed to be initiated on receipt of either strategic or tactical warning of attack, the potential for mistaken authorized use is by definition relatively high because such weapons might have to be launched despite the possibility that the indicators of incipient attack might ultimately turn out to be false.[546] The use of nuclear weapons in such instances would certainly be legitimate in that it would not contravene any standing orders custodians might have with respect to initiating nuclear operations in an emergency, and it would also be legitimate if the national command authority authorized nuclear release in situations where it genuinely believed that the country was under attack by virtue of "false positives" emerging from the sensors and early-warning system. During the Cold War, the United States sought to minimize the prospect of mistaken authorized use by requiring that positive confirmation of incipient attacks be derived from multiple sensors. In the later years of the Cold War, it used sensors with "dual phe-

---

[546]Thayer, "The Risk of Nuclear Inadvertence: A Review Essay," pp. 472–479.

nomenology"[547] so that all tactical warning indicators that could lead to the generation of heightened stages of alert and possibly to nuclear responses would be corroborated by separate detection systems that observed different physical signatures.

The Indian force-in-being resolves the problem of mistaken authorized use not so much through technical solutions as through organizational and doctrinal remedies. The most important safeguards here are India's commitment to a no-first-use policy and its refusal to allow the ultimate end user—the uniformed military—to maintain custody of completed nuclear weapons in peacetime. This no-first-use policy—which is more durable than Soviet variants of the same for all the reasons explicated in the previous chapter—effectively ensures that the Indian military will be unable to execute retaliation except in the aftermath of a nuclear attack. Only when such an attack takes place—and when these attacks are physically verified by multiple forms of reporting—would India's nuclear reserves be reconstituted into an arsenal for purposes of retaliation. Even if reconstitution itself does take place prior to nuclear attacks on India, retaliatory responses will certainly be delayed until information about the attacks is physically verified by multiple means. The dispersed posture of the force-in-being—together with the fact that important components are routinely maintained by organizations other than the uniformed military—implies that India's nuclear assets cannot be mistakenly used merely on receipt of tactical warning. It is in fact likely that at least in the near term, India will possess only thin tactical warning capabilities simply because it does not require any thick capabilities for the survivability of its deterrent: The operational doctrine of "delayed—but assured—retaliation" can be effectively executed without any tactical warning systems whatsoever and the doctrine's emphasis on delayed retaliation only implies that the kinds of hair-trigger response postures that increase the likelihood of mistaken authorized use can be avoided altogether. All these factors taken together suggest that the first notice Indian policymakers are likely to have of a nuclear attack would be when the incoming weapons actually detonate on their soil, but that is by no means vastly different from the situation currently obtaining, for example, in China today. When these attacks occur—assuming that they do

---

[547] Gottfried and Blair (eds.), *Crisis Stability and Nuclear War*, p. 56.

not totally devastate Indian society—even a relatively primitive system of report-back would ensure that Indian decisionmakers had the information they needed to fashion their own retaliatory response.[548]

While this scenario obviously represents the best outcome from the perspective of avoiding mistaken authorized use—since nuclear retaliation takes place only after incontrovertible evidence of nuclear attack is made available—even the more probable contingency of increased readiness under conditions of strategic warning embodies only a minimal prospect of mistaken authorized use. This is because so long as enhanced readiness mainly involves the relocation of nuclear reserves and components (although integration of fissile pits and SAFF components prior to absorbing an actual attack is not ruled out), the possibility of mistaken authorized use is still nonexistent so long as completed nuclear devices are not surrendered to the end user prior to the explicit authorization of retaliatory strikes. From all indications, this appears to be the preferred concept of operations currently associated with the force-in-being. Consequently, it is likely that the immunity to mistaken authorized use will continue to obtain even as Indian security managers look for better technical ways to preserve negative control while they increase the responsiveness of their nuclear assets during conditions of supreme emergency.[549]

Accidental Detonation. All technologies, including nuclear weapons, are susceptible to a variety of accidents. In the case of nuclear weapons, however, any accident leading to a chain reaction in

---

[548]It is important to recognize that the IRS-3 satellite system already in orbit can provide—though not instantaneously—information about nuclear attacks that may have been unleashed on India after they occur. As the new Test Evaluation Satellite and other follow-on systems become operational, the Indian capabilities for postattack confirmation will only improve further.

[549]Raj Chengappa has claimed that the Indian Prime Minister carries "the nuclear trigger in a tiny attache case that goes wherever the prime minister goes." If this claim is true, then the Indian command system could assume the posture illustrated in Figure 14 immediately, since completed nuclear weapons could be readily dispersed to their end users early in a crisis, with negative control maintained entirely through technical rather than organizational means. See Chengappa, *Weapons of Peace*, pp. xv–xvi. This description, however, has not been corroborated by any other source within or outside India and hence must be treated as a possible or, more likely, a speculative account.

the fissile core could have catastrophic consequences, depending on the type of nuclear weapon involved and the location of the accident. For this reason, the established nuclear powers, especially the United States, expended enormous amounts of time and resources to ensure that nuclear accidents—were they unfortunately to occur—would not lead to any accidental detonation caused by a chain reaction inadvertently triggered in the fissile core.[550] This emphasis makes it obvious that accidental nuclear detonations represent the limiting case and are a subset of a much larger category of nuclear weapon accidents that may in turn be broadly classified into three distinct categories of threat: dangers arising from the damage or destruction of inert nuclear weapons; dangers arising from an accidental or inadvertent nuclear detonation; and dangers arising from accidental nuclear war triggered as a result of an accidental or inadvertent nuclear detonation.[551] While all nuclear weapon accidents are no doubt unsettling, the last two dangers simply represent unacceptable kinds of threats. Therefore, it is not surprising that the established nuclear powers have devoted significant attention to developing a variety of "positive measures"[552]—technical design features and organizational procedures existing solely to provide weapon safety and security—intended to avoid just such contingencies.

Whether Indian nuclear weapons in particular or the force-in-being in general is safe is a critical question, but it is one that cannot be assessed at this point because the technical characteristics of New Delhi's weapon designs are not publicly known. In the absence of information about how Indian nuclear weapons are designed for immunity to heat, shock, pressure, and radiation and whether they include devices such as insensitive high explosive, weak-strong links, and PALs, conclusive judgments about the safety of such weapons must be deferred. For these reasons among others, it is also difficult to assess how susceptible to damage or destruction inert Indian

---

[550]The best overview of the technical safeguards incorporated into U.S. nuclear weaponry is Cotter, "Peacetime Operations: Safety and Security," pp. 17–74.

[551]Shaun Gregory, *The Hidden Cost of Deterrence* (London: Brassey's, 1990), pp. 82–103.

[552]U.S. General Accounting Office, *Observations on Navy Nuclear Weapons Safeguards and Nuclear Weapons Accident Emergency Planning*, GAO/NSIAD-85-123 (Washington, D.C.: USGPO, 1985), p. 5, and William A. Hodgson, "Nuclear Certification Program," *Combat Edge*, 4:4 (September 1995), pp. 28–29.

weapons actually are—a deficiency only compounded by the fact that little is publicly known about the handling procedures and human factors connected with their maintenance, stowage, and transportation. Despite this lack of information, it is not unreasonable to assume that—within the limitations of the available technology—Indian nuclear weapon designs would be biased toward ensuring safety; although there is no empirical evidence available to confirm or refute this hypothesis, the force-in-being's strong emphasis on negative as opposed to positive control makes this claim more reasonable than its antithesis.

More confident judgments can be made with respect to the dangers of accidental nuclear detonation as well as accidental nuclear war triggered as a result of an accidental nuclear detonation. The Indian force-in-being is likely to be highly resistant to an accidental nuclear detonation simply by virtue of its posture, which emphasizes separated weapon components. This pattern, which in fact replicates U.S. safety practices in the earliest years of the Cold War, implies that the prospect of an accidental nuclear detonation is minimal at least in the context of the peacetime disposition of the force-in-being. Whether the same condition obtains after the integration of weapon components takes place during an emergency is less clear because the design characteristics of Indian nuclear weapons are not publicly available. If the narrative in Chengappa's *Weapons of Peace* is to be believed, these assembled weapons *may* not have important safety features such as one-point safety, weak-strong links, and unique signal requirements—or at least that is the conclusion suggested by passages like "Sikka [the principal weapon designer during the May 1998 tests] and the others worried over the fact that if a bolt of lightning struck the 'Prayer House' [the code word used for the bunkers where the devices were assembled] it could mess up the device or even in an extreme case detonate one of them."[553] If these descriptions are in fact accurate depictions of the fragility of India's nuclear devices, the only saving grace may be that the integration of weapon components and of the completed weapon itself with the delivery system (depending on the degrees of separation maintained between these components) would most likely take place at assembly areas somewhat removed from major population centers. Since this is

---

[553]Chengappa, *Weapons of Peace*, p. 423.

likely to be the case, the otherwise catastrophic effects of an accidental nuclear detonation, should one occur, might be minimized—an outcome made all the more certain by the fact that India's standard fission devices have relatively low, 12- to 20-kt-class yields. While this is no doubt small consolation, the fact remains that the lack of authentic public information about India's nuclear weapon designs and about the handling practices associated with these weapons, especially during a crisis, makes any guesses about their safety—after systems integration is completed—hazardous indeed.

The prospect of an accidental nuclear detonation triggering an accidental nuclear war is in general rather low. This reassuring conclusion with respect to the third kind of nuclear accident cited above can be advanced in large measure because of the deployment postures maintained by all three South Asian states: China, India, and Pakistan. The nuclear capabilities resident in all three countries are not intended or designed for the conduct of prompt operations. Consequently, the danger that an accidental detonation occurring on the home territory of any of these countries might trigger a catalytic spasm of retaliatory violence by other competitors is minimal. If the surveillance capabilities existing at present are any indication, it is in fact likely that none of these three states would even know that an accidental nuclear detonation had occurred on the homeland of the other until they were so informed by the state that had suffered the accident, by the superpowers, or by the international media (which in turn would learn about the event from either the victim or the superpowers). This is because none of the South Asian states possesses GEO satellites with multispectral sensors of the kind deployed by the U.S. Nuclear Detection System aboard the NAVSTAR/GPS constellation.[554] Thus, an accidental nuclear detonation occurring on the homeland of one country could *not* be instantaneously detected by the others; at most, the others would immediately pick up seismic signals of an ambiguous nature depending on the yield and altitude of the detonation, and over time they might pick up more conclusive evidence in the form of radioactive debris, depending on the wind speed and flow patterns. None of these indicators, however, would

---

[554]The capabilities of this system are described in Blair, *Strategic Command and Control*, pp. 261–262.

be available immediately or in conclusive form through these states' own warning systems.

This limitation has stabilizing consequences in that none of the other states could respond even if they wanted to simply because they currently lack the real-time knowledge of what has actually occurred. These benefits accruing from the lack of tactical warning often go unappreciated by many Western commentators, who erroneously conclude that the absence of a "state-of-the-art early warning and intelligence-gathering capability" necessarily implies that "in the event of an accident" the South Asian states "might have little or no time to make an accurate assessment of what has happened or what to do next."[555] In fact, precisely the opposite is true: *Because* the South Asian states will not know what has actually happened, they will be freed from the burden of having to respond instantaneously. Even if they did know, however, they would be burdened mainly by the obligation to undertake prudential measures that enhance the survivability of their existing assets—through increased alert and emergency dispersal actions—in case the accident turned out to be the leading edge of an adversary's unfolding attack. There would nevertheless be little *objective* reason for any of the South Asian states to respond to such an ambiguous event with a prompt attack of its own, among other things because such a hasty action would not produce satisfactory damage limitation and would not be necessary for the preservation of that state's own strategic reserves given the opacity surrounding the nuclear forces on all sides.[556] At the very least, therefore, prudence and good judgment—in addition to objective calculations—would require that the victim investigate the circumstances surrounding such an ambiguous event, perhaps even soliciting the assistance of the international community, before any catastrophic actions that cannot be undone are unleashed in response. This generally sanguine conclusion about the potential for accidental war to be triggered by accidental detonations also holds in one other situation: an accidental nuclear detonation occurring on the territory of another state. This eventuality could materialize only

---

[555]Mann, "Subcontinent's Nuclear Duel Raises Miscalculation Risk," p. 58.

[556]This is in effect the answer to the questions posed by Gregory F. Giles, "Safeguarding the Undeclared Nuclear Arsenals," *Washington Quarterly*, 16:2 (Spring 1993), p. 183.

if aircraft or other delivery systems carrying nuclear payloads routinely operated over foreign (including adversary) territories as part of their preparations for nuclear attack. Since the Indian force-in-being will not be employed in the service of any such posture, these contingencies can be ruled out.

Terrorist Seizure. The last challenge that the force-in-being must successfully surmount is immunity to terrorist attacks and seizure. In a strict sense, this class of contingencies represents a subset of the threats posed by unauthorized use. The problems of terrorist attacks and seizure, however, are treated separately because of their two unique characteristics: Both involve a threat that usually emerges from outside as opposed to inside an organizational structure, and both are usually characterized by a high degree of systematic effort oriented toward advancing certain ends.[557] Traditionally, the established nuclear powers responded to the challenge of nuclear terrorism by ensuring that terrorists could never secure physical control over nuclear weapons to begin with and, even if they did, could never detonate them. Achieving the former objective required the development of complex systems for controlling physical access to nuclear weapons accompanied by stringent procedures for screening all personnel who enjoyed any access to such weapons during storage, transport, deployment, or operations. Achieving the latter objective required essentially the same technical systems developed to prevent other forms of unauthorized nuclear use.[558]

The Indian force-in-being is likely to enjoy a high degree of immunity to terrorist attacks and seizure despite the fact that the country is usually racked by several kinds of insurgencies at any given point in time. Indian insurgents, as a rule, have never distinguished themselves in terms of their ability to carry out focused special operations of the sort that would be required for nuclear terrorism; their usual accomplishments generally consist of harassing and

---

[557]For more on this issue, see Gavin Cameron, "Nuclear Terrorism: A Real Threat?" *Jane's Intelligence Review*, 8:9 (September 1996), pp. 422–425, and Fritz J. Barth, "Stemming Nuclear Terrorism," *U.S. Naval Institute Proceedings*, 115:12 (December 1989), pp. 54–59.

[558]Thomas A. Julian, "Nuclear Weapons Security and Control," in Paul Leventhal and Yonah Alexander (eds.), *Preventing Nuclear Terrorism* (Lexington, KY: Lexington Books, 1987), pp. 169–190.

threatening civilian populations, carrying out discrete attacks on police, military, and paramilitary pickets, and attacking thinly defended
symbolic sites. Thus far at least, no Indian insurgent group has yet
been identified as possessing the kind of sophisticated equipment
and weaponry necessary to carry out complex covert operations
against a trained and alerted defending force. In any event, successfully defending against terrorist attacks and seizures in the context of
the Indian force-in-being would require that strategic managers
safeguard both fixed installations—where nuclear weapons and delivery system components may be produced, stowed, or maintained—and mobile reserves such as missiles and TELs and their associated launch equipment, which may be dispersed from their
peacetime locations under conditions of crisis.[559]

Both types of assets are likely to be shielded by a defense-in-depth
approach in which multiple layers of opacity, strong local defenses,
and constant or intermittent movement would be used to frustrate
any effort at illegitimately capturing critical nuclear assets. The pervasive uncertainty about where components are stored thus represents the first and critical line of defense. This information is so
tightly held by the senior managers of India's strategic enclaves that
simply locating targets for seizure or attack would be a formidable
proposition. A successful solution to this problem would have to include insider information, but even such solutions are always beset
by the dangers of incompleteness and potential unreliability. In any
event, even if certain sites are identified, the local defenses must be
overwhelmed before their contents can be compromised. Yet all
fixed sites in India that are of any strategic value are heavily defended, and these defenses are always reinforced in times of crisis.
Obviously, there is always scope for improving security arrangements further, and it is most likely that New Delhi will pursue such
improvements as its force-in-being evolves over time. All such efforts
will no doubt encompass difficult trade-offs; enhancing security in a
visible way can, for example, increase the salience of the given facility and attract more attention from terrorist groups than is otherwise

---

[559]A useful survey of the challenges pertaining to nuclear terrorism in South Asia
and a review of some of the Indian responses to the same can be found in Paul Leventhal and Brahma Chellaney, "Nuclear Terrorism: Threat, Perception, and Response in
South Asia," *Terrorism*, 11 (1998), pp. 447–470.

likely. On the other hand, reducing visible security might weaken the security of a critical installation. Obviously, the best way out of this conundrum is to develop strong local defenses with minimal signatures, but operationalizing such solutions in a technical sense can often turn out to be difficult and costly. Irrespective of what solution is finally adopted, most competent observers today conclude that physical safety at all publicly known strategic facilities in India is fairly robust.[560]

Any discussion of the effectiveness of security arrangements with respect to mobile reserves would be premature at this point because India does not yet possess mobile missiles slated to carry nuclear payloads. When these systems are deployed several years hence, they will be maintained in protected garrisons during peacetime, and likely without their nuclear warheads. Under routine conditions, therefore, they will reap all the benefits accruing from the strong positional defenses surrounding them. It is most likely that when they are flushed from their garrisons during an emergency, they will be accompanied by dedicated military escorts, with other reserve elements available for reinforcement should that be required.[561] During this phase, however, their principal form of protection would derive from constant or intermittent movement so as to complicate the "targeting solutions" that would have to be derived by any terrorist group intent on seizing these assets. The great advantage of the force-in-being, finally, is that completed nuclear weapons not only are unlikely to exist in peacetime but are unlikely to be mated to the unalerted delivery systems in ordinary circumstances. Seizing a complete, usable weapon system would thus be difficult, since even success might involve merely the capture of a given part rather than custody of any integrated weapon system ready for use.

---

[560]Chari, *Protection of Fissile Materials: The Indian Experience*, and Lavoy, "Civil-Military Relations, Strategic Conduct, and the Stability of Nuclear Deterrence in South Asia," p. 84.

[561]A good description of how India's nuclear pits were transported during the May 1998 tests may be found in Chengappa, "The Bomb Makers," pp. 31–32. In contrast to this event, which focused on ensuring security principally through opacity, known (or recognizable) military assets in India are invariably moved or transferred under the protection of heavily armed convoys.

On balance, therefore, the Indian force-in-being—if operational-ized in the best possible form imaginable—would appear to be rela-tively effective in meeting many of the challenges associated with peacetime safety and security. Obviously, this conclusion will have to be revisited as the force-in-being evolves and as many of its key components are gradually inducted into the Indian arsenal. Until that point, however, it is reasonable to conclude that the force-in-being—at least when assessed as a concept advanced by Indian se-curity managers rather than as a completed material artifact—displays many desirable properties that make it potentially safer than several other conceivable deployment postures. So long as Indian se-curity managers maintain the preference schedule outlined in Table 6, the force-in-being should meet most of the standard criteria of successful deterrence even as it diminishes many of the difficult structural dilemmas associated with possession of a nuclear weapon capability.

The discussion thus far suggests that India's evolving force-in-being could meet many of the challenges posed by the presence of nuclear weapons in peacetime. The critical question facing any de-terrent, however—will it deter?—has been raised at different points in previous chapters but has not yet been systematically addressed. Whether a deterrent, however it is configured, can actually deter specific adversaries is an issue that cannot be conclusively resolved either in the abstract or in advance. In part, the problem is method-ological, because successful deterrence, which may be defined as averting potential attack, effectively requires accounting for some-thing that does not occur; as one analysis perceptively put it, "One

Table 6

Current Preference Schedule of Indian Security Managers with Respect to Nuclear Capabilities

	Relatively Unacceptable	Relatively Acceptable
Poor (prelaunch) systems integrity		√
Poor (postattack) responsiveness		√
Unauthorized use	√	
Mistaken authorized use	√	
Accidental detonation	√	
Terrorist seizure	√	

can know that deterrence has failed but never that it is succeeding."[562] In part, the problem is also substantive because it presumes a propensity on the part of an adversary to attack that may or may not exist in any given instance. While the substantive problem can be resolved in principle when deterrence effectiveness is examined in the context of past events, it is simply insurmountable when deterrence effectiveness against future threats is at issue.[563] For these reasons, the problem of effectiveness—or, put another way, the question of whether a given deterrent can deter—can be addressed only *a priori* by examining how it comports with some established formulations of rational deterrence theory.

This question is particularly interesting in India's case because even when the evolutionary process of developing the force-in-being is finally completed many years from now, New Delhi's deterrent will still be quite modest by the standards of the superpower arsenals maintained during the Cold War. If, for example, India's fissile materials are assessed ten years out, the country will certainly have a larger stockpile than it has today, but not one that is larger by orders of magnitude. Assuming that no FMCT constraints are enacted in the interim, India could add between 12–16 kg of Pu^{239} per annum—at its traditional rate of accumulation—and 45–90 kg of Pu^{239} per annum were it to greatly expand its production and separation capabilities. This implies that India could add between 120–160 and 450–900 kg of additional weapons-grade plutonium to its inventory by the end of the current decade—enough for roughly 20–26 to 75–150 simple fission weapons—if it is assumed that roughly 6 kg of Pu^{239} are used to fabricate a single weapon.[564] Many Indian analysts, however, discount the high-end estimates altogether. Brahma Chellaney, for example, actually concluded that "the possible maximum size of an Indian armoury before an FMCT is negotiated and brought into effect" is likely to be "less than 100 warheads."[565] All estimates con-

---

[562]Shlapak and Thaler, *Back to First Principles*, p. 14.

[563]Elli Lieberman, "The Rational Deterrence Theory Debate: Is the Dependent Variable Elusive?" *Security Studies*, 3:3 (Spring 1994), pp. 403–436.

[564]See the discussion on fissile materials earlier in this chapter.

[565]Brahma Chellaney, "After the Tests: India's Options," *Survival*, 40:4 (Winter 1998), p. 107. If it is assumed that FMCT constraints do not bar the continued physical production of weapons-usable materials, India might be able to regularly produce

sidered, therefore, New Delhi is unlikely to have a *gigantic* stockpile of weapons-grade materials even by the end of this decade: Assuming it had roughly 300 kg of Pu^{239} in the year 2000 and that it continues to add somewhere between its traditional and its expanded rates of annual accumulation, the Indian fissile-material stockpile in the year 2010 would stand at somewhere between 420–460 kg and 750–1200 kg of Pu^{239}, with some additional quantities of U^{235} thrown in for good measure. This would produce a force inventory of between 70–76 and 125–200 simple fission weapons—at a rate of 6 kg of Pu^{239} per warhead—some ten years hence. This stockpile would certainly be minuscule even in comparison to the 1997 estimate of China's fissile-material inventory, which has been assessed to consist of some 4000 kg of weapons-grade plutonium and 20,000 kg of HEU.[566]

If India were to sign the CTBT in the next few years without resuming its test program, New Delhi's fissile-material inventory would be useful primarily for the production of simple fission weapons alone. Even if the May 1998 tests were partially successful with regard to some elements of the advanced nuclear designs that were tested, India would not be able to migrate to an arsenal consisting even of boosted fission weapons without a resumption of hot testing.[567] To be sure, Indian nuclear scientists have claimed that their current technical capabilities allow them to develop warheads capable of producing yields in the region of 200 kt—but there is little empirical evidence to back up these declarations, and if New Delhi continues to abide by its self-imposed moratorium on field testing, it will be difficult for outside observers to believe that boosted fission weapons bearing such yields would in fact constitute the mainstay of

---

some annual quantity of Pu^{239}, but the inventory produced after the successful conclusion of the FMCT would certainly be subject to international safeguards and consequently would not be available for weapon purposes.

[566]David Albright, Lauren Barbour, Corey Gay, and Todd Lowery, "Ending the Production of Fissile Material for Nuclear Weapons: Background Information and Key Questions," available at http://www.isis-online.org/publications/fmct. This inventory would in theory yield some 1666 weapons of ~15-kt yield at the rate of 6 kg of Pu^{239} and 20 kg of HEU per weapon. Even if the Chinese fissile-material stockpile is only half the size it is usually assumed to be, this still implies that Beijing would have the capacity to produce 800-odd simple fission weapons. In practice, however, these weapons would not be simple fission weapons because China's relatively superior nuclear weapon technology allows Beijing to use its given fissile-material stockpile to produce a large number of high-yield boosted fission or thermonuclear weapons.

[567]Jones, *From Testing to Deploying Nuclear Forces*, pp. 7–8.

the Indian nuclear arsenal in the future. Of course, New Delhi could develop all sorts of new weapon designs, some capable of producing even higher yields in the interim, but in the absence of field testing the effectiveness of these designs could not be either verified experimentally by Indian scientists or credibly communicated to India's adversaries for purposes of deterrence. In any event, by the time the force-in-being is on the road to maturity some ten years from now, India will have many other strategic capabilities in place. At that point, for example, India should have completed the development of the Agni follow-on—a solid-fueled, rail-mobile IRBM capable of reaching some 3500 km—and may well be on its way to developing even longer-range missiles if these levels of performance are judged to be insufficient. It will also possess much of the supporting infrastructure and the procedural systems necessary to manage its nuclear deterrent in a relatively effective way.

Consequently, the force-in-being available by the end of this decade could consist of some 70 to 200 simple fission weapons carried by a mix of aircraft and missiles (the latter perhaps existing in larger numbers than the warheads themselves), complemented by a useful supporting infrastructure together with the necessary procedural systems. This force architecture would still not be oriented toward executing complex war-fighting operations, but if Indian judgments today are any indication, it would suffice for purposes of deterring blackmail and punishing any nuclear attacks on India.

The character of this hypothesized force architecture must, however, be qualified on two counts. First, descriptions of the size and structure of this deterrent are based on many assumptions—such as the continuation of India's moratorium against nuclear testing—primarily for heuristic reasons: They are not meant to be an accurate portrayal of what will exist 20 years from now. Instead, they are intended to convey an impression of what could exist primarily for the purpose of understanding whether such a force-in-being would be sufficient vis-à-vis Pakistan and China from the perspective of rational deterrence theory. Second, the exact size, quality, and disposition of the Indian nuclear force existing ten years out will be a state secret. Hence, the best that foreign observers—and India's adversaries—may be able to do in this regard is to infer what capabilities New Delhi possesses. The latter may even seek to verify these capabilities by clandestine means, but if Indian attempts at deception and denial are as successful as they have been thus far, there will always be a significant margin of uncertainty about the exact character of India's strategic capabilities. This is a significant issue from the perspective of deterrence efficacy because it implies that no matter how plausible the capabilities hypothesized above actually are, India's adversaries will always have to reckon with the possibility that New Delhi's nuclear prowess could turn out to be either larger or more effective than they themselves—or analysts standing on the outside—have assessed it to be.

Once these caveats are understood, it is easy to recognize that the question of whether India's nuclear capability can effectively deter its two major adversaries is not meant to be answered empirically but is intended to be addressed only at the level of principle. The question this issue embodies essentially pertains to the query made famous during the Cold War: "How much is enough?" And this question, when raised in the context of the Indian deterrent, often carries with it the explicit or implicit criticism that the capabilities represented by a small force-in-being—especially of the type referred to in the foregoing paragraphs—would be inadequate to provide the kinds of deterrence benefits India requires. This criticism of the evolving force-in-being has been vocalized most consistently by Indian hawks, though it has also found resonance among many Western analysts schooled in the classical conceptions of nuclear deterrence manifested during the Cold War.[568] At their root, the arguments these critics put forth boil down to three issues: The Indian stockpile of fissile materials is too small and, as a consequence, restricts the country to a fairly modest stockpile of nuclear weapons relative to its most significant adversaries, which "in effect would formalise the Sino-Indian asymmetry";[569] the size of the biggest Indian nuclear weapons is still too picayune and, as such, prevents the country from being able to levy the high absolute levels of punishment that those adversaries who are armed with thermonuclear weapons could inflict on India;[570] and finally, the size of the Indian delivery force is much too small and insufficiently diversified, resulting in a lower

---

[568]Karnad, "A Sucker's Payoff," pp. 45–50, and Jones, *From Testing to Deploying Nuclear Forces,* pp. 3–8 and 9–10.

[569]Chellaney, "India's Wrong Signal on Fissile Cut-Off."

[570]Karnad, "A Thermonuclear Deterrent," pp. 128–133.

overall balance of capabilities vis-à-vis New Delhi's most significant sources of threat.[571]

While the last criticism will lose some of its bite as new delivery systems come on line over time, the first two will endure so long as New Delhi does not increase its inventory of weapons-grade plutonium and remains reluctant to resume full-up testing of its nuclear weaponry. Even in this context, however, the second issue may turn out to be more significant than the first because a stockpile that consists of 100-odd weapons, while not gargantuan by any means, does not constitute a token arsenal. It could still be effectively used in a wide variety of contingencies, especially because the Chinese nuclear arsenal is not assessed by Indian security managers as being much larger than 350-odd weapons in size. While a force ratio approximating 100:350 is certainly not "balanced," it is not radically asymmetrical either.[572] Consequently, a force of 100-odd weapons may suffice for India's needs if the Chinese nuclear arsenal does not expand dramatically in terms of its weapon stockpile over time; Indian warheads and their delivery systems are reasonably survivable; and there continues to be enduring uncertainty about the true size and effectiveness of the Indian arsenal writ large. The disadvantages of relatively small yields may therefore turn out to be more salient from the perspective of deterrence sufficiency because the inability of fission weapons to inflict punishment comparable to that levied by thermonuclear warheads may suggest a disadvantage where the "balance of punishments" is concerned. If India does not return to the nuclear test ranges in the future, its ability to deploy advanced nuclear weapons, including thermonuclear devices, will certainly be stymied; at the very least, it will be unable to credibly communicate to its adversaries that it possesses such instruments for purposes of deterrence, even though it can continue to exploit those uncertainties in their decision calculus that would always arise from the ambiguities inherent in New Delhi's covert nuclear capability. The sufficiency of an Indian force-in-being without thermonuclear capabilities and subsisting at the kinds of modest force levels available

---

[571]Menon, *A Nuclear Strategy for India*, pp. 177–234.

[572]This issue is discussed in Chellaney, "After the Tests: India's Options," pp. 105–108.

ten years out is therefore an analytic issue that must be squarely addressed.

When the question of deterrence sufficiency is considered, it must first be understood that India's ability to deter a nuclear-armed Pakistan is not at issue: Irrespective of what Islamabad's nuclear arsenal might look like two decades from now, Pakistan ought to be deterrable even with relatively modest Indian nuclear forces simply because its geophysical limitations make it highly vulnerable even to relatively low levels of retaliation that New Delhi might unleash.[573] The most important political province in Pakistan, for example, the Punjab, can be effectively devastated simply by targeting the major population and industrial centers throughout this prosperous state. Thus, even if Pakistan is able to interdict and eliminate a substantial proportion of India's retaliatory capacity, New Delhi would still be able to inflict horrendous punishment on Pakistan—in terms of causing mass death—if it is capable of successfully delivering just a handful of ~15-kt weapons on these critical targets. If New Delhi can successfully deliver a larger number of such warheads, it should be able to ravage even more population centers throughout the Punjab and the Sind, thereby effectively disabling all the most productive centers within the Pakistani state. The sufficiency requirements for successful deterrence vis-à-vis Islamabad are therefore relatively low for India; even if Pakistan's own nuclear capabilities grow severalfold in the next two decades, India should be able to sustain relatively robust levels of nuclear deterrence stability so long as it can ensure that a small number of weapons can always be successfully detonated on critical Pakistani countervalue targets.[574] Given Pakistan's stark geophysical vulnerabilities, successful deterrence vis-à-vis Islamabad does not require either large numbers of nuclear weapons or extremely high-yield weapons, since modest retaliatory attacks

---

[573]This conclusion holds on the standard assumptions of rational deterrence theory—rationality, unitary actors, sensitivity to costs, etc.—and on the belief that whatever the handicaps afflicting India's deterrent may be, they will be resolved "eventually." If this conclusion therefore fails to hold over time, it will be mainly because one or both of these key assumptions do not survive robustly. Since the present analysis, however, is not about whether India can successfully deter Pakistan in all imaginable circumstances but only whether its capabilities are adequate prima facie *in terms of rational deterrence theory*, nothing more is claimed or suggested herein.

[574]Once again, this argument is constructed on the assumptions of rational deterrence theory.

can by themselves inflict so much damage as to provide India with effective "assured destruction" capabilities and, under some circumstances, even a kind of "escalation dominance" despite the possible presence of a small residual force. Since New Delhi will in all probability have a nuclear arsenal that is numerically larger than Pakistan's 10 to 20 years hence, and since this arsenal will enjoy greater survivability thanks to the increased uncertainty issuing from dispersal over a much larger landmass, the deterrence benefits accruing from Islamabad's physical vulnerability should be further magnified.

If the problem of generating effective deterrence vis-à-vis Pakistan is not a critical challenge from the perspective of sufficiency, the same argument does not hold where deterring China is concerned. This is because Beijing is and will continue to be a superior nuclear power whose lead both in numbers of weapons and in relative warhead yields is unlikely to be reduced by India's technical achievements during the next two decades. The constraints afflicting New Delhi in this regard are not produced by technical inferiority *simpliciter*; rather, they are fundamentally a product of both external pressures and internal preferences. If India were not encumbered by pressures relating to the CTBT, for example, it could continue to develop and test nuclear weapons until it was able to produce megaton-size warheads of the kind found in the Chinese arsenal today. This, of course, presumes that Indian policymakers would require high-yield warheads from their strategic enclaves—a presumption that has not yet been corroborated by any official statements emerging from the senior Indian leadership, who for all intents and purposes seem satisfied that their simple fission warheads are sufficient for effective deterrence. Similarly, India's own relatively small fissile-material inventory, combined with the looming restraints embodied by an FMCT, ensure that it will not produce fissile-material stocks anywhere close to those its larger rival possesses. Again, this presumes that Indian policymakers would demand a large fissile-material inventory from its nuclear estate, but the past record of Indian plutonium production and separation activity does not appear to bear out this assumption.

In any event, what all this suggests is that thanks to a variety of constraints—some external, some self-imposed—New Delhi is faced with the prospect of deterring a larger and more capable rival, China, with only modest nuclear capabilities of its own. These capabilities—

if the previously hypothesized Indian force structure is reiterated for the sake of argument—could materialize in the form of 100-plus long-range missiles, each armed with something resembling a ~12 to 20-kt simple fission warhead, facing more than 100 to 200 Chinese strategic missiles, each armed with a warhead that may be capable of producing yields as high as 3–5 Mt.[575] While these contending force structures obviously do not yet exist and may not even exist in this form 10 to 20 years hence, they are nonetheless useful for illustrating the nature of the deterrence problem India faces. Even if New Delhi produces the same number of long-range missiles as its largest adversary—something it may not do to begin with—it still cannot inflict equivalent levels of punishment on China because of asymmetries in the yield and number of warheads that both sides will possess.

Given this fact, how can New Delhi expect to deter Beijing? Many observers, drawing from the established architectures of nuclear deterrence made familiar during the Cold War, argue that India has no choice but to expand the number of nuclear weapons it possesses while increasing the yields of such weapons to levels comparable to those attained by China.[576] This argument would in effect require India to abjure signing the CTBT, resume hot testing of its nuclear weapons, and sharply accelerate the production of fissile materials. While it is possible that India might pursue one or more such initiatives in the future, it does not appear to be frenetically exploring any of them right now. This could imply either that New Delhi does not understand the requirements of sufficiency, especially as dictated by the classical model of deterrence exemplified during the Cold War, or that it believes effective deterrence can be obtained—even against asymmetrically powerful competitors—with relatively low levels of nuclear capability. If the writings of most Indian elites and the views of its strategic managers are any indication, the latter explana-

---

[575]China is currently believed to possess some 125 missiles with ranges ≥ 1700 km (see *SIPRI Yearbook 1997* [New York: Oxford University Press, 1997], p. 401). The number of Chinese strategic missiles a decade or so from now—200—is discussed in Myers, "Study Said to Find U.S. Missile Shield Might Incite China." Obviously, China would continue to possess many more missiles of shorter range that can be used in some contingencies against India—in addition to aircraft-delivered gravity bombs and tactical nuclear warheads.

[576]Jones, *From Testing to Deploying Nuclear Forces*, pp. 3–8.

tion accounts better than any other for the measured pace at which India's strategic capabilities are currently being developed.[577]

Even a cursory review of Indian strategic writings suggests that New Delhi's force-in-being will come much closer to the French model of "deterrence of the strong by the weak" (*dissuasion du faible au fort*) than to the American model of "deterrence by denial," which centered on the creation of large, diversified, and secure second-strike forces capable of achieving counterforce preeminence at various levels of conflict. The French vision of deterrence, exemplified by the *force de frappe*, underwrote the nuclear postures of at least three states during the Cold War—Great Britain, France, and China—and in each instance a relatively weak nuclear power was able to deter a superior adversary—the Soviet Union—from pursuing aggressive acts despite the latter's overwhelming predominance in nuclear capabilities. The effectiveness of deterrence in these situations of radically asymmetric capabilities constitutes a fascinating puzzle, and understanding it is important for the insights it may offer into how New Delhi might be able to garner comparable benefits in the Sino-Indian relationship without mimicking the U.S. solution of creating complex countervailing capabilities designed to frustrate the adversary at every rung of the escalatory ladder.

There were essentially three reasons the "deterrence of the strong by the weak" turned out to be relatively stable during the Cold War. First, the massive U.S. investments in deterrence vis-à-vis the Soviet Union created significant "positive externalities" that even relatively weaker powers could exploit to preserve their own security. This argument essentially implies that successful deterrence has some characteristics of a public good: It creates benefits that can be harvested by others who might not have contributed to producing it in the first place. Translated into the context of the Cold War, this public-good argument suggests that the same U.S. nuclear forces which prevented a Soviet assault on Washington's global interests simultaneously created niches of security which even states that did not produce any nuclear weapons could enjoy. This explanation, at any

---

[577] "India Not to Engage in a N-Arms Race: Jaswant," and Joshi, "India Must Have Survivable N-Arsenal."

rate, suggests why countries like Sweden could enjoy security from Soviet threats even while remaining outside the Atlantic alliance.[578]

Second, the weakness of small nuclear forces against the overwhelming Soviet threat was often mitigated by their tight coupling to the stronger nuclear capabilities of the United States. This argument asserts, in effect, that the possession of weak nuclear forces imposed no significant political penalties, since these instruments subsisted—for all practical purposes—as strategic appendages of a much stronger nuclear power. In the context of the Cold War, this implied that countries with minimal nuclear capabilities, like Great Britain, or countries with no nuclear capabilities whatsoever, like Germany, essentially overcame their disadvantages by tightly coupling their security needs to the massive nuclear reserves produced and maintained by the United States. By integrating British nuclear capabilities into the American SIOP and emplacing U.S. defensive, including nuclear, assets on German soil, the NATO alliance eliminated the disadvantages accruing to weakness by effectively transforming all its weaker constituents—both those with nuclear weapons and those without—into nuclear protectorates of the United States.[579]

While these two arguments can effectively explain why European neutrals and tightly coupled weaker allies were able to preserve their security in the face of overwhelming threats—even without nuclear weapons in some instances and with only weak nuclear capabilities in others—they do not completely account for how weak nuclear powers that were threatened by the Soviet Union but were not tightly coupled to the U.S. nuclear deterrent were also able to protect themselves more or less successfully. The two principal anomalies here were France and China: The former had a loose and idiosyncratic affinity to the U.S. deterrent, while the latter lay completely outside the formal ambit of American protection. Both were pervasively threatened by superior Soviet nuclear forces, and yet both managed to survive the Cold War—despite their conspicuously weak nuclear deterrents—without any serious mishaps. If the hypothesis of benign

---

[578]Cole, *Sweden Without the Bomb: The Conduct of a Nuclear-Capable Nation Without Nuclear Weapons.*

[579]See the discussion in Kenneth A. Myers (ed.), *NATO, the Next Thirty Years* (Boulder, CO: Westview Press, 1980).

Soviet intentions is excluded, the only credible explanation for this class of cases remains the French theory of "deterrence of the strong by the weak,"[580] and this argument constitutes the third explanation—actually rounding out the logic of the first—as to why relatively infirm powers were able to hold off much stronger adversaries.

The most common intuitive explanation for successful deterrence in these cases rests on the awesome power of nuclear weaponry—or, in other words, on the significance of the nuclear revolution. While this is certainly an important component of why weak nuclear powers were able to deter even stronger nuclear adversaries, it is insufficient. As one particularly insightful analysis has argued, successful nuclear deterrence of the strong by the weak ultimately "rests on the *possibility* that the latter will have at his disposal a deliverable devastating nuclear force *and* may prove to be an unsafe actor."[581] This conjoint requirement for the success of deterrence under conditions of radical asymmetry in capabilities can be satisfactorily explained in terms of rational deterrence theory.

In any contest between two asymmetrically capable nuclear powers, the weaker nuclear power can never rationally choose to make good on any of its retaliatory threats because the execution of these threats would invariably result in much greater pain for the weaker state. By this logic, a stronger nuclear state ought to be able to successfully blackmail a weaker one on every occasion simply because the consequences of being outgunned in the resulting exchange of punishments would always deter the latter. Even if the weaker state attempts to respond to blackmail with threats of limited use—in order to avoid the conclusive defeat that would be meted out as a result of threatening "massive retaliation"—the sequence of graduated escalation that could follow would inevitably end with the weaker power running out of limited options sooner or later, since the stronger state could respond to every such option with comparable if not higher levels of violence. In terms of rational deterrence

---

[580]This concept is discussed at length in David S. Yost, *France's Deterrent Posture and Security in Europe*, Part 1: *Capabilities and Doctrine*, and Part 2: *Strategic and Arms Control Implications*, Adelphi Paper Nos. 194 and 195 (London: IISS, 1984–1985).

[581]Avery S. Goldstein, "Robust and Affordable Security: Some Lessons from the Second-Ranking Powers During the Cold War," *Journal of Strategic Studies*, 15:4 (December 1992), p. 496.

theory, therefore, the weaker state must lose every time it engages in a contest of wills with a stronger nuclear power: Once it has run out of limited nuclear-use options, it must either surrender or engage in a massive "last roll of the dice" nuclear attack—an attack that is by definition suicidal in that the stronger power, which presumably was restrained until this point, loses every incentive to remain temperate in the aftermath. Faced with such choices, the alternative of suicide is invariably irrational for the weaker state, since the payoffs accruing to final and conclusive destruction are always less than the payoffs to surrender (because the latter at least embodies the hope that the consequences of defeat could someday be reversed if the conditions are propitious).[582]

If this logic was all there is to strategic deterrence, success in the nuclear realm would necessarily require all the competing actors to be equally robust, since weak nuclear states could never expect to successfully deter any threats issued by their stronger adversaries. Mercifully, there are in practice two variables that allow even weaker states to coexist with stronger nuclear powers, and it is the presence of these variables that arguably enables deterrence of the strong by the weak to survive as a reasonable alternative to deterrence produced by the rough equality of coercive capabilities.[583] The first variable is simply the enormous destructive power embodied by nuclear weaponry: This implies that even weaker powers can harm much stronger adversaries in a manner *disproportionate to their relative strength*, and unless the latter are confident of their ability to execute "splendid" disarming strikes, they must reckon with the prospect of suffering high absolute, even if only lower relative, levels of pain. The second variable is the unpredictability of decisionmaking entities under conditions of strategic threat. While rational deterrence theory presumes that political decisionmakers in the weaker state would perceive the hopelessness of their condition and, acting rationally on

---

[582]Robert Powell, "Nuclear Deterrence and the Strategy of Limited Retaliation," *American Political Science Review*, 83:2 (June 1989), pp. 503–519.

[583]This is not meant to imply that the former is to be preferred over the latter, but only that when the latter cannot be produced, the former could suffice in some specific circumstances. Also, the qualifier "arguably" is employed because it is difficult to establish conclusively whether "deterrence of the strong by the weak" could be effective independently if the positive externalities of American or some other great-power deterrence were absent.

that perception, invariably surrender to the stronger power, *there is no guarantee ensuring such an outcome will always occur in practice*: Thanks to imperfect information obtaining in any operating environment, security managers in the weaker state may in fact proceed to behave like "contingently unsafe actors"[584] and may choose to execute options that they might not otherwise have chosen were they omniscient about both their choices and the consequences of those choices. Since any use decision in the nuclear realm embodies high absolute costs—either because of the high costs of some kinds of discrete nuclear use or because of the high costs resulting from cumulative nuclear use—even stronger nuclear powers can be dissuaded from embarking on a course of strategic action that threatens the core interests of a relatively weaker state.

It is precisely this kind of calculus that underwrites New Delhi's belief that even relatively weak nuclear forces are sufficient to deter China—because so long as India's nuclear capabilities present more than just token opposition, and so long as Beijing cannot be certain that it can interdict India's nuclear reserves successfully and that a weaker India will always surrender rather than retaliate when faced with significant nuclear threats, China will in all likelihood be deterrable even in dyadic encounters characterized by a substantial asymmetry in relative nuclear capabilities. The late General Sundarji captured both components of this calculus succinctly when he wrote that because of India's weaknesses, "an Indian planner may not have the degree of assurance that he would like about the survival of the Indian second strike. However, with . . . [the] . . . deployment [of a force-in-being], no Chinese planner can be certain that no Indian second strike will survive, [especially if the residual elements] . . . could devastate a few major Chinese cities. [In such circumstances] there will be enormous reluctance [in Beijing] to go in for . . . a . . . first strike. That is what deterrence is all about."[585] Corroborating this insight further—and with more subtlety—K. Subrahmanyam noted that "India believes that in the present circumstances, there are very few objectives—political, strategic, economic—or ideologi-

---

[584]The term is Edward Rhodes' and is cited in Goldstein, "Robust and Affordable Security: Some Lessons from the Second-Ranking Powers During the Cold War," p. 488.

[585]Sundarji, "Indian Nuclear Doctrine—I: Notions of Deterrence."

cal reasons for which nations would be willing to accept [the] sacrifice of [even] two or three cities and, consequently, [the] projection of a capability to inflict that much hurt should deter any nation."[586] It is important to note that Subrahmanyam is not asserting that the ability to interdict "two or three cities" *always* suffices for purposes of deterrence but merely that "in present circumstances" there are "very few" situations facing India that would require nuclear forces capable of inflicting greater levels of damage.

The logic underlying Sundarji's vision of "deterrence of the strong by the weak" is therefore not centered on the claim that aggression by a stronger power will invariably be met by *a certain response that inflicts equivalent levels of damage*. Rather, it is predicated on the inherent *uncertainty* that the stronger power must always feel when it attempts to gauge both the kind of response that the weaker state might issue in a situation of extreme adversity *and* the high absolute costs even a ragged response would embody if it involved the use of nuclear weaponry. Any rejoinder to this argument based on the relative efficacy of thermonuclear versus other types of nuclear weapons risks missing the point. Indian security managers are well aware of the enormous differences in destructive capability inhering in different types of nuclear weaponry. They clearly recognize that thermonuclear weapons, with their vast destructive power, make splendid deterrents and that these weapons would perhaps be desirable if they could somehow be acquired today without the political costs associated with renewed testing. They would argue, however, that thermonuclear weapons, however advantageous they may be, are still not strictly necessary because even simple fission weapons could inflict all the damage required to enforce restraint on the part of a stronger state in the specific political circumstances India faces.[587] Restraint in this instance does not derive from the claim that India's simple fission weapons can destroy whole cities—they cannot—but rather from the fact that they will inflict enormous fatalities far out of proportion to the value of the disputed issues even if the cities tar-

---

[586]K. Subrahmanyam, "Articulating Our Nuclear Policy," *Economic Times*, June 15, 1994.

[587]The clearest and most explicit statement to this effect can be found in Sundarji, "Indian Nuclear Doctrine—I: Notions of Deterrence," and in Sundarji, "Imperatives of Indian Minimum Nuclear Deterrence."

geted by these weapons are not "entirely" destroyed as a result. Indian strategists have often pointed out in private conversations that the density of population concentrations in modern Chinese and Pakistani cities is often greater than that found in central Hiroshima and Nagasaki. Consequently, even the most pedestrian devices existing in the Indian arsenal today—simple fission weapons with yields of 12–20 kt—would cause much greater levels of death and injury than the atomic bombings in Japan even if large portions of the targeted Chinese and Pakistani cities remained immune to the lethal effects of India's nuclear weapons. Any nuclear use that involved multiple—spaced—detonations of simple fission weapons on a single countervalue target would only magnify these casualty levels.[588]

That deterrence might be successful because of the inherent lethality of nuclear weapons was well understood by the advocates of minimum deterrence even during the Cold War. In fact, these advocates, basing their claims on the horrendous destructive power embodied by the thermonuclear weapons present in the arsenals of all the established nuclear weapon states, often argued that small nuclear inventories were more than sufficient for strategic deterrence so long as the weapons and their associated delivery systems were survivable in terms of some standard measures used in operations analysis.[589] Some Western analysts, carrying this logic over to the Indian subcontinent, have argued that "where nuclear weapons are in play, [successful] deterrence requires only creating . . . 'first-strike uncertainty'"—that is, a situation where "one need only cause the adversary to worry that his first-strike may be less than fully successful."[590] This argument, replicating Sundarji's earlier claim, implies that India's modest nuclear reserves could provide stable and effective deterrence even against more powerful adversaries like China because the "absolute amounts of punishment that can be threatened are more important than [the] relative numbers of warheads or

---

[588]Sundarji, "CTBT and National Security: Options for India."

[589]Nicholas Wheeler, "Minimum Deterrence and Nuclear Abolition," in Regina Cowen Karp (ed.), *Security Without Nuclear Weapons?* (Oxford, UK: Oxford University Press, 1992), pp. 250–280.

[590]Avery Goldstein, "Scared Senseless? The South Asian Nuclear Tests," *E-Notes* (Philadelphia: Foreign Policy Research Institute), June 5, 1998.

launchers."[591] Although this formulation does not explicitly say so, it effectively implies that the types and numbers of weapons involved are less relevant for effective deterrence because so long as an adversary cannot be "COMPLETELY sure about the exact number and location of the [opponent's] nuclear forces and the effectiveness of [his] planned attack, the fear of devastating retaliation will continue to exert a powerful inhibiting effect on a decision-maker contemplating the use of military force in ways that risk escalation."[592]

Such arguments are logical prima facie because they highlight the powerful inhibiting effects that nuclear weapons can have on the war-or-peace calculus of states. They do not, however, establish that the relative balance of capabilities can be neglected in any standoff, irrespective of whether this balance is measured in terms of the numbers or the types of weapons involved. To be sure, many of the details pertaining to the nuclear balance can be less than arresting in peacetime because in the absence of strong political pressures, decisionmakers would most likely be hobbled by the kind of "first-strike uncertainty" that may be assumed to exist were they to fantasize about unleashing any unprovoked nuclear attacks "out of the blue." In the context of a crisis, however, an entirely different calculus could come into play: While security managers, pressed by the acute demands of necessity, might recognize that one consequence of "first-strike uncertainty" may be self-restraint leading to peace, they would also be forced to ponder the possibility that their self-restraint might result in preemptive attacks by an adversary. Such preemptive attacks would in fact be likely were an adversary, perceiving war to be a distinct possibility, to conclude that striking first was preferable to striking second. In other words, even if high levels of first-strike uncertainty were to exist in a given situation, preemptive nuclear attacks *might* still be deemed rational in the context of a crisis if an adversary were to conclude that striking first—even if only ineffectively by some notional standard of a "splendid" first strike—left it better off than waiting to absorb an attack that might be mounted by its antagonist. The optimists who propose a sufficiency criterion based on first-strike uncertainty alone often understate the acuteness of political pressures that could materialize in a crisis. These pressures

---

[591] Ibid.

[592] Ibid.

could force a state to initiate nuclear war even if such attacks could not effectively disarm its adversary's nuclear capabilities: So long as an initiator believed that war is inevitable and that striking first left it better off than striking second, initiating even a nuclear war could be a rational endeavor despite the high absolute levels of harm that would be sustained as a result of such an action.

If the adversary "forced" to "go first" in such a situation turned out to be China—purely for the prudential reason of limiting damage to itself in the context of some future Sino-Indian crisis—the fact that both Beijing and New Delhi were hobbled by high degrees of first-strike uncertainty in peacetime would be of comparatively little consequence where crisis stability was concerned. It is precisely in this context that the relative weakness of the Indian nuclear deterrent becomes a critical issue, because while the pressures leading to preemptive attack can materialize in *any* situation involving nuclear powers, they are (it is hoped) more effectively muted in those situations where even constrained preemption always and unambiguously invokes an "obviously dire, devastatingly clear and absolutely inescapable"[593] counterresponse. The inevitability of such a counterresponse is best personified by the presence of thermonuclear weaponry, because even a relatively small number of these residual weapons can effectively devastate most organized societies; consequently, it is not surprising that these instruments, which existed in large numbers during the Cold War, lent credence to the key claims of many Western devotees of minimum deterrence.[594] Given that New Delhi lacks comparable capabilities in terms of both the types and the numbers of weapons involved, the critical question from the perspective of deterrence sufficiency is whether India's simple fission weaponry would suffice to deter manifestly stronger adversaries like China in the context of an acute future crisis. In effect, this issue boils down to asking whether India's relatively modest nuclear capability would be able to prevent the worst imaginable outcome—a massive Chinese preemptive attack conducted with thermonuclear

---

[593]Shlapak and Thaler, *Back to First Principles*, p. 16.

[594]Wheeler, "Minimum Deterrence and Nuclear Abolition," pp. 250–280, and Lawrence Freedman, *The Evolution of Nuclear Strategy* (New York: St. Martin's Press, 1981), p. 207. The presence of thermonuclear weapons also underlay the concept of "existential deterrence" as elaborated in Bundy, "Existential Deterrence and Its Consequences," pp. 3–13.

weapons—even if all that New Delhi could offer in return would be a ragged nuclear response that sufficed only to partially destroy "two or three cities" of importance to Beijing. Obviously, India may be able to inflict even higher levels of pain in practice, but Subrahmanyam's metaphor of holding "two or three cities" at risk allows the question to be posed in its starkest and most illuminating form: Can a force-in-being capable of destroying only two or three Chinese cities suffice to deter Beijing in a future crisis with New Delhi?

Surprising as it may seem, the answer to this question *today* is a qualified "yes": New Delhi's nuclear deterrent, despite its presumed modesty, ought to be able to deter even an overwhelming Chinese preemptive attack in the context of a crisis not because of its ability to inflict horrendous retaliatory pain on Beijing but because the high absolute, albeit not overwhelming, levels of damage that even India's smaller nuclear weapons could inflict when employed in a counter-value mode would be far greater than the value of the assets China sought to secure through the use of force—especially any force that either involves nuclear employment or carries within it the potential for escalation to the nuclear level. The Indian force-in-being, when more mature some ten years from now, should thus be potentially sufficient not because of its intrinsic lethality, which will remain quite modest, or because it is superior in terms of the balance of capabilities vis-à-vis China (it is not) but only because even after absorbing a first strike it will be able to inflict more damage on China than any victory in the current political disputes with India is worth. Stated differently, there are simply no political issues at stake in the Sino-Indian dispute that would make the loss of even two or three Chinese cities palatable to Beijing, irrespective of what happens to many more Indian cities as a result of the probably asymmetrical nuclear exchange that would unfold between these two competitors. Despite its relative weakness, the modest Indian deterrent could therefore suffice so long as China does not become a rapacious political entity willing to accept any amount of nuclear punishment simply to seize control over territories it claims as its own and so long as New Delhi does not seek to conquer new territories that currently lie either unclaimed or outside the domain of its effective control. Since both China and India are currently status quo powers at least with respect to the territorial disputes that engulf them, neither state is likely to pursue any military action that would either involve the

employment of nuclear weapons or embody any real prospect of escalation to nuclear use. The challenge of crisis instability, with all the
attendant problems of preemptive-strike temptations, is thus neutralized in the Sino-Indian context simply by virtue of the political
pressures on both sides to avoid *any* recourse to force—particularly
because there are no worthwhile strategic objectives that could be
secured through the application of coercive instruments, including
nuclear weapons, that might be used in either a premeditated or an
anticipatory way. Since India's nuclear weapons have mostly political functions in this context—meaning that they exist principally as
insurance against the remote possibility of miscalculation by Beijing
while simultaneously serving to bolster political resolve in New
Delhi—the modest nuclear capabilities that India will evolve over
time should suffice for purposes of deterrence stability even against a
stronger power like China.

This preliminary judgment about the sufficiency of the Indian deterrent thus falls squarely between the claims made by two competing schools in the West. The optimists argue that nuclear weapons
simpliciter, with their horrendous destructive power, ought to suffice
for effective and stable deterrence in South Asia simply because first-
strike uncertainty makes all nuclear attacks improbable.[595] The pessimists, in contrast, argue that India's minimum deterrent would be
ineffective vis-à-vis stronger adversaries like China because the balance of capabilities and the inequalities in the exchange of punishments favor Beijing, thereby confronting India with the unpalatable
prospect of either facing disarming nuclear attacks or simply being
self-deterred as a result of its own weakness.[596] The judgment advanced here falls between these two positions: It credits the Indian
force-in-being with potential sufficiency because of the specific political objectives serviced by these weapons in the unique circumstances India faces in its competition with both Pakistan and China.
It does not derive this expectation of sufficiency simply from the
fearsome quality of India's nuclear weaponry, nor does it decry the
deterrence potential of this force-in-being simply because it turns
out to be admittedly modest in comparison to China's nuclear arse-

---

[595]Hagerty, "The Consequences of Nuclear Proliferation: Lessons from South
Asia," pp. 171–196.

[596]Jones, *From Testing to Deploying Nuclear Forces*, pp. 3–8.

nal. Rather, it argues that the force-in-being as it is currently conceived could be sufficient for India because it meets needs that are specific to New Delhi in a way that the optimists and certainly the pessimists do not always fully appreciate.[597]

The judgment that India's nuclear weaponry will successfully deter even stronger adversaries like China—in all the political circumstances deemed to be relevant to New Delhi—must therefore not be confused with the arguments advanced by Western devotees of minimum deterrence during the great strategic debates of the Cold War. This is an important point that must be borne in mind when the sufficiency of the hypothesized Indian deterrent is assessed. Most influential Indian elites, especially analysts like K. Subrahmanyam, Jasjit Singh, and other high-level officials in the Ministries of External Affairs and Defence (and even the late General K. Sundarji), believe that the confidence placed in India's modest deterrent derives not from the vast destructive power of nuclear weapons per se—because New Delhi may not possess the most ruinous devices imaginable—but rather from the costs that would be imposed on an adversary by even modest Indian nuclear use in relation to the political benefits that adversary sought to attain. This qualifier is essential to the success of the Indian variant of "deterrence of the strong by the weak" because it includes an inference that should be of importance to policymakers in the United States: New Delhi's emerging force-in-being, far from serving as a permanent solution for all time and against any imaginable adversary, is a narrow and specific antidote developed to further only those political interests thought to be both currently and prospectively at stake in the various South Asian disputes.[598]

---

[597]The most prominent Indian hawk who appears to have accepted this conclusion is Chellaney, "After the Tests: India's Options," pp. 105–108; the most prominent dissenter among Indian hawks remains Karnad, "A Thermonuclear Deterrent," pp. 108–149.

[598]This is a point that is often overlooked in India, with the result that justifications for thermonuclear weapons only become "unavoidable if India is to deploy a nuclear triad as envisaged by the nuclear doctrine . . . [that is] . . . not country-specific but possesses an all-azimuth character." See Chari, "Weaponisation and the CTBT." This argument, of course, raises the question of whether India requires an all-azimuth nuclear capability to begin with for purposes of its security.

In the context of China specifically, the modest Indian deterrent is premised on the belief that three critical asymmetries currently exist in favor of New Delhi.

First, the essential asymmetry of interests: India values the disputed territories it currently occupies because of their greater intrinsic worth to New Delhi more than China values the recovery of such territories through any use of force, including the employment of nuclear weapons.

Second, the essential asymmetry of capabilities: India can defend the disputed territories it currently occupies through conventional means alone, in contrast to China, which cannot reacquire these territories through use of comparable instruments.

Third, the essential asymmetry of resolve: India is likely to defend the territories it currently occupies with far greater resolution than China is inclined to display in recovering them, especially if any recovery operation involves the prospect of initial or eventual nuclear weapon use.

Despite Beijing's great advantage in nuclear capabilities, it is therefore not at all evident—given the kinds of asymmetries existing in India's favor—that China's advantages would actually have great utility in the face of the mismatch between the small contested objectives and the truly enormous power inherent in its strategic weaponry. Because the tensions in this mismatch would only be accentuated by the presence of even a modest Indian retaliatory force, it is not at all surprising that most Indian security managers, echoing the conclusion reached earlier, express confidence that their admittedly weak nuclear capabilities should suffice for purposes of deterrence in the specific conditions governing current and prospective security competition in Southern Asia.

The belief that even a relatively weak Indian deterrent will suffice to dissuade a stronger nuclear power like China is obviously not an absolute claim—i.e., one that holds with no exception—but rather an assertion that holds only so long as:

- Sino-Indian relations do not degenerate into high-intensity, zero-sum security competition across the board and in all issue areas;

- New Delhi continues to maintain existing levels of conventional superiority along the Himalayan border and in the Indian Ocean;

- India does not acquire any extended deterrence commitments along the "outer ring" of its traditional defensive periphery; and

- China remains a relatively risk-averse entity focused on internal economic regeneration rather than on the muscular pursuit of irredentist claims abroad.

If these conditions continue to obtain, India should be able to deter even a stronger adversary like China with a relatively limited nuclear force simply because the disputes between the two countries ultimately do not lend themselves to being advantageously resolved by the exploitation of nuclear assets on either side. When this fact is coupled with other stabilizing variables, such as uncertainty about India's true nuclear capabilities (especially as these appear to decisionmakers in Beijing and Islamabad), the opaqueness of India's nuclear assets (and the useful first-strike uncertainty resulting therefrom), and the fact that even relatively small Indian nuclear weapons could inflict far greater damage than the objectives sought by any competitor are worth, the viability of the modest Indian nuclear force only becomes more plausible, especially in a political environment that is increasingly defined by a strong and growing aversion to any nuclear use whatsoever.[599]

When viewed from a theoretical perspective, there is no doubt that this expectation of deterrence stability incorporates much lower levels of sufficiency, at least in comparison to the classical framework developed during the Cold War. Where the two superpowers were concerned, stability essentially derived from the certainty of nuclear retaliation, which in turn inevitably implied all-out—mutual—societal destruction through war. When second-rank nuclear states were arrayed against a superpower, a different criterion of sufficiency obtained: Stability derived from the uncertainty of retaliation on the part of the weaker power, which would nonetheless involve the

---

[599]Not surprisingly, then, India will continue to support all international, including U.S., efforts to strengthen the existing "nuclear taboo." For a useful discussion of the sources and durability of this phenomenon, see T. V. Paul, "Nuclear Taboo and War Initiation in Regional Conflicts," *Journal of Conflict Resolution*, 39:4 (December 1995), pp. 696–717.

meting out of high levels of absolute punishment. Deterrence involving third-rank proliferants such as India, Pakistan, and North Korea, which may have to contend with asymmetrically stronger nuclear powers in the foreseeable future, is likely to incorporate even weaker requirements relating to strategic sufficiency: Stability would still hinge on the uncertainty of retaliation on the part of the weaker state, but the levels of punishment inflicted may not even be high in absolute terms but only in comparison to the value of the disputed objectives the stronger adversary seeks to attain. Of course, there is no reason why, in any given case, the levels of punishment inflicted could not be both high in absolute terms and greater than the value of the disputed objectives simultaneously. But even if this condition does not obtain, the success of the deterrence posture will in these instances be measured not so much by the size and quality of the nuclear forces possessed by the weaker states or even by the relative nuclear balance obtaining across any given dyad—although both of these variables will continue to be relevant in specific ways—but rather by the ability of the weaker power to prevent the stronger adversary from embarking on a course of action that *could* result in an outcome that is far costlier than the value of the objectives sought to be secured by nuclear coercion or the use of force. One scholar captured this logic eloquently in the following words:

> Though both potential aggressor and victim are inhibited by the attendant risks in any confrontation between nuclear states, the key point about the robustness of the nuclear deterrent strategy [referring to the "deterrence of the strong by the weak"] is that it succeeds insofar as it makes it difficult for the aggressor [meaning the stronger nuclear power] to "go first." Where the victim is a nuclear power and cannot be completely disarmed, the onus of initiating a sequence of events that contain the possibility of disaster falls to the aggressor and exerts a powerful dissuasive effect. . . . Given incomplete information, the autonomous risk of disaster enable[s] a [weaker nuclear] power to deter a [superior] adversary. It instill[s] in the latter the fear of catastrophic nuclear retaliation despite its obvious irrationality given his clear superiority in limited nuclear options and the impossibility of the victim ever deliberately choosing the outcome of mutual nuclear suicide.[600]

---

[600]Goldstein, "Robust and Affordable Security: Some Lessons from the Second-Ranking Powers During the Cold War," p. 489.

In his study *India's Nuclear Bomb,* George Perkovich summed up the application of this logic in the Indian context when he stated that

> instead of building redundant nuclear arsenals on hair-trigger alert in the name of *certain* mutual destruction, the few Indians who attended to these issues believed that it was adequate to make an adversary *uncertain* that nuclear threats or attacks on India would *not* be met with nuclear reprisals. Nuclear weapons pose such horrifying threats, they argued, that this approach was adequate to deter a rational adversary. No greater capability would deter an irrational adversary.[601]

The continuing viability of this logic in the perception of Indian security managers highlights a critical element that ought not to be forgotten when the sufficiency of the Indian deterrent—or any other deterrent, for that matter—is examined. Nuclear deterrence is first and foremost a political phenomenon, not an abstract system of exchanging punishments designed by and for theorists residing in the rarefied atmosphere of a think tank. What constitutes sufficiency among new nuclear proliferants will therefore be influenced by the results of systems analysis but not determined by them. As Sundarji noted, there is a world of difference between what is required to ensure effective deterrence when measured by "a realistic political approach as against think-tank simulations."[602] In this "second coming of the nuclear age,"[603] when there exist high and ever-rising thresholds of nuclear use, states are likely to be even more sensitive than usual to the purported need for large nuclear arsenals, especially when these arsenals are considered necessary to address potentially problematic issues such as graduated escalation or nuclear war fighting.[604] Since political requirements rather than the abstract

---

[601] Perkovich, *India's Nuclear Bomb,* p. 3.

[602] Sundarji, "Indian Nuclear Doctrine—I: Notions of Deterrence."

[603] This phrase is borrowed from Iklé, "The Second Coming of the Nuclear Age," p. 119.

[604] Even during the Cold War, there was considerable skepticism among U.S. policymakers about the viability of such strategies despite the fact that the United States felt condemned to seek limited targeting options in order to minimize the catastrophe resulting from deterrence breakdown. As former Secretary of Defense Harold Brown once noted, "Counterforce and damage-limiting campaigns have been put forward as the nuclear equivalents of traditional warfare. But their proponents find it difficult to tell us what objectives an enemy would seek in launching such

claims of systems analysts are more likely to condition future notions of strategic sufficiency, political decisionmakers in newly proliferating states such as India will be extraordinarily sensitive to both context and costs where issues pertaining to the acquisition, deployment, and use of nuclear weapons are concerned. Because the value of these weapons "lies almost exclusively in what they help to avoid, rather than in what they can accomplish,"[605] the pursuit of any political goal involving the prospect of even a single nuclear weapon going off in anger is only likely to dampen—not heighten—the enthusiasm of state managers for securing these objectives.

It is precisely this condition that makes the Indian force-in-being a viable instrument of statecraft for certain narrow and clearly defined purposes such as increasing political confidence, preventing blackmail, and deterring nuclear use in the context of the relatively low levels of security competition with Pakistan and China. To that degree, the size, structure, and disposition of the evolving Indian arsenal must be clearly viewed as a *circumstantial* product that may not subsist as a stable equilibrium in perpetuity. This, in turn, implies that if the force-in-being currently desired by New Delhi is to survive more or less as a permanent end state, the three conditions referred to in earlier chapters would have to persist indefinitely. These include the gradual diminution in nuclear inventories worldwide coupled with high and ever-rising thresholds of nuclear use; the continued maintenance of robust U.S. hegemony; and the durable persistence of an offense-dominant global nuclear regime. All three conditions are critical for ensuring that New Delhi will remain satisfied with nuclear sufficiency even at low force levels.

The gradual reduction of nuclear arsenals worldwide remains an important evidentiary instrument testifying to the commitment of the Permanent Five to norms of global equity and their legal obligations under Article VI of the NPT. More important from New Delhi's perspective, it creates the structural preconditions that actually enhance Indian security under regional conditions while increasing India's status in the global order. The continued reinforcement of the

---

campaigns, how these campaigns would end, or how any resulting symmetries could be made meaningful." See Harold Brown, *Department of Defense Annual Report, Fiscal Year 1980* (Washington, D.C.: USGPO, 1979), p. 76.

[605]Shlapak and Thaler, *Back to First Principles*, p. 9.

tradition of nuclear nonuse additionally contributes to making the threats of nuclear employment against India even more remote and, by implication, further diminishes the necessity for New Delhi to contemplate dramatically enlarging its capabilities or engaging in heroic measures to cope with such contingencies.[606]

The continued maintenance of robust American hegemony also contributes to this outcome, but via a different route: It guarantees that India's regional competitor, China, will never become a preponderant power capable of coercing its neighbors without fear of countervailing responses mounted by the United States in Asia or beyond. To the degree that Indo-American relations also improve over time, it bequeaths to New Delhi all the deterrence advantages accruing from closer Indian collaboration with the most important power in the international system. Continued U.S. hegemony, in fact, ensures that the United States will be able to provide explicit or tacit extended guarantees to all states that may be threatened by a powerful and possibly bellicose China in the future while simultaneously allowing those states which may not seek such guarantees to enjoy them nonetheless because of the positive externalities created either by American deterrence of all its major and steadily growing rivals or by the promotion of a local Asian balance of power under the overall aegis of American hegemony at the core of the global system.[607]

Finally, the durable persistence of an offense-dominant global nuclear regime ensures that even relatively weak Indian nuclear forces will always be able to reach their targets in China and Pakistan without excessive difficulty. A shift to a "thick" defense-dominant nuclear

---

[606]Many of these issues are discussed in Perkovich, *India's Nuclear Bomb*, pp. 464–468.

[607]This is a point that Indian policymakers clearly recognize but are loath to admit publicly because they fear that continued American hegemony might turn out to be an impediment to the multipolarity that promises to assure India a role at the core of the global system. For this reason, Indian policymakers and analysts are more likely to argue for the creation of an Asian balance of power in which India becomes a prominent actor. For further details, see Ashley J. Tellis, "The Changing Political-Military Environment: South Asia," in Zalmay Khalilzad, David T. Orletsky, Jonathan D. Pollack, Kevin Pollpeter, Angel M. Rabasa, David A. Shlapak, Abram N. Shulsky, and Ashley J. Tellis (eds.), *The United States and Asia: Toward a New U.S. Strategy and Force Posture* (Santa Monica: RAND, 2001). See also Deepa M. Ollapally, "India and the New 'Asian' Balance of Power," *Strategic Analysis*, 22:4 (July 1998), pp. 515–526, and K. Subrahmanyam, "Son of Star Wars," *The Times of India*, February 12, 2001.

regime, on the other hand, would require greater exertions on New Delhi's part to ensure continued penetrativity of its strategic weaponry and, over time, may also require that India both improve the quality and increase the numbers of its nuclear weapons and delivery systems to levels far greater than were originally intended as part of the force-in-being.[608] To the degree that the offense-dominant global nuclear regime stays more or less intact, all the pressures for producing a larger, more capable, and more diversified Indian nuclear force will also remain relatively muted.

Should any of these three variables change systematically over time, the size, complexity, and character of the Indian force-in-being would also be progressively transformed. This would be particularly true:

- if China emerged as a true superpower in the future and, as a result of its changed status, dramatically expanded its strategic nuclear capabilities *and* transformed the current conventional balance vis-à-vis India to New Delhi's disadvantage;

- if Sino-Indian competition intensified over time as a result of growing national capabilities in both states and if the resulting struggle for power were to generate a high-intensity contest for influence in the middle eastern, southern, and southeastern rimlands of the Asian continent;

- if Sino-American relations were perceived in New Delhi as taking the form of coercive collusion manifested either through joint efforts at "ganging up" against India on political-strategic issues or through greater displays of laxity toward Pakistani efforts at increasing its strategic capabilities through proscribed international transactions; or

- if international politics were once again to radically change course and move in the direction of greater nuclearization and even stronger forms of dependence on nuclear weapons for ensuring order and security.

---

[608]Brahma Chellaney, "New Delhi's Dilemma," *Washington Quarterly*, 23:3 (Summer 2000), pp. 145–153.

If such circumstances come to pass, the Indian nuclear posture would change and could evolve into something resembling a traditional arsenal. In fact, the genius of the force-in-being is that it allows for such change to take place in a relatively evolutionary fashion. This is because the posture currently favored by India's security managers does not prevent the country from continually improving its delivery capabilities, supporting infrastructure, and procedural systems to levels that could support a variety of nuclear strategies other than delayed retaliation focused on simple punishment. Nor does it prevent India from continuing to accumulate weapons-grade plutonium and any other special nuclear materials that its evolving arsenal might need in the near term; in fact, depending on the final text of the FMCT, it is even possible, although not likely, that India and all other states might be permitted to continue producing fissile materials, albeit with the stipulation that all post-FMCT stocks of such material be maintained under safeguards. If such a position is actually agreed to in the Conference on Disarmament, India could continue to produce fissile materials, and these materials would remain in its custody, albeit under safeguards, and would be available to the Indian state for any purposes in an emergency. Even if this position does not survive the current negotiations relating to the FMCT, the fact remains that such a treaty is years away from completion, and given India's current refusal to accept a moratorium on the production of fissile materials, New Delhi could—and will—continue to produce weapons-usable nuclear materials until the last possible moment until prohibited from doing so by a multilateral FMCT.

The currently favored strategic posture also does not prevent the continued improvement of India's nuclear weapon designs through computer simulations and subcritical tests, and ultimately it would not prevent New Delhi from breaking out of any treaty commitments—assuming it signed on to the FMCT and CTBT in the first place—that prohibit either the production of fissile materials or the resumption of field testing for purposes of developing a larger number of more potent nuclear weapons.[609] As Indian Prime Minister

---

[609]Senior Indian policymakers have already indicated that India could withdraw its unilateral moratorium on explosive nuclear testing should that action comport with its national interests. See "India Can Still Conduct N-Tests, Says Jaswant," *Indian Express*, November 25, 2000.

Vajpayee noted in connection with the latter issue, "India could [always] carry out more nuclear tests if it perceived any threat to its national security in the future. There is nothing new about it. There is a provision in the CTBT . . . that if any country feels there is a threat to its security, it can act outside the provisions of the CTBT."[610] The solution embodied by the force-in-being thus carries within it the potential for transformation into some other, more lethal kind of nuclear posture—like a more robust force-in-being or different variants of a ready arsenal—if changes in India's strategic circumstances were to mandate that it embark on such a transition. In that sense, the force-in-being represents a continuation of the classic Indian preference for "keeping the option open."

What is never explicitly stated by Indian security managers but is always on their minds is that the currently favored solution represented by the force-in-being serves the specific purpose of ensuring Indian security in conditions that are best described as being "between the times"—that is, between the first nuclear era defined by the Cold War and the still-unclear but emerging reorganization of the international system. If the global order were really to change in a direction manifestly unfavorable to India, personified most simply by China's rise as a threatening superpower, Indian policymakers expect that the currently strong wave of American nonproliferation pressures on New Delhi—one of the factors that in fact contributes to maintaining their nuclear capabilities in the form of a force-in-being—would steadily abate and that India would then be free for the first time to return to the business of developing a more robust nuclear posture of the kind the altered strategic environment required. Under these conditions, they expect that the current U.S. attitude toward nuclear weapons may itself change and that Washington may return to emphasizing the acquisition of even more robust nuclear capabilities than are currently deployed by the United States.

Should such circumstances come to pass, whatever commitments India may have made in the interim to global regimes like the CTBT and the FMCT would slowly become irrelevant—just as U.S. com-

---

[610]Bishwanath Ghosh, "N-Tests Possible After CTBT: PM," *Asian Age*, August 23, 1998.

mitments to the ABM treaty threaten to become irrelevant today—
and New Delhi could find itself obligated to change course simply to
ensure its national security in the new strategic environment. If and
until such a point is reached, however, the force-in-being is seen to
serve India well—just as "maintaining the option" served it well for
over two decades—and this solution will in all likelihood subsist as
the new "punctuated equilibrium" for some time to come: a stable
way point, but not a permanent terminus in India's slow maturation
as a nuclear weapon power.

As Figure 19 graphically illustrates, the history of the Indian nuclear weapon program has in fact been little more than a series of se-
quentially punctuated equilibria. And if the past is any guide, the
defining changes in the character of India's currently preferred nuclear posture—although likely to materialize only after an extended

RAND MR1127-19

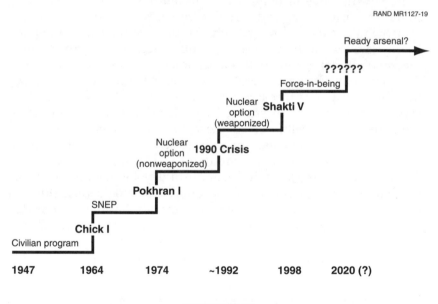

MR1127 fig 19

Figure 19—History of India's Nuclear Weapon Program

period of time—will likely be triggered by some sharp, specific external or internal stimulus that cannot yet be discerned with any clarity. What U.S. policymakers and the intelligence community can do in the interim, however, is continuously monitor the nature of the ongoing Indian strategic debate, especially with respect to the following questions, because the dominant answers accepted to these queries in the "official mind" of policymakers and strategic managers in New Delhi will—even more than technical intelligence about India's strategic programs—illuminate the prospect for future changes in India's nuclear posture:

What does effective deterrence entail in terms of the numbers of nuclear weapons?

What does effective deterrence entail in terms of the quality of nuclear weapons?

What does effective deterrence entail in terms of the numbers and quality of delivery systems?

What is the "dominant" solution to the problem of strategic force survivability?

How slow can "delayed retaliation" be without imperiling deterrence stability?

How formal do C³I systems have to be for effective deterrence?

How important is military custody of nuclear weapons in peacetime for effective deterrence?

Is stable deterrence best served by certainty or uncertainty of strategic outcomes?

Depending on how the answers to these questions change over time, the Indian strategic posture could mutate—and although previous discussions posited a ready arsenal as the "ideal-typical" alternative strategic managers in New Delhi might favor, this choice, like any other, may never be publicly announced or deliberately selected but may instead appear simply as the end point of a long process of creeping weaponization. It is thus worth noting—more from a policy standpoint than from a theoretical perspective—that there are some intermediate positions India may pause at along the way. If, for example, the currently favored posture is that of a force-in-being—that is, one defined by limited size, separated components, and centralized control—it is possible to imagine at least two subalternatives lying *between* the boundaries of a force-in-being and a ready arsenal.[611] At one end, India could continue to settle for a force-in-being, but one that is *not* limited in size. This posture—a robust force-in-being—would continue to be defined by separated components and centralized control, but it would seek to incorporate the largest and most capable nuclear force India could produce before it is constrained either by bilateral agreements or by multilateral treaties. At the other end, India could opt for a modest ready arsenal—that is, a force defined by highly integrated weapons ready for prompt operations as well as by a centralized but rapidly devolving command-and-control system, yet one that is nonetheless small at least in terms of the number and perhaps types of nuclear weapons it involves. Beyond these two subalternatives, of course, lies a true ready arsenal, which may be described as a large nuclear force that is fully integrated in disposition, with centralized but rapidly devolving command-and-control arrangements.

Since it is impossible to predict whether India will choose to move directly to a ready arsenal of this kind—once it feels compelled to go beyond its current preference for a force-in-being—or even if it will choose to move in decisive as opposed to incremental steps, Table 7 identifies some of the salient indicators that will help U.S. policymakers determine the status of India's nuclear posture as it evolves beyond its current disposition. In practice, none of these alternatives will be clearly associated with each of the indicators identified in the table—but taken in their totality, each set of indicators suggests a sufficiently different strategic orientation that warrants continued scrutiny by the United States.

---

[611]There are in principle many variants beyond the two alternatives discussed here. These variants can be derived by manipulating the following three variables—the size of the force, the degree of integration between weapon components, and the patterns of command, control, and custody—in different ways. The subalternatives identified here, however, are simply those believed to be most plausible in the Indian context, and no claims with respect to the exhaustiveness of all possible combinations are thereby implied.

Table 7

Signposts Indicating Future Shifts in India's Nuclear Posture

Variable	Force-in-Being *(Limited inventory size; separated weapon components; centralized control)*	Intermediate Posture I: Robust Force-in-Being *(Expanded inventory size; separated weapon components; centralized control)*	Intermediate Posture II: Modest Ready Arsenal *(Limited inventory size; integrated weapon systems; centralized but rapidly devolving control)*	Ready Arsenal *(Expanded inventory size; integrated weapon systems; centralized but rapidly devolving control)*
Fissile-material production	Production of weapons-grade plutonium at a traditional or marginally increasing rate in research reactors only	Production of weapons-grade plutonium at a highly increased rate in research reactors; use of civilian reactors for production of weapons-grade plutonium; accelerated enrichment of weapons-grade uranium	Production of weapons-grade plutonium at a traditional or marginally increasing rate in research reactors only	Production of weapons-grade plutonium at a highly increased rate in research reactors; use of civilian reactors for production of weapons-grade plutonium; accelerated enrichment of weapons-grade uranium
Nuclear weapon research, development, and production	Laboratory tests of nuclear weapon components; subcritical tests and other experiments	Resumption of hot testing for yield enhancement or for validation and weaponization of advanced nuclear designs; creation of a dedicated nuclear weapon assembly plant	Resumption of hot testing for validating warhead safety technologies	Resumption of hot testing for yield enhancement or for validation and weaponization of advanced nuclear designs or for validating warhead safety technologies; creation of a dedicated nuclear weapon assembly plant

Table 7 (continued)

Variable	Force-in-Being (Limited inventory size; separated weapon components; centralized control)	Intermediate Posture I: Robust Force-in-Being (Expanded inventory size; separated weapon components; centralized control)	Intermediate Posture II: Modest Ready Arsenal (Limited inventory size; integrated weapon systems; centralized but rapidly devolving control)	Ready Arsenal (Expanded inventory size; integrated weapon systems; centralized but rapidly devolving control)
Delivery system architecture	Dyad plus R&D on sea-based systems	Dyad plus R&D on sea-based systems; possible nuclear deployment on surface vessels	Triad with SSBNs/SSGNs	Triad with SSBNs/SSGNs
Procedural systems	Improving civil-military structures for planning nuclear requirements, regulating weapon integration and crisis management, and conducting nuclear operations; unified command responsible for managing tri-service nuclear delivery systems	Creation of formal military-dominated structure for planning nuclear requirements and operations; military dominance in joint civil-military structures for regulating weapon integration and crisis management; creation of independent command possessing autonomous ownership of nuclear delivery systems	Creation of formal military-dominated structure for planning nuclear requirements and operations; military dominance in joint civil-military structures for regulating weapon integration and crisis management; creation of a dedicated nuclear command manned and controlled by the military with autonomous ownership of nuclear delivery systems *and* peacetime custody of nuclear weapons; or routine peacetime custody of nuclear weapons with one or more Indian armed services	Creation of formal military-dominated structure for planning nuclear requirements and operations; military dominance in joint civil-military structures for regulating weapon integration and crisis management; creation of a dedicated nuclear command manned and controlled by the military with autonomous ownership of nuclear delivery systems *and* peacetime custody of nuclear weapons; or routine peacetime custody of nuclear weapons with one or more Indian armed services

Chapter Six

THE STRATEGIC IMPLICATIONS OF INDIA'S NUCLEAR POSTURE

The tumultuous events of May 1998 did not signify a dramatic change in New Delhi's strategic capabilities, but they did signal a critical shift in India's strategic direction: By transforming what was previously a "nuclear-capable state" into a "nuclear weapon power," the Vajpayee government committed the country to a new trajectory that is unlikely to be reversed by any succeeding regime. The pace of change with respect to nuclearization may vary depending on the external and internal circumstances India faces, but the strategic decisions already in place will not be rescinded by any future government—even one composed of parties utterly opposed to the BJP. Thus, so long as the regional and global nuclear environment remains similar to what it is now, India will not move in the opposite direction of denuclearization as the P-5, the G-8, and U.N. Resolution 1172 demanded in the aftermath of its nuclear tests. On this question, there is complete unanimity among all the major Indian political parties: Given that New Delhi has already claimed the status of a nuclear weapon state, the gradual development of its strategic capabilities will emerge as the new "consensus" position in national politics, and thanks to this fact, India will remain a nuclear weapon power for the foreseeable future. Its precise legal status, especially as this relates to the NPT, will be debated for many years to come, but what seems clear is that the multiple trends long under way in India will only be reinforced and formalized as a result of its decision to resume nuclear testing in May 1998. These trends include the continued covert research, development, and production of nuclear weapons for existing and new delivery vehicles; the continued research, development, testing, and slow production and acquisition of new delivery systems, including various ballistic and cruise missiles; and, in general, the continuation of creeping weaponization, understood here as the measured development of the technologies, plans, procedures, and organizations necessary for the conduct of effective nuclear operations in an emergency.

Inasmuch as these trends have been under way in India since the early 1980s, the country's 1998 nuclear tests portend an "equilibrium change"[1] rather than a radical transformation of the existing regional strategic environment. This evolutionary alteration, however, will be increasingly manifested through overt reminders such as periodic missile testing, continued acquisition of new delivery systems, steady modernization of supporting infrastructure, and perhaps increasingly vocal references to weaponization—understood now in the strict sense of developing nuclear payloads for the various delivery vehicles due to be inducted over time. None of this, obviously, translates into a new commitment to transparency on New Delhi's part: The Indian arsenal (like the Pakistani and Chinese arsenals, for that matter) will continue to be highly opaque with respect to the details of its architecture and operational policies, its command-and-control arrangements, and even some aspects of its declaratory doctrine. Despite continued opacity in these issue areas, however, New Delhi can be expected to episodically disclose certain elements of its nuclear capability. To be sure, some of these disclosures will be driven simply by the fact that many of the relevant technologies cannot be developed or acquired covertly. Consequently, announcing their presence is probably the best form of public diplomacy, especially if it allows India to garner certain deterrence benefits as a result. In other instances, however, public utterances about India's strategic programs will be grounded largely in the logic of "costly signaling."[2] This form of communication has a long and useful history

---

[1]The term "equilibrium change" is borrowed from Morton Kaplan's classic work *System and Process in International Politics* (New York: Wiley, 1957), pp. 6–8, where it refers to any movement that contributes to the achievement of new operating levels in an otherwise stable political system. "Equilibrium change" thus stands in contrast to "systems change," which refers to the complete transformation of the "system of action" itself.

[2]See A. M. Spence, "Job Market Signalling," *Quarterly Journal of Economics*, 87 (1973), pp. 355–374, and James Fearon, *Threats to Use Force: The Role of Costly Signals*

in South Asian regional politics because it serves as a means of "tacit bargaining"[3] with one's adversaries, while simultaneously helping reassure one's own populace about the efforts of state managers with respect to ensuring security.

Irrespective of why such public disclosures occur in a given instance, any notice of increasing Indian capabilities is bound to accentuate the triangular security dilemmas that already exist within the greater South Asian region. This unfortunate development cannot be avoided, since security dilemmas by their very nature materialize because the capabilities developed by one country for its own defense invariably threaten the safety of others. The only sure way to avoid security dilemmas is thus to forgo all defensive preparations entirely, but since such pacifist solutions are unlikely to appeal to any state, including those in South Asia, both the region and the world at large will have to either find ways to ameliorate these dilemmas or simply learn to live with all the jostling that will accompany the progressive nuclearization of the subcontinent. While India's "passage to nuclear power" will thus have strategic consequences for both Pakistan and China—many of which may be nettlesome—it is most likely that security competition in the Indo-Pakistani case will turn out to be much more discomfiting than any competition involving India and China. This judgment is vociferously contested by Indian hawks, who, while arguing that "Pakistan is not too weighty a nuclear threat,"[4] sometimes hold out the hope that Islamabad's nuclear forces "may even be complementary should the unitary strategic space of the subcontinent ever be reclaimed with the seeding of an *entente cordiale*."[5] While such sentiments may appear reasonable to some in New Delhi, they are disconcerting to state managers in Islamabad, who insist that Pakistan's nuclear capabilities are explicitly designed to prevent the re-creation of "the unitary strategic space"—however brought about—that characterized the Indian subcontinent prior to its partition in 1947. Precisely

---

in International Crises, unpublished doctoral dissertation, University of California, Berkeley, 1992, for different but complementary concepts of costly signaling.

[3]See Neil Joeck, "Tacit Bargaining and Stable Proliferation in South Asia," *Journal of Strategic Studies*, 13:3 (1990), pp. 77–91, for an excellent discussion of this phenomenon.

[4]Karnad, "A Thermonuclear Deterrent," p. 136.

[5]Ibid.

because this is the outcome to be avoided at all costs, Islamabad is likely to *overemphasize* the importance of nuclear weaponry, making the Indo-Pakistani pattern of nuclearization more troublesome than its Sino-Indian counterpart.

All things considered, however, the competitive nuclearization of the Indo-Pakistani dyad is likely to be unsettling simply because relations between New Delhi and Islamabad have been more competitive than cooperative during the last 50-odd years. The reasons for this state of affairs are complex and cannot be analyzed here in any detail, but suffice it to say that each country, as a result of history, has found itself in the unfortunate position of functioning as an objective constraint on the hopes, visions, and ambitions of the other, with the result that territorial, ideological, and power-political drivers of conflict all interact viciously to make the Indo-Pakistani rivalry much more acute than the Sino-Indian one has ever been.[6] This propensity for competition today is only magnified by the deformities of the Pakistani state, which manifest themselves in an excessive fear of Indian intentions and in an inordinate dread of Indian capabilities. There is good reason to believe that Islamabad's anxieties may be misplaced on both counts, even if they are otherwise understandable. Ever since 1991, New Delhi has consciously pursued a strategy of looking beyond South Asia to pursue the larger great-power capabilities that eluded it throughout the Cold War. Toward this end, it has attempted to "ignore" Pakistan to the maximum degree possible in order to focus on potentially more profitable policies such as embarking on internal economic reform, deepening its technological modernization, and seeking to revitalize its external relations with important countries like the United States and the rapidly growing economic centers in East and Southeast Asia.[7]

Unfortunately, important sections of the Pakistani elite, especially the military—trapped by their memory of defeat in the 1971 war—continue to believe that New Delhi's first order of business remains

---

[6]See Tellis, *Stability in South Asia*, pp. 8–11.

[7]For more on this strategy, see Tellis, "South Asia," pp. 283–307, and Walter Andersen, "India's Foreign Policy in the Post–Cold War World: Searching for a New Model," in Shalendra D. Sharma (ed.), *The Asia-Pacific in the New Millennium: Geopolitics, Security, and Foreign Policy* (Berkeley, CA: Institute of East Asian Studies, University of California, Berkeley, 2000), pp. 207–223.

the destruction of Pakistan and the undoing of Partition. India's larger conventional capabilities—which New Delhi maintains in order to service its security requirements along two fronts—reinforces Pakistan's deep-seated fear of India's intentions, and Islamabad's failure to see the constraints limiting the exercise of Indian military power only results in an exaggerated—and tremulous—assessment of New Delhi's martial prowess. A similar misperception about the robustness of the Indian nuclear program has led to the strong belief in Islamabad that New Delhi's strategic capabilities are much more sophisticated and effective than they actually are, and this has in turn fueled an intense Pakistani effort that, although initially aimed at catching up with India, has resulted in what may actually be a lead in some dimensions of strategic capability. The bottom line, therefore, is that Pakistan, for right or wrong, is likely to respond to continued Indian nuclearization with even more feverish efforts of its own: Believing that it faces an enormous task in catching up with its larger, more capable, and to its mind utterly hostile rival, Pakistani security managers are likely to ramp up their strategic efforts much more than the objective circumstances pertaining to the relative balance actually warrant. In so doing, they may precipitate a more resolute Indian counterreaction that could lead the process of competitive nuclearization to become even more interactive than might otherwise have been the case.

Even if such Indian counterreactions are not forthcoming—because New Delhi's strategic enclaves, remaining convinced of their own superiority, do not feel compelled to respond to Islamabad's innovations in kind—a significant danger exists that the multiple baronies that currently dominate the Pakistani nuclear and missile bureaucracies could stimulate the country's strategic programs far beyond the real requirements of national security.[8] The same dynamic, if it occurs in the context of weakening economic performance nationwide and decreasing state capacity, could also fuel the diffusion of strategic technologies well beyond the confines of Pakistan. In any event, internal bureaucratic competition coupled with exaggerated fears on the part of state managers about India are cer-

---

[8]The structure of the Pakistani nuclear program and the competition between the different baronies within it are well described in Shahid-ur-Rehman, *Long Road to Chagai* (Islamabad: Print Wise Publications, 1999).

tain to provoke a Pakistani response to Indian nuclearization that goes far beyond what most knowledgeable observers on the outside would view as either essential or prudent for Islamabad's security.[9] What is most tragic about this state of affairs, finally, is that its propelling forces are fundamentally rooted in a systematic misperception of the relative balance of capabilities existing in South Asia: India, the nominally stronger military power, is actually weaker than is commonly believed but may not know it, while Pakistan, the nominally weaker military power, is actually stronger than is commonly perceived but does not believe it.

The Indo-Pakistani dyad therefore bears careful observation in the years to come, as competitive pressures here are likely to become more acute, in part because the strategic research, development, test, and acquisition programs in both countries will proceed concurrently and, at least from Pakistan's point of view, may also be overly interactive insofar as Islamabad—seeing itself beleaguered—will bend over backward to expand its own strategic capabilities to match those it perceives to exist in India.[10] The strategic benefits of such an overwrought response are still uncertain, because expanded Pakistani nuclear capabilities will in no way diminish the country's geophysical vulnerability, although they would increase the quantum of deliverable punishments that Islamabad could threaten in any future face-off with India. In any event, the one factor that mitigates the potential for exacerbated competition between both countries remains their relatively strong economic constraints. At the Pakistani end, these constraints are simply structural: Islamabad simply has no discretionary resources to fritter away on an open-ended arms race and could not acquire resources for this purpose without fundamentally transforming the nature of the Pakistani state itself. At the Indian end, these constraints are more self-imposed: New Delhi has a much larger pool of economic resources that could be allocated to security instruments, but its desire to complete the technological modernization and development programs that have been under way for many decades prevents it from arbitrarily enlarging its budgetary allocations for nuclear programs. The fact that these constraints exist on

---

[9]See the apt remarks in Perkovich, "South Asia: A Bomb Is Born."

[10]See Shahi et al., "Securing Nuclear Peace," for a good statement summarizing Pakistani views on how Islamabad would respond to continued Indian nuclearization.

both sides therefore implies that future nuclearization in India and Pakistan is more likely to resemble an "arms crawl" than a genuine "arms race." The strategic capabilities on both sides will increase incrementally—and in India will have to traverse a longer distance because of its inferiority vis-à-vis China—but this process will manifest itself largely in slow motion, and that may be the best outcome from the standpoint of both the two South Asian competitors and the United States.[11]

In contrast to the frenetic response that Indian nuclearization has already evoked in Islamabad, Beijing's response to New Delhi's slowly maturing nuclear capabilities is more likely to be both muted and modest.[12] In part, this is because China historically has never viewed India as a "peer competitor," and any strategic reactions suggesting otherwise at this point would only undercut Beijing's traditional attitude of treating New Delhi as a parvenu that seeks to punch above its own weight. This is not to imply that China is oblivious to the potential threat that India could pose to it in some circumstances; rather, always being conscious of this possibility, it has traditionally coped with such challenges by refusing on the one hand to provoke India on any core issues of importance to New Delhi while on the other hand taking out sufficient insurance by targeting India, among other power centers in Asia, with a nontrivial fraction of its nuclear reserves. The larger and more sophisticated nuclear arsenal that China has deployed since the 1960s in fact provides Beijing with the ultimate reassurance against any threat that New Delhi might pose. Indeed, the gap in numbers and technological capabilities between the mature Chinese nuclear deterrent and New Delhi's evolving force-in-being is so large that Beijing does not have to respond in *any* way to India's incipient efforts at developing a minimum deterrent. Although some commentators have offered dire predictions of what China might do as India develops its nuclear assets, including a "nuclear buildup . . . [that involves] deployment of

---

[11]An Indian view confirming this judgment may be found in Chari, "India's Slow-Motion Nuclear Deployment."

[12]"Country Briefing: People's Republic of China," *Jane's Defence Weekly*, December 16, 1998, pp. 21–22.

missiles in Tibet and other bordering provinces,"[13] it is unlikely that Beijing will respond in such an intemperate fashion.

To be sure, Chinese nuclear capabilities will expand in the decades ahead, but this expansion will be driven more by its own modernization efforts (which were already under way for at least a decade prior to the Indian tests of May 1998), its perceptions of U.S. nuclear capabilities, and the future character of the nuclear regime in East Asia than by developments to the southwest of China. Chinese nuclear deterrence vis-à-vis India is in fact so robust that no capabilities India develops over the next decade will allow it to systematically interdict Beijing's nuclear forces for purposes of either ensuring damage limitation or achieving counterforce dominance. Given this fact, there is little China needs to do in the face of an evolving Indian nuclear capability except what it might choose to do purely for symbolic reasons; both the range of Beijing's missiles and the yields of its warheads already allow it to hold at risk numerous Indian targets from far outside the Chinese periphery, and consequently dramatic alterations in current Chinese deployment patterns or operating postures vis-à-vis India are both unnecessary and avoidable. Reaffirming this judgment, one of the most perceptive Western analysts of the subcontinent concluded that

> the kind of Indian [nuclear] force . . . [likely to be developed] . . . would not necessarily force China into any additional nuclear-related activity. Although India might eventually achieve a deterrent capability in relation to China, a threat capability is another matter. Unless Beijing were to come to see India as a threatening nuclear power—one that might catch up to China's capability—it is unlikely to be persuaded to proceed with its program of nuclear modernization more rapidly than would otherwise be the case.[14]

What is only likely to reinforce this propensity for an otiose response to India—the fulmination of Indian hawks notwithstanding—is the fact that Beijing's center of gravity will continue to remain northeast Asia (and Pacific Asia more generally) rather than the

---

[13]Barbara Opall-Rome, "India Moves May Spur China Nukes Buildup," *Defense News*, April 26, 1999, pp. 3 and 19.

[14]Sandy Gordon, "Can the South Asian Nuclear Equation Balance?" *Asia-Pacific Defense Reporter*, 24:6 (October–November 1998), p. 7.

Indian subcontinent. For most of the foreseeable future, China will continue to be obsessed with the political challenges posed by the possible independence of Taiwan, the uncertain future of Korea, the prospect of a remilitarized Japan, and the potential hostility of the United States. Given such complex challenges, one scholar has concluded that in the South Asian context, "China's apprehensions seem to turn mainly on being drawn into an arms race on its periphery that it would rather ignore. It has lived with far greater missiles than an Agni pointed at it."[15] At the same time, however, it must be recognized that China's foreign policy toward the South Asian states has always been much more subtle and multifaceted than it is usually given credit for. Beijing certainly seeks to avoid active interference in the affairs of the Indian subcontinent. Yet this preference historically has not translated into a neglect of its southwestern periphery. Rather, China has consistently sought to maintain and expand the autonomy of the smaller South Asian states while always avoiding any entreaties that could result in its having to lead and sustain a balancing coalition against New Delhi.[16]

Beijing's assistance to Islamabad's nuclear weapon program illustrates this dynamic clearly: While it is often asserted that "China seems to believe that it is not in its interest to assist any new nuclear weapons power along its borders, including Pakistan,"[17] there is little doubt that Beijing has repeatedly acted contrary to this belief when strategic assistance is seen as providing a useful means of avoiding potentially deeper political commitments to the security of the Pakistani state. China therefore covertly assisted Islamabad's nuclear and missile programs because it had the fortunate consequence of ensuring Pakistan's security at low cost to Beijing while simultaneously diverting New Delhi from its pursuit of a larger global role—precisely one of the preconditions that made China's relative neglect of India a viable strategy to begin with. If India's decision to

---

[15]Jeremy J. Stone, "Four Civilizations Gently Collide at Arms Control Conference," *FAS Public Interest Report*, 47:2 (March–April 1994), p. 1.

[16]Leo E. Rose, "India and China: Forging a New Relationship," in Shalendra D. Sharma (ed.), *The Asia-Pacific in the New Millennium: Geopolitics, Security, and Foreign Policy* (Berkeley, CA: Institute of East Asian Studies, University of California, Berkeley, 2000), pp. 224–238.

[17]Joseph Cirincione, "Foreword" in Ming Zhang (ed.), *China's Changing Nuclear Posture* (Washington, D.C.: Carnegie Endowment for International Peace, 1999), p. vii.

resume nuclear testing signals a greater commitment on New Delhi's part to actively reshaping its security environment, it is unlikely that China would want to compound the failures of its past strategy—the consolidation of new nuclear powers on its periphery and the rise of a nuclear-armed India levying political claims on the global stage—by engaging in an unnecessary arms race with India because no matter what such a race does to New Delhi over the long haul, it could prevent Beijing from dealing effectively with the more complex problems it confronts in northeast Asia and beyond. For all these reasons, continued Indian nuclearization is likely to evoke at best a muted response from China in the policy-relevant future.

If the consequences of continued Indian nuclearization are not likely to be provocative where China is concerned, a similarly hopeful conclusion may also carry over to the effects of India's nuclearization on the international nonproliferation regime. This is obviously not the view of many analysts in the nonproliferation community, who have argued not only that the South Asian nuclear tests constitute the iceberg that hit the Titanic but also that "the damage is more severe than it might look from the upper decks."[18] Other analysts have complained that nuclearization in South Asia would inexorably lead to the erosion of nonproliferation "norms" and, as a result, would make the world a more dangerous place.[19] While many of these claims reflect a frightened response rather than a dispassionate analysis, they do embody a profound disquiet that manifests itself in three separate but related claims: (1) that nuclearization in India (and in South Asia more generally) reflects a failure on the part of the international nonproliferation regime; (2) that nuclearization in India (and in South Asia more generally) will engender renewed efforts by other states to seek nuclear weapons; and (3) that nuclearization in India (and in South Asia more generally) will weaken global support for maintaining the existing international nonproliferation regime. Each of these issues will be briefly addressed below.

---

[18]Joseph Cirincione, "Viewpoint," *Aviation Week & Space Technology*, May 18, 1998, p. 102.

[19]Geoffrey Wiseman and Gregory F. Treverton, *Dealing with the Nuclear Dilemma in South Asia* (Los Angeles: Pacific Council on International Policy, 1998), p. 2.

Indian nuclearization (and nuclearization in South Asia more generally) represents a failure of the nonproliferation regime only if it is believed that maintaining a club of five de jure nuclear powers is the most sacrosanct objective in international politics. Fortunately, this is not the case: The American architects of the nonproliferation regime recognized from the beginning that India, Pakistan, and Israel would remain recalcitrant because these states were located in areas with high systemic insecurities, and Washington at least—for different reasons in each case—could offer no substitutes that would tempt them to forgo the acquisition of nuclear weaponry.[20] That these nuclear-capable states remained outside the ambit of NPT obligations no doubt created legal ambiguities about their status, but their nuclear capabilities were not viewed as radically subversive of the U.S.-dominated international order. As a result, a remarkably successful nonproliferation regime was constructed and maintained—and has now been indefinitely extended—despite the presence of these small exceptions.[21] The importance of this fact cannot be underestimated because the nonproliferation regime exists primarily as a corralling device intended to prevent the large-scale diffusion of those instruments which can dangerously threaten the interests of the great powers (and the United States in particular). The NPT regime, as it exists today, not only has fulfilled this objective but has actually been more successful than any of its creators expected it to be in 1967: It has managed to get every state in the international system—save three—to accept specific obligations with respect to the acquisition or presence of nuclear weaponry; it has actually managed to roll back, at various points in the past, the nuclear programs of at least seven major states; and, most important, it has provided the great powers with the requisite legitimacy to police all international behavior connected with the maintenance of the regime, including the use of diplomacy, economic coercion, and military force against any cheaters whenever necessary.

---

[20]For more on these issues, see T. V. Paul, *Power Versus Prudence: Why Nations Forgo Nuclear Weapons* (Montreal: McGill-Queen's University Press, 2000), pp. 14–34 and 125–141.

[21]Corroborating details can be found in George Perkovich, "Think Again: Nuclear Proliferation," *Foreign Policy*, 112 (Fall 1998), pp. 12–13.

All this suggests that the nuclear nonproliferation regime is actually a resounding success in that the worst nuclear threats to international (and particularly American) security—Iran, Iraq, Libya, and North Korea—are already bound by international obligations that require them to surrender their sovereign rights to weapons of mass destruction. So are numerous other states that might be tempted to acquire nuclear weapons in the future, all of which can be legitimately punished by the United States, in concert with other great powers, if they were ever to violate these obligations. Against this impressive tally stand three exceptions to the regime—India, Pakistan, and Israel—none of which is likely to either disturb the existing international order or threaten the extant hegemony of the United States. Ironically, all three of these countries would probably be inclined to assist Washington in preventing the dissolution of the existing nuclear nonproliferation order because any *further* diffusion of nuclear weaponry would be just as subversive to their security as it would be to that of the United States. If this does not define the accomplishment of an international regime, there is very little else that will.

The fear that nuclearization in India (and in South Asia more generally) would precipitate renewed efforts by other states to seek nuclear weapons is also based on an utterly tenuous, if not discredited, understanding of the mechanisms operating in international politics. While international anarchy may be seamless in theory, in practice it is usually contained within specific "security complexes." This implies that the actions initiated by a particular state usually evoke counteractions only by those states directly threatened by these actions and not others. When the states involved are not superpowers (that is, states whose ambit of influence extends over multiple security complexes), the action-reaction dynamic usually peters out at the edge of the geographic cluster defining the historical amity-enmity relations enjoyed by these states. This implies that nuclearization in India will precipitate responses from Pakistan and China but not from any other state located along its wider periphery. The "counterresponses" in both of these instances have already occurred: China was a nuclear power long before India became one and, as argued above, is unlikely to do much more than it already has in response to New Delhi's nuclear program; and Pakistan, in contrast, will respond to India's nuclearization but without necessarily *causing* any extended chain reaction because of its own decisions vis-à-vis India. This does not imply that further nuclearization in the greater Middle East or in the greater East Asian region cannot occur over time, but such nuclearization—if it does occur—will be the result of specific decisions made by countries such as Iran, Iraq, North Korea, Taiwan, and Japan in light of their own local security environment, their inherent technical capacity, and the cost-benefit attractiveness of nuclearization when compared to some other alternatives for preserving security. Any decision by these countries to go nuclear will not be an imitative—or even a causal—consequence of the Indian and Pakistani decisions to develop nuclear weaponry.[22]

Finally, the argument that nuclearization in India (and in South Asia more generally) will weaken global support for maintaining the existing nonproliferation architecture is greatly overstated because most of the existing great powers, including the United States as the chief enforcer of the nonproliferation regime, have demonstrated through their foreign policies that they recognize the difference in threat posed by nuclearization in South Asia compared with potential nuclearization elsewhere. Baldly stated, nuclear weapons in the hands of countries like Iran, Iraq, Libya, and North Korea are simply unacceptable from the perspective of U.S. security, whereas nuclear weapons in the hands of India and Pakistan, however undesirable they may be, plainly do not pose an equivalent threat either to the international order or to the United States. The concern that acquiescing to the existence of nuclear programs in South Asia automatically implies weakening global support for the existing nonproliferation regime thus fails to take into account two crucial realities in international politics: first, that there is no such thing as an "international regime" that exists outside the interests of the most important pow-

---

[22]For a perceptive argument about the invalidity of "demonstration effects" emerging from nuclearization in South Asia, see Muthiah Alagappa, "International Response to Nuclear Tests in South Asia: The Need for a New Policy Framework," *AsiaPacific Issues*, 38 (June 15, 1998), pp. 3–4. The causal consequences of Indian and Pakistani nuclearization are likely to be most relevant only in the case of proliferation decisions made in Iran, but even here it is hard to conclude that Iranian-Pakistani rivalry—which is currently exhibited, for example, in Afghanistan—lends itself to resolution through the acquisition of nuclear weaponry by Tehran. Should such an eventuality materialize, it will be owed more to Iran's fears of the United States and its desire to consolidate an Iranian hegemony in the Persian Gulf than to Indian and, by implication, Pakistani decisions to acquire nuclear weaponry.

ers who support it. In this age of unipolarity, this implies that the "international nonproliferation regime" is ultimately an American regime sustained by American power in the defense of what are primarily American interests. This does not in any way exclude the possibility that American interests here may be congruent with the interests of many other states, but it does imply that American power and efforts will be fundamentally responsible for generating the "global support" necessary to preserve the regime because its preservation fundamentally serves the interests of the United States. This very fact highlights a second important reality: The United States and other great powers, to the degree that they have congruent interests, can *choose* to safeguard the nonproliferation regime despite all the exceptions it contains. This implies that Indian nuclearization (and South Asian nuclearization more generally) can have a corrosive effect on the international regime only to the degree that the major powers allow it to. There is nothing that prevents the United States, for example, from pursuing all or some combination of the following policies to buttress the nonproliferation regime:

- denying India and Pakistan the formal status of being "nuclear weapon states" even as they are seriously treated as "nuclear weapon powers";

- expanding the surveillance, monitoring, and political pressure on undesirable candidate nuclear powers such as Iran, Iraq, and North Korea even as the United States moves to improve relations with India and Pakistan;

- increasing the pressure on key suppliers like Russia, China, France, and Germany to prevent further diffusion of strategic technology to all countries of proliferation concern;

- developing a range of counterproliferation plans and technologies that enable the United States to operate effectively even in the presence of suspected nuclear capabilities possessed by regional adversaries;

- accelerating existing plans to progressively reduce the nuclear arsenals possessed by all nuclear weapon powers; and

- working with India and Pakistan to limit the further spread of weapons of mass destruction even as all the other nuclear weapon states focus on marginalizing these weapons as instruments of high politics.

Obviously, all of these policies are already pursued to some degree or another, which only underscores the point that the United States can preserve the international nonproliferation regime successfully despite the nuclearization currently occurring in India and, more generally, in South Asia. By itself, the nuclearization of the subcontinent does not spell the doom of the international nonproliferation regime, and if the latter eventuality comes to pass, it may have to do more with how the United States responds to the challenge of proliferation globally than with any selective proliferation that has already occurred.[23] The nuclearization of South Asia suggests that Washington ought to intensify its nonproliferation efforts worldwide, but the best defense against further proliferation might be, as Richard Haass once put it, "a proliferation of proliferation policies"[24] in which states are targeted discriminatorily through a mix of policy instruments depending on their relative capabilities and the threat they pose to U.S. interests. Such a discriminatory strategy might seem duplicitous to nonproliferation purists, but there is no good reason to avoid duplicity in international politics if it enhances American interests. After all, the goal of U.S. grand strategy should first and foremost be the preservation of its security and the enhancement of its primacy—but because promoting nonproliferation is only a means to that end, its pursuit should not be absolutized to the neglect of alternative policies that may cement U.S. security and primacy far more effectively in some given case.

The above discussion suggests that the most obvious immediate implication of India's nuclearization (and of nuclearization in South Asia more generally) is the likelihood of a weak arms-race instability ensuing between India and Pakistan but not between India and China. India's nuclearization—and that in South Asia more generally—is also unlikely to have radically deleterious effects on the international nonproliferation regime because the "costs" of prolifera-

---

[23]For thoughtful comments on this question, see Perkovich, "Think Again: Nuclear Proliferation," p. 13.

[24]Cited in Miles A. Pomper, "As the Dust Settles in India, U.S. Rethinks Nuclear Policy," *Congressional Quarterly Weekly Report*, May 23, 1998.

tion here have already been absorbed by the regime's willingness to treat these states as exceptional since 1967. The future burdens on the regime will also be minimized by continued U.S. efforts to limit the exceptionalism permitted thus far, and so long as current non-proliferation efforts continue unabated, there is no reason other candidate proliferants should be able to escape the regime's constraints in a way that India, Pakistan, and Israel all did previously for unique historical reasons.

When these twin consequences of Indian nuclearization are considered, it is important to keep the first phenomenon in perspective. The low-grade arms-race instability that is predicted to obtain in the Indo-Pakistani dyad will occur mainly because *concurrent* nuclearization usually engenders problems of simultaneous competitive adjustment, whereas these instabilities are likely to be absent in the Sino-Indian case because the problem here is simply one of catching up at the Indian end. Even in the Indo-Pakistani case, however, the weak arms-race instability that is currently expected can be avoided if Islamabad focuses on developing a deterrent that is simply sufficient for its own needs rather than attempting to match India's capabilities across the board.[25] In the nuclear age, it is simply more profitable for a state to focus on increasing the survivability of its own deterrent rather than attempting to expand the threat posed to an adversary's assets: If Pakistan invests its resources in a manner consistent with this orientation, the weak form of arms-race instability that would otherwise ensue in the subcontinent could be diminished. In any event, the saving grace is that arms-race instability, even if it were to occur in strong form, cannot by itself cause deterrence breakdown. It may involve a waste of economic resources—always an undesirable outcome in South Asia—and may lead to an episodic upsurge in discordant "atmospherics" that may have the effect of fueling mutual suspicions about the political intentions of the two antagonists. This outcome, too, is undesirable, but if this is the worst consequence of nuclearization in South Asia, it is still better than many other outcomes that can be imagined for the region.

---

[25]For the dilemmas and tensions facing Pakistan in this regard, see Farah Zahra, "Pakistan's Road to a Minimum Nuclear Deterrent," *Arms Control Today*, 29:5 (July–August 1999), pp. 9–13.

At least two other issues require further analysis from the perspective of policy, and these relate to the effects of India's nuclearization on deterrence stability and crisis stability (especially on that subset known as "first-strike stability").[26] Although several previous discussions in this book have offered relatively optimistic prognoses of the prospects for both deterrence and crisis stability, these prognoses have been grounded almost entirely in abstract and *a priori* discussions of how these challenges might emerge in the region. Consequently, the conclusions advanced must be treated as indicative rather than determinative because they are based to a significant extent on deductive logic rather than on empirical scrutiny of the key issues. Thanks to this fact, no definitive conclusions about deterrence and crisis stability can be offered right now because any such assertions would require detailed analyses of the size, character, and disposition of conventional and nuclear forces (and strategic targets) in India, Pakistan, and China as well as some understanding of how conventional and nuclear deterrence interact in both individual countries and across various dyads. It is hoped that this work, which is currently under way at RAND, will be made publicly available in the future so as to corroborate the judgments advanced below and throughout the book. Until the fruits of that research are available, however, the following summary remarks will have to suffice.

Where deterrence stability is concerned, it is likely that both the Indo-Pakistani and the Sino-Indian dyads will experience reasonably high levels of stability in the policy-relevant future because the two most important states, China and India, are currently not locked into the pursuit of any revisionist objectives with regard to each other. Both India and China have also formally—and in practice—adopted a pacific posture with respect to their outstanding territorial disputes. Pakistan, in contrast, is both formally and materially the most

---

[26]For various views on these issues, see François Heisbourg, "The Prospects for Nuclear Stability Between India and Pakistan," *Survival*, 40:4 (1998–1999), pp. 77–92; Michael Quinlan, "Nuclear Tests in the Subcontinent: Prospects and Significance for the World," *International Relations*, 14:4 (1999), pp. 1–14; Chellaney, "After the Tests: India's Options," pp. 93–111; Ganguly, "India's Pathway to Pokhran II: The Prospects and Sources of New Delhi's Nuclear Weapons Program," pp. 148–177; and Brahma Chellaney, "Challenge of Nuclear Arms Control in South Asia," *Survival*, 35:3 (1993), pp. 121–136.

prominent revisionist entity in South Asia given its commitment to altering the prevailing status quo in Kashmir. Yet even Islamabad has for all practical purposes ruled out the alternative of securing political change through the pursuit of nuclear or conventional war even though it continues to engage in nuclear coercion at the subconventional level and could occasionally lapse into the temptation to engage in shallow cross-border operations in efforts to attract international attention to its claims on Kashmir. These actions might in turn invoke comparable Indian counterresponses, but such eventualities probably represent the current limits of premeditated war in South Asia. The prospects for deterrence stability are therefore high because no South Asian state is currently committed to securing any political objectives through the medium of major conventional and, by implication, nuclear war. This condition is only reinforced by the high levels of "defense dominance" obtaining at the military level, and thus it is not at all an exaggeration to say that deterrence stability in South Asia derives simply from the Indian, Pakistani, and Chinese inability to successfully prosecute quick and decisive conventional military operations, especially with respect to wars of unlimited aims. As research elsewhere has demonstrated, India's gross numerical superiorities vis-à-vis Pakistan are misleading and do not enable it to rapidly win a high-intensity land war even if it acquits itself favorably in the air and naval campaigns occurring in the theater.[27] Both India and Pakistan can defend their territorial integrity adequately with the forces they currently have in place but would be hard pressed to dramatically change the terrestrial status quo through a quick conventional or even nuclear attack. The Indo-Chinese balance along the Himalayas is similarly stable for now because the Chinese do not have the logistics capability to sustain any major conventional conflict in support of their more ambitious territorial claims, while the strong and refurbished Indian land defenses, coupled with India's superiority in airpower, enables New Delhi to defend its existing positions but not sustain any large-scale acquisition of new territory. Consequently, deterrence stability exists along this frontier as well.[28]

---

[27]Tellis, *Stability in South Asia*, pp. 5–22.

[28]This argument is based on Tellis et al., "Sources of Conflict in Asia," pp. 156–158.

In the final analysis, what makes this situation metastable is the fact that neither India nor Pakistan—nor, for that matter, China—has the strategic capabilities to execute those successful damage-limiting first strikes that might justify initiating nuclear attacks in a crisis. Even China, which of the three entities comes closest to possessing such capabilities, would find it difficult to conclude that the capacity for "splendid first strikes" lay truly within reach, and even if it could arrive at such a determination, the political justification for these actions would be substantially lacking given the nature of its current political disputes with India. On balance, then, it is reasonable to conclude—at the level of first approximation—that a reasonably high degree of deterrence stability currently exists within the greater South Asian region.

Obviously, these judgments say little about inadvertent wars or wars brought about by miscalculation or misperception, and should deterrence breakdown occur in the future, it is most likely to result from one or more of these possibilities.[29]. In this context, it is pertinent to note that the subcontinent historically has not witnessed any conflicts brought about through inadvertence or misperception, at least in their pure form, and while conflicts rooted either in miscalculation or in catalytic causes have indeed occurred—often because of Pakistan's desperate efforts at drawing international attention to its cherished cause, Kashmir—it is not unreasonable to expect that the acknowledged presence of nuclear weapons on all sides would inhibit any interactive sequences that could lead to serious forms of deterrence breakdown in the future. As Avery Goldstein argued, "Indians are likely to refrain from military operations that can escalate to the nuclear incineration of Pakistanis (and vice versa) not because they have mastered Brodie, Schelling, Waltz, and Jervis, nor because they care about their neighbors, but rather simply because they care about their own countrymen."[30]

Although this argument is both reasonable and reassuring, two gnawing uncertainties remain. The first uncertainty derives from the presence of weak state structures and, by implication, the possibility

---

[29]For different avenues toward deterrence breakdown, see Tellis, *Stability in South Asia*, pp. 55–62.

[30]See Goldstein, "Scared Senseless? The South Asian Nuclear Tests," p. 2.

of deficient strategic decisionmaking, especially in Pakistan. The severe motivational and cognitive biases that have historically afflicted Pakistan's higher decisionmaking institutions on matters of war and peace do raise fears about the prospect of extreme responses that might be precipitated in a crisis.[31] If overwhelming fear and helplessness combine with a suicidal destructiveness to overpower reason and inhibit the systematic processing of information during an emergency, it is possible that immoderate actions might occur irrespective of whether the objective circumstances warranted such decisions to begin with. These failures of rationality, which could be compounded by exigencies of domestic politics, civil-military discord, and biased and unreliable intelligence, could in principle occur both in India and in Pakistan, but if the historical record is any indication, the consequences of its occurrence are likely to be far more troublesome in the latter than in the former.[32] And although the fearsome potency of nuclear weapons is supposed to minimize the possibility of just such catastrophes, there is by now a sufficient margin of uncertainty to justify the fear that catastrophic deterrence breakdown in South Asia could arise as a result of various pathological forms of "cognitive closure."[33]

The second uncertainty derives from the possibility of catalytic wars. Catalytic wars are conflicts brought about either by the actions of third parties or by the principals involved with the intention of entrapping third parties into intervening in an ongoing conflict. Such wars have occurred with some frequency in South Asia, in at least one instance with disastrous consequences.[34] Catalytic wars are particularly problematic events from the perspective of deterrence

---

[31]For a trenchant review of these biases, see Altaf Gauhar, "Four Wars, One Assumption," *The Nation*, September 5, 1999.

[32]See Joeck, *Maintaining Nuclear Stability in South Asia*, pp. 28–33. See also Ahmad Faruqui, "Pakistan's Strategic Myopia," *RUSI Journal*, 145:2 (April 2000), pp. 49–54, and Faruqui, "Failure in Command: Lessons from Pakistan's Indian Wars," *Defense Analysis*, 17:1 (2001).

[33]The best analysis of this phenomenon in its many variants can be found in Robert Jervis, *Perception and Misperception in International Politics* (Princeton, NJ: Princeton University Press, 1976), pp. 117–406.

[34]For a good analysis of past South Asian conflicts, their causes, and their manifestations, see Sumit Ganguly, *The Origins of War in South Asia: The Indo-Pakistani Conflicts Since 1947*, 2nd ed. (Boulder, CO: Westview Press, 1994).

stability because they could occur first without the consent or control of the competing states, as "local insurgents or separatists may take initiatives that could be difficult to control,"[35] and second as a result of aggressive state actions that, despite the poor prospect of any lasting military success, are nonetheless pursued in the belief that "outside actors would intervene to stop the war before . . . [protracted conflict or irretrievable defeat] . . . was reached."[36] In any event, the greatest damper on the temptation to abet or initiate such wars, particularly from Pakistan's perspective, is the growing recognition in Islamabad—amply corroborated during the Kargil crisis—that neither the United States nor the other great powers, including China, Pakistan's most steadfast ally, have an interest in supporting any Pakistani revisionism involving the use of force initiated by Islamabad or by its surrogate allies battling India. This development, coupled with the fact that India's economic, political, and conventional military strength already bequeaths to it a large measure of safety against threats both to its external security and to its internal integrity, offers the best hope against the undermining of deterrence stability by threats of catalytic war over the long term.

There is, however, another more remote but nonetheless real threat that cannot be discounted where the issue of catalytic war is concerned. This contingency is rooted in the possibility that "Pakistan's inability to solve its internal problems [could] become a security problem for India."[37] If the events leading up to the 1971 war were to be replicated in Pakistan in the future, the South Asian region could well experience another episode of deterrence breakdown with even more catastrophic consequences this time around, as an imploding Pakistan could employ all the means at its disposal, including nuclear weapons, in a "Samson option" designed to punish what it perceived to be Indian aggression, irrespective of whether New Delhi was in fact behind the insurgent challenges leading up to Pakistan's potential breakup. The threats embodied by catalytic war in multiple ways—when conjoined with the challenges imposed by cognitive closure, especially in Pakistan—will thus continue to sub-

---

[35]Joeck, *Maintaining Nuclear Stability in South Asia*, p. 17.

[36]Ibid., p. 29.

[37]Ibid., p. 24.

vert the otherwise relatively high prospects of deterrence stability in South Asia.[38]

If the contours of deterrence stability in South Asia can be readily discerned, the same cannot be said with respect to crisis stability. In part, this is because the still-evolving Indian and Pakistani nuclear capabilities do not yet lend themselves to the kind of analytical modeling that would justify any strong claims about the first-strike stability of these deterrents. What can be said right now, however, is that the desired Indian force-in-being—if operationalized in the manner described in previous chapters—is heavily *biased* in support of crisis stability. The evolving Pakistani nuclear deterrent, though not analyzed in this volume, also appears to be biased in favor of crisis stability even though it does exemplify critically important differences in command-and-control arrangements, deployment patterns, and readiness rates in comparison to its Indian counterpart.[39] What completes this generally irenic picture is the highly slack operating posture of the Chinese deterrent: Beijing's nuclear capabilities are neither intended nor deployed for the conduct of prompt operations, and China's strategic forces as a whole are still incapable of executing the "limited deterrence"[40] missions attributed to them by some Western theorists. For at least another decade if not more, the

---

[38]These fears have acquired new currency in the post-Kargil era for three reasons: (1) in Pakistan, resolving the Kashmir dispute has now become the central and nonnegotiable issue to be tackled first in any future discussions with India; (2) in India, dealing with the Kashmir insurgency has moved beyond "reactive" strategies to a contemplation of various military operations conducted at if not beyond the Line of Control; and (3) in both countries there is now a new refusal to even initiate dialogue unless the other gives up its key bargaining levers held in anticipation of negotiations. See Paul Mann, "India Derides Nuclear 'Alarmism,'" *Aviation Week & Space Technology*, April 3, 2000, pp. 29–30.

[39]Unfortunately, no comprehensive analysis is yet available in the open literature on Pakistan's nuclear capabilities and its strategic posture. The best available analyses to date remain Cheema, "Pakistan's Nuclear Use Doctrine and Command and Control," pp. 158–181; Rodney W. Jones, "Pakistan's Nuclear Posture: Quest for Assured Nuclear Deterrence—A Conjecture," *Regional Studies*, 18:2 (Spring 2000), pp. 3–39; Rodney W. Jones, "Pakistan's Nuclear Posture: Arms Race Instabilities in South Asia," *Asian Affairs*, 25:2 (Summer 1998), pp. 67–87; Rodney W. Jones, "Pakistan's Nuclear Posture," *Dawn*, September 14, 1999; and Rodney W. Jones, "Pakistan's Nuclear Posture—II: Arms Control Diplomacy," *Dawn*, September 15, 1999.

[40]Johnston, "China's New 'Old Thinking': The Concept of Limited Deterrence," pp. 5–42.

Chinese nuclear deterrent will be oriented primarily toward conducting relatively simple forms of "delayed second strike," and that in effect implies that even China's strategic forces, although much more sophisticated in comparison to South Asian capabilities, actually share an important characteristic with the latter: a relatively relaxed routine operating posture that is heavily biased toward crisis stability.[41]

The fact that the nuclear capabilities of all three states—India, Pakistan, and China—are not structured for the conduct of prompt operations seems to have eluded many commentators in the United States, who, especially in the aftermath of the nuclear tests of May 1998, spewed forth several assertions that one scholar correctly described as "more visceral than thoughtful."[42] Examples of such assertions include claims that both sides "would . . . have weapons on aircraft or missiles capable of striking with as little as 3 min[utes] warning"[43] and that "India or Pakistan might opt to Launch on Warning (LoW) of attack."[44] Not only are such assertions misleading, but the evidence that ought to underwrite them simply does not exist. Consequently, the alarmist conclusions often derived about stability from raw geographic or technical facts are usually dubious and, more dangerously, could skew U.S. policy in directions that are either fruitless or counterproductive. As things stand today, there is simply no evidentiary basis for the claim advanced, for example, by Evan Medeiros that "the two sides [meaning India and Pakistan] are working themselves into just about as unstable a posture as you can imagine. . . . It's a nightmare."[45] If anything, the data available thus far suggest the opposite: The effort to develop a force-in-being in India—with a comparable sort of posture emerging in Pakistan—is more supportive of crisis stability than many other kinds of deterrent postures imaginable.

---

[41]This is well recognized by Indian observers of the Chinese military. See, for example, Savita Pande, "Chinese Nuclear Doctrine," *Strategic Analysis*, 23:12 (March 2000), pp. 2011–2036.

[42]Goldstein, "Scared Senseless? The South Asian Nuclear Tests" p. 1.

[43]Cirincione, "Viewpoint," p. 102.

[44]Withington, "Nuclear Dilemmas Seize Asia," p. 13.

[45]Cited in Tony Emerson, "Asia's Ground Zero," *Newsweek International Edition*, April 22, 1996.

Since this reality is often underappreciated, it is not surprising to find some analysts still arguing that "the United States must unequivocally demand that India and Pakistan join the Non-Proliferation Treaty as non-nuclear weapon states."[46] Still other have urged a "nuclear rollback in South Asia"[47] based at least initially on the lessons learned from previous nonproliferation successes elsewhere in the world. There are several reasons past examples of rollback have limited applicability to South Asia.[48] What is more to the point, however, is that the Clinton administration wisely chose not to pursue such chimerical goals but instead focused its attention on securing a more limited objective—namely, the institutionalization of a nuclear restraint regime covering both India and Pakistan. This search for a restraint regime is essentially based on the fact that nuclear capabilities in South Asia are here to stay, and while their eradication may be a distant goal to which Washington still aspires under the logic of the NPT, slowing down the pace of research, development, testing, and deployment of regional nuclear forces is perhaps the best alternative that the United States can hope to attain in the policy-relevant future. Pursuing this more circumscribed objective is eminently sensible and accords better with the prevailing realities in the region—but it must be borne in mind that even success here is not at all assured.

There are five broad components to the restraint regime that the United States government has advocated in its separate bilateral discussions with India and Pakistan. These involve (1) urging India and Pakistan to sign the CTBT and to support an early completion of the FMCT; (2) urging India and Pakistan to avoid nuclear weaponization and the creation of a ready arsenal; (3) urging India and Pakistan to avoid further missile testing, production, and deployment; (4) urging India and Pakistan to institutionalize strict export controls on the diffusion of strategic materials and technologies to other actors; and

---

[46]Samina Ahmed and David Cortright, *Preventing a Nuclear Arms Race in South Asia: U.S. Policy Options,* Policy Brief, No. 2 (Notre Dame, IN: The Kroc Institute for International Peace Studies, University of Notre Dame, January 2000).

[47]Toby F. Dalton, "Towards Nuclear Rollback in South Asia," *Current History,* 97:623 (December 1998), pp. 41–417.

[48]Joeck, "Nuclear Proliferation and Nuclear Reversal in South Asia," pp. 263–273.

(5) urging India and Pakistan to resume a diplomatic dialogue that leads to the resolution of their outstanding political differences.[49]

Defining the objectives of the restraint regime in this broad, generic way allows for a brief assessment of the critical issues involved with each of these goals—at least where India and its future deterrent are concerned. In the immediate aftermath of the May 1998 tests, the Vajpayee government announced that India would be prepared to convert its self-imposed moratorium on nuclear testing into a formal commitment. The conditions required for such a commitment were not specified but were presumably to be hammered out in negotiations with the United States. Just prior to the fall of the BJP government in May 1999, the Indian state began the arduous process of securing a "national consensus" in support of formally signing the CTBT—a demand issued by the United States in order to preserve the successes achieved thus far in the realm of global nonproliferation and to limit the emerging Indian (and Pakistani) nuclear arsenals to the lowest qualitative levels possible. The Indian efforts at creating a national consensus in favor of signing the treaty, however, appear to have foundered on two counts: the failure to secure a complete withdrawal of the U.S. sanctions imposed after the May 1998 tests prior to any Indian signature, and the U.S. Senate's own refusal to ratify the treaty prior to the review conference that was supposed to be held in September 1999. Both of these issues are important to New Delhi for different reasons: The former holds out the hope of consolidating the momentum in the improvement of U.S.-Indian relations, while the latter is critical by virtue of India's belief that the U.S. failure to ratify the CTBT would allow China to renege on its own commitments to the treaty—with all the consequent implications for Indian security. Thanks to the uncertainties currently clouding both issues, it would appear that a formal Indian accession to the CTBT is now farther off than ever despite the fact that several senior scientists, including the former Chairman of India's AEC, have publicly stated that signing the treaty would in no way crimp the country's ability to maintain an effective deterrent.[50] What

---

[49]Details about the restraint regime can be found in Chidanand Rajghatta, "U.S. Restraint Regime for India, Pak Covers N-Capable Aircraft," *Indian Express*, November 13, 1998.

[50]"Signing CTBT Will Not Weaken Country."

is more disquieting in this context is that several moderate Indian political parties that might otherwise have been expected to sign the treaty were they in power have now urged the government not to sign the CTBT if it cannot be linked to a specific time frame for global nuclear disarmament.[51] On balance, therefore, India is likely to maintain its self-imposed moratorium on testing in the near term but is unlikely to sign the CTBT at any time soon because withholding its consent is perceived as the only leverage India has with respect to both the withdrawal of U.S. sanctions and the surety of ratification by all the established nuclear weapon states. If India does not sign the CTBT soon—because issues such as the U.S. sanctions and U.S. failure to ratify the CTBT continue to intrude—then its temptation to resume nuclear testing could increase. A persistent delay in securing India's signature to the treaty will only encourage elements within the Indian nuclear and military establishment (and among its strategic elites) to push for renewed nuclear testing. Moreover, the Indian government, which thus far has been restrained, may give in to such pressures either prior to acceding to the treaty or simply because other strategic objectives—such as strengthening ties with the United States—have simply not borne the fruits expected in the interim.

In contrast to its diffidence over signing the CTBT, India has supported initiating the negotiations that would lead up to the FMCT.[52] On this issue, the Indian position is analogous to that of the United States, which argues that the FMCT should apply only to future stockpiles of fissile material and should involve no efforts at creating any transparency over past stockpiles owned by various nuclear powers. While the broad policies of the two countries are thus congruent, the devil, as usual, lies in the details, and it is still too early to tell whether India will sign the final version of the treaty if in fact one is negotiated over what may be objections to its specifics. In any case, having a draft treaty for signature is an event that lies many years away, and what India's position will be at that time is anyone's

---

[51]"Congress Not for CTBT Now," *Indian Express*, May 10, 1999. The intent of the Congress Party on this question is still unclear because the same report suggests that the refusal to back a national decision on signing the CTBT may also be linked to the exigencies of electoral politics.

[52]"Negotiating an FMCT," *The Hindu*, November 19, 1998.

guess. At the moment, Indian policymakers seem willing to support a treaty that complies with U.S. interests despite the fact that they may have a much smaller stockpile of fissile materials than many Western assessments suggest. This potentially anomalous conduct, however, does not support the inference that India's fissile-material inventory must therefore be bigger than is commonly believed. Rather, it must be remembered that India today appears willing to support a treaty that is still several years away from completion and, even then, might sign such an instrument only if it preserved complete opacity over past inventories: New Delhi's acquiescence here would derive not from the fact that it has larger-than-expected holdings of fissile materials but rather from its belief that continued uncertainty about the true size of its inventory provides greater deterrence benefits than could be garnered from a larger but completely transparent stockpile. Irrespective of what India's position on the final FMCT text may eventually be, however, New Delhi has already rejected Washington's interim demand that India declare a "voluntary" moratorium on the production of fissile materials pending the successful negotiation of the treaty.[53] This action indicates that New Delhi will continue to expand its fissile-material stockpile for all the strategic reasons described earlier even as it persists in maintaining a pervasive opacity over the size of that stockpile. And this, in turn, suggests that Washington is unlikely to secure part of its second goal in the ongoing dialogue with India despite the fact that there are in principle no differences between India and the United States on this issue.

While India's general stance with respect to the CTBT and the FMCT, when taken at face value, is not diametrically opposed to the interests of the United States, its position on the second and third components of the restraint regime—nuclear weaponization and missile development—stands greatly at variance with U.S. preferences. The rationale for pursuing these twin objectives at the U.S. end is ultimately based on two beliefs: first, that a nuclear-free South Asia is safer than a nuclear South Asia; and second, that the South Asian region is a volatile area that represents the most likely locale for a future war fought with nuclear weapons. While the first conviction may appear to be a natural consequence of the larger nonprolif-

---

[53]C. Raja Mohan, "India Rejects U.S. Suggestion for Moratorium on Fissile Material Production," *The Hindu*, September 13, 2000.

eration policy the United States has pursued, it does exemplify something more than just an ordinary nonproliferation prejudice. In many cases, it represents the private but considered judgment of many U.S. policymakers, who argue that the prevailing command structures, the acute resource constraints, and the limitations of rationality—all of which take on a special resonance in the case of Pakistan—conspire to make New Delhi's security hostage to the weakest links in Islamabad's security system and, as such, warrant ridding the region of nuclear weapons altogether.[54] The second notion, in contrast, is based on the more widely held impression that the ongoing disputes in the region, including the low-intensity war in Kashmir, present numerous opportunities for escalation that could spin out of control. While Indian policymakers are more likely to concede the legitimacy of the concerns underlying the first belief even as they reject the inferences inherent in the second (which are often based on the expectation that New Delhi might up the ante in an acute crisis), they are nonetheless unwilling to contemplate any alternative that involves eschewing the development of a nuclear deterrent of some kind at this point.[55] They will admit that a "ready arsenal," configured for the prompt conduct of nuclear operations, is not desirable from the viewpoint of Indian interests. On this score at least, they will acknowledge that nuclear capabilities ought to be arrayed only with a relatively long fuse, although the exact length of this fuse has not yet been publicly acknowledged. Different entities within the Indian establishment have proposed various desirable response times ranging from hours to days, and while both the urgency and the extent of actual retaliation in wartime may be conditioned more by adversary actions than by New Delhi's preferences, Indian security managers today remain adamant that their reluctance to deploy a "ready arsenal" does not translate into a termination of nuclear weaponization and missile development.[56]

---

[54]The best example of this argument in the public literature has been formulated by Stephen P. Cohen, "Nuclear Deterrence in South Asia: Strategic Considerations Reconsidered," report of the IPCS seminar held at the India International Centre, New Delhi, January 4, 1999, available at http://www.ipcs.org/issues/articles/166-ndi-cohen.htm.

[55]See Anita Katiyal, "No Freeze on N-Capability, U.S. Told," *The Times of India*, November 26, 1998.

[56]Rahul Bedi, "India Confirms Nuclear Policy," *Jane's Defence Weekly*, December 23, 1998, p. 7.

India will therefore continue to weaponize its nuclear capabilities despite whatever U.S. preferences on this score may be. Weaponization here will proceed in both senses of the term defined earlier: both in the loose sense, where it refers to the progressive development of the plans, procedures, technologies, and organizations necessary for the conduct of effective nuclear operations, and in the strict sense of developing, testing, and integrating nuclear payloads with specific delivery vehicles. In both instances, however, the processes of weaponization will remain primarily covert, as India's nuclear capabilities are at a stage where, so long as New Delhi does not revert to full-up nuclear testing in the field, most of its weaponization can be carried out clandestinely and with minimal notice (even though some activities will betray distinctive physical signatures that can be detected by national technical means). Washington's desire to have New Delhi commit to avoiding any weaponization is based on the belief that "latent nuclear capacities" alone ought to suffice for purposes of ensuring Indian security. Irrespective of whether this belief is true or not, the decisions arrived at in New Delhi after the May 1998 tests suggest a different vision of adequacy: For better or worse, India (and, for that matter, Pakistan) has decided that developing a "constitutable deterrent" rather than maintaining merely latent nuclear capacities is the most appropriate course of action. Consequently—and consistent with U.S. preferences—India will eschew developing a "standing force" of the sort represented by a ready arsenal, but it will move beyond the minimal posture represented by the American demand for maintaining latent nuclear capacities to something resembling a middling alternative—and this constitutable deterrent will take the form of a force-in-being that requires completed weaponization even if it precludes the deployment of actual, ready, standing nuclear forces. Since the weaponization required by this force-in-being will for the most part be completed surreptitiously, India will at best promise to carry out this process in as nonprovocative a fashion as possible if it chooses to offer any promises in this regard at all. Most likely, however, it will demur from complying with the U.S. demand for avoiding weaponization simply by pointing to the fact that a force-in-being—which the country believes is essential for its security today—requires the completion of weaponization in both the broad and narrow sense referred to earlier.

A similar judgment holds with respect to the demand that India cease missile development, testing, production, and deployment. Most analysts believe that this component of the restraint regime is predicated on the belief that aircraft-based deterrents are more stable than missile-delivered weapons because the short reaction times embodied by the latter, the inability to recall missiles once launched, and the deep concerns about the limitations of rationality and the character of the command-and-control systems in both countries, especially in Pakistan, all demand an effort to suppress the development and deployment of nuclear-armed missiles in South Asia. Irrespective of how valid these concerns may be, the United States government has correctly recognized that ballistic and cruise missiles *will* be developed or acquired, tested, produced, and deployed by both India and Pakistan, albeit for different reasons. Islamabad will acquire ballistic missile systems primarily because its air-breathing elements face severe constraints on penetrativity in any operations against India. India will develop ballistic missile systems primarily because none of its air-breathing platforms, currently or prospectively, has the required range to reach critical targets located deep within the Chinese landmass. Both states, appreciating the greater simplicity of missile attack operations, the lower probabilities of intercept associated with missile delivery, and the enhanced survivability enjoyed by mobile missiles in the field, will therefore continue to make nuclear-capable missile systems the mainstay of their strategic deterrents over time.

Recognizing just this fact, the United States government has focused not on getting India to eliminate its missile development program altogether—however preferable that might be for nonproliferation reasons—but rather on inducing India to terminate the development, testing, and production of new missiles after the current programs are concluded. In effect, the United States has sought to limit the possibility of an *open-ended* missile development program in South Asia where newer and more lethal missiles are continually developed not out of strategic necessity but rather out of bureaucratic momentum. At this point, however, it is unclear whether this objective can be successfully achieved. In part, this is because the missiles India requires for its force-in-being will not be available in operational form for at least five to seven years, and the number of missiles necessary may require production operations to persist for what may be the better part of the next decade, if not two. This development and production process may spawn better and more improved variants of the basic design, with the result that testing and production of newer systems may persist more or less continually for some time to come. Any promise made now by New Delhi to eschew the development of follow-on systems after the current R&D efforts are completed thus has uncertain credibility at best and at worst will be completely unenforceable. All that the United States can achieve at this juncture is to communicate the gravity of its concerns and, it is hoped, secure from New Delhi a better understanding of the limits of Indian ambitions. Acquiring such an understanding, then, would enable the United States to discuss how such capabilities may or may not comport with India's present desire for a "minimum" deterrent while simultaneously communicating to New Delhi that future improvements in U.S.-Indian strategic ties will always remain contingent on the degree to which India can be relied on to act in accordance with its own commitments.

In contrast to the knotty problems posed by nuclear weaponization and missile development, the last two components of the restraint regime urged by the United States face much better prospects of attainment. Without much difficulty, India will institute national controls on the diffusion of strategic technologies because it is in its own interests to do so. Many of these regulatory mechanisms already exist in Indian law, and wherever lacunae are discovered it is reasonable to expect that New Delhi will remedy them. It is clearly not in India's interests to encourage further proliferation, and for that reason India is most likely to comply with U.S. requests in this matter more than in any other out of sheer self-interest. Almost all the producers of strategic technology in India also happen to exist in the public sector, where New Delhi's writ runs firmly. None of these enterprises is controlled by authorities who enjoy any excessive autonomy within the Indian state; consequently, the chances that one or more of these organizations might pursue their parochial interests, irrespective of how that is reconciled with the objectives of the state writ large, is highly remote. In any event, the U.S. government would do well to carefully monitor India's activities with respect to its trade in critical materials with various countries of concern. It is entirely possible that New Delhi could occasionally succumb to the lure of engaging in such trade either because of the commercial benefits involved or because the commercial transactions in question happened to skirt the restrictive technology-control regimes maintained by the United States. Should such transactions be detected, Washington should chastise India both publicly and privately while simultaneously communicating to New Delhi that the evolving U.S.-Indian rapprochement will always be constrained if India cannot demonstrate due sensitivity to critical U.S. concerns about trade in strategic materials with potential adversaries of the United States.

In time, New Delhi is also likely to resume public dialogue with Pakistan on matters of mutual concern. India's dialogue with China, which was interrupted by the May 1998 nuclear tests, has now resumed—with hopeful portents.[57] Resumption of the dialogue with Pakistan will take somewhat longer, as New Delhi—upset by the events at Kargil and by continued violence in Kashmir—appears determined to isolate Pakistan and penalize it as long as it possibly can through a new policy of "malign neglect." Yet even Indian policymakers recognize that a dialogue with Pakistan must resume eventually if for no other reason than the fact that it serves the interests of all actors concerned. At the moment, New Delhi's precondition for resuming this dialogue has been a cessation of violence in Kashmir and a reduction in cross-border infiltration. If Pakistan is seen to embark on even tentative steps in this direction, India will have no choice but to resume the dialogue that was interrupted by the tragic events associated with Kargil and its aftermath.

At the very least, such a dialogue would help reduce the political temperatures at a time when all South Asian states could use the breathing room offered by these confidence-building measures to address the more pressing problems related to the continuation of economic reform or the preservation of order in domestic politics. Continued political dialogue would also help clarify the nature of strategic intentions on all sides with the objective of reducing surprises, assisting evolutionary change, and, over the long term, changing the antagonistic perceptions that are currently held by each side. In the near term, this dialogue would also allow each country to adjust to the changes in strategic capabilities that may be

---

[57]For a good assessment of these developments, see J. N. Dixit, "Beijing on Our Mind," *Hindustan Times*, August 2, 2000.

occurring on the opposite side without the need for an exaggerated response of one's own. Thus, it may even slow the pace of nuclearization at the margins or at least prevent the competitive action-reaction cycle from perniciously increasing in velocity.

It must be noted, however, that these benefits are unlikely to carry over into a resolution of the "core" disputes, especially in the case of India and Pakistan. The issue of disputed territories in the Sino-Indian case is a different matter; despite Beijing's general reluctance to specify the "line of actual control" along the Himalayan border, it is possible that China would move toward a satisfactory resolution of all of its border disputes with India once it was convinced that New Delhi posed no genuine threat to its fundamental interests.[58] Unlike the territorial disputes in the Indo-Pakistani case, the disputed Himalayan territories hold no emotive claims for China; their importance to Beijing is purely instrumental and, except for the Aksai Chin, which hosts the strategic lines of communication between Xinjiang and Tibet, serve primarily as useful instruments for intimidating India whenever necessary. In contrast, Indo-Pakistani territorial disputes—especially those relating to Kashmir—are highly emotive and involve claims that are considered to be intrinsically valuable on both sides: Indian and Pakistani claims over Kashmir in particular are in "absolute" conflict, and it is highly unlikely that any amount of dialogue will ever resolve the issue to the satisfaction of both. In a power-political sense, the Kashmir dispute is simply unresolvable because the side most committed to changing the status quo—Pakistan—also happens to be the weaker of the two disputants, while the stronger entity—India—not only feels uncompelled to alter its current claims but also can sustain the existing structure of political control in Kashmir indefinitely and at minimal cost to its body politic. For these reasons, the best that can be expected of the present Indo-Pakistani dialogue, at least where the outstanding territorial dispute relating to Kashmir is concerned, is the gradual diminution of violence and a return to civility in the disputed state; the evolution of a "working relationship" between New Delhi and

---

[58]Recent reports suggest that during meetings of the "experts group" in November 2000, China in fact agreed to exchange maps of the "middle sector" for the first time. See "Sino-Indian Ties Looking Up: Jaswant," *The Hindu*, November 25, 2000.

Islamabad; and a gradual accommodation in both India and Pakistan to the reality of divided control over the former Himalayan kingdom.

On balance, therefore, the restraint regime pursued by the United States since the May 1998 tests is likely to enjoy only mixed success, at least as far as India is concerned. New Delhi is likely to maintain its self-imposed moratorium on nuclear testing for a while longer even if it declines to sign the CTBT in the absence of normalized relations with the United States or in the face of incomplete ratification of the treaty by the established nuclear powers. It has supported the initiation of discussions leading up to the conclusion of an FMCT, although its final response to the draft treaty that may emerge from such a process obviously remains uncertain. In the interim, however, it will not agree to any moratorium on the production of fissile materials. New Delhi will continue to pursue both nuclear weaponization and the development and production of various missiles, especially the Agni series currently under way, although these efforts will not materialize in the form of ready and standing nuclear forces. India will comply with U.S. requests that it establish a rigorous national regime to prevent the external diffusion of strategic technologies, and it will resume a dialogue with Pakistan eventually (while continuing its current dialogue with China) even if these efforts do not end in a conclusive resolution of all the outstanding disputes that currently exist between these states. Whether Washington will be satisfied with the mixed achievements emerging from the U.S.-Indian dialogue is still unclear, in part because the strategic objective of improving U.S.-Indian relations has never been cogently articulated by the United States. There is no doubt, however, that the dialogue initiated by the Clinton administration in the aftermath of the May 1998 tests has resulted in the most intense and consistent conversation about national interests ever conducted in the history of bilateral relations between the two countries.

At the end of the day, therefore, the greatest achievement of this process may turn out to be the fact that the two sides have come to steadily appreciate the strategic concerns of the other somewhat better than they did before the dialogue began.[59] At the Indian end,

---

[59]This, at any rate, appears to be the Indian reading of current U.S. pronouncements on the nuclear issue. See "U.S. Recognises India's N-Concern," *The Hindu*, September 3, 2000.

the very fact that such a dialogue has occurred is itself important because it serves to redress in some way New Delhi's traditional grievance about being treated less than seriously by the United States. At the U.S. end, the dialogue has been useful insofar as it has allowed Washington to persuasively make the case for India's accession to the CTBT regime—an objective of great importance to U.S. global interests—even as it has enabled senior U.S. officials to catch a glimpse of India's ability and willingness to restrain its ongoing strategic programs. The general opacity about most details relating to New Delhi's desired nuclear force architecture and its operating posture remains a source of some anguish and frustration, and hence it is not surprising that several U.S. diplomats have gently urged New Delhi to display more transparency with respect to its nuclear deterrent. These calls have in most instances centered on understanding the question "How many missile systems and warheads does India need to have a minimum nuclear deterrent?"[60] U.S. requests for transparency on this issue have been driven in the first instance by a desire to prevent India and its neighbors from inadvertently locking themselves into an action-reaction cycle that inevitably degenerates into an arms race. However, these requests are also driven by the desire to avoid continual surprises and by the need to secure concrete and tangible manifestations of restraint, especially with respect to force levels, force composition, and force posture.[61]

Not surprisingly—and quite consistent with its prevailing practices on strategic matters—India has opposed these demands for transparency. This opposition has sometimes been articulated on the rhetorical grounds of defending sovereignty but may be rooted more substantially in the fact that India still does not know what its force-in-being will look like when it is eventually completed. This should not be surprising because as the analysis in this book reveals, the nuclear deterrent New Delhi desires is still several years and possibly up to two decades from completion. In any event, while the desire for greater transparency in Indian intentions and capabilities

---

[60]"Nukes: Mind Your Business, U.S. Told," *Economic Times*, January 7, 1999.

[61]These concerns were cogently articulated by U.S. Ambassador to India Richard Celeste in several statements made in New Delhi during December 1998 and January 1999. For a useful report of Celeste's argument, see K. V. Krishnaswamy, "Celeste Defends Demand on Deterrence," *The Hindu*, January 23, 1999.

is understandable, any transparency in force size, structure, and posture could become problematic if it brings the tensions between political restraint and first-strike stability to a head. This issue becomes relevant only when the nuclear deterrents in question are composed of relatively small and potentially weak forces that, however conducive they are to the objective of furthering restraint, could become dangerous magnets for attempted disarming strikes in the context of a crisis. Because Indian and Pakistani nuclear capabilities are relatively weak—the political pretensions and inflated rhetoric of their elites notwithstanding—it is probably better, from the perspective of larger U.S. interests, that these capabilities be kept continually hidden behind a dense veil of secrecy. Continued opaqueness represents their best defense against what may be even episodic temptations of preemptive attack, and to the degree that these temptations can be successfully neutralized through the institutionalization of pervasive uncertainty, the critical U.S. objective of preserving deterrence and crisis stability in the region will only be further enhanced even if some other local nonproliferation preferences must take a back seat in the process.

If the prevention of war, including nuclear war, ought to become the new goal of American nonproliferation policy in the region—an objective whose importance is matched only by the need to prevent the diffusion of strategic technologies to other potential proliferants—the United States should concentrate on shaping the character of the evolving Indian (and Pakistani) nuclear arsenals so that they comport with the following injunctions:

- *Keep 'em small*: A modest Indian arsenal suits American grand strategy more than a large arsenal so long as its constituent capabilities are safe, survivable, and reasonably effective.[62]

- *Keep 'em stealthy*: A surreptitious Indian force can avoid the high costs of ensuring survivability by means other than opacity, and since mobility is a special form of stealth, mobile delivery systems should be encouraged, not proscribed.[63]

---

[62]On the threats to stability posed by excessively small arsenals, see the pertinent admonitions in Michael Quinlan, "How Robust Is India-Pakistan Deterrence?" *Survival*, 42:4 (Winter 2000–2001), pp. 141–154.

[63]Shlapak and Thaler, *Back to First Principles*, pp. 69–71.

- *Keep 'em slow*: An Indian arsenal that embodies anything other than a rapid-response capability does not subvert either Indian or American interests because it helps dampen escalation and because if it has to be employed *in extremis*, "revenge is a dish best eaten cold."[64]

Although the United States cannot provide India with technical assistance to develop its force-in-being—nor should it seek to—it can play many other useful roles and can also influence the eventual size, shape, and disposition of India's evolving nuclear deterrent so as to reduce the threat it poses to larger American interests. To obtain this outcome, however, the United States must begin—paradoxical though it may seem—by truly accepting the fact that India will maintain a nuclear deterrent of some sort for some time to come. If Washington genuinely accepts this reality and internalizes it as a matter of policy, it may in fact create conditions that allow New Delhi to deemphasize the need for both a larger arsenal and a more provocative strategic posture.

There is no guarantee, however, that such an approach will work. What is nonetheless certain is that the opposing approach will fail. A policy that focuses on explicitly attempting to constrain the Indian nuclear weapon program—or one that explicitly holds the growth in U.S.-Indian relations hostage to securing Indian compliance with some proliferation benchmarks—will only increase resistance in New Delhi. It will, for example, strengthen the position of the hawks within India's domestic debate and will compel the government of India to pursue a far larger and more open-ended strategic weapon program than was its intention. Such reactions will in fact become inevitable because increased U.S. pressures are likely to be viewed as part of a hostile international environment that demands, among other things, expanded—not reduced—nuclear capabilities on the part of New Delhi.

If the net result of either increased American pressure or deepened American recalcitrance is a more extensive Indian strategic capability, the United States will have failed on two counts. First, it will

---

[64]James T. Quinlivan and Glenn C. Buchan, *Theory and Practice: Nuclear Deterrents and Nuclear Actors*, P-7902 (Santa Monica: RAND, 1995), p. 12.

have failed to constrain the size, shape, and disposition of the evolving Indian deterrent—presumably the first objective of pursuing such a policy. Second, it will have failed to entice a rising power into a strategic relationship that could provide larger advantages to both India and the United States on a variety of issues ranging from the evolving balance of power in Asia to the emerging challenges of global governance. In this context, it is important to recognize that left to its own devices, New Delhi will more likely than not pursue strategic programs that are more or less modest in their scope and orientation. In the face of external pressures or resistance, however, this native propensity for moderation could be transmuted into domestic decisions that have either the direct or the unintended effect of challenging both U.S. interests and the international order. At this point in the U.S.-Indian relationship, it is therefore likely that a genuine expansion of ties with New Delhi will promise more favorable outcomes for American interests across the board than the traditional U.S. policy—which, obsessed with resolving nonproliferation issues as a precondition to deepened bilateral relations, will result both in numerous lost opportunities along a much wider strategic canvas than just South Asia and in the defeat of every one of Washington's nonproliferation goals, if only on an installment plan.

Even as the United States countenances such a reorientation in its strategic attitude toward India (and, wherever applicable, toward Pakistan as well), there are three important policy initiatives Washington can undertake in the near term to influence New Delhi's strategic choices with respect to its evolving nuclear posture.

First, it can play the role of helpful critic. This contribution, however, is best made privately through sustained dialogue and through the various official mechanisms that are now in place at the highest levels for ongoing discussions between Indian and American policymakers. Such "intellectual assistance"—which would continually challenge India to think through the kinds of capabilities it needs, the forms in which they materialize, the posture in which they will be deployed, and the doctrine under which they may be utilized—will be more useful to India (and to Pakistan) over the long term than any quick fixes like transfers of technology. The tenor of these discussions, however, is as important as their substance; U.S. objectives must not consist of browbeating India into meeting certain political demands but must instead focus on understanding where India stands with respect to its strategic programs at any given point. This understanding ought to be premised on the recognition of an important fact: Indian nuclear weapons do not pose a threat to U.S. security, but Indian nuclear triumphalism could well damage important U.S. interests. Consequently, a continuing dialogue on nuclear issues must focus on eliminating the prospect of repeated Indian surprises in the strategic realm while helping identify those outcomes both sides could commonly strive toward because they serve U.S. and Indian interests simultaneously. Such discussions also provide a good opportunity to inform India about the American experience of managing nuclear forces, including the challenges and problems the United States faced during the Cold War—and to the degree that such discussions are found helpful, they should be further emphasized in the years ahead.

Second, it can begin to share its own assessments about the character of the strategic environment facing India. This contribution may not entail intelligence sharing of any sort but does require a willingness to share certain judgments based on intelligence information that the United States possesses. The utility of this contribution must not be underestimated: All the South Asian states today generally possess relatively poor information about the intentions and the capabilities of their competitors and are consequently apt to base programmatic decisions with respect to their strategic capabilities on a pervasive misreading of their threat environment. Given this problem, it is imperative that the United States search for ways to share its own appreciation of the regional strategic situation with each of the actors involved. In some instances, this may involve sharing bits of information—sometimes those available from commercial rather than governmental sources. Irrespective of the specifics involved, however, the objective of such discussions must be to help India (and other regional states where necessary) make strategic decisions that dampen, not heighten, the ongoing security competition in South Asia. Ultimately, the United States must prepare itself to play the role of an "umpire," especially in situations where deterrence breakdown or nuclear weapon use is plausible. This will require, among other things, a willingness to expose any attempts that regional states might make to disturb the status quo by means of military, including nuclear, instruments. The challenges associated with this task are numerous and complex, but Washington should prepare for them at least by assessing the nature of the demands involved, particularly if preventing war—especially nuclear war—is to become (as one can hope it will be) a new U.S. policy objective in South Asia.

Third, the United States can transform its stated preference for Indo-Pakistani reconciliation over Kashmir into a clear and articulated tenet of its regional policy. During President Clinton's visit to the region in March 2000, the United States began to affirm the proposition that disputed boundaries ought not to be redrawn in blood and that the existing Line of Control ought to be treated as sacrosanct by both sides.[65] Building on this foundation, the United States should encourage both India and Pakistan to negotiate the transformation of the existing Line of Control—with the appropriate modifications necessary to increase security—into a new international border. This solution is unlikely to fully satisfy either India or Pakistan, but since every other alternative is fraught with grave risks and could be obtained only through the medium of war, a future U.S. policy toward South Asia should strongly endorse the negotiated transformation of the Line of Control into an international border. Operationalizing this solution involves several other complicated predicates: It involves urging India to become more responsive to Kashmiri aspirations; it involves urging Pakistan to restrain both its official support for cross-border insurgency and the unofficial activities of various Islamist groups operating within its territory, if for no other reason than Pakistan's own continued stability; and it involves urging both India and Pakistan to engage in bilateral negotiations, conducted on the *a priori* understanding that the absence of politically viable alternatives to the current status quo requires both countries to prepare their citizenry for the compromises that acceptance of the Line of Control as an international border necessarily entails.

As the United States attempts to cope with the rapidly changing situation in Southern Asia—of which India's emerging nuclear capabilities are only one, albeit an important, component—it should not lose sight of the fact that bilateral U.S.-Indian relations still cry

---

[65]"Remarks of the President in Greeting to the People of Pakistan," March 25, 2000, available at http://www.whitehouse.gov/WH/New/SouthAsia/speeches/20000325.html.

out for a realistic strategic vision that could serve as the framework within which the sometimes competing interests of the two states may be reconciled. The lack of such a vision historically condemned both countries to a bitter "transactional" approach in which individual policy initiatives quickly became hostage to either transient political moods or bureaucratic pressures on both sides. Nowhere has this been seen more clearly than on the nuclear issue, a phenomenon that once led two prominent observers to remark that "of all the parts of the world where U.S. policy is held hostage by a single-issue constituency, South Asia is one of the worst."[66] During President Clinton's March 1998 trip to South Asia, the President and Prime Minister Vajpayee jointly signed a vision statement that elucidated the resolve "to create a closer and qualitatively new relationship between the United States and India."[67] With its soaring rhetoric and lofty goals, this statement represented a welcome first step in the long and delicate process of restoring equilibrium to the U.S.-Indian engagement. Yet for all its value, the statement remains incomplete to the extent that it fails to publicly articulate why engaging India—at some cost in American resources, energies, and attention—is necessary for the success of larger U.S. grand strategic objectives in Asia and beyond. Since it fails to amplify this critical issue, the vision statement cannot—and does not—establish either strategic priorities that could help guide bureaucratic choices in both countries or regulative principles that could influence decisionmakers when conflicts of interest are to be reconciled. Articulating such a vision, which embeds India multidimensionally in a larger framework defining American grand strategy, thus remains the most important task facing the new administration as far as U.S.-Indian relations are concerned—and until such a *strategic* vision is made evident, the U.S. response to future Indian nuclearization (and to nuclearization in South Asia in general) risks being disjointed and ineffective.

---

[66]Richard N. Haass and Gideon Rose, "Facing the Nuclear Facts in India and Pakistan," *Washington Post*, January 5, 1997.

[67]See "U.S.-India Relations: A Vision for the 21st Century," *Hindustan Times*, March 23, 2000.

BIBLIOGRAPHY

Abraham, Itty, "India's 'Strategic Enclave': Civilian Scientists and Military Technologies," *Armed Forces & Society*, 18:2 (Winter 1992).

Abraham, Itty, *The Making of the Indian Atomic Bomb: Science, Secrecy and the Post-Colonial State* (New York: Zed, 1998).

Abraham, Itty, "Science and Power in the Postcolonial State," *Alternatives*, 21 (1996).

"Address by Prime Minister Atal Bihari Vajpayee to the Joint Session of the United States Congress," Washington, D.C., September 14, 2000, available at http://www.meadev.gov.in/speeches/j-session.htm.

"Address to the Nation by Shri K.R. Narayanan, President of India, on the Occasion of the Closing Function of the Golden Jubilee of India's Independence, Central Hall of Parliament, New Delhi—August 15, 1998," *India News*, July 16–August 15, 1998.

"Agni-II Joins Nation's Missile Showcase," *Hindustan Times*, April 12, 1999.

"Agni 2 Test Soon?" *Hindustan Times*, March 4, 1999.

Ahmed, Samina, "Pakistan's Nuclear Weapons Program," *International Security*, 23:4 (Spring 1999).

Ahmed, Samina, and David Cortright, *Preventing a Nuclear Arms Race in South Asia: U.S. Policy Options*, Policy Brief No. 2 (Notre

Dame, IN: Kroc Institute for International Peace Studies, University of Notre Dame, January 2000).

Ahmedullah, Mohammed, "Prithvi and Beyond—India's Ballistic Missile Programmes," *Military Technology*, 23:4 (1999).

Ahuja, Dhiraj, "The Extra Terrestrial Connection," *Dataquest India*, November 15, 1996.

Aiyer, Mani Shankar, "A Bang or a Whimper?" *India Today*, June 1, 1998.

Alagappa, Muthiah (ed.), *Asian Security Practice* (Stanford, CA: Stanford University Press, 1998).

Alagappa, Muthiah, "International Response to Nuclear Tests in South Asia: The Need for a New Policy Framework," *AsiaPacific Issues*, 38 (June 15, 1998).

Albright, David, *Fact Sheet: India and Pakistan—Current and Potential Nuclear Arsenals* (Washington, D.C.: Institute for Science and International Security, May 13, 1998), available at http://www.isis-online.org/.

Albright, David, *India and Pakistan's Fissile Material and Nuclear Weapons Inventory, End of 1998* (Washington, D.C.: Institute for Science and International Security, October 27, 1999), available at http://www.isis-online.org/publications/southasia/stocks1099.html.

Albright, David, "India and Pakistan's Nuclear Arms Race: Out of the Closet but Not in the Street," *Arms Control Today*, 23:5 (June 1993).

Albright, David, Lauren Barbour, Corey Gay, and Todd Lowery, "Ending the Production of Fissile Material for Nuclear Weapons: Background Information and Key Questions," available at http://www.isis-online.org/publications/fmct.

Albright, David, and Kevin O'Neill, "ISIS Technical Assessment: Pakistan's Stock of Weapon-Grade Uranium," June 1, 1998, available at http://www.isis-online.org/.

Albright, David, William Walker, and Frans Berkhout, *Plutonium and Highly Enriched Uranium 1996: World Inventories, Capabilities and Policies* (Oxford, UK: Oxford University Press, 1997).

Albright, David, and Tom Zamora, "India, Pakistan's Nuclear Weapons: All the Pieces in Place," *Bulletin of the Atomic Scientists*, 45:5 (June 1989).

Albright, Madeleine K., "Op-Ed on the President's Trip to South Asia," printed in *Diario las Americas*, April 2, 2000, available at http://secretary.state.gov/www/statements/2000/000402.html.

Aldridge, Robert C., *First Strike!: The Pentagon's Strategy for Nuclear War* (Boston: South End Press, 1983).

"Alford Testimony in the House of Commons, Fourth Report from the Defence Committee, Session 1980–81," *Strategic Nuclear Weapons Policy* (London: HMSO, 1981).

Allen, Kenneth, and JoEllen Gorg, "Nuclear Weapons and Sino-Indian Relations," *South Asian Policy Brief* (Washington, D.C.: Henry L. Stimson Center, June 15, 1998), available at http://www.stimson.org/cbm/sapb/brief2.htm.

Andersen, Walter, "India's Foreign Policy in the Post–Cold War World: Searching for a New Model," in Shalendra D. Sharma (ed.), *The Asia-Pacific in the New Millennium: Geopolitics, Security, and Foreign Policy* (Berkeley, CA: Institute of East Asian Studies, University of California, Berkeley, 2000).

Anderson, John Ward, "Confusion Dominates Arms Race," *Washington Post*, June 1, 1998.

Anderson, John Ward, "Pakistan Claims It Has New Missile," *Washington Post*, June 2, 1998.

Aneja, Atul, "Army Gets Lion's Share of Funds," *The Hindu*, March 1, 2000.

Aneja, Atul, "GoM for Revamp of Defence Management," *The Hindu*, February 27, 2001.

Aneja, Atul, "Towards a New Security Architecture," *The Hindu*, February 28, 2001.

"Annexure II, Indian Memorial Submitted to the International Court of Justice, Status of Nuclear Weapons in International Law: Request for Advisory Opinion of the International Court of Justice," *Indian Journal of International Law*, 37:2 (April–June 1997).

Arkin, William M., "What's 'New?' " *Bulletin of the Atomic Scientists*, 53:6 (November–December 1997).

"Army Chief Calls for Steps to Counter N-Threats," *The Hindu*, April 21, 1998.

"Army Will Be Prepared to Tackle Nuclear Threat," *Hindustan Times*, September 29, 2000.

Arnett, Eric, "And the Loser Is . . . the Indian Armed Forces," *Economic and Political Weekly*, September 5–12, 1998.

Arnett, Eric, "Conventional Arms Transfers and Nuclear Stability in South Asia," in Eric Arnett (ed.), *Nuclear Weapons and Arms Control in South Asia After the Test Ban* (Oxford, UK: Oxford University Press, 1998).

Arnett, Eric, "The Future Strategic Balance in South Asia," in Herro Mustafa (ed.), *The Balance of Power in South Asia* (Abu Dhabi, UAE: Emirates Center for Strategic Studies and Research, 2000).

Arnett, Eric (ed.), *Military Capacity and the Risk of War* (Oxford, UK: Oxford University Press, 1997).

Arnett, Eric, "Military Research and Development in Southern Asia: Limited Capabilities Despite Impressive Resources," in Eric Arnett (ed.), *Military Capacity and the Risk of War* (Oxford, UK: Oxford University Press, 1997).

Arnett, Eric, "Military Technology: The Case of India," *SIPRI Yearbook 1994* (Oxford, UK: Oxford University Press, 1994).

Arnett, Eric (ed.), *Nuclear Weapons and Arms Control in South Asia After the Test Ban* (Oxford, UK: Oxford University Press, 1998).

Arnett, Eric, "What Threat?" *Bulletin of the Atomic Scientists*, 53:2 (March–April 1997).

Art, Robert J., "The United States: Nuclear Weapons and Grand Strategy," in Regina Cowen Karp (ed.), *Security with Nuclear Weapons?* (Oxford, UK: Oxford University Press, 1991).

"Atomic Energy Watchdog Won't Bark at BARC," *Indian Express*, June 1, 2000.

Ayoob, Mohammed, "Nuclear India and Indian-American Relations," *Orbis*, 43:1 (Winter 1999).

Babbage, Ross, and Sandy Gordon (eds.), *India's Strategic Future* (New York: St. Martin's Press, 1992).

Babbitt, Albert E., "Command Centers," in Ashton B. Carter, John D. Steinbruner, and Charles A. Zraket (eds.), *Managing Nuclear Operations* (Washington, D.C.: Brookings, 1987).

Badam, Ramola Talwar, "BARC Now Freed of Regulatory Control," *Asian Age*, May 31, 2000.

Badri-Maharaj, Sanjay, *The Armageddon Factor* (New Delhi: Lancer Publishers, 2000).

Badri-Maharaj, Sanjay, "The Nuclear Battlefield," *Indian Defence Review*, 14:2 (April–June 1999).

Badri-Maharaj, Sanjay, "Nuclear India's Status," *Indian Defence Review*, 15:2 (April–June 2000).

Badri-Maharaj, Sanjay, "World's Fourth Largest Air Force," *Indian Defence Review*, 14:4 (October–December 1999).

Bagla, Pallava, "Pokharan: DRDO Limelight Hurt DAE," *Indian Express*, December 10, 1998.

Bailey, Kathleen C., "Proliferation: Implications for U.S. Deterrence," in Kathleen C. Bailey (ed.), *Weapons of Mass Destruction: Costs Versus Benefits* (New Delhi: Manohar, 1994).

Bailey, Kathleen C. (ed.), *Weapons of Mass Destruction: Costs Versus Benefits* (New Delhi: Manohar, 1994).

Bailey, Kathleen, and Satoshi Morimoto, "A Proposal for a South Asian Intermediate Nuclear Forces Treaty," *Comparative Strategy*, 17:2 (1998).

Bain, William W., "Sino-Indian Military Modernization: The Potential for Destabilization," *Asian Affairs*, 21:3 (Fall 1994).

Bajpai, Kanti, "The Fallacy of an Indian Deterrent," in Amitabh Mattoo (ed.), *India's Nuclear Deterrent* (New Delhi: Har-Anand Publications, 1999).

Bajpai, Kanti, "A Flawed Doctrine," *The Times of India*, September 7, 1999.

Bajpai, Kanti, "The Great Indian Nuclear Debate," *The Hindu*, November 12, 1999.

Bajpai, Kanti, "India: Modified Structuralism," in Muthiah Alagappa (ed.), *Asian Security Practice* (Stanford, CA: Stanford University Press, 1998).

Bajpai, Kanti, "India's Diplomacy and Defence After Pokhran II," in *Post Pokhran II: The National Way Ahead* (New Delhi: India Habitat Centre, 1999).

Bajpai, Kanti, "India's Nuclear Posture After Pokhran II," *International Studies*, 37:4 (October–December 2000).

Bajpai, Kanti, "Secure Without the Bomb," *Seminar*, 444 (August 1996).

Baker, David (ed.), *Jane's Space Directory, 1999–2000* (Coulsdon, UK: Jane's Information Group Ltd., 1999).

Baker, John C., and Dana Johnson, "Security Implications," in John C. Baker, Kevin M. O'Connell, and Ray A. Williamson (eds.), *Commercial Observation Satellites: At the Leading Edge of Global Transparency*, MR-1229 (Santa Monica: RAND/ASPRS, 2001).

Baker, John C., Kevin M. O'Connell, and Ray A. Williamson (eds.), *Commercial Observation Satellites: At the Leading Edge of Global Transparency*, MR-1229 (Santa Monica: RAND/ASPRS, 2001).

Bakshi, Praful, "Nuclear Euphoria and Harsh Realities," *Hindustan Times*, July 14, 1998.

Balachandran, G., "A Consensus or a Sell-Off?" *The Hindu*, December 14, 1999.

Balachandran, G., "India's Nuclear Doctrine," available at http://www.ipcs.org/issues/articles/254-ndi-bala.htm.

Balachandran, G., "India's Nuclear Option: Economic Implications," *Strategic Analysis*, 19:2 (May 1996).

Balachandran, G., "Nuclear Weaponization in India," *Agni*, 5:1 (January–April 2000).

Balachandran, G., "What Is the Relevance of a Triad?" *The Hindu*, September 10, 1999.

Ball, Desmond, "The Development of the SIOP, 1960–1983," in Desmond Ball and Jeffrey Richelson (eds.), *Strategic Nuclear Targeting* (Ithaca, NY: Cornell University Press, 1986).

Ball, Desmond, *Signals Intelligence in the Post–Cold War Era: Developments in the Asia-Pacific Region* (Singapore: Institute of Southeast Asian Studies, 1993).

Ball, Desmond, *Signals Intelligence (SIGINT) in South Asia: India, Pakistan, Sri Lanka (Ceylon)* (Canberra: Strategic and Defence Studies Centre, Australian National University, 1996).

Ball, Desmond, *Targeting for Strategic Deterrence*, Adelphi Paper No. 185 (London: IISS, 1983).

Ball, Desmond, "U.S. Strategic Forces: How Would They Be Used?" *International Security*, 7:3 (Winter 1982–1983).

Ball, Desmond, and Jeffrey Richelson (eds.), *Strategic Nuclear Targeting* (Ithaca, NY: Cornell University Press, 1986).

Banerjee, D., "The Future of Chemical Warfare and India," *Combat Journal*, August 1989.

Banerjee, Dipankar, "The New Strategic Environment," in Amitabh Mattoo (ed.), *India's Nuclear Deterrent* (New Delhi: Har-Anand Publications, 1999).

Banerjee, Dipankar (ed.), *Security in the New World Order* (New Delhi: Institute for Defence Studies and Analyses, 1994).

Banerjie, Indranil, "The Integrated Guided Missile Development Programme," *Indian Defence Review*, 5:2 (July 1990).

Barker, Brian, Michael Clark, Peter Davis, Mark Fisk, Michael Hedlin, Hans Israelsson, Vitaly Khalturin, Won-Young Kim, Keith McLaughlin, Charles Meade, John Murphy, Robert North, John Orcutt, Chris Powell, Paul G. Richards, Richard Stead, Jeffry Stevens, Frank Vernon, and Terry Wallace, "Monitoring Nuclear Tests," *Science*, 282 (September 25, 1998).

Barth, Fritz J., "Stemming Nuclear Terrorism," *U.S. Naval Institute Proceedings*, 115:12 (December 1989).

Basu, Tarun, "Nuclear Doctrine Emerges, but Tension Mounts on Border," *India Abroad*, August 14, 1998.

Batra, Satkartar, *The Ports of India*, 3rd ed. (Kandla, India: Kandla Commercial Publications, 1982).

Baylis, John, and Robert O'Neill (eds.), *Alternative Nuclear Futures: The Role of Nuclear Weapons in the Post–Cold War World* (Oxford, UK: Oxford University Press, 2000).

Beaver, Paul, "Pakistan 'Faked Ghauri Missile Pictures,' " *Jane's Missiles & Rockets*, 2:6 (June 1998).

Beaver, Paul, "Pakistan's Missile 'Was a Nodong,' " *Jane's Missiles & Rockets*, 2:5 (May 1998).

Bedi, Rahul, "As Nuclear Test Preparations Avoid Detection," *Jane's Defence Weekly*, May 20, 1998.

Bedi, Rahul, "India Assesses Options on Future Nuclear Control," *Jane's Defence Weekly*, September 16, 1998.

Bedi, Rahul, "India Confirms Nuclear Policy," *Jane's Defence Weekly*, December 23, 1998.

Bedi, Rahul, "India Confirms Plans for Improved Agni and Naval Cruise Missile," *Jane's Missiles & Rockets*, 2:10 (October 1999).

Bedi, Rahul, "India Presses Ahead with SSN to Boost Navy's Nuclear Profile," *Jane's Defence Weekly*, July 22, 1998.

Bedi, Rahul, "India Seeks Mirage 2000 Nuclear Squadron," *Asian Age*, August 29, 1999.

Bedi, Rahul, "India Targets $1B Russian Air Defence Capability," *Jane's Defence Weekly*, April 2, 1997.

Bedi, Rahul, "India to Sign New 10-Year Defence Deal with Russia," *Jane's Defence Weekly*, July 1, 1998.

Bedi, Rahul, "Indian Forces to Be Restructured," *Jane's Defence Weekly*, October 21, 1998.

Bedi, Rahul, "India's Nuclear Prowess Remains on Paper, Official Rhetoric," *Asian Age*, November 8, 2000.

Bedi, Rahul, "Interview: Gen. Sunderajan Padmanabhan, India's Chief of Army Staff," *Jane's Defence Weekly*, January 17, 2001.

Bedi, Rahul, "Interview with George Fernandes," *Jane's Defence Weekly*, July 1, 1998.

Bedi, Rahul, "Tests Give Impetus to Agni Missile," *Jane's Defence Weekly*, May 20, 1998.

Bell, C., *The Conventions of Crisis: A Study in Diplomatic Management* (Oxford, UK: Oxford University Press, 1971).

Bendel, T. R., and W. S. Murray, "Response Is Assured," *U.S. Naval Institute Proceedings*, 125:6 (June 1999).

Benner, Jeffrey, *The Indian Foreign Policy Bureaucracy* (Boulder, CO: Westview Press, 1985).

Bennett, Bruce, "The Emerging Ballistic Missile Threat: Global and Regional Implications," in Natalie W. Crawford and Chung-In Moon (eds.), *Emerging Threats, Force Structures, and the Role of Air Power in Korea*, CF-152-AF (Santa Monica: RAND, 2000).

Benton, David, "MSS Systems Advance Telecommunications in India," *Satellite Communications*, November 1994.

Bertsch, Gary K., and Anupam Srivastava, "Weapons Proliferation and Export Controls in the Former Soviet Union: Implications for Strategic Stability in Asia," *AccessAsia Review*, 3:1 (December 1999).

Betts, Richard K., *Surprise Attack: Lessons for Defense Planning* (Washington, D.C.: Brookings, 1982).

Bhaduri, Shankar, "The One and a Half Front Scenario," *SAPRA India Monthly Bulletin*, April–May 1996.

Bhargava, G. S., "Nuclear Power in India," *Energy Policy*, 20:8 (August 1992).

Bhatia, Anita, "India's Space Program," *Asian Survey*, 25:10 (October 1985).

Bhatia, Shyam, *India's Nuclear Bomb* (Ghaiziabad, India: Vikas Publishing House, 1979).

Bhattacharyya, Suman, "Time to Crash Land," *Outlook*, March 13, 2000.

Bhimayya, Kotera, "Nuclear Deterrence in South Asia," *Asian Survey*, 34:7 (July 1994).

Bhushan, S. K., "Geology Around Pokhran Nuclear Sites," *Journal of the Geological Society of India*, 52:1 (July 1998).

Bhutto, Benazir, "Perspective on South Asia—Punishment: Make It Swift, Severe," *Los Angeles Times*, May 17, 1998.

Biddle, Stephen D., and Peter D. Feaver (eds.), *Battlefield Nuclear Weapons: Issues and Options*, CSIA Occasional Paper No. 5 (Boston: Center for Science and International Affairs, Harvard University, 1989).

Bidwai, Praful, "Beggared by the Bomb: Dangerous Shift in Nuclear Doctrine," *The Times of India*, April 21, 1998.

Bidwai, Praful, "BJP's Nuclear Stance Seen as Undermining Security," *India Abroad*, April 10, 1998.

Bidwai, Praful, "India and NPT Review: Grasping the Disarmament Nettle," *The Times of India*, September 22, 1994.

Bidwai, Praful, "Nuclear Policy in a Mess," *The Times of India*, November 27, 1991.

Bidwai, Praful, "Nuclear Weapons Seen as Having Enhanced Insecurity," *India Abroad*, July 16, 1999.

Bidwai, Praful, "Regaining Nuclear Sanity," *The Times of India*, June 6, 1998.

Bidwai, Praful, "Sign the Test Ban Treaty," *The Times of India*, July 14, 1998.

Blair, Bruce G., "Alerting in Crisis and Conventional War," in Ashton B. Carter, John D. Steinbruner, and Charles A. Zraket (eds.), *Managing Nuclear Operations* (Washington, D.C.: Brookings, 1987).

Blair, Bruce G., *The Logic of Accidental Nuclear War* (Washington, D.C.: Brookings, 1993).

Blair, Bruce G., *Strategic Command and Control: Redefining the Nuclear Threat* (Washington, D.C.: Brookings, 1985).

Blair, Bruce G., and John D. Steinbruner, *The Effects of Warning on Strategic Stability* (Washington, D.C.: Brookings, 1991).

Blake, Bernard, "Long-Range Air-Defense Systems: A Global Survey," *International Defense Review*, 27:5 (May 1994).

Blanche, Ed, "Nuclear Reactions," *Jane's Defence Weekly*, June 17, 1998.

Blechman, Barry M., and Stephen S. Kaplan (eds.), *Force Without War: U.S. Armed Forces as a Political Instrument* (Washington, D.C.: Brookings, 1978).

Bonds, Tim, Michael G. Mattock, Thomas Hamilton, Carl Rhodes, Michael Scheiern, Philip M. Feldman, David R. Frelinger, and

Robert Uy, *Employing Commercial Satellite Communications*, MR-1192-AF (Santa Monica: RAND, 2000).

Boryczka, Jocelyn M., M. K. Mohanan, and Jeffrey D. Weigand, "Cultural and Strategic Factors in South Asian Nuclear Arms Control," *Journal of Political and Military Sociology*, 25 (1997).

Bowen, Clayton P., and Daniel Wolven, "Command and Control Challenges in South Asia," *Nonproliferation Review*, 6:3 (Spring–Summer 1999).

Bower, J., and P. A. Goldberg, *British Directions in Hardening Missile Bases Against Electromagnetic Effects from Nuclear Explosions*, D-7226 (Santa Monica: RAND, 1960).

Boyer, Yves, "Questioning Minimum Deterrence," in Serge Sur (ed.), *Nuclear Deterrence: Problems and Perspectives in the 1990s* (New York: UNIDIR, 1993).

Bracken, Paul, *The Command and Control of Nuclear Forces* (New Haven, CT: Yale University Press, 1983).

Bracken, Paul, *Fire in the East* (New York: HarperCollins Publishers, 1999).

Bragin, Victor, and John Carlson, "Some Significant Divisions in the Scope Debate," *Disarmament Forum*, 2 (1999).

Brass, Paul R., *The Politics of India Since Independence*, 2nd ed. (Cambridge, UK: Cambridge University Press, 1994).

Broad, William J., "Monitors Picked Up Only 1 of 5 India Blasts," *New York Times*, May 15, 1998.

Brodie, Bernard, *The Absolute Weapon: Atomic Power and World Order* (New York: Harcourt, Brace, 1946).

Brodie, Bernard, "The Development of Nuclear Strategy," *International Security*, 2:4 (Spring 1978).

Brodie, Bernard, *Escalation and the Nuclear Option* (Princeton, NJ: Princeton University Press, 1966).

Brodie, Bernard, *Strategy in the Missile Age* (Princeton, NJ: Princeton University Press, 1959).

Brodie, Bernard, *War and Politics* (New York: Macmillan, 1973).

Brown, Harold, *Department of Defense Annual Report, Fiscal Year 1980* (Washington, D.C.: USGPO, 1979).

Brown, Harold, *Thinking About National Security: Defense and Foreign Policy in a Dangerous World* (Boulder, CO: Westview Press, 1983).

Brown, P. S., "Nuclear Weapons R&D and the Role of Nuclear Testing," *Energy and Technology Review*, UCRL-52000-86-9 (September 1986).

Buchan, Alastair (ed.), *A World of Nuclear Powers?* (Englewood Cliffs, NJ: Prentice-Hall, 1966).

Bundy, McGeorge, *Danger and Survival: Choices About the Bomb in the First Fifty Years* (New York: Random House, 1988).

Bundy, McGeorge, "Existential Deterrence and Its Consequences," in Douglas MacLean (ed.), *The Security Gamble: Deterrence Dilemmas in the Nuclear Age* (Totowa, NJ: Rowman & Allanheld, 1984).

Burns, John F., "In Nuclear India, Small Stash Does Not an Arsenal Make," *New York Times*, July 26, 1998.

Burns, John F., "India Calls for Talks on New Treaty Limiting Nuclear Arms," *New York Times*, June 1, 1998.

Burns, John F., "Indian Scientists Confirm They Detonated a Hydrogen Bomb," *New York Times*, May 18, 1998.

Burns, John F., "Nuclear Blasts Put India's Opposition Parties in a Bind," *New York Times*, May 14, 1998.

Burns, John F., "Pakistan, Answering India, Carries Out Nuclear Tests," *New York Times*, May 29, 1998.

Burns, Tom, and G. M. Stalker, *The Management of Innovation* (Oxford, UK: Oxford University Press, 1994).

Buzan, Barry, *People, States and Fear,* 2nd ed. (Boulder, CO: Lynne Rienner Publishers, 1991).

Buzan, Barry, *Strategic Studies: Military Technology and International Relations* (London: Macmillan, 1987).

Caldwell, John, and Alexander T. Lennon, "China's Nuclear Modernization Program," *Strategic Review,* 23:4 (Fall 1995).

Cambone, Stephen A., and Patrick J. Garrity, "The Future of U.S. Nuclear Policy," *Survival,* 36:4 (Winter 1994–1995).

Cameron, Gavin, "Nuclear Terrorism: A Real Threat?" *Jane's Intelligence Review,* 8:9 (September 1996).

Carlton, David, and Carlo Schaerf (eds.), *Arms Control and Technological Innovation* (New York: Wiley, 1976).

Carlton, D., and C. Schaerf (eds.), *Perspectives on the Arms Race* (London: Macmillan, 1989).

Carter, Ashton B., "Assessing Command System Vulnerability," in Ashton B. Carter, John D. Steinbruner, and Charles A. Zraket (eds.), *Managing Nuclear Operations* (Washington, D.C.: Brookings, 1987).

Carter, Ashton B., "BMD Applications: Performance and Limitations," in Ashton B. Carter and David N. Schwarz (eds.), *Ballistic Missile Defense* (Washington, D.C.: Brookings, 1984).

Carter, Ashton B., "The Command and Control of Nuclear War," *Scientific American,* 252 (January 1985).

Carter, Ashton B., "Communications Technologies," in Ashton B. Carter, John D. Steinbruner, and Charles A. Zraket (eds.), *Managing Nuclear Operations* (Washington, D.C.: Brookings, 1987).

Carter, Ashton B., "Introduction," in Ashton B. Carter, John D. Steinbruner, and Charles A. Zraket (eds.), *Managing Nuclear Operations* (Washington, D.C.: Brookings, 1987).

Carter, Ashton B., and David N. Schwarz (eds.), *Ballistic Missile Defense* (Washington, D.C.: Brookings, 1984).

Carter, Ashton B., John D. Steinbruner, and Charles A. Zraket (eds.), *Managing Nuclear Operations* (Washington, D.C.: Brookings, 1987).

Castells, Manuel, *The Informational City: Information Technology, Economic Restructuring, and the Urban-Regional Process* (Cambridge, UK: Blackwell, 1989).

Chakravarti, Sudeep, "Restless Rage," *India Today International*, May 18, 1998.

Challenges for U.S. National Security: Nuclear Strategy Issues of the 1980s: Strategic Vulnerabilities, Command, Control, Communications, and Intelligence, Theater Nuclear Forces: A Third Report, prepared by the staff of the Carnegie Panel on U.S. Security and the Future of Arms Control (Washington, D.C.: Carnegie Endowment for International Peace, 1982).

Chanda, Nayan, "The Perils of Power," *Far Eastern Economic Review*, February 4, 1999.

Chandran, Ramesh, "U.S. Has Not Accepted India's Need for Nuclear Deterrent: Holum," *The Times of India*, December 11, 1999.

Chandran, Suba, "Integration of Defence Apparatus," report of an IPCS seminar held on January 22, 1999, available at http://www.ipcs.org/issues/articles/T/1-mdi-Suba.htm.

Chandrashekar, S., "In Defense of Nukes," *Economic Times*, May 17, 1998.

Chant, Christopher, and Ian Hogg, *The Nuclear War File* (London: Ebury Press, 1983).

Chari, P. R., "BJP's Nuclear Agenda," February 20, 1998, available at http://www.ipcs.org/issues/articles/060-ndi-chari.html.

Chari, P. R., "Civil-Military Relations in India," *Armed Forces & Society*, 4:1 (November 1977).

Chari, P. R., "Command and Control Arrangements," in *Report of the Sixth IPCS Seminar on the Implications of Nuclear Testing in South Asia*, available at http://www.ipcs.org/issues/articles/135-ndi-chari.html.

Chari, P. R., "Defence Policy Formulation: The Indian Experience," *Indian Defence Review*, 11:1 (January–March 1996).

Chari, P. R., "India: The Policy Process," in James M. Roherty (ed.), *Defense Policy Formation* (Durham, NC: Carolina Academic Press, 1980).

Chari, P. R., "India's Global Nuclear Initiative," available at http://www.ipcs.org/issues/articles/157-ndi-chari.htm.

Chari, P. R., "India's Nuclear Option: Future Directions," in P. R. Chari, Pervaiz Iqbal Cheema, and Iftekharuzzaman (eds.), *Nuclear Non-Proliferation in India and Pakistan* (New Delhi: Manohar, 1996).

Chari, P. R., "India's Slow-Motion Nuclear Deployment," *Carnegie Endowment for International Peace Proliferation Brief*, 3:26 (September 7, 2000).

Chari, P. R., *Indo-Pak Nuclear Standoff: The Role of the United States* (New Delhi: Manohar, 1995).

Chari, P. R., "Misgivings on CTBT," *Hindustan Times*, January 4, 2000.

Chari, P. R., "Needed Radical Restructuring of the Defense Apparatus," *The Hindu*, February 16, 1999.

Chari, P. R., "The Nuclear Doctrine," August 24, 1999, available at http://www.ipcs.org/issues/articles/252-ndi-chari.htm.

Chari, P. R., *Protection of Fissile Materials: The Indian Experience*, ACDIS Occasional Paper (Urbana, IL: University of Illinois, September 1998).

Chari, P. R., "Weaponisation and the CTBT," *The Hindu*, July 5, 2000.

Chari, P. R., "What Is the Future of Nuclear India?" *The Times of India*, May 17, 1998.

Chari, P. R., Pervaiz Iqbal Cheema, and Iftekharuzzaman, *Nuclear Non-Proliferation in India and Pakistan* (New Delhi: Manohar, 1996).

Chatterjee, Patralekha, "Amid Blaring Headlines, India Mum on U.S. Nuclear Report," available at http://www.msnbc.com/news/418094.asp.

Chattopadhyay, Rupak, "The Indian Air Force: Flying into the 21st Century," *Bharat Rakshak Monitor*, 3:1 (July–August 2000), available at http://www.bharat-rakshak.com/MONITOR/ISSUE3-1/rupak.html.

Chaudhuri, Pramit Pal, "A Question of Strategy," *Hindustan Times*, November 6, 2000.

Chawla, Prabhu, "Interview: Atal Bihari Vajpayee," *India Today*, May 25, 1998.

Chawla, Prabhu, and Manoj Joshi, "Sunk!" *India Today*, January 11, 1999.

Cheema, Pervaiz Iqbal, "Pakistan's Quest for Nuclear Technology," *Australian Outlook*, 34:2 (1980).

Cheema, Zafar Iqbal, "Pakistan's Nuclear Policies: Attitudes and Posture," in P. R. Chari, Pervaiz Iqbal Cheema, and Iftekharuzzaman (eds.), *Nuclear Non-Proliferation in India and Pakistan* (New Delhi: Manohar, 1996).

Cheema, Zafar Iqbal, "Pakistan's Nuclear Use Doctrine and Command and Control," in Peter R. Lavoy, Scott D. Sagan, and James J. Wirtz (eds.), *Planning the Unthinkable* (Ithaca, NY: Cornell University Press, 2000).

Chellaney, Brahma, "After the Tests: India's Options," *Survival*, 40:4 (Winter 1998).

Chellaney, Brahma, "Caution on CTBT," *Hindustan Times*, November 3, 1999.

Chellaney, Brahma, "Challenge of Nuclear Arms Control in South Asia," *Survival*, 35:3 (1993).

Chellaney, Brahma, "Expert Comment: New Nuclear Clarity with Old Waffle," *Hindustan Times*, January 3, 1999.

Chellaney, Brahma, "For India, the Big Nuclear Breakthrough Has Fizzled," *International Herald Tribune*, May 13, 1999.

Chellaney, Brahma, "How Pokhran II Has Bombed," *Asian Age*, May 25, 1999.

Chellaney, Brahma, "India Demonstrates Its Missile Prowess," *Hindustan Times*, April 12, 1999.

Chellaney, Brahma, "An Indian Critique of U.S. Export Controls," *Orbis*, 38 (1994).

Chellaney, Brahma, "India's Crucial Role," *Indian Express*, April 21, 1995.

Chellaney, Brahma, "India's Hydrogen Bomb," *Hindustan Times*, January 13, 1999.

Chellaney, Brahma, "India's Nuclear Planning, Force Structure, Doctrine and Arms-Control Posture," *Australian Journal of International Affairs*, 53:1 (1999).

Chellaney, Brahma, "India's Strategic Depth Lies Shattered," *The Pioneer*, April 14, 1998.

Chellaney, Brahma, "India's Trial by Atom," *Hindustan Times*, November 4, 1998.

Chellaney, Brahma, "India's Trial by Fire," *Hindustan Times*, October 21, 1998.

Chellaney, Brahma, "India's Wrong Signal on Fissile Cut-Off," *Indian Express*, April 22, 1995.

Chellaney, Brahma, "New Delhi's Dilemma," *Washington Quarterly*, 23:3 (Summer 2000).

Chellaney, Brahma, "A New Nuclear Dividing Line," *The Pioneer*, June 4, 1997.

Chellaney, Brahma, "Nuclear-Deterrent Posture," in Brahma Chellaney (ed.), *Securing India's Future in the New Millennium* (New Delhi: Orient Longman, 1999).

Chellaney, Brahma, "Playing with Fire," *Hindustan Times*, March 10, 1999.

Chellaney, Brahma, "The Real Battle Has Just Begun," *The Pioneer*, May 13, 1998.

Chellaney, Brahma (ed.), *Securing India's Future in the New Millennium* (New Delhi: Orient Longman, 1999).

Chellaney, Brahma, "Shoring Up Indo-Russian Ties," *The Pioneer*, July 16, 1997.

Chellaney, Brahma, "South Asia's Passage to Nuclear Power," *International Security*, 16:1 (Summer 1991).

Chellaney, Brahma, "Woolly Diplomacy," *Hindustan Times*, May 5, 1999.

Chengappa, Bidanda M., "Playing Chinese Checkers," *Indian Express*, May 5, 1998.

Chengappa, Raj, "The Bomb Makers," *India Today International*, June 22, 1998.

Chengappa, Raj, "Boom for Boom," *India Today International*, April 26, 1999.

Chengappa, Raj, "Is India's H-Bomb a Dud?" *India Today International*, October 12, 1998.

Chengappa, Raj, "Moon Mission," *India Today International*, July 3, 2000.

Chengappa, Raj, "Pakistan Threatened India with Nuclear Attack During Kargil War: Army Chief," *The Newspaper Today*, January 12, 2001.

Chengappa, Raj, "Playing the Spoiler," *India Today*, September 15, 1996.

Chengappa, Raj, *Weapons of Peace* (New Delhi: HarperCollins Publishers, 2000).

Chengappa, Raj, "Worrying over Broken Arrows," *India Today International*, July 13, 1998.

Chengappa, Raj, and Manoj Joshi, "Future Fire," *India Today*, May 25, 1998.

Chenoy, Kamal Mitra, "India Should Beat the Nuclear Club, Not Join It," *Asian Age*, July 23, 1998.

Chidambaram R., and V. Ashok, "Embargo Regimes and Impact," in Deepa Ollapally and S. Rajagopal (eds.), *Nuclear Cooperation: Challenges and Prospects* (Bangalore, India: National Institute of Advanced Studies, 1997).

Childress, James F., "Just-War Criteria," in Thomas A. Shannon, *War or Peace? The Search for New Answers* (New York: Orbis Books, 1980).

China and Weapons of Mass Destruction: Implications for the United States, Conference Report (Washington, D.C.: National Intelligence Council, November 5, 1999).

"China's Missile Exports and Assistance to Pakistan," Center for Nonproliferation Studies, Monterey, CA, available at http://cns. miis.edu/research/india/china/mpakpos.htm.

"China's Missile Exports and Assistance to Pakistan—Statements and Developments," Center for Nonproliferation Studies, Monterey, CA, available at http://cns.miis.edu/research/india/china/ mpakchr.htm.

"China's Missile Exports and Assistance to South Asia," Center for Nonproliferation Studies, Monterey, CA, available at http://cns. miis.edu/research/india/china/msaspos.htm.

"China's Nuclear Exports and Assistance to Pakistan," Center for Nonproliferation Studies, Monterey, CA, available at http://cns. miis.edu/research/india/china/npakpos.htm.

"China's Nuclear Exports and Assistance to Pakistan—Statements and Developments," Center for Nonproliferation Studies, Monterey, CA, available at http://cns.miis.edu/research/india/china/ npakchr.htm.

"China's Nuclear Exports and Assistance to South Asia," Center for Nonproliferation Studies, Monterey, CA, available at http://cns. miis.edu/research/india/china/nsaspos.htm.

Choudhuri, Hirak, "Nuclear-Equipped Jaguars for IAF?" *The Statesman*, February 19, 1999.

Chow, Brian G., Richard H. Speier, and Gregory S. Jones, *The Proposed Fissile-Material Production Cut-Off: Next Steps*, MR-586-OSD (Santa Monica: RAND, 1995).

Chowdhury, Srinjoy, "Army Moots Nuclear Triad," *The Statesman*, April 6, 1999.

Chowdhury, Srinjoy, "Communication Network to Link Armed Forces with Ministries," *The Statesman*, August 11, 2000.

"Chronology of Indian Missile Development," Center for Nonproliferation Studies, Monterey, CA, available at http://cns.miis.edu/ india/indiachron2.html.

Cimbala, Stephen J., and Sidney R. Waldman (eds.), *Controlling and Ending Conflict* (New York: Greenwood Press, 1992).

Cirincione, Joseph, "Foreword," in Ming Zhang (ed.), *China's Changing Nuclear Posture* (Washington, D.C.: Carnegie Endowment for International Peace, 1999).

Cirincione, Joseph, "Viewpoint," *Aviation Week & Space Technology*, May 18, 1998.

Cochran, Thomas B., William M. Arkin, and Milton M. Hoenig, *Soviet Nuclear Weapons, Nuclear Weapons Databook*, Vol. 4 (Cambridge, MA: Ballinger Publishing Company, 1989).

Cochran, Thomas B., William M. Arkin, and Milton M. Hoenig, *U.S. Nuclear Forces and Capabilities, Nuclear Weapons Databook*, Vol. 1 (Cambridge, MA: Ballinger Publishing Company,1984).

Cochran, Thomas B., and Christopher E. Paine, *The Amount of Plutonium and Highly Enriched Uranium Needed for Pure Fission Nuclear Weapons* (Washington, D.C.: Natural Resources Defense Council, 1995).

Cohen, Stephen P., *The Indian Army: Its Contribution to the Development of a Nation* (Berkeley, CA: University of California Press, 1971).

Cohen, Stephen P., "Nuclear Deterrence in South Asia: Strategic Considerations Reconsidered," report of the IPCS seminar held at the India International Centre, New Delhi, January 4, 1999, available at http://www.ipcs.org/issues/articles/166-ndi-cohen.htm.

Cohen, Stephen P. (ed.), *Nuclear Proliferation in South Asia* (Boulder, CO: Westview Press, 1991).

Cohen, Stephen P., *The Pakistan Army, 1998 Edition* (Karachi, Pakistan: Oxford University Press, 1998).

Cohen, Stephen P., *Perception, Influence, and Weapons Proliferation in South Asia*, Report No. 1722-920184 (Washington, D.C.: Bureau of Intelligence and Research, U.S. Department of State, August 20, 1979).

Cohen, Stephen P., "A Way Out of the South Asia Arms Race," *Washington Post*, September 28, 1992.

Cole, Bernard D., and Paul H.B. Godwin, "Advanced Military Technology and the PLA: Priorities and Capabilities for the 21st Century," in Larry M. Wortzel (ed.), *The Chinese Armed Forces in the 21st Century* (Carlisle Barracks, PA: Strategic Studies Institute, 1999).

Cole, Paul M., *Sweden Without the Bomb: The Conduct of a Nuclear-Capable Nation Without Nuclear Weapons*, MR-460 (Santa Monica: RAND, 1994).

Collins, John M., *Imbalance of Power* (San Rafael, CA: Presidio Press, 1978).

Collins, John M., *U.S.-Soviet Military Balance: Concepts and Capabilities, 1960–1980* (New York: Aviation Week, 1980).

Collins, John M., *U.S./Soviet Military Balance Statistical Trends, 1970–1981* (Washington, D.C.: Congressional Research Service, Library of Congress, 1982).

Collins, John M., *U.S./Soviet Military Balance Statistical Trends, 1980–1989* (Washington, D.C.: Congressional Research Service, Library of Congress, 1990).

"Cong Parroting BJP on Minimum Nuclear Deterrent," *The Pioneer*, March 23, 2000.

"Congress Flays Nuclear Doctrine," *Asian Age*, August 19, 1999.

"Congress Not for CTBT Now," *Indian Express*, May 10, 1999.

Cook, Nick, "Re-arming the Dragon: The New People's Liberation Army Air Force," *Interavia*, 51:604 (November 1996).

Cooper, Kenneth J., "Indian Minister Warns Pakistan," *Washington Post*, May 19, 1998.

Cooper, Kenneth J., "Nuclear Dilemmas—India," *Washington Post*, May 25, 1998.

Cordesman, Anthony H., *Deterrence in the 1980s: Part I, American Strategic Forces and Extended Deterrence*, Adelphi Paper No. 175 (London: IISS, 1982).

Cortright, David, and Amitabh Mattoo, "Elite Public Opinion and Nuclear Weapons Policy in India," *Asian Survey*, 36:6 (June 1996).

Cosper, Amy C., "VSATs Find Their Voice," *Global Telephony*, 5:5 (September 1997).

Cotter, Donald, "Peacetime Operations: Safety and Security," in Ashton B. Carter, John D. Steinbruner, and Charles A. Zraket. (eds.), *Managing Nuclear Operations* (Washington, D.C.: Brookings, 1987).

"Country Briefing: People's Republic of China," *Jane's Defence Weekly*, December 16, 1998.

Covault, Craig, "Tibetan Air Operations—Part 1," *Aviation Week & Space Technology*, October 12, 1987.

Covault, Craig, "Tibetan Air Operations—Part 2, *Aviation Week & Space Technology*, October 19, 1987.

Crawford, Natalie W., and Chung-In Moon (eds.), *Emerging Threats, Force Structures, and the Role of Air Power in Korea*, CF-152-AF (Santa Monica: RAND, 2000).

Croft, Stuart, and Phil Williams, "The United Kingdom," in Regina Cowen Karp (ed.), *Security with Nuclear Weapons?* (Oxford, UK: Oxford University Press, 1991).

Crossette, Barbara, "Why India Thinks Atomic Equation Has Changed," *New York Times*, June 15, 1998.

Dadant, Philip M., *Why Go Deep Underground?* P-1675 (Santa Monica: RAND, 1959).

Dalton, Toby F., "Towards Nuclear Rollback in South Asia," *Current History*, 97:623 (December 1998).

Daniel, Donald C., *Anti-Submarine Warfare and Superpower Strategic Stability* (Urbana, IL: University of Illinois Press, 1986).

Das, Premvir, "A Simple Solution to CTBT Problem," *The Pioneer*, February 12, 2000.

"Dassault Mirage 2000," in Paul Jackson (ed.), *Jane's All the World's Aircraft, 1998–99* (Coulsdon, UK: Jane's Information Group Ltd., 1998).

Davis, Lynn Etheridge, *Limited Nuclear Options*, Adelphi Paper No. 121 (London: IISS, 1975–1976).

"A Decade of Economic Reforms: Political Discord and the Second Stage," *Doing Business in India*, 2:1 and 2:2 (Fall 1999).

"Declare Our Nuclear Capability to Deter Strike," *Asian Age*, December 26, 1998.

"Defence Intelligence Agency on the Anvil," *The Hindu*, October 19, 2000.

"Defence Research & Development Organisation," in R. K. Jasbir Singh (ed.), *Indian Defence Yearbook, 1997–98* (Dehra Dun, India: Natraj Publishers, 1997).

"Defending India's Frontiers," *Air International*, 33:6 (December 1987).

"Democracy of Science," *The Times of India*, January 7, 2000.

Department of Defense, *Dictionary of Military and Associated Terms* (Washington, D.C.: USGPO, 1984).

Department of Defense, *Soviet Military Power: An Assessment of the Threat, 1988*, 7th ed. (Washington, D.C.: USGPO,1988).

"Deterrence to Be Evaluated Time to Time: Govt," *Economic Times*, December 17, 1998.

Dhume, Sadanand, "Arming India," *Far Eastern Economic Review*, October 12, 2000.

Disarmament: India's Initiatives (New Delhi: Ministry of External Affairs, Government of India, 1988).

"Disarming Argument," *The Times of India*, May 11, 2000.

Dixit, Aabha, "Flying Tackle: Pakistan's Missile Program Now Represents a Serious Threat to India," *The Telegraph*, September 2, 1996.

Dixit, Aabha, "How Real Is the Ghauri Scare?" *The Pioneer*, January 24, 1998.

Dixit, J. N., "Beijing on Our Mind," *Hindustan Times*, August 2, 2000.

Dixit, J. N., "China-U.S. Equations," *The Hindu*, July 10, 1998.

Dixit, J. N., *India: Indian National Security Council Discussed*, FBIS-NES-98-147, May 27, 1998.

Dixit, J. N., "The Indian Dilemma," *Indian Express*, January 9, 1996.

Dixit, J. N., "Security Alert," *Hindustan Times*, December 7, 2000.

Dixit, J. N., "Stand Up or Put Up," *Indian Express*, April 16, 1996.

Dixit, Sharad, "IAF, the Pivot of Nuclear Power," *The Pioneer*, October 25, 1999.

Dixit, Sharad, "A Nuclear Strategy for India," *The Pioneer*, September 3, 1998.

Donald, David, and Jon Lake (eds.), *Encyclopedia of World Military Aircraft*, Vols. I and II (Westport, CT: AIRtime Publishers, 1994).

Donnelly, John, "Official: Pakistan's Nuclear Warheads Outpace India's," *Defense Week*, July 27, 1998.

"Don't Justify Nuclear Plan, Urges China," *Hindustan Times*, May 19, 1999.

"Draft Report of [the] National Security Advisory Board on Indian Nuclear Doctrine," *India News*, October 1, 1999.

Drell, Sidney (Chair), John Cornwall, Freeman Dyson, Douglas Eardley, Richard Garwin, David Hammer, John Kammerdiener, Robert LeLevier, Robert Peurifoy, John Richter, Marshall Rosenbluth, Seymour Sack, Jeremiah Sullivan, and Fredrik Zachariasen, "Nuclear Testing: Summary and Conclusions," *JASON Nuclear Testing Study*, JSR-95-320, August 3, 1995, available at http://www.fas.org/rlg/jsr-95-320.htm.

Drucquer, Seth, *Civil Defence in India* (Bombay: Oxford University Press, 1942).

Dubey, Muchkund, "The World Nuclear Order and India," *The Hindu*, May 27, 1998.

Dunn, Lewis A., *Controlling the Bomb: Nuclear Proliferation in the 1980s* (New Haven, CT: Yale University Press, 1982).

Dunn, Lewis A., and William H. Overholt, "The Next Phase in Nuclear Proliferation Research," in William H. Overholt (ed.), *Asia's Nuclear Future* (Boulder, CO: Westview Press, 1977).

Dutt, D. Som, *The Defense of India's Northern Borders*, Adelphi Paper No. 25 (London: IISS, 1966).

Dutt, D. Som, *India and the Bomb*, Adelphi Paper No. 30 (London: IISS, 1966).

Dutt, J. K., "The Army in the Nuclear Age," *The Statesman*, August 10, 1998.

Dutta, Bhaskar, "Beggars with the Bomb," *The Telegraph*, May 26, 1998.

Dutta, Rakesh, "Civil Defence Against Nuclear Attack," *Indian Defence Review*, 13:4 (October–December 1998).

"Early Solution to Nuclear Issues Will Help: Talbott," *The Hindu*, January 14, 2000.

Economy, Elizabeth, and Michel Oksenberg (eds.), *China Joins the World* (New York: Council on Foreign Relations Press, 1999).

Eden, Lynn, and Steven E. Miller (eds.), *Nuclear Arguments* (Ithaca, NY: Cornell University Press, 1989).

Eldridge, Francis R., *Protection of Communications and Electronic Systems*, P-1657 (Santa Monica: RAND, 1959).

Emerson, Tony, "Asia's Ground Zero," *Newsweek International Edition*, April 22, 1996.

Enthoven, Alain, and K. Wayne Smith, *How Much Is Enough? Shaping the Defense Program, 1961–69* (New York: Harper & Row, 1971).

"Epilogue to the 1998 Edition," in Stephen P. Cohen, *The Pakistan Army, 1998 Edition* (Karachi, Pakistan: Oxford University Press, 1998).

Erlanger, Steven, "U.S. Wary of Punishing China for Missile Help to Pakistan," *New York Times*, August 27, 1996.

Evangelista, Matthew, *Innovation and the Arms Race* (Ithaca, NY: Cornell University Press, 1988).

Evans, Peter, "Indian Informatics in the 1980s: The Changing Character of State Involvement," *World Development*, 20:1 (1992).

Evernden, Jack F., "Estimation of Yields of Underground Explosion with Emphasis on Recent Indian and Pakistani Explosions," *Physics and Society*, 27:4 (October 1998).

Fairall, Jon, "India's Global Aims," *Space*, January 1, 1995.

Farooq, Umer, "Pakistan Needs up to 70 Nuclear Warheads," *Jane's Defence Weekly*, June 10, 1998.

Farooq, Umer, "Pakistan Ready to Arm Ghauri with Warheads," *Jane's Defence Weekly*, June 3, 1998.

Farooq, Umer, "Pakistan Warned India of 'Massive' Retaliation," *Jane's Defence Weekly*, July 15, 1998.

Faruqui, Ahmad, "Failure in Command: Lessons from Pakistan's Indian Wars," *Defense Analysis*, 17:1 (2001).

Faruqui, Ahmad, "Pakistan's Strategic Myopia," *RUSI Journal*, 145:2 (April 2000).

Fearon, James, *Threats to Use Force: The Role of Costly Signals in International Crises*, unpublished doctoral dissertation, University of California, Berkeley, 1992.

Feaver, Peter D., "Command and Control in Emerging Nuclear Nations," *International Security*, 17:3 (Winter 1992–1993).

Feaver, Peter D., *Guarding the Guardians* (Ithaca, NY: Cornell University Press, 1992).

Federation of American Scientists, "Article-by-Article Analysis of the Comprehensive Nuclear Test Ban Treaty," available at http://www.fas.org/nuke/control/ctbt/text/artbyart/art01.htm.

Federation of American Scientists, "A View of Non-NPT Nuclear States from Space: Nuclear and Missile Facility Satellite Images and Their Implications for the NPT," available at http://www.fas.org/eye/3nws.htm.

Federation of American Scientists' websites on Pakistan and China at http://www.fas.org/spp/guide/pakistan/index.html and http://www.fas.org/spp/guide/china/index.html.

Feiveson, Harold, "Proliferation Resistant Nuclear Fuel Cycle," *Annual Review of Energy*, 3 (1978).

Feld, B. T., T. Greenwood, G. W. Rathjens, and S. Weinberg, *Impact of New Technologies on the Arms Race* (Cambridge, MA: MIT Press, 1971).

"Fernandes Sees No Threat from Ghauri," *The Hindu*, April 10, 1998.

Filkins, Dexter, "India Missile Test Raises Nuclear Bar for Rival," *Los Angeles Times*, April 12, 1999.

"Fissile Material: India Against Moratorium Now," *The Hindu*, April 2, 1999.

FitzGerald, Mary C., "Russia's New Military Doctrine," *Naval War College Review*, 46:2 (Spring 1993).

Foss, Christopher F., " 'Grumble' on Land—SA-10," *Jane's Intelligence Review*, 3:5 (May 1991).

Foss, Christopher F., "Update on SA-10b 'Grumble' Surface-to-Air Missile," *Jane's Intelligence Review*, 3:12 (December 1991).

Foster, Deborah J., "The Indian Space Program," in John C. Baker, Kevin M. O'Connell, and Ray A. Williamson (eds.), *Commercial Observation Satellites: At the Leading Edge of Global Transparency*, MR-1229 (Santa Monica: RAND/ASPRS, 2001).

Frankel, Francine (ed.), *Bridging the Nonproliferation Divide* (Lanham, MD: University Press of America, 1995).

Frazier, Mark W., "China-India Relations Since Pokhran-II: Assessing Sources of Conflict and Cooperation," *AccessAsia Review*, 3:2 (July 2000).

Freedman, Lawrence, "British Nuclear Targeting," in Desmond Ball and Jeffrey Richelson (eds.), *Strategic Nuclear Targeting* (Ithaca, NY: Cornell University Press, 1986).

Freedman, Lawrence, *The Evolution of Nuclear Strategy* (New York: St. Martin's Press, 1981).

"From Su-27 to Su-37: The Plane with Many Masks," *Vayu 2000 Aerospace Review*, III/1997.

From Surprise to Reckoning: The Kargil Review Committee Report (New Delhi: Sage Publications, 2000).

"The Future of Nuclear Weapons: A U.S.-India Dialogue," in *Proceedings of the Center for the Advanced Study of India, University of Pennsylvania,* held at the Wharton Sinkler Conference Center,

May 5–8, 1997, available at http://www.sas.upenn.edu/casi/nuclear97.html.

Gaddis, John Lewis, "Nuclear Weapons, the End of the Cold War, and the Future of the International System," in Patrick Garrity and Steven A. Maaranen (eds.), *Nuclear Weapons in a Changing World* (New York: Plenum Press, 1992).

"Gallery of U.S. Nuclear Tests," available at http://www.fas.org/nuke/hew/Usa/Tests/index.html.

Gandhi, Indira, *Statements on Foreign Policy, January–April 1983* (New Delhi: Government of India, Ministry of External Affairs, 1983).

Ganguly, Sumit, "India's Pathway to Pokhran II: The Prospects and Sources of New Delhi's Nuclear Weapons Program," *International Security*, 23:4 (Spring 1999).

Ganguly, Sumit, "Indo-Pakistani Nuclear Issues and the Stability/Instability Paradox," *Studies in Conflict & Terrorism*, 18:4 (1995).

Ganguly, Sumit, *The Origins of War in South Asia: The Indo-Pakistani Conflicts Since 1947*, 2nd ed. (Boulder, CO: Westview Press, 1994).

Ganguly, Sumit, "The Sino-Indian Border Talks, 1981–1989: A View from New Delhi," *Asian Survey*, 29:12 (December 1989).

Ganguly, Sumit, "Why India Joined the Nuclear Club," *Bulletin of the Atomic Scientists*, 39:4 (April 1983).

Garrett, Banning N., and Bonnie S. Glaser, *War and Peace: The Views from Moscow and Beijing*, Policy Paper in International Affairs No. 20 (Berkeley, CA: Institute of International Studies, University of California, 1984).

Garrity, Patrick, and Steven A. Maaranen (eds.), *Nuclear Weapons in a Changing World* (New York: Plenum Press, 1992).

Garwin, Richard L., "Effectiveness of Proposed National Missile Defense Against ICBMs from North Korea," March 17, 1999, available at http://www.fas.org/rlg/990317-nmd.htm.

Garwin, Richard L., "The Future of Nuclear Weapons Without Nuclear Testing," *Arms Control Today*, 27:8 (November–December 1997).

Garwin, Richard L., "Maintaining Nuclear Weapons Safe and Reliable Under a CTBT: What Types of Weapons Can Be Developed Without Nuclear Explosions?" available at http://www.fas.org/rlg/000531-ctbt.htm.

Garwin, Richard L., "Reactor-Grade Plutonium Can Be Used to Make Powerful and Reliable Nuclear Weapons: Separated Plutonium in the Fuel Cycle Must Be Protected as If It Were Nuclear Weapons," available at http://www.fas.org/rlg/980826-pu.htm.

Garwin, Richard L., "Technical Aspects of Ballistic Missile Defense," *APS Forum on Physics and Society*, 28:3 (July 1999).

Gauhar, Altaf, "Four Wars, One Assumption," *The Nation*, September 5, 1999.

Gause, Ken, "PLAAF (People's Liberation Army Air Force) Continues to Modernise at a Slow yet Steady Pace," *Jane's Intelligence Review*, 10:6 (June 1998).

Gelber, Harry, *Nuclear Weapons and Chinese Policy*, Adelphi Paper No. 99 (London: IISS, 1973).

George, Nirmala, "India Now Within CTBT Rules: Chidambaram," *Indian Express*, April 22, 1999.

George, Nirmala, "No More N-Tests Needed: AEC," *Indian Express*, February 4, 1999.

Gerardi, Greg J., "India's 333rd Prithvi Missile Group," *Jane's Intelligence Review*, 7:8 (August 1995).

Gertz, Bill, "China Summit Missile Pact Unlikely; 'Incremental Progress' Not Ruled Out," *Washington Times*, June 21, 1998.

Gertz, Bill, "China Targets Nukes at U.S.," *Washington Times*, May 1, 1998.

Gertz, Bill, "Crowding In on the High Ground," *Air Force Magazine*, April 1997.

Gertz, Bill, "New Chinese Missiles Target All of East Asia," *Washington Times*, June 10, 1997.

Gertz, Bill, "Scare Preceded Pakistan Nuke Test: Expected Strike by India, Israel," *Washington Times*, June 1, 1998.

Gertz, Bill, and Ernest Blazar, "Pakistan May Have Nuclear Tips for Rockets: New Test Blasts, Missile Firings Are Imminent," *Washington Times*, May 30, 1998.

Ghose, Arundhati, "Negotiating the CTBT: India's Security Concerns and Nuclear Disarmament," *Journal of International Affairs*, 51:1 (Summer 1997).

Ghosh, Amitav, "A Reporter at Large: Countdown," *The New Yorker*, October 26–November 2, 1998.

Ghosh, Amiya Kumar, *India's Defence Budget and Expenditure Management in a Wider Context* (New Delhi: Lancer Publishers, 1996).

Ghosh, Bishwanath, "N-Tests Possible After CTBT: PM," *Asian Age*, August 23, 1998.

Ghosh, Jayati, "The Bomb and the Economy," *Frontline*, May 8–21, 1999.

Ghosh, Partha S., "Bomb, Science and the State," *The Hindu*, June 9, 1998.

Giles, Gregory F., "Safeguarding the Undeclared Nuclear Arsenals," *Washington Quarterly*, 16:2 (Spring 1993).

Giles, Gregory F., and James E. Doyle, "Indian and Pakistani Views on Nuclear Deterrence," *Comparative Strategy*, 15:2 (1996).

Gill, Bates, and James Mulvenon, "The Chinese Strategic Rocket Forces: Transition to Credible Deterrence," in *China and Weapons of Mass Destruction: Implications for the United States, Conference Report* (Washington, D.C.: National Intelligence Council, November 5, 1999).

Gilpin, Robert, *War and Change in International Politics* (Cambridge, UK: Cambridge University Press, 1981).

"Give Up N-Programme, China Tells India," *The Hindu*, March 8, 2000.

Glaser, Charles L., *Analyzing Strategic Nuclear Policy* (Princeton, NJ: Princeton University Press, 1990).

Glaser, Charles L., "Disputes over the U.S. Military Requirements of Nuclear Deterrence," in Charles L. Glaser (ed.), *Analyzing Strategic Nuclear Policy* (Princeton, NJ: Princeton University Press, 1990).

Goldblat, Jozef, and David Cox (eds.), *Nuclear Weapons Tests: Prohibition or Limitation?* (Oxford, UK: Oxford University Press, 1998).

Goldstein, Avery, *Deterrence and Security in the 21st Century* (Stanford, CA: Stanford University Press, 2000).

Goldstein, Avery S., "Robust and Affordable Security: Some Lessons from the Second-Ranking Powers During the Cold War," *Journal of Strategic Studies*, 15:4 (December 1992).

Goldstein, Avery, "Scared Senseless? The South Asian Nuclear Tests," *E-Notes* (Philadelphia: Foreign Policy Research Institute), June 5, 1998.

Gole, C. V., "The Prithvi—Facts and Fancies," *Vayu Aerospace Review*, IV/1994.

Goodman, Glenn W., Jr., "Long-Distance Communications," *Armed Forces Journal International*, 137:8 (March 2000).

Gopalakrishnan, A., "How Credible Is Our Deterrence?" *The Hindu*, November 18, 1998.

Gordon, Sandy, "Can the South Asian Nuclear Equation Balance?" *Asia-Pacific Defense Reporter*, 24:6 (October–November 1998).

Gordon, Sandy, "Capping South Asia's Nuclear Weapons Programs: A Window of Opportunity?" *Asian Survey*, 34:7 (July 1994).

Gordon, Sandy, *India's Rise to Power* (New York: St. Martin's Press, 1995).

Gorwitz, Mark, "The Indian Strategic Nuclear Submarine Project: An Open Literature Analysis," December 1996, available at http://www.fas.org/nuke/guide/india/sub/ssn/index.html.

Gottfried, Kurt, and Bruce Blair (eds.), *Crisis Stability and Nuclear War* (Oxford, UK: Oxford University Press, 1988).

Government of India, *Indian Telecommunications,* Report by the Telecom Commission (New Delhi: Ministry of Commerce, 1994).

Government of India, *The Missile Development Programme, Backgrounder* (New Delhi: Public Information Bureau [Defence Wing]), June 25, 1992.

"Govt. to Purchase Tanker Planes," *The Hindu,* April 26, 2000.

"Govt. Will Not Bow to Pressure on N-Arms," *The Hindu,* July 24, 1998.

Gray, Colin, "Nuclear Strategy: The Case for a Theory of Victory," *International Security,* 4:1 (Summer 1979).

Gray, Colin, "Strategic Defense, Deterrence, and the Prospects for Peace," *Ethics,* 95:3 (April 1985).

Greenwood, Ted, Harold A. Feiveson, and Theodore B. Taylor, *Nuclear Proliferation: Motivations, Capabilities, Strategies for Control* (New York: McGraw-Hill, 1977).

Gregory, Shaun, *The Hidden Cost of Deterrence* (London: Brassey's, 1990).

Grimmett, Jeanne J., "Nuclear Sanctions: Section 102(b) of the Arms Export Control Act and Its Application to India and Pakistan," *CRS Report for Congress* (Washington, D.C.: Library of Congress, updated October 30, 1998).

Grover, V. K., "Nuclear Bluff," *The Pioneer,* February 12, 2000.

"Growing Pains," *Aviation Week & Space Technology,* October 13, 1997.

Guha, Ramachandra, "And Now, the Test of Sanity," *The Telegraph,* June 8, 1998.

Gunston, Bill, and Mike Spick, *Modern Air Combat* (New York: Crescent Books, 1983).

Gupta, Amit, "Fire in the Sky: The Indian Missile Program," *Defense and Diplomacy*, 8:10 (October 1990).

Gupta, Amit, "South Asian Nuclear Choices," *Armed Forces Journal International*, 136:2 (September 1998).

Gupta, Narendra, "Detonations Don't Make Deterrence," *Indian Express*, May 22, 1998.

Gupta, Narendra, "Nuclear Missiles in Tibet," *The Times of India*, March 24, 1988.

Gupta, S., and W.P.S. Sidhu, "The End Game Option," *India Today*, April 30, 1993.

Gupta, Shekhar, *India Redefines Its Role*, Adelphi Paper No. 293 (London: IISS, 1995).

Gupta, Shekhar, "Road to Resurgence," *Indian Express*, May 12, 1998.

Gupta, Shishir, "National Intelligence Board Mooted," *Hindustan Times*, October 1, 2000.

Gupta, Shishir, "Plan to Upgrade IAF, Navy, Intelligence Chiefs' Posts," *Hindustan Times*, October 19, 2000.

Gupta, Sisir, "The Indian Dilemma," in Alastair Buchan (ed.), *A World of Nuclear Powers?* (Englewood Cliffs, NJ: Prentice-Hall, 1966).

Gupta, Vipin, "Sensing the Threat—Remote Monitoring Technologics," in Stephen P. Cohen (ed.), *Nuclear Proliferation in South Asia* (Boulder, CO: Westview Press, 1991).

Haass, Richard N., and Gideon Rose, "Facing the Nuclear Facts in India and Pakistan," *Washington Post*, January 5, 1997.

Hagerty, Devin T., *The Consequences of Nuclear Proliferation: Lessons from South Asia* (Cambridge, MA: MIT Press, 1998).

Hagerty, Devin T., "The Power of Suggestion: Opaque Proliferation, Existential Deterrence, and the South Asian Nuclear Arms Competition," *Security Studies*, 2:3/4 (Spring–Summer 1993).

Haider, Ejaz, "No-First-Use vs. No-War-Pact, or Both?" *Friday Times*, October 20–26, 2000.

Haksar, A.N.D., "Parallel Seen Between Kosovo Crisis and Kashmir," *India Abroad*, May 21, 1999.

Hammer, J. G., C. A. Sandoval, and A. Laupa, *Installation Hardening Concepts for Manned Bomber Systems*, RM-3239-PR (Santa Monica: RAND, 1962).

Hannay, N. Bruce, and Robert E. McGinn, "The Anatomy of Modern Technology: Prolegomenon to an Improved Public Policy for the Social Management of Technology," *Daedalus*, 109:1 (Winter 1980).

Hansen, Chuck (ed.), *The Swords of Armageddon*, Vols. 1–8 (Sunnyvale, CA: Chukelea Publications, 1995).

Harrison, Selig S., "Cut a Regional Deal," *Foreign Policy*, 62 (Spring 1986).

Harrison, Selig S., "The United States and South Asia: Trapped by the Past?" *Current History*, 96:614 (December 1997).

Hart, David, *Nuclear Power in India* (Boston: G. Allen & Unwin, 1983).

Hashmi, Faraz, "Mass-Scale Production of Ghauri Begins," *Dawn*, June 1, 1998.

Heating, Ventilation, and Air Conditioning of Hardened Installations, Technical Manual, TM 5-855-4 (Washington, D.C.: Department of the Army, November 1986).

Heisbourg, François, "The Prospects for Nuclear Stability Between India and Pakistan," *Survival*, 40:4 (1998–1999).

Heppenheimer, T. A., *Anti-Submarine Warfare: The Threat, the Strategy, the Solution* (Arlington, VA: Pasha Publications, 1989).

Herken, Gregg, *The Winning Weapon: The Atomic Bomb in the Cold War, 1945–1950* (New York: Vintage Books, 1981).

Hersh, Seymour M., "On the Nuclear Edge," *The New Yorker*, March 29, 1993.

Hersh, Seymour M., *The Samson Option: Israel's Nuclear Arsenal and American Foreign Policy* (New York: Random House, 1991).

Heuser, Beatrice, "Warsaw Pact Military Doctrines in the 1970's and 1980's: Findings in the East German Archives," *Comparative Strategy*, 12:4 (1993).

Hibbs, Mark, "Because H-Bomb Fuel Didn't Burn, Iyengar Pleads for Second Test," *Nucleonics Week*, June 1, 2000.

Hibbs, Mark, "India May Test Again Because H-Bomb Failed, U.S. Believes," *Nucleonics Week*, November 26, 1998.

Hibbs, Mark, "Indian Pu Production Overstated, No Pit Production, Iyengar Says," *Nucleonics Week*, April 9, 1992.

Hodgson, William A., "Nuclear Certification Program," *Combat Edge*, 4:4 (September 1995).

Hodgson, William A., "Nuclear Weapons Personnel Reliability Program," *Combat Edge*, 4:1 (June 1995).

Hogendoorn, E. J., "A Chemical Weapons Atlas," *Bulletin of the Atomic Scientists*, 53:5 (September 1997).

Hollins, H. B., Averill L. Powers, and Mark Sommer, *The Conquest of War: Alternative Strategies for Global Security* (Boulder, CO: Westview Press, 1989).

Holum, John, speech to the DSWA International Conference on Controlling Arms, Philadelphia, Pennsylvania, June 10, 1998, available at http://www.acda.gov/speeches/holum/dswahol.htm.

Hopkins, John C., and Weixing Hu (eds.), *Strategic Views from the Second Tier: The Nuclear Weapons Policies of France, Britain, and China* (New Brunswick, NJ: Transaction Publishers, 1995).

Hughes, Wayne P., Jr., *Fleet Tactics: Theory and Practice* (Annapolis, MD: U.S. Naval Institute Press, 1986).

Hunter, Thomas C., Jr., "India: Set for Wireless," *Cellular and Mobile International*, January 1, 1997.

"IAF Draws Up Nuclear Strategy," *The Times of India*, October 8, 2000.

"IAF Jaguars to Get New Mission Computers," *Defence Systems Daily*, August 2, 2000.

"IAF Suggests Nuclear Air Command," *Hindustan Times*, November 28, 2000.

"ICBMs Any Day, Says Kalam," *Hindustan Times*, September 18, 2000.

Iklé, Fred Charles, "The Second Coming of the Nuclear Age," *Foreign Affairs* 75:1 (January–February 1996).

"Imaging Capability," *Aviation Week & Space Technology*, November 22, 1999.

"In Arms Way," *The Telegraph*, May 28, 1998.

"India," in David Baker (ed.), *Jane's Space Directory, 1999–2000* (Coulsdon, UK: Jane's Information Group Ltd., 1999).

"India Aborted 6th N-Test: Mishra," *The Pioneer*, October 4, 1999.

India and Disarmament: An Anthology of Selected Writings and Speeches (New Delhi: Ministry of External Affairs, Government of India, 1988).

"India and the Nuclear Question: An Interview with General K. Sundarji, PVSM (Retd)," *Trishul*, 7:2 (1994).

India: Article Views Posture on CWC, Real Case, FBIS-TAC-97-189, July 8, 1997.

"India Asks U.S. to Give Up Missile Testing," *The Hindu*, July 4, 2000.

India: BJP Demands "Two Nuclear Tests" to Develop Warheads, FBIS-NES-96-155, August 9, 1996.

"India Can Make 200 Kilotons of Nuke Weapons," *Hindustan Times,* October 31, 2000.

"India Can Produce N-Bomb of 220 Kiloton: Chidambaram," *The Times of India,* May 23, 1998.

"India Can Still Conduct N-Tests, Says Jaswant," *Indian Express,* November 25, 2000.

"India: Chemical Weapons," available at http://www.fas.org/nuke/guide/india/cw/.

"India–China–Pakistan Missile Ranges," in W.P.S. Sidhu, *Enhancing Indo-U.S. Strategic Cooperation,* Adelphi Paper No. 313 (Oxford, UK: Oxford University Press/IISS, 1997).

"India: The Commercial and Regulatory Environment," *Asia Pacific Telecommunications,* March 1, 1997.

India: Defense Experts Differ on Nuclear Deterrence, FBIS-NES-98-167, June 16, 1998.

India: Delhi: NSC Sets Up Missions for Strategic Defence Review, FBIS-TAC-99-020, January 20, 1999.

"India Drafts New N-Command, Control System," *Hindustan Times,* January 12, 2000.

India: DRDO Says 6–8 Tests Needed to Perfect Agni Missile, FBIS-NES-96-156, August 12, 1996.

India—Editorial: Pakistan's N-Tests "Pinpricks," FBIS-NES-98-152, June 1, 1998.

"India Evolves Nuclear Doctrine," *The Times of India,* August 5, 1998.

"India Eyes $3.75 Billion Nuclear Command Plan," *Defense News,* January 17, 2000.

India—Fixed Network: Voice and Data Services (Bucketty, Australia: Paul Budde Communication, 2000).

"India: Fixed Wireless Communications," *Tradeport,* available at http://www.tradeport.org/ts/countries/india/isa/isar0037.html.

"India, France to Expand Defence Co-operation," *Jane's Defence Weekly*, January 20, 1999.

India: Gujral Says Indians Cannot Give Up Nuclear Option, FBIS-TAC-97-002, December 2, 1996.

India: Indian Air Chief: War Success to Depend on Satellites, FBIS-NES-98-281, October 8, 1998.

India: Indian Army Trains for N-Contingencies, FBIS-TAC-98-194, July 13, 1998.

India: Indian Article Views Chinese Threat, FBIS-NES-98-131, May 10, 1998.

India: Indian Nuclear Tests Planned Since 1995, FBIS-NES-98-138, May 18, 1998.

India: India's Nuclear Weapons Plan Examined, FBIS-NES-98-190, July 9, 1998.

India, Its Space Program, and Opportunities for Collaboration with NASA (Arlington, VA: ANSER, 1999).

India: "Major" Indo-Russia Defense Pact Reported, FBIS-NES-98-174, June 23, 1998.

"India Must Test N-Bomb Before Signing CTBT," *The Hindu*, May 2, 2000.

"India Not Daunted by Pak Nuke Threat: PM," *The Times of India*, July 1, 1999.

"India Not to Engage in a N-Arms Race: Jaswant," *The Hindu*, November 29, 1999.

"India on U.S. Report," *The Statesman*, June 9, 2000.

"India-Pakistan Nuclear and Missile Proliferation: Background, Status, and Issues for U.S. Policy," *CRS Report for Congress*, Foreign Affairs and National Defense Division, Environment and Natural Resources Policy Division (Washington, D.C.: Library of Congress, December 16, 1996).

"India Rejects China's Call for Rollback," *Hindustan Times*, March 9, 2000.

India: Report Views Country's Stockpile of Chemical Weapons, FBIS-TAC-97-182, July 1, 1997.

India: Study Recommends Two-Person Rule for Using Nuclear Arms, FBIS-TAC-98-261, September 18, 1998.

India—Telecommunications Market and Regulatory Overview (Bucketty, Australia: Paul Budde Communication, 2000).

"India to Design ABM on U.S. Lines: Kalam," *The Times of India*, January 5, 2000.

"India to Produce Indigenous N-Submarine," *Hindustan Times*, July 27, 1999.

India—VSAT Overview and Major Players (Bucketty, Australia: Paul Budde Communication, 2000).

"India Will Cap Missiles with Nuclear Warheads: Minister," AFP Wire, May 12, 1998.

"India Will Have Plutonium for 50 N-Weapons by 2000 AD," *Hindustan Times*, October 27, 1997.

India—Wireless and Satellite Communications (Bucketty, Australia: Paul Budde Communication, 2000).

"India: Wireless Communications," *Tradeport*, available at http://www.tradeport.org/ts/countries/india/isa/isar0041.html.

"Indian Airports," available at http://civilaviation.nic.in/aai/airport.htm.

Indian Nuclear Tests Included Hydrogen Bomb, FBIS-NES-98-138, May 18, 1998.

"Indian Scientist Opposes Signing of CTBT," *Deccan Herald*, February 19, 2000.

"Indian Scientists Throw Questions at Pakistani Experiments," *Dawn*, May 30, 1998.

"Indian Space Program," U.S. Embassy Political Section, Cable to U.S. Department of Defense No. 30510, New Delhi, January 6, 1988, paragraph 62, cited in Timothy McCarthy, "India: Emerging Missile Power," in William C. Potter and Harlan W. Jencks (eds.), *The International Missile Bazaar: The New Suppliers' Network* (Boulder, CO: Westview Press, 1994).

"Indians Disparage Pakistan Missile Claim," *Washington Times*, April 11, 1998.

India's Malik Satisfied with N-Weaponry, FBIS-NES-98-149, May 29, 1998.

"India's Missile Move," *Washington Post*, June 9, 1997.

"India's Pies in the Sky," *India Today International*, October 20, 1997.

"India's Proposed Nuclear Doctrine Likely to Figure in Sino-Russian Talks," *Hindustan Times*, August 25, 1999.

"Information Technology Action Plan," *India News*, June 16–July 15, 1998.

International Air Forces and Military Aircraft Directory, 1991 (Essex, UK: Aviation Advisory Services, 1991).

"Interview: Atal Bihari Vajpayee," *India Today International*, May 25, 1998.

"Interview: I. K. Gujral," *India Today International*, September 15, 1996.

"Interview of the Week: Inder Kumar Gujral," *Sunday Observer*, September 20–26, 1998.

"Is India a N-Weapon State?" *The Hindu*, October 1, 2000.

"Israeli UAVs: Forces of the Future," *Vayu Aerospace Review*, IV/2000.

Ivanov, S. P., *The Initial Period of War: A Soviet View* (Washington, D.C.: USGPO, 1986).

Iyengar, P. K., "Nuclear Nuances," *The Times of India*, August 22, 2000.

Jackson, Paul (ed.), *Jane's All the World's Aircraft, 1998–99* (Coulsdon, UK: Jane's Information Group Ltd., 1998).

Jackson, Paul A., *Mirage* (Shepperton, UK: Ian Allan, 1985).

Jacobs, Keith, "Heavy Attack Aircraft," *Indian Defence Review*, 13:1 (January–March 1998).

Jain, B. M., *Nuclear Politics in South Asia* (New Delhi: Rawat Publications, 1994).

Jain, J. P., *Nuclear India*, Vols. 1 and 2 (New Delhi: Radiant, 1974).

Jaipal, Rikhi, "The Indian Nuclear Explosion," *International Security*, 1:4 (Spring 1977).

James, L. P. III, "No Silver Bullet in Missile Defense," *U.S. Naval Institute Proceedings*, 125:12 (December 1999).

"Jaswant Rejects U.S. Concern," *The Hindu*, August 20, 1999.

"Jawing About War," *The Times of India*, January 29, 2000.

Jayal, B. D., "India 2020: A Perspective on Air Power," *Indian Defence Review*, 13:4 (October–December 1998).

Jayanth, V., "India's 'Look East' Policy," *The Hindu*, April 2, 1998.

Jayaramu, P. S., "Nuclear Weapons–Free Zone, Non-Proliferation Treaty and South Asia," *IDSA Journal*, 13:1 (July–September 1980).

Jervis, Robert, *The Illogic of American Nuclear Strategy* (Ithaca, NY: Cornell University Press, 1984).

Jervis, Robert, *The Meaning of the Nuclear Revolution* (Ithaca, NY: Cornell University Press, 1989).

Jervis, Robert, *Perception and Misperception in International Politics* (Princeton, NJ: Princeton University Press, 1976).

Jervis, Robert, "Strategic Theory: What's New and What's True," *Journal of Strategic Studies*, 9:4 (December 1986).

Jervis, Robert, "Why Nuclear Superiority Doesn't Matter," *Political Science Quarterly*, 94 (Winter 1979–1980).

Jha, Prem Shankar, "India Must Resume N-Tests," *Hindustan Times*, April 18, 1998.

Jha, Prem Shankar, "Nuclear Blackmail," *Hindustan Times*, April 17, 1998.

Jhunjhunwala, Ashok, Bhaskar Ramamurthi, and Timothy A. Gonsalves, "The Role of Technology in Telecom Expansion in India," *IEEE Communications*, November 1998.

Joeck, Neil, *Maintaining Nuclear Stability in South Asia*, Adelphi Paper No. 312 (London: IISS, 1997).

Joeck, Neil, "Nuclear Developments in India and Pakistan," *Access Asia Review*, 2:2 (July 1999).

Joeck, Neil, "Nuclear Proliferation and Nuclear Reversal in South Asia," *Comparative Strategy*, 16 (1997).

Joeck, Neil, *Nuclear Relations in South Asia*, UCRL-JC-132729, December 1998.

Joeck, Neil, "Tacit Bargaining and Stable Proliferation in South Asia," *Journal of Strategic Studies*, 13:3 (1990).

Johnston, Alastair Iain, "China's New 'Old Thinking': The Concept of Limited Deterrence," *International Security*, 20:3 (Winter 1995–1996).

Joint Publications Research Service, *Worldwide Report: Nuclear Development and Proliferation*, 36 (March 28, 1980).

"Joint Statement by the Department of Atomic Energy and Defence Research and Development Organization," *India News*, May 16–June 15, 1998.

Jones, Gregory S., *From Testing to Deploying Nuclear Forces: The Hard Choices Facing India and Pakistan*, IP-192 (Santa Monica: RAND, 2000).

Jones, Rodney W., "Pakistan's Nuclear Posture," *Dawn*, September 14, 1999.

Jones, Rodney W., "Pakistan's Nuclear Posture—II: Arms Control Diplomacy," *Dawn*, September 15, 1999.

Jones, Rodney W., "Pakistan's Nuclear Posture: Arms Race Instabilities in South Asia," *Asian Affairs*, 25:2 (Summer 1998).

Jones, Rodney W., "Pakistan's Nuclear Posture: Quest for Assured Nuclear Deterrence—A Conjecture," *Regional Studies*, 18:2 (Spring 2000).

Jones, Rodney W., *Small Nuclear Forces*, Washington Paper No. 103 (New York: Praeger, 1984).

Jones, Rodney W. (ed.), *Small Nuclear Forces and U.S. Security Policy* (Lexington, KY: Lexington Books, 1984).

Joseph, Mallika, "India's Draft Nuclear Doctrine," report of the IPCS seminar held on August 27, 1999, available at http://www.ipcs.org/issues/articles/255-ndi-mallika.htm.

Joshi, J. P., "Employment of Prithvi Missiles," *Journal of the USI of India*, 126:526 (October–December 1996).

Joshi, Manoj, "The ABC and Whys of India's N-Doctrine," *The Times of India*, August 22, 1999.

Joshi, Manoj, "Chemical Confessions," *India Today*, July 7, 1997.

Joshi, Manoj, "Chemical Weapons Convention: Under Scrutiny," *India Today*, May 31, 1997.

Joshi, Manoj, "Deadly Option," *India Today International*, May 4, 1998.

Joshi, Manoj, "From Technology Demonstration to Assured Retaliation: The Making of an Indian Nuclear Doctrine," *Strategic Analysis*, 22:10 (January 1999).

Joshi, Manoj, "George in the China Shop," *India Today International*, May 18, 1998.

Joshi, Manoj, "In the Shadow of Fear," *India Today International*, July 21, 1997.

Joshi, Manoj, "India Must Have Survivable N-Arsenal," *The Times of India*, April 30, 2000.

Joshi, Manoj, "India's Nuclear Estate," *India Today International*, May 4, 1998.

Joshi, Manoj, "Marginal Costing," *India Today*, June 1, 1998.

Joshi, Manoj, "Missile Program on Hold," *Asia-Pacific Defense Reporter*, April–May 1994.

Joshi, Manoj, "The Nuclear Maharaja Has No Clothes," *The Times of India*, June 9, 2000.

Joshi, Manoj, "Nuclear Shock Waves," *India Today International*, May 25, 1998.

Joshi, Manoj, "Old Body, New Name," *India Today*, December 7, 1998.

Joshi, Manoj, "Operation Defreeze," *India Today*, August 11, 1997.

Joshi, Manoj, "Signal Wars: Indian Capability in Perspective," *Frontline*, September 10, 1993.

Julian, Thomas A., "Nuclear Weapons Security and Control," in Paul Leventhal and Yonah Alexander (eds.), *Preventing Nuclear Terrorism* (Lexington, KY: Lexington Books, 1987).

Kahan, Jerome H., *Security in the Nuclear Age* (Washington, D.C.: Brookings, 1975).

Kak, Kapil, "Command and Control of Small Nuclear Arsenals," in Jasjit Singh (ed.), *Nuclear India* (New Delhi: Knowledge World, 1998).

Kak, Kapil, "Direction of Higher Defence—II," *Strategic Analysis*, 22:4 (July 1998).

Kak, Kapil, "Management of India's Security and Higher Defence—I," *Strategic Analysis*, 22:3 (June 1998).

Kak, Kapil, "Strategic Template for Nuclear India," *The Times of India*, August 11, 1998.

Kalam, A.P.J. Abdul (with Y. S. Rajan), *India 2020* (New Delhi: Viking, 1998).

Kale, Pramod, "Future Space Communications System for India," *IETE Technical Review*, 8:5 (September 1991).

Kampani, Gaurav, "Prithvi: The Case for 'No-First-Deployment,' " *Rediff on the Net*, available at http://www.rediff.com/news/jul/10kamp.htm.

Kanwal, Gurmeet, "Command and Control of India's Nuclear Weapons," *World Focus*, 21:4 (April 2000).

Kanwal, Gurmeet, "Command and Control of Nuclear Weapons in India," *Strategic Analysis*, 23:10 (January 2000).

Kanwal, Gurmeet, "Defence Intelligence," *The Statesman*, November 20, 2000.

Kanwal, Gurmeet, "Does India Need Tactical Nuclear Weapons?" *Strategic Analysis*, 24:2 (May 2000).

Kanwal, Gurmeet, "India's Nuclear Force Structure," *Strategic Analysis*, 24:6 (September 2000).

Kanwal, Gurmeet, "'No First Use' Doctrine: India's Strategic Dilemma," *The Tribune*, July 15, 2000.

Kanwal, Gurmeet, "Nuclear Targeting Philosophy for India," *Strategic Analysis*, 24:3 (June 2000).

Kanwal, Gurmeet, "Pay-Back Time on the LOC," *Indian Express*, June 27, 2000.

Kapila, Subash, "India and Pakistan Nuclear Doctrine: A Comparative Analysis," available at http://www.ipcs.org/issues/articles/260-ndi-kapila.html.

Kaplan, Fred, *The Wizards of Armageddon* (New York: Simon and Schuster, 1983).

Kaplan, Morton, *The Strategy of Limited Retaliation*, Policy Memorandum No. 19 (Princeton, NJ: Woodrow Wilson School of Public and International Affairs, 1959).

Kaplan, Morton, *System and Process in International Politics* (New York: Wiley, 1957).

Kapur, Ashok, *India's Nuclear Option* (New York: Praeger Publishers, 1976).

Karan, Vijay, "Institutionalise Strategic Thinking," *Indian Express*, July 7, 1998.

Karan, Vijay, *War by Stealth* (New Delhi: Viking, 1997).

"Kargil Shouldn't Bias Western View of India's N-Policy: George," *The Times of India*, July 21, 1999.

Karnad, Bharat, "Contenting Scenarios," *Hindustan Times*, January 7, 1997.

Karnad, Bharat, "Cost-Effective Budgeting: Getting the Priorities Right," *Indian Defence Review*, 13:1 (January–March 1998).

Karnad, Bharat, "Fuelling Strategic Fatalism," *Hindustan Times*, May 7, 1999.

Karnad, Bharat (ed.), *Future Imperilled* (Delhi: Viking, 1994).

Karnad, Bharat, "Going Thermonuclear: Why, with What Forces, at What Cost," *Journal of the United Services Institution of India*, 127:533 (July–September 1998).

Karnad, Bharat, "India's Weak Geopolitics and What to Do About It," in Bharat Karnad (ed.), *Future Imperilled* (Delhi: Viking, 1994).

Karnad, Bharat, "Needed: An 'India First' Nuclear Policy," *The Pioneer*, July 27, 2000.

Karnad, Bharat, "Next, a Series of Thermonuclear Tests," *The Pioneer*, July 28, 2000.

Karnad, Bharat, "Policy on CTBT," *Hindustan Times*, November 4, 1999.

Karnad, Bharat, "Politics of 'Militarised' States," *Hindustan Times*, January 22, 1983.

Karnad, Bharat, "A Sucker's Payoff," *Seminar*, 485 (January 2000).

Karnad, Bharat, "A Thermonuclear Deterrent," in Amitabh Mattoo (ed.), *India's Nuclear Deterrent* (New Delhi: Har-Anand Publications, 1999).

Karp, Aaron, *Ballistic Missile Proliferation: The Politics and Technics* (Oxford, UK: Oxford University Press, 1996).

Karp, Jonathan, "India Faces Task of Creating Nuclear-Weapons Doctrine," *Wall Street Journal,* May 27, 1998.

Karp, Regina Cowen (ed.), *Security with Nuclear Weapons?* (Oxford, UK: Oxford University Press, 1991).

Karp, Regina Cowen (ed.), *Security Without Nuclear Weapons?* (Oxford, UK: Oxford University Press, 1992).

Kasturi, Bhashyam, *Intelligence Services: Analysis, Organization and Functions* (New Delhi: Lancer Publishers, 1995).

Kasturi, Bhashyam, "The Looming Chinese Threat," *The Pioneer,* August 19, 1995.

Kasturirangan, K., "Evolution of Space Based Remote Sensing in India," *IETE Technical Review,* 9:5 (1992).

Katiyal, Anita, "No Freeze on N-Capability, U.S. Told," *The Times of India,* November 26, 1998.

Katyal, K. K., "A Motivated Exercise?" *The Hindu,* August 23, 1999.

Keeny, Spurgeon M., Jr., and Wolfgang K.H. Panofsky, "MAD Versus NUTS: Can Doctrine or Weaponry Remedy the Mutual Hostage Relationship of the Superpowers?" *Foreign Affairs,* 60:2 (Winter 1981–1982).

Kent, Glenn A., and David E. Thaler, *First-Strike Stability: A Methodology for Evaluating Strategic Forces,* R-3765-AF (Santa Monica: RAND, 1989).

Keohane, Robert O. (ed.), *Neorealism and Its Critics* (New York: Columbia University Press, 1986).

Khalilzad, Zalmay (ed.), *Strategic Appraisal 1996,* MR-543-AF (Santa Monica: RAND, 1996).

Khalilzad, Zalmay, and Ian O. Lesser (eds.), *Sources of Conflict in the 21st Century*, MR-897-AF (Santa Monica: RAND, 1998).

Khalilzad, Zalmay, David T. Orletsky, Jonathan D. Pollack, Kevin Pollpeter, Angel M. Rabasa, David A. Shlapak, Abram N. Shulsky, and Ashley J. Tellis, *The United States and Asia: Toward a New U.S. Strategy and Force Posture*, MR-1315-AF (Santa Monica: RAND, 2001).

Khalilzad, Zalmay M., Abram N. Shulsky, Daniel Byman, Roger Cliff, David T. Orletsky, David Shlapak, and Ashley J. Tellis, *The United States and a Rising China: Strategic and Military Implications*, MR-1082-AF (Santa Monica: RAND, 1999).

Khan, A. Q., "The Spread of Nuclear Weapons Among Nations: Militarization or Development," in Sadruddin Agha Khan (ed.), *Nuclear War, Nuclear Proliferation and Their Consequences* (Oxford, UK: Clarendon Press, 1986).

Khan, Ayaz Ahmed, "Countering the Prithvi Threat," *The Nation*, June 30, 1997.

Khan, Munir Ahmed, "Future of Indian and Pakistani Nuclear/WMD Programmes," unpublished background paper prepared for the RAND-IRS Colloquium, February 25–26, 1996, Islamabad, Pakistan.

Khan, Sadruddin Agha (ed.), *Nuclear War, Nuclear Proliferation and Their Consequences* (Oxford, UK: Clarendon Press, 1986).

Khripunov, Igor, and Anupam Srivastava, "Russian-Indian Relations: Alliance, Partnership, Or?" *Comparative Strategy*, 18:2 (April–June 1999).

Kidder, Ray E., "Militarily Significant Nuclear Explosive Yields," *FAS Public Interest Report*, 38:7 (September 1985).

Kincade, William H., "The United States: Nuclear Decision Making, 1939–89," in Regina Cowen Karp (ed.), *Security with Nuclear Weapons?* (Oxford, UK: Oxford University Press, 1991).

King, John K. (ed.), *International Political Effects of the Spread of Nuclear Weapons* (Washington, D.C.: USGPO, 1979).

Kiran, Vijay, "Strategic Failure," *Hindustan Times*, July 25, 1998.

Kissinger, Henry, *Nuclear Weapons and Foreign Policy* (New York: Harper & Brothers, 1957).

Kitamura, Motoya, "Japan's Plutonium Program: A Proliferation Threat?" *Nonproliferation Review*, 3:2 (Winter 1996).

Klintworth, Gary, "Chinese Perspectives on India as a Great Power," in Ross Babbage and Sandy Gordon (eds.), *India's Strategic Future* (New York: St. Martin's Press, 1992).

Koblentz, Gregory, "Theater Missile Defense and South Asia: A Volatile Mix," *Nonproliferation Review*, 4:3 (Spring–Summer 1997).

Koch, Andrew R., "In Search of the Real Sagarika," *Jane's Intelligence Review*, 10:7 (July 1998).

Koch, Andrew R., "Nuclear-Powered Submarines: India's Strategic Trump Card," *Jane's Intelligence Review*, 10:6 (June 1998)

Koch, Andrew, "Pakistan Persists with Nuclear Procurement," *Jane's Intelligence Review*, 9:3 (March 1977).

Kohli, Atul, "Know India; Don't Overreact," *Christian Science Monitor*, May 18, 1998.

Koulik, Sergey, "The Soviet Union: Domestic and Strategic Aspects of Nuclear Weapon Policy," in Regina Cowen Karp (ed.), *Security with Nuclear Weapons?* (Oxford, UK: Oxford University Press, 1991).

Kramish, Arnold, "The Bombs of Balnibarbi," in Rodney W. Jones (ed.), *Small Nuclear Forces and U.S. Security Policy* (Lexington, KY: Lexington Books, 1984).

Krishnaswami, Sridhar, "N-Programme Not a Burden, Says Sinha," *The Hindu*, October 1, 1999.

Krishnaswamy, K. V., "Celeste Defends Demand on Deterrence," *The Hindu*, January 23, 1999.

Kristy, N. F., *Man in a Large Information Processing System—His Changing Role in SAGE*, RM-3206-PR (Santa Monica: RAND, 1963).

Kruzel, Joseph I., "Military Alerts and Diplomatic Signals," in Ellen P. Stern (ed.), *The Limits of Military Intervention* (Thousand Oaks, CA: Sage Publications, 1977).

Kukreja, Veena, *Civil-Military Relations in South Asia* (New Delhi: Sage Publications, 1991).

Kumar, Dinesh, "Government Set to Empower Armed Forces with Policy Ammunition," *The Times of India*, November 7, 2000.

Kumar, Dinesh, "IAF Still Lacks N-Capability," *The Times of India*, October 19, 1998.

Kumar, Dinesh, "Let's Be Stronger and Smarter, Says IAF Chief," *The Times of India*, May 16, 1999.

Kumar, Dinesh, "National Debate on N-Tests Hurts Security Concerns: Fernandes," *The Times of India*, October 12, 1998.

Kumar, Dinesh, "No Move Yet to Set Up Nuclear Command," *The Times of India*, July 2, 1998.

Kumar, Dinesh, "Nuclearization Calls for Strategic Command," *The Times of India*, May 16, 1998.

Kumar, Dinesh, "Sub-Kiloton Devices a Technological Leap," *The Times of India*, May 14, 1998.

Kumar, Girish, "Pokhran-II Is a Turning Point in Raising National Morale" (interview with Anil Kakodkar), *The Times of India*, July 30, 1998.

Kumar, Ranjit, *China's Military Designs*, FBIS-NES-98-131, May 11, 1998.

Kumaraswamy, P. R., *India and Israel: Evolving Strategic Partnership* (Ramat Gan, Israel: BESA Center for Strategic Studies, 1998).

Kwatra, R. D., "From Deterrence to Blackmail: Pakistan's Nuclear Agenda," *Indian Express*, January 20, 1996.

Lahiri, Dilip, "Formalizing Restraint: The Case of South Asia," *Strategic Analysis*, 23:4 (July 1999).

Lake, Jon, "Indian Air Power," *World Air Power Journal*, 12 (Spring 1993).

Lake, Jon, "Mikoyan Mig-25 'Foxbat' and Mig-31 'Foxhound' Variants," *World Air Power Journal*, 34 (Autumn–Fall 1998).

Lake, Jon, "Sukhoi Su-27 Variant Briefing, Part 1," *World Air Power Journal*, 28 (Spring 1997).

Langereux, Pierre (with Vivek Raghuvanshi), "Surprise: L'Inde teste sur 1200 km un nouveau missile strategique," *Air & Cosmos/ Aviation International*, 1463 (March 14–20, 1994).

Laskar, Rezaul H., "Navy to Get 4 Nuclear-Capable Bombers," *Asian Age*, February 14, 2000.

Lavoy, Peter R., "Civil-Military Relations, Strategic Conduct, and the Stability of Nuclear Deterrence in South Asia," in Scott Sagan (ed.), *Civil-Military Relations and Nuclear Weapons* (Stanford, CA: Center for International Security and Arms Control, Stanford University, 1994).

Lavoy, Peter R., *Learning to Live with the Bomb? India and Nuclear Weapons, 1947–1974*, unpublished doctoral dissertation, University of California, Berkeley, May 1997.

Lavoy, Peter R., Scott D. Sagan, and James J. Wirtz (eds.), *Planning the Unthinkable* (Ithaca, NY: Cornell University Press, 2000).

Lawrence, Robert M., and Joel Larus, *Nuclear Proliferation: Phase II* (Lawrence, KS: University Press of Kansas, 1974).

Laxman, Srinivas, "India Should Retain Option to Carry Out More N-Tests," *The Times of India*, November 1, 2000.

Lee, William T., "Soviet Nuclear Targeting Strategy," in Desmond Ball and Jeffrey Richelson (eds.), *Strategic Nuclear Targeting* (Ithaca, NY: Cornell University Press, 1986).

Legault, Albert, and George Lindsey, *The Dynamics of the Nuclear Balance* (Ithaca, NY: Cornell University Press, 1976).

Lennox, Duncan (ed.), *Jane's Strategic Weapons Systems* (Coulsdon, UK: Jane's Information Group Ltd., 1999), Issue 29, January 1999.

Leventhal, Paul, and Yonah Alexander (eds.), *Preventing Nuclear Terrorism* (Lexington, KY: Lexington Books, 1987).

Leventhal, Paul, and Brahma Chellaney, "Nuclear Terrorism: Threat, Perception, and Response in South Asia," *Terrorism*, 11 (1998).

Lewin, Guy, "La dissuasion française et la stratégie anti-cités," *Défense Nationale*, January 1980, cited in David Yost, "French Nuclear Targeting," in Desmond Ball and Jeffrey Richelson (eds.), *Strategic Nuclear Targeting* (Ithaca, NY: Cornell University Press, 1986).

Lewis, David, "Finite Counterforce," in H. Shue (ed.), *Nuclear Deterrence and Moral Restraint* (Cambridge, UK: Cambridge University Press, 1989).

Lewis, John Wilson, "China's Search for a Modern Air Force," *International Security*, 24:1 (Summer 1999).

Lewis, Kevin N., *Getting More Deterrence Out of Deliberate Capability Revelation*, N-2873-AF (Santa Monica: RAND, 1989).

Lieberman, Elli, "The Rational Deterrence Theory Debate: Is the Dependent Variable Elusive?" *Security Studies*, 3:3 (Spring 1994).

Little, I.M.D., and J. A. Mirrlees, *Project Appraisal and Planning for Developing Countries* (London: Heinemann, 1974).

Liu, Xuecheng, *The Sino-Indian Border Dispute and Sino-Indian Relations* (Lanham, MD: University Press of America, 1994).

Loeb, Vernon, "Hobbyists Track Down Spies in Sky," *Washington Post*, February 20, 1999.

Lovins, Amory B., "Nuclear Weapons and Power-Reactor Plutonium," *Nature*, 283 (February 1980).

Lynch, Allen, "The Soviet Union: Nuclear Weapons and Their Role in Security Policy," in Regina Cowen Karp (ed.), *Security with Nuclear Weapons?* (Oxford, UK: Oxford University Press, 1991).

Mack, Andrew, "What India Did Was Right for Indians," *Asian Age*, May 21, 1998.

MacKenzie, Debora, "Making Waves," *New Scientist,* June 13, 1998.

MacLean, Douglas (ed.*),* *The Security Gamble: Deterrence Dilemmas in the Nuclear Age* (Totowa, NJ: Rowman & Allanheld, 1984).

Mahapatra, Chintamani, "The U.S., China and the Ghauri Missile," *Strategic Analysis,* 22:3 (June 1998).

Mahmood, Afzal, "From the Pakistani Press: The Nuclear Option," *The Times of India,* July 18, 1999.

Mahmood, Afzal, "What Nuclear Sanity Demands," *Dawn,* May 31, 1999.

Makhijani, Arjun, "A Disarming Offer No One Can Refuse," *The Times of India,* September 3, 1998.

Malik, J. Mohan, "China and South Asian Nuclear-Free Zone," *China Report,* 25:2 (1989).

Mandelbaum, Michael, *The Nuclear Revolution* (New York: Cambridge University Press, 1981).

Mann, Paul, "India Derides Nuclear 'Alarmism,' " *Aviation Week & Space Technology,* April 3, 2000.

Mann, Paul, "Subcontinent Poised for Nuke Deployment," *Aviation Week & Space Technology,* August 3, 1998.

Mann, Paul, "Subcontinent's Nuclear Duel Raises Miscalculation Risk," *Aviation Week & Space Technology,* June 8, 1998.

Manning, Robert A., Ronald Montaperto, and Brad Roberts, *China, Nuclear Weapons, and Arms Control* (New York: Council on Foreign Relations, 2000).

Mannshaiya, Harbir K., "India's Prithvi," *International Defense Review,* 28:8 (August 1995).

Manohar, S. B., B. S. Tomar, S. S. Rattan, V. K. Shukla, V. V. Kulkarni, and Anil Kakodkar, "Post Shot Radioactivity Measurements on Samples Extracted from Thermonuclear Test Site," *BARC Newsletter,* 186 (July 1999).

Manor, James, "Collective Conflict in India," *Conflict Studies*, 212 (London: Centre for Security and Conflict Studies, 1988).

Manor, James, " 'Ethnicity' and Politics in India," *International Affairs*, 72:3 (1996).

Manor, James (ed.), *Nehru to the Nineties: The Changing Office of Prime Minister in India* (Vancouver, Canada: UBC Press, 1994).

Mansingh, Surjit, "India-China Relations in the Post–Cold War Era," *Asian Survey*, 34:3 (March 1994).

Mark, J. Carson, "Explosive Properties of Reactor-Grade Plutonium," *Science and Global Security*, 4 (1993).

Mark, J. Carson, "Nuclear Weapons Technology," in B. T. Feld, T. Greenwood, G. W. Rathjens, and S. Weinberg (eds.), *Impact of New Technologies on the Arms Race* (Cambridge, MA: MIT Press, 1971).

Marshall, Eliot, "Did Test Ban Watchdog Fail to Bark?" *Science*, 280 (June 26, 1998).

Martin, Lawrence, *Minimum Deterrence*, Faraday Discussion Paper No. 8 (London: Council for Arms Control, 1987).

Marwah, Onkar, "India's Nuclear Program: Decisions, Intent and Policy, 1950–1976," in William H. Overholt (ed.), *Asia's Nuclear Future* (Boulder, CO: Westview Press, 1977).

Marxism-Leninism on War and Army: A Soviet View (Washington, D.C.: USGPO, 1974).

Masood, Talat, "Evolving a Correct Nuclear Posture," *Dawn*, August 21, 1998.

Matinuddin, Kamal, "The Missile Threat," *The News*, March 2, 1997.

Matthews, Ron, *Defence Production in India* (New Delhi: ABC Publishing House, 1989).

Mattoo, Amitabh, "Chinese Takeaway," *The Telegraph*, August 8, 1997.

Mattoo, Amitabh, "Counsel for the Defence," *The Telegraph*, November 27, 1998.

Mattoo, Amitabh, "Enough Scientific Reasons Seen for Conducting Tests," *India Abroad*, May 15, 1996.

Mattoo, Amitabh (ed.), *India's Nuclear Deterrent* (New Delhi: Har-Anand Publications, 1999).

Mattoo, Amitabh, "India's Nuclear Policy in an Anarchic World," in Amitabh Mattoo (ed.), *India's Nuclear Deterrent* (New Delhi: Har-Anand Publications, 1999).

Mattoo, Amitabh, "Strategic Significance of the Agni-II Test Is Stressed," *India Abroad*, April 23, 1999.

McCarthy, Timothy V., "India: Emerging Missile Power," in William C. Potter and Harlan W. Jencks (eds.), *The International Missile Bazaar: The New Suppliers' Network* (Boulder, CO: Westview Press, 1994).

MccGwire, Michael, "Is There a Future for Nuclear Weapons?" *International Affairs*, 70:2 (April 1994).

McDowell, Stephen D., *Globalization, Liberalization and Policy Change: A Political Economy of India's Communications Sector* (New York: St. Martin's Press, 1997).

McEwan, A. C., "Environmental Effects of Underground Nuclear Explosions," in Jozef Goldblat and David Cox (eds.), *Nuclear Weapons Tests: Prohibition or Limitation?* (Oxford, UK: Oxford University Press, 1998).

Meade, Charles, "Surface Wave Magnitudes and Yield Estimates for the May 11, 1998 Indian Nuclear Test," unpublished memo.

Mearsheimer, John, *Conventional Deterrence* (Ithaca, NY: Cornell University Press, 1983).

Mecham, Michael, "Cost-Conscious Indians Find Profits in Imaging Satellites," *Aviation Week & Space Technology*, August 12, 1996.

Mecham, Michael, "India Builds a 'Crown Jewel,' " *Aviation Week & Space Technology*, August 12, 1996.

Mehta, Ashok K., "Case for a Nuclear Doctrine with Minimum Deterrence," *India Abroad*, August 28, 1998.

Mehta, Ashok K., "Need to Involve Services in Decision-Making Stressed," *India Abroad*, March 12, 1999.

Mehta, Ashok K., "Preparing for a Nuclear Future," *Hindustan Times*, June 19, 1998.

Mehta, Pratap B., "India: The Nuclear Politics of Self-Esteem," *Current History*, 97:623 (December 1998).

Mehta, V. R., *Foundations of Indian Political Thought* (New Delhi: Manohar, 1996).

Menon, N. C., "Subtleties of Sagarika," *Hindustan Times*, May 11, 1998.

Menon, Raja, "Deterrence Must Shift Underwater," *The Times of India*, March 23, 1995.

Menon, Raja, "Not in National Interest," *Hindustan Times*, January 5, 2000.

Menon, Raja, "The Nuclear Doctrine," *The Times of India*, August 26, 1999.

Menon, Raja, *A Nuclear Strategy for India* (New Delhi: Sage Publications, 2000).

Menon, Raja, "Strategic Decisionmaking," *Hindustan Times*, July 30, 1996.

Mian, Zia, and A. H. Nayyar, "A Time of Testing?" *Bulletin of the Atomic Scientists*, 52:4 (July–August 1996).

Mian, Z., A. H. Nayyar, and M. V. Ramana, "Bring Prithvi Down to Earth: The Capabilities and Potential Effectiveness of India's Prithvi Missile," *Science & Global Security*, 7 (1998)

The Military Balance, 1997–98 (Oxford, UK: Oxford University Press/ IISS, 1997).

Miller, Steven E. (ed.), *Strategy and Nuclear Deterrence* (Princeton, NJ: Princeton University Press, 1984).

Milovidov, A. S. (ed.), *The Philosophical Heritage of V. I. Lenin and Problems of Contemporary War: A Soviet View* (Washington, D.C.: USGPO, 1974).

Ministry of Communications, *VIII Five Year Plan (1992–1997): Industrial Development for Telecom Sector* (New Delhi: Government of India, 1991).

Mirchandani, G. G., *India's Nuclear Dilemma* (New Delhi: Popular Book Services, 1968).

"The Missile Race," *Hindustan Times*, April 8, 1998.

Mistry, Dinshaw, *India and the Comprehensive Test Ban Treaty*, ACDIS Research Report (Urbana, IL: University of Illinois, September 1998).

Mistry, Dinshaw, "India's Emerging Space Program," *Pacific Affairs*, 71:2 (Summer 1998).

Mistry, Dinshaw, "What If Deterrence Fails?" available at http://www.ipcs.org/issues/articles/132-ndi-dinshaw.html.

Mitra, Chandan, "Explosion of Self-Esteem," *The Pioneer*, May 12, 1998.

Mohan, C. Raja, "Beyond the Nuclear Obsession," *The Hindu*, November 25, 1999.

Mohan, C. Raja, "Fernandes Unveils 'Limited War' Doctrine," *The Hindu*, January 25, 2000.

Mohan, C. Raja, "Ghauri Missile: India in Denial," *The Hindu*, April 9, 1998.

Mohan, C. Raja, "Grand Strategy: Back to Basics," *The Hindu*, January 20, 2000.

Mohan, C. Raja, "India and the Nuclear Oligarchy," *The Hindu*, June 6, 1998.

Mohan, C. Raja, "India, China Power Equations Changing," *The Hindu*, December 2, 1996.

Mohan, C. Raja, "India Committed to Minimum N-Deterrence," *The Hindu*, December 7, 1998.

Mohan, C. Raja, "India in a Nuclear Limbo," *The Hindu*, August 21, 1997.

Mohan, C. Raja, "India Rejects U.S. Suggestion for Moratorium on Fissile Material Production," *The Hindu*, September 13, 2000.

Mohan, C. Raja, "India's Nuclear Options," *The Hindu*, December 20, 1995.

Mohan, C. Raja, "Living in a Nuclear South Asia," *The Hindu*, May 28, 1998.

Mohan, C. Raja, "Managing Indo-Japanese Nuclear Divergence," *The Hindu*, March 6, 1999.

Mohan, C. Raja, "Nuclear Balance in Asia," *The Hindu*, June 11, 1998.

Mohan, C. Raja, "Nuclear Free Zones: Illusion and Reality," in K. Subrahmanyam (ed.), *India and the Nuclear Challenge* (New Delhi: Lancer International, 1986).

Mohan, C. Raja, "Nuclear Politics—I: Playing Football with Nuclear Weapons," *The Hindu*, May 25, 1998.

Mohan, C. Raja, "Rethinking CTBT and FMCT," *The Hindu*, June 16, 1998.

Mohan, C. Raja, "Sundarji's Nuclear Doctrine," *The Hindu*, February 11, 1999.

Mohan, C. Raja, "Vajpayee's Nuclear Legacy," *The Hindu*, April 21, 1999.

Mohan, Saumitra, "The Agni Sermon," *The Pioneer*, May 1, 1999.

Mohapatra, Satyen, "Low Yield Reports Misleading: AEC Chief," *Hindustan Times*, January 5, 1999.

Molander, Roger C. , and Peter A. Wilson, *The Nuclear Asymptote: On Containing Nuclear Proliferation*, MR-214-CC (Santa Monica: RAND, 1993).

Moorthy, D. N., "AEC Chief Defends Pokharan Yields," *Indian Express*, November 30, 1999.

Moorthy, D. N., "Ambiguity Is India's New Nuclear Agenda," *Jane's Intelligence Review*, 11:11 (November 1999).

"Moratorium Will Not Affect N-Weaponisation: Fernandes," *The Times of India*, May 27, 1998.

"More Allocation for Para-Military Forces," *The Hindu*, March 1, 2000.

Morgenthau, Hans, "The Fallacy of Thinking Conventionally About Nuclear Weapons," in David Carlton and Carlo Schaerf (eds.), *Arms Control and Technological Innovation* (New York: Wiley, 1976).

Morrow, Daniel, and Michael Carriere, "The Economic Impacts of the 1998 Sanctions on India and Pakistan," *Nonproliferation Review*, 6:4 (Fall 1999).

Mow, C. C., and J. W. Workman, *Feasibility of Transportable Armored Command Posts*, RM-4422-ISA (Santa Monica: RAND, 1965).

Mozumber, Suman Guha, "Nation Not to Abandon Its Missile Program," *India Abroad*, June 19, 1998.

Mulvenon, James, "Chinese Nuclear and Conventional Weapons," in Elizabeth Economy and Michel Oksenberg (eds.), *China Joins the World* (New York: Council on Foreign Relations Press, 1999).

Murphy, J. R., "Seismic Yield Estimation for the Indian and Pakistani Nuclear Tests of May, 1998," paper presented at the 20th Annual Seismic Research Symposium on Monitoring a CTBT, Santa Fe, NM, September 23, 1998.

Mustafa, Herro (ed.), *The Balance of Power in South Asia* (Abu Dhabi, UAE: Emirates Center for Strategic Studies and Research, 2000).

Myers, Kenneth A. (ed.), *NATO, the Next Thirty Years* (Boulder, CO: Westview Press, 1980).

Myers, Steven Lee, "Russia Helping India Extend Range of Missiles, Aides Say," *New York Times*, April 27, 1998.

Myers, Steven Lee, "Study Said to Find U.S. Missile Shield Might Incite China," *New York Times*, August 10, 2000.

Nadkarni, Vidya, "India and Russia: The End of a Special Relationship?" *Naval War College Review*, 48:4 (Autumn 1995).

Naib, V. P., "The Nuclear Threat," *Indian Defence Review*, 8:1 (January 1993).

Naik, Niaz A., "Towards a Nuclear-Safe South Asia: A Pakistani Perspective," in David O. Smith (ed.), *From Containment to Stability: Pakistan–United States Relations in the Post–Cold War Era* (Washington, D.C.: National Defense University, 1993).

Naim, S. Rashid, "Aadhi Raat Ke Baad ('After Midnight')," in Stephen P. Cohen (ed.), *Nuclear Proliferation in South Asia* (Boulder, CO: Westview Press, 1991).

Naipaul, V. S., *India: A Million Mutinies Now* (London: Heinemann, 1990).

Nair, Vijai K., "Indian Nuclear Doctrine: Domestic and External Challenges," *Agni*, 4:2 (May 1999).

Nair, Vijai K., *Nuclear India* (New Delhi: Lancer International, 1992).

Nair, Vijai K., "Nuclear Proliferation: U.S. Aims and India's Response," *Studies in Conflict and Terrorism*, 17:2 (1994).

Nair, Vijai K., "Pak Weaponization Not So: Experts Doubt Blast Potency," *Sunday Observer*, May 31–June 6, 1998.

Nair, Vijai K., "The Structure of an Indian Nuclear Deterrent," in Amitabh Mattoo (ed.), *India's Nuclear Deterrent* (New Delhi: Har-Anand Publications, 1999).

Najeeb, Muhammed, "Indian H-Bomb Test a Failure, Say Pakistan Scientists," *India Abroad*, June 19, 1998.

Nalapat, M. D., "Eagle's Eye View: Isolating India to Help China," *The Times of India*, June 25, 1998.

Nalapat, M. D., "India Needs to Expand Scope of Nuclear Diplomacy," *The Times of India*, December 18, 1998.

Nalapat, M. D., "No More Waffling," *The Times of India*, January 18, 2000.

Nambiar, Satish, "Make the Army Fighting Fit, Paddy," *Hindustan Times*, August 20, 2000.

Nandy, Ashis (ed.), *Science, Hegemony and Violence: A Requiem for Modernity* (Delhi: Oxford University Press, 1988).

Narayanan, M. K., "It Takes More Than Two to Tango in Nuclear Club," *Asian Age*, May 31, 1998.

"N-Arms Alone Not Enough: Subrahmanyam Panel," *The Hindu*, October 29, 2000.

"National Command Authority Formed," *Dawn*, February 6, 2000.

The National Economic Atlas of China (New York: Oxford University Press, 1994).

National Intelligence Council, "Foreign Missile Developments and the Ballistic Missile Threats to the United States Through 2015," September 1999, available at http://www.cia.gov/cia/publications/nie/nie99msl.html.

Nayan, Rajiv, "Delivery Systems Seen as Aiding Nuclear Deterrence," *India Abroad*, June 26, 1998.

Nayar, Kuldip, "Between Welfare and Weapons," *Indian Express*, August 31, 1999.

Nayyar, A. H., A. H. Toor, and Zia Mian, "Fissile Material Production Potential in South Asia," *Science & Global Security*, 6 (1997).

"N-Deterrence a Must: PM," *The Pioneer*, May 13, 2000.

"N-Doctrine Adheres to Old Policy: Atal," *The Pioneer*, August 21, 1999.

"Need for ICBM Questioned," *The Times of India*, January 10, 1990.

Neelima, Kota, "Either You Will Be Dead or Crammed in a Bunker with 10,000 People," *Indian Express*, July 25, 1999.

"Negotiating an FMCT," *The Hindu*, November 19, 1998.

"New Delhi Plans Missile-Monitoring Satellite for '99," *Jane's Defence Weekly*, April 29, 1998.

"New Reactor Being Planned in Trombay," *The Hindu*, April 28, 1999.

"New Satellite Communication System for Army," *The Hindu*, April 20, 2000.

Nitze, Paul, "Deterring Our Deterrent," *Foreign Policy*, 25 (Winter 1976–1977).

"No Compromises on N-Power: AEC Chief," *Indian Express*, February 4, 1999.

"No Contradiction with Kalam's Views," *The Hindu*, September 24, 1998.

Nolan, Janne E., *Trappings of Power: Ballistic Missiles in the Third World* (Washington, D.C.: Brookings, 1991).

Noorani, A. G., "India's Quest for a Nuclear Guarantee," *Asian Survey*, 7:7 (July 1967).

Norbu, Dawa, "Strategic Developments in Tibet: Implications for Its Neighbors," *Asian Survey*, 19:3 (March 1979).

Norris, Robert S., "U.S. Nuclear Weapons Safety and Control Features," *Bulletin of the Atomic Scientists*, 47:8 (October 1991).

Norris, Robert S., Andrew S. Burrows, and Richard W. Fieldhouse, *British, French, and Chinese Nuclear Weapons, Nuclear Weapons Databook*, Vol. V (Boulder, CO: Westview Press, 1994).

Novak, Michael, *Moral Clarity in the Nuclear Age* (Nashville: Thomas Nelson, 1983).

"N-Sub Project on Course: Navy," *The Times of India*, July 27, 1999.

"N-Submarine Best Bet Against Nuclear Attack, Says Navy," *Indian Express*, December 12, 1999.

"Nuclear Afterglow," *India Today International*, May 25, 1998.

"Nuclear Follies," *The Times of India*, July 2, 1999.

"Nuclear Submarine Project Gets a New Head," *The Times of India,* September 30, 2000.

Nuclear Weapons and South Asian Security (Washington, D.C.: Carnegie Endowment for International Peace, 1988).

"Nukes: Mind Your Business, U.S. Told," *Economic Times,* January 7, 1999.

Office of the Secretary of Defense, *Proliferation: Threat and Response* (Washington, D.C.: USGPO, 1996).

Office of Technology Assessment, *The Effects of Nuclear War* (Montclair, NJ: Allanheld, Osmun, 1980).

Office of Technology Assessment, *MX Missile Basing* (Washington, D.C.: USGPO, 1981).

Office of Technology Assessment, *Nuclear Proliferation and Safeguards* (New York: Praeger, 1977).

Office of Technology Assessment, *Proliferation of Weapons of Mass Destruction: Assessing the Risks,* OTA-ISC-559 (Washington, D.C.: USGPO, 1993).

Ollapally, Deepa M., "India and the New 'Asian' Balance of Power," *Strategic Analysis,* 22:4 (July 1998).

Ollapally, Deepa M., "India's Strategic Doctrine and Practice: The Impact of Nuclear Testing," in Raju G.C. Thomas and Amit Gupta (eds.), *India's Nuclear Security* (Boulder, CO: Lynne Rienner Publishers, 2000).

Ollapally, Deepa, and S. Rajagopal (eds.), *Nuclear Cooperation: Challenges and Prospects* (Bangalore, India: National Institute of Advanced Studies, 1997).

Olsen, Mancur, Jr., and Richard Zechauser, "An Economic Theory of Alliances," *Review of Economics and Statistics,* 48:3 (August 1966).

" 'Only One Device at Pokhran-II Was a Weapon,' " *The Hindu,* June 22, 2000.

Opall-Rome, Barbara, "India Moves May Spur China Nukes Buildup," *Defense News*, April 26, 1999.

"Opening Remarks by National Security Adviser Mr. Brajesh Mishra at the Release of Draft Indian Nuclear Doctrine," available at http://www.meadev.gov.in/govt/opstm-indnucld.htm.

Osgood, Robert E., *Nuclear Control in NATO* (Washington, D.C.: Washington Center for Foreign Policy Research, 1962).

"Our India: Table of Precedence," available at http://www.ourindia.com/oi2.htm.

Overholt, William H. (ed.), *Asia's Nuclear Future* (Boulder, CO: Westview Press, 1977).

"Pak N-Threat Borders on Lunacy: Brajesh," *Hindustan Times*, July 5, 1999.

"Pak to Raise Nuclear Doctrine Issue at UN," *Asian Age*, August 28, 1999.

Pakistan: Beg Says Nuclear Program "Never Frozen," FBIS-NES-96-165, August 22, 1996.

Pakistan: Gohar Ayub on Next India-Pakistan War, FBIS-NES-98-228, August 16, 1998.

"Pakistan, India 'Have Not Moved Very Far' to Field Nukes: Cohen," *The News International*, May 13, 2000.

"Pakistan, India to Sign CTBT This Month," *The Muslim*, August 12, 1998.

"Pakistan May Use N-Weapons, Fears Fernandes," *Hindustan Times*, June 30, 1999.

Pakistan: "Nuclear and Missile Superiority" over India Claimed, FBIS-TAC-98-169, June 18, 1998.

"Pakistan Nuclear Development Leaves India No Choices," *The Times of India*, November 5, 1986.

Pakistan: Nuclear Scientist: Pakistan Can Hit Many Indian Cities, FBIS-NES-98-217, August 5, 1998.

"Pakistan Reacts Strongly to India's Assertion," *The Times of India*, August 19, 1999.

"Pakistan Starts Producing Plutonium," *The Nation*, November 17, 1998.

"Pakistan Used Sophisticated Technology, Says Qadeer," *Dawn*, June 1, 1998.

Pal, Sat, "Nuclear Onus on Navy," *The Pioneer*, October 11, 1999.

Palit, D. K., "War in the Deterrent Age," *United Services Institution of India Journal*, 124:535 (January–March 1999).

Panandiker, V.A. Pai, and Ajay K. Mehra, *The Indian Cabinet* (New Delhi: Konark Publishers, 1996).

Pande, Savita, "Chinese Nuclear Doctrine," *Strategic Analysis*, 23:12 (March 2000).

Pande, Savita, "It's a Bit of a Hogwash, This Doctrine," *Indian Express*, August 30, 1999.

"Panel Four: Nuclear Weapons and the Balance of Power," in *Proceedings of the Center for the Advanced Study of India, University of Pennsylvania*, held at the Wharton Sinkler Conference Center, May 5–8, 1997, available at http://www.sas.upenn.edu/casi/reports/nuclear/panel4.html.

Pant, N. K., "Ruling over the Skies," *The Pioneer*, February 8, 1997.

Pant, N. K., "SU-30s: Strategic Take-off into Next Century," available at http://www.ipcs.org/issues/articles/286-mi-pant.html.

"Paper Laid on the Table of the House on Evolution of India's Nuclear Policy," *India News*, May 16–June 15, 1998.

Parekh, Angana, "BJP Asks Centre to Review Move on CTBT, Moratorium," *Indian Express*, August 23, 1998.

Parker, Maynard, "Rajiv Gandhi's Bipolar World," *Newsweek*, June 3, 1985.

Pathak, D. C., "Security Concept," *The Pioneer*, December 11, 1998.

Paul, T. V., "Nuclear Taboo and War Initiation in Regional Conflicts," *Journal of Conflict Resolution*, 39:4 (December 1995).

Paul, T. V., "The Paradox of Power: Nuclear Weapons in a Changed World," *Alternatives*, 20:4 (October–December 1995).

Paul, T. V., *Power Versus Prudence: Why Nations Forgo Nuclear Weapons* (Montreal: McGill-Queen's University Press, 2000).

Perkovich, George, *India's Nuclear Bomb* (Berkeley, CA: University of California Press, 1999).

Perkovich, George, "A Nuclear Third Way in South Asia," *Foreign Policy*, 91 (Summer 1993).

Perkovich, George, "South Asia: A Bomb Is Born," *Newsweek*, January 24, 2000.

Perkovich, George, "Think Again: Nuclear Proliferation," *Foreign Policy*, 112 (Fall 1998).

Pipes, Richard, "Why the Soviet Union Thinks It Could Fight and Win a Nuclear War," *Commentary*, 64:1 (July 1977).

"Planned Series of Nuclear Tests Completed," *India News*, May 16–June 15, 1998.

"PM Declares No-First Strike," *Indian Express*, August 5, 1998.

"PM Will Decide on GoM Report: Fernandes," *The Hindu*, February 28, 2001.

Pollack, Jonathan, "China and Asia's Nuclear Future," in Francine Frankel (ed.), *Bridging the Nonproliferation Divide* (Lanham, MD: University Press of America, 1995).

Pomper, Miles A., "As the Dust Settles in India, U.S. Rethinks Nuclear Policy," *Congressional Quarterly Weekly Report*, May 23, 1998.

Posen, Barry R., *Inadvertent Escalation* (Ithaca, NY: Cornell University Press, 1991).

Post Pokhran II: The National Way Ahead (New Delhi: India Habitat Centre, 1999).

Potter, William C., and Harlan W. Jencks (eds.), *The International Missile Bazaar: The New Suppliers' Network* (Boulder, CO: Westview Press, 1994).

Powell, Robert, "Nuclear Deterrence and the Strategy of Limited Retaliation," *American Political Science Review*, 83:2 (June 1989).

Prakash, A. Surya, "All Were Party to the Nuclear Gatecrash," *The Pioneer*, May 25, 1998.

Prakash, Surya, "We Sleep Well Mr. Sebastian, Thank You," *The Pioneer*, July 28, 1999.

Prasad, Rajendra, *India's Civil Defence in the Nuclear Age* (Bareilly, India: Prakash Book Depot, 1988).

Press conference hosted by Dr. R. Chidambaram, Chairman, AEC, and Secretary, DAE; Dr. A.P.J. Kalam, Scientific Adviser to the Defence Minister and Secretary, Department of Defence Research and Development; Dr. Anil Kakodkar, Director, BARC; and Dr. K. Santhanam, Chief Advisor (Technologies), DRDO, May 17, 1998.

"Press Remarks on India and Pakistan," Secretary of State Madeleine K. Albright, Washington, D.C., June 3, 1998, available at http://secretary.state.gov/www/statements/1998/980603.html.

"Press Statements on India's Nuclear Tests Issued on May 11 and 13, 1998," *India News*, May 16–June 15, 1998.

"Prime Minister's Reply to the Discussion in Lok Sabha on Nuclear Tests on May 29, 1998," *India News*, May 16–June 15, 1998.

"Proposals for Establishing Nuclear-Free Zones," *Peking Review*, 50 (December 13, 1974).

Puri, Rakshat, "Another Approach to CTBT," *Hindustan Times*, August 14, 1996.

Quade, E. S., and W. I. Boucher (eds.), *Systems Analysis and Policy: Planning Applications in Defense* (New York: Elsevier, 1968).

Quanbeck, Alton H., and Archie L. Wood, *Modernizing the Strategic Bomber Force: Why and How* (Washington, D.C.: Brookings, 1976).

Quinlan, Michael, "How Robust Is India-Pakistan Deterrence?" *Survival*, 42:4 (Winter 2000–2001).

Quinlan, Michael, "Nuclear Tests in the Subcontinent: Prospects and Significance for the World," *International Relations*, 14:4 (1999).

Quinlivan, James T., and Glenn C. Buchan, *Theory and Practice: Nuclear Deterrents and Nuclear Actors*, P-7902 (Santa Monica: RAND, 1995).

Raghavan, V. R., "Dangerous Nuclear Uncertainties," *The Hindu*, March 13, 2000.

Raghavan, V. R., "The Indian Nuclear Gambit," *The Hindu*, August 5, 1998.

Raghavan, V. R., "India's Nuclear Dilemma," *The Hindu*, August 6, 1998.

Raghavan, V. R., "Limited War and Strategic Liability," *The Hindu*, February 2, 2000.

Raghavan, V. R., "Nuclear Insecurity," *Hindustan Times*, June 11, 1998.

Raghavan, V. R., "Where the NSC Has Failed," *The Telegraph*, December 11, 2000.

Raghavan, V. R., "Whither Nuclear Policy," *The Hindu*, July 1, 2000.

Raghuvanshi, Vivek, "India Moves Prithvi Missile Toward Serial Production," *Defense News*, September 11, 2000.

Raghuvanshi, Vivek, "India Starts Research on Satellite Project," *Defense News*, May 29–June 4, 1995.

Rai, Ranjit B., "Nuclear Strategy," *The Pioneer*, September 7, 1998.

Rajagopalan, Rajesh, "The Question of More Tests," *The Hindu*, December 17, 1999.

Rajagopalan, Rajesh, "'Restoring Normalcy': The Evolution of the Indian Army's Counterinsurgency Doctrine," *Small Wars and Insurgencies*, 11:1 (Spring 2000).

Rajaraman, R., "Delay Deployment: Towards Nuclear Risk Reduction," *The Times of India,* October 1, 1999.

Rajghatta, Chidanand, "The Country's Foreign and Military Policies Need to Be Disciplined," *The Times of India,* January 1, 1991.

Rajghatta, Chidanand, "U.S. Restraint Regime for India, Pak Covers N-Capable Aircraft," *Indian Express,* November 13, 1998.

Ramachandran, R., "Pokhran II: The Scientific Dimensions," in Amitabh Mattoo (ed.), *India's Nuclear Deterrent* (New Delhi: Har-Anand Publications, 1999).

Ramachandran, R., "Sanctions: The Bark and the Bite," *Frontline,* May 8–21, 1999.

Ramachandran, R., "Understanding Pokhran II & III: A Technical Appraisal," *Agni,* 3:3 (January–May 1998).

Ramana, M. V., "A Recipe for Disaster," *The Hindu,* September 9, 1999.

Ramanna, Raja, "Security, Deterrence, and the Future," *Journal of the United Services Institution of India,* 122:509 (July–September 1992).

Ramdas, L., "Pokhran-II and Its Fallout," *Frontline,* July 7–17, 1998.

Rao, M. A., *Indian Railways* (New Delhi: National Book Trust, 1975).

Rasgotra, Maharajakrishna, "Making India a Nuclear Eunuch," *The Pioneer,* April 1, 1999.

Rasgotra, Maharajakrishna, "Nuclear India Must Engage the U.S.," *The Times of India,* May 29, 1998.

Rauf, Tariq, "Fissile Material Treaty: Negotiating Approaches," *Disarmament Forum,* 2 (1999).

Ravi, N., "Telecommunications in India," *IEEE Communications,* March 1992.

Reconnaissance Handbook (McDonnell-Douglas Corporation, 1982).

Reddy, C. Rammanohar, "The Wages of Armageddon—I–III," *The Hindu*, August 31–September 2, 1998.

Reed, Arthur, *Sepecat Jaguar* (London: Ian Allan, 1982).

Reed, Michael I., *The Sociology of Organizations: Themes, Perspectives, and Prospects* (New York: Harvester Wheatsheaf, 1992).

Reiss, Mitchell, *Bridled Ambition: Why Countries Constrain Their Nuclear Capabilities* (Washington, D.C.: Woodrow Wilson Center Press, 1995).

"Remarks of the President in Greeting to the People of Pakistan," March 25, 2000, available at http://www.whitehouse.gov/WH/New/SouthAsia/speeches/20000325.html.

"Remarks to Stimson Center," Secretary of State Madeleine K. Albright, Washington, D.C., June 10, 1998, available at http://secretary.state.gov/www/statements/1998/980610.html.

"Report of the Carnegie Task Force on Non-Proliferation and South Asian Security," in *Nuclear Weapons and South Asian Security* (Washington, D.C.: Carnegie Endowment for International Peace, 1988).

Report of the Sixth IPCS Seminar on the Implications of Nuclear Testing in South Asia, available at http://www.ipcs.org/issues/articles/135-ndi-chari.html.

Rethinaraj, T.S. Gopi, "ATV: All at Sea Before It Hits the Water," *Jane's Intelligence Review*, 10:6 (June 1998).

Rethinaraj, T.S. Gopi, "In the Comfort of Secrecy," *Bulletin of the Atomic Scientists*, 55:6 (November 1999).

Rethinaraj, T.S. Gopi, "Indian Blasts Surprise the World, but Leave Fresh Doubts," *Jane's Intelligence Review*, 10:7 (July 1998).

Rethinaraj, T.S. Gopi, "Tritium Breakthrough Brings India Closer to an H-Bomb Arsenal," *Jane's Intelligence Review*, 10:1 (January 1998).

Richelson, Jeffrey, "The Dilemmas of Counterpower Targeting," *Comparative Strategy*, 2:3 (1980).

Richelson, Jeffrey, "Population Targeting and U.S. Strategic Doctrine," in Desmond Ball and Jeffrey Richelson (eds.), *Strategic Nuclear Targeting* (Ithaca, NY: Cornell University Press, 1986).

Rikhye, Ravi, "Pakistan N-Tests Seen as Having Little Military Value," *India Abroad*, July 24, 1998.

Rockwell, Mark, "Telecom in India: Bring Order from Chaos," *Telephony*, 218 (June 1990).

Roherty, James M. (ed.), *Defense Policy Formation* (Durham, NC: Carolina Academic Press, 1980).

Rose, Leo E., "India and China: Forging a New Relationship," in Shalendra D. Sharma (ed.), *The Asia-Pacific in the New Millennium: Geopolitics, Security, and Foreign Policy* (Berkeley, CA: Institute of East Asian Studies, University of California, Berkeley, 2000).

Rosen, Stephen Peter, *Societies and Military Power* (Ithaca, NY: Cornell University Press, 1996).

Rosenberg, David Alan, "The Origins of Overkill," in Steven E. Miller (ed.), *Strategy and Nuclear Deterrence* (Princeton, NJ: Princeton University Press, 1984).

Rostow, Eugene V., "Of Summitry and Grand Strategy," *Strategic Review*, 14 (Fall 1986).

Rudolph, Lloyd I., and Susanne Hoeber Rudolph, *In Pursuit of Lakshmi* (Chicago: University of Chicago Press, 1987).

Ruggie, John Gerard, "Continuity and Transformation in the World Polity: Toward a Neorealist Synthesis," in Robert O. Keohane (ed.), *Neorealism and Its Critics* (New York: Columbia University Press, 1986).

Sabherwal, O. P., "India's Nuclear Strategy: Peaceful and Weapon Capability," *World Focus*, 21:4 (April 2000).

Sagan, Scott (ed.), *Civil-Military Relations and Nuclear Weapons* (Stanford, CA: Center for International Security and Arms Control, Stanford University, 1994).

Sagan, Scott D., *The Limits of Safety: Organizations, Accidents, and Nuclear Weapons* (Princeton, NJ: Princeton University Press, 1993).

Sagan, Scott, "Nuclear Alerts and Crisis Management," *International Security*, 9:4 (Spring 1985)

Sagan, Scott, "The Origins of Military Doctrine and Command and Control Systems," in Peter R. Lavoy, Scott D. Sagan, and James J. Wirtz (eds.), *Planning the Unthinkable* (Ithaca, NY: Cornell University Press, 2000).

Sagan, Scott D., and Kenneth N. Waltz, *The Spread of Nuclear Weapons: A Debate* (New York: W. W. Norton, 1995).

Sahay, Anand K., "Emerging Power Equations," *The Pioneer*, July 8, 1998.

Sahgal, Arun, and Tejinder Singh, "Nuclear Threat from China: An Appraisal," *Trishul*, 6:2 (1993).

Salman, Michael, Kevin J. Sullivan, and Stephen van Evera, "Analysis or Propaganda? Measuring American Strategic Nuclear Capability, 1969–88," in Lynn Eden and Steven E. Miller (eds.), *Nuclear Arguments* (Ithaca, NY: Cornell University Press, 1989).

"SAPRA Backgrounder: The China Poser," *SAPRA India Monthly Bulletin*, April–May 1996.

Satyamurthy, T. V., "India's Post-Colonial Nuclear Estate," *Radical Science*, 14 (1984).

Savkin, V. E., *The Basic Principles of Operational Art and Tactics: A Soviet View* (Washington, D.C.: USGPO, 1974).

Sawhney, Pravin, "Himalayan Conflict Forges Artillery Doctrine," *Jane's International Defence Review*, 32:3 (1999).

Sawhney, Pravin, "How Inevitable Is an Asian Missile Race?" *Jane's Intelligence Review*, 12:1 (January 2000).

Sawhney, Pravin, "India's First Airpower Doctrine Takes Shape: An Aging Air Force Looks to the Future," *Jane's International Defence Review*, 30:6 (June 1997).

Sawhney, Pravin, "India's Missile Policy: Focus Must Shift to Agni," *The Times of India*, March 4, 1997.

Sawhney, Pravin, "Standing Alone," *Jane's International Defence Review*, 29:11 (November 1996).

Sawhney, Pravin, "To Test or Not to Test: The Challenge for India's Nuclear Credibility," *RUSI Journal*, 141:3 (June 1996).

Saxena, Rajendra Narain, *Four Decades of Indian Railways, 1950–1990* (Delhi: Academic Foundation, 1991).

Schelling, Thomas, *Arms and Influence* (New Haven, CT: Yale University Press, 1966).

Schelling, Thomas, *The Strategy of Conflict* (Cambridge, MA: Harvard University Press, 1960).

Schubert, Klaus, "France," in Regina Cowen Karp (ed.), *Security with Nuclear Weapons?* (Oxford, UK: Oxford University Press, 1991).

Schuster, S. (ed.), *The Air Force Manual for Design and Analysis of Hardened Structures*, Vols. I and II (Chatsworth, CA: California Research & Technology, Inc., 1987).

Schwartz, Stephen I. (ed.), *Atomic Audit* (Washington, D.C.: Brookings, 1998).

Schwarz, David N., "Past and Present: The Historical Legacy," in Ashton B. Carter and David N. Schwarz (eds.), *Ballistic Missile Defense* (Washington, D.C.: Brookings, 1984).

Schweitzer, J., F. Ringdal, and J. Fyen, "The Indian Nuclear Explosions of 11 and 13 May 1998," *NORSAR Semiannual Technical Summary*, NORSAR Scientific Report No. 2-97/98.

Scott, William B., "New Targeting Pods Deliver 'Litening Strikes,' " *Aviation Week & Space Technology*, August 21, 2000.

Seabury, Paul (ed.), *The Balance of Power* (San Francisco: Chandler, 1965).

Security Council Resolution 1172 (1998) on International Peace and Security, adopted by the Security Council at its 3890th meeting on

June 6, 1998, available at http://www.un.org/Docs/scres/1998/sres1172.htm.

Sehbai, Shaheen, "Pakistan Reassessing Position on CTBT," *Dawn*, July 1, 1998.

Senate Committee on Commerce, Science and Transportation, *NASA Authorization for Fiscal Year 1978*.

Seng, Jordan, *Strategy for Pandora's Children: Stable Nuclear Proliferation Among Minor States*, unpublished doctoral dissertation, University of Chicago, 1998.

"Service Chiefs to Plan on Control of N-Forces," *The Times of India*, March 5, 2001.

Seshagiri, N., *The Bomb! Fallout of India's Nuclear Explosion* (Delhi: Vikas Publishing House, 1975).

Sethi, Manpreet, "The Status of the Nuclear World at the Close of the Century," *Strategic Analysis*, 22:10 (January 1999).

Sethi, Manpreet, "The Struggle for Nuclear Disarmament," in Jasjit Singh (ed.), *Nuclear India* (New Delhi: Knowledge World, 1998).

Shahi, Agha, "Talbott's Visit: Would Delinking Pakistan's Signing of CTBT with India's Signing Serve the National Interest?" *Pakistan Link*, July 24, 1998.

Shahi, Agha, Zulfiqar Ali Khan, and Abdul Sattar, "Securing Nuclear Peace," *The News International*, October 5, 1999.

Shahid-ur-Rehman, *Long Road to Chagai* (Islamabad: Print Wise Publications, 1999).

Sharma, Dhirendra, *India's Nuclear Estate* (New Delhi: Lancer's, 1983).

Sharma, Sat Pal, "A Faulty Doctrine," *The Pioneer*, September 16, 1999.

Sharma, Shalendra D. (ed.), *The Asia-Pacific in the New Millennium: Geopolitics, Security, and Foreign Policy* (Berkeley, CA: Institute of East Asian Studies, University of California, Berkeley, 2000).

Shaver, R. D., *Range Enhancement Equations for Various Refueling Options*, N-1872-AF (Santa Monica: RAND, 1982).

Shenoy, T.V.R., "Why the Buddha Smiled," *Indian Express*, May 20, 1998.

Sheth, Ninad D., "Interview: The Depth of the Indian Navy," *India Today* Web Exclusive, available at http://www.india-today.com/webexclusive/interviews/20000520sushil.html.

Shlapak, David A., and David E. Thaler, *Back to First Principles: U.S. Strategic Forces in the Emerging Environment*, R-4260-AF (Santa Monica: RAND, 1993).

Shue, H. (ed.), *Nuclear Deterrence and Moral Restraint* (Cambridge, UK: Cambridge University Press, 1989).

Shuster, Mike, interview with Jaswant Singh, *All Things Considered*, National Public Radio, June 11, 1998.

Sibal, Kapil, "Toy Gun Security: Flaws in India's Nuclear Deterrence," *The Times of India*, January 13, 1999.

Siddharth, V., "NPT Extension: Safer World Only for U.S.," *Indian Express*, May 4, 1995.

Siddhartha, V., "Military Dimensions in the Future of the Indian Presence in Space," *Journal of the United Services Institution of India*, 130:540 (April–June 2000).

Siddiqi, A. R., "Balancing the Nuclear Debate," *Defence Journal*, 19:11–12 (1994).

Siddiqi, Rauf, "Khan Says India Has Plutonium to Make 50–70 Atom Bombs Anytime," *Nucleonics Week*, June 20, 1991.

Sidhu, W.P.S., *The Development of an Indian Nuclear Doctrine Since 1980*, unpublished doctoral dissertation, Emmanuel College, University of Cambridge, February 1997.

Sidhu, W.P.S., *Enhancing Indo-U.S. Strategic Cooperation*, Adelphi Paper No. 313 (London: IISS, 1997).

Sidhu, W.P.S., "India Sees Safety in Nuclear Triad and Second Strike Potential," *Jane's Intelligence Review*, 10:7 (July 1998).

Sidhu, W.P.S., "India's Nuclear Tests: Technical and Military Imperatives," *Jane's Intelligence Review*, 8:4 (April 1996).

Sidhu, W.P.S., "Pakistan's Bomb: A Quest for Credibility," *Jane's Intelligence Review*, 8:6 (June 1996).

Sidhu, W.P.S., "This Doctrine Is Full of Holes," *Indian Express*, September 8, 1999.

Sidhu, W.P.S., "A Virtual De-Alert in South Asia," *UNIDIR-Newsletter*, 38 (1998).

Sidorenko, A. A., *The Offensive: A Soviet View* (Washington, D.C.: US-GPO, 1973).

Sigal, Leon V., "Rethinking the Unthinkable," *Foreign Policy*, 34 (Spring 1979).

"Signing CTBT Will Not Weaken Country," *Indian Express*, May 10, 1999.

Sikka, S. K., and Anil Kakodkar, "Some Preliminary Results of May 11–13, 1998, Nuclear Detonations at Pokhran," *BARC Newsletter*, 172 (May 1998).

Sikka, S. K., F. Roy, and G. J. Nair, "Comment on the Paper 'Monitoring Nuclear Tests' by Barker et al.—*Science* 25 September 1998," unpublished manuscript.

Sikka, S. K., Falguni Roy, G. J. Nair, V. G. Kolvankar, and Anil Kakodkar, "Update on the Yield of May 11–13, 1998, Nuclear Detonations at Pokhran," *BARC Newsletter*, 178 (November 1998).

"Silent Thunder," *The Times of India*, October 13, 1998.

Singer, Clifford E., Jyotika Saksena, and Milind Thakar, "Feasible Deals with India and Pakistan After the Nuclear Tests," *Asian Survey*, 38:12 (December 1998).

Singh, Anita Inder, "A New Indo-Russian Connection," *International Affairs*, 71:1 (January 1995).

Singh, Harwant, "Only a N-Warhead!" *Vayu Aerospace Review,* IV/1994.

Singh, Jasjit, "Budgeting for Security Needs," *Frontline,* July 18–31, 1998.

Singh, Jasjit, "India, Europe and Non-Proliferation: Pokhran II and After," *Strategic Analysis,* 22:8 (November 1998).

Singh, Jasjit, "India's Nuclear Policy: The Year After," *Strategic Analysis,* 23:4 (July 1999).

Singh, Jasjit, "Nuclear Diplomacy," in Jasjit Singh (ed.), *Nuclear India* (New Delhi: Knowledge World, 1998).

Singh, Jasjit (ed.), *Nuclear India* (New Delhi: Knowledge World, 1998).

Singh, Jasjit, "The Nuclear Option," *Hindustan Times,* March 21, 1998.

Singh, Jasjit, "A Nuclear Strategy for India," in Jasjit Singh (ed.), *Nuclear India* (New Delhi: Knowledge World, 1998).

Singh, Jasjit, "Nukes Have No Prestige Value," *Indian Express,* June 4, 1998.

Singh, Jasjit, "Pakistan's Fourth War," *Strategic Analysis,* 23:5 (August 1999).

Singh, Jasjit, "Pakistan's Missiles: U.S. Turning a Nelson's Eye," *The Times of India,* July 19, 1995.

Singh, Jasjit, "South Asian Nuclear Scene," *The Times of India,* May 2, 1994.

Singh, Jasjit, "Why Nuclear Weapons?" in Jasjit Singh (ed.), *Nuclear India* (New Delhi: Knowledge World, 1998).

Singh, Jaswant, "Against Nuclear Apartheid," *Foreign Affairs,* 77:5 (September–October 1998).

Singh, Jaswant, *Defending India* (Chennai, India: Macmillan, 1999).

Singh, Jaswant, *What Constitutes National Security in a Changing World Order? India's Strategic Thought*, Occasional Paper No. 6 (Philadelphia: Center for the Advanced Study of India, 1998).

Singh, Manvendra, "Who Should Control Nuclear Button? Armed Forces Have a Proposal," *Indian Express*, September 1, 1998.

Singh, Pushpindar, "The Indian Army Today: Colour and Firepower," *Asian Defence Journal*, April 1987.

Singh, Pushpindar, Ravi Rikhye, and Peter Steinemann, *Fiza'ya* (New Delhi: Society for Aerospace Studies, 1991).

Singh, R.K. Jasbir (ed.), *Indian Defence Yearbook, 1997–98* (Dehra Dhun, India: Natraj Publishers, 1997).

Singh, Sampooran, *India and the Nuclear Bomb* (New Delhi: S. Chand, 1971).

Singh, Satinder, "Nuclear War in South Asia—The Worst Case," *Indian Defence Review*, 2:1 (January 1987).

"Sinha's Defence," *Indian Express*, March 2, 2000.

"Sino-Indian Ties Looking Up: Jaswant," *The Hindu*, November 25, 2000.

SIPRI Yearbook 1997 (New York: Oxford University Press, 1997).

Slocombe, Walter, "Preplanned Operations," in Ashton B. Carter, John D. Steinbruner, and Charles A. Zraket (eds.), *Managing Nuclear Operations* (Washington, D.C.: Brookings, 1987).

Smart, Ian, "The Great Engine: The Rise and Decline of a Nuclear Age," *International Affairs*, 51 (October 1975).

Smirnov, Victor, "Space Missile Defense Forces: Yesterday, Today, Tomorrow," *Military Parade*, 16 (July–August 1996), available at http://www.milparade.com/1996/16/72-73.htm.

Smith, Chris, *India's Ad Hoc Arsenal* (Oxford, UK: Oxford University Press, 1994).

Smith, David O. (ed.), *From Containment to Stability: Pakistan–United States Relations in the Post–Cold War Era* (Washington, D.C.: National Defense University, 1993).

Smith, R. Jeffrey, "India Moves Missiles Near Pakistani Border," *Washington Post*, June 3, 1997.

Smith, R. Jeffrey, "Report Cites China-Pakistan Missile Links," *Washington Post*, June 13, 1996.

Snyder, Glenn, "The Balance of Power and the Balance of Terror," in Paul Seabury (ed.), *The Balance of Power* (San Francisco: Chandler, 1965).

Snyder, Glenn H., *Deterrence and Defense* (Princeton, NJ: Princeton University Press, 1961).

Soviet Faculty of the General Staff Academy, *Dictionary of Basic Military Terms: A Soviet View* (Washington, D.C.: USGPO, 1976).

"Space Communications and Applications," in *Third United Nations Conference on the Exploration and Peaceful Uses of Outer Space*, Background Paper No. 5, A/CONF.184/BP/5, May 27, 1998.

"SPECAT/HAL Jaguar," available at http://www.bharat-rakshak.com/IAF/Info/Specs-Combat.html#SEPECAT%20Jaguar.

Spector, Leonard S., *The Undeclared Bomb* (Cambridge, MA: Ballinger Publishing Company, 1988).

Spector, Leonard S. (with Jacqueline R. Smith), *Nuclear Ambitions* (Boulder, CO: Westview Press, 1990).

Spector, Leonard S., and Mark G. McDonough (with Evan S. Medeiros), *Tracking Nuclear Proliferation* (Washington, D.C.: Carnegie Endowment for International Peace, 1995).

Spence, A. M., "Job Market Signalling," *Quarterly Journal of Economics*, 87 (1973).

" 'Spy Satellite' Launch by Year-End," *The Hindu*, July 2, 2000.

Srinivasan, M. R., "CTBT: A Phony Consensus?" *The Hindu*, January 19, 2000.

Srivastava, Anupam, "India's Growing Missile Ambitions: Assessing the Technical and Strategic Dimensions," *Asian Survey*, 40:2 (2000).

Srivastava, H. K., "Nuclear India: Problems and Praxises," *Combat Journal*, April 1987.

"SS-24 'Scalpel' (RS-22/RT-23U)" and "SS-27 (Topol-M, RS-12M1/-12M2)," in Duncan Lennox (ed.), *Jane's Strategic Weapons Systems* (Coulsdon, UK: Jane's Information Group Ltd., 1999), Issue 29, January 1999.

"Stale Tale," *The Times of India*, June 30, 1996.

Stanley, William, and Gary Liberson, *Measuring Effects of Payload and Range Differences of Fighter Aircraft*, DB-102-AF (Santa Monica: RAND, 1993).

Starsman, Raymond E., *Ballistic Missile Defense and Deceptive Basing: A New Calculus for the Defense of ICBMs* (Washington, D.C.: National Defense University Press, 1981).

Statement of Dr. John S. Foster, Director, Defense Research and Engineering, Department of Defense, before the Subcommittee on Arms Control, Senate Foreign Relations Committee, May 1, 1973, cited in Ray E. Kidder, "Militarily Significant Nuclear Explosive Yields," *FAS Public Interest Report*, 38:7 (September 1985).

Steer, Ian, "Asia's Rival Reactors a Cause for Concern," *Jane's Intelligence Review*, 10:10 (October 1998).

Stefanick, Tom, *Strategic Antisubmarine Warfare and Naval Strategy* (Lexington, KY: Lexington Books, 1987).

Steinbruner, John D., "Choices and Trade-offs," in Ashton B. Carter, John D. Steinbruner, and Charles A. Zraket (eds.), *Managing Nuclear Operations* (Washington, D.C.: Brookings, 1987).

Steinbruner, John D., "National Security and the Concept of Strategic Stability," *Journal of Conflict Resolution*, 22:3 (September 1978).

Steinbruner, John D., "Nuclear Decapitation," *Foreign Policy*, 45 (Winter 1981–1982).

Steinemann, Peter, "IAF Recce Intrusion," *Air Power International*, 2:3 (1998).

Stern, Ellen P. (ed.), *The Limits of Military Intervention* (Thousand Oaks, CA: Sage Publications, 1977).

Stokes, Mark, *China's Military Modernization: Implications for the United States* (Carlisle Barracks, PA: Strategic Studies Institute, 1999).

Stone, Jeremy J., "Four Civilizations Gently Collide at Arms Control Conference," *FAS Public Interest Report*, 47:2 (March–April 1994).

"Strategic Implications of the Atomic Bomb, August 29, 1947, United States Joint Chiefs of Staff Modern Military Section," in Gregg Herken, *The Winning Weapon: The Atomic Bomb in the Cold War, 1945–1950* (New York: Vintage Books, 1981).

Study Recommends Two-Person Rule for Using Nuclear Arms, FBIS-TAC-98-261, September 18, 1998.

Sublette, Carey, *Nuclear Weapons Frequently Asked Questions*, "Section 4.0: Engineering and Design of Nuclear Weapons," and "Section 4.3.1: Fusion Boosted Fission Weapons," available at http://www.fas.org/nuke/hew/Nwfaq/Nfaq4-3.html#Nfaq4.3.1.

Sublette, Carey, *Nuclear Weapons Frequently Asked Questions*, "Section 4.3: Fission-Fusion Hybrid Weapons," available at http://www.fas.org/nuke/hew/Nwfaq/Nfaq4-3.html#Nfaq4.3.

Sublette, Carey, *Nuclear Weapons Frequently Asked Questions*, "Section 4:4: Elements of Thermonuclear Weapons Design," available at http://www.fas.org/nuke/hew/Nwfaq/Nfaq4-4.html#Nfaq4.4.

Sublette, Carey, *Nuclear Weapons Frequently Asked Questions*, "Section 6.0: Nuclear Materials," available at http://www.fas.org/nuke/hew/Nwfaq/Nfaq6.html.

Subrahmanyam, K., "After Pokhran-II," *Economic Times*, May 14, 1998.

Subrahmanyam, K., "Arms Race Myth: Fallout of Overactive Minds," *The Times of India*, May 30, 1998.

Subrahmanyam, K., "Articulating Our Nuclear Policy," *Economic Times*, June 15, 1994.

Subrahmanyam, K., "Building Trust on the Bomb," *The Times of India*, July 7, 1985.

Subrahmanyam, K., "Challenges to Indian Security," Field Marshal K. C. Cariappa Memorial Lecture, New Delhi, October 28, 2000.

Subrahmanyam, K., "Countering Zia's Proposals," *The Times of India*, July 4, 1987.

Subrahmanyam, K., "A Credible Deterrent: Logic of The Nuclear Doctrine," *The Times of India*, October 4, 1999.

Subrahmanyam, K., "Dealing with Pakistan," *The Times of India*, June 26, 1990.

Subrahmanyam, K., "Educate India in Nuclear Strategy," *The Times of India*, May 22, 1998.

Subrahmanyam, K., "Global Watch: Pakistani Missile," *Economic Times*, February 20, 1998.

Subrahmanyam, K., "Hedging Against Hegemony: Gandhi's Logic in the Nuclear Age," *The Times of India*, June 16, 1998.

Subrahmanyam, K., "History Repeats Itself," *Economic Times*, July 27, 1998.

Subrahmanyam, K., "In Dubious Battle: How War Became Obsolete," *The Times of India*, May 9, 1995.

Subrahmanyam, K., "India and CTBT," *The Times of India*, February 21, 1996.

Subrahmanyam, K. (ed.), *India and the Nuclear Challenge* (New Delhi: Lancer International, 1986).

Subrahmanyam, K., "India: Keeping the Option Open," in Robert M. Lawrence and Joel Larus (eds.), *Nuclear Proliferation: Phase II* (Wichita, KS: University Press of Kansas, 1974).

Subrahmanyam, K., "Indian Nuclear Policy—1964–98," in Jasjit Singh (ed.), *Nuclear India* (New Delhi: Knowledge World, 1998).

Subrahmanyam, K., "India's Security: The North and North-East Dimension," *Conflict Studies*, 215 (London: Centre for Security and Conflict Studies, 1988).

Subrahmanyam, K., "Indo-Pak Nuclear Stand-Off," *The Times of India*, May 6, 1988.

Subrahmanyam, K., "Kashmir 1948–1998," *The Times of India*, June 26, 1998.

Subrahmanyam, K., "Missile Proliferation: U.S. Must Heed India's Concerns," *The Times of India*, July 13, 1995.

Subrahmanyam, K., "National Security Council," *Economic Times*, April 2, 1998.

Subrahmanyam, K., "Not a Numbers Game: Minimum Cost of N-Deterrence," *The Times of India*, December 7, 1998.

Subrahmanyam, K., "The Nuclear Bomb: Myths and Reality," *Economic Times*, June 22, 1998.

Subrahmanyam, K., "Nuclear Defence Philosophy: Not a Numbers Game Anymore," *The Times of India*, November 8, 1996.

Subrahmanyam, K., "Nuclear Force Design and Minimum Deterrence Strategy for India," in Bharat Karnad (ed.), *Future Imperilled* (New Delhi: Viking, 1994).

Subrahmanyam, K., "Nuclear India in Global Politics," *World Affairs*, 2:3 (July–September 1998).

Subrahmanyam, K., "Nuclear Option and Agenda," *Economic Times*, March 20, 1998.

Subrahmanyam, K., "Nuclear Policy and Political Culture," *Economic Times*, August 20, 1998.

Subrahmanyam, K., "Nuclear Policy, Arms Control and Military Co-operation," paper presented at the Carnegie Endowment for International Peace–India International Centre Conference on India and the United States after the Cold War, New Delhi, March 7–9, 1993.

Subrahmanyam, K., " Nuclear Tests: What Next?" *IIC Quarterly*, Summer/Monsoon 1998, p. 57.

Subrahmanyam, K., "Options for India," *Institute for Defence Studies and Analyses Journal*, 3 (1970).

Subrahmanyam, K., "Pak Nuclear Programme," *The Times of India*, February 28, 1987.

Subrahmanyam, K., "Planning for Security: Blueprint for an Apex Body," *The Times of India*, December 20, 1989.

Subrahmanyam, K., "Reform Decision-Making Process," *Economic Times*, April 16, 1998.

Subrahmanyam, K., "Restructuring Ministry of Defence," *Economic Times*, February 8, 1999.

Subrahmanyam, K., "The Smouldering Agni," *Economic Times*, March 18, 1999.

Subrahmanyam, K., "Son of Star Wars," *The Times of India*, February 12, 2000.

Subrahmanyam, K., "Talbott Is Stuck in Pre-'85 Nuclear Groove," *The Times of India*, November 17, 1998.

Subramanian, R. R., "India's Nuclear Weapons Capabilities: A Technological Appraisal," in P. R. Chari, Pervaiz Iqbal Cheema, and Iftekharuzzaman (eds.), *Nuclear Non-Proliferation in India and Pakistan* (New Delhi: Manohar, 1996).

Sugden, Robert, and Alan Williams, *The Principles of Practical Cost-Benefit Analysis* (Oxford, UK: Oxford University Press, 1978).

"Sukhoi Su-27," in Paul Jackson (ed.), *Jane's All the World's Aircraft, 1998–99* (Coulsdon, UK: Jane's Information Group Ltd., 1998).

"Sukhoi Su-30M," in Paul Jackson (ed.), *Jane's All the World's Aircraft, 1998–99* (Coulsdon, UK: Jane's Information Group Ltd., 1998).

Sukovic, O., "The Concept of Nuclear Free Zones," in D. Carlton and C. Schaerf (eds.), *Perspectives on the Arms Race* (London: Macmillan, 1989).

"Summary of Recommendations," presented at the Institute for Defence Studies and Analyses—Centre for Policy Research Joint Seminar, India International Centre, New Delhi, September 24, 1995.

Sundarji, K., *Blind Men of Hindoostan* (New Delhi: UBS Publishers, 1995).

Sundarji, K., "Changing Military Equations in Asia: The Role of Nuclear Weapons," in Francine Frankel (ed.), *Bridging the Nonproliferation Divide* (Lanham, MD: University Press of America, 1995).

Sundarji, K., "CTBT and National Security: Options for India," *Indian Express*, April 6, 1996.

Sundarji, K., "The CTBT Debate: Choice Before India," *Indian Express*, December 4, 1995.

Sundarji, K., "Declare Nuclear Status," *India Today*, December 31, 1990.

Sundarji, K., *Effects of Nuclear Asymmetry on Conventional Deterrence*, Combat Paper No. 1 (Mhow, India: College of Combat, 1981).

Sundarji, K., "Imperatives of Indian Minimum Nuclear Deterrence," *Agni*, 2:1 (May 1996).

Sundarji, K., "Indian Nuclear Doctrine—I: Notions of Deterrence," *Indian Express*, November 25, 1994.

Sundarji, K., "Indian Nuclear Doctrine—II: Sino-Indo-Pak Triangle," *Indian Express*, November 26, 1994.

Sundarji, K., "Meeting Nuclear Threat: A Plan for India," *Indian Express*, March 11, 1996.

Sundarji, K., "National Policy and Security Strategy," *The Hindu*, December 13, 1996.

Sundarji, K., "Nuclear Deterrence: Doctrine for India—Part 1," *Trishul*, 5:2 (1992).

Sundarji, K., "Nuclear Deterrence: Doctrine for India—Part 2," *Trishul*, 6:1 (1993).

Sundarji, K., *Nuclear Weapons in a Third World Context*, Combat Paper No. 2 (Mhow, India: College of Combat, 1981).

Sundarji, K., "Prithvi in the Haystack," *India Today International*, June 30, 1997.

"Suo Motu Statement by Prime Minister Atal Bihari Vajpayee in the Indian Parliament on May 27, 1998," *India News*, May 16–June 15, 1998.

Sur, Serge (ed.), *Nuclear Deterrence: Problems and Perspectives in the 1990s* (New York: UNIDIR, 1993).

Survey of India, *Railway Map of India*, 14th ed. (New Delhi: Survey of India, 1989).

Surveyor General of Pakistan, *Atlas of Pakistan* (Rawalpindi, Pakistan: Survey of Pakistan, 1990).

Swaine, Michael D., and Alastair Iain Johnston, "China and Arms Control Institutions," in Elizabeth Economy and Michel Oksenberg (eds.), *China Joins the World* (New York: Council on Foreign Relations Press, 1999).

Swaine, Michael D., and Ashley J. Tellis, *Interpreting China's Grand Strategy*, MR-1121-AF (Santa Monica: RAND, 2000).

Synnott, Hilary, *The Causes and Consequences of South Asia's Nuclear Tests*, Adelphi Paper No. 332 (London: IISS, 1999).

"Table of Precedence: Who, Exactly, Is What," available at http://www.indiavotes.com/reference/who.shtml.

Talbott, Strobe, "Address at Conference on Diplomacy and Preventive Defense," cosponsored by the Carnegie Commission on Preventing Deadly Conflict and the Stanford-Harvard Preventive Defense Project, Stanford University, Palo Alto, CA, January 16, 1999, available at http://www.state.gov/www/policy_remarks/1999/990116_talbott_sa.html.

Talbott, Strobe, "Dealing with the Bomb in South Asia," *Foreign Affairs*, 78:2 (March–April 1999).

Taneja, Abhinav, "A Phone in Every Village: Taking Telecom to Rural India," *New Telecom Quarterly*, October 11, 1997.

Tanham, George, and Marcy Agmon, *The Indian Air Force*, MR-424-AF (Santa Monica: RAND, 1995).

Telegram No. 31294, paragraph 96, U.S. Embassy, New Delhi, telegram to the U.S. State Department, in National Security Archives, Washington, D.C.

Tellis, Ashley J., "The Air Balance in the Indian Subcontinent: Trends, Constants, Contexts," *Defense Analysis*, 2:4 (Winter 1986).

Tellis, Ashley J., "The Changing Political-Military Environment: South Asia," in Zalmay Khalilzad, David T. Orletsky, Jonathan D. Pollack, Kevin Pollpeter, Angel M. Rabasa, David A. Shlapak, Abram N. Shulsky, and Ashley J. Tellis (eds.), *The United States and Asia: Toward a New U.S. Strategy and Force Posture*, MR-1315-AF (Santa Monica: RAND, 2001).

Tellis, Ashley J., "Hawkeyes for Pakistan: Rationale and Logic of the E-2C Request," *Journal of South Asian and Middle Eastern Studies*, 10:1 (Fall 1986).

Tellis, Ashley J., *India: Assessing Strategy and Military Capabilities in the Year 2000*, P-7978 (Santa Monica: RAND, 1996).

Tellis, Ashley J., "NATO and Theater Nuclear Force Modernization: Looking Backward, Looking Forward," *Journal of East and West Studies*, 15:2 (Fall–Winter 1986).

Tellis, Ashley J., "Nuclear Arms, Moral Questions, and Religious Issues," *Armed Forces & Society*, 13:4 (Summer 1987).

Tellis, Ashley J., "Securing the Barrack: The Logic, Structure and Objectives of India's Naval Expansion," Parts I and II, *Naval War College Review*, 43:3 and 43:4 (Summer and Autumn 1990).

Tellis, Ashley J., "South Asia," in Zalmay Khalilzad (ed.), *Strategic Appraisal 1996*, MR-543-AF (Santa Monica: RAND, 1996).

Tellis, Ashley J., *Stability in South Asia*, DB-185-A (Santa Monica: RAND, 1997).

Tellis, Ashley J., Chung Min Lee, James Mulvenon, Courtney Purrington, and Michael D. Swaine, "Sources of Conflict in Asia," in Zalmay Khalilzad and Ian O. Lesser (eds.), *Sources of Conflict in the 21st Century*, MR-897-AF (Santa Monica: RAND, 1998).

"Testing Reaction," *Far Eastern Economic Review*, June 8, 1989.

Thakur, Ramesh, "India and the United States: A Triumph of Hope over Experience?" *Asian Survey*, 36:6 (June 1996).

Thapan, M. L., "Nuclear Games," *The Statesman*, September 29, 1999.

Thayer, Bradley A., "The Risk of Nuclear Inadvertence: A Review Essay," *Security Studies*, 3:3 (Spring 1994).

Thomas, Raju G.C., "India's Nuclear and Space Programs: Defense or Development?" *World Politics*, 38 (1986).

Thomas, Raju G.C. (ed.), *The Nuclear Non-Proliferation Regime* (New York: St. Martin's Press, 1998).

Thomas, Raju G.C., "Security Relationships in Southern Asia: Difference in the Indian and American Perspectives," *Asian Survey*, 21:7 (July 1981).

Thomas, Raju G.C., "Should India Sign the NPT/CTBT?" in Raju G.C. Thomas (ed.), *The Nuclear Non-Proliferation Regime* (New York: St. Martin's Press, 1998).

Thomas, Raju G.C., and Amit Gupta (eds.), *India's Nuclear Security* (Boulder, CO: Lynne Rienner Publishers, 2000).

"Thrilled Experts Say Nation Has Strength to Take On World," *Economic Times*, May 12, 1998.

Till, Geoffrey, *Maritime Strategy and the Nuclear Age*, 2nd ed. (New York: St. Martin's Press, 1984).

Toomay, John C., "Warning and Assessment Sensors," in Ashton B. Carter, John D. Steinbruner, and Charles A. Zraket (eds.), *Managing Nuclear Operations* (Washington, D.C.: Brookings, 1987).

Trachtenberg, Marc, "The Influence of Nuclear Weapons in the Cuban Missile Crisis," *International Security*, 10:1 (Summer 1985).

Tripathi, Purnima S., "Agni III to Be Test Fired Soon, Says Fernandes," *Asian Age*, September 23, 2000.

Tsipis, Kosta, *Arsenal* (New York: Simon & Schuster, 1983).

Tucker, Jonathan B., "Strategic Command and Control Vulnerabilities: Dangers and Remedies," *Orbis*, 27:4 (Winter 1993).

Tyler, Patrick E., "China Raises Nuclear Stakes on the Subcontinent," *New York Times*, August 27, 1996.

"Unanswered Questions," *Financial Times*, October 26, 1998.

United States Air Force, *Systems Applications of Nuclear Technology: Effects of Airblast, Cratering, Ground Shock and Radiation on Hardened Structures*, AFSCM-500-8 (Washington, D.C.: Headquarters, Department of the Air Force, 1976).

United States Congress, House Committee on Armed Services, Panel on Nuclear Weapons Safety, *Nuclear Weapons Safety: Report of the Panel on Nuclear Weapons Safety of the Committee on Armed Services*, House of Representatives, 101st Congress, Second Session (Washington, D.C: USGPO, 1990).

United States Congress, Senate Committee on Foreign Relations, *Nuclear War Strategy*, Hearing before the Committee on Foreign Relations, 96th Congress, Second Session, on Presidential Directive 59, September 16, 1980 (Washington, D.C.: USGPO, 1981).

United States Congress, Senate Committee on Foreign Relations, Subcommittee on United States Security Agreements and Commitments Abroad, *Nuclear Weapons and Foreign Policy*, hearings before the Subcommittee on U.S. Security Agreements and Commitments Abroad and the Subcommittee on Arms Control, International Law and Organization of the Committee on Foreign Relations, United States Senate, 93rd Congress, Second Session, on U.S. Nuclear Weapons in Europe and U.S.-U.S.S.R. Strategic Doctrines and Policies, March 7, 14, and April 4, 1974 (Washington, D.C.: USGPO, 1974).

Uniyal, Mahesh, "Mixed Reviews Greet National Security Council," *India Abroad*, November 27, 1998.

Uniyal, Mahesh, "No Cap on Fissile Material, Says Vajpayee," *India Abroad*, December 25, 1998.

U.S. General Accounting Office, *Observations on Navy Nuclear Weapons Safeguards and Nuclear Weapons Accident Emergency Planning*, GAO/NSIAD-85-123 (Washington, D.C.: USGPO, 1985).

"U.S. High Tech to Remain 'Out of Bounds' for India," *Hindustan Times*, January 15, 1999.

"U.S.-India Relations: A Vision for the 21st Century," *Hindustan Times*, March 23, 2000.

"U.S. Recognises India's N-Concern," *The Hindu*, September 3, 2000.

van Cleave, William R., "The Nuclear Weapons Debate," *U.S. Naval Institute Proceedings*, 92:5 (May 1966).

van Cleave, William R., and S. T. Cohen, *Tactical Nuclear Weapons: An Examination of the Issues* (New York: Crane, Russak, 1978).

van der Vink, Gregory, Jeffrey Park, Richard Allen, Terry Wallace, and Christel Hennet, "False Accusations, Undetected Test and Implications for the CTB Treaty," *Arms Control Today*, 28:4 (May 1998).

Vanaik, Achin, "Danger of an Arms Race," *Hindustan Times*, May 14, 1998.

Vanaik, Achin, "Drawing New Lines," *The Hindu*, May 23, 1998.

Vanaik, Achin, "Hotter Than a Thousand Suns," *The Telegraph*, May 26, 1998.

Vanaik, Achin, "Since the Pokhran Tests," *Seminar*, 485 (January 2000).

Vas, E. A., "India's Nuclear Options in the 1990s and Its Effects on India's Armed Forces," *Indian Defence Review*, 1:1 (January 1986).

Vasudeva, P. K., "The Army Will Not Take Over," *The Hindu*, February 16, 1999.

Vaughn, Bruce, "The Use and Abuse of Intelligence Services in India," *Intelligence and National Security*, 8:1 (January 1993).

Venkataraman, Ganesan, *Bhabha and His Magnificent Obsessions* (Hyderabad, India: Universities Press, 1994).

Vertzberger, Yaccov, *China's Southwestern Strategy: Encirclement and Counterencirclement* (New York: Praeger, 1985).

Vick, Alan J., "Post-Attack Strategic Command and Control Survival: Options for the United States," *Orbis*, 29:1 (Spring 1985).

Vohra, A. M., chapter in K. Sundarji (ed.), *Nuclear Weapons in a Third World Context*, Combat Paper No. 2 (Mhow, India: College of Combat, 1981).

von Hippel, Frank N., "The FMCT and Cuts in Fissile Material Stockpiles," *Disarmament Forum*, 2 (1999).

"VSATs Are Very Competitive," *Indian Express*, February 4, 2000.

Walker, J. R., *Air-to-Ground Operations* (London: Brassey's, 1987).

Wallace, Terry, "The May 1998 India and Pakistan Nuclear Tests," *Seismological Research Letters*, 69:5 (September–October 1998).

Walter, William R., Arthur J. Rodgers, Kevin Mayeda, Stephen C. Myers, Michael Pasyanos, and Marvin Denny, *Preliminary Regional Seismic Analysis of Nuclear Explosions and Earthquakes in Southwest Asia*, UCRL-JC-130745 (Geophysics and Global Security Division, Lawrence Livermore National Laboratory, July 1998).

Waltz, Kenneth N., "What Will the Spread of Nuclear Weapons Do to the World?" in John K. King (ed.), *International Political Effects of the Spread of Nuclear Weapons* (Washington, D.C.: USGPO, 1979).

Wariavwalla, Bharat, "Are They Really MAD?" *Indian Express*, September 7, 1999.

Watman, Kenneth, Dean Wilkening, John Arquilla, and Brian Nichiporuk, *U.S. Regional Deterrence Strategies*, MR-490-A/AF (Santa Monica: RAND, 1995).

"We Have It, They Have It, That's All," *The Times of India*, May 16, 1998.

"Weaponization Now Complete, Say Scientists," *The Hindu*, May 18, 1998.

Weber, Max, *The Methodology of the Social Sciences*, translated and edited by Edward A. Shils and Henry A. Finch, eds. (New York: The Free Press, 1949).

Weiner, Stephen, "Systems and Technology," in Ashton B. Carter and David N. Schwarz (eds.), *Ballistic Missile Defense* (Washington, D.C.: Brookings, 1984).

Weir, Fred, "Can Russia Deliver on Arms Sales?" *Christian Science Monitor*, November 29, 2000.

Welch, Larry D., *John J. McCloy Roundtable on the Elimination of Nuclear Weapons* (New York: Council on Foreign Relations, 1998).

Westervelt,, Donald R., "Can Cold Logic Replace Cold Feet?" *Bulletin of the Atomic Scientists*, 35:2 (February 1979).

Westervelt, Donald R, "The Role of Laboratory Tests," in Jozef Goldblat and David Cox (eds.), *Nuclear Weapons Tests: Prohibition or Limitation?* (Oxford, UK: Oxford University Press, 1998).

"What More Do You Want? We've Got All the Scientific Data We Needed," *Indian Express*, December 4, 1999.

Wheeler, Nicholas, "Minimum Deterrence and Nuclear Abolition," in Regina Cowen Karp (ed.), *Security Without Nuclear Weapons?* (Oxford, UK: Oxford University Press, 1992).

Wilkening, Dean, and Kenneth Watman, *Nuclear Deterrence in a Regional Context*, MR-500-A/AF (Santa Monica: RAND, 1994).

Windrem, Robert, and Tammy Kupperman, "Pakistan Nukes Outstrip India's, Officials Say," *MSNBC International News*, June 6, 2000, available at http://www.msnbc.com/news/417106.asp.

Winner, Langdon, "Do Artifacts Have Politics?" *Daedalus*, 109:1 (Winter 1980).

Wiseman, Geoffrey, and Gregory F. Treverton, *Dealing with the Nuclear Dilemma in South Asia* (Los Angeles: Pacific Council on International Policy, 1998).

Wisner, Frank, "India's Nuclear Posture: Taking a Fresh Look," remarks delivered at the CII Round Table on Indo-U.S. Relations: Challenges and Opportunities, New Delhi, October 20, 1999.

Withington, Thomas, "Nuclear Dilemmas Seize Asia," *Jane's Intelligence Review–Pointer*, December 1998.

Wohlstetter, Albert, and Richard Brody, "Continuing Control as a Requirement for Deterring," in Ashton B. Carter, John D. Steinbruner, and Charles A. Zraket (eds.), *Managing Nuclear Operations* (Washington, D.C.: Brookings, 1987).

Wohlstetter, Albert J., and Henry Rowen, *Objectives of the United States Military Posture*, RM-2373-PR (Santa Monica: RAND, 1959).

Wohlstetter, Roberta, *"The Buddha Smiles": Absent-Minded Peaceful Aid and the Indian Bomb* (Los Angeles: Pan Heuristics, 1977).

Woolsey, R. James, Director, Central Intelligence Agency, U.S. Congress, Hearings of the Senate Governmental Affairs Committee on Nuclear Proliferation, 103rd Congress, 1st Session, February 24, 1993.

"Words, Words, Words," *India Today*, March 30, 1998.

Wortzel, Larry M. (ed.), *The Chinese Armed Forces in the 21st Century* (Carlisle Barracks, PA: Strategic Studies Institute, 1999).

Wright, David C., "An Analysis of the Pakistani Ghauri Missile Test of April 6, 1998," *Science and Global Security*, 7:2 (1998).

Yali, Chen, "Nuclear Arms Race Looms," *China Daily*, August 24, 1999.

Yasmeen, Samina, "Pakistan's Nuclear Tests: Domestic Debate and International Determinants," *Australian Journal of International Affairs*, 53:1 (1999).

Yost, David S., *France's Deterrent Posture and Security in Europe*, Part 1: *Capabilities and Doctrine* and Part 2: *Strategic and Arms Control Implications*, Adelphi Papers Nos. 194 and 195 (London: IISS, 1984–1985).

Yost, David S., "French Nuclear Targeting," in Desmond Ball and Jeffrey Richelson (eds.), *Strategic Nuclear Targeting* (Ithaca, NY: Cornell University Press, 1986).

Zachariah, Mini Pant, "Indian Scientist Says Ramanna Wrong About 1974 'Bomb,' " *Asian Age*, October 12, 1997.

Zahra, Farah, "Pakistan's Road to a Minimum Nuclear Deterrent," *Arms Control Today*, 29:5 (July–August 1999).

Zakaria, Fareed, "Becoming a Great Power, Cheap," *Newsweek*, May 25, 1998.

Zaloga, Steven J., " 'Grumble': Guardian of the Skies, Pt. 1," *Jane's Intelligence Review*, 9:3 (March 1997).

Zaloga, Steven J., " 'Grumble': Guardian of the Skies, Pt. 2," *Jane's Intelligence Review*, 9:4 (April 1997).

Zaloga, Steven J., "Russian Tactical Ballistic Missile Defence: The Antey S-300V," *Jane's Intelligence Review*, 5:2 (February 1993).

Zaloga, Steven J., "SA-15 'Gauntlet' Air Defence Missile System," *Jane's Intelligence Review*, 5:12 (December 1993).

Zhang, Ming (ed.), *China's Changing Nuclear Posture* (Washington, D.C.: Carnegie Endowment for International Peace, 1999).

Zimmerman, Peter D., "India's Testing: Something Doesn't Fit," *Los Angeles Times*, May 22, 1998.

Zuberi, Matin, "The Proposed Nuclear Doctrine," *World Focus*, 21:4 (April 2000).

Zutshi, Amar, "For a Strategic Defence," *The Pioneer*, May 1, 1998.